Smith and Roberson's Business Law

Richard A. Mann
Barry S. Roberts

CENGAGE
Learning™

Australia • Brazil • Japan • Korea • Mexico • Singapore • Spain • United Kingdom • United States

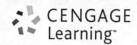

Smith and Roberson's Business Law

Executive Editors:
Maureen Staudt
Michael Stranz

Senior Project Development Manager:
Linda deStefano

Marketing Specialist:
Courtney Sheldon

Senior Production/Manufacturing Manager:
Donna M. Brown

PreMedia Manager:
Joel Brennecke

Sr. Rights Acquisition Account Manager:
Todd Osborne

Cover Image:
Getty Images*

*Unless otherwise noted, all cover images used by Custom
Solutions, a part of Cengage Learning, have been supplied
courtesy of Getty Images with the exception of the Earthview
cover image, which has been supplied by the National
Aeronautics and Space Administration (NASA).

Smith and Roberson's Business Law, Fourteenth Edition
Mann / Roberts
© 2009 Cengage Learning. All rights reserved.

For product information and technology assistance, contact us at
Cengage Learning Customer & Sales Support, 1-800-354-9706

For permission to use material from this text or product,
submit all requests online at **cengage.com/permissions**
Further permissions questions can be emailed to
permissionrequest@cengage.com

This book contains select works from existing Cengage Learning resources and
was produced by Cengage Learning Custom Solutions for collegiate use. As such,
those adopting and/or contributing to this work are responsible for editorial
content accuracy, continuity and completeness.

Compilation © 2011 Cengage Learning

ISBN-13: 978-1-133-15495-2

ISBN-10: 1-133-15495-6

Cengage Learning
5191 Natorp Boulevard
Mason, Ohio 45040
USA

Cengage Learning is a leading provider of customized learning solutions with
office locations around the globe, including Singapore, the United Kingdom,
Australia, Mexico, Brazil, and Japan. Locate your local office at:
international.cengage.com/region

Cengage Learning products are represented in Canada by Nelson Education, Ltd.
For your lifelong learning solutions, visit **www.cengage.com/custom**
Visit our corporate website at **www.cengage.com**

Printed in the United States of America

Contents in Brief

Contents

Contents

Contents

PART 2
Contracts

Introduction to Contracts

It is impossible to overestimate the importance of contracts in the field of business. Every business, whether large or small, must enter into contracts with its employees, its suppliers, and its customers to conduct its business operations. Contract law is, therefore, an important subject for the business manager. Contract law is also basic to other fields of law treated in other parts of this book, such as agency, partnerships, corporations, sales of personal property, commercial paper, and secured transactions.

Even the most common transaction may involve a multitude of contracts. For example, in a typical contract for the sale of land, the seller promises to transfer title to the land, and the buyer promises to pay an agreed-upon purchase price. In addition, the seller may promise to pay certain taxes or assessments; the buyer may promise to assume a mortgage on the property or may promise to pay the purchase price to a creditor of the seller. If attorneys represent the parties, they very likely do so on a contractual basis. If the seller deposits the proceeds of the sale in a bank, he enters into a contract with the bank. If the buyer leases the property, he enters into a contract with the tenant. When one of the parties leaves his car in a parking lot to attend to any of these matters, he assumes a contractual relationship with the proprietor of the lot. In short, nearly every business transaction is based upon contract and the expectations the agreed-upon promises create. Knowing the legal requirements for making binding contracts is, therefore, essential.

DEVELOPMENT OF THE LAW OF CONTRACTS

That law arises from social necessity is clearly true of the law of contracts. The vast and complicated institution of business can be conducted efficiently and successfully only upon the certainty that promises will be fulfilled. Business must be assured not only of supplies of raw materials or manufactured goods, but also of labor, management, capital, and insurance as well. Common experience has shown that promises based solely on personal honesty or integrity do not have the reliability essential to business. Hence the development of the law of contracts, which is the law of enforceable promises.

Contract law, like law as a whole, is not static. It has undergone—and is still undergoing—enormous changes. In the nineteenth century virtually absolute autonomy in forming contracts was the rule. The law imposed contract liability only where the parties strictly complied with the required formalities. The same principle also dictated that once a contract was formed it should be enforced according to its terms and that neither party should be lightly excused from performance.

During the twentieth century, contract law experienced tremendous changes. As will be discussed in the next ten chapters, many of the formalities of contract formation were relaxed. Today, the law usually recognizes contractual obligations whenever the parties manifest an intent to be bound. In addition, an increasing number of promises are now enforced in certain circumstances, even though they do not comply strictly with the basic requirements of a contract. While in the past contract liability was absolute and escape from liability, once assumed, was rare, presently the law allows a party to be excused from contractual duties where fraud, duress, undue influence, mistake, unconscionability, or impossibility is present. The law has expanded the nineteenth century's narrow view of contract damages to grant equitable remedies and restitution as remedies for breach of contract. The older doctrine of privity of contract, which sharply restricted which parties could enforce contract rights, has given way to the current view that permits intended third-party beneficiaries to sue in their own right.

In brief, the twentieth century left its mark on contract law by limiting the absolute freedom of contract and, at the same time, by relaxing the requirements of contract formation. Accordingly, it is now considerably easier to get into a contract and correspondingly less difficult to get out of one.

COMMON LAW

Contracts are primarily governed by State common law. An orderly presentation of this law is found in the Restatements of the Law of Contracts. The American Law Institute adopted and promulgated the first Restatement on May 6, 1932. On May 17, 1979, the institute adopted and promulgated a revised edition of the Restatement—the Restatement, Second, Contracts—which will be referred to as the Restatement. Regarded as a valuable authoritative reference work for more than seventy years, the Restatements have been extensively relied upon and quoted in reported judicial opinions.

THE UNIFORM COMMERCIAL CODE

The sale of personal property forms a substantial portion of commercial activity. Article 2 of the Uniform Commercial Code (the Code, or UCC) governs sales in all States except Louisiana. (Selected provisions of the UCC are set forth in *Appendix B* of this text.) A **sale** consists of the passing of title to goods from a seller to a buyer for a price. Section 2–106. A contract for sale includes both a present sale of goods and a contract to sell goods at a future time. Section 2–106. The Code essentially defines goods as movable personal property. Section 2–105(1). **Personal property** is any type of property other than an interest in real property (land). For example, the purchase of a television set, automobile, or textbook is considered a sale of goods. All such transactions are governed by Article 2 of the Code, but, where the Code has not specifically modified general contract law, the common law of contracts continues to apply. Section 1–103. In other words, the law of sales is a specialized part of the general law of contracts, and the law of contracts governs unless specifically displaced by the Code.

Amendments to Article 2 were promulgated in 2003 to accommodate electronic commerce and to reflect development of business practices, changes in other law, and interpretive difficulties of practical significance. To date no States have adopted them. However, at least thirty-seven States have adopted the 2001 Revisions to Article 1, which applies to all of the articles of the Code.

◆ **SEE FIGURE 9-1: Law Governing Contracts**

TYPES OF CONTRACTS OUTSIDE THE CODE

General contract law governs all contracts outside the scope of the Code. Such contracts play a significant role in commercial activities. For example, the Code does *not* apply to employment contracts, service contracts, insurance contracts, contracts involving **real property** (land and anything attached to it, including buildings), and contracts for the sale of intangibles such as patents and copyrights. These transactions continue to be governed by general contract law.

DEFINITION OF A CONTRACT

A **contract** is a binding agreement that the courts will enforce. Section 1 of the Restatement more precisely defines a contract as "a promise or a set of promises for the breach of which the law gives a remedy, or the performance of which the law in some way recognizes as a duty." The Restatement provides further insight by defining a **promise** as "a manifestation of the intention to act or refrain from acting in a specified way." Restatement, Section 2.

Those promises that meet all of the essential requirements of a binding contract are contractual and will be enforced. All other promises are not contractual, and usually no legal remedy is available for a **breach** (a failure to perform

◆ **FIGURE 9-1: Law Governing Contracts**

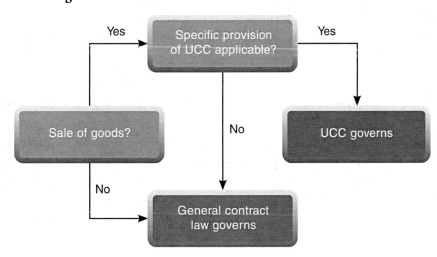

properly) of these promises. The remedies provided for breach of contract (discussed in *Chapter 18*) include compensatory damages, equitable remedies, reliance damages, and restitution. Thus, a promise may be contractual (and therefore binding) or noncontractual. In other words, all contracts are promises, but not all promises are contracts.

◆ **SEE FIGURE 9-2: Contractual and Noncontractual Promises**

In addition, though occasionally a contract must be evidenced by a writing to be enforceable, in most cases an oral contract is binding and enforceable. If all of these essentials are present, the promise is contractual and legally binding. If any is absent, however, the promise is noncontractual. These requirements will be separately considered in succeeding chapters.

◆ **SEE FIGURE 9-3: Validity of Agreements**

REQUIREMENTS OF A CONTRACT

The four basic requirements of a contract are as follows:

1. **Mutual Assent**. The parties to a contract must manifest by words or conduct that they have agreed to enter into a contract. The usual method of showing mutual assent is by offer and acceptance.
2. **Consideration**. Each party to a contract must intentionally exchange a legal benefit or incur a legal detriment as an inducement to the other party to make a return exchange.
3. **Legality of Object**. The purpose of a contract must not be criminal, tortious, or otherwise against public policy.
4. **Capacity.** The parties to a contract must have contractual capacity. Certain persons, such as those adjudicated (judicially declared) incompetent, have no legal capacity to contract, while others, such as minors, incompetent persons, and intoxicated persons, have limited capacity to contract. All others have full contractual capacity.

CLASSIFICATION OF CONTRACTS

Contracts can be classified according to various characteristics, such as method of formation, content, and legal effect. The standard classifications are (1) express or implied contracts; (2) unilateral or bilateral contracts; (3) valid, void, voidable, or unenforceable contracts; (4) executed or executory contracts; and (5) formal or informal contracts. These classifications are not mutually exclusive. For example, a contract may be express, bilateral, valid, executory, and informal.

EXPRESS AND IMPLIED CONTRACTS

Parties to a contract may indicate their assent either by express language or by conduct that implies such willingness. Thus, a contract may be (1) entirely oral; (2) partly oral and partly written; (3) entirely written; (4) partly oral or written and partly implied from the conduct of the parties; and (5) wholly implied from the conduct of the parties. The first three are known as express contracts, and the last two as implied

◆ **FIGURE 9-2: Contractual and Noncontractual Promises**

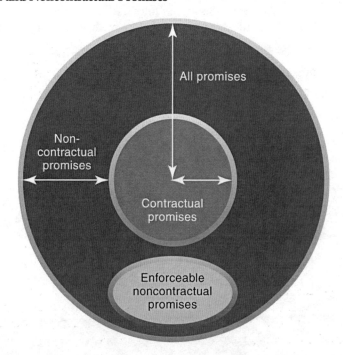

◆ **FIGURE 9-3: Validity of Agreements**

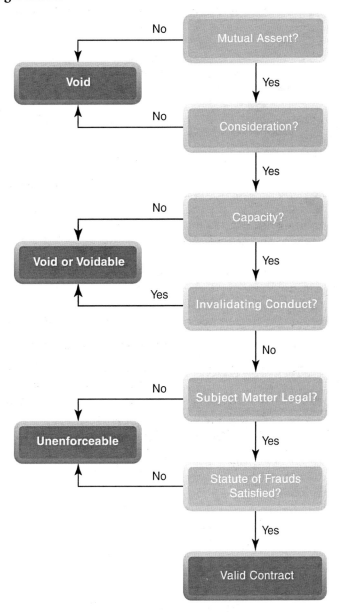

contracts. Both express and implied contracts are genuine contracts, equally enforceable. The difference between them is merely the manner in which the parties manifest assent.

An **express contract** is therefore one in which the parties have manifested their agreement by oral or written language, or both.

An **implied contract** is one that is inferred from the parties' conduct, not from spoken or written words. Implied contracts are also called implied in fact contracts. Thus, if Elizabeth orders and receives a meal in Bill's restaurant, a promise is implied on Elizabeth's part to pay Bill the price stated in the menu or, if none is stated, Bill's customary price. Likewise, when a passenger boards a bus, a wholly implied contract is formed by which the passenger undertakes

to pay the customary fare and the bus company undertakes to provide the passenger transportation.

UNILATERAL AND BILATERAL CONTRACTS

In the typical contractual transaction, each party makes at least one promise. For example, if Ali says to Ben, "If you promise to mow my lawn, I will pay you ten dollars," and Ben agrees to mow Ali's lawn, Ali and Ben have made mutual promises, each undertaking to do something in exchange for the promise of the other. When a contract comes into existence by the exchange of promises, each party is under a duty to the other. This kind of contract is called a

bilateral contract, because each party is both a *promisor* (a person making a promise) and a *promisee* (the person to whom a promise is made).

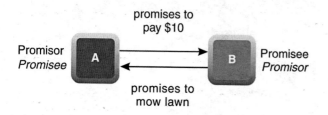

But suppose that only one of the parties makes a promise. Ali says to Ben, "If you will mow my lawn, I will pay you ten dollars." A contract will be formed when Ben has finished mowing the lawn and not before. At that time, Ali becomes contractually obligated to pay $10.00 to Ben. Ali's offer was in exchange for Ben's act of mowing the lawn, not for his promise to mow it. Because he never made a promise to mow the lawn, Ben was under no duty to mow it. This is a **unilateral contract** because only one of the parties made a promise.

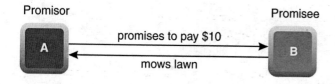

Thus, whereas a bilateral contract results from the exchange of a promise for a return promise, a unilateral contract results from the exchange of a promise either for an act or for a forbearance (refraining) from acting. If a contract is not clearly unilateral or bilateral, the courts presume that the parties intended a bilateral contract. Thus, in the above example, if Ali says to Ben, "I will pay you ten dollars if you will mow my lawn," and Ben replies, "OK, I will mow your lawn," a bilateral contract is formed.

VALID, VOID, VOIDABLE, AND UNENFORCEABLE CONTRACTS

By definition, a **valid contract** is one that meets all of the requirements of a binding contract. It is an enforceable promise or agreement.

A **void contract** is an agreement that does not meet all of the requirements of a binding contract. Thus, it is no contract at all; it is merely a promise or an agreement having no legal effect. An example of a void agreement is an agreement entered into by an adjudicated incompetent.

A voidable contract, on the other hand, is not wholly lacking in legal effect. A **voidable contract** is a contract, but because of the manner in which it was formed or a lack of capacity of a party to it, the law permits one or more of the parties to avoid the legal duties the contract creates. Restatement, Section 7. If the contract is avoided, both parties are relieved of their legal duties under the agreement. For instance, through intentional misrepresentation of a material fact (*fraud*), Thomas induces Regina to enter into a contract. Regina may, upon discovery of the fraud, notify Thomas that by reason of the misrepresentation she will not perform her promise, and the law will support Regina. Though not void, the contract induced by fraud is voidable at the election of Regina, the defrauded party. Thomas, the fraudulent party, has no such election. If Regina elects to avoid the contract, Thomas will be released from his promise under the agreement, although he may be liable under tort law for damages for fraud.

A contract that is neither void nor voidable may, nonetheless, be unenforceable. An **unenforceable contract** is one for the breach of which the law provides no remedy. Restatement, Section 8. For example, a contract may be unenforceable because of a failure to satisfy the requirements of the Statute of Frauds, which requires certain kinds of contracts to be evidenced by a writing to be enforceable. Also, the running of the time within which a suit may be filed, as provided in the Statute of Limitations, bars the right to bring a lawsuit for breach of contract. After that period has run, the contract is referred to as unenforceable, rather than void or voidable.

EXECUTED AND EXECUTORY CONTRACTS

The terms *executed* and *executory* pertain to the state of performance of a contract. A contract fully performed by all of the parties to it is an **executed contract**. Strictly, an executed contract is in the present tense no contract, as all duties under it have been performed; but it is useful to have a term for a completed contract. (The word *executed* is also used to mean "signed," as in to execute or sign a certain document.)

The term **executory**, which means "unperformed," applies to situations in which one or more promises by any party to the contract are as yet unperformed or where the contract is wholly unperformed by one or more of the parties. Thus, David and Carla make a contract under which David is to sell and deliver certain goods to Carla in ten days and Carla is to pay the agreed price in thirty days. Prior to the delivery of the goods by David on the tenth day, the contract is wholly executory. Upon David's delivery of the goods to Carla, the contract is executed as to David and executory as to Carla. When Carla duly pays for the goods, the contract is wholly executed and thereby completely fulfilled.

FORMAL AND INFORMAL CONTRACTS

A **formal contract** depends upon a particular form, or mode of expression, for its legal existence. For example, at common law a promise under seal (a particular symbol that serves to authenticate an instrument) is enforceable without anything more. Another formal contract is a negotiable instrument, such as a check, which has certain legal attributes resulting solely from the special form in which it is made. A letter of credit (a promise to honor drafts or other demands for payment) is also a formal contract. Recognizances, or formal acknowledgments of indebtedness made in court, are another example of formal contracts. All other contracts, whether oral or written, are simple or **informal contracts**, as they do not depend upon formality for their legal validity.

PROMISSORY ESTOPPEL

As a general rule, promises are unenforceable if they do not meet all the requirements of a contract. Nevertheless, to avoid injustice, in certain circumstances courts enforce noncontractual promises under the doctrine of promissory estoppel. A noncontractual promise is enforceable when it is made under circumstances that should lead the promisor reasonably to expect that the promise would induce the promisee to take definite and substantial action or forbearance in reliance on the promise, and the promisee does take such action or forbearance. See *Figure 9-2.* Section 90 of the Restatement provides:

A promise which the promisor should reasonably expect to induce action or forbearance on the part of the promisee or a third person and which does induce such action or forbearance is binding if injustice can be avoided only by enforcement of the promise. The remedy granted for breach may be limited as justice requires.

For example, Gordon promises Constance not to foreclose for a period of six months on a mortgage Gordon owns on Constance's land. Constance then expends $100,000 to construct a building on the land. His promise not to foreclose is binding on Gordon under the doctrine of promissory estoppel.

◆ **SEE FIGURE 9-4: Contracts, Promissory Estoppel, and Quasi Contracts**

QUASI CONTRACTS

In addition to implied in fact contracts, there are implied in law, or quasi, contracts, which were not included in the foregoing classification of contracts because a quasi (meaning "as if") contract is not a contract at all but based in restitution. The term *quasi contract* is used because the remedy granted for quasi contract is similar to one of the remedies available for breach of contract.

A quasi contract is *not* a contract because it is based on neither an express nor an implied promise. A **contract implied in law** or quasi contract is an obligation imposed by law to avoid injustice. For example, Anna by mistake delivers to Robert a plain, unaddressed envelope containing $100 intended for Claudia. Robert is under no contractual obligation to return it. However, Anna is permitted to recover the $100 from Robert. The law imposes a quasi-contractual obligation upon Robert to prevent his unjust enrichment at Anna's expense. The elements of such a recovery are (1) a benefit conferred upon the defendant (Robert) by the plaintiff (Anna); (2) an appreciation or knowledge by the defendant (Robert) of the benefit; and (3) acceptance or retention by the defendant (Robert) of the benefit under circumstances rendering inequitable the defendant's (Robert's) retention of the benefit without compensating the plaintiff for its value.

One court has summarized the doctrine of quasi contract as follows:

Quasi contracts are not contracts at all, although they give rise to obligations more akin to those stemming from contract than from tort. The contract is a mere fiction, a form imposed in order to adapt the case to a given remedy.... Briefly stated, a quasi-contractual obligation is one imposed by law where there has been no agreement or expression of assent, by word or act, on the part of either party involved. The law creates it, regardless of the intention of the parties, to assure a just and equitable result. *Bradkin v. Leverton*, 26 N.Y.2d 192, 309 N.Y.S.2d 192, 257 N.E.2d 643 (1970).

◆ **FIGURE 9-4: Contracts, Promissory Estoppel, and Quasi Contracts**

	Contract	Promissory Estoppel	Quasi Contract
Type of Promise	Contractual	Noncontractual	None Void Unenforceable Invalidated
Requirements	All of the essential elements of a contract	Detrimental and justifiable reliance	Benefit conferred and knowingly accepted
Remedies	Equitable Compensatory Reliance Restitution	Promise enforced to the extent necessary to avoid injustice	Reasonable value of benefit conferred

Not infrequently, courts use quasi contracts to provide a remedy when the parties have entered into a void contract, an unenforceable contract, or a voidable contract that is avoided. In such a case, the law of quasi contracts will determine the recovery permitted for any performance rendered by the parties under the invalid, unenforceable, or invalidated agreement.

◆ SEE FIGURE 9-4: **Contracts, Promissory Estoppel, and Quasi Contracts**

CHAPTER SUMMARY

LAW OF CONTRACTS	**Definition of Contract** a binding agreement that the courts will enforce **Common Law** most contracts are governed primarily by State common law, including contracts involving employment, services, insurance, real property (land and anything attached to it), patents, and copyrights **Uniform Commercial Code** Article 2 of the UCC governs the sales of goods • *Sale* the transfer of title from seller to buyer • *Goods* tangible personal property (personal property is all property other than an interest in land)
REQUIREMENTS OF A CONTRACT	**Mutual Assent** the parties to a contract must manifest by words or conduct that they have agreed to enter into a contract **Consideration** each party to a contract must intentionally exchange a legal benefit or incur a legal detriment as an inducement to the other party to make a return exchange **Legality of Object** the purpose of a contract must not be criminal, tortious, or otherwise against public policy **Capacity** the parties to a contract must have contractual capacity
CLASSIFICATION OF CONTRACTS	**Express and Implied Contracts** • *Express Contract* an agreement that is stated in words, either orally or in writing • *Implied in Fact Contract* a contract in which the agreement of the parties is inferred from their conduct **Unilateral Bilateral and Contracts** • *Bilateral Contract* a contract in which both parties exchange promises • *Unilateral Contract* a contract in which only one party makes a promise **Valid, Void, Voidable, and Unenforceable Contracts** • *Valid Contract* one that meets all of the requirements of a binding contract • *Void Contract* no contract at all; without legal effect • *Voidable Contract* a contract capable of being made void • *Unenforceable Contract* a contract for the breach of which the law provides no remedy **Executed and Executory Contracts** • *Executed Contract* a contract that has been fully performed by all of the parties • *Executory Contract* a contract that has yet to be fully performed **Formal and Informal Contracts** • *Formal Contract* an agreement that is legally binding because of its particular form or mode of expression • *Informal Contracts* all contracts other than formal contracts
PROMISSORY ESTOPPEL	**Definition** a doctrine enforcing some noncontractual promises **Requirements** a promise made under circumstances that should lead the promisor reasonably to expect that the promise would induce the promisee to take definite and substantial action, and the promisee does take such action **Remedy** a court will enforce the promise to the extent necessary to avoid injustice

QUASI CONTRACTS **Definition** an obligation not based on contract that is imposed to avoid injustice
Requirements a court will impose a quasi contract when (1) the plaintiff confers a benefit upon the defendant, (2) the defendant knows or appreciates the benefit, and (3) the defendant's retention of the benefit is inequitable
Remedy the plaintiff recovers the reasonable value of the benefit she conferred upon the defendant

Mutual Assent

Although each of the requirements for forming a contract is essential to its existence, mutual assent is so basic that frequently a contract is referred to as the agreement between the parties. The Restatement, Section 3, provides this definition: "An agreement is a manifestation of mutual assent on the part of two or more parties." Enforcing the contract means enforcing the agreement; indeed, the agreement between the parties is the very core of the contract.

The manner in which parties usually show mutual assent is by **offer** and **acceptance**. One party makes a proposal (offer) by words or conduct to the other party, who agrees by words or conduct to the proposal (acceptance). A contractual agreement always involves either a promise exchanged for a promise (*bilateral contract*) or a promise exchanged for an act or forbearance to act (*unilateral contract*), as manifested by what the parties communicate to one another.

An implied contract may be formed by conduct. Thus, though there may be no definite offer and acceptance, or definite acceptance of an offer, a contract exists if both parties have acted in a manner that manifests (indicates) a recognition by each of them of the existence of a contract. It may be impossible to determine the exact moment at which a contract was made.

To form the contract, the parties must manifest their agreement objectively. The important thing is what the parties indicate to one another by spoken or written words or by conduct. The law applies an **objective standard** and is, therefore, concerned only with the assent, agreement, or intention of a party as it reasonably appears from his words or actions. The law of contracts is not concerned with what a party may have actually thought or the meaning that he intended to convey, even if his subjective understanding or intention differed from the meaning he objectively indicated by word or conduct. For example, if Leslie seemingly offers to sell to Sam her Chevrolet automobile but intends to offer and believes that she is offering her Ford automobile, and Sam accepts the offer, reasonably believing it was for the Chevrolet, a contract has been formed for the sale of the Chevrolet. Subjectively, there is no agreement as to the subject matter, but objectively there is a manifestation of agreement, and the objective manifestation is binding.

The Uniform Commercial Code's (UCC or Code) treatment of mutual assent is covered in greater detail in *Chapter 21*.

OFFER

An offer is a definite proposal or undertaking made by one person to another which manifests a willingness to enter into a bargain. The person making the proposal is the **offeror**. The person to whom it is made is the **offeree**. Upon receipt, the offer confers on the offeree the power of acceptance, by which the offeree expresses her willingness to comply with the terms of the offer.

The communication of an offer to an offeree does not of itself confer any rights or impose any duties on either of the parties. The offeror, by making his offer, simply confers upon the offeree the power to create a contract by accepting the offer. Until the offeree exercises this power, the outstanding offer creates neither rights nor liabilities.

An offer may take several forms: (1) It may propose a promise for a promise. (This is an offer to enter into a bilateral contract.) An example is an offer to sell and deliver goods in thirty days in return for the promise to pay a stipulated amount upon delivery of the goods. If the offeree accepts this offer, the resulting contract consists of the parties' mutual promises, each made in exchange for the other. (2) An offer may be a promise for an act. (This is an offer to enter into a unilateral contract.) A common example is an offer of a reward for certain information or for the return of lost property. The offeree can accept such an offer only by the performance of the act requested. (3) An offer may be in the form of an act for a promise. (This is an offer to enter into an "inverted" unilateral contract.) For example, Maria offers the stated price to a clerk in a theater ticket office and

COLUMN: © PHOTOGRAPHEROLYMPUS CLOUDS: © KERTLIS

asks for a ticket for a certain performance. The clerk can accept this offer of an act only by delivery of the requested ticket, which amounts, in effect, to the theater owner's promise to admit Maria to the designated performance.

ESSENTIALS OF AN OFFER

An offer need not take any particular form to have legal validity. To be effective, however, it must (1) be communicated to the offeree, (2) manifest an intent to enter into a contract, and (3) be sufficiently definite and certain. If these essentials are present, an offer that has not terminated gives the offeree the power to form a contract by accepting the offer.

COMMUNICATION

To have the mutual assent required to form a contract, the offeree must have knowledge of the offer; he cannot agree to something of which he has no knowledge. Accordingly, the offeror must communicate the offer, in an intended manner, to the offeree.

For example, Andy signs a letter containing an offer to Bonnie and leaves it on top of the desk in his office. Later that day, Bonnie, without prearrangement, goes to Andy's office, discovers that Andy is away, notices the letter on his desk, reads it, and writes on it an acceptance which she dates and signs. No contract is formed because the offer never became effective; Andy never communicated it to Bonnie. If Andy had mailed the letter, and it had gone astray in the mail, the offer would likewise never have become effective.

Not only must the offer be communicated to the offeree, but the communication must also be made or authorized by the offeror. For instance, if Joanne tells Karlene that she plans to offer Larry $600 for his piano, and Karlene promptly informs Larry of this proposal, no offer has been made. There was no authorized communication of any offer by Joanne to Larry. By the same token, if Lance should offer to sell his diamond ring to Ed, an acceptance of this offer by Dianne would not be effective, because Lance made the offer to Ed, not to Dianne.

An offer need not be stated or communicated by words. Conduct from which a reasonable person may infer a proposal in return for either an act or a promise amounts to an offer.

An offer may be made to the general public. No person, however, can accept such an offer until and unless he has knowledge that the offer exists. For example, if a person, without knowing of an advertised reward for information leading to the return of a lost watch, gives information that leads to its return, he is not entitled to the reward. His act

was not an acceptance of the offer because he could not accept something of which he had no knowledge.

INTENT

To have legal effect an offer must manifest an intent to enter into a contract. The intent of an offer is determined objectively from the words or conduct of the parties. The meaning of either party's manifestation is based upon what a reasonable person in the other party's position would have believed. The courts sometimes consider subjective intention in interpreting the parties' communications (the interpretation of contracts is discussed in *Chapter 16*).

Occasionally, a person exercises her sense of humor by speaking or writing words that—taken literally and without regard to context or surrounding circumstances—a promisee could construe as an offer. The promisor intends the promise as a joke, however, and the promisee as a reasonable person should understand it to be such. Therefore, it is not an offer. Because the person to whom it is made realizes or should realize that it is not made in earnest, it should not create a reasonable expectation in his mind. No contractual intent exists on the part of the promisor, and the promisee is or reasonably ought to be aware of that fact. If, however, the intended jest is so successful that the promisee as a reasonable person under all the circumstances believes that the joke is in fact an offer, and so believing accepts, the objective standard applies and the parties have entered into a contract.

A promise made under obvious excitement or emotional strain is likewise not an offer. For example, Charlotte, after having her month-old Cadillac break down for the third time in two days, screams in disgust, "I will sell this car to anyone for $10.00!" Lisa hears Charlotte and hands her a ten-dollar bill. Under the circumstances, Charlotte's statement was not an offer, if a reasonable person in Lisa's position would have recognized it merely as an overwrought, nonbinding utterance.

It is important to distinguish language that constitutes an offer from that which merely solicits or invites offers. Such proposals, although made in earnest, lack intent and are therefore not deemed offers. As a result, a purported acceptance does not bring about a contract but operates only as an offer to accept. These proposals include preliminary negotiations, advertisements, and auctions.

PRELIMINARY NEGOTIATIONS If a communication creates in the mind of a reasonable person in the position of the offeree an expectation that his acceptance will conclude a contract, then the communication is an offer. If it does not, then the communication is a preliminary negotiation. Initial communications between potential parties to a contract often take the form of preliminary negotiations, through which the parties either request or supply the terms of an offer that may or may not be given. A statement that may indicate a willingness to make an offer is not in itself an offer. If Terri writes to Susan, "Will you buy my automobile for $3,000?" and Susan replies "Yes," no contract exists. Terri has not made an offer to sell her automobile to Susan for $3,000. The offer or must manifest an intent to enter into a contract, not merely a willingness to enter into negotiation.

ADVERTISEMENTS Merchants desire to sell their merchandise and thus are interested in informing potential customers about the goods, terms of sale, and the price. But if they make widespread promises to sell to each person on their mailing list, the number of acceptances and resulting contracts might conceivably exceed their ability to perform. Consequently, a merchant might refrain from making offers by merely announcing that he has goods for sale, describing the goods, and quoting prices. He is simply inviting his customers and, in the case of published advertisements, the public, to make offers to him to buy the goods. His advertisements, circulars, quotation sheets, and merchandise displays are *not* offers because (1) they do not contain a promise and (2) they leave unexpressed many terms that would be necessary to the making of a contract. Accordingly, his customers' responses are not acceptances because he has made no offer to sell.

Nonetheless, a seller is not free to advertise goods at one price and then raise the price once demand has been stimulated. Although, as far as contract law is concerned, the seller has made no offer, such conduct is prohibited by the Federal Trade Commission as well as by legislation in many States. (See *Chapter 42*.)

Moreover, in some circumstances a public announcement or advertisement may constitute an offer if the advertisement or announcement contains a definite promise of something in exchange for something else and confers a power of acceptance upon a specified person or class of persons. The typical offer of a reward is an example of a definite offer, as was shown in *Lefkowitz v. Great Minneapolis Surplus Store, Inc.* In this case, the court held that a newspaper advertisement was an offer because it contained a promise of performance in definite terms in return for a requested act.

AUCTION SALES The auctioneer at an auction sale does *not* make offers to sell the property that is being auctioned but invites offers to buy. The classic statement by the auctioneer is, "How much am I offered?" The persons attending the auction may make progressively higher bids for the property, and each bid or statement of a price or a figure is an offer to buy at that figure. If the bid is accepted—this customarily is indicated by the fall of the hammer in the auctioneer's hand—a contract results. A bidder is free to withdraw his bid at any time prior to its acceptance. The auctioneer is likewise free to withdraw the goods from sale *unless* the sale is advertised or announced to be without reserve.

If the auction sale is advertised or announced in explicit terms to be **without reserve**, the auctioneer may not withdraw an article or lot put up for sale unless no bid is made within a reasonable time. Unless so advertised or announced, the sale is with reserve. A bidder at either type of sale may retract his bid at any time prior to acceptance by the auctioneer. Such retraction, however, does not revive any previous bid.

DEFINITENESS

The terms of a contract, all of which the offer usually contains, must be reasonably certain so as to provide a court with a basis for determining the existence of a breach and for giving an appropriate remedy. Restatement, Section 33. It is a fundamental policy that contracts should be made by the parties and not by the courts; accordingly, remedies for breach must have their basis in the parties' contract.

However, where the parties have intended to form a contract, the courts will attempt to find a basis for granting a remedy. Missing terms may be supplied by course of dealing, usage of trade, or inference. Thus, uncertainty as to incidental matters will seldom be fatal so long as the parties intended to form a contract. Nevertheless, the more terms the parties leave open, the less likely it is that they have intended to form a contract. Because of the great variety of contracts, the terms essential to all contracts cannot be stated. In most cases, however, material terms would include the parties, subject matter, price, quantity, quality, and time of performance.

OPEN TERMS With respect to agreements for the sale of goods, the Code provides standards by which omitted terms may be determined, provided the parties intended to enter into a binding contract. The Code provides missing terms in a number of instances, where, for example, the contract fails to specify the price, the time or place of delivery, or payment terms. Sections 2–204(3), 2–305, 2–308, 2–309, and 2–310. The Restatement, Section 34, has adopted an approach similar to the Code's in supplying terms the parties have omitted from their contract.

Under the Code, an offer for the purchase or sale of goods may leave open particulars of performance to be specified by one of the parties. Any such specification must be made in good faith and within limits set by commercial reasonableness. Section 2–311(1). **Good faith** is defined as honesty in fact in the conduct or transaction concerned. Section 1–201(19). Under the 2001 Revised UCC Article 1, good faith means honesty in fact and the observance of reasonable commercial standards of fair dealing. Section 1–201(20). Commercial reasonableness is a standard determined in terms of the business judgment of reasonable persons familiar with the practices customary in the type of transaction involved and in terms of the facts and circumstances of the case.

If the price is to be fixed otherwise than by agreement and is not so fixed through the fault of one of the parties, the other party has an option to treat the contract as cancelled or to fix a reasonable price in good faith for the goods. However, where the parties intend not to be bound unless the price is fixed or agreed upon as provided in the agreement, and it is not so fixed or agreed upon, the Code provides in accordance with the parties' intent that no contractual liability exists. In such case the seller must refund to the buyer any portion of the price she has received, and the buyer must return the goods to the seller or, if unable to do so, pay the reasonable value of the goods. Section 2–305(4).

OUTPUT AND REQUIREMENTS CONTRACTS A buyer's agreement to purchase the entire output of a seller's factory for a stated period, or a seller's agreement to supply a buyer with all his requirements for certain goods, may appear to lack definiteness and mutuality of obligation. Such an agreement does not specify the exact quantity of goods; moreover, the seller may have some control over her output and the buyer over his requirements. Nonetheless, under the Code and the Restatement such agreements are enforceable by the application of an objective standard based upon the good faith of both parties. Thus, a seller who operated her factory for eight hours a day before entering an output agreement cannot operate her factory twenty-four hours a day and insist that the buyer take all of the output. Nor can the buyer expand his business abnormally and insist that the seller still supply all of his requirements.

DURATION OF OFFERS

An offer confers upon the offeree a power of acceptance, which continues until the offer terminates. The ways in which an offer may be terminated, *other than by acceptance*, are through (1) lapse of time; (2) revocation; (3) rejection; (4) counteroffer; (5) death or incompetency of the offeror or offeree; (6) destruction of the subject matter to which the offer relates; and (7) subsequent illegality of the type of contract the offer proposes.

LAPSE OF TIME

The offeror may specify the time within which the offer is to be accepted, just as he may specify any other term or condition in the offer. He may require that the offeree accept the offer immediately or within a **specified** period, such as a week or ten days. Unless otherwise terminated, the offer remains open for the specified period. Upon the expiration of that time, the offer no longer exists and cannot be accepted. Any subsequent purported acceptance will serve as a new offer.

If the offer states no time within which the offeree must accept, the offer will terminate after a **reasonable** time. Determining a "reasonable" period of time is a question of fact, depending on the nature of the contract proposed, the usages of business, and other circumstances of the case (including whether the offer was communicated by electronic means). Restatement, Section 41. For instance, an offer to sell a perishable good would be open for a far shorter time than an offer to sell undeveloped real estate.

REVOCATION

An offeror generally may withdraw an offer at any time before it has been accepted, even though he has definitely promised to keep it open for a stated time. To be effective, notice of revocation of the offer must actually reach the offeree before she has accepted. If the offeror originally promises that the offer will be open for thirty days, but after five days wishes to terminate it, he may do so merely by giving the offeree notice that he is withdrawing the offer. Notice, which may be given by any means of communication, effectively terminates the offer when **received** by the offeree. A very few States, however, have adopted a rule that treats revocations the same as acceptances, thus making them effective upon dispatch. An offeror, however, may revoke an offer made to the general public only by giving to the revocation publicity equivalent to that given the offer.

Notice of revocation may be communicated indirectly to the offeree through reasonably reliable information from a third person that the offeror has disposed of the goods which he has offered for sale or has otherwise placed himself in a position which indicates an unwillingness or inability to perform the promise contained in the offer. Restatement, Section 43. For example, Jane offers to sell her portable television set to Bruce and tells Bruce that he has ten days in which to accept. One week later, Bruce observes the television set in Carl's house and is informed that Carl had purchased it from Jane. The next day Bruce sends to Jane an acceptance of the offer. There is no contract, because Jane's offer was effectively revoked when Bruce learned of Jane's inability to sell the television set to him because she had sold it to Carl.

Certain limitations, however, restrict the offeror's power to revoke the offer at any time prior to its acceptance. These limitations apply to the following five situations.

OPTION CONTRACTS

An option is a contract by which the offeror is bound to hold open an offer for a specified period of time. It must comply with all of the requirements of a contract, including *consideration* being given to the offeror by the offeree. (Consideration is discussed in *Chapter 12*.) For example, if Ann, in return for the payment of $500 to her by Bobby, grants Bobby an option, exercisable at any time within thirty days, to buy Blackacre at a price of $80,000, Ann's offer is irrevocable. Ann is legally bound to keep the offer open for thirty days, and any communication by Ann to Bobby giving notice of withdrawal of the offer is ineffective. Bobby is not bound to accept the offer, but the option contract entitles him to thirty days in which to accept.

FIRM OFFERS UNDER THE CODE The Code provides that a *merchant* is bound to keep an offer to buy or sell **goods** open for a stated period (or, if no time is stated, for a reasonable time) not exceeding three months, if the merchant gives assurance in a **signed writing** that the offer will be held open. Section 2–205. The Code, therefore, makes a merchant's written promise not to revoke an offer for a stated period enforceable even though no consideration is given to the offeror for that promise. A **merchant** is defined as a person (1) who is a dealer in goods of a given kind, (2) who by his occupation holds himself out as having knowledge or skill peculiar to the goods or practices involved, or (3) who employs an agent or broker whom he holds out as having such knowledge or skill. Section 2–104.

STATUTORY IRREVOCABILITY Certain offers, such as bids made to the State, municipality, or other governmental body for the construction of a building or some other public work, are made irrevocable by statute. Another example is preincorporation stock subscription agreements, which are irrevocable for a period of six months under many State incorporation statutes. See Section 6.20 of the Model Business Corporation Act (Appendix D).

IRREVOCABLE OFFERS OF UNILATERAL CONTRACTS Where an offer contemplates a unilateral contract, that is, a promise for an act, injustice to the offeree may result if revocation is permitted after the offeree has started to perform the act requested in the offer and has substantially but not completely accomplished it. Traditionally, such an offer is not accepted and no contract is formed until the offeree has *completed* the requested act. By simply commencing performance, the offeree does not bind himself to complete performance; nor, historically, did he bind the offeror to keep the offer open. Thus, the offeror could revoke the offer at any time prior to the offeree's completion of performance. For example, Linda offers Tom $300 if Tom will climb to the top of the flagpole in the center of campus. Tom commences his ascent, and when he is five feet from the top, Linda yells to him, "I revoke."

The Restatement deals with this problem by providing that where the performance of the requested act necessarily requires the offeree to expend time and effort, the offeror is obligated not to revoke the offer for a reasonable time. This obligation arises when the offeree begins performance. If, however, the offeror does not know of the offeree's performance and has no adequate means of learning of it within a reasonable time, the offeree must exercise reasonable diligence to notify the offeror of the performance.

PROMISSORY ESTOPPEL As discussed in the previous chapter, a noncontractual promise may be enforced when it is made under circumstances that should lead the promisor reasonably to expect that the promise will induce the promisee to take action in reliance on it. This doctrine has been used in some cases to prevent an offeror from revoking an offer prior to its acceptance. The Restatement provides the following rule:

> An offer which the offeror should reasonably expect to induce action or forbearance of a substantial character on the part of the offeree before acceptance and which does induce such action or forbearance is binding as an option contract to the extent necessary to avoid injustice. Restatement, Section 87(2).

Thus, Ramanan Plumbing Co. submits a written offer for plumbing work to be used by Resolute Building Co. as part of Resolute's bid as a general contractor. Ramanan knows that Resolute is relying on Ramanan's bid, and in fact Resolute submits Ramanan's name as the plumbing subcontractor in the bid. Ramanan's offer is irrevocable until Resolute has a reasonable opportunity to notify Ramanan that Resolute's bid has been accepted.

REJECTION

An offeree is at liberty to accept or reject the offer as he sees fit. If the offeree decides not to accept it, he is not required to reject it formally but may simply wait until the offer terminates by the lapse of time. Through a **rejection** of an offer, the offeree manifests his unwillingness to accept. A communicated rejection terminates the power of acceptance. From the effective moment of rejection, which is the **receipt** of the rejection by the offeror, the offeree may no longer accept the offer. Rejection by the offeree may consist of express language or may be implied from language or from conduct.

COUNTEROFFER

A **counteroffer** is a counterproposal from the offeree to the offeror that indicates a willingness to contract but upon terms or conditions different from those contained in the offer. It is not an unequivocal acceptance of the original offer and, by indicating an unwillingness to agree to the terms of the offer, it operates as a rejection. It also operates as a new offer. For instance, assume that Jordan writes Chris a letter stating that he will sell to Chris a secondhand color television set for $300. Chris replies that she will pay Jordan $250 for the set. This is a counteroffer that, upon **receipt** by Jordan, terminates the original offer. Jordan may, if he wishes, accept the counteroffer and thereby create a contract for $250. If, on the other hand, Chris states in her reply that she wishes to consider the $300 offer but is willing to pay $250 at once for the set, she is making a counteroffer that does *not* terminate Jordan's original offer. In the first instance, after making the $250 counteroffer, Chris may not accept the $300 offer. In the second instance she may do so, as the manner in which she stated the counteroffer did not indicate an unwillingness to accept the original offer, and Chris therefore did not terminate it. In addition, a mere inquiry about the possibility of obtaining different or new terms is not a counteroffer and does not terminate the offer.

Another common type of counteroffer is the **conditional acceptance**, which purports to accept the offer but expressly makes the acceptance conditional upon the offeror's assent to additional or different terms. Nonetheless, it is a counteroffer and terminates the original offer. The Code's treatment of acceptances containing terms that vary from the offer are discussed later in this chapter.

DEATH OR INCOMPETENCY

The death or incompetency of either the offeror or the offeree ordinarily terminates an offer. Upon his death or incompetency the offeror no longer has the legal capacity to enter into a contract; thus, all his outstanding offers are terminated. Death or incompetency of the offeree likewise terminates the offer, because an ordinary offer is not assignable (transferable) and may be accepted only by the person to whom it was made. When the offeree dies or ceases to have legal capability to enter into a contract, no one else has the power to accept the offer. Therefore, the offer terminates.

The death or incompetency of the offeror or offeree, however, does *not* terminate an offer contained in an option.

DESTRUCTION OF SUBJECT MATTER

Destruction of the specific subject matter of an offer terminates the offer. The impossibility of performance prevents a contract from being consummated and thus terminates all outstanding offers with respect to the destroyed property. Suppose that Martina, owning a Buick automobile, offers to sell the car to Worthy and allows Worthy five days in which to accept. Three days later the car is destroyed by fire. On the following day, Worthy, without knowledge of the car's destruction, notifies Martina that he accepts her offer. There is no contract. Martina's offer was terminated by the destruction of the car.

SUBSEQUENT ILLEGALITY

One of the four essential requirements of a contract, as previously mentioned, is legality of purpose or subject matter. If performance of a valid contract is subsequently made illegal, the obligations of both parties under the contract are discharged. Illegality taking effect after the making of an offer but prior to acceptance has the same effect: the offer is legally terminated.

ACCEPTANCE

The acceptance of an offer is essential to the formation of a contract. Once an acceptance has been given, the contract is formed. An acceptance can only be made by an offeree. Acceptance of an offer for a bilateral contract requires some overt act by which the offeree manifests his assent to the terms of the offer, such as speaking or sending a letter, a telegram, or other explicit or implicit communication to the offeror. If the offer is for a unilateral contract, the offeree may refrain from acting as requested or may signify acceptance through performance of the requested act with the intention of accepting. For example, if Joy publishes an offer of a reward to anyone who returns the diamond ring which she has lost (a unilateral contract offer), and Steven, with knowledge of the offer, finds and returns the ring to Joy, Steven has accepted the offer. If, however, Steven returns the ring to Joy but in doing so disclaims the reward and says that he does not accept the offer, there is no contract. Without the intention of accepting the offer, merely doing the act requested by the offeror is not sufficient to form a contract.

A late or defective acceptance does not create a contract. After the offer has expired, it cannot be validly accepted. A late or defective acceptance, however, does manifest the offeree's willingness to enter into a contract and therefore constitutes a new offer. To create a contract based upon this offer, the original offeror must accept the new offer by manifesting his assent.

COMMUNICATION OF ACCEPTANCE

GENERAL RULE

Because acceptance manifests the offeree's assent to the offer, the offeree must communicate this acceptance to the offeror. This is the rule as to all offers to enter into bilateral contracts. In the case of an offer to enter into a unilateral contract, however, notice of acceptance to the offeror is usually not required. If, however, the offeree in a unilateral contract has reason to know that the offeror has no adequate means of learning of the performance with reasonable promptness and certainty, then the offeree must make reasonable efforts to notify the offeror of acceptance or lose the right to enforce the contract. Restatement, Section 54.

◆ **FIGURE 10-1: Mutual Assent**

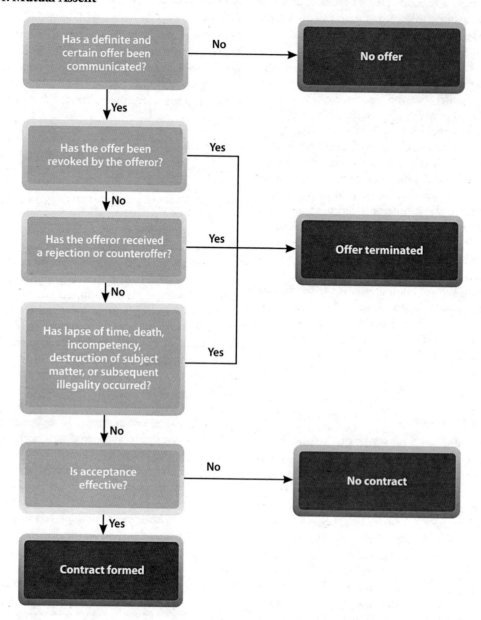

SILENCE AS ACCEPTANCE

An offeree is generally under no legal duty to reply to an offer. Silence or inaction, therefore, does *not* indicate acceptance of the offer. By custom, usage, or course of dealing, however, silence or inaction by the offeree may operate as an acceptance.

Thus, the silence or inaction of an offeree who fails to reply to an offer operates as an acceptance and causes a contract to be formed. Through previous dealings, the offeree has given the offeror reason to understand that the offeree will accept all offers unless the offeree sends notice to the contrary. Another example of silence operating as an acceptance occurs when the prospective member of a mail-order club agrees that his failure to return a notification card

rejecting offered goods will constitute his acceptance of the club's offer to sell the goods.

Furthermore, if an offeror sends unordered or unsolicited merchandise to a person stating that she may purchase the goods at a specified price and that the offer will be deemed to have been accepted unless the goods are returned within a stated period of time, the offer is one for an inverted unilateral contract (i.e., an act for a promise). This practice led to abuse, however, which has prompted the Federal government as well as most States to enact statutes which provide that in such cases the offeree-recipient of the goods may keep them as a gift and is under no obligation either to return them or to pay for them.

EFFECTIVE MOMENT

As previously discussed, an offer, a revocation, a rejection, and a counteroffer are effective when they are *received*. An acceptance, on the other hand, is generally effective upon **dispatch**. This is true unless the offer specifically provides otherwise, the offeree uses an unauthorized means of communication, or the acceptance follows a prior rejection.

STIPULATED PROVISIONS IN THE OFFER If the offer specifically stipulates the means of communication the offeree is to use, the acceptance, to be effective, must conform to that specification. Thus, if an offer states that acceptance must be made by registered mail, any purported acceptance not made by registered mail would be ineffective. Moreover, the rule that an acceptance is effective when dispatched or sent does not apply where the offer provides that the offeror must receive the acceptance. If the offeror states that a reply must be received by a certain date or that he must hear from the offeree or uses other language indicating that the acceptance must be received by him, the effective moment of the acceptance is when the offeror receives it, not when the offeree sends or dispatches it.

AUTHORIZED MEANS Historically, an authorized means of communication was the means the offeror expressly authorized in the offer, or, if none was authorized, it was the means the offeror used. For example, if in reply to an offer by mail, the offeree places in the mail a letter of acceptance properly stamped and addressed to the offeror, a contract is formed at the time and place that the offeree mails the letter. This assumes, of course, that the offer at that time was open and had not been terminated by any of the methods previously discussed. The reason for this rule is that the offeror, by using the mail, impliedly authorized the offeree to use the same method of communication. It is immaterial if the letter of acceptance goes astray in the mail and is never received.

The Restatement, Section 30, and the Code, Section 2–206(1)(a), both now provide that where the language in the offer or the circumstances do not otherwise indicate, an offer to make a contract shall be construed as authorizing acceptance in any **reasonable** manner. These provisions are intended to allow flexibility of response and the ability to keep pace with new modes of communication.

◆ **SEE FIGURE 10-1: Mutual Assent**

UNAUTHORIZED MEANS When the offeree uses an unauthorized method of communication, the traditional rule is that acceptance is effective when and if received by the offeror, provided that he receives it within the time during which the authorized means would have arrived. The Restatement, Section 67, provides that if these conditions are met, the effective time for the acceptance relates back to the moment of dispatch.

ACCEPTANCE FOLLOWING A PRIOR REJECTION An acceptance sent after a prior rejection is not effective when sent by the offeree, but is only effective when and if the offeror receives it before he receives the rejection. Thus, when an acceptance follows a prior rejection, the first communication to be received by the offeror is the effective one. For example, Anna in New York sends by mail to Fritz in San Francisco an offer that is expressly stated to be open for one week. On the fourth day, Fritz sends to Anna by mail a letter of rejection that is delivered on the morning of the sixth day. At noon on the fifth day, however, Fritz had dispatched a telegram of acceptance that is received by Anna before the close of business on that day. A contract was formed when Anna received Fritz's telegram of acceptance, as it was received before the letter of rejection.

◆ **SEE FIGURE 10-2: Offer and Acceptance**

VARIANT ACCEPTANCES

A variant acceptance—one that contains terms different from or additional to those in the offer—receives distinctly different treatment under the common law and the Code.

◆ **FIGURE 10-2: Offer and Acceptance**

	Time Effective	Effect
Communications by Offeror		
• Offer	Received by offeree	Creates power to form a contract
• Revocation	Received by offeree	Terminates offer
Communications by Offeree		
• Rejection	Received by offeror	Terminates offer
• Counteroffer	Received by offeror	Terminates offer
• Acceptance	Sent by offeree	Forms a contract
• Acceptance after prior rejection	Received by offeror	If received before rejection forms a contract

COMMON LAW

An acceptance must be *positive* and *unequivocal*. In that it may not change, add to, subtract from, or qualify in any way the provisions of the offer, it must be the **mirror image** of the offer. Any communication by the offeree that attempts to modify the offer is not an acceptance but is a counteroffer, which does not create a contract.

CODE

The Code modifies the common law "mirror image" rule, by which the acceptance cannot vary or deviate from the terms of the offer. This modification is necessitated by the realities of modern business practices. A vast number of business transactions use standardized business forms. For example, a merchant buyer sends to a merchant seller on the buyer's order form a purchase order for 1,000 dozen cotton shirts at $60.00 per dozen, with delivery by October 1 at the buyer's place of business. On the reverse side of this standard form are twenty-five numbered paragraphs containing provisions generally favorable to the buyer. When the seller receives the buyer's order, he agrees to the quantity, price, and delivery terms and sends to the buyer on his acceptance form an unequivocal acceptance of the offer. However, on the back of his acceptance form, the seller has thirty-two numbered paragraphs generally favorable to himself and in significant conflict with the buyer's form. Under the common law's *mirror image* rule, no contract would exist, for the seller has not accepted unequivocally all the material terms of the buyer's offer.

The Code in Section 2–207 attempts to alleviate this **battle of the forms** by focusing upon the intent of the parties. If the offeree expressly makes her acceptance conditioned upon assent to the additional or different terms, no contract is formed. If the offeree does not expressly make her acceptance conditional upon the offeror's assent to the additional or different terms, a contract is formed. The issue then becomes whether the offeree's different or additional terms may become part of the contract. If both offeror and offeree are merchants, such *additional* terms may become part of the contract, provided they do not materially alter the agreement and are not objected to either in the offer itself or within a reasonable period of time. If both parties are not merchants or if the additional terms materially alter the offer, then the additional terms are merely construed as proposals to the contract. *Different* terms proposed by the offeree will not become part of the contract unless the offeror accepts them. The courts are divided over what terms a contract includes when those terms differ or conflict. Some courts hold that the offeror's terms govern; other courts, holding that the terms cancel each other out, look to the Code to provide the missing terms. Some follow a third alternative and apply the additional terms test to different terms. (See *Figure 21-4* in *Chapter 21*.)

To apply Section 2–207 to the example above: because both parties are merchants and the acceptance was not conditional upon assent to the additional or different terms, (1) the contract will be formed without the seller's different terms unless the buyer specifically accepts them; (2) the contract will be formed without the seller's additional terms unless (a) the buyer specifically accepts them or (b) they do not materially alter the offer and the buyer does not object; and (3) depending upon the jurisdiction, either (a) the buyer's conflicting terms are included in the contract or (b) the Code provides the missing terms, as the conflicting terms cancel each other out, or (c) the additional terms test is applied.

CHAPTER SUMMARY

OFFER

ESSENTIALS OF AN OFFER	**Definition** indication of willingness to enter into a contract
	Communication offeree must have knowledge of the offer and the offer must be made by the offeror to the offeree
	Intent determined by an objective standard of what a reasonable offeree would have believed
	Definiteness offer's terms must be clear enough to provide a court with a basis for giving an appropriate remedy
DURATION OF OFFERS	**Lapse of Time** offer remains open for the time period specified or, if no time is stated, for a reasonable period of time
	Revocation generally, an offer may be terminated at any time before it is accepted, subject to the following exceptions
	• *Option Contract* contract that binds offeror to keep an offer open for a specified time
	• *Firm Offer* a merchant's irrevocable offer to sell or buy goods in a signed writing ensures that the offer will not be terminated for up to three months

- *Statutory Irrevocability* offer made irrevocable by statute
- *Irrevocable Offer of Unilateral Contract* a unilateral offer may not be revoked for a reasonable time after performance is begun
- *Promissory Estoppel* noncontractual promise that binds the promisor because she should reasonably expect that the promise will induce the promisee (offeree) to take action in reliance on it

Rejection refusal to accept an offer terminates the power of acceptance

Counteroffer counterproposal to an offer that generally terminates the original offer

Death or Incompetency of either the offeror or the offeree terminates the offer

Destruction of Subject Matter of an offer terminates the offer

Subsequent Illegality of the purpose or subject matter of the offer terminates the offer

ACCEPTANCE OF OFFER

REQUIREMENTS	**Definition** positive and unequivocal expression of a willingness to enter into a contract on the terms of the offer **Mirror Image Rule** except as modified by the Code, an acceptance cannot deviate from the terms of the offer
COMMUNICATION OF ACCEPTANCE	**General Rule** acceptance effective upon dispatch unless the offer specifically provides otherwise or the offeree uses an unauthorized means of communication **Stipulated Provisions** the communication of acceptance must conform to the specification in the offer **Authorized Means** the Restatement and the Code provide that unless the offer provides otherwise, acceptance is authorized to be in any reasonable manner **Unauthorized Means** acceptance effective when received, provided that it is received within the time within which the authorized means would have arrived **Acceptance Following a Prior Rejection** first communication received by the offeror is effective **Defective Acceptance** does not create a contract but serves as a new offer

CHAPTER 11

Conduct Invalidating Assent

The preceding chapter considered one of the essential requirements of a contract, namely, the objective manifestation of mutual assent by each party to the other. In addition to requiring that the offer and acceptance be satisfied, the law demands that the agreement be voluntary and knowing. If these requirements are not met, then the agreement is either voidable or void. This chapter deals with situations in which the consent manifested by one of the parties to the contract is not effective because it was not knowingly and voluntarily given. These situations are considered under the headings of duress, undue influence, fraud, nonfraudulent misrepresentation, and mistake.

DURESS

A person should not be held to an agreement into which she has not entered voluntarily. Accordingly, the law will not enforce any contract induced by **duress**, which in general is any wrongful or unlawful act or threat that overcomes the free will of a party.

PHYSICAL COMPULSION

There are two basic types of duress. The first occurs when one party compels another to manifest assent to a contract through actual **physical force**, such as pointing a gun at a person or taking a person's hand and compelling him to sign a written contract. This type of duress, while extremely rare, renders the agreement **void**. Restatement, Section 174(1).

IMPROPER THREATS

The second type of duress involves the use of improper threats or acts, *including economic and social coercion*, to compel a person to enter into a contract. The threat may be explicit or may be inferred from words or conduct; in either case, it must leave the victim with no reasonable alternative. This type of duress makes the contract **voidable** at the option of the coerced party. Restatement, Section 175(2).

For example, if Lance, a landlord, induces Tamara, an infirm, bedridden tenant, to enter into a new lease on the same apartment at a greatly increased rent by wrongfully threatening to terminate Tamara's lease and evict her, Tamara can escape or *avoid* the new lease by reason of the duress exerted upon her.

With respect to the second and more common type of duress, the fact that the act or threat would not affect a person of average strength and intelligence is not determinative if it places the particular person in fear and induces him to perform an action against his will. The test is *subjective*, and the question is, did the threat actually induce assent on the part of the person claiming to be the victim of duress? Threats that would suffice to induce assent by one person may not suffice to induce assent by another. All circumstances must be considered, including the age, background, and relationship of the parties. Restatement, Section 175. Indeed, as Comment c to this section of the Restatement states,

> Persons of a weak or cowardly nature are the very ones that need protection; the courageous can usually protect themselves. Timid and inexperienced persons are particularly subject to threats, and it does not lie in the mouths of the unscrupulous to excuse their imposition on such persons on the ground of their victims' infirmities.

Ordinarily, the acts or threats constituting duress are themselves crimes or torts. But this is not true in all cases. The acts need not be criminal or tortious to be *wrongful*; they merely need to be contrary to public policy or morally reprehensible. For example, if the threat involves a breach of a contractual duty of good faith and fair dealing or the use of the civil process in bad faith, it is improper.

Moreover, the courts have generally held that contracts induced by threats of criminal prosecution are voidable, regardless of whether the coerced party had committed an unlawful act. Likewise, threatening the criminal prosecution of a near relative, such as a son or husband, is duress, regardless of the guilt or innocence of the relative.

To be distinguished from such threats of prosecution are threats to resort to ordinary civil remedies to recover a debt due from another. Threatening to bring a civil suit against an individual to recover a debt is not wrongful. What is prohibited is threatening to bring a civil suit when bringing such a suit would be abuse of process.

UNDUE INFLUENCE

Undue influence is the unfair persuasion of a person by a party generally in a dominant position based upon a **confidential relationship**. The law very carefully scrutinizes contracts between those in a relationship of trust and confidence that is likely to permit one party to take unfair advantage of the other. Examples are the relationships of guardian-ward, trustee-beneficiary, principal-agent, spouses to each other, parent-child, attorney-client, physician-patient, and clergy-parishioner.

A transaction induced by unfair influence on the part of the dominant party is **voidable**. The ultimate question in undue influence cases is whether the dominant party induced the transaction by influencing a freely exercised and competent judgment or by dominating the mind or emotions of a submissive party. The weakness or dependence of the person persuaded is a strong indicator of the fairness or unfairness of the persuasion. For example, Ronald, a person without business experience, has for years relied in business matters on the advice of Nancy, who is experienced in business. Nancy, without making any false representations of fact, induces Ronald to enter into a contract with Nancy's confederate, George. The contract, however, is disadvantageous to Ronald, as both Nancy and George know. The transaction is voidable on the grounds of undue influence.

Undue influence, as previously mentioned, generally arises in the context of relationships in which one person is in a position of dominance, or is likely to be. Where such a relationship exists at the time of the transaction, and it appears that the dominant party has gained at the other party's expense, the transaction is presumed to be voidable. For example, in a legally challenged contract between a guardian and his ward, the law presumes that advantage was taken by the guardian. It is, therefore, incumbent upon the guardian to rebut this presumption. Important factors in determining whether a contract is fair are (1) whether the dominant party made full disclosure of all relevant information known to him, (2) whether the consideration was adequate, and (3) whether the dependent party received competent and independent advice before completing the transaction. Without limitation, in every situation in which a confidential relationship exists, the dominant party is held to utmost good faith in his dealings with the other.

FRAUD

Another factor affecting the validity of consent given by a contracting party is fraud, which prevents assent from being knowingly given. There are two distinct types of fraud: fraud in the execution and fraud in the inducement.

FRAUD IN THE EXECUTION

Fraud in the execution, which is extremely rare, consists of a misrepresentation that deceives the defrauded person as to the very nature of the contract. Such fraud occurs when a person does not know, or does not have reasonable opportunity to know, the character or essence of a proposed contract because the other party misrepresents its character or essential terms. Fraud in the execution renders the transaction **void**.

For example, Abigail delivers a package to Boris, requests that Boris sign a receipt for it, holds out a simple printed form headed "Receipt," and indicates the line on which Boris is to sign. This line, which to Boris appears to be the bottom line of the receipt, is actually the signature line of a promissory note cleverly concealed underneath the receipt. Boris signs where directed without knowing that he is signing a note. This is fraud in the execution. The note is void and of no legal effect because Boris has not actually given his assent, even though his signature is genuine and appears to manifest his assent to the terms of the note. The nature of Abigail's fraud precluded consent to the signing of the note because it prevented Boris from reasonably knowing what he was signing.

FRAUD IN THE INDUCEMENT

Fraud in the inducement, generally referred to as fraud or deceit, is an intentional misrepresentation of material fact by one party to the other, who consents to enter into a contract in justifiable reliance upon the misrepresentation. Fraud in the inducement renders the contract **voidable** by the defrauded party. For example, Ada, in offering to sell her dog to Ben, tells Ben that the dog won first prize in its class in a recent national dog show. In fact, the dog had not even been entered in the show. Nonetheless, Ada's statement induces Ben to accept the offer and pay a high price for the dog. A contract exists, but it is voidable by Ben because of Ada's fraud, which induced his assent.

The requisites for fraud in the inducement are as follows:

1. a false representation
2. of a fact
3. that is material and

4. made with knowledge of its falsity and the intention to deceive (scienter) and

5. which representation is justifiably relied upon.

FALSE REPRESENTATION A basic element of fraud is a false representation or misrepresentation; that is, an assertion not in accord with the facts, made through positive statement or conduct that misleads. **Concealment** is an action intended or known to be likely to keep another from learning of a fact of which he otherwise would have learned. Active concealment is a form of misrepresentation that can form the basis for fraud, as where a seller puts heavy oil or grease in a car engine to conceal a knock. Truth may be suppressed by concealment as much as by misrepresentation.

Expressly denying knowledge of a fact which a party knows to exist is a misrepresentation if it leads the other party to believe that the facts do not exist or cannot be discovered. Moreover, a statement of misleading half-truth is considered the equivalent of a false representation.

As a general rule, **silence** or nondisclosure alone does *not* amount to fraud. A seller generally is not obligated to tell a purchaser everything he knows about the subject of a sale. Thus, it is not fraud when a buyer possesses advantageous information about the seller's property, of which he knows the seller to be ignorant, and does not disclose such information to the seller. Likewise, a buyer is under no duty to inform a seller of the greater value or other advantages of his property. Assume that Sid owns a farm that, as a farm, is worth $10,000. Brenda knows that there is oil under Sid's farm and knows that Sid is ignorant of this fact. Brenda, without disclosing this information to Sid, makes an offer to Sid to buy the farm for $10,000. Sid accepts the offer, and a contract is duly made. Sid, on later learning the facts, can do nothing about the matter, either at law or in equity. As one case puts it, "a purchaser is not bound by our laws to make the man he buys from as wise as himself."

Although nondisclosure usually does not constitute a misrepresentation, in certain situations it does. One such situation arises when (1) a person fails to disclose a fact known to him, (2) he knows that the disclosure of that fact would correct a mistake of the other party as to a basic assumption on which that party is making the contract, and (3) nondisclosure of the fact amounts to a failure to act in a good faith and in accordance with reasonable standards of fair dealing. Restatement, Section 161. Accordingly, if the property at issue in the contract possesses a substantial latent (hidden) defect, one that the buyer would not discover by an ordinary examination, the seller may be obliged to reveal it. Suppose, for example, that Judith owns a valuable horse, which Judith knows is suffering from a disease only a competent veterinary surgeon might detect. Judith offers to sell this horse to Curt, but does not inform Curt about the condition of the horse. Curt makes a reasonable examination of the horse and, finding it in apparently normal condition, purchases it from Judith. Curt, on later discovering the disease in question, can have the sale set aside. Judith's silence, under the circumstances, was a misrepresentation.

There are other situations in which the law imposes a duty of disclosure. For example, one may have a duty of disclosure because of prior representations, innocently made before entering into the contract, which are later discovered to be untrue. Another instance in which silence may constitute fraud is a transaction involving a fiduciary. A **fiduciary** is a person in a confidential relationship who owes a duty of trust, loyalty, and confidence to another. For example, an agent owes a fiduciary duty to his principal, as does a trustee to the beneficiary of a trust and a partner to her copartners. A fiduciary may not deal at *arm's length* but rather owes a duty to make full disclosure of all relevant facts when entering into a transaction with the other party to the relationship. In contrast, in most everyday business or market transactions, the parties are said to deal at "arm's length," meaning that they deal with each other on equal terms.

FACT The basic element of fraud is the misrepresentation of a material fact. A **fact** is an event that actually took place or a thing that actually exists. Suppose that Dale induces Mike to purchase shares in a company unknown to Mike at a price of $100 per share by representing that she had paid $150 per share for them during the preceding year, when in fact she had paid only $50. This representation of a past event is a misrepresentation of fact.

Actionable fraud rarely can be based on what is merely a statement of **opinion**. A representation is one of opinion if it expresses only the uncertain belief of the representer as to the existence of a fact or his judgment as to quality, value, authenticity, or other matters of judgment.

The line between fact and opinion is not an easy one to draw and in close cases presents an issue for the jury. The solution will often turn on the superior knowledge of the person making the statement and the information available to the other party. Thus, if Dale said to Mike that the shares were "a good investment," she is merely stating her opinion, and in the usual case Mike ought to regard it as no more than that. Other common examples of opinion are statements of value, such as "This is the best car for the money in town" or "This deluxe model will give you twice the wear of a cheaper model." Such exaggerations and commendations of articles offered for sale are to be expected from dealers, who are merely puffing their wares with sales talk. If, however, the representer is a professional advising a client, the courts are more likely to regard as actionable an untrue statement of opinion. When the person expressing the opinion is one who holds himself out as having expert knowledge, the tendency is to grant relief to those who have sustained loss through reasonable reliance upon the expert evaluation.

Also to be distinguished from a representation of fact is a **prediction** of the future. Predictions, which are similar to opinions in that no one can know with certainty what will happen in the future, normally are not regarded as factual statements. Likewise, promissory statements ordinarily do not constitute a basis of fraud, as a breach of promise does not necessarily indicate that the promise was fraudulently made. A promise that the promisor, at the time of making, had no intention of keeping, however, is a misrepresentation of fact. Most courts take the position that a misrepresented state of mind "is as much a fact as the state of a person's digestion." *Edgington v. Fitzmaurice,* 29 Ch.D. 459 (1885). If a dealer promises, "I will service this machine free for the next year," but at the time has no intention of doing so, his conduct is actionable if the other elements of fraud are present.

Historically, courts held that representations of **law** were not statements of fact but rather of opinion. The present trend is to recognize that a statement of law may have either the effect of a statement of fact or a statement of opinion. Restatement, Torts, Section 545. For example, a statement of law asserting that a particular statute has been enacted or repealed has the effect of a statement of fact. On the other hand, a statement as to the legal consequences of a particular set of facts is a statement of opinion. Nonetheless, such a statement may imply that the facts known to the maker are consistent with the legal conclusion stated. For example, an assertion that a company has the legal right to do business in a State may include the assurance that the company has taken all the steps required to be duly qualified. Moreover, a statement by one who is learned in the law, such as a practicing attorney, may be considered a statement of fact.

MATERIALITY In addition to being a misrepresentation of fact, a misrepresentation also must be material. A misrepresentation is **material** if (1) it would be likely to induce a reasonable person to manifest his assent or (2) the maker knows that it would be likely to induce the recipient to do so. Restatement, Section 162. In the sale of a racehorse, whether a certain jockey rode the horse in its most recent race may not be material, but its running time for the race probably would be. The Restatement of Contracts provides that a contract justifiably induced by a misrepresentation is voidable if the misrepresentation is either fraudulent *or* material. Therefore, a fraudulent misrepresentation does not have to be material for the recipient to obtain rescission, but it must be material if she is to recover damages. Restatement, Section 164; Restatement, Torts, Section 538.

KNOWLEDGE OF FALSITY AND INTENTION TO DECEIVE To establish fraud, the misrepresentation must have been known by the one making it to be false and must have been made with an intent to deceive. This element of fraud is known as *scienter.* Knowledge of falsity can consist of (1) actual knowledge, (2) lack of belief in the statement's truthfulness, or (3) reckless indifference as to its truthfulness.

JUSTIFIABLE RELIANCE A person is not entitled to relief unless he has justifiably relied upon the misrepresentation. If the misrepresentation in no way influenced the complaining party's decision, he must abide by the terms of the contract. He is not deceived if he does not rely. Justifiable reliance requires that the misrepresentation contribute substantially to the misled party's decision to enter into the contract. If the complaining party knew or it was obvious that the defendant's representation was untrue, but he still entered into the contract, he has not justifiably relied. Moreover, where the misrepresentation is fraudulent, the party who relies on it is entitled to relief even though he does not investigate the statement or is contributorily negligent in relying on it. Restatement, Torts, Sections 540, 545A. Not knowing or discovering the facts before making a contract does not constitute unjustified reliance unless it amounts to a failure to act in good faith and in accordance with reasonable standards of fair dealing. Restatement, Section 172. Thus, most courts will not allow a person who concocts a deliberate and elaborate scheme to defraud—one that the defrauded party should readily detect—to argue that the defrauded party did not justifiably rely upon the misrepresentation.

NONFRAUDULENT MISREPRESENTATION

Nonfraudulent misrepresentation is a material, false statement that induces another to rely justifiably but is made without *scienter.*

Negligent misrepresentation is a false representation that is made without due care in ascertaining its truthfulness. **Innocent misrepresentation** is a false representation made without knowledge of its falsity but with due care. To obtain relief for nonfraudulent misrepresentation, all of the other elements of fraud must be present *and* the misrepresentation must be material. The remedies that may be available for nonfraudulent misrepresentation are rescission and damages (see *Chapter 18*).

◆ **SEE FIGURE 11-1: Misrepresentation**

MISTAKE

A **mistake** is a belief that is not in accord with the facts. Where the mistaken facts relate to the basis of the parties' agreement, the law permits the adversely affected party to

◆ **FIGURE 11-1: Misrepresentation**

	Fraudulent	Negligent	Innocent
False statement of fact	Yes	Yes	Yes
Materiality	Yes for damages No for rescission	Yes	Yes
Fault	Scienter	Without due care (knowledge and intent)	Without due care and knowledge
Reliance	Yes	Yes	Yes
Injury	Yes for damages No for rescission	Yes for damages No for rescission	Yes for damages No for rescission
Remedies	Damages Rescission	Damages Rescission	Damages Rescission

avoid or reform the contract under certain circumstances. But because permitting avoidance for mistake undermines the objective approach to mutual assent, the law has experienced considerable difficulty in specifying those circumstances that justify permitting the subjective matter of mistake to invalidate an otherwise objectively satisfactory agreement. As a result, establishing clear rules to govern the effect of mistake has proven elusive.

The Restatement and modern cases treat mistakes of law in existence at the time of making a contract no differently than mistakes of fact. For example, Susan contracts to sell a parcel of land to James with the mutual understanding that James will build an apartment house on the land. Both Susan and James believe that such a building is lawful. Unknown to them, however, the town in which the land is located had enacted an ordinance precluding such use of the land three days before they entered into the contract. This mistake of law, which the courts would treat as a mistake of fact, would lead to the consequences discussed below.

MUTUAL MISTAKE

Mutual mistake occurs when *both* parties are mistaken as to the same set of facts. If the mistake relates to a basic assumption on which the contract is made and has a material effect on the agreed exchange, then it is **voidable** by the adversely affected party unless he bears the risk of the mistake. Restatement, Section 152.

Usually, market conditions and the financial situation of the parties are not considered basic assumptions. Thus, if Gail contracts to purchase Pete's automobile under the belief that she can sell it at a profit to Jesse, she is not excused from liability if she is mistaken in this belief. Nor can she rescind the agreement simply because she was mistaken as to her estimate of what the automobile was worth. These are the ordinary risks of business, and courts do not undertake to relieve against them. But suppose that the parties contract upon the assumption that the automobile is a 1993 Cadillac with fifteen thousand miles of use, when in fact the engine is that of a cheaper model and has been run in excess of fifty thousand miles. Here, a court would likely allow a rescission because of mutual mistake of a material fact. Another example of mutual mistake of fact was presented in a California case where a noted violinist purchased two violins from a collector for $8,000, the bill of sale reading, "I have on this date sold to Mr. Efrem Zimbalist one Joseph Guarnerius violin and one Stradivarius violin dated 1717." Actually, unknown to either party, neither violin was genuine. Taken together they were worth no more than $300. The sale was voidable by the purchaser for mutual mistake. In a New Zealand case, the plaintiff purchased a "stud bull" at an auction. There were no express warranties as to "sex, condition, or otherwise." Actually, the bull was sterile. Rescission was allowed, with the court observing that it was a "bull in name only."

UNILATERAL MISTAKE

Unilateral mistake occurs when only one of the parties is mistaken. Courts have been hesitant to grant relief for unilateral mistake even though it relates to a basic assumption on which the party entered into the contract and has a material effect on the agreed exchange. Nevertheless, relief will be granted where the nonmistaken party knows, or reasonably should know, that such a mistake has been made (palpable unilateral mistake) or where the mistake was caused by the fault of the nonmistaken party. For example, suppose a building contractor makes a serious error in his computations and as a result submits a bid on a job that is one-half the amount it should be. If the other party knows that he made such an error, or reasonably should have known, she cannot, as a general rule, take advantage of the other's mistake by accepting the offer. In addition, many courts and the Restatement allow rescission where the effect of the unilateral mistake makes enforcement of the contract unconscionable. Section 153.

ASSUMPTION OF RISK OF MISTAKE

A party who has undertaken to bear the risk of a mistake will be unable to avoid the contract, even though the mistake (which may be either mutual or unilateral) otherwise would have permitted her to do so. This allocation of risk may occur by agreement of the parties. For instance, a ship at sea may be sold "lost or not lost." In such case the buyer is liable whether the ship was lost or not lost at the time the contract was made. There is no mistake; instead, there is a conscious allocation of risk.

Conscious ignorance may serve to allocate the risk of mistake when the parties recognize that they have limited knowledge of the facts. For example, the Supreme Court of Wisconsin refused to set aside the sale of a stone for which the purchaser paid one dollar, but which was subsequently discovered to be an uncut diamond valued at $700. The parties did not know at the time of sale what the stone was and knew they did not know. Each consciously assumed the risk that the value might be more or less than the selling price.

EFFECT OF FAULT UPON MISTAKE

The Restatement provides that a mistaken party's fault in not knowing or discovering a fact before making a contract does not prevent him from avoiding the contract "unless his fault amounts to a failure to act in good faith and in accordance with reasonable standards of fair dealing." Restatement, Section 157. This rule does not, however, apply to a failure to read a contract. As a general proposition, a party is held to what she signs. Her signature authenticates the writing, and she cannot repudiate that which she has voluntarily approved. Generally, one who assents to a writing is presumed to know its contents and cannot escape being bound by its terms merely by contending that she did not read them; her assent is deemed to cover unknown as well as known terms. Restatement, Section 157, Comment b.

MISTAKE IN MEANING OF TERMS

Somewhat related to mistakes of facts is the situation in which the parties misunderstand the meaning of one another's manifestations of mutual assent. A famous case involving this problem is *Raffles v. Wichelhaus*, 2 Hurlstone & Coltman 906 (1864), popularly known as the "*Peerless* Case." A contract of purchase was made for 125 bales of cotton to arrive on the *Peerless* from Bombay. It happened, however, that there were two ships by the name of *Peerless*, each sailing from Bombay, one in October and the other in December. The buyer had in mind the ship that sailed in October, while the seller reasonably believed the agreement referred to the *Peerless* sailing in December. Neither party was at fault, but both believed in good faith that a different ship was intended. The English court held that no contract existed. The Restatement, Section 20, is in accord.

There is no manifestation of mutual assent in cases in which the parties attach materially different meanings to their manifestations and neither party knows or has reason to know the meaning attached by the other. If blame can be ascribed to either party, however, that party will be held responsible. Thus, if the seller knew of two ships by the name of *Peerless* sailing from Bombay, then he would be at fault, and the contract would be for the ship sailing in October as the buyer expected. If neither party is to blame or both are to blame, there is no contract at all; that is, the agreement is void.

CHAPTER SUMMARY

DURESS	**Definition** wrongful or unlawful act or threat that overcomes the free will of a party **Physical Compulsion** coercion involving physical force renders the agreement void **Improper Threats** improper threats or acts, including economic and social coercion, render the contract voidable	
UNDUE INFLUENCE	**Definition** taking unfair advantage of a person by reason of a dominant position based on a confidential relationship **Effect** renders a contract voidable	
FRAUD	**Fraud in the Execution** a misrepresentation that deceives the other party as to the nature of a document evidencing the contract renders the agreement void	

Fraud in the Inducement renders the agreement voidable if the following elements are present:
* *False Representation* positive statement or conduct that misleads
* *Fact* an event that occurred or thing that exists
* *Materiality* of substantial importance
* *Knowledge of Falsity and Intention to Deceive* called *scienter* and includes (1) actual knowledge, (2) lack of belief in statement's truthfulness, or (3) reckless indifference to its truthfulness
* *Justifiable Reliance* a defrauded party is reasonably influenced by the misrepresentation

NONFRAUDULENT MISREPRESENTATION	**Negligent Misrepresentation** misrepresentation made without due care in ascertaining its truthfulness; renders agreement voidable **Innocent Misrepresentation** misrepresentation made without knowledge of its falsity but with due care; renders contract voidable
MISTAKE	**Definition** an understanding that is not in accord with existing fact **Mutual Mistake** both parties have a common but erroneous belief forming the basis of the contract; renders the contract voidable by either party **Unilateral Mistake** courts are unlikely to grant relief unless the error is known or should be known by the nonmistaken party **Assumption of Risk** a party may assume the risk of a mistake **Effect of Fault upon Mistake** not a bar to avoidance unless the fault amounts to a failure to act in good faith

Consideration

Consideration is the primary—but not the only—basis for the enforcement of promises in our legal system. Consideration is the inducement to make a promise enforceable. The doctrine of consideration ensures that promises are enforced only in cases in which the parties have exchanged something of value in the eye of the law. Gratuitous (gift) promises, accordingly, are legally enforceable only under certain circumstances, which are discussed later in the chapter.

Consideration, or that which is exchanged for a promise, is present only when the parties intend an exchange. The consideration exchanged for the promise may be an act, a forbearance to act, or a promise to do either of these. In like manner, Section 71 of the Restatement defines consideration for a promise as (1) an act other than a promise, (2) a forbearance, (3) the creation, modification, or destruction of a legal relation, or (4) a return promise if any of these are bargained for and given in exchange for the promise.

Thus, consideration comprises two basic elements: (1) legal sufficiency (something of value) and (2) bargained-for exchange. Both must be present to satisfy the requirement of consideration. The consideration may be given to the promisor or to some other person; likewise, it may be given by the promisee or by some other person.

LEGAL SUFFICIENCY

To be legally sufficient, the consideration exchanged for the promise must be either a legal detriment to the promisee *or* a legal benefit to the promisor. In other words, in return for the promise the promisee must give up something of legal value or the promisor must receive something of legal value.

Legal detriment means (1) doing (or undertaking to do) that which the promisee was under no prior legal obligation to do or (2) refraining from doing (or the undertaking to refrain from doing) that which he was previously under no legal obligation to refrain from doing. On the other hand, **legal benefit** means the obtaining by the promisor of

that which he had no prior legal right to obtain. Most, if not all, cases involving legal detriment to the promisee also will involve a legal benefit to the promisor. Nonetheless, the presence of either is sufficient.

ADEQUACY

Legal sufficiency has nothing to do with adequacy of consideration. Restatement, Section 79. The subject matter that the parties agree to exchange does not need to have the same or equal value; rather, the law will regard consideration as adequate if the parties have freely agreed to the exchange. The requirement of legally sufficient consideration is, therefore, not at all concerned with whether the bargain was good or bad, or whether one party received disproportionately more or less than what he gave or promised in exchange. Such facts, however, may be relevant to the availability of certain defenses (such as fraud, duress, or undue influence) or certain remedies (such as specific performance). The requirement of legally sufficient consideration is simply (1) that the parties have agreed to an exchange and (2) that, with respect to each party, the subject matter exchanged, or promised in exchange, either imposed a legal detriment upon the promisee or conferred a legal benefit upon the promisor. If the purported consideration is clearly without value, however, such that the transaction is a sham, many courts would hold that consideration is lacking.

UNILATERAL CONTRACTS

In a unilateral contract, a promise is exchanged for a completed act or a forbearance to act. Because only one promise exists, only one party, the **offeror**, makes a promise and is therefore the **promisor** while the other party, the **offeree**, is the person receiving the promise and thus is the **promisee**. For example, A promises to pay B $2,000 if B paints A's house. B paints A's house.

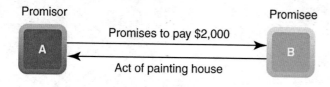

For A's promise to be binding, it must be supported by consideration consisting of either a legal detriment to B, the promisee (offeree), or a legal benefit to A, the promisor (offeror). B's having painted the house is a legal detriment to B, the promisee, because she was under no prior legal duty to paint A's house. Also, B's painting A's house is a legal benefit to A, the promisor, because A had no prior legal right to have his house painted by B.

A unilateral contract may also consist of a promise exchanged for a forbearance. To illustrate, A negligently injures B, for which B may recover damages in a tort action. A promises to pay B $5,000 if B forbears from bringing suit. B accepts by not filing suit.

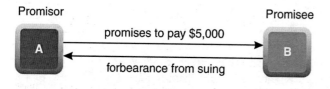

A's promise to pay B $5,000 is binding because it is supported by consideration: B, the promisee (offeree), has incurred a legal detriment by refraining from bringing suit, which he was under no prior legal obligation to refrain from doing. A, the promisor (offeror), has received a legal benefit because she had no prior legal right to B's forbearance from bringing suit.

BILATERAL CONTRACTS

In a bilateral contract, the parties exchange promises. Thus, each party is *both* a promisor and a promisee. For example, if A (the offeror) promises (offers) to purchase an automobile from B (the offeree) for $15,000 and B promises to sell the automobile to A for $15,000 (accepts the offer), the following relationship exists:

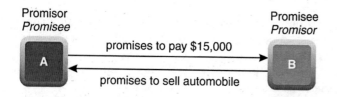

A's promise (the offer) to pay B $15,000 is binding and therefore enforceable by B, if that promise is supported by

legal consideration from B (offeree), which may consist of either a legal detriment to B, the promisee, or a legal benefit to A, the promisor. B's promise to sell A the automobile is a legal detriment to B because he was under no prior legal duty to sell the automobile to A. Moreover, B's promise is also a legal benefit to A because A had no prior legal right to that automobile. Consequently, A's promise to pay $15,000 to B is supported by consideration and is enforceable.

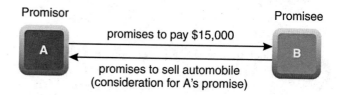

For **B's promise** (the acceptance) to sell the automobile to A to be binding, it likewise must be supported by consideration from A (offeror), which may be either a legal detriment to A, the promisee, or a legal benefit to B, the promisor. A's promise to pay B $15,000 is a legal detriment to A because he was under no prior legal duty to pay $15,000 to B. At the same time, A's promise is also a legal benefit to B because B had no prior legal right to the $15,000. Thus, B's promise to sell the automobile is supported by consideration and is enforceable.

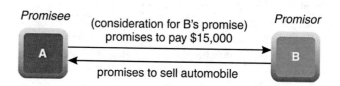

To summarize, for A's promise to B to be binding, B must support the promise with legally sufficient consideration, which requires that the promise A receives in exchange from B provide either a legal benefit to A (the promisor) or a legal detriment to B (the promisee). A, in turn, must support B's return promise with consideration for that promise to be binding on B.

Thus, in a bilateral contract each promise is the consideration for the other, a relationship that has been referred to as **mutuality of obligation**. A general consequence of mutuality of obligation is that each promisor in a bilateral contract must be bound, or neither is bound.

◆ **SEE FIGURE 12-1: Consideration in Unilateral and Bilateral Contracts**

◆ FIGURE 12-1: **Consideration in Unilateral and Bilateral Contracts**

Type of Contract	Offer	Acceptance	Consideration
Unilateral	Promise by A	Performance of requested act or forbearance by B	*Promise* by A *Performance* of requested act or forbearance by B
Bilateral	Promise by A	Return promise by B to perform requested act or forbearance	*Promise* by A Return *promise* by B to perform requested act or forbearance

ILLUSORY PROMISES

Words of promise that make the performance of the purported promisor entirely optional constitute no promise at all. Consequently, they cannot serve as consideration. In this section, such illusory promises will be distinguished from promises that impose obligations of performance upon the promisor and thus can be legally sufficient consideration. An **illusory promise** is a statement that is in the form of a promise but imposes no obligation upon the maker of the statement. An illusory promise is not consideration for a return promise. Thus, a statement committing the promisor to purchase such quantity of goods as she may "desire," "want," or "wish to buy" is an illusory promise because its performance is entirely optional. For example, if ExxonMobil, Inc., agrees to sell to Barnes Co. as many barrels of oil as Barnes shall choose at $40 per barrel, there would be no consideration: Barnes may wish or desire to buy none of the oil, yet in buying none it would fulfill its promise. An agreement containing such a promise as that made by Barnes, although accepted by both parties, does not create a contract because the promise is illusory—performance by Barnes is entirely optional, and the offer places no constraint upon its freedom. Barnes is not bound to do anything, nor can Ames reasonably expect to receive any performance. Thus, Barnes, by its promise, suffers no legal detriment and confers no legal benefit. Consequently, Barnes's promise does not provide legally sufficient consideration for ExxonMobil's promise; thus, ExxonMobil's promise is not binding upon ExxonMobil.

Many courts have transformed otherwise illusory promises into actual promises by implying an obligation of good faith or fair dealing. Under this approach, courts have held to be nonillusory a promise "to spend such time as he personally sees fit in developing" a business and a clause "specifying that leases 'satisfactory' to plaintiff must be secured before he would be bound to perform."

OUTPUT AND REQUIREMENTS CONTRACTS A seller's agreement to sell her entire production to a particular purchaser is called an **output contract**. It affords the seller an ensured market for her product. Conversely, a **requirements contract**, or a purchaser's agreement to buy from a particular seller all the materials of a particular kind he needs, ensures the buyer of a ready source of inventory or supplies. These contracts may or may not be accompanied by an estimate of the quantity to be sold or to be purchased. Nevertheless, these promises are not illusory. The buyer under a requirements contract does not promise to buy as much as she desires to buy but, rather, to buy as much as she *needs*. Similarly, under an output contract the seller promises to sell to the buyer the seller's entire production, not merely as much as the seller desires.

Furthermore, the Code, Section 2–306(1), imposes a good faith limitation upon the quantity to be sold or purchased under an output or requirements contract. Thus, a contract of this type involves such actual output or requirements as may occur in good faith, except that no quantity unreasonably disproportionate to any stated estimate or, in the absence of a stated estimate, to any normal prior output or requirements may be tendered or demanded. Therefore, after contracting to sell to Adler, Inc., its entire output, Benevito Company cannot increase its production from one eight-hour shift per day to three eight-hour shifts per day.

EXCLUSIVE DEALING CONTRACTS Where a manufacturer of goods grants an exclusive right to a distributor to sell its products in a designated territory, unless otherwise agreed, the manufacturer is under an implied obligation to use its best efforts to supply the goods, and the distributor must use his best efforts to promote their sale. Uniform Commercial Code (UCC) Section 2–306(2). The obligations that arise upon acceptance of an **exclusive dealing agreement** are sufficient consideration to bind both parties to the contract.

CONDITIONAL PROMISES A conditional promise is a promise the performance of which depends upon the happening or nonhappening of an event not certain to occur (the condition). A conditional promise is sufficient consideration *unless* the promisor knows at the time of making the promise that the condition cannot occur. Restatement, Section 76.

Thus, if Debbie offers to pay John $8,000 for John's automobile, provided that Debbie receives such amount as an inheritance from the estate of her deceased uncle, and John accepts the offer, the duty of Debbie to pay $8,000 to John is *conditioned* upon her receiving $8,000 from her deceased uncle's estate. The consideration moving from John to Debbie is the promise to transfer title to the automobile. The consideration moving from Debbie to John is the promise of $8,000 subject to the condition.

PREEXISTING OBLIGATION

The law does not regard the performance of, or the promise to perform, a preexisting legal duty, public or private, as either a legal detriment to the party under the prior legal obligation or a benefit to the other party. A **public duty** does not arise out of a contract; rather, it is imposed upon members of society by force of the common law or by statute. As illustrated in the law of torts, public duty includes the duty not to commit an assault, battery, false imprisonment, or defamation. The criminal law also imposes numerous public duties. Thus, if Cleon promises to pay Spike, the village ruffian, $100 not to abuse him physically, Cleon's promise is unenforceable because both tort and criminal law impose on Spike a preexisting public obligation to refrain from so acting.

By virtue of their public office, public officials, such as the mayor of a city, members of a city council, police officers, and firefighters, are under a preexisting obligation to perform their duties.

The performance of, or the promise to perform, a **preexisting contractual duty**, a duty the terms of which are neither doubtful nor the subject of honest dispute, is also legally insufficient consideration because the doing of what one is legally bound to do is neither a detriment to the promisee nor a benefit to the promisor. For example, Leigh and Associates employs Jason for one year at a salary of $2,000 per month and at the end of six months promises Jason that, in addition to the salary, it will pay him $3,000 if he remains on the job for the remainder of the period originally agreed upon. Leigh's promise is not binding because Jason's promise does not constitute legally sufficient consideration. If Jason's duties were changed in nature or amount, however, Leigh's promise would be binding because Jason's new duties are a legal detriment.

MODIFICATION OF A PREEXISTING CONTRACT A modification of a contract occurs when the parties to the contract mutually agree to change one or more of its terms. Under the common law, a modification of an existing contract must be supported by mutual consideration to be enforceable. In other words, the modification must be supported by some new consideration beyond that which is already owing (thus, there must be a separate and distinct modification contract). For example, Fred and Jodie agree that Fred shall put in a gravel driveway for Jodie at a cost of $2,000. Subsequently, Jodie agrees to pay an additional $1,000 if Fred will blacktop the driveway. Because Fred was not bound by the original contract to provide blacktopping, he would incur a legal detriment in doing so and is therefore entitled to the additional $1,000.

The Code has modified the common law rule for contract modification by providing that the parties can effectively modify a contract for the sale of goods without new consideration, though the Comments to this section make the modification subject to the requirement of good faith. Moreover, the Restatement has moved toward this position by providing that a modification of an executory contract is binding if it is fair and equitable in light of surrounding facts that the parties did not anticipate when the contract was made. Restatement, Section 89. A few States have followed the Code's rule by statutorily providing that the parties need provide no new consideration when modifying any contract. These States vary, however, as to whether the modification must be in writing and whether the original contract must be executory.

◆ **SEE FIGURE 12-2: Modification of a Preexisting Contract**

SUBSTITUTED CONTRACTS A substituted contract results when the parties to a contract mutually agree to rescind their original contract and enter into a new one. This situation involves separate contracts: the original contract, the agreement of rescission, and the substitute contract. Substituted contracts are perfectly valid, allowing the parties effectively to discharge the original contract and to impose obligations under the new one. The rescission is binding in that each party, by giving up his rights under the original contract, has provided consideration to the other, as long as each party still has rights under the original contract. Where the rescission and new agreement are simultaneous, the effect is the same as a contractual modification. The Restatement takes the position that the substitute contract is *not* binding unless it is fair and equitable in view of circumstances the parties did not anticipate when they made the original contract. Section 89, Comment b.

SETTLEMENT OF A LIQUIDATED DEBT A **liquidated debt** is an obligation the existence or amount of which is undisputed. Under the common law, the partial payment of a sum of money in consideration of a promise to discharge a fully matured, undisputed debt is legally *insufficient* to support the promise of discharge. To illustrate, assume that Pamela

◆ **FIGURE 12-2: Modification of a Preexisting Contract**

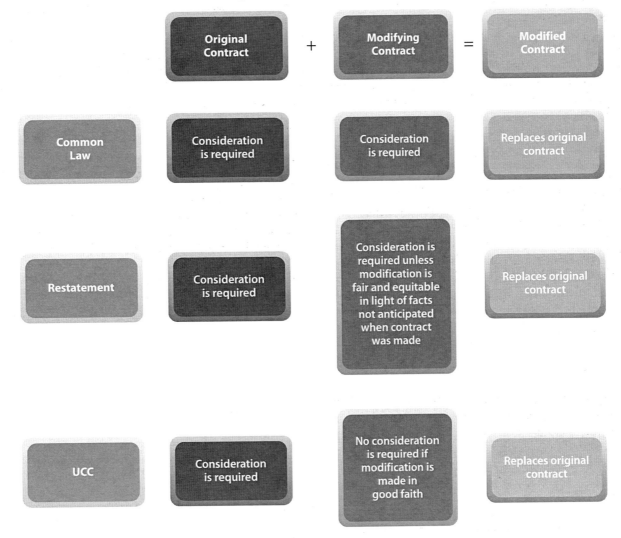

owes Julie $100, and in consideration of Pamela's paying Julie $50, Julie agrees to discharge the debt. In a subsequent suit by Julie against Pamela to recover the remaining $50, at common law Julie is entitled to judgment for $50 on the ground that Julie's promise of discharge is not binding because Pamela's payment of $50 was no legal detriment to the promisee, Pamela, as she was under a preexisting legal obligation to pay that much and more. Consequently, the consideration for Julie's promise of discharge was legally insufficient, and Julie is not bound on her promise. If, however, Julie had accepted from Pamela any new or different consideration, such as the sum of $40 and a fountain pen worth $10 or less, or even the fountain pen with no payment of money, in full satisfaction of the $100 debt, the consideration moving from Pamela would be legally sufficient inasmuch as Pamela was under no legal obligation to give a fountain pen to Julie. In this example, considera-

tion would also exist if Julie had agreed to accept $50 before the debt became due, in full satisfaction of the debt. Pamela was under no legal obligation to pay any of the debt before its due date. Consequently, Pamela's early payment would represent a legal detriment to Pamela as well as a legal benefit to Julie. The law is not concerned with the amount of the discount, as that is simply a question of adequacy for the courts to decide. Likewise, Pamela's payment of a lesser amount on the due date at an agreed-upon different place of payment would be legally sufficient consideration. The Restatement requires that the new consideration "differs from what was required by the duty in a way which reflects more than a pretense of bargain." Section 73.

SETTLEMENT OF AN UNLIQUIDATED DEBT An **unliquidated debt** is an obligation disputed as to either its existence or its amount. A promise to settle a validly disputed claim in exchange for an agreed payment or other performance is supported by consideration. Where the dispute is based upon contentions that are nonmeritorious or not made in good faith, however, the debtor's surrender of such a claim is no legal detriment to the claimant. The Restatement adopts a different position by providing that the settlement of a claim that proves invalid is consideration if at the time of the settlement (1) the claimant honestly believed that the claim was valid, or (2) the claim was in fact doubtful because of uncertainty as to the facts or the law. Section 74.

For example, where a person has requested professional services from an accountant or a lawyer and the parties reached no agreement with respect to the amount of the fee to be charged, the accountant or lawyer is entitled to receive from her client a reasonable fee for the services rendered. As no definite amount has been agreed upon, the client's obligation is uncertain; nevertheless, his legal obligation is to pay the reasonable worth of the services performed. When the accountant or lawyer sends the client a bill for services rendered, even though the amount stated in the bill is an estimate of the reasonable value of the services, the debt does not become undisputed until and unless the client agrees to pay the amount of the bill. If the client honestly disputes the amount that is owed and tenders in full settlement an amount less than the bill, acceptance of the lesser amount by the creditor discharges the debt. Thus, if Ted sends to Betty, an accountant, a check for $120 in payment of his debt to Betty for services rendered, which services Ted considered worthless but for which Betty billed Ted $600, Betty's acceptance of the check releases Ted from any further liability. Ted has given up his right to dispute the billing further, while Betty has forfeited her right to further collection. Thus, there is mutuality of consideration.

BARGAINED-FOR EXCHANGE

The central idea behind consideration is that the parties have intentionally entered into a bargained exchange with one another and have given to each other something in exchange for a promise or performance. "A performance or return promise is bargained for if it is sought by the promisor in exchange for his promise and is given by the promisee in exchange for that promise." Restatement, Section 71. Thus, a promise to give someone a birthday present is without consideration, as the promisor received nothing in exchange for his promise of a present.

PAST CONSIDERATION

Consideration is the inducement for a promise or performance. The element of bargained-for exchange is absent where a promise is given for a past transaction. Therefore, unbargained-for past events are not consideration, despite their designation as "past consideration." A promise made on account of something that the promisee has already done is not enforceable. For example, Noel gives emergency care to Tim's adult son while the son is ill. Tim subsequently promises to pay Noel for her services, but his promise is not binding because there is no bargained-for exchange.

THIRD PARTIES

Consideration to support a promise may be given to a person other than the promisor if the promisor bargains for that exchange. For example, A promises to pay B $15 if B delivers a specified book to C.

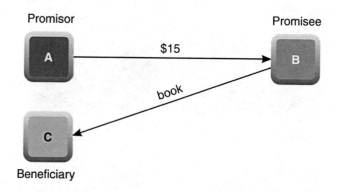

A's promise is binding because B incurred a legal detriment by delivering the book to C, as B was under no prior legal obligation to do so, and A had no prior legal right to have the book given to C. A and B have bargained for A to pay B $15 in return for B's delivering the book to C. A's promise to pay $15 is also consideration for B's promise to give the book to C.

Conversely, consideration may be given by some person other than the promisee. For example, A promises to pay B $25 in return for D's promise to give a radio to A.

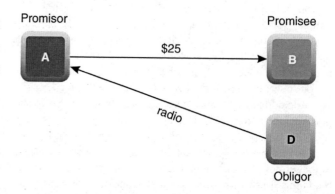

A's promise to pay $25 to B is consideration for D's promise to give a radio to A and vice versa.

CONTRACTS WITHOUT CONSIDERATION

Certain transactions are enforceable even though they are not supported by consideration. Such transactions include (1) promises to perform prior unenforceable obligations, (2) promises that induce detrimental reliance (promissory estoppel), (3) promises made under seal, and (4) promises made enforceable by statute.

PROMISES TO PERFORM PRIOR UNENFORCEABLE OBLIGATIONS

In certain circumstances the courts will enforce new promises to perform an obligation that originally was not enforceable or has become unenforceable by operation of law. These situations include promises to pay debts barred by the statute of limitations, debts discharged in bankruptcy, and voidable obligations. In addition, as previously indicated, some courts will enforce promises to pay moral obligations.

PROMISE TO PAY DEBT BARRED BY THE STATUTE OF LIMITATIONS Every State has a statute of limitations, which provides that legal actions must be initiated within a prescribed period after the right to bring the action arose. Actions not commenced within the specified time period, which varies among the States and also with the nature of the legal action, will be dismissed.

An exception to the past consideration rule extends to promises to pay all or part of a contractual or quasi-contractual debt barred by the statute of limitations. The new promise is binding according to its terms without consideration for a second statutory period. Any recovery under the new promise is limited to the terms contained in the new promise. Most States require that new promises falling under this rule, except those indicated by part payment, be in writing to be enforceable.

PROMISE TO PAY DEBT DISCHARGED IN BANKRUPTCY Another exception to the requirement that consideration be given in exchange for a promise to make it binding is a promise to pay a debt that has been discharged in bankruptcy. Restatement, Section 83. The Bankruptcy Act, however, imposes a number of requirements before a promise to pay a debt discharged in bankruptcy may be enforced. These requirements are discussed in *Chapter 39*.

VOIDABLE PROMISES Another promise that is enforceable without new consideration is a new promise to perform a voidable obligation that has not previously been avoided. Restatement, Section 85. The power of avoidance may be based on lack of capacity, fraud, misrepresentation, duress, undue influence, or mistake. For instance, a promise to perform an antecedent obligation made by a minor upon reaching the age of majority is enforceable without new consideration. To be enforceable, the promise itself must not be voidable. For example, if the new promise is made without knowledge of the original fraud or by a minor before reaching the age of majority, then the new promise is not enforceable.

MORAL OBLIGATION Under the common law, a promise made to satisfy a preexisting moral obligation is made for past consideration and therefore is unenforceable for lack of consideration. Instances involving such obligations include promises to pay for board and lodging previously furnished to a needy relative of the promisor, promises to pay debts owed by a relative, and an employer's promises to pay a completely disabled former employee a sum of money in addition to an award the employee has received under a workers' compensation statute. Although in many cases the moral obligation may be strong by reason of the particular facts and circumstances, no liability generally attaches to the promise.

The Restatement and a minority of States give considerable recognition to moral obligations as consideration. The Restatement provides that a promise made for "a benefit previously received by the promisor from the promisee is binding to the extent necessary to prevent injustice." Section 86. For instance, Tim's subsequent promise to Noel to reimburse her for the expenses she incurred in rendering emergency services to Tim's son is binding even though it is not supported by new consideration.

The Restatement also provides for enforcement of a moral obligation when a person promises to pay for a mistakenly conferred benefit. For example, Pam hires Elizabeth to pave her driveway, and Elizabeth mistakenly paves Chuck's driveway next door. Chuck subsequently promises to pay Pam $1,000 for the benefit conferred. Under the Restatement, Chuck's promise to pay the $1,000 is binding.

PROMISSORY ESTOPPEL

As discussed in *Chapter 9*, in certain circumstances in which detrimental reliance has occurred, the courts will enforce noncontractual promises under the doctrine of promissory estoppel. When applicable, the doctrine makes gratuitous promises enforceable to the extent necessary to avoid injustice. The doctrine applies when a promise that the promisor reasonably should expect to induce detrimental reliance does induce such action or forbearance.

Promissory estoppel does not mean that every gratuitous promise is binding simply because it is followed by a change of position on the part of the promisee. To create liability, the promisee must make the change of position in justifiable reliance on the promise. For example, Smith promises to Barclay not to foreclose on a mortgage Smith holds on Barclay's factory for a period of six months. In justifiable reliance on Smith's promise, Barclay expends $900,000 on expanding the factory. Smith's promise not to foreclose is binding on Smith under the doctrine of promissory estoppel.

The most common application of the doctrine of promissory estoppel is to charitable subscriptions. Numerous churches, memorials, college buildings, hospitals, and other structures used for religious, educational, and charitable purposes have been built with the assistance of contributions fulfilling pledges or promises to contribute to particular worthwhile causes. Although the pledgor regards herself as making a gift for a charitable purpose and gift promises generally are not enforceable, the courts tend to enforce charitable subscription promises. Numerous reasons and theories have been advanced in support of liability: the most accepted argues that the subscription has induced a change of position by the promisee (the church, school, or charitable organization) in reliance on the promise. The Restatement, moreover, has relaxed the reliance requirement for charitable subscriptions so that actual reliance need not be shown; the probability of reliance is sufficient.

PROMISES MADE UNDER SEAL

Under the common law, when a person desired to bind himself by bond, deed, or solemn promise, he executed his promise under seal. He did not have to sign the document, his delivery of a document to which he had affixed his seal being sufficient. No consideration for his promise was necessary. In some States the courts still hold a promise under seal to be binding without consideration.

Nevertheless, most States have abolished by statute the distinction between contracts under seal and written unsealed contracts. In these States, the seal is no longer recognized as a substitute for consideration. The Code has also adopted this position, specifically eliminating the use of seals in contracts for the sale of goods.

PROMISES MADE ENFORCEABLE BY STATUTE

Some gratuitous promises that otherwise would be unenforceable have been made binding by statute. Most significant among these are (1) contract modifications, (2) renunciations, and (3) irrevocable offers.

CONTRACT MODIFICATIONS As mentioned previously, the UCC has abandoned the common law rule requiring that a modification of an existing contract be supported by consideration to be valid. The Code provides that a contract for the sale of goods can be effectively modified without new consideration, provided the modification is made in good faith. Section 2–209.

RENUNCIATION Under the Code, Section 1–107, any claim or right arising out of an alleged breach of contract can be discharged in whole or in part without consideration by a written waiver or renunciation signed and delivered by the aggrieved party. Under the 2001 Revised UCC Article 1, a claim or right arising out of an alleged breach may be discharged in whole or in part without consideration by agreement of the aggrieved party in an authenticated record. Section 1–306. This section is subject to the obligation of good faith and, as with all sections of Article 1, applies to a transaction to the extent that it is governed by one of the other article of the UCC. Section 1–102.

IRREVOCABLE OFFERS Under the Code, a *firm offer*, a written offer signed by a merchant offeror promising to keep open an offer to buy or sell goods, is not revocable for lack of consideration during the time stated, not to exceed three months, or if no time is stated, for a reasonable time. Section 2–205.

CHAPTER SUMMARY

CONSIDERATION **Definition** the inducement to enter into a contract
Elements legal sufficiency and bargained-for exchange

LEGAL SUFFICIENCY **Definition** consists of either a benefit to the promisor or a detriment to the promisee
- *Legal Benefit* obtaining something to which one had no prior legal right
- *Legal Detriment* doing an act one is not legally obligated to do or not doing an act that one has a legal right to do

Adequacy not required where the parties have freely agreed to the exchange
Illusory Promise promise that imposes no obligation on the promisor; the following promises are *not* illusory:
- *Output Contract* agreement to sell all of one's production to a single buyer
- *Requirements Contract* agreement to buy all of one's needs from a single producer
- *Exclusive Dealing Contract* grant to a franchisee or licensee by a manufacturer of the sole right to sell goods in a defined market
- *Conditional Promise* a contract in which the obligations are contingent upon the occurrence of a stated event

Preexisting Public Obligations public duties such as those imposed by tort or criminal law are neither a legal detriment nor a legal benefit

Preexisting Contractual Obligation performance of a preexisting contractual duty is not consideration

- *Modification of a Preexisting Contract* under the common law a modification of a preexisting contract must be supported by mutual consideration; under the Code a contract can be modified without new consideration
- *Substituted Contracts* the parties agree to rescind their original contract and to enter into a new one; rescission and new contract are supported by consideration
- *Settlement of an Undisputed Debt* payment of a lesser sum of money to discharge an undisputed debt (one whose existence or amount is not contested) does not constitute legally sufficient consideration
- *Settlement of a Disputed Debt* payment of a lesser sum of money to discharge a disputed debt (one whose existence or amount is contested) is legally sufficient consideration

BARGAINED-FOR EXCHANGE	**Definition** a mutually agreed-upon exchange
	Past Consideration an act done before the contract is made is not consideration

CONTRACTS WITHOUT CONSIDERATION	**Promises to Perform Prior Unenforceable Obligations**

- *Promise to Pay Debt Barred by the Statute of Limitations* a new promise by the debtor to pay the debt renews the running of the statute for a second statutory period
- *Promise to Pay Debt Discharged in Bankruptcy* may be enforceable without consideration
- *Voidable Promises* a new promise to perform a voidable obligation that has not been previously avoided is enforceable
- *Moral Obligation* a promise made to satisfy a preexisting moral obligation is generally unenforceable for lack of consideration

Promissory Estoppel doctrine that prohibits a party from denying her promise when the promisee takes action or forbearance to his detriment reasonably based upon the promise

Promises under Seal where still recognized, the seal acts as a substitute for consideration

Promises Made Enforceable by Statute some gratuitous promises have been made enforceable by statute; the Code makes enforceable (1) contract modifications, (2) renunciations, and (3) firm offers

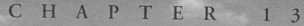

Illegal Bargains

An essential requirement of a binding promise or agreement is legality of objective. When the formation or performance of an agreement is criminal, tortious, or otherwise contrary to public policy, the agreement is illegal and unenforceable (as opposed to being void). The law does not provide a remedy for the breach of an unenforceable agreement and thus "leaves the parties where it finds them." It is preferable to use the term *illegal bargain* or *illegal agreement* rather than *illegal contract*, because the word *contract*, by definition, denotes a legal and enforceable agreement. The illegal bargain is made unenforceable (1) to discourage such undesirable conduct and (2) to preclude the inappropriate use of the judicial process in carrying out such socially undesirable bargains.

The Restatement avoids defining the term *illegal bargain*, instead focusing upon whether public policy should bar enforcement of the agreement. By relying upon the concept of public policy, the Restatement provides the courts with greater flexibility in determining the enforceability of questioned agreements by weighing the strength of legally recognized policies against the effect that declaring a particular bargain to be against public policy would have on the contracting parties and on the public.

This chapter will discuss (1) agreements in violation of a statute, (2) agreements contrary to public policy, and (3) the effect of illegality upon agreements.

VIOLATIONS OF STATUTES

The courts will not enforce an agreement declared illegal by statute. For example, wagering or gambling contracts are specifically declared unenforceable in most States. In addition, an agreement to violate a statute prohibiting crimes, such as murder, robbery, embezzlement, forgery, and price fixing, is unenforceable. Likewise, an agreement that is induced by criminal conduct will not be enforced. For example, if Alice enters into an agreement with Brent Co.

through the bribing of Brent Co.'s purchasing agent, the agreement would be unenforceable.

LICENSING STATUTES

Every jurisdiction has laws requiring a license for those who engage in certain trades, professions, or businesses. Common examples are licensing statutes which apply to lawyers, doctors, dentists, accountants, brokers, plumbers, and contractors. Some licensing statutes mandate schooling and/or examination, while others require only financial responsibility and/or good moral character. Whether or not a person may recover for services rendered if he has failed to comply with a licensing requirement depends upon the terms or type of licensing statute. This rule pertains only to the rights of the unlicensed party to enforce the obligations of the other party.

The statute itself may expressly provide that an unlicensed person engaged in a business or profession for which a license is required shall not recover for services rendered. Absent such statutory provision, the courts commonly distinguish between those statutes or ordinances that are **regulatory** in character and those that are enacted merely to raise **revenue** through the issuance of licenses. If the statute is regulatory, a person cannot recover for professional services unless he has the required license, as long as the public policy behind the regulatory purpose clearly outweighs the person's interest in being paid for his services. Restatement, Section 181. Some courts have gone further by balancing the penalty the unlicensed party suffers against the benefit the other party receives. In contrast, if the law is for revenue purposes only, agreements for such services are enforceable.

A regulatory license, including those issued under statutes prescribing standards for those wishing to practice law or medicine, is a measure designed to protect the public against unqualified persons. A revenue license, on the other hand, does not seek to protect against incompetent or unqualified practitioners but simply to furnish revenue. An example is a statute requiring a license of plumbers but not establishing standards of competence for those who seek to follow the trade. The courts regard such legislation as a taxing measure lacking any expression of legislative intent to preclude unlicensed plumbers from enforcing their business contracts.

GAMBLING STATUTES

In a wager the parties stipulate that one shall win and the other lose depending upon the outcome of an event in which their sole "interest" arises from the possibility of such gain or loss. All States have legislation pertaining to gambling or wagering, and U.S. courts generally refuse to recognize the enforceability of a gambling agreement. Thus, if Arnold makes a bet with Bernice on the outcome of a ball game, the agreement is unenforceable by either party. Some States, however, now permit certain kinds of regulated gambling. Wagering conducted by governmental agencies, principally State-operated lotteries, has come to constitute an increasingly important source of public revenues.

To be distinguished from wagers are ordinary insurance contracts in which the insured, having an "insurable interest" (discussed in *Chapter 49*), pays a certain sum of money or premium in exchange for an insurance company's promise to pay a larger amount upon the occurrence of some event, such as a fire, which causes loss to the insured. Here, the agreement compensates for loss under an existing risk; it does not create an entirely new risk. In a wager, the parties contemplate gain through mere chance, whereas in an insurance contract they seek to distribute possible loss. Furthermore, most games at fast-food restaurants and grocery store drawings have been upheld because the participants need not make a purchase to be eligible for the prize.

USURY STATUTES

A **usury statute** is a law establishing a maximum rate of permissible interest for which a lender and borrower of money may contract. Though, historically, every State had a usury law, a recent trend has been to limit or relax usury statutes. The maximum rates permitted vary greatly from State to State and among types of transactions. These statutes typically are general in their application, although certain specified types of transactions are exempted. For example, numerous States impose no limit on the rate of interest that may be charged on loans to corporations. Furthermore, some States permit the parties to contract for any rate of interest on loans made to individual proprietorships or partnerships for the purpose of carrying on a business. Moreover, there are not many protections remaining for typical consumer transactions, including those involving credit cards. (More than half of the States have no interest rate limits on credit card transactions.)

In addition to the exceptions accorded certain designated types of borrowers, a number of States have exempted specific lenders. For example, the majority of the States have enacted installment loan laws, which permit eligible lenders a return on installment loans that is higher than the applicable general interest statute would permit. These specific lender usury statutes, which have all but eliminated general usury statutes, vary greatly but generally have included small consumer loans, corporate loans, loans by small lenders, real estate mortgages, and numerous other transactions.

For a transaction to be usurious, courts usually require evidence of the following factors: (1) a loan or forbearance (2) of money (3) which is repayable absolutely and in all events (4) for which an interest charge is exacted in excess of the interest rate allowed by law. Transactions that are really loans may not be clothed with the trappings of a sale for the purpose of avoiding the usury laws.

The legal effect to be given a usurious loan varies from State to State. In a few States, the lender forfeits both principal and interest. In some jurisdictions, the lender can recover the principal but forfeits all interest. In other States, only that portion of interest exceeding the permitted maximum is forfeited. In several States, the amount forfeited is a multiple (double or treble) of the interest charged. Disposition of usurious interest already paid also varies. Some States do not allow any recovery of usurious interest paid; others allow recovery of such interest or a multiple of it.

SUNDAY STATUTES

In the absence of a statutory prohibition, the common law does not prohibit entering into contracts on Sunday. Some States, however, have legislation, referred to as **Blue Laws**, modifying this common law rule and prohibiting certain types of commercial activity on Sunday. Even in a State which prohibits contracts on Sunday, a court nonetheless will enforce a subsequent weekday ratification of a loan made on Sunday or a promise to pay for goods sold and delivered on Sunday. In addition, Blue Laws usually do not apply to activities of "necessity" and "charity."

VIOLATIONS OF PUBLIC POLICY

The reach of a statute may extend beyond its language. Sometimes, the courts, by analogy, use the statute and the policy it seeks to serve as a guide in determining the private contract rights of one harmed by a violation of the statute. In addition, the courts must frequently articulate the "public policy" of the State without significant help from statutory sources. This judicially declared public policy is very broad in scope, it often being said that agreements having "a tendency to be injurious to the public or the public good" are contrary to public policy. Thus, the term *public policy* eludes precise definition. Contracts raising questions of public policy include agreements that (1) restrain trade, (2) exempt or exculpate a party from liability for his own tortious conduct, (3) are unconscionable, (4) involve tortious conduct, (5) tend to obstruct the administration of justice, (6) tend to corrupt public officials or impair the legislative process, or (7) impair family relationships. This section will focus on the first four of these types of agreements.

COMMON LAW RESTRAINT OF TRADE

A **restraint of trade** is any contract or agreement that eliminates or tends to eliminate competition or otherwise obstructs trade or commerce. One type of restraint is a **covenant not to compete**, which is an agreement to refrain from entering into a competing trade, profession, or business.

An agreement to refrain from a particular trade, profession, or business is enforceable if (1) the purpose of the restraint is to protect a property interest of the promisee and (2) the restraint is no more extensive than is reasonably necessary to protect that interest. Restraints typically arise in two situations: the sale of a business and employment contracts.

SALE OF A BUSINESS As part of an agreement to sell a business, the seller frequently promises not to compete in that particular type of business in a *defined area* for a stated *time*. To protect the business's goodwill (an asset that the buyer has purchased), the buyer must be allowed to enforce such a covenant (promise) by the seller not to compete with the purchaser within reasonable limitations. Most litigation on this subject has involved the requirement that the restraint be no greater than is reasonably necessary. Whether the restraint is reasonable or not depends on the geographic area it covers, the time period for which it is to be effective, and the hardship it imposes on the promisor and the public.

For example, the promise of a person selling a service station business in Detroit not to enter the service station business in Michigan for the next twenty-five years is unreasonable, both as to area and time. The business interest to be protected would not include the entire State, so it is not necessary to the protection of the purchaser that the seller be prevented from engaging in the service station business in the entire State or perhaps, for that matter, in the entire city of Detroit. Limiting the area to the neighborhood in which the station is located or to a radius of a few miles probably would be adequate.

The same type of inquiry must be made about time limitations. In the sale of a service station, a twenty-five-year ban on competition from the seller would be unreasonable; a one-year ban probably would not. The court, in determining what is reasonable under particular circumstances, must consider each case on its own facts.

EMPLOYMENT CONTRACTS Salespeople, management personnel, and other employees frequently are required to sign employment contracts prohibiting them from competing with their employers during their time of employment and for some additional stated period after termination. The same is also frequently true among corporations or partnerships involving professionals, such as accountants, lawyers, investment brokers, stockbrokers, or doctors. Although the courts readily enforce a covenant not to compete during the period of employment, the promise not to compete after termination is subjected to an even stricter test of reasonableness than that applied to noncompetition promises included in a contract for the sale of a business. One reason for this is that the employer is in a stronger bargaining position than the employee.

A court order enjoining a former employee from competing in a described territory for a stated time is the usual method by which an employer seeks to enforce the employee's promise not to compete. Before granting such injunctions, the courts insist that the employer demonstrate that the restriction is *necessary* to protect his legitimate interests, such as trade secrets or customer lists. Because issuing the injunction may place the employee out of work, the courts must carefully balance the public policy favoring the employer's right to protect his business interests against the public policy favoring full opportunity for individuals to gain employment.

Thus, one court has held unreasonable a covenant in a contract requiring a travel agency employee, after termination of her employment, to refrain from engaging in a like business in any capacity in either of two named towns or within a sixty-mile radius of those towns for two years. There was no indication that the employee had enough influence over customers to cause them to move their business to her new agency, nor was it shown that any trade secrets were involved. *United Travel Service, Inc. v. Weber*, 108 Ill. App.2d 353, 247 N.E.2d 801 (1969). Instead of refusing to enforce an unreasonable covenant, some courts, considering the action justifiable under the circumstances of the case, will reform the agreement to make it reasonable and enforceable.

Due to the rapid evolution of business practices in the Internet industry, it has been argued that noncompete agreements for Internet company employees need their own rules. *National Business Services, Inc. v. Wright* addressed the geographic scope of an Internet noncompete agreement, upholding a one-year time restriction and a territorial clause that prevented the employee from taking another Internet-related job anywhere in the United States. The court stated, "Transactions involving the Internet, unlike traditional 'sales territory' cases, are not limited by state boundaries."

EXCULPATORY CLAUSES

Some contracts contain an exculpatory clause that excuses one party from liability for her own tortious conduct. The courts generally agree that exculpatory clauses relieving a person from tort liability for harm caused intentionally or recklessly are unenforceable as violating public policy. On the other hand, exculpatory clauses that excuse a party from liability for harm caused by negligent conduct are scrutinized carefully by the courts, which often require that the clause be conspicuously placed in the contract and clearly written. Accordingly, an exculpatory clause on the reverse side of a parking lot claim check, which attempts to relieve the parking lot operator of liability for negligently damaging the customer's automobile, will generally be held unenforceable as against public policy.

The Restatement provides that exculpatory clauses excusing negligent conduct are unenforceable on grounds of public policy if they exempt (1) an employer from liability to an employee, (2) a public service business (such as a common carrier) from liability to a customer, or (3) a person from liability to a party who is a member of a protected class. Restatement, Section 195. For example, a railroad company will not be permitted to avoid liability for the negligent operation or maintenance of its trains.

A similar rule applies to a contractual provision unreasonably exempting a party from the legal consequences of a misrepresentation. Restatement, Section 196. Such a term is unenforceable on the grounds of public policy with respect to both fraudulent and nonfraudulent misrepresentations.

Further, where the superior bargaining position of one party has enabled him to impose upon the other party such a provision, the courts are inclined to nullify the provision. Such a situation may arise in residential leases exempting a landlord from liability for his negligence. Moreover, an exculpatory clause may be unenforceable for unconscionability.

UNCONSCIONABLE CONTRACTS

The court may scrutinize every contract of sale to determine whether it is, in its commercial setting, purpose, and effect, **unconscionable**. The court may refuse to enforce an unconscionable contract in its entirety or any part it finds to be unconscionable. Section 2–302 of the UCC provides:

> If the court as a matter of law finds the contract or any clause of the contract to have been unconscionable at the time it was made the court may refuse to enforce the contract, or it may enforce the remainder of the contract without the unconscionable clause, or it may so limit the application of any unconscionable clause as to avoid any unconscionable result.

Similarly, Section 208 of the Restatement parallels this provision and provides:

> If a contract or term thereof is unconscionable at the time the contract is made a court may refuse to enforce the contract, or may enforce the remainder of the contract without the unconscionable term, or may so limit the application of any unconscionable term as to avoid any unconscionable result.

Neither the Code nor the Restatement defines the word *unconscionable*; however, the *New Webster's Dictionary* (Deluxe Encyclopedic Edition) defines the term as "contrary to the dictates of conscience; unscrupulous or unprincipled; exceeding that which is reasonable or customary; inordinate, unjustifiable."

The doctrine of unconscionability has been justified on the basis that it permits the courts to resolve issues of unfairness explicitly as regards that unfairness without recourse to formalistic rules or legal fictions. In policing contracts for fairness, the courts have again demonstrated their willingness to limit freedom of contract to protect the less advantaged from overreaching by dominant contracting parties. The doctrine of unconscionability has evolved through its application by the courts to include both procedural and substantive unconscionability.

Procedural unconscionability involves scrutiny for the presence of "bargaining naughtiness." In other words, was the negotiation process fair, or were there procedural irregularities, such as burying important terms of the agreement in fine print or obscuring the true meaning of the contract with impenetrable legal jargon?

Substantive unconscionability, which involves the actual terms of the contract, consists of oppressive or grossly unfair provisions, such as an exorbitant price or an unfair exclusion or limitation of contractual remedies. An all-too-common example is that involving a necessitous buyer in an unequal bargaining position with a seller, who consequently obtains an exorbitant price for his product or service. In one case, a court held unconscionable a price of $749 ($920 on time) for a vacuum cleaner that cost the seller $140. In another case the buyers, welfare recipients, purchased by time payment contract a home freezer unit for $900 which, when added to time credit charges, credit life insurance, credit property insurance, and sales tax, amounted to $1,235. The purchase resulted from a visit to the buyer's home by a salesman representing Your Shop At Home Service, Inc.; the maximum retail value of the freezer unit at time of purchase was $300. The court held the contract unconscionable and reformed it by reducing the price to the total payment ($620) the buyers had managed to make.

Some courts hold that in order for a contract to be unenforceable both substantive and procedural unconscionability must be present. Nevertheless, they need not exist to the same degree; the more oppressive one is, the less evidence of the other is required.

Closely akin to the concept of unconscionability is the doctrine of contracts of adhesion. A standard-form contract prepared by one party, an **adhesion contract** generally involves the preparer's offering the other party the contract on a "take-it-or-leave-it" basis. Such contracts are not automatically unenforceable but are subject to greater scrutiny for procedural or substantive unconscionability.

TORTIOUS CONDUCT

"A promise to commit a tort or to induce the commission of a tort is unenforceable on grounds of public policy." Restatement, Section 192. The courts will not permit contract law to violate the law of torts. Any agreement attempting to do so is considered contrary to public policy. For example, Andrew and Barlow Co. enter into an agreement under which Andrew promises Barlow that in return for $5,000 he will disparage the product of Barlow Co.'s competitor Cosmo, Inc., in order to provide Barlow Co. with a competitive advantage. Andrew's promise is to commit the tort of disparagement and is unenforceable as contrary to public policy.

EFFECT OF ILLEGALITY

As a general rule, illegal contracts are unenforceable. In a few instances, however, one of the parties may be permitted to enforce all or part of the contract; whereas, under other circumstances, the courts will allow one party to recover in restitution for his performance of the illegal contract.

GENERAL RULE: UNENFORCEABILITY

In most cases when an agreement is illegal, neither party can successfully sue the other for breach or recover for any performance rendered. Whichever party is plaintiff is immaterial to the courts. As is frequently said in these cases, the court will leave the parties where it finds them.

EXCEPTIONS

The courts recognize several exceptions to the general rule regarding the effect of illegality on a contract and may, after considering the circumstances surrounding a particular contract, grant relief to one of the parties, though not to the other. The following sections will consider these exceptions.

PARTY WITHDRAWING BEFORE PERFORMANCE A party to an illegal agreement may, prior to performance, withdraw from the transaction and recover whatever she has contributed, if the party has not engaged in serious misconduct. Restatement, Section 199. A common example is recovery of money left with a stakeholder pursuant to a wager before it is paid over to the winner.

PARTY PROTECTED BY STATUTE Sometimes an agreement is illegal because it violates a statute designed to protect persons in the position of one of the parties. For example, State "Blue Sky Laws" prohibiting the sale of unregistered securities are designed primarily for the protection of investors. In such cases, even though there is an unlawful agreement, the statute usually expressly gives the purchaser the right to rescind the sale and recover the money paid.

PARTY NOT EQUALLY AT FAULT Where one of the parties is less at fault than the other, he will be allowed to recover payments made or property transferred. Restatement, Section 198. For example, this exception would apply where one party induces the other to enter into an illegal bargain through fraud, duress, or undue influence.

EXCUSABLE IGNORANCE An agreement that appears on its face to be entirely permissible may, nevertheless, be illegal by reason of facts and circumstances of which one of the parties is completely unaware. For example, a man and woman make mutual promises to marry, but unknown to the woman, the man is already married. This is an agreement to commit the crime of bigamy, and the marriage, if entered into, is void. In such case the courts permit the party who is ignorant of the illegality to maintain a lawsuit against the other party for damages.

A party may also be excused for ignorance of relatively minor legislation. Restatement, Section 180. For instance, Jones and Old South Building Co. enter into a contract to build a factory that contains specifications in violation of the town's building ordinance. Jones did not know of the violation and had no reason to know. Old South's promise to build would not be rendered unenforceable on grounds of public policy, and Jones would have a claim against Old South for damages for breach of contract.

PARTIAL ILLEGALITY A contract may be partly unlawful and partly lawful. The courts view such a contract in one of two ways. First, the partial illegality may be held to taint the entire contract with illegality, so that it is wholly unenforceable. Second, it may be possible to separate the illegal from the legal part, in which case the court will hold the illegal part unenforceable but will enforce the legal part. For example, if a contract contains an illegal covenant not to compete, the covenant will not be enforced, though the rest of the contract may be.

CHAPTER SUMMARY

VIOLATIONS OF STATUTES	**General Rule** the courts will not enforce agreements declared illegal by statute **Licensing Statutes** require formal authorization to engage in certain trades, professions, or businesses • *Regulatory License* licensing statute that is intended to protect the public against unqualified persons; an unlicensed person may not recover for services she has performed • *Revenue License* licensing statute that seeks to raise money; an unlicensed person may recover for services he has performed **Gambling Statutes** prohibit wagers, which are agreements that one party will win and the other lose depending upon the outcome of an event in which their only interest is the gain or loss **Usury Statutes** establish a maximum rate of interest **Sunday Statutes** prohibition of certain types of commercial activity on Sunday (also called Blue Laws)
VIOLATIONS OF PUBLIC POLICY	**Common Law Restraint of Trade** unreasonable restraints of trade are not enforceable • *Sale of a Business* the promise by the seller of a business not to compete in that particular business in a reasonable geographic area for a reasonable period of time is enforceable • *Employment Contracts* an employment contract prohibiting an employee from competing with his employer for a reasonable period following termination is enforceable provided the restriction is necessary to protect legitimate interests of the employer **Exculpatory Clauses** the courts generally disapprove of contractual provisions excusing a party from liability for her own tortious conduct **Unconscionable Contracts** unfair or unduly harsh agreements are not enforceable • *Procedural Unconscionability* unfair or irregular bargaining • *Substantive Unconscionability* oppressive or grossly unfair contractual terms **Tortious Conduct** an agreement that requires a person to commit a tort is unenforceable **Corrupting Public Officials** agreements that corrupt public officials are not enforceable
EFFECT OF ILLEGALITY	**Unenforceability** neither party may recover under an illegal agreement where both parties are *in pari delicto* (in equal fault) **Exceptions** permit one party to recover payments • *Party Withdrawing before Performance* • *Party Protected by Statute* • *Party Not Equally at Fault* • *Excusable Ignorance* • *Partial Illegality*

Contractual Capacity

A binding promise or agreement requires that the parties to the agreement have contractual capacity. Everyone is regarded as having such capacity unless the law for reasons of public policy holds that the individual lacks such capacity. This essential ingredient of a contract will be discussed by considering those classes and conditions of persons who are legally limited in their capacity to contract: (1) minors, (2) incompetent persons, and (3) intoxicated persons.

MINORS

A **minor**, also called an infant, is a person who has not attained the age of legal majority. At common law, a minor was a person who was under twenty-one years of age. Today the age of majority has been changed in nearly all jurisdictions by statute, usually to age eighteen. Almost without exception, a minor's contract, whether executory or executed, is **voidable** at his or his guardian's option. Restatement, Section 14. Thus, the minor is in a favored position by having the option to disaffirm the contract or to enforce it. The adult party to the contract cannot avoid her contract with a minor. Even an "emancipated" minor, one who because of marriage or other reason is no longer subject to strict parental control, may avoid contractual liability in most jurisdictions. Consequently, businesspeople deal at their peril with minors and in situations of consequence generally require an adult to cosign or guarantee the performance of the contract. Nevertheless, most States recognize special categories of contracts that cannot be avoided (such as student loans or contracts for medical care) or that have a lower age for capacity (such as bank account, marriage, and insurance contracts).

LIABILITY ON CONTRACTS

A minor's contract is not entirely void and of no legal effect; rather, it is *voidable* at the minor's option. The exercise of this power of avoidance, called a **disaffirmance**, ordinarily releases the minor from any liability on the contract. On the other hand, after the minor becomes of age, she may choose to adopt or **ratify** the contract, in which case she surrenders her power of avoidance and becomes bound.

DISAFFIRMANCE As previously stated, a minor's contract is voidable at his or his guardian's option, conferring upon him a power to avoid liability. He, or in some jurisdictions his guardian, may, through words or conduct manifesting an intention not to abide by the contract, exercise the power to disaffirm.

In general, a minor's disaffirmance must come either during his minority or within a reasonable time after he reaches majority, as long as he has not already ratified the contract. In most States, defining a reasonable time depends upon such circumstances as the nature of the transaction, whether either party has caused the delay, and the extent to which either party has been injured by the delay. Some States, however, statutorily prescribe a time period, generally one year, in which the minor may disaffirm the contract.

A notable exception is that a sale of land by a minor cannot be disaffirmed until after he reaches his majority. But must he disaffirm immediately upon becoming an adult? In the case of a sale of land, there is a strong precedent that the minor may wait until the period of the statute of limitations has expired, if the sale involves no questions of fairness and equity.

Disaffirmance may be either *express* or *implied*. No particular form of words is essential, so long as they show an intention not to be bound. This intention also may be manifested by acts or by conduct. For example, a minor agrees to sell property to Alice and then sells that property to Brian. The sale to Brian would constitute a disaffirmance of the contract with Alice.

A troublesome yet important problem in this area, upon which the courts are not in agreement, pertains to the minor's duty upon disaffirmance. The majority hold that the minor must return any property he has received from the other party, provided he has it in his possession at the time of disaffirmance. Nothing more is required. If the minor disaffirms the purchase of an automobile and the vehicle has been wrecked, he need only return the wrecked vehicle. Other States require at least the payment of a reasonable amount for the use of the property or the amount of its depreciation while in the hands of the minor. A few States, either by statute or court ruling, recognize a duty upon the part of the minor to make *restitution*, that is, return an equivalent of what has been received in order to place the seller in approximately the same position she would have occupied had the sale not occurred.

Finally, can a minor disaffirm and recover property that his buyer has transferred to a good faith purchaser for value? Traditionally, the minor could avoid the contract and recover the property, despite the fact that the third person gave value for it and had no notice of the minority. Thus, in the case of the sale of real estate, a minor may rescind her deed of conveyance even against a good faith purchaser of the land who did not know of the minority. Regarding the sale of goods, however, this principle has been changed by Section 2–403 of the Uniform Commercial Code (UCC), which provides that a person with voidable title (e.g., the person buying goods from a minor) has power to transfer valid title to a good faith purchaser for value. For example, a minor sells his car to an individual who resells it to a used car dealership, a good faith purchaser for value. The used car dealer would acquire legal title even though he bought the car from a seller who had only voidable title.

RATIFICATION A minor has the option of ratifying a contract after reaching the age of majority. Ratification makes the contract binding *ab initio* (from the beginning). That is, the result is the same as if the contract had been valid and binding from its inception. Ratification, once effected, is final and cannot be withdrawn. Further, it must be in total, validating the entire contract. The minor can ratify the contract only as a whole, both as to burdens and benefits. He cannot, for example, ratify so as to retain the consideration he received and escape payment or other performance on his part, nor can he retain part of the contract and disaffirm the rest.

Ratification may be express, implied from conduct, or result from the failure to make a timely disaffirmance. Suppose that a minor makes a contract to buy property from an adult. The contract is voidable by the minor, and she can escape liability. But suppose that after reaching her majority, she promises to go through with the purchase. Because she has *expressly* ratified the contract she entered when she was a minor, her promise is binding, and the adult can recover for breach upon her failure to perform. In the absence of a statutory provision to the contrary, an express ratification may be oral.

Note that a minor has no power to ratify a contract while he remains a minor. A ratification cannot be based on words or conduct occurring while a minor is still underage, for his ratification at that time would be no more effective than his original contractual promise. The ratification must take place after the individual has acquired contractual capacity by attaining his majority.

Ratification, as previously stated, need not be express; it may be *implied* from the minor's conduct. Suppose that the minor, after attaining her majority, uses the property involved in the contract, undertakes to sell it to someone else, or performs some other act showing an intention to affirm the contract. She may not thereafter disaffirm the contract but is bound by it. Perhaps the most common form of implied ratification occurs when a minor, after attaining her majority, continues to use the property which she purchased as a minor. This use is obviously inconsistent with the nonexistence of the contract, and whether the contract is performed or still partly executory, it will amount to a ratification and prevent a disaffirmance by the minor. Simply keeping the goods for an unreasonable time after attaining majority also has been construed as a ratification. Although the courts are divided on the issue, payments by the minor upon reaching majority, either on principal or interest or on the purchase price of goods, have been held to amount to a ratification. Some courts require additional evidence of an intention to abide by the contract, such as an express promise to that effect or the actual use of the subject matter of the contract.

LIABILITY FOR NECESSARIES

Contractual incapacity does not excuse a minor from an obligation to pay for necessaries, those things that suitably and reasonably supply his personal needs, such as food, shelter, medicine, and clothing. Even here, however, the minor is liable not for the agreed price but for the *reasonable* value of the items furnished. Recovery is based on quasi contract. Thus, if a clothier sells a minor a suit that the minor needs, the clothier can successfully sue the minor. The clothier's recovery is limited, however, to the reasonable value of the suit, even if this amount is much less than the agreed-upon selling price.

Defining necessaries is a difficult problem. In general, the States regard as **necessary** those things that the minor needs to maintain himself in his particular station in life. Items necessary for subsistence and health—such as food, lodging, clothing, medicine, and medical services—are obviously included. But other less essential items, such as textbooks, school instruction, and legal advice, may be included as well. Further, many States enlarge the concept of necessaries to include articles of property and services that a minor needs to earn the money required to provide the necessities of life for himself and his dependents. Nevertheless, many States limit necessaries to items that are not provided to the minor. Thus, if a minor's guardian provides her with an adequate wardrobe, a blouse the minor purchased would not be considered a necessary. In addition, a minor is *not* liable for anything on the grounds that it is necessary unless it has been actually furnished to him and used or consumed by him. In other words, a minor may disaffirm his executory contracts for necessaries and refuse to accept the clothing, lodging, or other items or services.

Ordinarily, luxury items such as cameras, tape recorders, stereo equipment, television sets, and motorboats seldom qualify as necessaries. Whether automobiles and trucks are necessaries has caused considerable controversy, but some courts have recognized that under certain circumstances an automobile may be necessary when it is used by the minor for his business activities.

LIABILITY FOR MISREPRESENTATION OF AGE

The States do not agree on whether a minor who has fraudulently misrepresented her age when entering into contract has the power to disaffirm. Suppose a contracting minor says that she is eighteen years of age (or twenty-one if that is the year of attaining majority) and actually looks that old or even older. By the prevailing view in this country, the minor may nevertheless disaffirm the contract. Some States, however, prohibit disaffirmance if a minor misrepresents her age and the adult party, in good faith, reasonably relied upon the misrepresentation. Other States not following the majority rule either (1) require the minor to restore the other party to the position she occupied before the making of the contract or (2) allow the defrauded party to recover damages against the minor in tort.

LIABILITY FOR TORT CONNECTED WITH CONTRACT

It is well settled that minors are generally liable for their torts. There is, however, a legal doctrine providing that if a tort and a contract are so "interwoven" that the court must enforce the contract to enforce the tort action, the minor is not liable in tort. Thus, if a minor rents an automobile from an adult, he enters into a contractual relationship obliging him to exercise reasonable care and diligence to protect the property from injury. By negligently damaging the automobile, he breaches that contractual undertaking. But his contractual immunity protects him from an action by the adult based on the contract. Can the adult nonetheless recover damages on a tort theory? By the majority view, he cannot. For, it is reasoned, a tort recovery would, in effect, be an

enforcement of the contract and would defeat the protection that contract law affords the minor.

A different result arises, however, when the minor departs from the terms of the agreement, as by using a rental automobile for an unauthorized purpose and in so doing negligently causing damage to the automobile. In that event, most courts would hold that the tort is independent, and the adult can collect from the minor. Such a situation would not involve the breach of a contractual duty, but rather the commission of a tort while performing an activity completely beyond the scope of the rental agreement.

INCOMPETENT PERSONS

This section discusses the contract status of incompetent persons who are under court-appointed guardianship and those who are not adjudicated incompetents.

PERSON UNDER GUARDIANSHIP

If a person is under guardianship by court order, her contracts are void and of no legal effect. Restatement, Section 13. A *guardian* is appointed by a court, generally under the terms of a statute, to control and preserve the property of a person (the *ward*) whose impaired capacity prevents her from managing her own property. Nevertheless, a party dealing with an individual under guardianship may be able to recover the fair value of any necessaries provided to the incompetent. Moreover, the contracts of the ward may be ratified by her guardian or by herself upon termination of the guardianship.

MENTAL ILLNESS OR DEFECT

A contract is a consensual transaction; therefore, for a contract to be valid, it is necessary that the parties have a certain level of mental capacity. If a person lacks such capacity (is mentally incompetent), he may avoid liability under the agreement (because the contract is **voidable**).

Under the traditional, cognitive ability test, a person who is lacking in sufficient mental capacity to enter into a contract is one unable to comprehend the subject of the contract, its nature, and probable consequences. To avoid the contract, he need not be proved permanently incompetent, but his mental defect must be something more than a weakness of intellect or a lack of average intelligence. In short, a person is competent unless he is unable to understand the nature and effect of his act in entering a contract. Restatement, Section 15. In this situation, the incompetent may disaffirm the contract even if the other party did not know, or had no reason to know, of the incompetent's mental condition.

A second type of mental incompetence recognized by the Restatement and some States is a mental condition that impairs a person's ability to act in a reasonable manner. Section 15. In other words, the person understands what he is doing but cannot control his behavior in order to act in a reasonable and rational way. If the contract he enters is entirely executory or grossly unfair, it is voidable. If, however, the contract is executed and fair, and the competent party had no reason to suspect the incompetency of the other, the incompetent must restore the competent party to the *status quo* by returning the consideration he has received or its equivalent in money. If restoration to the *status quo* is impossible, avoidance will depend upon the equities of the situation.

Like minors and persons under guardianship, an incompetent person is liable for necessaries furnished him on the principle of quasi contract, the amount of recovery being the reasonable value of the goods or services. Moreover, an incompetent person may ratify or disaffirm his voidable contracts when he becomes competent or during a lucid period.

INTOXICATED PERSONS

A person may avoid any contract that he enters into if the other party has reason to know that, because of intoxication, he is unable either to understand the nature and conse-

quences of his actions or to act in a reasonable manner. Restatement, Section 16. Such contracts are voidable, although they may be ratified when the intoxicated person regains his capacity. Slight intoxication will not destroy one's contractual capacity, but neither is it essential that one be so drunk as to be totally without reason or understanding.

The effect of intoxication on contractual capacity is similar to that accorded contracts that are voidable because of the second type of incompetency, although the courts are even more strict with contracts a party enters while intoxicated, given the idea that the condition is voluntary. Most courts, therefore, require that the intoxicated person on regaining his capacity must act promptly to disaffirm and must generally offer to restore the consideration received. Individuals who are taking prescribed medication or who are involuntarily intoxicated are treated the same as those who are incompetent under the cognitive ability test. As with incompetent persons, intoxicated persons are liable in quasi contract for necessaries furnished them during their incapacity.

Figure 14-1 summarizes the voidability of contracts made by persons with contractual incapacity.

◆ **SEE FIGURE 14-1: Incapacity: Minors, Nonadjudicated Incompetents, and Intoxicated**

◆ **FIGURE 14-1: Incapacity: Minors, Nonadjudicated Incompetents, and Intoxicated**

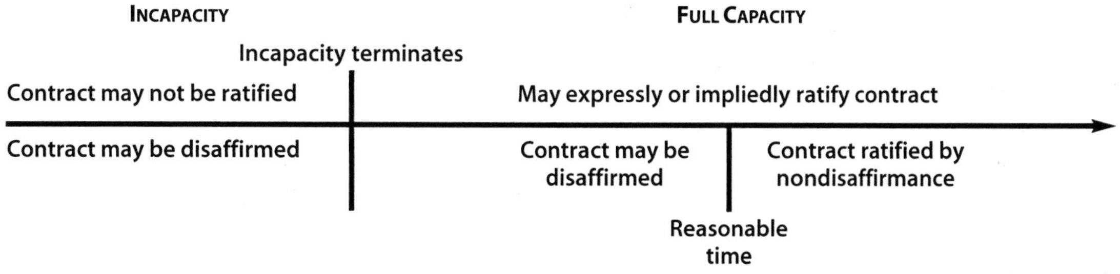

CHAPTER SUMMARY

MINORS   **Definition** persons who are under the age of majority (usually 18 years)
Liability on Contracts a minor's contracts are voidable at the minor's option
- *Disaffirmance* avoidance of the contract; may be done during minority and for a reasonable time after reaching majority
- *Ratification* affirmation of the entire contract; may be done upon reaching majority

Liability for Necessaries a minor is liable for the reasonable value of necessary items (those that reasonably supply a person's needs)

Liability for Misrepresentation of Age prevailing view is that a minor may disaffirm the contract

Liability for Tort Connected with Contract if a tort and a contract are so intertwined that to enforce the tort the court must enforce the contract, the minor is not liable in tort

---

INCOMPETENT AND INTOXICATED PERSONS

Person under Guardianship contracts made by a person placed under guardianship by court order are void

Mental Illness or Defect a contract entered into by a mentally incompetent person (one who is unable to understand the nature and consequences of his acts) is voidable

Intoxicated Persons a contract entered into by an intoxicated person (one who cannot understand the nature and consequence of her actions) is voidable

CHAPTER 15

Contracts in Writing

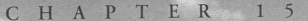

An **oral** contract, that is, one not written, is in every way as enforceable as a written contract unless otherwise provided by statute. Although most contracts are not required to be in writing to be enforceable, it is highly desirable that significant contracts be written. Written contracts avoid the numerous problems that proving the terms of oral contracts inevitably involves. The process of setting down the contractual terms in a written document also tends to clarify the terms and to reveal problems the parties might not otherwise foresee. Moreover, the terms of a written contract do not change over time, while the parties' recollections of the terms might.

When the parties do reduce their agreement to a complete and final written expression, the law (under the parol evidence rule) honors this document by not allowing the parties to introduce any evidence in a lawsuit that would alter, modify, or vary the terms of the written contract. Nevertheless, the parties may differ as to the proper or intended meaning of language contained in the written agreement where such language is ambiguous or susceptible to different interpretations. To ascertain the proper meaning requires an interpretation, or construction, of the contract. The rules of construction permit the parties to introduce evidence to resolve ambiguity and to show the meaning of the language employed and the sense in which both parties used it.

This chapter will examine (1) the types of contracts that must be in writing to be enforceable, (2) the parol evidence rule, and (3) the rules of contractual interpretation.

STATUTE OF FRAUDS

The statute of frauds requires that certain designated types of contracts be evidenced by a writing to be enforceable. The original statute became law in 1677, when the English Parliament adopted "An Act for Prevention of Frauds and Perjuries," commonly referred to as the statute of frauds. From the early days of U.S. history practically every State had and continues to have a statute of frauds patterned upon the original English statute.

The statute of frauds has no relation whatever to any kind of fraud practiced in the making of contracts. The common law rules relating to such fraud are discussed in *Chapter 11*. The purpose of the statute is to prevent perjured testimony in court from creating fraud in the proof of certain oral contracts, which purpose the statute accomplishes by requiring that certain contracts be evidenced by a signed writing. On the other hand, the statute does not prevent the performance of oral contracts if the parties are willing to perform. In brief, the statute relates only to the proof or evidence of a contract. It has nothing to do with the circumstances surrounding the making of a contract or with a contract's validity.

CONTRACTS WITHIN THE STATUTE OF FRAUDS

Many more types of contracts are *not* subject to the statute of frauds than are subject to it. Most oral contracts, as previously indicated, are as enforceable and valid as a written contract. If, however, a given contract is subject to the statute of frauds, the contract is said to be **within** the statute; to be enforceable, it must comply with the statute's requirements. All other types of contracts are said to be "not within" or "outside" the statute and need not comply with its requirements to be enforceable.

The following kinds of contracts are within the original English statute and remain within most State statutes; compliance requires a writing signed by the party to be charged (the party against whom the contract is to be enforced).

1. Promises to answer for the duty of another
2. Promises of an executor or administrator to answer personally for a duty of the decedent whose funds he is administering
3. Agreements upon consideration of marriage
4. Agreements for the transfer of an interest in land
5. Agreements not to be performed within one year

COLUMN: © PHOTOGRAPHEROLYMPUS CLOUDS: © KERTLIS

A sixth type of contract within the statute applied to contracts for the sale of goods. Section 2–201 of the Uniform Commercial Code (UCC) now governs the enforceability of contracts of this kind.

The various provisions of the statute of frauds apply independently. Accordingly, a contract for the sale of an interest in land may also be a contract in consideration of marriage, a contract not to be performed in one year, *and* a contract for the sale of goods.

In addition to those contracts specified in the original statute, most States require that other contracts be evidenced by a writing as well; for example, a contract to make a will, to authorize an agent to sell or purchase real estate, or to pay a commission to a real estate broker. Moreover, Article 1 of the UCC requires that a contract for the sale of securities, contracts creating certain types of security interests, and contracts for the sale of other personal property for more than $5,000 also be in writing. The 2001 Revision to Article 1 has deleted this requirement.

ELECTRONIC RECORDS

One significant impediment to e-commerce has been the questionable enforceability of contracts entered into through electronic means such as the Internet or e-mail because of the writing requirements under contract and sales law (statute of frauds). In response, the **Uniform Electronic Transactions Act (UETA)** was promulgated by the National Conference of Commissioners on Uniform State Laws (NCCUSL) in July 1999, and has been adopted by almost all of the States and introduced in a number of others. UETA applies only to transactions between parties each of which has agreed to conduct transactions by electronic means. It gives full effect to electronic contracts, encouraging their widespread use, and develops a uniform legal framework for their implementation. UETA protects electronic signatures and contracts from being denied enforcement because of the statute of frauds. Section 7 of UETA accomplishes this by providing the following:

1. A record or signature may not be denied legal effect or enforceability solely because it is in electronic form.
2. A contract may not be denied legal effect or enforceability solely because an electronic record was used in its formation.
3. If a law requires a record to be in writing, an electronic record satisfies the law.
4. If a law requires a signature, an electronic signature satisfies the law.

Section 14 of UETA further validates contracts formed by machines functioning as electronic agents for parties to a transaction: "A contract may be formed by the interaction of electronic agents of the parties, even if no individual was aware of or reviewed the electronic agents' actions or the resulting terms and agreements." The Act excludes from its coverage wills, codicils, and testamentary trusts as well as all Articles of the UCC except Articles 2 and 2A.

In addition, Congress in 2000 enacted the **Electronic Signatures in Global and National Commerce (E-Sign)**. The Act, which uses language very similar to that of UETA, makes electronic records and signatures valid and enforceable across the United States for many types of transactions in or affecting interstate or foreign commerce. E-Sign does not generally preempt UETA. E-Sign does not require any person to agree to use or accept electronic records or electronic signatures. The Act defines transactions quite broadly to include the sale, lease, exchange, and licensing of personal property and services, as well as the sale, lease, exchange, or other disposition of any interest in real property. E-Sign defines an electronic record as "a contract or other record created, generated, sent, communicated, received, or stored by electronic means." It defines an electronic signature as "an electronic sound, symbol, or process, attached to or logically associated with a contract or other record and executed or adopted by a person with the intent to sign the record." Like UETA, E-Sign ensures that Internet and e-mail agreements will not be unenforceable because of the statute of frauds by providing that

1. a signature, contract, or other record relating to such transaction may not be denied legal effect, validity, or enforceability solely because it is in electronic form; and
2. a contract relating to such transaction may not be denied legal effect, validity, or enforceability solely because an electronic signature or electronic record was used in its formation.

To protect consumers, E-Sign provides that they must consent *electronically* to conducting transactions with electronic records after being informed of the types of hardware and software required. Prior to consent, consumers must also receive a "clear and conspicuous" statement informing consumers of their right to (1) have the record provided on paper or in nonelectronic form; (2) after consenting to electronic records, receive paper copies of the electronic record; and (3) withdraw consent to receiving electronic records.

As defined by E-Sign, an electronic agent is a computer program or other automated means used independently to initiate an action or respond to electronic records or performances in whole or in part without review or action by an individual at the time of the action or response. The Act validates contracts or other records relating to a transaction in or affecting interstate or foreign commerce formed by electronic agents so long as the action of each electronic agent is legally attributable to the person to be bound.

E-Sign specifically excludes certain transactions, including (1) wills, codicils, and testamentary trusts; (2) adoptions, divorces, and other matters of family law; and (3) the UCC other than sales and leases of goods.

SURETYSHIP PROVISION

The **suretyship** provision applies to a contractual promise by a surety (*promisor*) to a **creditor** (*promisee*) to perform the duties or obligations of a third person (**principal debtor**) if the principal debtor does not perform. Thus, if a mother tells a merchant to extend $1,000 worth of credit to her son and says, "If he doesn't pay, I will," the promise must be in writing (or have a sufficient electronic record) to be enforceable. The factual situation can be reduced to the simple statement, "If X doesn't pay, I will." The promise is said to be **collateral**, in that the promisor is not primarily liable. The mother does not promise to pay in any event; her promise is to pay only if the one primarily obligated, her son, defaults.

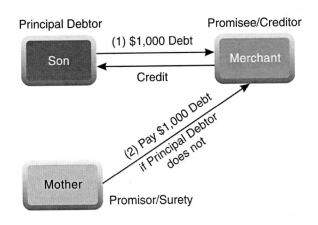

The rule applies only to cases involving three parties and two contracts. The primary contract, between the principal debtor and the creditor, creates the indebtedness. The collateral contract is made by the third person (surety) directly with the creditor, whereby the surety promises to pay the debt to the creditor in case the principal debtor fails to do so. For a complete discussion of suretyship see *Chapter 38*.

ORIGINAL PROMISE If the promisor makes an **original promise** by undertaking to become primarily liable, then the statute of frauds does not apply. For example, a father tells a merchant to deliver certain items to his daughter and says, "I will pay $400 for them." The father is not promising to answer for the debt of another; rather, he is making the debt his own. It is to the father, and the

father alone, that the merchant extends credit; only from the father may the creditor seek payment. The statute of frauds does not apply, and the promise may be oral.

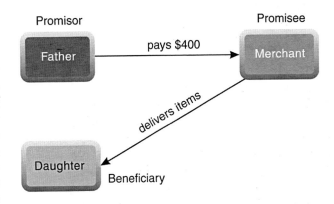

MAIN PURPOSE DOCTRINE The courts have developed an exception to the suretyship provision based on the purpose or object of the promisor, called the "main purpose doctrine" or "leading object rule." Where the object or purpose of the promisor is to obtain an economic benefit for himself, the promise is *not* within the statute. Restatement, Section 116. The expected benefit to the surety "must be such as to justify the conclusion that his main purpose in making the promise is to advance his own interest." Restatement, Section 116, Comment b. The fact that the surety received consideration for his promise or that he might receive a slight and indirect advantage is insufficient to bring the promise within the main purpose doctrine.

Suppose that a supply company has refused to furnish materials upon the credit of a building contractor. Facing a possible slowdown in the construction of his building, the owner of the land promises the supplier that if he will extend credit to the contractor, the owner will pay if the contractor does not. Here, the primary purpose of the promisor is to serve his own economic interest, even though the performance of the promise would discharge the duty of another. The intent to benefit the contractor is at most incidental, and courts will uphold oral promises of this type.

PROMISE MADE TO DEBTOR The suretyship provision has been interpreted not to include promises made to a debtor. For example, D owes a debt to C. S promises D that she will pay D's debt in return for valid consideration from D. Because S made the promise to the debtor (D), not the creditor, the promise may be oral. The promise is not a collateral promise to pay C if D fails to pay and thus is not a promise to discharge the obligation of another.

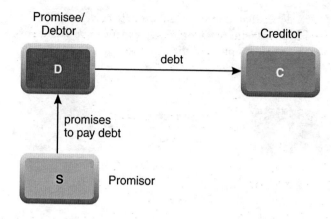

EXECUTOR-ADMINISTRATOR PROVISION

The executor-administrator provision applies to the contractual promises of an executor of a decedent's will, or to those of the administrator of his estate if the decedent dies without a will, to answer personally for a duty of the decedent. An **executor** or **administrator** is a person appointed by a court to carry on, subject to order of court, the administration of the estate of a deceased person. If the will of a decedent nominates a certain person as executor, the court customarily appoints that person. (For a more detailed discussion of executors and administrators, see *Chapter 52*.) If an executor or administrator promises to pay personally a debt of the decedent, the promise must be in writing—or in proper electronic form—to be enforceable. For example, Brian, who is Ann's son and executor of her will, recognizing that Ann's estate will not provide funds sufficient to pay all of her debts, orally promises Curtis, one of Ann's creditors, that he, Brian, will personally pay all of his mother's creditors in full in return for valid consideration from Curtis. Brian's oral promise is not enforceable. This provision does not apply to promises to pay debts of the deceased out of assets of the estate.

The executor-administrator provision is thus a specific application of the suretyship provision. Accordingly, the exceptions to the suretyship provision apply to this provision as well.

MARRIAGE PROVISION

The notable feature of the marriage provision is that it does *not* apply to mutual promises to marry. The provision applies only if a promise to marry is made in consideration for some promise other than a reciprocal promise to marry. Restatement, Section 124. If, for example, Greg and Betsy each orally promise and agree to marry each other, their agreement is not within the statute and is a binding contract between them. If, however, Greg promises to convey title to a certain farm to Betsy if she accepts

his proposal of marriage, their agreement would fall within the statute of frauds.

LAND CONTRACT PROVISION

The land contract provision covers promises to transfer "any interest in land," which includes any right, privilege, power, or immunity in real property. Restatement, Section 125. Thus, all promises to transfer, buy, or pay for an interest in land, including ownership interests, leases, mortgages, options, and easements, are within the provision.

The land contract provision does not include contracts to transfer an interest in personal property. It also does not cover short-term leases, which by statute in most States are those for one year or less; contracts to build a building on a piece of land; contracts to do work on the land; or contracts to insure a building on the land.

The courts may enforce an oral contract for the transfer of an interest in land if the party seeking enforcement has so changed his position in reasonable reliance upon the contract that injustice can be prevented only by enforcing the contract. Restatement, Section 129. In applying this **part performance** exception, many States require that the transferee has paid a portion or all of the purchase price *and* either has taken possession of the real estate or has started to make valuable improvements on the land. For example, Aaron orally agrees to sell land to Barbara for $30,000. With Aaron's consent, Barbara takes possession of the land, pays Aaron $10,000, builds a house on the land, and occupies it. Several years later, Aaron repudiates the contract. The courts will enforce the contract against Aaron. On the other hand, the courts will not enforce the promise unless equity so demands.

An oral promise by a purchaser is also enforceable if the seller fully performs by conveying the property to the purchaser. As previously indicated, however, payment of part or all of the price is not sufficient in itself to remove the contract from the scope of the statute.

ONE-YEAR PROVISION

The statute of frauds requires all contracts that *cannot* be fully performed within one year of their making to be in writing or in proper electronic form. Restatement, Section 130.

THE POSSIBILITY TEST To determine whether a contract can be performed within a year, the courts ask whether it is *possible* to complete its performance within a year. The **possibility test** does not ask whether the agreement is likely to be performed within one year from the date it was formed; nor does it ask whether the parties think that performance will be within the year. The enforceability of the contract depends not on probabilities or on the actuality of subsequent events but on whether the terms of the contract make it possible for performance to occur within one year. For example, an oral contract between Alice and Bill for Alice to build a bridge, which should reasonably take three years, is enforceable if it is possible, although extremely unlikely and difficult, for Alice to perform the contract in one year. Similarly, if Alice agrees to employ Bill for life, this contract also is not within the statute of frauds. Given the possibility that Bill may die within the year (in which case the contract would be completely performed), the contract is therefore one that is *fully performable* within a year. Contracts of indefinite duration are likewise excluded from the provision. On the other hand, an oral contract to employ another person for thirteen months could not possibly be performed within a year and is unenforceable.

COMPUTATION OF TIME The year runs from the time the agreement is made, not from the time when the performance is to begin. For example, on January 1, 2010, A orally hires B to work for eleven months starting on May 1, 2010. That contract will be fully performed on March 31, 2011, which is more than one year after January 1, 2010, the date the contract was made. Consequently, it is *within* the statute of frauds and unenforceable as it is oral.

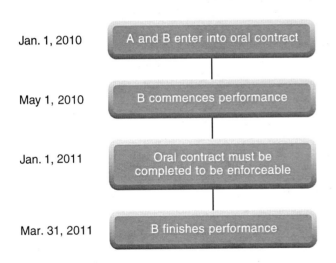

Jan. 1, 2010	A and B enter into oral contract
May 1, 2010	B commences performance
Jan. 1, 2011	Oral contract must be completed to be enforceable
Mar. 31, 2011	B finishes performance

Similarly, a contract for a year's performance, which is to begin three days after the date on which the contract is made, is within the statute and, if oral, is unenforceable. If, however, the performance is to begin the following day or, under the terms of the agreement, could have begun the following day, the contract is not within the statute and need not be in writing, as the one year's performance would be completed on the anniversary date of the making of the contract.

FULL PERFORMANCE BY ONE PARTY Where one party to a contract has fully performed, most courts hold that the promise of the other party is enforceable, even though by its terms the performance of the contract was not possible within the period of a year. Restatement, Section 130. For example, Vince borrows $4,800 from Julie, orally promising to pay Julie $4,800 in three annual installments of $1,600. Vince's promise is enforceable, notwithstanding the one-year provision, because Julie has fully performed by making the loan.

SALE OF GOODS

The original statute of frauds, which applied to contracts for the sale of goods, has been used as a prototype for the UCC Article 2 statute of frauds provision. Section 2–201 of the UCC provides that a contract for the sale of goods for the price of **$500 or more** is not enforceable unless there is some writing or record sufficient to indicate that the parties have made a contract for sale. **Goods**, as previously indicated, are defined as movable personal property. Section 2–105(1). The definition expressly includes growing crops and unborn animals.

ADMISSION The Code permits an oral contract for the sale of goods to be enforced against a party who in his pleading, testimony, or otherwise in court admits that a contract was made, but limits enforcement to the quantity of goods so admitted. Section 2–201(3)(b). The language "otherwise in court" may include pretrial deposition and written interrogatories of the defendant. Some courts now apply this exception to other statute of frauds provisions.

SPECIALLY MANUFACTURED GOODS The Code permits a seller to enforce an oral contract for goods specially manufactured for a buyer, but only if evidence indicates that the goods were made for the buyer and the seller can show that he made a *substantial beginning* of their manufacture prior to receiving any notice of repudiation. Section 2–201(3)(a). If goods manufactured on special order are nonetheless readily marketable in the ordinary course of the seller's business, this exception does not apply.

For example, if Jim brings an action against Robin alleging breach of an oral contract under which Robin agreed to purchase from Jim three million balloons with Robin's trademark imprinted on them at a price of $30,000, the action is not subject to the defense of the statute of frauds unless Robin can show (1) that the balloons are suitable for sale to other buyers, which is highly improbable in view of the trademark, or (2) that Jim received notice of repudiation before he had made a substantial start on the production of the balloons or had otherwise substantially committed himself to procuring them.

DELIVERY OR PAYMENT AND ACCEPTANCE Prior to the Code, delivery and acceptance of part of the goods or payment of part of the price made the entire oral contract enforceable

◆ **FIGURE 15-1: The Statute of Frauds**

Contracts within the Statute of Frauds	Exceptions
Suretyship—a promise to answer for the duty of another	• Main purpose rule • Original promise • Promise made to debtor
Executor-Administrator—a promise to answer personally for debt of decedent	• Main purpose rule • Original promise • Promise made to debtor
Agreements made upon consideration of marriage	• Mutual promises to marry
Agreements for the transfer of an interest in land	• Part performance plus detrimental reliance • Seller conveys property
Agreements not to be performed within one year	• Full performance by one party • Possibility of performance within one year
Sale of goods for $500 or more	• Admission • Specially manufactured goods • Delivery or payment acceptance

against the buyer who had received part delivery or against the seller who had received part payment. Under the Code, such "partial performance" validates the contract only for the goods that have been accepted or for which payment has been accepted. Section 2–201(3)(c). To illustrate, Johnson orally agrees to buy one thousand watches from Barnes for $15,000. Barnes delivers three hundred watches to Johnson, who receives and accepts the watches. The oral contract is enforceable to the extent of three hundred watches ($4,500)—those received and accepted—but is unenforceable to the extent of seven hundred watches ($10,500).

But what if the contract, such as one for the sale of an automobile, is indivisible so that the making of part payment creates only a choice between not enforcing the contract or enforcing it as a whole? Presently, authority is divided on this issue, although the better rule appears to be that such part payment and acceptance makes the entire contract enforceable.

◆ **SEE FIGURE 15-1: The Statute of Frauds**

MODIFICATION OR RESCISSION OF CONTRACTS WITHIN THE STATUTE OF FRAUDS

Oral contracts modifying previously existing contracts are unenforceable if the resulting contract is within the statute of frauds. The reverse is also true: an oral modification of a prior contract is enforceable if the new contract is not within the statute. Thus, examples of unenforceable oral contractual modifications include an oral promise to guarantee additional duties of another, an oral agreement to substitute different land for that described in the original contract, and an oral agreement to extend an employee's contract for six months to a total of two years. On the other hand, an oral agreement to modify an employee's contract from two years to six months at a higher salary is not within the statute of frauds and is enforceable.

By extension, an oral rescission is effective and discharges all unperformed duties under the original contract. For example, Linda and Donald enter into a written contract of employment for a two-year term. Later they orally agree to rescind the contract. The oral agreement is effective, and the written contract is rescinded. Where, however, land has been transferred, an agreement to rescind the transaction constitutes a contract to retransfer the land and is within the statute of frauds.

Under the UCC, the decisive point is the contract price *after* the modification. Section 2–209(3). If the parties enter into an oral contract to sell for $450 a motorcycle to be delivered to the buyer and later, prior to delivery, orally agree that the seller shall paint the motorcycle and install new tires and that the buyer shall pay a price of $550, the modified contract is unenforceable. Conversely, if the parties have a written contract for the sale of two hundred bushels of wheat at a price of $4 per bushel and later orally agree to decrease the quantity to one hundred bushels at the same price per bushel, the agreement, as modified, is for a total price of $400 and thus is enforceable.

COMPLIANCE WITH THE STATUTE OF FRAUDS

Even though a contract is within the statute of frauds, a sufficient *writing*, *memorandum*, or *record* may justify its enforcement. The writing or record need not be in any specific form, nor be an attempt by the parties to enter into a binding contract, nor represent their entire agreement: it need only comply with the requirements of the statute of frauds.

GENERAL CONTRACTS PROVISIONS

The English statute of frauds and most modern statutes of frauds require that the agreement be evidenced by a writing or record to be enforceable. The note, memorandum, or record, which may be formal or informal, must

1. specify the parties to the contract;
2. specify with reasonable certainty the subject matter and the essential terms of the unperformed promises; and
3. be signed by the party to be charged or by his agent.

The statute's purpose in requiring a writing or record is to ensure that the parties have entered into a contract. The writing or record, therefore, need not exist at the time of the litigation; showing that the memorandum once existed is sufficient.

The memorandum may be a receipt or a check. It may be such that the parties themselves view the memorandum as having no legal significance whatever, as, for example, a personal letter between the parties, an interdepartmental communication, an advertisement, or the record books of a business. The writing or record need not have been delivered to the party who seeks to take advantage of it, and it may even contain a repudiation of the oral agreement. For example, Adrian and Joseph enter into an oral agreement that Adrian will sell Blackacre to Joseph for $5,000. Adrian subsequently receives a better offer and sends Joseph a signed letter, which begins by reciting all the material terms of the oral agreement. The letter concludes, "Since my agreement to sell Blackacre to you for $5,000 was oral, I am not bound by my promise. I have since received a better offer and will accept that one." Adrian's letter constitutes a sufficient memorandum for Joseph to enforce Adrian's promise to sell Blackacre. It should be recognized that because Joseph did not sign the memorandum, the writing does not bind him. Thus, a contract may be enforceable against only one of the parties.

The "signature" may be initials or may even be typewritten or printed, so long as the party intended it to authenticate the writing or record. Furthermore, the signature need not be at the bottom of the page or at the customary place for a signature. The memorandum may consist of *several* papers or documents, none of which would be sufficient by itself. The several memoranda, however, must together satisfy all of the requirements of a writing or record to comply with the statute of frauds and must clearly indicate that they relate to the same transaction. Restatement, Section 132. The latter requirement can be satisfied if (1) the writings are physically attached, (2) the writings refer to each other, or (3) an examination of the writings shows them to be in reference to each other.

SALE OF GOODS

The statute of frauds provision under Article 2 is more liberal. For a sale of goods, Section 2–201 of the Code requires merely some writing or record

1. sufficient to indicate that a contract has been made between the parties;
2. specifying the quantity of goods to be sold; and
3. signed by the party against whom enforcement is sought or by her authorized agent or broker.

The writing or record is sufficient even if it omits or incorrectly states an agreed-upon term; however, where the quantity term is misstated, the contract can be enforced only to the extent of the quantity stated in the writing or record.

As with general contracts, several related documents may satisfy the writing or record requirement. Moreover, the signature again may be by initials or even typewritten or printed, so long as the party intended thereby to authenticate the writing or record.

In addition, the Code provides relief to a merchant who, within a reasonable time after entering into the oral contract, confirms the contract for the sale of goods by a letter or signed writing to the other party if he too is a merchant. As between **merchants**, the **written confirmation**, if sufficient against the sender, is also sufficient against the recipient unless he gives written notice of his objection within ten days after receiving the confirmation. Section 2–201(2). This means that if these requirements have been met, the recipient of the writing or record is in the same position he would have assumed by signing it; and the confirmation, therefore, is enforceable against him.

For example, Brown Co. and ATM Industries enter into an oral contract that provides that ATM will deliver twelve thousand shirts to Brown at $6 per shirt. Brown sends a letter to ATM acknowledging the agreement. The letter, containing the quantity term but not the price, is signed by

Brown's president and is mailed to ATM's vice president for sales. Brown was bound by the contract once its authorized agent signs the letter; ATM cannot raise the defense of the statute of frauds if ATM does not object to the letter within ten days after receiving it. Therefore, it is extremely important for merchants to examine their mail carefully and promptly to make certain that any written confirmations conform to their understanding of their outstanding contractual agreements.

EFFECT OF NONCOMPLIANCE

The English statute provided that "no action shall be brought" upon a contract to which the statute of frauds applied *and* which did not comply with its requirements. The Code, by comparison, states that the contract "is not enforceable by way of action or defense." Despite the difference in language the basic legal effect is the same: a contracting party has a defense to an action by the other party to enforce an oral contract that is within the statute and that does not comply with its requirements. In short, the oral contract is **unenforceable**.

For example, if Tia, a painter, and James, a homeowner, make an oral contract under which James is to give Tia a certain tract of land in return for her painting his house, the contract is unenforceable under the statute of frauds. It is a contract for the sale of an interest in land. Either party can repudiate and has a defense to an action by the other to enforce the contract.

FULL PERFORMANCE

After all the promises of an oral contract have been performed by all the parties, the statute of frauds no longer applies. Accordingly, neither party can have the contract set aside on the grounds that it should have been in writing. The purpose of the statute is not to prohibit the performance of oral contracts but simply to exclude oral evidence of contracts within its provisions. Courts, in other words, will not "unscramble" a fully performed contract merely because it was not in writing or a proper record. In short, the statute applies to executory contracts only.

RESTITUTION

A party to a contract that is unenforceable because of the statute of frauds may have, nonetheless, acted in reliance upon the contract. In such a case the party may recover in restitution the benefits he conferred upon the other in relying upon the unenforceable contract. Thus, if Wilton makes an oral contract to furnish services to Rochelle that are not to be performed within a year and Rochelle discharges Wilton after three months, Wilton may recover as restitution the value of the services he rendered during the three

months. Most courts require, however, that the party seeking restitution not be in default.

PROMISSORY ESTOPPEL

A growing number of courts have used the doctrine of promissory estoppel to displace the requirement of a writing by enforcing oral contracts within the statute of frauds where the party seeking enforcement has reasonably and foreseeably relied upon a promise in such a way that injustice can be avoided only by enforcing the promise. Restatement, Section 139. This section is essentially identical to Section 90 of the Restatement, which, as discussed in *Chapter 12*, dispenses with the requirement of consideration, although the comments to Section 139 state that "the requirement of consideration is more easily displaced than the requirement of a writing." The remedy granted is limited, as justice requires, and depends upon such factors as the availability of other remedies; the foreseeability, reasonableness, and substantiality of the reliance; and the extent to which reliance corroborates evidence of the promise.

PAROL EVIDENCE RULE

A contract reduced to writing and signed by the parties is frequently the result of many conversations, conferences, proposals, counterproposals, letters, and memoranda and sometimes is the product of negotiations conducted, or partly conducted, by agents of the parties. Any given stage in the negotiations may have produced tentative agreements that were superseded (or regarded as such by one of the parties) by subsequent negotiations. Offers may have been made and withdrawn, either expressly or by implication, or forgotten in the give-and-take of negotiations. Ultimately, though, the parties prepare and sign a final draft of the written contract, which may or may not include all of the points that were discussed and agreed upon during the negotiations. By signing the agreement, however, the parties have declared it to be their contract; and the terms it contains represent the contract they have made. As a rule of substantive law, neither party is later permitted to show that the contract they made differs from the terms and provisions that appear in the written agreement. This rule, which also applies to wills and deeds, is called the parol evidence rule.

THE RULE

When a contract is expressed in a writing that is intended to be the complete and final expression of the rights and duties of the parties, parol evidence of *prior* oral or written negotiations or agreements of the parties, or their *contemporaneous* oral agreements that vary or change the written contract, are not admissible. The word *parol* means literally "speech" or "words." The term **parol evidence** refers to any evidence, whether oral or in writing, which is outside the written contract and not incorporated into it either directly or by reference.

The parol evidence rule applies only to an *integrated* contract; that is, one contained in a certain writing or writings to which the parties have assented as the statement of the complete agreement or contract between them. When a contract is thus integrated, the courts will not permit parol evidence of any prior or contemporaneous agreement to vary, change, alter, or modify any of the terms or provisions of the written contract. Restatement, Section 213.

A writing may contain a **merger clause**, which states that the writing is intended to be the complete and final expression of the agreement between the parties. Most courts consider a merger clause to be conclusive proof of an integrated contract, while a few courts view a merger clause only as evidence of an integrated contract.

The reason for the parol evidence rule is that the parties, by reducing their entire agreement to writing, are regarded as having intended the writing that they signed to include the whole of their agreement. The terms and provisions contained in the writing are there because the parties intended them to be there. Conversely, any provision not in the writing is regarded as having been omitted because the parties intended that it should not be a part of their contract. In safeguarding the contract as made by the parties, the rule excluding evidence that would tend to change, alter, vary, or modify the terms of a written agreement applies to all integrated written contracts and deals with what terms are part of the contract. The rule differs from the statute of frauds, which governs what contracts must be evidenced by a writing to be enforceable.

SITUATIONS TO WHICH THE RULE DOES NOT APPLY

The parol evidence rule, in spite of its name, is neither an exclusionary rule of evidence nor a rule of construction or interpretation; rather, it is a rule of substantive law that defines the limits of a contract. Bearing this in mind, as well as the reason underlying the rule, it should be clear that the rule does **not** apply to any of the following:

1. A contract that is partly written and partly oral; that is, one in which the parties do not intend the writing to be their entire agreement.
2. A clerical or *typographical error* that obviously does not represent the agreement of the parties. Where, for example, a written contract for the services of a skilled mining engineer provides that his rate of compensation is to be $7 per day, a court of equity would permit reformation (correction) of the contract to rectify the mistake upon a showing that both parties intended the rate to be $700 per day.

3. Evidence showing the lack of *contractual capacity* of one of the parties, such as proof of minority, intoxication, or mental incompetency. Such evidence would not tend to vary, change, or alter any of the terms of the written agreement, but rather would show that the written agreement was voidable or void.
4. A *defense* of fraud, misrepresentation, duress, undue influence, mistake, illegality, or unconscionability. Though evidence establishing any of these defenses would not purport to vary, change, or alter any of the terms of the written agreement, it would show such agreement to be voidable, void, or unenforceable.
5. A *condition precedent* to which the parties agreed orally at the time they executed the written agreement and to which they made the entire agreement subject. Again, such evidence does not tend to vary, alter, or change any of the terms of the agreement, but rather shows whether the entire written agreement, unchanged and unaltered, ever became effective. For example, if John signs a subscription agreement to buy stock in a corporation to be formed and delivers the agreement to Thompson with the mutual understanding that it is not to be binding unless the other persons financially responsible under it shall each agree to buy at least an equivalent amount of such stock, John is permitted to show by parol evidence this condition.
6. A *subsequent mutual rescission or modification* of the written contract. Parol evidence of a later agreement does not tend to show that the integrated writing did not represent the contract between the parties at the time it was made. Parties to an existing contract, whether written or oral, may agree to change the terms of their contract as they see fit, or to cancel it completely, if they so desire.
7. Parol evidence is admissible to explain *ambiguous* terms in the contract. To enforce a contract, it is necessary to understand its intended meaning. Nevertheless, such interpretation is not to alter, change, or vary the terms of the contract.
8. The rule does not prevent a party from proving the existence of a separate, distinct contract between the same parties.

SUPPLEMENTAL EVIDENCE

Although a written agreement may not be contradicted by evidence of a prior agreement or of a contemporaneous agreement, under the Restatement, Section 216, and the Code, Section 2–202, a written contract may be explained or supplemented by (1) course of dealing between the parties, (2) usage of trade, (3) course of performance, or (4) evidence of consistent additional terms, unless the parties intended the writing to be a complete and exclusive statement of their agreement.

A **course of dealing** is a sequence of previous conduct between the parties under an agreement that the court reasonably may

◆ **FIGURE 15-2: Parol Evidence Rule**

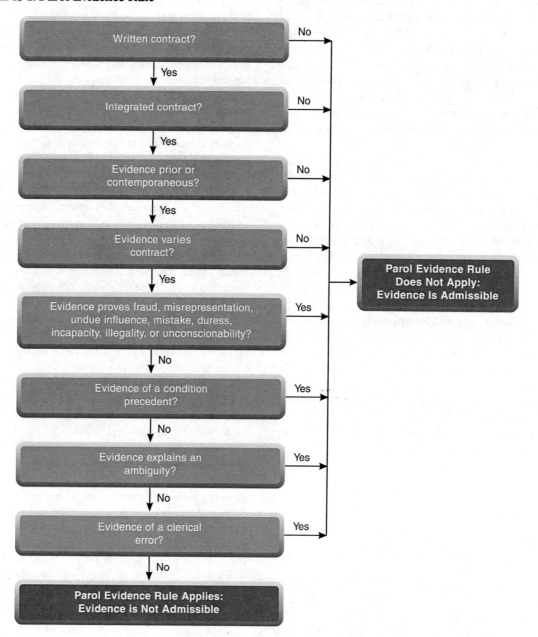

regard as establishing a common basis of understanding for interpreting their expressions and other conduct.

A **usage of trade** is a practice or method of dealing, regularly observed and followed in a place, vocation, or trade.

Course of performance refers to the manner and extent to which the respective parties to a contract have accepted without objection successive tenders of performance by the other party.

The Restatement and the Code permit *supplemental consistent evidence* to be introduced into a court proceeding, but only if it does not contradict a term or terms of the original agreement and would probably not have been included in the original contract.

◆ **SEE FIGURE 15-2: Parol Evidence Rule**

INTERPRETATION OF CONTRACTS

Although the written words or language in which the parties embodied their agreement or contract may not be changed by parol evidence, the ascertainment (determination) of the meaning to be given the written language is outside the scope of the parol evidence rule. Though written words embody the terms of the contract, words are but symbols. If their meaning is unclear, the courts may clarify this meaning by applying rules of interpretation or construction and by using extrinsic (external) evidence, where necessary.

The Restatement, Section 200, defines **interpretation** as the ascertainment of the meaning of a promise or agreement or a term of the promise or agreement. Where the language in a contract is unambiguous, the courts will not accept extrinsic evidence tending to show a meaning different from that which the words clearly convey. Its function being to interpret and construe written contracts and documents, the court adopts rules of interpretation to apply a legal standard to the words contained in the agreement. The courts will attempt to interpret a contract in accordance with the intent of the parties. If the subjective intent of the parties fails to provide a clear interpretation, the courts will make an objective interpretation. Among the rules that aid interpretation are the following:

1. Words and other conduct are interpreted in the light of all the circumstances, and the principal purpose of the parties, if ascertainable, is given great weight.
2. A writing is interpreted as a whole, and all writings that are part of the same transaction are interpreted together.
3. Unless a different intention is manifested, language that has a commonly accepted meaning is interpreted in accordance with that meaning.
4. Unless a different intention is manifested, technical terms and words of art are given their technical meanings.
5. Wherever reasonable, the manifestations of intention of the parties to a promise or agreement are interpreted as consistent with each other and with any relevant course of performance, course of dealing, or usage of trade.
6. An interpretation that gives a reasonable, lawful, and effective meaning to all the terms is preferred over an interpretation that leaves a part unreasonable, unlawful, or of no effect.
7. Specific terms and exact terms are given greater weight than general language.
8. Separately negotiated or added terms are given greater weight than standardized terms or other terms not separately negotiated.
9. Express terms, course of performance, course of dealing, and usage of trade are weighted in that order.
10. Where a term or promise has several possible meanings, it will be interpreted against the party who supplied the contract or the term. Restatement, Sections 201, 202, and 203.
11. Where written provisions are inconsistent with typed or printed provisions, the written provision is given preference. Likewise, typed provisions are given preferences to printed provisions.
12. If the amount payable is set forth in both figures and words and the amounts differ, the words control the figures.

It may be observed that, through the application of the parol evidence rule (where properly applicable) and the above rules of interpretation and construction, the law not only enforces a contract but, in so doing, exercises great care that the contract being enforced is the one the parties made and that the sense and meaning of the parties' intentions are carefully ascertained and given effect.

CHAPTER SUMMARY

STATUTE OF FRAUDS

CONTRACTS WITHIN THE STATUTE OF FRAUDS	**Rule** contracts within the statute of frauds must be evidenced by a writing to be enforceable **Electronic Records** full effect is given to electronic contracts and signatures **Suretyship Provision** applies to promises to pay the debts of others • *Promise Must Be Collateral* promisor must be secondarily, not primarily, liable • *Main Purpose Doctrine* if primary object is to provide an economic benefit to the surety, then the promise is not within the statute **Executor-Administrator Provision** applies to promises to answer personally for duties of decedents **Marriage Provision** applies to promises made in consideration of marriage but not to mutual promises to marry **Land Contract Provision** applies to promises to transfer any rights, privileges, powers, or immunities in real property **One-Year Provision** applies to contracts that cannot be performed within one year • *The Possibility Test* the criterion is whether it is possible, not likely, for the agreement to be performed within one year • *Computation of Time* the year runs from the time the agreement is made

- *Full Performance by One Party* makes the promise of the other party enforceable under majority view

Sale of Goods a contract for the sale of goods for the price of $500 or more must be evidenced by a writing or record to be enforceable

- *Admission* an admission in pleadings, testimony, or otherwise in court makes the contract enforceable for the quantity of goods admitted
- *Specially Manufactured Goods* an oral contract for specially manufactured goods is enforceable
- *Delivery or Payment and Acceptance* validates the contract only for the goods that have been accepted or for which payment has been accepted

Modification or Rescission of Contracts within the Statute of Frauds oral contracts modifying existing contracts are unenforceable if the resulting contract is within the statute of frauds

METHODS OF COMPLIANCE	**General Contract Law** the writing(s) or record must - specify the parties to the contract - specify the subject matter and essential terms - be signed by the party to be charged or by her agent **Sale of Goods** provides a general method of compliance for all parties and an additional one for merchants - *Writing(s) or Record* must (1) be sufficient to indicate that a contract has been made between the parties, (2) be signed by the party against whom enforcement is sought or by her authorized agent, and (3) specify the quantity of goods to be sold - *Written Confirmation* between merchants, a written confirmation that is sufficient against the sender is also sufficient against the recipient unless the recipient gives written notice of his objection within ten days
EFFECT OF NONCOMPLIANCE	**Oral Contract within Statute of Frauds** is unenforceable **Full Performance** statute does not apply to executed contracts **Restitution** is available in quasi contract for benefits conferred in reliance on the oral contract **Promissory Estoppel** oral contracts will be enforced where the party seeking enforcement has reasonably and justifiably relied on the promise and the court can avoid injustice only by enforcement

PAROL EVIDENCE RULE AND INTERPRETATION OF CONTRACTS

PAROL EVIDENCE RULE	**Statement of Rule** when parties express a contract in a writing that they intend to be the complete and final expression of their rights and duties, evidence of their prior oral or written negotiations or agreements of their contemporaneous oral agreements that vary or change the written contract are not admissible *Situations to Which the Rule Does Not Apply* - a contract that is not an integrated document - correction of a typographical error - showing that a contract was void or voidable - showing whether a condition has in fact occurred - showing a subsequent mutual rescission or modification of the contract **Supplemental Evidence** may be admitted - *Course of Dealing* previous conduct between the parties - *Usage of Trade* practice engaged in by the trade or industry - *Course of Performance* conduct between the parties concerning performance of the particular contract - *Supplemental Consistent Evidence*

INTERPRETATION OF CONTRACTS

Definition the ascertainment of the meaning of a promise or agreement or a term of the promise or agreement

Rules of Interpretation include the following:

- all the circumstances are considered and the principal purpose of the parties is given great weight
- a writing is interpreted as a whole
- commonly accepted meanings are used unless the parties manifest a different intention
- wherever possible, the intentions of the parties are interpreted as consistent with each other and with course of performance, course of dealing, or usage of trade
- technical terms are given their technical meaning
- specific terms are given greater weight than general language
- separately negotiated terms are given greater weight than standardized terms or those not separately negotiated
- the order for interpretation is express terms, course of performance, course of dealing, and usage of trade
- where a term has several possible meanings, the term will be interpreted against the party who supplied the contract or term
- written provisions are given preference over typed or printed provisions, and typed provisions are given preference over printed provisions
- if an amount is set forth in both words and figures and they differ, words control figures

C H A P T E R 1 6
Third Parties to Contracts

Whereas prior chapters considered contractual situations essentially involving only two parties, this chapter deals with the rights or duties of third parties, namely, persons who are not parties to the contract but who have a right to, or an obligation for, its performance. These rights and duties arise either by (1) an assignment of the rights of a party to the contract, (2) a delegation of the duties of a party to the contract, or (3) the express terms of a contract entered into for the benefit of a third person. In an assignment or delegation, the third party's rights or duties arise after the contract is made, whereas in the third situation, the third-party beneficiary's rights arise at the time the contract was formed. We will consider these three situations in that order.

ASSIGNMENT OF RIGHTS

Every contract creates both rights and duties. A person who owes a duty under a contract is an **obligor**, while a person to whom a contractual duty is owed is an **obligee**. For instance, Ann promises to sell to Bart an automobile for which Bart promises to pay $10,000 in monthly installments over the next three years. Ann's right under the contract is to receive payment from Bart, whereas Ann's duty is to deliver the automobile. Bart's right is to receive the automobile; his duty is to pay for it.

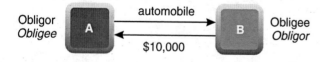

An **assignment of rights** is the voluntary transfer to a third party of the rights arising from the contract. In the above example, if Ann were to transfer her right under the contract (the installment payments due from Bart) to Clark for $8,500 in cash, this would constitute a valid assignment

of rights. In this case, Ann would be the **assignor**, Clark would be the **assignee**, and Bart would be the **obligor**.

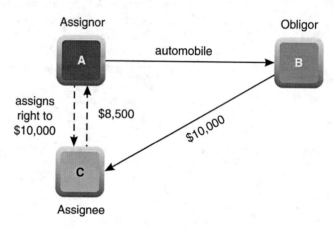

An effective assignment terminates the assignor's right to receive performance by the obligor. After an assignment, only the assignee has a right to the obligor's performance.

On the other hand, if Ann and Doris agree that Doris should deliver the automobile to Bart, this would constitute a delegation, not an assignment, of duties between Ann and Doris. A **delegation of duties** is a transfer to a third party of a contractual obligation. In this instance, Ann would be the **delegator**, Doris would be the **delegatee**, and Bart would be the **obligee**. Delegations of duties are discussed later in this chapter.

LAW GOVERNING ASSIGNMENTS

The law governing assignments arises principally from the common law of contracts, Article 2 of the Uniform Commercial Code (UCC), and Article 9 of the UCC. Article 2 applies to assignments of rights under a contract for the sale of goods. Article 9 covers all assignments made to secure the performance of an obligation *and* all assignments involving rights to payment for goods sold or leased or for services rendered.

REQUIREMENTS OF AN ASSIGNMENT

The Restatement defines an assignment of a right as a "manifestation of the assignor's intention to transfer it by virtue of which the assignor's right to performance by the obligor is extinguished in whole or in part and the assignee acquires a right to such performance." Section 317(1). No special form or particular words are necessary to create an assignment. Any words that fairly indicate an intention to make the assignee the owner of the right are sufficient. For instance, Eve delivers to Harold a writing addressed to Mary stating, "Pay Harold for his own use $1,000 out of the amount you owe me." This writing is a legally sufficient assignment. Restatement, Section 325, Illustration 1.

Unless otherwise provided by statute, an assignment may be oral. The UCC imposes a writing requirement on all assignments beyond $5,000. Section 1–206. The 2001 Revision to Article 1, however, has deleted this requirement. In addition, Article 9 requires certain assignments to be in writing.

Consideration is not required for an effective assignment. Consequently, gratuitous assignments are valid and enforceable. By giving value for the assignment, the assignee manifests his assent to the assignment as part of the bargained-for exchange. On the other hand, when the assignment is gratuitous, the assignee's assent is not always required. Any assignee who has not assented to an assignment may, however, disclaim the assignment within a reasonable time after learning of its existence and terms. Restatement, Section 327. No particular formality is required for the disclaimer, which renders the assignment inoperative from the beginning.

REVOCABILITY OF ASSIGNMENTS When the assignee gives consideration in exchange for an assignment, a contract exists between the assignor and the assignee. Consequently, the assignor may not revoke the assignment without the assignee's assent. A gratuitous assignment, in contrast, is revocable by the assignor and is terminated by her death, incapacity, or subsequent assignment of the right, unless she has made an effective delivery of the assignment to the assignee by transferring a deed or other document evidencing the right, such as a stock certificate or savings passbook. Delivery may also consist of physically delivering a signed, written assignment of the contract right.

A gratuitous assignment is also rendered irrevocable if, prior to the attempted revocation, the donee-assignee receives payment of the claim from the obligor, obtains a judgment against the obligor, or obtains a new contract with the obligor. For example, Nancy owes Howard $50,000. Howard signs a written statement granting Paul a gratuitous assignment of his rights from Nancy but dies prior to delivering to Paul the signed, written assignment of the contract right. The assignment is terminated and therefore ineffective. On the other hand, had Howard delivered the signed, written assignment to Paul before he died, the assignment would have been effective and irrevocable.

PARTIAL ASSIGNMENTS A partial assignment is a transfer of a portion of the contractual rights to one or more assignees. Although partial assignments were not enforceable at early common law, such assignments now are permitted and are enforceable. The obligor, however, may require all the parties entitled to the promised performance to litigate the matter in one action, thus ensuring that all parties are present and thereby avoiding the undue hardship of multiple lawsuits. For example, Jack owes Richard $2,500. Richard assigns $1,000 to Mildred. Neither Richard nor Mildred can maintain an action against Jack if Jack objects, unless the other is joined in the lawsuit against Jack.

RIGHTS THAT ARE ASSIGNABLE

As a general rule, most contract rights, including rights under an option contract, are assignable. The most common contractual right that may be assigned is the right to the payment of money, such as an account receivable or interest due or to be paid. The right to property other than money, such as goods or land, is also frequently assignable.

RIGHTS THAT ARE NOT ASSIGNABLE

To protect the obligor or the public interest, some contract rights are not assignable. These nonassignable contract rights include those that (1) materially change the obligor's duty or materially increase the risk or burden upon the obligor, (2) transfer highly personal contract rights, (3) are validly prohibited by the contract, or (4) are prohibited by statute or public policy. Restatement, Section 317(2).

ASSIGNMENTS THAT MATERIALLY INCREASE THE DUTY, RISK, OR BURDEN An assignment is ineffective where performance by the obligor to the assignee would differ materially from her performance to the assignor; that is, where the assignment would significantly change the nature or extent of the obligor's duty. Thus, an automobile liability insurance policy issued to Alex is not assignable by Alex to Betty. The risk assumed by the insurance company was liability for Alex's negligent operation of the automobile. Liability for operation of the same automobile by Betty would be a risk entirely different from the one that the insurance company had assumed. Similarly, Alex would not be allowed to assign to Cynthia, the owner of a twenty-five-room mansion, his contractual right to have Betty paint his small, two-bedroom house. Clearly, such an assignment would materially increase Betty's duty of performance. By comparison, the right to receive monthly payments under a contract may be assigned; for mailing the check to the assignee costs no more than mailing it to the assignor. Moreover, if a contract explicitly provides that it may be assigned, then rights under it are assignable even if the assignment would change the duty, risk, or burden of performance on the obligor. Restatement, Section 323(1).

ASSIGNMENTS OF PERSONAL RIGHTS Where the rights under a contract are highly personal, in that they are limited to the person of the obligee, such rights are not assignable. An extreme example of such a contract is an agreement of two persons to marry one another. The prospective groom obviously cannot transfer to some third party the prospective bride's promise to marry him. A more typical example of a contract involving personal rights would be a contract between a teacher and a school. The teacher could not assign to another teacher her right to a faculty position. Similarly, a student who is awarded a scholarship cannot assign his right to some other person.

EXPRESS PROHIBITION AGAINST ASSIGNMENT Contract terms prohibiting assignment of rights under the contract are strictly construed. Moreover, most courts interpret a general prohibition against assignments as a mere promise not to assign. As a consequence, the prohibition, if violated, gives the obligor a right to damages for breach of the terms forbidding assignment but does *not* render the assignment ineffective.

Section 322(1) of the Restatement provides that, unless circumstances indicate the contrary, a contract term prohibiting assignment of the contract bars only the delegation to the assignee (delegatee) of the assignor's (delegator's) duty of performance, not the assignment of rights. Thus, Abe and Bill contract for the sale of land by Bill to Abe for $30,000 and provide in their contract that Abe may not assign his rights under it. Abe pays Bill $30,000 and thereby fully performs his obligations under the contract. Abe then assigns his rights to Cheryl, who is entitled to receive the land from Bill (the obligor) despite the contractual prohibition of assignment.

UCC Section 2–210(2) provides that a right to damages for breach of the whole contract or a right arising out of the assignor's due performance of his entire obligation can be assigned despite a contractual provision to the contrary. UCC Section 2–210(3) provides that, unless circumstances indicate the contrary, a contract term prohibiting assignment of the contract bars only the delegation to the assignee (delegatee) of the assignor's (delegator's) duty of performance, not the assignment of rights. UCC Section 9-408 makes ineffective any term in a contract prohibiting the assignment of a security interest arising out of a sale of any right to payment for goods sold or leased or for services rendered.

ASSIGNMENTS PROHIBITED BY LAW Various Federal and State statutes, as well as public policy, prohibit or regulate the assignment of certain types of contract rights. For instance, assignments of future wages are subject to statutes, some of which prohibit such assignments altogether while others require them to be in writing and subject to certain restrictions. Moreover,

an assignment that violates public policy will be unenforceable even in the absence of a prohibiting statute.

RIGHTS OF THE ASSIGNEE

OBTAINS RIGHTS OF ASSIGNOR The general rule is that an assignee **stands in the shoes** of the assignor. He acquires the rights of the assignor, but no new or additional rights, and takes the assigned rights with all of the defenses, defects, and infirmities to which they would be subject, were the assignor to bring an action against the obligor. Thus, in an action brought by the assignee against the obligor, the obligor may plead fraud, duress, undue influence, failure of consideration, breach of contract, or any other defense against the assignor arising out of the original contract. The obligor also may assert rights of setoff or counterclaim arising against the assignor out of entirely separate matters, provided they arose prior to his receiving notice of the assignment.

The Code permits the buyer under a contract of sale to agree as part of the contract that he will not assert against an assignee any claim or defense that the buyer may have against the seller if the assignee takes the assignment for value, in good faith, and without notice of conflicting claims or of certain defenses. UCC Section 9–403. Such a provision in an agreement renders the seller's rights more marketable. The Federal Trade Commission, however, has invalidated such waiver of defense provisions in consumer credit transactions. (This rule is discussed more fully in *Chapter 28*.) Article 9 reflects this rule by essentially rendering waiver-of-defense clauses ineffective in consumer transactions. UCC Section 9–403(d). Most States also have statutes protecting buyers in consumer transactions by prohibiting waiver of defenses.

NOTICE To be valid, notice of an assignment does not have to be given to the obligor. Nonetheless, giving such notice is advisable because an assignee will lose his rights against an obligor who pays the assignor without notice of the assignment: to compel an obligor to pay a claim a second time, when she was not notified that a new party was entitled to payment would be unfair. For example, Donald owes Gary $1,000 due on September 1. Gary assigns the debt to Paula on August 1, but neither he nor Paula informs Donald. On September 1, Donald pays Gary. Donald is fully discharged from his obligation, whereas Gary is liable for $1,000 to Paula. On the other hand, if Paula had given notice of the assignment to Donald before September 1 and Donald had paid Gary nevertheless, Paula would then have the right to recover the $1,000 from either Donald or Gary.

Furthermore, notice cuts off any defenses based on subsequent agreements between the obligor and assignor. Moreover, as already indicated, notice precludes subsequent setoffs and counterclaims of the obligor that arise out of entirely separate matters.

IMPLIED WARRANTIES OF ASSIGNOR

An implied warranty is an obligation imposed by law upon the transfer of property or contract rights. In the absence of an express intention to the contrary, an assignor who receives value makes the following implied warranties to the assignee with respect to the assigned right:

1. that he will do nothing to defeat or impair the assignment;
2. that the assigned right actually exists and is subject to no limitations or defenses other than those stated or apparent at the time of the assignment;
3. that any writing evidencing the right delivered to the assignee or exhibited to him as an inducement to accept the assignment is genuine and what it purports to be; and
4. that the assignor has no knowledge of any fact that would impair the value of the assignment.

Thus, Eric has a right against Julia and assigns it for value to Gwen. Later, Eric gives Julia a release. Gwen may recover damages from Eric for breach of the first implied warranty.

EXPRESS WARRANTIES OF ASSIGNOR

An **express warranty** is an explicitly made contractual promise regarding property or contract rights transferred. The assignor is further bound by any express warranties he makes to the assignee with respect to the right assigned. The assignor does not, however, guarantee that the obligor will pay the assigned debt or otherwise perform, unless such a guarantee is explicitly stated.

SUCCESSIVE ASSIGNMENTS OF THE SAME RIGHT

The owner of a right could conceivably make successive assignments of the same claim to different persons. Assume that B owes A $1,000. On June 1, A for value assigns the debt to C. Thereafter, on June 15, A assigns it to D, who in good faith gives value and has no knowledge of the prior assignment by A to C. If the assignment is subject to Article 9, then that article's priority rules will control, as discussed in *Chapter 38*. Otherwise, the priority is determined by the common law. The majority rule in the United States is that the **first assignee in point of time** (here, C) prevails over subsequent assignees. By comparison, in England and in a minority of the States, the first assignee to notify the obligor prevails.

The Restatement adopts a third view: a prior assignee is entitled to the assigned right and its proceeds to the exclusion of a subsequent assignee, *except* where the prior assignment is revocable or voidable by the assignor or where the subsequent assignee in good faith and without knowledge of the prior assignment gives value and obtains one of the following: (1) payment or satisfaction of the obligor's duty, (2) a judgment against the obligor, (3) a new contract with the obligor, or (4) possession of a writing of a type customarily accepted as a symbol or evidence of the right assigned. Restatement, Section 342.

DELEGATION OF DUTIES

As indicated, contractual duties are *not* assignable, but their performance generally may be *delegated* to a third person. A **delegation of duties** is a transfer of a contractual obligation to a third party. For example, A promises to sell B a new automobile, for which B promises to pay $10,000 by monthly installments over the next three years. If A and D agree that D should deliver the automobile to B, this would not constitute an assignment but would be a delegation of duties between A and D. In this instance, A would be the **delegator**, D would be the **delegatee**, and B would be the **obligee**.

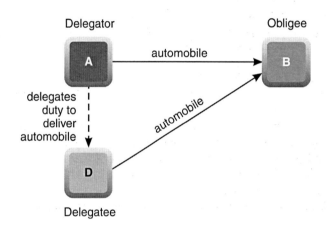

A delegation of duty does not extinguish the delegator's obligation to perform, because A remains liable to B. When the delegatee accepts, or assumes, the delegated duty, both the delegator and delegatee are held liable to the obligee for performance of the contractual duty.

DELEGABLE DUTIES

Although contractual duties generally are delegable, a delegation will not be permitted if

1. the nature of the duties is personal in that the obligee has a substantial interest in having the delegator perform the contract;
2. the performance is expressly made nondelegable; or
3. the delegation is prohibited by statute or public policy.

Restatement, Section 318 and UCC Section 2–210. The courts will examine a delegation more closely than an assignment because a delegation compels the nondelegating party to the contract (the obligee) to receive performance from a party with whom she has not dealt.

For example, a schoolteacher may not delegate her performance to another teacher, even if the substitute is equally competent; for this is a contract that is personal in nature. In the frequently quoted words of an English case: "You have a right to the benefit you contemplate from the character, credit and substance of the person with whom you contract." On the other hand, under a contract in which performance involves no peculiar or special skill and in which no personal trust or confidence is involved, the party may delegate the performance of his duty. For example, the duty to pay money, to deliver fungible goods such as corn, or to mow a lawn is usually delegable.

DUTIES OF THE PARTIES

Even when permitted, a delegation of a duty to a third person still leaves the delegator bound to perform. If the delegator desires to be discharged of the duty, she is allowed to enter into an agreement by which she obtains the consent of the obligee to substitute a third person (the delegatee) in her place. This is a **novation**, whereby the delegator is discharged and the third party becomes directly bound upon his promise to the obligee.

Though a delegation authorizes a third party to perform a duty for the delegator, a delegatee becomes liable for performance only if he assents to perform the delegated duties. Thus, if Frank owes a duty to Grace, and Frank delegates that duty to Henry, Henry is not obligated to either Frank or Grace to perform the duty unless Henry agrees to do so. Nevertheless, if Henry promises either Frank (the delegator) or Grace (the obligee) that he will perform Frank's duty, Henry is said to have **assumed the delegated duty** and becomes liable to both Frank and Grace for nonperformance. Accordingly, when duties are both delegated and assumed, both the delegator and the delegatee are liable to the obligee for proper performance of the original contractual duty. The delegatee's promise to perform creates contract rights in the obligee who may bring an action against the delegatee as a third party beneficiary of the contract between the delegator and the delegatee. (Third-party contracts are discussed later in this chapter.)

The question of whether a delegatee has assumed delegated duties frequently arises in the following ambiguous situation: Marty and Carol agree to an assignment of Marty's contract with Bob. The Code clearly resolves this ambiguity by providing that, unless the language or circumstances indicate the contrary, an assignment of "the contract," or of "all my rights under the contract," or an assignment in similar general terms is an assignment of rights *and* a delegation of performance of the assignor's duties; its acceptance by the assignee constitutes a promise by her to perform those duties. Section 2–210(4). The

Restatement, Section 328, has also adopted this position. For example, Cooper Oil Co. has a contract to deliver oil to Halsey. Cooper Oil Co. delivers to Lowell Oil Co. a writing assigning to Lowell Oil Co. "all Cooper Oil Co.'s rights under the contract." Lowell Oil Co. is under a duty to Halsey to deliver the oil called for by the contract, and Cooper Oil Co. is liable to Halsey if Lowell Oil Co. does not perform. It should also be recalled that the Restatement and the Code provide that a clause prohibiting an assignment of "the contract" is to be construed as barring only the delegation to the assignee (delegatee) of the assignor's (delegator's) performance, unless the circumstances indicate the contrary.

THIRD-PARTY BENEFICIARY CONTRACTS

A contract in which a party (the **promisor**) promises to render a certain performance not to the other party (the **promisee**) but to a third person (the **beneficiary**) is called a third-party beneficiary contract. The third person is not a party to the contract but is merely a beneficiary of it. Such contracts may be divided into two types: (1) intended beneficiary and (2) incidental beneficiary. An **intended beneficiary** is intended by the two parties to the contract (the promisor and promisee) to receive a benefit from the performance of their agreement. Accordingly, the courts generally permit intended beneficiaries to enforce third-party contracts. For example, Abbott promises Baldwin to deliver an automobile to Carson if Baldwin promises to pay $10,000. Carson is the intended beneficiary.

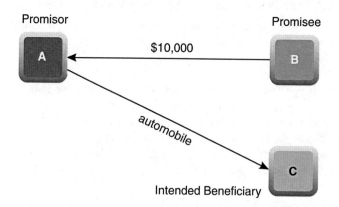

In an **incidental beneficiary** contract, the third party is not intended to receive a benefit under the contract. Accordingly, courts do not enforce the third party's right to the benefits of the contract. For example, Abbott promises to purchase and deliver to Baldwin an automobile for $10,000. In all probability, Abbott would acquire the automobile from Davis. Davis would be an incidental beneficiary and would have no enforceable rights against either Abbott or Baldwin.

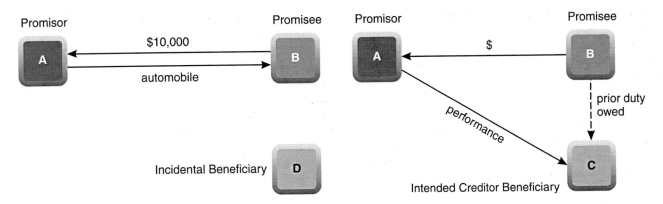

INTENDED BENEFICIARY

Unless otherwise agreed between the promisor and promisee, a beneficiary of a promise is an intended beneficiary if the parties intended this to be the result of their agreement. Restatement, Section 302. There are two types of intended beneficiaries: (1) donee beneficiaries and (2) creditor beneficiaries.

DONEE BENEFICIARY A third party is an intended donee beneficiary if the promisee's purpose in bargaining for and obtaining the agreement with the promisor is to make a gift of the promised performance to the beneficiary. The ordinary life insurance policy illustrates this type of contract. The insured (the promisee) makes a contract with an insurance company (the promisor) that promises, in consideration of premiums paid to it by the insured, to pay upon the death of the insured a stated sum of money to the named beneficiary, who is an intended donee beneficiary.

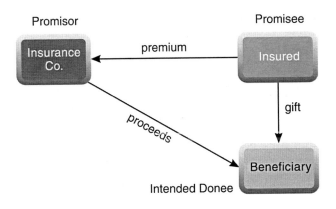

CREDITOR BENEFICIARY A third person is also an intended beneficiary if the promisee intends the performance of the promise to satisfy a legal duty he owes to the beneficiary, who is a creditor of the promisee. The contract involves consideration moving from the promisee to the promisor in exchange for the promisor's engaging to pay a debt or to discharge an obligation the promisee owes to the third person.

To illustrate, in a contract for the sale by Wesley of his business to Susan, Susan promises Wesley that she will pay all of his outstanding business debts, as listed in the contract. Here, Wesley's creditors are creditor beneficiaries. Similarly, in the classic *Lawrence v. Fox*, 20 N.Y. 268 (1859), Holly loaned Fox $300 in consideration for Fox's promise to pay that sum to Lawrence, a creditor of Holly. Fox failed to pay Lawrence, who sued Fox for the $300. The court held for Lawrence, who was permitted to recover as a third-party creditor beneficiary to the contract between Holly and Fox.

RIGHTS OF INTENDED BENEFICIARY An intended *donee* beneficiary may enforce the contract only against the promisor. He cannot maintain an action against the promisee, as the promisee was under no legal obligation to him. An intended *creditor* beneficiary, however, may enforce the contract against either or both parties. If Willard owes Lola $500, and Julie contracts with Willard to pay this debt to Lola, Willard is not thereby relieved of his liability to Lola. If Julie breaks the contract, Lola, as a creditor beneficiary, may sue her. In addition, Lola may sue Willard as her debtor. If Lola should obtain judgments against both Julie and Willard, she is, of course, entitled to collect only one judgment. If Lola recovers against Willard, Willard has a right of reimbursement from Julie, the promisor. Restatement, Section 310.

VESTING OF RIGHTS A contract for the benefit of an intended beneficiary confers upon that beneficiary rights that she may enforce. Until these rights **vest** (take effect), however, the promisor and promisee may, by later agreement, vary or completely discharge them. The States vary considerably as to when vesting occurs. Some hold that vesting takes place immediately upon the making of the contract. In others, vesting occurs when the third party learns of the contract and assents to it. In another group of States, vesting requires the third party to change his position in reliance upon the promise made for his benefit. The Restatement has adopted the following position: If the contract between the promisor and promisee provides that they may not vary its terms without the consent of the beneficiary, such a provision is effective. Otherwise, the parties to the contract may rescind or vary the contract unless the intended beneficiary (1) has brought an action upon the promise, (2) has changed her position in reliance upon it, or (3) has assented to the promise at the request of the promisor or promisee. Restatement, Section 311.

On the other hand, the promisor and promisee may provide that the benefits will *never* vest. For example, Mildred purchases an insurance policy on her own life, naming her husband as beneficiary. Her policy, as such policies commonly do, reserves to Mildred the right to change the beneficiary or even to cancel the policy entirely.

DEFENSES AGAINST BENEFICIARY In an action by the intended beneficiary of a third-party contract to enforce the promise, the promisor may assert any defense that would be available to her if the action had been brought by the promisee. The rights of the third party are based upon the promisor's contract with the promisee. Thus, the promisor may assert the absence of mutual assent or consideration, lack of capacity, fraud, mistake, and the like against the intended beneficiary. Once an intended beneficiary's rights have vested, however, the promisor may not assert the defense of contractual modification or rescission.

INCIDENTAL BENEFICIARY

An incidental third-party beneficiary is a person whom the parties to a contract did not intend to benefit but who nevertheless would derive some benefit from its performance. For instance, a contract to raze an old, unsightly building and replace it with a costly, modern house would benefit the owner of the adjoining property by increasing his property's value. He would have no rights under the contract, however, as the benefit to him would be unintended and incidental.

A third person who may benefit incidentally from the performance of a contract to which he is not a party has no rights under the contract. Neither the promisee nor the promisor intended that the third person benefit. Assume that for a stated consideration George promises Kathy that he will purchase and deliver to Kathy a brand-new Sony television of the latest model. Kathy pays in advance for the television. George does not deliver the television to Kathy. As an incidental beneficiary, Cosmos Appliances, Inc., the local exclusive Sony dealer, has no rights under the contract, although performance by George would produce a sale from which Cosmos would benefit.

CHAPTER SUMMARY

ASSIGNMENT OF RIGHTS

Definition of Assignment voluntary transfer to a third party of the rights arising from a contract so that the assignor's right to performance is extinguished
- *Assignor* party making an assignment
- *Assignee* party to whom contract rights are assigned
- *Obligor* party owing a duty to the assignor under the original contract
- *Obligee* party to whom a duty of performance is owed under a contract

Requirements of an Assignment include intent but not consideration
- *Revocability of Assignment* when the assignee gives consideration, the assignor may not revoke the assignment without the assignee's consent
- *Partial Assignment* transfer of a portion of contractual rights to one or more assignees

Assignability most contract rights are assignable, except
- assignments that materially increase the duty, risk, or burden upon the obligor
- assignments of personal rights
- assignments expressly forbidden by the contract
- assignments prohibited by law

Rights of Assignee the assignee stands in the shoes of the assignor
- *Defenses of Obligor* may be asserted against the assignee
- *Notice* is not required but is advisable

Implied Warranty obligation imposed by law upon the assignor of a contract right

Express Warranty explicitly made contractual promise regarding contract rights transferred

Successive Assignments of the Same Right the majority rule is that the first assignee in point of time prevails over later assignees; minority rule is that the first assignee to notify the obligor prevails

DELEGATION OF DUTIES	**Definition of Delegation** transfer to a third party of a contractual obligation • *Delegator* party delegating his duty to a third party • *Delegatee* third party to whom the delegator's duty is delegated • *Obligee* party to whom a duty of performance is owed by the delegator and delegatee **Delegability** most contract duties may be delegated, *except* • duties that are personal • duties that are expressly nondelegable • duties whose delegation is prohibited by statute or public policy **Duties of the Parties** • *Delegation* delegator is still bound to perform original obligation • *Novation* contract, to which the obligee is a party, substituting a new promisor for an existing promisor, who is consequently no longer liable on the original contract and is not liable as a delegator
THIRD-PARTY BENEFICIARY CONTRACTS	**Definition** a contract in which one party promises to render a performance to a third person (the beneficiary) **Intended Beneficiaries** third parties intended by the two contracting parties to receive a benefit from their contract • *Donee Beneficiary* a third party intended to receive a benefit from the contract as a gift • *Creditor Beneficiary* a third person intended to receive a benefit from the agreement to satisfy a legal duty owed to her • *Rights of Intended Beneficiary* an intended donee beneficiary may enforce the contract against the promisor; an intended creditor beneficiary may enforce the contract against either or both the promisor and the promisee • *Vesting of Rights* if the beneficiary's rights vest, the promisor and promisee may not thereafter vary or discharge these vested rights • *Defenses against Beneficiary* in an action by the intended beneficiary of a third-party contract to enforce the promise, the promisor may assert any defense that would be available to her if the action had been brought by the promisee **Incidental Beneficiary** third party whom the two parties to the contract have no intention of benefiting by their contract and who acquires no rights under the contract

Performance, Breach, and Discharge

The subject of discharge of contracts concerns the termination of contractual duties. In earlier chapters we have seen how parties may become bound to a contract. It is also important to know how a person may become unbound from a contract. For although contractual promises are made for a purpose, and the parties reasonably expect this purpose to be fulfilled by performance, performance of a contractual duty is only one method of discharge.

Whatever causes a binding promise to cease to be binding constitutes a discharge of the contract. In general, there are four kinds of discharge: (1) performance by the parties, (2) material breach by one or both of the parties, (3) agreement of the parties, and (4) operation of law. Moreover, many contractual promises are not absolute promises to perform but rather are conditional; that is, they are dependent upon the happening or nonhappening of a specific event. After a discussion of conditions, the four kinds of discharge will be covered.

CONDITIONS

A **condition** is an event whose happening or nonhappening affects a duty of performance under a contract. Some conditions must be satisfied before any duty to perform arises; others terminate the duty to perform; still others either limit or modify the duty to perform. A promisor inserts conditions into a contract for her protection and benefit. Furthermore, the more conditions to which a promise is subject, the less content the promise has. For example, a promise to pay $8,000, provided that such sum is realized from the sale of an automobile, provided the automobile is sold within sixty days, and provided that the automobile, which has been stolen, can be found, is clearly different from, and worth considerably less than, an unconditional promise by the same promisor to pay $8,000.

A fundamental difference exists between the breach or nonperformance of a contractual promise and the failure or nonhappening of a condition. A breach of contract subjects the promisor to liability. It may or may not, depending upon its materiality, excuse nonperformance by the nonbreaching party of his duty under the contract. The happening or nonhappening of a condition, on the other hand, either prevents a party from acquiring a right to performance by the other party or deprives him of such a right, but subjects neither party to any liability.

Conditions may be classified by *how* they are imposed: express conditions, implied-in-fact conditions, or implied-in-law conditions (also called constructive conditions). They also may be classified by *when* they affect a duty of performance: conditions concurrent, conditions precedent, or conditions subsequent. These two ways of classifying conditions are not mutually exclusive; for example, a condition may be constructive and concurrent or express and precedent.

EXPRESS CONDITION

An **express condition** is explicitly set forth in language. No particular form of words is necessary to create an express condition, so long as the event to which the performance of the promise is made subject is clearly expressed. An express condition is usually preceded by such words as "provided that," "on condition that," "if," "subject to," "while," "after," "upon," or "as soon as."

The basic rule applied to express conditions is that they must be fully and literally performed before the conditional duty to perform arises. Where application of the full and literal performance test would result in a forfeiture, however, the courts usually apply to the completed portion of the condition a *substantial satisfaction* test, as discussed later in this chapter under the section titled "Substantial Performance."

SATISFACTION OF A CONTRACTING PARTY The parties to a contract may agree that performance by one of them will be to the satisfaction of the other, who will not be obligated to pay for such performance unless he is satisfied. This is an express condition to the duty to pay for the performance. Assume that tailor Melissa contracts to make a suit of clothes to Brent's satisfaction, and that Brent promises to pay Melissa $350 for the suit if he is satisfied with it when completed. Melissa completes the suit using materials ordered by Brent. Though the suit fits Brent beautifully, he tells Melissa that he is not satisfied with it and refuses to acceptor pay for it. If Brent's dissatisfaction is honest and in good faith, even if it is unreasonable, Melissa is not entitled to recover $350 or any amount from Brent by reason of the nonhappening of the express condition. Where satisfaction relates to a matter of personal taste, opinion, or judgment, the law applies the **subjective satisfaction** standard: if the promisor in good faith is dissatisfied, the condition has not occurred.

If the contract does not clearly indicate that satisfaction is subjective, or if the performance contracted for relates to mechanical fitness or utility, the law assumes an **objective satisfaction** standard. For example, the objective standard would apply to the sale of a building or standard goods, such as steel, coal, or grain. In such cases, the question would not be whether the promisor was actually satisfied with the performance by the other party but whether, as a reasonable person, he ought to be satisfied.

Satisfaction of a Third Party A contract may condition the duty of one contracting party to accept and pay for the performance of the other contracting party upon the approval of a third party who is not a party to the contract. For example, building contracts commonly provide that before the owner is required to pay, the builder shall furnish a certificate of the architect stating that the building has been constructed according to the plans and specifications. For although the owner is paying for the building, not for the certificate, he must have both the building and the certificate before he is obligated to pay. The duty of payment was made expressly conditional upon the presentation of the certificate.

IMPLIED-IN-FACT CONDITIONS

Implied-in-fact conditions are similar to express conditions, in that they must fully and literally occur and in that the parties understand them to be part of the agreement. They differ in that they are not stated in express language; rather, they are necessarily inferred from the terms of the contract, the nature of the transaction, or the conduct of the parties. Thus, if Fernando, for $750, contracts to paint Peggy's house any color Peggy desires, it is necessarily implied in fact that Peggy will inform Fernando of the desired color before Fernando begins to paint. The notification of choice of color is an implied-in-fact condition, an operative event that must occur before Fernando is subject to the duty of painting the house.

IMPLIED-IN-LAW CONDITIONS

An **implied-in-law condition**, or a **constructive condition**, is imposed by law to accomplish a just and fair result. It differs from an express condition and an implied-in-fact condition in two ways: (1) it is not contained in the language of the contract or necessarily inferred from the contract, and (2) it need only be substantially performed. For example, Melinda contracts to sell a certain tract of land to Kelly for $18,000, but the contract is silent as to the time of delivery of the deed and payment of the price. The law will imply that the respective performances are not independent of one another; consequently, the courts will treat the promises as mutually dependent and will therefore hold that a delivery or tender of the deed by Melinda to Kelly is a condition to Kelly's duty to pay the price. Conversely, Melinda's duty to deliver the deed to Kelly is conditioned upon the payment or tender of $18,000 by Kelly to Melinda. If the contract specifies a sale on credit, however, giving Kelly thirty days after delivery of the deed within which to pay the price, these conditions are not implied by law because the parties have expressly agreed to make their respective duties of performance independent of each other.

CONCURRENT CONDITIONS

Concurrent conditions occur when the mutual duties of performances are to take place simultaneously. As indicated in the previous section, in the absence of an agreement to the contrary, the law assumes that the respective performances under a contract are concurrent conditions.

CONDITIONS PRECEDENT

A **condition precedent** is an event that must occur before performance under a contract is due. For instance, if Gail is to deliver shoes to Mike on June 1, with Mike's duty to pay for the shoes on July 15, Gail's delivery of the shoes is a condition precedent to Mike's performance. Similarly, if Seymour promises to buy Edna's land for $50,000, provided Seymour can obtain financing in the amount of $40,000 at 10 percent interest or less for thirty years within sixty days of signing the contract, Seymour's obtaining the specified financing is a condition precedent to his duty. If the condition is satisfied, Seymour is bound to perform; if it is not, he is not so bound. Seymour, however, is under an implied-in-law duty to use his best efforts to obtain financing under these terms.

CONDITIONS SUBSEQUENT

A **condition subsequent** is an event that terminates an existing duty. For example, where goods are sold under terms of "sale or return," the buyer has the right to return the goods to the seller within a stated period but is under an immediate duty to pay the price unless she and the seller have agreed upon credit. A return of the goods, which operates as a condition subsequent, terminates the duty to pay the price. Conditions subsequent occur very infrequently in contract law, while conditions precedent are quite common.

DISCHARGE BY PERFORMANCE

Discharge by performance is undoubtedly the most frequent method of discharging a contractual duty. If a promisor exactly performs his duty under the contract, he is no longer subject to that duty.

Every contract imposes upon each party a duty of good faith and fair dealing in its performance and its enforcement. Restatement, Section 205. As discussed in *Chapter 21*, the Uniform Commercial Code (UCC) imposes a comparable duty. Section 1–203; Revised Section 1–304.

Tender is an offer by one party—who is ready, willing, and able to perform—to the other party to perform his obligation according to the terms of the contract. Under a bilateral contract, the refusal or rejection of a tender of performance may be treated as a repudiation that excuses or discharges the tendering party from further duty of performance under the contract. For example, on the due date of contractual performance, George arrives at Thelma's house prepared to do plumbing work under their contract. Thelma, however, refuses to allow George to enter the premises. George is therefore discharged from performing the contract and has a legal claim against Thelma for material breach.

If a debtor owes money on several accounts and tenders to his creditor less than the total amounts due, the debtor has the right to designate the account or debt to which the payment is to be applied, and the creditor must accept this direction. If the debtor does not direct the application of the payment, the creditor may apply it to any account owing to him by the debtor or distribute it among several such accounts.

DISCHARGE BY BREACH

Breach of contract is the unexcused failure of a party to perform her promise. While breach of contract always gives rise to a cause of action for damages by the aggrieved (injured) party, it may have a more important effect: an uncured (uncorrected) *material* breach by one party operates as an excuse for nonperformance by the other party and discharges the aggrieved party from any further duty under the contract. If, on the other hand, the breach is not material, the aggrieved party is not discharged from the contract, although she may recover money damages. Under the Code, *any* deviation discharges the aggrieved party.

MATERIAL BREACH

An unjustified failure to perform *substantially* the obligations promised in a contract constitutes a **material breach**. The key is whether, despite the breach, the aggrieved party obtained substantially what he bargained for or whether the breach significantly impaired his rights under the contract. A material breach discharges the aggrieved party from his duty of performance. For instance, Esta orders a custom-made, tailored suit from Stuart to be made of wool; but Stuart instead makes the suit of cotton. Assuming that the labor component of this contract predominates and thus the contract is not considered a sale of goods, Stuart has materially breached the contract. Consequently, Esta not only is discharged from her duty to pay for the suit but may also recover money damages from Stuart due to his breach.

Although there are no clear-cut rules as to what constitutes a material breach, the Restatement, Section 241, lists a number of relevant factors:

In determining whether a failure to render or to offer performance is material, the following circumstances are significant:

(a) the extent to which the injured party will be deprived of the benefit which he reasonably expected;

(b) the extent to which the injured party can be adequately compensated for the part of that benefit of which he will be deprived;

(c) the extent to which the party failing to perform or to offer to perform will suffer forfeiture;

(d) the likelihood that the party failing to perform or to offer to perform will cure his failure, taking account of all the circumstances including any reasonable assurances;

(e) the extent to which the behavior of the party failing to perform or to offer to perform comports with standards of good faith and fair dealing.

An *intentional* breach of contract is generally held to be material. Moreover, a failure to perform a promise promptly is a material breach if "**time is of the essence,**" that is, if the parties have clearly indicated that a failure to perform by the stated time is material; otherwise, the aggrieved party may recover damages only for the loss caused by the delay.

Finally, the parties to a contract may, within limits, specify what breaches are to be considered material.

PREVENTION OF PERFORMANCE One party's substantial interference with or **prevention of performance** by the other generally constitutes a material breach that discharges the other party to the contract. For instance, Craig prevents an architect from giving Maud a certificate that is a condition to Craig's liability to pay Maud a certain sum of money. Craig may not then use Maud's failure to produce a certificate as an excuse for his nonpayment. Likewise, if Harold has contracted to grow a certain crop for Rafael, and Rafael plows the field and destroys the seedlings after Harold has planted the seed, his interference with Harold's performance discharges Harold from his duty under the contract. It does not, however, discharge Rafael from his duty under the contract.

PERFECT TENDER RULE The Code greatly alters the common law doctrine of material breach by adopting what is known as the **perfect tender rule**. This rule, which is discussed more fully in *Chapter 22*, essentially provides that *any* deviation from the promised performance in a sales contract under the Code constitutes a material breach of the contract and discharges the aggrieved party from his duty of performance. Thus, if a seller of camera accessories delivers to a buyer ninety-nine of the one hundred ordered pieces, or ninety-nine correct accessories and one incorrect accessory, the buyer may rightfully reject the improper delivery.

SUBSTANTIAL PERFORMANCE

If a party substantially, but not completely, performs her obligations under a contract, the common law generally will allow her to obtain the other party's performance, less any damages caused by the partial performance. Thus, in the specially ordered suit illustration discussed in the previous section, if Stuart, the tailor, used the correct fabric but improperly used black buttons instead of blue, Stuart would be permitted to collect from Esta the contract price of the suit less the damage, if any, caused to Esta by the substitution of the wrongly colored buttons. The doctrine of substantial performance assumes particular importance in the construction industry in cases in which a structure is built on the aggrieved party's land. Consider the following: Kent Construction Co. builds a $300,000 house for Martha but deviates from the specifications, causing Martha $10,000 in damages. If this breach were considered material, then Martha would not have to pay for the house that is now on her land. This would clearly constitute an unjust forfeiture on Kent's part. Therefore, because Kent's performance is substantial, the courts would probably not deem the breach material. As a result, Kent would be able to collect $290,000 from Martha.

ANTICIPATORY REPUDIATION

A breach of contract, as previously discussed, is a failure to perform the terms of a contract. Although it is logically and physically impossible to fail to perform a duty before the date on which that performance is due, a party nonetheless may announce before the due date that she will not perform, or she may commit an act that makes her unable to perform. Either act repudiates the contract, which notifies the other party that a breach is imminent. Such repudiation before the performance date fixed by the contract is called an **anticipatory repudiation**. The courts, as shown in the leading case of *Hochster v. De La Tour*, view it as a breach that discharges the nonrepudiating party's duty to perform and permits her to bring suit immediately. Nonetheless, the nonbreaching party may wait until the time the performance is due, to see whether the repudiator will retract his repudiation and perform his contractual duties. To be effective, the retraction must come to the attention of the injured party before she materially changes her position in reliance on the repudiation or before she indicates to the repudiator that she considers the repudiation to be final. If the retraction is effective and the repudiator does perform, then there is a discharge by performance; if he does not perform, there is a material breach.

MATERIAL ALTERATION OF WRITTEN CONTRACT

An unauthorized alteration or change of any of the material terms or provisions of a written contract or document is a discharge of the entire contract. To be a discharge, the alteration must be material and fraudulent and must be the act of a party to the contract or someone acting on his behalf. An alteration is material if it would vary any party's legal relations with the maker of the alteration or would adversely affect that party's legal relations with a third person. Restatement, Section 286. An unauthorized change in the terms of a written contract by a person who is not a party to the contract does not discharge the contract.

DISCHARGE BY AGREEMENT OF THE PARTIES

The parties to a contract may by agreement discharge each other from performance under the contract. They may do this by rescission, substituted contract, accord and satisfaction, or novation.

MUTUAL RESCISSION

A **mutual rescission** is an agreement between the parties to terminate their respective duties under the contract. Literally a contract to end a contract, it must contain all the essentials of a contract. In rescinding an executory, bilateral contract, each party furnishes consideration in giving up his rights under the contract in exchange for the other party's relinquishment of his rights under the contract. Where one party has already fully performed, a mutual rescission may not be binding at common law because of lack of consideration.

SUBSTITUTED CONTRACT

A **substituted contract** is a new contract accepted by both parties in satisfaction of their duties under the original contract. Restatement, Section 279. A substituted contract immediately discharges the original duty and imposes new obligations. For example, the Restatement, Section 279, gives the following illustration:

> A and B make a contract under which A promises to build on a designated spot a building, for which B promises to pay $100,000. Later, before this contract is performed, A and B make a new contract under which A is to build on the same spot a different building, for which B is to pay $200,000. The new contract is a substituted contract and the duties of A and B under the original contract are discharged.

ACCORD AND SATISFACTION

An **accord** is a contract by which an obligee promises to accept a stated performance in satisfaction of the obligor's existing contractual duty. Restatement, Section 281. The performance of the accord is called a **satisfaction**, and it discharges the original duty. Thus, if Ted owes Alan $500 and the parties agree that Ted shall paint Alan's house in satisfaction of the debt, the agreement is an accord. The debt, however, is not discharged until Ted performs the accord by painting Alan's house.

NOVATION

A **novation** is a substituted contract that involves an agreement among *three* parties to substitute a new promisee for the existing promisee, or to replace the existing promisor with a new one. Restatement, Section 280. A novation discharges the old obligation by creating a new contract in which there is either a new promisee or a new promisor. Thus, if B owes A $500, and A, B, and C agree that C will pay the debt and B will be discharged, the novation is the substitution of the new promisor C for B. Alternatively, if the three parties agree that B will pay $500 to D instead of to A, the novation is the substitution of a new promisee (D for A). In each instance, the debt B owes to A is discharged.

DISCHARGE BY OPERATION OF LAW

This chapter has considered various ways by which contractual duties may be discharged. In all of these cases, the discharge resulted from the action of one or both of the parties to the contract. This section examines discharge brought about by the operation of law.

IMPOSSIBILITY

"Contract liability is strict liability ... [and an] obligor is therefore liable for in damages breach of contract even if he is without fault and even if circumstances have made the contract more burdensome or less desirable than he had anticipated." Restatement, Introductory Note to Chapter 11. Historically, the common law excused a party from contractual duties for **objective impossibility**; that is, where no one could render the performance. If, by comparison, a particular contracting party is unable to perform because, for instance, of financial inability or lack of competence, this **subjective impossibility** does not excuse the promisor from liability for breach of contract. For example, the Christys entered into a written contract to purchase an apartment house from Pilkinton for $30,000. Pilkinton tendered a deed to the property and demanded payment of the unpaid balance of $29,000 due on the purchase price. Because of a decline in their used car business, the Christys, who did not possess and could not borrow the unpaid balance, asserted that it was impossible for them to perform their contract. The court held for Pilkinton, identifying a distinction between objective impossibility, which amounts to saying, "the thing cannot be done," and subjective impossibility— "I cannot do it." The latter, which is illustrated by a promisor's financial inability to pay, does not discharge the contractual duty. *Christy v. Pilkinton*, 224 Ark. 407, 273 S.W.2d 533 (1954).

The **death** or **incapacity** of a person who has contracted to render *personal services* discharges his contractual duty due to objective impossibility. Restatement, Section 262. For example, a singer unable to perform a contractual engagement because of a severe cold is excused from performance, as is a pianist or violinist who is unable to perform because of a hand injury.

DESTRUCTION OF SUBJECT MATTER Destruction of the subject matter or of the agreed-upon means of performance of a contract, without the fault of the promisor, is also excusable impossibility. "Subject matter" here means specific subject matter. Suppose that Alice contracts to sell to Gary five office chairs at an agreed price. Alice has one hundred of these chairs in stock, out of which she expects to deliver five to Gary. Before she can do so, fire destroys the entire stock of one hundred chairs. Though not at fault, Alice is not excused from performance. This was not a contract for the sale of specific goods; consequently, Alice could perform the contract by delivering to Gary any five chairs of the kind and grade specified in the contract. Her failure to do so will render her liable to Gary for breach of contract. Suppose, now, that Alice and Gary make a contract for Alice to manufacture these five chairs in her factory but that prior to their manufacture, fire destroys the factory. Again, Alice is not at fault. Although the chairs are available from other manufacturers, the destruction of the factory discharges Alice's duty to deliver the chairs. Suppose further that Alice and Gary enter into a contract under which Alice is to sell to Gary the particular desk that she uses in her private office. This desk, and no other, is the specific subject matter of the contract. If, before the sale is completed, this desk is destroyed by fire without Alice's fault, it is then impossible for Alice to perform. The contract is therefore discharged.

SUBSEQUENT ILLEGALITY If the performance of a contract that was legal when formed becomes illegal or impractical by reason of a subsequently enacted law, the duty of performance is discharged. Restatement, Section 264. For example, Jill contracts to sell and deliver to Fred ten cases of a certain whiskey each month for one year. A subsequent prohibition law makes the manufacture, transportation, or sale of intoxicating liquor unlawful. The contractual duties that Jill has yet to perform are discharged.

FRUSTRATION OF PURPOSE Where, after a contract is made, a party's principal purpose is substantially frustrated without his fault by the occurrence of an event the nonoccurrence of which was a basic assumption on which the contract was made, his remaining duties to render performance are discharged, unless the party has assumed the risk. Restatement, Second 265. This rule developed from the so-called coronation cases. When, upon the death of his mother, Queen Victoria, Edward VII became King of England, impressive coronation ceremonies were planned, including a procession along a designated route through certain streets in London. Owners and lessees of buildings along the route made contracts to permit the use of rooms with a view on the date scheduled for the procession. The King, however, became ill, and the procession did not take place. The purpose for using the rooms having failed, the rooms were not used. Numerous suits were filed, some by landowners seeking to hold the would-be viewers liable on their promises, and some by the would-be viewers seeking to recover money they paid in advance for the rooms. The principle involved

was novel, but from these cases evolved the **frustration of purpose doctrine**, under which a contract is discharged if supervening circumstances make impossible the fulfillment of the purpose that both parties had in mind, unless one of the parties has contractually assumed that risk.

COMMERCIAL IMPRACTICABILITY The Restatement, Section 261, and the Code, Section 2–615, have relaxed the traditional test of objective impossibility by providing that performance need not be actually or literally impossible, but that commercial impracticability will excuse nonperformance. This does not mean mere hardship or an unexpectedly increased cost of performance. A party will be discharged from performing his duty only when a supervening event not caused by his fault makes his performance impracticable. Moreover, the nonoccurrence of the subsequent event must have been a "basic assumption" both parties made when entering into the contract, neither party having assumed the risk that the event would occur. Commercial impracticability could include

> a severe shortage of raw materials or of supplies due to a contingency such as war, embargo, local crop failure, unforeseen shutdown of major sources of supply or the like, which either causes a marked increase in cost or altogether prevents the seller from securing supplies necessary to his performance. UCC Section 2–615, Comment 4.

BANKRUPTCY

Bankruptcy is a discharge of a contractual duty by operation of law available to a debtor who, by compliance with the requirements of the Bankruptcy Code, obtains an order of discharge by the bankruptcy court. It is applicable only to obligations that the Code provides are dischargeable in bankruptcy. The subject of bankruptcy is treated in *Chapter 39.*

STATUTE OF LIMITATIONS

At common law a plaintiff was not subject to any time limitation within which to bring an action. Now, however, all States have statutes providing such a limitation. The majority of courts hold that the running of the period of the statute of limitations does not operate to discharge the obligation, but only to bar the creditor's right to bring an action.

◆ **SEE FIGURE 17-1: Discharge of Contracts**

◆ FIGURE 17-1: **Discharge of Contracts**

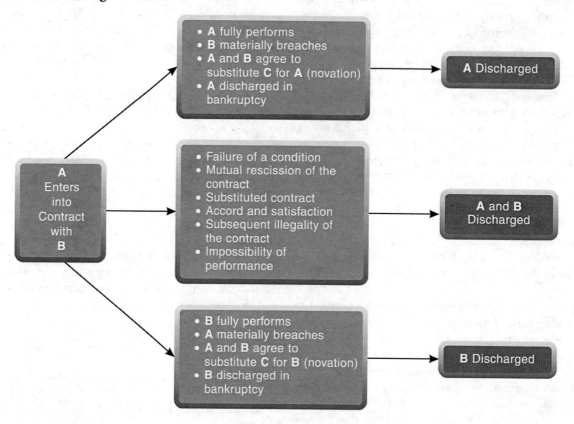

CHAPTER SUMMARY

CONDITIONS	**Definition of a Condition** an event whose happening or nonhappening affects a duty of performance

Express Condition contingency explicitly set forth in language
- *Satisfaction* express condition making performance contingent upon one party's approval of the other's performance
- *Subjective Satisfaction* approval based upon a party's honestly held opinion
- *Objective Satisfaction* approval based upon whether a reasonable person would be satisfied

Implied-in-Fact Conditions contingency understood by the parties to be part of the agreement, though not expressed

Implied-in-Law Conditions contingency not contained in the language of the contract but imposed by law; also called a constructive condition

Concurrent Conditions conditions that are to take place at the same time

Conditions Precedent an event that must or must not occur before performance is due

Conditions Subsequent an event that terminates a duty of performance

DISCHARGE BY PERFORMANCE	**Discharge** termination of a contractual duty

Performance fulfillment of a contractual obligation resulting in a discharge

DISCHARGE BY BREACH	**Definition of Breach** a wrongful failure to perform the terms of a contract that gives rise to a right to damages by the injured party **Material Breach** nonperformance that significantly impairs the injured party's rights under the contract and discharges the injured party from any further duty under the contract • *Prevention of Performance* one party's substantial interference with or prevention of performance by the other; constitutes a material breach and discharges the other party to the contract • *Perfect Tender Rule* standard under the Uniform Commercial Code that a seller's performance under a sales contract must strictly comply with contractual duties and that any deviation discharges the injured party **Substantial Performance** performance that is incomplete but that does not defeat the purpose of the contract; does not discharge the injured party but entitles him to damages **Anticipatory Repudiation** an inability or refusal to perform, before performance is due, that is treated as a breach, allowing the nonrepudiating party to bring suit immediately **Material Alteration of Written Contract** a material and fraudulent alteration of a written contract by a party to the contract; discharges the entire contract
DISCHARGE BY AGREEMENT OF THE PARTIES	**Mutual Rescission** an agreement between the parties to terminate their respective duties under the contract **Substituted Contract** a new contract accepted by both parties in satisfaction of the parties' duties under the original contract **Accord and Satisfaction** substituted duty under a contract (accord) and the discharge of the prior contractual obligation by performance of the new duty (satisfaction) **Novation** a substituted contract involving a new third-party promisor or promisee
DISCHARGE BY OPERATION OF LAW	**Impossibility** performance of contract cannot be done • *Subjective Impossibility* the promisor—but not all promisors—cannot perform; does not discharge the promisor • *Objective Impossibility* no promisor is able to perform; generally discharges the promisor • *Destruction of Subject Matter* will discharge contract if it occurs without the promisor's fault • *Subsequent Illegality* if performance becomes illegal or impractical as a result of a change in the law, the duty of performance is discharged • *Frustration of Purpose* principal purpose of a contract cannot be fulfilled because of a subsequent event • *Commercial Impracticability* where performance can be accomplished only under unforeseen and unjust hardship, the contract is discharged under the Code and the Restatement **Bankruptcy** discharge available to a debtor who obtains an order of discharge by the bankruptcy court **Statute of Limitations** after the statute of limitations has run, the debt is not discharged, but the creditor cannot maintain an action against the debtor

CHAPTER 18
Contract Remedies

When one party to a contract breaches the contract by failing to perform his contractual duties, the law provides a remedy for the injured party. Although the primary objective of contract remedies is to compensate the injured party for the loss resulting from the breach, it is impossible for any remedy to equal the promised performance. To an injured party a court can give as relief what it regards as an equivalent of the promised performance.

This chapter will examine the most common judicial remedies available for breach of contract: (1) monetary damages, (2) the equitable remedies of specific performance and injunction, and (3) restitution. Sales of goods are governed by Article 2 of the Uniform Commercial Code (UCC), which provides specialized remedies that are discussed in *Chapter 25*.

INTERESTS PROTECTED BY CONTRACT REMEDIES

Contract remedies are available to protect one or more of the following interests of the injured party:

1. the **expectation interest**, which is his interest in having the benefit of his bargain by being put in a position as good as the one he would have occupied had the contract been performed;
2. the **reliance interest**, which is his interest in being reimbursed for loss caused by reliance on the contract by being put in a position as good as the one he would have been in had the contract not been made; or
3. the **restitution interest**, which is his interest in having restored to him any benefit that he has conferred on the other party. Restatement, Section 344.

The expectation interest is protected by the contract remedies of compensatory damages, specific performance, and injunction. The reliance interest is protected by the contractual remedy of reliance damages, while the restitution interest is protected by the contractual remedy of restitution.

MONETARY DAMAGES

A judgment awarding monetary damages is the most frequently granted judicial remedy for breach of contract. Monetary damages, however, will be awarded only for losses that are foreseeable, established with reasonable certainty, and unavoidable. The equitable remedies discussed in this chapter are discretionary and are available only if monetary damages are inadequate.

COMPENSATORY DAMAGES

The right to recover compensatory money damages for breach of contract is always available to the injured party. Restatement, Section 346. The purpose in allowing **compensatory damages** is to place the injured party in a position as good as the one she would have occupied had the other party performed under the contract. This involves compensating the injured party for the dollar value of the benefits she would have received had the contract been performed less any savings she experienced by not having to perform her own obligations under the contract. Because these damages are intended to protect the injured party's expectation interest, or the value he expected to derive from the contract, the amount of compensatory damages is generally computed as follows:

> **Loss of value**
> **+ Incidental damages**
> **+ Consequential damages**
> **− Loss or cost avoided by injured party**
>
> **= Compensatory damages**

LOSS OF VALUE In general, loss of value is the *difference between the value of the promised performance* of the breaching party *and the value of the actual performance* rendered by the breaching party.

> **Value of promised performance**
> **− Value of actual performance**
>
> **= Loss of value**

If the breaching party renders no performance at all, then the loss of value is the value of the promised performance. If defective or partial performance is rendered, the loss of value is the difference between the value that the full performance would have had and the value of the performance actually rendered. Thus, where there has been a breach of warranty, the injured party may recover the difference between the value the goods would have had, if they had been as warranted, and the value of the goods in the condition in which the buyer received them. To illustrate, Victor sells an automobile to Joan and expressly warrants that it will get forty-five miles per gallon, but the automobile gets only twenty miles per gallon. The automobile would have been worth $14,000 had it been as warranted, but it is worth only $10,000 as delivered. Joan would recover $4,000 in damages for loss of value.

In addition to loss of value, the injured party may also recover for all other losses actually suffered, subject to the limitation of foreseeability discussed below. These damages include incidental and consequential damages.

INCIDENTAL DAMAGES **Incidental damages** are damages that arise directly out of the breach, such as costs incurred to acquire the nondelivered performance from some other source. For example, Agnes employs Benton for nine months for $40,000 to supervise construction of a factory, but fires him without cause after three weeks. Benton, who spends $850 in reasonable fees attempting to find comparable employment, may recover $850 in incidental damages, in addition to any other actual loss he may suffer.

CONSEQUENTIAL DAMAGES **Consequential damages** include lost profits and injury to person or property resulting from defective performance. Thus, if Tracy leases to Sean a defective machine that causes him $40,000 in property damage and $120,000 in personal injuries, Sean may recover, in addition to damages for loss of value and incidental damages, $160,000 as consequential damages.

COST AVOIDED The recovery by the injured party, however, is reduced by any cost or loss she has avoided by not having to perform. For example, Clinton agrees to build a hotel for Debra for $11,250,000 by September 1. Clinton breaches by not completing construction until October 1. As a consequence, Debra loses revenues for one month in the amount of $400,000 but saves operating expenses of $60,000. She therefore may recover damages for $340,000. Similarly, in a contract in which the injured party has not fully performed, the injured party's recovery is reduced by the value to him of the performance he promised but did not render. For example, Clinton agrees to convey land to Debra in return for Debra's promise to work for Clinton for two years, but she repudiates the contract before Clinton has conveyed the land. Clinton's recovery for loss from Debra is reduced by the value to Clinton of the land.

NOMINAL DAMAGES

An action to recover damages for breach of contract may be maintained even though the plaintiff has not sustained or cannot prove any injury or loss resulting from the breach. Restatement, Section 346. In such a case, he will be permitted to recover **nominal damages**—a small sum fixed without regard to the amount of loss. For example, Edward contracts to sell and deliver goods to Florence for $1,000. Edward refuses to deliver the goods as agreed, and so breaks the contract. Florence, however, is able to purchase goods of the same kind and quality elsewhere for $1,000 without incurring any incidental damages. As a result, although Edward has violated Florence's rights under the contract, Florence has suffered no actual loss. Consequently, if Florence, as she may, should sue Edward for breach of contract, she would recover a judgment for nominal damages only. Nominal damages are also available where loss is actually sustained but cannot be proved with reasonable certainty.

RELIANCE DAMAGES

As an alternative to compensatory damages, the injured party may seek reimbursement for foreseeable loss caused by his reliance upon the contract. The purpose of **reliance damages** is to place the injured party in a position as good as the one he would have held, had the contract *not been made*. Reliance damages include expenses incurred in preparing to perform, in actually performing, or in forgoing opportunities to enter into other contracts. An injured party may prefer damages for reliance to compensatory damages when he is unable to establish his lost profits with reasonable certainty. For example, Donald agrees to sell his retail store to Gary, who spends $750,000 acquiring inventory and fixtures. Donald then repudiates the contract, and Gary sells the inventory and fixtures for $735,000. Neither party can establish with reasonable certainty what profit Gary would have made; Gary, therefore, may recover from Donald as damages the loss of $15,000 he sustained on the sale of the inventory and fixtures plus any other costs he incurred in entering into the contract. An injured party may choose reliance damages instead of compensatory damages when the contract is itself unprofitable. In such a case, however, if the breaching party can prove with reasonable certainty the amount of the loss, it will be subtracted from the injured party's reliance damages.

DAMAGES FOR MISREPRESENTATION

The basic remedy for misrepresentation is rescission (avoidance) of the contract, though when appropriate, the courts also will require restitution. At common law, an alternative remedy to rescission is a suit for damages. The Code liberalizes the common law by not restricting a defrauded party to an election of remedies; that is, the injured party may both rescind the contract by restoring the other party to the status quo and recover damages or obtain any other remedy available under the Code. UCC Section 2–721. In most States, the measure of damages for misrepresentation depends upon whether the misrepresentation was fraudulent or nonfraudulent.

Fraud A party induced by fraud to enter into a contract may recover general damages in a tort action. A minority of States allows the injured party to recover, under the "**out-of-pocket**" rule, general damages equal to the difference between the value of what she has received and the value of what she has given for it. The great majority of States, however, under the "**benefit-of-the-bargain**" rule, permits the intentionally defrauded party to recover general damages that are equal to the difference between the value of what she has received and the value of the fraudulent party's performance as represented. The Restatement of Torts provides the fraudulently injured party with the option of either out-of-pocket or benefit-of-the-bargain damages. Section 549. To illustrate, Emily intentionally misrepresents the capabilities of a printing press and thereby induces Melissa to purchase the machine for $20,000. The value of the press as delivered is $14,000, but if the machine had performed as represented, it would be worth $24,000. Under the out-of-pocket rule, Melissa would recover $6,000, whereas under the benefit-of-the-bargain rule, she would recover $10,000.

In addition to a recovery of general damages under one of the measures just discussed, consequential damages may be recovered to the extent they are proved with reasonable certainty and to the extent they do not duplicate general damages. Moreover, where the fraud is gross, oppressive, or aggravated, punitive damages are permitted.

Nonfraudulent Misrepresentation Where the misrepresentation is negligent, the deceived party may recover general damages—under the out-of-pocket measure—and consequential damages. Restatement of Torts, Section 552B. Some States, however, permit the recovery of general damages under the benefit-of-the-bargain measure for negligent misrepresentation. Where the misrepresentation is neither fraudulent nor negligent, however, the Restatement limits damages to the out-of-pocket measure. Section 552C.

PUNITIVE DAMAGES

Punitive damages are monetary damages in addition to compensatory damages awarded to a plaintiff in certain situations involving willful, wanton, or malicious conduct. Their purpose is to punish the defendant and thus discourage him and others from similar wrongful conduct. The purpose of allowing contract damages, on the other hand, is to compensate the plaintiff for the loss that he has sustained because of the defendant's breach of contract. Accordingly, the

Restatement provides that punitive damages are *not* recoverable for a breach of contract unless the conduct constituting the breach is also a tort for which the plaintiff may recover punitive damages. Restatement, Section 355.

LIQUIDATED DAMAGES

A contract may contain a **liquidated damages** provision by which the parties agree in advance to the damages to be paid in event of a breach. Such a provision will be enforced if it amounts to a reasonable forecast of the loss that may or does result from the breach. If, however, the sum agreed upon as liquidated damages bears no reasonable relationship to the amount of probable loss that may or does result from breach, it is unenforceable as a penalty. (A penalty is a contractual provision designed to deter a party from breaching her contract and to punish her for doing so.) Restatement, Section 356, Comment a states,

> The parties to a contract may effectively provide in advance the damages that are to be payable in the event of breach as long as the provision does not disregard the principle of compensation. The enforcement of such provisions for liquidated damages saves the time of courts, juries, parties and witnesses and reduces the expense of litigation. This is especially important if the amount in controversy is small. However, the parties to a contract are not free to provide a penalty for its breach. The central objective behind the system of contract remedies is compensatory, not punitive.

By examining the substance of the provision, the nature of the contract, and the extent of probable harm to the promisee that a breach may reasonably be expected to cause, the courts will determine whether the agreed amount is proper as liquidated damages or unenforceable as a penalty. If a liquidated damage provision is not enforceable, the injured party nevertheless is entitled to the ordinary remedies for breach of contract.

To illustrate, Reliable Construction Company contracts with Equerry to build a grandstand at Equerry's racecourse at a cost of $1,330,000, to have it completed by a certain date, and to pay Equerry, as liquidated damages, $5,000 per day for every day's delay beyond that date in completing the grandstand. The stipulated sum for delay is liquidated damages and not a penalty because the amount is reasonable. If, instead, the sum stipulated had been $40,000 per day, it would obviously have been unreasonable and therefore a penalty. Provisions for liquidated damages are sometimes found in contracts for the sale of a business, in which the seller agrees not to reenter the same business within a reasonable geographic area and time period. Actual damages resulting from the seller's breach of his agreement would ordinarily be difficult to ascertain, and the sum stipulated, if reasonable, would be enforced as liquidated damages.

LIMITATIONS ON DAMAGES

To accomplish the basic purposes of contract remedies, the law imposes the limitations of foreseeability, certainty, and mitigation upon monetary damages. These limitations are intended to ensure that damages can be taken into account at the time of contracting, that damages are compensatory and not speculative, and that damages do not include loss that could have been avoided by reasonable efforts.

FORESEEABILITY OF DAMAGES A contracting party is generally expected to consider foreseeable risks when entering into the contract. Therefore, compensatory or reliance damages are recoverable only for loss that the party in breach had reason to foresee as a *probable* result of such breach when the contract was made; conversely, the breaching party is not liable for loss that was not foreseeable when the parties entered into the contract. The test of foreseeability is *objective*, based upon what the breaching party had reason to foresee. Loss may be deemed foreseeable as a probable result of a breach by following from the breach (1) in the ordinary course of events or (2) as a result of special circumstances, beyond the ordinary course of events, which the party in breach had reason to know. Restatement, Section 351(2). Moreover, "[a] court may limit damages for foreseeable loss by excluding recovery for loss of profits, by allowing recovery only for loss incurred in reliance, or otherwise if it concludes that in the circumstances justice so requires in order to avoid disproportionate compensation." Restatement, Section 351(3).

The leading case on the subject of foreseeability of damages is *Hadley v. Baxendale*, decided in England in 1854. In this case, the plaintiffs operated a flour mill at Gloucester. Their mill was compelled to cease operating because of a broken crankshaft attached to the steam engine that furnished power to the mill. It was necessary to send the broken shaft to a foundry located at Greenwich so that a new shaft could be made. The plaintiffs delivered the broken shaft to the defendants, who were common carriers, for immediate transportation from Gloucester to Greenwich, but did not inform the defendants that operation of the mill had ceased because of the nonfunctioning crankshaft. The defendants received the shaft, collected the freight charges in advance, and promised to deliver the shaft for repairs the following day. The defendants, however, did not make delivery as promised; as a result, the mill did not resume operations for several days, causing the plaintiffs to lose profitable sales. The defendants contended that the loss of profits was too remote, and therefore unforeseeable, to be recoverable. Nonetheless, the jury, in awarding damages to the plaintiffs, was permitted to take into consideration the loss of these profits. The appellate court reversed the decision and ordered a new trial on the ground that the plaintiffs had never communicated to the defendants the special circumstances that caused the loss of profits, namely, the continued stoppage of the mill while awaiting the return of the repaired crankshaft. A common carrier, the court reasoned, would not reasonably have foreseen that the plaintiffs' mill would be shut down as a result of delay in transporting the broken crankshaft.

On the other hand, if the defendants in *Hadley v. Baxendale* had been informed that the shaft was necessary for the operation of the mill, or otherwise had reason to know this fact, they would be liable for the plaintiffs' loss of profit during that period of the shutdown caused by their delay. Under these circumstances, the loss would be the "foreseeable" and "natural" result of the breach.

Should a plaintiff's expected profit be extraordinarily large, the general rule is that the breaching party will be liable for such special loss only if he had reason to know of it. In any event, the plaintiff may recover for any ordinary loss resulting from the breach. Thus, if Madeline breaches a contract with Jane, causing Jane, due to special circumstances, $10,000 in damages where ordinarily such a breach would result in only $6,000 in damages, Madeline would be liable to Jane for $6,000, not $10,000, provided that Madeline was unaware of the special circumstances causing Jane the unusually large loss.

CERTAINTY OF DAMAGES Damages are not recoverable for loss beyond an amount that the injured party can establish with reasonable certainty. Restatement, Section 352. If the injured party cannot prove a particular element of her loss with reasonable certainty, she nevertheless will be entitled to recover the portion of her loss that she can prove with reasonable certainty. The certainty requirement creates the greatest challenge for plaintiffs seeking to recover consequential damages for lost profits on related transactions. Those attempting to prove lost profits caused by breach of a contract to produce a sporting event or to publish a new book experience similar difficulties.

MITIGATION OF DAMAGES Under the doctrine of mitigation of damages, the injured party may not recover damages for loss that he could have avoided with reasonable effort and without undue risk, burden, or humiliation. Restatement, Section 350. Thus, if James is under a contract to manufacture goods for Kathy, and Kathy repudiates the contract after James has commenced performance, James will not be allowed to recover for losses he sustains by continuing to manufacture the goods if to do so would increase the amount of damages. The amount of loss that James could reasonably have avoided is deducted from the amount that would otherwise be recoverable as damages. On the other hand, if the goods were almost completed when Kathy repudiated the contract, completing the goods might mitigate the damages, because the finished goods may be resalable whereas the unfinished goods may not. UCC Section 2–704(2).

Similarly, if Harvey contracts to work for Olivia for one year for a weekly salary and is wrongfully discharged by Olivia after two months, Harvey must use reasonable efforts to mitigate his damages by seeking other employment. If, after such efforts, he cannot obtain other employment of the same general character, he is entitled to recover full pay for the contract period that he is unemployed. He is not obliged to accept a radically different type of employment or to accept work at a distant place. For example, a person employed as a school-teacher or accountant who is wrongfully discharged is not obliged, in order to mitigate damages, to accept available employment as a chauffeur or truck driver. If Harvey does *not* seek other employment, then if Olivia proves with reasonable certainty that employment of the same general character was available, Harvey's damages are reduced by the amount he could have earned.

REMEDIES IN EQUITY

At times, damages based on the expectation interest, reliance interest, or restitution interest will not adequately compensate an injured party. In these cases, equitable relief in the form of specific performance or an injunction may be available to protect the injured party's interest.

The remedies of specific performance and an injunction are not a matter of right but rest in the discretion of the court. Consequently, they will not be granted where:

1. there is an adequate remedy at law;
2. it is impossible to enforce them, as where the seller has already conveyed the subject matter of the contract to an innocent third person;
3. the terms of the contract are unfair;
4. the consideration is grossly inadequate;
5. the contract is tainted with fraud, duress, undue influence, mistake, or unfair practices;
6. the terms of the contract are not sufficiently certain; or
7. the relief would cause unreasonable hardship.

A court may grant specific performance or an injunction despite a provision for liquidated damages. Restatement, Section 361. Moreover, a court will grant specific performance or an injunction even though a term of the contract prohibits equitable relief, if denying such relief would cause unreasonable hardship to the injured party. Restatement, Section 364(2).

Another equitable remedy is **reformation**, a process whereby the court "rewrites" or "corrects" a written contract to make it conform to the true agreement of the parties. The purpose of reformation is not to make a new contract for the parties but rather to express adequately the contract they have made for themselves. The remedy of reformation is granted when the parties agree on a contract but write it in a way that inaccurately reflects their actual agreement. For example, Acme Insurance Co. and Bell agree that for good consideration Acme will issue an annuity paying $500 per month. Through a clerical error, the annuity policy is issued for $50 per month. A court of equity, upon satisfactory proof of the mistake, will reform the policy to provide for the correct amount—$500 per month. In addition, as discussed in *Chapter 13*, where a covenant not to compete is unreasonable, some courts will reform the agreement to make it reasonable and enforceable.

SPECIFIC PERFORMANCE

Specific performance is an equitable remedy that compels the defaulting party to perform her contractual obligations. Ordinarily, where a seller breaches her contract for the sale of **personal property**, the buyer has a sufficient remedy at law. If, however, the personal property contracted for is rare or unique, this remedy is inadequate. Examples of such property would include a famous painting or statue, an original manuscript or a rare edition of a book, a patent, a copyright, shares of stock in a closely held corporation, or an heirloom. Articles of this kind cannot be purchased elsewhere. Accordingly, should the seller breach her contract for the sale of any such article, money damages will not adequately compensate the buyer. Consequently, in these instances, the buyer may avail herself of the equitable remedy of specific performance.

Although courts of equity will grant specific performance in connection with contracts for the sale of personal property only in exceptional circumstances, they will always grant it in cases involving breach of contract for the sale of **real property**. The reason for this is that every parcel of land is considered unique. Consequently, if the seller refuses to convey title to the real estate contracted for, the buyer may seek the aid of a court of equity to compel the seller to convey the title. Most courts of equity will likewise compel the buyer in a real estate contract to perform at the suit of the seller. Courts of equity will not grant specific performance of contracts for personal services. In the first place, enforcing such a decree may be difficult if not impossible. In the second place, it is against the policy of the courts to force one person to work for or to serve another against his will, even though the person has contracted to do so, in that such enforcement would closely resemble involuntary servitude. For example, if Carmen, an accomplished concert pianist, agrees to appear at a certain time and place to play a specified program for Rudolf, a court would not issue a decree of specific performance upon her refusal to appear.

INJUNCTIONS

The **injunction**, as used as a contract remedy, is a formal court order enjoining (commanding) a person to refrain from doing a specific act or to cease engaging in specified conduct. A court of equity, at its discretion, may grant an injunction against breach of a contractual duty where damages for a breach would be inadequate. For example, Clint enters into a written contract to give Janice the right of first refusal on a tract of land he owns. Clint, however, subsequently offers the land to Blake without first offering it to Janice. A court of equity may properly enjoin Clint from selling the land to Blake. Similarly, valid covenants not to compete may be enforced by an injunction.

An employee's promise of exclusive personal services may be enforced by an injunction against serving another employer as long as the probable result will not be to deprive the employee of other reasonable means of making a living. Restatement, Section 367. Suppose, for example, that Allan makes a contract with Marlene, a famous singer, under which Marlene agrees to sing at Allan's theater on certain dates for an agreed fee. Before the date of the first performance, Marlene makes a contract with Craig to sing for Craig at his theater on the same dates. Although, as already discussed, Allan cannot secure specific performance of his contract by Marlene, a court of equity will, on suit by Allan against Marlene, issue an injunction against her, ordering her not to sing for Craig.

Where the services contracted for are not unusual or extraordinary, the injured party cannot obtain injunctive relief. His only remedy is an action at law for damages.

RESTITUTION

One remedy that may be available to a party to a contract is restitution. **Restitution** is the act of returning to the aggrieved party the consideration, or its value, which he gave to the other party. The purpose of restitution is to restore the injured party to the position he occupied before the contract was made. Therefore, the party seeking restitution must return what he has received from the other party.

Restitution is available in several contractual situations: (1) as an alternative remedy for a party injured by breach; (2) for a party in default; (3) for a party who may not enforce a contract because of the statute of frauds; and (4) for a party wishing to rescind (avoid) a voidable contract.

PARTY INJURED BY BREACH

A party is entitled to restitution if the other party totally breaches the contract by nonperformance or repudiation. Restatement, Section 373. For example, Benedict agrees to sell land to Beatrice for $60,000. After Beatrice makes a partial payment of $15,000, Benedict wrongfully refuses to transfer title. As an alternative to damages or specific performance, Beatrice may recover the $15,000 in restitution.

PARTY IN DEFAULT

Where a party, after having partly performed, commits a breach by nonperformance or repudiation that discharges the other party's duty to perform, the party in default is entitled to restitution for any benefit she has conferred in excess of the loss she has caused by her breach. Restatement, Section 374. For example, Nathan agrees to sell land to Lilly for $60,000, and Lilly makes a partial payment of $15,000. Lilly then repudiates the contract. Nathan sells the land to Murray in good faith for $55,000. Lilly may recover from Nathan in restitution the part payment of the $15,000 *less* the $5,000 damages Nathan sustained because of Lilly's breach, which equals $10,000.

STATUTE OF FRAUDS

A party to a contract that is unenforceable because of the statute of frauds may, nonetheless, have acted in reliance upon the contract. In such a case, that party may recover in restitution the benefits she conferred upon the other in relying upon the unenforceable contract. In most States, the party seeking restitution must not be in default. Thus, if Wilton makes an oral contract to furnish services to Rochelle that are not to be performed within a year, and Rochelle discharges Wilton after three months, Wilton may recover as restitution the value of the services he rendered during the three months.

VOIDABLE CONTRACTS

A party who has rescinded or avoided a contract for lack of capacity, duress, undue influence, fraud in the inducement, nonfraudulent misrepresentation, or mistake is entitled to restitution for any benefit he has conferred upon the other party. Restatement, Section 376. For example, Samuel fraudulently induces Edith to sell land for $60,000. Samuel pays the purchase price, and Edith conveys the land. Discovering the fraud, Edith may disaffirm the contract and recover the land as restitution. Generally, the party seeking restitution must return any benefit that he has received under the agreement; however, as discussed in *Chapter 14* (which deals with contractual capacity), this is not always the case.

◆ **SEE FIGURE 18-1: Contract Remedies**

LIMITATIONS ON REMEDIES

ELECTION OF REMEDIES

If a party injured by a breach of contract has more than one remedy available to him, his manifesting a choice of one of them, such as bringing suit, does not prevent him from

◆ **FIGURE 18-1: Contract Remedies**

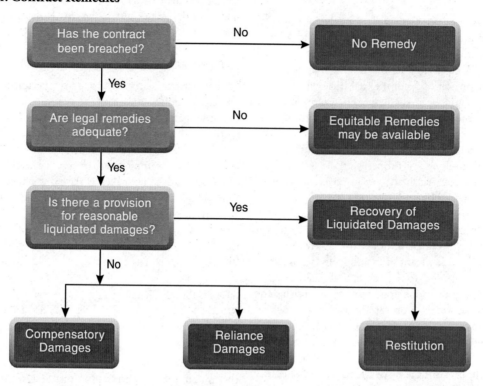

seeking another remedy unless the remedies are inconsistent and the other party materially changes his position in reliance on the manifestation. Restatement, Section 378. For example, a party who seeks specific performance, an injunction, or restitution may be entitled to incidental damages for delay in performance. Damages for *total breach*, however, are inconsistent with the remedies of specific performance, injunction, and restitution. Likewise, the remedy of specific performance or an injunction is inconsistent with that of restitution.

With respect to contracts for the sale of goods, the Code rejects any doctrine of election of remedies. Thus, the remedies it provides are essentially cumulative, including all of the available remedies for breach. Whether one remedy precludes another depends on the facts of the individual case. UCC Section 2–703, Comment 1.

LOSS OF POWER OF AVOIDANCE

A party with a power of avoidance for lack of capacity, duress, undue influence, fraud, misrepresentation, or mistake may lose that power if (1) she affirms the contract; (2) she delays unreasonably in exercising the power of disaffirmance; or (3) the rights of third parties intervene.

AFFIRMANCE A party who has the power to avoid a contract for lack of capacity, duress, undue influence, fraud in the inducement, nonfraudulent misrepresentation, or mistake will lose that power by affirming the contract. Affirmance occurs when the party, with full knowledge of the facts, either declares his intention to proceed with the contract or takes some other action from which such intention may reasonably be inferred. Thus, suppose that Pam was induced to purchase a ring from Sally through Sally's fraudulent misrepresentation. If, after learning the truth, Pam undertakes to sell the ring to Janet or else does something that is consistent only with her ownership of the ring, she may no longer rescind the transaction with Sally. In the case of incapacity, duress, or undue influence, affirmance is effective only after the circumstances that made the contract voidable cease to exist. Where there has been fraudulent misrepresentation, the defrauded party may affirm only after he knows of the misrepresentation. If the misrepresentation is nonfraudulent or a mistake is involved, the defrauded or mistaken party may affirm only after he knows or should know of the misrepresentation or mistake.

DELAY The power of avoidance may be lost if the party who has the power does not rescind within a reasonable time after the circumstances that made the contract voidable have ceased to exist. Determining a reasonable time depends upon all the circumstances, including the extent to which the delay enables the party with the power of avoidance to speculate at the other party's risk. To illustrate, a defrauded purchaser of stock cannot wait unduly to see if the market price or value of the stock appreciates sufficiently to justify retaining the stock.

RIGHTS OF THIRD PARTIES The intervening rights of third parties further limit the power of avoidance and the accompanying right to restitution. If A transfers property to B in a transaction that is voidable by A, and B sells the property to C (a good faith purchaser for value) before A exercises her power of avoidance, A will lose the right to recover the property.

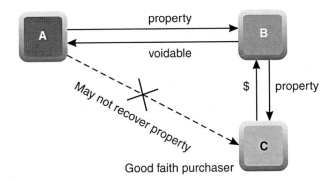

property

voidable

$ | property

May not recover property

Good faith purchaser

Thus, if C, a third party who is a good faith purchaser, acquires an interest in the subject matter of the contract before A has elected to rescind, no rescission is permitted. Because the transaction is voidable, B acquires a voidable title to the property. Upon a sale of the property by B to C, who is a purchaser in good faith and for value, C obtains good title and is allowed to retain the property. As both A and C are innocent, the law will not disturb the title held by C, the good faith purchaser. In this case, as in all cases in which rescission is not available, A's only recourse is against B.

The one notable exception to this rule is the situation involving a sale, *other than a sale of goods*, by a minor who subsequently wishes to avoid the transaction, in which the property has been retransferred to a good faith purchaser. Under this special rule, a good faith purchaser is deprived of the protection generally provided such third parties. Therefore, the third party in a transaction not involving goods, real property being the primary example, is no more protected from the minor's disaffirmance than is the person dealing directly with the minor.

CHAPTER SUMMARY

MONETARY DAMAGES

Compensatory Damages contract damages placing the injured party in a position as good as the one he would have held had the other party performed; equals loss of value minus loss avoided by injured party plus incidental damages plus consequential damages
* *Loss of Value* value of promised performance minus value of actual performance
* *Cost Avoided* loss or costs the injured party avoids by not having to perform
* *Incidental Damages* damages arising directly out of a breach of contract
* *Consequential Damages* damages not arising directly out of a breach but arising as a foreseeable result of the breach

Nominal Damages a small sum awarded where a contract has been breached but the loss is negligible or unproved

Reliance Damages contract damages placing the injured party in as good a position as she would have been in had the contract not been made

Damages for Misrepresentation
* *Benefit-of-the-Bargain Damages* difference between the value of the fraudulent party's performance as represented and the value the defrauded party received
* *Out-of-Pocket Damages* difference between the value given and the value received

Punitive Damages are generally *not* recoverable for breach of contract

Liquidated Damages reasonable damages agreed to in advance by the parties to a contract

Limitations on Damages
* *Foreseeability of Damages* potential loss that the party now in default had reason to know of when the contract was made
* *Certainty of Damages* damages are not recoverable beyond an amount that can be established with reasonable certainty
* *Mitigation of Damages* injured party may not recover damages for loss he could have avoided by reasonable effort

REMEDIES IN EQUITY	**Availability** only in cases in which there is no adequate remedy at law
	Types
	• *Specific Performance* court decree ordering breaching party to render promised performance
	• *Injunction* court order prohibiting a party from doing a specific act
	• *Reformation* court order correcting a written contract to conform with the original intent of the contracting parties

RESTITUTION	**Definition of Restitution** restoration of the injured party to the position she was in before the contract was made
	Availability
	• *Party Injured by Breach* if the other party totally breaches the contract by nonperformance or repudiation
	• *Party in Default* for any benefit conferred in excess of the loss caused by the breach
	• *Statute of Frauds* where a contract is unenforceable because of the statute of frauds, a party may recover the benefits conferred on the other party in reliance on the contract
	• *Voidable Contracts* a party who has avoided a contract is entitled to restitution for any benefit conferred on the other party

LIMITATIONS ON REMEDIES	**Election of Remedies** if remedies are not inconsistent, a party injured by a breach of contract may seek more than one
	Loss of Power of Avoidance a party with the power to avoid a contract may lose that power by
	• affirming the contract
	• delaying unreasonably in exercising the power of avoidance
	• being subordinated to the intervening rights of third parties

PART 3
Agency

CHAPTER 19
Relationship of Principal and Agent

CHAPTER 20
Relationship with Third Parties

COLUMN: © PHOTOGRAPHEROLYMPUS CLOUDS: © KERTLIS

Relationship of Principal and Agent

By using agents, one person (the principal) may enter into any number of business transactions as though he had personally carried them out, thus multiplying and expanding his business activities. The law of agency, like the law of contracts, is basic to almost every other branch of business law. Practically every type of contract or business transaction can be created or conducted through an agent. Therefore, the place and importance of agency in the practical conduct and operation of business cannot be overemphasized.

This is particularly true in the case of partnerships, corporations, and other business associations. Partnership is founded on the agency of the partners. Each partner is an agent of the partnership and, as such, has the authority to represent and bind the partnership in all usual transactions of the partnership. A corporation, being an artificial legal entity, must act through the agency of its officers and employees. Limited liability companies act through the actions of their members, managers, or both. Thus, practically and legally, agency is an essential part of partnerships, corporations, and other business associations. In addition, sole proprietors also may employ agents in the operations of their business. Business, therefore, is largely conducted not by owners themselves but by their agents or representatives.

The law of agency divides broadly into two main and somewhat overlapping parts: the internal and the external. An agent functions as an agent by dealing with third persons, thereby establishing legal relationships between the principal and those third persons. These relationships, which constitute the external part of agency law, are discussed in the next chapter. This chapter will cover the internal relationship between principal and agent, including the nature of agency, the creation of an agency, the duties of agent to principal, the duties of principal to agent, and the termination of agency.

Agency is primarily governed by State common law. An orderly presentation of this law was found in the Restatement (Second) of the Law of Agency, published in 1958 by the American Law Institute (ALI). Regarded as a valuable authoritative reference work, the Restatement is extensively cited and quoted in reported judicial opinions and by legal scholars. In 2006, the ALI published the Restatement of the Law Third, Agency, which completely replaced the ALI's Restatement Second of Agency. This chapter and the next chapter will refer to the Third Restatement as the Restatement.

NATURE OF AGENCY

Agency is a consensual relationship in which one person (the agent) acts as a representative of or otherwise acts on behalf of another person (the principal) with power to affect the legal rights and duties of the principal. Moreover, the principal has a right to control the actions of the agent. Restatement, Section 1.01.

An agent, therefore, is one who represents another, the principal, in business dealings with a third person; the operation of agency therefore involves three persons: the principal, the agent, and a third person who deals with the agent. In dealing with a third person, the agent acts for and in the name and place of the principal, who, along with the third person, is, if properly entered into, a party to the transaction. When the agent is dealing with the third person, the principal, in legal effect, is present in the person of the agent; and the result of the agent's functioning is exactly the same as if the principal had dealt directly with the third person. If, moreover, the existence and identity of the principal are disclosed, the agent acts not as a party but simply as an intermediary.

Within the scope of the authority granted to her by her principal, the agent may negotiate the terms of contracts with others and bind her principal to such contracts. In addition, the negligence of an agent who is an employee in conducting the business of her principal exposes the principal to tort liability for injury and loss suffered by third persons. The old maxim "*qui facit per alium, facit per se*" (he who acts through another, acts himself) accurately describes the relationship between principal and agent. The rights and liabilities of the parties where an agent enters into a contract with a third party or commits a tort against a third party are discussed in the next chapter.

SCOPE OF AGENCY PURPOSES

As a general rule, a person may do through an agent whatever business activity he may accomplish personally. Conversely, whatever he cannot legally do himself, he cannot authorize another to do for him. Thus, a person may not validly authorize another to commit an illegal act or crime. Any such agreement is illegal and therefore unenforceable. Also, a person may not appoint an agent to perform acts that are so personal that their performance may not be delegated to another, as in the case of a contract for personal services. For example, Howard, a painter, contracts to paint a portrait of Doris. But Howard has one of his students execute the painting and tenders it to Doris. This is not a valid tender because the duty to paint Doris's portrait is not delegable.

OTHER LEGAL RELATIONSHIPS

Two other legal relationships overlap with agency: employer-employee and principal-independent contractor. In the **employment relationship** (historically referred to as the master-servant relationship), for the purposes of vicarious liability discussed in the next chapter, an employee is an agent whose principal controls or has the right to control the manner and means of the agent's performance of work. Restatement, Section 7.07(3). All employees are agents, even those employees not authorized to contract on behalf of the employer or otherwise to conduct business with third parties. Thus, an assembly-line worker in a factory is an agent of the company employing her since she is subject to the employer's control, thereby consenting to act "on behalf" of the principal, but she does not have the right to bind the principal in contracts with third parties.

Although all employees are agents, not all agents are employees. Agents who are not employees are generally referred to as **independent contractors**. (The Third Restatement does not use this term.) In these cases, although the principal has the right of control over the agent, the principal does not control the manner and means of the agent's performance. For instance, an attorney retained to handle a particular transaction would be an independent contractor-agent regarding that particular transaction because the attorney is hired by the principal to perform a service, but the manner of the attorney's performance is not controlled by the principal. Other examples are auctioneers, brokers, and factors.

Finally, not all independent contractors are agents because the person hiring the independent contractor has no right of control over the independent contractor. For example, a taxicab driver hired to carry a person to the airport is not an agent of that person. Likewise, if Pam hires Bill to build a stone wall around her property, Bill is an independent contractor who is not an agent.

In determining whether an agent is an employee, the courts consider numerous factors, including the following:

(a) the extent of control that the agent and the principal have agreed the principal may exercise—or has exercised in practice—over details of the work;

(b) whether the agent is engaged in a distinct occupation or business;

(c) whether the type of work done by the agent is customarily done under a principal's direction or without supervision;

(d) the skill required in the agent's occupation;

(e) whether the agent or the principal supplies the tools and other instrumentalities required for the work and the place in which to perform it;

(f) the length of time during which the agent is engaged by a principal;

(g) whether the agent is paid by the job or by the time worked;

(h) whether the agent's work is part of the principal's regular business;

(i) whether the principal and the agent believe that they are creating an employment relationship; and

(j) whether the principal is or is not in business.

Restatement, Section 7.07.

The distinction between employee and independent contractor has several important legal consequences. For example, as discussed in the next chapter, a principal is liable for the torts committed by an employee within the scope of his employment but ordinarily is not liable for torts committed by an independent contractor. In addition, the obligations of a principal under numerous Federal and State statutes apply only to agents who are employees. These statutes cover such matters as labor relations, employment discrimination, disability, employee safety, workers' compensation, social security, minimum wage, and unemployment compensation. These and other statutory enactments affecting the employment relationship are discussed in *Chapter 43*.

CREATION OF AGENCY

As previously stated, agency is a consensual relationship that the principal and agent may form by contract *or* agreement. The Restatement defines an agency relationship as "the fiduciary relationship that arises when one person (a 'principal') manifests assent to another person (an 'agent') that the agent shall act on the principal's behalf and subject to the principal's control, and the agent manifests assent or otherwise consents so to act." Section 1.01. Thus the agency relationship involves three basic elements: assent, control by the principal, and the agent's acting on behalf of the principal. A person can manifest assent or intention through written or spoken words or other conduct. Restatement, Section 1.03. Thus, whether an agency relationship has been created is determined by an *objective test*. If the principal requests another to act for him with respect to a matter and indicates that the other is to act without further communication, and the other consents to act, the relation of principal and agent exists. For example, Paula writes to Austin, a factor whose business is purchasing goods for others, telling him to select described goods and ship them at once to Paula. Before answering Paula's letter, Austin does as directed, charging the goods to Paula. He is authorized to do this because an agency relationship exists between Paula and Austin.

The principal has the right to control the conduct of the agent with respect to the matters entrusted to the agent. Restatement, Section 1.01.

The principal's right to control continues throughout the duration of the agency relationship. The relationship of principal and agent is consensual and not necessarily contractual; therefore, it may exist without consideration. Restatement, Section 1.04(3). Even though the agency relationship is consensual, how the parties label the relationship does not determine whether it is an agency. Section 1.02. An agency created without an agent's right to compensation is a **gratuitous agency**. For example, Patti asks her friend Andrew to return for credit goods recently purchased from a store. If Andrew consents, a gratuitous agency has been created. The power of a gratuitous agent to affect the principal's relationships with third persons is the same as that of a paid agent, and his liabilities to and rights against third persons also are the same. Nonetheless, agency by contract, the most usual method of creating the relationship, must satisfy all the requirements of a contract.

In some circumstances a person is held liable as a principal, even though no actual agency has been created, in order to protect third parties who justifiably rely on a reasonable belief that a person is an agent and who act on that belief to their detriment. Called **agency by estoppel**, apparent agency, or ostensible agency, this liability arises when (1) a person ("principal") intentionally or carelessly causes a third party to believe that another person (the "agent") has authority to act on the principal's behalf; (2) the principal has notice of the third party's belief and does not take reasonable steps to notify the third party; (3) the third party reasonably and in good faith relies on the appearances created by the principal; and (4) the third party justifiably and detrimentally changes her position in reliance on the agent's apparent authority. Restatement, Section 2.05. When these requirements are met, the principal is liable to the third party for the loss the third party suffered by changing her position. The doctrine is applicable when the person against whom estoppel is asserted has made no manifestation that an actor has authority as an agent but is responsible for the third party's belief that an actor is an agent, and the third party has justifiably been induced by that belief to undergo a detrimental change in position. Restatement, Section 2.05.

FORMALITIES

As a general rule, a contract of agency requires no particular formality. Usually the contract is express or inferred from the conduct of the principal. In some cases, however, the contract must be in writing. For example, the appointment of an agent for a period of more than a year comes within the one-year clause of the statute of frauds and thus must be in writing to be enforceable. In some States, the authority of an agent to sell land must be stated in a writing signed by the principal. Many States have "equal dignity" statutes providing that a principal must grant his agent in a written instrument the authority to enter into any contract required to be in writing. Restatement, Section 3.02. See *Chapter 15* for a discussion of State and Federal legislation giving electronic records and signatures the legal effect of traditional writings and signatures.

A **power of attorney** is an instrument that states an agent's authority. Restatement, Section 1.04(7). A power of attorney is a formal manifestation from principal to agent, who is known as "an attorney in fact," as well as to third parties that evidences the agent's appointment and the nature or extent of the agent's authority. Under a power of attorney, a principal may, for example, appoint an agent not only to execute a contract for the sale of the principal's real estate, but also to execute the deed conveying title to the real estate to the third party. A number of States have created an optional statutory short-form power of attorney based on the Uniform Statutory Form Power of Attorney Act. In 2006, a new Uniform Power of Attorney Act was promulgated to replace the Uniform Statutory Form Power of Attorney Act. To date, only five States have adopted the 2006 Act.

CAPACITY

The capacity of an individual to be a principal, and thus to act through an agent, depends upon the capacity of the principal to do the act herself. Restatement, Section 3.04(1). For example, contracts entered into by a minor or an incompetent not under a guardianship are voidable. Consequently, the appointment of an agent by a minor or an incompetent not under a guardianship and any resulting contracts are voidable, regardless of the agent's contractual capacity. The capacity of a person that is not an individual, such as a government or business association, is determined by the law governing that entity. Restatement, Section 3.04(2).

Almost all of the States have adopted the Uniform Durable Power of Attorney Act providing for a durable power of attorney under which an agent's power survives or is triggered by the principal's loss of mental competence. (In 2006, a new Uniform Power of Attorney Act was promulgated to replace Uniform Durable Power of Attorney Act. To date, only five States have adopted the 2006 Act.) A **durable power of attorney** is a written instrument that expresses the principal's intention that the agent's authority will not be affected by the principal's subsequent incapacity or that the agent's authority will become effective upon the principal's subsequent incapacity.

Any person able to act, including individuals, corporations, partnerships, and other associations, ordinarily has the capacity to act as an agent. Restatement, Section 3.05. Because the act of the agent is considered the act of the principal, the incapacity of an agent to bind himself by contract does not disqualify him from making a contract that is binding on his principal. The agent's liability, however, depends upon the agent's capacity to contract. Thus, although the contract of agency may be voidable, an authorized contract between the principal and the third person who dealt with the agent is valid.

An "electronic agent" is a computer program or other automated means used independently to initiate an action or respond to electronic records or performances in whole or in part without review or action by an individual. Electronic agents are not persons and, therefore, are not considered agents. In 2000, Congress enacted the Electronic Signatures in Global and National Commerce (E-Sign). The Act makes electronic records and signatures valid and enforceable across the United States for many types of transactions in or affecting interstate or foreign commerce. The Act validates contracts or other records relating to a transaction in or affecting interstate or foreign commerce formed by electronic agents so long as the action of each electronic agent is legally attributable to the person to be bound. E-Sign specifically excludes certain transactions, including (1) wills, codicils, and testamentary trusts; (2) adoptions, divorces, and other matters of family law; and (3) the Uniform Commercial Code other than sales and leases of goods.

DUTIES OF AGENT TO PRINCIPAL

The duties of the agent to the principal are determined by the express and implied terms of any contract between the agent and the principal. Restatement, Section 8.07. In addition to these contractual duties, the agent is subject to various other duties imposed by law, unless the parties agree otherwise. Normally, a principal bases the selection of an agent on the agent's ability, skill, and integrity. Moreover, the principal not only authorizes and empowers the agent to bind her on contracts with third persons, but also frequently places the agent in possession of her money and other property. As a result, the agent is in a position, either through negligence or dishonesty, to injure the principal. Accordingly, an agent as a **fiduciary** (a person in a position of trust and confidence) owes his principal the duties of obedience, good conduct, diligence, and loyalty; the duty to inform; and the duty to provide an accounting. Moreover, the agent is subject to liability for loss caused to the principal by any breach of duty.

A gratuitous agent is subject to the same duty of loyalty that is imposed upon a paid agent and is liable to the principal for the harm he causes by his careless performance. Although the lack of consideration usually places a gratuitous agent under no duty to perform for the principal, such an agent may be liable to the principal for failing to perform a promise on which the principal has relied if the agent should have realized that his promise would induce reliance. Restatement, Section 8.07, comment c.

DUTY OF OBEDIENCE

The duty of obedience requires the agent to act in the principal's affairs only as actually authorized by the principal and to obey all lawful instructions and directions of the principal. Restatement, Section 8.09. If an agent exceeds her actual authority, she is subject to liability to the principal for loss caused the principal. An agent is also liable to the principal for unauthorized acts that are the result of the agent's unreasonable interpretations of the principal's directions. An agent is not, however, under a duty to follow orders to perform illegal or tortious acts, such as misrepresenting the quality of his principal's goods or those of a competitor. Still, he may be subject to liability to his principal for breach of the duty of obedience (1) because he entered into an unauthorized contract for which his principal is liable, (2) because he has improperly delegated his authority, or (3) because he has committed a tort for which the principal is liable. Thus, an agent who sells on credit in violation of his principal's explicit instructions has breached the duty of obedience and is liable to the principal for any amounts the purchaser does not pay. Moreover, an agent who violates his duty of obedience materially breaches the agency contract and loses his right to compensation.

DUTY OF GOOD CONDUCT

An agent has a duty, within the scope of the agency relationship, to act reasonably and to avoid conduct that is likely to damage the principal's interests. Restatement, Section 8.10. This duty reflects the fact that the conduct of agents can have a significant effect on the principal's reputation. A breach of this duty makes the agent liable to the principal and subject to rightful discharge or termination.

DUTY OF DILIGENCE

Subject to any agreement with the principal, an agent has a duty to the principal to act with the care, competence, and diligence normally exercised by agents in similar circumstances. Special skills or knowledge possessed by an agent are circumstances to be taken into account in determining whether the agent acted with due care and diligence. Moreover, if the agent claims to possess special skill or knowledge, the agent has a duty to act with the care, competence, and diligence normally exercised by agents with such skill or knowledge. Restatement, Section 8.08. By failing to exercise the required care, competence, and diligence, she is liable to the principal for any resulting harm. For example, Peg appoints Alvin as her agent to sell goods in markets where the highest price can be obtained. Although by carefully obtaining information he could have obtained a higher price in a nearby market, Alvin sells goods in a glutted market, receiving only a low price. Consequently, he is liable to Peg for breach of the duty of diligence.

A gratuitous agent owes a standard of care that is reasonable to expect under the circumstances, which include the skill and experience that the agent possesses. Thus, providing a service gratuitously may subject an agent to duties of competence and diligence to the principal that do not differ from the duties owed by a compensated agent. Restatement, Section 8.08, comment e.

DUTY TO INFORM

An agent has a duty to use reasonable effort to provide the principal with facts that the agent knows, has reason to know, or should know if (1) the agent knows, or has reason to know, that the principal would wish to have the facts; or (2) the facts are material to the agent's duties to the principal. However, this duty does not apply to facts if providing them to the principal would violate a superior duty owed by the agent to another person. Restatement, Section 8.11. The rule of agency providing that notice to an agent is notice to his principal makes this duty imperative. Restatement, Section 5.02. An agent who breaches this duty is subject to liability to the principal for loss caused the principal by the agent's breach and may also be subject to termination of the agency relationship. Moreover, if the agent's breach of this duty constitutes a breach of the contract between the agent and the principal, the agent is also liable for breach of contract.

Examples of information that an agent is under a duty to communicate to his principal include the following: (1) that a customer of the principal has become insolvent; (2) that a debtor of the principal has become insolvent; (3) that a partner of a firm with which the principal has previously dealt, and with which the principal or agent is about to deal, has withdrawn from the firm; or (4) that property which the principal has authorized the agent to sell at a specified price can be sold at a higher price.

DUTY TO ACCOUNT

Subject to any agreement with the principal, an agent has a duty to keep and render accounts to the principal of money or other property received or paid out on the principal's account. Moreover, the agent may not mingle the principal's property with any other person's property and may not deal with the principal's property so that it appears to be the agent's property. Restatement, Section 8.12.

FIDUCIARY DUTY

A **fiduciary duty** arises out of a relationship of trust and confidence and requires the utmost loyalty and good faith. An agent has a fiduciary duty to act loyally for the principal's benefit in all matters connected with the agency relationship. Restatement, Section 8.01. This duty is imposed by law upon the agent and is also owed by an employee to his employer. The principal may agree that conduct by an agent that would otherwise constitute a breach of the fiduciary duty shall not constitute a breach of that duty provided that in obtaining the principal's consent, the agent (1) acts in good faith, (2) discloses all material facts that the agent knows, has reason to know, or should know would reasonably affect the principal's judgment, and (3) otherwise deals fairly with the principal. Restatement, Section 8.06.

An agent's fiduciary duty to a principal generally begins with the formation of the agency relationship and ends with its termination. Restatement, Section 8.01. However, as discussed below, an agent may be subject to duties after termination applicable to the agent's use of the principal's property and confidential information provided by the principal.

The fiduciary duty arises most frequently in the following situations involving principals and their agents although it is by no means limited to these situations.

CONFLICTS OF INTEREST An agent has a duty not to deal with the principal as, or on behalf of, an adverse party in a transaction connected with the agency relationship. Restatement, Section 8.03. An agent must act solely in the interest of his principal, not in his own interest or in the interest of another. In addition, an agent may not represent his principal in any transaction in which the agent has a personal interest. Nor may he act on behalf of adverse parties to a transaction without both principals' approval to the dual agency. An agent may take a position that conflicts with the interest of his principal only if the principal, with full knowledge of all of the facts, consents. For example, A, an agent of P who desires to purchase land, agrees with C, who represents B, a seller of land, that A and C will endeavor to effect a transaction between their principals and will pool their commissions. A and C have committed a breach of fiduciary duty to P and B.

SELF-DEALING An agent has a duty not to deal with the principal as an adverse party in a transaction connected with the agency relationship. Restatement, Section 8.03. The courts closely scrutinize transactions between an agent and her principal. Because the agent may not deal at arm's length with her principal, she thus owes her principal a duty of full disclosure of all relevant facts that affect the transaction. Moreover, the transaction must be fair. Thus, an agent who is employed to buy may not buy from himself without the principal's consent. Restatement, Section 8.06. For example, Penny employs Albert to purchase for her a site suitable for a shopping center. Albert owns such a site and sells it to Penny at the fair market value, but does not disclose to Penny that he had owned the land. Penny may rescind the transaction. An agent who is employed to sell may not become the purchaser nor may he act as agent for the purchaser without the consent of the principal. The agent's loyalty must be undivided, and he must devote his actions exclusively to represent and promote the interests of his principal.

DUTY NOT TO COMPETE During the agency relationship an agent must not compete with his principal or act on behalf or otherwise assist any of the principal's competitors. Restatement, Section 8.04. After the agency terminates without breach by the agent, however, unless otherwise agreed, the agent may compete with his former principal. The courts will enforce by injunction a contractual agreement by the agent not to compete after the agency terminates if the restriction is reasonable as to time and place and is necessary to protect the principal's legitimate interest. Contractual agreements not to compete are discussed in *Chapter 13* where it is noted that such noncompete contracts may be subject to different standards for Internet companies and their employees.

MISAPPROPRIATION An agent may not use property of the principal for the agent's own purposes or for the benefit of a third party. Restatement, Section 8.05(1). Unless the principal consents, an agent who has possession of the principal's property has a duty to use it only on the principal's behalf even if the agent's use of the property does not cause harm to the principal. An agent is liable to the principal for any profit the agent made while using the principal's property or for the value of the agent's use of the principal's property. An agent's duties regarding the principal's property continue after the agency terminates, and a former agent has a duty to return any of the principal's property she still possesses.

CONFIDENTIAL INFORMATION An agent may not use or disclose confidential information obtained in the course of the agency for his own benefit or those of a third party. Restatement, Section 8.05(2). Confidential information is information that, if disclosed, would harm the principal's business or that has a value because it is not generally known. Such information includes unique business methods, trade secrets, business plans, personnel, nonpublic financial results, and customer lists. An agent may, however, reveal confidential information that the principal is committing, or is about to commit, a crime. Many statutes provided protection to employees who "whistle-blow."

Unless otherwise agreed, even after the agency terminates, the agent may not use or disclose to third persons confidential information. The agent may, however, utilize the generally known skills, knowledge, and information she acquired during the agency relationship.

DUTY TO ACCOUNT FOR FINANCIAL BENEFITS Unless otherwise agreed, an agent has a duty not to acquire any financial or other material benefits in connection with transactions conducted on behalf of the principal. Restatement, Section 8.02. Such benefits would include bribes, kickbacks, and gifts. Moreover, an agent may not profit secretly from any transaction subject to the agency. All material benefits, including secret profits, belong to the principal, to whom the agent must account. In addition, the principal may recover any damages caused by the agent's breach. Thus, if an agent, authorized to sell certain property of his principal for $1,000, sells it for $1,500, he may not secretly pocket the additional $500. Further, suppose Peabody employs real estate broker Anderson to sell his land for a commission of 6 percent of the sale price. Anderson, knowing that Peabody is willing to sell for $20,000, agrees secretly with a prospective buyer who is willing to pay $22,000 for the land that he will endeavor to obtain Peabody's consent to sell for $20,000, in which event the buyer will pay Anderson $1,000, or one-half of the amount that the buyer believes she is saving on the price. The broker has violated his fiduciary duty and must pay to Peabody the secret profit of $1,000. Furthermore, Anderson loses the right to any commission on the transaction.

PRINCIPAL'S REMEDIES An agent who violates his fiduciary duty is liable to his principal for breach of contract, in tort for losses caused and possibly punitive damages, and in restitution for profits he made or property he received in breach of the fiduciary duty. Moreover, he loses the right to compensation. The principal may avoid a transaction in which the agent breached his fiduciary duty, even though the principal suffered no loss. A breach of fiduciary duty may also constitute just cause for discharge of the agent. Restatement, Section 8.01, comment d.

DUTIES OF PRINCIPAL TO AGENT

Although both principal and agent have rights and duties arising out of the agency relationship, more emphasis is placed on the duties of the agent. This is necessarily so because of the nature of the agency relationship. First, the acts and services to be performed, both under the agency contract and as may be required by law, are to be performed mostly by the agent. Second, the agent is a fiduciary and as such is subject to the duties discussed earlier. Nonetheless, an agent has certain rights against the principal, both under the contract and by the operation of law. Correlative to these rights are certain duties, based in contract and tort law, which the principal owes to the agent.

◆ **SEE FIGURE 19-1: Duties of Principal and Agent**

CONTRACTUAL DUTIES

An agency relationship may exist in the absence of a contract between the principal and agent. However, many principals and agents do enter into contracts, in which case a principal has a duty to act in accordance with the express and implied terms of any contract between the principal and the agent. Restatement, Section 8.13. The contractual duties owed by a principal to an agent are the duties of compensation, reimbursement, and indemnification; each may be excluded or modified by agreement between the principal and agent. Although a gratuitous agent is not owed a duty of compensation, she is entitled to reimbursement and indemnification.

As with any party to a contract, a principal is under a duty to perform his part of the contract according to its terms. The most important duty of the principal, from the standpoint of the agent, is to compensate the agent as specified in the contract. It is also the duty of the principal not to terminate the agency wrongfully. Whether the principal must furnish the agent with the means of employment or the opportunity for work will depend upon the particular case. For example, a principal who employs an agent to sell his goods must supply the agent with conforming goods, whereas in other cases, the agent must create his own opportunity for work, as in the case of a broker employed to procure a buyer for his principal's house. How far, if at all, the principal must assist or cooperate with the agent will depend on the particular agency. Usually, cooperation on the part of the principal is more necessary where the agent's compensation is contingent upon the success of his efforts than where the agent is paid a fixed salary regularly over a period of permanent employment.

COMPENSATION A principal has a duty to compensate her agent unless the agent has agreed to serve gratuitously. If the agreement does not specify a definite compensation, a principal is under a duty to pay the reasonable value of the authorized services her agent has performed. Restatement, Section 8.13, comment d. An agent loses the right to compensation by (1) breaching the duty of obedience, (2) breaching the duty of loyalty, or (3) willfully and deliberately breaching the agency contract. Furthermore, an agent whose compensation depends upon her accomplishing a specific result is entitled to the agreed compensation only if she achieves the result within the time specified or within a reasonable time, if no time is stated. A common example is a listing agreement between a seller and a real estate broker providing for a commission to the broker if he finds a buyer ready, willing, and able to buy the property on the terms specified in the agreement. A principal also has a duty to maintain and provide to the agent a true and complete account of the money or property due to her.

◆ **FIGURE 19-1: Duties of Principal and Agent**

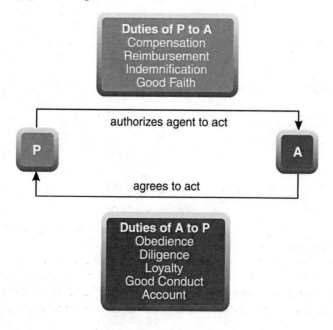

INDEMNIFICATION AND REIMBURSEMENT In general, a principal has an obligation to **indemnify** (compensate for a loss) an agent whenever the agent makes a payment or incurs an expense or other loss while acting as authorized on behalf of the principal. The contract between the principal and agent may specify the extent of this duty. In the absence of any contractual provisions, a principal has a duty to **reimburse** the agent when the agent makes a payment within the scope of the agent's actual authority. Restatement, Section 8.14. For example, an agent who reasonably and properly pays a fire insurance premium for the protection of her principal's property is entitled to reimbursement for the payment.

A principal also has a duty to indemnify the agent when the agent suffers a loss that fairly should be borne by the principal in light of their relationship. Restatement, Section 8.14. For example, suppose that Perry, the principal, has in his possession goods belonging to Margot. Perry directs Alma, his agent, to sell these goods. Alma, believing Perry to be the owner, sells the goods to Turner. Margot then sues Alma for the conversion of her goods and recovers a judgment, which Alma pays to Margot. Alma is entitled to indemnification from Perry for her loss, including the amount she reasonably expended in defense of the action brought by Margot.

TORT AND OTHER DUTIES A principal owes to any agent the same duties under tort law that the principal owes to all parties. Moreover, a principal has a duty to deal with the agent fairly and in good faith. This duty requires that the principal provide the agent with information about risks of physical harm or monetary loss that the principal knows, has reason to know, or should know are present in the agent's work but are unknown to the agent. Restatement, Section 8.15. For instance, in directing his agent to collect rent from a tenant who is known to have assaulted rent collectors, the principal has a duty to warn the agent of the risk involved.

Where the agent is an employee, the principal owes the agent additional duties. Among these is the duty to provide reasonably safe conditions of employment and to warn the employee of any unreasonable risk involved in the employment. A negligent employer is also liable to her employees for injury caused by the negligence of other employees and of other agents doing work for her. The duties an employer owes to an employee are discussed more fully in *Chapter 43.*

TERMINATION OF AGENCY

Because the authority of an agent is based upon the consent of the principal, the agency is terminated when such consent is withdrawn or otherwise ceases to exist. Upon termination of the agency, the agent's actual authority ends, and he is not entitled to compensation for services subsequently rendered. However, some of the agent's fiduciary duties may continue. The termination of *apparent* authority will be discussed in the next chapter. Termination may take place by the acts of the parties or by operation of law.

ACTS OF THE PARTIES

Termination by the acts of the parties may occur by the provisions of the original agreement, by the subsequent acts of both principal and agent, or by the subsequent act of either one of them.

LAPSE OF TIME An agent's actual authority terminates as agreed by the agent and the principal. Restatement, Section 3.09. Authority conferred upon an agent for a specified time terminates when that period expires. If no time is specified, authority terminates at the end of a reasonable period. Restatement, Section 3.09, comment d. For example, Palmer authorizes Avery to sell a tract of land for him. After ten years pass without communication between Palmer and Avery, though Avery purports to have sold the tract, his authorization has terminated due to lapse of time.

MUTUAL AGREEMENT OF THE PARTIES The agency relationship is created by agreement and may be terminated at any time by mutual agreement of the principal and the agent. Restatement, Section 3.09(1).

REVOCATION OF AUTHORITY A principal may revoke an agent's authority at any time by notifying the agent. Restatement, Section 3.10. If, however, such revocation constitutes a breach of contract, the agent may recover damages from the principal. For example, Patrick, in consideration of Alice's agreement to advertise and give her best energies to the sale of Patrick's property, Blackacre, grants to Alice "a power of attorney, irrevocable for one year." Alice advertises and spends time trying to sell Blackacre. At the end of three months, Patrick informs Alice that he is revoking the power of attorney. Although her authority is terminated, Alice may recover damages from Patrick. Restatement, Section 3.10, Illustration 2. Nonetheless, where the agent has seriously breached the agency contract, willfully disobeyed, or violated the fiduciary duty, the principal is not liable for terminating the agency relationship. In addition, a principal ordinarily may revoke a gratuitous agency without liability to the agent.

RENUNCIATION BY THE AGENT The agent also has the power to end the agency by notifying the principal that she renounces the authority given her. Restatement, Section 3.10. If the parties have contracted for the agency to continue for a specified time, an unjustified renunciation prior to the expiration of that time is a breach of contract. If the agency is gratuitous, however, the agent ordinarily may renounce it without liability to the principal.

OPERATION OF LAW

The occurrence of certain events will automatically terminate an agency relationship by the operation of law. These events either make it impossible for the agent to perform or unlikely that the principal would want the agent to act. As a matter of law, the occurrence of any of the following events ordinarily terminates agency.

DEATH Because the authority given to an agent by a principal is strictly personal, the death of an individual agent terminates the agent's actual authority. The death of an individual principal also terminates the actual authority of the agent when the agent has notice of the principal's death. Restatement, Section 3.07. This is contrary to the Second Restatement, which took the position that the principal's death terminated the agent's actual authority whether the agent had notice or not. Section 120. For example, Polk employs Allison to sell Polk's line of goods under a contract specifying Allison's commission and the one-year period for which the employment is to continue. Without Allison's knowledge, Polk dies. Under the Second Restatement Allison no longer has authority to sell Polk's goods, even though the contract specified that she would be employed for one year. The death of Polk, the principal, terminated the authority of Allison the agent. Under the Third Restatement, on the other hand, Allison would continue to have actual authority until she received notice of Polk's death. A person has **notice** of a fact if the person knows the fact, has reason to know the fact, has received an effective notification of the fact, or should know the fact to fulfill a duty owed to another person. Restatement, Section 1.04(4). Moreover, the Uniform Durable Power of Attorney Act allows the holder of *any* power of attorney, durable or otherwise, to exercise it on the death of the principal, if its exercise is in good faith and without knowledge of the principal's death. Almost all of the States have adopted this act.

When an agent or principal is not an individual, the organizational statutes typically determine when authority terminates upon the cessation of the existence of that organization. (This will be discussed further in *Parts 6* and *7* of this book.) When the organizational statute does not specify, the Restatement provides the agent's actual authority terminates when the nonindividual principal or agent ceases to exist or begins a process that will lead to the cessation of its existence. Restatement, Section 3.07.

INCAPACITY Incapacity of the principal that occurs after the formation of the agency terminates the agent's actual authority when the agent has notice of the principal's incapacity. Restatement, Section 3.08. This is contrary to the Second Restatement, which took the position that the principal's incapacity terminated the agent's actual authority without notice to the agent. Section 122. To illustrate, Powell authorizes Anna to sell in the next ten months an apartment complex for not less than $2 million. Without Anna's knowledge, Powell is adjudicated incompetent two months later. Under the Second Restatement Anna's authority to sell the apartment complex is terminated. Under the Third Restatement Anna would continue to have actual authority until she received notice of Powell's incapacity.

If an agent is appointed under a durable power of attorney, the authority of an agent survives, or is triggered by, the incapacity or disability of the principal. Moreover, the Uniform Durable Power of Attorney Act allows the holder of a power of attorney that is *not* durable to exercise it on the incapacity of the principal, if its exercise is in good faith and without knowledge of the principal's incapacity.

CHANGE IN CIRCUMSTANCES An agent's actual authority terminates whenever the agent should reasonably conclude that the principal no longer would assent to the agent's taking action on the principal's behalf. Restatement, Section 3.09(2). Thus, Patricia authorizes Aaron to sell her eighty acres of farmland for $800 per acre. Subsequently, oil is discovered on nearby land, which causes Patricia's land to increase greatly in value. Because Aaron knows of this, but Patricia does not, Aaron's authority to sell the land is terminated.

The Second Restatement specified a number of subsequent changes in circumstances that would terminate an agent's actual authority, including accomplishment of authorized act, bankruptcy of principal or agent, change in business conditions, loss or destruction of subject matter, disloyalty of agent, change in law, and outbreak of war. The Third Restatement takes a different approach by providing a basic rule that an agent acts with actual authority "when, *at the time of taking action* that has legal consequences for the principal, the agent reasonably believes, in accordance with the principal's manifestations to the agent, that the principal wishes the agent so to act." Section 2.01 (emphasis added). Thus, if circumstances have changed such that, at the time the agent takes action, it is not reasonable for the agent to believe that the principal at that time consents to the action being taken on the principal's behalf, then the agent lacks actual authority so to act even though she would have had actual authority prior to the change in circumstances.

IRREVOCABLE POWERS

A **power given as security** "is a power to affect the legal relations of its creator that is created in the form of a manifestation of actual authority and held for the benefit of the holder or a third person." Restatement, Section 3.12. A power given as security creates neither a relationship of agency nor actual authority, although the power enables its holder to affect the legal relations of the creator of the power. Restatement, Section 3.12, comment b. The power arises from a manifestation of assent by its creator that the holder of the power may, for example, dispose of property or other interests of the creator. To illustrate: Pillsbury owns Blackacre, which is situated next to Whiteacre, on which Pillsbury operates a restaurant. To finance renovations and expansions, Pillsbury borrows money from Ashton. A written agreement between Pillsbury and Ashton provides that Ashton shall irrevocably have Pillsbury's authority to transfer ownership of Blackacre to Ashton in the event Pillsbury defaults on the loan. Ashton has a power given as security. Restatement, Section 3.12, Illustration 1.

The Restatement's definition includes, but is more extensive than, the rule in some States regarding an **agency coupled with an interest**, in which the holder (agent) has a security interest in the power conferred upon him by the creator (principal). For example, an agency coupled with an interest would arise where an agent has advanced funds on behalf of the principal and the agent's power to act is given as security for the loan.

Unless otherwise agreed, a power given as security may *not* be revoked. In addition, the incapacity of the creator or of the holder of the power does not terminate the power. Nor will the death of the creator terminate the power, unless the duty for which the power was given terminates with the death of the creator. Restatement, Section 3.13(2). A power given as security *is* terminated by an event that discharges the obligation secured by it or that makes execution of the power illegal or impossible. Restatement, Section 3.13(1). Thus, in the example above, when the creator repays the loan, the power is terminated.

CHAPTER SUMMARY

NATURE OF AGENCY	**Definition of Agency** consensual relationship authorizing one party (the agent) to act on behalf of the other party (the principal) subject to the principal's control **Scope of Agency Purposes** generally, whatever business activity a person may accomplish personally he may do through an agent **Other Legal Relationships** • *Employment Relationship* one in which the employer has the right to control the manner and means of the employee's performance of work • *Independent Contractor* a person who contracts with another to do a particular job and who is not subject to the other's control over the manner and means of conducting the work
CREATION OF AGENCY	**Formalities** though agency is a consensual relationship that may be formed by contract or agreement between the principal and agent, agency may exist without consideration • *Requirements* no particular formality usually is required in a contract of agency, although appointments of agents for a period of more than one year must be in writing • *Power of Attorney* written, formal appointment of an agent **Capacity** • *Principal* if the principal is a minor or an incompetent not under a guardianship, his appointment of another to act as an agent is voidable, as are any resulting contracts with third parties • *Agent* any person able to act may act as an agent, as the act of the agent is considered the act of the principal
DUTIES OF AGENT TO PRINCIPAL	**Duty of Obedience** an agent must act in the principal's affairs only as actually authorized by the principal and must obey all lawful instructions and directions of the principal **Duty of Good Conduct** within the scope of the agency relationship, an agent must act reasonably and refrain from conduct that is likely to damage the principal's interests **Duty of Diligence** an agent must act with reasonable care, competence, and diligence in performing the work for which he is employed **Duty to Inform** an agent must use reasonable efforts to give the principal information material to the affairs entrusted to her **Duty to Account** an agent must maintain and provide the principal with an accurate account of money or other property that the agent has received or expended on

behalf of the principal; an agent must not mingle the principal's property with any other person's property

Fiduciary Duty an agent owes a duty of utmost loyalty and good faith to the principal; it includes:

- *Conflicts of Interest*
- *Self-dealing*
- *Duty Not to Compete*
- *Misappropriation*
- *Confidential Information*
- *Duty to Account for Financial Benefits*

DUTIES OF PRINCIPAL TO AGENT

Contractual Duties

- *Compensation* a principal must compensate the agent as specified in the contract, or for the reasonable value of the services provided, if no amount is specified
- *Reimbursement* the principal must pay back to the agent authorized payments the agent has made on the principal's behalf
- *Indemnification* the principal must pay the agent for losses the agent incurred while acting as directed by the principal

Tort and Other Duties include (1) the duty to provide an employee with reasonably safe conditions of employment and (2) the duty to deal with the agent fairly and in good faith

---

TERMINATION OF AGENCY

Acts of the Parties

- *Lapse of Time*
- *Mutual Agreement of the Parties*
- *Revocation of Authority*
- *Renunciation by the Agent*

Operation of Law

- *Death* of either the principal or the agent
- *Incapacity* of either the principal or the agent
- *Change in Circumstances*

Irrevocable Powers a power given as security—including an agency coupled with an interest—is irrevocable

Relationship with Third Parties

T he purpose of an agency relationship is to allow the principal to extend his business activities by authorizing agents to enter into contracts with third persons on the principal's behalf. Accordingly, it is important that the law balance the competing interests of principals and third persons. The principal wants to be liable *only* for those contracts he actually authorizes the agent to make for him. The third party, on the other hand, wishes the principal bound on *all* contracts that the agent negotiates on the principal's behalf. As this chapter discusses, the law has adopted an intermediate outcome: the principal and the third party are bound to those contracts the principal *actually* authorizes *plus* those the principal has *apparently* authorized.

While pursuing her principal's business, an agent may tortiously injure third parties, who then may seek to hold the principal personally liable. Under what circumstances should the principal be held liable? Similar questions arise concerning a principal's criminal liability for an agent's violation of the criminal law. The law of agency has established rules to determine when the principal is liable for the torts and crimes his agents commit. These rules are discussed in this chapter.

Finally, what liability to the third party should the agent incur, and what rights should she acquire against the third party? Usually, the agent has no liability for, or rights under, the contracts she makes on behalf of her principal. As discussed in this chapter, however, in some situations the agent has contractually created obligations or rights or both.

RELATIONSHIP OF PRINCIPAL AND THIRD PERSONS

This section will first consider the contract liability of the principal; then it will examine the principal's potential tort liability.

CONTRACT LIABILITY OF THE PRINCIPAL

The power of an agent is his ability to change the legal status of his principal. An agent having either actual or apparent authority has the power to bind his principal. Thus, whenever an agent, acting within his authority, makes a contract for his principal, he creates new rights or liabilities for his principal, thereby changing his principal's legal status. This power of an agent to act for his principal in business transactions is the basis of agency.

A principal's contract liability also depends upon whether the principal is disclosed, unidentified, or undisclosed. The principal is a **disclosed principal** if, when an agent and a third party interact, the third party has notice that the agent is acting for a principal and also has notice of the principal's identity. The principal is an **unidentified principal** if, when an agent and a third party interact, the third party has notice that the agent is acting for a principal but does not have notice of the principal's identity. (Some courts refer to an unidentified principal as a "partially disclosed principal.") An example is an auctioneer who sells on behalf of a seller who is not identified: the seller is an unidentified principal (or a partially disclosed principal) since it is understood that the auctioneer acts as an agent. The principal is an **undisclosed principal** if, when an agent and a third party interact, the third party has no notice that the agent is acting for a principal. Restatement, Section 1.04(2).

TYPES OF AUTHORITY

Authority is of two basic types: actual and apparent. **Actual authority** depends upon consent that the principal manifests to the agent. Section 2.01. It may be either express or implied. In either case, such authority is binding and confers upon the agent both the power and the right to create or affect the principal's legal relations with third persons. Actual express authority does not depend on the third party having knowledge of the manifestations or statements made by the principal to the agent.

Apparent authority is based upon acts or conduct of the principal that lead a third person to believe that the agent, or supposed agent, has actual authority, upon which belief the third person *justifiably* relies. Section 2.03. This manifestation, which confers upon the agent the power to create a legal relationship between the principal and a third party, may consist of words or actions of the principal as well as other facts and circumstances that induce the third person reasonably to rely upon the existence of an agency relationship.

ACTUAL EXPRESS AUTHORITY The express authority of an agent, found in the spoken or written words the principal communicates to the agent, is actual authority stated in language directing or instructing the agent to do something specific. "As commonly used, the term 'express authority' often means actual authority that a principal has stated in very specific or detailed language." Restatement, Section 2.01, comment b. Thus, if Perkins, orally or in writing, requests his agent Abbott to sell Perkins's automobile for $6,500, Abbott's authority to sell the car for this sum is actual and express.

ACTUAL IMPLIED AUTHORITY Implied authority is not found in express or explicit words of the principal but is inferred from words or conduct that the principal manifests to the agent. An agent has implied authority to do that which she reasonably believes the principal wishes her to do, based on the agent's reasonable interpretation of the principal's manifestations to her and all other facts she knows or should know. Restatement, Section 2.02. Implied authority may arise from customs and usages of the principal's business. In addition, the authority granted to an agent to accomplish a particular purpose necessarily includes the implied authority to employ the means reasonably required to accomplish it. Restatement, Section 2.02. For example, Pearson authorizes Arlington to manage her eighty-two-unit apartment complex but says nothing about expenses. In order to manage the building, Arlington must employ a janitor, purchase fuel for heating, and arrange for ordinary maintenance. Even though Pearson has not expressly granted him the authority to incur such expenses, Arlington may, because such expenses are necessary to proper apartment management, reasonably infer the authority to incur them from the express authority to manage the building. On the other hand, suppose Paige employs Arthur, a real estate broker, to find a purchaser for her residence at a stated price. Arthur has no authority to contract for its sale.

◆ **SEE FIGURE 20-1: Contract Liability of Disclosed Principal**

APPARENT AUTHORITY Apparent authority is power arising from words or conduct of a disclosed or unidentified principal that, when manifested to third persons, reasonably induce

them to rely upon the assumption that actual authority exists. Restatement, Section 2.03. Apparent authority depends upon the principal's manifestations to the third party; an agent's own statements about the agent's authority do not by themselves create apparent authority. Apparent authority confers upon the agent, or supposed agent, the power to bind the disclosed or unidentified principal in contracts with third persons and precludes the principal from denying the existence of actual authority. Thus, when authority is apparent but not actual, the disclosed or unidentified principal is nonetheless bound by the act of the agent. By exceeding his actual authority, however, the agent violates his duty of obedience and is liable to the principal for any loss the principal suffers as a result of the agent's acting beyond his actual authority.

Common ways in which apparent authority may arise include the following:

1. When a principal appoints an agent to a position in an organization, third parties may reasonably believe that the agent has the authority to do those acts customary of an agent in such a position. (Apparent authority for agents of various business associations is discussed in *Parts 6* and *7.*)
2. If a principal has given an agent general authority to engage in a transaction, subsequently imposed limitations or restrictions will not affect the agent's apparent authority to engage in that transaction until third parties are notified of the restrictions.
3. The principal's acquiescence in prior similar transactions between the agent and a third party may create a basis for the third party reasonably to believe that the agent has apparent authority.
4. The agent shows the third party a document, such as a power of attorney, from the principal authorizing the agent to enter into such a transaction.
5. As discussed below, after many terminations of authority an agent has lingering apparent authority until the third party has actual knowledge or receives notice of the termination.

For example, Peter writes a letter to Alice authorizing her to sell his automobile and sends a copy of the letter to Thomas, a prospective purchaser. On the following day, Peter writes a letter to Alice revoking the authority to sell the car but does not send a copy of the second letter to Thomas, who is not otherwise informed of the revocation. Although Alice has no actual authority to sell the car, she continues to have apparent authority with respect to Thomas. Or suppose that Arlene, in the presence of Polly, tells Thad that Arlene is Polly's agent to buy lumber. Although this statement is not true, Polly does not deny it, as she easily could. Thad, in reliance upon the statement, ships lumber to Polly on Arlene's order. Polly is obligated to pay for the lumber because Arlene had apparent authority to act on Polly's behalf. This apparent authority of Arlene exists only with respect to Thad. If Arlene were to give David an

◆ **FIGURE 20-1: Contract Liability of Disclosed Principal**

Agent Has Actual Authority

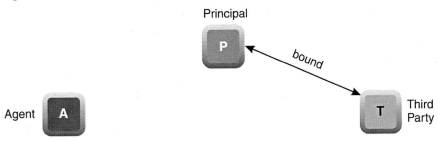

Agent Has Apparent Authority But Not Actual Authority

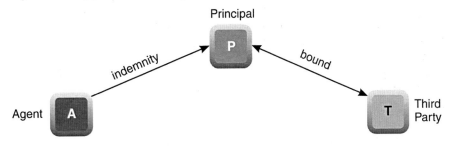

Agent Has No Actual or Apparent Authority

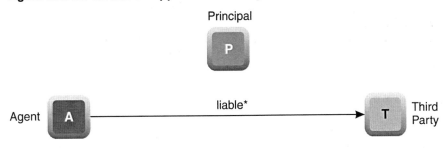

*Agent is liable for breach of implied warranty of authority or misrepresentation, as discussed later in this chapter.

order for a shipment of lumber to Polly, David would be unable to hold Polly liable. Arlene would have had neither actual authority nor, as to David, apparent authority.

Because apparent authority is the power resulting from acts that appear to the third party to be authorized by the principal, apparent authority cannot exist where the principal is undisclosed. Nor can apparent authority exist where the third party knows that the agent has no actual authority.

◆ **SEE FIGURE 20-2: Contract Liability of Unidentified Principal**

◆ **SEE FIGURE 20-3: Contract Liability of Undisclosed Principal**

DELEGATION OF AUTHORITY

A **subagent** is a person appointed by an agent to perform functions that the agent has consented to perform on behalf of the agent's principal and for whose conduct the appointing agent is responsible to the principal. Restatement, Section 3.15(1). Because the appointment of an agent reflects the principal's confidence in and reliance upon the agent's personal skill, integrity, and other qualifications, an agent may appoint a subagent only if the agent has actual or apparent authority to do so. Restatement, Section 3.15(2).

◆ **FIGURE 20-2: Contract Liability of Unidentified Principal**

Agent Has Actual Authority

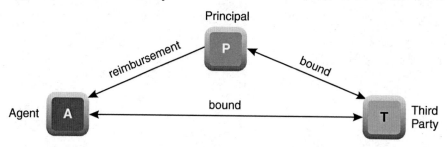

Agent Has Apparent Authority But Not Actual Authority

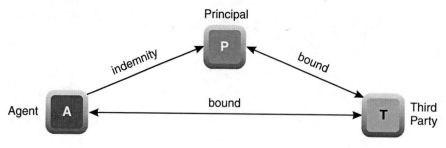

Agent Has No Actual or Apparent Authority

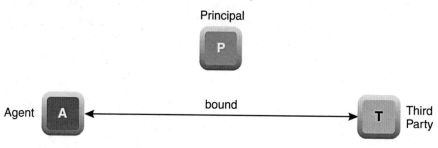

If an agent is authorized to appoint subagents, the acts of the subagent are as binding on the principal as those performed by the agent. Restatement, Section 3.15, comment b. As an agent of both the principal and the agent, the subagent owes a fiduciary duty to both. For example, P contracts with A, a real estate broker (agent), to sell P's house. P knows that A employs salespersons to show houses to prospective purchasers and to make representations about the property. The salespersons are A's employees and P's subagents.

If an agent having no authority to delegate her authority does so nevertheless, the acts of the subagent do not impose upon the principal any obligations or liability to third persons. Likewise, the principal acquires no rights against such third persons.

EFFECT OF TERMINATION OF AGENCY ON AUTHORITY

As discussed in *Chapter 19*, when an agency terminates, the agent's *actual authority* ceases. The Second and Third

Restatements differ, however, regarding when an agent's *apparent authority* ceases.

SECOND RESTATEMENT Where the performance of an authorized transaction becomes impossible, such as when the subject matter of the transaction is destroyed or the transaction is made illegal, the agent's *apparent authority* also expires and notice of such termination to third persons is *not* required. The bankruptcy of the principal terminates without notice the power of an agent to affect the principal's property, which has passed to the bankruptcy trustee.

When the termination is by the death or incapacity of the principal or agent, the Second Restatement provides that the agent's *apparent authority* also expires and notice of such termination to third persons is not required. However, with respect to the death or incapacity of the principal, this rule has been legislatively changed in more than forty States that have adopted the Uniform Durable Power of Attorney Act. This Act provides that the death of a principal, who has executed a

◆ **FIGURE 20-3: Contract Liability of Undisclosed Principal**

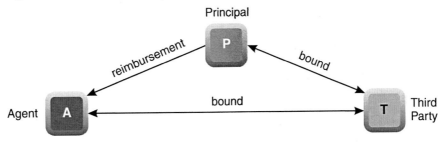

Agent Has Actual Authority

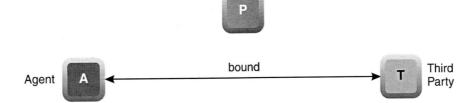

Agent Has No Actual Authority

written power of attorney, whether or not it is durable, does not terminate the agency as to the attorney in fact (agent) or a third person who without actual knowledge of the principal's death acts in good faith under the power. Moreover, the Act provides that the incapacity of a principal, who has previously executed a written power of attorney that is *not* durable, does not terminate the agency as to the attorney in fact or a third person who without actual knowledge of the principal's incapacity acts in good faith under the power. If an agent is appointed under a durable power of attorney, the *actual* authority of an agent survives the incapacity of the principal.

In other cases, *apparent authority* continues until the third party has actual knowledge or receives actual notice, if that third party is one (1) with whom the agent had previously dealt on credit, (2) to whom the agent has been specially accredited, or (3) with whom the agent has begun to deal, as the principal should know. **Actual notice** requires a communication to the third party, either oral or written. If notice is given by mail, it is effective as actual notice upon delivery, not upon dispatch. All other third parties as to whom there was apparent authority must have actual knowledge or be given **constructive notice** through, for example, publication in a newspaper of general circulation in the area where the agency is regularly carried on.

THIRD RESTATEMENT Section 3.11 of the Third Restatement applies the same rule to *all* causes of termination of agency— it applies a reasonableness standard.

(1) The termination of actual authority does not by itself end any apparent authority held by an agent.

(2) Apparent authority ends when it is no longer reasonable for the third party with whom an agent deals to believe that the agent continues to act with actual authority.

The general rule of the Third Restatement is that it is reasonable for third parties to assume that an agent's actual authority continues ("lingers"), unless and until a third party has notice of circumstances that make it unreasonable to continue that assumption. These circumstances include notice that (1) the principal has revoked the agent's actual authority, (2) the agent has renounced it, or (3) circumstances otherwise have changed such that it is no longer reasonable to believe that the principal consents to the agent's act on the principal's behalf. Restatement, Section 3.11, comment c. A person has **notice** of a fact if the person knows the fact, has reason to know the fact, has received an effective notification of the fact, or should know the fact to fulfill a duty owed to another person. Restatement, Section 1.04(4).

For example, if the principal tells a third party that the agent's authority has terminated, the former agent's lingering apparent authority with respect to that third party has terminated. Moreover, if a third party has notice of facts that call the agent's authority into question, and these facts would prompt a reasonable person to make inquiry of the principal before dealing with the agent, the agent no longer acts with apparent authority. In addition, suppose that a principal has furnished an agent with a power of attorney stating the extent, nature, and duration of the agent's actual authority. Prior to the stated expiration of the power of attorney the principal terminates the agent's actual authority.

At this time the agent has a duty to return the power of attorney to the principal. If, however, the agent does not return the power of attorney to the principal, third parties to whom the agent shows the power of attorney would still be protected by apparent authority until the third parties have notice that actual authority had been terminated.

Consistent with this general rule—but contrary to the rule under the Second Restatement—a principal's death or loss of capacity does *not* automatically end the agent's apparent authority. In these instances, apparent authority terminates when the third party has (1) notice of the principal's death or (2) has notice that the principal's loss of capacity is permanent or that the principal has been adjudicated to lack capacity. Restatement, Sections 3.07 and 3.08. The Third Restatement's rule is consistent with the Uniform Durable Power of Attorney Act.

RATIFICATION

Ratification is the confirmation or affirmance by one person of a prior unauthorized act performed by another who is his agent or who purports to be his agent. Restatement, Sections 4.01(1) and 4.03. The ratification of such act or contract binds the principal and the third party as if the agent or purported agent had been acting initially with actual authority. Restatement, Section 4.02(1). Once made, a valid ratification is irrevocable. Restatement, Section 4.02, comment b.

REQUIREMENTS OF RATIFICATION Ratification may relate to acts that have exceeded the authority granted to an agent, as well as to acts that a person without any authority performs on behalf of an alleged principal. To effect a ratification, the principal must manifest an intent to do so with knowledge of all material facts concerning the transaction. Restatement, Section 4.06. The principal does not need to communicate this intent, which may be manifested by express language or implied from her conduct, such as accepting or retaining the benefits of a transaction. Thus, if Amanda, without authority, contracts in Penelope's name for the purchase of goods from Tate on credit, and Penelope, having learned of Amanda's unauthorized act, accepts the goods from Tate, she thereby impliedly ratifies the contract and is bound on it. Furthermore, a principal may ratify an unauthorized action by failing to repudiate it once the principal knows the material facts about the agent's action. Restatement, Section 4.01, comment f. If formalities are required for the authorization of an act, the same formalities apply to a ratification of that act. Restatement, Section 4.01, comment e. In any event, the principal must ratify the entire act or contract. Restatement, Section 4.07.

A person may ratify an act if the actor acted *or* purported to act as an agent on the person's behalf. Restatement, Section 4.03. Under this section and a number of relatively recent cases, an undisclosed principal may ratify an agent's unauthorized act. This is *contrary* to the Second Restatement's rule, which requires that the actor must have indicated to the third person that he was acting on a principal's behalf. Thus, under the Second Restatement there can be no ratification by an undisclosed principal. To illustrate: Archie, without any authority, contracts to sell to Tina an automobile belonging to Pierce. Archie states that the auto is his. Tina promises to pay $5,500 for the automobile. Pierce subsequently learns of the agreement and affirms. Under the Third Restatement Pierce's affirmation of Archie's action *would* be a ratification because Archie had acted on behalf of Pierce. On the other hand, under the Second Restatement it would *not* be a ratification because Archie did not indicate he was acting on behalf of a principal.

To be effective, ratification must occur before the third party gives notice of his withdrawal to the principal or agent. Restatement, Section 4.05(1). If the affirmance of a transaction occurs when the situation has so materially changed that it would be inequitable to subject the third party to liability, the third party may elect to avoid liability. Restatement, Section 4.05(2). For example, Alex has no authority, but, purporting to act for Penny, contracts to sell Penny's house to Taylor. The next day, the house burns down. Penny then affirms. Taylor is not bound. Moreover, the power to ratify is terminated by the death or loss of capacity of the third party and by the lapse of a reasonable time. Restatement, Section 4.05, comment b.

For ratification to be effective, the purported principal must have been in existence when the act was done. Restatement, Section 4.04(1)(a). For example, a promoter of a corporation not yet in existence may enter into contracts on behalf of the corporation. In the vast majority of States, however, the corporation cannot ratify these acts because it did not exist when the contracts were made. Instead, the corporation may **adopt** the contract. Adoption differs from ratification because it is not retroactive and does not release the promoter from liability. See *Chapter 34*.

If a principal's lack of capacity entitles her to avoid transactions, the principal may also avoid any ratification made when under the incapacity. Restatement, Section 4.04(2). The principal, however, may ratify a contract that is voidable because of her incapacity when the incapacity no longer exists. Thus, after she reaches majority, a principal may ratify an unauthorized contract made on her behalf during her minority. She may also avoid any ratification made prior to attaining majority.

EFFECT OF RATIFICATION Ratification retroactively creates the effects of actual authority. Restatement, Section 4.02(1). Ratification is equivalent to prior authority, which means that the effect of ratification is substantially the same as if the agent or purported agent had been actually authorized when she performed the act. The respective rights, duties, and remedies of the principal and the third party are the same as if the agent had originally possessed actual authority. Both the principal and the agent are in the same position as they would have been if the principal had actually authorized the act originally. The agent is entitled to her due compensation and, moreover, is exonerated (freed) from liability to the principal for acting as his agent without authority or for exceeding her authority, as the case may be. Between the agent and the third party, the agent is released from any liability she may have to the third party by reason of her having induced the third party to enter into the contract without the principal's authority.

FUNDAMENTAL RULES OF CONTRACTUAL LIABILITY

The following rules summarize the contractual relations between the principal and the third party:

1. A disclosed principal and the third party are parties to the contract if the agent acts within her actual or apparent authority in making the contract on the principal's behalf. Restatement, Section 6.01(1). See *Figure 20-1.*

2. An unidentified (partially disclosed) principal and the third party are parties to the contract if the agent acts within her actual or apparent authority in making the contract on the principal's behalf. Restatement, Section 6.02(1). See *Figure 20-2.*

3. An undisclosed principal and the third party are parties to the contract if the agent acts within her actual authority in making the contract on the principal's behalf unless (a) the terms of the contract exclude the principal or (b) his existence is fraudulently concealed. Restatement, Sections 6.03 and 6.11(4). See *Figure 20-3.*

4. No principal is a party to a contract with a third party if the agent acts without any authority in making the contract on the principal's behalf, unless the principal ratifies the contract. Restatement, Section 4.02. Under the Second Restatement the principal must have been either disclosed or unidentified.

TORT LIABILITY OF THE PRINCIPAL

In addition to being contractually liable to third persons, a principal may be liable in tort to third persons because of the acts of her agent. Tort liability may arise directly or indirectly (vicariously) from authorized or unauthorized acts of an agent. Also, a principal is liable for the unauthorized torts an agent commits in connection with a transaction that the purported principal, with full knowledge of the tort, subsequently ratifies. Restatement, Sections 4.01 and 7.04. Cases involving unauthorized but ratified torts are extremely rare. Of course, in all of these situations the wrongdoing agent is personally liable to the

injured persons because he committed the tort. Restatement, Section 7.01.

◆ **SEE FIGURE 20-4: Tort Liability**

DIRECT LIABILITY OF PRINCIPAL

A principal is liable for his own tortious conduct involving the use of agents. Such liability primarily arises in one of two ways. First, a principal is directly liable in damages for harm resulting from his directing an agent to commit a tort. Second, the principal is directly liable if he fails to exercise reasonable care in employing competent agents.

AUTHORIZED ACTS OF AGENT A principal who authorizes his agent to commit a tortious act with respect to the property or person of another is liable for the injury or loss that person sustains. This liability also extends to unauthorized tortious conduct that the principal subsequently ratifies. Restatement, Section 7.04(1). The authorized act is that of the principal. Thus, if Phillip directs his agent, Anthony, to enter upon Clark's land and cut timber, which neither Phillip nor Anthony has any right to do, the cutting of the timber is a trespass, and Phillip is liable to Clark. A principal may be subject to tort liability because of an agent's conduct even though the agent is not subject to liability. Restatement, Section 7.04(2). For example, Phillip instructs his agent, Anthony, to make certain representations as to Phillip's property, which Anthony is authorized to sell. Phillip knows these representations are false, but Anthony does not know and has no reason or duty to know. Such representations by Anthony to Tammy, who buys the property in reliance on them, constitute a deceit for which Phillip is liable to Tammy. Anthony, however, would not be liable to Tammy.

UNAUTHORIZED ACTS OF AGENT A principal who negligently conducts activities through an employee or other agent is liable for harm resulting from such conduct. Restatement, Section 7.05(1). For example, a principal is liable if he negligently (1) selects agents, (2) retains agents, (3) trains agents, (4) supervises agents, or (5) otherwise controls agents.

The liability of a principal under this provision—called **negligent hiring**—arises when the principal does not exercise proper care in selecting an agent for the job to be done. For example, if Patricia lends to her employee, Art, a company car with which to run a business errand knowing that Art is incapable of driving the vehicle, Patricia would be liable for her own negligence to anyone injured through Art's unsafe driving. The negligent hiring doctrine has also been used to impose liability on a principal for intentional torts committed by an agent against customers of the principal or members of the public, where the principal either knew or should have known that the agent was violent or aggressive.

◆ **FIGURE 20-4: Tort Liability**

Agent's Tort Authorized

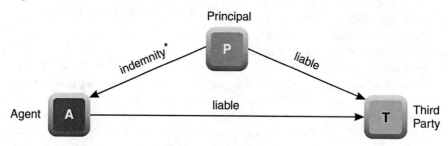

Employee's Tort Unauthorized But Within Scope of Employment

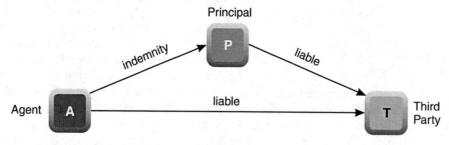

Employee's Tort Outside Authority and Scope of Employment or Independent Contractor's Tort Unauthorized

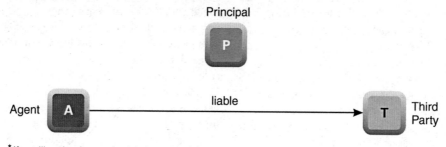

*If not illegal or known by A to be wrongful.

VICARIOUS LIABILITY OF PRINCIPAL FOR UNAUTHORIZED ACTS OF AGENT

The vicarious liability of a principal for the unauthorized torts of an agent depends primarily on whether the agent is an employee or not. In this context, an employee is an agent whose principal controls or has the right to control the manner and means of the agent's performance of work. Restatement, Section 7.07(3)(a). By comparison, if the principal does *not* control the manner and means of the agent's performance of the work, the agent is not an employee and is often referred to as an "independent contractor." The general rule is that a principal is not liable for physical harm caused by the tortious conduct of an agent who is an independent contractor if the principal did not intend or authorize the result or the manner of performance. Conversely, a principal is liable for an unauthorized tort committed by an employee acting within the scope of his employment. Restatement, Section 7.07(1).

RESPONDEAT SUPERIOR An employer is subject to vicarious liability for an unauthorized tort committed by his employee, even one that is in flagrant disobedience of his instructions, if the employee committed the tort within the scope of his employment. This form of employer liability without fault is based upon the doctrine of *respondeat superior* (let the superior respond). It does not matter how carefully the employer selected the employee, if in fact the latter tortiously injures a third party while engaged in the scope of employment. Moreover, an *undisclosed* principal–employer is liable for the torts committed by her employee within the scope of employment. Furthermore, the principal is liable even if the work is performed gratuitously so long as the principal controls or has the right to control the manner and means of the agent's performance of work. Restatement, Section 7.07(3)(b).

The doctrine of *respondeat superior* is fundamental to the operation of tort law in the United States. The rationale for this doctrine is that a person who conducts his business activities through the use of employees should be liable for the employees' tortious conduct in carrying out those activities. The employer is more likely to insure against liability and is more likely to have the assets to satisfy a tort judgment than the employee. Moreover, *respondeat superior* creates an economic incentive for employers to exercise care in choosing, training, and supervising employees.

The liability of the principal under *respondeat superior* is vicarious or derivative and depends upon proof of wrongdoing by the employee *within the scope of his employment.* Restatement, Section 7.07. The employer's vicarious liability to the third party is in *addition* to the agent's liability to the third party. Frequently both principal and employee are joined as defendants in the same suit. Because the liability of the employer is based upon the employee's tortious conduct, if the employee is not held liable, the principal is not liable either. A principal who is held liable for her employee's tort has a right of **indemnification** against the employee, or the right to be reimbursed for the amount that she was required to pay as a result of the employee's wrongful act. Frequently, however, an employee is unable to reimburse his employer, who then must bear the brunt of the liability.

The wrongful act of the employee must be connected with his employment and within its scope if the principal is to be held liable for injuries or damage resulting to third persons. Section 7.07(2) of the Restatement provides a general rule for determining whether the conduct of an employee is within the scope of employment:

> An employee acts within the scope of employment when performing work assigned by the employer or engaging in a course of conduct subject to the employer's control. An employee's act is not within the scope of employment when it occurs within an independent course of conduct not intended by the employee to serve any purpose of the employer.

For example, Eugene, while delivering gasoline for Packer Oil Co., lights his pipe and negligently throws the blazing match into a pool of gasoline that has dripped onto the ground during the delivery. The gasoline ignites, burning Ray's filling station. Packer is subject to liability for the resulting harm because the negligence of the employee who delivered the gasoline relates directly to the manner in which he handled the goods in his custody. But if a chauffeur, while driving his employer's car on an errand for his employer, suddenly decides to shoot his pistol at pedestrians for target practice, the employer would not be liable to the pedestrians. This willful and intentional misconduct is not related to the performance of the services for which the chauffeur was employed, nor is it expectable by the employer.

To further illustrate, if Page employs Earl to deliver merchandise to Page's customers in a given city, and while driving a delivery truck to or from a place of delivery Earl negligently causes the truck to hit and injure Fred, Page is liable to Fred for the injuries he sustains. But if, after making the scheduled deliveries, Earl drives the truck to a neighboring city to visit a friend and while so doing negligently causes the truck to hit and injure Dottie, Page is not liable. In the latter case, Earl is said to be on a "frolic of his own." By using the truck to accomplish his own purposes, not those of his employer, he has deviated from serving any purpose of his employer.

A principal may be held liable for the intentional torts of his employee if the commission of the tort is so reasonably connected with the employment as to be within its scope. For example, a principal would be liable if his employee were to make fraudulent statements about the products she is selling, defame a competitor, or disparage the competitor's product.

AGENT ACTS WITH APPARENT AUTHORITY "A principal is subject to vicarious liability for a tort committed by an agent in dealing or communicating with a third party on or purportedly on behalf of the principal when actions taken by the agent with apparent authority constitute the tort or enable the agent to conceal its commission." Restatement, Section 7.08. This liability applies to (1) agents, whether or not they are employees, and (2) agents who are employees but whose tortious conduct is not within the scope of employment under *respondeat superior.* The torts to which this rule applies include fraudulent and negligent misrepresentations, defamation, wrongful institution of legal proceedings, and conversion of property. For example, Pillsbury engages Adams as an agent to sell some land. While negotiating with Trent, Adams states that a stream running through the property has not overflowed its banks during the past ten years. Adams knows that this is false. In reliance upon this false statement, Trent purchases the land. Pillsbury is liable to Trent for fraudulent misrepresentation.

TORTS OF INDEPENDENT CONTRACTOR As previously indicated, an independent contractor is not the employee of the person for whom he is performing work or rendering services. Hence, the doctrine of *respondeat superior* generally does not apply to torts committed by an independent contractor. For example, Parnell authorizes Bob, his broker, to sell land for him. Parnell, Teresa, and Bob meet in Teresa's office, where Bob arranges the sale to Teresa. While Bob is preparing the deed for Parnell to sign, he negligently knocks over an inkstand and ruins a valuable rug belonging to Teresa. Bob, but not Parnell, is liable to Teresa. Similarly, Patty employs Igor, a roofer, as an independent contractor to repair her roof. Igor drops a hammer upon Wanda, a pedestrian walking by on the public sidewalk. Igor, but not Patty, is liable to Wanda.

Nonetheless, the principal may be *directly* liable if she fails to exercise reasonable care in selecting an independent contractor. For example, Melanie employs Gordon, whom she knows to be an alcoholic, as an independent contractor to repair her roof. Gordon attempts the repairs while heavily intoxicated and negligently drops a fifty-pound bundle of shingles upon Eric, a pedestrian walking on the sidewalk. Both Gordon and Melanie are liable to Eric.

Moreover, under some circumstances a principal will be *vicariously* liable for torts committed by a carefully selected independent contractor. Certain duties imposed by law are nondelegable, and a person may not escape the consequences of their nonperformance by having entrusted them to another person, whether or not that person is an agent. Restatement, Section 7.06. For example, a landowner who permits an independent contractor to maintain a dangerous condition on his premises, such as an excavation, neither surrounded by a guardrail nor lit at night, adjoining a public sidewalk is liable to a member of the public who is injured by falling into the excavation.

A principal is also vicariously liable for an independent contractor's conduct in carrying on an abnormally dangerous activity, such as using fire or high explosives, or spraying crops.

CRIMINAL LIABILITY OF THE PRINCIPAL

A principal is liable for the authorized criminal acts of his agents only if the principal directed, participated in, or approved of the acts. For example, if an agent, at his principal's direction or with his principal's knowledge, fixes prices with the principal's competitors, both the agent and the principal have criminally violated the antitrust laws. Otherwise, a principal ordinarily is not liable for the unauthorized criminal acts of his agents. One of the elements of a crime is mental fault, and this element is absent, so far as the criminal responsibility of the principal is concerned, in cases in which the principal did not authorize the agent's act.

An employer may, nevertheless, be subject to a criminal penalty for the act of an advisory or managerial person acting in the scope of employment. Moreover, an employer may be criminally liable under liability without fault statutes for certain unauthorized acts of an employee, whether the employee is managerial or not. These statutes, which usually are regulatory, do not require mental fault. For example, many States have statutes that punish "every person who by himself or his employee or agent sells anything at short weight," or "whoever sells liquor to a minor and any sale by

an employee shall be deemed the act of the employer as well." Another example is a statute prohibiting the sale of unwholesome or adulterated food. See *Chapter 6* for a more detailed discussion of this topic.

RELATIONSHIP OF AGENT AND THIRD PERSONS

The function of an agent is to assist in the conduct of the principal's business by carrying out his orders. Generally, the agent acquires no rights against third parties and likewise incurs no liabilities to them. There are, however, several exceptions to this general proposition. In certain instances, an agent may become personally liable to the third party for contracts she made on behalf of her principal. In some of these situations, the agent also may acquire rights against the third party. In addition, an agent who commits a tort is personally liable to the injured third party. These circumstances involving the personal liability of an agent, as well as those in which an agent may acquire rights against third persons, will be covered in this section.

CONTRACT LIABILITY OF AGENT

The agent normally is not a party to the contract he makes with a third person on behalf of a disclosed principal. An agent who exceeds his actual and apparent authority, however, may be personally liable to the third party. In addition, an agent acting for a disclosed principal may become liable if he expressly assumes liability on the contract. When an agent enters into a contract on behalf of an unidentified (partially disclosed) principal or an undisclosed principal, the agent becomes personally liable to the third party on the contract. Furthermore, an agent who knowingly enters into a contract on behalf of a nonexistent or completely incompetent principal is personally liable to the third party on that contract.

DISCLOSED PRINCIPAL

As explained earlier, the principal is a disclosed principal if, when an agent and a third party interact, the third party has notice that the agent is acting for a principal and also has notice of the principal's identity. The liability of an agent acting for a disclosed principal depends on whether the agent acts within her authority in making the contract or otherwise assumes liability on the contract.

AUTHORIZED CONTRACTS When an agent acting with actual or apparent authority makes a contract with a third party on behalf of a disclosed principal, the agent is not a party to the contract unless she and the third party agree otherwise. Restatement, Section 6.01(2). The third person is on notice that he is transacting business with an agent who is acting for an identified principal and that the agent is not personally undertaking to perform the contract, but is simply negotiating on behalf of her principal. The resulting contract, if within the agent's actual authority, is between the third person and the principal, and the agent ordinarily incurs no liability on the contract to either party. Thus, Angela, who has actual authority to sell circuit boards manufactured by Pinter, writes to Toni, "On behalf of Pinter, I offer to sell you 5,000 circuit boards for $15,000." Toni accepts; consequently, a contract exists between Toni and Pinter. Angela is not a party to that contract and has no liability to Pinter or Toni. This is also true of unauthorized contracts that are subsequently ratified by the principal. If, however, the agent has apparent authority but no actual authority, he has no liability to the third party but is liable to the principal for any loss he causes by exceeding his actual authority.

◆ **SEE FIGURE 20-1: Contract Liability of Disclosed Principal**

UNAUTHORIZED CONTRACTS If an agent exceeds his actual *and* apparent authority, the principal is not bound. The fact that the principal is not bound does not, however, make the agent a party to the contract unless the agent had agreed to be a party to the contract. The agent's liability, if any, arises from express or implied representations about his authority that he makes to the third party. For example, an agent may give an **express warranty of authority** by stating that he has authority and that he will be personally liable to the third party if he does not in fact have the authority to bind his principal.

Moreover, a person who undertakes to make a contract on behalf of another gives an **implied warranty of authority** that he is in fact authorized to make the contract on behalf of the party whom he purports to represent. If the agent does not have authority to bind the principal, the agent is liable to the third party for damages unless the principal ratifies the contract or the third party knew that the agent was unauthorized. Restatement, Section 6.10. No implied warranty of authority exists, however, if the agent expressly states that the agent gives no warranty of authority or if the agent, acting in good faith, discloses to the third person all of the facts upon which his authority rests. For example, agent Larson has received an ambiguous letter of instruction from his principal, Dan. Larson shows it to Carol, stating that it represents all of the authority that he has to act, and both Larson and Carol rely upon its sufficiency. Larson has made no implied or express warranty of his authority to Carol.

The Restatement provides that breach of the implied warranty of authority subjects the agent to liability to the third party for damages caused by breach of that warranty, including loss of the benefit expected from performance by the principal. Restatement, Section 6.10. Some courts, however, limit the third party's recovery to the damage or loss the third party suffered and exclude the third party's expected gain from the contract.

If a purported agent **misrepresents** to a third person that he has authority to make a contract on behalf of a principal whom he has no power to bind, he is liable in a tort action to the third person for the loss she sustained in reliance upon the misrepresentation. If the third party knows, however, that the representation is false, then the agent is not liable.

AGENT ASSUMES LIABILITY An agent for a disclosed principal may agree to become liable on a contract between the principal and the third party (1) by making the contract in her own name, (2) by co-making the contract with the principal, or (3) by guaranteeing that the principal will perform the contract between the third party and the principal. In each situation, the agent's liability is separate unless the parties agree otherwise. Therefore, the third party may sue the agent separately without joining the principal and may obtain a judgment against either the principal or the agent or both. If the principal satisfies the judgment, the agent is discharged. If the agent pays the judgment, he usually will have a right of reimbursement from the principal. This right is based upon the principles of suretyship, discussed in *Chapter 38*.

UNIDENTIFIED PRINCIPAL

As previously discussed, the principal is an unidentified principal (partially disclosed principal) if, when an agent and a third party interact, the third party has notice that the agent is acting for a principal but does not have notice of the principal's identity. The use of an unidentified principal may be helpful where, for example, the third party might inflate the price of property he was selling if he knew the principal's identity. Partial disclosure also may occur inadvertently, when the agent fails through neglect to inform the third party of the principal's identity.

Unless otherwise agreed, when an agent makes a contract with actual or apparent authority on behalf of an unidentified principal, the agent is a party to the contract. Restatement, Section 6.02. For example, Ashley writes to Terrence offering to sell a rare painting on behalf of its owner, who wishes to remain unknown. Terrence accepts. Ashley is a party to the contract.

Whether the particular transaction is authorized or not, an agent for an unidentified principal is liable to the third party. If the agent is actually or apparently authorized to make the contract, then both the agent and the unidentified principal are liable. If the agent has no actual and no apparent authority, the agent is liable either as a party to the contract or for breach of the implied warranty of authority. Restatement, Section 6.02, comment b. In any event, the agent is separately liable, and the third party may sue her individually without joining the principal and may obtain a judgment against either the principal or the agent or both. If the principal satisfies the judgment, the agent is also discharged. Restatement, Section 6.09. If the agent pays the judgment, the principal is discharged from liability to the third party, but the agent has the right to be reimbursed by the principal.

◆ **SEE FIGURE 20-2: Contract Liability of Unidentified Principal**

UNDISCLOSED PRINCIPAL

The principal is an undisclosed principal if, when an agent and a third party interact, the third party has no notice that the agent is acting for a principal. Thus, when an agent acts for an undisclosed principal, she appears to be acting in her own behalf and the third person with whom she is dealing has no knowledge that she is acting as an agent. The principal has instructed the agent to conceal not only the principal's identity but also the agency relationship. Such concealment can also occur if the agent simply neglects to disclose the existence and identity of her principal. Thus, the third person is dealing with the agent as though she were a principal.

The agent is personally liable upon a contract she enters into with a third person on behalf of an undisclosed principal. Restatement, Section 6.03(2). The agent is liable because the third person has relied upon the agent individually and has accepted the agent's personal undertaking to perform the contract. Obviously, where the principal is undisclosed, the third person does not know of the interest of anyone in the contract other than that of himself and the agent.

The Second Restatement and many cases hold that after the third person has learned of the identity of the undisclosed principal, he may obtain performance of the contract from either the principal or the agent, but not both; and his choice, once made, binds him irrevocably. Nevertheless, to avoid the possibility that evidence at trial will fail to establish the agency relationship, the third person may bring suit against both the principal and agent. In most States following this approach, this act of bringing suit and proceeding to trial against both is not an election, but before the entry of any judgment, the third person is compelled to make an election because he is not entitled to a judgment against both. A judgment against the agent by a third party who knows the identity of the previously undisclosed principal discharges the liability of the principal. In this case, the agent would have the right to be reimbursed by the principal. If,

however, the third party obtains a judgment against the agent before learning the principal's identity, the principal is not discharged. Finally, the agent is discharged from liability if the third party gets a judgment against the principal.

The Third Restatement and a number of States have recently rejected the election rule, holding that a third party's rights against the principal are *additional* and not alternative to the third party's rights against the agent. Section 6.09 provides, "When an agent has made a contract with a third party on behalf of a principal, unless the contract provides otherwise, the liability, if any, of the principal or the agent to the third party is not discharged if the third party obtains a judgment against the other." However, the liability, if any, of the principal or the agent to the third party *is* discharged to the extent a judgment against the other is satisfied.

◆ **SEE FIGURE 20-3: Contract Liability of Undisclosed Principal**

NONEXISTENT OR INCOMPETENT PRINCIPAL

Unless the third party agrees otherwise, if a person who purports to act as an agent knows or has reason to know that the person purportedly represented does not exist or completely lacks capacity to be a party to contract, the person purporting to act as agent will become a party to the contract. Restatement, Section 6.04. Complete lack of capacity to contract includes an individual person who has been adjudicated incompetent. An example of a nonexistent principal is a corporation or limited liability corporation (LLC) that has not yet been formed. Thus, a promoter of a corporation who enters into contracts with third persons in the name of a corporation yet to be organized is personally liable on such contracts. Not yet in existence, and therefore unable to authorize the contracts, the corporation is not liable. If, after coming into existence, the corporation affirmatively adopts a preincorporation contract made on its behalf, it, in addition to the promoter, becomes bound. If the corporation enters into a new contract with such a third person, however, the prior contract between the promoter and the third person is discharged, and the liability of the promoter is terminated. This is a novation.

◆ **SEE FIGURE 34-1: Promoter's Preincorporation Contracts Made in Corporation's Name**

An agent who makes a contract for a disclosed principal whose contracts are *voidable* for lack of contractual capacity is *not* liable to the third party. Restatement, Section 6.04, comment b. There are two exceptions to this rule: (1) if the agent warrants or represents that the principal has capacity; or (2) if the agent has reason to know both of the principal's lack of capacity and of the third party's ignorance of that incapacity.

TORT OF LIABILITY OF AGENT

An agent is personally liable for his tortious acts that injure third persons, whether the principal authorizes such acts or not and whether or not the principal may also be liable. Restatement, Section 7.01. For example, an agent is personally liable if he converts the goods of a third person to his principal's use. An agent is also liable for making representations that he knows to be fraudulent to a third person who in reliance sustains a loss.

RIGHTS OF AGENT AGAINST THIRD PERSON

An agent who makes a contract with a third person on behalf of a disclosed principal usually has no right of action against the third person for breach of contract. Restatement, Section 6.01. The agent is not a party to the contract. An agent for a disclosed principal may sue on the contract, however, if it provides that the agent is a party to the contract. Furthermore, an agent for an undisclosed principal or an unidentified (partially disclosed) principal may maintain in her own name an action against the third person for breach of contract. Restatement, Sections 6.02 and 6.03.

CHAPTER SUMMARY

RELATIONSHIP OF PRINCIPAL AND THIRD PERSONS

CONTRACT LIABILITY OF PRINCIPAL	
	Types of Principals

CONTRACT LIABILITY OF PRINCIPAL

Types of Principals
- *Disclosed Principal* principal whose existence and identity are known
- *Unidentified (Partially Disclosed) Principal* principal whose existence is known but whose identity is not known
- *Undisclosed Principal* principal whose existence and identity are not known

Authority power of an agent to change the legal status of the principal
- *Actual Authority* power conferred upon the agent by actual consent manifested by the principal to the agent
- *Actual Express Authority* actual authority derived from written or spoken words of the principal communicated to the agent
- *Actual Implied Authority* actual authority inferred from words or conduct manifested to the agent by the principal
- *Apparent Authority* power conferred upon the agent by acts or conduct of the principal that reasonably lead a third party to believe that the agent has such power

Delegation of Authority is usually not permitted unless actually or apparently authorized by the principal; if the agent is authorized to appoint other subagents, the acts of these subagents are as binding on the principal as those of the agent

Effect of Termination of Agency on Authority ends *actual* authority
- *Second Restatement* if the termination is by operation of law, *apparent* authority also ends without notice to third parties; if the termination is by an act of the parties, *apparent* authority ends when third parties have actual knowledge or when appropriate notice is given to third parties: actual notice must be given to third parties with whom the agent has previously dealt on credit, has been specially accredited, or has begun to deal; all other third parties as to whom there was apparent authority need be given only constructive notice
- *Third Restatement* termination of actual authority does not by itself end any apparent authority held by an agent; *apparent* authority ends when it is no longer reasonable for the third party with whom an agent deals to believe that the agent continues to act with actual authority

Ratification affirmation by one person of a prior unauthorized act that another has done as her agent or as her purported agent

Fundamental Rules of Contractual Liability
- *Disclosed Principal* is contractually bound with the third party if the agent acts within her actual or apparent authority in making the contract on the principal's behalf
- *Partially Disclosed Principal* is contractually bound with the third party if the agent acts within her actual or apparent authority in making the contract on the principal's behalf
- *Undisclosed Principal* is contractually bound with the third party if the agent acts within her actual authority in making the contract on the principal's behalf

TORT LIABILITY OF PRINCIPAL	**Direct Liability of Principal** a principal is liable for his own tortious conduct involving the use of agents

- *Authorized Acts of Agent* a principal is liable for torts that she authorizes another to commit or that she ratifies
- *Unauthorized Acts of Agent* a principal is liable for failing to exercise reasonable care in employing agents whose unauthorized acts cause harm

Vicarious Liability of Principal for Unauthorized Acts of Agent
- **Respondeat Superior** an employer is liable for unauthorized torts committed by an employee in the scope of his employment
- *Agent Acts with Apparent Authority* a principal is liable for torts committed by an agent in dealing with third parties while acting within the agent's apparent authority
- *Independent Contractor* a principal is usually not liable for the unauthorized torts of an independent contractor

CRIMINAL LIABILITY OF PRINCIPAL	**Authorized Acts** the principal is liable if he directed, participated in, or approved the criminal acts of his agents **Unauthorized Acts** the principal may be liable either for a criminal act of a managerial person or under liability without fault statutes

RELATIONSHIP OF AGENT AND THIRD PERSONS

CONTRACT LIABILITY OF AGENT	**Disclosed Principal**

- *Authorized Contracts* the agent is not normally a party to the contract she makes with a third person if she has actual or apparent authority or if the principal ratifies an unauthorized contract
- *Unauthorized Contracts* if an agent exceeds her actual and apparent authority, the principal is not bound but the agent may be liable to the third party for breach of warranty or for misrepresentation
- *Agent Assumes Liability* an agent may agree to become liable on a contract between the principal and the third party

Unidentified (Partially Disclosed) Principal an agent who acts for a partially disclosed principal is a party to the contract with the third party unless otherwise agreed

Undisclosed Principal an agent who acts for an undisclosed principal is personally liable on the contract to the third party

Nonexistent or Incompetent Principal a person who purports to act as an agent for a principal whom the agent knows to be nonexistent or completely incompetent is personally liable on a contract entered into with a third person on behalf of such a principal

TORT LIABILITY OF AGENT	**Authorized Acts** the agent is liable to the third party for his own torts **Unauthorized Acts** the agent is liable to the third party for his own torts

[Citations.] Moreover, the authority must be founded upon some word or act of the principal, not on the acts or words of the agent. [Citations.]

* * * Both Hogan and Bonner, ZuChristian's superiors, testified that ZuChristian had no actual authority to either make an offer of a specific salary to Schoenberger or to make any promise of additional compensation. Furthermore, ZuChristian's testimony corroborated the testimony that he lacked the authority to make formal offers. From this evidence, it is clear that the trial court properly determined that ZuChristian lacked the actual authority to bind the C.T.A. for the additional $500 in compensation to Schoenberger.

Nor can it be said that the C.T.A. clothed ZuChristian with the apparent authority to make Schoenberger a promise of compensation over and above that formally offered by the Placement Department. The general rule to consider in determining whether an agent is acting within the apparent authority of his principal was stated in [citation] in this way:

> Apparent authority in an agent is such authority as the principal knowingly permits the agent to assume or which he holds his agent out as possessing—it is such authority as a reasonably prudent man, exercising diligence and discretion, in view of the principal's conduct, would naturally suppose the agent to possess.

* * *

Here, Schoenberger's initial contact with the C.T.A. was with the Placement Department where he filled out an application and had his first interview. There is no evidence that the C.T.A. did anything to permit ZuChristian to assume authority nor did they do anything to hold him out as having the authority to hire and set salaries. ZuChristian was not at a management level in the C.T.A. nor did his job title of Principal Communications Analyst suggest otherwise. The mere fact that he was allowed to interview prospective employees does not establish that the C.T.A. held him out as possessing the authority to hire employees or set salaries. Moreover, ZuChristian did inform Schoenberger that the formal offer of employment would be made by the Placement Department.

* * *

Our final inquiry concerns the plaintiff's contention that irrespective of ZuChristian's actual or apparent authority, the C.T.A. is bound by ZuChristian's promise because it ratified his acts. Ratification may be express or inferred and occurs where "the principal, with knowledge of the material facts of the unauthorized transaction, takes a position inconsistent with nonaffirmation of the transaction." [Citations.] Ratification is the equivalent to an original authorization and confirms that which was originally unauthorized. [Citation.] Ratification occurs where a principal attempts to seek or retain the benefits of the transaction. [Citations.]

Upon review of the evidence, we are not convinced that the C.T.A. acted to ratify ZuChristian's promise. * * *

* * *

For the reasons we have indicated, the judgment of the circuit court of Cook County granting judgment in favor of the defendant, C.T.A., is affirmed.

PART 4

Sales

COLUMN: © PHOTOGRAPHEROLYMPUS   CLOUDS: © KERTLIS

Introduction to Sales and Leases

Sales are the most common and important of all commercial transactions. In an exchange economy such as ours, sales are the essential means by which the various units of production exchange their outputs, thereby providing the opportunity for specialization and enhanced productivity. An advanced, complex, industrialized economy with highly coordinated manufacturing and distribution systems requires a reliable mechanism for ensuring that *future* exchanges can be entered into today and fulfilled at a later time. Because practically everyone in our economy is a purchaser of both durable and consumable goods, the manufacture and distribution of goods involve numerous sales transactions. The law of sales establishes a framework in which these present and future exchanges may take place in a predictable, certain, and orderly fashion with a minimum of transaction costs.

Until the early 1900s, sales transactions were completely governed by general contract law. In 1906, the Uniform Sales Act was promulgated and eventually adopted by thirty-six States. By the end of the 1930s, however, dissatisfaction with this and other uniform commercial statutes brought about the development of the Uniform Commercial Code (UCC). Article 2 of the Code deals with transactions in sales and has been adopted in all of the States (except Louisiana) plus the District of Columbia and the Virgin Islands. The UCC appears in Appendix B. Amendments to Article 2 and 2A were promulgated in 2003 to accommodate electronic commerce and to reflect development of business practices, changes in other law, and interpretive difficulties of practical significance. To date no States have adopted them. However, at least thirty-seven States have adopted the 2001 Revisions to Article 1, which applies to all of the articles of the Code.

Leases of personal property, which are of great economic significance, exceed $100 billion annually. Leases range from a consumer renting an automobile or a lawn mower to a Fortune 500 corporation leasing heavy industrial machinery. Despite the frequent and widespread use of personal property leases, the law governing these transactions had been patched together from the common law of personal property, real estate leasing law, and Articles 2 and 9 of the UCC. Although containing several applicable provisions, the UCC did not directly relate to leases. Some courts have held, nevertheless, that the UCC is applicable to leases of goods because a lease is a transaction in goods; other courts have refused to apply the Code to leases because actual title to the goods never passed. Still other courts have applied the Code to lease by analogy. Even in States where Article 2 was extended to leases, which provisions were to be applied remained unclear. In any event, no unified or uniform statutory law governed leases of personal property for most of the twentieth century.

To fill this void, the drafters of the Code approved Article 2A—Leases in 1987 and subsequently amended the Article in 1990. An analogue of Article 2, the new Article adopts many of the rules contained in Article 2. Article 2A is an attempt to codify in one statute all the rules governing the leasing of personal property. South Dakota has enacted the 1987 version of Article 2A while the District of Columbia and all the other States except Louisiana have adopted the 1990 version.

This section of the book covers both the sale and the lease of goods. All of the chapters will cover Article 2A in addition to Article 2 by stating the Article 2A section number wherever Article 2A's provision is either identical to or essentially the same as the Article 2 provision. Where Article 2A significantly deviates from Article 2, both rules will generally be discussed. This chapter will discuss the nature and formation of sales and lease contracts as well as the fundamental principles of Article 2 and Article 2A.

NATURE OF SALES AND LEASES

The law of sales, which governs contracts involving the sale of goods, is a specialized branch of both the law of contracts (discussed previously in *Chapters 9–18*) and the law of personal property (discussed later in *Chapter 48*). This section will cover the definition of sales and lease contracts and the fundamentals of Article 2 and Article 2A.

◆ **SEE FIGURE 21-1: Law of Sales and Leases**

DEFINITIONS

GOODS

Goods are essentially defined as movable, tangible personal property. For example, the purchase of a bicycle, CD player, or this textbook is considered a sale of goods. "Goods" also include the unborn young of animals, growing crops, and, if removed by the seller, timber, minerals, or a building attached to real property. Section 2–105(1). Under Article 2A, minerals cannot be leased prior to their extraction. Section 2A–103(1)(h).

SALE

The Code defines a sale as the transfer of title to goods from seller to buyer for a price. Section 2–106. The price can be money, other goods, real estate, or services.

LEASE

Article 2A defines a lease of goods as a "transfer of the right to possession and use of goods for a term in return for consideration, but … retention or creation of a security interest is not a lease." Section 2A–103(1)(j). A transaction within this definition of a lease is governed by Article 2A, but if the transaction is a security interest disguised as a lease, it is governed by Article 9. Categorizing a transaction as a lease has significant implications not only for the parties to the lease but for third parties as well. If the transaction is deemed to be a lease, then the residual interest in the goods belongs to the lessor, who need not file publicly to protect this interest. On the other hand, if the transaction is a security interest, then the provisions of Article 9 regarding enforceability, perfection, priority, and remedies apply (see *Chapter 38*). UCC Section 1–201(37) and Revised Section 1–203 provide rules that govern the determination of whether a transaction in the form of a lease creates a security interest.

CONSUMER LEASES Article 2A affords special treatment for consumer leases. The definition of a consumer lease requires that (1) the transaction meet the definition of a lease under Article 2A; (2) the lessor be regularly engaged in the business of leasing *or* selling goods; (3) the lessee be an individual, not an organization; (4) the lessee take the lease interest primarily for a personal, family, or household purpose; and (5) the total payments under the lease do not exceed $25,000. Section 2A–103(1)(e). Although consumer protection for lease transactions is primarily left to other State and Federal law, Article 2A does contain a number of provisions that apply to consumer leases and that may *not* be varied by agreement of the parties.

FINANCE LEASES A finance lease is a special type of lease transaction generally involving three parties instead of two. Whereas in the typical lease situation the lessor also supplies the goods, in a finance lease arrangement the lessor and the supplier are separate parties. The lessor's primary function in a finance lease is to provide financing to the lessee for a lease of goods provided by the supplier. For example, under a finance lease arrangement a manufacturer supplies goods pursuant to the lessee's instructions or specifications. The

◆ **FIGURE 21-1: Law of Sales and Leases**

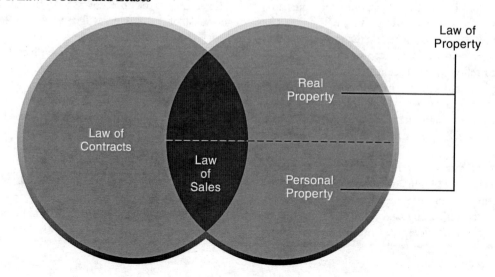

party functioning as the lessor will then either purchase those goods from the supplier or act as the prime lessee in leasing them from the supplier. In turn, the lessor will lease or sublease the goods to the lessee. Comment g to Section2A–103. Because the finance lessor functions merely as a source of credit, she typically will have no special expertise as to the goods. Due to the limited role the finance lessor usually plays, Article 2A treats finance leases differently from ordinary leases.

GOVERNING LAW

Though sales transactions are governed by Article 2 of the Code, general contract law continues to apply where the Code has not specifically modified such law. Nevertheless, although principles of common law and equity may supplement provisions of the Code, they may not be used to supplant its provisions. Thus the law of sales is a specialized part of the general law of contracts, and the law of contracts continues to govern unless specifically displaced by the Code.

General contract law also continues to govern all contracts outside the scope of the Code. Transactions not within the scope of Article 2 include employment contracts, service contracts, insurance contracts, contracts involving real property, and contracts for the sale of intangibles such as stocks, bonds, patents, and copyrights. For an illustration of the relationship between the law of sales and the general law of contracts, see *Figure 9-1*. In determining whether a contract containing both a sale of goods and a service is a UCC contract or a general contract, the majority of States follow the predominant purpose test. This test holds that if the predominant purpose of the whole transaction is a sale of goods, then Article 2 applies to the entire transaction. If, on the other hand, the predominant purpose is the nongood or service portion, then Article 2 does not apply at all. A few States apply Article 2 to the goods part of a transaction and general contract law to the nongoods or service part of the transaction.

◆ **SEE FIGURE 9-1: Law Governing Contracts**

Although Article 2 governs sales, the drafters of the Article have invited the courts to extend Code principles to non-sale transactions in goods. To date, a number of courts have accepted this invitation and have applied Code provisions by analogy to other transactions in goods not expressly included within the Act, most frequently to leases and bailments. The Code has also greatly influenced the revision of the Restatement, Second, Contracts, which, as previously discussed, has great effect upon all contracts.

Although lease transactions are governed by Article 2A of the Code, general contract law continues to apply where the

Code has not specifically modified such law. In other words, the law of leases is a specialized part of the general law of contracts, and the law of contracts continues to govern unless specifically displaced by the Code.

CISG The United Nations Convention on Contracts for the International Sale of Goods (CISG), which has been ratified by the United States and more than forty other countries, governs all contracts for the international sales of goods between parties located in different nations that have ratified the CISG. Because treaties are Federal law, the CISG supersedes the UCC in any situation to which either could apply. The CISG includes provisions dealing with interpretation, trade usage, contract formation, obligations and remedies of sellers and buyers, and risk of loss. Parties to an international sales contract may, however, expressly exclude CISG governance from their contract. The CISG specifically excludes sales of (1) goods bought for personal, family, or household use; (2) ships or aircraft; and (3) electricity. In addition, it does not apply to contracts in which the primary obligation of the party furnishing the goods consists of supplying labor or services.

FUNDAMENTAL PRINCIPLES OF ARTICLE 2 AND ARTICLE 2A

The purpose of Article 2 is to modernize, clarify, simplify, and make uniform the law of sales. Furthermore, the Article is to be interpreted in accordance with these underlying principles and not according to some abstraction such as the passage of title. The Code

is drawn to provide flexibility so that, since it is intended to be a semi-permanent piece of legislation, it will provide its own machinery for expansion of commercial practices. It is intended to make it possible for the law embodied in this Act to be developed by the courts in the light of unforeseen and new circumstances and practices. However, the proper construction of the Act requires that its interpretation and application be limited to its reason. Section 1–102, Comment 1; Revised Section 1-103, Comment 1.

This open-ended drafting includes the following fundamental concepts.

CISG The CISG governs only the formation of the contract of sales and the rights and obligations of the seller and buyer arising from such contract. It does not cover the validity of the contract or any of its provisions. In addition, one of the purposes of the CISG is to promote uniformity of the law of sales.

GOOD FAITH

All parties who enter into a contract or duty within the scope of the Code must perform their obligations in good faith. The Code defines **good faith** as "honesty in fact in the conduct or transaction concerned." Section 1–201(19). For a merchant (defined later), good faith also requires the observance of reasonable commercial standards of fair dealing in the trade. Section 2–103(1)(b); Section 2A–103(3). Revised Section 1–201(19) provides that "good faith means honesty in fact in the conductor transaction concerned and the observance of reasonable commercial standards of fair dealing," thus adopting the broader definition of good faith and making it applicable to both merchants and nonmerchants. For instance, if the parties agree that the seller is to set the price term, the seller must establish the price in good faith.

> **CISG** The CISG is also designed to promote the observation of good faith in international trade.

UNCONSCIONABILITY

The court may scrutinize every contract of sale to determine whether in its commercial setting, purpose, and effect it is unconscionable. The court may refuse to enforce an unconscionable contract or any part of it found to be unconscionable or may limit its application to prevent an unconscionable result. Section 2–302. Though the Code itself does not define *unconscionable*, the *New Webster's Dictionary* (Deluxe Encyclopedic Edition) defines the term as "contrary to the dictates of conscience; unscrupulous or unprincipled; exceeding that which is reasonable or customary; inordinate, unjustifiable."

The Code denies or limits enforcement of an unconscionable contract for the sale of goods to promote fairness and decency and to correct harshness or oppression in contracts resulting from inequality in the bargaining positions of the parties.

The doctrine of unconscionability has been justified on the basis that it permits the courts to resolve issues of unfairness explicitly on that basis without recourse to formalistic rules or legal fictions. In policing contracts for fairness, the courts have again demonstrated their willingness to limit freedom of contract to protect the less advantaged from overreaching by dominant contracting parties. Accordingly, most cases concerning unconscionability have involved low-income consumers.

The doctrine of unconscionability has evolved through its application by the courts to include both procedural and substantive unconscionability. **Procedural unconscionability** involves scrutiny for the presence of "bargaining naughtiness." In other words, was the negotiation process fair? Or were there procedural irregularities such as burying important terms of the agreement in fine print or obscuring the true meaning of the contract with impenetrable legal jargon?

In checking for **substantive unconscionability**, the court examines the actual terms of the contract for oppressive or grossly unfair provisions such as an exorbitant price or an unfair exclusion or limitation of contractual remedies. An all-too-common example places a necessitous buyer in an unequal bargaining position with a seller who consequently obtains an exorbitant price for his product or service. In one case, a price of $749 ($920 on time payments) for a vacuum cleaner that cost the seller $140 was held unconscionable. In another case, the buyers, welfare recipients, purchased by time payment contract a home freezer unit for $900 plus time credit charges, credit life insurance, credit property insurance, and sales tax for a total price of $1,235. The maximum retail value of the freezer unit at the time of purchase was $300. The court held the contract unconscionable and reformed it by changing the price to the total payment ($620) the buyers had managed to make. *Jones v. Star Credit Corp.*, 59 Misc.2d 189, 298 N.Y.S.2d 264 (1969).

As to leases, Article 2A provides that a court faced with an unconscionable contract or clause may refuse to enforce either the entire contract or just the unconscionable clause, or may limit the application of the unconscionable clause to avoid an unconscionable result. This is similar to Article 2's treatment of unconscionable clauses in sales contracts. A lessee under a consumer lease, however, is provided with additional protection against unconscionability. In the case of a consumer lease, if a court as a matter of law finds that any part of the lease contract has been induced by unconscionable conduct, the court is expressly empowered to grant appropriate relief. Section 2A–108(2). The same is true when unconscionable conduct occurs in the collection of a claim arising from a consumer lease contract. The explicit availability of relief for consumers subjected to unconscionable conduct (procedural unconscionability)—in addition to a provision regarding unconscionable contracts (substantive unconscionability)—represents a departure from Article 2. An additional remedy that Article 2A provides for consumers is the award of attorney's fees. If the court finds unconscionability with respect to a consumer lease, it shall award reasonable attorney's fees to the lessee. Section 2A–108(4)(a).

EXPANSION OF COMMERCIAL PRACTICES

An underlying policy of the Code is "to permit the continued expansion of commercial practices through custom, usage and agreement of the parties." Section 1–102(2)(b). In particular, the Code emphasizes the course of dealings and the usage of trade in interpreting agreements.

A **course of dealing** is a sequence of previous conduct between the parties that may fairly be regarded as establishing a common basis of understanding for interpreting their expressions and agreement. Section 1–205(1); Revised Section 1–303(b). For example, Plaza, a sugar company, enters into a written agreement with Brown, a grower of sugar beets, by which Brown agrees to raise and deliver and Plaza agrees to purchase specified quantities of beets during the coming season. No price is fixed. The agreement is on a standard form used by Plaza for Brown and many other growers in prior years. Plaza's practice is to pay all growers uniformly according to a formula based on Plaza's established accounting system. Unless otherwise agreed, the established pricing pattern is part of the agreement between Plaza and Brown as a course of dealing.

A **usage of trade** is a practice or method of dealing regularly observed and followed in a place, vocation, or trade. Section 1–205(2); Revised Section 1–303(c). To illustrate: Tamara contracts to sell Seth one thousand feet of San Domingo mahogany. By usage of dealers in mahogany, known to Tamara and Seth, good mahogany of a certain density is known as San Domingo mahogany, though it does not come from San Domingo. Unless otherwise agreed, the usage is part of the contract.

CISG The parties are bound by any usage or practices that they have agreed to or established between themselves. In addition, the parties are considered, unless otherwise agreed, to be bound by any usage of international trade that is widely known and regularly observed in the particular trade.

SALES BY AND BETWEEN MERCHANTS

The Code establishes separate rules that apply to transactions transpiring between merchants or involving a merchant as a party. A **merchant** is defined as a person who (1) is a dealer in the type of goods the transaction involves, (2) by his occupation holds himself out as having knowledge or skill peculiar to the goods or practices involved, or (3) employs an agent or broker whom he holds out as having such knowledge or skill. Section 2–104(1); Section 2A–103(3). These rules exact a higher standard of conduct from merchants because of their knowledge of trade and commerce and because merchants as a class generally set these standards for themselves. The most significant of these merchant rules are listed in *Figure 21-2*.

◆ **SEE FIGURE 21-2: Selected Rules Applicable to Merchants**

LIBERAL ADMINISTRATION OF REMEDIES

Section 1–106 and Revised Section 1–305 of the Code provide that its remedies shall be liberally administered to place the aggrieved party in a position as good as the one she would have occupied had the defaulting party fully

◆ **FIGURE 21-2: Selected Rules Applicable to Merchants**

Section of UCC	Merchant Rules	Chapter in Text Where Discussed
2-103(1)(b), 2-103(3)	Good faith	21
2-201	Confirmation of oral contracts	15, 21
2-205, 2A-205	Firm offers	10, 21
2-207(2)	Battle of the forms	10, 21
2-312(3), 2A-211(2)	Warranty against infringement	24
2-314(1), 2A-212	Warranty of merchantability	24
2-327(1)(c)	Sales on approval	23
2-402(2)	Retention of possession of goods by seller	23
2-403(2), 2A-304(2), 2A-305(2)	Entrusting of goods	23
2-509(3), 2A-219(2)(c)	Risk of loss	23
2-603(1), 2A-511(1)	Duties after rightful rejection	22

performed. The Code states clearly, however, that remedies are limited to compensation and do not include consequential or punitive damages, unless specifically provided by the Code. Nevertheless, the Code provides that even in cases in which it does not expressly provide a remedy for a right or obligation, the courts should provide an appropriate remedy. Remedies are discussed in *Chapter 25*.

FREEDOM OF CONTRACT

Most of the Code's provisions are not mandatory but permit the parties by agreement to vary or displace them altogether. The parties may not, however, disclaim by agreement the obligations of good faith, diligence, reasonableness, and care the Code prescribes, though they may by agreement determine the standards by which to measure the performance of these obligations, so long as such standards are not obviously unreasonable. Section 1–102(3); Revised Sections 1–103(a)(2) and 1–302. Through this approach, the Code not only maximizes freedom of contract but also permits the continued expansion of commercial practices through private agreement.

VALIDATION AND PRESERVATION OF SALES CONTRACTS

One of the requirements of commercial law is the establishment of rules that determine when an agreement is valid. The Code approaches this requirement by minimizing formal requisites and attempting to preserve agreements whenever the parties manifest an intent to enter into a contract.

FORMATION OF SALES AND LEASE CONTRACTS

The Code's basic approach to validation is to recognize contracts whenever the parties manifest such an intent. This is so whether or not the parties can identify a precise moment at which the contract was formed. Section 2–204(2); Section 2A–204(2).

As already noted, the law of sales and leases is a subset of the general law of contracts and is governed by general contract law unless particular provisions of the Code displace the general law. Although the Code leaves most issues of contract formation to general contract law, it has modified the general law of contract formation in several significant respects. These modifications serve to modernize contract law, to relax the validation requirements of contract formation, and to promote fairness.

MANIFESTATION OF MUTUAL ASSENT

For a contract to exist, there must be an objective manifestation of mutual assent: an offer and an acceptance. This section examines the UCC rules that affect offers and acceptances.

DEFINITENESS OF AN OFFER

At common law, the terms of a contract were required to be definite and complete. The Code has rejected the strict approach of the common law by recognizing an agreement as valid, despite missing terms, if there is any reasonably certain basis for granting a remedy. Accordingly, the Code provides that even a contract from which one or more terms have been omitted need not fail for indefiniteness. Section 2–204(3); Section 2A–204(3). The Code provides standards by which the courts may ascertain and supply omitted essential terms, provided the parties intended to enter into a binding agreement. Nevertheless, the more terms the parties leave open, the less likely their intent to enter into a binding contract. Article 2A generally does not provide the same gap-filling provisions.

CISG An offer to contract is sufficiently definite if it indicates the goods and fixes or makes provision, expressly or implicitly, for determining price and quality.

OPEN PRICE The parties may enter into a contract for the sale of goods even though they have reached no agreement on the price (that is, left open the price term). Under the Code, the price is reasonable at the time for delivery where the agreement (1) says nothing as to price, (2) provides that the parties shall agree later as to the price and they fail to so agree, or (3) fixes the price in terms of some agreed market or other standard as set by a third person or agency, and the price is not so set. Section 2–305(1). An agreement that the price is to be fixed by the seller or buyer means that it must be fixed in good faith.

OPEN DELIVERY Unless otherwise agreed, the place of delivery is the seller's place of business. Moreover, in the absence of specific instructions, the delivery must be made within a reasonable time and in a single delivery. Section 2–308.

OPEN QUANTITY: OUTPUT AND REQUIREMENT CONTRACTS A buyer's agreement to purchase a seller's entire output for a stated period, or a seller's agreement to fulfill a buyer's need for certain goods used in her business operations, may appear to lack definiteness and mutuality of obligation. In neither case do the parties specify the exact quantity of goods, and the seller and the buyer may have some control over their respective output and requirements. Nonetheless, such agreements are enforceable by the application of an objective standard based upon the good faith of both parties, and the quantities may not be disproportionate to any stated estimate or the prior output or requirements. Section 2–306(1). For example, the seller cannot operate his factory twenty-four hours a day and insist that the buyer take all of the output when the seller operated the factory only eight hours a day at the time the agreement was made. Nor can the buyer unilaterally triple the size of her business and insist that the seller supply all of her requirements.

OTHER OPEN TERMS The Code further provides rules, where the parties do not agree, as to the terms of payment, the duration of the contract, and the particulars of performance. Sections 2–310, 2–309, 2–307, 2–311.

IRREVOCABLE OFFERS

An offeror generally may withdraw an offer at any time prior to its acceptance. To be effective, notice of revocation must reach the offeree before he has accepted the offer.

An **option** is a *contract* by which the offeror is bound to hold open an offer for a specified time. It must comply with all the requirements of a contract, including consideration. Option contracts apply to all types of contracts, including those for sales of goods.

The Code has made certain offers—called **firm offers**—irrevocable without any consideration being given for the promise to keep the offer open. The Code provides that a merchant who gives assurance in a signed writing that an offer will be held open is bound to keep the offer open for a maximum of three months. Section 2–205; Section 2A–205. The Code, therefore, makes a merchant's written promise not to revoke an offer for a stated time enforceable even though no consideration is given the merchant-offeror for that promise.

For example, Ben's Brewery approached Flora Flooring, Inc., to purchase tile for Ben's floor. Ben's employees would install the tile after it was delivered by Flora. On June 6, Flora sent Ben a written, signed offer to provide the tile according to Ben's specifications for $26,000 and promised that "the offer will remain open until July 17." Flora is bound by her firm offer to keep the offer open until July 17. The result would differ, however, if Flora had merely stated that the "offer terminates on July 17" or that "the offer will terminate if not accepted on or before July 17." In both of these instances, there is no assurance to keep the offer open: because it is not a firm offer, Flora could revoke it at any time prior to Ben's acceptance.

Any firm offer on a form supplied by the offeree must be separately signed by the offeror.

CISG An offer may not be revoked if it indicates that it is irrevocable; it need not be in writing.

VARIANT ACCEPTANCES

The realities of modern business practices have necessitated the modification by the Code of the common law's "**mirror**

image" rule, by which the acceptance cannot vary or deviate from the terms of the offer. A vast number of business transactions use standardized business forms, resulting in what has been termed the **battle of the forms**. For example, a merchant buyer sends to the merchant seller on the buyer's order form a purchase order for 1,000 dozen cotton shirts at $60 per dozen with delivery by October 1 at the buyer's place of business. On the reverse side of this standard form are twenty-five numbered paragraphs containing provisions generally favorable to the buyer. When the seller receives the buyer's order, he sends to the buyer an unequivocal acceptance of the offer on his acceptance form. Although the seller agrees to the buyer's quantity, price, and delivery terms, on the back of the form the seller utilizes in sending his unequivocal acceptance to the buyer are thirty-two numbered paragraphs generally favorable to the seller and in significant conflict with the buyer's form. Under the common law's "mirror image" rule, no contract would exist, for the seller has not in fact accepted unequivocally all of the material terms of the buyer's offer.

By comparison, Section 2–207 of the Code addresses variant acceptances by providing:

1. A definite and seasonable expression of acceptance or a written confirmation which is sent within a reasonable time operates as an acceptance even though it states terms additional to or different from those offered or agreed upon, unless acceptance is expressly made conditional on assent to the additional or different terms.

2. The additional terms are to be construed as proposals for addition to the contract. Between merchants such terms become part of the contract unless:
   (a) the offer expressly limits acceptance to the terms of the offer;
   (b) they materially alter it; or
   (c) notification of objection to them has already been given or is given within a reasonable time after notice of them is received.

3. Conduct by both parties which recognizes the existence of a contract is sufficient to establish a contract for sale although the writings of the parties do not otherwise establish a contract. In such case the terms of the particular contract consist of those terms on which the writings of the parties agree, together with any supplementary terms incorporated under any other provisions of this Act.

Thus, the Code attempts to settle the battle of the forms by focusing upon the intent of the parties. If the offeree expressly makes his acceptance conditioned upon the offeror's assent to the additional or different terms, no contract is formed. If the offeree does not expressly make his acceptance conditional upon such assent, a contract is formed. The issue then becomes whether the offeree's different or additional terms should become part of the contract. If both offeror and offeree are merchants, **additional** terms (terms the offeree proposed for the contract for the first time) will become part of the contract, provided they do not materially alter the agreement and are not objected to either in the offer itself or within a reasonable time. If either of the parties is not a merchant, or if the additional terms materially alter the offer, then the terms are merely construed as proposals for addition to the contract. **Different** terms (terms that contradict terms of the offer) proposed by the offeree generally will not become part of the contract unless specifically accepted by the offeror. The courts are divided over what terms are included when the terms conflict. The majority of courts hold that the terms cancel each other out and look to the Code to provide the missing terms; other courts hold that the offeror's terms govern. Some States follow a third alternative and apply the additional terms test to different terms.

Applying Section 2–207 to the example above: because both parties are merchants and the seller did not condition his acceptance upon the buyer's assent to the additional or different terms, (1) the contract will be formed without the *seller's different terms* unless the buyer specifically accepts them; (2) the contract will be formed without the *seller's additional terms* unless (a) the buyer specifically accepts or (b) the additional terms do not materially alter the offer and the buyer does not object to them; and (3) depending upon the jurisdiction, either (a) the conflicting (different) terms cancel each other out and the Code provides the missing terms or (b) the buyer's conflicting terms are included in the contract or (c) the additional terms test is applied.

CISG A reply to an offer that contains additions, limitations, or other modifications is a counteroffer that rejects the original offer. Nevertheless, a purported acceptance that contains additional or different terms acts as an acceptance if the terms do not materially alter the contract unless the offeror objects to the change. Changes in price, payment, quality, quantity, place and time of delivery, terms of delivery, liability of the parties, and settlement of a dispute are always considered to be material alterations.

Finally, subsection 3 of 2–207 deals with those situations in which the writings do not form a contract, but the conduct of the parties recognizes the existence of one. For instance, Ernest makes an offer to Gwen, who replies with a conditional acceptance. Although no contract has been formed, Gwen ships the ordered goods and Ernest accepts the goods. Subsection 3 provides that in this instance the contract consists of the written terms to which both parties agreed together with supplementary provisions of the Code.

♦ **SEE FIGURE 21-3: Battle of the Forms**

MANNER OF ACCEPTANCE

As with the common law, the offeror may specify the manner in which the offer must be accepted. If the offeror does not and the circumstances do not otherwise clearly indicate, an offer to make a contract invites acceptance in any manner and by any medium reasonable under the circumstances. Section 2–206(1)(a); Section 2A–206(1). The Code, therefore, allows flexibility of response and the ability to keep pace with new modes of communication.

An offer to buy goods for prompt or current shipment may be accepted either by a prompt promise to ship or by prompt shipment. Section 2–206(1)(b). Acceptance by performance requires notice within a reasonable time, or the offer may be treated as lapsed. Section 2–206(2); Section 2A–206(2).

AUCTIONS

The Code provides that if an auction sale is advertised or announced in explicit terms to be **without reserve**, the auctioneer may not withdraw the article put up for sale unless no bid is made within a reasonable time. Unless the sale is advertised as being without reserve, the sale is **with reserve**, and the auctioneer may withdraw the goods at any time until he announces completion of the sale. Whether the sale is with or without reserve, a bidder may retract his bid at anytime prior to acceptance by the auctioneer. Such retraction does not, however, revive any previous bid. Section 2–328.

If the auctioneer knowingly receives a bid by or on behalf of the seller, and notice has not been given that the seller reserves the right to bid at the auction sale, the bidder to whom the goods are sold can either avoid the sale or take the goods at the price of the last good faith bid.

CISG The CISG does not apply to sales by auctions.

CONSIDERATION

The Code has abandoned the common law rule requiring that a modification of an existing contract be supported by consideration to be valid. The Code provides that a contract for the sale of goods can be effectively modified without new consideration, provided the modification is made in good faith. Section 2–209(1); Section 2A–208(1).

In addition, any claim of right arising out of an alleged breach of contract can be discharged in whole or in part

◆ **FIGURE 21-3: Battle of the Forms**

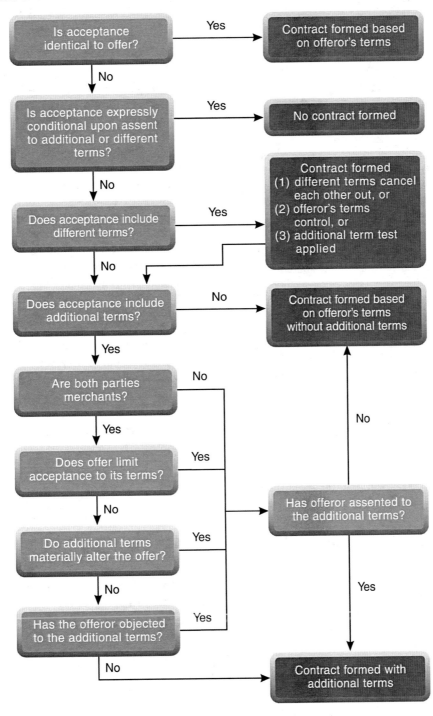

without consideration by a written waiver or renunciation signed and delivered by the aggrieved party. Section 1–107. Under the Revised UCC Article 1, a claim or right arising out of an alleged breach may be discharged in whole or in part without consideration by agreement of the aggrieved party in an authenticated record. Section 1–306. Moreover,

as previously noted, a firm offer is not revocable for lack of consideration.

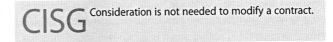

CISG   Consideration is not needed to modify a contract.

FORM OF THE CONTRACT

STATUTE OF FRAUDS

The original statute of frauds, which applied to contracts for the sale of goods, has been used as a prototype for the Article 2 statute of frauds provision. Section 2–201 of the Code provides that a contract for the sale of goods costing *$500 or more* is not enforceable unless there is some writing or record sufficient to evidence the existence of a contract between the parties ($1,000 or more for leases, Section 2A–201). As discussed in *Chapter 15*, almost all of the States have adopted the **Uniform Electronic Transactions Act (UETA)**, which gives full effect to contracts formed by electronic records and signatures. The Act applies to contracts governed by Articles 2 and 2A. In addition, Congress in 2000 enacted the **Electronic Signatures in Global and National Commerce (E-Sign)**. The Act, which uses language very similar to that of UETA, makes electronic records and signatures valid and enforceable across the United States for many types of transactions in or affecting interstate or foreign commerce.

CISG A contract need not be evidenced by a writing, unless one of the parties has her place of business in a country that provides otherwise.

MODIFICATION OF CONTRACTS An agreement modifying a contract must be evidenced by a writing or record if the resulting contract is within the statute of frauds. Section 2–209(3) (Article 2A omits this provision). Conversely, if a contract that was previously within the statute of frauds is modified so as to no longer fall within it, the modification is enforceable even if it is oral. Thus, if the parties enter into an oral contract to sell for $450 a dining room table to be delivered to the buyer and later, prior to delivery, orally agree that the seller shall stain the table and that the buyer shall pay a price of $550, the modified contract is unenforceable. In contrast, if the parties have a written contract for the sale of 150 bushels of wheat at a price of $4.50 per bushel and later, upon oral agreement, decrease the quantity to 100 bushels at the same price per bushel, the agreement, as modified, is enforceable.

A signed agreement that requires modifications or rescissions to be in a signed writing cannot be otherwise modified or rescinded. Section 2–209(2); Section 2A–208(2). If this requirement is on a form provided by a merchant, the other party must separately sign it unless the other party is a merchant.

WRITING(S) OR RECORD The statute of frauds compliance provisions under the Code are more liberal than the rules under general contract law. The Code requires merely some writing or record (1) sufficient to indicate that a contract has

been made between the parties, (2) signed by the party against whom enforcement is sought or by her authorized agent or broker, that (3) includes a term specifying the quantity of goods the agreement involves. Whereas general contract law requires that a writing include all essential terms, even a writing or record that omits or incorrectly states a term agreed upon may be sufficient under the Code. This is consistent with other provisions of the Code stating that contracts may be enforced despite the omission of material terms. Nevertheless, the contract is enforceable only to the extent of the quantity set forth in the writing or record. Given proof that a contract was intended and a signed writing describing the goods, their quantity, and the names of the parties, under the Code the court can supply omitted terms such as price and particulars of performance. Many courts have concluded, however, that the Code does not require a clear and precise quantity term in a requirements or output contract. Moreover, several related documents may satisfy the writing or record requirement.

Between merchants, if within a reasonable time a writing in confirmation of the contract is received, the **written merchant confirmation**, if sufficient against the sender, is also sufficient against the recipient unless he gives written notice of his objection within ten days after receiving the confirmation. Section 2–201(2). (Article 2A does not have a comparable rule.) This means that if these requirements have been met, the recipient of the writing or record is in the same position he would have assumed by signing it; and the confirmation, therefore, is enforceable against him. For example, Brown Co. and ATM Industries enter into an oral contract providing that ATM will deliver 1,000 dozen shirts to Brown at $6 per shirt. The next day, Brown sends to ATM a letter signed by Brown's president confirming the agreement. The letter contains the quantity term but does not mention the price. Brown is bound by the contract when its authorized agent sends the letter, whereas ATM is bound by the oral contract ten days after receiving the letter, unless it objects in writing within that time. Therefore, it is essential that merchants examine their mail carefully and promptly to make certain that any written confirmations conform to their understanding of their outstanding contractual agreements. Where one or both of the parties is not a merchant, however, this rule does not apply.

EXCEPTIONS A contract that does not satisfy the writing requirement but is otherwise valid is enforceable in the following instances.

The Code permits an oral contract for the sale of goods to be enforced against a party who in his pleading, testimony, or otherwise in court **admits** that a contract was made, but limits enforcement to the quantity of goods so admitted. Section 2–201(3)(b); Section 2A–201(4)(b). This provision recognizes that the policy behind the statute of frauds does not apply when the party seeking to avoid the oral contract admits under oath the existence of the contract.

The Code also permits enforcement of an oral contract for goods **specially manufactured** for the buyer. Section 2–201(3)(a); Section 2A–201(4)(a). Nevertheless, if the goods, although manufactured on special order, are readily marketable in the ordinary course of the seller's business, the contract is not enforceable unless in writing.

In most States, prior to the Code, delivery and acceptance of part of the goods or payment of part of the price and acceptance of the payment made the entire oral contract enforceable against the buyer who had received part delivery or against the seller who had received part payment. Under the Code such "partial performance" validates the contract only for the goods that have been **delivered and accepted** or for which **payment** has been **accepted**. Section 2–201(3)(c); Section 2A–201 (4)(c). To illustrate, Debra orally agrees to buy one thousand watches from Brian for $15,000. Brian delivers three hundred watches to Debra, who receives and accepts them. The oral contract is enforceable to the extent of three hundred watches ($4,500)—those received and accepted—but is unenforceable to the extent of seven hundred watches ($10,500).

But what if part payment under an indivisible contract, such as one for the sale of an automobile, presents a choice between not enforcing the contract or enforcing it as a whole?

Presently, there is a division of authority on this issue, although the better rule appears to be that such part payment and acceptance makes the entire contract enforceable.

PAROL EVIDENCE

Contractual terms that the parties set forth in a writing that they intend as a final expression of their agreement may not be contradicted by evidence of any prior agreement or of a contemporaneous agreement. Nevertheless, under the Code, the terms may be explained or supplemented by (1) course of dealing, usage of trade, or course of performance; and (2) evidence of consistent additional terms, unless the writing was intended as the complete and exclusive statement of the terms of the agreement. Section 2–202; Section 2A–202.

For a comparison of general contract law and the law governing sales and leases of goods, see *Figure 21-4*.

CISG   The CISG permits a court to consider all relevant circumstances of the agreement, including the negotiations, any course of performance between the parties, trade usages, and any subsequent conduct.

◆ **SEE FIGURE 21-4: Contract Law Compared with Law of Sales**

◆ FIGURE 21-4: **Contract Law Compared with Law of Sales**

Section of UCC	Contract Law	Law of Sales/Leases
Definiteness	Contract must include all material terms.	Open terms permitted if parties intend to make contract. Section 2-204; 2A-204.
Counteroffers	Acceptance must be a mirror image of offer. Counteroffer and conditional acceptance are rejections.	Battle of forms. Section 2-207. See *Figure 21-3*.
Modification of Contract	Consideration is required.	Consideration is not required. Section 2-209; 2A-208.
Irrevocable Offers	Options.	Options. Firm offers up to three months binding without consideration. Section 2-205; 2A-205.
Statute of Frauds	Writing must include all material terms.	Writing must include quantity term. Specially manufactured goods. Confirmation by merchants. Delivery or payment and acceptance. Admissions. Section 2-201; 2A-201 (except merchant confirmation).

CHAPTER SUMMARY

NATURE OF SALES AND LEASES

DEFINITIONS

Goods movable personal property

Sale transfer of title to goods from seller to buyer for a price

Lease a transfer of right to possession and use of goods in return for consideration

- *Consumer Leases* leases by a merchant to an individual who leases for personal, family, or household purposes for no more than $25,000
- *Finance Leases* special type of lease transaction generally involving three parties: the lessor, the supplier, and the lessee

Governing Law

- *Sales Transactions* governed by Article 2 of the Code, but where general contract law has not been specifically modified by the Code, general contract law continues to apply
- *Lease Transactions* governed by Article 2A of the Code, but where general contract law has not been specifically modified by the Code, general contract law continues to apply
- *Transactions outside the Code* include employment contracts, service contracts, insurance contracts, contracts involving real property, and contracts for the sale of intangibles

FUNDAMENTAL PRINCIPLES OF ARTICLE 2 AND ARTICLE 2A

Purpose to modernize, clarify, simplify, and make uniform the law of sales and leases

Good Faith the Code requires all sales and lease contracts to be performed in good faith, which means honesty in fact in the conduct or transaction concerned; in the case of a merchant (and a nonmerchant under Revised Article 1), it also includes the observance of reasonable commercial standards

Unconscionability a court may refuse to enforce an unconscionable contract or any part of a contract found to be unconscionable

- *Procedural Unconscionability* unfairness of the bargaining process
- *Substantive Unconscionability* oppressive or grossly unfair contractual provisions

Expansion of Commercial Practices

- *Course of Dealing* a sequence of previous conduct between the parties establishing a common basis for interpreting their agreement
- *Usage of Trade* a practice or method of dealing regularly observed and followed in a place, vocation, or trade

Sales by and between Merchants the Code establishes separate rules that apply to transactions between merchants or involving a merchant (a dealer in goods or a person who by his occupation holds himself out as having knowledge or skill peculiar to the goods or practice involved, or who employs an agent or broker whom he holds out as having such knowledge or skill)

Liberal Administration of Remedies

Freedom of Contract most provisions of the Code may be varied by agreement

Validation and Preservation of Sales Contract the Code reduces formal requisites to the bare minimum and attempts to preserve agreements whenever the parties manifest an intention to enter into a contract

FORMATION OF SALES AND LEASE CONTRACTS

MANIFESTATION OF MUTUAL ASSENT

Definiteness of an Offer the Code provides that a sales or lease contract does not fail for indefiniteness even though one or more terms may have been omitted; the Code provides standards by which missing essential terms may be supplied for sales of goods

Irrevocable Offers
- *Option* a contract to hold open an offer
- *Firm Offer* a signed writing by a merchant to hold open an offer for the purchase or sale of goods for a maximum of three months

Variant Acceptances the inclusion of different or additional terms in an acceptance is addressed by focusing on the intent of the parties

Manner of Acceptance an acceptance can be made in any reasonable manner and is effective upon dispatch

Auction auction sales are generally with reserve, permitting the auctioneer to withdraw the goods at any time prior to sale

---

CONSIDERATION

Contractual Modifications the Code provides that a contract for the sale or lease of goods may be modified without new consideration if the modification is made in good faith

Firm Offers are not revocable for lack of consideration

FORM OF THE CONTRACT

Statute of Frauds sale of goods costing $500 or more (or lease of goods for $1,000 or more) must be evidenced by a signed writing to be enforceable
- *Writing or Record* the Code requires some writing(s) or record sufficient to indicate that a contract has been made between the parties, signed by the party against whom enforcement is sought or by her authorized agent or broker, and including a term specifying the quantity of goods
- *Alternative Methods of Compliance* written confirmation between merchants, admission, specially manufactured goods, and delivery or payment and acceptance

Parol Evidence contractual terms that are set forth in a writing intended by the parties as a final expression of their agreement may not be contradicted by evidence of any prior agreement or of a contemporaneous oral agreement, but such terms may be explained or supplemented by course of dealing, usage of trade, course of performance, or consistent additional evidence

Performance is the process of discharging contractual obligations by carrying out those obligations according to the terms of the contract. The basic obligation of the seller in a contract for the sale of goods is to transfer and deliver goods that conform to the terms of the contract. The basic obligation of the buyer is to accept and pay for conforming goods in accordance with the contract. The basic obligation of the lessor is to transfer possession of the goods for the lease term, and that of the lessee is to pay the agreed rent. Section 2A–103(1)(j). Unless the parties have agreed otherwise, a tender (offer) of performance by one party is a condition to performance by the other party. A contract of sale also requires that each party not impair the other party's expectation of having the contract performed.

The obligations of the parties are determined by their contractual agreement. For example, the contract of sale may expressly provide that the seller must deliver the goods before receiving payment of the price or that the buyer must pay the price before receiving the goods. If the contract does not sufficiently cover the particulars of performance, these terms will be supplied by the Code, common law, course of dealing, usage of trade, and course of performance. (Article 2A provides only a few gap-fillers.) In all events, both parties to the sales contract must perform their contractual obligations in good faith.

This chapter will examine the performance obligations of the seller and the buyer as well as the contractual obligations that apply to both of them.

PERFORMANCE BY THE SELLER

Tender of conforming goods by the seller entitles him to acceptance of them by the buyer and to payment of the contractually agreed-upon price. Nonetheless, the rights of the parties may be otherwise fixed by the terms of the contract. For example, if the seller has agreed to sell goods on sixty or ninety days' credit, he is required to perform his part of the contract before the buyer performs.

Tender of delivery requires that the seller put and hold goods that conform to the contract at the buyer's disposition and that he give the buyer reasonable notification to enable her to take delivery. Section 2–503. Tender must also be made at a reasonable time and be kept open for a reasonable period. For example, Robert agrees to sell Barbara a home theater system composed of a speaker system (consisting of four identical, small speakers for the front and rear, a center channel speaker, and a subwoofer speaker), a Blu-Ray disc player and an audio-video receiver. Each component is specified by manufacturer and model number, and delivery is to be at Robert's store. Robert obtains the ordered equipment in accordance with the contractual specifications and notifies Barbara that she may pick up the system at her convenience. Robert has now tendered and thus has performed his obligations under the sales contract: he holds goods that conform to the contract, he has reasonably placed them at the buyer's disposal, and he has notified the buyer of their readiness.

CISG As specified by the contract and the CISG, the seller must deliver the goods, hand over any documents relating to them, and transfer the property in the goods.

TIME AND MANNER OF TENDER

Tender must be at a *reasonable* time, and the goods tendered must be kept available for the period reasonably necessary to enable the buyer to take possession of them. Unless otherwise agreed, the buyer must furnish facilities reasonably suited to the receipt of the goods tendered by the seller. Section 2–503.

If the terms of the contract do not fix a definite time for delivery, the seller is allowed a reasonable time after entering into the contract within which to tender the goods to the buyer. Likewise, the buyer has a reasonable time within which to accept delivery. What length of time is reasonable depends upon the facts and circumstances of each case. If the goods can be delivered immediately, a reasonable time would be very short. Where the goods must be constructed or manufactured, however, "reasonable" would take into account the usual length of time required to make the goods.

A contract may not be performed piecemeal or in installments unless the parties specifically agree. If such performance is not so specified, all of the goods the contract specifies must be tendered in a single delivery, and payment is due on such tender.

> CISG The seller must deliver the goods: (1) if a date is fixed by or determinable from the contract, on that date; (2) if a period of time is fixed by or determinable from the contract, at any time within that period unless circumstances indicate that the buyer is to choose a date; or (3) in any other case, within a reasonable time after the conclusion of the contract.

PLACE OF TENDER

If the contract does not specify the place for delivery of the goods, the place for delivery is the *seller's place of business* or, if he has none, his residence. The seller must hold the goods for the buyer's disposition and notify her that the goods are being held for her to pick up. Section 2–308(a). If the contract is for the sale of identified goods that the parties know at the time of making the contract are located neither at the seller's place of business nor at his residence, the *location* of the goods is then the place for delivery. Section 2–308. For example, George, a boat builder in Chicago, contracts to sell to Chris a certain yacht that both parties know is anchored at Milwaukee. The place of delivery would be Milwaukee. On the other hand, if the contract provides that George shall overhaul the motor at his shipyard in Chicago, George would have to return the yacht to Chicago, and the place of delivery would be George's Chicago shipyard.

The parties frequently agree expressly upon the place of tender, typically by using one of various *delivery terms*. These terms specify whether the contract is a shipment or destination contract and determine the place where the seller must tender delivery of the goods.

> CISG If the seller is not bound to deliver the goods at any other particular place and the contract of sale does not involve carriage of the goods, his obligation to deliver consists: (1) if the contract relates to specific goods, or unidentified goods to be drawn from a specific stock or to be manufactured or produced, and at the time of the conclusion of the contract the parties knew that the goods were at, or were to be manufactured or produced at, a particular place, in placing the goods at the buyer's disposal at that place; and (2) in other cases, in placing the goods at the buyer's disposal at the place where the seller had his place of business at the time of the conclusion of the contract.

SHIPMENT CONTRACTS The delivery terms *F.O.B. (free on board) place of shipment, F.A.S. (free alongside ship) port of shipment, C.I.F. (cost, insurance, and freight)*, and *C.&F. (cost and freight)* are all "shipment contracts." Under a shipment contract, the seller is required or authorized to send the goods to the buyer, but the contract does not obligate her to deliver them at a particular destination. In these cases, the seller's tender of performance occurs at the point of shipment, provided the seller meets certain specified conditions designed to protect the interests of the absent buyer. A contract is assumed to be a shipment contract unless otherwise indicated.

Under the Uniform Commercial Code (UCC), the initials "F.O.B." and "F.A.S." are delivery terms, even though they are used only in connection with a stated price. Section 2–319(1)(a). A contract providing that the sale is **F.O.B. place of shipment** or **F.A.S. port of shipment** is a shipment contract. For example, Linda, whose place of business is in New York, enters into a contract with Holly, the buyer, who is located in San Francisco. The contract calls for delivery of the goods F.O.B. New York. This would be a shipment contract. Under a **C.I.F.** ("cost, insurance, and freight") contract, in consideration for an agreed unit price for the goods, the seller agrees to pay all costs of transportation, insurance, and freight to the destination. The amount of the agreed unit price of the goods will, of course, reflect these costs. By comparison, under a **C.&F.** contract, the seller would pay "cost and freight." The unit price in such a contract is understandably less than in a C.I.F. contract as the C.&F. contract does not include the cost of insurance.

Under a shipment contract, the seller is required to (1) deliver the goods to a carrier; (2) make a contract for their transportation that is reasonable given the nature of the goods and other circumstances; (3) obtain and promptly deliver or tender to the buyer any document necessary to enable the buyer to obtain possession of the goods from the carrier; and (4) promptly notify the buyer of the shipment. Section 2–504. Failing either to make a proper contract for transportation or to notify the buyer of the shipment is a ground for rejection *only* if material loss or delay results. Section 2–504.

> CISG If the seller is not bound to deliver the goods at any other particular place and if the contract of sale involves carriage of the goods, his obligation to deliver consists of handing the goods over to the first carrier for delivery to the buyer.

DESTINATION CONTRACTS The delivery terms *F.O.B. city of buyer, ex-ship*, and *no arrival, no sale* are destination contracts. Because a destination contract requires the seller to tender delivery of conforming goods at a specified destination, the seller must place the goods at the buyer's disposition and give the buyer reasonable notice to enable him to take delivery. In addition, if the destination contract involves documents of title, the seller must tender the necessary documents. Section 2–503.

Where the contract provides that the sale is **F.O.B. place of destination**, the seller must at his own expense and risk transport the goods to that place and there tender delivery of them to the buyer. Section 2–319(1)(b). For example, if the buyer is in Boston and the seller is in Chicago, a contract providing F.O.B. Boston is a destination contract under which the seller must tender the goods at the designated place in Boston at his own expense and risk. A contract that provides for delivery "**ex-ship**," or from the ship, is also a destination contract, requiring the seller to unload the goods from the carrier at the named destination. Finally, where the contract contains the terms "**no arrival, no sale**," the title and risk of loss do not pass to the buyer until the seller makes a tender of the goods after they arrive at their destination. The major significance of the "no arrival, no sale" term is that it excuses the seller from any liability to the buyer for the goods' failure to arrive, unless the seller has caused their nonarrival.

GOODS HELD BY BAILEE Where goods are in the possession of a bailee and are to be delivered without being moved, in most instances the seller may either tender to the buyer a document of title or obtain an acknowledgment by the bailee of the buyer's right to possess the goods. Section 2–503(4). This acknowledgment permits the buyer to obtain the goods directly from the bailee.

◆ **SEE FIGURE 22-1: Tender of Performance by the Seller**

PERFECT TENDER RULE

The Code imposes upon the seller the obligation to conform her tender of goods *exactly* to the requirements of the contract. The seller's tender cannot deviate in any way from the terms of the contract. Thus, a buyer may rightfully reject the delivery of 110 dozen shirts under an agreement calling for delivery of 100 dozen shirts. The size or extent of the breach does not affect the right to reject.

If the goods or the tender of delivery fail in any respect to conform to the contract, the buyer may (1) reject the whole lot, (2) accept the whole lot, or (3) accept any commercial unit or units and reject the rest. Section 2–601; Section 2A–509(1). A commercial unit means such a unit of goods as by commercial usage is a single unit and which, if divided, would be materially impaired in character or value. A **commercial unit** may be a single item (such as a machine), a set of articles (such as a suite of furniture or an assortment of sizes), a quantity (such as a bale, gross, or carload), or any other unit treated in use or in the relevant market as a whole. Section 2–105(6); Section 2A–103(1)(c).

CISG The CISG does not follow the perfect tender rule. The buyer may declare the contract avoided if the failure by the seller to perform any of his obligations under the contract or the CISG amounts to a fundamental breach of contract. A breach of contract committed by one of the parties is fundamental if it results in such detriment to the other party as substantially to deprive her of what she is entitled to expect under the contract, unless the party in breach did not foresee and a reasonable person of the same kind in the same circumstances would not have foreseen such a result.

The buyer's right to reject the goods upon the seller's failure to comply with the perfect tender rule is subject to three basic qualifications: (1) agreement between the parties limiting the buyer's right to reject nonconforming goods, (2) cure by the seller, and (3) the existence of an installment contract. In addition, as previously discussed, the perfect tender rule does not apply to a seller's breach of her obligation under a shipment contract to make a proper contract for transportation or to give proper notice of the shipment. A failure to perform either of these obligations is a ground for rejection only if material loss or delay results. Section 2–504.

AGREEMENT BY THE PARTIES The parties may contractually agree to limit the operation of the perfect tender rule. For example, they may agree that the seller shall have the right to repair or replace any defective parts or goods. Such contractual limitations are discussed in *Chapter 25*.

CURE BY THE SELLER The Code recognizes two situations in which a seller may cure or correct a nonconforming tender of goods. This relaxation of the seller's obligation to make a perfect tender gives the seller an opportunity to make either a second delivery or a substitute tender. Whereas the first opportunity for cure occurs when the time for performance under the contract has not expired, the second opportunity is available after the time for performance has expired, but only if the seller had reasonable grounds to believe that the nonconforming tender would be acceptable to the buyer, with or without monetary adjustment.

Where the buyer refuses to accept a tender of goods that do not conform to the contract, the seller, by acting promptly and within the time allowed for performance, may make a proper tender or delivery of conforming goods and thereby cure his defective tender or performance. Section 2–508(1); Section 2A–513(1). Upon notice of the buyer's rightful rejection, the seller must first give the buyer reasonable notice of her intention to cure the defect and then must make a proper tender according to the *original* contract. This rule, which predates the Code, is fair to both parties. It gives the seller the full contractual period in which to perform while causing no harm to the buyer, who receives full

◆ **FIGURE 22-1: Tender of Performance by the Seller**

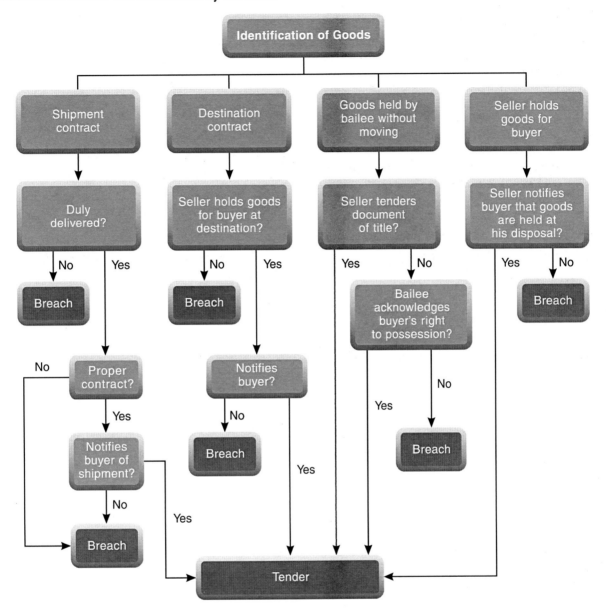

performance within the time agreed to in the contract. For example, Conroy is to deliver to Elizabeth twenty-five blue shirts and fifty white shirts by October 15. On October 1, Conroy delivers twenty-nine blue shirts and forty-six white shirts, which Elizabeth rejects as not conforming to the contract. Elizabeth notifies Conroy of her rejection and the reasons for it. Conroy has until October 15 to cure the defect by making a perfect tender, provided he seasonably notifies Elizabeth of his intention to do so.

The Code also provides the seller an opportunity after the time for performance has expired to cure a nonconforming tender, which the seller had reasonable grounds to believe would be acceptable to the buyer, with or without money allowance. Section 2–508(2); Section 2A–513(2). This Code-created opportunity to cure a nonconforming tender after the date set for performance is conditioned on the seller's satisfying the following requirements: (1) the seller had reasonable grounds for believing that the nonconforming tender would be acceptable to the buyer, (2) the seller, after being informed of the buyer's rightful rejection, seasonably notifies the buyer of his intention to cure the defect, and (3) the seller cures the defect within a reasonable time. The principal difficulty in applying this rule is whether or not the first requirement has been satisfied.

For example, Vanessa orders from Gary a model 110X S.C.A. television to be delivered on January 20. The 110X is unavailable, but Gary can obtain last year's model of the same television, a model 110, which lists for 5 percent less than the 110X. On January 20, Gary delivers to Vanessa the 110 at a discount price of 10 percent less than the contract price for the 110X. Vanessa rejects the substituted television set. Gary, who promptly notifies Vanessa that he will obtain and deliver a model 110X, will most likely have a reasonable time beyond the January 20 deadline in which to deliver the 110X television set to Vanessa, because under these facts Gary appeared to have reasonable grounds to believe the model 110 would be acceptable with the money allowance.

CISG If the seller has delivered goods before the date for delivery, the seller may, up to the delivery date, cure any deficiency, provided that the exercise of this right does not cause the buyer unreasonable inconvenience or unreasonable expense. However, the buyer retains any right to claim damages as provided for in the CISG. If the seller does not perform on time, the buyer may fix an additional period of time of reasonable length for performance by the seller of his obligations. Unless the buyer has received notice from the seller that the seller will not perform within the period so fixed, the buyer may not, during that period, resort to any remedy for breach of contract. However, the buyer retains any right he may have to claim damages for delay in performance. If the seller does not deliver the goods within the additional period of time or declares that he will not deliver within the period so fixed, the buyer may declare the contract avoided.

The seller may, even after the date for delivery, cure a defective performance, if she can do so without unreasonable delay and without causing the buyer unreasonable inconvenience. However, the buyer retains any right to claim damages for delay in performance. If the seller requests the buyer to make known whether he will accept performance and the buyer does not comply with the request within a reasonable time, the seller may perform within the time indicated in his request.

INSTALLMENT CONTRACTS Unless the parties have otherwise agreed, the buyer does not have to pay any part of the price of the goods until the seller has delivered or tendered the entire quantity specified in the contract. Section 2–307. An installment contract is an instance in which the parties have otherwise agreed. It expressly provides for delivery of the goods in separate lots or installments and usually provides for payment of the price in installments. If the contract is silent about payment, the Code provides that the price, if it can be apportioned, may be demanded for each lot. Section 2–307.

The buyer may reject any nonconforming installment if the nonconformity *substantially* impairs the value of that installment and cannot be cured. Section 2–612(2); Section 2A–510(1). When, however, the installment substantially impairs the value of the installment but not the value of the entire contract, the buyer cannot reject the installment if the seller gives adequate assurance of the installment's cure. Section 2–612(2); Section 2A–510(1). Whenever the nonconformity or default with respect to one or more of the installments substantially impairs the value of the whole contract, however, the buyer can treat the breach as a breach of the *whole contract*. Section 2–612(3); Section 2A–510(2).

CISG When a contract calls for delivery of goods by installments, if the seller's failure to perform any of his obligations with respect to any installment constitutes a fundamental breach of contract with respect to that installment, the buyer may declare the contract avoided with respect to that installment. A buyer who declares the contract avoided with respect to any delivery may, at the same time, declare it avoided with respect to deliveries already made or to future deliveries if, by reason of their interdependence, those deliveries could not be used for the purpose contemplated by the parties at the time of the conclusion of the contract. If the seller's failure to perform any of his obligations with respect to any installment gives the buyer good grounds to conclude that a fundamental breach of contract will occur with respect to future installments, he may declare the contract avoided for the future, provided that he does so within a reasonable time.

PERFORMANCE BY THE BUYER

The buyer is obligated to accept conforming goods and to pay for them according to the contract terms. Section 2–301; Section 2A–103(1)(j). Payment or tender of payment by the buyer, unless otherwise agreed, is a condition to the seller's duty to tender and to complete delivery. Section 2–507(1).

The buyer is not obliged to accept a tender or delivery of goods that do not conform to the contract. Upon determining that the tender or delivery is nonconforming, the buyer has three choices. He may (1) reject all of the goods, (2) accept all of the goods, or (3) accept any commercial unit or units of the goods and reject the rest. Section 2–601; Section 2A–509(1). The buyer must pay the contract rate for the commercial units he accepts.

CISG The buyer must pay the price for the goods and take delivery of them as required by the contract and the CISG.

INSPECTION

Unless the parties otherwise agree, the buyer has a right to inspect the goods before payment or acceptance. Section 2–513(1). (Section 2A–515(1) provides for the right to inspect before acceptance.) This **inspection** enables him to ascertain whether the goods tendered or delivered conform to the contract. If the contract requires payment before acceptance (where, for example, the contract provides for shipment C.O.D. [collect on delivery]), payment must be made prior to inspection unless the nonconformity appears without inspection. Section 2–512. Payment, however, in such a case is not an acceptance of the goods and impairs neither the buyer's right to inspect nor any of his remedies.

The buyer, allowed a reasonable time in which to inspect the goods, may lose the right to reject or revoke acceptance of nonconforming goods by failing to inspect them in a timely manner. The expenses of inspection must be borne by the buyer but may be recovered from the seller if the goods do not conform and are rejected. Section 2–513(2); Section 2A–520(1).

CISG The buyer is not bound to pay the price until he has had an opportunity to examine the goods, unless the parties have agreed otherwise. The buyer must examine the goods within as short a period of time as is practicable in the circumstances. The buyer loses the right to rely on a lack of conformity of the goods if he does not give notice to the seller of the nonconformity within a reasonable time after he has discovered it or ought to have discovered it.

REJECTION

Rejection is a manifestation by the buyer of his unwillingness to become the owner of the goods. It must be made within a reasonable time after the goods have been tendered or delivered and is not effective unless the buyer seasonably notifies the seller. Section 2–602(1); Section 2A–509(2).

The rejection of tendered or delivered goods may be rightful or wrongful, depending on whether the goods conform to the contract. The buyer's rejection of nonconforming goods or tender is rightful under the perfect tender rule. Nonetheless, if the buyer refuses a tender of goods or rejects it as nonconforming without disclosing to the seller the nature of the defect, she may not assert such defect as an excuse for not accepting the goods or as a breach of contract by the seller if the defect is curable. Section 2–605(1); Section 2A–514(1).

After the buyer has rejected the goods, any attempt she makes to exercise ownership of the goods is wrongful as against the seller. (Because the lessor retains title in a lease, this does not apply to leases.) If the buyer has possession of the rejected goods but does not have a security interest in

them, she is obliged to hold them with reasonable care for a time sufficient to permit the seller to remove them. Section 2–602(2)(b); Section 2A–512(1). The buyer who is not a merchant is under no further obligation with regard to goods rightfully rejected. Section 2–602(2); Section 2A–512(1)(c). If the seller gives no instructions within a reasonable time after notification of rejection, the buyer may (1) store the goods for the seller's account, (2) reship them to the seller, or (3) resell them for the seller's account. Such action is not an acceptance or conversion of the goods. Section 2–604; Section 2A–511(2). A *merchant* buyer of goods who has rightfully rejected them has additional duties: she is obligated to follow reasonable instructions from the seller with respect to the disposition of the goods in her possession or control when the seller has no agent or business at the place of rejection. Section 2–603(1); Section 2A–511(1). If the merchant buyer receives no instructions from the seller within a reasonable time after giving notice of the rejection, and the rejected goods are perishable or threaten to decline in value speedily, she is obligated to make reasonable efforts to sell them for the seller's account. Section 2–603(1); Section 2A–511(1).

When the buyer sells the rejected goods, she is entitled to reimbursement for the reasonable expenses of caring for and selling them and a reasonable selling commission not to exceed 10 percent of the gross proceeds. Section 2–603(2); Section 2A–511(2).

CISG If the goods do not conform to the contract and the nonconformity constitutes a fundamental breach of contract, the buyer may require delivery of substitute goods. If the buyer has received the goods and intends to exercise any right under the contract or the CISG to reject them, she must take such steps to preserve them as are reasonable in the circumstances. She is entitled to retain them until she has been reimbursed her reasonable expenses by the seller.

ACCEPTANCE

Acceptance of goods means a willingness by the buyer to become the owner of the goods tendered or delivered to him by the seller. Acceptance of the goods, which includes overt acts or conduct manifesting such willingness, precludes any subsequent rejection of the goods. Section 2–607(2); Section 2A–516(2). Acceptance may be indicated by express words, by the presumed intention of the buyer through his failure to act, or by conduct of the buyer that is inconsistent with the seller's ownership of the goods. More specifically, acceptance occurs when the buyer, after a reasonable opportunity to inspect the goods, (1) signifies to the seller that the goods conform to the contract, (2) signifies to the seller that he will take the goods or retain them in spite of their nonconformity to the contract, or (3) fails to make an effective rejection of the goods. Section 2–606(1); Section 2A–515(1).

Acceptance, as previously noted, of any part of a commercial unit is acceptance of the entire unit. Section 2–606(2); Section 2A–515(2). Although the buyer must pay at the contract rate for those commercial units he accepts, he is entitled, after giving the seller timely notice of the breach, to recover from the seller or to deduct from the purchase price the amount of damages for nonconformity of the commercial units he has accepted and for nondelivery of the commercial units he has rejected. Sections 2–714 and 2–717; Sections 2A–516(1) and 2A–508(6) (except for finance leases in some situations). For example, Nancy agrees to deliver to Paul five hundred light bulbs of 100 watts each for $300 and one thousand light bulbs of 60 watts each for $500. Nancy delivers on time, but the shipment contains only four hundred of the 100-watt bulbs and eight hundred of the 60-watt bulbs. If Paul accepts the shipment, he must pay Nancy $240 for the 100-watt bulbs accepted and $400 for the 60-watt bulbs accepted, less the amount of damages Nancy's nonconforming delivery caused him.

When goods are rejected by the buyer, the burden is on the seller to establish their conformity to the contract; but the burden is on the buyer to establish any breach of contract (including warranty) with regard to goods accepted. Section 2–607(4); Section 2A–516(3)(c).

REVOCATION OF ACCEPTANCE

A buyer might accept defective goods either because discovering the defect by inspection was difficult or because the buyer reasonably assumed that the seller would correct the defect. In either instance the buyer may revoke his acceptance of the goods if the uncorrected defect substantially impairs the value of the goods to him. With respect to the goods, **revocation of acceptance** gives the buyer rights and duties that are the same as if he had rejected them. Section 2–608(3); Section 2A–517(5).

More specifically, the buyer may revoke his acceptance of goods that do not conform to the contract when such nonconformity *substantially* impairs the value of the goods to him, provided that his acceptance was (1) premised on the reasonable assumption that the seller would cure the nonconformity, and it was not seasonably cured; or (2) made without discovery of the nonconformity, and such acceptance was reasonably induced by the difficulty of discovery before acceptance or by the seller's assurances. Section 2–608(1); Section 2A–517(1).

Revocation of acceptance is not effective until notification is given to the seller. This must be done within a reasonable time after the buyer discovers or should have discovered the grounds for revocation and before the goods

have undergone any substantial change not caused by their own defects. Section 2–608(2); Section 2A–517(4).

OBLIGATION OF PAYMENT

The terms of the contract may expressly state the time and place at which the buyer is obligated to pay for the goods. If so, these terms are controlling. Thus, if the buyer has agreed to pay either the seller or a carrier for the goods in advance of delivery, his duty to pay is not conditioned upon performance or a tender of performance by the seller. Furthermore, where the sale is on credit, the buyer is not obligated to pay for the goods when he receives them, as the credit provision in the contract will control the time of payment. Unless the parties agree otherwise, payment is due at the time and place at which the buyer is to receive the goods, even though the place of shipment is the place of delivery. Section 2–310(a). This rule is understandable in view of the buyer's right, in the absence of agreement to the contrary, to inspect the goods before being obliged to pay for them.

Tender of payment in the ordinary course of business is sufficient when made by any means or in any manner current, such as a check, unless the seller demands cash and allows the buyer a reasonable time within which to obtain it. Payment by personal check is defeated as between seller and buyer, however, if the check is not paid when the seller attempts to cash it. Section 2–511(3).

CISG Unless the buyer is bound to pay the price at any other specific time, he must pay it when the seller places either the goods or documents controlling their disposition at the buyer's disposal in accordance with the contract and the CISG. The seller may make such payment a condition for handing over the goods or documents. If the buyer is not bound to pay the price at any other particular place, he must pay it to the seller: (1) at the seller's place of business; or (2) if the payment is to be made against the handing over of the goods or of documents, at the place where the handing over takes place.

◆ **SEE FIGURE 22-2: Performance by the Buyer**

OBLIGATIONS OF BOTH PARTIES

Contracts for the sale of goods necessarily involve risks concerning future events that may or may not occur. In some instances, the parties explicitly allocate these risks; in most instances, they do not. The Code contains three sections that allocate these risks when the parties fail to do so. Each provision, when applicable, relieves the parties from the obligation of full performance under the sales contract. The first

◆ **FIGURE 22-2: Performance by the Buyer**

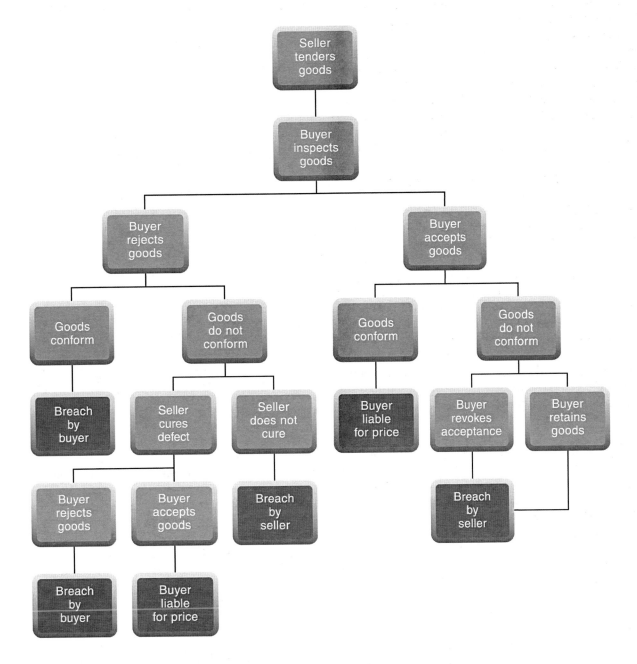

section deals with casualty to identified goods, the second with the nonhappening of presupposed conditions, and the third with substituted performance.

Related to the subject of whether the Code will excuse performance is the question of whether both parties are able and willing to perform. Should one party seem unwilling or unable, the Code allows the other party to seek reasonable assurance of the potentially defaulting party's willingness and ability to perform. In addition, if one of the parties

clearly indicates an unwillingness or inability to perform, the Code protects the other party.

CASUALTY TO IDENTIFIED GOODS

If goods are destroyed before an offer to sell or buy them is accepted, the offer is terminated by general contract law. But what if the goods are destroyed after the sales contract is formed? The rules for the passage of risk of loss (as discussed in *Chapter 23*) apply with one exception: the contract is for goods that are identified when the contract was made and the goods suffer damage without fault of either party *before* the risk of loss passes to the buyer. The outcome of this situation depends upon the degree of damage. (1) If these goods are *totally* lost or damaged, the contract is avoided. Section 2–613(a); Section 2A–221(a). This means that each party is excused from his performance obligation under the contract: the seller is no longer obligated to deliver and the buyer need not pay the price.

(2) In the case of a *partial* destruction or deterioration of the goods, the buyer may avoid the contract or may accept the goods with due allowance or deduction from the contract price sufficient to account for the deterioration or deficiency. Section 2–613(b); Section 2A–221(b) (except in a finance lease that is not a consumer lease). Thus, Adams agrees to sell to Taylor a specific lot of wheat containing one thousand bushels at a price of $4 per bushel. Without the fault of Adams or Taylor, fire destroys three hundred bushels of the wheat. Taylor does not have to take the remaining seven hundred bushels of wheat, but he has the option to do so upon paying $2,800, the price of seven hundred bushels.

On the other hand, if the destruction or damage to the goods, whether total or partial, occurs *after* risk of loss has passed to the buyer, the buyer has no option but must pay the entire contract price of the goods.

NONHAPPENING OF PRESUPPOSED CONDITION

The ability to perform a contract for the sale of goods is subject to a number of possible hazards, such as strikes, lockouts, the unforeseen shutdown of supply sources, or the loss of a plant or machinery by fire or other casualty. Ordinarily such difficulties do not operate as an excuse on the ground of impossibility of performance, unless the contract expressly so provides. Both parties may have understood when they made the contract, however, that its performance depended upon the existence of certain facilities or that the purpose of the contract and the value of performance depended entirely upon the happening of a specific future event. In such a case, the seller is excused from her duty of performance upon the nonoccurrence of presupposed conditions which were a basic assumption of the contract, unless the seller has expressly assumed the risk. Section 2–615(a); Section 2A–405(a). Although the nonhappening of presupposed conditions may relieve the seller of her contractual duty, if the contingency affects only a part of the seller's capacity to perform, she must, to the extent of her remaining capacity, allocate delivery and production in a fair and reasonable manner among her customers. Section 2–615(b); Section 2A–405(b).

Central to the Code's approach to impossibility is the concept of **commercial impracticability**, through which the

Code will excuse performance that, while not actually or literally impossible, is commercially impracticable. This, however, requires more than mere hardship or increased cost of performance. For a party to be discharged, performance must be rendered impracticable as a result of an unforeseen supervening event not within the contemplation of the parties at the time of contracting. Moreover, the nonoccurrence of the event must have been a "basic assumption" that both parties made when entering into the contract.

Increased production cost alone does not excuse performance by the seller, nor does a collapse of the market for the goods excuse the buyer. But a party to a contract for the sale of programs for a scheduled but subsequently canceled yacht regatta, or for the sale of tin horns for export, which become subject to embargo, or for the production of goods at a designated factory that suffers extensive fire damage would be excused from performance on the basis of commercial impracticability.

SUBSTITUTED PERFORMANCE

The Code provides that where neither party is at fault and the agreed manner of delivering the goods becomes commercially impracticable, as by the failure of loading or unloading facilities or the unavailability of an agreed type of carrier, a substituted manner of performance, if commercially reasonable, must be tendered and accepted. Section 2–614(1); Section 2A–404(1). Where a practical alternative or substitute exists, the Code excuses neither seller nor buyer on the ground that delivery in the express manner provided in the contract is impossible.

RIGHT TO ADEQUATE ASSURANCE OF PERFORMANCE

A contract of sale also requires that each party not impair the other party's expectation of having the contract performed. While the essential purpose of a contract is actual performance, an important feature of such performance is a secure and continuing sense that performance will occur when due. If, after contracting but before the time for performance, either the willingness or ability of a party to perform is put in doubt, the other party is threatened with the loss of a substantial part of what he has bargained for.

Therefore, when reasonable grounds for insecurity arise regarding either party's performance, the other party may demand written assurance and suspend his own performance until he receives that assurance. The failure to provide adequate assurance of performance within a reasonable time not exceeding thirty days constitutes a repudiation of the contract. Section 2–609; Section 2A–401.

CISG A party may suspend the performance of his obligations if, after the conclusion of the contract, it becomes apparent that the other party will not perform a substantial part of his obligations. A party suspending performance must immediately notify the other party of the suspension and must continue with performance if the other party provides adequate assurance of his performance.

RIGHT TO COOPERATION

Where one party's cooperation is necessary to the agreed performance but is not timely forthcoming, the other party is excused with regard to any resulting delay in her own performance. The nonbreaching party either may proceed to perform in any reasonable manner or, if the time for her performance has occurred, may treat the other's failure to cooperate as a breach. In either event, the nonbreaching party has access to any other remedies the Code may provide, as discussed in *Chapter 25*.

ANTICIPATORY REPUDIATION

While a repudiation is a clear indication by either party that he is unwilling or unable to perform his obligations under the contract, an **anticipatory repudiation** is a repudiation made *before* the time to perform occurs. It may occur by express communication or by the repudiating party's taking an action that makes performance impossible, such as selling unique goods to a third party. A repudiation also may result from a party's failure to give timely assurance of performance after a justifiable demand. If an anticipatory repudiation substantially impairs the value of the contract, the aggrieved party may (1) await performance for a commercially reasonable time or (2) resort to any remedy for breach. In either case, he may suspend his own performance. Section 2–610; Section 2A–402. The repudiating party may retract his anticipatory repudiation and thereby reinstate the contract unless the aggrieved party has canceled the contract, materially changed his position, or otherwise indicated that she considers the anticipatory repudiation final. Section 2–611; Section 2A–403.

CISG If prior to the date for performance of the contract it is clear that one of the parties will commit a fundamental breach of contract, the other party may declare the contract avoided.

CHAPTER SUMMARY

PERFORMANCE BY THE SELLER

Tender of Delivery the seller makes available to the buyer goods conforming to the contract and so notifies the buyer
- *Buyer* is obligated to accept conforming goods
- *Seller* is entitled to receive payment of the contract price

Time and Manner of Tender tender must be made at a reasonable time and kept open for a reasonable period of time

Place of Tender if none is specified, place for delivery is the seller's place of business or, if he has no such place, his residence
- *Shipment Contracts* seller is required to tender delivery of the goods to a carrier for delivery to buyer; shipment terms include the following: *F.O.B. place of shipment, F.A.S. port of shipment, C.I.F., C.&F.*
- *Destination Contracts* seller is required to tender delivery of the goods at a named destination; destination terms include the following: *F.O.B. place of destination, ex-ship*, and *no arrival, no sale*
- *Goods Held by Bailee* seller must either tender to the buyer a document of title or obtain an acknowledgment from the bailee

Perfect Tender Rule the seller's tender of performance must conform exactly to the contract, subject to the following qualifications:
- *Agreement by the Parties* the parties may contractually limit the operation of the perfect tender rule

- *Cure by the Seller* when the time for performance under the contract has not expired or when the seller has shipped nonconforming goods in the belief that the nonconforming tender would be acceptable, a seller may cure or correct her nonconforming tender
- *Installment Contracts* when the contract calls for the goods to be delivered in separate lots, the buyer may reject a nonconforming installment if it substantially impairs the value of that installment and cannot be cured; but if nonconformity or default of one or more of the installments substantially impairs the value of the whole contract, the buyer can treat the breach as a breach of the whole contract

PERFORMANCE BY THE BUYER	**Inspection** unless otherwise agreed, the buyer has a reasonable time in which to inspect the goods before payment or acceptance to determine whether they conform **Rejection** buyer's manifestation of unwillingness to become the owner of the goods; must be made within a reasonable time after the goods have been tendered or delivered and gives the buyer the right to (1) reject all of the goods, (2) accept all of the goods, or (3) accept any commercial unit(s) and reject the rest **Acceptance** buyer's express or implied manifestation of willingness to become the owner of the goods **Revocation of Acceptance** rescission of buyer's acceptance of the goods if nonconformity of the goods substantially impairs their value, provided that the acceptance was (1) premised on the assumption that the nonconformity would be cured by the seller and it was not, or (2) the nonconformity was an undiscovered hidden defect **Obligation of Payment** in the absence of an agreement, payment is due at the time and place the buyer is to receive the goods
OBLIGATIONS OF BOTH PARTIES	**Casualty to Identified Goods** if the contract is for goods that were identified when the contract was made and those goods are totally lost or damaged without fault of either party and before the risk of loss has passed to the buyer, the contract is avoided **Nonhappening of Presupposed Condition** the seller is excused from the duty of performance on the nonoccurrence of presupposed conditions that were a basic assumption of the contract, unless the seller has expressly assumed the risk **Substituted Performance** where neither party is at fault and the agreed manner of goods becomes commercially impracticable, a substituted manner of performance must be tendered and accepted **Right to Adequate Assurance of Performance** when reasonable grounds for insecurity arise regarding either party's performance, the other party may demand written assurance and suspend his own performance until he receives that assurance **Right to Cooperation** where one party's required cooperation is untimely, the other party is excused from any resulting delay in her own performance **Anticipatory Repudiation** if either party clearly indicates an unwillingness or inability to perform before the performance is due, the other party may await performance for a reasonable time or resort to any remedy for breach

Transfer of Title and Risk of Loss

Historically, title governed nearly every aspect of the rights and duties of the buyer and seller arising out of a sales contract. In an attempt to add greater precision and certainty to sales contracts, the Uniform Commercial Code (UCC or Code) has abandoned the common law's reliance upon title. Instead, the Code approaches each legal issue arising out of a sales contract on its own merits and provides separate and specific rules to control the various transactional situations. This chapter covers the Code's approach to the transfer of title and other property rights, the passage of risk of loss, and the transfer of goods sold in bulk.

TRANSFER OF TITLE

As previously stated, a sale of goods is defined as the transfer of title from the seller to the buyer for a price. Section 2–106. Transfer of title is, therefore, fundamental to a sale of goods. Title, however, cannot pass under a contract for sale until existing goods have been identified as those to which the contract refers. Section 2–401(1). Future goods (goods that are not both existing and identified) cannot constitute a present sale. Section 2–105. If the buyer rejects the goods, whether justifiably or not, title revests to the seller. Section 2–401(4).

In a lease, title does not pass. Instead, the lessee obtains the right to possess and use the goods for a period of time in return for consideration. Section 2A–103(1)(j).

IDENTIFICATION

After formation of the contract, the seller normally takes steps to obtain, manufacture, prepare, or select goods with which to fulfill her obligation under the contract. At some stage in the process the seller will have identified existing goods that she intends to ship, deliver, or hold for the buyer. Identification may be made by either the seller or the buyer and can be made at any time and in any manner agreed

upon by the parties. In the absence of explicit agreement, **identification** takes place as provided in Section 2–501(1) (Section 2A–217 contains similar, but not identical, provisions):

1. upon the making of the contract if it is for goods already existing and identified;
2. if the contract is for all other future goods, when the seller ships, marks, or otherwise designates existing goods as those to which the contract refers; or
3. if the contract is (a) for crops to be grown within twelve months or at the time of the next normal harvest, when the crops are planted or start growing, or (b) for the offspring of animals to be born within twelve months, when the young animals are conceived.

To illustrate, suppose Barringer contracts to purchase a particular Buick automobile from Stevenson's car lot. Identification occurs as soon as the contract is entered into. If, however, Barringer agrees to purchase a television set from Stevenson, whose storeroom is filled with such televisions, identification will not occur until either Barringer or Stevenson selects a particular television to fulfill the contract.

Fungible goods are goods of which any unit, by nature, agreement, or usage of trade, is the equivalent of any other like unit. Section 1–201(17); Revised Section 1–201(b)(18). If the goods are fungible, identification of a share of undivided goods occurs when the contract is entered into. Thus, if Barringer agrees to purchase one thousand gallons of gasoline from Stevenson, who owns a five-thousand-gallon tank of gasoline, identification occurs as soon as the contract is formed.

INSURABLE INTEREST For a contract or policy of insurance to be valid, the insured must have an insurable interest in the subject matter (see *Chapter 48*). At common law only a person with title or a lien (a legal claim of a creditor on property) could insure his interest in specific goods. The Code extends this right to a buyer's interest in goods that have been identified as goods to which the contract refers. Section 2–501(1); Section 2A–218(1). This **special property**

interest of the buyer enables her to purchase insurance protection on goods that she does not presently own but that she will own upon delivery by the seller.

So long as he has title to them or any security interest in them, the seller also has an insurable interest in the goods. Section 2–501(2). Nothing prevents both seller and buyer from simultaneously carrying insurance on goods in which they both have a property interest, whether it be title, a security interest, or a special property interest. In a lease, the lessor retains an insurable interest in the goods until an option to buy, if included in the lease, has been exercised by the lessee. Section 2A–218(3).

SECURITY INTEREST The Code defines a security interest as an interest in personal property or fixtures that ensures payment or performance of an obligation. Section 1–201(37); Revised Section 1–201(b)(35). Any reservation by the seller of title to goods delivered to the buyer is limited in effect to a reservation of a security interest. Section 2–401(1). As mentioned above, the seller retains an insurable interest in goods for which he holds title or any security interest. Section 2–501(2). Security interests in goods are governed by Article 9 of the Code (discussed in *Chapter 38*).

PASSAGE OF TITLE

Title passes when the parties *intend* it to pass, provided the goods are in existence and have been identified. Where the parties have no explicit agreement as to transfer of title, the Code provides rules that determine when title passes to the buyer. Section 2–401.

PHYSICAL MOVEMENT OF THE GOODS When delivery is to be made by moving the goods, title passes at the time and place the seller completes his performance with reference to delivery of the goods. Section 2–401(2). When and where delivery occurs depends on whether the contract is a shipment contract or a destination contract.

A **shipment contract** requires or authorizes the seller to send the goods to the buyer but does not require the seller to deliver them to a particular destination. Under a shipment contract, title passes to the buyer at the time and place that the seller *delivers* the goods to the carrier for shipment to the buyer.

A **destination contract** requires the seller to deliver the goods to a particular destination. Under a destination contract, title passes to the buyer upon *tender* of the goods at that destination. Tender, as discussed in *Chapter 22*, requires that the seller (1) put and hold conforming goods at the buyer's disposition, (2) give the buyer reasonable notice that the goods are available, and (3) keep the goods available for a reasonable time. Section 2–503.

NO MOVEMENT OF THE GOODS When delivery is to be made without moving the goods, unless otherwise agreed, title passes (1) upon delivery of a document of title, if the contract calls for delivery of such document (documents of title are documents that evidence a right to receive specified goods—they are discussed more fully in *Chapter 48*); or (2) at the time and place of contracting, if the goods at the time have been identified and no documents are to be delivered. Section 2–401(3). Where the goods are not identified at the time of contracting, title passes when the goods are identified.

For a summary of passage of title in the absence of an agreement by the parties, see *Figure 23-1*.

◆ **SEE FIGURE 23-1: Passage of Title in Absence of Agreement by Parties**

POWER TO TRANSFER TITLE

It is important to understand under what circumstances a seller has the right or power to transfer title to a buyer. If the seller is the rightful owner of goods or is authorized to sell the goods for the rightful owner, then the seller has the **right** to transfer title. But when a seller is in possession of goods that he neither owns nor has authority to sell, then the sale is not rightful. In some situations, however, these unauthorized sellers may have the **power** to transfer good title to certain buyers. This section pertains to such sales by a person in possession of goods that he neither owns nor has authority to sell.

The fundamental rule of property law protecting existing ownership of goods is the starting point for any discussion of a sale of goods by a nonowner. A basic tenet of the law is that a purchaser of goods obtains such title as his transferor had or had power to transfer, and the Code expressly so states. Section 2–403; Sections 2A–304 and 2A–305. Likewise, the purchaser of a limited interest in goods acquires rights only to the extent of the interest that he purchased. By the same token, no one can transfer what he does not have. A purported sale by a thief or finder or ordinary bailee of goods does not transfer title to the purchaser.

The principal reason underlying the policy of the law in protecting existing ownership of goods is that a person should not be required to retain possession at all times of all the goods that he owns in order to maintain his ownership of them. Incidental to the ownership of goods is the owner's freedom to make a bailment of his goods as desired; the mere possession of goods by a bailee does not authorize the bailee to sell them.

A second policy, one concerning the protection of the good faith purchaser, conflicts with the policy protecting existing ownership of goods. Protecting the expectations of good faith transactions in goods is of paramount importance in trade and commerce. To encourage and make safe good faith acquisitions of goods, *bona fide* (good faith) purchasers for value must be protected under certain circumstances. A **good faith purchaser** is defined as one who acts honestly,

◆ **FIGURE 23-1: Passage of Title in Absence of Agreement by Parties**

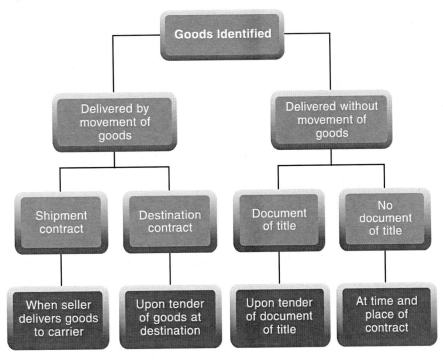

gives value, and takes the goods without notice or knowledge of any defect in the title of his transferor.

VOID AND VOIDABLE TITLE TO GOODS A **void title** is no title. A person claiming ownership of goods by an agreement that is void obtains no title to the goods. Thus, a thief or a finder of goods or a person who acquires goods from someone under physical duress or under guardianship has no title to them and can transfer none.

A **voidable title** is one acquired under circumstances that permit the former owner to rescind the transfer and revest herself with title, as in the case of mistake, common duress, undue influence, fraud in the inducement, misrepresentation, mistake, or sale by a person without contractual capacity (other than an individual under guardianship). In these situations, the buyer has acquired legal title to the goods, which may be divested by action of the seller. If, however, before the seller has rescinded the transfer of title, the buyer were to resell the goods to a good faith purchaser for value, the right of rescission in the seller is cut off, and the good faith purchaser for value acquires good title. The Code defines good faith as "honesty in fact in the conduct or transaction concerned"; for merchants, and all parties under Revised Article 1, good faith also requires the observance of reasonable commercial standards of fair dealing. Section 1–201. The Code defines value to include a consideration sufficient to support a simple contract. Section 1–201; Revised Section 1–204.

The distinction between a void and voidable title is, therefore, extremely important in determining the rights of good faith purchasers of goods. The good faith purchaser for value always believes that she is buying the goods from the owner or from one with authority to sell. Otherwise she would not be acting in good faith. In each situation, the party selling the goods appears to be the owner whether his title is valid, void, or voidable. Given a transaction involving two innocent persons—the true owner and the good faith purchaser for value, who have done nothing wrong—the law will not disturb the *legal title* but will rule in favor of the one who has it. Thus, where A transfers possession of goods to B under such circumstances that B acquires no title or a void title, and B thereafter sells the goods to C, a good faith purchaser for value, B has nothing except possession to transfer to C. In a lawsuit between A and C involving the right to the goods, A will win because she has the legal title. C's only recourse is against B for breach of warranty of title, discussed in *Chapter 24*.

If, however, B acquired voidable title from A and resold the goods to C, in a suit between A and C over the goods, C would win. In this case, B had title, although it was voidable, which she transferred to the good faith purchaser for value. The title thus acquired by C will be protected. The voidable title in B, which is title until it has been avoided, may not be avoided after transfer to a good faith purchaser. A's only recourse is against B for restitution or damages.

◆ **FIGURE 23-2: Void Title**

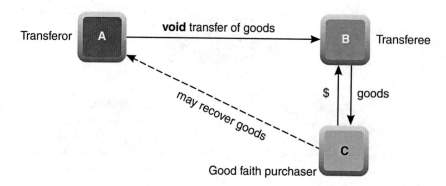

The Code has enlarged this common law doctrine by providing that a good faith purchaser for value obtains valid title from one possessing voidable title even if that person obtained voidable title by (1) fraud as to her identity; (2) exchange for a subsequently dishonored check; (3) an agreement that the transaction was to be a cash sale, and the sale price has not been paid; or (4) criminal fraud punishable as larceny. Section 2–403(1); (Sections 2A–304 and 2A–305 are similar).

In addition, the Code has expanded the rights of good faith purchasers with respect to sales by **minors**. While the common law permitted a minor seller of goods to disaffirm the sale and to recover the goods from a third person who had purchased them in good faith from the party who acquired the goods from the minor, the Code has changed this rule by no longer permitting a minor seller of goods to prevail over a good faith purchaser for value. Section 2–403.

◆ **SEE FIGURE 23-2: Void Title**

◆ **SEE FIGURE 23-3: Voidable Title**

ENTRUSTING OF GOODS TO A MERCHANT

Frequently, an owner of goods entrusts (transfers possession of) the goods to a bailee for resale, repair, cleaning, or some other use. In some instances, the bailee violates this entrusting by selling the goods to a third party. Although the "true" owner has a right of recourse against the bailee for the value of the goods, what right, if any, should the true owner of the goods have against the third party? Once again the law must balance the right of ownership against the rights of market transactions.

The Code takes the position of protecting a buyer of goods in the ordinary course of business from a merchant who deals in goods of the kind involved in the sale, where the owner has entrusted possession of the goods to the merchant. The Code defines **buyer in ordinary course of business** as a person that buys goods in good faith, without knowledge that the sale violates the rights of another person in the goods, and in the ordinary course of business from a person, other than a pawnbroker, in the business of selling goods of that kind. Section 1–201(9); Revised Section 1–201(b)(9). Because the merchant who deals in goods of

◆ **FIGURE 23-3: Voidable Title**

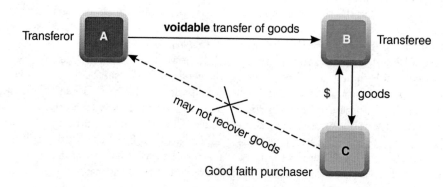

that kind is cloaked with the appearance of ownership or apparent authority to sell, the Code seeks to protect the innocent third-party purchaser. Any such entrusting of possession bestows upon the merchant the power to transfer all rights of the entruster to a buyer in the ordinary course of business. Section 2–403(2); (Sections 2A–304(2) and 2A–305(2) are similar). For example, A brings her stereo for repair to B, who also sells both new and used stereo equipment. C purchases A's stereo from B in the ordinary course of business. The Code protects the rights of C and defeats the rights of A. A's only recourse is against B.

The Code, however, does not go so far as to protect the buyer in the ordinary course of business from a merchant to whom a thief, a finder, or a completely unauthorized person has entrusted the goods. It merely grants the buyer in the ordinary course of business the rights of the entruster.

Where a buyer of goods to whom title has passed leaves the seller in possession of the goods, the buyer has "entrusted the goods" to the seller. Section 2–403(3). If that seller is a merchant and resells and delivers the goods to another buyer in the ordinary course of business, this second buyer acquires good title to the goods. Thus, Marianne sells certain goods to Martin, who pays the price but allows possession to remain with Marianne. Marianne thereafter sells the same goods to Carla, a buyer in the ordinary course of business. Carla takes delivery of the goods. Martin does not have any rights against Carla or to the goods. Martin's only remedy is against Marianne.

◆ **SEE FIGURE 23-4: Entrusting of Goods to a Merchant**

RISK OF LOSS

Risk of loss, as the term is used in the law of sales, addresses the question of allocation of loss between seller and buyer where the goods have been damaged, destroyed, or lost *without the fault* of either the seller or the buyer. If the loss is placed on the buyer, he is under a duty to pay the price for the goods even though they were damaged or he never received them. If loss is placed upon the seller, he has no right to recover the purchase price from the buyer and is usually liable to the buyer for damages for nondelivery unless he tenders a performance in replacement of the lost or destroyed goods.

> **CISG** Loss of or damage to the goods after the risk of loss has passed to the buyer does not discharge the buyer from his obligation to pay the purchase price.

In determining which party carries the risk of loss, the Code provides definite rules for specific situations, a sharp departure from the common law concept of risk of loss, which was determined by ownership of the goods and which depended upon the transfer of title. The transactional approach under the Code is necessarily detailed and for this reason is probably more understandable and meaningful than the common law's reliance upon the abstract concept of title. The Code has adopted rules for determining the risk of loss in the absence of breach separate from those that apply where the sales contract has been breached.

Except in a finance lease, risk of loss is retained by the lessor and does not pass to the lessee. Section 2A–219(1). In a finance lease, risk of loss passes to the lessee.

RISK OF LOSS WHERE THERE IS A BREACH

Where one party breaches the contract, the Code places the risk of loss on the breaching party. Nevertheless, where the nonbreaching party is in control of the goods, the Code places the risk of loss on him to the extent of his insurance coverage.

BREACH BY THE SELLER If the seller ships nonconforming goods to the buyer, the risk of loss remains on the seller until the buyer has accepted the goods or the seller has remedied the defect. Section 2–510(1); Section 2A–220(1)(a).

◆ **FIGURE 23-4: Entrusting of Goods to a Merchant**

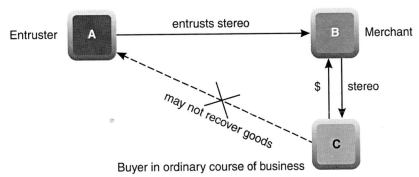

Where the buyer has accepted nonconforming goods, and thereafter by timely notice to the seller rightfully revokes his acceptance (discussed in *Chapter 22*), he may treat the risk of loss, to the extent of any deficiency in his effective insurance coverage, as resting from the beginning on the seller. Section 2–510(2); Section 2A–220(1)(b). For example, Heidi delivers to Gary nonconforming goods, which Gary accepts. Subsequently, Gary discovers a hidden defect in the goods and rightfully revokes his prior acceptance. If the goods are destroyed through no fault of either party, and Gary has insured the goods for 60 percent of their fair market value of $10,000, then the insurance company will cover $6,000 of the loss and Heidi will bear the remainder of the loss, or $4,000. Had the buyer's insurance coverage been $10,000, the seller would not bear any of the loss.

BREACH BY THE BUYER Where conforming goods have been identified to a contract that the buyer repudiates or breaches before risk of loss has passed to him, the seller may treat the risk of loss as resting on the buyer "for a commercially reasonable time" to the extent of any deficiency in the seller's effective insurance coverage. Section 2–510(3); Section 2A–220(2). For example, Susan agrees to sell forty thousand pounds of plastic resin to Bernie, F.O.B. (free on board) Bernie's factory, delivery by March 1. On February 1, Bernie wrongfully repudiates the contract by telephoning Susan and telling her that he does not want the resin. Susan immediately seeks another buyer, but before she is able to locate one, and within a commercially reasonable time, the resin is destroyed by a fire through no fault of Susan's. The fair market value of the resin is $35,000. Because Susan's insurance covers only $15,000 of the loss, Bernie is liable for $20,000.

RISK OF LOSS IN ABSENCE OF A BREACH

Where there is no breach of contract, the parties may by agreement allocate the risk of loss. Where there is no breach, and the parties have not otherwise agreed, the Code places the risk of loss, for the most part, upon the party who is more likely to have greater control over the goods, is more likely to insure the goods, or is better able to prevent their loss.

AGREEMENT OF THE PARTIES The parties, by agreement, not only may shift the allocation of risk of loss but also may divide the risk between them. Section 2–303. Such agreement is controlling. Thus, the parties may agree, for example, that the seller shall retain the risk of loss even though the buyer is in possession of the goods or has title to them. Or the agreement may provide that the buyer bears 60 percent of the risk and the seller bears 40 percent.

TRIAL SALES Some sales are made with the understanding that the buyer can return the goods even though they conform to the contract. Such trial sales permit a buyer to try

goods to determine whether she wishes to keep them or to try to resell them. The Code recognizes two types of trial sales, a sale on approval and a sale or return, and provides a test for distinguishing between them: unless otherwise agreed, if the goods are delivered primarily for the buyer's use, the transaction is a sale on approval; if they are delivered primarily for resale by the buyer, it is a sale or return. Section 2–326(1).

In a **sale on approval**, possession of, but not title to, the goods is transferred to the buyer for a stated time or, if no time is stated, for a reasonable time, during which the buyer may use the goods to determine whether she wishes to buy them. Both title and risk of loss remain with the *seller* until the buyer approves, or accepts, the goods. Section 2–327(1)(a). Until acceptance by the buyer, the sale is a bailment with an option to purchase.

Although use of the goods consistent with the purpose of approval is not acceptance, the buyer's failure to notify the seller within a reasonable time of her election to return the goods *is* an acceptance. The buyer also may manifest approval by exercising over the goods any dominion or control that is inconsistent with the seller's ownership. Upon approval, title and risk of loss passes to the buyer, who then becomes liable to the seller for the purchase price of the goods. If the buyer elects to return the goods and so notifies the seller, the return is at the seller's risk and expense.

In a **sale or return**, the goods are sold and delivered to the buyer with an option to return them to the seller. The risk of loss is on the *buyer*, who also has title until she revests it in the seller by returning the goods. The return of the goods is at the buyer's risk and expense.

A **consignment** is a delivery of possession of personal property to an agent for sale by the agent. Under the Code, a sale on consignment is regarded as a sale or return. Therefore, creditors of the consignee (the agent who receives the merchandise for sale) prevail over the consignor and may obtain possession of the consigned goods, provided the consignee maintains a place of business where he deals in goods of the kind involved under a name other than the name of the consignor. Nevertheless, under Section 2–326(3) the consignor will prevail if he (1) complies with applicable State law requiring a consignor's interest to be evidenced by a sign, (2) establishes that the consignee is generally known by his creditors to be substantially engaged in selling the goods of others, or (3) complies with the filing provisions of Article 9 (Secured Transactions). Section 2–326(3).

CONTRACTS INVOLVING CARRIERS Sales contracts frequently contain terms that indicate the agreement of the parties as to delivery by a carrier. These terms identify the contract as a shipment contract or a destination contract and, by implication, indicate when the risk of loss will pass. If the contract does not require the seller to deliver the goods to a particular destination but merely to the carrier (a **shipment contract**), risk of loss passes to the buyer upon *delivery* of the goods to the common carrier. If the seller is required to deliver them to a particular destination (a **destination contract**), risk of loss passes to the buyer at destination upon *tender* of the goods to the buyer. Section 2–509(1); Section 2A–219(2)(a).

Windows, Inc. v. Jordan Panel Systems Corp. deals with the question of when the risk of loss passes between parties whose contract makes no specific provision and contains no delivery term. The case demonstrates that if the contract is not clearly a destination contract or a shipment contract, the law assumes that it is a shipment contract.

CISG If the sales contract involves the carriage of the goods and the seller is not obligated to hand them over at a particular destination, the risk of loss passes to the buyer when the goods are handed over to the first carrier. If the contract requires the seller to deliver the goods to a carrier at a particular destination, the risk of loss passes when the goods are handed over to the carrier at that place.

GOODS IN POSSESSION OF BAILEE

In some sales, the goods, at the time the contract is made, are held by a bailee and are to be delivered without being moved. For instance, a seller may contract with a buyer to sell grain that is located in a grain elevator and that the buyer intends to leave in the same elevator. In such situations, Sections 2–509(2) and 2A–219(2)(b) provide that the risk of loss passes to the buyer when one of the following occurs:

1. If a negotiable document of title (discussed in *Chapter 48*; 1–201(15); Revised Section 1–201(b)(16)) is involved, the risk of loss passes upon the buyer's receipt of the document.
2. If a nonnegotiable document of title is involved, the risk passes when the document is tendered to the buyer.
3. If no documents of title are employed, risk passes upon either (a) the seller's tender to the buyer of written directions to the bailee to deliver the goods to the buyer or (b) the bailee's acknowledgment of the buyer's right to possession of the goods.

In situations 2 and 3(a), if the buyer seasonably objects, the risk of loss remains upon the seller until the buyer has had a reasonable time to present the document or direction to the bailee.

CISG If the buyer is bound to take over the goods at a place other than the seller's place of business, the risk of loss passes when the buyer is aware of the fact that the goods are placed at her disposal at that location.

ALL OTHER SALES

If the buyer possesses the goods when the contract is formed, risk of loss passes to the buyer at that time. Section 2–509(3); Section 2A–219(2)(c).

All other sales not involving breach are covered by Section 2–509(3). This catchall provision applies when the buyer picks up the goods at the seller's place of business or when the seller delivers the goods using her own transportation. In these cases, risk of loss depends on whether or not the seller is a **merchant**. If the seller is a merchant, risk of loss passes to the buyer upon the buyer's *receipt* of the goods. If the seller is **not a merchant**, it passes on *tender* of the goods from the seller to the buyer. Section 2–509(3); Section 2A–219(2)(c). The policy behind this rule is that so long as the merchant seller is making delivery at her place of business or with her own vehicle, she continues to control the goods and can be expected to insure them. The buyer, on the other hand, has no control over the goods and is not likely to have insurance on them.

Suppose Belinda goes to Sidney's furniture store, selects a particular set of dining room furniture, and pays Sidney the agreed price of $1,800 for it upon Sidney's agreement to stain the set a darker color and deliver it. Sidney stains the furniture and notifies Belinda that he will deliver it the following day. That night, the furniture is accidentally destroyed by fire. Belinda can recover from Sidney the $1,800 payment. The risk of loss is on seller Sidney as he is a merchant and the goods were not received by Belinda but were only tendered to her.

CISG If the sales contract does not involve the carriage of the goods, the risk of loss passes to the buyer when he takes over the goods, or, if the buyer does not take over the goods in due time, from the time when the goods are placed at his disposal.

On the other hand, suppose Georgia, an accountant, prior to moving to a different city, contracts to sell her household furniture to Nina for $3,000. Though Georgia notifies Nina that the furniture is available for her to pickup, Nina delays picking up the furniture for several days. In the interim, the furniture is stolen from Georgia's residence without her fault. Georgia may recover from Nina the $3,000 purchase price. The risk of loss is on the buyer (Nina), as the seller is not a merchant and tender is sufficient to transfer the risk.

◆ **SEE FIGURE 23-5: Passage of Risk of Loss in Absence of Breach**

◆ **FIGURE 23-5: Passage of Risk of Loss in Absence of Breach**

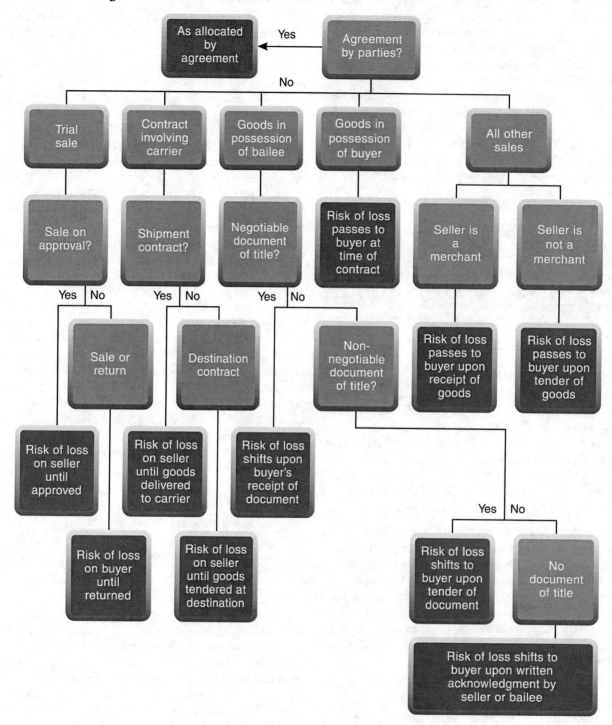

SALES OF GOODS IN BULK

Because a debtor may secretly liquidate all or a major part of his tangible assets by a bulk sale and conceal or divert the proceeds of the sale without paying his creditors, creditors have an obvious interest in a merchant's bulk disposal of his merchandise made not in the ordinary course of business. The central purpose of bulk sales law is to deter two common forms of commercial fraud, namely (1) when the merchant, owing debts, sells out his stock in trade to a friend for a low price, pays his creditors less than he owes them, and hopes to come back into the business "through the back door" sometime in the future; and (2) when the merchant, owing debts, sells out his stock in trade to anyone for any price, pockets the proceeds, and disappears without paying his creditors.

Article 6 of the Code, which applies to such sales, defines a **bulk transfer** as "any transfer in bulk and not in the ordinary course of the transferor's business of a major part of the materials, supplies, merchandise or other inventory." Section 6–102. The transfer of a substantial part of equipment is a bulk transfer only if made in connection with a bulk transfer of inventory. Those subject to Article 6 of the Code are merchants whose principal business is the sale of merchandise from stock, including those who manufacture what they sell.

In 1988, the National Conference of Commissioners on Uniform State Laws and the American Law Institute jointly issued a recommendation stating "that changes in the business and legal contexts in which sales are conducted have made regulation of bulk sales unnecessary." They, therefore, recommended the repeal of Article 6 or, for those States that felt the need to continue the regulation of bulk sales, the adoption of a revised Article 6 designed to afford better protection to creditors while minimizing the obstacles to good faith transactions. At least forty-five States have repealed Article 6, while only a few States have adopted Revised Article 6.

CHAPTER SUMMARY

TRANSFER OF TITLE

Identification designation of specific goods as goods to which the contract of sale refers
- *Insurable Interest* buyer obtains an insurable interest and specific remedies in the goods by the identification of existing goods as goods to which the contract of sale refers
- *Security Interest* an interest in personal property or fixtures that ensures payment or performance of an obligation

Passage of Title title passes when the parties intend it to pass; when the parties do not specifically agree, the Code provides rules to determine when title passes
- *Physical Movement of the Goods* when delivery is to be made by moving the goods, title passes at the time and place where the seller completes his performance with reference to delivery
- *No Movement of the Goods*

Power to Transfer Title the purchaser of goods obtains such title as her transferor either has or had the power to transfer; however, to encourage and make secure good faith acquisitions of goods, it is necessary to protect certain third parties under certain circumstances
- *Void Title* no title can be transferred
- *Voidable Title* the good faith purchaser acquires good title
- *Entrusting of Goods to a Merchant* buyers in the ordinary course of business acquire good title when buying from merchants

RISK OF LOSS

Definition allocation of loss between seller and buyer where the goods have been damaged, destroyed, or lost without the fault of either party

Risk of Loss Where There Is a Breach
- *Breach by the Seller* if the seller ships to the buyer goods that do not conform to the contract, the risk of loss remains on the seller until the buyer has accepted the goods or until the seller has remedied the defect
- *Breach by the Buyer* the seller may treat the risk of loss as resting on the buyer for a commercially reasonable time to the extent of any deficiency in the seller's effective insurance coverage

Risk of Loss in Absence of a Breach
- *Agreement of the Parties* the parties may by agreement allocate the risk of loss
- *Trial Sales* unless otherwise agreed, if the goods are delivered primarily for the buyer's use, the transaction is a sale on approval (risk of loss remains with the

seller until "approval" or acceptance of the goods by the buyer); if they are delivered primarily for resale by the buyer, it is a sale or return (the risk of loss is on the buyer until she returns the goods)
- ***Contracts Involving Carriers*** in shipment contracts, the seller bears the risk of loss and expense until the goods are delivered to the carrier for shipment; in destination contracts, the seller bears the risk of loss and expense until tender of the goods at a particular destination
- ***Goods in Possession of Bailee***
- ***All Other Sales*** for merchant seller, risk of loss passes to buyer on the buyer's receipt of the goods; for nonmerchant seller, risk of loss passes to buyer upon tender of goods

BULK SALES   **Definition** a transfer, not in the ordinary course of the transferor's business, of a major part of inventory

Requirements of Article 6 transfer is ineffective against any creditor of the transferor, unless certain requirements are met

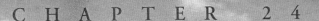

Products Liability: Warranties and Strict Liability in Tort

This chapter considers the liability of manufacturers and sellers of goods to buyers, users, consumers, and bystanders for damages caused by defective products. The rapidly expanding development of case law has established products liability as a distinct field of law that combines and enforces rules and principles of contracts, sales, negligence, strict liability in tort, and statutory law.

One reason for the expansion of this liability is the modern method of distributing goods. Today, retailers serve principally as conduits of prepackaged goods that are widely advertised by the manufacturer or distributor. This has brought about the extension of product liability coverage to include manufacturers and other parties along the chain of distribution. The extension of product liability to manufacturers, however, has not lessened the liability of the retailer to his immediate purchaser. Rather, it has broadened the base of liability through the development and application of new principles of law.

The entire area of products liability has attracted a great deal of public attention. According to the U.S. Consumer Product Safety Commission, deaths, injuries, and property damage from consumer product incidents cost the United States more than $800 billion annually. The resultant cost of maintaining product liability insurance has skyrocketed, causing great concern in the business community. In response to the clamor over this insurance crisis, almost all of the States have revised their tort laws to make successful tort (including product liability) lawsuits more difficult to bring. These tort reforms include legislation dealing with joint and several liability, punitive damages, noneconomic damages, and class actions. Nevertheless, repeated efforts to pass Federal product liability legislation have been unsuccessful.

The liability of manufacturers and other sellers of goods for a defective product, or for its failure to perform adequately, may be based upon one or more of the following: (1) negligence, (2) misrepresentation, (3) violation of statutory duty, (4) warranty, and (5) strict liability in tort. The first three causes of actions have been covered in *Chapters 8* and *11*.

Chapter 8 also covered traditional strict liability—where liability is imposed regardless of the defendant's negligence or intent to cause harm. In this chapter we will cover a specialized type of strict liability—strict liability in tort for products. This chapter will also explore warranty liability.

WARRANTIES

A **warranty**, under the Uniform Commercial Code (UCC or Code), creates a duty on the part of the seller that the goods she sells will conform to certain qualities, characteristics, or conditions. A seller, however, is not required to warrant the goods; and, in general, she may, by appropriate words, disclaim, exclude, negate, or modify a particular warranty or even all warranties.

In bringing a warranty action, the buyer must prove that (1) a warranty existed, (2) the warranty has been breached, (3) the breach of the warranty proximately caused the loss suffered, and (4) notice of the breach was given to the seller. The seller has the burden of proving defenses based on the buyer's conduct. If the seller breaches his warranty, the buyer may reject or revoke acceptance of the goods. Moreover, whether he has accepted or rejected the goods, the buyer may recover a judgment against the seller for damages. Harm for which damages are recoverable include personal injury, damage to property, and economic loss. Economic loss most commonly involves damages for loss of bargain and consequential damages for lost profits. (Damages for breach of warranty are discussed in the next chapter.) This section will examine the various types of warranties as well as the obstacles to a cause of action for breach of warranty.

TYPES OF WARRANTIES

A warranty may arise out of the mere existence of a sale (a warranty of title), any affirmation of fact or promise made by the seller to the buyer (an express warranty), or the circumstances under which the sale is made (an implied warranty). In a contract for the sale of goods, it is possible to have all three types of warranties. All warranties are construed as consistent with each other and cumulative, unless such a construction is unreasonable. A purchaser, as discussed in previous chapters, means a person who takes by sale, lease, lien, security interest, gift, or any other voluntary transaction creating an interest in property. Revised Article 1–201(b)(29), (30). (Prior Article 1 did not include leases.)

Article 2A carries over the warranty provisions of Article 2 with relatively minor revision to reflect differences in style, leasing terminology, or leasing practices. The creation of express warranties and, except for finance leases, the imposition of the implied warranties of merchantability and fitness for a particular purpose are virtually identical to their Article 2 analogues. Article 2 and Article 2A diverge somewhat in their treatment of the warranties of title and infringement as well as in their provisions for the exclusion and modification of warranties.

WARRANTY OF TITLE

Under the Code's warranty of title, the seller implicitly warrants (1) that the title conveyed is good and its transfer rightful and (2) that the goods have no security interest or other lien (a claim on property by another for payment of debt) of which the buyer was not aware at the time of purchase. Section 2–312(1). In a lease, title does not transfer to the lessee. Accordingly, Article 2A's analogous provision protects the lessee's right to possession and use of the goods from the claims of other parties arising from an act or omission of the lessor. Section 2A–211(1).

For example, Iris acquires goods from Sherman in a transaction that is void and then sells the goods to Brenda. Sherman brings an action against Brenda and recovers the goods. Iris has breached the warranty of title: because she did not have good title to the goods, her transfer of the goods to Brenda was not rightful. Accordingly, Iris is liable to Brenda for damages.

The Code does *not* label the warranty of title as an implied warranty, even though it arises from the sale and not from any particular words or conduct. Consequently, the Code's general disclaimer provision for implied warranties does not apply to a warranty of title, which instead is subject to its own disclaimer provision. Nevertheless, a seller of goods does implicitly warrant title to those goods.

A seller who is a merchant makes an additional warranty in sales of goods of the kind in which he regularly deals: that such goods shall be delivered free of the rightful claim of any third person that the goods infringe (use without authorization) upon any existing patent. Section 2–312(3); Section 2A–211(2).

EXPRESS WARRANTIES

An express warranty is an explicit undertaking by the seller with respect to the quality, description, condition, or performability of the goods. The undertaking may consist of an affirmation of fact or a promise that relates to the goods, a description of the goods, or a sample or model of the goods. In each of these instances, the undertaking must become or be made part of the basis of the bargain in order for an express warranty to be created. The seller need not, however, have a specific intention to make a warranty or use formal words such as "warrant" or "guarantee." Moreover, to be liable for a breach of express warranty a seller need not know that she has made a false statement; the seller may be acting in good faith. For example, if John mistakenly asserts to Sam that a rope will easily support three hundred pounds and Sam is injured when the rope breaks while supporting only two hundred pounds, John is liable for breach of an express warranty.

CREATION The seller can create an express warranty either orally or in writing. One of the ways in which an express warranty can be created is through an **affirmation of fact** or a **promise** relating to the goods that becomes part of the basis of the bargain. Section 2–313(1)(a); Section 2A–210(1)(a). The statement can be in regard to the quality, condition, capacity, performability, or safety of the goods. For example, a statement made by a seller that an automobile will get forty-two miles to the gallon of gasoline or that a camera has automatic focus is an express warranty.

The Code further provides that a statement affirming the **value** of the goods or purporting merely to be the seller's **opinion** or recommendation of the goods does not create a warranty. Section 2–313(2); Section 2A–210(2). Such statements are not factual and do not deceive the ordinary buyer, who accepts them merely as opinions or as puffery (sales talk). For example, a statement by a salesperson that "this is one terrific deal" would likely be considered puffery. On the other hand, a statement that "this car gets thirty miles to the gallon" would be considered an express warranty, given its specificity. A statement of value may be an express warranty, however, where the seller states the price at which the goods were purchased from a former owner, or where she gives market figures relating to sales of similar goods. As statements of events, not mere opinions, these are statements of facts; and the seller is liable for breach of warranty if they are untrue. Moreover, although a statement of opinion by the seller is not ordinarily a warranty, if the seller is an expert and gives her opinion as such, she may be liable for breach of warranty. Thus, if an art expert states that a certain painting is a genuine Rembrandt, and this becomes part of the basis of the bargain, then the expert warrants the accuracy of her professional opinion.

An express warranty also can be created by the use of a **description** of the goods that becomes part of the basis of the bargain. Section 2–313(1)(b); Section 2A–210(1)(b). Under such a warranty, the seller expressly warrants that the goods shall conform to the description. Examples include statements regarding a particular brand or type of goods, technical specifications, and blueprints.

The use of a **sample** or model is another means of creating an express warranty. Section 2–313(1)(c); Section 2A–210(1)(c). If a sample or model is part of the basis of the bargain, the seller expressly warrants that the entire lot of goods sold shall conform to the sample or model. A sample is a good drawn from the bulk of goods comprising the subject matter of the sale. A model, by comparison, is offered for inspection when the subject matter is not at hand; it is not drawn from the bulk. Section 2–313, Comment 6.

CISG — The seller must deliver goods that conform to quality and description required by the contract. In addition, the goods must possess the qualities of any sample or model used by the seller.

BASIS OF BARGAIN The Code does not require that the buyer rely on the affirmations, promises, descriptions, samples, or models the seller makes or uses but only that they constitute a part of the basis of the bargain. If they are part of the buyer's assumption underlying the sale, then reliance by the buyer is presumed. Some courts merely require that the buyer know of the affirmation or promise for it to be presumed to be part of the basis of the bargain. Relaxing the reliance requirement more often forces sellers to live up to their express warranties than does a rule requiring reliance.

Because they may constitute part of the basis of the bargain just as much as statements in advertisements or catalogs would, statements or promises the seller makes to the buyer prior to the sale may be express warranties. Furthermore, under the Code, statements or promises made by the seller subsequent to the contract of sale may become express warranties even though no new consideration is given. Sections 2–209(1) and 2A–208(1) provide that an agreement modifying a sale or lease needs no consideration to be binding. Thus, a statement, promise, or assurance with respect to the goods that the seller makes to the buyer at the time of delivery may be considered a binding modification of the prior contract of sale and held to be an express warranty basic to the bargain.

IMPLIED WARRANTIES

An implied warranty, unlike an express warranty, is not found in the language of the sales contract or in a specific affirmation or promise by the seller. Instead, an **implied warranty** is an obligation imposed by operation of law upon the transfer of property or contract rights. This warranty, which arises out of the circumstances under which the parties enter into their contract, depends on factors such as the type of contract or sale entered into, the seller's merchant or non-merchant status, the conduct of the parties, and the applicability of other statutes. The law has developed implied warranties not as something to which the parties must agree but as a departure from the early rule of *caveat emptor*.

MERCHANTABILITY At early common law, a seller was not held to any implied warranty as to the quality of goods. Under the Code, however, a **merchant seller** impliedly warrants the merchantability of goods that are of the kind in which she deals. The implied warranty of **merchantability** provides that the goods are reasonably fit for the ordinary purposes for which they are used, pass without objection in the trade under the contract description, and are of fair, average quality. Section 2–314; Section 2A–212. Because the warranty arises as a matter of law, the buyer does not need to prove that she relied on the warranty or that the warranty formed a basis of the bargain. The warranty applies automatically unless disclaimed by the seller. The official Comments to the Code further provide that a contract for the sale of secondhand goods "involves only such obligation as is appropriate to such goods for that is their description."

The Code in Sections 2–314(3) and 2A–212(3) expressly provides that implied warranties may arise from course of dealing or usage of trade. Thus, where the seller of a new automobile failed to lubricate it before delivery to the buyer, and the evidence established that it was the regular custom and usage of new car dealers to do so, the seller was held liable to the buyer for the resulting damages to the automobile in an action for breach of implied warranty.

The Code further provides that the serving for value of food or drink to be consumed on the premises or elsewhere is a sale. Section 2–314(1). Where a nonedible substance in food causes an injury, however, an implied warranty may not exist if the substance is natural to the food. A minority of jurisdictions distinguish between natural objects in food, such as fish bones in fish, and foreign objects such as a pebble, a piece of wire, or glass. The modern and majority test is the reasonable expectation of the consumer. That a substance is natural to a product in one stage of preparation does not necessarily imply that the consumer will reasonably anticipate or expect it to be in the final product.

CISG — The seller must deliver goods, unless otherwise agreed, that are fit for any particular purpose expressly or impliedly made known to the seller by the buyer, except where the buyer did not rely on the seller's skill and judgment or when it was unreasonable for the buyer to rely on the seller.

FITNESS FOR PARTICULAR PURPOSE Unlike the warranty of merchantability, the implied warranty of fitness for a particular purpose applies to *any* seller, whether he is a merchant or not. The **implied warranty of fitness for a particular purpose** arises if at the time of sale the seller had reason to know the buyer's particular purpose and that the buyer was relying upon the seller's skill and judgment to select suitable goods. Section 2–315; Section 2A–213.

The implied warranty of fitness for a particular purpose does not require any specific statement by the seller. Rather, the warranty requires only that the seller know that the buyer is relying on the seller's expertise in selecting a product for the buyer's specific purpose. The buyer need not specifically inform the seller of her particular purpose; it is sufficient if the seller has reason to know it. On the other hand, the implied warranty of fitness for a particular purpose would not arise if the buyer were to insist on a particular product and the seller simply conveyed it to her.

In contrast to the implied warranty of merchantability, the implied warranty of fitness for a particular purpose pertains to the *specific* purpose of the goods. The courts disagree whether an ordinary purpose of goods can be a particular purpose. Goods that are fit for ordinary purposes, and therefore are merchantable, may nonetheless be unfit for a particular purpose. A particular purpose may be a specific use or relate to a special situation in which the buyer intends to use the goods. Thus, if Miller has reason to know that Levine is purchasing a pair of shoes for mountain climbing and that Levine is relying upon Miller's judgment to furnish shoes suitable for this purpose, an implied warranty of fitness for a particular purpose would arise in this sale. If Miller sold Levine shoes suitable only for ordinary walking purposes, Miller would breach this implied warranty. Likewise, a buyer indicates to a seller that she needs a stamping machine to stamp ten thousand packages in an eight-hour period and that she relies on the seller to select an appropriate machine. By selecting the machine, the seller impliedly warrants that the machine selected will stamp ten thousand packages in an eight-hour period.

Reliance is therefore required for this warranty, unlike an express warranty, which requires only that the affirmation meet the broad "basis of the bargain" test, or the implied warranty of merchantability, which requires no proof of reliance. In order to prevail in a case involving an implied warranty of fitness for a particular purpose, the buyer must be able to demonstrate specifically that she relied on the seller's skill or judgment in selecting or furnishing suitable goods.

CISG The seller must deliver goods, unless otherwise agreed, that are fit for the purposes for which goods of the same description would ordinarily be used.

OBSTACLES TO WARRANTY ACTIONS

In certain respects, warranty claims offer injured persons many advantages. Generally, a plaintiff need only establish the existence and breach of a warranty, an injury resulting from the breach, and the giving of notice in order to recover in a warranty action. This makes warranty claims easier to bring than negligence cases, which require the plaintiff to show that the defendant failed to act with due care—often a difficult task. Nonetheless, a number of technical obstacles limit the effectiveness of warranty as a basis for recovery. These include disclaimers of warranties, limitations or modifications of warranties, privity, notice of breach, and the conduct of the plaintiff. These obstacles vary considerably from jurisdiction to jurisdiction.

DISCLAIMER OF WARRANTIES

The Code calls for a reasonable construction of words or conduct to **disclaim** (negate) or limit warranties. Section 2–316; Section 2A–214. The Code makes clear that the seller should not rely on a time-honored formula of words and expect to obtain a disclaimer that may go unnoticed by the buyer. To be effective, disclaimers must be positive, explicit, unequivocal, and conspicuous.

EXPRESS EXCLUSIONS A **warranty of title** may be excluded only by specific language or by certain circumstances, including judicial sales or sales by sheriffs, executors, or foreclosing lienors. Section 2–312(2); Section 2A–214(4). In the latter cases the seller is manifestly offering to sell only such right or title as he or a third person might have in the goods, as it is apparent that the goods are not the property of the person selling them.

In general, a seller cannot provide an **express warranty** and then disclaim it. A seller can avoid making an express warranty, however, by carefully refraining from making any promise or affirmation of fact relating to the goods, refraining from making a description of the goods, or refraining from using a sample or model. Section 2–313; Section 2A–210. A seller also may be able to negate an express warranty by *clear, specific, unambiguous* language. The Code, however, provides that words or conduct relevant to the creation of an express warranty and words or conduct negating a warranty shall be construed wherever reasonable as consistent with each other and that a negation or limitation is inoperative to the extent that such construction is unreasonable. Section 2–316; Section 2A–214. For example, a seller and a buyer enter into a written contract for the sale of a camera in which the seller warrants that the camera being sold is free of defects. This express warranty renders inoperative another provision in the contract that attempts to disclaim liability for any repairs necessitated by defects in the camera. The inconsistency between the two contractual provisions makes the disclaimer ineffective. Moreover, if the seller's disclaimer attempts to negate "all express warranties," this general disclaimer would be ineffective against the specific express warranty providing that the camera is free of defects. Finally, oral warranties made prior to the execution of a written agreement that contains an express disclaimer are subject to the parol evidence rule. Thus, as discussed in *Chapter 15*, if the parties intend the written contract to be the final and complete statement of the agreement between them, oral evidence of warranties that contradict the terms of the written contract is inadmissible.

To exclude an **implied warranty of merchantability**, the language of disclaimer must mention merchantability and, in the case of a writing, must be *conspicuous*. Section 2–316(2). Article 2A requires that a disclaimer of an implied warranty of merchantability mention merchantability, be in writing, and be conspicuous. Section 2A–214(2). For example, Bart wishes to buy a used refrigerator from Ben's Used Appliances Store for $100. Given the low purchase price, Ben is unwilling to guarantee the refrigerator's performance. Bart agrees to buy it with no warranty protection. To exclude the warranty, Ben writes conspicuously on the contract, "This refrigerator carries no warranties, including no warranty of MERCHANTABIL-ITY." Ben has effectively disclaimed the implied warranty of merchantability. Some courts, however, do not require the disclaimer to be conspicuous where a *commercial* buyer has actual knowledge of the disclaimer. The Code's test for whether a provision is *conspicuous* is whether a reasonable person against whom the disclaimer is to operate ought to have noticed it. Section 1–201(10); Revised Section 1–201(b)(10). Revised Article 1 provides that conspicuous terms include (1) a heading in capitals equal to or greater in size than the surrounding text; or in contrasting type, font, or color to the surrounding text of the same or lesser size; and (2) language in the body of a record or display in larger type than the surrounding text; or in contrasting type, font, or color to the surrounding text of the same size; or set off from surrounding text of the same size by symbols or other marks that call attention to the language. Revised Section 1–201(b)(10). Whether a term is conspicuous is an issue for the court. Revised Section 1–201, Comment.

To exclude or to modify an **implied warranty of fitness** for the particular purpose of the buyer, the disclaimer must be in *writing* and *conspicuous*. Section 2–316(2); Section 2A–214(2).

All implied warranties, unless the circumstances indicate otherwise, are excluded by expressions like *as is, with all faults*, or other language plainly calling the buyer's attention to the exclusion of warranties. Section 2–316(3)(a); Section 2A–214(3)(a). Most courts require the "as is" clause to be conspicuous. Implied warranties also may be excluded by course of dealing, course of performance, or usage of trade. Section 2–316(3)(c); Section 2A–214(3)(c).

The courts will invalidate disclaimers they consider unconscionable. Sections 2–302 and 2A–108 of the Code,

as discussed in *Chapter 21*, permit a court to limit the application of any contract or provision of a contract that it finds unconscionable.

BUYER'S EXAMINATION OR REFUSAL TO EXAMINE If the buyer inspects the goods before entering into the contract, *implied warranties* do not apply to defects that are apparent upon examination. The particular buyer's skill and the normal method of examining goods in the circumstances determine what defects are excluded by examination. Section 2–316, Comment 8. Moreover, no implied warranty exists as to defects that an examination ought to have revealed, not only where the buyer has examined the goods as fully as she desired, but also where the buyer has *refused* to examine the goods. Section 2–316(3)(b); Section 2A–214(3)(b).

A mere failure or omission to examine the goods is not a refusal to examine them. It is not enough that the goods were available for inspection and the buyer did not see fit to inspect them. In order for the buyer to have "refused to examine the goods," the seller *must* first have demanded that the buyer examine them.

CISG If at the time of entering into the sales contract the buyer knew or could not have been unaware of the lack of conformity, the seller is not liable for the warranty of particular purpose, ordinary purpose, or sale by sample or model.

FEDERAL LEGISLATION RELATING TO WARRANTIES OF CONSUMER GOODS To protect purchasers of consumer goods (defined as "tangible personal property normally used for personal, family, or household purposes"), Congress enacted the **Magnuson-Moss Warranty Act**. The purpose of the Act is to prevent deception and to make available to consumer purchasers adequate information with respect to warranties. Some courts have applied the Act to leases.

The Federal Trade Commission administers and enforces the Act. The commission's guidelines regarding the type of information a seller must set forth in warranties of consumer products are aimed at providing the consumer with clear and useful information. More significantly, the act provides that a seller who makes a written warranty cannot disclaim *any* implied warranty. For a complete discussion of the Act, see *Chapter 42*.

◆ **SEE FIGURE 24-1: Warranties**

LIMITATION OR MODIFICATION OF WARRANTIES

Sometimes a seller is willing to give some warranty protection but wishes to limit the scope or type of protection she gives. For example, a seller who is willing to repair or replace

◆ **FIGURE 24-1: Warranties**

Type of Warranty	How Created	What is Warranted	How Disclaimed
Title (Section 2–312)/Use and Possession (2A–211)	• Seller contracts to sell goods	• Good title • Rightful transfer • Not subject to lien	• Specific language • Circumstances giving buyer reason to know that seller does not claim title
Express (Section 2–313; Section 2A–210)	• Affirmation of fact • Promise • Description • Sample or model	• Conform to affirmation • Conform to promise • Conform to description • Conform to sample or model	• Specific language (extremely difficult)
Merchantability (Section 2–314; Section 2A–212*)	• Merchant sells goods	• Fit for ordinary purpose • Adequately contained, packaged, and labeled	• Must mention "merchantability" • If in writing must be conspicuous/in lease must be in writing and conspicuous • As-is sale • Buyer examination • Course of dealing, course of performance, usage of trade
Fitness for a particular purpose (Section 2–315; Section 2A–213*)	• Seller knows buyer is relying upon seller to select goods suitable for buyer's particular purpose	• Fit for particular purpose	• No buzzwords necessary • Must be in writing and conspicuous • As-is sale • Buyer examination • Course of dealing, course of performance, usage of trade

* except in a finance lease

a defective product may not be willing to pay consequential damages, such as the buyer's lost profits, arising from any product defects. Sections 2–719 and 2A–503 of the Code permit a seller to *limit* or *modify* the buyer's remedies for breach of warranty. Two important exceptions to the seller's right are Sections 2–719(3) and 2A–503(3), which prohibit "unconscionable" limitations or exclusions of consequential damages. Specifically, the limitation of consequential damages for injury to the person in the case of consumer goods is prima facie unconscionable.

In some cases, a seller may choose not to limit the buyer's rights to seek damages for breach of warranty but to impose time limits within which the warranty is effective. Except for instances of unconscionability, the Code permits such clauses; it does not, however, permit any attempt to shorten to less than one year the time period for filing an action for personal injury.

PRIVITY OF CONTRACT

Because of the association of warranties with contracts, a principle of law in the nineteenth century established that a plaintiff could not recover for breach of warranty unless he was in a contractual relationship with the defendant. This relationship is known as privity of contract.

Horizontal privity pertains to noncontracting parties who are injured by the defective goods; this group would include users, consumers, and bystanders who are not the contracting purchaser. Horizontal privity determines who benefits from a warranty and who may, therefore, sue for its breach.

Under this rule, a warranty by seller Ingrid to buyer Sylvester, who resells the goods to purchaser Lyle under a similar warranty, gives Lyle no rights against Ingrid. There is no privity of contract between Ingrid and Lyle. In the event of breach of warranty, Lyle may recover only from his seller, Sylvester, who in turn may recover from Ingrid.

The Code relaxes the requirement of horizontal privity of contract by permitting recovery on a seller's warranty, at a minimum, to members of the buyer's family or household or to guests in his home. Section 2–318 of the Code provides three alternative sections from which the States may select. *Alternative A*, the least comprehensive and most widely adopted, provides that a seller's warranty, whether express or implied, extends to any natural person who is in the family or household of the buyer or who is a guest in his home, if it is reasonable to expect that such person may use, consume, or be affected by the goods, and who is injured in person by breach of the warranty. *Alternative B* extends Alternative A to any natural person who may reasonably be expected to use, consume, or be affected by the goods. *Alternative C* further expands the coverage of the section to any person, not just natural persons, and to property damage as well as personal injury. (A natural person would not include artificial entities such as corporations.) A seller may not exclude or limit the operation of this section for injury to a person. Section 2A–216 provides the same alternatives with slight modifications.

Nonetheless, the Code merely sets a minimum standard that the States may expand through case law. Most States have judicially accepted the Code's invitation to relax the requirements of horizontal privity and, for all practical purposes, have *eliminated* horizontal privity in warranty cases.

Vertical privity, in determining who is liable for breach of warranty, pertains to remote sellers within the chain of distribution, such as manufacturers and wholesalers, with whom the consumer purchaser has not entered into a contract. Although the Code adopts a neutral position regarding vertical privity, the courts in most States have eliminated the requirement of vertical privity in warranty actions.

NOTICE OF BREACH OF WARRANTY

When a buyer has accepted a tender of goods that are not as warranted by the seller, she is required to notify the seller of any breach of warranty within a reasonable time after she has discovered or should have discovered it. If the buyer fails to notify the seller of any breach within a reasonable time, she is barred from any remedy against the seller. Section 2–607(3)(a); Section 2A–516(3)(a).

The purpose of the reasonable notice requirement is (1) to enable the seller to cure the defect or to minimize the buyer's loss, (2) to provide the seller an opportunity to prepare for conflict resolution and litigation, and (3) to provide the seller with an end point to liability. In determining whether notice was provided within a reasonable time, commercial standards apply to a merchant buyer whereas standards designed to preserve a good faith consumer's right to his remedy apply to a retail consumer.

PLAINTIFF'S CONDUCT

Because warranty liability developed in the law of sales and contracts, in most States, contributory negligence of the buyer is no defense to an action against the seller for breach of warranty. In a number of States, however, comparative negligence statutes apply to warranty actions. (Comparative negligence is discussed more fully later in this chapter.)

If the buyer discovers a defect in the goods that may cause injury and then proceeds to make use of the goods, he will not be permitted to recover damages from the seller for loss or injuries caused by such use. This is not contributory negligence but **voluntary assumption** of a known risk.

STRICT LIABILITY IN TORT

The most recent and far-reaching development in the field of products liability is that of strict liability in tort. All but a very few States have now accepted the concept, which is embodied in **Section 402A** of the Restatement, Second, of Torts. In 1997 a new Restatement of the Law, Third, Torts: Products Liability (the Restatement Third) was promulgated. It is far more comprehensive than the second Restatement in dealing with the liability of commercial sellers and distributors of goods for harm caused by their products. (This revision will be discussed more fully later in this chapter.)

Section 402A imposes **strict liability in tort** on merchant sellers for both personal injuries and property damage resulting from selling a product in a **defective condition, unreasonably dangerous** to the user or consumer. Section 402A applies even though "the seller has exercised all possible care in the preparation and sale of his product." Thus, negligence is not the basis of liability in strict liability cases. The essential distinction between the two doctrines is that actions in strict liability do not require the plaintiff to prove that the injury-producing defect resulted from any specific act of negligence of the seller. Strict liability actions focus on the product, not on the conduct of the manufacturer. Courts in strict liability cases are interested in the fact that a product defect arose—not in how it arose. Thus, even an "innocent" manufacturer—one who has not been negligent—may be liable if his product contains a defect that injures a consumer.

The reasons asserted in support of imposing strict liability in tort upon manufacturers and assemblers of products include the following: (1) consumers should be given maximum protection against dangerous defects in products; (2) manufacturers are in the best position to prevent or reduce the hazards to life and health in defective products; (3) manufacturers, who realize the most profit from the total sales of their goods, are best able to carry the financial burden of such liability by distributing it among the public as a cost of doing business; (4) manufacturers utilize wholesalers and retailers merely as conduits in the marketing of their products and should not be permitted to avoid liability simply because they have no contract with the user or consumer; and (5) because the manufacturer is liable to his purchaser who may be a wholesaler who in turn is liable to the retailer who in turn is liable to the ultimate purchaser, time and expense is saved by making liability direct rather than a chain reaction.

Although liability for personal injuries caused by a product in an unreasonably dangerous defective condition is usually associated with sales of goods, such liability also exists with respect to **leases** and **bailments** of defective goods. The extension of liability to lessors and bailors of goods is not surprising in view of the rationale the courts have developed in imposing strict liability in tort upon manufacturers and sellers of products. The danger to which the public is exposed by defectively manufactured cars and trucks traveling on the highways, for example, does not differ greatly from the hazards of defective cars and trucks leased to operators.

REQUIREMENTS OF STRICT LIABILITY

Section 402A imposes strict liability in tort on merchant sellers for both personal injuries and property damage that result from selling a product in a defective condition unreasonably dangerous to the user or consumer. Specifically, this section provides:

1. One who sells any product in a defective condition unreasonably dangerous to the user or consumer or to his property is subject to liability for physical harm thereby caused to the ultimate user or consumer, or to his property, if (a) the seller is engaged in the business of selling such a product, and (b) it is expected to and does reach the user or consumer without substantial change in the condition in which it is sold.
2. The rule stated in Subsection (1) applies although (a) the seller has exercised all possible care in the preparation and sale of his product, and (b) the user or consumer has not bought the product from or entered into any contractual relation with the seller.

Negligence, as previously stated, is not the basis of this liability; it applies even though "the seller has exercised all possible care in the preparation and sale of his product." The seller is not an insurer of the goods that he manufactures or sells, however; and the essential requirements for strict product liability are that (1) the defendant was engaged in the business of selling such a product; (2) the defendant sold the product in a defective condition; (3) the defective condition was one that made the product unreasonably dangerous to the user or consumer or to his property; (4) the defect in the product existed at the time it left the hands of the defendant; (5) the plaintiff sustained physical harm or property damage by use or consumption of the product; and (6) the defective condition was the proximate cause of such injury or damage.

This liability is imposed by law as a matter of public policy and does not depend upon contract, either express or implied. It does not require reliance by the injured user or consumer upon any statements made by the manufacturer or seller. The liability is not limited to persons in a buyer-seller relationship; thus, neither vertical nor horizontal privity is required. No notice of the defect is required to have been given by the injured user or consumer. The liability, furthermore, is generally not subject to disclaimer, exclusion, or modification by contractual agreement. Rather, the liability is solely in tort and arises out of the common law; it is not governed by the provisions of the UCC.

The majority of courts considering the question have held that Section 402A imposes liability for injury to person and damage to property (the economic loss doctrine) but not for commercial loss (such as loss of bargain or profits), which is recoverable in an action for breach of warranty. A minority of States have held, however, that commercial loss may be recovered in tort where the defect creates an unreasonable risk of personal injury or property damage, even though the only damage resulting is to the defective goods themselves.

MERCHANT SELLERS

Section 402A imposes liability only upon a person who is in the *business* of selling the product involved. It does *not* apply to an occasional seller, such as a person who trades in his used car or who sells his lawn mower to a neighbor. In this respect, the section is similar to the implied warranty of merchantability, which applies only to sales by a merchant with respect to goods of the type in which he deals. A growing number of jurisdictions recognize the applicability of strict liability in tort to merchant sellers of *used* goods.

DEFECTIVE CONDITION

In an action against a defendant manufacturer or other seller to recover damages under the rule of strict liability in tort, the plaintiff must prove a defective condition in the product, but she is not required to prove how or why the product became defective. In an action based on Section 402A, the reason for or cause of the defect is not material, although it would be in an action based on negligence. Under a strict liability approach, a manufacturer will be held liable even though it did not act negligently. For example, if the Quality Bottling Company, despite its having the most stringent quality control program in the industry, through no negligence of its own manufactures a bottle that explodes in the hands of a consumer, the company would be liable to the consumer under Section 402A. Whether or not Quality Bottling Company acted negligently is irrelevant. The plaintiff, however, must show that at the time she was injured the condition of the product was not substantially changed from the condition in which the manufacturer or seller sold it. In general, defects may arise through faulty manufacturing, faulty product design, or inadequate warning, labeling, packaging, or instructions. Some States, however, and the Restatement Third do not impose strict liability for a design defect or a failure to provide proper warnings or instructions.

MANUFACTURING DEFECT A manufacturing defect occurs when the product is not properly made; that is, it fails to meet its own manufacturing specifications. For instance, suppose a chair is manufactured with legs designed to be attached by four screws and glue. If such a chair were produced without the required screws, this would constitute a manufacturing defect.

DESIGN DEFECT A product contains a design defect when, despite its being produced as specified, the product is dangerous or hazardous because of inadequate design. Design defects can result from a number of causes, including poor engineering and poor choice of materials. An example of a design defect that received great notoriety was the Ford Pinto. A number of courts found the car to be inadequately designed because its fuel tank had been placed too close to its rear axle, causing the tank to rupture upon impact from the rear.

Section 402A provides no guidance in determining which injury-producing designs should give rise to strict liability and which should not; consequently, the courts have adopted widely varying approaches in applying 402A to defective design cases.

At one extreme, a few courts have taken a very literal approach to Section 402A by ruling that a manufacturer is strictly liable for injuries caused by a design that a reasonable person would not have produced had he known of the design's harmful character at the time it was made. Whether the manufacturer did or could have known of the risk associated with the design, or of an alternative design that could have avoided the risk, is deemed irrelevant for purposes of strict liability. Manufacturers, in effect, are held liable for hazards that were unknowable at the time they manufactured their products.

A slightly larger number of courts, although still a minority, have taken the opposite approach: recognizing no difference between negligence and strict liability principles in defective design cases, they apply negligence principles to such cases. Unless the plaintiff can demonstrate that the manufacturer knew, or should have known, of a safer, cost-effective design, these courts will not hold the manufacturer liable.

The majority of courts have ostensibly adopted a middle-of-the-road approach, stating that strict liability cases should be viewed differently from negligence cases. Beyond reciting that strict liability cases focus on the product, not on the manufacturer's conduct, these courts have yet to clarify what

the different view implies. Nevertheless, virtually none of them has upheld a judgment in a strict liability case in which the defendant demonstrated that the "**state of the art**" was such that the manufacturer (1) neither knew nor could have known of a product hazard, or (2) if he knew of the product hazard, could have designed a safer product given existing technology. Thus, almost all courts evaluate the design of a product on the basis of the dangers that could have been known when the product was produced or sold.

In deciding design defect cases, courts identify any government safety standards applicable to the design involved in the product liability lawsuit. If such a standard exists and the manufacturer's failure to follow it caused the plaintiff's injury, the courts tend to impose liability automatically. On the other hand, a manufacturer's compliance with safety standards does not equal automatic relief from liability. If a plaintiff can demonstrate that a safer, cost-effective design was available to the manufacturer, the plaintiff can still prevail in a product liability lawsuit even though the manufacturer complied with a government safety standard.

FAILURE TO WARN A seller is under a duty to provide adequate warning of possible danger, to provide appropriate directions for safe use, and to package the product safely. Warnings do not, however, always protect sellers from liability. A seller who could have designed or manufactured a product in a safe but cost-effective manner, but who instead chooses to produce the product cheaply and to provide a warning of the product's hazards, cannot escape liability simply through the warning. Warnings usually will avoid liability only if there are no cost-effective designs or manufacturing processes available to reduce a risk of injury.

The duty to give a warning arises out of a foreseeable danger of physical harm resulting from the normal or probable use of the product and out of the likelihood that, unless warned, the user or consumer will not ordinarily be aware of such danger or hazard. For example, a seller may reasonably assume that those with allergies to products such as eggs or strawberries will know of their allergies and therefore need not be warned of this risk. On the other hand, if a product contains an ingredient to which a substantial number of persons are allergic, and the ingredient is one whose danger is not generally known or, if known, is one that the consumer would not reasonably expect to find in the product, the seller is required to give a warning about it. Under strict liability principles, sellers are generally required to provide warnings against uses for which a product is not marketed, including certain instances of consumer misuse, if such uses are foreseeable by the manufacturer and the consumer is unlikely to recognize the hazard.

Section 402A imposes liability in failure-to-warn cases only where the seller "has knowledge, or by the application of reasonable, developed human skill and foresight should have knowledge, of the … danger." Comment j. In effect, the seller is held to the knowledge and skill of an expert in the field. Some courts have ruled that this means a manufacturer not only must keep abreast of scientific knowledge, discoveries, and advances, but also must conduct research to determine whether his product contains hazards. Most courts today require proof that the manufacturer knew, or could have known, of a product hazard before imposing liability for a failure to warn.

UNREASONABLY DANGEROUS

Section 402A liability applies only if the defective product is **unreasonably dangerous** to the user or consumer. An unreasonably dangerous product is one that contains a danger beyond that which the ordinary consumer, who purchases the product with common knowledge of its characteristics, would contemplate. Thus,

> good whiskey is not unreasonably dangerous merely because it will make some people drunk, and is especially dangerous to alcoholics; but bad whiskey, containing a dangerous amount of fuel oil, is unreasonably dangerous. Good tobacco is not unreasonably dangerous merely because the effects of smoking may be harmful; but tobacco containing something like marijuana may be unreasonably dangerous. Good butter is not unreasonably dangerous merely because, if such be the case, it deposits cholesterol in the arteries and leads to heart attacks; but bad butter, contaminated with poisonous fish oil, is unreasonably dangerous. Comment i to Section 402A.

Most courts have left the question of reasonable consumer expectations to the jury.

OBSTACLES TO RECOVERY

Few of the obstacles to recovery in warranty cases present serious problems to plaintiffs in strict liability actions brought pursuant to Section 402A because this section was drafted largely to avoid such obstacles.

DISCLAIMERS AND NOTICE

Comment m to Section 402A provides that the basis of strict liability rests solely in tort and therefore is not subject to contractual defenses. The comment specifically states that strict product liability is not governed by the Code, that it is not affected by contractual limitations or disclaimers, and

that it is not subject to any requirement that the injured party gives notice to the seller within a reasonable time. Nevertheless, most courts have allowed clear and specific disclaimers of Section 402A liability in *commercial* transactions between merchants of relatively equal economic power.

PRIVITY

With respect to horizontal privity, the majority of States hold that the strict liability in tort of manufacturers and other sellers extends not only to buyers, users, and consumers, but also to injured bystanders. Bystanders to whom such liability has extended include the occupants of an automobile injured in a collision with another car due to the other car's having defective brakes; a golfer killed by a runaway golf cart that started due to a faulty transmission system; a bystander injured by a runaway truck started by a short circuit; a bystander injured by the explosion of a defective beer keg; a neighbor injured by the explosion of a propane gas tank; and a bystander injured by the explosion of a shotgun barrel caused by a defective shell. Some States, however, limit liability to foreseeable purchasers or users of the product.

In terms of **vertical privity**, strict liability in tort imposes liability on any seller who is engaged in the business of selling the product, including a wholesaler or distributor as well as the manufacturer and retailer. The rule of strict liability in tort also applies to the manufacturer of a defective component that has been incorporated into a larger product where the manufacturer of the finished product has made no essential change in the component.

PLAINTIFF'S CONDUCT

Many product liability defenses relate to the conduct of the plaintiff. The contention common to all of them is that the plaintiff's improper conduct so contributed to the plaintiff's injury that it would be unfair to blame the product or its seller.

CONTRIBUTORY NEGLIGENCE Contributory negligence is conduct on the part of the plaintiff that falls below the standard to which he should conform for his own protection and that is the legal cause of the plaintiff's harm. Under traditional negligence law principles, if the negligence of the plaintiff together with that of the defendant proximately caused the plaintiff's injury, the plaintiff could not recover *any* damages from the defendant. It did not matter whether the plaintiff's contributory negligence was slight or extensive. Because strict liability is designed to assess liability without fault, Section 402A rejects contributory negligence as a defense. Thus, a seller cannot defend a strict liability lawsuit on the basis of a plaintiff's negligent failure to discover a defect or to guard against its possibility. But, as discussed below, contributory negligence in the form of an assumption of the risk can bar recovery under Section 402A.

COMPARATIVE NEGLIGENCE The harshness of the contributory negligence doctrine has caused all but a few States to reject the all-or-nothing rule of contributory negligence and to substitute the doctrine of **comparative negligence**. Under comparative negligence, damages are apportioned between the parties in proportion to the degree of fault or negligence found against them.

Despite Section 402A's bar of contributory negligence in strict liability cases, some courts apply comparative negligence to strict liability cases. (Some courts use the term **comparative responsibility** rather than *comparative negligence*.) There are two basic types of comparative negligence or comparative responsibility. One is **pure comparative responsibility**, which simply reduces the plaintiff's recovery in proportion to her fault, whatever that may be. Thus, the recovery of a plaintiff found to be 80 percent at fault in causing an accident in which she suffered a $100,000 loss would be limited to 20 percent of her damages, or $20,000. By comparison, under **modified comparative responsibility**, the plaintiff recovers according to the general principles of comparative responsibility *unless* she is more than 50 percent responsible for her injuries, in which case she recovers nothing. The majority of comparative negligence States follow the modified comparative responsibility approach.

VOLUNTARY ASSUMPTION OF THE RISK Under the Second Restatement of Torts, assumption of risk is a defense in an action based on strict liability in tort. Basically, **assumption of risk** is the plaintiff's express or implied consent to encounter a known danger. The user or consumer who voluntarily uses goods in an unusual, inappropriate, or improper manner for which they were not intended, such use being, under the circumstances, unreasonable, assumes the risk of injuries that result from such use. Thus, a person who drives an automobile after realizing that the brakes are not working or an employee who attempts to remove a foreign object from a high-speed roller press without shutting off the power has assumed the risk of his own injury. In a comparative negligence or comparative responsibility State, assumption of the risk would either reduce or bar recovery, depending on the degree to which it contributed to the plaintiff's injury.

To establish such a defense, the defendant must show that (1) the plaintiff actually knew and appreciated the particular risk or danger the defect created, (2) the plaintiff voluntarily encountered the risk while realizing the danger, and (3) the plaintiff's decision to encounter the known risk was unreasonable.

The Third Restatement of Torts: Apportionment of Liability has abandoned the doctrine of implied voluntary assumption of risk in tort actions generally; it is no longer a defense that the plaintiff was aware of a risk and voluntarily confronted it. This new Restatement limits the defense of assumption of risk to express assumption of risk, which consists of a contract between the plaintiff and another person to absolve the other person from liability for future harm. Section 2.

MISUSE OR ABUSE OF THE PRODUCT Closely connected to voluntary assumption of the risk is the valid defense of misuse or abuse of the product by the injured party. **Misuse** or **abuse** occurs when the injured party knows, or should know, that he is using the product in a manner not contemplated by the seller. The major difference between misuse or abuse and assumption of the risk is that the former includes actions that the injured party does not know to be dangerous, whereas the latter does not. Instances of such misuse or abuse include standing on a rocking chair to change a light bulb or using a lawn mower to trim hedges.

The courts, however, have significantly limited this defense by requiring that the misuse or abuse not be foreseeable by the seller. If a use is foreseeable, then the seller must take measures to guard against it. For example, if William stands on a rocking chair to change a light bulb and is injured when the chair tilts and tips over, his misuse of the chair would bar his recovery. Similarly, if Jenny hammers a nail with a hair dryer and suffers an eye injury when a chip flies from the dryer, she will be unsuccessful in a claim against the manufacturer.

SUBSEQUENT ALTERATION

Section 402A provides that liability exists only if the product reaches "the user or consumer without substantial change in the condition in which it is sold." Accordingly, most, but not all, courts would not hold a manufacturer liable for a faulty oil pump if a car dealer were to remove the part and make significant changes in it prior to reinstalling it in an automobile.

STATUTE OF REPOSE

Numerous lawsuits have been brought against manufacturers many years after a product was first sold. In one case, a manufacturer was successfully sued twenty-two years after a defective water meter was first purchased and fourteen years after it was installed in the plaintiff's home. In another case, Volkswagen of America was ordered to pay $1.8 million in damages in an accident case centering around a missing door latch costing $0.35. The accident occurred ten years after the car had been manufactured and nine years after Volkswagen had informed its dealers about the defect.

In response, many States have adopted **statutes of repose**. These enactments limit the time period—typically to between six and twelve years—for which a manufacturer is liable for injury caused by a defective product. After the statutory period has elapsed, a manufacturer ceases to be liable for such harm.

LIMITATIONS ON DAMAGES

More than half of the States have limited the punitive damages that a plaintiff can collect in a product liability lawsuit. They have done this by a number of means, including the following:

1. Placing caps on the amount of damages that can be awarded, with caps ranging from $50,000 to $5 million;
2. Providing for the State to receive all or a portion of any punitive damages awarded with the State's share ranging from 35 percent to 100 percent in order to reduce the plaintiff's incentive to bring products liability suits;
3. Providing for bifurcated trials; that is, separate hearings to determine liability and punitive damages;
4. Increasing the plaintiff's burden of proof for recovery of punitive damages, with most states adopting the "clear and convincing" evidence standard;
5. Requiring proportionality between compensatory and punitive damages by specifying an acceptable ratio between the two types of damages.

◆ SEE FIGURE 24-2: **Products Liabilities**

RESTATEMENT OF TORTS (THIRD): PRODUCTS LIABILITY

The Restatement (Third) of Torts: Products Liability makes some significant changes in product liability. The adoption of the new Restatement by the States has been a slow process and the great majority of States continue to follow Section 402A of the Second Restatement of Torts.

The new Restatement expands Section 402A into an entire treatise of its own, comprising more than twenty sections. The Restatement Third does not use the term strict liability but instead defines separate liability standards for each type of defect. The new Restatement continues to cover anyone engaged in the business of selling or distributing a defective product if the defect causes harm to persons or property. Its major provision (Section 2) defines a product as defective "when, at the time of sale or distribution, it contains a manufacturing defect, is defective in design, or is defective because of inadequate instructions or warnings." Thus, Section 2 explicitly recognizes the three types of product defects discussed above: manufacturing defects, design defects, and failure to warn. However, as discussed below, strict liability is imposed

◆ **FIGURE 24-2: Products Liabilities**

Type of Warranty	Warranty of Merchantability*	Strict Liability in Tort (§402A)
Condition of Goods Creating Liability	Not fit for ordinary purposes	Defective condition, unreasonably dangerous
Type of Transaction Covered	Sales and leases (except finance leases); some courts apply to bailments of goods	Sales, leases, and bailments of goods
Disclaimer	Must mention "merchantability" If in writing, must be conspicuous (lease must be in writing) Must not be unconscionable Sales subject to Magnuson-Moss Act/leases may be subject	Not possible in consumer transactions; may be permitted in commercial transactions
Notice to Seller	Required within reasonable time	Not required
Causation	Required	Required
Who May Sue	In some States, buyer and the buyer's family or guests in home; in other States, any person who may be expected to use, consume, or be affected by goods	Any user or consumer of product; also, in most States, any bystander
Compensable Harms	Personal injury, property damage, economic loss	Personal injury, property damage
Who May Be Sued	Seller or lessor who is a merchant with respect to the goods sold	Seller who is a merchant with respect to the goods sold

* The warranty of fitness for a particular purpose differs from the warranty of merchantability in the following respects: (1) the condition that triggers liability is the failure of the goods to perform according to the particular purpose of the warranty, (2) a disclaimer need not mention "fitness for a particular purpose" but must be in writing, and (3) applies to any seller.

only on the first of these, while liability for inadequate design or warning is imposed only for foreseeable risks of harm that could have been avoided by the use of an alternative *reasonable* design, warning, or instruction.

MANUFACTURING DEFECT

Section 2(a) provides that "A product … contains a manufacturing defect when the product departs from its intended design even though all possible care was exercised in the preparation and marketing of the product." Therefore, sellers and distributors of products remain strictly liable for manufacturing defects, although a plaintiff may seek to recover based upon allegations and proof of negligent manufacture. In actions against the manufacturer, the plaintiff ordinarily must prove that the defect existed in the product when it left the manufacturer.

DESIGN DEFECT

Section 2(b) states:

A product … is defective in design when the foreseeable risks of harm posed by the product could have been reduced or avoided by the adoption of a reasonable alternative design by the seller or other distributor, or a predecessor in the commercial chain of distribution, and the omission of the reasonable alternative design renders the product not reasonably safe.

This rule pulls back from a strict liability standard and imposes a negligence-like standard by requiring that the defect be reasonably foreseeable and that it could have been avoided by a reasonable alternative design. The Comments explain that this standard involves resolving "whether a reasonable alternative design would, at a reasonable cost, have reduced the foreseeable risk of harm posed by the product and, if so, whether the omission of the alternative design by the seller … rendered the product not reasonably safe." The burden rests upon the plaintiff to demonstrate the existence of a reasonable alternative safer design that would have reduced the foreseeable risks of harm. However, consumer expectations do not constitute an independent standard for judging the defectiveness of product designs.

FAILURE TO WARN

Section 2(c) provides:

A product … is defective because of inadequate instructions or warnings when the foreseeable risks of harm posed by the product could have been reduced or avoided by the provision of reasonable instructions or warnings by the seller or other distributor, or a predecessor in the commercial chain of distribution and the omission of the instructions or warnings renders the product not reasonably safe.

Commercial product sellers must provide reasonable instructions and warnings about risks of injury associated with their products. The omission of warnings sufficient to allow informed decisions by reasonably foreseeable users or consumers renders the product not reasonably safe at time of sale. A seller, however, is under a duty to warn only if it knew or should have known of the risks involved. Moreover, warning about risks is effective only if an alternative design to avoid the risk cannot reasonably be implemented. Whenever safer products can be reasonably designed at a reasonable cost, adoption of the safer design is required rather than using a warning or instructions.

CHAPTER SUMMARY

WARRANTIES

TYPES OF WARRANTIES	**Definition of Warranty** an obligation of the seller to the buyer concerning title, quality, characteristics, or condition of goods
	Warranty of Title the obligation of a seller to convey the right to ownership without any lien (in a lease the warranty protects the lessee's right to possess and use the goods)
	Express Warranty an affirmation of fact or promise about the goods or a description, including a sample, of the goods that becomes part of the basis of the bargain
	Implied Warranty a contractual obligation, arising out of certain circumstances of the sale, imposed by operation of law and not found in the language of the sales contract
	• *Merchantability* warranty by a merchant seller that the goods are reasonably fit for the ordinary purpose for which they are manufactured or sold, pass without objection in the trade under the contract description, and are of fair, average quality

- *Fitness for Particular Purpose* warranty by any seller that goods are reasonably fit for a particular purpose if, at the time of contracting, the seller had reason to know the buyer's particular purpose and that the buyer was relying on the seller's skill and judgment to furnish suitable goods

OBSTACLES TO WARRANTY ACTIONS	**Disclaimers of Warranties** negations of warranties

Disclaimers of Warranties negations of warranties
- *Express Warranty* not usually possible to disclaim
- *Warranty of Title* may be excluded or modified by specific language or by certain circumstances, including judicial sale or a sale by a sheriff, executor, or foreclosing lienor
- *Implied Warranty of Merchantability* the disclaimer must mention "merchantability" and, in the case of a writing, must be conspicuous (in a lease the disclaimer must be in writing)
- *Implied Warranty of Fitness for a Particular Purpose* the disclaimer must be in writing and conspicuous
- *Other Disclaimers of Implied Warranties* the implied warranties of merchantability and fitness for a particular purpose may also be disclaimed (1) by expressions like "as is," "with all faults," or other similar language; (2) by course of dealing, course of performance, or usage of trade; or (3) as to defects an examination ought to have revealed where the buyer has examined the goods or where the buyer has refused to examine the goods
- *Federal Legislation Relating to Warranties of Consumer Goods* the Magnuson-Moss Warranty Act protects purchasers of consumer goods by providing that warranty information be clear and useful and that a seller who makes a written warranty cannot disclaim any implied warranty

Limitation or Modification of Warranties permitted as long as it is not unconscionable

Privity of Contract a contractual relationship between parties that was necessary at common law to maintain a lawsuit
- *Horizontal Privity* doctrine determining who benefits from a warranty and who therefore may bring a cause of action; the Code provides three alternatives
- *Vertical Privity* doctrine determining who in the chain of distribution is liable for a breach of warranty; the Code has not adopted a position on this

Notice of Breach if the buyer fails to notify the seller of any breach within a reasonable time, she is barred from any remedy against the seller

Plaintiff's Conduct
- *Contributory Negligence* is not a defense
- *Voluntary Assumption of the Risk* is a defense

STRICT LIABILITY IN TORT

NATURE	**General Rule** imposes tort liability on merchant sellers for both personal injuries and property damage for selling a product in a defective condition unreasonably dangerous to the user or consumer

General Rule imposes tort liability on merchant sellers for both personal injuries and property damage for selling a product in a defective condition unreasonably dangerous to the user or consumer

Defective Condition
- *Manufacturing Defect* by failing to meet its own manufacturing specifications, the product is not properly made
- *Design Defect* the product, though made as designed, is dangerous because the design is inadequate
- *Failure to Warn* failure to provide adequate warnings of possible danger or to provide appropriate directions for use of a product

Unreasonably Dangerous contains a danger beyond that which would be contemplated by the ordinary consumer

OBSTACLES TO RECOVERY	**Contractual Defenses** defenses such as privity, disclaimers, and notice generally do not apply to tort liability
	Plaintiff's Conduct
	• *Contributory Negligence* not a defense in the majority of States
	• *Comparative Negligence* most States have applied the rule of comparative negligence to strict liability in tort
	• *Voluntary Assumption of the Risk* express assumption of risk is a defense to an action based upon strict liability; some States apply implied assumption of risk to strict liability cases
	• *Misuse or Abuse of the Product* is a defense
	Subsequent Alteration liability exists only if the product reaches the user or consumer without substantial change in the condition in which it is sold
	Statute of Repose limits the time period for which a manufacturer is liable for injury caused by its product
	Limitations on Damages many States have limited the punitive damages that a plaintiff can collect in a product liability lawsuit
RESTATEMENT (THIRD) OF TORTS: PRODUCTS LIABILITY	**General Rule** one engaged in the business of selling products who sells a defective product is subject to liability for harm to persons or property caused by the defect
	Manufacturing Defect a seller is held to strict liability when the product departs from its intended design
	Design Defect a product is defective when the foreseeable risks of harm posed by the product could have been reduced or avoided by the adoption of a reasonable alternative design
	Failure to Warn a product is defective because of inadequate instructions or warnings when the foreseeable risks of harm posed by the product could have been reduced or avoided by the provision of reasonable instructions or warnings

Sales Remedies

A contract for the sale of goods may require total performance at one time or part performance in stages, according to the agreement of the parties. At any stage, one of the parties may repudiate the contract, may become insolvent, or may breach the contract by failing to perform his obligations under it. In a sales contract, breach may consist of the seller's delivering defective goods, too few goods, the wrong goods, or no goods. The buyer may breach by not accepting conforming goods or by failing to pay for conforming goods that he has accepted. Breach may occur when the goods are in the possession of the seller, in the possession of a bailee, in transit to the buyer, or in the possession of the buyer.

Remedies, therefore, need to address not only the type of breach of contract but also the situation with respect to the goods. Consequently, the Uniform Commercial Code (UCC) provides distinct remedies for the seller and for the buyer, each specifically keyed to the factual situation.

In all events, the purpose of the Code is to put the aggrieved party in a position as good as the one he would have occupied, had the other party fully performed. To accomplish this purpose, the Code has provided that its remedies should be liberally administered. Moreover, damages do not have to be "calculable with mathematical precision": they need only be proved with "whatever definiteness and accuracy the facts permit, but no more." Comment 1 to Section 1–106. The purpose of remedies under the Code is compensation; therefore, punitive damages generally are not available.

Finally, the Code has rejected the doctrine of election of remedies, essentially providing that remedies for breach are cumulative in nature. Whether one remedy bars another depends entirely on the facts of the individual case.

CISG Damages for breach of contract by one party consist of a sum equal to the loss, including loss of profit, suffered by the other party as a consequence of the breach. Such damages may not exceed the loss that the party in breach foresaw or should have foreseen at the time of the conclusion of the contract as a possible consequence of the breach of contract. The aggrieved party must take such measures as are reasonable in the circumstances to mitigate the loss, including loss of profit, resulting from the breach. If he fails to take such measures, the party in breach may claim a reduction in the damages in the amount by which the loss should have been mitigated.

REMEDIES OF THE SELLER

A buyer's default in performing any of his contractual obligations deprives the seller of the rights for which he bargained. Such default may consist of any of the following acts: wrongfully rejecting the goods, wrongfully revoking acceptance of the goods, failing to make a payment due on or before delivery, or repudiating (indicating an intention not to perform) the contract in whole or in part. Section 2–703; Section 2A–523(1). The Code catalogs the seller's remedies for each of these defaults. Section 2–703. (Section 2A–523(1) contains a comparable set of remedies for the lessor.) These remedies allow the seller to—

1. withhold delivery of the goods;
2. stop delivery of the goods by a carrier or other bailee;
3. identify to the contract conforming goods not already identified;
4. resell the goods and recover damages;
5. recover damages for nonacceptance of the goods or repudiation of the contract;
6. recover the price;
7. recover incidental damages;
8. cancel the contract; and
9. reclaim the goods on the buyer's insolvency (Section 2–702).

Under Article 2A a lessor also may recover compensation for any loss of or damage to the lessor's residual interest in the goods caused by the lessee's default. Section 2A–532.

COLUMN: © PHOTOGRAPHEROLYMPUS   CLOUDS: © KERTLIS

The first three and the ninth remedies indexed above are **goods-oriented**—that is, they relate to the seller's exercising control over the goods. The fourth through seventh remedies are money-oriented because they provide the seller with the opportunity to recover monetary damages. The eighth remedy is obligation-oriented because it allows the seller to avoid his obligation under the contract.

Moreover, if the seller delivers goods on credit and the buyer fails to pay the price when due, the seller's sole remedy, unless the buyer is insolvent, is to sue for the unpaid price. If, however, the buyer received the goods on credit while insolvent, the seller may be able to reclaim the goods. The Code defines **insolvency** to include both its equity meaning and its bankruptcy meaning. Section 1–201(23); Revised Section 1–201(b)(23). The **equity** meaning of insolvency is the inability of a person to pay his debts in the ordinary course of business or as they become due. The **bankruptcy** meaning of insolvency is that total liabilities exceed the total value of all assets.

As noted above, the Code's remedies are *cumulative*. Thus, by way of example, an aggrieved seller may (1) identify goods to the contract; *and* (2) withhold delivery; *and* (3) resell or recover damages for nonacceptance or recover the price; *and* (4) recover incidental damages; *and* (5) cancel the contract.

| CISG | If the buyer fails to perform any of her obligations under the contract or the CISG, the seller (1) may require the buyer to pay the price or (2) may fix an additional period of time of reasonable length for performance by the buyer of his obligations. Unless the seller has received notice from the buyer that she will not perform within the period so fixed, the seller may not, during that period, resort to any remedy for breach of contract. Moreover, if the buyer's breach is fundamental or the buyer fails to perform within the additional time granted by the seller, the seller may avoid the contract. In addition to these remedies, the seller also has the right to damages. |

TO WITHHOLD DELIVERY OF THE GOODS

A seller may withhold delivery of goods to a buyer who has wrongfully rejected or revoked acceptance of the goods, who has failed to make a payment due on or before delivery, or who has repudiated the contract. Section 2–703; Section 2A–523(1). This right is essentially that of a seller to withhold or discontinue performance of her side of the contract because of the buyer's breach.

Where the contract calls for installments, any breach of an installment that impairs the value of the *whole* contract will permit the seller to withhold the entire undelivered balance of the goods. In addition, upon discovery of the buyer's insolvency, the seller may refuse to deliver the goods except for cash, including payment for all goods previously delivered under the contract. Section 2–702. (Section 2A–525(1) is similar.)

TO STOP DELIVERY OF THE GOODS

An extension of the right to withhold delivery is the right of an aggrieved seller to stop the delivery of goods in transit to the buyer or in the possession of a bailee. A seller who discovers that the buyer is insolvent may stop *any* delivery. If the buyer is not insolvent but repudiates or otherwise breaches the contract, the seller may stop carload, truckload, planeload, or larger shipments. Section 2–705(1); Section 2A–526(1). To stop delivery, the seller must notify the carrier or other bailee soon enough for the bailee to prevent delivery of the goods. After this notification, the carrier or bailee must hold and deliver the goods according to the directions of the seller, who is liable to the carrier or bailee for any charges or damages incurred. If a negotiable document of title has been issued for the goods, the bailee need not obey a notification until the document is provided. Section 2–705(3).

The seller's right to stop delivery ceases when (1) the buyer receives the goods; (2) the bailee of the goods, except a carrier, acknowledges to the buyer that he holds them for the buyer; (3) the carrier acknowledges to the buyer that he holds them for the buyer by reshipment or as warehouseman; or (4) a negotiable document of title covering the goods is negotiated to the buyer. Section 2–705(2); Section 2A–526(2) is similar.

TO IDENTIFY GOODS TO THE CONTRACT

Upon a breach of the contract by the buyer, the seller may proceed to identify to the contract conforming goods in her possession or control that were not so identified at the time she learned of the breach. Section 2–704(1); Section 2A–524(1). This enables the seller to exercise the remedy of resale of goods (discussed below). Furthermore, the seller may resell any unfinished goods demonstrably intended to fulfill the particular contract. The seller may either complete the manufacture of unfinished goods and identify them to the contract or cease their manufacture and resell the unfinished goods for scrap or salvage value. Section 2–704(2); Section 2A–524(2). In so deciding, the seller must exercise reasonable commercial judgment to minimize her loss.

TO RESELL THE GOODS AND RECOVER DAMAGES

Under the same circumstances that permit the seller to withhold delivery of goods to the buyer (i.e., wrongful rejection or revocation, repudiation, or failure to make timely payment), the seller may resell the goods or the undelivered balance. If the resale is made in good faith and is commercially reasonable, the seller may recover from the buyer the difference between the contract price and the resale price, plus any incidental damages (discussed below), minus expenses saved because of the buyer's breach. Section 2–706(1). For example, Floyd agrees to sell goods to Beverly for a contract price of $8,000 due on delivery. Beverly wrongfully rejects the goods and refuses to pay Floyd anything. Floyd resells the goods in strict compliance with the Code for $6,000, incurring incidental damages for sales commissions of $500 but saving $200 in transportation costs. Floyd would recover from Beverly the difference between the contract price ($8,000) and the resale price ($6,000), plus incidental damages ($500), minus expenses saved ($200), which equals $2,300.

In a lease, the comparable recovery is the **difference between the present values** of the **old rent** due under the original lease and the **new rent** due under the new lease. More specifically, the lessor may recover (1) the accrued and unpaid rent as of the date of commencement of the new lease; (2) the present value as of that date of total rent for the then remaining term of the original lease minus the present value, as of the same date, of the rent under the new lease applicable to a comparable time period; and (3) any incidental damages, less expenses saved because of the lessee's breach. Section 2A–527(2).

The resale may be a public or private sale, and the goods may be sold as a unit or in parcels. The goods resold must be identified as those related to the contract, but where an anticipatory repudiation has occurred, for example, the goods need be neither in existence nor identified to the contract before the buyer's breach. Section 2–706(2).

Where the resale is at a private sale, the seller must give the buyer reasonable notice of his intention to resell. Section 2–706(3). The seller or a broker may carry out a private sale by negotiations or solicitations. Where the resale is at a public sale (such as an auction), only identified goods can be sold, except where a recognized market exists for a public sale of future goods of the kind involved. The public sale must be made at a usual place or market for public sale, if one is reasonably available, and the seller must give the buyer reasonable notice of the time and place of the resale unless the goods are perishable or threaten to decline in value speedily. Prospective bidders must be given an opportunity for reasonable inspection of the goods before the sale. Moreover, the seller may be a purchaser of the goods at the public sale. Section 2–706(4). In choosing between a public and private sale, the seller must observe relevant trade practices and usages and take into account the character of the goods.

The seller is not accountable to the buyer for any profit made on any resale of the goods. Section 2–706(6); Section 2A–527(5). Moreover, a *bona fide* purchaser at a resale takes the goods free of any rights of the original buyer, even if the seller has failed to comply with one or more of the require-ments of the Code in making the resale. Section 2–706(5); Section 2A–524(4).

Failure to act in good faith and in a commercially reasonable manner deprives the seller of this remedy and relegates him to the remedy of recovering damages for nonacceptance or repudiation (discussed below). Section 2–706, Comment 2; Section 2A–527(3).

CISG If the contract is avoided and the seller has resold the goods in a reasonable manner and within a reasonable time after avoidance, he may recover the difference between the contract price and the resale price. In addition, he may recover consequential damages.

TO RECOVER DAMAGES FOR NONACCEPTANCE OR REPUDIATION

In the event of the buyer's wrongful rejection or revocation, repudiation, or failure to make timely payment, the seller may recover damages from the buyer equal to the **difference between the unpaid contract price and the market price** at the time and place of tender of the goods, plus incidental damages, less expenses saved because of the buyer's breach. Section 2–708(1). This remedy is an alternative to the remedy of reselling the goods.

In a lease the comparable recovery is the **difference between the present values** of the **old rent due** under the original lease and the **market rent**. Section 2A–528(1).

For example, Joan in Seattle agrees to sell goods to Nelson in Chicago for $20,000 F.O.B. ("free on board") Chicago, with delivery by June 15. Nelson wrongfully rejects the goods. The market price would be ascertained as of June 15 in Chicago because F.O.B. Chicago is a destination contract in which the place of tender would be Chicago. The market price of the goods on June 15 in Chicago is $15,000. Joan, who incurred $1,000 in incidental expenses while saving $500 in expenses, would recover from Nelson the difference between the contract price ($20,000) and the market price ($15,000), plus incidental damages ($1,000), minus expenses saved ($500), which equals $5,500.

If the difference between the contract price and the market price will not place the seller in as good a position as performance would have, then the measure of damages is the **lost profit**; that is, the profit, including reasonable overhead, that the seller would have realized from full performance by the buyer, plus any incidental damages, less expenses saved because of the buyer's breach. Section 2–708(2). For example, Green, an automobile dealer, enters into a contract to sell a large, fuel-inefficient luxury car to Holland for $22,000. The price of gasoline increases 20 percent, and Holland repudiates. The market value of the car is still $22,000, but because Green cannot sell as many cars as he can obtain, his sales volume has decreased by one as a result of Holland's breach. Therefore, Green would be permitted to recover the profits he lost on the sale to Holland (computed as the contract price minus what the car cost Green, plus an allocation of overhead), plus any incidental damages.

Article 2A has a comparable provision, except the profit is reduced to its present value as the lessor would have received it over the term of the lease. Section 2A–528(2).

> **CISG** If the contract is avoided and the seller has not made a resale, she may recover the difference between the contract price and the current price at the time of avoidance and at the place where delivery of the goods should have been made. In addition, he may recover consequential damages.

TO RECOVER THE PRICE

The Code permits the seller to recover the price plus incidental damages in only three situations: (1) where the buyer has accepted the goods; (2) where conforming goods have been lost or damaged after the risk of loss has passed to the buyer; and (3) where the goods have been identified to the contract and there is no ready market available for their resale at a reasonable price. Section 2–709(1). For example, Kelly, in accordance with her agreement with Sally, prints ten thousand letterheads and envelopes with Sally's name and address on them. Sally wrongfully rejects the stationery, which Kelly is unable to resell at a reasonable price. Kelly is entitled to recover the price plus incidental damages from Sally.

Article 2A has a similar provision except that the lessor is entitled to (1) accrued and unpaid rent as of the date of the judgment; (2) the present value as of the judgment date of the rent for the then remaining lease term; and (3) incidental damages less expenses saved. Section 2A–529(1).

A seller who sues for the price must hold for the buyer any goods identified to the contract that are still in her control. Section 2–709(2); Section 2A–529(2). If resale becomes possible, the seller may resell the goods at any time prior to the collection of the judgment, and the net proceeds of such resale must be credited to the buyer. Payment of the judgment entitles the buyer to any goods not resold. Section 2–709(2). In a lease, payment of the judgment entitles the lessee to the use and possession of the goods for the remaining lease term. Section 2A–529(4).

> **CISG** The seller may require the buyer to pay the price, take delivery or perform her other obligations, unless the seller has resorted to a remedy that is inconsistent with this requirement.

TO RECOVER INCIDENTAL DAMAGES

In addition to recovering damages for the difference between the contract price and the resale price, recovering damages for nonacceptance or repudiation, or recovering the price, the seller may in the same action recover her incidental damages in order to recoup expenses she reasonably incurred as a result of the buyer's breach. Section 2–710 defines a seller's **incidental damages** as follows:

> Incidental damages to an aggrieved seller include any commercially reasonable charges, expenses or commissions incurred in stopping delivery, in the transportation, care and custody of goods after the buyer's breach, in connection with return or resale of the goods or otherwise resulting from the breach.

Section 2A–530 has an analogous definition.

TO CANCEL THE CONTRACT

Where the buyer wrongfully rejects or revokes acceptance of the goods, fails to make a payment due on or before delivery, or repudiates the contract in whole or in part, the seller may cancel the contract with respect to the goods directly affected. If the breach is of an installment contract and it substantially impairs the whole contract, the seller may cancel the entire contract. Section 2–703(f); Section 2A–523(1)(a).

The Code defines **cancellation** as one party's putting an end to the contract by reason of a breach by the other. Section 2–106(4); Section 2A–103(1)(b). The obligation of the canceling party for any future performance under the contract is discharged, although she retains any remedy for breach of the whole contract or any unperformed balance. Section 2–720; Section 2A–505(1). Thus, if the seller has the right to cancel, she may recover damages for breach without having to tender any further performance.

> **CISG** The seller may declare the contract avoided if (1) the buyer commits a fundamental breach, or (2) the buyer does not, within the additional period of time fixed by the seller, perform his obligation to pay the price or take delivery of the goods. Avoidance of the contract releases both parties from their obligations under it, subject to any damages that may be due. Avoidance does not affect any provision of the contract for the settlement of disputes or any other provision of the contract governing the rights and obligations of the parties consequent upon the avoidance of the contract. A party who has performed the contract either wholly or in part may claim restitution from the other party. If both parties are bound to make restitution, they must do so concurrently.

TO RECLAIM THE GOODS UPON THE BUYER'S INSOLVENCY

In addition to the right of an unpaid seller to withhold and stop delivery of the goods, he may reclaim them from an insolvent buyer by demand upon the buyer within ten days after the buyer has received the goods. Section 2–702(2). Where, however, the buyer has committed fraud by misrepresenting her solvency to the seller in writing within three months prior to delivery of the goods, the ten-day limitation does not apply.

The seller's right to reclaim the goods is subject to the rights of a buyer in the ordinary course of business or to the rights of any other good faith purchaser. Furthermore, upon reclaiming the goods from an insolvent buyer, the seller is excluded from all other remedies with respect to those goods. Section 2–702(3).

A lessor retains title to the goods and therefore has the right to recover possession of them upon default by the lessee. Section 2A–525(2).

◆ **SEE FIGURE 25-1: Remedies of the Seller**

REMEDIES OF THE BUYER

Basically, a seller may default in three different ways: he may repudiate, he may fail to deliver the goods, or he may deliver or tender goods that do not conform to the contract. Section 2–711; Section 2A–508. The Code provides remedies for each of these breaches. Some remedies are available for all three types; others are not. Moreover, the availability of some remedies depends on the buyer's actions. For example, if the seller tenders nonconforming goods, the buyer may reject or accept them. If the buyer rejects them, he can choose from a number of remedies. On the other hand, if the buyer accepts the nonconforming goods and does not justifiably revoke his acceptance, he limits himself to recovering damages.

Where the seller fails to make delivery or repudiates, or where the buyer rightfully rejects or justifiably revokes acceptance, the buyer may, with respect to any goods involved, or with respect to the whole if the breach goes to the whole contract, (1) cancel *and* (2) recover payments made. In addition, the buyer may (3) "cover" and obtain damages *or*

◆ **FIGURE 25-1: Remedies of the Seller**

Buyer's Breach	Seller's Remedies		
	Obligation-oriented	Goods-oriented[1]	Money-oriented[2]
Buyer wrongfully rejects goods	Cancel	• Withhold delivery of goods • Stop delivery of goods in transit • Identify conforming goods to the contract	• Resell and recover damages • Recover difference between unpaid contract and market prices *or* lost profits • Recover price
Buyer wrongfully revokes acceptance	Cancel	• Withhold delivery of goods • Stop delivery of goods in transit • Identify conforming goods to the contract	• Resell and recover damages • Recover difference between unpaid contract and market prices *or* lost profits • Recover price
Buyer fails to make payment	Cancel	• Withhold delivery of goods • Stop delivery of goods in transit • Identify conforming goods to the contract • Reclaim goods upon buyer's insolvency	• Resell and recover damages • Recover difference between unpaid contract and market prices *or* lost profits • Recover price
Buyer repudiates	Cancel	• Withhold delivery of goods • Stop delivery of goods in transit • Identify conforming goods to the contract	• Resell and recover damages • Recover difference between unpaid contract and market prices *or* lost profits • Recover price

[1] In a lease, the lessor has the right to recover possession of the goods upon default by the lessee.
[2] In a lease, the lessor's recovery of damages for future rent payments is reduced to their present value.

(4) recover damages for nondelivery. Where the seller fails to deliver or repudiates, the buyer, where appropriate, may also (5) recover identified goods if the seller is insolvent, *or* (6) replevy the goods, *or* (7) obtain specific performance. Moreover, upon rightful rejection or justifiable revocation of acceptance, the buyer (8) has a security interest in the goods. Where the buyer has accepted goods and notified the seller of their nonconformity, the buyer may (9) recover damages for breach of warranty. Finally, in addition to the remedies listed above, the buyer may, where appropriate, (10) recover incidental damages, and (11) recover consequential damages. Article 2A provides for essentially the same remedies for the lessee. Section 2A–508.

The first remedy cataloged above is **obligation-oriented**; the second through fourth and ninth through eleventh are **money-oriented**; and the fifth through eighth are **goods-oriented**.

The buyer may deduct from the price due any damages resulting from any breach of contract by the seller. The buyer must, however, give notice to the seller of her intention to withhold such damages from payment of the price due. Section 2–717; Section 2A–508(6).

CISG If the seller fails to perform any of his obligations under the contract or the CISG, the buyer (1) may require the seller to perform his contractual obligations or (2) may fix an additional period of time of reasonable length for performance by the seller of his obligations. Unless the buyer has received notice from the seller that he will not perform within the period so fixed, the buyer may not, during that period, resort to any remedy for breach of contract. Moreover, if the seller's breach is fundamental or the seller fails to perform within the additional time granted by the buyer, the buyer may avoid the contract. In addition to these remedies, the buyer also has the right to damages. If the goods do not conform with the contract, the buyer may reduce the price in the same proportion as the value that the goods actually delivered had at the time of the delivery bears to the value that conforming goods would have had at that time.

TO CANCEL THE CONTRACT

Where the seller fails to make delivery or repudiates the contract, or where the buyer rightfully rejects or justifiably revokes acceptance of goods tendered or delivered to him, the buyer may cancel the contract with respect to any goods involved; and if the breach by the seller concerns the whole contract, the buyer may cancel the entire contract. Section 2–711(1); Section 2A–508(1)(a). The buyer, who must give the seller notice of his cancellation, is excused from further performance or tender on his part. Section 2–106; Section 2A–505(1).

CISG The buyer may declare the contract avoided if (1) the seller commits a fundamental breach or (2) the seller does not deliver the goods within the additional period of time fixed by the buyer. Avoidance of the contract releases both parties from their obligations under it, subject to any damages that may be due. Avoidance does not affect any provision of the contract for the settlement of disputes or any other provision of the contract governing the rights and obligations of the parties consequent upon the avoidance of the contract. A party who has performed the contract either wholly or in part may claim restitution from the other party. If both parties are bound to make restitution, they must do so concurrently.

TO RECOVER PAYMENTS MADE

The buyer, upon the seller's breach, also may recover as much of the price as he has paid. Section 2–711(1). For example, Jonas and Sheila enter into a contract for a sale of goods for a contract price of $3,000, and Sheila, the buyer, has made a down payment of $600. Jonas delivers nonconforming goods to Sheila, who rightfully rejects them. Sheila may cancel the contract and recover the $600 plus whatever other damages she can prove. Under Article 2A, the lessee may recover so much of the rent and security as has been paid and is just under the circumstances. Section 2A–508(1)(b).

TO COVER

Upon the seller's breach, the buyer may protect himself by obtaining cover. Cover means that the buyer may in good faith and without unreasonable delay proceed to purchase needed goods or make a contract to purchase such goods in substitution for those due under the contract from the seller. Section 2–712(1). In a lease, the lessee may purchase or lease substitute goods. Section 2A–518(1).

Upon making a reasonable contract of cover, the buyer may recover from the seller the **difference between the cost of cover and the contract price**, plus any incidental and consequential damages (discussed below), less expenses saved because of the seller's breach. Section 2–712(2). For example, Doug, whose factory is in Oakland, agrees to sell goods to Velda, in Atlanta, for $22,000 F.O.B. Oakland. Doug fails to deliver, and Velda covers by purchasing substitute goods in Atlanta for $25,000, incurring $700 in sales commissions but suffering no other damages as a consequence of Doug's breach. Shipping costs from Oakland to Atlanta for the goods are $1,300. Velda would recover the difference between the cost of cover ($25,000) and the contract price ($22,000), plus incidental damages ($700 in sales commissions), plus consequential damages ($0 in this example), minus expenses saved ($1,300 in shipping costs that Velda need not pay under the contract of cover), which equals $2,400.

In a lease, the comparable recovery is the **difference between the present values** of the **new rent** due under the new lease and the **old rent** due under the original lease. Section 2A–518(2).

The buyer is not required to obtain cover, and his failure to do so does not bar him from any other remedy the Code provides. Section 2–712(3); 2A–519(1). The buyer may not, however, recover consequential damages that he could have prevented by cover. Section 2–715(2)(a); Section 2A–520(2)(a).

CISG If the contract is avoided and the buyer has bought goods in replacement in a reasonable manner and within a reasonable time after avoidance, she may recover the difference between the contract price and the price paid in the substitute transaction. In addition, she may recover consequential damages.

TO RECOVER DAMAGES FOR NONDELIVERY OR REPUDIATION

If the seller repudiates the contract or fails to deliver the goods, or if the buyer rightfully rejects or justifiably revokes acceptance of the goods, the buyer is entitled to recover damages from the seller equal to the **difference between** the **market price** at the time when the buyer learned of the breach and the contract price, together with incidental and consequential damages, less expenses saved because of the seller's breach. Section 2–713(1). This remedy is a complete alternative to the remedy of cover and, as such, is available only to the extent the buyer has not covered. As previously indicated, the buyer who elects this remedy may not recover consequential damages that she could have avoided by cover.

In a lease, the comparable recovery is the **difference between** the **present values** of the **market rent** and the **old rent** due under the original lease. Section 2A–519(1).

The market price is to be determined either as of the place for tender or, in the event that the buyer has rightfully rejected the goods or has justifiably revoked his acceptance of them, as of the place of arrival. Section 2–713(2). For example, Janet, in Portland, agrees to sell goods to Laura, in Minneapolis, for $7,000 C.O.D. (collect on delivery), with delivery by November 15. Janet fails to deliver. As a consequence, Laura suffers incidental damages of $1,500 and consequential damages of $1,000. In the case of nondelivery or repudiation, market price is determined as of the place of tender. Because C.O.D. is a shipment contract, the place of tender would be the seller's city. Therefore, the market price

must be the market price in Portland, the seller's city, on November 15, the date when Laura learned of the breach. At this time and place the market price is $8,000. Laura would recover the difference between the market price ($8,000) and the contract price ($7,000), plus incidental damages ($1,500), plus consequential damages ($1,000), minus expenses saved ($0 in this example), which equals $3,500.

In the example above, if Janet had instead delivered nonconforming goods that Laura rejected, then the market price would be determined at Laura's place of business in Minneapolis. If Janet had repudiated the contract on November 1 rather than November 15, then the market price would be determined as of November 1.

In a lease, market rent is to be determined as of the place for tender or, in cases of rejection after arrival or revocation of acceptance, as of the place of arrival. Section 2A–519(2).

CISG If the contract is avoided and the buyer has not made a replacement purchase, he may recover the difference between the contract price and the current price at the time of avoidance and at the place where delivery of the goods should have been made. In addition, he may recover consequential damages.

TO RECOVER IDENTIFIED GOODS UPON THE SELLER'S INSOLVENCY

Where existing goods are identified to the contract of sale, the buyer acquires a *special property interest* in the goods. Section 2–501. This special property interest exists even though the goods are nonconforming, and the buyer therefore has the right to return or reject them. Either the buyer or the seller may identify the goods to the contract.

The Code gives the buyer a right, which does not exist at common law, to recover from an insolvent seller the goods in which the buyer has a special property interest and for which he has paid part or all of the price. This right exists where the seller, who is in possession or control of the goods, becomes insolvent within ten days after receiving the first installment of the price. To exercise it, the buyer must tender to the seller any unpaid portion of the price. If the special property interest exists by reason of an identification made by the buyer, he may recover the goods only if they conform to the contract for sale. Section 2–502; Section 2A–522.

TO SUE FOR REPLEVIN

Replevin is an action at law to recover from a defendant's possession specific goods that are being unlawfully withheld from the plaintiff. Where the seller has repudiated or breached the contract, the buyer may maintain against the seller an action for replevin for goods that have been identified to the contract if the buyer after a reasonable effort is unable to effect cover for such goods. Section 2–716(3); Section 2A–521(3). Article 2 also provides the buyer with the right to replevin if the goods have been shipped under reservation of a security interest in the seller and satisfaction of this security interest has been made or tendered. Section 2–716(3).

TO SUE FOR SPECIFIC PERFORMANCE

Specific performance is an equitable remedy compelling the party in breach to perform the contract according to its terms. At common law, specific performance is available only if legal remedies are inadequate. For example, where the contract is for the purchase of a unique item, such as a work of art, a famous racehorse, or an heirloom, money damages may not be an adequate remedy. In such a case, a court of equity has the discretion to order the seller specifically to deliver to the buyer the goods described in the contract upon payment of the price.

The Code not only has continued the availability of specific performance but also has sought to encourage a more liberal attitude toward its use. Accordingly, it does not expressly require that the remedy at law be inadequate. Instead, the Code states that specific performance may be granted where "the goods are unique or in other proper circumstances." Section 2–716(1); Section 2A–521(1). As the Comment to Section 2–716 explains, the test of uniqueness under the Code must be made in view of the total situation that characterizes the contract.

CISG The buyer may require the seller to perform his contractual obligations. If the goods do not conform to the contract and the nonconformity constitutes a fundamental breach of contract, the buyer may require delivery of substitute goods. If the goods do not conform to the contract, the buyer may require the seller to remedy the lack of conformity by repair, unless this is unreasonable having regard to all the circumstances. Nevertheless, a court is not bound to enter a judgment for specific performance unless a court would do so under its own law in respect of similar contracts of sale not governed by the CISG.

TO ENFORCE A SECURITY INTEREST IN THE GOODS

A buyer who has rightfully rejected or justifiably revoked acceptance of goods that remain in his possession or control has a security interest in these goods to the extent of any payment of the price that he has made and for any expenses he reasonably has incurred in their inspection, receipt, transportation, care, and custody. The buyer may hold such goods and resell them in the same manner as an aggrieved seller may resell goods. Section 2–711(3); Section 2A–508(5). In the event of resale the buyer is accountable to the seller for any amount of the net proceeds of the resale that exceeds the amount of his security interest. Section 2–706(6); Section 2A–527(5).

TO RECOVER DAMAGES FOR BREACH IN REGARD TO ACCEPTED GOODS

Where the buyer has accepted nonconforming goods and has timely notified the seller of the breach of contract, the buyer is entitled to recover from the seller the damages resulting in the ordinary course of events from the seller's breach, as determined in any reasonable manner. Section 2–714(1); Section 2A–519(3). Where appropriate, the buyer may also recover incidental and consequential damages. Section 2–714(3); Section 2A–519(3). Nonconformity includes breaches of warranty as well as any failure of the seller to perform according to her obligations under the contract. Thus, even if a seller cures a nonconforming tender, the buyer may recover under this section for any injury he suffered because the original tender was nonconforming.

In the event of breach of warranty, the measure of damages is the **difference** at the time and place of acceptance **between** the **value of the goods that have been accepted** and the **value** that the goods would have had if they had been **as warranted**, unless special circumstances show proximate damages of a different amount. Section 2–714(2). Article 2A has a comparable provision, except the recovery is for the **present value** of the difference between the value of the use of the goods accepted and the value if they had been as warranted for the lease term. Section 2A–519(4).

The contract price of the goods does not figure in this computation because the buyer is entitled to the benefit of his bargain, which is to receive goods that are as warranted. For example, Max agrees to sell goods to Stanley for $1,000. The value of the goods accepted is only $800; had they been as warranted, their value would have been $1,200. Stanley's damages for breach of warranty are $400, which he may deduct from any unpaid balance due on the purchase price upon notice to Max of his intention to do so. Section 2–717; Section 2A–508(6).

TO RECOVER INCIDENTAL DAMAGES

In addition to remedies such as covering, recovering damages for nondelivery or repudiation, or recovering damages for breach in regard to accepted goods, including breach of warranty, the buyer may recover **incidental damages**. A buyer's incidental damages provide reimbursement for the buyer who incurs reasonable expenses in handling rightfully rejected goods or in effecting cover. Section 2–715(1) of the Code defines the buyer's incidental damages as follows:

Incidental damages resulting from the seller's breach include expenses reasonably incurred in inspection, receipt, transportation and care and custody of goods rightfully rejected, any commercially reasonable charges, expenses or commissions in connection with effecting cover and any other reasonable expense incident to the delay or other breach.

Article 2A has an analogous definition. Section 2A–520(1).

For example, the buyer of a racehorse who justifiably revokes acceptance because the horse does not conform to the contract will be allowed to recover as incidental damages the cost of caring for the horse from the date the horse was delivered until the buyer returns it to the seller.

TO RECOVER CONSEQUENTIAL DAMAGES

In many cases, the remedies discussed above will not fully compensate the aggrieved buyer for her losses. For example, nonconforming goods that are accepted may in some way damage or destroy the buyer's warehouse and its contents, or undelivered goods may have been the subject of a lucrative contract of resale, the profits from which are now lost. The Code responds to this problem by providing the buyer with the opportunity to recover **consequential damages** resulting from the seller's breach, including (1) any loss resulting from the buyer's requirements and needs of which the seller at the time of contracting had reason to know and which the buyer could not reasonably prevent by cover or otherwise; and (2) injury to person or property proximately resulting from any breach of warranty. Section 2–715(2); Section 2A–520(2).

With respect to the first type of consequential damages, *particular* needs of the buyer usually must be made known to the seller, whereas *general* needs usually need not be. In the case of a buyer who is in the business of reselling goods, resale is one requirement of which the seller has reason to know. For example, Supreme Machine Co., a manufacturer, contracts to sell Allied Sales, Inc., a dealer in used machinery, a used machine that Allied plans to resell. When Supreme repudiates and Allied is unable to obtain a similar machine elsewhere, Allied's damages include the net profit that it would have made on resale of the machine. A buyer may not, however, recover consequential damages he could have prevented by cover. Section 2–715(2); Section 2A–520(2)(a). For instance, Supreme Machine Co. contracts for $10,000 to sell Capitol Manufacturing Co. a used machine to be delivered at Capitol's factory by June 1. Supreme repudiates the contract on May 1. By reasonable efforts, Capitol could buy a similar machine from United Machinery, Inc., for $11,000 in time for a June 1 delivery. Capitol fails to do so, thereby losing a $5,000 profit that it would have made from the resale of the machine. Though Capitol can recover

$1,000 from Supreme, its damages do not include the loss of the $5,000 profit.

An example of the second type of consequential damages would be the following: Federal Machine Co. sells a machine to Southern Manufacturing Co., warranting its suitability for Southern's purpose. The machine is not suitable for Southern's purpose, however, and causes $10,000 in damage to Southern's property and $15,000 in personal injuries. Southern can recover the $25,000 consequential damages in addition to any other loss suffered.

◆ **SEE FIGURE 25-2: Remedies of the Buyer**

CONTRACTUAL PROVISIONS AFFECTING REMEDIES

Within specified limits, the Code permits the parties to a sales contract to modify, exclude, or limit by agreement the remedies or damages that will be available for breach of that contract. Two basic types of contractual provisions affect remedies: (1) liquidation or limitation of damages, and (2) modification or limitation of remedy.

LIQUIDATION OR LIMITATION OF DAMAGES

The parties may provide for liquidated damages in their contract by specifying the amount or measure of damages that either party may recover in the event of a breach by the other. The amount of such damages must be reasonable in light of the anticipated or actual loss resulting from a breach, the difficulties of proof of loss, and the inconvenience or lack of feasibility of otherwise obtaining an adequate remedy. A contractual provision fixing unreasonably large liquidated damages is void as a penalty. Section 2–718(1). An unreasonably small amount, on the other hand, might be stricken on the grounds of unconscionability. Comment 1 to Section 2–718.

To illustrate, Sterling Cabinetry Company contracts to build and install shelves and cabinets for an office building being constructed by Baron Construction Company. The contract price is $120,000, and the contract provides that Sterling would be liable for $100 per day for every day's delay beyond the completion date specified in the contract. The stipulated sum of $100 per day is reasonable and commensurate with the anticipated loss. Therefore, it is enforceable as liquidated damages. If, instead, the sum stipulated had been $5,000 per day, it would be unreasonably large and therefore would be void as a penalty.

Section 2A–504(1) authorizes liquidated damages payable by either party for default, or any other act or omission. The amount of, or formula for, liquidated damages must be reasonable in light of the then anticipated harm caused by default or other act or omission. Section 2A–504(1).

◆ **FIGURE 25-2: Remedies of the Buyer**

	Buyer's Remedies		
Seller's Breach	**Obligation-oriented**	**Goods-oriented**	**Money-oriented***
Buyer rightfully rejects goods	Cancel	Have a security interest	• Recover payments made • Cover and recover damages • Recover damages for nondelivery
Buyer justifiably revokes acceptance	Cancel	Have a security interest	• Recover payments made • Cover and recover damages • Recover damages for nondelivery
Seller fails to deliver	Cancel	• Recover identified goods if seller is insolvent • Replevy goods • Obtain specific performance	• Recover payments made • Cover and recover damages • Recover damages for nondelivery
Seller repudiates	Cancel	• Recover identified goods if seller is insolvent • Replevy goods • Obtain specific performance	• Recover payments made • Cover and recover damages • Recover damages for nondelivery
Buyer accepts nonconforming goods			Recover damages for breach of warranty

* In a lease, the lessee's recovery of damages for future rent payments is reduced to their present value.

Where the seller justifiably withholds delivery of the goods because of the buyer's breach, and the buyer has made payments on the price, the buyer is entitled to restitution of the amount by which the sum of his payments exceeds the amount of liquidated damages to which the seller is entitled under the contract. In the absence of a provision for liquidated damages, the buyer may recover the difference between the amounts that he has paid on the price and 20 percent of the value of the total performance for which he is obligated under the contract, or $500, whichever is smaller. Section 2–718(2)(b). Article 2A has a comparable provision, except the $500 provision applies only to consumer leases. Section 2A–504(3)(b). The buyer's right to restitution is offset by the seller's right to recover other damages provided in the Code and by the value of any benefits the buyer has received by reason of the contract. Section 2–718(3); Section 2A–504(4).

Thus, if a buyer, after depositing $1,500 with the seller on a $10,000 contract for goods, breaches the contract and the seller withholds delivery, in the absence of a provision for liquidated damages and in the absence of the seller's establishing greater actual damages resulting from the breach, the buyer is entitled to restitution of $1,000 ($1,500 less $500). If the deposit were $250 on a $500 contract, the buyer would be entitled to $150 ($250 less $100, which is 20 percent of the price).

MODIFICATION OR LIMITATION OF REMEDY BY AGREEMENT

The contract between the seller and buyer may expressly provide for remedies in addition to or instead of those provided in the Code and may limit or change the measure of damages recoverable in the event of breach. Section 2–719(1); Section 2A–503(1). For instance, the contract may validly limit the buyer's remedy to a return of the goods and a refund of the price, or to the replacement of nonconforming goods or parts.

A contractual remedy is deemed optional, however, unless the parties expressly agree that it is to be exclusive of other remedies, in which event it becomes the sole remedy. Section 2–719(1)(b); Section 2A–503(2). Moreover, where circumstances cause an exclusive or limited remedy to fail in its essential purpose, the parties may resort to the remedies provided by the Code. Section 2–719(2); Section 2A–503(2).

The contract may expressly limit or exclude consequential damages unless such limitation or exclusion would be unconscionable. Limitation of consequential damages for personal injuries resulting from breach of warranty in the sale of consumer goods is *prima facie* unconscionable, whereas limitation of such damages for commercial loss is not. Section 2–719(3); Section 2A–503(3). For example, Ace Motors, Inc., sells a pickup truck to Brenda, a consumer. The contract of sale excludes liability for all consequential damages. The next day, the truck explodes, causing

Brenda serious personal injury. Brenda would recover for her personal injuries unless Ace could prove that the exclusion of consequential damages was not unconscionable.

STATUTE OF LIMITATIONS

Any action for breach of a sales contract must be begun within four years after the cause of action has accrued. Section 2–725(1); Section 2A–506(1). The parties may reduce the period of limitation to not less than one year. Section 2–725(1); Section 2A–506(1). In a sale, they may not, however, extend the period. Article 2A does not include this limitation.

A cause of action accrues when the breach occurs without regard to the injured party's knowledge of the breach. Section 2–725(2). A breach of warranty occurs upon tender of delivery, except where the warranty extends to future performance. In that event, the cause of action occurs when the breach is or should have been discovered. In a lease, a cause of action for default accrues when the act or omission is discovered or should have been discovered by the aggrieved party, or when the default occurs, whichever is later. Section 2A–506(2).

CHAPTER SUMMARY

REMEDIES OF THE SELLER

Buyer's Default the seller's remedies are triggered by the buyer's actions in wrongfully rejecting or revoking acceptance of the goods, in failing to make payment due on or before delivery, or in repudiating the contract

To Withhold Delivery

To Stop Delivery if the buyer is insolvent (one who is unable to pay his debts as they become due or one whose total liabilities exceed his total assets), the seller may stop any delivery; if the buyer repudiates or otherwise breaches, the seller may stop carload, truckload, planeload, or larger shipments

To Identify Goods

To Resell the Goods the seller may resell the goods concerned or the undelivered balance of the goods and recover the difference between the contract price and the resale price, together with any incidental damages, less expenses saved
* *Type of Resale* may be public or private
* *Manner of Resale* must be made in good faith and in a commercially reasonable manner

To Recover Damages for Nonacceptance or Repudiation
* *Market Price Differential* the seller may recover damages from the buyer measured by the difference between the unpaid contract price and the market price at the time and place of tender of the goods, plus incidental damages, less expenses saved
* *Lost Profit* in the alternative, the seller may recover the lost profit, including reasonable overhead, plus incidental damages, less expenses saved

To Recover the Price the seller may recover the price
* where the buyer has accepted the goods
* where the goods have been lost or damaged after the risk of loss has passed to the buyer
* where the goods have been identified to the contract and a ready market is not available for their resale

To Recover Incidental Damages incidental damages include any commercially reasonable charges, expenses, or commissions directly resulting from the breach

To Cancel the Contract

To Reclaim the Goods upon the Buyer's Insolvency an unpaid seller may reclaim goods from an insolvent buyer under certain circumstances

REMEDIES OF THE BUYER	**Seller's Default** the buyer's remedies arise in cases (1) in which the seller fails to make delivery or repudiates the contract or (2) in which the buyer rightfully rejects or justifiably revokes acceptance of goods tendered or delivered

To Cancel the Contract

To Recover Payments Made

To Cover the buyer may obtain cover by proceeding in good faith and without unreasonable delay to purchase substitute goods; the buyer may recover the difference between the cost of cover and the contract price, plus any incidental and consequential damages, less expenses saved

To Recover Damages for Nondelivery or Repudiation the buyer may recover the difference between the market price at the time the buyer learned of the breach and the contract price, together with any incidental and consequential damages, less expenses saved

To Recover Identified Goods on the Seller's Insolvency for which he has paid all or part of the price

To Sue for Replevin the buyer may recover goods identified to the contract if (1) the buyer is unable to obtain cover, or (2) the goods have been shipped under reservation of a security interest in the seller

To Sue for Specific Performance the buyer may obtain specific performance in cases in which the goods are unique or in other proper circumstances

To Enforce a Security Interest a buyer who has rightfully rejected or justifiably revoked acceptance of goods that remain in her possession has a security interest in these goods for any payments that she has made on their price and for any expenses she has reasonably incurred

To Recover Damages for Breach in Regard to Accepted Goods the buyer may recover damages resulting in the ordinary course of events from the seller's breach; in the case of breach of warranty, such recovery is the difference between the value the goods would have had if they had been as warranted and the value of the nonconforming goods that have been accepted

To Recover Incidental Damages the buyer may recover incidental damages, which include any commercially reasonable expenses connected with the delay or other breach

To Recover Consequential Damages the buyer may recover consequential damages resulting from the seller's breach, including (1) any loss resulting from the buyer's requirements and needs of which the seller at the time of contracting had reason to know and which the buyer could not reasonably prevent by cover or otherwise, and (2) injury to person or property proximately resulting from any breach of warranty

CONTRACTUAL PROVISIONS AFFECTING REMEDIES	**Liquidation or Limitation of Damages** the parties may specify the amount or measure of damages that may be recovered in the event of a breach if the amount is reasonable

Modification or Limitation of Remedy by Agreement the contract between the parties may expressly provide for remedies in addition to those in the Code, or it may limit or change the measure of damages recoverable for breach

PART 5
Negotiable Instruments

CHAPTER 26

Form and Content

In 1990, the American Law Institute and the National Conference of Commissioners on Uniform Laws approved a Revised Article 3 to the Uniform Commercial Code (UCC). Named "Negotiable Instruments," the new Article maintains the basic scope and content of prior Article 3 (Commercial Paper). In 2002, the American Law Institute and the National Conference of Commissioners on Uniform Law completed updates to Articles 3 and 4. Thirty-nine States have adopted the 1990 version of Article 3, ten States have adopted the 2002 version, and New York has retained the original version of Article 3 (Commercial Paper). This part of the text will discuss Revised Article 3 but will also point out the major changes from prior Article 3. The 1990 version of Revised Article 3 is presented in *Appendix C*.

Negotiable instruments, also referred to simply as instruments, include checks, promissory notes, drafts, and certificates of deposit. These instruments are crucial to the sale of goods and services as well as to the financing of most businesses. The use of negotiable instruments has increased to such an extent that payments made with these instruments, with checks in particular, are now many times greater than payments made with cash, which now is used primarily for smaller transactions. In the United States, approximately seventy billion checks are written each year for a total value of $42 trillion. However, the number of checks written is lower than in previous years due to the increased use of electronic payments. In addition, as of the end of 2009, in the United States $1.1 trillion of outstanding commercial paper in the form of promissory notes had been issued by corporations to fund operating expenses or current assets. Moreover, in the United States in 2007, almost $6 trillion of corporate long-term promissory notes (bonds) were outstanding. Accordingly, the vital importance of negotiable instruments and electronic transfers as methods of payment and financing cannot be overstated.

To accomplish its social and economic objectives, the payment system must be quick, sure, and efficient. The use of cash can never satisfy all of these requirements because

(1) it is inconvenient to maintain large quantities of cash; (2) the risk of loss or theft is far too great; (3) the risk in sending cash is likewise too high, as is the cost of postage and insurance in shipping cash over long distances; and (4) the costs to the Federal government of maintaining an adequate supply of currency would be prohibitive. In addition, negotiable instruments used for payment provide a convenient receipt as well as a record for accounting and tax purposes. Although negotiable instruments closely approximate cash for the purpose of payment, they are not exactly equivalent because, for example, negotiable instruments may be forged, they may be drawn on insufficient funds, payment may be stopped, or the instrument may be materially altered. Nevertheless, these risks (which are real but very infrequent—more than 99 percent of all checks are paid) are slight compared with the advantages that negotiable instruments provide for payment. Consequently, a major objective of the law of negotiable instruments and the bank collection process is to reduce these risks by increasing the safety, soundness, and operating efficiency of the entire payment system.

Moreover, the credit function of negotiable instruments is indispensable. Promissory notes and drafts serve an important business purpose, not only in areas of high finance but also at the level of the small business and individual consumer. In recent years, individuals have increasingly used certificates of deposit instead of savings accounts.

NEGOTIABILITY

Negotiability is a legal concept that makes written instruments more freely transferable and therefore a readily accepted form of payment in substitution for money.

DEVELOPMENT OF LAW OF NEGOTIABLE INSTRUMENTS

The starting point for an understanding of negotiable instruments is recognizing that four or five centuries ago in England a contract right to the payment of money was not assignable because a contractual promise ran to the promisee. The fact that performance could be rendered only to him constituted a hardship for the owner of the right because it prevented him from selling or disposing of it. Eventually, however, the law permitted recovery upon an assignment by the assignee against the obligor.

An innocent assignee bringing an action against the obligor was subject to all defenses available to the obligor. Such an action would result in the same outcome whether it was brought by the assignee or assignor. Thus, a contract right became assignable but not very marketable because merchants had little interest in buying paper that may be subject to a defense. This remains the law of **assignments**: *the assignee stands in the shoes of his assignor.* For a discussion of assignments, see *Chapter 16.*

With the flourishing of trade and commerce, it became essential to develop a more effective means of exchanging contractual rights for money. For example, a merchant who sold goods for cash might use the cash to buy more goods for resale. If he were to make a sale on credit in exchange for a promise to pay money, why should he not be permitted to sell that promise to someone else for cash with which to carry on his business? One difficulty was that the buyer of the goods gave the seller only a promise to pay money to him. The seller was the only person to whom performance or payment was promised. If, however, the seller obtained from the buyer a promise in writing to pay money to anyone in possession (a *bearer*) of the writing (the *paper* or *instrument*) or to anyone the seller (or *payee* in this case) designated, then the duty of performance would run directly to the holder (the bearer of the paper or to the person to whom the payee ordered payment to be made). This is one of the essential distinctions between negotiable and nonnegotiable instruments. Although a negotiable instrument has other formal requirements, this particular one eliminates the limitations of a promise to pay money only to a named promisee.

Moreover, if the promise to pay were not subject to all of the defenses available against the assignor, a transferee would not only be more willing to acquire the promise but also would pay more for it. Accordingly, the law of negotiable instruments developed the concept of the **holder in due course**, whereby certain good faith transferees who gave value acquired the right to be paid, free of most of the defenses to which an assignee would be subject. By reason of this doctrine, a transferee of a negotiable instrument could acquire *greater* rights than his transferor, whereas an assignee would acquire *only* the rights of his assignor. With these basic innovations, negotiable instruments enabled merchants to sell their contractual rights more readily and thereby keep their capital working.

ASSIGNMENT COMPARED WITH NEGOTIATION

Negotiability invests negotiable instruments with a high degree of marketability and commercial utility. It allows negotiable instruments to be freely transferable and enforceable by a person with the rights of a holder in due course against any person obligated on the instrument, subject only to a limited number of defenses. To illustrate, assume that George sells and delivers goods to Elaine for $50,000 on sixty days' credit and that, a few days later, George assigns this account to Marsha. Unless Elaine is duly notified of this assignment, she may safely pay the $50,000 to George on the due date without incurring any liability to Marsha, the assignee. Assume next that the goods were defective and that Elaine, accordingly, has a defense against George to the extent of $20,000. Assume also that Marsha duly notified Elaine of the assignment. The result is that Marsha can recover only $30,000, not $50,000, from Elaine because Elaine's defense against George is equally available against George's assignee, Marsha. In other words, an assignee of contractual rights merely "steps into the shoes" of her assignor and, hence, acquires only the same rights as her assignor—and no more.

Assume, instead, that upon the sale by George to Elaine, Elaine executes and delivers her negotiable note to George for $50,000 payable to George's order in sixty days and that, a short time later, George duly negotiates (transfers) the note to Marsha. In the first place, Marsha is not required to notify Elaine that she has acquired the note from George, because one who issues a negotiable instrument is held to know that the instrument may be negotiated and is generally obligated to pay the holder of the instrument, whoever that may be. In the second place, Elaine's defense is not available against Marsha if Marsha acquired the note in good faith and for value and had no knowledge of Elaine's defense against George and took it without reason to question its authenticity. Marsha, therefore, is entitled to hold Elaine for the full face amount of the note at maturity, namely, $50,000. In other words, Marsha, by the negotiation of the negotiable note to her, acquired rights greater than those George had, because, by keeping the note, George could have recovered only $30,000 on it because Elaine successfully could have asserted her defense in the amount of $20,000 against him.

To have the full benefit of negotiability, negotiable instruments not only must meet the requirements of negotiability but also must be acquired by a holder in due course. This chapter discusses the formal requirements instruments must satisfy to be negotiable. *Chapter 27* deals with the manner in which a negotiable instrument must be negotiated to preserve its advantages. *Chapter 28* covers the requisites and rights of a holder in due course. *Chapter 29* examines the liability of all the parties to a negotiable instrument.

◆ **FIGURE 26-1: Order to Pay: Draft or Check**

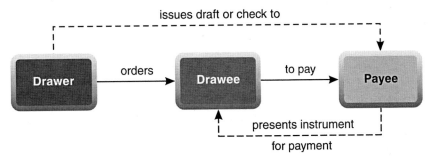

TYPES OF NEGOTIABLE INSTRUMENTS

There are four types of negotiable instruments: drafts, checks, notes, and certificates of deposit. Section 3–104. The first two contain **orders** or directions to pay money; the last two involve **promises** to pay money.

DRAFTS

A **draft** involves three parties, each in a distinct capacity. One party, the **drawer**, *orders* a second party, the **drawee**, to pay a fixed amount of money to a third party, the **payee**. Thus, the drawer "draws" the draft on the drawee. The drawee is ordinarily a person or entity that either is in possession of money belonging to the drawer or owes money to him. A sample draft is reproduced as *Figure 26-2*. The same party may appear in more than one capacity; for instance, the drawer may also be the payee.

Drafts may be either "time" or "sight." A **time draft** is one payable at a specified future date, whereas a **sight draft** is payable on demand (i.e., immediately upon presentation to the drawee). A form of time draft known as a trade acceptance is frequently used as a credit device in commercial transactions. A **trade acceptance** is a time draft, drawn by the seller (drawer) on the buyer (drawee), that names the seller or some third party as the payee.

◆ **SEE FIGURE 26-1: Order to Pay: Draft or Check**

◆ **SEE FIGURE 26-2: Draft**

CHECKS

A check is a specialized form of draft, namely, an order to pay money drawn on a *bank* and payable on *demand* (i.e., upon the payee's request for payment). Section 3–104(f). Once again, parties are involved in three distinct capacities: the **drawer**, who orders the **drawee**, a bank, to pay the payee on demand. Checks are by far the most widely used form of negotiable instruments. Each year more than ten billion checks are written in the United States for a total of more than $5 trillion. The Check Clearing for the 21st Century Act (also called Check 21 or the Check Truncation Act), which went into effect in late 2004, creates a new negotiable instrument called a substitute check or image replacement document (IRD). The law permits banks to truncate original checks, to process check information electronically, and to deliver substitute checks to banks that want to continue receiving paper checks. A substitute check would be the legal equivalent of the original check and would include all the information contained on the original check. The law does not require banks to accept checks in electronic form nor does it require banks to use the new authority granted by the act to create substitute checks. This newly authorized document is more fully discussed in *Chapter 30*.

A **cashier's check** is a check drawn by a bank upon itself to the order of a named payee. Section 3–104(g).

◆ **SEE FIGURE 26-3: Check**

◆ **FIGURE 26-2: Draft**

Two years from date pay to the order of   St. Louis, Missouri Perry Payee   May 1, 2011 $50,000 Fifty Thousand . . . Dollars   To: DEBRA DRAWEE   (Signed) Donald Drawer 50 Main St.   DONALD DRAWER Louisville, Kentucky

◆ **FIGURE 26-3: Check**

NOTES

A **promissory note** is an instrument involving two parties in two capacities. One party, the **maker**, promises to pay a second party, the payee, a stated sum of money, either on demand or at a stated future date. The note may range from a simple "I promise to pay $X to the order of Y" form to more complex legal instruments such as installment notes, collateral notes, mortgage notes, and judgment notes. *Figure 26-5* is a note payable at a definite time—six months from the date of April 7, 2011—and hence is referred to as a **time note**. A note payable upon the request or demand of the payee or holder is a **demand note**

◆ **SEE FIGURE 26-4: Promise to Pay: Promissory Note or Certificate of Deposit**

◆ **SEE FIGURE 26-5: Note**

CERTIFICATES OF DEPOSIT

A certificate of deposit, or CD as it is frequently called, is a specialized form of *promise* to pay money given by a *bank*. A **certificate of deposit** is a written acknowledgment by a bank of the receipt of money that it promises to repay. Section 3–104(j). The issuing party, the **maker**, which is always a bank, promises to pay a second party, the payee, who is named in the CD.

◆ **SEE FIGURE 26-6: Certificate of Deposit**

FORMAL REQUIREMENTS OF NEGOTIABLE INSTRUMENTS

To perform its function in the business community effectively, a negotiable instrument must be able to pass freely from person to person. The fact that *negotiability* is wholly a matter of form makes such freedom possible. The instrument must contain within its "four corners" all the information required to determine whether it is negotiable. No reference to any other source is permitted. For this reason, a negotiable instrument is called a "courier without luggage." In addition, indorsements **cannot** create or destroy negotiability.

To be negotiable, the **instrument** must—

1. be in writing,
2. be signed,
3. contain a promise or order to pay,
4. be unconditional,

◆ **FIGURE 26-4: Promise to Pay: Promissory Note or Certificate of Deposit**

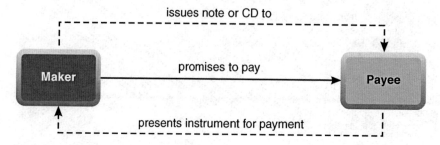

◆ **FIGURE 26-5: Note**

$10,000	Albany, NY	April 7, 2011

Six months from date I promise to pay to the order of Pat Payee ten thousand dollars.

(signed) Matthew Maker

---

5. be for a fixed amount,
6. be for money,
7. contain no other undertaking or instruction,
8. be payable on demand or at a definite time, and
9. be payable to order or to bearer.

Section 3–104(a). If these requirements are not met, the undertaking is not negotiable (nor is it a negotiable instrument or simply an instrument), and the rights of the parties are governed by the law of contract (assignment).

WRITING

The requirement that the instrument be a writing (Sections 3–103(a)(6), (9)) is broadly construed. Printing, typewriting, handwriting, or any other intentional tangible expression is sufficient to satisfy the requirement. Section 1–201; Revised Section 1-201. Most negotiable instruments, of course, are written on paper, but this is not required. For example, a check in one instance was reportedly written on the back of a cow and in another written on a coconut.

SIGNED

A note or certificate of deposit must be signed by the maker; a draft or check must be signed by the drawer. As in the case of a writing, extreme latitude is granted in determining what constitutes a **signature**, which is any symbol a party executes or adopts with the present *intention* to authenticate a writing. Section 1–201(39). Revised Article 1 changes the word "authenticate" to "adopt or accept." Revised Section 1–201(b)(37). Moreover, it may consist of any word or mark used in place of a written signature, Section 3–401(b), such as initials, an X, or a thumbprint. It may be a trade name or an assumed name. Even the location of the signature on the document is unimportant. Normally, a maker or drawer signs in the lower right corner of the instrument, but this is not required. Negotiable instruments are frequently signed by an agent for her principal. For a discussion of the appropriate way in which an agent should sign a negotiable instrument, see *Chapter 29*.

PROMISE OR ORDER TO PAY

A negotiable instrument must contain either a promise to pay money, in the case of a note or certificate of deposit, or an order to pay, in the case of a draft or check.

PROMISE TO PAY A promise to pay is an undertaking and must be more than the mere acknowledgment or recognition of an existing obligation or debt. Section 3–103(a)(9). The so-called due bill or I.O.U. is not a promise but merely

◆ **FIGURE 26-6: Certificate of Deposit**

NEGOTIABLE CERTIFICATE OF DEPOSIT

The Mountain Bank

No. 13900	Mountain, N.Y.	June 1, 2011

THIS CERTIFIES THAT THERE HAS BEEN DEPOSITED
with the undersigned the sum of $200,000.00
Two hundred thousand................................Dollars
Payable to the order of Pablo Payee on December 1, 2011 with interest only to maturity at the rate of Seven percent (7%) per annum upon surrender of this certificate properly indorsed.

The Mountain Bank
By (Signature) Malcolm Maker, Vice President
Authorized Signature

---

an acknowledgment of indebtedness. Accordingly, an instrument reciting "due Adam Brown $100" or "I.O.U., Adam Brown, $100" is not negotiable because it does not contain a promise to pay.

ORDER TO PAY An order to pay is an instruction to pay. It must be more than an authorization or request and must identify with reasonable certainty the person to be paid. Section 3–103(a)(6). The usual way to express an order is by use of the word *pay*: "Pay to the order of John Jones" or "Pay bearer." The addition of words of courtesy, such as "please pay" or "kindly pay," will not destroy the negotiability. Nonetheless, caution should be exercised in employing words that modify the prototypically correct "Pay." For example, the use of the words "I wish you would pay" has been held to destroy the negotiability of an instrument and to render its transfer a contractual assignment.

UNCONDITIONAL

The requirement that the promise or order be unconditional is to prevent the inclusion of any term that could reduce the promisor's obligation to pay. Conditions limiting a promise would diminish the payment and credit functions of negotiable instruments by necessitating costly and time-consuming investigations to determine the degree of risk such conditions imposed. Moreover, if the holder (transferee) had to take an instrument subject to certain conditions, her risk factor would be substantial, and this would lead to limited transferability. Substitutes for money must be capable of rapid circulation at minimum risk.

A promise or order to pay is **unconditional** if it is absolute and not subject to any contingencies or qualifications. Thus, an instrument would not be negotiable if it stated that "ABC Corp. promises to pay $100,000 to the order of Johnson provided the helicopter sold meets all contractual specifications." On the other hand, suppose that upon delivering an instrument that provided, "ABC Corp. promises to pay $100,000 to the order of Johnson," Meeker, the president of ABC, stated that the money would be paid only if the helicopter met all contractual specifications. The instrument would be negotiable because negotiability is determined solely by examining the instrument itself and is not affected by matters beyond the instrument's face.

A promise or order is unconditional unless it states (1) that there is an express condition to payment, (2) that the promise or order is subject to or governed by another writing, or (3) that rights or obligations concerning the order or promise are stated in another writing. A mere reference to another writing, however, does not make the promise or order conditional. Section 3–106(a).

An instrument is not made conditional by the fact that it is subject to implied or constructive conditions; the condition must be expressed to destroy negotiability. Section 3–106(a). Implications of law or fact are not to be considered in deciding whether an instrument is negotiable. Thus, a statement in an instrument that it is given for an executory promise does not imply that the instrument is conditioned upon performance of that promise.

REFERENCE TO OTHER AGREEMENTS The restriction against reference to another agreement is to enable any person to determine the right to payment provided by the instrument without having to look beyond its four corners. If such right is made subject to the terms of another agreement, the instrument is nonnegotiable. Section 3–106(a)(ii).

A distinction is to be made between a mere recital of the *existence* of a separate agreement (this does not destroy negotiability) and a recital that makes the instrument *subject* to the terms of another agreement (this does destroy negotiability).

A statement in a note such as "This note is given in partial payment for a color TV set to be delivered two weeks from date in accordance with a contract of this date between the payee and the maker" does not impair negotiability. It merely describes the consideration and the transaction giving rise to the note. It does not place any restriction or condition on the maker's obligation to pay. The promise is not made subject to any other agreement.

Added words that would impair negotiability are "This note is subject to all terms of said contract." Such words make the promise to pay conditional upon the adequate performance of the television set in accordance with the terms of the contract and thus render the instrument nonnegotiable.

THE PARTICULAR FUND DOCTRINE Revised Article 3 eliminates the particular fund doctrine by providing that a promise or order is not made conditional because payment is to be made only out of a particular fund. Section 3–106(b)(ii).

Under prior Article 3 an order or promise to pay only out of a particular fund was conditional and destroyed negotiability because payment depended upon the existence and sufficiency of the particular fund. On the other hand, a promise or order to pay that merely indicated a particular fund out of which reimbursement was to be made or a particular account to be debited with the amount did not impair negotiability because the promise or order relied on the drawer's or maker's general credit and the notation charging a particular account was merely a bookkeeping entry to be followed after payment.

FIXED AMOUNT

The purpose of the requirement of a fixed amount in money is to enable the person entitled to enforce the instrument to determine from the instrument itself the amount that he is entitled to receive.

The requirement that payment be of a "fixed amount" must be considered from the point of view of the person entitled to enforce the instrument, not the maker or drawer. (Prior Article 3 used the term "sum certain," which means fundamentally the same as "fixed amount.") The holder must be assured of a determinable minimum payment, although provisions of the instrument may increase the recovery under certain circumstances. Revised Article 3, however, applies the fixed amount requirement only to the *principal*. Section 3–112, Comment 1. Thus, the fixed amount portion does not apply to interest or to other charges, such as collection fees or attorneys' fees. Moreover, negotiability of an instrument is not affected by the inclusion or omission of a stated rate of interest. If the instrument does not state a rate of interest, it is payable without interest. Section 3–112(a). If the instrument states that it is payable "with interest" but does not specify a rate, the judgment rate of interest applies.

Most significantly, Revised Article 3 provides that "Interest may be stated in an instrument as a fixed or variable amount of money or it may be expressed as a fixed or variable rate or rates." Section 3–112(b). Moreover, determination of the rate of interest "may require reference to information not contained in the instrument." Section 3–112(b). Variable rate mortgages, therefore, may be negotiable; this result is consistent with the rule that the fixed amount requirement applies only to the principal.

Under prior Article 3, both principal and interest had to be determined from the face of the instrument. Thus, courts held that variable interest rate provisions destroyed negotiability because the interest rate was tied to a published index external to the instrument.

A sum payable is a fixed amount even though it is payable in installments or payable with a fixed discount, if paid before maturity, or with a fixed addition, if paid after maturity. This is because it is always possible to use the instrument itself to compute the amount due at any given time.

MONEY

The term **money** means a medium of exchange authorized or adopted by a sovereign government as part of its currency. Section 1–201(24). (Revised Section 1–201(b)(24) adds that the authorized or adopted currency must be the current official currency of the government.) Consequently, even though local custom may make gold or diamonds a medium of exchange, an instrument payable in such commodities would be nonnegotiable because of the lack of governmental sanction of such media as legal tender. On the other hand, an instrument paying a fixed amount in Swiss francs, English pounds, Australian dollars, Japanese yen, Nigerian naira, or other foreign currency is negotiable. Section 3–107.

NO OTHER UNDERTAKING OR INSTRUCTION

A negotiable instrument must contain a promise or order to pay money, but it may not "state any other undertaking or instruction by the person promising or ordering payment to do any act in addition to the payment of money." Section 3–104(a)(3). Accordingly, an instrument containing an order or promise to do an act in addition to or in lieu of the payment of money is not negotiable. For example, a promise to pay $100 "and a ton of coal" would be nonnegotiable.

The Code sets out a list of terms and provisions that may be included in instruments without adversely affecting negotiability. Among these are (1) an undertaking or power to give, maintain, or protect collateral in order to secure payment, (2) an authorization or power to confess judgment (written authority by the debtor to allow the holder to enter judgment against the debtor in favor of the holder) on the instrument, (3) an authorization or power to sell or dispose of collateral upon default, and (4) a waiver of the benefit of any law intended for the advantage or protection of the obligor. It is important to note that the Code does not render any of these terms legal or effective; it merely provides that their inclusion will not affect negotiability.

PAYABLE ON DEMAND OR AT A DEFINITE TIME

A negotiable instrument must "be payable on demand or at a definite time." Section 3–104. This requirement, like the other formal requirements of negotiability, is designed to promote certainty in determining the present value of a negotiable instrument.

DEMAND "Payable upon demand" means that the money owed under the instrument must be paid upon the holder's request. **Demand paper** always has been considered sufficiently certain as to time of payment to satisfy the requirements of negotiability because it is the person entitled to enforce the instrument who makes the demand and who thus sets the time for payment. Any instrument in which no time for payment is stated—a check, for example—is payable on demand. An instrument also qualifies as being payable on demand if it is payable at sight or on presentment. Section 3–108(a).

DEFINITE TIME Instruments payable at a definite time are called **time paper**. A promise or order is payable at a definite time if it is payable—

1. at a fixed date or dates,
2. at a definite period of time after sight or acceptance, or
3. at a time readily ascertainable at the time the promise or order is issued.

Section 3–108(b). An instrument is payable at a definite time if it is payable "on or before" a stated date. The person entitled to enforce the instrument is thus assured that she will have her money by the maturity date at the latest, although she may receive it sooner. This right of anticipation enables the obligor, at his option, to pay before the stated maturity date (*prepayment*) and thereby stop the further accrual of interest or, if interest rates have gone down, to refinance at a lower rate of interest. Nevertheless, it constitutes sufficient certainty so as not to impair negotiability. Section 3–108(b)(i).

Frequently, instruments are made payable at a fixed period after a stated date. For example, the instrument may be made payable "thirty days after date." This means it is payable thirty days after the date of issuance, which is recited on the instrument. Such an instrument is payable at a definite time, for its exact maturity date can be determined by simple math.

An undated instrument payable "thirty days after date" is not payable at a definite time, because the date of payment cannot be determined from its face. It is therefore nonnegotiable until it is completed.

An instrument that by its terms is otherwise payable only upon an act or event whose time of occurrence is uncertain is *not* payable at a definite time. An example would be a note providing for payment to the order "when X dies." However, as previously stated, a time that is readily ascertainable at the time the promise or order is issued is a definite time. Section 3–108(b). This changes prior Article 3 and seemingly would permit a note reading "payable on the day of the next presidential election." As long as the scheduled event is certain to happen, Revised Article 3 appears to be satisfied.

The clause "at a fixed period after sight" is frequently used in drafts. Because a fixed period after sight means a fixed period after acceptance, a simple mathematical calculation makes the maturity date certain; and the instrument is, therefore, negotiable.

An instrument payable at a fixed time subject to **acceleration** by the holder also satisfies the requirement of being payable at a definite time. Section 3–108(b)(ii). Indeed, such an instrument would seem to have a more certain maturity date than a demand instrument because it at least states a definite maturity date. In addition, the acceleration may be contingent upon the happening of some act or event.

Finally, a provision in an instrument granting the holder an option to extend the maturity of the instrument for a definite or indefinite period does not impair its negotiability. Section 3–108(b)(iii). Nor does a provision permitting the obligor of an instrument to extend the maturity date to a further definite time. Section 3–108(b)(iv). For example, a provision in a note, payable one year from date, that the maker may extend the maturity date six months does not impair negotiability. If the obligor is given an option to extend the maturity of the instrument for an indefinite period, however, his promise is illusory; and there is no certainty regarding time of payment. Such an instrument is nonnegotiable. If the obligor's right to extend is limited to a definite time, the extension clause is no more indefinite than an acceleration clause with a time limitation.

In addition, extension may be made automatic upon or after a specified act or event, provided a definite time limit is stated. An example of such an extension clause is, "I promise to pay to the order of John Doe the sum of $2,000 on December 1, 2011, but it is agreed that if the crop of sections 25 and 26 of Twp. 145 is below eight bushels per acre for the 2011 season, this note shall be extended for one year."

AT A DEFINITE TIME AND ON DEMAND If the instrument, payable at a fixed date, *also* provides that it is payable on demand made before the fixed date, it is still a negotiable instrument. Revised Article 3 provides that the instrument is payable on demand until the fixed date and, if demand is not made prior to the specified date, becomes payable at a definite time on the fixed date. Section 3–108(c).

PAYABLE TO ORDER OR TO BEARER

A negotiable instrument must contain words indicating that the maker or drawer intends that it may pass into the hands of someone other than the payee. Although the "magic" **words of negotiability** typically are *to the order of* or *to bearer*, other clearly equivalent words also may fulfill this requirement. The use of synonyms, however, only invites trouble. Moreover, as noted above, indorsements cannot create or destroy negotiability, which must be determined from the "face" of the instrument. Words of negotiability must be present when the instrument is issued or first comes into possession of a holder. Section 3–104(a)(1).

Revised Article 3 provides that a *check* that meets all requirements of being a negotiable instrument except that it is not payable to bearer or order is nevertheless a negotiable instrument. Section 3–104(c). This rule does *not* apply to instruments other than checks and does not exist under prior Article 3.

PAYABLE TO ORDER An instrument is payable to order if it is payable (a) to the order of an identified person or (b) to an identified person or order. Section 3–109(b). If an instrument is payable to bearer, it cannot be payable to order; an instrument that is ambiguous as to this point is payable to bearer. Prior Article 3 provided that use of the word *assigns* met the requirement of words of negotiability; Revised Article 3, however, does not so provide.

Moreover, in every instance the person to whose order the instrument is payable must be designated with reasonable certainty. Within this limitation a broad range of payees is possible, including an individual, two or more payees, an office, an estate, a trust or fund, a partnership or unincorporated association, and a corporation.

This requirement should not be confused with the requirement that the instrument contain an order or promise to pay. An order to pay is an instruction to a third party to pay the instrument as drawn. The word *order* in terms of an "order instrument," on the other hand, pertains to the transferability of the instrument rather than to instructions directing a specific party to pay.

A writing, other than a *check*, that names a specified person without indicating that it is payable to order—for example, "Pay to Justin Matthew"—is not payable to order or to bearer. Such a writing is not a negotiable instrument and is not covered by Article 3. On the other hand, a check that meets all of the requirements of a negotiable instrument, except that it does not provide the words of negotiability, is still a negotiable instrument and falls within the purview of Article 3. Section 3–104(c). Thus, a check payable to Justin Matthew is a negotiable check.

PAYABLE TO BEARER Section 3–109(a) of the Code states that an instrument fulfills the requirements of being **payable to bearer** if it (1) states it is payable to bearer or the order of bearer, (2) does not state a payee or (3) states it is payable to "cash" or to the order of "cash." Section 3–109(a). An instrument made payable both to order and to bearer, that is, "pay to the order of Mildred Courts or bearer," is payable to bearer. Section 3–109, Comment 2.

An instrument that does not state a payee is payable to bearer. Thus, if a drawer leaves blank the "pay to order of" line of a check or the maker of a note writes "pay to_____," the instrument is a negotiable bearer instrument. Section 3–109(a)(2).

TERMS AND OMISSIONS AND THEIR EFFECT ON NEGOTIABILITY

The negotiability of an instrument may be questioned because of an omission of certain provisions or because of ambiguity. Problems may also arise in connection with the interpretation of an instrument, whether or not negotiability is called into question. Accordingly, the Code contains rules of construction that apply to every instrument.

DATING OF THE INSTRUMENT The negotiability of an instrument is not affected by the fact that it is antedated, or postdated. Section 3–113(a). If the instrument is undated, its date is the date of its issuance. If it is unissued, its date is the

date it first comes into the possession of a holder. Section 3–113(b).

INCOMPLETE INSTRUMENTS Occasionally, a party will sign a paper that clearly is intended to become an instrument but that, either by intention or through oversight, is incomplete because of the omission of a necessary element such as a promise or order, a designated payee, an amount payable, or a time for payment. Section 3–115 provides that such an instrument is not negotiable until completed.

If, for example, an undated instrument is delivered on November 1, 2011, payable "thirty days after date," the payee has implied authority to fill in "November 1, 2011." Until he does so, however, the instrument is not negotiable because it is not payable at a definite time. If the payee completes the instrument by inserting an erroneous date, the rules as to material alteration, covered in *Chapter 29*, apply.

AMBIGUOUS INSTRUMENTS Rather than commit the parties to the use of parol evidence to establish the interpretation of an instrument, Article 3 establishes rules to resolve common ambiguities. This promotes negotiability by providing added certainty to the holder.

Where it is doubtful whether the instrument is a draft or note, the holder may treat it as either and present it for payment to the drawee or the person signing it. Section 3–104(e). For example, an instrument reading

> To X: On demand I promise to pay $500 to the order of Y.
> 　　Signed, Z

may be presented for payment to X as a draft or to Z as a note.

An instrument naming no drawee but stating

> On demand, pay $500 to the order of Y.
> 　　Signed, Z

although in the form of a draft, may be treated as a note and presented to Z for payment.

If a printed form of note or draft is used and the party signing it inserts handwritten or typewritten language that is inconsistent with the printed words, the handwritten words control the typewritten and the printed words, and the typewritten words control the printed words. Section 3–114.

If the amount payable is set forth on the face of the instrument in both figures and words and the amounts differ, the words control the figures. It is presumed that the maker or drawer would be more careful with words. If the words are ambiguous, however, then the figures control. Section 3–114.

CHAPTER SUMMARY

NEGOTIABILITY	**Rule** invests instruments with a high degree of marketability and commercial utility by conferring upon certain good faith transferees immunity from most defenses to the instrument **Formal Requirements** negotiability is wholly a matter of form, and all the requirements for negotiability must be met within the four corners of the instrument
TYPES OF NEGOTIABLE INSTRUMENTS	**Orders to Pay** • *Drafts* a draft involves three parties: the drawer orders the drawee to pay a fixed amount of money to the payee • *Checks* a specialized form of draft that is drawn on a bank and payable on demand; the drawer orders the drawee (bank) to pay the payee on demand (upon the request of the holder) **Promises to Pay** • *Notes* a written promise by a maker (issuer) to pay a payee • *Certificates of Deposit* a specialized form of note that is given by a bank or thrift association
FORMAL REQUIREMENTS OF NEGOTIABLE INSTRUMENTS	**Writing** any intentional reduction to tangible form is sufficient **Signed** any symbol executed or adopted by a party with the present intention to authenticate/adopt or accept a writing **Promise or Order to Pay** • *Promise to Pay* an undertaking to pay, which must be more than a mere acknowledgment or recognition of an existing debt • *Order to Pay* instruction to pay **Unconditional** an absolute promise to pay that is not subject to any contingencies • *Reference to Other Agreements* does not destroy negotiability unless the recital makes the instrument subject to or governed by the terms of another agreement • *The Particular Fund Doctrine* an order or promise to pay only out of a particular fund no longer is conditional and does not destroy negotiability **Fixed Amount** the holder must be assured of a determinable minimum principal payment although provisions in the instrument may increase the amount of recovery under certain circumstances **Money** legal tender authorized or adopted by a sovereign government as part of its currency **No Other Undertaking or Instruction** a promise or order to do an act in addition to the payment of money destroys negotiability **Payable on Demand or at a Definite Time** an instrument is demand paper if it must be paid upon request; an instrument is time paper if it is payable at a definite time **Payable to Order or to Bearer** a negotiable instrument must contain words indicating that the maker or drawer intends that it pass into the hands of someone other than the payee • *Payable to Order* payable to the "order of" (or other words which mean the same) a named person or anyone designated by that person • *Payable to Bearer* payable to the holder of the instrument; includes instruments (1) payable to bearer or the order of bearer, (2) that do not specify a payee, or (3) payable to "cash" or to order of "cash"

The primary advantage of negotiable instruments is their ease of transferability. Nonetheless, although both negotiable instruments and nonnegotiable undertakings are transferable by assignment, only negotiable instruments can result in the transferee becoming a holder. This distinction is highly significant. If the transferee of a negotiable instrument is entitled to payment by the terms of the instrument, he is a holder of the instrument. Only holders may be holders in due course and thus may be entitled to greater rights in the instrument than the transferor may have possessed. These rights, discussed in the next chapter, are the reason why negotiable instruments move freely in the marketplace. This chapter discusses the methods by which negotiable instruments may be transferred.

NEGOTIATION

A holder, under the Uniform Commercial Code (UCC), is broadly defined in Section 1–201(20) as "a person who is in possession of … an instrument … drawn, issued, or indorsed to him or his order or to bearer or in blank." Revised Article 1 has a similar definition: "the person in possession of a negotiable instrument that is payable either to bearer or to an identified person that is the person in possession." Revised Section 1–201(b)(21). **Negotiation** is the transfer of possession, whether voluntary or involuntary, by a person other than the issuer of a negotiable instrument in such a manner that the transferee becomes a holder. Section 3–201(a). An instrument is transferred when a person other than its issuer delivers it for the purpose of giving the recipient the right to enforce the instrument. Section 3–203(a). Accordingly, to qualify as a holder a person must have possession of an instrument that runs to him. Thus, there are two ways in which a person can be a holder: (1) the instrument has been issued to that person, or (2) the instrument has been transferred to that person by negotiation.

The transfer of a nonnegotiable promise or order operates as an assignment, as does the transfer of a negotiable instrument by a means that does not render the transferee a holder. As discussed in *Chapter 16*, an **assignment** is the voluntary transfer to a third party of the rights arising from a contract.

Whether a transfer is by assignment or by negotiation, the transferee acquires the rights his transferor had. Section 3–203(b). The transfer need not be for value: if the instrument is transferred as a gift, the donee acquires all the rights of the donor. If the transferor was a holder in due course, the transferee acquires the rights of a holder in due course, which rights he in turn may transfer. This rule, sometimes referred to as the *shelter rule*, existed at common law and still exists under the UCC. The shelter rule is discussed more fully in *Chapter 28*.

The requirements for negotiation depend on whether the instrument is bearer paper or order paper.

NEGOTIATION OF BEARER PAPER

If an instrument is payable to bearer, it may be negotiated by transfer of possession alone. Section 3–201(b). Because bearer paper (an instrument payable to bearer) runs to whoever is in possession of it, a finder or a thief of bearer paper would be a holder even though he did not receive possession by voluntary transfer. Section 3–201(a). For example, P loses an instrument payable to bearer that I had issued to her. F finds it and delivers it to B, who thus receives it by negotiation and is a holder. F also qualified as a holder because he was in possession of bearer paper. As a holder, F had the power to negotiate the instrument, and B, the transferee, may be a holder in due course if he meets the Code's requirements for such a holder (discussed in *Chapter 28*). See *Figure 27-1* for an illustration of this example. Because a bearer instrument is negotiated by mere *possession*, it is comparable to cash.

◆ **SEE FIGURE 27-1: Bearer Paper**

NEGOTIATION OF ORDER PAPER

If the instrument is order paper (an instrument payable to order), both (1) transfer of its *possession* and (2) its *indorsement* (signature) by the appropriate parties are necessary for the

◆ **FIGURE 27-1: Bearer Paper**

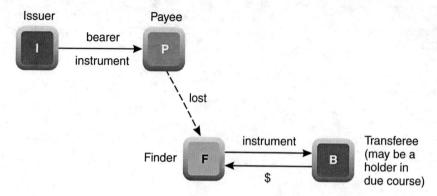

transferee to become a holder. Section 3–201(b). *Figure 27-2* compares the negotiation of bearer and order paper.

Any transfer for *value* of order paper gives the transferee the specifically enforceable right to have the unqualified indorsement of the transferor, unless the parties agree otherwise. Section 3–203(c). The parties may agree that the transfer is to be an assignment rather than a negotiation, in which case no indorsement is required. Absent such agreement, the courts presume that negotiation was intended where value is given. Where a transfer is not for value (i.e., a gift), the transaction is normally noncommercial; thus, the courts do not presume the intent to negotiate.

Until the necessary indorsement has been supplied, the transferee has nothing more than the contract rights of an assignee. Negotiation takes effect only when a proper indorsement is made, at which time the transferee becomes a holder of the instrument.

If a customer deposits a check or other instrument for collection without properly indorsing the item, the depository bank becomes a holder when it accepts the item for deposit if the depositor is a holder. Section 4–205(i). It no longer needs to supply the customer's indorsement.

◆ **SEE FIGURE 27-2: Negotiation of Bearer and Order Paper**

THE IMPOSTOR RULE Negotiation of an order instrument requires a valid indorsement by the person to whose order the instrument is payable. The impostor rule governing unauthorized signatures is an *exception* to this general rule. Usually, the impostor rule comes into play in situations involving a confidence man who impersonates a respected citizen and who deceives a third party into delivering a negotiable instrument to the impostor in the name of the respected citizen. For instance, John Doe, falsely representing himself as Richard Roe, a prominent citizen, induces Ray Davis to loan him $10,000. Davis draws a check payable to the order of Richard Roe and delivers it to Doe, who then forges Roe's name to the check and presents it to the drawee for payment. The drawee pays it. Subsequently, Davis, the drawer, denies the drawee's right of reimbursement upon the ground that the drawee did not pay in accordance with his order: Davis ordered payment to Roe or to Roe's order. Roe did not order payment to anyone; therefore, the drawee would not acquire a right of reimbursement against Davis. The general rule governing unauthorized signatures supports this argument in favor of the drawer.

Nevertheless, Section 3–404(c) provides that the indorsement of the impostor (Doe) or of any other person in the name of the named payee is **effective** as the indorsement of the payee if the impostor has induced the maker or drawer

◆ **FIGURE 27-2: Negotiation of Bearer and Order Paper**

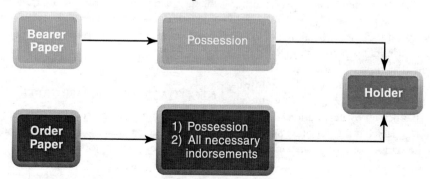

(Davis) to issue the instrument to him or his confederate using the name of the payee (Roe). It is as if the named payee had indorsed the instrument. The reason for this rule is that the drawer or maker is to blame for failing to detect the impersonation by the impostor. Thus, in the above example, the drawee would be able to debit the drawer's account. Moreover, Revised Article 3 expands the impostor rule by extending its coverage to include an impostor who is impersonating an agent. Section 3–404(a). Thus, if an impostor impersonates Jones and induces the drawer to draw a check to the order of Jones, the impostor can negotiate the check. Moreover, under the Revision, if an impostor impersonates Jones, the president of Jones Corporation, and the check is to the order of Jones Corporation, the impostor can negotiate the check. Comment 1 to Section 3–404.

If the person paying the instrument fails to exercise ordinary care, the issuer may recover from the payor to the extent the payor's negligence contributed to the loss. If the issuer is also negligent, comparative negligence would apply.

THE FICTITIOUS PAYEE RULE The rule just discussed also applies when a person who does not intend the payee to have an interest in the instrument signs as or on behalf of a maker or drawer. Section 3–404(b). In such a situation, any person's indorsement in the name of the named payee is **effective** if the person identified as the payee is a fictitious person. For instance, Palmer gives Albrecht, her employee, authority to write checks to pay Palmer's debts. Albrecht writes a check for $2,000 to Foushee, a fictitious payee, which Albrecht takes and indorses in Foushee's name to Albrecht. Albrecht cashes the check at Palmer's bank, which can debit Palmer's account because Albrecht's signature in Foushee's name is effective against Palmer. Palmer should bear the risk of her unscrupulous employees.

In a similar situation also involving a disloyal employee, a drawer's employee falsely tells the drawer that money is owed to Leon, and the drawer writes a check payable to the order of Leon and hands it to the agent for delivery to him. The agent forges Leon's name to the check and obtains payment from the drawee bank. The drawer then denies the bank's claim to reimbursement upon the ground that the bank did not comply with her order; that the drawer had ordered payment to Leon or order; that the drawee did not make payment either to Leon or as ordered by him, inasmuch as the forgery of Leon's signature is wholly inoperative; and that the drawee paid in accordance with the scheme of the faithless agent and not in compliance with the drawer's order. Under Section 3–405, an employer has liability on the instrument when one of its employees, who is entrusted with responsibility with respect to such an instrument, makes a fraudulent indorsement if (1) the instrument is payable to the employer and the employee forges the indorsement of the employer or (2) the instrument is issued by the employer and the employee forges the indorsement of the person identified as the payee. The example above falls under the second part of the rule just stated. Accordingly, the employee's indorsement is effective as that of the unintended payee, and the drawee bank will be able to debit the drawer's (employer's) account.

Section 3–405 also applies to a situation (the first part of the rule stated above) not involving a fictitious payee: a fraudulent indorsement made by an employee entrusted with responsibility with respect to an instrument payable to the employer. For example, an employee, whose job involves posting amounts of checks payable to her employer, steals some of the checks and forges her employer's indorsement. The indorsement is effective as the employer's indorsement because the employee's duties included processing checks for bookkeeping purposes.

Section 3–405 provides, however, that the employer may recover from the drawee bank to the extent the loss resulted from the bank's failure to exercise ordinary care. If the employer is also negligent, a rule of comparative negligence applies.

NEGOTIATIONS SUBJECT TO RESCISSION

A negotiation conforming to the requirements discussed above is effective to transfer the instrument even if it is—

1. made by an infant, a corporation exceeding its powers, or a person without capacity; or
2. obtained by fraud, duress, or mistake; or
3. made in breach of a duty or as part of an illegal transaction. Section 3–202(a).

Thus, a negotiation is valid even though the transaction in which it occurs is voidable or even void. In all of these instances, the transferor loses all rights in the instrument until he regains possession of it. His right to do so, determined by State law, is valid against the immediate transferee and all subsequent holders, but not against a subsequent holder in due course or a person paying the instrument in good faith and without notice. Section 3–202(b).

INDORSEMENTS

An **indorsement** is

a signature, other than that of a signer as maker, drawer, or acceptor, that alone or accompanied by other words is made on an instrument for the purpose of (i) negotiating the instrument, (ii) restricting payment of the instrument, or (iii) incurring indorser's liability on the instrument, but regardless of the intent of the signer, a signature and its accompanying words is an indorsement unless the accompanying words, terms of the instrument, place of the signature, or other circumstances unambiguously indicate that the signature was made for a purpose other than indorsement. Section 3–204(a).

An indorsement may be complex or simple. It may be dated and may indicate where it is made, but neither date nor place is required to be shown. The simplest type is merely the signature of the indorser. The indorser undertakes certain obligations, as explained later, by merely signing her name. A forged or otherwise unauthorized signature necessary to negotiation is inoperative and thus breaks the chain of title to the instrument. Section 3–403(a).

The type of indorsement used in first negotiating an instrument affects its subsequent negotiation. Every indorsement is (1) either blank or special, (2) either restrictive or nonrestrictive, and (3) either qualified or unqualified. These categories are not mutually exclusive. Indeed, each indorsement may be placed within three of these six categories because all indorsements disclose three things: (1) the method to be employed in making subsequent negotiations (this depends upon whether the indorsement is blank or special); (2) the kind of interest that is being transferred (this depends upon whether the indorsement is restrictive or nonrestrictive); and (3) the liability of the indorser (this depends upon whether the indorsement is qualified or unqualified). For instance, an indorser who merely signs her name on the back of an instrument is making a blank, nonrestrictive, unqualified indorsement. See *Figure 27-3* for further illustrations.

Revised Article 3 identifies an additional type of indorsement—an anomalous indorsement. An anomalous indorsement is "an indorsement made by a person that is not the holder of the instrument." Section 3–205(d). The only effect of an anomalous indorsement is to make the signer liable on the instrument as an indorser. Such an

indorsement does not affect the manner in which the instrument may be negotiated.

The effectiveness of an indorsement as well as the rights of the transferee and transferor depend upon whether the indorsement meets certain formal requirements. This section will cover the different kinds of indorsements and the formal requirements of each.

◆ **SEE FIGURE 27-3: Indorsements**

BLANK INDORSEMENTS

A **blank indorsement**, which specifies no indorsee, may consist solely of the signature of the indorser or her authorized agent. Section 3–205(b). Such an indorsement converts order paper into bearer paper and leaves bearer paper as bearer paper. Thus, an instrument indorsed in blank may be negotiated by delivery alone without further indorsement. Hence, the holder should treat it with the same care as cash.

SPECIAL INDORSEMENTS

A **special indorsement** specifically identifies the person to whom or to whose order the instrument is to be payable. Section 3–205(a). Thus, if Peter, the payee of a note, indorses it "Pay to the order of Andrea," or even "Pay Andrea," the indorsement is special because it names the transferee. Words of negotiability—"pay to order or bearer"—are *not* required in an indorsement. Thus, an indorsement reading "Pay Edward" is interpreted as meaning "Pay to the order of Edward." Any further negotiation of the instrument would require Edward's indorsement.

Moreover, a holder of an instrument with a blank indorsement may protect himself by converting the blank indorsement to a special indorsement by writing over the signature of the indorser words identifying the person to

◆ **FIGURE 27-3: Indorsements**

Indorsement	Type of Indorsement	Interest Transferred	Liability of Indorser
1. "John Doe"	Blank	Nonrestrictive	Unqualified
2. "Pay to Richard Roe, John Doe"	Special	Nonrestrictive	Unqualified
3. "Without Recourse, John Doe"	Blank	Nonrestrictive	Qualified
4. "Pay to Richard Roe in trust for John Roe, without recourse, John Doe"	Special	Restrictive	Qualified
5. "For collection only, without recourse, John Doe"	Blank	Restrictive	Qualified
6. "Pay to XYZ Corp., on the condition that it delivers goods ordered this date, John Doe"	Special	Nonrestrictive	Unqualified

whom the instrument is payable. Section 3–205(c). For example, on the back of a negotiable instrument appears the blank indorsement "Sally Seller." Harry Holder, who receives the instrument from Seller, may convert this bearer instrument into order paper by inserting above Seller's signature "Pay Harry Holder" or other similar words.

RESTRICTIVE INDORSEMENTS

As the term implies, a **restrictive indorsement** attempts to restrict the rights of the indorsee in some fashion. It limits the purpose for which the proceeds of the instrument can be applied. Section 3–206. The Code discusses four types of indorsements as restrictive: conditional indorsements, indorsements prohibiting further transfer, indorsements for deposit or collection, and indorsements in trust. Section 3–206. Only the last two are effective. An **unrestrictive indorsement**, in contrast, does not attempt to restrict the rights of the indorsee.

INDORSEMENTS FOR DEPOSIT OR COLLECTION The most frequently used form of restrictive indorsement is that designed to place the instrument in the banking system for deposit or collection. Indorsements of this type, collectively referred to as "collection indorsements," include "for collection," "for deposit," and "pay any bank." Such an indorsement *effectively limits* further negotiation to those consistent with its limitation and binds (1) all nonbanking persons, (2) a depository bank that purchases the instrument or takes it for collection, and (3) a payor bank that is also the depository bank or that takes the instrument for immediate payment over the counter from a person other than a collecting bank. Section 3–206(c). Thus, a collection indorsement binds all parties except an intermediary bank (discussed in *Chapter 30*) or a payor bank that is not also the depository bank.

INDORSEMENTS IN TRUST Another common kind of restrictive indorsement is that in which the indorser creates a trust for the benefit of himself or others. If an instrument is indorsed "Pay Thelma in trust for Barbara," "Pay Thelma for Barbara," "Pay Thelma for account of Barbara," or "Pay Thelma as agent for Barbara," Thelma is a fiduciary, subject to liability for any breach of her obligation to Barbara. Trustees commonly and legitimately sell trust assets, and, consequently, a trustee has power to negotiate an instrument. The first taker under an indorsement to her in trust (in this case Thelma) is under a duty to pay or apply, in a manner consistent with the indorsement, all the funds she receives. Thelma's immediate transferee may safely pay Thelma for the instrument if he does not have *notice* of any breach of fiduciary duty. Section 3–206(d)(1). Subsequent indorsees or transferees are not bound by such indorsement unless they *know* that the trustee negotiated the instrument for her own benefit or otherwise in breach of her fiduciary duty. Section 3–206(d)(2).

INDORSEMENTS WITH INEFFECTIVE RESTRICTIONS A **conditional indorsement** is one by which the indorser makes the rights of the indorsee subject to the happening or nonhappening of a specified event. Suppose Marcin makes a note payable to Parker's order. Parker indorses it "Pay Rodriguez, but only if the good ship *Jolly Jack* arrives in Chicago harbor by November 15, 2011." If Marcin had used this language in the instrument itself, it would be nonnegotiable because her promise to pay must be unconditional to satisfy the formal requisites of negotiability. Revised Article 3 makes such indorsements ineffective by providing that an indorsement stating a condition to the right of a holder to receive payment does not affect the right of the indorsee to enforce the instrument. Section 3–206(b).

An indorsement may by its express terms attempt to prohibit further transfer by stating "Pay [name] only" or language to similar effect. Such an indorsement, or any other purporting to prohibit further transfer, is designed to restrict the rights of the indorsee. To remove any doubt as to the effect of such a provision, the Code provides that *no* indorsement limiting payment to a particular person or otherwise prohibiting further transfer is effective. Section 3–206(a). As a result, an indorsement that purports to prohibit further transfer of the instrument is given the same effect as an unrestricted indorsement.

QUALIFIED AND UNQUALIFIED INDORSEMENTS

Unqualified indorsers promise that they will pay the instrument according to its terms at the time of their indorsement to the holder or to any subsequent indorser who paid it. Section 3–415(a). In short, an unqualified indorser guarantees payment of the instrument if certain conditions are met.

An indorser may disclaim her liability on the contract of indorsement, but only if the indorsement so declares and the disclaimer is written on the instrument. The customary manner of disclaiming an indorser's liability is to add the words "without recourse," either before or after her signature. Section 3–415(b). A "**without recourse**" indorsement, called a qualified indorsement, does not, however, eliminate all of an indorser's liability. As discussed in *Chapter 29*, a **qualified** indorsement disclaims contract liability but does not entirely remove the warranty liability of the indorser. A qualified indorsement and delivery is a negotiation and transfers legal title to the indorsee, but the indorser does not guarantee payment of the instrument. Furthermore, a qualified indorsement does not destroy negotiability or prevent further negotiation of the instrument. For example, assume that an attorney receives a check payable to her order in payment of a client's claim. She may indorse the check to the client without recourse, thereby disclaiming liability as a guarantor of payment of the check. The qualified indorsement plus delivery would transfer title to the client.

FORMAL REQUIREMENTS OF INDORSEMENTS

PLACE OF INDORSEMENT An indorsement must be written on the instrument or on a paper, called an **allonge**, affixed to the instrument. Section 3–204(a). An allonge may be used even if the instrument contains sufficient space for the indorsement.

Customarily, indorsements are made on the back or reverse side of the instrument, starting at the top and continuing down. Under Federal Reserve Board guidelines, indorsements of checks must be in ink of an appropriate color, such as blue or black, and must be made within one

and one-half inches of the trailing (left) edge of the back of the check. The remaining space is reserved for bank indorsements. Nevertheless, failure to comply with the guidelines does not destroy negotiability, and there are no penalties for violating the standard.

Occasionally, however, a signature may appear on an instrument in such a way that it is impossible to tell with certainty the nature of the liability the signer intended to undertake. In such an event, the Code specifies that the signer is to be treated as an indorser. Section 3–204(a). In keeping with the rule that a transferee must be able to determine her rights from the face of the instrument, the person who signed in an ambiguous capacity may not introduce parol evidence to establish that she intended to be something other than an indorser.

◆ **SEE FIGURE 27-4: Placement of Indorsement**

◆ **FIGURE 27-4: Placement of Indorsement**

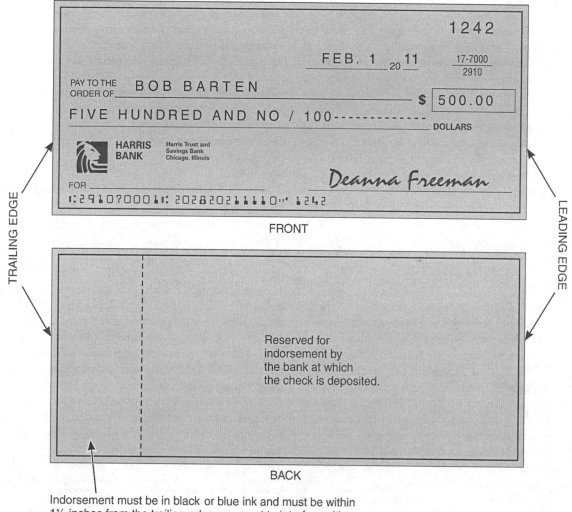

Indorsement must be in black or blue ink and must be within 1½ inches from the trailing edge so as not to interfere with indorsements from the bank.

INCORRECT OR MISSPELLED INDORSEMENTS If an instrument is payable to a payee or indorsee under a misspelled name or a name different from that of the holder, the holder may require the indorsement in the name stated or in the holder's correct name or both. Section 3–204(d). Nevertheless, the person paying or taking the instrument for value may require the indorser to sign both names.

CHAPTER SUMMARY

NEGOTIATION
Holder possessor of an instrument with all necessary indorsements
Shelter Rule transferee gets rights of transferor
Negotiation of Bearer Paper transferred by mere possession
Negotiation of Order Paper transferred by possession and indorsement by all appropriate parties
- *The Impostor Rule* an indorsement of an impostor or of any other person in the name of the named payee is effective if the impostor has induced the maker or drawer to issue the instrument to him using the name of the payee
- *The Fictitious Payee Rule* an indorsement by any person in the name of the named payee is effective if an agent of the maker or drawer has supplied her with the name of the payee for fraudulent purposes

Negotiations Subject to Rescission negotiation is valid even though a transaction is void or voidable

INDORSEMENTS
Definition signature (on the instrument) of a payee, drawee, accommodation party, or holder
Blank Indorsement one specifying no indorsee and making the instrument bearer paper
Special Indorsement one identifying an indorsee to be paid and making the instrument order paper
Unrestrictive Indorsement one that does not attempt to restrict the rights of the indorsee
Restrictive Indorsement one attempting to limit the rights of the indorsee
- *Indorsements for Deposit or Collection* effectively limit further negotiation to those consistent with the indorsement
- *Indorsements in Trust* effectively require the indorsee to pay or apply all funds in accordance with the indorsement
- *Indorsements with Ineffective Restrictions* include conditional indorsements and indorsements attempting to prohibit further negotiation

Unqualified Indorsement one that imposes liability on the indorser
Qualified Indorsement without recourse, one that limits the indorser's liability
Formal Requirements of Indorsements
- *Place of Indorsement*
- *Incorrect or Misspelled Indorsement*

Holder in Due Course

The unique and most significant aspect of negotiability is the concept of the holder in due course. While a mere holder or assignee acquires a negotiable instrument subject to all claims and defenses to it, a holder in due course, except in consumer credit transactions, takes the instrument free of all claims of other parties and free of all defenses to the instrument except for a very limited number. The law has conferred this preferred position upon the holder in due course to encourage the free transferability of negotiable instruments by minimizing the risks assumed by an innocent purchaser of the instrument. The transferee of a negotiable instrument wants payment for it; he does not want to be subject to any dispute between the obligor and the obligee (generally the original payee). This chapter discusses the requirements of becoming a holder in due course and the benefits conferred upon a holder in due course.

REQUIREMENTS OF A HOLDER IN DUE COURSE

To acquire the preferential rights of a holder in due course, a person either must meet the requirements of Section 3–302 of the Uniform Commercial Code (UCC or Code) or must "inherit" these rights under the shelter rule, Section 3–203(b) (discussed later in this chapter). To satisfy the requirements of Section 3–302, a transferee must—

1. be a holder of a negotiable instrument;
2. take it for value;
3. take it in good faith; and
4. take it without notice
   (a) that it is overdue or has been dishonored, or
   (b) that the instrument contains an unauthorized signature or an alteration, or
   (c) that any person has any defense against or claim to it; and
5. take it without reason to question its authenticity due to apparent evidence of forgery, alteration, incompleteness, or other irregularity.

Figure 28-1 illustrates the various requirements of becoming a holder in due course and the consequence of meeting or not meeting these requirements.

◆ **SEE FIGURE 28-1: Rights of Transferees**

HOLDER

To become a holder in due course, the transferee must first be a holder. A holder, as discussed in *Chapter 27*, is a person who is in possession of a negotiable instrument that is "payable to bearer or, in the case of an instrument payable to an identified person, if the identified person is in possession." Section 1–201(20). Revised Article 1 has a similar definition: "the person in possession of a negotiable instrument that is payable either to bearer or to an identified person that is the person in possession." Revised Section 1–201(b)(21). In other words, a holder is a person who has both possession of an instrument and all indorsements necessary to it. Whether the holder is the owner of the instrument or not, he may transfer it, negotiate it, enforce payment of it (subject to valid claims and defenses), or, with certain exceptions, discharge it.

The following factual situation, illustrated in *Figure 28-2*, defines the significance of being a holder. Poe indorsed her paycheck in blank and cashed it at a hardware store where she was a well-known customer. Shortly thereafter, a burglar stole the check from the hardware store. The owner of the hardware store immediately notified Poe's employer, who gave the drawee bank a stop payment order (an order not to pay the instrument). The burglar indorsed the check in a false name and transferred it to a grocer who took it in good faith and for value. The check was dishonored (not paid) when presented to the drawee bank. The paycheck became bearer paper when Poe indorsed it in blank. It retained this character in the hands of the owner of the hardware store, in the hands of the burglar, and in the hands of the grocer, who became a holder in due course even though he had received it from a thief who had indorsed it with a false name. Because an

◆ **FIGURE 28-1: Rights of Transferees**

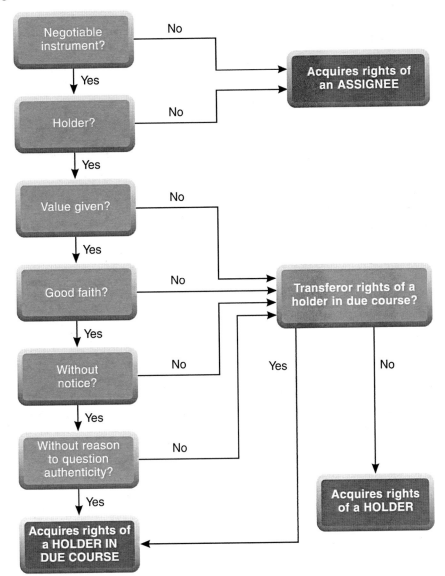

indorsement is not necessary to the negotiation of bearer paper, the fact that the indorsement was forged was immaterial. The thief was a "holder" of the check within the definition of Section 1–201 and may negotiate an instrument "whether or not he is the owner." Accordingly, one who, like the grocer, takes from a holder for value, in good faith, without notice, and without reason to question its authenticity, becomes a holder in due course. Furthermore, in the absence of a real defense, discussed later in this chapter, the grocer will be entitled to payment from the drawer.

◆ **SEE FIGURE 28-2: Stolen Bearer Paper**

This rule does not apply to a stolen order instrument. In the prior example, assume that the thief had stolen the paycheck from Poe prior to indorsement. The thief then forged Poe's signature and transferred the check to the grocer, who again took it in good faith, for value, without notice, and without reason to question its authenticity. Negotiation of an order instrument requires a valid indorsement by the person to whose order the instrument is payable, in this case Poe. A forged indorsement is not valid. Consequently, the grocer has not taken the instrument with all necessary indorsements, and, therefore, he could not be a holder and, as a result, could not be a holder in due course. The grocer's only recourse would be to collect the amount of the check from the thief. *Figure 28-3* illustrates this example.

◆ **SEE FIGURE 28-3: Stolen Order Paper**

◆ **FIGURE 28-2: Stolen Bearer Paper**

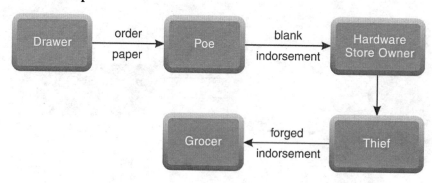

Grocer is a holder in due course because he
(1) Was a holder of a negotiable instrument,
(2) Gave value,
(3) Took in good faith,
(4) Took without notice, and
(5) Took without reason to question its authenticity.

In addition, certain other persons are entitled to enforce an instrument even though the person is not the owner of the instrument or is in wrongful possession of the instrument. Section 3–301. These other persons entitled to enforce an instrument include a nonholder in possession of the instrument who has the rights of a holder, and a person not in possession of the instrument who is entitled to enforce the instrument pursuant to special situations, such as where the instrument has been lost, destroyed, or stolen (Section 3–309) or where the instrument has been paid or accepted by mistake and the payor or acceptor has recovered the money or revoked acceptance (Section 3–418(d)).

VALUE

The law requires a holder in due course to give value. An obvious case of the failure to do so is where the holder makes a gift of the instrument to a third person.

The concept of value in the law of negotiable instruments is not the same as that of consideration under the law of contracts. **Value**, for purposes of negotiable instruments, is defined as (1) the actual *performing* of the agreed promise (executory promises are excluded because they have not been performed); (2) the acquiring of a security interest or other lien in the instrument other than a judicial lien; (3) the taking of the instrument in payment of or as security for an antecedent debt; (4) the giving of a negotiable instrument; and (5) the giving of an irrevocable obligation to a third party. Section 3–303(a).

EXECUTORY PROMISE An executory promise, though clearly valid consideration to support a contract, is *not* the giving of value to support holder in due course status because such a promise has yet to be performed. A purchaser of a note or draft who has not yet given value may rescind the transaction if she learns of a defense to the instrument. A person who has given value, however, cannot do this; to recover value, she needs the protection accorded a holder in due course.

◆ **FIGURE 28-3: Stolen Order Paper**

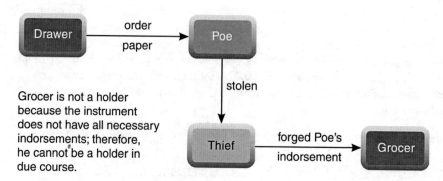

Grocer is not a holder because the instrument does not have all necessary indorsements; therefore, he cannot be a holder in due course.

For example, Mike executes and delivers a $1,000 note payable to the order of Pat, who negotiates it to Henry, who promises to pay Pat for it a month later. During the month, Henry learns that Mike has a defense against Pat. Henry can rescind the agreement with Pat and return or tender the note back to her. Because this makes him whole, Henry has no need to cut off Mike's defense. Assume, on the other hand, that Henry has paid Pat for the note before he learns of Mike's defense. Because he may be unable to recover his money from Pat, Henry needs holder in due course protection, which permits him to recover on the instrument from Mike.

A holder therefore takes an instrument for value to the extent that the agreed promise of performance has been performed provided that performance was given prior to the holder's learning of any defense or claim to the instrument. Assume that in the previous example Henry had agreed to pay Pat $900 for the note. If Henry had paid Pat $600, he could be a holder in due course to the extent of $666.67 (600 ÷ 900 × $1000), and if a defense were available, it would be valid against him only to the extent of the balance. Section 3–302(d). When Henry paid the $300 balance to Pat, he would become a holder in due course as to the full $1,000 face value of the note, provided payment was made prior to Henry's discovery of Mike's defense. If he made the $300 payment after discovering the defense or claim, Henry would be a holder in due course only to the extent of $666.67. A holder in due course, to give value, need pay only the amount he agreed to pay, not the face amount of the instrument.

The Code provides an exception to the executory promise rule in two situations: (1) the giving of a negotiable instrument and (2) the making of an irrevocable obligation to a third party. Section 3–303(a)(4), (5).

SECURITY INTEREST Where an instrument is given as security for an obligation, the lender is regarded as having given value to the extent of his security interest. Sections 3–302(e) and 3–303(a). For example, Pedro is the holder of a $1,000 note payable to his order, executed by Monica, and due in twelve months. Pedro uses the note as security for a $700 loan made to him by Larry. Larry has advanced $700; therefore, he has met the requirement of value to the extent of $700.

Likewise, a bank gives value when a depositor is allowed to withdraw funds against a deposited item. Sections 4–210 and 4–211. The provisional or temporary crediting of a depositor's account (discussed in *Chapter 30*) is not sufficient. If a number of checks have been deposited, and some but not all of the funds have been withdrawn, the Code traces the deposit by following the "FIFO" or "first-in, first-out" method of accounting.

ANTECEDENT DEBT Under general contract law, an antecedent debt (a preexisting obligation) is not consideration.

Under Section 3–303(a)(3) of the Code, however, a holder gives value when she takes an instrument in payment of or as security for an antecedent debt. Thus, Martha makes and delivers a note for $1,000 to the order of Penny, who indorses the instrument and delivers it to Howard in payment of an outstanding debt of $970 which she owes him. Howard has given value.

GOOD FAITH

Revised Article 3 defines **good faith** as "honesty in fact and the observance of reasonable commercial standards of fair dealing." Section 3–103(4). Thus, Revised Article 3 adopts a definition of good faith that has both a subjective and objective component. (This is the same definition adopted by Revised Article 1.) The subjective component ("honesty in fact") measures good faith by what the purchaser knows or believes. The objective component ("the observance of reasonable commercial standards of fair dealing") is comparable to the definition of good faith applicable to merchants under Article 2 in that it includes the requirement of the observance of reasonable commercial standards of fairness. Buying an instrument at a discounted price does not demonstrate lack of good faith.

LACK OF NOTICE

To become a holder in due course, a holder must also take the instrument without notice that it is (1) overdue, (2) dishonored, (3) forged or altered (see discussion of these later in the chapter), or (4) subject to any claim or defense. Notice of any of these matters should alert the purchaser that she may be buying a lawsuit and consequently may not be accorded the favored position of a holder in due course. Section 1–201(25) defines *notice* as follows: "A person has 'notice' of a fact when (a) he has actual knowledge of it; or (b) he has received a notice or notification of it; or (c) from all the facts and circumstances known to him at the time in question he has reason to know that it exists." Revised Section 1–202(a) is substantially the same. Whereas the first two clauses of this definition impose a wholly subjective standard, the last clause provides a partially objective one: the presence of suspicious circumstances does not adversely affect the purchaser, unless he has reason to recognize them as suspicious. Because the applicable standard is "actual notice," "notice received," or "reason to know," constructive notice through public filing or recording is not of itself sufficient notice to prevent a person from being a holder in due course.

To be effective, notice must be received at a time and in a manner that the recipient will have a reasonable opportunity to act on it. Section 3–302(f).

NOTICE AN INSTRUMENT IS OVERDUE To be a holder in due course, the purchaser must take the instrument without notice that it is overdue. This requirement is based on the idea that overdue paper conveys a suspicion that something is wrong. **Time paper** is due on its stated due date if the stated date is a business day or, if not, on the next business day. It "becomes overdue on the day after the due date." Section 3–304(b)(2). Thus, if an instrument is payable on July 1, a purchaser cannot become a holder in due course by buying it on July 2, provided that July 1 was a business day. In addition, in the case of an installment note or of several notes issued as part of the same transaction with successive specified maturity dates, the purchaser has notice that an instrument is overdue if he has reason to know that any part of the principal amount is overdue or that there is an uncured default in payment of another instrument of the same series. Sections 3–302(a)(2) and 3–304(b).

Demand paper is overdue for purposes of preventing a purchaser from becoming a holder in due course if the purchaser has notice that she is taking the instrument on a day after demand has been made or after it has been outstanding for an unreasonably long time. Section 3–304(a). The Code provides that for checks a reasonable time is ninety days after its date. For all other demand instruments the reasonable period of time varies depending upon the facts of the particular case. Thus, the particular situation, business custom, and other relevant factors must be considered in determining whether an instrument is overdue: No hard-and-fast rules are possible.

Acceleration clauses have caused problems. If an instrument's maturity date has been accelerated, the instrument becomes overdue on the day after the accelerated due date even though the holder may be unaware that it is past due. Section 3–304(b)(3).

NOTICE AN INSTRUMENT HAS BEEN DISHONORED **Dishonor** is the refusal to pay or accept an instrument when it becomes due. If a transferee has notice that an instrument has been dishonored, he cannot become a holder in due course. Section 3–302(a)(2)(iii). For example, a person who takes a check stamped "NSF" (not sufficient funds) or "no account" has notice of dishonor and will not be a holder in due course.

NOTICE OF A CLAIM OR DEFENSE A purchaser of an instrument cannot become a holder in due course if he purchases it with notice of "any claim to the instrument described in Section 3–306" or "a defense or claim in recoupment described in Section 3–305(a)." Section 3–302(a)(2). A **defense** protects a person from liability on an instrument, whereas a **claim** to an instrument asserts ownership of it.

Claims covered by Section 3–306 "include not only claims to ownership but also any other claim of a property

or possessory right. It includes the claim to a lien or the claim of a person in rightful possession of an instrument who was wrongfully deprived of possession." Section 3–306, Comment. Claims to instruments may be made against thieves, finders, or possessors with void or voidable title. In many instances, both a defense and claim will be involved. For example, Donna is fraudulently induced to issue a check to Pablo. Donna has a claim to ownership of the instrument as well as a defense to Pablo's demand for payment.

Section 3–305(a), which is more fully discussed later in this chapter, provides that personal defenses are valid against a holder, while real defenses are effective against both holders and holders in due course. In addition, a person without the rights of a holder in due course is subject to an obligor's claim in recoupment "against the original payee of the instrument if the claim arose from the transaction that gave rise to the instrument." Section 3–305(a)(3). For example, Buyer gives Seller a negotiable note in exchange for Seller's promise to deliver certain goods. Seller delivers nonconforming goods that Buyer elects to accept. Buyer has a cause of action under Article 2 for breach of warranty under the contract, which "claim may be asserted against Seller … to reduce the amount owing on the note. It is not relevant whether Seller knew or had notice that Buyer had the warranty claim." Section 3–305, Comment 3.

Buying an instrument at a discount or for a price less than face value does not mean that the buyer had notice of any defense or claim against the instrument. Nonetheless, a court may construe an unusually large discount as notice of a claim or defense.

WITHOUT REASON TO QUESTION ITS AUTHENTICITY

Under prior Article 3, a purchaser had notice of a claim or defense if the instrument was so incomplete, contained such visible evidence of forgery or alteration, or was otherwise so irregular as to call into question its validity. Courts differed greatly as to how irregular an instrument had to be for a holder to have notice. Revised Article 3 provides that a party may become a holder in due course only if the instrument issued or negotiated to the holder "does not bear such apparent evidence of forgery or alteration or is not otherwise so irregular or incomplete as to call into question its authenticity." Section 3–302(a)(1). According to the comments to this section, the term "authenticity" clarifies the idea that the irregularity or incompleteness must indicate that the instrument may not be what it purports to be. The Revision takes the position that persons who purchase such instruments do so at their own peril and should not be protected against defenses of the obligor or claims of prior owners. In addition, the Revision takes the position that it makes no difference if the holder does not have notice of such irregularity or incompleteness; it depends only on whether the instrument's defect is apparent and whether the taker should have reason to know of the problem.

HOLDER IN DUE COURSE STATUS

A holder who meets the requirements discussed in the previous section obtains the preferred position of holder in due course status. This section discusses whether a payee may become a holder in due course. It also addresses the rights of a transferee from a holder in due course under the shelter rule. Finally, it identifies those special circumstances that prevent a transferee from acquiring holder in due course status.

A PAYEE MAY BE A HOLDER IN DUE COURSE

A payee may be a holder in due course. Section 3–302, Comment 4. This does not mean that a payee automatically is a holder in due course but that he *may* be one if he satisfies the requirements for such status. For example, if a seller delivers goods to a buyer and accepts a current check in payment, the seller will be a holder in due course if he acted in good faith and had no notice of defenses or claims and no reason to question its authenticity. The most common example is where the transaction involves three parties, and the defense involves the parties other than the payee. For example, after purchasing goods from Punky, Robin fraudulently obtains a check from Clem payable to the order of Punky and forwards it to Punky. Punky takes it for value and without any knowledge that Robin had defrauded Clem into issuing the check. In such a case, the payee, Punky, is a holder in due course and takes the instrument free and clear of Clem's defense of fraud in the inducement.

THE SHELTER RULE

Through operation of the shelter rule, the transferee of an instrument acquires the *same* rights in the instrument as the transferor had. Section 3–203(b). Therefore, even a holder who does not comply fully with the requirements for being a holder in due course nevertheless acquires all the rights of a holder in due course if some previous holder of the instrument had been a holder in due course. For example, Prosser induces Mundheim, by fraud in the inducement, to make a note payable to her order and then negotiates it to Henn, a holder in due course. After the note is overdue, Henn gives it to Corbin, who has notice of the fraud. Corbin is not a holder in due course, because he took the instrument when overdue, did not pay value, and had notice of Mundheim's defense. Nonetheless, through the operation of the shelter rule, Corbin acquires Henn's rights as a holder in due course, and Mundheim cannot successfully assert his defense against Corbin. The purpose of the shelter provision is not to benefit the transferee but to assure the holder in due course of a free market for the negotiable instruments he acquires.

The shelter rule, however, provides that a transferee who has been a party to any fraud or illegality affecting the instrument cannot subsequently acquire the rights of a holder in due course. For example, Parker induces Miles, by fraud in the inducement, to make an instrument payable to the order of Parker, who subsequently negotiates the instrument to Henson, a holder in due course. If Parker later reacquires it from Henson, Parker will not succeed to Henson's rights as a holder in due course and will remain subject to the defense of fraud.

THE PREFERRED POSITION OF A HOLDER IN DUE COURSE

In a nonconsumer transaction a holder in due course takes the instrument (1) free from all *claims* on the part of any person and (2) free from all *defenses* of any party with whom he has not dealt, except for a limited number of defenses that are available against anyone, including a holder in due course. Such defenses that are available against all parties are referred to as **real defenses**. In contrast, defenses that may not be asserted against a holder in due course are referred to as **personal** or **contractual defenses**.

REAL DEFENSES

The real defenses available against all holders, including holders in due course, are:

1. infancy, to the extent that it is a defense to a simple contract, Section 3–305(a)(1)(i);
2. any other incapacity, duress, or illegality of the transaction that renders the obligation void, Section 3–305(a)(1)(ii);
3. fraud in the execution, Section 3–305(a)(1)(iii);
4. discharge in insolvency proceedings, Section 3–305(a)(1)(iv);
5. any other discharge of which the holder has notice when he takes the instrument, Section 3–601(b);
6. unauthorized signature, Section 3–401(a); and
7. fraudulent alteration, Section 3–407(b), (c).

INFANCY All States have a firmly entrenched public policy of protecting minors from persons who might take advantage of them through contractual dealings. The Code does not state when minority (infancy) is available as a defense or the conditions under which it may be asserted. Rather, it provides that minority is a defense available against a holder in due course to the extent that it is a defense to a contract under the laws of the State involved. See *Chapter 14*.

VOID OBLIGATIONS Where the obligation on an instrument originates in such a way that it is *void* or null under the law of the State involved, the Code authorizes the use of this defense against a holder in due course. This follows from the idea that where the party was never obligated, it is unreasonable to permit an event over which he has no control—negotiation to a holder in due course—to convert a nullity into a valid claim against him.

Incapacity, duress, and the illegality of a transaction are defenses that may render the obligation of a party either voidable or void, depending upon the law of the State involved as applied to the facts of a given transaction. To the extent the obligation is rendered void (because of duress by physical force, because the party is a person under guardianship, or, in some cases, because the contract is illegal) the defense may be asserted against a holder in due course. To the extent it is voidable, which is generally the case, the defense (other than minority, discussed above) is not effective against a holder in due course.

FRAUD IN THE EXECUTION Fraud in the execution of the instrument renders the instrument void and therefore is a defense valid against a holder in due course. The Code describes this type of fraud as misrepresentation that induced the party to sign the instrument with neither knowledge nor reasonable opportunity to learn of its character or its essential terms. For example, Francis is asked to sign a receipt and does so without realizing or having the opportunity of learning that her signature is going on a promissory note cleverly concealed under the receipt. Because her signature has been obtained by fraud in the execution, Francis would have a valid defense against a holder in due course.

DISCHARGE IN INSOLVENCY PROCEEDINGS If a party's obligation on an instrument is discharged in a proceeding for bankruptcy or for any other insolvency, he has a valid defense in any action brought against him on the instrument, including one brought by a holder in due course. Thus, a debtor whose obligation on a negotiable instrument is discharged in an insolvency proceeding (bankruptcy) is relieved of payment, even to a holder in due course.

DISCHARGE OF WHICH THE HOLDER HAS NOTICE Any holder, including a holder in due course, takes the instrument subject to *any* discharge of which she has notice at the time of taking. If only some, but not all, of the parties to the instrument have been discharged, the purchaser can still become a holder in due course. The discharged parties, however, have a real defense against a holder in due course who had notice of their discharge. For example, Harris, who is in possession of a negotiable instrument, strikes out the indorsement of Jones. The instrument is subsequently negotiated to Stephen, a holder in due course, against whom Jones has a real defense.

UNAUTHORIZED SIGNATURE A person's signature on an instrument is unauthorized when it is made without express, implied, or apparent authority. A person whose signature is unauthorized or forged cannot be held liable on the instrument in the absence of estoppel or ratification, even if the instrument is negotiated to a holder in due course. Similarly, if Joan's signature were forged on the back of an instrument, Joan could not be held as an indorser, because she has not made a contract. Thus, any unauthorized signature is totally invalid as that of the person whose name is signed unless she ratifies it or is precluded from denying it; the unauthorized signature operates only as the signature of the unauthorized signer. Section 3–403(a).

An unauthorized signature may be **ratified** and thereby become valid so far as its effect as a signature. Section 3–403(a). Thus, Kathy forges Laura's indorsement on a promissory note and negotiates it to Allison. Laura subsequently ratifies Kathy's act. As a result, Kathy is no longer liable to Allison on the note, although Laura is. Nonetheless, Laura's ratification does not relieve Kathy from civil liability to Laura; nor does it in any way affect Kathy's criminal liability for the forgery.

A party is precluded from denying the validity of his signature if his **negligence** substantially contributes to the making of the unauthorized signature. The most obvious case is that of a drawer who uses a mechanized or other automatic signing device and is negligent in safeguarding it. In such an instance, the drawer would not be permitted to assert an unauthorized signature as a defense against a holder in due course. Section 3–406(c). Under Revised Article 3, if the person seeking to enforce the instrument is also negligent, then comparative negligence applies. Section 3–406(b).

A person may also be precluded from asserting a defense by estoppel if his conduct in the matter has caused reliance by a third party to his loss or damage.

FRAUDULENT ALTERATION An alteration is (1) an unauthorized change that modifies the obligation of any party to the instrument or (2) an unauthorized addition or change to an incomplete instrument concerning the obligation of a party.

An alteration that is fraudulently made discharges a party whose obligation is affected by the alteration except where that party assents or is precluded by his own negligence from raising the defense. Section 3–407(b). All other alterations do not discharge any party, and the instrument may be enforced according to its original terms. Section 3–407(b). Thus, if an instrument has been nonfraudulently altered, it may be enforced, but only to the extent of its original tenor (i.e., according to its initially written terms).

A discharge under Section 3–407(b) for fraudulent alteration, however, is not effective against a holder in due course who took the instrument without notice of the alteration. Such a subsequent holder in due course may always enforce the instrument according to its original terms and, in the case of an incomplete instrument, may enforce it as completed. Section 3–407(c). (Under this section of the Code a person taking the instrument for value, in good faith, and without notice of the alteration is accorded the same protection as a holder in due course.) The following examples demonstrate the operation of these rules (*Figure 28-5* illustrates these examples).

1. M executes and delivers a note to P for $2,000, which P subsequently indorses and transfers to A for $1,900. A intentionally and skillfully changes the figure on the note to $20,000 and then negotiates it to B, who takes it, in good faith, without notice of any wrongdoing and without reason to question its authenticity, for $19,000. B is a holder in due course and, therefore, can collect the original amount of the note ($2,000) from M or P and the full amount ($20,000) from A, less any amount paid by the other parties.

2. Assume the facts in (1) except that B is not a holder in due course. M and P are both discharged by A's fraudulent alteration. B's only recourse is against A for the full amount ($20,000).

3. M issues his blank check to P, who is to complete it when the exact amount is determined. Though the correct amount is set at $2,000, P fraudulently fills in $4,000 and then negotiates the check to T. If T is a holder in due course, she can collect the amount as completed ($4,000) from either M or P. If T is not a holder in due course, however, she has no recourse against M but may recover the full amount ($4,000) from P.

4. Assume the facts in (3) except that P filled in the $4,000 amount in good faith. No party is discharged from liability on the instrument because the alteration was not

◆ FIGURE 28-4: Effects of Alterations

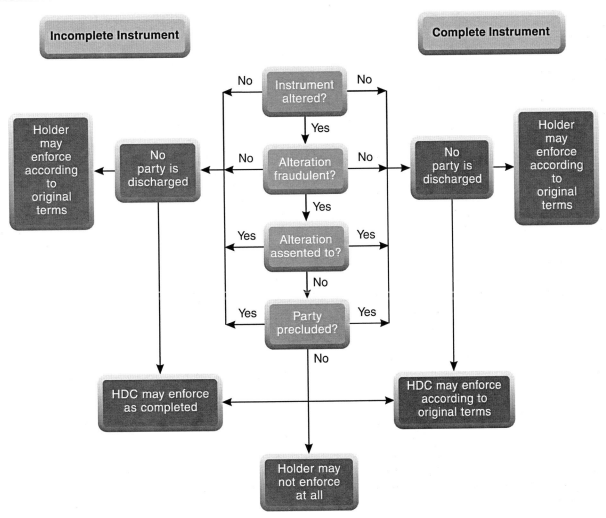

◆ **FIGURE 28-5: Material Alteration**

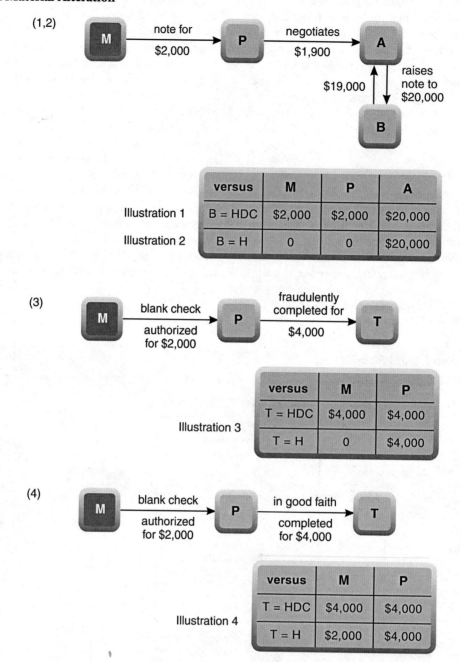

fraudulent. If T is not a holder in due course, M is liable for the correct amount ($2,000). If T is a holder in due course, T is entitled to receive $4,000 from M because she can enforce an incomplete instrument as completed. Whether or not T is a holder in due course, T may recover $4,000 from P.

◆ **SEE FIGURE 28-4: Effects of Alterations**

◆ **SEE FIGURE 28-5: Material Alteration**

PERSONAL DEFENSES

Defenses to an instrument may arise in many ways, either when the instrument is issued or later. In general, the numerous defenses to liability on a negotiable instrument, which are similar to those that may be raised in an action for breach of contract, are available against any holder of the instrument unless he has the rights of a holder in due course. Among the personal defenses are (1) lack of consideration; (2) failure of consideration; (3) breach of contract; (4) fraud

◆ FIGURE 28-6: Availability of Defenses against Holders in Due Course

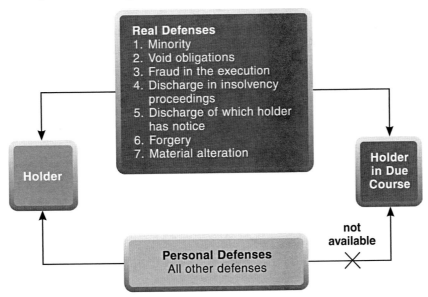

in the inducement; (5) illegality that does not render the transaction void; (6) duress, undue influence, mistake, misrepresentation, or incapacity that does not render the transaction void; (7) setoff or counterclaim; (8) discharge of which the holder in due course does not have notice; (9) nondelivery of an instrument, whether complete or incomplete; (10) unauthorized completion of an incomplete instrument; (11) payment without obtaining surrender of the instrument; (12) theft of a bearer instrument or of an instrument payable to the thief; and (13) lack of authority of a corporate officer, agent, or partner as to the particular instrument, where such officer, agent, or partner had general authority to issue negotiable paper for his principal or firm.

These situations are the most common examples, but others exist. Indeed, the Code does not attempt to detail defenses that may be cut off. It simply states that a holder in due course takes the instrument free and clear of all claims and defenses, except those listed as real defenses.

◆ SEE FIGURE 28-6: Availability of Defenses against Holders in Due Course

LIMITATIONS UPON HOLDER IN DUE COURSE RIGHTS

The preferential position enjoyed by a holder in due course has been severely limited by a Federal Trade Commission (FTC) rule restricting the rights of a holder in due course of an instrument concerning a debt arising out of a consumer credit contract, which includes negotiable instruments. The rule, entitled "Preservation of Consumers' Claims and Defenses," applies to sellers and lessors of consumer goods, which are goods for personal, household, or family use. It also applies to lenders who advance money to finance a consumer's purchase of consumer goods or services. The rule is intended to prevent consumer purchase transactions from being financed in such a manner that the purchaser is legally obligated to make full payment of the price to a third party, even though the dealer from whom she bought the goods committed fraud or the goods were defective. Such obligations arise when a purchaser executes and delivers to a seller a negotiable instrument that the seller negotiates to a holder in due course. The buyer's defense that the goods were defective or that the seller committed fraud, although valid against the seller, is not valid against the holder in due course.

To correct this situation, the FTC rule preserves claims and defenses of consumer buyers and borrowers against holders in due course. The rule states that no seller or creditor can take or receive a consumer credit contract unless the contract contains this conspicuous provision:

NOTICE: ANY HOLDER OF THIS CONSUMER CREDIT CONTRACT IS SUBJECT TO ALL CLAIMS AND DEFENSES WHICH THE DEBTOR COULD ASSERT AGAINST THE SELLER OF THE GOODS OR SERVICES OBTAINED PURSUANT HERETO OR WITH THE PROCEEDS HEREOF. RECOVERY HEREUNDER BY THE DEBTOR SHALL NOT EXCEED AMOUNTS PAID BY THE DEBTOR HEREUNDER.

◆ FIGURE 28-7: **Rights of Holder in Due Course under FTC Rule**

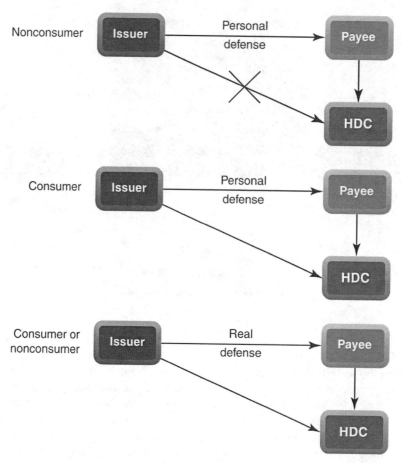

The purpose of this notice is to inform any holder in due course of a paper or negotiable instrument that he takes the instrument subject to all claims and defenses that the buyer could assert against the seller. The effect of the rule is to place the holder in due course in the position of an assignee.

◆ SEE FIGURE 28-7: **Rights of Holder in Due Course under FTC Rule**

CHAPTER SUMMARY

REQUIREMENTS OF A HOLDER IN DUE COURSE

Holder a person who has both possession of an instrument and all indorsements necessary to it

Value differs from contractual consideration and consists of any of the following:
- the timely performance of legal consideration (which excludes executory promises);
- the acquisition of a security interest in or a lien on the instrument;
- taking the instrument in payment of or as security for an antecedent debt;
- the giving of a negotiable instrument; or
- the giving of an irrevocable commitment to a third party

Good Faith honesty in fact and the observance of reasonable commercial standards of fair dealing

Lack of Notice
- *Notice an Instrument Is Overdue* time paper is overdue after its stated date; demand paper is overdue after demand has been made or after it has been outstanding for an unreasonable period of time

- *Notice an Instrument Has Been Dishonored* dishonor is the refusal to pay or accept an instrument when it becomes due
- *Notice an Instrument Has Been Forged or Altered*
- *Notice of a Claim or Defense* a defense protects a person from liability, while a claim is an assertion of ownership

Without Reason to Question Its Authenticity instrument cannot bear such apparent evidence of forgery or alteration or otherwise be so irregular or incomplete as to call into question its authenticity

HOLDER IN DUE COURSE STATUS	**A Payee May Be a Holder in Due Course** the payee's rights as a holder in due course are limited to defenses of persons with whom he has not dealt **The Shelter Rule** the transferee of an instrument acquires the same rights that the transferor had in the instrument
THE PREFERRED POSITION OF A HOLDER IN DUE COURSE	**Real Defenses** real defenses are available against all holders, including holders in due course; such defenses are as follows: • *Infancy* • *Void Obligations* • *Fraud in the Execution* • *Discharge in Insolvency Proceedings* • *Discharge of Which the Holder Has Notice* • *Unauthorized Signature* • *Fraudulent Alteration* **Personal Defenses** all other defenses that might be asserted in the case of any action for breach of contract **Limitations upon Holder in Due Course Rights** the preferential position of a holder in due course has been severely limited by a Federal Trade Commission rule that applies to consumer credit contracts: under this rule, a transferee of consumer credit contracts cannot take as a holder in due course

Liability of Parties

The preceding chapters discussed the requirements of negotiability, the transfer of negotiable instruments, and the preferred position of a holder in due course. When parties issue negotiable instruments they do so with the expectation that they, either directly or indirectly, will satisfy their obligation under the instrument. Likewise, when a person accepts, indorses, or transfers an instrument, he incurs liability for the instrument under certain circumstances. This chapter examines the liability of parties arising out of negotiable instruments and the ways in which liability may be terminated.

Two types of potential liability are associated with negotiable instruments: contractual liability and warranty liability. The law imposes **contractual liability** on those who **sign**, or have a representative agent sign, a negotiable instrument. Because some parties to a negotiable instrument never sign it, they never assume contractual liability. Section 3–401(a).

Warranty liability, on the other hand, is not based on signature; thus, it may be imposed on both signers and nonsigners. **Warranty liability** applies (1) to persons who transfer an instrument and (2) to persons who obtain payment or acceptance of an instrument.

CONTRACTUAL LIABILITY

All parties whose signatures appear on a negotiable instrument incur certain contractual obligations, unless they disclaim liability. No person is liable on an instrument unless she signs it herself or has it signed by a person whose signature binds her. Once the person signs the instrument, the person has *prima facie* liability on the instrument. The *maker* of a promissory note and the *acceptor* of a draft assume primary, or unconditional, liability, subject to valid claims and defenses, to pay according to the terms of the instrument at the time he signs it or as completed according to the rules for incomplete instruments, discussed in *Chapter 28*. **Primary liability** means that a party is legally obligated to pay

without the holder's having to resort first to another party. *Indorsers* of all instruments incur secondary, or conditional, liability if the instrument is not paid. **Secondary liability** means that a party is legally obligated to pay only after another party, who is expected to pay, fails to do so. The liability of drawers of drafts and checks is also conditional because it is generally contingent upon the drawee's dishonor of the instrument. A *drawee* has *no* liability on the instrument until he accepts it.

An **accommodation party** signs the instrument to lend her credit to another party to the instrument and is a direct beneficiary of the value received. Section 3–419(a). The liability of an accommodation party, who generally signs as a comaker, or anomalous indorser, is determined by the capacity in which she signs. Section 3–419(b). If she signs as a maker, she incurs primary liability; if she signs as an anomalous indorser, she incurs secondary liability.

SIGNATURE

The word *signature*, as discussed in *Chapter 26*, is broadly defined to include any name, word, or mark, whether handwritten, typed, printed, or in any other form, made with the intention of authenticating an instrument. Sections 3–401(b) and 1–201(39); Revised Section 1–201(b)(37). The signature may be made by the individual herself or on her behalf by the individual's authorized agent.

AUTHORIZED SIGNATURES

A person is obligated by a signature if the signature is her own or if it is signed by an agent with authority. Authorized agents often execute negotiable instruments on behalf of their principals. The agent is not liable if she is authorized to execute the instrument and does so properly (e.g., "Prince, principal, by Adams, agent"). If these two conditions are met, then only the principal is liable on the instrument. (For a comprehensive discussion of the principal–agent relationship, see *Chapters 19* and *20*.)

Occasionally, however, the agent, although fully authorized, uses an inappropriate form of signature that may mislead holders or prospective holders as to the identity of the obligor. Although incorrect signatures by agents assume many forms, they can be conveniently sorted into three groups. In each of these instances the intention of the original parties to the instrument is that the principal is to be liable on the instrument and the agent is not.

The first type occurs when an agent signs only his own name to an instrument, neither indicating that he is signing in a representative capacity nor stating the name of the principal. For example, Adams, the agent of Prince, makes a note on behalf of Prince but signs it "Adams." The signature does not indicate that Adams has signed in a representative capacity or that he has made the instrument on behalf of Prince. The second type of incorrect form occurs when an authorized agent indicates that he is signing in a representative capacity but does not disclose the name of his principal. For example, Adams, executing an instrument on behalf of Prince, merely signs it "Adams, agent." The third type of inappropriate signature occurs when an agent reveals both her name and her principal's name, but does not indicate that she has signed in a representative capacity. For example, Adams, signing an instrument on behalf of Prince, signs it "Adams, Prince."

In all three situations, the agent is liable on the instrument only to a holder in due course without notice that Adams was not intended to be liable. Because Prince's liability on the instrument is determined by contract and agency law, Prince is liable to all holders. Under Revised Article 3, if a representative (an agent) signs his name as the drawer of a *check* without indicating his representative status and the check is payable from an account of the represented person (the principal) who is identified on the check, the representative is not liable on the check if he is an authorized agent. Some courts reached this result under prior Article 3.

UNAUTHORIZED SIGNATURES

An unauthorized signature, with two exceptions, is totally ineffective and does not bind anybody. Unauthorized signatures include both forgeries and signatures made by an agent without authority. Though generally not binding on the person whose name appears on the instrument, the unauthorized signature is binding upon the unauthorized signer, whether her own name appears on the instrument or not, to any person who in good faith pays or gives value for the instrument. Section 3–403(a). Thus, if Adams, without authority, signed Prince's name to an instrument, Adams, not Prince, would be liable on the instrument. The rule, therefore, is an exception to the principle that only those whose names appear on a negotiable instrument can be liable on it.

RATIFICATION OF UNAUTHORIZED SIGNATURE An unauthorized signature may be **ratified** by the person whose name appears on the instrument. Section 3–403(a). Although the ratification may relieve the actual signer from liability on the instrument, it does not of itself affect any rights the person ratifying the signature may have against the actual signer.

NEGLIGENCE CONTRIBUTING TO FORGED SIGNATURE Any person who by his **negligence** substantially contributes to the making of a forged signature may *not* assert the lack of authority as a defense against a holder in due course or a person who in good faith pays the instrument or takes it for value or for collection. Section 3–406. For example, Ingrid employs a signature stamp to sign her checks and carelessly leaves it accessible to third parties. Lisa discovers the stamp and uses it to write a number of checks without Ingrid's authorization. Norman, a person who takes the instrument for value and in good faith, will not be subject to Ingrid's defense of unauthorized signature and will be able to recover the amount of the check from Ingrid, due to Ingrid's negligence in storing the signature stamp. Nevertheless, if the person asserting the preclusion also fails to exercise reasonable care, Revised Section 3–406(b) adopts a comparative negligence standard.

LIABILITY OF PRIMARY PARTIES

There is a primary party on every note: the *maker*. The maker's commitment is unconditional. Section 3–412. No one, however, is unconditionally liable on a draft or check as issued. A *drawee* is not liable on the instrument unless he accepts it. Section 3–408. If, however, the drawee accepts the draft, after which he is known as the *acceptor*, he becomes primarily liable on the instrument. **Acceptance** or, in the case of a check, certification is the drawee's signed promise to pay a draft as presented. Section 3–409(a), (d). Presentment (i.e., a demand for payment) is not a condition to the holder's right to recover from parties with primary liability.

MAKERS

The maker of a note is obligated to pay the instrument according to its terms at the time of issuance or, if the instrument is incomplete, according to its terms when completed, as discussed in *Chapter 28*. Section 3–412. The obligation of the maker is owed to a person entitled to enforce the instrument or to an indorser who paid the instrument.

Primary liability also applies to issuers of cashier's checks and to issuers of drafts drawn on the drawer (i.e., where the issuer is both the drawee and the drawer). Section 3–412.

ACCEPTORS

A **drawee** has no liability on the instrument until she accepts it, at which time she becomes an acceptor and, like a maker, primarily liable. The acceptor becomes liable on the draft according to its terms at the time of acceptance or as completed according to the rules for incomplete instruments as discussed in *Chapter 28*. Section 3–413(a). Nevertheless, if the acceptor does not state the amount accepted and the amount of the draft is later raised, a subsequent holder in due course can enforce the instrument against the acceptor according to the terms at the time the holder in due course took possession. Section 3–413(b). Thus, an acceptor should always indicate on the instrument the amount that it is accepting. The acceptor owes the obligation to pay to a person entitled to enforce the instrument or to the drawer or an indorser who paid the draft under drawer's or indorser's liability. Section 3–413(a).

An acceptance must be written on the draft. Section 3–409(a). Having met this requirement, it may take many forms. It may be printed on the face of the draft, ready for the drawee's signature. It may consist of a rubber stamp, with the signature of the drawee added. It may be the drawee's signature, preceded by a word or phrase such as "Accepted," "Certified," or "Good." It may consist of nothing more than the drawee's signature. Normally, but by no means necessarily, an acceptance is written vertically across the face of the draft. It must not, however, contain any words indicating an intent to refuse to honor the draft. Furthermore, no writing separate from the draft and no oral statement or conduct of the drawee will convert the drawee into an acceptor.

Checks, when accepted, are said to be certified. **Certification** is a special type of acceptance consisting of the drawee bank's promise to pay the check when subsequently presented for payment. Section 3–409(d).

The drawee bank has no obligation to certify a check, and its refusal to certify does not constitute dishonor of the instrument. If the drawee refuses to accept or pay the instrument, he may be liable to the drawer for breach of contract.

LIABILITY OF SECONDARY PARTIES

Parties with secondary (conditional) liability do not unconditionally promise to pay the instrument; rather, they engage to pay the instrument if the party expected to pay does not do so. The drawer is liable if the drawee dishonors the instrument. Indorsers (including the payee if he indorses) of an instrument are also conditionally liable; their liability is subject to the conditions of dishonor and notice of dishonor. If an instrument is *not* paid by the party expected to pay and

the conditions precedent to the liability of a secondary party are satisfied, a secondary party is liable unless he has disclaimed his liability or he possesses a valid defense to the instrument.

DRAWERS

A drawer of a draft orders the drawee to pay the instrument and does not expect to pay the draft personally. The drawer is obligated to pay the draft only if the drawee fails to pay the instrument. The drawer of an *unaccepted draft* is obligated to pay the instrument upon its dishonor according to its terms at the time it was issued or, in the case of an incomplete instrument, according to the rules discussed in *Chapter 28*. Under Revised Article 3, the drawer's liability is contingent only upon dishonor and does not require notice of dishonor. The drawer's obligation on an unaccepted draft is owed to a person entitled to enforce the instrument or to an indorser who paid the instrument under indorser's liability.

If the draft has been accepted and the acceptor is not a bank, the obligation of the drawer to pay the instrument is then contingent upon both dishonor of the instrument and notice of dishonor; the drawer's liability in this instance is equivalent to that of an indorser. Sections 3–414(d), 3–503.

INDORSERS

An indorser promises that upon dishonor of the instrument *and* notice of dishonor she will pay the instrument according to the terms of the instrument at the time it was indorsed or, if an incomplete instrument when indorsed, according to its terms when completed, as discussed in *Chapter 28*. Sections 3–415, 3–503. Once again, this obligation is owed to a person entitled to enforce the instrument or to a subsequent indorser who paid the instrument under indorser's liability.

EFFECT OF ACCEPTANCE

Where a draft is accepted by a *bank*, the drawer and all prior indorsers are discharged. Sections 3–414(c), 3–415(d). The liability of indorsers subsequent to certification is not affected. When the bank accepts a draft, it should withhold from the drawer's account funds sufficient to pay the instrument. Because the bank is primarily liable on its acceptance and has the funds, whereas the drawer does not, the discharge is reasonable.

DISCLAIMER OF LIABILITY BY SECONDARY PARTIES

Both drawers and indorsers may disclaim their normal conditional liability by drawing or indorsing an instrument "**without recourse**." Sections 3–414(e), 3–415(b). However, drawers of checks may not disclaim contractual liability. Section 3–414(e). The use of the qualifying words *without recourse* is understood to place purchasers on notice that they may not rely on the credit of the person using this language. A person drawing or indorsing an instrument in this manner does not incur the normal contractual liability of a drawer or indorser to pay the instrument, but he may nonetheless be liable for breach of warranty.

CONDITIONS PRECEDENT TO LIABILITY

A **condition precedent** is an event or events that must occur before liability arises. The condition precedent to the liability of the drawer of an *unaccepted* draft is dishonor. Conditions precedent to the liability of any indorser or the drawer of an *accepted* draft by a nonbank are dishonor and notice of dishonor. If the conditions to secondary liability are not met, a party's conditional obligation on the instrument is discharged, unless the conditions are excused.

DISHONOR Dishonor generally involves the refusal to pay an instrument when it is presented. **Presentment** is a demand made by or on behalf of a person entitled to enforce the instrument for (1) **payment** by the drawee or other party obligated to pay the instrument or (2) **acceptance** by the drawee of a draft. Section 3–501(a). The return of any instrument for lack of necessary indorsements or for failure of the presentment to comply with the terms of the instrument, however, is not a dishonor. Section 3–501(b)(3).

What constitutes dishonor varies depending upon the type of instrument and whether presentment is required.

1. **Note**—A *demand note* is dishonored if the maker does not pay it on the day of presentment. Section 3–502(a)(1). If the note is payable at a *definite time* and (a) the terms of the note require presentment or (b) the note is payable at or through a bank, the note is dishonored if it is not paid on the date it is presented or its due date, whichever is later. Section 3–502(a)(2). All *other time notes* need not be presented and are dishonored if they are not paid on their due dates. Section 3–502(a)(3). Nevertheless, because makers are primarily liable on their notes, their liability is not affected by failure of proper presentment.

2. **Drafts**—An *unaccepted draft* (other than a check, discussed later) that is payable on *demand* is dishonored if presentment is made and it is not paid on the date presented. Section 3–502(b)(2). A *time draft* presented for *payment* is due on the due date or presentment date, whichever is later. Section 3–502(b)(3). A *time draft* presented for *acceptance* prior to its due date is dishonored if it is not accepted on the day presented. Section 3–502(b)(3). Refusal to accept a demand instrument is not a dishonor, although acceptance may be requested. Of course, if an instrument is payable at a certain time period

after acceptance or sight, a refusal to accept the draft on the day presented is a dishonor. Section 3–502(b)(4).

An accepted demand draft is dishonored if the acceptor (who is primarily liable on the instrument) does not pay it on the day presented for payment. Section 3–502(d)(1). An accepted time draft is dishonored if it is not paid on the due date for payment or on the presentment date, whichever is later. Section 3–502(d)(2).

Drawers, with the exception of drafts accepted by a bank, are not discharged from liability by a delay in presentment. Once an instrument has been properly presented and dishonored, a drawer becomes liable to pay the instrument. As previously indicated, drawers and prior indorsers are discharged from liability when a draft is accepted by a bank. Sections 3–414, 3–415.

3. **Checks**—If a check is presented for payment directly to the payor/drawee bank for immediate payment, a refusal to pay the check on the day presented constitutes dishonor. Section 3–502(b)(2). In the more common situation of a check being presented through the normal collection process, a check is dishonored if the payor bank makes timely return of the check, sends timely notice of dishonor or nonpayment, or becomes accountable for the amount of the check (until that payment has been made the check is dishonored, Comment 4). Section 3–502(b)(1). As more fully explained in *Chapter 30*, under Article 4 a bank in most instances has a midnight deadline (before midnight of the next banking day) in which to decide whether to honor or dishonor an instrument. Thus, depending on the number of banks involved in the collection process, the time for dishonor can greatly vary.

Delay in presentment discharges an *indorser* only if the instrument is a check and it is not presented for payment or given to a depositary bank for collection within thirty days after the day the indorsement was made. Section 3–415(e). The same rule does not apply, however, to a drawer. If a person entitled to enforce a check fails to present a check within thirty days after its date, the drawer will be discharged only if the delay deprives the drawer of funds because of the suspension of payments by the drawee bank such as would result from a bank failure. Section 3–414(f). This discharge is quite unlikely because of Federal bank insurance but would be available when an account is not fully insured because it exceeds $100,000 or because the account does not qualify for deposit insurance. Section 3–414, Comment 6.

NOTICE OF DISHONOR

The obligation of an indorser of any instrument and of a drawer of a draft accepted by a nonbank is not enforceable unless the indorser or drawer is given notice of dishonor or the notice is otherwise excused. Sections 3–503(a), 3–415(c). Thus, lack of proper notice discharges the liability of an indorser; for this purpose a drawer of a draft accepted by a party other than a bank is treated as an indorser. Notice of dishonor is *not* required to retain the liability of drawers of unaccepted drafts. In addition, as previously mentioned a drawer is discharged when a draft is accepted by a *bank*. Section 3–414. In short, a drawer's liability usually is not contingent upon receiving notice of dishonor, whereas an indorser's liability is.

Notice of dishonor is normally given by the holder or by an indorser who has himself received notice. For example, Michael makes a note payable to the order of Phyllis; Phyllis indorses it to Arthur; Arthur indorses it to Bambi; and Bambi indorses it to Henry, the last holder. Henry presents it to Michael within a reasonable time, but Michael refuses to pay. Henry may give notice of dishonor to all secondary parties: Phyllis, Arthur, and Bambi. If he is satisfied that Bambi will pay him or if he does not know how to contact Phyllis or Arthur, he may notify only Bambi, who then must see to it that Arthur or Phyllis is notified, or she will have no recourse. Bambi may notify either or both. If she notifies Arthur only, Arthur will have to see to it that Phyllis is notified, or Arthur will have no recourse. When properly given, notice benefits all parties who have rights on the instrument against the party notified. Section 3–503(b). Thus, Henry's notification to Phyllis operates as notice to Phyllis by both Arthur and Bambi. Likewise, if Henry notifies only Bambi and Bambi notifies Arthur and Phyllis, then Henry has the benefit of Bambi's notification of Arthur and Phyllis. Nonetheless, it would be advisable for Henry to give notice to all prior parties because Bambi may be insolvent and thus may not bother to notify Arthur or Phyllis.

If, in the above example, Henry were to notify Phyllis alone, Arthur and Bambi would be discharged. Because she has no claim against Arthur or Bambi, who indorsed after she did, Phyllis would have no ground for complaint. It cannot matter to Phyllis that she is compelled to pay Henry rather than Arthur. Therefore, subsequent parties are permitted to skip intermediate indorsers if they want to discharge them and are willing to look solely to prior indorsers for recourse.

Any necessary notice must be given by a bank before midnight on the *next* banking day following the banking day on which it receives notice of dishonor. Any nonbank with respect to an instrument taken for collection must give notice within thirty days following the day on which it received notice. In all other situations, notice of dishonor must be within thirty days following the day on which dishonor occurred. Section 3–503(c). For instance, Donna draws a check on Youngstown Bank payable to the order of Pablo; Pablo indorses it to Andrea; Andrea deposits it to her account in Second Chicago National Bank; Second Chicago National Bank properly presents it to Youngstown Bank, the drawee; and Youngstown dishonors it because the drawer, Donna, has insufficient funds on deposit to cover it. Youngstown has until midnight of the following day to notify Second Chicago National, Andrea, or Pablo of the dishonor. Second Chicago National then has until midnight on the day after receipt of notice of dishonor to notify Andrea or Pablo. That is, if Second Chicago National received the notice of dishonor on Monday, it would have until midnight on Tuesday to notify Andrea or Pablo. If it failed to notify Andrea, it could not charge the item back to her. Andrea, in turn, has thirty days after receipt of notice of dishonor to notify Pablo. Donna, a drawer of an unaccepted draft, is not discharged from liability for failure to receive notice of dishonor.

Frequently, notice of dishonor is given by returning the unpaid instrument with an attached stamp, ticket, or memorandum stating that the item was not paid and requesting that the recipient make good on it. But because the purpose of notice is to give knowledge of dishonor and to inform the secondary party that he may be held liable on the instrument, any kind of notice which informs the recipient of his potential liability is sufficient. No formal requisites are imposed—notice may be given by any commercially reasonable means, including oral, written, or electronic communication. Section 3–503(b). An oral notice, while sufficient, is inadvisable because it may be difficult to prove. Notice of dishonor must reasonably identify the instrument. Section 3–503(b).

PRESENTMENT AND NOTICE OF DISHONOR EXCUSED The Uniform Commercial Code excuses *presentment* for payment or acceptance if (1) the person entitled to enforce the instrument cannot with reasonable diligence present the instrument, (2) the maker or acceptor of the instrument has repudiated the obligation to pay, is dead, or is in insolvency proceedings, (3) the terms of the instrument do not require presentment to hold the indorsers or drawer liable, (4) the drawer or indorser has waived the right of presentment, (5) the drawer instructed the drawee not to pay or accept the draft, or (6) the drawee was not obligated to the drawer to pay the draft. Section 3–504(a).

Notice of dishonor is excused if the terms of the instrument do not require notice to hold the party liable or if notice has been waived by the party whose obligation is being enforced. Moreover, a waiver of presentment is also a waiver of notice of dishonor. Section 3–504(b). Finally, delay in giving notice of dishonor is excused if the delay is caused by circumstances beyond the control of the person giving notice and that person exercised reasonable diligence in giving notice after the cause of the delay ceased to exist. Section 3–504(c).

◆ **SEE FIGURE 29-1: Contractual Liability**

◆ **FIGURE 29-1: Contractual Liability**

Party	Instrument	Liability	Conditions
Maker	Note	Unconditional	None
Acceptor	Draft	Unconditional	None
Drawer	Unaccepted Draft	Conditional	Dishonor
	Draft accepted by a nonbank	Conditional	Dishonor and notice
	Cashier's check	Unconditional	None
	Draft drawn on drawer	Unconditional	None
	Draft accepted by a bank	None	
	Draft (not check) drawn without recourse	None	
Indorser	Note or draft	Conditional	Dishonor and notice
	Draft subsequently accepted by a bank	None	
	Note or draft indorsed without recourse	None	
Drawee	Draft	None	

LIABILITY FOR CONVERSION

Conversion is a tort by which a person becomes liable in damages because of his wrongful control over the personal property of another. The law applicable to conversion of personal property applies to instruments. Section 3–420(a). An instrument is so converted if the instrument "is taken by transfer, other than by negotiation, from a person not entitled to enforce the instrument or a bank makes or obtains payment with respect to the instrument for a person *not* entitled to enforce the instrument or receive payment." Section 3–420(a) (emphasis added). Examples of conversion thus would include a drawee bank that pays an instrument containing a forged indorsement or a bank that pays an instrument containing only one of two required indorsements.

TERMINATION OF LIABILITY

Eventually, every commercial transaction must end, terminating the potential liabilities of the parties to the instrument. The Code specifies the various methods by and extent to which the liability of *any* party, primary or secondary, is discharged. "Discharge" means that the obligated individual is released from liability on the instrument due to either Article 3 or contract law. The Code also specifies when the liability of *all* parties is discharged. No discharge of a party is effective against a subsequent holder in due course, however, unless she has notice of the discharge when she takes the instrument. Section 3–601(b). In addition, discharge of liability is not always final; liability under certain circum-

stances (e.g., coming into possession of a subsequent holder in due course) can be revived. Discharge applies to the individual and not the instrument, and discharge of individuals may occur at different points in time. Moreover, a person's liability may be discharged with regard to one party but not to another.

PAYMENT

The most obvious and common way for a party to discharge liability on an instrument is to pay a party entitled to enforce the instrument. Section 3–602. An instrument is paid to the extent that payment is made by or for a person obligated to pay the instrument and to a person entitled to enforce the instrument. Section 3–602(a). Subject to three exceptions, such payment results in a discharge even though it is made with knowledge of another person's claim to the instrument, unless such other person either supplies adequate indemnity or obtains an injunction in a proceeding to which the holder is made a party. It should be noted, however, that the discharge is only to the extent of the payment.

The person making payment should, of course, take possession of the instrument or have it canceled—marked "paid" or "canceled"—so that it cannot pass to a subsequent holder in due course against whom his discharge would be ineffective.

TENDER OF PAYMENT

Any party liable on an instrument who makes proper tender of full payment to a person entitled to enforce the instrument when or after payment is due is discharged from liability for interest after the due date. Section 3–603(c). If her tender is refused, she is not discharged from liability for the face amount of the instrument or for any interest accrued until the time of tender. Moreover, if an instrument requires presentment and the obligor is ready and able to pay the instrument when it is due at the place of payment specified in the instrument, such readiness is the equivalent of tender. Section 3–603(c).

Occasionally a person entitled to enforce an instrument will refuse a tender of payment for reasons known only to himself. It may be that he believes his rights exceed the amount of the tender or that he desires to enforce payment against another party. In any event, his refusal of the tender wholly discharges to the extent of the amount of tender every party who has a right of recourse against the party making tender. Section 3–603(b).

CANCELLATION AND RENUNCIATION

Section 3–604 provides that a person entitled to enforce an instrument may discharge the liability of any party to an instrument by an intentional voluntary act, such as by canceling the instrument or the signature of the party or parties to be discharged, by mutilating or destroying the instrument, by obliterating a signature, or by adding words indicating a discharge. Section 3–604(a). A party entitled to enforce an instrument may also renounce his rights by a writing, signed and delivered, promising not to sue or otherwise renouncing rights against the party. Like other discharges, however, a written renunciation is of no effect against a subsequent holder in due course who takes without knowledge of the renunciation. Section 3–601(b).

Cancellation or renunciation is effective even without consideration.

LIABILITY BASED ON WARRANTY

Article 3 imposes two types of implied warranties: (1) transferor's warranties and (2) presenter's warranties. Sections 3–416 and 3–417. Although these warranties are effective whether or not the transferor or presenter signs the instrument, the extension of the transferor's warranty to subsequent holders does depend on whether one or the other has indorsed the instrument. Like other warranties, these may be disclaimed by agreement between immediate parties. In the case of an indorser, his disclaimer of transfer warranties and presentment warranties must appear in the indorsement itself and is effective, except with respect to checks. Sections 3–416(c), 3–417(e). Such disclaimers must be specific, such as "without warranty." The use of "without recourse" will disclaim only contract liability, not warranty liability.

WARRANTIES ON TRANSFER

Any person who transfers an instrument, whether by negotiation or assignment, and receives *consideration* makes certain **transferor's warranties**. Section 3–416. Any consideration sufficient to support a contract will support transfer warranties. If transfer is by delivery alone, warranties on transfer run only to the immediate transferee. If the transfer is made by indorsement, whether qualified or unqualified, the transfer warranty runs to "any subsequent transferee." *Transfer* means that the delivery of possession is voluntary. Sections 3–201(a), 1–201(14). The warranties of the transferor are as follows.

ENTITLEMENT TO ENFORCE

The first warranty that the Code imposes on a transferor is that the transferor is a person entitled to enforce the instrument. Section 3–416(a)(1). This warranty "is in effect a warranty that there are no unauthorized or missing indorsements that prevent the transferor from making the transferee a person entitled to enforce the instrument." Section 3–416, Comment 2. The following example illustrates this rule. Mitchell makes a note payable to the order of Penelope. A thief steals the note from Penelope, forges Penelope's indorsement, and sells the instrument to Aaron. Aaron is not entitled to enforce the instrument because the break in the indorsement chain prevents him from being a holder. If Aaron transfers the instrument to Judith for consideration, Judith can hold Aaron liable for breach of warranty. The warranty action is important to Judith because it enables her to hold Aaron liable, even if Aaron indorsed the note "without recourse."

AUTHENTIC AND AUTHORIZED SIGNATURES

The second warranty imposed by the Code is that all signatures are authentic and authorized. In the example presented above, this warranty would also be breached. Section 3–416(a)(2). If, however, the signature of a maker, drawer, drawee, acceptor, or indorser not in the chain of title is unauthorized, there is a breach of this warranty but no breach of the warranty of entitlement to enforce.

NO ALTERATION

The third warranty is the warranty against alteration. Section 3–416(a)(3). Suppose that Maureen makes a note payable to the order of the payee in the amount of $100. The payee, without authority, alters the note so that it appears to be drawn for $1,000 and negotiates the instrument to Lois, who buys it without knowledge of the alteration. Lois, indorsing "without recourse," negotiates the instrument to Kyle for consideration. Kyle presents the instrument to Maureen, who refuses to pay more than $100 on it. Kyle can collect the difference from Lois, for although her qualified indorsement saves Lois from liability to Kyle on the indorsement contract, she is liable to him for breach of warranty. If Lois had not qualified her indorsement, Kyle would be able to recover against her on the basis of either warranty or the indorsement contract.

NO DEFENSES

The fourth transferor's warranty imposed by the Code is that the instrument is not subject to a defense or claim in recoupment of any party. Section 3–416(a)(4). A claim in recoupment, as discussed in *Chapter 28*, is a counterclaim that arose from the transaction that gave rise to the instrument. Suppose that Madeline, a minor and a resident of a State where minors' contracts for non-necessaries are voidable, makes a note payable to bearer in payment of a motorcycle. Pierce, the first holder, negotiates it to Iola by mere delivery. Iola indorses it and negotiates it to Justin, who unqualifiedly indorses it to Hector. All negotiations are made for consideration. Because of Madeline's minority (a real defense), Hector cannot recover upon the instrument against Madeline. Hector therefore recovers against Justin or Iola on either the breach of warranty that no valid defenses exist to the instrument or the indorsement contract. Justin, if he is forced to pay Hector, can in turn recover against Iola on either a breach of warranty or the indorsement contract. Justin, however, cannot recover against Pierce. Pierce is not liable to Justin as an indorser because he did not indorse the instrument. Although Pierce, as a transferor, warrants that there are no defenses good against him, this warranty extends only to his immediate transferee, Iola. Therefore, Justin cannot hold Pierce liable. Iola, however, can recover from Pierce on a breach of warranty.

NO KNOWLEDGE OF INSOLVENCY

Any person who transfers a negotiable instrument warrants that he has no knowledge of any insolvency proceedings instituted with respect to the maker, acceptor, or drawer of an unaccepted instrument. Section 3–416(a)(5). Insolvency proceedings include bankruptcy and "any assignment for the benefit of creditors or other proceedings intended to liquidate or rehabilitate the estate of the person involved." Section 1–201(22). Thus, if Marcia makes a note payable to bearer, and the first holder, Taylor, negotiates it for consideration without indorsement to Ursula, who then negotiates it for consideration by qualified indorsement to Valerie, both Taylor and Ursula warrant that they do not know that Marcia is in bankruptcy. Valerie could not hold Taylor liable for breach of warranty, however, because Taylor's warranty runs only in favor of her immediate transferee, Ursula, because Taylor transferred the instrument without indorsement. If Valerie could hold Ursula liable on her warranty, Ursula could thereupon hold Taylor, her immediate transferor, liable.

◆ **SEE FIGURE 29-2: Liability on Transfer**

WARRANTIES ON PRESENTMENT

Any party who pays or accepts an instrument must do so in strict compliance with the orders that instrument contains. For example, the payment or acceptance must be made to a person entitled to receive payment or acceptance, the amount paid or accepted must be the correct amount, and the instrument must be genuine and unaltered. If the payment or acceptance is incorrect, the payor or acceptor potentially will incur a loss. In the case of a note, a maker who pays the wrong person will not be discharged from his obligation to pay the correct person. If the maker pays too much, the excess comes out of his pocket. If a drawee pays the wrong person, he generally cannot charge the drawer's account; if he pays too much, he generally cannot charge the drawer's account for the excess. Indorsers who pay an instrument may make similar incorrect payments.

After paying or accepting an instrument to the wrong person, for the wrong amount, or in some other incorrect way, does the person who incorrectly paid or accepted have any recourse against the person who received the payment or acceptance? Section 3–418 addresses this critical question by providing that

> if an instrument has been paid or accepted by mistake … the person paying or accepting may, to the extent permitted by the law governing mistake and restitution, (i) recover the payment from the person to whom or for whose benefit payment was made or (ii) in the case of acceptance, may revoke the acceptance. Section 3–418(b).

Nevertheless, this payment or acceptance is *final* and may not be asserted against a person who took the instrument in good faith and for value or who in good faith changed position in reliance on the payment or acceptance, unless there has been a breach of the implied **warranties on presentment**. Section 3–418(c). What warranties are given by presenters depends upon who is the payor or acceptor. The greatest protection is given to drawees of unaccepted drafts, while all other payors receive significantly less protection.

DRAWEES OF UNACCEPTED DRAFTS

A drawee of an unaccepted draft (including uncertified checks), who pays or accepts in good faith, receives a

◆ **FIGURE 29-2: Liability on Transfer**

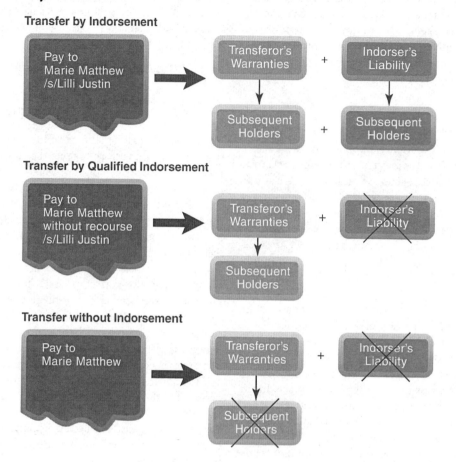

presentment warranty from the person obtaining payment or acceptance and from all prior transferors of the draft. These parties warrant to the drawee making payment or accepting the draft in good faith that (1) the warrantor is a person entitled to enforce the draft, (2) the draft has not been altered, and (3) the warrantor has no knowledge that the drawer's signature is unauthorized. Section 3–417(a).

ENTITLED TO ENFORCE Presenters of unaccepted checks give the same warranty of entitlement to enforce to persons who pay or accept as is granted to transferees under the transferor's warranty. Thus, the presenter warrants that she is a person entitled to enforce the instrument. As explained above, this warranty extends to the genuineness and completeness of the indorser's signatures but not to the signature of the drawer or maker. It is "in effect a warranty that there are no unauthorized or missing indorsements." Section 3–417, Comment 2.

For example, if Donnese draws a check to Peter or order, and Peter's indorsement is forged, the bank does not follow Donnese's order in paying such an item and therefore cannot charge her account (except in the impostor or fictitious payee situations discussed in *Chapter 27*). The bank, however, can recover for breach of the presenter's warranty of entitlement to enforce the instrument from the person who obtained payment of the check from the bank. Although it should know the signatures of its own customers, the bank should not be expected to know the signatures of payees or other indorsers of checks; the bank, therefore, should not have to bear this loss.

NO ALTERATION Presenters also give a warranty of no alteration. For example, if Dolores makes a check payable to Porter's order in the amount of $30, and the amount is fraudulently raised to $30,000, the drawee bank cannot charge to the drawer's account the $30,000 it pays out on the check. The drawee bank can charge the drawer's account only $30, because that is all the drawer ordered the drawee bank to pay. Nonetheless, because the presenter's warranty of no alteration has been breached, the drawee bank can collect the difference from all warrantors. Section 3–417(a)(2), (b).

GENUINENESS OF DRAWER'S SIGNATURE Presenters lastly warrant that they have no knowledge that the signature of the

◆ **FIGURE 29-3: Liability Based on Warranty**

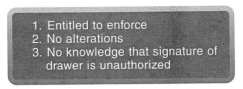

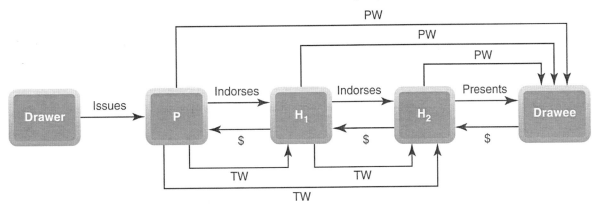

drawer is unauthorized. Thus, unless the presenter has knowledge that the drawer's signature is unauthorized, the drawee bears the risk that the drawer's signature is unauthorized.

◆ **SEE FIGURE 29-3: Liability Based on Warranty**

ALL OTHER PAYORS

In all instances other than a drawee of an unaccepted draft or uncertified check, the only presentment warranty that is given is that the warrantor is a person entitled to enforce the instrument or is authorized to obtain payment on behalf of the person entitled to enforce the instrument. Section 3–417(d). This warranty is given by the person obtaining pay-ment and prior transferors and applies to the presentment of notes and accepted drafts for the benefit of any party obliged to pay the instrument, including an indorser. It also applies to presentment of dishonored drafts if made to the drawer or an indorser.

The warranties of no alteration and authenticity of the drawer's signature are not given to all other payors. These warranties are not necessary for makers and drawers because they should know their own signature and the terms of their instruments. Similarly, indorsers have already warranted the authenticity of signatures and that the instrument was not altered. Finally, acceptors should know the terms of the instrument when they accepted it; moreover, they did receive the full presentment warranties when they as a drawee accepted the draft upon presentment.

CHAPTER SUMMARY

CONTRACTUAL LIABILITY

GENERAL PRINCIPLES

Liability on the Instrument no person has contractual liability on an instrument unless her signature appears on it

Signature a signature may be made by the individual herself or by her authorized agent

- *Authorized Signatures* an agent who executes a negotiable instrument on behalf of his principal is not liable if the instrument is executed properly and as authorized
- *Unauthorized Signatures* include forgeries and signatures made by an agent without proper power; are generally not binding on the person whose name appears on the instrument but are binding on the unauthorized signer

LIABILITY OF PRIMARY PARTIES

Primary Liability absolute obligation to pay a negotiable instrument

Makers the maker guarantees that he will pay the note according to its original terms

Acceptors a drawee has no liability on the instrument until she accepts it; she then becomes primarily liable

- *Acceptance* a drawee's signed engagement to honor the instrument
- *Certification* acceptance of a check by a bank

LIABILITY OF SECONDARY PARTIES

Secondary (Conditional) Liability obligation to pay a negotiable instrument that is subject to conditions precedent

Indorsers and Drawers if the instrument is not paid by a primary party and if the conditions precedent to the liability of secondary parties are satisfied, indorsers and drawers are secondarily (conditionally) liable unless they have disclaimed their liability or have a valid defense to the instrument

Effect of Acceptance when a draft is accepted by a bank, the drawer and all prior indorsers are discharged from contractual liability

Disclaimer by Secondary Parties a drawer (except of a check) or indorser may disclaim liability by a qualified drawing or indorsing ("without recourse")

Conditions Precedent to Liability

- *Drawer* liability is generally only contingent upon dishonor and does not require notice
- *Indorser* liability is contingent upon dishonor and notice of dishonor

LIABILITY FOR CONVERSION

Tort Liability conversion occurs (1) when a drawee refuses to return a draft that was presented for acceptance, (2) when any person refuses to return an instrument after he dishonors it, or (3) when an instrument is paid on a forged indorsement

TERMINATION OF LIABILITY

Effect of Discharge potential liability of parties to the instrument is terminated

Discharge

- *Performance*
- *Tender of Payment* for interest, costs, and attorneys' fees
- *Cancellation*
- *Renunciation*

LIABILITY BASED ON WARRANTY

WARRANTIES ON TRANSFER

Parties

- *Warrantor* any person who transfers an instrument and receives consideration gives the transferor's warranties

- *Beneficiary* if the transfer is by delivery, the warranties run only to the immediate transferee; if the transfer is by indorsement, the warranties run to any subsequent holder who takes the instrument in good faith

Warranties
- *Entitled to Enforce*
- *All Signatures Are Authentic and Authorized*
- *No Alteration*
- *No Defenses*
- *No Knowledge of Insolvency*

WARRANTIES ON PRESENTMENT	**Parties**

- *Warrantor* all people who obtain payment or acceptance of an instrument as well as all prior transferors give the presenter's warranties
- *Beneficiary* the presenter's warranties run to any person who in good faith pays or accepts an instrument

Warranties
- *Entitled to Enforce*
- *No Alteration*
- *Genuineness of Drawer's Signature*

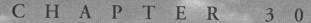

Bank Deposits, Collections, and Funds Transfers

I n today's 21st-century society, most goods and services are bought and sold without a physical transfer of "money." Credit cards, charge accounts, and various deferred payment plans have made cash sales increasingly infrequent. But even credit sales must ultimately be settled—when they are, payment is usually made by check rather than with cash. If the parties to a sales transaction happen to have accounts at the same bank, a transfer of credit is easily accomplished. In the vast majority of cases, however, the parties have accounts at different banks. Then the buyer's check must journey from the seller-payee's bank (the depositary bank), where the check is deposited by the seller for credit to his account, to the buyer-drawer's bank (the payor bank) for payment. In this collection process, the check frequently passes through one or more other banks (intermediary banks), each of which must accurately record its passing, before it may be collected. Our banking system has developed a network to handle the collection of checks and other instruments.

In recent years, payments by electronic funds transfers have increased at an astounding rate. The dollar amount of commercial payments made by wire transfer far exceeds the dollar amount made by checks or credit cards. In addition, electronic funds transfers have become exceedingly popular with consumers. Consumer electronic funds transfers are covered by the Federal Electronic Fund Transfer Act (EFTA); nonconsumer (wholesale) electronic transfers are covered by Article 4A of the Uniform Commercial Code (UCC).

This chapter will cover both the bank deposit–collection system and electronic funds transfers.

BANK DEPOSITS AND COLLECTIONS

Article 4 of the UCC, entitled "Bank Deposits and Collections," provides the principal rules governing the bank collection process. The end result of the collection process is either the payment of the check or the dishonor (refusal to pay) of the check by the drawee bank. As items in the bank collection process are essentially those covered by Article 3, "Commercial Paper," and to a lesser extent by Article 8, "Investment Securities," these Articles often apply to a bank collection problem. In addition, Articles 3 and 4 are supplemented and, at times, preempted by Federal law: the Expedited Funds Availability Act and its implementing Federal Reserve Regulation (Regulation CC). This section will cover the collection of an item through the banking system and the relationship between the payor bank and its customer.

COLLECTION OF ITEMS

When a person deposits a check in his bank (the depositary bank), the bank credits his account by the amount of the check. This initial crediting is **provisional**. Normally, a bank does not permit a customer to draw funds against a provisional credit; by permitting its customer to thus draw, the bank will have given *value* and, provided it meets the other requirements, will be a holder in due course. Under the customer's contract with his bank, the bank is obligated to make a reasonable effort to obtain payment of all checks deposited for collection. When the amount of the check has been collected from the payor bank (the drawee), the credit becomes a **final credit**.

The Competitive Equality Banking Act has expedited the availability of funds by establishing maximum time periods for which a bank may hold (and thereby deny a customer access to the funds represented by) various types of instruments. Under the Act, (1) cash deposits, wire transfers, government checks, the first $100 of a day's check deposits, cashier's checks, and checks deposited in one branch of a depositary institution and drawn on the same or another branch of the same institution must clear by the next business day; (2) local checks must clear within one intervening business day; and (3) nonlocal checks must clear in no more than four intervening business days.

◆ **FIGURE 30-1: Bank Collections**

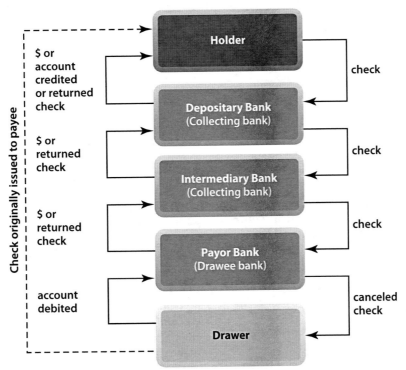

If the payor bank (the drawee bank) does not pay the check for some reason, such as a stop payment order or insufficient funds in the drawer's account, the depositary bank reverses the provisional credit to the account, debits his account for that amount, and returns the check to him with a statement of the reason for nonpayment. If, in the meantime, the customer has been permitted to draw against the provisional credit, the bank may recover the payment from him.

In some cases, the bank involved is both the depositary bank and the payor bank. In most cases, however, the depositary and payor banks are different, in which event the bank collection aspects of Article 4 come into play. Where the depositary and payor banks differ, it is necessary for the item to pass from one to the other, either directly through a clearinghouse or through one or more **intermediary banks** (banks, other than the depositary payor bank, that are involved in the collection process, such as one of the twelve Federal Reserve Banks). A **clearinghouse** is an association, composed of banks or other payors, whose members settle accounts with each other on a daily basis. Each member of the clearinghouse forwards all deposited checks drawn on other members and receives from the clearinghouse all checks drawn on it. Balances are adjusted and settled each day.

◆ **SEE FIGURE 30-1: Bank Collections**

COLLECTING BANKS

A **collecting bank** is any bank, other than the payor bank, handling an item for payment. In the usual situation, where

the depositary and payor banks are different, the depositary bank gives a provisional credit to its customer, transfers the item to the next bank in the chain, and receives a provisional credit or "settlement" from it; the process repeats until the item reaches the payor bank, which gives a provisional settlement to its transferor. When the item is paid, all the provisional settlements given by the respective banks in the chain become final, and the particular transaction has been completed. Because this procedure simplifies bookkeeping by necessitating only one entry if the item is paid, no adjustment is necessary on the books of any of the banks involved.

If, however, the payor bank does not pay the check, it returns the item, and each intermediary or collecting bank reverses the provisional settlement or credit it previously gave to its forwarding bank. Ultimately, the depositary bank will charge (remove the provisional credit from) the account of the customer who deposited the item. The customer must then seek recovery from the indorsers or the drawer.

A collecting bank is an **agent** or subagent of the owner of the item until the settlement becomes final. Section 4–201(a). Unless otherwise provided, any credit given for the item initially is provisional. Once settled, the agency relationship changes to one of **debtor-creditor**. The effects of this agency rule are that the risk of loss remains with the owner and any chargebacks go to her, not to the collecting bank.

All collecting banks have certain responsibilities and duties in collecting checks and other items. These will now be discussed.

DUTY OF CARE A collecting bank must exercise ordinary care in handling an item transferred to it for collection. Section 4–202(a). The steps it takes in presenting an item or sending it for presentment are of particular importance. It must act within a reasonable time after receipt of the item and must choose a reasonable method of forwarding the item for presentment. It also is responsible for using care in routing and in selecting intermediary banks or other agents.

DUTY TO ACT TIMELY Closely related to the collecting bank's duty of care is its duty to act in a timely manner. A collecting bank acts timely in any event if it takes proper action, such as forwarding or presenting an item before the "midnight deadline" following its receipt of the item, notice, or payment. If the bank adheres to this standard, the timeliness of its action cannot be challenged; should it, however, take a reasonably longer time, the bank bears the burden of proof in establishing timeliness. Section 4–202(b). The **midnight deadline** is the midnight of the banking day following the banking day on which the bank received the item or notice. Section 4–104(a)(10). Thus, if a bank receives a check on Monday, it must take proper action by midnight on the next banking day, or Tuesday. A banking day means the part of a day on which a bank is open to the public for carrying on substantially all of its banking functions. Section 4–104(a)(3). The midnight deadline presents a problem because it takes time to process an item through a bank—whether it be the depositary, intermediary, or payor bank. If a day's transactions are to be completed without overtime work, the bank must either close early or fix an earlier cutoff time for the day's work. Accordingly, the Code provides that for the purpose of allowing time to process items, prove balances, and make the bookkeeping entries necessary to determine its position for the day, a bank may fix an afternoon hour of 2:00 P.M. or later as a cutoff point for handling money and items and for making entries on its books. Section 4–108. Items received after the cutoff hour fixed as the close of the banking day are considered to have been received at the opening of the next banking day, and the time for taking action and for determining the bank's midnight deadline begins to run from that point.

Recognizing that everyone involved will be greatly inconvenienced if an item is not paid, Section 4–109 provides that unless otherwise instructed, a collecting bank in a good faith effort to secure payment may, in the case of a specific item drawn on a payor other than a bank, waive, modify, or extend the time limits, but not in excess of two additional banking days. This extension may be made without the approval of the parties involved and without discharging drawers or indorsers. This section does not apply to checks and other drafts drawn on a bank. The Code also authorizes delay when communications or computer facilities are interrupted as a result of blizzard, flood, hurricane, or other disaster; the suspension of payments by another bank; war; emergency conditions; failure of equipment; or other circumstances beyond the bank's control. Nevertheless, such delay will be excused only if the bank exercises such diligence as the circumstances require.

INDORSEMENTS An item restrictively indorsed with words such as "pay any bank" is locked into the bank collection system, and only a bank may acquire the rights of a holder. When forwarding an item for collection, a bank normally indorses the item "pay any bank," regardless of the type of indorsement, if any, that the item carried at the time of receipt. This protects the collecting bank by making it impossible for the item to stray from regular collection channels.

If the item had no indorsement when the depositary bank received it, the bank nonetheless becomes a holder of the item at the time it takes possession of the item for collection if the customer was a holder at the time of delivery to the bank and, if the bank satisfies the other requirements of a holder in due course, it will become a holder in due course in its own right. Section 4–205(1). In return, the bank warrants to the collecting banks, the payor, and the drawer that it has paid the amount of the item to the customer or deposited that amount to the customer's account. Section 4–205(2). This rule speeds up the collection process by eliminating the necessity of returning checks for indorsement when the depositary bank knows they came from its customers.

WARRANTIES Customers and collecting banks give substantially the same warranties as those given by parties under Article 3 upon presentment and transfer, which were discussed in *Chapter 29*. In addition, under Article 4 customers and collecting banks may give encoding warranties. Each customer or collecting bank who transfers an item and receives a settlement or other consideration warrants to his transferee and any subsequent collecting bank that (1) he is a person entitled to enforce the item; (2) *all* signatures are authentic and authorized; (3) the item has not been altered; (4) he is not subject to any defense or claim in recoupment; and (5) he has no knowledge of any insolvency proceeding involving the maker or acceptor or the drawer of an unaccepted draft. Section 4–207(a). Moreover, each customer or collecting bank who obtains payment or acceptance from a drawee on a draft as well as each prior transferor warrants to the drawee who pays or accepts the draft in good faith that (1) she is a person entitled to enforce the draft; (2) the item has not been altered; and (3) she has no knowledge that the signature of the drawer is unauthorized. Section 4–208.

Processing of checks is now done by Magnetic Ink Character Recognition (MICR). When a check is deposited, the depositary bank magnetically encodes the check with the amount of the check (all checks are pre-encoded with the drawer's account number and the designation of the drawee bank), after which the processing occurs automatically, without further human involvement. Despite its efficiency, the magnetic encoding of checks has created several problems. The first is the problem a bank encounters when paying a postdated instrument prior to its date. The Revision changes prior law by providing that the drawee may debit the drawer's account, unless the drawer timely informs the drawee that the check is postdated. Section 4–401(c). A second difficulty arises when a depositing bank or its customer who encodes her own checks miscodes a check. Revised Article 4 provides that such an encoder **warrants** to any subsequent collecting bank and to the payor that information on a check is properly encoded. Section 4–209(a). If the customer does the encoding, the depository bank also makes the warranty. Section 4–209(a).

FINAL PAYMENT The provisional settlements made in the collection chain are all directed toward final payment of the item by the payor bank. From this turnaround point in the collection process, the proceeds of the item begin their return flow, and provisional settlements become final. For example, a customer of the California Country State Bank may deposit a check drawn on the State of Maine Country National Bank. The check may then take a course such as follows: from the California Country State Bank to a correspondent bank in San Francisco, to the Federal Reserve Bank of San Francisco, to the Federal Reserve Bank of Boston, to the payor bank. Provisional settlements are made at each step. When the payor bank finally pays the item, the proceeds begin to flow back over the same course.

The critical question, then, is the point at which the payor bank has **paid** the item, as this not only commences the payment process but also affects questions of priority between the payment of an item and actions such as the filing of a stop payment order against it. Under the Code, *final payment* occurs when the payor bank first does any of the following: (1) pays an item in cash; (2) settles an item and does not have the right to revoke the settlement through statute, clearinghouse rule, or agreement; or (3) makes a provisional settlement and does not revoke it within the time and in the manner permitted by statute, clearinghouse rule, or agreement. Section 4–215(a).

PAYOR BANKS

The **payor** or drawee **bank**, under its contract of deposit with the drawer, agrees to pay to the payee or his order a check issued by the drawer, provided that the order is not countermanded and that there are sufficient funds in the drawer's account.

The tremendous increase in volume of bank collections has necessitated deferred posting procedures, whereby items are sorted and proved on the day of receipt but are not posted to customers' accounts or returned until the next banking day. The UCC not only approves such procedures but also establishes specific standards to govern their application to the actions of payor banks.

When a payor bank that is not also a depository bank receives a demand item other than for immediate payment over the counter, it must either return the item or give its transferor a provisional settlement before **midnight** of the banking day on which the item is received. Otherwise, the bank becomes liable to its transferor for the amount of the item, unless it has a valid defense, such as breach of a presentment warranty. Section 4–302.

If the payor bank gives the provisional settlement as required, it has until the midnight deadline to return the item or, if the item is held for protest or is otherwise unavailable for return, to send written notice of dishonor or nonpayment. Section 4–301(a). After doing this, the bank is entitled to revoke the settlement and recover any payment it has made. Should it fail to return the item or send notice before its midnight deadline, the payor bank will be accountable for the amount of the item unless it has a valid defense for its inaction. If a check is for $2,500 or more, Federal law (Regulation CC) requires special notice of nonpayment—the paying bank must give notice to the depository bank by 4:00 P.M. on the second business day following the banking day on which the check was presented to the paying bank. This regulation does not, however, relieve the paying bank of returning the check in compliance with Article 4.

A bank may dishonor an item and return it or send notice for innumerable reasons. The following situations are the most common: the drawer or maker may have no account or may have funds insufficient to cover the item, a signature on the item may be forged, or the drawer or maker may have stopped payment of the item.

If the funds in a customer's account are insufficient to pay all of the items that the bank receives on that account on any given day, the bank may charge them against the account in any order it deems convenient. The owner of the account from which the item was payable also has no basis for complaint when the bank pays one item rather than another. It is his responsibility to have enough funds on deposit to pay all of the items chargeable to his account at any time.

RELATIONSHIP BETWEEN PAYOR BANK AND ITS CUSTOMER

The relationship between a payor bank and its checking account customer is primarily the product of their contractual arrangement. Although the parties have relatively broad latitude in establishing the terms of their agreement and in altering the provisions of the Code, a bank may not validly (1) disclaim responsibility for its lack of good faith, (2) disclaim responsibility for its failure to exercise ordinary care, or (3) limit its damages for a breach comprising such lack or failure. Section 4–103(a). The parties by agreement, however, may determine the standards by which the bank's responsibility is to be measured, if these standards are not clearly unreasonable.

PAYMENT OF AN ITEM

A payor bank owes a duty to its customer, the drawer, to pay checks properly drawn by him on an account having funds sufficient to cover the items. A check or draft, however, is not an assignment of the drawer's funds that are in the drawee's possession. Moreover, as discussed in *Chapter 29*, the drawee is not liable on a check until it accepts the item. Section 3–408. Therefore, the *holder* of a check has no right to require the drawee bank to pay it, whether the drawer's account contains sufficient funds or not. But if a payor bank improperly refuses payment when presented with an item, it will incur a liability to the *customer* from whose account the item should have been paid. Section 4–402. If the customer has adequate funds on deposit, and there is no other valid basis for the refusal to pay, the bank is liable to its customer for damages proximately caused by the *wrongful dishonor*. Liability is limited to actual damages proved and may include damages for arrest, prosecution, or other consequential damages. Section 4–402.

When a payor bank receives an item properly payable from a customer's account but the funds in the account are insufficient to pay it, the bank may (1) dishonor the item and return it or (2) pay the item and charge its customer's account, even though the actions create an overdraft. Section 4–401(a). The item authorizes or directs the bank to make the payment and hence carries with it an enforceable implied promise to reimburse the bank. Furthermore, the customer may be liable to pay the bank a service charge for its handling of the overdraft or to pay interest on the amount of the overdraft. A customer, however, is not liable for an overdraft if the customer did not sign the item or benefit from the proceeds of the item. Section 4–401(b).

A payor bank is under no obligation to its customer to pay an uncertified check that is more than six months old. Section 4–404. This rule reflects the usual banking practice of consulting a depositor before paying a "*stale*" item (one more than six months old) on her account. The bank is not required to dishonor such an item, however; and if the bank makes payment in good faith, it may charge the amount of the item to its customers' account.

SUBSTITUTE CHECK

The Check Clearing for the 21st Century Act (also called Check 21 or the Check Truncation Act) permits banks to truncate original checks, which means removing an original paper check from the check collection or return process and sending in lieu of it (1) a substitute check or, (2) *by*

agreement, information relating to the original check (including data taken from the MICR line of the original check or an electronic image of the original check). The Act sets forth a statutory framework under which a substitute check is the legal equivalent of an original check for all purposes, if the substitute check (1) accurately represents all of the information on the front and back of the original check as of the time the original check was truncated; and (2) bears the legend, "This is a legal copy of your check. You can use it the same way you would use the original check." The Act defines a **substitute check** as a paper reproduction of the original check that (1) contains an image of the front and back of the original; (2) bears an MICR containing all the information appearing on the MICR line of the original check; (3) conforms, in paper stock, dimension, and otherwise, with generally applicable industry standards for substitute checks; and (4) is suitable for automated processing in the same manner as the original. Thus, a substitute check is basically a copy of the original check that shows both the front and back of the original check.

The law does not require banks to accept checks in electronic form nor does it require banks to use the new authority granted by the Act to create substitute checks. On the other hand, parties cannot refuse to accept a substitute check that meets the Act's requirements.

The Act permits banks to replace paper checks during the check collection process with either digital or paper substitutes. Thus, banks can employ digital images or image replacement documents (IRDs), which are documents that include the front, rear, and all MICR data in one image. However, the Act does not provide legal equivalence for electronic check or image presentment.

The ultimate objective of the Act is to make the collection process more efficient and much faster (transferring digital files within seconds rather than days) and to enhance fraud detection by accelerating return of dishonored checks.

STOP PAYMENT ORDERS

A check drawn on a bank is an order to pay a sum of money and an authorization to charge the amount to the drawer's account. The customer, or any person authorized to draw on the account, may countermand this order, however, by means of a **stop payment order**. Section 4–403. If the order does not come too late, the bank is bound by it. If the bank inadvertently pays a check over a valid stop order, it is *prima facie* liable to the customer, but only to the extent of the customer's loss resulting from the payment. The burden of establishing the fact and amount of loss is on the customer.

To be effective, a stop payment order must be received in time to provide the bank a reasonable opportunity to act on it. Section 4–403(a). An oral stop order is binding on the bank for only fourteen calendar days. Section 4–403(b). If the customer confirms an oral stop order in writing within the fourteen-day period, the order is effective for six months and may be renewed in writing for additional six-month periods.

The fact that a drawer has filed a stop payment order does not automatically relieve her of liability. If the bank honors the stop payment order and returns the check, the holder may bring an action against the drawer. If the holder qualifies as a holder in due course, personal defenses that the drawer might have to such an action would be of no avail.

BANK'S RIGHT TO SUBROGATION ON IMPROPER PAYMENT

If a payor bank pays an item over a stop payment order, after an account has been closed, or otherwise in violation of its contract with the drawer or maker, the payor bank is subrogated to (obtains) the rights of (1) any holder in due course on the item against the drawer or maker, (2) the payee or any other holder against the drawer or maker, and (3) the drawer or maker against the payee or any other holder. Section 4–407. For instance, over the drawer's stop payment order a bank pays a check presented to the bank by a holder in due course. The drawer's defense is that the check was obtained by fraud in the inducement. The drawee bank is subrogated to the rights of the holder in due course, who would not be subject to the drawer's personal defense, and thus can debit the drawer's account. Section 4–407(1). The same would be true if the presenter were the payee, against whom the drawer did not have a valid defense. Section 4–407(2).

DISCLOSURE REQUIREMENTS

Congress enacted the Truth in Savings Act, which requires all depositary institutions (including commercial banks, savings and loan associations, savings banks, and credit unions) to disclose in great detail to consumers the terms and conditions of their deposit accounts. The stated purpose of the Act is to allow consumers to make informed decisions regarding deposit accounts by mandating standardized disclosure of rates of interest and fees to facilitate meaningful comparison of different deposit products.

More specifically, the Act provides that the disclosures must be made in a clear and conspicuous writing and must be given to the consumer when an account is opened or service is provided. These disclosures must include the following: (1) the annual percentage yield (APY) and the percentage rate; (2) how variable rates are calculated and when the rates may be changed; (3) balance information (including how the balance is calculated); (4) when and how interest is calculated and credited; (5) the amount of fees that may be charged and how they are calculated; and (6) any limitation on the number or amount of withdrawals or deposits. In addition, the Act requires the depository institution to disclose the following information with periodic statements it sends to its customers: (1) the APY earned; (2) any fees debited during the covered period; (3) the dollar amount of the interest earned during the covered period; and (4) the dates of the covered period.

CUSTOMER'S DEATH OR INCOMPETENCE

The general rule is that death or incompetence revokes all agency agreements. Furthermore, adjudication of incompetency by a court is regarded as notice to the world of that fact. Actual notice is not required. Section 4–405 of the Code modifies these stringent rules in several ways with respect to bank deposits and collections.

First, if either a payor or collecting bank does not know that a customer has been adjudicated incompetent, the existence of such incompetence at the time an item is issued or its collection is undertaken does not impair either bank's authority to accept, pay, or collect the item or to account for proceeds of its collection. The bank may pay the item without incurring any liability.

Second, neither death nor adjudication of incompetence of a customer revokes a payor or collecting bank's authority to accept, pay, or collect an item until the bank knows of the condition and has a reasonable opportunity to act on this knowledge.

Finally, even though a bank knows of the death of its customer, it may for ten days after the date of his death pay or certify checks drawn by the customer unless a person claiming an interest in the account, such as an heir, executor, or administrator, orders the bank to stop making such payments. Section 4–405(b).

CUSTOMER'S DUTIES

The Code imposes certain affirmative duties on bank customers and fixes time limits within which they must assert their rights. The duties arise and the time starts to run from the point at which the bank either sends or makes available to its customer a statement of account showing payment of items against the account. The statement of account will suffice provided it describes by item the number of the item, the amount, and the date of payment. The customer must exercise reasonable promptness in examining the bank statement or the items to discover whether any payment was unauthorized due to an *unauthorized signature* on or any *alteration* of an item. Section 4–406(c). Because he is not presumed to know the signatures of payees or indorsers, this duty of prompt and careful examination applies only to alterations and the customer's own signature, both of which he should be able to detect immediately. If he discovers an unauthorized signature or an alteration, he must notify the bank promptly. Section 4–406(c). A failure to fulfill these duties of prompt examination and notice precludes the customer from asserting against the bank his unauthorized signature or any alteration if the bank establishes that it suffered a loss by reason of such failure. Section 4–406(d).

Furthermore, the customer will lose his rights in a potentially more serious situation. Occasionally a forger, possibly an employee who has access to his employer's checkbook, carries out a series of transactions involving the account of the same individual. He may forge one or more checks each month until he is finally detected. The bank, noticing nothing suspicious, might pay one or more of the customer's checks bearing the false signatures before the customer detects the forgery, months or even years later. Section 4–406(d) of the Code deals with these situations by stating that once the statement and items become available to him, the customer must examine them within a reasonable period—which in no event may exceed thirty calendar days and which may, under certain circumstances, be less—and notify the bank. Any instruments containing alterations or unauthorized signatures by the same wrongdoer that the bank pays during that period will be the bank's responsibility, but any paid thereafter but before the customer notifies the bank may not be asserted against it. This rule is based on the concept that the loss involved is directly traceable to the customer's negligence and that, as a result, he should stand the loss.

These rules depend, however, on the bank's exercising ordinary care in paying the items involved. If it does not, and that failure by the bank substantially contributed to the loss, the loss will be allocated between the bank and the customer based on their comparative negligence. Section 4–406(e). But whether the bank exercised due care or not, the customer must in all events report any alteration or his unauthorized signature within one year from the time the statement or items are made available to him or be barred from asserting them against the bank. Section 4–406(f). Any *unauthorized indorsement* must be asserted within three years under the Article's general Statute of Limitations provisions. Section 4–111.

Consistent with modern automated methods for processing checks, Articles 3 and 4 provide that "ordinary care" does not require a bank to examine every check if the failure to do so does not vary unreasonably from general banking usage. Section 3–103(7).

ELECTRONIC FUNDS TRANSFERS

As previously mentioned, the use of negotiable instruments for payment has greatly reduced the use of *cash* in the United States. The advent and technological advances of interconnected computers have resulted in electronic fund transfer systems (EFTS) that have greatly reduced the use of *checks*. Financial institutions seek to substitute EFTS for checks for two principal reasons. The first is to eliminate the ever-increasing paperwork involved in processing the billions of checks issued annually. The second is to eliminate the "float" that a drawer of a check currently enjoys by maintaining the use of his funds during the processing period between the time at which he issues the check and final payment.

An electronic fund transfer (EFT) has been defined as "any transfer of funds, other than a transaction originated by check, draft, or similar paper instrument, which is initiated through an electronic terminal, telephonic instrument, or computer or magnetic tape so as to order, instruct or authorize a financial institution to debit or credit an account." For example, with an EFT, William in New York would be able to pay a debt he owes to Yvette in Illinois by entering into his computer an order to his bank to pay Yvette. The drawee bank would then instantly debit William's account and transfer the credit to Yvette's bank, where Yvette's account would immediately be credited in that amount. The entire transaction would be completed in minutes.

The use of EFTs generated considerable confusion concerning the legal rights of customers and financial institutions. Congress provided a partial solution to the legal issues affecting consumer EFTs by enacting the EFTA, discussed below. Transactions not covered by the EFTA—primarily wholesale electronic transfers—are covered by Article 4A—Funds Transfers of the UCC.

TYPES OF ELECTRONIC FUNDS TRANSFERS

Although new EFTs may appear in the coming years, six main types of EFTs are currently in use: (1) automated teller machines, (2) point-of-sale systems, (3) direct deposit and withdrawal of funds, (4) pay-by-phone systems, (5) personal computer (online) banking, and (6) wholesale EFTs.

AUTOMATED TELLER MACHINES

Automated teller machines (ATMs) permit customers to conduct various transactions with their banks through the use of electronic terminals. After activating an ATM with a plastic identification card and a personal identification number, or PIN, a customer can deposit and withdraw funds from her account, transfer funds between accounts, obtain cash advances, and make payments on loan accounts.

POINT-OF-SALE SYSTEMS

Computerized point-of-sale (POS) systems permit consumers to transfer funds from their bank accounts to a merchant automatically. The POS machines, located within the merchant's store and activated by the consumer's identification card and code, instantaneously debit the consumer's account and credit the merchant's account.

DIRECT DEPOSITS AND WITHDRAWALS

Another type of EFT involves deposits, authorized in advance by a customer, that are made directly to his account. Examples include direct payroll deposits, deposits of Social Security payments, and deposits of pension payments. Conversely, automatic withdrawals are preauthorized EFTs from the customer's account for regular payments to some party other than the financial institution at which the funds are deposited. Automatic withdrawals to pay insurance premiums, utility bills, or automobile loan payments are common examples of this type of EFT.

PAY-BY-PHONE SYSTEMS

Financial institutions provide a service that permits customers to pay bills by telephoning the bank's computer system and directing a transfer of funds to a designated third party. This service also permits customers to transfer funds between accounts.

PERSONAL COMPUTER (ONLINE) BANKING

Personal computer (online) banking enables the customer to execute many banking transactions via an Internet-connected computer. For instance, customers may view account balances, request transfers between accounts, and pay bills electronically.

WHOLESALE ELECTRONIC FUNDS TRANSFERS

Wholesale EFTs, commonly called wholesale wire transfers, involve the movement of funds between financial institutions, between financial institutions and businesses, and between businesses. More than $1 *trillion* is transferred this way each business day over the two major transfer systems—the Federal Reserve wire transfer network system (Fedwire) and the New York Clearing House Interbank Payment System (CHIPS). In addition, a number of private wholesale wire systems exist among the large banks. Limited aspects of wholesale wire transfers are governed by uniform rules promulgated by the Federal Reserve, CHIPS, and the National Automated Clearing House Association.

CONSUMER FUNDS TRANSFERS

Congress determined that the use of electronic systems to transfer funds provided the potential for substantial benefits to consumers. Existing consumer protection legislation failed to account for the unique characteristics of such systems, however, leaving the rights and obligations of consumers and financial institutions undefined. Accordingly, Congress

enacted Title IX of the Consumer Protection Act, the EFTA, to "provide a basic framework establishing the rights, liabilities, and responsibilities of participants in electronic fund transfers" with primary emphasis on "the provision of individual consumer rights." Because the EFTA deals exclusively with the protection of **consumers**, it does not govern electronic transfers between financial institutions, between financial institutions and businesses, and between businesses. The Act is similar in many respects to the Fair Credit Billing Act (see *Chapter 42*), which applies to credit card transactions. The EFTA is administered by the Board of Governors of the Federal Reserve System, which is mandated to prescribe regulations to carry out the purposes of the Act. Pursuant to this congressional mandate, the Federal Reserve has issued Regulation E.

The Dodd-Frank Wall Street Reform and Consumer Protection Act of 2010 (CFPA), discussed in *Chapter 42*, requires that the amount of any interchange transaction fee that an issuer may receive or charge with respect to an electronic debit transaction must be reasonable and proportional to the cost incurred by the issuer, as determined by the Federal Reserve. Debit cards issued by small banks and prepaid reloadable cards are exempt from this rule.

DISCLOSURE

The EFTA is primarily a disclosure statute and as such requires that the terms and conditions of electronic funds transfers involving a consumer's account be disclosed in readily understandable language at the time the consumer contracts for such services. Included among the required disclosure are the consumer's liability for unauthorized transfers, the kinds of EFTs allowed, the charges for transfers or for the right to make transfers, the consumer's right to stop payment of preauthorized EFTs, the consumer's right to receive documentation of EFTs, rules concerning disclosure of information to third parties, procedures for correcting account errors, and the financial institution's liability to the consumer under the Act.

DOCUMENTATION AND PERIODIC STATEMENTS

The Act requires the financial institution to provide the consumer with written documentation of each transfer made from an electronic terminal at the time of transfer—a receipt. The receipt must clearly state the amount involved, the date, the type of transfer, the identity of the account(s) involved, the identity of any third party involved, and the location of the terminal involved.

In addition, the financial institution must provide each consumer with a periodic statement for each account of the consumer that may be accessed by means of an EFT. The statement must describe the amount, date, and location for each transfer; the fee, if any, to be charged for the transaction;

and an address and phone number for questions and information.

PREAUTHORIZED TRANSFERS

A preauthorized transfer from a consumer's account must be authorized in advance and in writing by the consumer, and a copy of the authorization must be provided to the consumer when the transfer is made. Up to three business days before the scheduled date of the transfer, a consumer may stop payment of a preauthorized EFT by notifying the financial institution orally or in writing, though the financial institution may require the consumer to provide written confirmation of an oral notification within fourteen days.

ERROR RESOLUTION

The consumer has sixty days after the financial institution sends a periodic statement in which to notify the institution of any errors appearing on that statement. The financial institution is required to investigate alleged errors within ten business days and to report its findings within three business days after completing the investigation. If the financial institution needs more than ten days to investigate, it may take up to forty-five days, provided it recredits the consumer's account for the amount alleged to be in error. The institution must correct an error within one business day after determining that the error has occurred. Failure to investigate in good faith makes the financial institution liable to the consumer for treble damages (three times the amount of provable damages).

CONSUMER LIABILITY

A consumer's liability for an unauthorized electronic fund transfer is limited to a maximum of $50 if the consumer notifies the financial institution within two days after he learns of the loss or theft. If the consumer does not report the loss or theft within two days, he is liable for losses up to $500 but no more than $50 for the first two days. If the consumer fails to report the unauthorized use within sixty days of transmittal of a periodic statement, he is liable for losses resulting from any unauthorized EFT that appeared on the statement if the financial institution can show that the loss would not have occurred had the consumer reported the loss within sixty days; thus there is unlimited liability on unauthorized transfers made after sixty days following the bank's sending the periodic statement.

LIABILITY OF FINANCIAL INSTITUTION

A financial institution is liable to a consumer for all damages proximately caused by its failure to make an EFT in accordance with the terms and conditions of an account, in the correct amount, or in a timely manner when properly instructed to do so by the consumer. There are, however, exceptions to such liability. The financial institution will not be liable if—

1. the consumer's account has insufficient funds through no fault of the financial institution,
2. the funds are subject to legal process,
3. the transfer would exceed an established credit limit,
4. an electronic terminal has insufficient cash, or
5. circumstances beyond the financial institution's control prevent the transfer.

The financial institution is also liable for failure to stop payment of a preauthorized transfer from a consumer's account when instructed to do so in accordance with the terms and conditions of the account.

WHOLESALE FUNDS TRANSFERS

Article 4A, Funds Transfers, is designed to provide a statutory framework for payment systems that are not covered by existing Articles of the UCC or by the EFTA. The typical wholesale wire transfer involves sophisticated parties who desire great speed in transferring large sums of money. Article 4A has been universally adopted by the States and Territories. In general, "Article 4A governs a method of payment in which the person making payment (the 'originator') directly transfers an instruction to a bank to either make a payment to the person receiving the payment (the 'beneficiary') or to instruct some other bank to make payment to the beneficiary." Article 4A–102, Comment 1.

Although checks and credit cards are more common forms of payment as measured by number of transactions per day, commercial electronic transfers (commercial or wholesale wire transfers) far exceed these transactions as measured by their dollar volume, which is much greater than $1 trillion a day.

Article 4A provides that the parties to a funds transfer generally may by agreement vary their rights and obligations. Moreover, funds-transfer system rules governing banks that use the system may be effective even if such rules conflict with Article 4A. Section 4A–501. Rights and obligations under Article 4A can also be changed by Federal Reserve regulations and operating circulars of Federal Reserve Banks. Section 4A–107.

SCOPE OF ARTICLE 4A

Article 4A, which covers wholesale funds transfers, defines a funds transfer as a

> series of transactions, beginning with the originator's payment order, made for the purpose of making payment to the beneficiary of the order. The term includes any payment order issued by the originator's bank or an intermediary bank intended to carry out

the originator's payment order. A funds transfer is completed by acceptance by the beneficiary's bank of a payment order for the benefit of the beneficiary of the originator's payment order. Section 4A–104(a).

The Article, therefore, covers the transfers of credit that move from an originator to a beneficiary through the banking system. If any step in the process is governed by the EFTA, however, the entire transaction is excluded from the Article's coverage. Section 4A–108.

The following examples illustrate the coverage of the Article:

1. Johnson Co. instructs its bank, First National Bank (FNB), to pay $2 million to West Co., also a customer of FNB. FNB executes the payment order by crediting West's account with $2 million and notifying West that the credit has been made and is available.
2. Assume the same facts as those in the first example except that West's bank is Central Bank (CB). FNB will execute the payment order of Johnson Co. by issuing to CB its own payment order instructing CB to credit the account of West.
3. Assume the facts presented in the second example with the added fact that FNB does not have a correspondent relationship with CB. In this instance, FNB will have to issue its payment order to Northern Bank (NB), a bank that does have a correspondent relationship with CB, and NB will then issue its payment order to CB.

PAYMENT ORDER **Payment order** is a sender's instruction to a receiving bank to pay, or to cause another bank to pay, a fixed or determinable amount of money to a beneficiary. Section 4A–103. The instruction may be communicated orally, electronically, or in writing. To be a payment order, the instruction must—

1. not contain a condition to payment other than the time of payment;
2. be sent to a receiving bank that is to be reimbursed either by debiting an account of the sender or by otherwise receiving payment from the sender; and
3. be transmitted by the sender directly to the receiving bank or indirectly through an agent, a funds-transfer system, or a communication system.

The payment order is issued when sent and, if more than one payment is to be made, each payment represents a separate payment order. Section 4A–104(b)(c). In the examples above, one payment order is issued in the first example (from Johnson Co.), two in the second example (from Johnson Co. and from First National Bank), and three in the third example (from Johnson Co., from First National Bank, and from Northern Bank).

PARTIES The **originator** is either the sender of the payment order or, in a series of payment orders, the sender of the first payment order. Section 4A–104(c). A **sender** is the party who gives an instruction to the **receiving bank**, or the bank to which the sender's instruction is addressed. Section 4A–103(4). The receiving bank may be the **originator's bank**, an intermediary bank, or the **beneficiary's bank**. The originator's bank is either the bank that receives the original payment order or the originator if the originator is a bank. Section 4A–104(d). The beneficiary's bank, the last bank in the chain of a funds transfer, is the bank instructed in the payment order to credit the beneficiary's account. Section 4A–103(a)(3). The **beneficiary** is the person to be paid by the beneficiary bank. Section 4A–103(a)(2). An **intermediary bank** is any receiving bank, other than the originator's bank or the beneficiary's bank, that receives the payment order. Section 4A–104(b). Thus, in the above examples,

1. Johnson Co. is the *originator* in all three examples;
2. Johnson Co. is a *sender* in all three examples, FNB is a sender in examples 2 and 3, and NB is a sender in example 3;
3. FNB is the *receiving bank* of Johnson Co.'s payment order in all three examples; in example 2, CB is the receiving bank of FNB's payment order; and, in example 3, CB is the receiving bank of NB's payment order and NB is the receiving bank of FNB's payment order;
4. FNB is the *originator's bank* in all three examples;
5. FNB is the *beneficiary's bank* in example 1; CB is the beneficiary's bank in examples 2 and 3;
6. West is the *beneficiary* in all three examples; and
7. NB is an *intermediary bank* in example 3.

See *Figure 30-2* for a summary of the parties in these three examples. In some instances, the originator and the beneficiary may be the same party. For example, a corporation may wish to transfer funds from one account to another account that is in the same or a different bank.

◆ **SEE FIGURE 30-2: Parties to a Funds Transfer**

EXCLUDED TRANSACTIONS As previously mentioned, Section 4A–108 provides that if any part of a funds transfer is governed by the EFTA, then the transfer is excluded from Article 4A coverage. In addition, Article 4A covers only credit transactions; it therefore excludes debit transactions. If the person making the payment gives the instruction, the transfer is a credit transfer. If, however, the person receiving the payment gives the instruction, the transfer is a debit transfer. For example, a seller of goods obtains authority from the purchaser to debit the purchaser's account after the seller ships the goods. Article 4A does not cover this transaction because the instructions to make payment issue from the beneficiary (the seller), not from the party whose account is to be debited (the purchaser).

◆ **SEE FIGURE 30-3: Credit Transaction**

◆ **FIGURE 30-2: Parties to a Funds Transfer**

	Example 1	Example 2	Example 3
Originator	Johnson Co.	Johnson Co.	Johnson Co.
Sender(s)	Johnson Co.	Johnson Co.	Johnson Co.
		FNB	FNB
			NB
Receiving Bank(s)	FNB	FNB	FNB
		CB	CB
			NB
Originator's Bank	FNB	FNB	FNB
Beneficiary's Bank	FNB	CB	CB
Beneficiary	West	West	West
Intermediary Bank	—	—	NB

Note: CB = Central Bank; FNB = First National Bank; NB = Northern Bank.

ACCEPTANCE

Rights and obligations arise as a result of a receiving bank's acceptance of a payment order. The effect of acceptance depends upon whether the payment order was issued to the beneficiary's bank or to a receiving bank other than the beneficiary's bank.

If a receiving bank is not the beneficiary's bank, the receiving bank does not subject itself to any liability until it accepts the instrument. Acceptance by a receiving bank other than the beneficiary's bank occurs when the receiving bank executes the sender's order. Section 4A–209(a). Such execution occurs when the receiving bank "issues a payment order intended to carry out" the sender's payment order. Section 4A–301(a). When the receiving bank executes the sender's payment order, the bank is entitled to payment from the sender and can debit the sender's account. Section 4A–402(c).

The beneficiary's bank may accept an order in any of three ways, and acceptance occurs at the earliest of these events: (1) when the bank (a) pays the beneficiary or (b) notifies the beneficiary that the bank has received the order or has credited the beneficiary's account with the funds; (2) when the bank receives payment of the sender's order; or (3) the opening of the next funds-transfer business day of the bank after the payment date of the order if the order was not rejected and funds are available for payment. Section 4A–209(b).

If a beneficiary's bank accepts a payment order, the bank is obliged to pay the beneficiary the amount of the order. Section 4A–404(a). The bank's acceptance of the payment order does not, however, create any obligation to either the sender or the originator.

ERRONEOUS EXECUTION OF PAYMENT ORDERS

If a receiving bank mistakenly executes a payment order for an amount greater than the amount authorized, the bank is entitled to payment only in the amount of the sender's correct order. Section 4A–303(a). To the extent allowed by the law governing mistake and restitution, the receiving bank may then recover from the beneficiary of the erroneous order the amount in excess of the authorized amount. If the

◆ **FIGURE 30-3: Credit Transaction**

wrong beneficiary is paid, however, the bank that issued the erroneous payment order is entitled to payment neither from its sender nor from prior senders and has the burden of recovering the payment from the improper beneficiary. Section 4A–303(c).

UNAUTHORIZED PAYMENT ORDERS

If a bank wishing to prevent unauthorized transactions establishes commercially reasonable security measures, to which a customer agrees, and the bank properly follows the process it has established, the customer must pay an order even if it was unauthorized. Section 4A–202. The customer, however, can avoid liability by showing that the unauthorized order was not caused directly or indirectly by (1) a person with access to confidential security information who was acting for the customer or (2) a person who obtained such information from a source controlled by the customer. Section 4A–203.

CHAPTER SUMMARY

BANK DEPOSITS AND COLLECTIONS

COLLECTION OF ITEMS	**Depositary Bank** the bank in which the payee or holder deposits a check for credit
	Provisional Credit tentative credit for the deposit of an instrument until final credit is given
	Final Credit payment of the instrument by the payor bank; if the payor bank (drawee) does not pay the check, the depositary bank reverses the provisional credit
	Intermediary Bank a bank, other than the depositary or payor bank, involved in the collection process
	Collecting Bank any bank (other than the payor bank) handling the item for payment
	• *Agency* a collecting bank is an agent or subagent of the owner of the check until the settlement becomes final
	• *Duty of Care* a collecting bank must exercise ordinary care in handling an item
	• *Duty to Act Timely* a collecting bank acts timely if it takes proper action before its midnight deadline (midnight of the next banking day)
	• *Indorsements* if an item is restrictively indorsed "for deposit only," only a bank may be a holder
	• *Warranties* customers and collecting banks give warranties on transfer, presentment, and encoding
	• *Final Payment* occurs when the payor bank does any of the following, whichever happens first: (1) pays an item in cash; (2) settles and does not have the right to revoke the settlement; or (3) makes a provisional settlement and does not properly revoke it
	Payor Bank under its contract with the drawer, the payor or drawee bank agrees to pay to the payee or his order checks that are issued by the drawer, provided the order is not countermanded by a stop payment order and provided there are sufficient funds in the drawer's account
RELATIONSHIP BETWEEN PAYOR BANK AND ITS CUSTOMER	**Contractual Relationship** the relationship between a payor bank and its checking account customer is primarily the product of their contractual arrangement
	Payment of an Item when a payor receives an item for which the funds in the account are insufficient, the bank may either dishonor the item and return it or pay the item and charge the customer's account even though an overdraft is created

Substitute Check a paper reproduction of the original check that is the legal equivalent of an original check for all purposes

Stop Payment Orders an oral stop payment order (a command from a drawer to a drawee not to pay an instrument) is binding for fourteen calendar days; a written order is effective for six months and may be renewed in writing

Bank's Right to Subrogation on Improper Payment if a payor bank pays an item over a stop payment order or otherwise in violation of its contract, the payor bank is subrogated to (obtains) the rights of (1) any holder in due course on the item against the drawer or maker; (2) the payee or any other holder against the drawer or maker; and (3) the drawer or maker against the payee or any other holder

Disclosure Requirement all depositary institutions must disclose in great detail to their consumers the terms and conditions of their deposit account

Customer's Death or Incompetence a bank may pay an item if it does not know of the customer's incompetency or death

Customer's Duties the customer must examine bank statements and items carefully and promptly to discover any unauthorized signatures or alterations

ELECTRONIC FUNDS TRANSFERS

NATURE AND TYPES OF ELECTRONIC FUNDS TRANSFERS

Definition any transfer of funds, other than a transaction originated by check, draft, or similar paper instrument, which is initiated through an electronic terminal, telephonic instrument, or computer or magnetic tape so as to order, instruct, or authorize a financial institution to debit or credit an account

Purpose to eliminate the paperwork involved in processing checks and the "float" available to a drawer of a check

Types of Electronic Funds Transfers
- *Automated Teller Machines*
- *Point-of-Sale Systems*
- *Direct Deposits and Withdrawals*
- *Pay-by-Phone Systems*
- *Personal Computer (Online) Banking*
- *Wholesale Electronic Funds Transfers*

CONSUMER FUNDS TRANSFERS

Electronic Fund Transfer Act provides a basic framework establishing the rights, liabilities, and responsibilities of participants in consumer electronic funds transfers

Financial Institution Responsibility liable to a consumer for all damages proximately caused by its failure to properly handle an electronic fund transfer transaction

WHOLESALE FUNDS TRANSFERS

Scope of Article 4A
- *Wholesale Funds Transfers* the movement of funds through the banking system; excludes all transactions governed by the Electronic Fund Transfer Act
- *Payment Order* an instruction of sender to a receiving bank to pay, or to cause another bank to pay, a fixed amount of money to a beneficiary
- *Parties* include originator, sender, receiving bank, originator's bank, beneficiary's bank, beneficiary, and intermediary banks

Acceptance rights and obligations that arise as a result of a receiving bank's acceptance of a payment order

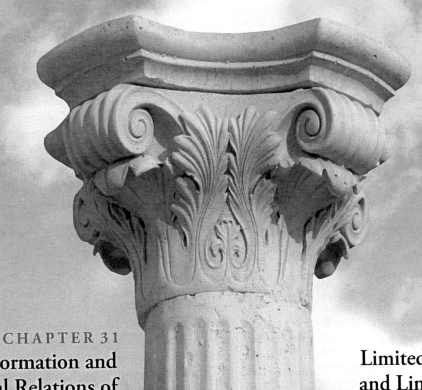

PART 6

Unincorporated Business Associations

CHAPTER 31
Formation and
Internal Relations of
General Partnerships

CHAPTER 32
Operation and
Dissolution of
General Partnerships

CHAPTER 33
Limited Partnerships
and Limited Liability
Companies

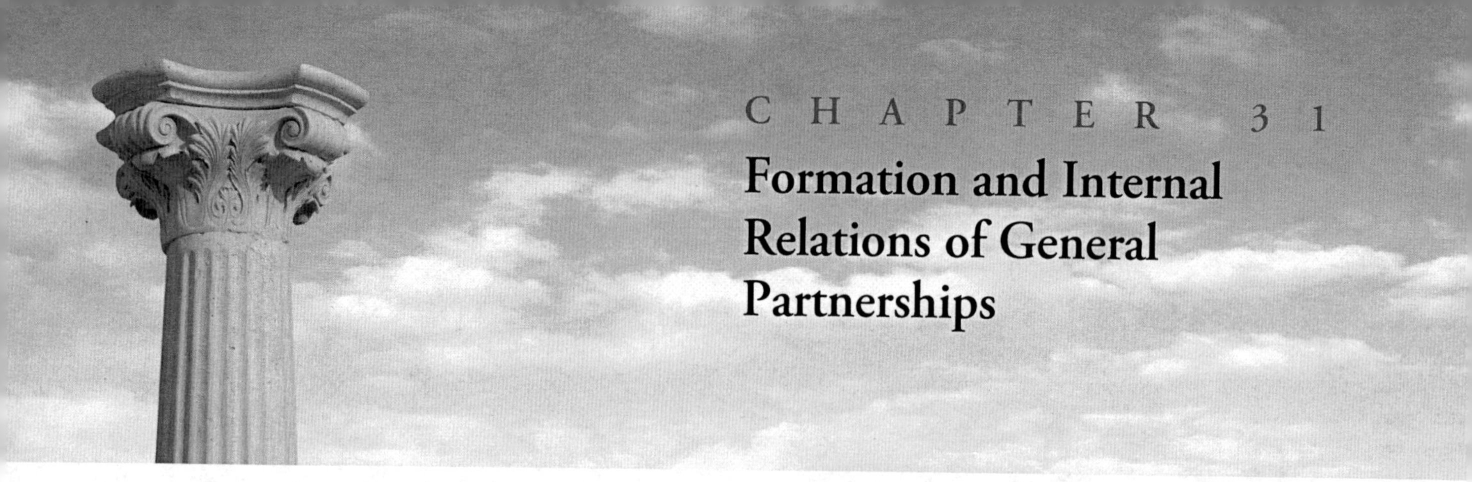

C H A P T E R 31

Formation and Internal Relations of General Partnerships

A business enterprise may be operated or conducted as a sole proprietorship, an unincorporated business association (such as a general partnership, a limited partnership, or a limited liability company [LLC]), or a corporation. The choice of the most appropriate form cannot be determined in a general way but depends on the particular circumstances of the owners. We will begin this chapter with a brief overview of the various types of business associations and the factors that are relevant to deciding which form to use. The rest of this chapter and the next chapter will examine general partnerships. *Chapter 33* will cover other types of unincorporated business associations. *Part 7 (Chapters 34* through *37)* will address corporations.

CHOOSING A BUSINESS ASSOCIATION

The owners of an enterprise determine the form of business unit they wish to use based upon their specific circumstances. In the United States there are more than 32 million business entities, with annual receipts of more than $34 trillion. There are approximately 23 million sole proprietorships, 5.9 million corporations, 1.8 million limited liability companies, 740,000 general partnerships, and 530,000 limited partnerships. Unincorporated business associations are common in a number of areas. General partnerships, for example, are used frequently in finance, insurance, accounting, real estate, law, and other service-related fields. Joint ventures have enjoyed popularity among major corporations planning to engage in cooperative research; in the exploitation of land and mineral rights; in the development, promotion, and sale of patents, trade names, and copyrights; and in manufacturing operations in foreign countries. Limited partnerships have been widely used for enterprises such as real estate investment and development, motion picture and theater productions, oil and gas ventures, and equipment leasing. In the last few years the States have authorized the formation of limited liability companies. This form of business organization will probably appeal to a number of businesses including real estate ventures, high-technology enterprises, businesses in which transactions involve foreign investors, professional organizations, corporate joint ventures, start-up businesses, and venture capital projects.

First to be discussed are the most important factors to consider in choosing a form of business association. This is followed by a brief description of the various forms of business associations and how they differ with respect to these factors.

◆ SEE FIGURE 31-1: **General Partnership, Limited Partnership, Limited Liability Company, and Corporation**

FACTORS AFFECTING THE CHOICE

In choosing the form in which to conduct business the owners should consider a number of factors, including ease of formation, Federal and State income tax laws, external liability, management and control, transferability of ownership interests, and continuity. The relative importance of each factor will vary with the specific needs and objectives of the owners.

EASE OF FORMATION

Business associations differ as to the formalities and expenses of formation. Some can be created with no formality, while others require the filing of documents with the State.

TAXATION

Some business associations are not considered to be separate taxable entities, and taxation is on a "pass-through" basis. In these cases, the income of the business is conclusively presumed to have been distributed to the owners, who must pay taxes on that income. Losses receive comparable treatment and can be used to offset some of the owners' income. In contrast, some business forms, most significantly corporations, are considered separate tax entities and are directly taxed. When such an entity distributes income to the

COLUMN: © PHOTOGRAPHEROLYMPUS CLOUDS: © KERTLIS

◆ **FIGURE 31-1: General Partnership, Limited Partnership, Limited Liability Company, and Corporation**

	General Partnership	Limited Partnership	Limited Liability Company	Corporation
Transferability	Financial interest may be assigned; membership requires consent of all partners	Financial interest may be assigned, and assignee may become limited partner if all partners consent	Financial interest may be assigned; membership requires consent of all members	Freely transferable unless shareholders agree otherwise
Liability	Partners have unlimited liability[1]	General partners have unlimited liability[2]; Limited partners have limited liability	All members have limited liability	Shareholders have limited liability
Control	By all partners	By general partners, not limited partners	By all members	By board of directors elected by shareholders
Continuity	RUPA: Usually unaffected by death, bankruptcy, or—in a term partnership—withdrawal of partner; UPA: Dissolved by death, bankruptcy, or withdrawal of partner	Dissolved by death, bankruptcy, or withdrawal of general partner; Unaffected by death, bankruptcy, or withdrawal of limited partner	In many States death, bankruptcy, or withdrawal of member does *not* dissolve LLC	Unaffected by death, bankruptcy, or withdrawal of shareholder
Taxation	May elect that only partners are taxed	May elect that only partners are taxed	May elect that only members are taxed	Corporation taxed unless Subchapter S applies; Shareholders taxed

Note: RUPA = Revised Uniform Partnership Act; UPA = Uniform Partnership Act.

[1] In an LLP, the partners' liability is limited for some or all of the partnership's obligations
[2] In an LLLP, the partners' liability is limited for some or all of the partnership's obligations

owners, that income is separately taxed to the recipients. Thus, these funds are taxed twice: once to the entity and once to the owners. Unincorporated business entities can elect whether or not to be taxed as a separate entity. All businesses that have publicly traded ownership interests must be taxed as a corporation.

EXTERNAL LIABILITY

External liability arises in a variety of ways, but the crucial and most commonly occurring are tort and contract liability. Owners of some business forms have unlimited liability for all of the obligations of the business. Thus, if the business does not have sufficient funds to pay its debts, each and every owner has personal liability to the creditors for the full amount of the debts. In brief, owners of interests in businesses with unlimited liability place their entire estates at risk. In some types of entities, the owners have unlimited liability for some but not all of the entity's obligations. Finally, in some types of business associations, the owners enjoy limited liability, which means their liability is limited to the extent of their capital contribution. It should be

noted, however, that creditors often require that the owners of small businesses guarantee personally loans made to the businesses. Moreover, an owner of *any* type of business does not have limited liability for his own tortious conduct; the person is liable as an individual tortfeasor.

MANAGEMENT AND CONTROL

In some entities, the owners can fully share in the control of the business. In other types of business associations, the owners are restricted as to their right to take part in control.

TRANSFERABILITY

An ownership interest in a business consists of a financial interest, which is the right to share in the profits of the business, and a management interest, which is the right to participate in control of the business. In some types of business associations, the owners may freely transfer their financial interest but may not transfer their management interest without the consent of all of the other owners. In other types of business associations, the entire ownership interest is freely transferable.

CONTINUITY

Some business associations have low continuity, which means that the death, bankruptcy, or withdrawal of an owner results in the dissolution of the association. Other types have high continuity and are not affected by the death, bankruptcy, or withdrawal of owners.

FORMS OF BUSINESS ASSOCIATIONS

This section contains a brief description of the various types of business associations and how they differ with respect to the factors just discussed. In addition, general partnerships, limited partnerships, LLCs, limited liability partnerships (LLPs), and corporations will be discussed more extensively in this and the next part of the book.

SOLE PROPRIETORSHIP

A sole proprietorship is an unincorporated business consisting of one person who owns and completely controls the business. It is formed without any formality, and no documents need be filed. Moreover, if one person conducts a business and does not file with the State to form an LLC or corporation, a sole proprietorship will result by default. A sole proprietorship is not a separate taxable entity and only the sole proprietor is taxed. Sole proprietors have unlimited liability for the sole proprietorship's debts. The sole proprietor's interest in the business is freely transferable. The death of a sole proprietor dissolves the sole proprietorship.

GENERAL PARTNERSHIP

A general partnership is an unincorporated business association consisting of two or more persons who co-own a business for profit. It is formed without any formality, and no documents need be filed. Thus, if two or more people conduct a business and do not file with the State to form another type of business organization, a general partnership will result by default. A partnership may elect not to be a separate taxable entity, in which case only the partners are taxed. Partners have unlimited liability for the partnership's debts. Each partner has an equal right to control of the partnership. Partners may assign their financial interest in the partnership, but the assignee may become a member of the partnership only if all of the members consent. Under the Revised Partnership Act the death or bankruptcy of a partner usually does not dissolve a partnership; the same is also true in a term partnership for the withdrawal of a partner.

JOINT VENTURE

A joint venture is an unincorporated business association composed of persons who combine their property, money, efforts, skill, and knowledge for the purpose of carrying out a particular business enterprise for profit. Usually, although not necessarily, it is of short duration. A joint venture, therefore, differs from a partnership, which is formed to carry on a business over a considerable or indefinite period of time. Nonetheless, except for a few differences, the law of partnerships generally governs a joint venture. An example of a joint venture is a securities underwriting syndicate or a syndicate formed to acquire a certain tract of land for subdivision and resale. Other common examples involve joint research conducted by corporations, the exploitation of mineral rights, and manufacturing operations in foreign countries.

LIMITED PARTNERSHIP

A limited partnership is an unincorporated business association consisting of at least one general partner and at least one limited partner. It is formed by filing a certificate of limited partnership with the State. A limited partnership may elect not to be a separate taxable entity, in which case only the partners are taxed. Publicly traded limited partnerships, however, are subject to corporate income taxation. General partners have unlimited liability for the partnership's debts; limited partners have limited liability. Each general partner has an equal right to control of the partnership; limited partners have no right to participate in control. Partners may assign their financial interest in the partnership, but the assignee may become a limited partner only if all of the members consent. The death, bankruptcy, or withdrawal of a general partner dissolves a limited partnership; the limited partners have neither the right nor the power to dissolve the limited partnership.

LIMITED LIABILITY COMPANY

An LLC is an unincorporated business association that provides limited liability to all of its owners (members) and permits all of its members to participate in management of the business. It may elect not to be a separate taxable entity, in which case only the members are taxed. As noted previously, publicly traded LLCs are subject to corporate income taxation. If an LLC has only one member, then it will be taxed as a sole proprietorship, unless separate entity tax treatment is elected. Thus, the LLC provides many of the advantages of a general partnership plus limited liability for all its members. Its benefits outweigh those of a limited partnership in that all members of an LLC not only enjoy limited liability but also may participate in management and control of the business. In most States members may assign their financial interest in the LLC, but the assignee may become a member of the LLC only if all of the members consent or the LLC's operating agreement provides otherwise. In some States the death, bankruptcy, or withdrawal of a member dissolves an LLC; in others they do not. Every State has adopted an LLC statute.

LIMITED LIABILITY PARTNERSHIP

A registered LLP is a general partnership that, by making the statutorily required filing, limits the liability of its partners for some or all of the partnership's obligations. To become an LLP, a general partnership must file with the State an application containing specified information. All of the States have enacted LLP statutes. Except for the filing requirements and the partners' liability shield, the law governing LLPs is identical to the law governing general partnerships.

LIMITED LIABILITY LIMITED PARTNERSHIP

A limited liability limited partnership (LLLP) is a limited partnership in which the liability of the general partners has been limited to the same extent as in an LLP. A growing number of States authorize LLLPs enabling the general partners in an LLLP to obtain the same degree of liability limitation that general partners can achieve in LLPs. Where available, a limited partnership may register as an LLLP without having to form a new organization, as would be the case in converting to an LLC.

CORPORATION

A corporation is a legal entity separate and distinct from its owners. It is formed by filing its articles of incorporation with the State. A corporation is taxed as a separate entity, and shareholders are taxed on corporate earnings that are distributed to them. (Some corporations are eligible to elect to be taxed as Subchapter S corporations, which results in only the shareholders being taxed.) The shareholders have limited liability for the corporation's obligations. The board of directors elected by the shareholders manages the corporation. Shares in a corporation are freely transferable. The death, bankruptcy, or withdrawal of a shareholder does not dissolve the corporation.

BUSINESS TRUSTS

The business trust, sometimes called a Massachusetts trust, was devised to avoid the burdens of corporate regulation, particularly the formerly widespread prohibition denying to corporations the power to own and deal in real estate. The business trust is used today primarily for asset securitization ventures in which income-generating assets, such as mortgages, are pooled in a trust. Like an ordinary trust between natural persons, a business trust may be created by a voluntary agreement without any authorization or consent of the State. A business trust has three distinguishing characteristics: (1) the trust estate is devoted to the conduct of a business; (2) by the terms of the agreement, each beneficiary is entitled to a certificate evidencing his ownership of a beneficial interest in the trust, which he is free to sell or otherwise transfer; and (3) the trustees have the exclusive right to manage and control the business free from control of the beneficiaries. If the third condition is not met, the trust may fail; the beneficiaries, by participating in control, would become personally liable as partners for the obligations of the business.

The trustees are personally liable for the debts of the business unless, in entering into contractual relations with others, it is expressly stated or definitely understood between the parties that the obligation is incurred solely upon the responsibility of the trust estate. To escape personal liability on the contractual obligations of the business, the trustee must obtain the agreement or consent of the other contracting party to look solely to the assets of the trust. The personal liability of the trustees for their own torts or the torts of their agents and servants employed in the operation of the business stands on a different footing. Although this liability cannot be avoided, the risk involved may be reduced substantially or eliminated altogether by insurance. In most jurisdictions, the beneficiaries of a business trust have no liability for obligations of the business trust.

FORMATION OF GENERAL PARTNERSHIPS

The form of business association known as partnership can be traced to ancient Babylonia, classical Greece, and the Roman Empire. It was also used in Europe and England during the Middle Ages. Eventually the English common law recognized partnerships. In the nineteenth century, partnerships were widely used in England and the United States, and the common law of partnership developed considerably during this period. Partnerships are important in that they allow individuals with different expertise, backgrounds, resources, and interests to form a more competitive enterprise by combining their various skills. This part of the chapter will cover the nature of general partnerships and how they are formed. It should be recalled that except for the filing requirements and the partners' liability shield, the law governing LLPs is identical to the law governing general partnerships.

NATURE OF PARTNERSHIP

In 1914, the National Conference of Commissioners on Uniform State Laws promulgated the Uniform Partnership Act (UPA). Since then it had been adopted in all States (except Louisiana) as well as by the District of Columbia, the Virgin Islands, and Guam. (The UPA is reprinted in Appendix C.)

In August 1986, the UPA Revision Subcommittee of the Committee on Partnerships and Unincorporated Business Organizations of the American Bar Association's Section of Corporation, Banking, and Business Law and the National Conference of Commissioners on Uniform State Laws decided to undertake a complete revision of the UPA. The revision was approved in August 1992 and was amended in 1993, 1994, 1996, and 1997. More than thirty-five States have adopted the Revised Act. This chapter will discuss the Revised Uniform Partnership Act or RUPA. (Selected provisions of the RUPA are reprinted in Appendix D.) Where the RUPA has made significant changes, the original 1914 UPA will also be discussed. (References to provisions of the RUPA will state the section number only; references to the original UPA will include the "UPA" designation.) The chapter summary reflects the RUPA.

Though fairly comprehensive, the RUPA and UPA do not cover all legal issues concerning partnerships. Accordingly, both the RUPA (Section 104) and the UPA (Section 5) provide that unless displaced by particular provisions of this Act, the principles of law and equity supplement this Act.

DEFINITION

The RUPA defines a **partnership** as "an association of two or more persons to carry on as co-owners a business for profit." Section 101(6). The RUPA broadly defines "person" to include "individuals, partnerships, corporations, joint ventures, business trusts, estates, trusts, and any other legal or commercial entity." Section 101(10). The comments indicate that this definition would include an LLC. Also defined by Section 101, a business includes every trade, occupation, and profession. The UPA has similar definitions. UPA Sections 2 and 6.

ENTITY THEORY

A **legal entity** is a unit capable of possessing legal rights and of being subject to legal duties. A legal entity may acquire, own, and dispose of property. It may enter into contracts, commit wrongs, sue, and be sued. For example, each business corporation is a legal entity having a legal existence separate from that of its shareholders.

A partnership was regarded by the common law as a legal aggregate, a group of individuals having no legal existence apart from that of its members. The Revised Act has greatly increased the extent to which partnerships are treated as entities. It applies aggregate treatment to very few aspects of partnerships, the most significant of which is that partners still have unlimited liability for the partnership's obligations. The UPA treats partnerships as legal entities for some purposes and as aggregates for others.

PARTNERSHIP AS A LEGAL ENTITY The RUPA Section 201 states: "A partnership is an entity distinct from its partners." The Revised Act embraces the entity treatment of partnerships, particularly in matters concerning title to partnership property, legal actions by and against the partnership, and continuity of existence. Examples of entity treatment include

the following: (1) The assets of the firm are treated as those of the business and are considered to be distinct from the individual assets of the members. Section 203. (2) A partner is accountable as a fiduciary to the partnership. Section 404. (3) Every partner is considered an agent of the partnership. Section 301. (4) A partnership may sue and be sued in the name of the partnership. Section 307.

PARTNERSHIP AS A LEGAL AGGREGATE The Revised Act has retained the aggregate characteristic of a partner's unlimited liability for partnership obligations, unless the partnership has filed a statement of qualification to become an LLP. Section 306. Thus, if Meg and Mike enter into a partnership that becomes insolvent, as does Meg, Mike is fully liable for the partnership's debts. Likewise, although a partner's interest in the partnership may be assigned, the assignee does not become a partner without the consent of all the partners. Sections 401(i), 502. Moreover, a partner's dissociation results in dissolution, although only in limited circumstances. Section 801.

Under the UPA, because a partnership is considered an aggregate for some purposes, it can neither sue nor be sued in the firm name unless a statute specifically allows such an action. In addition, a partnership generally lacks continuity of existence: whenever any partner ceases to be associated with the partnership, it is dissolved. UPA Section 29.

FORMATION OF A PARTNERSHIP

RUPA Section 202 provides that the association of two or more persons to carry on as co-owners a business for profit forms a partnership, whether or not the parties intend to form a partnership. The formation of a partnership is relatively simple and may be done consciously or unconsciously. A partnership may result from an oral or written agreement between the parties, from an informal arrangement, or from the conduct of the parties, who become partners by associating themselves in a business as co-owners. Consequently, if two or more individuals share the control and profits of a business, the law may deem them partners without regard to how they themselves characterize their relationship. Thus, associates frequently discover, to their chagrin, that they have inadvertently formed a partnership and have thereby subjected themselves to the duties and liabilities of partners. The legal existence of the relationship depends merely upon the parties' explicit or implicit agreement and their association in business as co-owners.

PARTNERSHIP AGREEMENT

The RUPA defines a "partnership agreement" as "the agreement, whether written, oral, or implied, among the partners concerning the partnership, including amendments to the partnership agreement." Section 101(7). This definition does not include other agreements between some or all of the partners, such as a lease or a loan agreement.

Except as otherwise provided by the RUPA, the partnership agreement governs relations among the partners and between the partners and the partnership. Section 103. Thus, the RUPA gives almost total freedom to the partners to provide whatever provisions they agree upon in their partnership agreement. In essence, RUPA is primarily a set of "default rules" that apply only when the partnership agreement does not address the issue. Nevertheless, the RUPA makes some duties mandatory; these cannot be waived or varied by the partnership agreement. Section 103(b).

To render their understanding more clear, definite, and complete, partners are advised, though not usually required, to put their partnership agreement in writing. A partnership agreement can provide almost any conceivable arrangement of capital investment, control sharing, and profit distribution that the partners desire. Unless the agreement provides otherwise, the partners may amend it only by unanimous consent. Any partnership agreement should include the following:

1. The firm name and the identity of the partners;
2. The nature and scope of the partnership business;
3. The duration of the partnership;
4. The capital contributions of each partner;
5. The division of profits and sharing of losses;
6. The managerial duties of each partner;
7. A provision for salaries, if desired;
8. Restrictions, if any, upon the authority of particular partners to bind the firm;
9. Any desired variations from the partnership statute's default provisions governing dissolution; and
10. A statement of the method or formula for determining the value of a partner's interest in the partnership.

STATUTE OF FRAUDS Because the statute of frauds does not apply expressly to a contract for the formation of a partnership, usually no writing is required to create the relationship. A contract to form a partnership to continue for a period longer than one year is within the statute, however, as is a contract for the transfer of an interest in real estate to or by a partnership; consequently, both of these contracts require a writing in order to be enforceable.

FIRM NAME In the interest of acquiring and retaining goodwill, a partnership should have a firm name. Although the name selected by the partners may not be identical or deceptively similar to the name of any other existing business concern, it may be the name of the partners or of any one of them; or the partners may decide to operate the business under a fictitious or assumed name, such as "Peachtree Restaurant," "Globe Theater," or "Paradise Laundry." A partnership may not use a name that would be likely to indicate to the public that it is a corporation. Nearly all of the States have enacted statutes that require any person or persons conducting business under an assumed or fictitious name to file in a designated public office a certificate setting forth the name under which the business is conducted and the real names and addresses of all persons conducting the business as partners or proprietors.

TESTS OF PARTNERSHIP EXISTENCE

Partnerships can be formed without the slightest formality. Consequently, it is important that the law establish a test for determining whether or not a partnership has been formed. Two situations most often require this determination. The most common involves a creditor who has dealt only with one person but who wishes to hold another liable as well by asserting that the two were partners. Less frequently, a person seeks to share profits earned and property held by another by claiming that they are partners.

As previously mentioned, Section 202 of the UPA provides the operative rule for formation of a partnership: an association of two or more persons to carry on as co-owners a business for profit. Thus, three components are essential to the existence of a partnership: (1) an association of two or more persons, (2) conducting a business for profit, (3) which they co-own.

◆ **SEE FIGURE 31-2: Tests for Existence of a Partnership**

ASSOCIATION A partnership must consist of two or more persons who have agreed to become partners. Any natural person having full *capacity* may enter into a partnership. A corporation is defined as a "person" by Section 101 of the RUPA and is, therefore, legally capable of entering into a partnership in those States whose incorporation statutes authorize a corporation to do so. Furthermore, as previously noted, a partnership, joint venture, business trust, estate, trust, and any other legal or commercial entity may be a member of a partnership. Section 101.

BUSINESS FOR PROFIT The RUPA provides that co-ownership does not in itself establish a partnership, even if the co-owners share profits made by the use of the property. Section 202(c). For a partnership to exist, there must be co-ownership of a business. Thus, passive co-ownership of property by itself, as distinguished from the carrying on of a business, does not establish a partnership. Moreover, to be a partnership, the business carried on by the association of two or more persons must be "for profit." This requirement excludes unincorporated nonprofit organizations from being partnerships. State common law and statutes govern such unincorporated nonprofit organizations. These laws, however, generally do not address the issues facing nonprofit associations in a systematic or integrated fashion. Consequently, in

◆ **FIGURE 31-2: Tests for Existence of a Partnership**

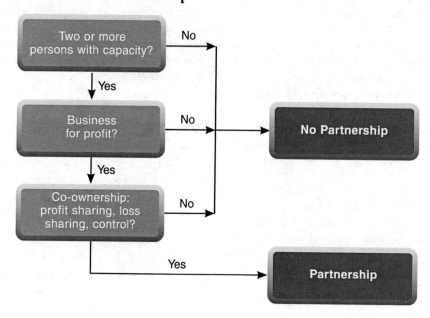

1996, the National Conference of Commissioners on Uniform State Laws promulgated a Uniform Unincorporated Nonprofit Association Act to reform the common law concerning unincorporated nonprofit associations in a limited number of major issues, including ownership of property, authority to sue and be sued, and the contract and tort liability of officers and members of the association. At least ten States have adopted the act.

Nor does a partnership exist in situations in which persons associate for mutual financial gain on a temporary or limited basis involving a single transaction or a few isolated transactions: such persons are not engaged in the continuous series of commercial activities necessary to constitute a business. Co-ownership of the means or instrumentality of accomplishing a single business transaction or a limited series of transactions may result in a joint venture but not in a general partnership.

For example, Katherine and Edith have joint ownership of shares of the capital stock of a corporation, have a joint bank account, and have inherited or purchased real estate as joint tenants or tenants in common. They share the dividends paid on the stock, the interest on the bank account, and the net proceeds from the sale or lease of the real estate. Nevertheless, Katherine and Edith are not partners. Although they are co-owners and share profits, they are not engaged in carrying on a business; hence, no partnership exists. On the other hand, if Katherine and Edith continually bought and sold real estate over a period of time and conducted a business of trading in real estate, a partnership relation would exist between them, regardless of whether they considered themselves partners or not.

To illustrate further: Alec, Laura, and Shirley each inherit an undivided one-third interest in a hotel and, instead of selling the property, decide by an informal agreement to continue operating the hotel. The operation of a hotel is a business; as co-owners of a hotel business, Alec, Laura, and Shirley are partners and are subject to all of the rights, duties, and incidents arising from the partnership relation.

CO-OWNERSHIP Although the co-ownership of *property* used in a business is a condition neither necessary nor sufficient for the existence of a partnership, the co-ownership of a *business* is essential. In identifying business co-ownership, the two most important factors are the sharing of profits and the right to manage and control the business.

A person who receives a share of the **profits** from a business is presumed to be a partner in the business. This means that persons who share profits are deemed to be partners unless they can prove otherwise. Section 202(c)(3) of the RUPA, however, provides that the existence of a partnership relation shall not be presumed where such profits were received in payment:

1. of a debt, by installments or otherwise;
2. for services as an independent contractor or of wages or other compensation to an employee;
3. of rent;
4. of an annuity or other retirement or health benefit to a beneficiary, representative, or designee of a deceased or retired partner;
5. of interest or other charge on a loan, even if the amount of payment varies with the profits of the business; or

6. for the sale of the goodwill of a business or other property by installments or otherwise.

These transactions do not give rise to a presumption that the party is a partner because the law assumes that the creditor, employee, landlord, or other recipient of such profits is unlikely to be a co-owner. It is possible, nonetheless, to establish that such a person is a partner by proof of other facts and circumstances, such as the sharing of control.

The sharing of *gross returns*, in contrast to profits, does *not* of itself establish a partnership. Section 202(c)(2). This is so whether or not the persons sharing the gross returns have a joint or common right or interest in property from which the returns are derived. Thus, two brokers who share commissions are not necessarily partners, or even presumed to be. Similarly, an author who receives royalties (a share of gross receipts from the sales of a book) is not a partner with her publisher.

By itself, evidence as to participation in the *management* or **control** of a business is not conclusive proof of a partnership relation, but it is persuasive. Limited voice in the management and control of a business may be accorded to an employee, a landlord, or a creditor. On the other hand, an actual partner may choose to take no active part in the affairs of the firm and may, by agreement with his copartners, forgo all right to exercise any control over the ordinary affairs of the business. In any event, the right to participate in control is an important factor considered by the courts in conjunction with other factors, particularly with profit sharing.

PARTNERSHIP CAPITAL AND PROPERTY

The total money and property that the partners contribute and dedicate to use in the enterprise is the partnership capital. Partnership capital represents the partners' equity in the partnership. No minimum amount of capitalization is necessary before a partnership may commence business.

Partnership property is property acquired by a partnership. Section 203. Property acquired by the partnership is conclusively deemed to be partnership property. Property becomes partnership property if acquired in the name of the partnership, which includes a transfer to (1) the partnership in its name or (2) one or more partners in their capacity as partners in the partnership, if the name of the partnership is indicated in the instrument transferring title to the property. Section 204. Property also may be partnership property even if it is not acquired in the name of the partnership. Property is partnership property if acquired in the name of one or more of the partners with an indication in the instrument transferring title of either (1) their capacity as partners or (2) of the existence of a partnership, even if the name of the partnership is not indicated. Section 204(a)(2).

Even if the instrument transferring title to one or more of the partners does not indicate their capacity as a partner or the existence of a partnership, the property nevertheless may be partnership property. Ultimately, the partners' intention controls whether property belongs to the partnership or to one or more of the partners in their individual capacities. The RUPA sets forth two rebuttable presumptions that apply when the partners have failed to express their intent. First, under Section 204(c), property purchased with partnership funds is presumed to be partnership property, without regard to the name in which title is held. The presumption applies not only when partnership cash or property is used for payment but also when partnership credit is used to obtain financing.

Second, under Section 204(d), property acquired in the name of one or more of the partners, without an indication of their capacity as partners and without use of partnership funds or credit, is presumed to be the partners' separate property, even if used for partnership purposes. In this last case it is presumed that only the *use* of the property is contributed to the partnership.

As discussed later, who owns the property—an individual partner or the partnership—determines (1) who gets it upon dissolution of the partnership, (2) who shares in any loss or gain upon its sale, (3) who shares in income from it, and (4) who may sell it or transfer it by will.

A question may arise regarding whether property that was owned by a partner before formation of the partnership and was used in the partnership business is a capital contribution and hence an asset of the partnership. For example, a partner who owns a store building may contribute to the partnership the use of the building but not the building itself. The building is, therefore, not partnership property, and the amount of capital contributed by this partner is the reasonable value of the rental of the building.

The fact that legal title to property remains unchanged is not conclusive evidence that such property has not become a partnership asset. The intent of the partners controls the question of who owns the property. Without an express agreement, an intention to consider property as partnership property may be inferred from any of the following facts: (1) the property was improved with partnership funds; (2) the property was carried on the books of the partnership as an asset; (3) taxes, liens, or expenses, such as insurance or repairs, were paid by the partnership; (4) income or proceeds of the property were treated as partnership funds; or (5) the partners declared or admitted the property to be partnership property.

RELATIONSHIPS AMONG PARTNERS

When parties enter into a partnership, the law imposes certain duties upon them and also grants them specific rights. Except as otherwise provided by the RUPA, the partnership agreement governs relations among the partners and between the partners and the partnership. Section 103. Thus, the RUPA gives almost total freedom to the partners to provide whatever provisions they agree upon in their partnership agreement. Nevertheless, the RUPA makes some duties mandatory; these cannot be waived or varied by the partnership agreement. Section 103(b).

DUTIES AMONG PARTNERS

The principal legal duties imposed upon partners in their relations with one another are (1) the fiduciary duty (the duty of loyalty), (2) the duty of obedience, and (3) the duty of care. In addition, each partner has a duty to inform his copartners and a duty to account to the partnership. (These additional duties are discussed later, in a section covering the rights of partners.) All of these duties correspond precisely with those duties owed by an agent to his principal and reflect the fact that much of the law of partnership is the law of agency.

FIDUCIARY DUTY

The extent of the fiduciary duty or duty of loyalty has been most eloquently expressed by the often-quoted words of Judge (later Justice) Cardozo:

> Joint adventurers, like copartners, owe to one another, while the enterprise continues, the duty of the *finest loyalty*. Many forms of conduct permissible in a workaday world for those acting at arm's length, are forbidden to those bound by fiduciary ties. A trustee is held to something stricter than the morals of the market place. *Not honesty alone, but the punctilio of an honor the most sensitive, is then the standard of behavior.* As to this there has developed a tradition that is unbending and inveterate. Uncompromising rigidity has been the attitude of courts of equity when petitioned to undermine the rule of undivided loyalty by the "disintegrating erosion" of particular exceptions. Only thus has the level of conduct for fiduciaries been kept at a level higher than that trodden by the crowd. It will not consciously be lowered by any judgment of this court. *Meinhard v. Salmon*, 249 N.Y. 458, 459, 164 N.E. 545, 546 (1928) [emphasis added].

The RUPA's provision regarding the fiduciary duty is both comprehensive and exclusive. Section 404. "In that regard, it is structurally different from the UPA which touches only sparingly on a partner's duty of loyalty and leaves any further development of the fiduciary duties of partners to the common law of agency." Comment 1 to Section 404. The RUPA completely and exclusively states the components of the duty of loyalty by specifying that a

partner has a duty not to appropriate partnership benefits without the consent of her partners, to refrain from self-dealing, and to refrain from competing with the partnership. Section 404(b). More specifically, Section 404(b) of the RUPA provides that a partner's duty of loyalty to the partnership and the other partners is limited to the following:

1. to account to the partnership and hold as trustee for it any property, profit, or benefit derived by the partner in the conduct and winding up of the partnership business or derived from a use by the partner of partnership property, including the appropriation of a partnership opportunity;
2. to refrain from dealing with the partnership in the conduct or winding up of the partnership business as, or on behalf of, a party having an interest adverse to the partnership; and
3. to refrain from competing with the partnership in the conduct of the partnership business before the dissolution of the partnership.

In addition, the Revised Act provides that a partner does not violate the duty of loyalty merely because the partner's conduct furthers the partner's own interest. Section 404(e).

For example, a partner committed a breach of fiduciary duty when he retained a secret discount on purchases of petroleum that he obtained through acquisition of a bulk plant, and the partnership was entitled to the entire amount of the discount.

Within the demands of the fiduciary duty, a partner cannot acquire for herself a partnership asset or opportunity without the consent of all the partners. Thus, a partner may not renew a partnership lease in her name alone. A partner cannot, without the permission of her partners, engage in any other business within the scope of the partnership enterprise. Should she participate in a competing or similar business, the disloyal partner not only must surrender any profit she has acquired from such business but must compensate the existing partnership for any damage it may have suffered as a result of the competition. A partner, however, may enter into any business neither in competition with nor within the scope of the partnership's business. For example, a partner in a law firm may, without violating her fiduciary duty, act as an executor or administrator of an estate. Furthermore, she need not account for her fees where it cannot be shown that her service in this other capacity impaired her duty to the partnership (for example, by monopolizing her attention).

The fiduciary duty does *not* extend to the formation of the partnership, when, according to the comments to RUPA Section 404, the parties are really negotiating at arm's length. The duty not to compete terminates upon dissociation, and the dissociated partner may immediately engage in a competitive business, without any further consent. Section 603(b)(2). The partner's other fiduciary duties continue only with regard to matters arising and events occurring before the partner's dissociation, unless the partner participates in winding up the partnership's business. Section 603(b)(3). Thus, upon a partner's dissociation, a partner may appropriate to his own benefit any *new* business opportunity coming to his attention after dissociation, even if the partnership continues, and a partner may deal with the partnership as an adversary with respect to *new* matters or events. A dissociated partner is not, however, free to use confidential partnership information after dissociation.

The Revised Act imposes a duty of good faith and fair dealing when a partner discharges duties to the partnership and the other partners under the RUPA or under the partnership agreement and exercises any rights. Section 404(d). The comments to this section state:

> The obligation of good faith and fair dealing is a contract concept, imposed on the partners because of the consensual nature of a partnership. . . . It is not characterized, in RUPA, as a fiduciary duty arising out of the partners' special relationship. Nor is it a separate and independent obligation. It is an ancillary obligation that applies whenever a partner discharges a duty or exercises a right under the partnership agreement or the Act.

The partnership agreement may not eliminate the duty of loyalty or the obligation of good faith and fair dealing. However, the partnership agreement may identify specific types or categories of activities that do not violate the duty of loyalty, if not clearly unreasonable. In addition, the other partners may consent to a specific act or transaction that otherwise violates the duty of loyalty, if there has been full disclosure of all material facts regarding the act or transaction as well as the partner's conflict of interest. Similarly, the partnership agreement may prescribe the standards by which the performance of the obligation of good faith and fair dealing is to be measured, if the standards are not manifestly unreasonable. Section 103(b).

The fiduciary duty under the UPA differs in some respects from that of the RUPA. First, the partner's fiduciary duty under the UPA applies to the formation of the partnership. Second, it applies to the winding up of the partnership. The UPA states that every partner must account to the partnership for any benefit he receives and must hold as trustee for it any profits he derives without the consent of the other partners from any transaction connected with the formation, conduct, or liquidation of the partnership or from any use he makes of its property. UPA Section 21. A partner may not prefer himself over the firm, nor may he even deal at arm's length with his partners, to whom his duty is one of undivided and continuous loyalty. The fiduciary duty also

applies to the purchase of a partner's interest from another partner. Each partner owes the highest duty of honesty and fair dealing to the other partners, including the obligation to disclose fully and accurately all material facts.

DUTY OF OBEDIENCE

A partner owes his partners a duty to act in obedience to the partnership agreement and to any business decisions properly made by the partnership. Any partner who violates this duty is liable individually to his partners for any resulting loss. For example, a partner who, in violation of a specific agreement not to extend credit to relatives, advances money from partnership funds and sells goods on credit to an insolvent relative would be held personally liable to his partners for the unpaid debt.

DUTY OF CARE

Whereas under the fiduciary duty a partner "is held to something stricter than the morals of the market place," he is held to something less than the skill of the marketplace. Each partner owes the partnership a duty of faithful service to the best of his ability. Nonetheless, he need not possess the degree of knowledge and skill of an ordinary paid agent. Under the Revised Act, a partner's duty of care to the partnership and the other partners in the conduct and winding up of the partnership business is limited to refraining from engaging in grossly negligent or reckless conduct, intentional misconduct, or a knowing violation of law. RUPA Section 404(c). For example, a partner assigned to keep the partnership books uses an overly complicated bookkeeping system and consequently produces numerous mistakes. Because these errors result simply from poor judgment, not an intent to defraud, and are not intended to and do not operate to the personal advantage of the negligent bookkeeping partner, she is *not* liable to her copartners for any resulting loss. The duty of care may not be eliminated entirely by agreement, but the standard may be reasonably reduced. Section 103(b)(4). The standard may be increased by agreement to one of ordinary care or an even higher standard of care. Comment 6 to RUPA Section 103.

RIGHTS AMONG PARTNERS

The law provides partners with certain rights, which include (1) their right to use and possess partnership property for partnership purposes, (2) their transferable interest in the partnership, (3) their right to share in distributions (part of their transferable interest), (4) their right to participate in management, (5) their right to choose associates, and (6) their enforcement rights.

RIGHTS IN SPECIFIC PARTNERSHIP PROPERTY

In adopting the entity theory, the Revised Act abolishes the UPA's concept of tenants in partnership: partnership property is owned by the partnership entity and not by the individual partners. Section 203. Moreover, RUPA Section 501 provides, "A partner is not a co-owner of partnership property and has no interest in partnership property which can be transferred, either voluntarily or involuntarily." A partner may use or possess partnership property only on behalf of the partnership. Section 401(g).

Under the UPA, a partner's ownership interest in any specific item of partnership property is that of a **tenant in partnership**. UPA Section 25. The UPA's tenancy in partnership reaches a similar entity result to the RUPA but states that result in aggregate terms. This type of ownership, which exists only in a partnership, has the following principal characteristics:

1. Each partner has a right equal to that of his copartners to possess partnership property for partnership purposes, but he has no right to possess it for any other purpose without his copartners' consent.
2. A partner may not make an individual assignment of his right in specific partnership property.
3. A partner's interest in specific partnership property is not subject to attachment or execution by his individual creditors. It is subject to attachment or execution only on a claim against the partnership.
4. Upon the death of a partner, his right in specific partnership property vests in the surviving partner or partners. Upon the death of the last surviving partner, his right in such property vests in his legal representative.

PARTNER'S TRANSFERABLE INTEREST IN THE PARTNERSHIP

Each partner has an **interest in the partnership**, which is defined as "all of a partner's interests in the partnership, including the partner's transferable interest and all management and other rights." Section 101(9). A **partner's transferable interest** is a more limited concept; it is the partner's share of the profits and losses of the partnership and the partner's right to receive distributions. This interest is personal property. Section 502. A partner's transferable interest is discussed here; a partner's management and other rights are discussed later in this chapter.

ASSIGNABILITY A partner may voluntarily transfer, in whole or in part, his transferable interest in the partnership. Section 503. The transfer does not by itself cause the partner's dissociation or a dissolution and winding up of the partnership business. (Dissolution is discussed in *Chapter 32*.) The transferee, however, is not entitled to (1) participate in the management or conduct of the partnership business, (2) require access to any information concerning partnership transactions, or (3) inspect or copy the partnership books or records. She is merely entitled to receive, in accordance with the terms of the assignment, any distributions to which the assigning partner would have been entitled under the partnership agreement before dissolution. After dissolution, the transferee is entitled to receive the net amount that would have been distributed to the transferring partner upon the winding up of the business. Moreover, the assignee may apply for a court-ordered dissolution. Section 801(6). The assigning partner remains a partner with all of a partner's rights and duties other than the transferred interest in distributions.

Under Section 601(4)(ii), however, the other partners by a unanimous vote may expel a partner who has transferred substantially all of his transferable partnership interest, other than as security for a loan. The partner may be expelled, nevertheless, upon *foreclosure* of the security interest.

Under Section 103(a), the partners may agree among themselves to restrict the right to transfer their partnership interests.

CREDITORS' RIGHTS A partner's transferable interest (the right to distributions from the partnership and the right to seek court-ordered dissolution of the partnership) is subject to the claims of that partner's creditors, who may obtain a **charging order** (a type of judicial lien) against the partner's transferable interest. Section 504. On application by a judgment creditor of a partner, a court may charge the transferable interest of the partner to satisfy the judgment. A charging order is also available to the judgment creditor of a *transferee* of a partnership interest. A charging order is the judgment creditor's exclusive remedy against a partner's transferable interest in the partnership. The court may appoint a receiver of the debtor's share of the distributions due or to become due. The court may order a foreclosure of the interest subject to the charging order at any time. The purchaser at the foreclosure sale has the rights of a transferee. At any time before foreclosure, an interest charged may be redeemed by (1) the partner who is the judgment debtor; (2) other partners with nonpartnership property; or (3) other partners with partnership property, but only with the consent of all of the remaining partners.

Neither the judgment creditor, the receiver, nor the purchaser at foreclosure becomes a partner, and thus none is entitled to participate in the partnership's management or to have access to information. Furthermore, neither the charging order nor its sale upon foreclosure causes a dissolution, though the other partners may dissolve the partnership or redeem the charged interest. Section 601(4)(ii) provides that a partner may be expelled by a unanimous vote of the other partners upon foreclosure of a judicial lien charging a partner's interest.

◆ **FIGURE 31-3: Partnership Property Compared with Partner's Interest**

	Partnership Property		Partner's Interest
	RUPA	**UPA**	
Definition	A partner is *not* a co-owner of partnership property	Tenant in partnership	Share of profits and surplus
Possession	For partnership purposes, not individual ones	For partnership purposes, not individual ones	Intangible, personal property right
Assignability	Partner has *no* interest in partnership property which can be transferred	If all other partners assign their rights in the property	Assignee does not become a partner
Attachment	Only for a claim against the partnership	Only for a claim against the partnership	By a charging order
Inheritance	Partner has *no* interest in partnership property which can be transferred	Goes to surviving partner(s)	Passes to the personal representative of deceased partner

Note: RUPA = Revised Uniform Partnership Act; UPA = Uniform Partnership Act.

◆ **SEE FIGURE 31-3: Partnership Property Compared with Partner's Interest**

RIGHT TO SHARE IN DISTRIBUTIONS

A **distribution** is a transfer of money or other partnership property from the partnership to a partner in the partner's capacity as a partner. Section 101(3). Distributions include a division of profits, a return of capital contributions, a repayment of a loan or advance made by a partner to the partnership, and a payment made to compensate a partner for services rendered to the partnership. The RUPA's rules regarding distribution are subject to contrary agreement of the partners. Section 103. A partner has no right to receive, and may not be required to accept, a distribution in kind. Section 402. The RUPA provides that each partner is deemed to have an account that is credited with the partner's contributions and share of the partnership profits and charged with distributions to the partner and the partner's share of partnership losses. Section 401.

RIGHT TO SHARE IN PROFITS Because a partnership is an association to carry on a business for profit, each partner is entitled, unless otherwise agreed, to a share of the profits. Absent an agreement to the contrary, however, a partner does not have a right to receive a current distribution of the profits credited to his account, the timing of the distribution of profits being a matter arising in the ordinary course of business to be decided by majority vote of the partners. In the absence of an agreement regarding the division of profits, the partners share the profits *equally*, regardless of the ratio of their financial contributions or the degree of their participation in management. Thus, under this default rule, partners share profits per capita and not in proportion to their capital contributions.

Conversely, each partner is chargeable with a share of any losses the partnership sustains. Section 401(b). A partner, however, is not obligated to contribute to partnership losses before his withdrawal or the liquidation of the partnership, unless the partners agree otherwise. The partners bear losses in a proportion *identical* to that in which they share profits. Section 401(b). The partnership agreement may, however, validly provide for bearing losses in a proportion different from that in which profits are shared.

For example, Alice, Betty, and Carol form a partnership, with Alice contributing $10,000; Betty, $20,000; and Carol, $30,000. They could agree that Alice would receive 20 percent of the profits and assume 30 percent of the losses; that Betty would receive 30 percent of the profits and assume 50 percent of the losses; and that Carol would receive 50 percent of the profits and assume 20 percent of the losses. If their agreement is silent as to the sharing of profits and losses, however, each would have an equal one-third share of both profits and losses.

RIGHT TO RETURN OF CAPITAL Absent an agreement to the contrary, a partner does not have a right to receive a distribution of the capital contributions in his account before his withdrawal or the liquidation of the partnership.

Under the UPA after all the partnership's creditors have been paid, each partner is entitled to repayment of his capital contribution during the winding up of the firm. UPA Section 18(a). Unless otherwise agreed, a partner is not entitled to interest on his capital contribution; however, a delay in the return of his capital contribution entitles the partner to interest at the legal rate from the date when it should have been repaid. UPA Section 18(d).

RIGHT TO INDEMNIFICATION A partner who makes an advance beyond his agreed capital contribution is entitled to reimbursement from the partnership. Section 401(d). An advance is treated as a loan to the partnership that accrues interest. Section 401(e). In addition, the partnership must reimburse a partner for payments made and indemnify a partner for liabilities incurred by the partner in the ordinary course of the business of the partnership or for the protection of the partnership business or property. Section 401(c). Under the Revised Act, a loan from a partner to the partnership is treated the same as loans of a person not a partner, subject to other applicable law, such as fraudulent transfer law, the law of avoidable preferences under the Bankruptcy Act, and general debtor-creditor law. RUPA Section 404(f) and Comment 6.

Under the UPA, a partner's claim as a creditor of the firm, though subordinate to the claims of nonpartner creditors, is superior to the partners' rights to the return of capital.

RIGHT TO COMPENSATION The RUPA provides that, unless otherwise agreed, *no* partner is entitled to payment for services performed for the partnership. Section 401(h). Even a partner who works disproportionately harder than the others to conduct the business is entitled to no salary but only to his share of the profits. A partner may, however, by agreement among all of the partners, receive a salary. Moreover, a partner is entitled to reasonable compensation for services rendered in winding up the business of the partnership. Section 401(h).

RIGHT TO PARTICIPATE IN MANAGEMENT

Each of the partners, unless otherwise agreed, has *equal* rights in the management and conduct of the partnership business. Section 401(f). The majority governs the actions and decisions of the partnership with respect to matters in the ordinary course of partnership business. Section 401(j). *All* the partners must consent to any act outside the ordinary course of partnership business and to any amendment of the partnership agreement. Section 401(j). In their partnership agreement, the partners may provide for unequal voting rights. For example, Jones, Smith, and Williams form a partnership, agreeing that Jones will have two votes, Smith four votes, and Williams five votes. Large partnerships commonly concentrate most or all management authority in a committee of a few partners or even in just one partner. Classes of partners with different management rights also may be

created. This practice is common in accounting and law firms, which may have two classes (for example, junior and senior partners) or three classes (for example, junior, senior, and managing partners).

RIGHT TO CHOOSE ASSOCIATES

No partner may be forced to accept as a partner any person of whom she does not approve. This is partly because of the fiduciary relationship between the partners and partly because each partner has a right to take part in the management of the business, to handle the partnership's assets for partnership purposes, and to act as an agent of the partnership. An ill-chosen partner, through negligence, poor judgment, or dishonesty, may bring financial loss or ruin to her copartners. Because of this danger and because of the close relationship among the members, partnerships must necessarily be founded on mutual trust and confidence. All this finds expression in the term *delectus personae* (literally, "choice of the person"), which indicates the right one has to choose her partners. This principle is embodied in Section 401(i) of the RUPA, which provides: "A person may become a partner only with the consent of *all* of the partners." [Emphasis added.] It is because of *delectus personae* that a purchaser (assignee) of a partner's interest does not become a partner and is not entitled to participate in management. The partnership agreement may provide, however, for admission of a new partner by a less-than-unanimous vote.

ENFORCEMENT RIGHTS

As discussed, the partnership relationship creates a number of duties and rights among partners. Accordingly, partnership law provides partners and the partnership with the means to enforce these rights and duties.

RIGHT TO INFORMATION AND INSPECTION OF THE BOOKS The RUPA provides that if a partnership maintains books and records, they must be kept at its chief executive office. Section 403. A partnership must provide partners access to its books and records to inspect and copy them during ordinary business hours. Section 403(b). Former partners are given a similar right, although limited to the books and records pertaining to the period during which they were partners. A duly authorized agent on behalf of a partner may also exercise this right. A partnership may impose a reasonable charge, covering the costs of labor and material, for copies of documents furnished. The partnership agreement may *not* unreasonably restrict a partner's right of access to partnership books and records. Section 103(b)(2).

Each partner and the partnership must affirmatively disclose to a partner, *without demand*, any information concerning the partnership's business and affairs reasonably required for the proper exercise of the partner's rights and duties under the partnership agreement or the Act. Section 403(c)(1).

(In addition, under some circumstances, a disclosure duty may arise from the obligation of good faith and fair dealing.) Moreover, *on demand*, each partner and the partnership must furnish to a partner any other information concerning the partnership's business and affairs, except to the extent the demand or the information demanded is unreasonable or otherwise improper under the circumstances. The rights to receive and demand information extend also to the legal representative of a deceased partner. They may, however, be waived or varied by agreement of the partners.

Legal Action Under the RUPA a partner may maintain a direct suit against the partnership or another partner for legal or equitable relief, with or without an accounting as to partnership business, to enforce the partner's rights under the partnership agreement and the Revised Act. Section 405(b). Thus, under the RUPA, an accounting is not a prerequisite to the availability of the other remedies a partner may have against the partnership or the other partners. Since general partners are not passive investors, the RUPA does not authorize derivative actions. Reflecting the entity theory of partnership, the RUPA provides that the partnership itself may maintain an action against a partner for any breach of the partnership agreement or for the violation of any duty owed to the partnership, such as a breach of fiduciary duty. Section 405(a).

The UPA grants to each partner the right to an account whenever (1) his copartners wrongfully exclude him from the partnership business or possession of its property, (2) the partnership agreement so provides, (3) a partner makes a profit in violation of his fiduciary duty, or (4) other circumstances render it just and reasonable. UPA Section 22. If a partner does not receive or is dissatisfied with a requested account, she may bring an enforcement action, called an accounting. Designed to produce and evaluate all testimony relevant to the various claims of the partners, an accounting is an equitable proceeding for a comprehensive and effective settlement of partnership affairs.

CHAPTER SUMMARY

FORMATION OF GENERAL PARTNERSHIPS

NATURE OF PARTNERSHIP	**Definition** an association of two or more persons to carry on as co-owners a business for profit **Entity Theory** • *Partnership as a Legal Entity* an organization having a legal existence separate from that of its members; the Revised Act considers a partnership a legal entity for nearly all purposes • *Partnership as a Legal Aggregate* a group of individuals not having a legal existence separate from that of its members; the Revised Act considers a partnership a legal aggregate for few purposes
FORMATION OF PARTNERSHIP	**Partnership Agreement** it is preferable, although not usually required, that the partners enter into a written partnership agreement **Tests of Existence** the formation of a partnership requires all of the following: • *Association* two or more persons with legal capacity who agree to become partners • *Business for Profit* • *Co-ownership* includes sharing of profits and control of the business **Partnership Capital** total money and property contributed by the partners for use by the partnership **Partnership Property** sum of all of the partnership's assets, including all property acquired by the partnership

RELATIONSHIPS AMONG PARTNERS

DUTIES AMONG PARTNERS	**Fiduciary Duty** duty of utmost loyalty, fairness, and good faith owed by partners to each other and to the partnership; includes duty not to appropriate partnership opportunities, not to compete, not to have conflicts of interest, and not to reveal confidential information **Duty of Obedience** duty to act in accordance with the partnership agreement and any business decisions properly made by the partners **Duty of Care** duty owed by partners to manage the partnership affairs without gross negligence, reckless conduct, intentional misconduct, or knowing violation of law
RIGHTS AMONG PARTNERS	**Rights in Specific Partnership Property** partners have the right to use and possess partnership property for partnership purposes **Transferable Interest in Partnership** the partner's share of the profits and losses of the partnership and the partner's right to receive distributions • *Assignability* a partner may sell or assign his transferable interest in the partnership; the new owner becomes entitled to the assigning partner's right to receive distributions but does not become a partner • *Creditors' Rights* a partner's transferable interest is subject to the claims of creditors, who may obtain a charging order (judicial lien) against the partner's transferable interest **Distributions** transfer of partnership property from the partnership to a partner • *Profits* each partner is entitled to an equal share of the profits unless otherwise agreed • *Capital* a partner does not have a right to receive a distribution of the capital contributions in his account before his withdrawal or the liquidation of the partnership • *Indemnification* if a partner makes an advance (loan) to the partnership, he is entitled to repayment of the advance plus interest; a partner is entitled to reimbursement for payments made and indemnification for liabilities incurred by the partner in the ordinary course of the business • *Compensation* unless otherwise agreed, no partner is entitled to payment for services rendered to the partnership **Management** each partner has equal rights in management of the partnership unless otherwise agreed **Choice of Associates** under the doctrine of *delectus personae*, no person can become a member of a partnership without the consent of all of the partners **Enforcement Rights** • *Information* each partner has the right (1) *without demand*, to any information concerning the partnership and reasonably required for the proper exercise of the partner's rights and duties and (2) *on demand*, to any other information concerning the partnership • *Legal Action* a partner may maintain a direct suit against the partnership or another partner for legal or equitable relief to enforce the partner's rights; the partnership itself may maintain an action against a partner for any breach of the partnership agreement or for the violation of any duty owed to the partnership

Operation and Dissolution of General Partnerships

T he operation and management of a general partnership involve interactions among the partners as well as their interactions with third persons. The previous chapter covered the rights and duties of the partners among themselves. The first part of this chapter focuses on the relations among the partnership, the partners, and third persons who deal with the partnership. These relations are governed by the laws of agency, contracts, and torts as well as by the partnership statute. The second part of the chapter addresses the dissociation and dissolution of general partnerships.

RELATIONSHIP OF PARTNERSHIP AND PARTNERS WITH THIRD PARTIES

In the course of transacting business, the partnership and the partners also may acquire rights over and incur duties to third parties. For example, under the law of agency, a principal is liable upon contracts that his duly authorized agents make on his behalf and is liable in tort for the wrongful acts his employees commit in the course of their employment. Because much of the law of partnership is the law of agency, most problems arising between partners and third persons require the application of principles of agency law. The Revised Uniform Partnership Act (RUPA) makes this relationship explicit by stating that "[e]ach partner is an agent of the partnership for the purpose of its business." Section 301(1). In addition, the RUPA provides that unless displaced by particular provisions of the RUPA, the principles of law and equity supplement the RUPA. Section 104. The law of agency is discussed in *Chapters 19* and *20*.

When a partnership becomes liable to a third party, each partner has **unlimited personal liability** for that partnership obligation.

CONTRACTS OF PARTNERSHIP

The act of every partner binds the partnership to transactions *within* the scope of the partnership business unless the partner does not have actual or apparent authority to so act. If the partnership is bound, then each general partner has unlimited, personal liability for that partnership obligation unless the partnership is a limited liability partnership (LLP) and the LLP statute shields contract obligations. Under the Revised Act, the partners are jointly and severally liable for all contract obligations of the partnership. Section 306(a). **Joint and several liability** means that all of the partners may be sued jointly in one action or that separate actions, leading to separate judgments, may be maintained against each of them. Judgments obtained are enforceable, however, against property of only the defendant or defendants named in the suit; and payment of any one of the judgments satisfies all of them. The Revised Act, in keeping with its entity treatment of partnerships, requires the judgment creditor to exhaust the partnership's assets before enforcing a judgment against the separate assets of a partner. Section 307(d).

The Uniform Partnership Act (UPA) provides that partners are jointly liable on all debts and contract obligations of the partnership. UPA Section 15(b). Under **joint liability**, a creditor must bring suit against all of the partners as a group, and the judgment must be against all of the obligors. Therefore, any suit in contract against the partners must name all of them as defendants.

◆ **SEE FIGURE 32-1: Contract Liability**

AUTHORITY TO BIND PARTNERSHIP

A partner may bind the partnership by her act if (1) she has actual authority, express or implied, to perform the act; or (2) she has apparent authority to perform the act. If the act is not apparently for carrying on in the ordinary course the partnership business, then the partnership is bound only where the partner has actual authority. In such a case, the third person dealing with the partner assumes the risk that such actual authority exists. Section 301(2). Where there is neither actual authority nor apparent authority, the partnership is bound only if it ratifies the act. Ratification is discussed in *Chapter 20*.

◆ FIGURE 32-1: Contract Liability

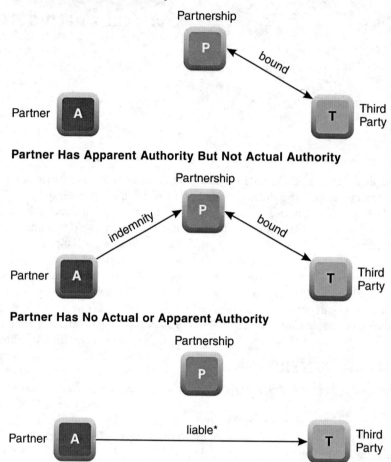

Partner Has Actual Authority

Partnership

Partner

Partner Has Apparent Authority But Not Actual Authority

Partnership

Partner

Partner Has No Actual or Apparent Authority

Partnership

Partner

*Partner is liable for breach of implied warranty of authority or misrepresentation

ACTUAL EXPRESS AUTHORITY The actual express authority of partners may be written or oral; it may be specifically set forth in the partnership agreement or in an additional agreement between the partners. In addition, it may arise from decisions made by a majority of the partners regarding ordinary matters connected with the partnership business. Section 401(j).

A partner who does not have actual authority from *all* of her partners may not bind the partnership by any act that does not apparently carry on in the ordinary course the partnership business. Sections 301(2) and 401(j). Acts outside the ordinary course of the partnership business would include the following: (1) execution of contracts of guaranty or suretyship in the firm name, (2) sale of partnership property not held for sale in the usual course of business, and (3) payment of an individual partner's debts out of partnership assets.

The Revised Act also authorizes the optional, central filing of a statement of partnership authority specifying the names of the partners authorized to execute instruments transferring real property held in the name of the partnership. A statement may also limit the authority of a partner or partners to transfer real property. In addition, a statement may grant extraordinary authority to some or all the partners, or limit their ordinary authority, to enter into transactions on behalf of the partnership. A filed statement is effective for up to five years. Section 303. A partner, or other person named as a partner, may file a statement denying any fact asserted in a statement of partnership authority, including a denial of a person's status as a partner or of another person's authority as a partner. Section 304. A statement of denial is a limitation on authority.

Section 9(3) of the UPA provides that the following acts do **not** bind the partnership unless authorized by **all** of the partners: (1) assignment of partnership property for the benefit of its creditors; (2) disposal of the goodwill of the business; (3) any act which would make it impossible to carry on the ordinary business of the partnership; (4) confession of a judgment; or (5) submission of a partnership claim or liability to arbitration or reference.

ACTUAL IMPLIED AUTHORITY Actual implied authority is neither expressly granted nor expressly denied but is reasonably deduced from the nature of the partnership, the terms of the partnership agreement, or the relations of the partners. For example, a partner has implied authority to hire and fire employees whose services are necessary to carry on the partnership business. In addition, a partner has implied authority to purchase property necessary for the business, to receive performance of obligations due to the partnership, and to bring legal actions to enforce claims of the partnership.

APPARENT AUTHORITY Apparent authority (which may or may not be actual) is authority that a third person, in view of the circumstances, the conduct of the parties, and a lack of knowledge or notification to the contrary, may reasonably believe to exist. Section 301(1) of the RUPA provides

> Each partner is an agent of the partnership for the purpose of its business. An act of a partner, including the execution of an instrument in the partnership name, for apparently carrying on in the ordinary course the partnership business or business of the kind carried on by the partnership binds the partnership, unless the partner had no authority to act for the partnership in the particular matter and the person with whom the partner was dealing knew or had received a notification that the partner lacked authority.

This section characterizes a partner as a general managerial agent having both actual and apparent authority within the scope of the firm's ordinary business. For example, a partner has apparent authority to indorse checks and notes, to make representations and warranties in selling goods, and to enter into contracts for advertising. A third person, however, may not rely upon apparent authority in any situation in which he already knows, or has received notification, that the partner does not have actual authority. A person knows a fact if the person has actual knowledge of it. A person receives a notification when the notification comes to the person's attention or is duly delivered at the person's place of business or at any other place held out by the person as a place for receiving communications. Section 102.

PARTNERSHIP BY ESTOPPEL

Partnership by estoppel imposes partnership duties and liabilities upon a nonpartner who has either represented himself or consented to be represented as a partner. It extends to a third person to whom such a representation is made

and who justifiably relies upon the representation. Section 308(a).

For example, Marks and Saunders are partners doing business as Marks and Company. Marks introduces Patterson to Taylor, describing Patterson as a member of the partnership. Patterson verbally confirms the statement made by Marks. Believing that Patterson is a member of the partnership and relying upon Patterson's good credit standing, Taylor sells goods on credit to Marks and Company. In an action by Taylor against Marks, Saunders, and Patterson as partners to recover the price of the goods, Patterson is liable although he is not a partner in Marks and Company. Taylor had justifiably relied upon the representation that Patterson was a partner in Marks and Company, to which Patterson actually consented. If, however, Taylor had known at the time of the sale that Patterson was not a partner, his reliance on the representation would not have been justified, and Patterson would not be liable.

Except in situations in which the representation of membership in a partnership has been made publicly, no person is entitled to rely upon a representation of partnership unless it is made directly to him. For example, Patterson falsely tells Dillon that he is a member of the partnership Marks and Company. Dillon casually relays this statement to Taylor, who in reliance sells goods on credit to Marks and Company. Taylor cannot hold Patterson liable, as he was not justified in relying on the representation made privately by Patterson to Dillon, which Patterson did not consent to have repeated to Taylor.

Where Patterson, however, knowingly consents to his name appearing publicly in the firm name or in a list of partners, or to be used in public announcements or advertisements in a manner which indicates that he is a partner in the firm, Patterson is liable to any member of the public who relies on the purported partnership, whether or not Patterson is aware of being held out as a partner to such person. Section 308(a).

TORTS AND CRIMES OF PARTNERSHIP

As discussed in *Chapter 20*, under the doctrine of *respondeat superior* a partnership, like any employer, may be liable for an unauthorized tort committed by its employee if the employee committed the tort in the scope of his employment. With respect to a *partner's* conduct, the RUPA provides that a partnership is liable for the loss or injury any partner causes by any wrongful act or omission, or other actionable conduct, while acting within the ordinary course of the partnership business or with the authority of the partnership. Section 305(a).

Tort liability of the partnership may include not only the negligence of the partners but also trespass, fraud, defamation, and breach of fiduciary duty, so long as the tort is committed in the course of partnership business. Moreover, though the fact that a tort is intentional does not necessarily remove it from the course of business, it is a factor to be considered. The Revised Act makes the partnership liable for no-fault torts by the addition of the phrase, "or other actionable conduct." Comment to Section 305. A partnership is also liable if a partner in the course of the partnership's business or while acting with authority of the partnership breaches a trust by receiving money or property of a person not a partner, and the partner misapplies the money or property. Section 305(b).

If the partnership is liable, each partner has **unlimited, personal liability** for the partnership obligation unless the partnership is an LLP. The liability of partners for a tort or breach of trust committed by any partner or by an employee of the firm in the course of partnership business is joint and several. Section 306. As mentioned earlier, the Revised Act requires the judgment creditor to exhaust the partnership's assets before enforcing a judgment against the separate assets of a partner. RUPA Section 307(d).

The partner who commits the tort or breach of trust is directly liable to the third party and must also **indemnify** the partnership for any damages it pays to the third party. Section 405(a).

A partner is not criminally liable for the crimes of her partners unless she authorized or participated in them. Nor is a partnership criminally liable for the crimes of individual partners or employees unless a statute imposes vicarious liability. Even under such a statute, a partnership usually is liable only in those States that have adopted the entity theory or if the statute itself expressly imposes liability upon

partnerships. Otherwise, the vicarious liability statute renders the partners liable as individuals.

◆ **SEE FIGURE 32-2: Tort Liability**

NOTICE TO A PARTNER

A partner's knowledge, notice, or receipt of a notification of a fact relating to the partnership is effective immediately as knowledge by, notice to, or receipt of a notification by the partnership, except in the case of a fraud on the partnership committed by or with the consent of that partner. Section 102(f). A person has notice of a fact if the person (1) knows of it, (2) has received a notification of it, or (3) has reason to know it exists from all of the facts known to the person at the time in question. Section 102(b).

LIABILITY OF INCOMING PARTNER

A person admitted as a partner into an existing partnership is *not* personally liable for any partnership obligations incurred before the person's admission as a partner. Section 306(b). This means that the liability of an incoming partner for **antecedent debts** and obligations of the firm is limited to his capital contribution. This restriction does not apply, of course, to **subsequent debts** (obligations arising after his admission into the partnership), for which obligations his liability is *unlimited*. For example, Nash is admitted to Higgins, Cooke, and White Co., a partnership. Nash's capital contribution is $7,500, which she paid in cash upon her

◆ **FIGURE 32-2: Tort Liability**

Tort Within Authority or Ordinary Course of Business

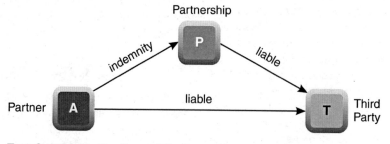

Tort Outside Authority and Ordinary Course of Business

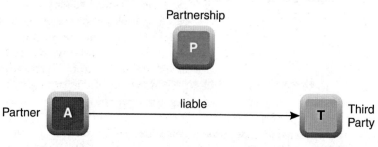

admission to the partnership. A year later, when liabilities of the firm exceed its assets by $40,000, the partnership is dissolved. Porter had lent the firm $15,000 eight months before Nash was admitted; Skinner lent the firm $20,000 two months after Nash was admitted. Nash has no liability to Porter *except* to the extent of her capital contribution, but she is *personally* liable to Skinner.

In an LLP, an incoming partner does not have personal liability for both antecedent debts *and* those subsequent debts that are shielded by that State's LLP statute.

DISSOCIATION AND DISSOLUTION OF GENERAL PARTNERSHIPS UNDER RUPA

Dissociation occurs when a partner ceases to be associated in the carrying on of the business. **Dissolution** refers to those situations when the Revised Act requires a partnership to wind up and terminate. A dissociation of a partner results in dissolution only in limited circumstances. In many instances, dissociation will result merely in a buyout of the withdrawing partner's interest rather than a winding up of the partnership. When dissociation or other cause results in dissolution, the partnership *is not terminated* but continues until the winding up of its affairs is complete. During winding up, unfinished business is completed, receivables are collected, payments are made to creditors, and the remaining assets are distributed to the partners. Termination occurs when the process is finished.

DISSOCIATION

Dissociation occurs when a partner ceases to be associated in the carrying on of the business. A number of events that were considered causes of dissociation or dissolution under the common law are no longer considered so under the RUPA. For example, the assignment of a partner's interest, a creditor's charging order on a partner's interest, and an accounting are not considered a dissociation or dissolution.

A partner has the *power* to dissociate at any time, rightfully or wrongfully, by expressing an intent to withdraw. Section 602(a). A partner does not, however, always have the *right* to dissociate. A partner who wrongfully dissociates is liable to the partnership for damages caused by the dissociation. Section 602(c). In addition, if the wrongful dissociation results in the dissolution of the partnership, the wrongfully dissociating partner is not entitled to participate in winding up the business.

WRONGFUL DISSOCIATIONS

A partner's dissociation is wrongful if it breaches an express provision of the partnership agreement. In addition, dissoci-

ation is wrongful in a *term partnership* if before the expiration of the term or the completion of the undertaking (1) the partner voluntarily withdraws by express will unless the withdrawal follows within ninety days after another partner's dissociation by death, bankruptcy, or wrongful dissociation; (2) the partner is expelled for misconduct by judicial determination; (3) the partner becomes a debtor in bankruptcy; or (4) the partner is an entity (other than a trust or estate) and is expelled or otherwise dissociated because its dissolution or termination was willful. Section 602(b). A **term partnership** is a partnership for a specific term or particular undertaking. The partnership agreement may eliminate or expand the dissociations that are wrongful or modify the effects of wrongful dissociation, except for the power of a court to expel a partner for misconduct.

RIGHTFUL DISSOCIATIONS

The RUPA provides that a partner's dissociation is wrongful only if it results from one of the events just discussed. Section 602(b). All other dissociations are rightful, including (1) in **any** partnership the death of partner, (2) in a **partnership at will** the withdrawal of a partner, (3) in **any** partnership an event occurs that was agreed to in the partnership agreement as causing dissociation, and (4) in **any** partnership a court determines that a partner has become incapable of performing the partner's duties under the partnership agreement. The RUPA defines a **partnership at will** as a partnership in which the partners have not agreed to remain partners until the expiration of a definite term or the completion of a particular undertaking. Section 101(8).

EFFECTS OF DISSOCIATION

Upon a partner's dissociation, the partner's right to participate in the management and conduct of the partnership business terminates. Section 603(b). If, however, the dissociation results in a dissolution and winding up of the business, all of the partners who have not wrongfully dissociated may participate in winding up the business. Section 804(a). The duty not to compete terminates upon dissociation, and the dissociated partner may immediately engage in a competitive business, without any further consent. The partner's other fiduciary duties and duty of care continue only with regard to matters arising and events occurring before the partner's dissociation, unless the partner participates in winding up the partnership's business. For example, a partner who leaves a partnership providing consulting services may immediately compete with the firm for new clients, but must exercise care in completing current transactions with clients and must account to the firm for any fees received from the old clients on account of those transactions.

DISSOLUTION

In accordance with the Revised Act's emphasis on the entity treatment of partnerships, only a limited subset of dissociations requires the dissolution of a partnership. In addition, some events other than dissociation can bring about the dissolution of a partnership under RUPA. The following sections discuss the causes and effects of dissolution.

CAUSES OF DISSOLUTION

The basic rule under the RUPA is that a partnership is dissolved and its business must be wound up only if one of the events listed in Section 801 occur. The events causing dissolution may be brought about by (1) an act of the partners (i.e., some dissociations), (2) operation of law, or (3) court order. The provisions of Section 801 that involve an act of the parties are default provisions: the partners may by agreement modify or eliminate these grounds. The partners may *not* vary or eliminate the grounds for dissolution based on operation of law or court order. Section 103.

DISSOLUTION BY ACT OF THE PARTNERS These causes of dissolution make up a subset of dissociations. In a **partnership at will**, a partner's giving notice of intent to withdraw will result in dissolution of a partnership. Section 801. Thus, any member of a partnership at will has the right to force a liquidation of the partnership. (The death or bankruptcy of a partner does *not* dissolve a partnership at will.)

No partner by herself has the power to dissolve a term partnership. Section 801 provides for three ways in which a **term partnership** will be dissolved.

1. The term of the partnership expires or the undertaking is complete. It should be noted that if the partners continue a term partnership after the expiration of the term or completion of the undertaking, the partnership will be treated as a partnership at will. Section 406.
2. All of the partners expressly agree to dissolve. This reflects the principle that the partners can unanimously amend the partnership agreement.
3. A partner's dissociation caused by a partner's death or incapacity, bankruptcy or similar financial impairment, or wrongful dissociation will bring on a dissolution if within ninety days after dissociation at least half of the remaining partners express their will to wind up the partnership business. Thus, if a term partnership has eight partners and one of the partners wrongfully dissociates before the end of the term, the partnership will be dissolved only if four of the remaining seven partners vote in favor of liquidation.

In **all partnerships** dissolution occurs upon the happening of an event that was specified in the partnership agreement as resulting in dissolution. The partners may, however, agree to continue the business.

DISSOLUTION BY OPERATION OF LAW A partnership is dissolved by operation of law if an event occurs that makes it unlawful to continue all or substantially all of the partnership's business. For example, a law prohibiting the production and sale of alcoholic beverages would dissolve a partnership formed to manufacture liquor. A cure of such illegality within ninety days after notice to the partnership of the event is effective retroactively. The partnership agreement cannot vary the requirement that an uncured illegal business must be dissolved and liquidated. Section 103(b)(8).

DISSOLUTION BY COURT ORDER On application by a **partner**, a court may order dissolution on grounds of another partner's misconduct or upon a finding that (1) the economic purpose of the partnership is likely to be unreasonably frustrated; (2) another partner has engaged in conduct relating to the partnership business that makes it not reasonably practicable to carry on the business in partnership with that partner; or (3) it is not otherwise reasonably practicable to carry on the partnership business in conformity with the partnership agreement. On application of a **transferee** of a partner's transferable interest or a purchaser at foreclosure of a charging order, a court may order dissolution if it determines that it is equitable to wind up the partnership business (1) at any time in a partnership at will or (2) after the term of a term partnership has expired. The partners may *not* by agreement vary or eliminate the court's power to wind up a partnership. Section 103(b)(8).

EFFECTS OF DISSOLUTION

A partnership continues after dissolution only for the purpose of winding up its business. The partnership is terminated when the winding up of its business is completed. Section 802. The remaining partners have the right, however, to continue the business after dissolution if **all** of the partners, including any dissociating partner other than a wrongfully dissociating partner, waive the right to have the partnership's business wound up and the partnership terminated. Section 802(b). In that event the partnership resumes carrying on its business as if dissolution had not occurred.

AUTHORITY Upon dissolution, the *actual authority* of a partner to act for the partnership terminates, except so far as is appropriate to wind up partnership business. Section 804. Actual authority to wind up includes the authority to complete existing contracts, to collect debts, to sell partnership assets, and to pay partnership obligations. A person winding up a partnership's business also has the authority to preserve the partnership business or property as a going concern for a reasonable time, bring and defend legal actions, settle and close the partnership's business, distribute the assets of the partnership pursuant to the RUPA, settle disputes by mediation or arbitration, and perform other necessary acts. Section 803(c).

With respect to apparent authority, the partnership is bound in a transaction not appropriate for winding up only if the partner's act would have bound the partnership before dissolution and the other party to the transaction did not have notice of the dissolution. Section 804(2). A person has notice of a fact if the person (1) knows of it, (2) has received a notification of it, or (3) has reason to know it exists from all of the facts known to the person at the time in question. Section 102(b). Moreover, RUPA Section 805 provides that, after an event of dissolution, any partner who has not wrongfully dissociated may file a statement of dissolution on behalf of the partnership and that ninety days after the filing of the statement of dissolution nonpartners are deemed to have notice of the dissolution and the corresponding limitation on the authority of all partners. Thus, after ninety days the statement of dissolution operates as constructive notice conclusively limiting the apparent authority of partners to transactions that are appropriate for winding up the business.

LIABILITY Partners are liable for their share of partnership liabilities incurred after dissolution. Section 806(a). That includes not only obligations that are appropriate for winding up the business, but also obligations that are inappropriate but within the partner's apparent authority. A partner, however, who, with knowledge of the dissolution nevertheless incurs a liability binding on the partnership by an act that is not appropriate for winding up the partnership business, is liable to the partnership for any damage caused to the partnership by the liability. Section 806(b).

WINDING UP

Whenever a dissolved partnership is not to be continued, the partnership must be liquidated. The process of liquidation, called **winding up**, involves completing unfinished business, collecting debts, taking inventory, reducing assets to cash, auditing the partnership books, paying creditors, and distributing the remaining assets to the partners. During this period, the fiduciary duties of the partners continue in effect except the duty not to compete.

PARTICIPATION IN WINDING UP After dissolution, a partner who has not wrongfully dissociated may participate in winding up the partnership's business. Section 803(a). On application of any partner, partner's legal representative, or transferee, the court may order judicial supervision of the winding up if good cause is shown. Any partner winding up the partnership is entitled to reasonable compensation for services rendered in the winding up. Section 401(h).

DISTRIBUTION OF ASSETS After all the partnership assets have been collected and reduced to cash, they are distributed to creditors and the partners. When the partnership has been profitable, the order of distribution is not critical; however, when liabilities exceed assets, the order of distribution has great importance. In winding up a partnership's business, the "assets" of the partnership include all required contributions of partners. Section 807(a).

The RUPA provides that the partnership must apply its assets first to discharge the obligations of partners who are creditors on *parity* with other creditors, subject to any other laws, such as fraudulent conveyance laws and voidable transfers under the Bankruptcy Act. Second, any surplus must be applied to pay a liquidating distribution equal to the net amount distributable to partners in accordance with their right to distributions. Section 807. (This does not distinguish between amounts owing to partners for return of capital and amounts owing to partners for profits.) The partnership agreement may vary the RUPA's rules for distributing the surplus among the partners. For example, it may distinguish between capital and operating losses, as the original UPA does.

Each partner is entitled to a settlement of all partnership accounts upon winding up. In settling accounts among the partners, profits and losses that result from the liquidation of the partnership assets must be credited and charged to the partners' accounts according to their respective shares of profits and losses. Then, the partnership must make a final liquidating distribution to those partners with a positive account balance in an amount equal to any excess of the credits over the charges in the partner's account. Any partner with a negative account balance must contribute to the partnership an amount equal to any excess of the charges over the credits in the partner's account. Section 807(b). (In an LLP a partner is *not* required to contribute for any partnership obligations for which that partner is not personally liable under the LLP statute's shield.)

Partners share proportionately in the shortfall caused by partners who fail to contribute their proportionate share. The partnership may enforce a partner's obligation to contribute. A partner is entitled to recover from the other partners any contributions in excess of that partner's share of the partnership's liabilities. After the settlement of accounts, each partner must contribute, in the proportion in which the partner shares partnership losses, the amount necessary to satisfy partnership obligations that were not known at the time of the settlement. The estate of a deceased partner is liable for the partner's obligation to contribute to the partnership.

MARSHALING OF ASSETS The Revised Act abolishes the marshaling of assets doctrine—which segregates and considers separately the assets and liabilities of the partnership and the respective assets and liabilities of the individual partners—

and the dual priority rule. Section 807. (These are discussed later in this chapter.) Under the RUPA, like the UPA, partnership creditors are entitled to be satisfied first out of partnership assets. Unlike the UPA, the Revised Act provides that unsatisfied partnership creditors may recover any deficiency out of the individually owned assets of the partners on equal footing with the partners' creditors.

DISSOCIATION WITHOUT DISSOLUTION

As already mentioned, the RUPA uses the term "dissociation," instead of the UPA term "dissolution," to denote the change in the relationship caused by a partner's ceasing to be associated in the carrying on of the business. Under the RUPA, a dissociation of a partner results in dissolution only in limited circumstances, discussed previously. Thus in many instances, dissociation will result merely in a buyout of the withdrawing partner's interest rather than a winding up of the partnership.

DISSOCIATIONS NOT CAUSING DISSOLUTION

In a **partnership at will**, a partner will be dissociated from the partnership without dissolution upon specified causes, including that partner's death, bankruptcy, or incapacity; the expulsion of that partner; or, in the case of an entity-partner, its termination. RUPA Sections 601 and 801. (As covered earlier, a partnership at will is *dissolved* upon notice of a partner's intent to withdraw.)

In a **term partnership**, if within ninety days after any specified cause of dissolution occurs, fewer than half of the remaining partners express their will to wind up the partnership business, then the partnership will not dissolve. These causes include the following: a partner's dissociation by death, bankruptcy, or incapacity; the distribution by a trust-partner of its entire partnership interest; the termination of an entity-partner; or a partner's wrongful dissociation. (A wrongful dissociation includes a partner's voluntary withdrawal in violation of the partnership agreement and the judicial expulsion of a partner.) Section 801.

With three exceptions, the partners may by agreement modify or eliminate any of the grounds for dissolution. The three exceptions are (1) carrying on an illegal business, (2) a court-ordered dissolution on application of a partner, and (3) a court-ordered dissolution on application of a transferee of a partner's interest. Section 103. Moreover, at any time after the dissolution of a partnership and before the winding up of its business is completed, all of the partners, including any dissociating partner other than a wrongfully dissociating partner, may waive the right to have the partnership's business wound up and the partnership terminated. In that event, the partnership resumes carrying on its business as if dissolution had never occurred. Section 802(b).

CONTINUATION AFTER DISSOCIATION

If a partner is dissociated from a partnership without resulting in dissolution, the remaining partners have the right to continue the business. Creditors of the partnership remain creditors of the continued partnership. Moreover, the dissociated partner remains liable for partnership obligations incurred before dissociation. Section 703(a).

The partnership must purchase the dissociated partner's interest in the partnership. Section 701. The partnership agreement can vary these rights. Section 103. The buyout price of a dissociated partner's interest is the amount that would have been distributable to the dissociating partner in a winding up of the partnership if, on the date of dissociation, the assets of the partnership were sold at a price equal to the greater of liquidation value or going concern value without the dissociated partner. The partnership must offset against the buyout price all other amounts owing from the dissociated partner to the partnership, including damages for wrongful dissociation. RUPA Section 701. These rules, however, are merely default rules, and the partnership agreement may specify the method or formula for determining the buyout price and all of the other terms and conditions of the buyout right.

A partner in a term partnership who wrongfully dissociates before the expiration of a definite term or the completion of a particular undertaking is not entitled to payment of any portion of the buyout price until the expiration of the term or completion of the undertaking, unless the partner establishes to the satisfaction of the court that earlier payment will not cause undue hardship to the business of the partnership. Section 701(h).

A partnership must indemnify a dissociated partner whose interest is being purchased against all partnership liabilities, whether incurred before or after the dissociation, except liabilities incurred by an act of the dissociated partner after dissociation that binds the partnership, as discussed later.

◆ **SEE FIGURE 32-3: Dissociation and Dissolution under RUPA**

DISSOCIATED PARTNER'S POWER TO BIND THE PARTNERSHIP

A dissociated partner has no actual authority to act for the partnership. Section 603(b)(1). With respect to apparent authority, Section 702 provides that for two years after a partner dissociates without resulting in a dissolution of the partnership business, the partnership is bound by an act of the dissociated partner which would have bound the partnership before dissociation but *only if* at the time of entering into the transaction the other party:

1. reasonably believed that the dissociated partner was then a partner;

◆ **FIGURE 32-3: Dissociation and Dissolution under RUPA**

Cause	Effects			
	Partnership at Will		Term Partnership	
	Dissociation	Dissolution	Dissociation	Dissolution
ACTS OF PARTNERS				
Assignment of partner's interest				
Accounting				
Withdrawal	•	•	•	*
Bankruptcy	•		•	*
Incapacity	•		•	*
Death	•		•	*
Expulsion of partner	•		•	
Expiration of term				•
Event specified in partnership agreement	•	•	•	•
Unanimous agreement to dissolve	•	•	•	•
OPERATION OF LAW				
Illegality		•		•
COURT ORDER				
Judicial expulsion of partner	•		•	*
Judicial determination of partner's incapacity to perform partnership duties	•		•	*
Judicial determination of economic frustration or impracticability		•		•
Application by transferee of partner's interest if equitable		•		•

* Dissolution will occur if, within ninety days after dissociation, at least half the remaining partners express their will to wind up the partnership business.

2. did not have notice of the partner's dissociation; *and*

3. is not deemed to have had constructive notice from a filed statement of dissociation.

A dissociated partner is liable to the partnership for any damage caused to the partnership arising from an obligation improperly incurred by the dissociated partner after dissociation for which the partnership is liable. Section 702(b). The dissociated partner is also personally liable to the third party for the unauthorized obligation.

A person has *notice* of a fact if he knows or has reason to know it exists from all the facts that are known to him or he has received a notification of it. Section 102(b). The RUPA provides that ninety days after a statement of dissociation is filed, nonpartners are deemed to have constructive notice of the dissociation thereby conclusively terminating a dissociated partner's apparent authority. Section 704(c). Thus, under the RUPA a partnership should notify all known creditors of a partner's dissociation and file a statement of dissociation, which will conclusively limit a dissociated partner's continuing agency power to ninety days after filing. Conversely, third parties dealing with a partnership should check for partnership filings at least every ninety days.

DISSOCIATED PARTNER'S LIABILITY TO THIRD PERSONS

A partner's dissociation does not of itself discharge the partner's liability for a partnership obligation incurred before dissociation. Section 703(a). A dissociated partner is not liable for a partnership obligation incurred more than two years after dissociation. For partnership obligations incurred within two years after a partner dissociates without resulting in a dissolution of the partnership business, a dissociated partner is liable for a partnership obligation if, at the time of entering into the transaction, the other party (1) reasonably believed that the dissociated partner was then a partner; (2) did not have notice of the partner's dissociation; *and* (3) is not deemed to have had constructive notice from a filed statement of dissociation. Section 703(b).

By agreement with the partnership creditor and the partners continuing the business, a dissociated partner may be released from liability for a partnership obligation. Section 703(c). Moreover, a dissociated partner is released from liability for a partnership obligation if a partnership creditor, with notice of the partner's dissociation but without the partner's consent, agrees to a material alteration in the nature or time of payment of a partnership obligation. Section 703(d).

DISSOLUTION OF GENERAL PARTNERSHIPS UNDER UPA

The extinguishment of a partnership consists of three stages: (1) dissolution, (2) winding up or liquidation, and (3) termination. Dissolution occurs when the partners cease to carry on the business together. Upon dissolution, the partnership is not terminated but continues until the winding up of its affairs is complete. During winding up, unfinished business is completed, receivables are collected, payments are made to creditors, and the remaining assets are distributed to the partners. Termination occurs when the process is finished.

DISSOLUTION

The UPA defines **dissolution** as the change in the relation of the partners caused by any partner's ceasing to be associated in the carrying on, as distinguished from the winding up, of the business. UPA Section 29. The following sections discuss the causes and effects of dissolution.

CAUSES OF DISSOLUTION

Dissolution may be brought about by (1) an act of the partners, (2) operation of law, or (3) court order. UPA Section 31. A number of events that were considered causes of dissolution under the common law are no longer considered so under the UPA. For example, the assignment of a partner's interest, a creditor's charging order (judicial lien) on a partner's interest, and an accounting no longer trigger dissolution.

DISSOLUTION BY ACT OF THE PARTNERS Because a partnership is a personal relationship, a partner always has the power to dissolve it by his actions, but whether he has the right to do so is determined by the partnership agreement. A partner who has withdrawn from the partnership in violation of the partnership agreement is liable to the remaining partners for damages resulting from the **wrongful dissolution**.

A partnership is **rightfully dissolved**, that is, dissolved in such a manner that the partner's or partners' act does not violate the partnership agreement (1) when all of those partners who have not assigned their interests or permitted their interests to be charged expressly agree to dissolve the partnership; (2) when the time period provided in the agreement has ended or the purpose for which the partnership was formed has been accomplished; (3) when a partner withdraws from a partnership at will, that is, a partnership with no definite term or specific undertaking; or (4) when a partner is expelled in accordance with a power to expel conferred by the partnership agreement. UPA Section 31.

DISSOLUTION BY OPERATION OF LAW A partnership is dissolved by operation of law upon (1) the death of a partner, (2) the bankruptcy of a partner or of the partnership, or (3) the subsequent illegality of the partnership, which includes any event that makes it unlawful for the partnership business to be carried on or for the members to carry on the business in partnership form. Section 31.

DISSOLUTION BY COURT ORDER Upon application by or for a partner, a court will order a dissolution if it finds that (1) a partner has been adjudicated mentally incompetent or suffers some other incapacity that prevents him from functioning as a partner; (2) a partner has engaged in conduct prejudicial to the business, has willfully or persistently breached the partnership agreement, or has conducted himself so that it is impracticable to carry on business; (3) the business can be carried on only at a loss; or (4) other circumstances render a dissolution equitable. UPA Section 32. An assignee of a partner's interest or a partner's personal creditor who has obtained a charging order against the partner's interest is entitled to a dissolution by court decree. If the partnership is not at will, however, the partnership will not be dissolved until the term or particular undertaking specified in the partnership agreement is complete.

EFFECTS OF DISSOLUTION

On dissolution, the partnership is not terminated but continues until the winding up of its affairs is complete. UPA Section 30. Moreover, dissolution does not discharge the existing liability of any partner, though it does restrict her authority to act for the partnership.

Upon dissolution, the *actual authority* of a partner to act for the partnership terminates, except so far as may be necessary to wind up partnership affairs. UPA Section 33. Actual authority to wind up includes the authority to complete existing contracts, to collect debts, to sell partnership assets, and to pay partnership obligations.

Although actual authority terminates upon dissolution, *apparent authority* continues to bind the partnership for acts within the scope of the partnership business unless the third party is given notice of the dissolution. UPA Section 35. A third party who extended credit to the partnership before dissolution may hold the partnership liable for any transaction that would have bound the partnership had dissolution not occurred, unless the third party had knowledge or actual notice of the dissolution. **Actual notice** requires a verbal statement to the third party or actual delivery of a written statement. UPA Section 3(2). On the other hand, a third party who knew of or had dealt with the partnership but who had not extended credit to it before its dissolution can hold the partnership liable unless he had knowledge, actual notice, or constructive notice of the dissolution.

Constructive notice consists of advertising a notice of dissolution in a newspaper of general circulation in the places at which the partnership regularly conducted its business. UPA Section 35(1)(b)(II). No notice need be given to third parties who had no knowledge of the partnership before its dissolution.

WINDING UP

Whenever a dissolved partnership is not to be continued, the partnership must be liquidated. The process of liquidation, called winding up, involves completing unfinished business, collecting debts, taking inventory, reducing assets to cash, auditing the partnership books, paying creditors, and distributing the remaining assets to the partners. During this period, the fiduciary duties of the partners continue in effect.

THE RIGHT TO WIND UP

Upon dissolution any partner who has not wrongfully dissolved the partnership or been rightfully expelled according to the terms of the partnership agreement has the right to insist on the winding up of the partnership unless the partnership agreement provides otherwise. Unless otherwise agreed, all nonbankrupt partners who have not wrongfully dissolved the partnership have the right to wind up the partnership affairs. UPA Section 37.

DISTRIBUTION OF ASSETS

After all the partnership assets have been collected and reduced to cash, they are distributed to creditors and the partners. When the partnership has been profitable, the order of distribution is not critical; however, when liabilities exceed assets, the order of distribution has great importance.

Section 40 of the UPA sets forth the rules for settling accounts between the parties after dissolution. It states that the liabilities of a partnership are to be paid out of partnership assets in the following order: (1) amounts owing to nonpartner creditors, (2) amounts owing to partners other than for capital and profits (loans or advances), (3) amounts owing to partners for capital, and (4) amounts owing to partners for profits. The partners may by agreement among themselves change the internal priorities of distribution (numbers 2, 3, and 4) but not the preferred position of third parties (number 1). The UPA defines partnership assets to include all partnership property as well as the contributions necessary for the payment of all partnership liabilities, which consist of numbers 1, 2, and 3. UPA Section 40(a).

In addition, the UPA provides that, in the absence of any contrary agreement, each partner shall share equally in the profits and surplus remaining after all liabilities (numbers 1, 2, and 3) are satisfied and must contribute toward the partnership's losses, capital or otherwise, according to his share in the profits. UPA Section 18(a). Thus, the proportion in which the partners bear losses depends not on their relative capital contributions but on their agreement. If no specific agreement exists, the partners bear losses in the same proportion in which they share profits.

If the partnership is insolvent, the partners individually must contribute their respective share of the losses to pay the creditors. Furthermore, if one or more of the partners is insolvent or bankrupt or is out of the jurisdiction and refuses to contribute, the other partners must contribute the additional amount necessary to pay the firm's liabilities in the relative proportions in which they share the profits. UPA Section 40(d). Any partner who pays an amount in excess of his proper share of the losses has a right of contribution against the partners who have not paid their share. UPA Section 40(f).

MARSHALING OF ASSETS

The doctrine of marshaling of assets applies only in situations in which a court of equity is administering the assets of a partnership and of its members. **Marshaling of assets** means segregating and considering separately the assets and liabilities of the partnership and the respective assets and liabilities of the individual partners. Partnership creditors are entitled to be satisfied first out of partnership assets and may recover any deficiency out of the individually owned assets of the partners. This right is subordinate, however, to the rights of nonpartnership creditors to those assets. Conversely, the nonpartnership creditors have first claim to the individually owned assets of their respective debtors, whereas their claims to partnership assets are subordinate to the claims of partnership creditors. This approach is called the "dual priority" rule.

Finally, the assets of an insolvent partner are distributed in the following order: (1) debts and liabilities owing to her nonpartnership creditors, (2) debts and liabilities owing to partnership creditors, and (3) contributions owing to other partners who have paid more than their respective share of the firm's liabilities to partnership creditors. UPA Section 40(i).

This rule, however, is no longer followed if the partnership is a debtor under the Bankruptcy Code. In a proceeding under the Federal bankruptcy law, a trustee is appointed to administer the estate of the debtor. If the partnership property is insufficient to pay all the claims against the partnership, the statute directs the trustee to seek recovery of the deficiency first from the general partners who are not bankrupt. The trustee may then seek recovery against the estates of bankrupt partners on the same basis as other creditors of the bankrupt partner. Bankruptcy Code, Section 723. This provision, although contrary to the UPA's doctrine of marshaling of assets, governs whenever partnership assets are being administered by a bankruptcy court.

CONTINUATION AFTER DISSOLUTION

Dissolution produces one of two outcomes: either the partnership is liquidated or the remaining partners continue the partnership. Whereas liquidation sacrifices the value of a going concern, continuation of the partnership after dissolution avoids this loss. The UPA, nonetheless, gives each partner the right to have the partnership liquidated except in a few instances in which the remaining partners have the right to continue the partnership. UPA Section 37.

RIGHT TO CONTINUE PARTNERSHIP

After dissolution, the remaining partners have the right to continue the partnership when (1) the partnership has been dissolved in contravention of the partnership agreement, (2) a partner has been expelled in accordance with the partnership agreement, or (3) all the partners agree to continue the business. Nevertheless, the noncontinuing partner, or his legal representative, has a right to an account of his interest against the person or partnership continuing the business as of the date of dissolution, unless otherwise agreed. UPA Section 43. Moreover, when a partner dies or retires and the surviving partners continue the business, the retired partner or the legal representative of the deceased partner is entitled to be paid the value of his interest as of the date of the dissolution as an ordinary creditor of the partnership. In addition, he is entitled to receive interest on this amount or, at his option, in lieu of interest, the profits of the business attributable to the use of his right in the property of the dissolved partnership. His rights are subordinate, however, to those of creditors of the dissolved partnership. UPA Section 42.

CONTINUATION AFTER WRONGFUL DISSOLUTION A partner who causes dissolution by wrongfully withdrawing cannot force the liquidation of the firm. The aggrieved partners may either liquidate the firm and recover damages for the breach of the partnership agreement or continue the partnership by buying out the withdrawing partner, who is entitled to realize his interest in the partnership less the amount of the damages that the other partners have sustained because of his breach. The withdrawing partner's interest is computed without considering the goodwill of the business. In addition, the remaining partners may use the capital contributions of the wrongdoing partner for the unexpired period of the partnership agreement. They must, however, indemnify the former partner against all present and future partnership liabilities. UPA Section 38(2).

CONTINUATION AFTER EXPULSION A partner expelled pursuant to the partnership agreement cannot force the liquidation of the partnership. He is entitled only (1) to be discharged from all partnership liabilities either by payment or by a novation with the creditors, and (2) to receive in cash the net amount due him from the partnership. UPA Section 38(1).

CONTINUATION AGREEMENT OF THE PARTNERS By far the best and most reliable tool for preserving a partnership business after dissolution is through a continuation agreement. Frequently used to ensure continuity in the event of a partner's death or retirement, continuation agreements permit remaining partners to keep partnership property, carry on partnership business, and specify settlements for outgoing partners.

RIGHTS OF CREDITORS

Any change in membership dissolves a partnership and forms a new one, despite the fact that the new combination may include a majority of the old partners. The creditors of the old partnership may pursue their claims against the new partnership and also may proceed to hold all of the members of the dissolved partnership personally liable. UPA Section 41. If a withdrawing partner has made arrangements with those who continue the business whereby they assume and pay all debts and obligations of the firm, the partner is still liable to creditors whose claims arose before the dissolution. If compelled to pay such debts, the withdrawing partner nonetheless has a right of indemnity against her former partners, who agreed to pay the debts but failed to do so.

A retiring partner may be discharged from his existing liabilities by entering into a novation with the continuing partners and the creditors. A creditor must agree to a novation, although his consent may be inferred from his course of dealing with the partnership after dissolution. UPA Section 36(2). Whether such dealings with a continuing partnership constitute an implied novation is a factual question of intent.

A withdrawing partner may protect herself against liability upon contracts the firm enters subsequent to her withdrawal by giving notice that she is no longer a member of the firm. Otherwise, she will be liable for debts thus incurred to creditors who had no notice or knowledge of the partner's withdrawal. Persons who had extended credit to the partnership prior to its dissolution must receive actual notice, whereas constructive notice by newspaper publication will suffice for those who knew of the partnership but had not extended credit to it before its dissolution. UPA Section 35.

CHAPTER SUMMARY

RELATIONSHIP OF PARTNERSHIP AND PARTNERS WITH THIRD PARTIES

CONTRACTS OF PARTNERSHIP	**Partners' Liability** • *Personal Liability* if the partnership is contractually bound, each partner has joint and several unlimited personal liability • *Joint and Several Liability* a creditor may sue the partners jointly as a group or separately as individuals **Authority to Bind Partnership** a partner who has actual authority (express or implied) or apparent authority may bind the partnership • *Actual Express Authority* authority set forth in the partnership agreement, in additional agreements among the partners, or in decisions made by a majority of the partners regarding the ordinary business of the partnership • *Actual Implied Authority* authority that is reasonably deduced from the nature of the partnership, the terms of the partnership agreement, or the relations of the partners • *Apparent Authority* an act of a partner for apparently carrying on in the ordinary course the partnership business or business of the kind carried on by the partnership binds the partnership, so long as that third person has no knowledge or notice of the lack of actual authority **Partnership by Estoppel** imposes partnership duties and liabilities on a nonpartner who has either represented himself or consented to be represented as a partner
TORTS AND CRIMES OF PARTNERSHIP	**Torts** the partnership is liable for loss or injury caused by any wrongful act or omission or other actionable conduct of any partner while acting within the ordinary course of the business or with the authority of her copartners; the partners are jointly and severally liable **Breach of Trust** the partnership is liable if a partner in the course of the partnership's business or while acting with authority of the partnership breaches a trust by misapplying money or property entrusted by a third person; the partners are jointly and severally liable **Crimes** a partner is not criminally liable for the crimes of her partners unless she authorized or participated in them

NOTICE TO A PARTNER	**Binds Partnership** a partnership is bound by a partner's knowledge, notice, or receipt of a notification of a fact relating to the partnership
	Notice a person has notice of a fact if the person (1) knows of it, (2) has received a notification of it, or (3) has reason to know it exists from all of the facts known to the person at the time in question
LIABILITY OF INCOMING PARTNER	**Antecedent Debts** the liability of an incoming partner for antecedent debts of the partnership is limited to her capital contribution
	Subsequent Debts the liability of an incoming partner for subsequent debts of the partnership is unlimited

DISSOCIATION AND DISSOLUTION OF GENERAL PARTNERSHIPS UNDER RUPA

DISSOCIATION	**Definition of Dissociation** change in the relation of partners caused by any partner's ceasing to be associated in carrying on of the business
	• *Term Partnership* partnership for a specific term or particular undertaking
	• *Partnership at Will* partnership in which the partners have not agreed to remain partners until the expiration of a definite term or the completion of a particular undertaking
	Wrongful Dissociation a dissociation that breaches an express provision of the partnership agreement or in a term partnership if before the expiration of the term or the completion of the undertaking (1) the partner voluntarily withdraws by express will, (2) the partner is judicially expelled for misconduct, (3) the partner becomes a debtor in bankruptcy, or (4) the partner is an entity (other than a trust or estate) and is expelled or otherwise dissociated because its dissolution or termination was willful
	Rightful Dissociation all other dissociations are rightful including the death of a partner in *any* partnership and the withdrawal of a partner in a *partnership at will*
	Effects of Dissociation terminates the dissociating partner's right to participate in the management of the partnership business and duties to partnership
DISSOLUTION	**Causes of Dissolution**
	• *Dissolution by Act of the Partners* **partnership at will**: withdrawal of a partner; **term partnership**: (1) the term ends, (2) all partners expressly agree to dissolve, or (3) a partner's dissociation is caused by a partner's death or incapacity, bankruptcy or similar financial impairment, or wrongful dissociation if within ninety days after dissociation at least half of the remaining partners express their will to wind up the partnership business; **any partnership**: an event occurs that was specified in the partnership agreement as resulting in dissolution
	• *Dissolution by Operation of Law* a partnership is dissolved by operation of law upon the subsequent illegality of the partnership business
	• *Dissolution by Court Order* a court will order dissolution of a partnership under certain conditions
	Effects of Dissolution upon dissolution a partnership is not terminated but continues until the winding up is completed
	• *Authority* a partner's actual authority to act for the partnership terminates, except so far as may be appropriate to wind up partnership affairs; apparent authority continues unless notice of the dissolution is given to a third party
	• *Liability* dissolution does not in itself discharge the existing liability of any partner; partners are liable for their share of partnership liabilities incurred after dissolution
	Winding Up completing unfinished business, collecting debts, and distributing assets to creditors and partners; also called liquidation

- *Winding Up Required* a dissolved partnership must be wound up and terminated when the winding up of its business is completed unless all of the partners, including any rightfully dissociating partner, waive the right to have the partnership's business wound up and the partnership terminated
- *Participation in Winding Up* any partner who has not wrongfully dissociated may participate in winding up the partnership's business
- *Distribution of Assets* the assets of the partnership include all required contributions of partners; the liabilities of a partnership are to be paid out of partnership assets in the following order: (1) amounts owing to nonpartner and partner creditors and (2) amounts owing to partners on their partners' accounts
- *Partnership Creditors* are entitled to be first satisfied out of partnership assets
- *Nonpartnership Creditors* share on equal footing with unsatisfied partnership creditors in the individually owned assets of their respective debtor-partners

DISSOCIATION WITHOUT DISSOLUTION	**Dissociations not Causing Dissolution**

- *Partnership at Will* a partner's death, bankruptcy, or incapacity, the expulsion of a partner, or the termination of an entity-partner results in a dissociation of that partner but does not result in a dissolution
- *Term Partnership* if within ninety days after any of the following causes of dissolution occurs, fewer than half of the remaining partners express their will to wind up the partnership business, then the partnership will not dissolve: a partner's dissociation by death, bankruptcy, or incapacity, the distribution by a trust-partner of its entire partnership interest, the termination of an entity-partner, or a partner's wrongful dissociation

Continuation after Dissociation the remaining partners have the right to continue the partnership with a mandatory buyout of the dissociating partner; the creditors of the partnership have claims against the continued partnership

Dissociated Partner's Power to Bind the Partnership a dissociated partner's actual authority to act for the partnership terminates; apparent authority continues for two years unless notice of the dissolution is given to a third party

Dissociated Partner's Liability to Third Persons a partner's dissociation does not of itself discharge the partner's liability for a partnership obligation incurred before dissociation; a dissociated partner is liable for a partnership obligation incurred within two years after a partner dissociates unless notice of the dissolution is given to a third party

Limited Partnerships and Limited Liability Companies

This chapter will consider other types of unincorporated business associations: limited partnerships, limited liability companies, limited liability partnerships, and limited liability limited partnerships. These organizations have developed to meet special business and investment needs. Consequently, each has characteristics that make it appropriate for certain purposes.

LIMITED PARTNERSHIPS

The limited partnership has proved to be an attractive vehicle for a variety of investments because of its tax advantages and the limited liability it confers upon limited partners. Unlike general partnerships, limited partnerships are statutory creations. Before 1976, the governing statute in all States except Louisiana was the Uniform Limited Partnership Act (ULPA), which was promulgated in 1916. At that time, most limited partnerships were small and had only a few limited partners. But over time, limited partnerships became much larger, typically involving a small number of major investors and a relatively large group of widely distributed investors who purchase limited partnership interests. This type of organization has evolved to attract substantial amounts of investment capital. As a result, limited partnerships have been used to muster the sizable investments necessary in areas such as real estate, oil and gas, motion pictures, professional sports, and research and development. The large scale and multistate operations of the modern limited partnership, however, have severely burdened the framework established by the ULPA.

These shortcomings prompted the National Conference of Commissioners on Uniform State Laws to develop a Revised Uniform Limited Partnership Act (RULPA), which was promulgated in 1976. According to its preface, the RULPA is "intended to modernize the prior uniform law while retaining the special character of limited partnerships as compared with corporations." In 1985, the National Conference revised the RULPA "for the purpose of more effectively modernizing, improving and establishing

uniformity in the law of limited partnerships." The 1985 Act is substantially similar to the 1976 RULPA, preserving the philosophy of the older Act and making almost no change in its basic structure. All of the States except Louisiana had adopted either the 1976 Act or the 1985 Act with a large majority of these States adopting the 1985 version.

In 2001 the National Conference of Commissioners on Uniform State Laws promulgated a new revision of the 1985 Revised Uniform Limited Partnership Act (the 2001 ReRULPA). The new Act has been drafted to reflect that limited liability partnerships and limited liability companies can meet many of the needs formerly met by limited partnerships. Accordingly, the 2001 ReRULPA adopts as default rules provisions that strongly favor current management and treat limited partners as passive investors with little control over or right to exit the limited partnership. To date, at least fifteen States have adopted the 2001 ReRULPA.

This chapter will discuss the 1985 RULPA. The ULPA, the 1976 RULPA, and the 1985 RULPA are supplemented by the Uniform Partnership Act, which applies to limited partnerships in any case for which the Limited Partnership Act does not provide. The 2001 ReRULPA is a stand-alone statute and is not linked to the Uniform Partnership Act.

◆ **SEE FIGURE 31-1: General Partnership, Limited Partnership, Limited Liability Company, and Corporation**

In addition, limited partnership interests are almost always considered to be securities, and their sale is therefore subject to State and Federal securities regulation, as discussed in *Chapter 44*.

DEFINITION

A **limited partnership** is a partnership formed by two or more persons under the laws of a State and having one or more general partners and one or more limited partners. Section 101(7). A *person* includes a natural person, partnership, limited partnership, trust, estate, association, or corporation. Section 101(11). A limited partnership differs from a general partnership in several respects, three of which are fundamental:

1. a statute providing for the formation of limited partnerships must be in effect;
2. the limited partnership must substantially comply with the requirements of that statute; and
3. the liability of a limited partner for partnership debts or obligations is limited to the extent of the capital he has contributed or has agreed to contribute.

FORMATION

Although the formation of a general partnership calls for no special procedures, the formation of a limited partnership requires substantial compliance with the limited partnership statute. Failure to so comply may result in the limited partners' not obtaining limited liability.

FILING OF CERTIFICATE Section 201 of the RULPA provides that two or more persons desiring to form a limited partnership shall file in the office of the Secretary of State of the State in which the limited partnership is to have its principal office a signed certificate of limited partnership. The certificate must include the following information:

1. the name of the limited partnership;
2. the address of the office and the name and address of the agent for service of process;
3. the name and the business address of each general partner;
4. the latest date upon which the limited partnership is to dissolve; and
5. any other matters the general partners decide to include in the certificate.

The certificate of limited partnership must be amended if a new general partner is admitted, a general partner withdraws, or a general partner becomes aware that any statement in the certificate was or has become false. Section 202. In addition, the certificate may be amended at any time for any other purpose the general partners deem proper. As discussed later, false statements in a certificate or amendment that cause loss to third parties who rely on the statements may result in liability for the general partners.

NAME The inclusion of the surname of a limited partner in the partnership name is prohibited unless it is also the name of a general partner or unless the business had operated under that name before the admission of the limited partner. A limited partner who knowingly permits his name to be used in violation of this provision is liable to any creditor who did not know that he was a limited partner. Section 303(d). In addition, a limited partnership cannot use a name that is the same as, or deceptively similar to, the name of

any corporation or other limited partnership. Section 102. Finally, the name of the limited partnership must contain the unabbreviated words "limited partnership."

CONTRIBUTIONS The contribution of a partner may be cash, property, services rendered, or a promissory note or other obligation to contribute cash or property or to perform services. Section 501. A promise by a limited partner to contribute to the limited partnership is not enforceable unless it is in a signed writing. Should a partner fail to make a required capital contribution described in a signed writing, the limited partnership may hold her liable to contribute the cash value of the stated contribution.

DEFECTIVE FORMATION A limited partnership is formed when a certificate of limited partnership that substantially complies with the requirements of the statute is filed. Therefore, the formation is defective if no certificate is filed or if the certificate filed does not substantially meet the statutory requirements. In either case, the limited liability of limited partners is jeopardized. The RULPA provides that a person who has contributed to the capital of a business (an "equity participant"), erroneously and in good faith believing that he has become a limited partner in a limited partnership, is not liable as a general partner, provided that on ascertaining the mistake he either (1) withdraws from the business and renounces future profits or (2) files a certificate or an amendment curing the defect. Section 304. The equity participant will be liable, however, to any third party who transacted business with the enterprise before the withdrawal or amendment and who in good faith believed that the equity participant was a general partner at the time of the transaction.

The 1985 RULPA does not require that the limited partners be named in the certificate. This greatly reduces the risk that an inadvertent omission of such information will expose a limited partner to liability.

FOREIGN LIMITED PARTNERSHIPS A limited partnership is considered "foreign" in any State other than the one in which it was formed. The laws of the State in which a foreign limited partnership is organized govern its organization, its internal affairs, and the liability of its limited partners. Section 901. In addition, the RULPA requires all foreign limited partnerships to register with the Secretary of State before transacting any business in a State. Section 902. Any foreign limited partnership transacting business without so registering may not bring enforcement actions in the State's courts until it registers, although it may defend itself in the State's courts. Section 907.

RIGHTS

Because limited partnerships are organized pursuant to statute, the rights of the parties are usually set forth in the certificate of limited partnership and the limited partnership agreement. Unless otherwise agreed or provided in the Act, a general partner of a limited partnership has all the rights and powers of a partner in a partnership without limited partners. Section 403. A general partner also may be a limited partner; as such, he shares in profits, losses, and distributions both as a general partner and as a limited one. Section 404.

Control The general partners of a limited partnership have almost exclusive control and management of the limited partnership. A limited partner, on the other hand, is not permitted to share in this management or control; if he does, he may forfeit his limited liability. A limited partner who participates in the control of the business is liable only to those persons who transact business with the limited partnership reasonably believing, based upon the limited partner's conduct, that the limited partner is a general partner. Section 303(a).

In addition, Section 303(b) of the RULPA provides a "safe harbor" by enumerating activities that a limited partner may perform without being deemed to have taken part in control of the business. They are the following:

1. being a contractor for, or an agent or employee of, the limited partnership or of a general partner or being an officer, director, or shareholder of a general partner that is a corporation;
2. consulting with and advising a general partner with respect to the business of the limited partnership;
3. acting as surety for the limited partnership;
4. bringing a derivative action in the right of the limited partnership;
5. requesting or attending a meeting of partners;
6. voting on one or more of the following matters:
   (a) the dissolution and winding up of the limited partnership;
   (b) the sale, exchange, lease, mortgage, pledge, or other transfer of all or substantially all of the assets of the limited partnership;
   (c) the incurrence of indebtedness by the limited partnership other than in the ordinary course of its business;
   (d) a change in the nature of the business;
   (e) the admission or removal of a general partner;
   (f) the admission or removal of a limited partner;
   (g) a transaction involving an actual or potential conflict of interest between a general partner and the limited partnership or the limited partners;
   (h) an amendment to the partnership agreement or certificate of limited partnership; or
   (i) other matters related to the business of the limited partnership which the partnership agreement states in writing may be subject to the approval or disapproval of limited partners;
7. winding up the limited partnership; or
8. exercising any other right or power permitted to limited partners under the Act.

Voting Rights The partnership agreement may grant to all or a specified group of general or limited partners the right to vote on any matter. Sections 302 and 405. If, however, the agreement grants limited partners voting powers beyond the safe harbor of Section 303, a court may hold that the limited partners have participated in control of the business. The RULPA does not require that limited partners have the right to vote on matters as a class separate from the general partners, although the partnership agreement may provide such a right.

Choice of Associates After the formation of a limited partnership, the admission of additional limited partners requires the written consent of all partners, unless the partnership agreement provides otherwise. Section 301. The admission of the new limited partner is not effective until the records of the limited partnership have been amended to reflect that fact. Regarding the admission of additional general partners, the written partnership agreement determines the procedure for authorizing their admission. The written consent of all partners is required only if the partnership agreement fails to deal with this issue. Section 401.

Withdrawal A general partner may withdraw from a limited partnership at any time by giving written notice to the other partners. Section 602. If the withdrawal violates the partnership agreement, the limited partnership may recover damages from the withdrawing general partner. A limited partner may withdraw as provided in the written partnership agreement. If the agreement does not specify when a limited partner may withdraw or a definite time for the limited partnership's dissolution, a limited partner may withdraw upon giving at least six months' prior written notice to each general partner. Section 603. Upon withdrawal, a withdrawing partner is entitled to receive any distribution to which she is entitled under the partnership agreement, subject to the restrictions on amount discussed below. If the partnership agreement makes no provision, the partner is entitled to receive the fair value of her interest in the limited partnership as of the date of withdrawal, based upon her right to share in distributions from the limited partnership. Section 604.

Assignment of Partnership Interest A partnership interest is a partner's share of the profits and losses of a limited partnership and the right to receive distributions of partnership assets. Section 101(10). A partnership interest is personal property. Section 701. Unless otherwise provided in the partnership agreement, a partner may assign his partnership interest. An assignment does not dissolve the limited partnership. The assignee, who does not become a partner, may exercise none of the rights of a partner: the assignment entitles the assignee only to receive, to the extent of the assignment, the assigning partner's share of distributions. Except as otherwise provided in the partnership agreement, a partner ceases to be a partner upon assignment of all his partnership interest. Section 702.

An assignee of a partnership interest, including an assignee of a general partner, may, however, become a *limited* partner if all the other partners consent or if the assigning partner, having such power provided in the partnership agreement, grants the assignee this right. Section 704. An assignee who becomes a limited partner is liable for the obligation of his assignor to make or return contributions, except for those liabilities unknown to the assignee at the time he became a limited partner. Section 704(b). Upon the death of a partner, her executor or administrator has all the rights of the partner for the purpose of settling her estate, including any power the deceased partner had to make her assignee a substituted limited partner. Section 705.

A creditor of a partner may obtain a charging order against a partner's interest in the partnership. To the extent of the charging order, the creditor has the rights of an assignee of the partnership interest. Section 703.

PROFIT AND LOSS SHARING Profits and losses are allocated among the partners as provided in the partnership agreement. If the agreement makes no such provision in writing, then the profits and losses are allocated on the basis of the value of the contributions each partner actually has made. Section 503. Nonetheless, limited partners usually are not liable for losses beyond their capital contribution. Section 303(a).

DISTRIBUTIONS The partners share distributions of cash or other assets of the limited partnership as provided in writing in the partnership agreement. The RULPA allows partners to share in distributions in a proportion different from that in which they share in profits. If the partnership agreement does not provide for allocation in writing, then distributions are based on the value of contributions each partner actually made. Section 504. Unless otherwise provided in writing, a partner has no right to demand a distribution in any form other than cash. Once a partner becomes entitled to a distribution, he has the status of a creditor with respect to that distribution. Section 606. A partner may not receive a distribution from a limited partnership unless the assets remaining after the distribution are sufficient to pay all partnership liabilities other than liabilities to partners on account of their partnership interests. Section 607.

LOANS Both general and limited partners may be secured or unsecured creditors of the partnership with the same rights as a person who is not a partner, subject to applicable State

and Federal bankruptcy and fraudulent conveyance statutes. Section 107.

INFORMATION The partnership must continuously maintain within the State an office at which it keeps basic organizational and financial records. Section 105. Each partner has the right to inspect and copy any of the partnership records. Each limited partner may obtain from the general partners upon reasonable demand (1) complete and accurate information regarding the business and financial condition of the limited partnership, (2) copies of the limited partnership's Federal, State, and local income tax returns for each year, and (3) any other reasonable information regarding the affairs of the limited partnership. Section 305.

DERIVATIVE ACTIONS A limited partner has the right to bring an action on behalf of a limited partnership to recover a judgment in its favor if the general partners having authority to bring the action have refused to do so. Section 1001. The Act also establishes standing and pleading requirements similar to those imposed in shareholder's derivative actions and permits the court to award reasonable expenses, including attorneys' fees, to a successful plaintiff. Section 1002.

DUTIES AND LIABILITIES

The duties and liabilities of general partners in a limited partnership are quite different from those of limited partners. A general partner is subject to all the duties and restrictions of a partner in a partnership without limited partners, whereas a limited partner is subject to few, if any, duties and enjoys limited liability.

DUTIES A *general partner* of a limited partnership owes a **fiduciary** duty to her general and limited partners. The existence of this duty is extremely important to the limited partners because of their circumscribed role in the control and management of the business enterprise. Conversely, whether a limited partner owes a fiduciary duty either to his general partners or to the limited partnership remains unclear. The very limited judicial authority on this question seems to indicate that the limited partner does not.

The RULPA does not distinguish between the duty of care owed by a general partner to a general partnership and that owed by a general partner to a limited partnership. Thus, although a general partner owes her partners a duty not to be grossly negligent (as discussed in *Chapter 31*), some courts have imposed upon general partners a higher duty of care toward *limited partners*. On the other hand, a limited partner owes no duty of care to a limited partnership as long as she remains a limited partner.

LIABILITIES One of the most appealing features of a limited partnership is the limited personal liability it offers limited partners. **Limited liability** means that a limited partner who has paid her contribution has no further liability to the limited partnership or its creditors. Thus, if a limited partner buys a 25 percent share of a limited partnership for $50,000 and does not forfeit her limited liability, her liability is limited to the $50,000 she contributed, even if the limited partnership suffers losses of $500,000. This protection is subject to three conditions discussed earlier:

1. that the partnership has substantially complied in good faith with the requirement that a certificate of limited partnership be filed;
2. that the surname of the limited partner does not appear in the partnership name; and
3. that the limited partner does not participate in control of the business.

In addition, if the certificate contains a false statement, anyone who suffers loss by reliance on that statement may hold liable any party to the certificate who knew the statement to be false when the certificate was executed. Section 207. As long as the limited partner abides by these conditions, his liability for any and all obligations of the partnership is limited to his capital contribution.

At the same time, the general partners of a limited partnership have unlimited external liability, unless the limited partnership is a limited liability limited partnership discussed later in this chapter. Also, any general partner who knew or should have known that the limited partnership certificate contained a false statement is liable to anyone who suffers loss by reliance on that statement. Moreover, a general partner is liable if he knows or should know that a statement has become false and he does not amend the certificate within a reasonable time. Accordingly, it has become a common practice for limited partnerships to be formed with a corporation or other limited liability entity as the sole general partner.

Any partner to whom any part of her contribution has been returned without violation of the partnership agreement or of the limited partnership act is liable for one year to the limited partnership, to the extent necessary to pay creditors who extended credit during the period the partnership held the contribution. Section 608. In contrast, any partner to whom any part of her contribution was returned in violation of the partnership agreement or the limited partnership act is liable to the limited partnership for six years for the amount of the contribution wrongfully returned.

◆ **SEE FIGURE 33-1: Comparison of General and Limited Partners**

DISSOLUTION

As with a general partnership, extinguishing a limited partnership involves three steps: (1) dissolution, (2) winding up or liquidation, and (3) termination. The causes of dissolution and the priorities for distributing the assets, however, differ somewhat from those in a general partnership.

CAUSES In a limited partnership, the limited partners have no right or power to dissolve the partnership, except by court decree. The death or bankruptcy of a limited partner does not dissolve the partnership. Section 801 of the RULPA specifies those events that will trigger a dissolution, after which the affairs of the partnership must be liquidated:

1. the expiration of the time period specified in the certificate;
2. the happening of events specified in writing in the partnership agreement;
3. the unanimous written consent of all the partners;
4. the withdrawal of a general partner unless either
   (a) there is at least one other general partner and the written provisions of the partnership agreement permit the remaining general partners to continue the business or (b) within ninety days all partners agree in writing to continue the business; or

◆ **FIGURE 33-1: Comparison of General and Limited Partners**

	General Partner	Limited Partner
Control	Has all the rights and powers of a partner in a partnership without limited partners	Has no right to take part in management or control
Liability	Unlimited	Limited, unless partner takes part in control or partner's name is used
Agency	Is an agent of the partnership	Is not an agent of the partnership
Fiduciary Duty	Yes	No
Duty of Care	Yes	No

5. a decree of judicial dissolution, which may be granted whenever it is not reasonably practicable to carry on the business in conformity with the partnership agreement.

A general partner's withdrawal occurs upon his retirement, assignment of all his general partnership interest, removal, bankruptcy, death, or adjudication of incompetency.

A certificate of cancellation must be filed when the limited partnership dissolves and winding up commences. Section 203.

WINDING UP Unless otherwise provided in the partnership agreement, the general partners who have not wrongfully dissolved the limited partnership may wind up its affairs. Section 803. The limited partners may wind up the limited partnership if all the general partners have wrongfully dissolved the partnership. But any partner, his legal representative, or his assignee may obtain a winding up by court order if cause is shown.

DISTRIBUTION OF ASSETS Section 804 sets forth the priorities in distributing the assets of a limited partnership:

1. to creditors, including partners who are creditors, except with respect to liabilities for distributions;

2. to partners and ex-partners in satisfaction of liabilities for unpaid distributions;

3. to partners for the return of their contributions, except as otherwise agreed; and

4. to partners for their partnership interests in the proportions in which they share in distributions, except as otherwise agreed.

General and limited partners rank equally unless the partnership agreement provides otherwise.

LIMITED LIABILITY COMPANIES

A limited liability company (LLC) is another form of unincorporated business association. Prior to 1990, only two States had statutes permitting LLCs. Now all States have enacted LLC statutes. Until 1995, there was no uniform statute on which States might base their LLC legislation, and since its promulgation twelve States have adopted the Uniform Limited Liability Company Act (ULLCA), which was amended in 1996. (In 2006 the Revised ULLCA was completed but to date only four States have adopted it. The Revised ULLCA will *not* be covered in this chapter.) Therefore, the enabling legislation varies from State to State. Nevertheless, the LLC statutes generally share certain characteristics.

A **limited liability company** is a noncorporate business organization that provides limited liability to *all* of its owners (members) and permits all of its members to participate in management of the business. It may elect not to be a sep-

arate taxable entity, in which case only the members are taxed. (Publicly traded LLCs, however, are subject to corporate income taxation.) If an LLC has only one member, then it will be taxed as a sole proprietorship, unless separate entity tax treatment is elected. Thus, the LLC provides many of the advantages of a general partnership plus limited liability for all its members. Its benefits outweigh those of a limited partnership in that all members of an LLC not only enjoy limited liability but also may participate in management and control of the business. LLCs have become the most popular and widely used unincorporated business form that provides limited liability for its members. The most frequent use of LLCs has been in real estate transactions (about one-half of all LLCs), professional services, construction, finance, and retail. Ownership interests in an LLC may be considered to be securities, especially interests in those LLCs operated by managers. If a particular LLC interest is considered a security, its sale would be subject to State and Federal securities regulation, as discussed in *Chapter 44.*

◆ **SEE FIGURE 31-1: General Partnership, Limited Partnership, Limited Liability Company, and Corporation**

FORMATION

The formation of an LLC requires substantial compliance with a State's LLC statute. All States permit an LLC to have only one member. Once formed, an LLC is a separate legal entity that is distinct from its members, who are normally not liable for its debts and obligations. An LLC can contract in its own name and is generally permitted to carry on any lawful purpose, although some statutes restrict the permissible activities of LLCs.

FILING The LLC statutes generally require the central public filing of articles of organization in a designated State office. The States vary regarding the information they require the articles to include, but all require at least the following: (1) the name of the firm, (2) the address of the principal place of business or registered office, and (3) the name and address of the agent for service of process. Most LLC statutes provide that the acceptance for filing is conclusive evidence that the LLC has been properly formed, except against the State in an involuntary dissolution or certificate revocation proceeding. Most LLC statutes require the articles to state whether the LLC will be managed by managers. Most States provide that LLCs have perpetual existence unless the members agree otherwise. The articles of organization may be amended by filing articles of amendment. In most States LLCs must file annual reports with the State.

NAME LLC statutes generally require the name of the LLC to include the words *limited liability company* or the abbreviation

LLC. A number of States also permit the use of the name *limited company* and the abbreviation *LC.* The name of each LLC must be distinguishable from other firms doing business within the State.

CONTRIBUTION The contribution of a member to an LLC may be cash, property, services rendered, a promissory note, or other obligation to contribute cash, property, or to perform services. Most LLC statutes require both a written agreement to make a contribution and a written record of contributions. Members are liable to the LLC for failing to make an agreed contribution.

OPERATING AGREEMENT The members of most LLCs adopt an **operating agreement**, which is the basic contract among the members governing the affairs of an LLC and stating the various rights and duties of the members and any managers. The operating agreement is subordinate to Federal and State law. LLC statutes generally do not require the operating agreement to be in writing, although some statutes permit modification of certain statutory rules to be only by written provision in an operating agreement. Unless the operating agreement provides otherwise, the members may amend it only by unanimous consent.

FOREIGN LIMITED LIABILITY COMPANIES An LLC is considered "foreign" in any State other than that in which it was formed. LLC statutes typically provide that the laws of the State in which a foreign LLC is organized govern its organization, its internal affairs, and the liability of its members and managers. Foreign LLCs must register with the Secretary of State before transacting any business in a State. Any foreign LLC transacting business without so registering may not bring enforcement actions in the State's courts until it registers, although it may defend itself in the State's courts.

RIGHTS OF MEMBERS

A member has no property interest in property owned by the LLC. On the other hand, a member does have an interest in the LLC, which is personal property. A member's interest in the LLC includes two components:

1. the **financial interest**, which is the right to share profits and losses and to receive distributions, and
2. the **management interest**, which consists of all other rights granted to a member by the LLC operating agreement and the LLC statute. The management interest typically includes the right to manage, vote, obtain information, and bring enforcement actions.

PROFIT AND LOSS SHARING The LLC's operating agreement determines how the partners allocate the profits and losses. If the LLC's operating agreement makes no such provision, the profits and losses are typically allocated on the basis of the value of the members' contributions. The ULLCA's default rule and a few States follow the partnership model under which profits are divided equally. Section 405.

DISTRIBUTIONS LLC statutes do not provide LLC members the right to distributions before withdrawal from the LLC. Therefore, the members share distributions of cash or other assets of an LLC as provided in the operating agreement. If the LLC's operating agreement does not allocate distributions, they are typically made on the basis of the contributions each member made. Almost all LLC statutes give creditors a remedy against members who receive wrongful distributions and many also impose liability on members and managers who approved the wrongful distributions. The statutes vary in defining what constitutes a wrongful distribution, but most make a distribution wrongful if the LLC is insolvent or if the distribution would make the LLC insolvent.

WITHDRAWAL Some statutes permit a member to withdraw and demand payment of her interest upon giving the notice specified in the statute or the LLC's operating agreement. Some of the statutes permit the operating agreement to deny members the right to withdraw from the LLC.

MANAGEMENT Nearly all LLC statutes provide that, in the absence of a contrary agreement, each member has equal rights in the management of the LLC. All LLC statutes permit LLCs to be managed by one or more managers who may, but need not, be members. In a member-managed LLC, the members have actual and apparent authority to bind the LLC. In a manager-managed LLC, the managers have this authority, while the members have no actual or apparent authority to bind the manager-managed LLC. Most statutes require a publicly filed document to elect a manager-managed structure; a few statutes permit the operating agreement to make that election.

VOTING Most of the LLC statutes specify the voting rights of members, subject to a contrary provision in an LLC's operating agreement. In some States the default rule for voting follows a partnership approach (each member has equal voting rights), while the other States take a corporate approach (voting is based on the financial interests of members). Typically, members have the right to vote on proposals to (1) adopt or amend the operating agreement, (2) admit any person as a member, (3) sell all or substantially all of the LLC's assets prior to dissolution, and (4) merge the LLC with another LLC or other business entity. Some LLC statutes authorize voting by proxy. A **proxy** is a member's authorization to an agent to vote for the member.

INFORMATION The LLC must keep basic organizational and financial records. Each member has the right to inspect the LLC records.

DERIVATIVE ACTIONS A member has the right to bring an action on behalf of an LLC to recover a judgment in its favor if the managers or members with authority to bring the action have refused to do so.

ASSIGNMENT OF LLC INTEREST Unless otherwise provided in the LLC's operating agreement, a member may assign his financial interest in the LLC. An assignment does not dissolve the LLC. The assignment only entitles the assignee to receive, to the extent of the assignment, the assigning member's share of distributions. A judgment creditor of a member may obtain a charging order against the member's financial interest in the LLC. The charging order gives the creditor the same rights as an assignee to the extent of the interest charged.

The assignee does not become a member and may not exercise any management rights of a member. However, an assignee of a financial interest in an LLC may acquire the other rights by being admitted as a member of the company by all the remaining members. (Some States allow admission by majority vote.) In most States this unanimous acceptance rule is now a default rule, and the operating agreement may eliminate or modify it. For example, the ULLCA provides, "A transferee of a [financial] interest may become a member of a limited liability company if and to the extent that the transferor gives the transferee the right in accordance with authority described in the operating agreement or all other members consent." Section 503(a).

DUTIES

As with general partnerships and limited partnerships, the duties of care and loyalty also apply to LLCs. In a number of States, the LLC statute expressly imposes these duties. In other States, the common law imposes these duties. Some statutes also expressly impose an obligation of good faith and fair dealing. Who has these duties in an LLC depends upon whether the LLC is a manager-managed LLC (analogous to a limited partnership) or a member-managed LLC (analogous to a partnership).

MANAGER-MANAGED LLCs Most LLC statutes impose upon the managers of an LLC a duty of care. In some States, this is a duty to refrain from grossly negligent, reckless, or intentional conduct; in other States, it is a duty to act in good faith and as a prudent person would in similar circumstances. Managers also have a fiduciary duty, although the statutes vary in how they specify that duty. Usually, members of manager-managed LLCs have no duties to the LLC or its members by reason of being a member.

MEMBER-MANAGED LLCs Members of member-managed LLCs have the same duties of care and loyalty that managers have in manager-managed LLCs.

◆ **SEE FIGURE 33-2: Comparison of Member-Managed and Manager-Managed LLCs**

LIABILITIES

One of the most appealing features of an LLC is the limited personal liability it offers to all its members and managers. Statutes typically provide that no member or manager of an LLC shall be obligated personally for any debt, obligation, or liability of the LLC solely by reason of being a member or acting as a manager of the LLC. The limitation on liability, however, will not affect the liability of a member or manager who committed the wrongful act. A member or manager is also personally liable for any LLC obligations guaranteed by the member or manager.

As mentioned earlier, a member who fails to make an agreed contribution is liable to the LLC for the deficiency.

◆ **FIGURE 33-2: Comparison of Member-Managed and Manager-Managed LLCs**

	Member of Member-Managed LLC / Manager of Manager-Managed LLC	Member of Manager-Managed LLC
Control	Full	None
Liability	Limited	Limited
Agency	Is an agent of the LLC	Is not an agent of the LLC
Fiduciary Duty	Yes	No
Duty of Care	Yes	No

Note: LLC = limited liability company.

Moreover, under the great majority of statutes, any member who receives a distribution or return of her contribution in violation of the LLC's operating agreement or the LLC statute is liable to the LLC for the amount of the contribution wrongfully returned. Under a few of the statutes, even members who receive a return of their capital contribution without violating the LLC agreement or the LLC statute remain liable to the LLC for a specified time to the extent necessary to pay creditors.

DISSOLUTION

LLC statutes generally provide that an LLC will automatically dissolve upon the following:

1. the expiring of the LLC's agreed duration or the happening of any of the events specified in the articles,
2. the written consent of all the members, or
3. a decree of judicial dissolution typically on the grounds that "it is not reasonably practicable to carry on the LLC's activities in conformity with the articles of organization and the operating agreement" or, under some statutes, the members or managers have acted illegally, fraudulently, or oppressively.

LLC statutes require a public filing in connection with dissolution. For example, after winding up the company, the ULLCA and some LLC statutes provide for the filing of articles of termination stating (1) the name of the company, (2) the date of the dissolution, and (3) that the company's business has been wound up and the legal existence of the company has been terminated. Other statutes require either (1) a public filing of the intent to dissolve at the time of dissolution or (2) filings at both the time of dissolution and after winding up.

DISSOCIATION Dissociation means that a member has ceased to be associated with the company through voluntary withdrawal, death, incompetence, expulsion, or bankruptcy. Initially, many LLC statutes required an LLC to be dissolved upon the dissociation of a member. Most statutes permitted the nondissociating members by unanimous consent to continue the LLC after a member dissociates. Some allowed continuation by majority vote. Although some States still retain these provisions, an increasing number of States (currently about half of the States) and the amended ULLCA have eliminated a member's dissociation as a mandatory cause of dissolution.

WINDING UP An LLC continues after dissolution only for the purpose of winding up its business, which involves completing unfinished business, collecting debts, disposing of inventory, reducing assets to cash, paying creditors, and distributing the remaining assets to the members. During this period, the fiduciary duties of members and managers continue.

AUTHORITY Upon dissolution, the *actual authority* of a member or manager to act for the LLC terminates, except so far as is appropriate to wind up LLC business. Actual authority to wind up includes the authority to complete existing contracts, to collect debts, to sell LLC assets, and to pay LLC obligations. In addition, some statutes expressly provide that after dissolution, members and managers continue to have *apparent* authority to bind the company that they had prior to dissolution provided that the third party did not have notice of the dissolution.

DISTRIBUTION OF ASSETS Most statutes provide default rules for distributing the assets of an LLC as follows:

1. to creditors, including members and managers who are creditors, except with respect to liabilities or distributions;
2. to members and former members in satisfaction of liabilities for unpaid distributions, except as otherwise agreed;
3. to members for the return of their contributions, except as otherwise agreed; and
4. to members for their LLC interests in the proportions in which members share in distributions, except as otherwise agreed.

PROTECTION OF CREDITORS Many LLC statutes establish procedures to safeguard the interests of the LLC's creditors. Such procedures typically include the required mailing of notice of dissolution to known creditors, a general publication of notice, and the preservation of claims against the LLC for a specified time. For example, the ULLCA provides that a claim against the LLC is barred unless a proceeding to enforce the claim is commenced within five years after publication of the notice of dissolution.

MERGERS AND CONVERSIONS

Most LLC statutes expressly provide for mergers. A **merger** of two or more entities is the combination of all of their assets. One of the entities, known as the *surviving entity*, receives title to all the assets. The other party or parties to the merger, known as the *merged entity* or entities, is merged into the surviving entity and ceases to exist as a separate entity. Thus, if Alpha LLC and Beta LLC combine into the Alpha LLC, Alpha is the surviving LLC and Beta is the merged LLC. The ULLCA provides that an LLC may be merged with or into one or more limited liability companies, corporations, partnerships, limited partnerships, or other entities.

The LLC statutes vary with respect to the voting rights of the members regarding approval of a merger. Some provide for a majority or unanimous vote; others leave it to the operating agreement. Some statutes require the filing of articles of merger; others require a merged LLC to file articles of dissolution. Upon the required filing the merger is effective, and the separate existence of each merged entity terminates. All property owned by each of the merged entities vests in the surviving entity, and all debts, liabilities, and other obligations of each merged entity become the obligations of the surviving entity.

Many LLC statutes provide for the conversion of another business entity into an LLC. LLC statutes and other business association statutes also provide for an LLC to be converted into another business entity. The converted entity remains the same entity that existed before the conversion.

OTHER TYPES OF UNINCORPORATED BUSINESS ASSOCIATIONS

LIMITED LIABILITY PARTNERSHIPS

All of the States have enacted statutes enabling the formation of limited liability partnerships (LLPs). Until 1997 there was no uniform LLP statute, so the enabling statutes vary from State to State. In 1997 the Revised Uniform Partnership Act (RUPA) was amended to add provisions enabling general partnerships to elect to become LLPs, and more than thirty States have adopted this version of the RUPA. A registered **LLP** is a general partnership that, by making the statutorily required filing, limits the liability of its partners for some or all of the partnership's obligations.

FORMALITIES To become an LLP, a general partnership must file with the Secretary of State an application containing specified information. The RUPA requires the partnership to file a statement of qualification. RUPA Section 1001(c). Most of the statutes require only a majority of the partners to authorize registration as an LLP; others require unanimous approval. The RUPA requires unanimity unless the partnership agreement provides otherwise. RUPA Section 1001(b). Some statutes require renewal of registrations annually; other statutes require periodic reports; and a few require no renewal. The RUPA requires filing annual reports. RUPA Section 1003. Some statutes require a new filing after any change in membership of the partnership, but a few of the statutes do not. The RUPA does not.

DESIGNATION All statutes require LLPs to designate themselves as such. Most statutes require the name of the LLP to include the words *limited liability partnership* or *registered limited liability partnership*, or the abbreviation *LLP* or *RLLP*. Most statutes provide that the laws of the jurisdiction under which a foreign LLP is registered shall govern its organization, internal affairs, and the liability and authority of its partners. Many, but not all, of the statutes require a foreign

LLP to register or obtain a certificate of authenticity. The RUPA requires a foreign LLP to qualify and file annual reports. RUPA Sections 1102 and 1003.

LIABILITY LIMITATION LLP statutes have taken three different approaches to limiting the liability of partners for the partnership's obligations. The earliest statutes limited liability for negligent acts only; they retained unlimited liability for all other obligations. The next generation of statutes extended limited liability to any partnership tort or contract obligation that arose from negligence, malpractice, wrongful acts, or misconduct committed by any partner, employee, or agent of the partnership. Unlimited liability remained for ordinary contract obligations, such as those owed to suppliers, lenders, and landlords. The first two generations of LLP statutes are called "partial shield" statutes. Many of the more recent statutes (called "full shield" statutes) have provided limited liability for all debts and obligations of the partnership, including Section 306(c) of the RUPA. Most States have now adopted full shield statutes although some States still provide only a partial shield.

The statutes, however, generally provide that the limitation on liability will not affect the liability of (1) a partner who committed the wrongful act giving rise to the liability and (2) a partner who supervised the partner, employee, or agent of the partnership who committed the wrongful act. A partner is also personally liable for any partnership obligations guaranteed by the partner. The statutes also provide that the limitations on liability will apply only to claims that arise while the partnership was a registered LLP. Accordingly, partners would have unlimited liability for obligations that either arose before registration or after registration lapses.

◆ **SEE FIGURE 33-3: Liability Limitations in LLPs**

LIMITED LIABILITY LIMITED PARTNERSHIPS

A **limited liability limited partnership** (LLLP) is a limited partnership in which the liability of the general partners has been limited to the same extent as in an LLP. A growing number of States allow limited partnerships to become LLLPs. A number of States have statutes expressly providing for LLLPs. In other States, by operation of the provision in the RULPA that a general partner in a limited partnership assumes the liabilities of a general partner in a general partnership, the LLP statute may provide limited liability to general partners in a limited partnership that registers as an LLLP under the LLP statute. Where authorized, the general partners in an LLLP will obtain the same degree of liability limitation that general partners can achieve in LLPs. Where available, a limited partnership may register as an LLLP without having to form a new organization, as would be the case in converting to an LLC.

◆ **FIGURE 33-3: Liability Limitations in LLPs**

LLP Statutes	Limited Liability	Unlimited Liability
First Generation	Negligent acts	• All other obligations • Wrongful partner • Supervising partner
Second Generation	Tort and contract obligations arising from wrongful acts	• All other obligations • Wrongful partner • Supervising partner
Third Generation	All obligations	• Wrongful partner • Supervising partner

Note: LLP = limited liability partnership.

The new revision of the RULPA promulgated in 2001, which has been adopted by at least fifteen States, provides that an LLLP "means a limited partnership whose certificate of limited partnership states that the limited partnership is a limited liability limited partnership." Section 102(9). The revision provides a full shield for general partners in LLLPs:

An obligation of a limited partnership incurred while the limited partnership is a limited liability limited partnership, whether arising in contract, tort, or otherwise, is solely the obligation of the limited partnership. A general partner is not personally liable . . . for such an obligation solely by reason of being or acting as a general partner.

Section 404(c). Moreover, under the revision, a *limited* partner cannot be held liable for the partnership debts even if he participates in the management and control of the limited partnership.

CHAPTER SUMMARY

LIMITED PARTNERSHIPS

Definition of a Limited Partnership a partnership formed by two or more persons under the laws of a State and having one or more general partners and one or more limited partners

Formation a limited partnership can be formed only by substantial compliance with a State limited partnership statute
- *Filing of Certificate* two or more persons must file a signed certificate of limited partnership
- *Name* inclusion of a limited partner's surname in the partnership name in most instances will result in the loss of the limited partner's limited liability
- *Contributions* may be cash, property, services, or a promise to contribute cash, property, or services
- *Defective Formation* if no certificate is filed or if the one filed does not substantially meet the statutory requirements, the formation is defective and the limited liability of the limited partners is jeopardized
- *Foreign Limited Partnerships* a limited partnership is considered "foreign" in any State other than that in which it was formed

Rights a general partner in a limited partnership has all the rights and powers of a partner in a general partnership
- *Control* the general partners have almost exclusive control and management of the limited partnerships; a limited partner who participates in the control of the limited partnership may lose limited liability

- *Voting Rights* the partnership agreement may grant to all or a specified group of general or limited partners the right to vote on any matter
- *Choice of Associates* no person may be added as a general partner or a limited partner without the consent of all partners
- *Withdrawal* a general partner may withdraw from a limited partnership at any time by giving written notice to the other partners; a limited partner may withdraw as provided in the limited partnership certificate
- *Assignment of Partnership Interest* unless otherwise provided in the partnership agreement, a partner may assign his partnership interest; an assignee may become a substituted limited partner if all other partners consent
- *Profit and Loss Sharing* profits and losses are allocated among the partners as provided in the partnership agreement; if the partnership agreement has no such provision, then profits and losses are allocated on the basis of the contributions each partner actually made
- *Distributions* the partners share distributions of cash or other assets of a limited partnership as provided in the partnership agreement
- *Loans* both general and limited partners may be secured or unsecured creditors of the partnership
- *Information* each partner has the right to inspect and copy the partnership records
- *Derivative Actions* a limited partner may sue on behalf of a limited partnership if the general partners refuse to bring the action

Duties and Liabilities
- *Duties* general partners owe a duty of care and loyalty (fiduciary duty) to the general partners, the limited partners, and the limited partnership; limited partners do not
- *Liabilities* the general partners have unlimited liability; the limited partners have limited liability (liability for partnership obligations only to the extent of the capital that they contributed or agreed to contribute)

Dissolution
- *Causes* the limited partners have neither the right nor the power to dissolve the partnership, except by decree of the court; the following events trigger a dissolution: (1) the expiration of the time period; (2) the withdrawal of a general partner, unless all partners agree to continue the business; or (3) a decree of judicial dissolution
- *Winding Up* unless otherwise provided in the partnership agreement, the general partners who have not wrongfully dissolved the partnership may wind up its affairs
- *Distribution of Assets* the priorities for distribution are as follows: (1) creditors, including partners who are creditors; (2) partners and ex-partners in satisfaction of liabilities for unpaid distributions; (3) partners for the return of contributions, except as otherwise agreed; and (4) partners for their partnership interests in the proportions in which they share in distributions, except as otherwise agreed

---

LIMITED LIABILITY COMPANIES

Definition a limited liability company is a noncorporate business organization that provides limited liability to all of its owners (members) and permits all of its members to participate in management of the business

Formation the formation of an LLC requires substantial compliance with a State's LLC statute
- *Filing* the LLC statutes generally require the central filing of articles of organization in a designated State office
- *Name* LLC statutes generally require the name of the LLC to include the words *limited liability company* or the abbreviation *LLC*

- *Contribution* the contribution of a member to an LLC may be cash, property, services rendered, a promissory note, or other obligation to contribute cash, property, or to perform services
- *Operating Agreement* the basic contract governing the affairs of an LLC and stating the various rights and duties of the members
- *Foreign Limited Liability Companies* an LLC is considered "foreign" in any State other than that in which it was formed

Rights of Members a member's interest in the LLC includes the financial interest (the right to distributions) and the management interest (which consists of all other rights granted to a member by the LLC operating agreement and the LLC statute)

- *Profit and Loss Sharing* the LLC's operating agreement determines how the partners allocate the profits and losses; if the LLC's operating agreement makes no such provision, the profits and losses are typically allocated on the basis of the value of the members' contributions
- *Distributions* the members share distributions of cash or other assets of an LLC as provided in the operating agreement; if the LLC's operating agreement does not allocate distributions, they are typically made on the basis of the contributions each member made
- *Withdrawal* a member may withdraw and demand payment of her interest upon giving the notice specified in the statute or the LLC's operating agreement
- *Management* in the absence of a contrary agreement, each member has equal rights in the management of the LLC, but LLCs may be managed by one or more managers who may be members
- *Voting* LLC statutes usually specify the voting rights of members, subject to a contrary provision in an LLC's operating agreement
- *Information* LLCs must keep basic organizational and financial records; each member has the right to inspect the LLC records
- *Derivative Actions* a member has the right to bring an action on behalf of an LLC to recover a judgment in its favor if the managers or members with authority to bring the action have refused to do so
- *Assignment of LLC Interest* Unless otherwise provided in the LLC's operating agreement, a member may assign his financial interest in the LLC; an assignee of a financial interest in an LLC may acquire the other rights by being admitted as a member of the company if all the remaining members consent or the operating agreement so provides

Duties

- *Manager-Managed LLCs* The managers of a manager-managed LLC have a duty of care and loyalty; usually, members of a manager-managed LLC have no duties to the LLC or its members by reason of being members
- *Member-Managed LLCs* members of member-managed LLCs have the same duties of care and loyalty that managers have in manager-managed LLCs

Liabilities no member or manager of an LLC is obligated personally for any debt, obligation, or liability of the LLC solely by reason of being a member or acting as a manager of the LLC

Dissolution an LLC will automatically dissolve upon (1) in some States, the dissociation of a member, (2) the expiration of the LLC's agreed duration or the happening of any of the events specified in the articles, (3) the written consent of all the members, or (4) a decree of judicial dissolution

- *Dissociation* means that a member has ceased to be associated with the company through voluntary withdrawal, death, incompetence, expulsion, or bankruptcy
- *Winding Up* completing unfinished business, collecting debts, and distributing assets to creditors and members; also called liquidation

- *Authority* the actual authority of a member or manager to act for the LLC terminates, except so far as may be appropriate to wind up LLC affairs; apparent authority continues unless notice of the dissolution is given to a third party
- *Distribution of Assets* the default rules for distributing the assets of an LLC are (1) to creditors, including members and managers who are creditors, except with respect to liabilities for distributions; (2) to members and former members in satisfaction of liabilities for unpaid distributions, except as otherwise agreed; (3) to members for the return of their contributions, except as otherwise agreed; and (4) to members for their LLC interests in the proportions in which members share in distributions, except as otherwise agreed

Mergers
- *Definition* the combination of the assets of two or more business entities into one of the entities
- *Effect* the surviving entity receives title to all of the assets of the merged entities and assumes all of their liabilities; the merged entities cease to exist

---

OTHER TYPES OF UNINCORPORATED BUSINESS ASSOCIATIONS

Limited Liability Partnership a general partnership that, by making the statutorily required filing, limits the liability of its partners for some or all of the partnership's obligations
- *Formalities* most statutes require only a majority of the partners to authorize registration as an LLP; others require unanimous approval
- *Designation* the name of the LLP must include the words *limited liability partnership* or *registered limited liability partnership* or the abbreviation *LLP*
- *Liability Limitation* some statutes limit liability only for negligent acts; others limit liability to any partnership tort or contract obligation that arose from negligence, malpractice, wrongful acts, or misconduct committed by any partner, employee, or agent of the partnership; most provide limited liability for all debts and obligations of the partnership

Limited Liability Limited Partnership a limited partnership in which the liability of the general partners has been limited to the same extent as in an LLP

COLUMN: © PHOTOGRAPHEROLYMPUS   CLOUDS: © KERTLIS

Nature, Formation, and Powers

A corporation is an entity created by law whose existence is distinct from that of the individuals whose initiative, property, and control enable it to function. In the opinion of the Supreme Court in *Dartmouth College v. Woodward*, 17 U.S. (4 Wheat.) 518, 4 L.Ed. 629 (1819), Chief Justice Marshall stated,

A corporation is an artificial being, invisible, intangible, and existing only in contemplation of law. Being the mere creature of law, it possesses only those properties which the charter of its creation confers upon it, either expressly or as incidental to its very existence. These are such as are supposed best calculated to effect the object for which it was created. Among the most important are immortality, and, if the expression may be allowed, individuality; properties by which a perpetual succession of many persons are considered as the same, so that they may act as a single individual. A corporation manages its own affairs, and holds property without the hazardous and endless necessity of perpetual conveyances for the purpose of transmitting it from hand to hand.

The corporation is the dominant form of business organization in the United States, accounting for 85 percent of the gross revenues of all business entities. Approximately 6 million domestic corporations, with annual revenues approaching $30 trillion and assets exceeding $50 trillion, are currently doing business in the United States. Approximately 50 percent of American households own stock directly or indirectly through institutional investors, such as mutual funds, pension funds, banks, and insurance companies. Corporations have achieved this dominance because their attributes of limited liability, free transferability of shares, and continuity have attracted great numbers of widespread investors. Moreover, the centralized management of corporations has facilitated the development of large organizations that employ great quantities of invested capital, thereby utilizing economies of scale.

Use of the corporation as an instrument of commercial enterprise has made possible the vast concentrations of wealth and capital that have largely transformed this country's economy from an agrarian to an industrial one. Due to its size, power, and impact, the business corporation is a key institution not only in the American economy but also in the world power structure.

In 1946, a committee of the American Bar Association, after careful study and research, submitted a draft of a Model Business Corporation Act (MBCA). The MBCA has been amended frequently since then. Although the provisions of the Act do not become law until enacted by a State, its influence has been widespread; and a majority of the States had adopted it in whole or in part.

In 1984, the Committee on Corporate Laws of the Section of Corporation, Banking, and Business Law of the American Bar Association approved a Revised Model Business Corporation Act (RMBCA). The Revised Act is the first complete revision of the Model Act in more than thirty years, although the Act had been amended frequently since it was first published. More than half of the States have adopted it in whole or in part. The Revised Act is "designed to be a convenient guide for revision of state business corporation statutes, reflecting current views as to the appropriate accommodation of the various commercial and social interests involved in modern business corporations." One of the tasks of the revision was to organize the provisions of the Model Act more logically and to revise the language to make the Act more consistent. In addition, substantive changes were made in a number of areas. More than half of the States have adopted the Revised Act in whole or in part, although Delaware and seven of the ten most populous States have *not* adopted either the Model Act or the Revised Act. Moreover, many States have adopted selected provisions of the Revised Act. Since 1984, a number of sections of the Revised Act have been amended. The Revised Act as amended will be used throughout the chapters on corporations in this text and will be referred to as the Revised

Act or the RMBCA. Appendix E contains the RMBCA as amended.

NATURE OF CORPORATIONS

To understand corporations, it is helpful to examine their common attributes and their various types. Both of these topics will be discussed in this section.

CORPORATE ATTRIBUTES

The principal attributes of a corporation are as follows: (1) it is a legal entity; (2) it owes its existence to a State, which also regulates it; (3) it provides limited liability to its shareholders; (4) its shares of stock are freely transferable; (5) its existence may be perpetual; (6) its management is centralized; and it is considered, for some purposes, (7) a person and (8) a citizen.

◆ **SEE FIGURE 31-1: General Partnership, Limited Partnership, Limited Liability Company, and Corporation**

LEGAL ENTITY

A corporation is a legal entity separate from its shareholders, with rights and liabilities entirely distinct from theirs. It may sue or be sued by, as well as contract with, any other party, including any one of its shareholders. A transfer of stock in the corporation from one individual to another has no effect upon the legal existence of the corporation. Title to corporate property belongs not to the shareholders but to the corporation. Even where a single individual owns all of the stock of a corporation, the existence of the shareholder is distinct from that of the corporation.

CREATURE OF THE STATE

A corporation may be formed only by substantial compliance with a State incorporation statute. Every State has a general incorporation statute authorizing the Secretary of State to issue a certificate of incorporation or charter upon compliance with its provisions.

A corporation's charter and the provisions of the statute under which it is formed constitute a contract between it and the State. Article I, Section 10, of the U.S. Constitution provides that no State shall pass any law "impairing the obligation of contracts," and this prohibition applies to contracts between a State and a corporation. See *Chapter 4*.

To avoid the impact of this provision, incorporation statutes reserve to the State the power to establish such regulations, provisions, and limitations as it deems advisable and to amend or repeal the statute at its pleasure. Section 1.02.

This reservation is a material part of the contract between the State and a corporation formed under the statute; consequently, because the contract expressly permits them, amendments or modifications regulating or altering the structure of the corporation do not impair the obligation of contract.

LIMITED LIABILITY

A corporation is a legal entity and therefore is liable out of its own assets for its debts. Generally, the shareholders have **limited liability** for the corporation's debts—their liability does not extend beyond the amount of their investment—although, as discussed later in this chapter, under certain circumstances a shareholder may be personally liable. The limitation on liability, however, will not affect the liability of a shareholder who committed the wrongful act. A shareholder is also liable for any corporate obligations personally guaranteed by the individual member or manager.

FREE TRANSFERABILITY OF CORPORATE SHARES

In the absence of contractual restrictions, shares in a corporation may be freely transferred by way of sale, gift, or pledge. The ability to transfer shares is a valuable right and may enhance their market value. Article 8 of the Uniform Commercial Code, Investment Securities, governs transfers of shares of stock.

PERPETUAL EXISTENCE

A corporation's existence is perpetual unless otherwise stated in its articles of incorporation. Section 3.02. Consequently, the death, withdrawal, or addition of a shareholder, director, or officer does not terminate the existence of a corporation. A corporation's existence will terminate upon its dissolution or merger into another business.

CENTRALIZED MANAGEMENT

The shareholders of a corporation elect a board of directors to manage the business of the corporation. The board in turn appoints officers to run the day-to-day operations of the business. As neither the directors nor the officers (collectively referred to as *management*) need be shareholders, it is entirely possible, and in large corporations quite typical, for ownership and management to be separate. The management structure of corporations is discussed in *Chapter 36*.

AS A PERSON

Whether a corporation is a "person" within the meaning of a constitution or statute is a matter of construction based upon the intent of the lawmakers in using the word. For example, a corporation is considered a person within the provision in the Fifth and Fourteenth Amendments to the U.S. Constitution that no "person" shall be "deprived of life, liberty, or property without due process of law"; and in the provision in the Fourteenth Amendment that no State shall "deny to any person within its jurisdiction the equal protection of the laws." A corporation also enjoys the right of a person to be secure against unreasonable searches and seizures, as provided for in the Fourth Amendment. On the other hand, a corporation is not considered to be a person within the Fifth Amendment's clause that protects a "person" against self-incrimination.

AS A CITIZEN

A corporation is considered a citizen for some purposes but not for others. A corporation is not deemed to be a citizen as the term is used in the Fourteenth Amendment, which provides, "No State shall make or enforce any law which shall abridge the privileges or immunities of citizens of the United States."

A corporation is, however, regarded as a citizen of the State of its incorporation and of the State in which it has its principal office for the purpose of identifying diversity of citizenship between the parties to a lawsuit and thereby providing a basis for Federal court jurisdiction.

CLASSIFICATION OF CORPORATIONS

Corporations may be classified as public or private, profit or nonprofit, domestic or foreign, publicly held or closely held, Subchapter S, and professional. As will be seen, these classifications are not mutually exclusive. For example, a corporation may be a closely held, professional, private, profit, domestic corporation.

PUBLIC OR PRIVATE

A **public corporation** is one that is created to administer a unit of local civil government, such as a county, city, town, village, school district or park district, or one created by the United States to conduct public business, such as the Tennessee Valley Authority or the Federal Deposit Insurance Corporation. A public corporation usually is created by specific legislation, which determines the corporation's purpose and powers. Many public corporations are also referred to as municipal corporations.

A **private corporation** is founded by and composed of private persons for private purposes and has no governmental duties. A private corporation may be for profit or nonprofit.

PROFIT OR NONPROFIT

A **profit corporation** is one founded for the purpose of operating a business for profit from which payments are made to the corporation's shareholders in the form of dividends.

Although a **nonprofit** (or not-for-profit) **corporation** may make a profit, the profit may not be distributed to members, directors, or officers but must be used exclusively for the charitable, educational, or scientific purpose for which the corporation was organized. Examples of nonprofit corporations include private schools, library clubs, athletic clubs, fraternities, sororities, and hospitals. Most States have special incorporation statutes governing nonprofit corporations, most of which are patterned after the Model Nonprofit Corporation Act.

DOMESTIC OR FOREIGN

A corporation is a **domestic corporation** in the State in which it is incorporated. It is a **foreign corporation** in every other State or jurisdiction. A corporation may not do business, except for acts in interstate commerce, in a State other than the State of its incorporation without the permission and authorization of the other State. Every State, however, provides for the issuance of certificates of authority that allow foreign corporations to do business within its borders and for the taxation of such foreign businesses. Obtaining a certificate (called "qualifying") usually involves filing certain information with the Secretary of State, paying prescribed fees, and designating a resident agent. Doing or transacting business within a particular State makes the corporation subject to local litigation, regulation, and taxation.

DOING BUSINESS The Revised Act does not attempt to fully define what constitutes the transaction of business. Instead, the Act provides a definition by exclusion by listing activities that do *not* constitute the transaction of business. Section 15.01. Generally, any conduct more regular, systematic, or extensive than that described in this section constitutes the transaction of business and requires a corporation to obtain a certificate of authority. Conduct typically requiring a certificate of authority includes maintaining an office to conduct local intrastate business, selling personal property not in interstate commerce, entering into contracts relating to local business or sales, and owning or using real estate for general corporate purposes. Section 15.01, Comment.

The Revised Act, as stated, provides a *nonexclusive* list of "safe harbors," that is, activities in which a foreign corporation may engage without being considered to have transacted intrastate business. The list includes the following:

1. maintaining bank accounts;
2. selling through independent contractors;
3. soliciting or obtaining orders, whether by mail or through employees or agents or otherwise, if such orders require acceptance outside the State before they become contracts;
4. owning, without more, real or personal property;

5. conducting an isolated transaction that is completed within thirty days and that is not one of a number of repeated transactions of like nature; and
6. transacting business in interstate commerce.

SCOPE OF REGULATION It is a common and accepted principle that local courts will not interfere with the internal affairs of a foreign corporation. To this end, the Revised Act states that "this Act does not authorize this state to regulate the organization or internal affairs of a foreign corporation." Section 15.05(c). Nevertheless, subjecting foreign corporations to reasonable regulation need not violate due process or constitute a burden on interstate commerce. A few States—most notably California and New York—regulate some of the internal affairs of foreign corporations that conduct a majority of their business in those States.

SANCTIONS A foreign corporation that transacts business without having first qualified may be subject to a number of penalties. Statutes in many States provide that an unlicensed foreign corporation doing business in a State shall not be entitled to maintain a suit in the State's courts until such corporation obtains a certificate of authority to transact business in that State. Failure to obtain such a certificate does not, however, impair the validity of a contract entered into by the corporation or prevent such corporation from defending any action or proceeding brought against it in the State. Section 15.02. In addition, most States impose fines upon an unqualified corporation, while a few States also impose fines upon the corporation's officers and directors, as well as holding them personally liable on contracts made within the State.

PUBLICLY HELD OR CLOSELY HELD

A **publicly held corporation** is one whose shares are owned by a large number of people and are widely traded. There is no accepted minimum number of shareholders, but any corporation required to register under the Federal Securities and Exchange Act of 1934 is considered to be publicly held. In addition, corporations that have issued securities subject to a registered public distribution under the Federal Securities Act of 1933 usually are also considered publicly held. The Federal securities laws are discussed in *Chapter 44*. To distinguish publicly held corporations from other corporations, the Revised Act was amended to define the term "public corporation" as "a corporation that has shares listed on a national securities exchange or regularly traded in a market maintained by one or more members of a national securities association." Section 1.40(18A).

A **corporation** is described as **closely held** or **close** when its outstanding shares of stock are held by a small number of persons who often are family, relatives, or friends. In most closely held corporations, the shareholders are active in the management and control of the business. Accordingly, they are concerned about the identities of their fellow shareholders, a concern that frequently leads shareholders to restrict the transfer of shares to prevent "outsiders" from obtaining stock in a closely held corporation. See the discussion of *Galler v. Galler* in *Chapter 36*. Although a vast majority of corporations in the United States are closely held, they account for only a small fraction of corporate revenues and assets.

In most States, closely held corporations are subject to the general incorporation statute that governs all corporations. The Revised Act includes a number of liberalizing provisions for closely held corporations. In addition, about twenty States have enacted special legislation to accommodate the needs of such corporations, and a Statutory Close Corporation Supplement to the Model and Revised Acts was promulgated. The Supplement applies only to those eligible corporations that elect statutory close corporation status. To be eligible, a corporation must have fewer than fifty shareholders. A corporation may voluntarily terminate statutory close corporation status. Other provisions of the Supplement will be discussed in this and other chapters.

In 1991 the Revised Act was amended to authorize shareholders in closely held corporations to adopt unanimous shareholders' agreements that depart from the statutory norms by altering (1) the governance of the corporation, (2) the allocation of the economic return from the business, and (3) other aspects of the relationship among shareholders, directors, and the corporation. Section 7.32. Such a shareholder agreement is valid for ten years unless the agreement provides otherwise but terminates automatically if the corporation's shares become publicly traded. Shareholder agreements validated by Section 7.32 bind only the shareholders and the corporation; they do not bind the State, creditors, or other third parties. The provisions of Section 7.32 will be discussed in this and other chapters.

SUBCHAPTER S CORPORATION

Subchapter S of the Internal Revenue Code permits a corporation meeting specified requirements to elect to be taxed essentially as though it were a partnership. (Approximately two-thirds of all corporations in the United States are Chapter S corporations, but they account for only 20 percent of total corporate revenues and less than 5 percent of total corporate assets.) Under subchapter S, a corporation's income is taxed only once at the individual shareholder level. The requirements for a corporation to elect subchapter S treatment are (1) it must be a domestic corporation; (2) it must have no more than one hundred shareholders; (3) each shareholder must be an individual, or an estate, or certain types of trusts;

(4) no shareholder may be a nonresident alien; and (5) it may have only one class of stock, although classes of common stock differing only in voting rights are permitted.

PROFESSIONAL CORPORATIONS

All of the States have professional association or corporation statutes that permit duly licensed individuals to practice their professions within the corporate form. Some statutes apply to all professions licensed to practice within the State, while others apply only to specified professions. There is a Model Professional Corporation Supplement to the MBCA.

FORMATION OF A CORPORATION

The formation of a corporation under a general incorporation statute requires the action of various groups, individuals, and State officials. The procedure to organize a corporation begins with the promotion of the proposed corporation by its organizers, also known as promoters, who procure offers by interested persons, known as subscribers, to buy stock in the corporation, once created, and who prepare the necessary incorporation papers. The incorporators then execute the articles of incorporation and file them with the Secretary of State, who issues the charter or certificate of incorporation. Finally, an organizational meeting is held.

ORGANIZING THE CORPORATION

PROMOTERS

A **promoter** is a person who brings about the "birth" of a corporation by arranging for capital and financing; assembling the necessary assets, equipment, licenses, personnel, leases, and services; and attending to the actual legal formation of the corporation. Upon incorporation, the promoter's organizational task is finished.

PROMOTERS' CONTRACTS In addition to procuring subscriptions and preparing the incorporation papers, promoters often enter into contracts in anticipation of the creation of the corporation. The contracts may be ordinary agreements necessary for the eventual operation of the business, such as leases, purchase orders, employment contracts, sales contracts, or franchises. If the promoter executes these contracts in her own name and there is no further action, the promoter is liable on such contracts; the corporation, when created, is not liable. Moreover, a preincorporation contract made by a promoter in the name of the corporation and on its behalf does not bind the corporation. The promoter, in executing such contracts, may do so in the corporate name even if incorporation has yet to occur. Before its formation,

a corporation has no capacity to enter into contracts or to employ agents or representatives. After its formation, it is not liable at common law upon any prior contract, even one made in its name, unless it adopts the contract expressly, impliedly, or by knowingly accepting benefits under it.

A promoter who enters into a preincorporation contract in the name of the corporation usually remains liable on that contract even if the corporation adopts it. This liability results from the rule of agency law stating that to be able to ratify a contract, a principal must be in existence at the time the contract is made. A promoter will be relieved of liability, however, if the contract provides that adoption shall terminate the promoter's liability or if the promoter, the third party, and the corporation enter into a novation substituting the corporation for the promoter.

◆ **SEE FIGURE 34-1: Promoter's Preincorporation Contracts Made in Corporation's Name**

PROMOTERS' FIDUCIARY DUTY The promoters of a corporation owe a fiduciary duty to one another as well as to the corporation, its subscribers, and its initial shareholders. This duty requires good faith, fair dealing, and full disclosure to an independent board of directors. If an independent board has not been elected, then full disclosure must be made to all shareholders. Accordingly, the promoters are under a duty to account for any *secret* profit they realize. Failure to disclose also may constitute a violation of Federal or State securities laws.

SUBSCRIBERS

A **preincorporation subscription** is an offer to purchase capital stock in a corporation yet to be formed. The offeror is called a "subscriber." Courts traditionally have viewed subscriptions in one of two ways. The majority regard a subscription as a continuing offer to purchase stock from a nonexisting entity, incapable of accepting the offer until it exists. Under this view, a subscription may be revoked at any time prior to its acceptance. In contrast, a minority of jurisdictions treat a subscription as a contract among the various subscribers, rendering the subscription irrevocable except with the subscribers' unanimous consent. Most incorporation statutes have adopted an intermediate position making preincorporation subscriptions irrevocable for a stated period without regard to whether they are supported by consideration. For example, the Revised Act provides that a preincorporation subscription is irrevocable for six months, unless the subscription agreement provides a different period or all of the subscribers consent to the revocation. Section 6.20. If the corporation accepts the subscription during the period of

◆ **FIGURE 34-1: Promoter's Preincorporation Contracts Made in Corporation's Name**

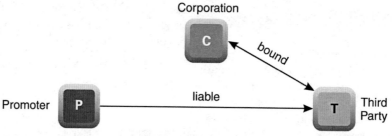

Corporation Does NOT Adopt Preincorporation Contract

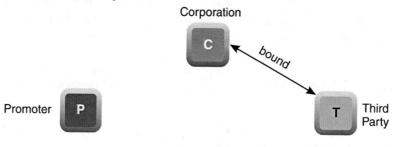

Corporation Does Adopt Preincorporation Contract

Corporation, Promoter, and Third Party Enter into a Novation or Preincorporation Contract Provides That Adoption Will Terminate Promoter's Liability

irrevocability, the subscription becomes a contract binding on both the subscriber and the corporation.

A **postincorporation subscription** is a subscription agreement entered into after incorporation. It is treated as a contract between the subscriber and the corporation. RMBCA Section 6.20(e). Unlike preincorporation subscriptions, the subscriber may withdraw her offer to enter into a postincorporation subscription anytime before the corporation accepts it. She cannot, however, withdraw the offer after the corporation has accepted it as the acceptance forms a contract.

SELECTION OF STATE FOR INCORPORATION

A corporation is usually incorporated in the State in which it intends to be located and to transact all or the principal part of its business. Nevertheless, a corporation may be formed in one State and have its principal place of business and conduct all or most of its operations in another State or States

by duly qualifying and obtaining a certificate of authority to transact business in those States. The principal criteria in selecting a State for incorporation include the flexibility accorded management, the rights granted to shareholders, the protection provided against takeovers, the limitations imposed upon the issuance of shares, the restrictions placed upon the payment of dividends, and organizational costs such as fees and taxes.

FORMALITIES OF INCORPORATION

Although the procedure involved in organizing a corporation varies somewhat from State to State, typically the incorporators execute and deliver articles of incorporation to the Secretary of State or another designated official. The Revised Act provides that after incorporation, the board of directors named in the articles of incorporation shall hold an organizational meeting for the purpose of adopting bylaws, appointing officers, and carrying on any other business brought before the meeting. Section 2.05. After completion of these organizational details, the corporation's officers and board of directors manage its business and affairs. Several States require that a corporation have a minimum amount of capital, usually $1,000, before doing any business. The Revised Act and most States have eliminated this requirement.

SELECTION OF NAME

Most general incorporation laws require that a corporate name contain a word or words that clearly identify the organization as a corporation, such as *corporation, company, incorporated, limited, Corp., Co., Inc.,* or *Ltd.* Section 4.01. Furthermore, the name must be distinguishable from the name of any domestic corporation or any foreign corporation authorized to do business within the State. Section 4.01.

INCORPORATORS

The **incorporators** are the persons who sign the articles of incorporation, which are filed with the Secretary of State of the State of incorporation. Although they perform a necessary function, in many States their services as incorporators are perfunctory and short-lived, ending with the organizational meeting. Furthermore, modern statutes have greatly relaxed the qualifications of incorporators and also have reduced the number required. The Revised Act and all States provide that only one person need act as the incorporator or incorporators, though more may do so. Section 2.01. The Revised Act and most States permit artificial entities to serve as incorporators. For example, the Revised Act defines a person to include individuals and entities, with an entity defined to include domestic and foreign corporations, not-for-profit corporations, profit and not-for-profit unincorporated associations, business trusts, estates, partnerships, and trusts. Section 1.40.

ARTICLES OF INCORPORATION

The articles of incorporation, or **charter**, is generally a rather simple document that under the Revised Act must include the name of the corporation, the number of authorized shares, the street address of the registered office and the name of the registered agent, and the name and address of each incorporator. Section 2.02(a). The Act also permits the charter to include optional information such as the identities of the corporation's initial directors, corporate purposes, procedures for managing internal affairs, powers of the corporation, the par value of shares, and any provision required or permitted to be set forth in the bylaws. Some optional provisions may be elected *only* in the charter, including cu-

mulative voting, supermajority voting requirements, preemptive rights, and limitations on the personal liability of directors for breach of their duty of care.

To form a corporation, the charter, once it is drawn up, must be executed and filed with the Secretary of State. The articles of incorporation then become the basic governing document of the corporation, so long as its provisions are consistent with State and Federal law.

◆ **SEE FIGURE 34-2: Sample Articles of Incorporation**

ORGANIZATIONAL MEETING

The Revised Act and most States require that an organizational meeting be held to adopt the new corporation's bylaws, appoint officers, and carry on any other business brought before it. If the articles do not name the corporation's initial directors, the incorporators hold the organizational meeting to elect directors, after which either the incorporators or the directors complete the organization of the corporation. Section 2.05. Additional business that may be brought before the meeting typically includes authorization to issue shares of stock, approval of preincorporation contracts made by promoters, selection of a bank, and approval of a corporate seal and the form of stock certificates.

BYLAWS

The **bylaws** of a corporation are the rules and regulations that govern its internal management. Because bylaws are necessary to the organization of the corporation, their adoption is one of the first items of business at the organizational meeting held promptly after incorporation. Under the Revised Act, either the incorporators or the board of directors may adopt the bylaws. Section 2.06.

The bylaws may contain any provision for managing the business and regulating the affairs of the corporation that is not inconsistent with law or the articles of incorporation. Section 2.06. In contrast to the articles of incorporation, the bylaws do not have to be publicly filed. Under the Revised Act, the shareholders may amend or repeal the bylaws, as may the board of directors, unless (1) the articles of incorporation or other sections of the RMBCA reserve that power exclusively to the shareholders in whole or in part, or (2) the shareholders in amending, repealing, or adopting a bylaw expressly provide that the board of directors may not amend, repeal, or reinstate that bylaw. Section 10.20.

The Statutory Close Corporation Supplement (Section 22) permits close corporations to avoid the adoption of bylaws by including either in a shareholder agreement or in the articles of incorporation all information required in corporate bylaws.

◆ **SEE FIGURE 34-3: Comparison of Charter and Bylaws**

◆ **FIGURE 34-2: Sample Articles of Incorporation**

ARTICLES OF INCORPORATION OF [CORPORATE NAME]

The undersigned, acting as incorporator(s) of a corporation under the _____ Business Corporation Act, adopt(s) the following Articles of Incorporation for such corporation:

First: The name of the corporation is _____

_____

Second: The period of its duration is _____

_____

Third: The purpose or purposes for which the corporation is organized are _____

_____

Fourth: The aggregate number of shares which the corporation shall have authority to issue is _____

_____

Fifth: Provisions granting preemptive rights are _____

_____

Sixth: Provisions for the regulation of the internal affairs of the corporation are ____

_____

Seventh: The address of the initial registered office of the corporation is _____

and the name of its initial registered agent at such address is _____

Eighth: The number of directors constituting the initial board of directors of the corporation is _____, and the names and addresses of the persons who are to serve as directors until the first annual meeting of shareholders or until their successors are elected and shall qualify are

Name	Address
_____	_____
_____	_____
_____	_____

Ninth: The name and address of each incorporator is

Name	Address
_____	_____
_____	_____
_____	_____

Dated _____, 20 _____.   _____

_____

_____

Source: Reprinted from *Corporations*, 3rd ed., by Henn & Alexander, copyright 1983 with permission of the West Group.

RECOGNITION OR DISREGARD OF CORPORATENESS

Business associates choose to incorporate to obtain one or more corporate attributes—primarily limited liability and perpetual existence. Because a corporation is a creature of the State, such attributes are recognized when the enterprise complies with the State's requirements for incorporation. Although the formal procedures are relatively simple, errors or omissions sometimes occur. In some cases the mistakes may be trivial, such as incorrectly stating an incorporator's address; in other instances the error may be more significant, such as a complete failure to file the articles of incorporation. The consequences of procedural noncompliance depend upon the seriousness of the error. Conversely, even when a corporation has been formed in strict compliance with the incorporation statute, a court may disregard the corporateness of the enterprise if justice requires. This section addresses these two complementary issues.

DEFECTIVE INCORPORATION

Although modern incorporation statutes have greatly simplified incorporation procedures, defective incorporations do occur. The possible consequences of a defective incorporation include the following: (1) the State brings an action against the association for involuntary dissolution, (2) the associates are held personally liable to a third party, (3) the association asserts that it is not liable on an obligation, or (4) a third party asserts that it is not liable to the association. Corporate statutes addressing this issue have taken an approach considerably different from that of the common law.

COMMON LAW APPROACH

Under the common law, a defectively formed corporation was, under certain circumstances, accorded corporate attri-

butes. The courts developed a set of doctrines granting corporateness to *de jure* (of right) corporations, *de facto* (of fact) corporations, and corporations by estoppel but denying corporateness to corporations that were too defectively formed.

CORPORATION *DE JURE* A corporation *de jure* is one that has been formed in substantial compliance with the incorporation statute and the required organizational procedure. Once such a corporation is formed, its existence may not be challenged by anyone, even by the State in a direct proceeding for this purpose.

CORPORATION *DE FACTO* Though it fails to comply substantially with the incorporation statute (and therefore is not *de jure*), a corporation *de facto* nevertheless is recognized for most purposes as a corporation. A failure to form a *de jure* corporation may result in the formation of a *de facto* corporation if the following requirements are met: (1) the existence of a general corporation statute, (2) a *bona fide* attempt to comply with that law in organizing a corporation under the statute, and (3) the actual exercise of corporate power by conducting business in the belief that a corporation has been formed. If the corporation sues to collect a debt, the fact that the corporation is not *de jure* is not a defense. Furthermore, the existence of the *de facto* corporation can be challenged only by the State, though not even the State can question its existence collaterally (in a proceeding involving some other issue). The State must bring an independent suit against the corporation for this express purpose, known as an action of *quo warranto* ("by what right").

CORPORATION BY ESTOPPEL The doctrine of corporation by estoppel is distinct from that of corporation *de facto*. Estoppel does not create a corporation. It operates only to prevent a person or persons under the facts and circumstances of a particular case from questioning a corporation's existence or its capacity to act or to own property. Corporation by estoppel requires a holding out by a purported corporation or its

◆ **FIGURE 34-3: Comparison of Charter and Bylaws**

	Charter	Bylaws
Filing	Publicly	Not publicly
Amendment	Requires board and shareholder approval	Requires only board approval
Availability	Must include certain mandatory provisions; may include optional provisions although some optional provisions may be elected only in the charter	Must include certain provisions unless they are included in the charter
Validity	May include any provision not inconsistent with law	May include any provision not inconsistent with law and the charter

associates and reliance by a third party. In addition, application of the doctrine depends on equitable considerations. A person who has dealt with a defectively organized corporation may be precluded or estopped from denying its corporate existence where the necessary elements of holding out and reliance are present. The doctrine can be applied not only to third parties but also to the purported corporation and to the associates who held themselves out as a corporation.

Defective Corporation If the associates who purported to form a corporation so fail to comply with the requirements of the incorporation statute that neither a *de jure* nor a *de facto* corporation is formed and the circumstances do not justify applying the corporation by estoppel doctrine, the courts generally deny the associates the benefits of incorporation. This results in some or all of the associates being held unlimitedly liable for the obligations of the business.

STATUTORY APPROACH

While the common law approach to defective incorporation is cumbersome both in theory and in application, incorporation statutes now address the issue more simply. All States provide that corporate existence begins either upon the filing of the articles of incorporation or their acceptance by the Secretary of State. Moreover, the Revised Act and most States provide the *filing* or acceptance of the articles of incorporation by the Secretary of State is conclusive proof that the incorporators have satisfied all conditions precedent to incorporation, except in a proceeding brought by the State. Section 2.03(b). This applies even if the articles of incorporation contain mistakes or omissions.

With respect to the attribute of limited liability, the original Model Act and a few States provide that "[a]ll persons who assume to act as a corporation without authority so to do shall be jointly and severally liable for all debts and liabilities incurred or arising as a result thereof." Section 146. The Revised Act, however, imposes liability *only* on persons who purport to act as or on behalf of a corporation, knowing that there was no incorporation. Section 2.04.

Consider the following two illustrations: First, Smith had been shown executed articles of incorporation some months before he invested in the corporation and became an officer and director. He was also told by the corporation's attorney that the articles had been filed; however, because of confusion in the attorney's office, the filing had not in fact occurred. Under the Revised Act and many court decisions, Smith would not be held personally liable for the obligations of the defective corporation. Second, Jones represents that a corporation exists and enters into a contract in the corporate name when she knows that no corporation has been formed because no attempt has been made to file articles of incorporation. Jones would be held liable for the obligations of the defective corporation under the Model Act, the Revised Act,

and most court decisions involving similar situations. RMBCA Section 2.04 and Comment.

PIERCING THE CORPORATE VEIL

If substantial compliance with the incorporation statute results in a *de jure* or *de facto* corporation, the courts generally will recognize corporateness and its attendant attributes, including limited liability. Nonetheless, the courts will disregard the corporate entity when it is used to defeat public convenience, commit a wrongdoing, protect fraud, or circumvent the law. Going behind the corporate entity to confront those seeking to insulate themselves from personal accountability and the consequences of their wrongdoing is known as piercing the corporate veil. Courts will pierce the corporate veil where they deem such action necessary to remedy wrongdoing. However, there is no commonly accepted test used by the courts. They have done so most frequently in regard to closely held corporations and parent-subsidiary relationships. It should be noted that piercing the corporate veil is the exception, and in most cases courts uphold the separateness of corporations.

CLOSELY HELD CORPORATIONS

The joint and active management by all the shareholders of closely held corporations frequently results in a tendency to forgo corporate formalities, such as holding meetings of the board and shareholders, while the small size of close corporations often renders creditors unable to fully satisfy their claims against the corporation. Such frustrated creditors often ask the court to disregard an organization's corporateness and to impose personal liability for the corporate obligations upon the shareholders. Courts have responded by piercing the corporate veil in cases in which the shareholders (1) have not conducted the business on a corporate basis, (2) have not provided an adequate financial basis for the business, or (3) have used the corporation to defraud. For example, in *D.I. Felsenthal Co. v. Northern Assurance Co.* 284 Ill. 343, 120 N.E. 268 (1918), Felsenthal Company sued the Northern Assurance Company to collect on its fire insurance policy. Northern claimed that it was not liable under the policy because Felsenthal's property had been destroyed by a fire instigated by Fox, the president, director, creditor, and principal shareholder of Felsenthal. The court ruled in favor of Northern Assurance because the instigator of the fire, Fox, was the beneficial owner of almost all of Felsenthal's stock as well as the corporation's president and director. Under those circumstances, the corporation could not recover because to allow such a recovery would allow a wrongdoer to benefit from his own illegal act. The corporate form could not be used in this case to protect Fox and to aid him in his plan to defraud the insurance company.

Conducting the business on a corporate basis involves separately maintaining the corporation's funds and the shareholders' funds, maintaining separate financial records, holding regular directors' meetings, and generally observing corporate formalities. Adequate capitalization requires that the shareholders invest capital or purchase liability insurance sufficient to meet the reasonably anticipated requirements of the enterprise.

The Revised Act validates unanimous shareholder agreements by which the shareholders may relax traditional corporate formalities. Section 7.32. The Revised Act further provides that the existence or performance of an agreement authorized by Section 7.32

> shall not be grounds for imposing personal liability on any shareholder for the acts or the debts of the corporation even if the agreement or its performance treats the corporation as if it were a partnership or results in failure to observe the corporate formalities otherwise applicable to the matters governed by the agreement.

Thus, this section narrows the grounds for imposing personal liability on shareholders for the liabilities of a corporation for acts or omissions authorized by a shareholder agreement validated by Section 7.32.

The Statutory Close Corporation Supplement validates several arrangements whereby the shareholders may relax traditional corporate formalities. Section 25 of the Supplement provides: "The failure of a statutory close corporation to observe the usual corporate formalities or requirements relating to the exercise of its corporate powers or management of its business and affairs is not a ground for imposing personal liability on the shareholders for liabilities of the corporation." Courts may still pierce the corporate veil of a statutory close corporation if the same circumstances would justify imposing personal liability on the shareholders of a general business corporation. The Supplement simply prevents a court from piercing the corporate veil just because the corporation is a statutory close corporation.

PARENT-SUBSIDIARY CORPORATIONS

A corporation wishing to risk only a portion of its assets in a particular enterprise may choose to form a **subsidiary corporation**. A subsidiary corporation is one in which another corporation, the **parent corporation**, owns at least a majority of the shares and over which the other corporation therefore has control. Courts may pierce the corporate veil and hold the parent liable for the debts of its subsidiary if any of the following criteria are met:

1. both corporations are not adequately capitalized, *or*

2. the formalities of separate corporate procedures are not observed, *or*
3. each corporation is not held out to the public as a separate enterprise, *or*
4. the funds of the two corporations are commingled, *or*
5. the parent corporation completely dominates the subsidiary solely to advance its own interests.

So long as a parent and a subsidiary avoid these pitfalls, the courts generally will recognize the subsidiary as a separate entity, even if the parent owns all the subsidiary's stock and the two corporations share facilities, employees, directors, and officers.

CORPORATE POWERS

Because a corporation derives its existence and all of its powers from its State of incorporation, it possesses only those powers that the State confers on it. These powers consist of those expressly set forth in the statute unless limited by the articles of incorporation.

SOURCES OF CORPORATE POWERS

STATUTORY POWERS

Typical of the general corporate powers granted by incorporation statutes are those provided by Section 3.02 of the Revised Act, which include the following:

1. to have perpetual succession;
2. to sue and be sued in the corporate name;
3. to have a corporate seal;
4. to make and amend bylaws for managing the business and regulating the affairs of the corporation;
5. to acquire, own, improve, use, and dispose of real or personal property;
6. to own, vote, and dispose of shares or other interests in, or obligations of, any other entity;
7. to make contracts and guarantees; incur liabilities; borrow money; issue notes, bonds, and other obligations; and secure any corporate obligations;
8. to lend money, invest and reinvest funds, and receive and hold real and personal property as security for repayment;
9. to be a promoter, partner, member, associate, or manager of any partnership, joint venture, trust, or other entity;
10. to conduct business, locate offices, and exercise the powers granted by the Act within or without the State of incorporation;
11. to elect directors and appoint officers, employees, and agents; define their duties; fix their compensation; and lend them money and credit;

12. to pay pensions and establish pension plans, pension trusts, profit sharing plans, share bonus plans, share option plans, and benefit or incentive plans for any or all current or former directors, officers, employees, and agents;

13. to make donations for the public welfare or for charitable, scientific, or educational purposes;

14. to transact any lawful business that will aid governmental policy; and

15. to make payments or donations or do any other act, not inconsistent with law, that furthers the business and affairs of the corporation.

In most States this list is not exclusive. Moreover, the Revised Act also grants to all corporations the same powers as individuals have to do all things necessary or convenient to carry out their business and affairs. Section 3.02.

PURPOSES

All State incorporation statutes provide that a corporation may be formed for any lawful purposes. The Revised Act permits a corporation's articles of incorporation to state a more limited purpose. Many State statutes, but not the RMBCA, require that the articles of incorporation specify the corporation's purposes although they usually permit a general statement that the corporation is formed to engage in any lawful purpose.

ULTRA VIRES ACTS

Because a corporation has authority to act only within its powers, any action or contract that is not within the scope and type of acts which the corporation is legally empowered to perform is *ultra vires*. The doctrine of *ultra vires* is less significant today because modern statutes permit incorporation for any lawful purpose, and most articles of incorporation do not limit corporate powers. Consequently, far fewer acts are *ultra vires*.

EFFECT OF ULTRA VIRES ACTS

Traditionally, *ultra vires* contracts were unenforceable as null and void. Under the modern approach, courts allow the *ultra vires* defense where the contract is wholly executory on both sides. A corporation having received full performance from the other party to the contract is not permitted to escape liability by a plea of *ultra vires*. Conversely, the defense of *ultra vires* is unavailable to a corporation suing for breach of a contract which has been fully performed on its side.

Almost all statutes have abolished the defense of *ultra vires* in an action by or against a corporation. The Revised

Act provides that "the validity of corporate action may not be challenged on the ground that the corporation lacks or lacked the power to act." Section 3.04. This section extends beyond contract actions to encompass any corporate action, including conveyances of property. Thus, under this section, persons dealing with a corporation need not examine its articles of incorporation for limitations upon its purposes or powers. The section does not, however, validate illegal corporate actions.

REMEDIES FOR ULTRA VIRES ACTS

Although *ultra vires* under modern statutes may no longer be used as a shield against liability, corporate activities that are *ultra vires* may be redressed in any of three ways, as provided by Section 3.04(b) of the Revised Act:

1. in a proceeding by a shareholder against the corporation to enjoin the unauthorized act, if such an injunction is equitable and if all affected persons are parties to the proceeding, and the court may award damages for losses suffered by the corporation or another party because of enjoining the unauthorized act;

2. in a proceeding by the corporation, or a shareholder derivatively (in a representative capacity), against the incumbent or former directors or officers for exceeding their authority; or

3. in a proceeding by the Attorney General of the State of incorporation to dissolve the corporation or to enjoin it from transacting unauthorized business.

LIABILITY FOR TORTS AND CRIMES

A corporation is liable for the torts its agents commit in the course of their employment. The doctrine of *ultra vires*, even in those jurisdictions where it is permitted as a defense, does not apply to wrongdoing by the corporation. The doctrine of *respondeat superior* imposes full liability upon a corporation for the torts its agents and employees commit during the course of their employment. For example, Robert, a truck driver employed by the Webster Corporation, negligently runs over Pamela, a pedestrian, while on a business errand. Both Robert and the Webster Corporation are liable to Pamela in her action to recover damages for the injuries she sustained. A corporation also may be found liable for fraud, false imprisonment, malicious prosecution, libel, and other torts, though some States hold the corporation liable for *punitive* damages only if it authorized or ratified the agent's act.

Historically, corporations were not held criminally liable because, under the traditional view, a corporation could not possess the criminal intent requisite to committing a crime. Dramatic growth in the size and importance of corporations has changed this view. Under the modern approach, a corporation may be liable for violating statutes that impose liability without fault. In addition, a corporation may be liable for an offense perpetrated by a high corporate officer or by its board of directors. Punishment of a corporation for crimes is necessarily by fine, not imprisonment.

CHAPTER SUMMARY

NATURE OF CORPORATIONS

CORPORATE ATTRIBUTES	**Legal Entity** a corporation is an entity apart from its shareholders, with entirely distinct rights and liabilities **Creature of the State** a corporation may be formed only by substantial compliance with a State incorporation statute **Limited Liability** a shareholder's liability is limited to the amount invested in the business enterprise **Free Transferability of Corporate Shares** unless otherwise specified in the charter **Perpetual Existence** unless the charter provides otherwise **Centralized Management** shareholders of a corporation elect the board of directors to manage its business affairs; the board appoints officers to run the day-to-day operations of the business **As a Person** a corporation is considered a person for some but not all purposes **As a Citizen** a corporation is considered a citizen for some but not all purposes
CLASSIFICATION OF CORPORATIONS	**Public or Private** • *Public Corporation* one created to administer a unit of local civil government or one created by the United States to conduct public business • *Private Corporation* one founded by and composed of private persons for private purposes; has no governmental duties **Profit or Nonprofit** • *Profit Corporation* one founded to operate a business for profit • *Nonprofit Corporation* one whose profits must be used exclusively for charitable, educational, or scientific purposes **Domestic or Foreign** • *Domestic Corporation* one created under the laws of a given State • *Foreign Corporation* one created under the laws of any other State or jurisdiction; it must obtain a certificate of authority from each State in which it does intrastate business **Publicly Held or Closely Held** • *Publicly Held Corporation* one whose shares are owned by a large number of people and are widely traded • *Closely Held Corporation* one that is owned by few shareholders and whose shares are not actively traded **Subchapter S Corporation** eligible corporation electing to be taxed as a partnership under the Internal Revenue Code **Professional Corporations** corporate form under which duly licensed individuals may practice their professions

FORMATION OF A CORPORATION

ORGANIZING THE CORPORATION	**Promoter** person who takes the preliminary steps to organize a corporation • *Promoters' Contracts* promoters remain liable on preincorporation contracts made in the name of the corporation unless the contract provides otherwise or unless a novation is effected

- *Promoters' Fiduciary Duty* promoters owe a fiduciary duty among themselves and to the corporation, its subscribers, and its initial shareholders

Subscribers persons who agree to purchase the initial stock in a corporation
- *Preincorporation Subscription* an offer to purchase capital stock in a corporation yet to be formed which under many incorporation statutes is irrevocable for a specified time period
- *Postincorporation Subscription* a subscription agreement entered into after incorporation; an offer to enter into such a subscription is revocable anytime before the corporation accepts it

FORMALITIES OF INCORPORATION	**Selection of Name** the name must clearly designate the entity as a corporation **Incorporators** the persons who sign the articles of incorporation **Articles of Incorporation** the charter or basic organizational document of a corporation **Organizational Meeting** the first meeting, held to adopt the bylaws and appoint officers **Bylaws** rules governing a corporation's internal management

RECOGNITION OR DISREGARD OF CORPORATENESS

DEFECTIVE INCORPORATION	**Common Law Approach** • *Corporation* de Jure one formed in substantial compliance with the incorporation statute and having all corporate attributes • *Corporation* de Facto one not formed in compliance with the statute but recognized for most purposes as a corporation • *Corporation by Estoppel* prevents a person from raising the question of a corporation's existence • *Defective Corporation* the associates are denied the benefits of incorporation **Statutory Approach** the filing or acceptance of the articles of incorporation is generally conclusive proof of proper incorporation • *Revised Model Business Corporation Act (RMBCA)* liability is imposed only on persons who act on behalf of a defectively formed corporation knowing that there was no incorporation • *Model Business Corporation Act (MBCA)* unlimited personal liability is imposed on all persons who act on behalf of a defectively formed corporation
PIERCING THE CORPORATE VEIL	**General Rule** the courts may disregard the corporate entity when it is used to defeat public convenience, commit a wrongdoing, protect fraud, or circumvent the law **Application** most frequently applied to • *Closely Held Corporations* • *Parent-Subsidiary Corporations*

CORPORATE POWERS

SOURCES OF CORPORATE POWERS	**Statutory Powers** typically include perpetual existence, right to hold property in the corporate name, and all powers necessary or convenient to effect the corporation's purposes **Purposes** a corporation may be formed for any lawful purposes unless its articles of incorporation state a more limited purpose

ULTRA VIRES ACTS	**Definition of *Ultra Vires* Acts** any action or contract that goes beyond a corporation's express and implied powers **Effect of *Ultra Vires* Acts** under RMBCA, *ultra vires* acts and conveyances are not invalid **Remedies for *Ultra Vires* Acts** the RMBCA provides three possible remedies
LIABILITY FOR TORTS AND CRIMES	**Torts** under the doctrine of *respondeat superior*, a corporation is liable for torts committed by its employees within the course of their employment **Crimes** a corporation may be criminally liable for violations of statutes imposing liability without fault or for an offense perpetrated by a high corporate officer or its board of directors

CHAPTER 35

Financial Structure

Capital is necessary for any business to function. Two principal sources for corporate financing involve debt and equity investment securities. While equity securities represent an ownership interest in the corporation and include both common and preferred stock, corporations finance most of their operations through debt securities. Debt securities, which include notes and bonds, do not represent an ownership interest in the corporation but rather create a debtor-creditor relationship between the corporation and the bondholder. The third principal way in which a corporation may meet its financial needs is through retained earnings.

All States have statutes regulating the issuance and sale of corporate shares and other securities. Popularly known as **blue-sky laws**, these statutes typically have provisions prohibiting fraud in the sale of securities. In addition, a number of States require the registration of securities, and some States also regulate brokers, dealers, and others who engage in the securities business.

In 1933, Congress passed the first Federal statute for the regulation of securities offered for sale and sold through the use of the mails or otherwise in interstate commerce. The statute requires a corporation to disclose certain information about a proposed security in a registration statement and in its **prospectus** (an offer a corporation makes to interest people in buying securities). Although the Securities and Exchange Commission (SEC) does not examine the merits of the proposed security and although registration does not guarantee the accuracy of the facts presented in the registration statement or prospectus, the law does prohibit false and misleading statements under penalty of fine or imprisonment or both.

Under certain conditions, a corporation may receive an exemption from the requirement of registration under the blue-sky laws of most States and the Securities Act of 1933. If no exemption is available, a corporation offering for sale or selling its shares of stock or other securities, as well as any person selling such securities, is subject to court injunction,

possible criminal prosecution, and civil liability in damages to the persons to whom securities are sold in violation of the regulatory statute. A discussion of Federal regulation of securities appears in *Chapter 44*.

An investor has the right to transfer her investment securities by sale, gift, or pledge. The right to transfer is a valuable one, and easy transferability augments the value and marketability of investment securities. The availability of a ready market for any security affords liquidity and makes the security both attractive to investors and useful as collateral. The Uniform Commercial Code (UCC), Article 8, Investment Securities, contains the statutory rules applicable to transfers of investment securities; these rules are similar to those in Article 3, which concern negotiable instruments. In 1994 a revision to Article 8 was promulgated, and all of the States have adopted the revision. The Federal securities laws also regulate several aspects of the transfer of investment securities, as discussed in *Chapter 44*.

This chapter will discuss debt and equity securities as well as the payment of dividends and other distributions to shareholders.

DEBT SECURITIES

Corporations frequently find it advantageous to use debt as a source of funds. **Debt securities** (also called **bonds**) generally involve the corporation's promise to repay the principal amount of a loan at a stated time and to pay interest, usually at a fixed rate, while the debt is outstanding. Thus, a debt security creates a debtor-creditor relationship between the corporation and the holder of the security. In addition to bonds, a corporation may finance its operations through other forms of debt, such as credit extended by its suppliers and short-term commercial paper. Some State statutes, but not the Revised Act, permit the articles of incorporation to confer voting rights on debt security holders; a few States allow other shareholder rights to be conferred on bondholders.

AUTHORITY TO USE DEBT SECURITIES

The Revised Act provides that every corporation has the power "to make contracts and guarantees, incur liabilities, borrow money, issue its notes, bonds, and other obligations (which may be convertible into or include the option to purchase other securities of the corporation), and secure any of its obligations by mortgage or pledge of any of its property, franchises, or income." Section 3.02. The board of directors may issue bonds without the authorization or consent of the shareholders.

TYPES OF DEBT SECURITIES

Debt securities can be classified into various types according to their characteristics. The variants and combinations possible within each type are limited only by a corporation's ingenuity. Debt securities are typically issued under an **indenture** or debt agreement, which specifies in great detail the terms of the loan. The Federal Trust Indenture Act of 1939 applies to indentures covering bonds issued for $10 million or more.

In addition, a **high-yield bond (non-investment-grade bond** or **junk bond)** is a bond that is rated below investment grade at the time of purchase. These bonds have a greater risk of default than investment-grade bonds but typically pay higher yields than higher grade bonds to make them attractive to investors.

UNSECURED BONDS

Unsecured bonds, usually called **debentures**, have only the obligation of the corporation behind them. Debenture holders are thus unsecured creditors and rank equally with other general creditors. To protect the unsecured bondholders, indentures frequently impose limitations on the corporation's borrowing, its payment of dividends, and its redemption and reacquisition of its own shares. They also may require the corporation to maintain specified minimum reserves.

SECURED BONDS

A secured creditor is one whose claim not only is enforceable against the general assets of the corporation but also is a lien upon specific property. Thus, **secured** or mortgage **bonds** provide the security of specific corporate property in addition to the general obligation of the corporation. After resorting to the specified security, the holder of secured bonds becomes a general creditor for any unpaid amount of the debt.

INCOME BONDS

Traditionally, debt securities bear a fixed interest rate that is payable without regard to the financial condition of the corporation. **Income bonds**, on the other hand, condition the payment of interest to some extent upon corporate earnings. This provision lessens the burden of the debt upon the issuer during periods of financial adversity. **Participating bonds** call for a stated percentage of return regardless of earnings, with additional payments dependent upon earnings.

CONVERTIBLE BONDS

Convertible bonds may be exchanged, usually at the option of the holder, for other securities of the corporation at a specified ratio. For example, a convertible bond may provide that the bondholder shall have the right for a specified time to exchange each bond for twenty shares of common stock.

CALLABLE BONDS

Callable bonds are bonds subject to a redemption provision that permits the corporation to redeem or call (pay off) all or part of the issue before maturity at a specified redemption price. This provision enables the corporation to reduce fixed costs, to improve its credit rating, to refinance at a lower interest rate, to free mortgaged property, or to reduce its proportion of debt.

EQUITY SECURITIES

An **equity security** is a source of capital creating an ownership interest in the corporation. The holders of equity security, as owners of the corporation, occupy a position financially riskier than that of creditors; they, more than any other class of investor, bear the impact of changes in the corporation's fortunes and general economic conditions.

Though **shares** of equity securities describe a proportionate proprietary interest in a corporate enterprise, they do not in any way vest their owner with title to any of the corporation's property. Shares do, however, confer on their owner a threefold interest in the corporation: (1) the right to participate in control, (2) the right to participate in the earnings of the corporation, and (3) the right to participate in the residual assets of the corporation upon dissolution. The shareholder's interest is usually evidenced by a certificate of ownership and is recorded by the corporation.

ISSUANCE OF SHARES

The State of incorporation regulates the issuance of shares by determining the type of shares that may be issued, the kinds and amount of consideration for which shares may be issued, and the rights of shareholders to purchase a proportionate part of additionally issued shares. Moreover, the

Federal government and each State in which the shares are issued or sold regulate the issuance and sale of shares.

AUTHORITY TO ISSUE

The initial amount of shares to be issued is determined by the promoters or incorporators and is generally governed by practical business considerations and financial needs. A corporation is limited, however, to selling only the amount of shares that has been authorized in its articles of incorporation. Section 6.03. Unauthorized shares of stock that a corporation purportedly issues are void. The rights of parties entitled to these overissued shares are governed by Article 8 of the UCC, which provides that the corporation must either obtain an identical security, if it is reasonably available, for the person entitled to the security or pay that person the price he (or the last purchaser for value) paid for it, with interest from the date of that person's demand. UCC Section 8–210.

Once the amount of shares that the corporation is authorized to issue has been specified in the charter, it cannot be increased or decreased without amending the articles of incorporation. This means that the shareholders, who must approve any amendment to the articles of incorporation, have residual authority over increases in the amount of authorized capital stock. Consequently, articles of incorporation commonly specify more shares than are to be issued initially.

PREEMPTIVE RIGHTS

A shareholder's proportionate interest in a corporation can be changed by either a disproportionate issuance of additional shares or a disproportionate reacquisition of outstanding shares. In either transaction, management owes both the shareholder and the corporation a fiduciary duty. Moreover, when additional shares are issued, a shareholder may have the **preemptive right** to purchase a proportionate part of the new issue. Preemptive rights are used far more frequently in closely held corporations than in publicly traded corporations. Without such rights, a shareholder may be unable to prevent a dilution of his ownership interest in the corporation. For example, Leonard owns two hundred shares of stock of the Fordham Company, which has a total of one thousand shares outstanding. The company decides to increase its capital stock by issuing one thousand additional shares of stock. If Leonard has preemptive rights, he and every other shareholder will be offered one share of the newly issued stock for every share they own. If he accepts the offer and buys the stock, he will have four hundred shares out of a total of two thousand outstanding, and his relative interest in the corporation will be unchanged. Without preemptive rights, however, he would have only two hundred out of the two thousand shares outstanding; instead of owning 20 percent of the stock, he would own 10 percent.

Most statutes expressly authorize articles of incorporation to deny or limit preemptive rights to the issuance of additionally authorized shares. In about half of the States, preemptive rights exist unless denied by the charter (**opt-out**); in about half of the States, they do not exist unless the charter so provides (**opt-in**).

Certain shares are not subject to preemptive rights. In some States preemptive rights do not apply to the reissue of previously issued shares. In addition, preemptive rights generally do not apply to shares issued for noncash consideration or shares issued in connection with a merger or consolidation. Moreover, preemptive rights do not apply to the issuance of unissued shares that were originally authorized if the shares represent part of the initial capitalization.

The Revised Act adopts the opt-in approach: preemptive rights are nonexistent unless the charter provides for them. Section 6.30. If the charter simply states that "the corporation elects to have preemptive rights," then the shareholders have a preemptive right to acquire proportional amounts of the corporation's unissued shares, but they have no preemptive rights with respect to (1) shares issued as compensation to directors, officers, and employees; (2) shares issued within six months of incorporation; and (3) shares issued for consideration other than money. In addition, holders of nonvoting preferred stock have no preemptive rights with respect to *any* class of shares, and holders of voting common shares have no preemptive rights with respect to preferred stock unless the preferred stock is convertible into common stock. Section 6.30(b). The articles of incorporation may expressly modify any or all of these limitations.

AMOUNT OF CONSIDERATION FOR SHARES

The board of directors usually determines the price for which the corporation will issue shares, although the charter may reserve this power to the shareholders. Section 6.21. Shares are deemed fully paid and nonassessable when the corporation receives the consideration for which the board of directors authorized their issuance. Section 6.21(d). The amount of that consideration depends upon the kind of shares being issued.

PAR VALUE STOCK In some States a corporation must specify in the articles of incorporation either a par value for its shares or that the shares are no par. Par value shares may be issued for any amount, not less than par, set by the board of directors or shareholders. The par value of a share of stock can be an arbitrary value selected by the corporation and may or may not reflect either the actual value of the share or the actual price paid to the corporation. It indicates only the *minimum price* that the corporation must receive for the share. The par value of stock must be stated in the articles of incorporation. The consideration received constitutes *stated capital* to the extent of the par value of the shares; any consideration in excess of par value constitutes *capital surplus*. It is common practice to authorize *low* or *nominal* par shares, such as $1 per share, and issue these shares at a considerably higher price, thereby providing ample capital surplus. By doing so the corporation, in some jurisdictions, obtains greater flexibility in declaring subsequent distributions to shareholders.

The Revised Act, the 1980 amendments to the Model Business Corporation Act (MBCA), and at least twenty-eight States have eliminated the concepts of par value, stated capital, and capital surplus. Under these acts, all shares may be issued for such consideration as authorized by the board of directors or, if the charter so provides, the shareholders. Section 6.21. A corporation, however, may elect to issue shares with par value. Section 2.02(b).

NO PAR VALUE STOCK Shares without par value may be issued for any amount set by the board of directors or shareholders. Under incorporation statutes recognizing par value, stated value, and capital surplus, the entire consideration the corporation receives for such stock constitutes stated capital unless the board of directors allocates a portion of the consideration to capital surplus. MBCA Section 21, repealed in 1980. (As noted above, the Revised Act and the 1980 amendments to the MBCA eliminated the concepts of par value, stated capital, and capital surplus.) The directors are free to allocate any or all of the consideration received, unless the no par stock has a liquidation preference. In that event, only the consideration in excess of the amount of liquidation preference may be allocated to capital surplus. No par shares provide the directors with great latitude in establishing capital surplus, which can, in some jurisdictions, provide greater flexibility in declaring subsequent distributions to shareholders.

TREASURY STOCK Treasury stock consists of shares that the corporation has issued and subsequently reacquired. Treasury shares are issued *but not* outstanding, in contrast to shares owned by shareholders, which are issued *and* outstanding. A corporation may sell treasury shares for any amount the board of directors determines, even if the shares have a par value that is more than the sale price. Treasury shares provide neither voting rights nor preemptive rights; furthermore, no dividend may be paid upon them.

The Revised Act advances the 1980 amendments to the MBCA, which eliminated the concept of treasury shares. Under the Revised Act, all shares reacquired by a corporation constitute authorized but unissued shares, unless the articles of incorporation prohibit reissue, in which event the authorized shares are reduced by the number of shares reacquired. Section 6.31.

◆ **SEE FIGURE 35-1: Issuance of Shares**

PAYMENT FOR SHARES

Two major issues arise regarding payment for shares. First, what type of consideration may the corporation validly accept in payment for shares? Second, who shall determine the value to be placed upon the consideration the corporation receives in payment for shares?

TYPE OF CONSIDERATION In terms of the issuance of capital stock, consideration receives a more limited definition than it does under contract law. In about twenty-five States, cash, property, and services actually rendered to the corporation are generally acceptable as valid consideration, but promissory notes and promises regarding the performance of future services are not. Some States permit shares to be issued for preincorporation services; other States do not.

The Revised Act greatly liberalized these rules by specifically validating for the issuance of shares consideration consisting of any tangible or intangible property or *benefit* to the corporation, including cash, services performed, *contracts for future services*, and *promissory notes*. Section 6.21(b). To guard against possible abuse, the corporation may place the shares in escrow or otherwise restrict their transfer until the services are performed, the note is paid, or the benefits are received. If the services are not performed, the note is not paid, or the benefits are not received, the shares escrowed or restricted may be canceled. Section 6.21(e). Moreover, the Revised Act requires that corporations annually inform their shareholders in writing of all shares issued during the previous year for promissory notes or promises of future services. Section 16.21.

VALUATION OF CONSIDERATION Determining the value to be placed on the consideration that stock purchasers will exchange for shares is the responsibility of the directors. Many jurisdictions hold that this valuation is a matter of opinion and that, in the absence of fraud in the transaction, the judgment of the board of directors as to the value of the consideration actually or to be received for shares shall be conclusive. For example, assume that the directors of Elite Corporation authorize the issuance of two thousand shares of common stock for $10 per share to Kramer for property that the directors purportedly value at $20,000. The valuation is fraudulent, however, and the property is actually worth only $10,000. Kramer is liable to Elite Corporation and its creditors for $10,000. If, on the other hand, the directors had made the valuation without fraud and in good faith, Kramer would not be liable, even though the property is actually worth less than $20,000.

Under the Revised Act, the directors simply determine whether or not the consideration received (or to be received) for shares is *adequate*. Their determination is "conclusive insofar as the adequacy of consideration for the issuance of shares relates to whether the shares are validly issued, fully

◆ **FIGURE 35-1: Issuance of Shares**

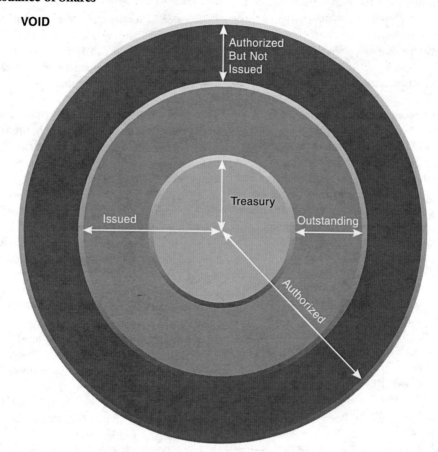

paid, and nonassessable." Section 6.21(c). Under the Revised Act, the articles of incorporation may reserve to the shareholders the powers granted to the board regarding the issuance of shares. Section 6.21(a).

LIABILITY FOR SHARES

A purchaser of shares has no liability to the corporation or its creditors with respect to the shares except to pay the corporation either the consideration for which the shares were authorized to be issued or the consideration specified in the preincorporation stock subscription. Section 6.22(a). When the corporation receives that consideration, the shares are fully paid and nonassessable. Section 6.21(d). A transferee who acquires these shares in good faith and without knowledge or notice that the full consideration had not been paid is not personally liable to the corporation or its creditors for the unpaid portion of the consideration.

CLASSES OF SHARES

Corporations are generally authorized by statute to issue different classes of stock, which may vary with respect to their rights to dividends, their voting rights, and their right to share in the assets of the corporation upon liquidation. The usual classifications of stock are common and preferred shares. Although the Revised Act has eliminated the terms *preferred* and *common*, it permits the issuance of shares with different preferences, limitations, and relative rights. Section 6.01. The Revised Act explicitly requires that the charter authorize "(1) one or more classes of shares that together have unlimited voting rights, and (2) one or more classes of shares (which may be the same class or classes as those with voting rights) that together are entitled to receive the net assets of the corporation upon dissolution." Section 6.01(b). In most States, however, even nonvoting shares may vote on certain mergers, share exchanges, and other fundamental changes which affect that class of shares as a class. See *Chapter 37*.

COMMON STOCK

Common stock does not have any special contract rights or preferences. Often the only class of stock outstanding, it generally represents the greatest proportion of the corporation's capital structure and bears the greatest risk of loss should the enterprise fail.

Common stock may be divided into one or more classes bearing designations, limitations, or relative rights stated in the articles of incorporation. Section 6.01. The Revised Act and some States permit common stock to be redeemable or convertible. Section 6.01(c)(2). The articles also may limit or deny the voting rights of classes of common shares, but at least one or more classes of shares must together have unlimited voting rights. Section 6.01(b). For example, Class A common may be entitled to three times the dividends per share to which Class B common is entitled. Or Class A common may be entitled to elect six directors while Class B common elects three directors. Or Class A common may have two votes per share while Class B common has no votes per share.

PREFERRED STOCK

Stock generally is considered preferred stock if it has contractual rights superior to those of common stock with regard to dividends, assets upon liquidation, or both. (Most preferred stock has both dividend and liquidation preferences.) Other special rights or privileges generally do not remove stock from the common stock classification. The articles of incorporation must provide for the contractual rights and preferences of an issue of preferred stock. Section 6.01(c).

Notwithstanding the special rights and preferences that distinguish preferred from common stock, both represent a contribution of capital. Preferred stock is no more a debt than common, and until a dividend is declared, the holder of preferred shares is not a creditor of the corporation. Furthermore, the rights of preferred shareholders are subordinate to the rights of the corporation's creditors.

DIVIDEND PREFERENCES Though the holders of an issue of preferred stock with a dividend preference will receive full dividends before any dividend may be paid to holders of common stock, no dividend is payable upon any class of stock, common or preferred, unless such dividend has been declared by the board of directors. The dividend preference may be described in terms of dollars per share ("$3.00 preferred") or as a percentage of par value ("10 percent preferred").

Preferred stock may provide that dividends are cumulative, noncumulative, or cumulative to the extent earned. For **cumulative** stock, if the board does not declare regular dividends on the preferred stock, such omitted dividends cumulate, and no dividend may be declared on common stock until all dividend arrearages on the preferred stock are declared and paid. For **noncumulative** stock, regular dividends do not cumulate upon the board's failure to declare them, and all rights to a dividend for the period omitted are gone forever. Accordingly, noncumulative stock has a prior-

ity over common only during a fiscal period in which a dividend on common stock is declared. Unless the charter expressly makes the dividends on preferred stock noncumulative, the courts generally hold them to be cumulative. **Cumulative-to-the-extent-earned** stock cumulates unpaid dividends only to the extent that funds were legally available to pay such dividends during that fiscal period.

Preferred stock also may be participating, although generally it is not. **Participating preferred** shares are entitled to their original dividend, and after the common shares receive a specified amount, the participating preferred stock shares with the common stock in any additional dividends. The manner in which preferred stock participates in dividends with common stock must be specified in the articles of incorporation. For example, a class of participating preferred stock could be entitled to share at the same rate with the common stock in any additional distribution of earnings for a given year *after* provision has been made for paying the prior preferred dividend and for paying dividends on the common at a rate equal to the fixed rate of the preferred.

LIQUIDATION PREFERENCES After a corporation has been dissolved, its assets liquidated, and the claims of its creditors satisfied, the remaining assets are distributed *pro rata* among the shareholders according to their priority as provided in the articles of incorporation. In the event that a class of stock with a dividend preference does not expressly provide for a preference of any kind upon dissolution and liquidation, its holders share *pro rata* with the common shareholders.

When the articles provide a liquidation preference, preferred stock has priority over common stock to the extent the articles state. In addition, if specified, preferred shares may participate beyond the liquidation preference in a stated ratio with other classes of shares. Such shares are said to be participating preferred with reference to liquidation. Preferred shares not so specified do not participate beyond the liquidation preference.

ADDITIONAL RIGHTS AND LIMITATIONS Preferred stock may have additional rights, designations, and limitations. For instance, it may be expressly denied voting rights if the incorporation statute so permits, or it may be redeemable by the corporation or convertible into shares of another class. Sections 6.01(c) and 7.21(a). Preferred stock is typically nonvoting.

STOCK OPTIONS

A corporation may issue **stock options** entitling their holders to purchase from the corporation shares of a specified class or classes. A **stock warrant** is a type of stock option that typically has a longer term and is freely transferable. A **stock right** is a short-term warrant. The board of directors determines the terms upon which stock rights, options, or warrants are issued; their form and content; and the consideration for which the shares are to be issued. Section 6.24. Stock options or warrants are used in incentive compensation plans for directors, officers, and employees. Corporations also use them in raising capital to make one class of securities more attractive by including in it the right to purchase shares in another class immediately or at a later date.

◆ **SEE FIGURE 35-2: Debt and Equity Securities**

DIVIDENDS AND OTHER DISTRIBUTIONS

The board of directors, in its discretion, determines when and in what amount to declare distributions and dividends. The corporation's working capital requirements, shareholder expectations, tax consequences, and other factors influence the board as it creates distribution policy. In addition, the conditions under which the earnings of a business may be paid out in the form of dividends or other distributions of corporate assets will depend upon the contractual rights of those who hold the particular shares involved or shares having superior rights, provisions in the charter and bylaws of the corporation, and provisions of the State incorporation statute that are designed to protect creditors and shareholders from the dissipation of corporate assets. Creditors

receive more significant protection under contractual restrictions typically included in their loan agreements, as well as under State fraudulent conveyance laws and Federal bankruptcy law.

TYPES OF DIVIDENDS AND OTHER DISTRIBUTIONS

The Revised Act defines a **distribution** as

> a direct or indirect transfer of money or other property (except its own shares) or incurrence of indebtedness by a corporation to or for the benefit of its shareholders in respect of any of its shares. A distribution may be in the form of a declaration or payment of a dividend; a purchase, redemption, or other acquisition of shares; a distribution of indebtedness; or otherwise. Section 1.40(6).

The comments to this section explain that the term *indirect* is intended to include any other transaction the substance of which is clearly the same as that of a typical dividend or share repurchase, without regard to how the transaction is labeled or structured. Stock dividends and stock splits, which are not included in this definition, will also be covered in this section.

The Revised Act validates in close corporations unanimous shareholder agreements by which the shareholders

◆ **FIGURE 35-2: Debt and Equity Securities**

		Equity	
	Debt	Preferred	Common
Ownership Interest	No	Yes	Yes
Obligation to Repay Principal	Yes	No	No
Fixed Maturity	Yes	No	No
Obligation to Pay Income	Yes	No	No
Preference on Income	Yes	Yes	No
Preference on Liquidation	Yes	Yes	No
Voting Rights	Some States	Yes, unless denied	Yes, unless denied
Redeemable	Yes	Yes	In some States
Convertible	Yes	Yes	In some States

may relax traditional corporate formalities. Section 7.32. This section, for example, expressly authorizes shareholder agreements that permit making distributions not in proportion to share ownership.

CASH DIVIDENDS

The most customary type of dividend is a cash dividend, declared and paid at regular intervals from legally available funds. These dividends may vary in amount, depending upon the policy of the board of directors and the earnings of the enterprise.

PROPERTY DIVIDENDS

Although dividends are almost always paid in cash, shareholders occasionally receive a property dividend, a distribution of earnings in the form of property. On one occasion, a distillery declared and paid a dividend in bonded whiskey.

STOCK DIVIDENDS

A stock or share dividend is a proportional distribution of additional shares of the capital stock of a corporation to its shareholders. The practical and legal significance of a stock dividend differs greatly from that of a dividend payable in cash or property. Following the payment of a stock dividend, the assets of the corporation are no less than they were before, and the shareholder's relative interest in the net worth of the corporation is no greater than it was before, except possibly where the dividend is paid in shares of a different class. His shares will each represent a smaller proportionate interest in the corporation's assets, but by reason of the increase in the number of shares, his total investment will remain the same. Accordingly, a stock dividend is *not* considered a distribution. Under incorporation statutes recognizing par value and stated capital, a stock dividend results in the transfer from surplus to stated capital of an amount equal to the par value of the stock dividend.

STOCK SPLITS

In a stock split, the corporation simply breaks each of the issued and outstanding shares into a greater number of shares, each representing a proportionately smaller interest in the corporation. Under incorporation statutes recognizing par value and stated capital, the par value of the shares to be split is divided among the new shares. The usual purpose of a stock split is to lower the price per share to a more marketable price and thus increase the number of potential shareholders. Like a stock dividend, a stock split is not a distribution; unlike a stock dividend, a split entails no transfer of surplus to stated capital.

LIQUIDATING DIVIDENDS

Although dividends ordinarily are identified with the distribution of profits, a distribution of capital assets to shareholders is referred to as a liquidating dividend in some jurisdictions. Incorporation statutes usually require that the shareholder be informed when a distribution is a liquidating dividend.

REDEMPTION OF SHARES

Redemption is the repurchase by the corporation of its own shares, usually at its own option. The Model Act and the statutes of many States permit corporations to redeem preferred shares but not common stock; the Revised Act, in contrast, does not prohibit redeemable common stock. The articles of incorporation must expressly provide for the power of redemption.

ACQUISITION OF SHARES

A corporation may acquire its own shares. Such shares, unless canceled, are referred to as treasury shares. Under the Revised Act, such shares are considered authorized but unissued. Section 6.31. As with redemption, the acquisition of shares constitutes a distribution to shareholders and has an effect similar to a dividend.

LEGAL RESTRICTIONS ON DIVIDENDS AND OTHER DISTRIBUTIONS

Several legal restrictions limit the amount of distributions a board of directors may declare. Though all States have statutes restricting the funds that are legally available for dividends and other distributions of corporate assets, lender-imposed contractual restrictions often limit the declaration of dividends and distributions even more stringently.

States restrict the payment of dividends and other distributions to protect creditors. All States impose the **equity insolvency test**, which prohibits the payment of any dividend or other distribution when the corporation either is insolvent or would become so through the payment of the dividend or distribution. **Insolvent** in the equity sense indicates the inability of a corporation to pay its debts as they become due in the usual course of business. In addition, almost all States impose further restrictions regarding the funds that are legally available to pay dividends and other distributions. These additional restrictions are based upon the corporation's assets or balance sheet, whereas the equity insolvency test is based upon the corporation's cash flow.

DEFINITIONS

The legal, asset-based restrictions upon the payment of dividends or other distributions involve the concepts of earned surplus, surplus, net assets, stated capital, and capital surplus.

Earned surplus consists of the corporation's undistributed net profits, income, gains, and losses, computed from its date of incorporation.

Surplus is the amount by which the net assets of a corporation exceed its stated capital.

Net assets equal the amount by which the total assets of a corporation exceed its total debts.

Stated capital is the sum of the consideration the corporation has received for its issued stock, excepting the consideration properly allocated to capital surplus but including any amount transferred to stated capital when a stock dividend is declared. In the case of par value shares, the amount of stated capital is the total par value of all the issued shares. In the case of no par stock, it is the consideration the corporation has received for all the no par shares that it has issued, except that amount allocated to capital surplus or paid-in surplus.

Capital surplus means the entire surplus of a corporation other than its earned surplus. It may result from an allocation of part of the consideration received for no par shares, from any consideration in excess of par value received for par shares, or from a higher reappraisal of certain corporate assets.

◆ **SEE FIGURE 35-3: Key Concepts in Legal Restrictions upon Distributions**

LEGAL RESTRICTIONS ON CASH DIVIDENDS

Each State imposes an equity insolvency test on the payment of dividends. The States differ regarding the asset-based or balance sheet test they apply. Some apply the earned surplus test, others use the surplus test, and the Revised Act adopts a net assets test.

EARNED SURPLUS TEST Unreserved and unrestricted earned surplus is available for dividends in all jurisdictions. Many States permit dividends to be paid *only* from earned surplus; corporations in these jurisdictions may not pay dividends out of capital surplus or stated capital. In addition, the corporation may not pay dividends if it is or would be rendered insolvent in the equity sense by the payment. The MBCA used this test until 1980.

SURPLUS TEST A number of less-restrictive States permit dividends to be paid out of any surplus—earned or capital. Some of these States express this test by prohibiting dividends that impair stated capital. Moreover, dividends may not be paid if the corporation is or would be rendered insolvent in the equity sense by the payment.

NET ASSETS TEST The MBCA, as amended in 1980, and the Revised Act have adopted a net assets test. Section 6.40 of the Revised Act as amended states,

(c) No distribution may be made if, after giving it effect:

(1) the corporation would not be able to pay its debts as they become due in the usual course of business; or
(2) the corporation's total assets would be less than the sum of its total liabilities plus (unless the articles of incorporation permit otherwise) the amount that would be needed, if the corporation were to be dissolved at the time of the distribution, to satisfy the preferential rights upon dissolution of shareholders

◆ **FIGURE 35-3: Key Concepts in Legal Restrictions upon Distributions**

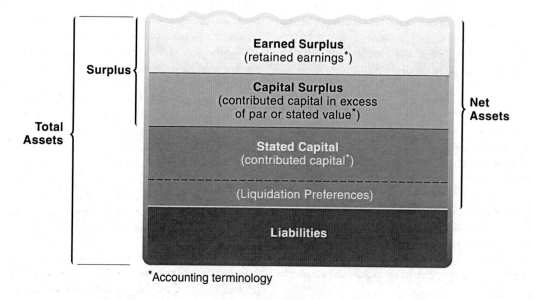

*Accounting terminology

whose preferential rights are superior to those receiving the distribution.

LEGAL RESTRICTIONS ON LIQUIDATING DISTRIBUTIONS

Even those States that do not permit cash dividends to be paid from capital surplus usually will permit distributions, or dividends, in partial liquidation from that source. Before 1980, the Model Act had such a provision. A distribution paid out of such surplus is a return to the shareholders of part of their investment.

The corporation may make no such distribution, however, when it is insolvent or when the distribution would render it so. Distributions from capital surplus are also restricted to protect the liquidation preference and cumulative dividend arrearages of preferred shareholders. Unless provided for in the articles of incorporation, a liquidating dividend must be authorized not only by the board of directors but also by the affirmative vote of the holders of a majority of the outstanding shares of stock of each class.

Because the Revised Act does not distinguish between cash and liquidating dividends, it therefore imposes upon liquidating dividends the same limitations it imposes upon cash dividends, discussed above. Section 6.40.

LEGAL RESTRICTIONS ON REDEMPTION AND ACQUISITION OF SHARES

To protect creditors and holders of other classes of shares, most States place statutory restrictions upon redemption. A corporation may not redeem or purchase its redeemable shares when insolvent or when such redemption or purchase would render it insolvent or would reduce its net assets below the aggregate amount payable upon shares having prior or equal rights to the assets of the corporation upon involuntary dissolution.

A corporation may purchase its own shares only out of earned surplus or, if the articles of incorporation permit or if the shareholders approve, out of capital surplus. As with redemption, the corporation may make no purchase of shares when insolvent or when such purchase would make it insolvent.

The Revised Act permits a corporation to purchase, redeem, or otherwise acquire its own shares unless (1) the corporation's total assets after the distribution would be less than the sum of its total liabilities and the maximum amount that then would be payable for all outstanding shares having preferential rights in liquidation, or (2) the corporation would be unable to pay its debts as they become due in the usual course of its business. Section 6.40.

Additional restrictions may apply to a corporation's acquisition of its own shares. In close corporations, for example, courts may scrutinize acquisitions for compliance with the good faith and fair dealing requirements of the fiduciary duty.

DECLARATION AND PAYMENT OF DISTRIBUTIONS

The declaration of dividends and other distributions is within the discretion of the board of directors and may not be delegated. If the charter clearly and expressly provides for mandatory dividends, however, the board must comply with the provision. Nonetheless, such provisions are extremely infrequent, and shareholders cannot usurp the board's power in any other way, although it is in their power to elect a new board. Moreover, the board cannot discriminate in its declaration of dividends among shareholders of the same class.

SHAREHOLDERS' RIGHT TO COMPEL A DIVIDEND

Should the directors fail to declare a dividend, a shareholder may bring a suit in equity against them and the corporation to seek a mandatory injunction requiring the directors to declare a dividend. Courts of equity are reluctant to order an injunction of this kind, which involves substituting the business judgment of the court for that of the directors elected by the shareholders. Where the evidence shows noncorporate motives or personal animosity as the basis for a refusal to declare dividends, however, a court may require the directors to distribute an apparently reasonable portion of the earnings. This is not a frequent occurrence; *Dodge v. Ford Motor Co.* is a landmark example.

With respect to the directors' discretion regarding the declaration of dividends, a preferred shareholder having prior rights with respect to dividends occupies a position identical to that of a holder of common shares. In the absence of special contractual or statutory rights, the holder of preferred shares, like the holder of common ones, must abide by the directors' decision.

EFFECT OF DECLARATION

Once lawfully and properly declared, a cash dividend is considered a debt the corporation owes to the shareholders. It follows from this debtor-creditor relationship that, once declared, a dividend cannot be rescinded without the shareholders' consent; a stock dividend, however, may be revoked unless actually distributed.

LIABILITY FOR IMPROPER DIVIDENDS AND DISTRIBUTIONS

The Revised Act imposes personal liability upon the directors of a corporation who vote for or assent to the declaration of a dividend or other distribution of corporate assets contrary to the incorporation statute or the articles of

◆ **FIGURE 35-4: Liability for Improper Distributions**

	Corporation Solvent	Corporation Insolvent
Nonbreaching Director	No	No
Breaching Director	Yes	Yes
Knowing Shareholder	Yes	Yes
Innocent Shareholder	No	Yes

incorporation. Section 8.33(a). The measure of damages is the amount of the dividend or distribution in excess of the amount that the corporation lawfully may have paid.

A director is not liable if she acted in accordance with the relevant standard of conduct: in good faith, with reasonable care, and in a manner she reasonably believed to be in the best interests of the corporation. Sections 8.30 and 8.33. (This standard of conduct is discussed in the next chapter.) In discharging this duty, a director is entitled to rely in good faith upon financial statements presented by the corporation's officers, public accountants, or finance committee. Such statements must be prepared on the basis of "accounting practices and principles that are reasonable in the circumstances or on a fair valuation or other method that is reasonable in the circumstances." Section 6.40(d). According to the Comments to this section, generally accepted accounting principles are *always* reasonable in the circumstances; other accounting principles *may* be acceptable under a general standard of reasonableness.

A shareholder's obligation to repay an illegally declared dividend depends upon a variety of factors, which may include the good or bad faith in which the shareholder accepted the dividend, his knowledge of the facts, the solvency or insolvency of the corporation, and, in some instances, special statutory provisions. Statutory liability on the part of directors does not relieve shareholders of the duty to make repayment.

A shareholder who receives illegal dividends with knowledge of their illegality is under a duty to refund them. See Section 8.33(b). Where the corporation is insolvent, the shareholder may retain not even a dividend he received in good faith, as the assets of an insolvent corporation are regarded as a trust fund for its creditors. Where an unsuspecting shareholder receives an illegal dividend from a solvent corporation, however, the majority rule is that the corporation cannot compel a refund.

◆ **SEE FIGURE 35-4: Liability for Improper Distributions**

CHAPTER SUMMARY

DEBT SECURITIES

AUTHORITY TO ISSUE DEBT SECURITIES	**Definitions** • *Debt Security* source of capital creating no ownership interest and involving the corporation's promise to repay funds lent to it • *Bond* a debt security **Rule** each corporation has the power to issue debt securities as determined by the board of directors
TYPES OF DEBT SECURITIES	**Unsecured Bonds** called debentures; have only the obligation of the corporation behind them **Secured Bonds** are claims against a corporation's general assets and also liens on specific property **Income Bonds** condition to some extent the payment of interest on corporate earnings

Participating Bonds call for a stated percentage of return regardless of earnings, with additional payments dependent upon earnings
Convertible Bonds may be exchanged for other securities
Callable Bonds bonds subject to redemption

EQUITY SECURITIES

ISSUANCE OF SHARES	**Definitions** • *Equity Security* source of capital creating an ownership interest in the corporation • *Share* a proportionate ownership interest in a corporation • *Treasury Stock* shares reacquired by a corporation **Authority to Issue** only those shares authorized in the articles of incorporation may be issued **Preemptive Rights** right to purchase a *pro rata* share of new stock offerings **Amount of Consideration for Shares** shares are deemed fully paid and nonassessable when a corporation receives the consideration for which the board of directors authorized the issuance of the shares, which in the case of par value stock must be at least par **Payment for Newly Issued Shares** may be cash, property, and services actually rendered, as determined by the board of directors; under the Revised Act, promises to contribute cash, property, or services are also permitted
CLASSES OF SHARES	**Common Stock** stock not having any special contract rights **Preferred Stock** stock having contractual rights superior to those of common stock • *Dividend Preferences* must receive full dividends before any dividend may be paid on common stock • *Liquidation Preferences* priority over common stock in corporate assets upon liquidation **Stock Options** contractual right to purchase stock from a corporation

DIVIDENDS AND OTHER DISTRIBUTIONS

TYPES OF DIVIDENDS AND OTHER DISTRIBUTIONS	**Distributions** transfers of property by a corporation to any of its shareholders with respect to its shares **Cash Dividends** the most common type of distribution **Property Dividends** distribution in the form of property **Stock Dividends** a proportional distribution of additional shares of stock **Stock Splits** each of the outstanding shares is broken into a greater number of shares **Liquidating Dividends** a distribution of capital assets to shareholders **Redemption of Shares** a corporation's exercise of the right to purchase its own shares **Acquisition of Shares** a corporation's repurchase of its own shares
LEGAL RESTRICTIONS ON DIVIDENDS AND OTHER DISTRIBUTIONS	**Legal Restrictions on Cash Dividends** dividends may be paid only if the cash flow and applicable balance sheet tests are satisfied • *Cash Flow Test* a corporation must not be or become insolvent (unable to pay its debts as they become due in the usual course of business) • *Balance Sheet Test* varies among the States and includes the earned surplus test (available in all States), the surplus test, and the net assets test (used by the Model and Revised Acts) **Legal Restrictions on Liquidating Distributions** States usually permit distribution in partial liquidation from capital surplus unless the company is insolvent

Legal Restrictions on Redemptions of Shares in most States, a corporation may not redeem shares when insolvent or when such redemption would render it insolvent

Legal Restrictions on Acquisition of Shares restrictions similar to those on cash dividends usually apply

DECLARATION AND PAYMENT OF DISTRIBUTIONS	**Shareholders' Right to Compel a Distribution** the declaration of distributions is within the discretion of the board of directors, and only rarely will a court substitute its business judgment for that of the board's **Effect of Declaration** once properly declared, a distribution is considered a debt the corporation owes to the shareholders
LIABILITY FOR IMPROPER DIVIDENDS AND DISTRIBUTIONS	**Directors** the directors who assent to an improper dividend are liable for the unlawful amount of the dividend **Shareholders** a shareholder must return illegal dividends if he knew of the illegality, if the dividend resulted from his fraud, or if the corporation is insolvent

Management Structure

The corporate management structure, as required by State incorporation statutes, is pyramidal. At the base of the pyramid are the *shareholders*, who are the residual owners of the corporation. Basic to their role in controlling the corporation is the right to elect representatives to manage the ordinary business matters of the corporation and the right to approve all extraordinary matters.

The *board of directors*, as the shareholders' elected representatives, are delegated the power to manage the business of the corporation. Directors exercise dominion and control over the corporation, hold positions of trust and confidence, and determine questions of operating policy. Because they are not expected to devote their time completely to the affairs of the corporation, directors have broad authority to delegate power to agents and to *officers* who hold their offices at the will of the board and who, in turn, hire and fire all necessary operating personnel and run the day-to-day affairs of the corporation.

◆ **SEE FIGURE 36-1: Management Structure of Corporations: The Statutory Model**

CORPORATE GOVERNANCE

The statutory model of corporate management, although required by most States, accurately describes the actual governance of only a few corporations. A great majority of corporations are closely held; they have a small number of stockholders and no ready market for their shares, and most of the shareholders actively participate in the management of the business. Typically, the shareholders of a closely held corporation are also its directors and officers.

Although the statutory model and the actual governance of closely held corporations diverge, in most States **closely held corporations** must adhere to the general corporate statutory model. One of the greatest burdens conventional general business corporation statutes impose on closely held corporations is a set of rigid corporate formalities. Although

these formalities may be necessary and desirable in publicly held corporations, where management and ownership are separate, in a closely held corporation, where the owners are usually the managers, many of these formalities are unnecessary and meaningless. Consequently, shareholders in closely held corporations tend to disregard corporate formalities, sometimes forfeiting their limited liability as a result. In response to this problem, the 1969 Amendments to the Model Business Corporation Act (MBCA) included several liberalizing provisions for closely held corporations. The amendments were carried over to the Revised Act. Moreover, about twenty States have enacted special legislation to accommodate the needs of closely held corporations. These statutes vary considerably but they are all optional and must be specifically elected by eligible corporations. Eligibility is generally based on the corporation having fewer than a specified maximum number of shareholders. These special close corporation statutes permit operation without a board of directors and authorize broad use of shareholder agreements, including their use in place of bylaws. Some prohibit courts from denying limited liability simply because an electing corporation engages in informal conduct.

As noted in *Chapter 34*, a Statutory Close Corporation Supplement (the Supplement) to the Model and Revised Acts has been promulgated. The Supplement relaxes the most nonessential corporate formalities by permitting operation without a board of directors, authorizing broad use of shareholder agreements (including their use in place of bylaws), making annual meetings optional, and authorizing one person to execute documents in more than one capacity. Most important, it prevents courts from denying limited liability simply because the corporation is a statutory close corporation. The general incorporation statute applies to closely held corporations except to the extent that it is inconsistent with the Supplement.

The Revised Act was amended to authorize shareholders in closely held corporations to adopt unanimous shareholders' agreements that depart from the statutory norms. Section 7.32. The section requires that the agreement is set forth either (1) in the articles of incorporation or bylaws and approved by all persons who are shareholders at the time of the agreement or (2) in a written agreement that is signed by all persons who are shareholders at the time of the agreement and is made known to the corporation. Section 7.32(b). Under this section, shareholder agreements are valid for ten years unless the agreement provides otherwise. The section *specifically* validates a number of provisions, including those (1) eliminating or restricting the powers of the board of directors; (2) establishing who shall be directors or officers; (3) specifying how directors or officers will be selected or removed; (4) governing the exercise or division of voting power by or between the shareholders and directors; (5) permitting the use of weighted voting rights or director proxies; and (6) transferring the authority of the board of directors to one or more shareholders or other persons. The section also *generally* authorizes any provision that governs the exercise of the corporate powers or the management of the business and affairs of the corporation or the relationship among the shareholders, the directors and the corporation, or among any of them, so long as it is not contrary to public policy. There are limits, however, and a shareholder agreement that provides that the directors of the corporation have no duties of care or loyalty to the corporation or the shareholders would be beyond the authorization of Section 7.32. To the extent that an agreement authorized by this section limits the discretion or powers of the board of directors, it relieves the directors of liability while imposing that liability upon the person or persons in whom such discretion or powers are vested.

In sharp contrast is the large, **publicly held corporation** with a vast market for its shares. These shares typically are widely dispersed, and very few are owned by management. Approximately two-thirds are held by institutional investors, such as insurance companies, pension and retirement funds, mutual funds, and university endowments; the remaining shares are owned directly by individual investors. Whereas a great majority of institutional investors exercise their right to vote their shares, most individual investors do not. Nonetheless, virtually all shareholders who vote for the directors do so through the use of a **proxy**—an authorization by a shareholder to an agent (usually the chief executive officer [CEO] of the corporation) to vote his shares. The majority of shareholders who return their proxies vote as management advises. As a result, the nominating committee of the board of directors actually determines the board's membership.

Thus, the 500 to 1,000 largest, publicly held corporations—which own the great bulk of the industrial wealth of the United States—are controlled by a small group of corporate officers. This great concentration of control over wealth, and the power that results from it, raises social, policy, and ethical issues concerning the governance of these corporations and the accountability of their management. The actions (or inactions) of these powerful corporations greatly affect the national economy, employment policies, the health and safety of the workplace and the environment, product quality, and the effects of overseas operations.

Accordingly, the accountability of management is a critical issue. In particular, what obligations should the large, publicly held corporation and its management have to (1) the corporation's shareholders, (2) its employees, (3) its customers, (4) its suppliers, (5) the communities in which the corporation is located, and (6) the rest of society? These critical questions remain mostly unanswered. Some corporate statutes now provide that the board of directors, committees of the board, individual directors, and individual officers *may*, in determining the corporation's best interests, consider the effects of any action upon employees, suppliers, creditors, and customers of the corporation; the communities in which the corporation maintains offices or other establishments; the economy of the State and nation; societal considerations; and all other pertinent factors.

In response to the business scandals involving companies such as Enron, WorldCom, Global Crossing, Adelphia, and Arthur Andersen, in 2002 Congress passed the Sarbanes-Oxley Act, which is further discussed in *Chapter 44*, Securities Regulation, as well as in *Chapters 6* and *45*. The legislation seeks to prevent these types of scandals by increasing corporate responsibility; adding new financial disclosure requirements; creating new criminal offenses; increasing the penalties for existing federal crimes; and creating a five-person Accounting Oversight Board with authority to review and discipline auditors. Several provisions of the Act impose governance requirements on publicly held corporations and will be discussed in this chapter.

In July 2010, President Obama signed into law the Dodd-Frank Wall Street Reform and Consumer Protection Act (CFPA), the most significant change to U.S. financial regulation since the New Deal. One of the many stand-alone statutes included in the CFPA is the Investor Protection and Securities Reform Act of 2010, which imposes new corporate governance rules on publicly held companies. These corporate governance provisions of the CFPA will be discussed in this chapter, *Chapter 37*, and *Chapter 44*.

The structure and governance of corporations must adhere to incorporation statute requirements. Therefore, this chapter will discuss the rights, duties, and liabilities of shareholders, directors, and officers under these statutes.

◆ **SEE FIGURE 36-2: Management Structure of Typical Closely Held Corporation**

◆ **SEE FIGURE 36-3: Management Structure of Typical Publicly Held Corporation**

ROLE OF SHAREHOLDERS

The role of the shareholders in managing the corporation is generally restricted to the election of directors, the approval of certain extraordinary matters, the approval of corporate transactions that are void or voidable unless ratified, and the right to bring suits to enforce these rights.

VOTING RIGHTS OF SHAREHOLDERS

The shareholder's right to vote is fundamental both to the corporate concept and to the corporation's management structure. In most States, a shareholder is entitled to one vote for each share of stock that she owns, unless the articles of incorporation provide otherwise. In addition, incorporation

◆ FIGURE 36-1: **Management Structure of Corporations: The Statutory Model**

Officers
Run the day-to-day
operations of the corporation

Board of Directors
Declare dividends
Delegate authority to officers
Manage the business of the corporation
Select, remove, and determine compensation
of officers

Shareholders
Elect and remove directors
Approve fundamental changes

◆ FIGURE 36-2: **Management Structure of Typical Closely Held Corporation**

Shareholders = Directors = Officers

◆ FIGURE 36-3: **Management Structure of Typical Publicly Held Corporation**

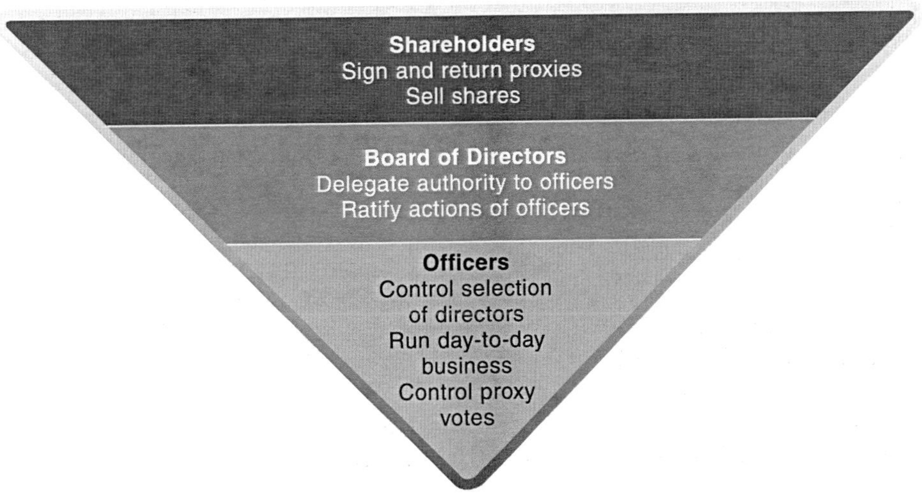

Shareholders
Sign and return proxies
Sell shares

Board of Directors
Delegate authority to officers
Ratify actions of officers

Officers
Control selection
of directors
Run day-to-day
business
Control proxy
votes

statutes generally permit the issuance of one or more classes of nonvoting stock, so long as at least one class of shares has voting rights. Section 6.01. The articles of incorporation may provide for more or less than one vote for any share. For example, in *Providence & Worcester Co. v. Baker*, 378 A.2d 121 (Del. 1977), the court upheld articles of incorporation which provided that each shareholder was entitled to one vote per share for each of fifty or fewer shares that he owned and one vote for every twenty shares in excess of fifty, but no shareholder was entitled to vote more than one-fourth of the whole number of outstanding shares.

SHAREHOLDER MEETINGS

Shareholders may exercise their voting rights at both annual and special shareholder meetings. **Annual meetings** are required and must be held at a time fixed by the bylaws. Section 7.01. If the annual shareholder meeting is not held within the earlier of six months after the end of the corporation's fiscal year or fifteen months after its last annual meeting, any shareholder may petition and obtain a court order requiring such meeting to be held. Section 7.03. The Revised Act further provides that the failure to hold an annual meeting does not affect the validity of any corporate action. Section 7.01(c). In contrast, the Close Corporation Supplement provides that no annual meeting of shareholders need be held unless a shareholder makes a written request at least thirty days in advance of the date specified for the meeting. The date may be established in the articles of incorporation, the bylaws, or a shareholders' agreement.

Special meetings may be called by the board of directors, by holders of at least 10 percent of the shares, or by other persons authorized to do so in the articles of incorporation. Section 7.02. As amended, the Revised Act permits a corporation's articles of incorporation to lower or raise the 10 percent requirement, but the corporation cannot raise the requirement to more than 25 percent of the shares.

Written notice, stating the date, time, and place of the meeting and, in the case of a special meeting, the purposes for which it is called, must be given in advance of the meeting. Section 7.05. Notice, however, may be waived in writing by any shareholder entitled to notice. Section 7.06.

A number of States permit shareholders to conduct business without a meeting if they consent unanimously in writing to the action taken. Section 7.04. Some States have further relaxed the formalities of shareholder action by permitting shareholders to act without a meeting simply by obtaining the written consent of the number of shares required to act on the matter.

QUORUM AND VOTING

To effectuate corporate business, a quorum of shares must be represented at the meeting, either in person or by proxy.

Unissued shares and treasury stock may not be voted or counted in determining whether a quorum exists. The majority view is that once a quorum is present at a meeting, it is deemed present for the rest of the meeting, even if shareholders withdraw in an effort to break it. Unless the articles of incorporation otherwise provide, a majority of shares entitled to vote constitutes a quorum. In most States and under the Model Act, a quorum may not consist of less than one-third of the shares entitled to vote; the Revised Act and some States do not provide a statutory minimum for a quorum. State statutes do not impose an upper limit upon a quorum, so it may be set higher than a majority and may even require *all* the outstanding shares.

Most States require shareholder actions to be approved by a majority of shares represented at the meeting and entitled to vote if a quorum exists. The Revised Act and some States, however, provide a different rule: if a quorum exists, a shareholder action (other than the election of directors) is approved if the votes cast for the action exceed the votes cast against it. Section 7.25(c). Moreover, virtually all States permit the articles of incorporation to increase the percentage of shares required to take any action that is subject to shareholder approval. Section 7.27. A provision that increases voting requirements is commonly called a "supermajority provision." Close corporations frequently have used supermajority shareholder voting requirements to protect minority shareholders from oppression by the majority, while some publicly held corporations recently have used them to defend against hostile takeover bids.

ELECTION OF DIRECTORS

Directors are elected each year at the annual meeting of the shareholders. Most States provide that where a corporation's board consists of nine or more directors, the charter or bylaws may provide for a **classification** or staggering of directors, that is, a division into two or three classes to be as nearly equal in number as possible and to serve for staggered terms. Under the Revised Act as amended there is no minimum-size board required. Section 8.06. If the directors are divided into two classes, the members of each class are elected once a year in alternate years for a two-year term; if divided into three classes, they are elected for three-year terms. This permits one-half of the board to be elected every two years or one-third to be elected every three years, thus lending continuity to the board's membership. Moreover, where there are two or more classes of shares, the courts generally have held that each class may elect a specified number of directors, if the articles of incorporation so provide. The Revised Act makes this explicit. Section 8.04.

STRAIGHT VOTING Normally, each shareholder has one vote for each share owned, and under the Revised Act and many State statutes directors are elected by a *plurality* of the votes.

Section 7.28(a). In other States directors are elected by a *majority* of the votes. The charter may increase the percentage of shares required for the election of directors. Thus, under straight voting shareholders owning a majority of the voting shares can always elect the *entire* board of directors.

CUMULATIVE VOTING In certain States shareholders have the right of cumulative voting when electing directors. In most of these States and under the Revised Act, cumulative voting is permissive, not mandatory. Section 7.28(b). **Cumulative voting** entitles the shareholders to multiply the number of votes they are entitled to cast by the number of directors for whom they are entitled to vote and to cast the product for a single candidate or distribute the product among two or more candidates. Cumulative voting permits a minority shareholder, or a group of minority shareholders acting together, to obtain minority representation on the board if they own a certain minimum number of shares. In the absence of cumulative voting, the holder or holders of 51 percent of the voting shares can elect all of the members of the board.

The formula for determining how many shares a minority shareholder with cumulative voting rights must own, or have proxies to vote, to secure representation on the board is as follows:

$$X = \frac{ac}{b+1} + 1$$

where

a = number of shares voting
b = number of directors to be elected
c = number of directors desired to be elected
X = number of shares necessary to elect the number of directors desired to be elected

For example, Gray Corporation has two shareholders, Stephanie with sixty-four shares and Thomas with thirty-six shares. The board of directors of Gray Corporation consists of three directors. Under "straight" or noncumulative voting, Stephanie could cast sixty-four votes for each of her three candidates, and Thomas could cast thirty-six votes for his three candidates. As a result, all three of Stephanie's candidates would be elected. On the other hand, if cumulative voting were in force, Thomas could elect one director:

$$X = \frac{ac}{b+1} + 1$$

$$X = \frac{100(1)}{3+1} + 1 = 26 \text{ shares}$$

This result indicates that Thomas would need at least twenty-six shares to elect one director. Because Thomas has the right to vote thirty-six shares, he would be able to elect one director. Stephanie, of course, with her sixty-four shares, could elect the remaining two directors.

The effect of cumulative voting for directors may be diluted by classification, by staggering elections, or by reducing the size of the board. For example, if nine directors are each elected annually, only 11 percent of the shares are needed to elect one director; if the nine directors' elections are staggered and three are elected annually, 26 percent of the shares are required to elect one director.

REMOVAL OF DIRECTORS

By a majority vote, shareholders may remove any director or the entire board of directors, with or without cause, in a meeting called for that purpose. In the case of a corporation having cumulative voting, however, a director may be removed only if the number of votes opposing his removal would be insufficient to elect him. Section 8.08(c). Removal of directors is discussed more fully later in this chapter.

APPROVAL OF FUNDAMENTAL CHANGES

The board of directors manages the ordinary business affairs of the corporation. Extraordinary matters involving fundamental changes in the corporation require shareholder approval; such matters include amendments to the articles of incorporation, a sale or lease of all or substantially all of the corporate assets not in the regular course of business, most mergers, consolidations, compulsory share exchanges, and dissolution. Fundamental changes are discussed in *Chapter 37.*

CONCENTRATIONS OF VOTING POWER

Certain devices enable groups of shareholders to combine their voting power for purposes such as obtaining or maintaining control or maximizing the impact of cumulative voting. The most important methods of concentrating voting power are proxies, voting trusts, and shareholder voting agreements.

◆ **SEE FIGURE 36-4: Concentrations of Voting Power**

PROXIES A shareholder may vote either in person or by written proxy. Section 7.22(a). As mentioned earlier, a proxy is simply a shareholder's authorization to an agent to vote his shares at a particular meeting or on a particular question. Generally, proxies must be in writing to be effective; furthermore, statutes typically limit the duration of proxies to no more than eleven months, unless the proxy specifically provides otherwise. Section 7.22(c). Some States limit all proxy appointments to a period of eleven months. Because a proxy is the appointment of an agent, it is revocable, as all agencies are, unless conspicuously stated to be irrevocable *and* coupled with an interest, such as shares held as collateral. Section 7.22(d). The solicitation of proxies by publicly held corporations is also regulated by the Securities Exchange Act of 1934, as discussed in *Chapter 44.*

◆ FIGURE 36-4: **Concentrations of Voting Power**

	Proxy	Voting Trust	Shareholder Agreement
Definition	Authorization of an agent to vote shares	Conferral of voting rights on trustee	Agreement among shareholders on voting of shares
Formalities	Signed writing delivered to corporation	Signed writing delivered to corporation	Signed writing
Duration	Eleven months, unless otherwise agreed	Ten years; may be extended	No limit
Revocability	Yes, unless coupled with an interest	No	Only by unanimous agreement
Prevalence	Publicly held	Publicly and closely held	Closely held

As discussed above, in large, publicly held corporations, virtually all shareholders who vote for the directors do so through the use of proxies. Because the majority of shareholders who return their proxies vote as management advises, the nominating committee of the board of directors almost always determines the board's membership. In 2009, the Revised Model Business Corporation Act (RMBCA) was amended to authorize the directors or shareholders of corporations to establish procedures in the corporate bylaws that (1) require the corporation to include in the corporation's proxy statement one or more individuals nominated by a shareholder in addition to individuals nominated by the board of directors and (2) require the corporation to reimburse shareholders for reasonable expenses incurred in soliciting proxies in an election of directors. Section 2.06(c).

Moreover, the CFPA authorizes the Securities and Exchange Commission (SEC) to issue rules requiring that a publicly held company's proxy solicitation include nominations for the board of directors submitted by shareholders. The SEC has issued a new such rule. See *Chapter 44*.

VOTING TRUSTS Voting trusts, which are designed to concentrate corporate control in one or more persons, have been used in both publicly held and closely held corporations. A voting trust is a device by which one or more shareholders separate the voting rights of their shares from the ownership of those shares. Under a voting trust, one or more shareholders confer on a trustee the right to vote or otherwise act for them by signing a written agreement setting out the provisions of the trust and transferring their shares to the trustee. Section 7.30(a). In most States, voting trusts are permitted by statute but usually are limited in duration to ten years. The Revised Act and many States permit all or some of the parties to a voting trust to extend it for an additional term of up to ten years by signing an extension agreement and obtaining the voting trustee's written consent. Section 7.30(c). The extension runs from the time the first shareholder signs the agreement but binds only those shareholders who consent to it.

SHAREHOLDER VOTING AGREEMENTS In most jurisdictions, shareholders may agree in writing to vote in a specified manner for the election or removal of directors or on any other matter subject to shareholder approval. Section 7.31(a). The Revised Act and some State statutes expressly provide that shareholder voting agreements are enforceable by a decree of specific performance. Section 7.31(b). Unlike voting trusts, shareholder voting agreements are usually not limited in duration. Shareholder voting agreements are used frequently in closely held corporations, especially in conjunction with restrictions on the transfer of shares, to provide each shareholder with greater control and *delectus personae* (the right to choose those who will become shareholders).

Galler v. Galler, 32 Ill.2d 16, 203 N.E.2d 577 (1964), provides a well-known example of the effect a shareholder agreement may have within a close corporation. In 1927, two brothers, Benjamin and Isadore Galler, incorporated the Galler Drug Co., a wholesale drug business that they had operated as equal partners since 1919. The company continued to grow, and in 1955 the two brothers and their wives, Emma and Rose Galler, entered into a written shareholder agreement to leave the corporation in equal control of each family after the death of either brother. Specifically, the agreement provided that the corporation would continue to provide income for the support and maintenance of their immediate families and that the parties would vote for directors so as to give the estate and heirs of a deceased shareholder the same representation as before. Benjamin died in 1957, and shortly thereafter his widow, Emma, requested that Isadore, the surviving brother, comply with the terms of the agreement. When he refused, instead proposing that certain changes be made in the agreement, Emma brought an action seeking specific performance of the agreement.

Isadore and his wife, Rose, defended on the ground that the shareholder agreement was against public policy and the State's corporation law. The court decided in favor of Emma Galler, explaining that a close corporation is one in which the stock is held in a few hands and is rarely traded. In contrast to a shareholder in a public corporation, who may easily trade his shares on the open market when he disagrees with management over corporate policy, the shareholder of a closely held corporation often has no ready market in which to sell his shares should he wish to do so. Moreover, the shareholder in a closely held corporation often has most of his capital invested in the corporation and, therefore, views himself not only as an investor but also as a participant in the management of the business. Without a shareholder agreement subject to specific performance by the courts, the minority shareholder might find himself at the mercy of the controlling majority shareholder. In short, the detailed shareholder voting agreement is the only sound means by which the minority shareholder can protect himself. Therefore, the court concluded, because the agreement was reasonable in its scope and purpose of providing continuing support for the Galler brothers' families, it should be enforced.

RESTRICTIONS ON TRANSFER OF SHARES

In the absence of a specific agreement, shares of stock are freely transferable. Although free transferability of shares is usually considered an advantage of the corporate form, in some situations the shareholders may prefer to restrict the transfer of shares. In closely held corporations, for example, stock transfer restrictions are used to control who may become shareholders, thereby achieving the corporate equivalent of *delectus personae* (choice of the person). They are also used to maintain statutory close corporation status or S Corporation status by restricting the number of persons who may become shareholders. In publicly held corporations, restrictions on the transfer of shares are used to preserve exemptions under State and Federal securities laws. (These are discussed in *Chapter 44*.)

Most incorporation statutes have no provisions governing share transfer restrictions. The common law validates such restrictions if they are adopted for a lawful purpose and do not unreasonably restrain or prohibit transferability. In addition, the Uniform Commercial Code provides that an otherwise valid share transfer restriction is ineffective against a person without actual knowledge of it unless the restriction is conspicuously noted on the share certificate. Section 8–204. The Revised Act and the statutes of several States permit the articles of incorporation, bylaws, or a shareholder agreement to impose transfer restrictions but require that the restriction be noted conspicuously on the stock certificate. The Revised Act authorizes restrictions for any reasonable purpose, including maintaining statutory close corporation status and preserving exemptions under Federal and State securities law. Section 6.27.

ENFORCEMENT RIGHTS OF SHAREHOLDERS

To protect a shareholder's interests in the corporation, the law provides shareholders with certain enforcement rights, including the right to obtain information, the right to sue the corporation directly or to sue on the corporation's behalf, and the right to dissent.

RIGHT TO INSPECT BOOKS AND RECORDS

Most States have enacted statutory provisions granting shareholders the right to inspect for a *proper purpose* books and records in person or through an agent and to make extracts from them. The right generally covers all records relevant to the shareholder's legitimate interest. The Revised Act extends the right to copy records to include, if reasonable, the right to receive copies made by photographic, xerographic, or other means. Section 16.03. The Act provides that every shareholder is entitled to examine *specified* corporate records upon prior written request if the demand is made in good faith, for a proper purpose, and during regular business hours at the corporation's principal office. Section 16.02. Many States, however, limit this right to shareholders who own a minimum number of shares or to those who have been shareholders for a specified minimum time. For example, the MBCA requires that a shareholder either must own 5 percent of the outstanding shares or must have owned his shares for at least six months; a court, however, may order an inspection even when neither condition is met.

A **proper purpose** for inspection is one that is reasonably relevant to a shareholder's interest in the corporation. Proper purposes include determining the financial condition of the corporation, the value of shares, the existence of mismanagement or improper transactions, or the names of other shareholders in order to communicate with them about corporate affairs. The right of inspection is subject to abuse and will be denied a shareholder who is seeking information for an improper purpose. Examples of improper purposes include obtaining proprietary information for use by a competing company or obtaining a list of shareholders in order to offer it for sale.

The Revised Act requires that a voting list of shareholders be prepared and that it be made available to shareholders upon request. Section 7.20. In addition, unlike many States, the Act requires every corporation to prepare and submit to its shareholders annual financial statements. Section 16.20.

SHAREHOLDER SUITS

The ultimate recourse of a shareholder, short of selling her shares, is to bring suit against or on behalf of the corporation. Shareholder suits are essentially of two kinds: direct suits or derivative suits.

◆ **SEE FIGURE 36-5: Shareholder Suits**

DIRECT SUITS A shareholder may bring a direct suit to enforce a claim that he has *against* the corporation, based upon his ownership of shares. Any recovery in a direct suit goes to the shareholder plaintiff. Examples of direct suits include shareholder actions to compel payment of dividends properly declared, to enforce the right to inspect corporate records, to enforce the right to vote, to protect preemptive rights, and to compel dissolution. Shareholders also may bring a class suit or class action. A **class suit** is a direct suit in which one or more shareholders purport to represent a class of shareholders in order to recover for injuries to the entire class. Such a suit is a direct suit because the representative claims that all similarly situated shareholders were injured by an act that did not injure the corporation.

DERIVATIVE SUITS A derivative suit is a cause of action brought by one or more shareholders *on behalf* of the corporation to enforce a right belonging to the corporation. Shareholders may bring such an action when the board of directors refuses to so act on the corporation's behalf. Recovery usually goes to the corporation's treasury, so that all shareholders can benefit proportionately. Examples of derivative suits are actions to recover damages from management for an *ultra vires* act, to recover damages for a managerial breach of duty, and to recover improper dividends. In such situations, the board of directors may well be hesitant to bring suit against the corporation's officers or directors. Consequently, a shareholder derivative suit is the only recourse.

In most States, a shareholder must have owned his shares at the time the complained-of transaction occurred in order to bring a derivative suit. Section 7.41. In addition, under the Revised Act and some State statutes, the shareholder must first make demand upon the board of directors to enforce the corporate right. Section 7.42. In a number of States demand is excused in limited situations. The statutes of some States require a plaintiff to give security for reasonable expenses, including attorneys' fees, if his holdings of shares are not of a specified size or value. The Revised Act does not have this requirement.

SHAREHOLDER'S RIGHT TO DISSENT

A shareholder has the right to dissent from certain corporate actions that require shareholder approval. These actions include most mergers, consolidations, compulsory share exchanges, and a sale or exchange of all or substantially all the assets of the corporation not in the usual and regular

◆ **FIGURE 36-5: Shareholder Suits**

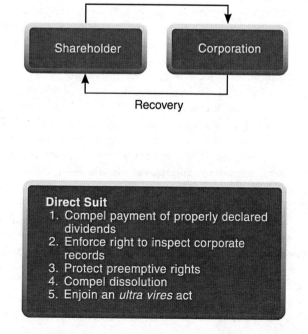

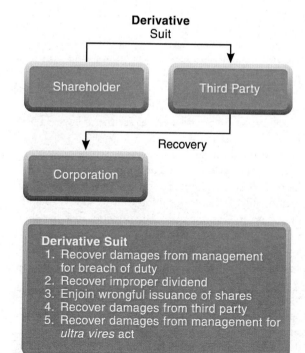

course of business. The shareholder's right to dissent is discussed in *Chapter 37*.

ROLE OF DIRECTORS AND OFFICERS

Management of a corporation is vested by statute in its board of directors, which determines general corporate policy and appoints officers to execute that policy and to administer day-to-day corporate operations. Both the directors and the officers owe certain duties to the corporate entity as well as to the corporation's shareholders and are liable for breaching these duties.

The following sections will discuss the roles of corporate directors and officers. In some instances, controlling shareholders, or those owning a number of shares sufficient to allow them effective control over the corporation, are held to duties the same as those of directors and officers, which are discussed later in this chapter. Moreover, in close corporations, many courts impose upon *all* the shareholders a fiduciary duty similar to that imposed upon partners.

FUNCTION OF THE BOARD OF DIRECTORS

Although the directors are elected by the shareholders to manage the corporation, the directors are neither trustees nor agents of the shareholders or the corporation. The directors are, however, fiduciaries who must perform their duties in good faith, in the best interests of the corporation, and with due care.

The Revised Act and the statutes of many States provide that "[a]ll corporate powers shall be exercised by or under the authority of, and the business and affairs of the corporation managed under the direction of, its board of directors, subject to any limitation set forth in the articles of incorporation." Section 8.01(b). In some corporations, the members of the board all are actively involved in the management of the business. In these cases, the corporate powers are exercised *by* the board of directors. On the other hand, in publicly held corporations, most board members are unlikely to be actively involved in management. Here, the corporate powers are exercised *under* the authority of the board, which formulates major management policy and monitors management's performance but does not involve itself in day-to-day management.

In publicly held corporations, the directors who are also officers or employees of the corporation are **inside directors**, while the directors who are not officers or employees are **outside directors**. Outside directors who have no business contacts with the corporation are **unaffiliated directors**; outside directors who do have such contacts with the corporation—such as investment bankers, lawyers, or suppliers—are **affiliated directors**. Historically, the boards of many publicly held corporations consisted mainly or entirely of inside directors. During the past two decades, however, the number and influence of outside directors have increased substantially, and now boards of the great majority of publicly held corporations consist primarily of outside directors.

Under the CFPA, the SEC must issue rules requiring publicly held companies to disclose in annual proxy statements the reasons why the company has chosen to separate or combine the positions of chairman of the board of directors and CEO.

In those States with special close corporation statutes, electing corporations can operate without a board of directors. Moreover, under the Revised Act as originally enacted, a corporation having fifty or fewer shareholders may dispense with or limit the authority of a board of directors by describing in its articles of incorporation those who will perform some or all of the duties of a board. The Revised Act as amended permits any corporation to dispense with a board of directors by a written agreement executed by all of the shareholders. Sections 7.32 and 8.01.

Under incorporation statutes the board has the responsibility for determining corporate policy in a number of areas, including (1) selecting and removing officers, (2) determining the corporation's capital structure, (3) initiating fundamental changes, (4) declaring dividends, and (5) setting management compensation.

SELECTION AND REMOVAL OF OFFICERS

In most States, the board of directors is responsible for choosing the corporation's officers and may remove any officer at any time. Sections 8.40 and 8.43. Officers are corporate agents who are delegated their responsibilities by the board of directors.

CAPITAL STRUCTURE

The board of directors determines the capital structure and financial policy of the corporation. For example, the board of directors has the power to—

1. fix the selling price of newly issued shares unless the articles reserve this power to the shareholders;
2. determine the value of the consideration the corporation will receive in payment for the shares it issues;
3. purchase, redeem, or otherwise acquire shares of the corporation's equity securities;
4. borrow money; issue notes, bonds, and other obligations; and secure any of the corporation's obligations by mortgage or pledge of any or all of the corporation's property; and
5. sell, lease, or exchange assets of the corporation in the usual and regular course of business.

FUNDAMENTAL CHANGES

The board of directors has the power to amend or repeal the bylaws, unless the articles of incorporation reserve this power exclusively to the shareholders. Section 10.20. In a few States directors may not repeal or amend bylaws adopted by the shareholders. In addition, the board initiates certain actions that require shareholder approval. For instance, the board initiates proceedings to amend the articles of incorporation; to effect a merger, consolidation, compulsory share exchange, or the sale or lease of all or substantially all of the assets of the corporation other than in the usual and regular course of business; and to dissolve the corporation.

DIVIDENDS

The board of directors declares the amount and type of dividends, subject to restrictions in the State incorporation statute, the articles of incorporation, and corporate loan and preferred stock agreements. Section 6.40. The board also fixes a record date for the purpose of determining the shareholders who are entitled to receive dividends. Section 6.40(b).

MANAGEMENT COMPENSATION

The board of directors usually determines the compensation of officers. Moreover, a number of States allow the board to fix the compensation of its members. Section 8.11. In addition to fixed salaries, executive compensation may include (1) cash bonuses, (2) share bonuses, (3) share options, (4) share purchase plans, (5) insurance benefits, (6) deferred compensation, (7) retirement plans, and (8) a variety of other fringe benefits.

The CFPA requires that, at least once every three years, publicly held companies include a provision in certain proxy statements for a nonbinding shareholder vote on the compensation of executives. In a separate resolution, shareholders determine whether this "say on pay" vote should be held every one, two, or three years.

Under the Sarbanes-Oxley Act, if a publicly held company is required to issue an accounting restatement due to a material violation of securities law, the CEO and the chief financial officer must forfeit certain bonuses and compensation received, as well as any profit realized from the sale of the company's securities, during the twelve-month period following the original issuance of the noncomplying financial document.

These "clawback" requirements of the Sarbanes-Oxley Act have been greatly expanded by the CFPA. Under the CFPA, the SEC must issue rules directing the national securities exchanges to require each listed company to disclose and implement a policy regarding any incentive-based compensation that is based on financial information that must be reported under the securities laws. In the event that a company is required to prepare an accounting restatement due to the material noncompliance with any financial reporting requirement under the securities laws, the company must recover from any current or former executive officers who received excess incentive-based compensation (including stock options awarded as compensation) during the three-year period preceding the date on which the company is required to prepare an accounting restatement. The amount of the recovery is the incentive-based compensation in excess of what would have been paid to the CEO under the accounting restatement.

ELECTION AND TENURE OF DIRECTORS

The incorporation statute, articles of incorporation, and bylaws determine the qualifications essential for those who would be directors of the corporation. They also determine the election, number, tenure, and compensation of directors. Only individuals may serve as directors. Section 8.03(a).

ELECTION, NUMBER, AND TENURE OF DIRECTORS

The initial board of directors generally is named in the articles of incorporation and serves until the first meeting of the shareholders at which directors are elected. Section 8.05(a). Thereafter, directors are elected at annual meetings of the shareholders and hold office for one year unless their terms are staggered. If the shares represented at a meeting in person or by proxy are insufficient to constitute a quorum, however, or if the shareholders are deadlocked and unable to elect a new board, the incumbent directors continue in office as "holdover" directors until their successors are duly elected and qualified. Section 8.05(e). Although State statutes traditionally required each corporation to have three or more directors, most States permit the board to consist of one or more members. Section 8.03(a). Moreover, the number of directors may be increased or decreased, within statutory limits, by amendment to the bylaws or charter.

VACANCIES AND REMOVAL OF DIRECTORS

The Revised Act provides that a vacancy in the board may be filled either by the shareholders or by the affirmative vote of a majority of the remaining directors, even if they constitute less than a quorum of the board. Section 8.10(a). When shareholders fill a vacant office which was held by a director elected by a class of shares, only the holders of that class of shares have the right to vote to fill that vacancy. The term of a director elected to fill a vacancy expires at the next shareholders' meeting at which directors are elected. Section 8.05(d).

Some States have no statutory provision for the removal of directors, although a common law rule permits removal for cause by action of the shareholders. The Revised Act and an increasing number of other statutes permit the shareholders to remove one or more directors or the entire board, with or without cause, at a special meeting called for that purpose, subject to cumulative voting rights, if applicable. Section 8.08. Nevertheless, the Revised Act permits the articles of incorporation to provide that directors may be removed only for cause. Section 8.08(a). In addition, however, the Revised Act and a number of States authorize a court to remove a director in a proceeding brought by the corporation or by shareholders who own at least 10 percent of the outstanding shares of any class of shares, if the court finds that (1) the director engaged in fraudulent or dishonest conduct or gross abuse of authority or discretion and (2) removal is in the best interests of the corporation. Section 8.09.

COMPENSATION OF DIRECTORS

Traditionally, directors did not receive salaries for their directorial services, although they usually collected a fee or honorarium for attendance at meetings. The Revised Act and many incorporation statutes now specifically authorize the board of directors to fix the compensation of directors unless there is a contrary provision in the articles of incorporation or bylaws. Section 8.11.

EXERCISE OF DIRECTORS' FUNCTIONS

Although they are powerless to bind the corporation when acting individually, directors can exert this power when acting as a board. Nevertheless, the board may act only through a meeting of the directors or with the written, unanimously signed consent of the directors, if written consent without a meeting is authorized by the statute and not contrary to the charter or bylaws. Section 8.21.

Meetings either are held at a regular time and place fixed in the bylaws or are called at special times. Notice of meetings must be given as prescribed in the bylaws. A director's attendance at any meeting is a waiver of such notice, unless the director attends only to object to the holding of the meeting or to the transacting of business at it and does not vote for or assent to action taken at the meeting. Section 8.23(b). Waiver of notice also may be given in a signed writing. Most modern statutes provide that meetings of the board may be held either in or outside the State of incorporation. Section 8.20(a).

QUORUM AND VOTING

A majority of board members constitutes a quorum (the minimum number of members that must be present at a meeting in order to transact business). Although most States do not permit a quorum to be set at less than a majority, the Revised Act and some States allow the articles of incorporation or the bylaws to authorize a quorum consisting of as few as one-third of a board's members. Section 8.24(b). In contrast, however, in all States the articles of incorporation or bylaws may require a number greater than a simple majority. Section 8.24(a). If a quorum is present at any meeting, the act of a majority of the directors in attendance is the act of the board, unless the articles of incorporation or bylaws require the act of a greater number. Section 8.24(c).

Closely held corporations sometimes impose supermajority or unanimous quorum requirements. In addition, they may require a supermajority or unanimous vote of the board for some or all matters. The use of either or both of these provisions, however, creates the possibility of deadlock at the director level.

By requiring a quorum to be present when "a vote is taken," the Revised Act makes it clear that the board may act only when a quorum is present. Section 8.24(c) and Comment 2. This rule is in contrast to the rule governing shareholder meetings: once obtained, a quorum of shareholders cannot be broken by the withdrawal of shareholders. Many State statutes, however, do not have this provision. In any event, directors may not vote by proxy, although most States permit directors to participate in meetings through teleconference. See Section 8.20.

A director who is present at a board meeting at which action on any corporate matter is taken is deemed to have assented to such action unless, in addition to dissenting or abstaining from it, he (1) has his dissent or abstention entered in the minutes of the meeting, (2) files his written dissent or abstention to such action with the presiding officer before the meeting adjourns, or (3) delivers his written dissent or abstention to the corporation immediately after adjournment. Section 8.24(d).

ACTION TAKEN WITHOUT A MEETING

The Revised Act and most States provide that, unless the articles of incorporation or bylaws provide otherwise, any action the statute requires or permits to be taken at a meeting of the board may be taken without a meeting if consent in writing is signed by all of the directors. Section 8.21. Such consent has the same effect as a unanimous vote.

DELEGATION OF BOARD POWERS

Unless otherwise provided by the articles of incorporation or bylaws, the board of directors may, by majority vote of the full board, appoint one or more committees, all of whose members must be directors. Section 8.25. Many State statutes, however, permit the board to form committees only if the charter expressly authorizes such action; furthermore, the Revised Act and many States require that the creation of a committee and appointment of members to it must be

In addition, a common question is whether officers possess implied authority merely by virtue of their positions. The courts have been circumspect in granting such implied or inherent authority. Traditionally, the courts tended to hold that the president had no implied authority by virtue of his office, although more recent decisions tend to recognize his authority to bind the corporation in ordinary business transactions. Any act requiring board approval, such as issuing stock, however, is clearly beyond the implied authority of the president or any other officer. In most jurisdictions, implied authority of position does not extend to any officer other than the president.

APPARENT AUTHORITY Apparent authority arises from acts of the corporation that lead third parties to believe reasonably and in good faith that an officer has the required authority. Apparent authority might arise when a third party relies on the fact that an officer has exercised the same authority in the past with the consent of the board of directors.

RATIFICATION A corporation may ratify the unauthorized acts of its officers. Equivalent to the corporation's having granted the officer prior authority, ratification relates back to the original transaction and may either be express or implied from the corporation's acceptance of contractual benefits with full knowledge of the facts.

DUTIES OF DIRECTORS AND OFFICERS

Generally, directors and officers owe the duties of obedience, diligence, and loyalty to the corporation. These duties are for the most part judicially imposed. State and Federal statutes supplement the common law by imposing liability upon directors and officers for specific acts, but the common law remains the most significant source of duties.

A corporation may not recover damages from its directors and officers for losses resulting from their poor business judgment or honest mistakes of judgment. Directors and officers are not insurers of business success. They are required only to be obedient, reasonably diligent, and completely loyal. In 1999 an amendment to the Revised Act was adopted refining the Act's standards of conduct and liability for directors.

DUTY OF OBEDIENCE

Directors and officers must act within their respective authority. For any loss the corporation suffers because of their unauthorized acts, they are in some jurisdictions held strictly liable; in others, they are held liable only if they exceeded their authority intentionally or negligently.

DUTY OF DILIGENCE

In discharging their duties, directors and officers must exercise ordinary care and prudence. Some States interpret this standard to mean that directors and officers must exercise "the same degree of care and prudence that [those] promoted by self-interest generally exercise in their own affairs." *Hun v. Cary*, 82 N.Y. 65 (1880). The great majority of States and the Revised Act, however, hold that the test requires a director or officer to discharge her duties—

1. in good faith;
2. with the care an ordinarily prudent person in a like position would exercise under similar circumstances; and
3. in a manner she reasonably believes to be in the best interests of the corporation.

Sections 8.30 and 8.42. A director or officer who has performed the duties of his office in compliance with these requirements is liable neither for any action he has taken as a director or officer nor for any failure to act. Sections 8.30(d) and 8.42(d).

So long as the directors and officers act in good faith and with due care, the courts will not substitute their judgment for that of the board or officer—the so-called **business judgment** rule. Directors and officers will, nonetheless, be held liable for bad faith or negligent conduct. Moreover, they may be liable for failing to act. In one instance, a bank director, who in the five-and-one-half years that he had been on the board had never attended a board meeting or made any examination of the books and records, was held liable for losses resulting from the unsupervised acts of the president and cashier, who had made various improper loans and had permitted large overdrafts.

In 1999 an amendment to the Revised Act was adopted refining the Act's standards of conduct and liability for directors. It substituted a different duty of care standard for the second point above (prudent person): When becoming informed in connection with their decision-making function or devoting attention to their oversight function, directors shall discharge their duties with the care that a person in a like position would reasonably believe appropriate under similar circumstances. Section 8.30(b) as amended. While some aspects of a director's role will be performed individually, such as preparing for meetings, this reformulation explicitly recognizes that directors perform most of their functions as a unit.

RELIANCE UPON OTHERS Directors and officers are, nevertheless, permitted to entrust important work to others, and if they have selected employees with care, they are not personally liable for the negligent acts or willful wrongs of those selected. A reasonable amount of supervision is required, however; and an officer or director who knew or should have known or suspected that an employee was incurring losses through carelessness, theft, or embezzlement will be held liable for such losses.

A director also may rely in good faith upon *information* provided him by officers and employees of the corporation;

legal counsel, public accountants, or other persons as to matters the director reasonably believes are within the person's professional or expert competence; and a committee of the board of directors of which the director is not a member if the director reasonably believes the committee merits confidence. Section 8.30 of the Revised Act. A director is not acting in good faith if he has knowledge concerning the matter in question that makes reliance unwarranted. The 1999 amendments to the Revised Act added a provision entitling a director to rely on the *performance* of board functions properly delegated by the board to officers, employees, or a committee of the board of directors of which the director is not a member unless the director has knowledge that makes reliance unwarranted. Section 8.30(c) as amended.

An officer is also entitled to rely upon this information, but this right may, in many circumstances, be more limited than a director's right to so rely because of the officer's greater familiarity with the corporation's affairs. Section 8.42 and Comment.

BUSINESS JUDGMENT RULE Directors and officers are continually called upon to make decisions that require balancing benefits and risks to the corporation. Although hindsight may reveal that some of these decisions were less than optimal, the business judgment rule precludes imposing liability upon the directors or officers for honest mistakes of judgment. To subsequently benefit from the business judgment rule, a director or officer must make an informed decision, in good faith without any conflict of interests, and have a rational basis for believing it was in the best interests of the corporation. (With respect to *directors*, the 1999 amendments to the Revised Act added a new Section 8.31 codifying much of the business judgment rule and providing guidance as to its application.) Moreover, when a director or officer fails to satisfy this standard of conduct, it must be shown that her action (or inaction) is the proximate cause of damage to the corporation.

Hasty or ill-advised action also can render directors liable. The Supreme Court of Delaware has held directors liable for approving the terms of a cash-out merger because the directors did not adequately inform themselves of the company's intrinsic value and were grossly negligent in approving the terms of the merger upon two hours' consideration and without prior notice. *Smith v. Van Gorkom*, 488 A.2d 858 (1985).

DUTY OF LOYALTY

The officers and directors of a corporation owe a duty of loyalty (a **fiduciary duty**) to the corporation and to its shareholders. The essence of a fiduciary duty is the subordination of self-interest to the interest of the person or persons to whom the duty is owing. It requires officers and directors to be constantly loyal to the corporation, which they both serve and control.

An officer or director is required to disclose fully to the corporation any financial interest that he may have in any contract or transaction to which the corporation is a party. (This is a corollary to the rule that forbids fiduciaries from making secret profits.) He must eschew self-interest in his business conduct, and he may not advance his personal interests at the corporation's expense. Moreover, he may not represent conflicting interests; his duty is one of strict allegiance to the corporation.

The remedy for breach of fiduciary duty is a suit in equity by the corporation, or more often a derivative suit instituted by a shareholder, to require the fiduciary to pay to the corporation the profits that he obtained through breach of his fiduciary duty. It need not be shown that the corporation could otherwise have made the profits that the fiduciary has realized. The object of the rule is to discourage breaches of duty by taking from the fiduciary all of the profits he has made. Though enforcing the rule may result in a windfall to the corporation, this is incidental to the rule's deterrent objective. Whenever a director or officer breaches his fiduciary duty, he forfeits his right to compensation during the period he engaged in the breach.

CONFLICT OF INTERESTS A contract or other transaction between an officer or a director and the corporation inherently involves a conflict of interest. Contracts between officers and the corporation are covered under the law of agency. (See *Chapter 19*.) Early on, the common law viewed all director–corporation transactions as automatically void or voidable but eventually regarded this rule as unreasonable because it would prevent directors from entering into contracts beneficial to the corporation. Now, therefore, if such a contract is honest and fair, the courts will uphold it. In the case of contracts between corporations having an interlocking directorate (corporations whose boards of directors share one or more members), the courts subject the contracts to scrutiny and will set them aside unless the transaction is shown to have been entirely fair and entered in good faith.

Most States and the original version of the Revised Act address these related problems by providing that such transactions are neither void nor voidable if, after full disclosure, they are approved by either the board of disinterested directors or the shareholders, or if they are fair and reasonable to the corporation.

The Revised Act was amended in 1988 to adopt a more specific approach to a director's conflict-of-interest transactions, which it defines as transactions between a corporation (or a subsidiary of it or an entity controlled by it) and one of the corporation's directors, a close relative of the director, or approved by the greater of (1) a majority of all the directors in office when the action is taken or (2) the number of directors required by the articles of incorporation or bylaws to take action. Section 8.25(b). The Revised Act as amended and some statutes permit a committee to have as few as one member, whereas the statutes of many States require that a committee consist of at least two directors.

Committees may exercise all of the authority of the board, except with regard to certain matters specified in the incorporation statute, such as declaring dividends and other distributions, filling vacancies in the board or in any of its committees, amending the bylaws, or proposing actions that require approval by shareholders. Section 8.25(e). Delegating authority to a committee does not relieve any board member of his duties to the corporation. Commonly used committees include executive committees, audit committees (to recommend and oversee independent public accountants), compensation committees, finance committees, nominating committees, and investment committees.

The Sarbanes-Oxley Act confers on the audit committee of every publicly held corporation direct responsibility for the appointment, compensation, and oversight of the work of the public accounting firm employed by the company to perform audit services. Moreover, the public accounting firm must report directly to the audit committee, and the lead auditor must rotate every five years. Each member of the audit committee must be independent, and at least one member must qualify as a financial expert. The Act requires that the company provide appropriate funding for the audit committee to compensate the auditors, independent counsel, and other advisers. The audit committee is responsible for resolving disagreements between management and the auditor regarding the company's financial reporting. The audit committee must establish procedures for addressing complaints regarding accounting, internal accounting controls, or auditing matters.

Under the CFPA, the SEC must issue rules directing the national securities exchanges to require that each member of a listed company's compensation committee be an independent director.

DIRECTORS' INSPECTION RIGHTS

So that they can perform their duties competently and fully, directors have the right to inspect corporate books and records. This right is considerably broader than a shareholder's right to inspect. Nevertheless, it is subject to limitations.

OFFICERS

In most States, the officers of a corporation are appointed by the board of directors to hold the offices provided in the bylaws, which set forth the respective duties of each officer.

Statutes generally require as a minimum that the officers consist of a president, one or more vice presidents as prescribed by the bylaws, a secretary, and a treasurer. A person may hold more than one office, with the exception that the same person may not hold the office of president and secretary at the same time.

The Revised Act and other modern statutes permit every corporation to designate whatever officers it wants. Although the Act specifies no particular number of officers, one of them must be delegated responsibility for preparing the minutes of directors' and shareholders' meetings and authenticating corporate records. The Revised Act permits the same individual to hold *all* of the offices of a corporation. Section 8.40(d).

SELECTION AND REMOVAL OF OFFICERS

Most State statutes provide that officers be appointed by the board of directors and that they serve at the pleasure of the board. Accordingly, the board may remove officers with or without cause. Section 8.43(b). Of course, if the officer has an employment contract that is valid for a specified time, removing the officer without cause before that time expires would constitute a breach of the employment contract. The board also determines the compensation of officers.

ROLE OF OFFICERS

The officers are, like the directors, fiduciaries to the corporation. On the other hand, unlike the directors, they are agents of the corporation. The roles of officers are set forth in the corporate bylaws.

AUTHORITY OF OFFICERS

The Revised Act provides that each officer has the authority provided in the bylaws or prescribed by the board of directors, to the extent that such prescribed authority is consistent with the bylaws. Section 8.41. Like that of other agents, the authority of an officer to bind the corporation may be (1) actual express, (2) actual implied, or (3) apparent.

ACTUAL EXPRESS AUTHORITY Actual express authority results when the corporation manifests its assent to the officer that the officer should act on its behalf. Actual express authority arises from the incorporation statute, the articles of incorporation, the bylaws, and resolutions of the board of directors. The last represent the principal source of such authority. The Revised Act further provides that the board of directors may authorize an officer to prescribe the duties of other officers. Section 8.41. This provision empowers officers to delegate authority to subordinates.

ACTUAL IMPLIED AUTHORITY Officers, as agents of the corporation, have actual implied authority to do what is reasonably necessary to perform their actual, delegated authority.

a person to whom the director owes a fiduciary duty. Section 8.60. The Revised Act establishes more clearly prescribed safe harbors to validate conflict-of-interest transactions. Section 8.61. The Revised Act provides two alternative safe harbors, each of which is available before or after the transaction: approval by "qualified" (disinterested) directors or approval by the shareholders. In either case, the interested director must make full disclosure to the approving group. Full disclosure requires the director to disclose both the existence of the conflicting interest and all material facts known to her regarding the subject matter of the transaction.

If neither of the safe harbor provisions is satisfied, then the transaction is subject to appropriate judicial action unless the transaction is fair to the corporation. The comments to Section 8.61 explain that fairness requires that (1) the terms of the transaction, including the price, are fair; (2) the transaction benefits the corporation; and (3) the course of dealing or process of the transaction is fair.

LOANS TO DIRECTORS AND OFFICERS The Model Act and some States permit a corporation to lend money to its directors only with its shareholders' authorization for each loan. The statutes in most States permit such loans either on a general or on a limited basis. The Revised Act initially permitted such loans if each was approved (1) by a majority of disinterested shareholders or (2) by the board of directors after its determination that the loan would benefit the corporation. Section 8.32. The 1988 amendments to the Revised Act deleted this section, instead subjecting director loans to the procedure that applies to a director's conflict-of-interest transactions.

The Sarbanes-Oxley Act prohibits any publicly held corporation from making personal loans to its directors or its executive officers, although it does provide certain limited exceptions.

CORPORATE OPPORTUNITY Directors and officers may not usurp any corporate opportunity that in all fairness should belong to the corporation. A corporate opportunity is one in which the corporation has a right, property interest, or expectancy; whether or not such an opportunity exists depends on the facts and circumstances of each case.

A corporate opportunity should be promptly offered to the corporation, which, in turn, should promptly accept or reject it. Rejection may be based on one or more of several factors, such as the corporation's lack of interest in the opportunity, its financial inability to acquire the opportunity, legal restrictions on its ability to accept the opportunity, or a third party's unwillingness to deal with the corporation. Section 8.70 was added to the Revised Act to deal with business opportunities and to provide safe-harbor protection for directors considering involvement with a business opportunity that might be considered a corporate opportunity.

For instance, a party proposes a business arrangement to a corporation through its vice president, who personally accepts the arrangement without offering it to the corporation. The vice president has usurped a corporate opportunity. On the other hand, a corporate opportunity generally would not include one that the corporation was unable to accept or one that the corporation expressly rejected by a vote of disinterested directors after full disclosure. In both of these instances, a director or officer is free to take personal advantage of the opportunity.

TRANSACTIONS IN SHARES The issuance of shares at favorable prices to management by excluding other shareholders normally will constitute a violation of the fiduciary duty. So might the issuance of shares to a director at a fair price if the purpose of the issuance is to perpetuate corporate control rather than to raise capital or to serve some other interest of the corporation.

Officers and directors have access to inside advance information, unavailable to the public, which may affect the future market value of the corporation's shares. Federal statutes have attempted to deal with this trading advantage by prohibiting officers and directors from purchasing or selling shares of their corporation's stock without adequately disclosing all material facts in their possession that may affect the stock's actual or potential value. See *Chapter 44* for a discussion of these matters.

Although the imposition of liability upon officers and directors for secret, profitable use of inside information has been inconsistent under State law, the trend is toward holding them liable for breach of fiduciary duty to shareholders from whom they purchase stock without disclosing facts that give the stock added potential value. They are also held liable to the corporation for profits realized upon a sale of the stock when undisclosed conditions of the corporation make a substantial decline in value practically inevitable.

DUTY NOT TO COMPETE As fiduciaries, directors and officers owe to the corporation the duty of undivided loyalty, which means they may not compete with the corporation. A director or officer who breaches his fiduciary duty by competing with the corporation is liable for the damages he thus causes to the corporation. Although directors and officers may engage in their own business interests, courts will closely scrutinize any interest that competes with the corporation's business. Moreover, an officer or director may not use corporate personnel, facilities, or funds for her own benefit nor disclose trade secrets of the corporation to others.

INDEMNIFICATION OF DIRECTORS AND OFFICERS

Directors and officers incur personal liability for breaching any of the duties they owe to the corporation and its shareholders. Under many modern incorporation statutes, a corporation *may* indemnify a director or officer for liability incurred if he acted in good faith and in a manner he reasonably believed to be in the best interests of the corporation, so long as he has not been adjudged negligent or liable for misconduct. The Revised Act provides for *mandatory* indemnification of directors and officers for reasonable expenses they incur in the wholly successful defense of any proceeding brought against them because they are or were directors or officers. Sections 8.52 and 8.56. These provisions, however, may be limited by the articles of incorporation. In addition, a corporation may purchase insurance to indemnify officers and directors for liability arising out of their corporate activities, including liabilities against which the corporation is not empowered to indemnify directly. Section 8.57.

LIABILITY LIMITATION STATUTES

Virtually all States have enacted legislation limiting the liability of directors. Most of these States, including Delaware, have authorized corporations—with shareholder approval—to limit or eliminate the liability of directors for some breaches of duty. (A few States permit shareholders to limit the liability of officers.) The Delaware statute provides that the articles of incorporation may contain a provision eliminating or limiting the personal liability of a director to the corporation or its stockholders for monetary

damages for breach of her directorial duty, provided that such provision does not eliminate or limit the liability of a director (1) for any breach of the director's duty of loyalty to the corporation or its stockholders, (2) for acts or omissions lacking good faith or involving intentional misconduct or a knowing violation of law, (3) for liability for unlawful dividend payments or redemptions, or (4) for any transaction from which the director derived an improper personal benefit.

A few States have directly limited personal liability for directors, subject to certain exceptions, without requiring an amendment to the articles of incorporation. Other States adopt a third approach by limiting the amount of money damages that may be assessed against a director or officer.

The Revised Act authorizes the articles of incorporation to include a provision eliminating or limiting—with certain exceptions—the liability of a director to the corporation or its shareholders for any action that he, as a director, has taken or has failed to take. The exceptions, for which liability would be unaffected, are (1) the amount of any financial benefit the director receives to which he is not entitled, such as a bribe, kickback, or profits from a usurped corporate opportunity; (2) an intentional infliction of harm on the corporation or the shareholders; (3) liability under Section 8.33 for unlawful distributions; and (4) an intentional violation of the criminal law. Section 2.02(b)(4).

CHAPTER SUMMARY

ROLE OF SHAREHOLDERS

VOTING RIGHTS OF SHAREHOLDERS
Management Structure of Corporations see *Figures 36-1, 36-2,* and *36-3* for illustrations of the statutory model of corporate governance, the structure of the typical closely held corporation, and the structure of the typical publicly held corporation

Shareholder Meetings shareholders may exercise their voting rights at both annual and special shareholder meetings

Quorum minimum number necessary to be present at a meeting in order to transact business

Election of Directors the shareholders elect the board at the annual meeting of the corporation
* *Straight Voting* directors are elected by a plurality of votes
* *Cumulative Voting* entitles shareholders to multiply the number of votes they are entitled to cast by the number of directors for whom they are entitled to vote and to cast the product for a single candidate or to distribute the product among two or more candidates

Removal of Directors the shareholders may by majority vote remove directors with or without cause, subject to cumulative voting rights

Approval of Fundamental Changes shareholder approval is required for charter amendments, most acquisitions, and dissolution

Concentrations of Voting Power
- *Proxy* authorization to vote another's shares at a shareholder meeting
- *Voting Trust* transfer of corporate shares' voting rights to a trustee
- *Shareholder Voting Agreement* used to provide shareholders with greater control over the election and removal of directors and other matters
- *Restrictions on Transfer of Shares* must be reasonable and conspicuously noted on stock certificate

ENFORCEMENT RIGHTS OF SHAREHOLDERS	**Right to Inspect Books and Records** if the demand is made in good faith and for a proper purpose **Shareholder Suits** • *Direct Suits* brought by a shareholder or a class of shareholders against the corporation based upon the ownership of shares • *Derivative Suits* brought by a shareholder on behalf of the corporation to enforce a right belonging to the corporation • *Shareholder's Right to Dissent* a shareholder has the right to dissent from certain corporate actions that require shareholder approval

ROLE OF DIRECTORS AND OFFICERS

FUNCTION OF THE BOARD OF DIRECTORS	**Selection and Removal of Officers** **Capital Structure** **Fundamental Changes** the directors have the power to make, amend, or repeal the bylaws, unless this power is exclusively reserved to the shareholders **Dividends** directors declare the amount and type of dividends **Management Compensation** **Vacancies in the Board** may be filled by the vote of a majority of the remaining directors
EXERCISE OF DIRECTORS' FUNCTIONS	**Meeting** directors have the power to bind the corporation only when acting as a board **Action Taken without a Meeting** permitted if a consent in writing is signed by all of the directors **Delegation of Board Powers** committees may be appointed to perform some but not all of the board's functions **Directors' Inspection Rights** directors have the right to inspect corporate books and records
OFFICERS	**Role of Officers** officers are agents of the corporation **Authority of Officers** • *Actual Express Authority* arises from the incorporation statute, the charter, the bylaws, and resolutions of the directors • *Actual Implied Authority* authority to do what is reasonably necessary to perform actual authority • *Apparent Authority* acts of the principal that lead a third party to believe reasonably and in good faith that an officer has the required authority • *Ratification* a corporation may ratify the unauthorized acts of its officers
DUTIES OF DIRECTORS AND OFFICERS	**Duty of Obedience** must act within respective authority **Duty of Diligence** must exercise ordinary care and prudence **Duty of Loyalty** requires undeviating loyalty to the corporation **Business Judgment Rule** precludes imposing liability on directors and officers for honest mistakes in judgment if they act with due care, in good faith, and in a manner reasonably believed to be in the best interests of the corporation

Indemnification a corporation may indemnify a director or officer for liability incurred if he acted in good faith and was not adjudged negligent or liable for misconduct

Liability Limitation Statutes many States now authorize corporations—with shareholder approval—to limit or eliminate the liability of directors for some breaches of duty

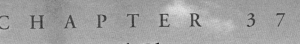

Certain extraordinary changes exert such a fundamental effect on a corporation by altering the corporation's basic structure that they fall outside the authority of the board of directors and require shareholder approval. Such fundamental changes include charter amendments, mergers, consolidations, compulsory share exchanges, dissolution, and the sale or lease of all or substantially all of the corporation's assets, other than those in the regular course of business. Although each of these actions is authorized by State incorporation statutes, which impose specific procedural requirements, they are also subject to equitable limitations imposed by the courts. In 1999 substantial revisions were made to the Revised Act's treatment of fundamental changes.

Because shareholder approval for fundamental changes usually does not need to be unanimous, such changes frequently will be approved despite opposition by minority shareholders. Shareholder approval means a majority (or some other specified fraction) of *all votes entitled* to be cast, rather than a majority (or other fraction) of votes represented at a shareholders' meeting at which a quorum is present. (The 1999 amendments to the Revised Act significantly changed the voting rule: fundamental changes need only be approved by a majority of the shares present at a meeting at which a quorum is present.) In some instances, minority shareholders have the right to dissent and to recover the fair value of their shares if they follow the prescribed procedure for doing so. This right is called the appraisal remedy. The legal aspects of fundamental changes will be discussed in this chapter.

CHARTER AMENDMENTS

Shareholders do not have a vested property right resulting from any provision in the articles of incorporation. Section 10.01(b). Accordingly, corporate charters may be amended if proper procedures are followed. The amended articles of incorporation, however, may contain only those provisions that the articles of incorporation might lawfully contain at the time of the amendment. Section 10.01(a).

APPROVAL BY DIRECTORS AND SHAREHOLDERS

Under the Revised Act and most statutes, the typical procedure for amending the articles of incorporation requires the board of directors to adopt a resolution setting forth the proposed amendment, which must then be approved by a majority vote of the shareholders entitled to vote, although some older statutes require a two-thirds shareholder vote. Moreover, a class of shares is entitled to vote as a class on certain proposed amendments, whether the articles of incorporation provide such entitlement or not. In some States shareholders may approve charter amendments without a prior board of directors' resolution.

After the shareholders approve the amendment, the corporation executes articles of amendment and delivers them to the Secretary of State for filing. Section 10.06. The amendment does not affect the existing rights of nonshareholders. Section 10.09.

Under Section 13.02(a)(4) of the Revised Act, dissenting shareholders may obtain the appraisal remedy only if an amendment materially and adversely affects their rights by—

1. altering or abolishing a preferential right of the shares;
2. creating, altering, or abolishing a right involving the redemption of the shares;
3. altering or abolishing a preemptive right of the holder of the shares;
4. excluding or limiting the shareholder's right to vote on any matter or to cumulate his votes; or
5. reducing to a fraction of a share the number of shares the shareholder owns, if the fractional share is to be acquired for cash.

The 1999 amendments to the Revised Act eliminate the appraisal remedy for virtually all charter amendments.

Under the Revised Act, the shareholder approval required for an amendment depends upon the nature of the amendment. An amendment that would give rise to dissenters' rights must be approved by a majority of all votes entitled to be cast on the amendment, unless the act, the charter, or the board of directors requires a greater vote. All other amendments must be approved by a majority of all votes cast on the amendment at a meeting where a quorum exists, unless the act, the charter, or the board of directors requires a greater vote. Sections 10.03, 7.25.

APPROVAL BY DIRECTORS

The Revised Act permits the board of directors to adopt certain amendments without shareholder action, unless the articles of incorporation provide otherwise. Section 10.02. These amendments include (1) extending the duration of the corporation if it was incorporated when limited duration was required by law, (2) changing each issued and unissued authorized share of an outstanding class into a greater number of whole shares if the corporation has only one class of shares, and (3) making minor name changes.

COMBINATIONS

Acquiring all or substantially all of the assets of another corporation or corporations may be both desirable and profitable. A corporation may accomplish this through (1) purchase or lease of other corporations' assets, (2) purchase of a controlling stock interest in other corporations, (3) merger with other corporations, or (4) consolidation with other corporations. A few States have and the 1999 amendments to the Revised Act contain provisions authorizing a corporation to merge into another type of business organization, such as a limited partnership (LP), limited liability company (LLC), or a limited liability partnership (LLP).

Any method of combination that involves the issuance of shares, proxy solicitations, or tender offers may be subject to Federal securities regulation, as discussed in *Chapter 44*. Moreover, a combination that is potentially detrimental to competition may be subject to Federal antitrust laws, as discussed in *Chapter 41*.

In July 2010, President Obama signed into law the Dodd-Frank Wall Street Reform and Consumer Protection Act (CFPA), the most significant change to U.S. financial regulation since the New Deal. One of the many stand-alone statutes included in the CFPA is the Investor Protection and Securities Reform Act of 2010, which imposes new corporate governance rules on publicly held companies. (This Act is also discussed in *Chapters 36, 44,* and *47*.) One of these provisions of the CFPA applies to proxy solicitations asking shareholders to approve an acquisition, merger, consolidation, or proposed sale or other disposition of all or substantially all the assets of a publicly held company issuer. In these proxy solicitations, publicly held companies must disclose, and provide shareholders with a nonbinding vote to approve, any type of compensation that is based on or relates to these specified combinations.

PURCHASE OR LEASE OF ALL OR SUBSTANTIALLY ALL OF THE ASSETS

When one corporation purchases or leases all or substantially all of the assets of another corporation, the legal personality of neither corporation changes. The purchaser or lessee corporation simply acquires ownership or control of additional physical assets. The selling or lessor corporation, in exchange for its physical properties, receives cash, other property, or a stipulated rental. Having altered only the form or extent of its assets, each corporation continues its separate existence.

Generally, a corporation that purchases the assets of another corporation does not assume the other's liabilities unless (1) the purchaser expressly or impliedly agrees to assume the seller's liabilities; (2) the transaction amounts to a consolidation or merger of the two corporations; (3) the purchaser is a mere continuation of the seller; or (4) the sale is for the fraudulent purpose of avoiding the liabilities of the seller. Some courts recognize a fifth exception (called the "product line" exception), which imposes strict tort liability upon the purchaser for defects in products manufactured and distributed by the seller corporation when the purchaser corporation continues the product line.

REGULAR COURSE OF BUSINESS If the sale or lease of all or substantially all of its assets is in the selling or lessor corporation's usual and regular course of business, approval by its board of directors is required but shareholder authorization is not. Similarly, a mortgage or pledge of any or all of a corporation's property and assets—whether or not in the usual or regular course of business—requires only the approval of the board of directors. Section 12.01. The Revised Act considers a transfer of any or all of a corporation's assets to a wholly owned subsidiary to be a sale in the regular course of business. Section 12.01(a)(3). Under the Revised Act, a sale of assets in the regular course of business does not require shareholder approval unless the articles of incorporation provide otherwise. Section 12.01(b).

OTHER THAN IN REGULAR COURSE OF BUSINESS Shareholder approval is necessary *only if* a sale or lease of all or substantially all of its assets is *not* in the corporation's usual and regular course of business. (The 1999 amendments to the Revised Act adopt an objective test for determining when shareholder approval is required.) The selling corporation, by liquidating its assets, or the lessor corporation, by placing its physical assets beyond its control, has significantly changed its position and perhaps its ability to carry on the type of business contemplated in its charter. For this reason, such sale or lease must be approved not only by action of the directors but also by the affirmative vote of the holders of a majority of the corporation's shares entitled to vote at a shareholders' meeting called for this purpose. Section 12.02. In most States, dissenting shareholders of the selling corporation are given an appraisal remedy. Section 13.02(a)(3).

PURCHASE OF SHARES

An alternative to purchasing another corporation's assets is to purchase its stock. When one corporation acquires all of, or a controlling interest in, the stock of another corporation, the legal existence of neither corporation changes. The acquiring corporation acts through its board of directors, whereas the corporation that becomes a subsidiary does not act at all, because the decision to sell stock is made not by the corporation but by its individual shareholders. The capital structure of the subsidiary remains unchanged, and that of the parent is usually not altered unless financing the acquisition of the stock necessitates a change in capital. Because the action of neither corporation requires formal shareholder approval, there is no appraisal remedy.

SALE OF CONTROL When a controlling interest is owned by one or a few shareholders, a privately negotiated transaction is possible, though the courts require that these sales be made with due care. The controlling shareholders must make a reasonable investigation so as not to transfer control to purchasers who wrongfully plan to steal or "loot" the corporation's assets or to act against its best interests. In addition, purchasers frequently are willing to pay a premium for a block of shares that conveys control. Although historically some courts required that this so-called control premium inure to the benefit of the corporation, virtually all courts now permit the controlling shareholders to retain the full amount of the control premium.

TENDER OFFER When a controlling interest is not held by one or a few shareholders, the acquisition of a corporation through the purchase of shares may take the form of a tender offer. A tender offer is a general invitation to all the shareholders of a target company to tender their shares for sale at a specified price. The offer may be for all of the target company's shares or for just a controlling interest. Tender offers for publicly held companies, which are subject to Federal securities regulation, are discussed in *Chapter 44*.

COMPULSORY SHARE EXCHANGE

The Revised Act and some State statutes provide different procedures for which a corporation to acquire shares through a **compulsory share exchange**, a transaction by which the corporation becomes the owner of *all* the outstanding shares of one or more classes of another corporation by an exchange that is compulsory on all owners of the acquired shares. Section 11.02. The corporation may acquire the shares with its or any other corporation's shares, obligations, or other securities or for cash or other property. For example, if A corporation acquires all of the outstanding shares of B corporation through a compulsory exchange, then B becomes a wholly owned subsidiary of A. A compulsory share exchange affects the separate existence of neither corporate party to the transaction. Although they produce results similar to mergers, as discussed below, compulsory share exchanges are used instead of mergers where preserving the existence of the acquired corporation is essential or desirable, as, for example, in the formation of holding company systems for insurance companies and banks.

A compulsory share exchange requires approval from the board of directors of each corporation and from the shareholders of the corporation whose shares are being acquired. Sections 11.02 and 11.03. Each included class of shares must vote separately on the exchange. The shareholders of the acquiring corporation need not approve the transaction. Once the shareholders of the corporation whose shares are to be acquired have adopted and approved a compulsory share exchange plan, it is binding on all who hold shares of the class to be acquired. Dissenting shareholders are given an appraisal remedy. Section 13.02(a)(2).

MERGER

A **merger** of two or more corporations is the combination of all of their assets. One of the corporations, known as the **surviving corporation**, receives title to the combined assets. The other party or parties to the merger, known as the **merged corporation** or corporations, are merged into the surviving corporation and cease their separate existence. Thus, if A Corporation and B Corporation combine into the A Corporation, A is the surviving corporation and B is the merged corporation. Under the Revised Act and most statutes, the shareholders of the merged corporation may receive stock or other securities issued by the surviving corporation or other consideration *including cash*, as provided in the merger agreement. Moreover, the surviving corporation assumes all debts and other liabilities of the merged corporation. Section 11.06.

A merger requires the approval of each corporation's board of directors, as well as the affirmative vote of the holders of a majority of the shares of each corporation that are entitled to vote. Sections 11.01 and 11.03. A dissenting shareholder of any corporate party to the merger has an appraisal remedy if shareholder approval is required and the shareholder is entitled to vote on the merger. Section 13.02(a)(1). Many States and the 1999 amendments to the Revised Act permit the vote of the shareholders of the surviving corporation to be eliminated when a merger increases the number of outstanding shares by no more than 20 percent.

In a **short-form merger**, a corporation that owns a statutorily specified percentage of the outstanding shares of each class of a subsidiary may merge the subsidiary into itself without approval by the shareholders of either corporation. The Revised Act and most States specify 90 percent. Section 11.04. Obtaining approval from the subsidiary's shareholders or from the subsidiary's board of directors is unnecessary because the parent's 90 percent ownership ensures approval of the merger plan. All the merger requires is a resolution by the board of directors of the parent corporation. The dissenting shareholders of the subsidiary have the right to obtain payment from the parent for their shares. Section 13.02(a)(1). The shareholders of the parent do not have this appraisal remedy because the transaction has not materially changed their rights. Instead of indirectly owning 90 percent of the subsidiary's assets, the parent now directly owns 100 percent of the same assets.

CONSOLIDATION

A consolidation of two or more corporations is the combination of all of their assets, the title to which is taken by a newly created corporation known as the **consolidated corporation**. Each constituent corporation ceases to exist, and all of its debts and liabilities are assumed by the new corporation. The shareholders of the constituent corporations receive stock or other securities, not necessarily of the same class, issued to them by the new corporation or other consideration provided in the plan of consolidation. A consolidation requires the approval of each corporation's board of directors, as well as the affirmative vote of the holders of a majority of the shares of each corporation that are entitled to vote. Dissenting shareholders have an appraisal remedy.

The Revised Act has deleted all references to consolidations, as explained by the comment to Section 11.01: "In modern corporate practice consolidation transactions are obsolete since it is nearly always advantageous for one of the parties in the transaction to be the surviving corporation."

DOMESTICATION AND CONVERSION

The Revised Act was amended in 2002 to provide for domestication and conversion into other entities without a merger. The **domestication** procedures permit a corporation to change its State of incorporation, thus allowing a domestic business corporation to become a foreign business corporation or a foreign business corporation to become a domestic business corporation. The **conversion** procedures permit a domestic business corporation to become a domestic or foreign partnership, LLC, or other entity, and also permit a domestic or foreign partnership, LLC, or other entity to become a domestic business corporation. In both of these transactions a domestic business corporation must be present immediately before or after the transaction.

GOING PRIVATE TRANSACTIONS

Corporate combinations are sometimes used to take a publicly held corporation private in order to eliminate minority interests, to reduce the burdens of certain provisions of the Federal securities laws, or both. One method of going private is for the corporation or its majority shareholder to acquire the corporation's shares through purchases on the open market or through a tender offer for the shares. Other methods include a cash-out combination, a merger with or sale of assets to a corporation controlled by the majority shareholder. If the majority shareholder is a corporation, it may arrange a cash-out combination with itself or, if it owns enough shares, use a short-form merger. In recent years, a new type of going private transaction—a management buyout—has become much more frequent. This section will examine cash-out combinations and management buyouts.

CASH-OUT COMBINATIONS Cash-out combinations are used to eliminate minority shareholders by forcing them to accept cash or property for their shares. A cash-out combination often follows the acquisition, by a person, group, or company, of a large interest in a target company (T) through a tender offer. The tender offeror (TO) then seeks to eliminate all other shareholders, thereby achieving complete control of T. To do so, TO might form a new corporation (Corporation N) and take 100 percent of its stock. A cash-out merger of T into N is then arranged, with all the shareholders of T other than TO to receive cash for their shares. Because TO owns all the stock of N and a controlling interest in T, the shareholders of both companies will approve the merger. Alternatively, TO could purchase for cash or notes the assets of T, leaving the minority shareholders with only an interest in the proceeds of the sale. The use of cash-out combinations has raised questions concerning their purpose and their fairness to minority shareholders. Some States require that cash-out combinations have a valid business purpose and that they be fair to all concerned. Fairness, in this context, includes both fair dealing (which involves the procedural aspects of the transaction) and fair price (which involves the financial considerations of the merger). Other States require only the transaction to be fair.

MANAGEMENT BUYOUT A management buyout is a transaction by which existing management increases its ownership of a corporation while eliminating the entity's public shareholders. The typical procedure is as follows. The management of an existing company (Corporation A) forms a new corporation (Corporation B) in which the management owns some of the stock and institutional investors own the rest. Corporation B issues bonds to institutional investors to raise cash, with which it purchases the assets or stock of Corporation A. The assets of Corporation A are used as security for the bonds issued by Corporation B. (Because of the extensive use of borrowed funds, a management buyout is commonly called a **leveraged buyout** [LBO].) The result of this transaction is twofold: the public shareholders of Corporation A no longer have any proprietary interest in the assets of Corporation A, and management's equity interest in Corporation B is greater than its interest was in Corporation A.

A critical issue is the fairness of the management buyout to the shareholders of Corporation A. The transaction inherently presents a potential conflict of interest to those in management, who owe a fiduciary duty to represent the interests of the shareholders of Corporation A. As substantial shareholders of Corporation B, however, those in management are apt to have personal and probably adverse financial interests in the transaction.

DISSENTING SHAREHOLDERS

The shareholder's right to dissent, a statutory right to obtain payment for shares, is accorded to shareholders who object to certain fundamental changes in the corporation. The Introductory Comment to Chapter 13 of the Revised Act explains the purpose of dissenters' rights:

> Chapter 13 deals with the tension between the desire of the corporate leadership to be able to enter new fields, acquire new enterprises, and rearrange investor rights and the desire of investors to adhere to the rights and the risks on the basis of which they invested. Most contemporary corporation codes in the United States attempt to resolve this tension through a combination of two devices. On the one hand, the majority is given an almost unlimited power to change the nature and shape of the enterprise and the rights of its members. On the other hand, the members who dissent from these changes are given a right to withdraw their investment at a fair value.

TRANSACTIONS GIVING RISE TO DISSENTERS' RIGHTS States vary considerably with respect to which transactions give rise to dissenters' rights. Some include transactions not covered by the Revised Act, and other States omit transactions included in the Revised Act.

The Revised Act grants dissenters' rights to (1) dissenting shareholders of a corporation selling or leasing all or substantially all of its property or assets not in the usual or regular course of business; (2) dissenting shareholders of each corporate party to a merger, except in a short-form merger, where only the dissenting shareholders of the subsidiary have dissenters' rights; (3) any plan of compulsory share exchange in which their corporation is to be the one acquired; (4) any amendment to the articles of incorporation that materially and adversely affects a dissenter's rights regarding her shares; and (5) any other corporate action taken pursuant to a shareholder vote with respect to which the articles of incorporation, the bylaws, or a resolution of the board of directors provides that shareholders shall have a right to dissent and obtain payment for their shares. Section 13.02. The 1999 amendments to the Revised Act narrowed the scope of the appraisal remedy: in a merger, only shareholders whose shares have been exchanged have dissenters' rights, and the appraisal remedy for virtually all charter amendments has been eliminated.

Many States have a stock market exception to the appraisal remedy. Under these statutes, a shareholder has no right to dissent if an established market, such as the New York Stock Exchange, exists for the shares. The Revised Act does not contain this exception but the 1999 amendments to the Revised Act have added it.

PROCEDURE The corporation must notify the shareholders of the existence of dissenters' rights before taking the vote on the corporate action. A dissenting shareholder who strictly complies with the provisions of the statute is entitled to receive the fair value of his shares. Unless he makes written demand within the prescribed time, however, the dissenting shareholder is not entitled to payment for his shares.

APPRAISAL REMEDY A dissenting shareholder who complies with all applicable requirements is entitled to an appraisal remedy, which is payment by the corporation of the **fair value** of his shares, plus accrued interest. The fair value is the value immediately preceding the effectuation of the corporate action to which the dissenter objects, excluding any appreciation or depreciation that occurs in anticipation of such corporate action, unless such exclusion would be inequitable.

A shareholder who has a right to obtain payment for his shares does not have the right to attack the validity of the corporate action that gives rise to his right to obtain payment or to have the action set aside or rescinded, except when the corporate action is unlawful or fraudulent with regard to the complaining shareholder or to the corporation. Section 13.02(b). Where the corporate action is not unlawful or fraudulent, the appraisal remedy is usually exclusive, and the shareholder may not challenge the action. Some States, however, make the appraisal remedy exclusive in all cases; others make it nonexclusive in certain cases.

DISSOLUTION

Although a corporation may have perpetual existence, its life may be terminated in a number of ways. Incorporation statutes usually provide for both voluntary dissolution and involuntary dissolution. Dissolution does not in itself terminate the corporation's existence but does require that the corporation wind up its affairs and liquidate its assets.

VOLUNTARY DISSOLUTION

Voluntary dissolution may be brought about through a board resolution approved by the affirmative vote of the holders of a majority of the corporation's shares entitled to vote at a shareholders' meeting duly called for this purpose. Section 14.02. Although shareholders who object to dissolution usually have no right to dissent and recover the fair value of their shares, the Revised Act grants dissenters' rights in connection with a sale or exchange of all or substantially all of a corporation's assets not made in the usual or regular course of business, including a sale in dissolution. Nevertheless, the Act excludes such rights in sales by court order and sales for cash on terms requiring that all or substantially all of the net proceeds be distributed to the shareholders within one year. Section 13.02(a)(3). In addition, in many States, but not the Revised Act, dissolution without action by the directors may be effected by unanimous consent of the shareholders.

The Revised Act authorizes shareholders in closely held corporations to adopt unanimous shareholders' agreements requiring dissolution of the corporation at the request of one or more shareholders or upon the occurrence of a specified event or contingency.

The Statutory Close Corporation Supplement gives the shareholders, if they elect such a right in the articles of incorporation, the power to dissolve the corporation. Unless the charter specifies otherwise, an amendment to include, modify, or delete a power to dissolve must be approved by all of the shareholders. The power to dissolve may be conferred upon any shareholder or holders of a specified number or percentage of shares of any class and may be exercised either at will or upon the occurrence of a specified event or contingency.

◆ **SEE FIGURE 37-1: Fundamental Changes under Pre-1999 RMBCA**

INVOLUNTARY DISSOLUTION

A corporation may be involuntarily dissolved by administrative dissolution or by judicial dissolution.

ADMINISTRATIVE DISSOLUTION The Secretary of State may commence an administrative proceeding to dissolve a corporation if (1) the corporation does not pay within sixty days after they are due any franchise taxes or penalties; (2) the corporation does not deliver its annual report to the Secretary of State within sixty days after it is due; (3) the corporation is without a registered agent or registered office in the State for sixty days or more; (4) the corporation does not notify the Secretary of State within sixty days that it has changed its registered agent or registered office, that its registered agent has resigned, or that it has discontinued its registered office; or (5) the corporation's period of duration stated in its articles of incorporation expires. Section 14.20.

JUDICIAL DISSOLUTION The State, a shareholder, or a creditor may bring a proceeding seeking judicial dissolution. A court may dissolve a corporation in a proceeding brought by the Attorney General if it is proved that the corporation obtained its charter through fraud or has continued to exceed or abuse the authority conferred upon it by law. Section 14.30(1).

A court may dissolve a corporation in a proceeding brought by a shareholder if it is established that (1) the directors are deadlocked in the management of the corporate affairs, the shareholders are unable to break the deadlock, and the corporation is threatened with or suffering irreparable injury; (2) the acts of the directors or those in control of the corporation are illegal, oppressive, or fraudulent; (3) the corporate assets are being misapplied or wasted; or (4) the shareholders are deadlocked and have failed to elect directors for at least two consecutive annual meetings. Section 14.30(2). The Revised Act as amended provides a *closely held* corporation or the remaining shareholders a limited right to purchase at fair value the shares of a shareholder who has brought a proceeding for involuntary dissolution. Section 14.34.

A creditor may bring a court action for dissolution upon a showing that the corporation has become unable to pay its debts and obligations as they mature in the regular course of its business and that either (1) the creditor has reduced his claim to a judgment and an execution issued on it has been returned unsatisfied or (2) the corporation has admitted in writing that the claim of the creditor is due and owing. Section 14.30(3).

LIQUIDATION

Dissolution, as mentioned earlier, requires that the corporation devote itself to winding up its affairs and liquidating its assets. After dissolution, the corporation must cease carrying on its business except as is necessary to wind up. Section 14.05. When a corporation is dissolved, its assets are liquidated and used first to pay the expenses of liquidation and its creditors according to their respective contract or lien rights. Any remainder is distributed proportionately to shareholders according to their respective contract rights; stock with a liquidation preference has priority over common stock. Voluntary liquidation is carried out by the board of directors, who serve as trustees; a court-appointed receiver may conduct involuntary liquidation. Section 14.32.

PROTECTION OF CREDITORS

The statutory provisions governing dissolution and liquidation usually prescribe procedures to safeguard the interests of the corporation's creditors. Such procedures typically include a required mailing of notice to known creditors, a general publication of notice, and the preservation of claims

◆ **FIGURE 37-1: Fundamental Changes under Pre-1999 RMBCA**

Change	Board of Directors Resolution Required	Shareholder Approval Required	Shareholder's Appraisal Remedy Available
A amends its articles of incorporation	A: Yes	A: Yes	A: No, unless amendment materially and adversely affects rights of shares
B sells its assets in usual and regular course of business to A	B: Yes	B: No	B: No
B sells its assets not in usual and regular course of business to A	B: Yes	B: Yes	B: Yes
A voluntarily purchases shares of B	A: Yes B: No	A: No B: No, individual shareholders decide	A: No B: No
A acquires shares of B through a compulsory exchange	A: Yes B: Yes	A: No B: Yes	A: No B: Yes
A and B merge	A: Yes B: Yes	A: Yes B: Yes	A: Yes B: Yes
A merges its 90 percent subsidiary B into A	A: Yes B: No	A: No B: No	A: No B: Yes
A and B consolidate	A: Yes B: Yes	A: Yes B: Yes	A: Yes B: Yes
A voluntarily dissolves	A: Yes	A: Yes	A: No (usually)

Note: RMBCA = Revised Model Business Corporation Act.

against the corporation. The Revised Act provides a three-year period within which an otherwise barred claim may be enforced for (1) a claimant who did not receive notice, (2) a claimant on whose timely claim the corporation failed to act, or (3) a claimant whose claim is contingent on an event occurring after dissolution. Section 14.07.

CHAPTER SUMMARY

CHARTER AMENDMENTS | **Authority to Amend** statutes permit charters to be amended
Procedure the board of directors adopts a resolution that must be approved by a majority vote of the shareholders

COMBINATIONS | **Purchase or Lease of All or Substantially All of the Assets** results in no change in the legal personality of either corporation
- *Regular Course of Business* approval by the selling corporation's board of directors is required, but shareholder authorization is not
- *Other Than in Regular Course of Business* approval by the board of directors and shareholders of selling corporation is required

Purchase of Shares a transaction by which one corporation acquires all of or a controlling interest in the stock of another corporation; no change occurs in the legal existence of either corporation, and no formal shareholder approval of either corporation is required

Compulsory Share Exchange a transaction by which a corporation becomes the owner of all of the outstanding shares of one or more classes of stock of another corporation by an exchange that is compulsory on all owners of the acquired shares; the board of directors of each corporation and the shareholders of the corporation whose shares are being acquired must approve

Merger the combination of the assets of two or more corporations into one of the corporations

- *Procedure* requires approval by the board of directors and shareholders of each corporation
- *Short-Form Merger* a corporation that owns at least 90 percent of the outstanding shares of a subsidiary may merge the subsidiary into itself without approval by the shareholders of either corporation
- *Effect* the surviving corporation receives title to all of the assets of the merged corporation and assumes all of its liabilities; the merged corporation ceases to exist

Consolidation the combination of two or more corporations into a new corporation

- *Procedure* requires approval of the board of directors and shareholders of each corporation
- *Effect* each constituent corporation ceases to exist; the new corporation assumes all of their debts and liabilities

Domestication Revised Act permits a corporation to change its State of incorporation

Conversion Revised Act permits (1) a domestic business corporation to become a domestic or foreign partnership, LLC, or other entity; and (2) a domestic or foreign partnership, LLC, or other entity to become a domestic business corporation

Going Private Transactions a combination that makes a publicly held corporation a private one; includes cash-out combinations and management buyouts

Dissenting Shareholder one who opposes a fundamental change and has the right to receive the fair value of her shares

- *Availability* dissenters' rights arise in (1) mergers, (2) consolidations, (3) sales or leases of all or substantially all of the assets of a corporation not in the regular course of business, (4) compulsory share exchanges, and (5) amendments that materially and adversely affect the rights of shares
- *Appraisal Remedy* the right to receive the fair value of one's shares (the value of shares immediately before the corporate action to which the dissenter objects takes place, excluding any appreciation or depreciation in anticipation of such corporate action unless such exclusion would be inequitable)

DISSOLUTION

Voluntary Dissolution may be brought about by a resolution of the board of directors that is approved by the shareholders

Involuntary Dissolution may occur by administrative or judicial action taken (1) by the Attorney General, (2) by shareholders under certain circumstances, or (3) by a creditor on a showing that the corporation has become unable to pay its debts and obligations as they mature in the regular course of its business

Liquidation when a corporation is dissolved, its assets are liquidated and used first to pay its liquidation expenses and its creditors according to their respective contract or lien rights; any remainder is proportionately distributed to shareholders according to their respective contract rights

Debtor and Creditor Relations

CHAPTER 38
**Secured Transactions
and Suretyship**

CHAPTER 39
Bankruptcy

Secured Transactions and Suretyship

"Neither a borrower nor a lender be"—Shakespeare's well-known line in *Hamlet*—reflects an earlier view of debt, for today borrowed funds are both essential and honorable under our economic system. In fact, the absence of loans would severely restrict the availability of goods and services and would greatly limit consumers in the quantities they would be able to purchase.

The public policy and social issues created by today's enormous use of debt center on certain tenets; among them are the following:

1. The means by which debt is created and transferred should be as simple and as inexpensive as possible.
2. The risks to lenders should be minimized.
3. Lenders should have a way to collect unpaid debts.

A lender typically incurs two basic collection risks: the borrower may be unwilling to repay the loan even though he is able to, or the borrower may prove to be unable to repay the loan. In addition to the remedies dealing with the first of these risks, the law has developed several devices to maximize the likelihood of repayment. These devices, which we will discuss in this chapter, include consensual security interests (also called secured transactions) and suretyships.

In addition, debtors of all sorts—wage earners, sole proprietorships, partnerships, unincorporated associations, and corporations—sometimes accumulate debts far in excess of their assets or suffer financial reverses that make it impossible for them to meet their obligations. In such an event, it is an important policy of the law to treat all creditors fairly and equitably and to provide the debtor with relief from these debts so that he may continue to contribute to society. These are the two basic purposes of the federal bankruptcy law, which we will briefly discuss in this chapter and discuss more fully in *Chapter 39*.

SECURED TRANSACTIONS IN PERSONAL PROPERTY

An obligation or debt can exist without security if the creditor deems adequate the integrity, reputation, and net worth of the debtor. Often, however, businesses or individuals cannot obtain credit without giving adequate security, or, in some cases, even if the borrower can obtain an unsecured loan, he can negotiate more favorable terms by giving security.

Transactions involving security in personal property are governed by Article 9 of the Uniform Commercial Code (UCC). This chapter will cover revised Article 9, which is in effect in all the States. This article provides a simple and unified structure within which a tremendous variety of secured financing transactions can take place with less cost and with greater certainty than was possible before the article's enactment. Moreover, the article's flexibility and simplified formalities allow new forms of secured financing to fit comfortably under its provisions. In addition, the revised article recognizes and provides coverage for electronic commerce.

ESSENTIALS OF SECURED TRANSACTIONS

Article 9 governs a secured transaction in personal property in which the debtor *consents* to provide a security interest in personal property to secure the payment of a debt. A security interest in property cannot exist apart from the debt it secures, and discharging the debt in any manner terminates the security interest in the property. Article 9 also applies to the *sales* of certain types of collateral (accounts, chattel paper, payment intangibles, and promissory notes). Article 9 does *not* apply to nonconsensual security interests that arise by operation of law, such as mechanics' or landlords' liens, although it does cover nonpossessory statutory agricultural liens.

A common type of consensual secured transaction covered by Article 9 occurs when a person wanting to buy goods has neither the cash nor a sufficient credit standing to obtain the goods on open credit, and the seller, to secure payment of all or part of the price, obtains a security interest in the goods. Alternatively, the buyer may borrow the purchase price from a third party and pay the seller in cash. The third-party lender may then take a security interest in the goods to secure repayment of the loan.

Every consensual secured transaction involves a debtor, a secured party, collateral, a security agreement, and a security interest. Some Article 9 definitions follow:

A **security interest** is "an interest in personal property or fixtures which secures payment or performance of an obligation." Section 1–201.

A **security agreement** is an agreement that creates or provides for a security interest. Section 9–102(a)(73).

Collateral is the property subject to a security interest or agricultural lien. Section 9–102(a)(12).

A **secured party** is the person in whose favor a security interest in the collateral is created or provided for under a security agreement. Section 9–102(a)(72). The definition of a secured party includes lenders, credit sellers, consignors, purchasers of certain types of collateral (accounts, chattel paper, payment intangibles, or promissory notes), and other specified persons.

A **debtor** is a person (1) having an interest in the collateral other than a security interest or lien, whether or not the person is an obligor; (2) a seller of accounts, chattel paper, payment intangibles, or promissory notes; or (3) a consignee. Section 9–102(a)(28).

An **obligor** is a person who, with respect to an obligation secured by a security interest in or an agricultural lien on the collateral, (1) owes payment or other performance, (2) has provided property other than the collateral to secure payment or performance, or (3) is otherwise accountable for payment or performance. Section 9–102(a)(59).

A **secondary obligor** is usually a guarantor or surety of the debt. Section 9–102(a)(71).

A **purchase money security interest** (PMSI) is created in goods when a seller retains a security interest in the goods sold on credit by a security agreement. Similarly, a third-party lender who advances funds to enable the debtor to purchase goods has a PMSI in goods if she has a security agreement and the debtor in fact uses the funds to purchase the goods.

In most secured transactions, the debtor is an obligor with respect to the obligation secured by the security interest. Thus, a security interest is created when an automobile dealer sells and delivers a car to an individual (the *debtor*) under a retail installment contract (a *security agreement*) that provides that the dealer (the *secured party*) obtains a *security interest* (a *PMSI*) in the car (the *collateral*) until the price is paid.

◆ **SEE FIGURE 38-1: Fundamental Rights of Secured Party and Debtor**

CLASSIFICATION OF COLLATERAL

Although most of the provisions of Article 9 apply to all kinds of personal property, some provisions state special rules that apply only to particular kinds of collateral. Under the Code, collateral is classified according to its nature and its use. The classifications according to nature are (1) goods, (2) indispensable paper, and (3) intangibles.

GOODS

Goods are all things that are movable when a security interest attaches and include fixtures, standing timber to be cut, the unborn young of animals, crops grown, growing, or to be grown, and manufactured homes. Section 9–102(a)(44). The Revised Act also includes computer programs embedded in goods if the software becomes part of the goods. (When software maintains its separate state it is considered a general intangible.) Goods are further classified according to their use.

Goods are subdivided into (1) consumer goods, (2) farm products, (3) inventory, (4) equipment, (5) fixtures, and (6) accessions. Depending on its primary use or purpose, the

◆ **FIGURE 38-1: Fundamental Rights of Secured Party and Debtor**

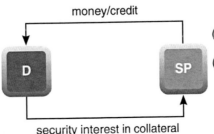
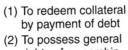

money/credit

(1) To redeem collateral by payment of debt
(2) To possess general rights of ownership as limited by security agreement

D

SP

(1) To recover amount of debt
(2) To have collateral applied to payment of the debt on default

security interest in collateral

same item of goods may fall into different classifications. For example, a refrigerator purchased by a physician to store medicines in his office is classified as equipment, while the same refrigerator would be classified as consumer goods if the physician purchased it for home use. In the hands of a refrigerator dealer or manufacturer, the refrigerator would be classified as inventory. If goods are used for multiple purposes, such as by a physician in both her office and her home, their classification is dependent upon their predominant use.

CONSUMER GOODS Goods used or bought primarily for personal, family, or household purposes are consumer goods. Section 9–102(a)(23).

FARM PRODUCTS The Code defines farm products as goods, other than standing timber, which are part of a farming operation and which are crops grown, growing, or to be grown, including crops produced on trees, vines, and bushes, and aquatic goods. In addition, farm products include livestock, born or unborn, including aquatic goods such as fish raised on a fish farm as well as supplies used or produced in a farming operation. Section 9–102(a)(34). Thus, farm products would include wheat growing on the farmer's land; the farmer's pigs, cows, and hens; and the hens' eggs. When such products become the possessions of a person not engaged in farming operations, they cease to be farm products.

INVENTORY The term inventory includes nonfarm product goods (1) held for sale, held for lease, or to be furnished under a service contract; or (2) that consist of raw materials, work in process, or materials used or consumed in a business. Section 9–102(a)(33). Thus, a retailer's or a wholesaler's merchandise, as well as a manufacturer's raw materials, are inventory.

EQUIPMENT Goods not included in the definition of inventory, farm products, or consumer goods are classified as equipment. Section 9–102(a)(33). This category is broad enough to include a lawyer's library, a physician's office furniture, or a factory's machinery.

FIXTURES Goods and personal property that have become so related to particular *real property* that an interest in them arises under real estate law are called fixtures. Section 9–102 (a)(41). Thus, State law other than the Code determines whether and when goods become fixtures. In general terms, fixtures are goods so firmly affixed to real estate that they are considered part of such real estate. Examples are furnaces, central air-conditioning units, and plumbing fixtures. See *Chapter 48* for a further discussion of fixtures. A security interest in fixtures may arise under Article 9, and, under certain circumstances, a perfected security interest in fixtures

will have priority over a conflicting security interest or mortgage in the real property to which the goods are attached.

ACCESSION Goods installed in or firmly affixed to *personal property* are accessions if the identity of the original goods is not lost. Section 9–102(a)(1). Thus, a new engine placed in an old car automobile is an accession.

INDISPENSABLE PAPER

Four kinds of collateral involve rights evidenced by indispensable paper: (1) chattel paper, (2) instruments, (3) documents, and (4) investment property.

CHATTEL PAPER Chattel paper is a record or records that evidence both a monetary obligation and a security interest in or a lease of specific goods. Section 9–102(a)(11). A record is information inscribed on a tangible medium (written on paper) or stored in an electronic or other medium and retrievable in perceivable form (electronically stored). Section 9–102(a)(69). Thus, chattel paper can be either tangible chattel paper or electronic chattel paper.

For example, Dealer sells goods on credit to Buyer who uses the goods as equipment. Dealer retains a PMSI in the goods. Dealer then borrows against (or sells) the security agreement of Buyer along with Dealer's security interest in the collateral. The collateral provided by Dealer to his lender in this type of transaction (consisting of the security agreement and the security interest) is chattel paper.

INSTRUMENTS The definition of an instrument includes negotiable instruments (drafts, checks, promissory notes, and certificate of deposits) as well as any other writing that evidences a right to payment of money that is transferable by delivery with any necessary indorsement or assignment and that is not of itself a security agreement or lease. Section 9–102(a)(47). Negotiable instruments are covered in *Chapters 26* through *30*. An instrument does not include an investment property, a letter of credit, or writings evidencing a right to payment from a credit or charge card.

DOCUMENTS The term document includes documents of title, such as bills of lading and warehouse receipts, which may be either negotiable or nonnegotiable. Section 9–102(a)(30). A document of title is negotiable if by its terms the goods it covers are deliverable to the bearer or to the order of a named person. Any other document is nonnegotiable. Documents of title are covered in *Chapter 48*.

INVESTMENT PROPERTY The term investment property means an investment security, such as stocks and bonds, as well as securities accounts, commodity contracts, and commodity accounts. Section 9–102(a)(49). A **certificated security** is an investment security that is represented by a certificate.

Section 8–102(a)(4). An **uncertificated security** is not represented by a certificate. Section 8–102(a)(18). **A security entitlement** means the rights and property interests of a person who holds securities or other financial assets through a securities intermediary such as a bank, broker, or clearing house, which in the ordinary course of business maintains security accounts for others. A security entitlement thus includes both the rights against the securities intermediary and an interest in the property held by the securities intermediary. Section 8–102(7), (14), (17).

INTANGIBLES

The Code also recognizes two kinds of collateral that are neither goods nor indispensable paper, namely, accounts and general intangibles. These types of intangible collateral are not evidenced by any indispensable paper, such as a stock certificate or a negotiable bill of lading.

ACCOUNTS The term account includes the right to monetary payment, whether or not such right has been earned by performance, for (1) goods sold, leased, licensed, or otherwise disposed of, or (2) services rendered. Section 9–102(a)(2). Accounts include credit card receivables and health-care-insurance receivables. Section 9–102(a)(2). An example of an account is a business's accounts receivable.

GENERAL INTANGIBLES The term general intangibles applies to any personal property *other than* goods, accounts, chattel paper, commercial tort claims, deposit accounts, documents, instruments, investment property, letter-of-credit rights, money, and oil, gas, and other minerals before extraction. Section 9–102(a)(42). Included in the definition are software, goodwill, literary rights, and interests in patents, trademarks, and copyrights to the extent they are not regulated by Federal statute. Also included is a payment intangible, which is a general intangible under which the account debtor's principal obligation is the payment of money. Section 9–102(a)(61).

OTHER KINDS OF COLLATERAL

Proceeds include whatever is received upon the sale, lease, license, exchange, or other disposition of collateral; whatever is collected on, or distributed on account of, collateral; or other rights arising out of collateral. Section 9–102(a)(64). For example, an automobile dealer grants a security interest in its inventory to the automobile manufacturer that sold the inventory. When the dealer sells a car to Henry and receives from Henry a used car and the remainder of the purchase price in a monetary payment, the used car and the money are both proceeds from the sale of the new car. Unless otherwise agreed, a security agreement gives the secured party

(the manufacturer in this example) the rights to proceeds. Section 9–203(f).

Additional types of collateral include timber to be cut, minerals, motor vehicles, mobile goods (goods used in more than one jurisdiction), and money. Revised Article 9 also adds the following kinds of collateral: commercial tort claim, letter-of-credit rights, and deposit accounts (a demand, savings, time, or similar account maintained with a bank). In consumer transactions, however, deposit accounts may not be taken as *original* collateral. Section 9–109(d)(13).

ATTACHMENT

Attachment is the Code's term to describe the creation of a security interest that is enforceable against the *debtor*. Attachment is also a prerequisite to rendering a security interest enforceable against third parties, though in some instances attachment in itself is sufficient to create such enforceability. Perfection, which provides the greatest enforceability against third parties who assert competing interests in the collateral, is discussed later.

Until a security interest "attaches," it is *ineffective* against the debtor. Under Section 9–203 of the Code, the security interest created by a security agreement attaches to the described collateral once the following events have occurred:

1. the secured party has given value;
2. the debtor has acquired rights in the collateral or has the power to transfer such rights to a secured party; and
3. the debtor and secured party have an agreement, which in most instances must be authenticated by the debtor, although in some cases alternative evidence, such as possession by the secured party pursuant to agreement, will suffice.

The parties may, however, by explicit agreement postpone the time of attachment. Section 9–203(a).

VALUE

The term **value** is broadly defined and includes consideration under contract law, a binding commitment to extend credit, and an antecedent debt. Section 1–201(44) and Revised Section 1–204. For example, Buyer purchases equipment from Seller on credit. When Buyer fails to make timely payment, Seller and Buyer enter into a security agreement that grants Seller a security interest in the equipment. By entering into the agreement, Seller has given value, even though he relies upon an antecedent debt—the original transfer of goods to Buyer—instead of providing new consideration. Moreover, Seller is not limited to acquiring a security interest in the equipment he sold to Buyer but also may obtain a security interest in other personal property of Buyer.

DEBTOR'S RIGHTS IN COLLATERAL

The elusive concept of the debtor's rights in collateral is not specifically defined by the Code. As a general rule, the debtor is deemed to have **rights in collateral** that she owns or is in possession of as well as in those items that she is in the process of acquiring from the seller. Section 9–203(b)(2). For example, if Adrien borrows money from Richard and grants him a security interest in corporate stock that she owns, then Adrien had rights in the collateral before entering into the secured transaction. Likewise, if Sally sells goods to Benjamin on credit and he provides Sally a security interest in the goods, Benjamin will acquire rights in the collateral upon identification of the goods to the contract. In addition, Section 9–203(b)(2) adds the words "or the power to transfer rights in the collateral to a secured party." The comments to this section state "[h]owever, in accordance with basic personal property conveyancing principles, the baseline rule is that a security interest attaches only to whatever rights a debtor may have, broad or limited as those rights may be." Comment 6.

SECURITY AGREEMENT A security interest cannot attach unless an agreement (contract) between the debtor and creditor creates or provides the creditor with a security interest in the debtor's collateral. Sections 9–203, 9–102(a)(73). With certain exceptions (discussed below), the agreement must (1) be authenticated by the debtor and (2) contain a reasonable description of the collateral. Section 9–203(b)(3)(A). In addition, if the collateral is timber to be cut, the agreement must contain a reasonable description of the land concerned. A description of personal or real property is sufficient if it reasonably identifies what is described. Section 9–108(a). A description of personal property may identify the collateral by specific listing, category, or in most cases a type of collateral defined in the Code (e.g., inventory or farm equipment). Section 9–108(b). The description, however, may not be a super generic description, such as "all my personal property." Section 9–108(c).

The Code provides the parties with a great deal of freedom to draft the security agreement, although this freedom is limited by good faith, diligence, reasonableness, and care. Section 1–102(3) and Revised Section 1–302(b). Moreover, security agreements frequently contain a provision for acceleration at the secured party's option of all payments upon the default in any payment by the debtor, the debtor's bankruptcy or insolvency, or the debtor's failure to meet other requirements of the agreement. Sometimes security agreements require the debtor to furnish additional collateral if the secured party becomes insecure about the prospects of future payments.

AUTHENTICATING RECORD In most instances there must be a record of the security agreement authenticated by the debtor. Section 9–203(b)(3)(A). Authentication can occur in one of two ways. First, the debtor can sign a written security agreement. Section 9–102(a)(7)(A). A writing can include any printing, typewriting, or other intentional reduction to tangible form. Section 1–201. To sign includes any symbol executed or adopted by a party with the present intention to authenticate a writing. Section 1–201(39). Revised Article 1 substitutes "adopt or accept" for "authenticate." Revised Section 1-201(b)(37).

Second, in recognition of e-commerce and electronic security agreements, Revised Article 9 provides that a debtor can authenticate a security agreement by executing or otherwise adopting a symbol, or by encrypting or similarly processing a record in whole or in part, with the present intent of the authenticating party to adopt or accept the record. Section 9–102(a)(7)(B). As already mentioned, a record means information (1) on a tangible medium or (2) that is stored in an *electronic* or other medium and is retrievable in perceivable form. According to the Code "[e]xamples of current technologies commercially used to communicate or store information include, but are not limited to, magnetic media, optical discs, digital voice messaging systems, electronic mail, audio tapes, and photographic media, as well as paper. 'Record' is an inclusive term that includes all of these methods." Section 9–102, Comment 9. It does not, however, include any oral or other communication that is not stored or preserved.

AUTHENTICATING RECORD NOT REQUIRED Under the Code, a record of a security agreement is not mandated in some situations. A record of a security agreement is not required when some types of collateral are pledged or are in the possession of the secured party pursuant to an agreement. Sections 9–203(b)(3)(B), 9–310(b)(6), 9–313. This rule applies to a security interest in negotiable documents, goods, instruments, money, and tangible chattel paper. A **pledge** is the delivery of personal property to a creditor as security for the payment of a debt. A pledge requires that the secured party (the pledgee) and the debtor agree to the pledge of the collateral and that the collateral be *delivered* to the pledgee. Other situations in which a secured party does not need a record authenticated by the debtor include the following: (1) The collateral is a certificated security in registered form which has been delivered to the secured party. Section 9–203(b)(3)(C). (2) The collateral is a deposit account, electronic chattel paper, investment property, or letter-of-credit rights, and the secured party has control over the collateral. Section 9–203(b)(3)(D). Control is discussed below.

CONSUMER GOODS Federal regulation prohibits a credit seller or lender from obtaining a consumer's grant of a nonpossessory security interest in household goods. This rule does not apply to PMSIs or to pledges. Rather, it prevents a lender or seller from obtaining a nonpurchase money security interest covering the consumer's household goods, which are defined to include clothing, furniture, appliances, kitchenware, personal effects, wedding rings, one radio, and one television. (These hard-to-sell items are also referred to as "junk" collateral.) The definition of household goods specifically excludes works of art, other electronic entertainment equipment, antiques, and jewelry.

AFTER-ACQUIRED PROPERTY "[A] security agreement may create or provide for a security interest in after-acquired collateral." Section 9–204(a). After-acquired property is property that the debtor presently does not own or have rights to but may acquire at some time. For example, an after-acquired property clause in a security agreement may include all present and subsequently acquired inventory, accounts, or equipment of the debtor. This clause would provide the secured party with a valid security interest not only in the typewriter, desk, and file cabinet that the debtor currently owns, but also in a personal computer she purchases later. Article 9 therefore accepts the concept of a "continuing general lien," or a *floating lien*, though the Code limits the operation of an after-acquired property clause against consumers by providing that no such interest can be claimed as additional security in consumer goods, except accessions, if the goods are acquired more than ten days after the secured party gives value. Section 9–204(b)(1).

FUTURE ADVANCES The obligations covered by a security agreement may include future advances. Section 9–204(c). Frequently, a debtor obtains a line of credit from a creditor for advances to be made at some later time. For instance, a manufacturer may provide a retailer with a $60,000 line of credit, only $20,000 of which the retailer initially uses. Nevertheless, the manufacturer and the retailer may enter a security agreement granting to the manufacturer a security interest in the retailer's inventory that covers not only the initial $20,000 advance but also any future advances.

PERFECTION

To be effective against third parties who assert competing interests in the collateral (including other creditors of the debtor, the debtor's trustee in bankruptcy, and transferees of the debtor), the security interest must be perfected. **Perfection** of a security interest occurs when it has attached *and* when all the applicable steps required for perfection have been satisfied. Section 9–308(a). If these steps precede attachment, the security interest is perfected at the time it attaches. Once a security interest becomes perfected, it "may still be or become subordinate to other interests… [h]owever, in general, after perfection the secured party is

protected against creditors and transferees of the debtor and, in particular, against any representative of creditors in insolvency proceedings instituted by or against the debtor." Section 9–308, Comment 2. Thus, in most instances a perfected secured party will prevail over a subsequent perfected security interest, a subsequent lien creditor or a representative of creditors (e.g., a trustee in bankruptcy), and subsequent buyers of the collateral.

Depending on the type of collateral, a security interest may be perfected:

1. by the secured party filing a financing statement in the designated public office;
2. by the secured party taking or retaining possession of the collateral;
3. automatically, on the attachment of the security interest;
4. temporarily, for a period specified by the Code; or
5. by the secured party taking control of the collateral.

A security interest or agricultural lien is perfected continuously if it is originally perfected by one method and is later perfected by another if there is no period when it was unperfected. Section 9–308(c).

Many States have adopted certificate of title statutes for automobiles, trailers, mobile homes, boats, and farm tractors. A **certificate of title** is an official representation of ownership. In these States, Article 9's filing requirements do not apply to perfecting a security interest in such collateral except when the collateral is inventory held by a dealer for sale. Section 9–311(a),(d).

◆ **SEE FIGURE 38-2: Requisites for Enforceability of Security Interests**

FILING A FINANCING STATEMENT

Filing a financing statement is the most common method of perfecting a security interest under Article 9. Filing is *required* to perfect a security interest in general intangibles and accounts except for assignments of isolated accounts. Filing *may* be used to perfect a security interest in any other kind of collateral, with the general *exception* of deposit accounts, letter-of-credit rights, and money. Section 9–312(b). A financing statement may be filed before or after the security interest attaches. The form of the **financing statement**, which is filed to give public notice of the security interest, may vary from State to State.

WHAT TO FILE The Revised Act continues to adopt a system of "notice filing": it indicates merely that a person may have a security interest in the collateral. It also authorizes and encourages filing financing statements electronically. Though it need not be highly detailed, the financing statement must include the name of the debtor, the name of the secured party or a representative of the secured party, and an

◆ FIGURE 38-2: Requisites for Enforceability of Security Interests

Attachment	Perfection
A. Value given by secured party	**A.** Secured party files a financing statement
B. Debtor has rights in collateral	**B.** Secured party takes possession
C. Agreement	**C.** Automatically
1. record authenticated by debtor (except for most pledges)	**D.** Temporarily, or
2. providing a security interest	**E.** Control
3. in described collateral	

indication of the collateral covered by the financing statement. Section 9–502(a). If the financing statement substantially complies with these requirements, minor errors that do not seriously mislead will not render the financing statement ineffective. Section 9–506(a). Significantly, the Revised Act no longer requires the debtor's signature on the financing statement in order to facilitate **paperless or electronic filing.** Section 9–502, Comment 3. Since a signature is not required, the Revised Act attempts to deter unauthorized filings by imposing statutory damages of $500 in addition to damages for any loss caused. Section 9–625(b),(e)(3).

Financing statements are indexed under the debtor's name so it is particularly important that the financing statement provide the debtor's name. Section 9–503 provides rules for what names must appear for registered organizations (such as corporations, limited partnerships, and limited liability companies), trusts, and other organizations. If the organization does not have a name, the names of the partners, members, associates, or other persons comprising the debtor must appear on the financing statement. Section 9–503(a)(4). A financing statement that includes only the trade name is insufficient. Section 9–503(c). A financing statement that does not comply with these requirements is considered to be seriously misleading. Section 9–506(b).

The description of the collateral is sufficient if it meets the requirements for a security agreement discussed above or if it indicates that the financing statement covers all assets or all personal property. Section 9–504(1),(2). Thus, the use of super generic descriptions is permitted in financing statements but is *not* permitted in security agreements. In **real-property-related filings** (collateral involving fixtures, timber to be cut, or minerals to be extracted), a description of the real property must be included sufficient to reasonably identify the real property. Section 9–502(b).

Section 9–516(b) further provides a list of grounds upon which the filing officer rejects a record of the financing statement. These reasons include the following: (1) if the statement does not indicate whether the debtor is an individual

or an organization, (2) the statement does not include the addresses of the debtor and secured party, (3) the record is not communicated by a method or medium authorized, and (4) the record does not provide a sufficient description of the real property. None of these reasons, however, render an accepted financing statement ineffective, unlike those listed in Section 9–502(a) above. If the filing officer rejects the financing statement, the secured interest is not perfected; if the filing officer accepts the statement, the security interest is perfected.

◆ SEE FIGURE 38-3: Sample Financing Statement

DURATION OF FILING A financing statement is generally effective for five years from the date of filing. Section 9–515(a). A continuation statement filed by the secured party within six months prior to expiration will extend the effectiveness of the filing for another five years. Section 9–515(d),(e). If the financing statement lapses, the security interest is no longer perfected unless it is perfected by another method. Section 9–515(c).

In many States, security interests in motor vehicles and other specified collateral must be perfected by making a notation on the certificate of title rather than by filing a financing statement. Nevertheless, as previously indicated, certificate of title laws do not apply if the collateral is held as inventory for sale by a dealer.

PLACE OF FILING Revised Article 9 greatly simplifies the place or places of filing: except for real-estate-related collateral financing, statements must be filed in a central location designated by the State. Section 9–501(a)(2). With respect to real-estate-related collateral, the financing statement is to be filed in the office designated for the filing or recording of mortgages on the related real property, which is usually local. Section 9–501(a)(1). If the debtor is an individual, the financing statement is to be filed in the State of the individual's principal residence; for a registered organization, the place of filing is the State where the debtor is organized.

◆ **FIGURE 38-3: Sample Financing Statement**

UCC FINANCING STATEMENT
FOLLOW INSTRUCTIONS (front and back) CAREFULLY

A. NAME & PHONE OF CONTACT AT FILER [optional]

B. SEND ACKNOWLEDGMENT TO: (Name and Address)

THE ABOVE SPACE IS FOR FILING OFFICE USE ONLY

1. DEBTOR'S EXACT FULL LEGAL NAME - insert only one debtor name (1a or 1b) - do not abbreviate or combine names

1a. ORGANIZATION'S NAME			

OR

1b. INDIVIDUAL'S LAST NAME	FIRST NAME	MIDDLE NAME	SUFFIX

1c. MAILING ADDRESS	CITY	STATE	POSTAL CODE	COUNTRY

1d. TAX ID #: SSN OR EIN	ADD'L INFO RE ORGANIZATION DEBTOR	1e. TYPE OF ORGANIZATION	1f. JURISDICTION OF ORGANIZATION	1g. ORGANIZATIONAL ID #, if any ☐ NONE

2. ADDITIONAL DEBTOR'S EXACT FULL LEGAL NAME - insert only one debtor name (2a or 2b) - do not abbreviate or combine names

2a. ORGANIZATION'S NAME			

OR

2b. INDIVIDUAL'S LAST NAME	FIRST NAME	MIDDLE NAME	SUFFIX

2c. MAILING ADDRESS	CITY	STATE	POSTAL CODE	COUNTRY

2d. TAX ID #: SSN OR EIN	ADD'L INFO RE ORGANIZATION DEBTOR	2e. TYPE OF ORGANIZATION	2f. JURISDICTION OF ORGANIZATION	2g. ORGANIZATIONAL ID #, if any ☐ NONE

3. SECURED PARTY'S NAME (or NAME of TOTAL ASSIGNEE of ASSIGNOR S/P) - insert only one secured party name (3a or 3b)

3a. ORGANIZATION'S NAME			

OR

3b. INDIVIDUAL'S LAST NAME	FIRST NAME	MIDDLE NAME	SUFFIX

3c. MAILING ADDRESS	CITY	STATE	POSTAL CODE	COUNTRY

4. This FINANCING STATEMENT covers the following collateral:

5. ALTERNATIVE DESIGNATION [if applicable]: ☐ LESSEE/LESSOR ☐ CONSIGNEE/CONSIGNOR ☐ BAILEE/BAILOR ☐ SELLER/BUYER ☐ AG. LIEN ☐ NON-UCC FILING

6. ☐ This FINANCING STATEMENT is to be filed [for record] (or recorded) in the REAL ESTATE RECORDS.   Attach Addendum   [if applicable] 7. Check to REQUEST SEARCH REPORT(S) on Debtor(s) [ADDITIONAL FEE]   [optional] ☐ All Debtors ☐ Debtor 1 ☐ Debtor 2

8. OPTIONAL FILER REFERENCE DATA

FILING OFFICE COPY — NATIONAL UCC FINANCING STATEMENT (FORM UCC1) (REV. 07/29/98)

SUBSEQUENT CHANGE OF DEBTOR'S LOCATION After a secured party has properly filed a financing statement, the debtor may change the place of his residence or business or the location or use of the collateral and thus render the information in the filing incorrect. A change in the use of the collateral or a move within the State (intrastate) does not impair the effectiveness of the original filing. If the debtor moves to another State after the initial filing, the security interest remains perfected until the earliest of (1) the time the security interest would have terminated in the State in which perfection occurred; (2) four months after the debtor moved to the new State; or (3) the expiration of one year after the debtor transfers the collateral to a person, who becomes the debtor, in another State. Section 9–316(a).

POSSESSION

Possession by the secured party perfects a security interest in goods (e.g., those in the possession of pawnbrokers), instruments, money, negotiable documents, or tangible chattel paper. Section 9–313(a). Moreover, a secured party may perfect a security interest in a certificated security by taking delivery of it. Sections 8–301 and 9–313(a). Possession is *not* available, however, as a means of perfecting a security interest in accounts, general intangibles, commercial tort claims, deposit accounts, other types of investment property, letter-of-credit rights, or oil, gas, and other minerals before extraction. Section 9–313, Comment 2.

A **pledge**, which is a possessory security interest, is the delivery of personal property to a creditor, or to a third party acting as an agent or bailee for the creditor, as security for the payment of a debt. No pledge occurs where the debtor retains possession of the collateral. In making a pledge, the debtor is not legally required to sign a written security agreement; an oral agreement granting the secured party a security interest is sufficient. In any situation not involving a pledge, however, the Code requires an authenticated record of the security agreement. Section 9–203(b)(3)(B).

One type of pledge is the **field warehouse**. This common arrangement for financing inventory allows the debtor access to the pledged goods and provides the secured party with control over the pledged property at the same time. In this arrangement, a professional warehouseman generally establishes a warehouse on the debtor's premises—usually by enclosing a portion of those premises and posting appropriate signs—to store the debtor's unsold inventory. The warehouseman then typically issues nonnegotiable receipts for the goods to the secured party, who may then authorize the warehouseman to release a portion of the goods to the debtor as the goods are sold, at a specified quantity per week, or at any rate on which the parties agree. Thus, the secured party legally possesses the goods while allowing the debtor easy access to her inventory.

AUTOMATIC PERFECTION

In some situations, a security interest is automatically perfected on attachment. The most important situation to which automatic perfection applies is a PMSI in consumer goods. A partial or isolated assignment of accounts that transfers a less-than-significant portion of the assignor's outstanding accounts is also automatically perfected. Sections 9–309(2), 9–310(b)(2).

A PMSI in consumer goods, with the exception of motor vehicles, is perfected automatically upon attachment; filing a financing statement is unnecessary. Sections 9–309(1), 9–310(b)(2). For example, Doris purchases a refrigerator from Carol on credit for Doris's personal, family, or household use. Doris takes possession of the refrigerator and then grants Carol a security interest in the refrigerator pursuant to a written security agreement. Upon Doris's granting Carol the security interest, Carol's security interest attaches and is automatically perfected. The same would be true if Doris purchased the refrigerator for cash but borrowed the money from Logan, to whom Doris granted a security interest in the refrigerator pursuant to a written security agreement. Logan's security interest would attach and would be automatically perfected when she received the security agreement from Doris. Nevertheless, because an automatically perfected PMSI in consumer goods protects the secured party less fully than a filed PMSI, secured parties frequently file a financing statement, rather than rely solely on automatic perfection.

TEMPORARY PERFECTION

Security interests in certain types of collateral are automatically, but only temporarily, perfected. Section 9–312(e) provides that a security interest in a certificated security, negotiable document, or instrument is perfected upon attachment for a period of twenty days. This provision, however, is applicable only to the extent that the security interest arises for new value given under an authenticated security agreement. Section 9–312(e). A perfected security interest in a certificated security or an instrument also remains perfected for twenty days if the secured party delivers the security certificate or instrument to the debtor for the purpose of (1) sale or exchange or (2) presentation, collection, enforcement, renewal, or registration of transfer. Section 9–312(g). After the temporary period expires, the security interest becomes unperfected unless it is perfected by other means. Section 9–312(h).

PERFECTION BY CONTROL

A security interest in investment property, deposit accounts (not including consumer deposit accounts), electronic chattel paper, and letter-of-credit rights may be perfected by control of the collateral. Section 9–314. A security interest in deposit accounts and letter-of-credit rights may be perfected *only* by control. What constitutes control varies with the type of collateral involved. For example, control of a commercial deposit account (e.g., a checking account) is acquired if (1) the secured party is the bank with which the checking account is maintained or (2) the debtor, secured party, and bank agree in an authenticated record that the bank will comply with the secured party's instructions. Section 9–104. The rules for control for other collateral are somewhat different as provided in the following sections: investment property (Section 9–106), electronic chattel paper (Section 9–105), and letter-of-credit rights (Section 9–107).

◆ **SEE FIGURE 38-4: Methods of Perfecting Security Interests**

PRIORITIES AMONG COMPETING INTERESTS

Revised Article 9 makes only minor changes to old Article 9 concerning the priorities of competing interests. As previously noted, a security interest must be perfected to be most effective against the debtor's other creditors, her trustee in bankruptcy, and her transferees. Nonetheless, perfection of a security interest does *not* provide the secured party with a **priority** over *all* third parties with an interest in the collateral. On the other hand, even an unperfected but attached security interest has priority over a limited number of third parties and is enforceable against the debtor. Article 9 establishes a complex set of rules that determine the relative priorities among these parties.

AGAINST UNSECURED CREDITORS

Once a security interest *attaches*, it has priority over claims of other creditors who do not have a security interest or a lien. This priority does not depend upon perfection. If a security interest does not attach, the creditor is merely an unsecured or general creditor of the debtor.

AGAINST OTHER SECURED CREDITORS

The rights of a secured creditor against other secured creditors depend upon the security interests perfected, when they are perfected, and the type of collateral. Notwithstanding the rules of priority, a secured party entitled to priority may subordinate her interest to that of another secured creditor. The parties may do this by agreement, and nothing need be filed.

◆ **FIGURE 38-4: Methods of Perfecting Security Interests**

| Collateral | Applicable Method of Perfection | | | | |
	Filing	Possession	Automatic	Temporary (for twenty days)	Control
Goods					
Consumer goods	•	•	PMSI		
Farm products	•	•			
Inventory	•	•			
Equipment	•	•			
Fixtures	•	•			
Indispensable Paper					
Chattel paper	•	Tangible			Electronic
Instruments	•	•		•	
Documents	Negotiable	Negotiable		Negotiable	
Investment property	•	Certificated		Certificated	•
Intangibles					
Accounts	•		Isolated assignment		
General intangibles	•				
Deposit Accounts					Commercial
Letter of Credit Accounts					•
Money		•			

Note: PMSI = purchase money security interest.

PERFECTED VERSUS UNPERFECTED A creditor with a perfected security interest or agricultural lien has superior rights in the collateral over a creditor with an unperfected security interest or agricultural lien, whether or not the unperfected security interest has attached. Section 9–322(a)(2).

PERFECTED VERSUS PERFECTED Two parties each having a perfected security interest or agricultural lien rank according to priority in *time of filing or perfection*. This general rule is stated in Section 9–322(a)(1), which provides:

> Conflicting perfected security interests and agricultural liens rank according to priority in time of filing or perfection. Priority dates from the earlier of the time a filing covering the collateral is first made or the security interest or agricultural lien is first perfected, if there is no period thereafter when there is neither filing nor perfection.

This rule favors filing, as it can occur prior to attachment and thus grant priority from a time that may precede perfection. Generally, the original time for filing or perfection of a security interest in collateral is also the time of filing or perfection for a security interest in proceeds from that collateral. Section 9–322(b)(1).

For example, Debter Store and Leynder Bank enter into a loan agreement (assume there is no binding commitment to extend credit) under the terms of which Leynder agrees to lend $5,000 on the security of Debter's existing store equipment. A security agreement is executed and a financing statement is filed, but no funds are advanced. One week later, Debter enters into a loan agreement with Reserve Bank, and Reserve agrees to lend $5,000 on the security of the same store equipment. The funds are advanced, a security agreement is executed, and a financing statement is filed. One week later, Leynder Bank advances the agreed sum of $5,000. Debter Store defaults on both loans. Between Leynder Bank and Reserve Bank, Leynder has priority, because priority among security interests perfected by filing is determined by the order in which they were filed. Reserve Bank should have checked the financing statements on file. Had it done so, it would have discovered that Leynder Bank claimed a security interest in the equipment. Conversely, after filing its financing statement, with no prior secured party of record, Leynder had no need to check the files before advancing funds to Debter Store in accordance with its loan commitment.

To further illustrate, assume that Marc grants a security interest in a Chagall painting to Miro Bank and that the bank advances funds to Marc in accordance with the loan agreement. A financing statement is filed. Later, Marc wants more money and goes to Brague, an art dealer, who advances funds to Marc upon a pledge of the painting. Marc defaults on both loans. As between Miro and Brague, Miro has priority because its financing statement was filed before Brague's perfection by possession. By checking the financing statement on file, Brague would have discovered that Miro had a prior security interest in the painting.

There are several exceptions to the general rules just discussed:

1. A **PMSI in noninventory goods** (except livestock) takes priority over a conflicting security interest if the PMSI is perfected when the debtor receives possession of the collateral *or* within twenty days of receiving possession. Section 9–324(a). Thus, the secured party has a twenty-day grace period in which to perfect.

   For example, Dawkins Manufacturing Co. enters into a loan contract with Larkin Bank, which loans money to Dawkins on the security (as provided in the security agreement) of Dawkins's existing and future equipment and files a financing statement stating that the collateral is "all equipment presently owned and subsequently acquired" by Dawkins. At a later date, Dawkins buys new equipment from Parker Supply Co., paying 25 percent of the purchase price, with Parker retaining a security interest (as provided in the security agreement) in the equipment to secure the remaining balance. If Parker files a financing statement within ten days of Dawkins's obtaining possession of the equipment, Parker's PMSI in the new equipment purchased from Parker has priority over Larkin's interest. If, however, Parker files one day beyond the statutory grace period, Parker's interest is subordinate to Larkin's.

2. A **PMSI in inventory** has priority over earlier-filed security interests in inventory if the following requirements are met. The purchase money security holder must perfect his interest in the inventory at the time the debtor receives the inventory and send an authenticated notification to the holder of a conflicting security interest. The holder of the conflicting security interest must receive the notification within five years before the debtor receives possession of the inventory, and the notification must state that the person sending the notification has or will acquire a PMSI in the debtor's inventory and must describe the inventory. Section 9–324(b).

   For example, Dodger Store and Lyons Bank enter into a loan agreement in which Lyons agrees to finance Dodger's entire inventory of stoves, refrigerators, and other kitchen appliances. A security agreement is executed and a financing statement is filed, and Lyons advances funds to Dodger. Subsequently, Dodger enters into an agreement under which Rodger Stove Co. will supply Dodger with stoves, retaining a PMSI in this inventory. Rodger will have priority as to the inventory it supplies to Dodger, provided that Rodger files a financing statement by the time Dodger receives the goods and notifies Lyons that it is going to engage in this purchase money financing of the described stoves. If Rodger fails either to give the required notice or to file timely a financing statement, Lyons will have priority over Rodger as to the stoves Rodger supplies to Dodger. As noted, the Code adopts a system of notice filing, and secured parties who fail to check the financing statements on file proceed at their peril.

3. A **security interest perfected by control** in deposit accounts, letter-of-credit rights, or investment property has priority over a conflicting perfected security interest held by a secured party who does not have control. Sections 9–327(1), 9–328(1), 9–329(1). If both conflicting security interests are perfected by control, they rank according to priority in time of obtaining control.

Unperfected versus Unperfected If neither security interest or agricultural lien is perfected, then the first to attach has priority. Section 9–322(a)(3). If neither attach, both of the creditors are general, unsecured creditors.

AGAINST BUYERS

A security interest or agricultural lien continues even in collateral that is sold, leased, licensed, exchanged, or otherwise disposed of unless the secured party authorizes the sale. Section 9–315. Thus, following a sale, lease, license, exchange, or other disposition of collateral, a secured party who did not authorize the transaction does not have to file a new financing statement to continue her perfected interest. The security interest also attaches to any identifiable proceeds from the sale, including proceeds in consumer deposit accounts. Sections 9–315(a)(2), 9–109(d)(13).

In many instances, however, buyers of collateral sold without the secured party's authorization take it free of an **unperfected** security interest. A buyer of goods, tangible chattel paper, documents, instruments, or certificated securities who gives value and receives delivery of the collateral without knowledge of the security interest *before* it is perfected takes free of the security interest. Section 9–317(b). Similarly, a buyer of accounts, electronic chattel paper, general intangibles, or investment property other than certificated securities takes free of a security interest if the buyer gives value without knowledge of the security interest and does so *before* it is perfected. Section 9–317(d). Thus, with respect to all of these types of collateral, an unperfected security interest prevails over a buyer who does *not* give value or has *knowledge* of the security interest.

In addition, in some instances, purchasers take the collateral free of a **perfected** security interest. The most significant of these instances are as follows:

Buyers in the Ordinary Course of Business A buyer in the ordinary course of business takes collateral (other than farm products) free of any security interest created by *the buyer's* seller, even if the security interest is perfected and the buyer *knows* of its existence. Section 9–320(a). A buyer in the ordinary course of business is a person who, without knowledge that the sale violates a security interest of a third party, buys in good faith and in ordinary course from a person in the business of selling goods of that kind. Section 1–201(9); Revised Section 1-201(b)(9). Thus, this rule applies primarily to purchasers of inventory. For example, a consumer who purchases a sofa from a furniture dealer and the dealer who purchases the sofa from another dealer are both buyers in the ordinary course of business. On the other hand, a person who purchases a sofa from a dentist who used the sofa in his waiting room or from an individual who used the sofa in his home is not a buyer in the ordinary course of business.

To illustrate further, a person who in the ordinary course of business buys an automobile from an automobile dealership will take free and clear of a security interest created by the dealer from whom she purchased the car. That same buyer in the ordinary course of business will not, however, take clear of a security interest created by any person who owned the automobile prior to the dealer. A leading case on this point is *National Shawmut Bank of Boston v. Jones,* 108 N.H. 386, 236 A.2d 484 (1967). In that case, Wever bought a 1964 Dodge Dart from Wentworth Motor Company for his own personal use and granted a security interest in the car to Wentworth. Wentworth later assigned the security interest to National Shawmut Bank, which properly perfected it. Without Shawmut's consent, Wever sold the car to Hanson-Rock, another automobile dealer. Hanson-Rock then sold the car to Jones. Even though Jones was a buyer in the ordinary course of business from Hanson-Rock, he took the automobile subject to Shawmut's security interest, as that interest had not been created by Jones's seller, Hanson-Rock.

Buyers of Farm Products Buyers in the ordinary course of business of **farm products**, although not protected by Section 9–320, may be protected by the Federal Food Security Act. This Act defines a buyer in the ordinary course of business as "a person who, in the ordinary course of business, buys farm products from a person engaged in farming operations who is in the business of selling farm products." The Act provides that such a buyer shall take free of most security interests created by the seller, even if the security interest is perfected and the buyer knows of its existence.

Buyers of Consumer Goods In the case of consumer goods, a buyer who buys without knowledge of a security interest, for value, and primarily for personal, family, or household purposes takes the goods free of any PMSI *automatically* perfected, but takes the goods subject to a security interest perfected by filing. Section 9–320(b). For example,

Ann purchases on credit a refrigerator from Sean for use in her home and grants Sean a security interest in the refrigerator. Sean does not file a financing statement but has a security interest perfected by attachment. Ann subsequently sells the refrigerator to her neighbor, Juwan, for use in his home. Juwan does not know of Sean's security interest and therefore takes the refrigerator free of that interest. If Sean had filed a financing statement, however, his security interest would continue in the collateral, even in Juwan's hands.

Buyers of Other Collateral To the extent provided by UCC Articles 3, 7, and 8, a secured party who has a perfected security interest in a negotiable instrument, a negotiable document of title, or a security has a *subordinate* interest to a purchaser of (1) the instrument who has the rights of a holder in due course, (2) the document of title to whom it has been duly negotiated, or (3) the security who is a protected purchaser. Section 9–331. In addition, in certain instances a secured party who has a perfected security interest in chattel paper also may have subordinate rights to a purchaser of such collateral. Section 9–330.

AGAINST LIEN CREDITORS

A **lien creditor** is a creditor who has acquired a lien in the property by judicial decree ("attachment garnishment, or the like"), an assignee for the benefit of creditors, a receiver in equity, or a **trustee in bankruptcy**. Section 9–102(a)(52). (A trustee in bankruptcy is a representative of an estate in bankruptcy who is responsible for collecting, liquidating, and distributing the debtor's assets.) Whereas a **perfected** security interest or agricultural lien has priority over lien creditors who acquire their liens after perfection, an **unperfected** security interest or agricultural lien is subordinate to the rights of one who becomes a lien creditor before (1) its perfection or (2) a financing statement covering the collateral is filed and either (a) the debtor has authenticated a properly drawn security agreement, (b) if the collateral is a certificated security, the certificate has been delivered to the secured party, or (c) if the collateral is an uncertificated security, it is in possession of the secured party. Section 9–317(a)(2). If a secured party files with respect to a *PMSI* within twenty days after the debtor receives possession of the collateral, however, the secured party takes priority over the rights of a lien creditor that arise between the time the security interest attaches and the time of filing. Section 9–317(e). Nonetheless, a lien securing claims arising from services or materials furnished in the ordinary course of a person's business with respect to goods (an artisan's or mechanic's lien) has priority over a security interest in the goods unless the lien is created by a statute that expressly provides otherwise. Section 9–333.

AGAINST TRUSTEE IN BANKRUPTCY

The Bankruptcy Act empowers a trustee in bankruptcy to invalidate secured claims in certain instances. It also imposes some limitations on the rights of secured parties. This section will examine the power of a trustee in bankruptcy to (1) take priority over an unperfected security interest and (2) avoid preferential transfers.

Priority over Unperfected Security Interest A trustee in bankruptcy may invalidate any security interest that is voidable by a creditor who obtained a judicial lien on the date the bankruptcy petition was filed. Bankruptcy Act, Section 544. Under the Code and the Bankruptcy Act, the trustee, as a hypothetical **lien creditor**, has priority over a creditor whose security interest was not perfected when the bankruptcy petition was filed. A creditor with a PMSI interest who files within the Code's statutory grace period of twenty days after the debtor receives the collateral will defeat the trustee, even if the bankruptcy petition is filed before the creditor perfects and after the security interest is created. For example, David borrowed $5,000 from Cynthia on September 1 and gave her a security interest in the equipment he purchased with the borrowed funds. On October 3, before Cynthia perfected her security interest, David filed for bankruptcy. The trustee in bankruptcy can invalidate Cynthia's security interest because it was unperfected when the bankruptcy petition was filed. If, however, David had filed for bankruptcy on September 8 and Cynthia had perfected the security interest within the Code's statutory grace period of twenty days, Cynthia would prevail.

Avoidance of Preferential Transfers Section 547 of the Bankruptcy Act provides that a trustee in bankruptcy may invalidate any transfer of property—including the granting of a security interest—from the debtor, provided that the transfer (1) was to or for the benefit of a creditor; (2) was made on account of an antecedent debt; (3) was made when the debtor was insolvent; (4) was made on the date of or within ninety days before the filing of the bankruptcy petition or, if made to an insider, was made within one year before the date of the filing; and (5) enabled the transferee to receive more than he would have received in bankruptcy. (An insider includes a relative or general partner of a debtor, as well as a partnership in which the debtor is a general partner or a corporation of which the debtor is a director, officer, or person in control.) In determining whether the debtor is insolvent, the Act establishes a rebuttable presumption of insolvency for the ninety days prior to the filing of the bankruptcy petition. To avoid a transfer to an insider that occurred more than one year before bankruptcy, the trustee must prove that the debtor was insolvent when the transfer was made. If a security interest is invalidated as a preferential transfer, the creditor may still make a claim for the unpaid debt, but the creditor's claim is unsecured.

To illustrate the operation of this rule, consider the following. On May 1, Debra bought and received merchandise from Stuart and gave him a security interest in the goods for the unpaid price of $20,000. On June 5, Stuart filed a financing statement. On August 1, Debra filed a petition for bankruptcy. The trustee in bankruptcy may avoid the perfected security interest as a preferential transfer because (1) the transfer of the perfected security interest on June 5 was to benefit a creditor (Stuart); (2) the transfer was on account of an antecedent debt (the $20,000 owed from the sale of the merchandise); (3) the debtor was insolvent at the time (the Act presumes that the debtor is insolvent for the ninety days preceding the date the bankruptcy petition was filed—August 1); (4) the transfer was made within ninety days of bankruptcy (June 5 is less than ninety days before August 1); and (5) the transfer enabled the creditor to receive more than he would have received in bankruptcy (Stuart would have a secured claim on which he would recover more than he would on an unsecured claim).

Nevertheless, not all transfers made within ninety days of bankruptcy are voidable. As amended in 2005, the Bankruptcy Code makes exceptions for certain prebankruptcy transfers. If the creditor gives the debtor new value which the debtor uses to acquire property in which he grants the creditor a security interest, the resulting PMSI is not voidable if the creditor perfects it within thirty days after the debtor receives possession of the property. For example, if within ninety days of the filing of the petition, the debtor purchases a refrigerator on credit and grants the seller or lender a PMSI in the refrigerator, the transfer of that interest is not voidable if the secured party perfects within thirty days after the debtor receives possession of the property.

◆ **SEE FIGURE 38-5: Priorities**

DEFAULT

Because the Code does not define or specify what constitutes default, general contract law or the agreement between the parties will determine when a default occurs. After default, the security agreement and the applicable provisions of the Code govern the rights and remedies of the parties. In general, the secured party may reduce his claim to judgment, foreclose, or otherwise enforce the claim, security interest, or

◆ **FIGURE 38-5: Priorities**

Versus	Unsecured creditor	Creditor with unperfected security interests	Creditor with perfected security interest	Creditor with perfected money security interest
Unsecured creditor	=	↑	↑	↑
Creditor with unperfected security interest	←	first to attach	↑	↑
Creditor with perfected security interest	←	←	first to file or perfect	↑ if PMSI perfected within grace period
Creditor with perfected PMSI	←	←	first to file or perfect	↑ if PMSI gives notice and perfects by time debtor gets possession
Buyer in ordinary course of business	←	←	← if created by immediate seller	←
Consumer buyer of consumer goods	←	←	↑	← if not filed
Lien creditor (including trustee in bankruptcy)	←	←	first in time	first in time but PMSI has grace period
Trustee in bankruptcy— voidable preferences	←	←	↑ if secured party perfects within grace period	↑ if PMSI perfects within grace period

Note: PMSI = purchase money security interest.

agricultural lien by any available judicial procedure. Section 9–601(a)(1). If the collateral consists of documents, the secured party may proceed against the documents or the goods they cover. Section 9–601(a)(2). These rights and remedies of the creditor are cumulative. Section 9–601(c).

Unless the debtor has waived his rights in the collateral after default, he has a right of **redemption** (to free the collateral of the security interest by fulfilling all obligations securing the collateral and paying reasonable expenses and attorneys' fees) at any time before the secured party has collected the collateral, has disposed of the collateral, has entered a contract to dispose of it, or has discharged the obligation by accepting the collateral. Section 9–623.

REPOSSESSION

Unless the parties have agreed otherwise, the secured party may take possession of the collateral on default. If it can be done without a breach of the peace, such taking may occur without judicial process. Section 9–609. The Code leaves the term *breach of the peace* for the courts to define. Some States have defined such a breach to require either the use of violence or the threat of violence, while others require merely an entry without consent. Most States require permission for entry to a residence or garage. On the other hand, the courts do permit the repossession of motor vehicles from driveways or streets. Some courts, however, do not permit a creditor to repossess if the debtor has orally protested the repossession.

After default, instead of removing the collateral, the secured party may render it unusable and leave it on the debtor's premises until disposing of it. It also may be done without judicial process if accomplished without a breach of peace. Section 9–609.

SALE OF COLLATERAL

The secured party may sell, lease, license, or otherwise dispose of any collateral in its existing condition at the time of default or following any commercially reasonable preparation or processing. Section 9–610(a). A secured party's disposition of the collateral after default (1) transfers to a transferee for value all of the debtor's rights in the collateral, (2) discharges the security interest under which the disposition occurred, and (3) discharges any subordinate security interests and liens. Section 9–617(a).

The collateral may be disposed of at public sale (auction) or private sale, so long as all aspects of the disposition, including its method, manner, time, place, and other terms, are "commercially reasonable." Section 9–610(b). The secured party may buy at a public sale and at a private sale if the collateral is customarily sold in a recognized market or is the subject of widely distributed standard price quotations. Section 9–610(c). The collateral, if it is commercially

reasonable, may be disposed of by one or more contracts or as a unit or in parcels. Section 9–610(b). The Code favors private sales since they generally garner a higher price for the collateral. Section 9–610, Comment 2. The fact that the secured party could have received a greater amount is not of itself sufficient to establish that the sale was not made in a commercially reasonable manner. Section 9–627(a). Unless the collateral is perishable or threatens to decline speedily in value or is of a type customarily sold on a recognized market, the secured party must send a reasonable authenticated notification of disposition to the debtor, any secondary obligor (surety or guarantor) and, except in the case of consumer goods, other parties who have sent an authenticated notice of a claim or any secured party or lien holder who has filed a financing statement at least ten days before the notification date. Section 9–611.

Section 9–615(a) provides that the proceeds from the sale of the collateral are to be applied in the following order:

1. paying the reasonable expenses of retaking and disposing of the collateral,
2. paying the debt owed to the secured party,
3. paying any subordinate interests in the collateral, and
4. paying a secured party that is a consignor.

The debtor is entitled to any *surplus* and is liable for any *deficiency*, except in the case of a sale of accounts, chattel paper, payment intangibles, or promissory notes for which he is neither entitled nor liable unless the security agreement so provides. Section 9–615(d)(e). If the goods are consumer goods, the secured party must give the debtor an explanation of how the surplus or deficiency was calculated. Section 9–616.

ACCEPTANCE OF COLLATERAL

Acceptance of collateral (strict foreclosure) is a way for a secured party to acquire the debtor's interests without the need for a sale or other disposition. The secured party may, after default and repossession if the debtor consents in a record authenticated after default, keep the collateral in full or partial satisfaction of the obligation. Section 9–620(a)(1)(c). In addition, the secured party may accept the collateral in *full* satisfaction of the obligation if she sends an unconditional proposal to the debtor to accept the collateral in full satisfaction of the obligation and she does not receive a notice of objection authenticated by the debtor within twenty days. Section 9–620(c)(2). If there is an objection, however, the secured party must dispose of the collateral as provided in the Code. Section 9–620. Silence is not consent to a *partial* satisfaction of the obligation. The debtor's consent, however, will not permit the secured party to accept the collateral in satisfaction of the obligation if a person holding a junior interest (secured party or lien holder) lodges a proper objection to the proposal. Section 9–620(a)(2), Comment 3.

In the case of *consumer goods*, if the debtor has paid 60 percent or more of the obligation, the secured party who has taken possession of the collateral must dispose of it by sale within ninety days after repossession unless the debtor and all secondary obligors have agreed in a record authenticated after default to a longer period of time. Section 9–620(e),(f). Additionally, with a consumer debt, the secured party may not accept collateral in *partial* satisfaction of the obligation it secures. Section 9–620(g).

The acceptance of collateral in full or partial satisfaction discharges the obligation to the extent consented to by the debtor, transfers all of the debtor's rights to the secured party, and terminates all subordinate interests in the collateral. Section 9–622.

SURETYSHIP

In many business transactions involving the extension of the credit, the creditor will require that someone in addition to the debtor promise to fulfill the obligation. This promisor generally is known as a surety. In a contract involving a minor, a surety commonly will act as a party with full contractual capacity who can be held responsible for the obligations arising from the contract. Sureties are often used in addition to security to further reduce the risks involved in the extension of credit and are used instead of security interests when security is unavailable or when the use of a secured transaction is too expensive or inconvenient. Employers frequently use sureties to protect against losses caused by employees' embezzlement, while property owners use sureties to bond the performance of contracts for the construction of commercial buildings. Similarly, statutes commonly require that contracts for work to be done for governmental entities have the added protection of a surety. Premiums for compensated sureties exceed $1 billion annually in the United States.

NATURE AND FORMATION

A **surety** promises to answer for the payment of a debt or the performance of a duty owed to one person (called the **creditor**) by another (the **principal debtor**) upon the *failure* of the principal debtor to make payment or otherwise perform the obligation. Thus, the suretyship relationship involves three parties—the principal debtor, the creditor, and the surety—and three contractual obligations. Two or more persons bound for the same debt of a principal debtor are **cosureties**.

The creditor's rights against the principal debtor are determined by the contract between them. The creditor also may realize upon any collateral securing the principal debtor's performance that the creditor or the surety holds. In addition, the creditor may proceed against the surety if the principal debtor defaults. If the surety is an **absolute surety**, then the creditor may hold the surety liable as soon as the principal debtor defaults. The creditor need *not* proceed first against the principal debtor. In contrast, a surety who is a **conditional guarantor of collection** is liable only upon the creditor's first exhausting his legal remedies against the principal debtor. Thus, a conditional guarantor of collection is liable if the creditor first obtains, but is unable to collect, a judgment against the principal debtor.

A surety who is required to pay the creditor for the principal debtor's obligation is entitled to be exonerated (relieved of liability) and reimbursed by the principal debtor. In addition, the surety is subrogated to (assumes) the rights of the creditor and has a right of contribution from cosureties. These rights of sureties are discussed more fully later in this chapter.

Although in theory a surety and a guarantor are distinct entities, the two terms are nearly synonymous in common usage. Strictly speaking, a surety is bound with the principal debtor as a primary obligor, usually, although not necessarily, on the same instrument, whereas the guarantor is separately or collaterally bound to pay if the principal debtor does not. For convenience, and because the rights and duties of a surety are almost indistinguishable from those of a guarantor, the term surety will be used to include both terms.

◆ **SEE FIGURE 38-6: Suretyship Relationship**

TYPES OF SURETIES

Creditors seeking to reduce the risk of default by their debtors frequently use a suretyship arrangement. For example, Philco Developers, a closely held corporation, applies to Caldwell Bank, a lending institution, for a loan. After scrutinizing the assets and financial prospects of Philco, the lender refuses to extend credit unless Simpson, the sole shareholder of Philco, promises to repay the loan if Philco does not. Simpson agrees, and Caldwell Bank makes the loan. Simpson's undertaking is that of a surety. Similarly, Philco wishes to purchase goods on credit from Bird Enterprises, the seller, who agrees to extend credit only if Philco obtains an acceptable surety. Simpson agrees to pay Bird Enterprises for the goods if Philco does not. Simpson is a surety. In each of these examples, the surety's promise gives the creditor recourse for payment against two persons—the principal debtor and the surety—instead of one, thereby reducing the creditor's risk of loss.

Another common suretyship relation arises when an owner of property subject to a mortgage sells the property to a purchaser who expressly **assumes the mortgage**. Although by assuming the obligation the purchaser becomes the principal debtor and therefore personally obligated to pay the seller's

◆ **FIGURE 38-6: Suretyship Relationship**

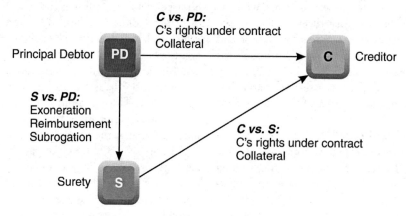

debt to the lender, the seller nevertheless remains liable to the lender and is a surety on the obligation the purchaser has assumed. If, however, the purchaser does not assume the mortgage but simply takes the property "**subject to**" the mortgage, he is neither personally liable for the mortgage nor a surety for the mortgage obligation. In this case, the purchaser's potential loss is limited to the value of the property; for although the mortgagee creditor may foreclose against the property, he may not hold the purchaser personally liable for the debt.

In addition to the more general types of sureties, there are numerous specialized kinds of suretyship, the most important of which are (1) fidelity, (2) performance, (3) official, and (4) judicial. A surety undertakes a **fidelity bond** to protect an employer against employee dishonesty. **Performance bonds** guarantee the performance of the terms and conditions of a contract. These bonds are used frequently in the construction industry to protect an owner from losses that may result from a contractor's failure to perform under a building contract. **Official bonds** arise from a common statutory requirement that public officers furnish bonds for the faithful performance

of their duties. Such bonds obligate a surety for all losses that an officer causes through negligence or through nonperformance of her duties. Judicial bonds are provided on behalf of a party to a judicial proceeding to cover losses caused by delay or by deprivation of the use of property resulting from the institution of the action. In criminal proceedings, the purpose of a judicial bond, called a bail bond, is to ensure the appearance of the defendant in court.

◆ **SEE FIGURE 38-7: Assumption of Mortgage**

FORMATION

The suretyship relationship is contractual and must satisfy all the usual elements of a contract, including offer and acceptance, consideration, capacity of the parties, and legality of object. No particular words are required to constitute a contract of suretyship or guaranty.

As discussed in *Chapter 15*, the contractual promise of a surety to the creditor must be in writing to be enforceable under the statute of frauds. This requirement, which applies only to collateral promises, is subject to the exception

◆ **FIGURE 38-7: Assumption of Mortgage**

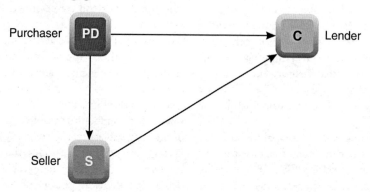

known as the *main purpose doctrine*. Under this doctrine, if the leading object (main purpose) of the promisor (surety) is to obtain an economic benefit that he did not previously enjoy, the promise is not within the statute of frauds.

The promise of a surety is *not* binding without consideration. Because the surety generally makes her promise to induce the creditor to confer a benefit upon the principal debtor, the same consideration that supports the principal debtor's promise usually supports the surety's promise as well. Thus, if Constance lends money to Philip upon Sally's promise to act as a surety, Constance's extension of credit is the consideration to support not only Philip's promise to repay the loan but also Sally's suretyship undertaking. In contrast, a surety's promise made *subsequent* to the principal debtor's receipt of the creditor's consideration must be supported by new consideration. Accordingly, if Constance has already sold goods on credit to Philip, a subsequent guaranty by Sally will not be binding unless new consideration is given.

RIGHTS OF SURETY

Upon the principal debtor's default, the surety has a number of rights against the principal debtor, third parties, and cosureties. These rights include (1) exoneration, (2) reimbursement, (3) subrogation, and (4) contribution. As discussed above, a surety or absolute guarantor has *no* right to compel the creditor to collect from the principal debtor or to realize upon collateral provided by the principal debtor. Nor is the creditor required to give the surety notice of the principal debtor's default unless the contract of suretyship provides otherwise. A conditional guarantor of collection, on the other hand, faces no liability until the creditor first exhausts his legal remedies of collection against the principal debtor.

EXONERATION

The ordinary expectation in a suretyship relation is that the principal debtor will perform the obligation and the surety will not be required to perform. Therefore, the surety has the right to require that her principal debtor pay the creditor when the obligation is due. This right of the surety against the principal debtor, called the right of **exoneration**, is enforceable at equity. If the principal debtor fails to pay the creditor when the debt is due, the surety may obtain a decree ordering the principal debtor to pay the creditor. The remedy of exoneration against the principal debtor does not, however, impair the creditor's right to proceed against the surety.

A surety also has a right of exoneration against his cosureties. When the principal debtor's obligation becomes due, each surety owes every other cosurety the duty to pay her proportionate share of the principal debtor's obligation to the creditor. Accordingly, a surety may bring an action in equity

to obtain an order requiring his cosureties to pay their share of the debt to the creditor.

REIMBURSEMENT

When a surety pays the creditor upon the default of the principal debtor, the surety has the right of **reimbursement** (repayment) against the principal debtor. The surety, however, has no right to reimbursement until he actually has made payment, and then only to the extent of the payment. Thus, a surety who advantageously negotiates a defaulted obligation down to a compromise figure less than the original sum may recover from the principal debtor only the sum he actually paid, not the sum before negotiation.

SUBROGATION

Upon payment of the principal debtor's *entire* obligation, the surety "steps into the shoes" of the creditor. This process of substitution, called **subrogation**, confers upon the surety all the rights the creditor has against or through the principal debtor. These include the creditor's rights:

1. against the principal debtor, including the creditor's priorities in a bankruptcy proceeding;
2. in security of the principal debtor;
3. against third parties, such as co-makers, who are also obligated on the principal debtor's obligation; and
4. against cosureties.

CONTRIBUTION

Up to the amount of their individual undertakings, cosureties are jointly and severally liable for the principal debtor's default. The creditor may proceed against any or all of the cosureties and collect from any of them the amount that the surety has agreed to guarantee, which may be the entire amount of the principal debtor's obligation.

A surety who pays her principal debtor's obligation may require her cosureties to pay her their proportionate shares of the obligation she has paid. This right of **contribution** arises when a surety has paid more than her proportionate share of a debt, even if the cosureties originally were unaware of each other or were bound on separate instruments. They need only be sureties for the same principal debtor and the same obligation. The right and extent of contribution is determined by contractual agreement among the cosureties. If no agreement exists, sureties obligated for equal amounts share equally; where they are obligated for varying amounts, the proportion of the debt that each surety must contribute is determined by proration according to each surety's undertaking. For example, if X, Y, and Z are cosureties for PD to C in the amounts of $5,000, $10,000, and $15,000, respectively, which totals $30,000, then X's contributive share is one-sixth ($5,000/$30,000), Y's share is one-third

($10,000/$30,000), and Z's share is one-half ($15,000/$30,000).

DEFENSES OF SURETY AND PRINCIPAL DEBTOR

The obligations the principal debtor and the surety owe to the creditor arise out of contracts. Accordingly, those in surety relationships can assert the usual contractual defenses, such as those resulting from (1) the nonexistence of the principal debtor's obligation, (2) a discharge of the principal debtor's obligation, (3) a modification of the principal debtor's contract, or (4) a variation of the surety's risk. Some of these defenses are available only to the principal debtor, some only to the surety, and others are available to both parties.

◆ **SEE FIGURE 38-8: Defenses of Surety and Principal Debtor**

PERSONAL DEFENSES OF PRINCIPAL DEBTOR

The defenses available only to a principal debtor are known as the personal defenses of the principal debtor. For exam-

ple, the principal debtor's **incapacity** due to infancy or mental incompetency may serve as a defense for the principal debtor but not for the surety. If, however, the principal debtor disaffirms the contract and returns the consideration he received from the creditor, then the surety is discharged from his liability. In contrast, a discharge of the principal debtor's obligation in **bankruptcy** does not in turn discharge the surety's liability to the creditor on that obligation. In addition, the surety may not use as a **setoff** any claim that the principal debtor has against the creditor.

PERSONAL DEFENSES OF SURETY

Those defenses that *only* the surety may assert are called personal defenses of the surety. The surety may use as a defense his own **incapacity**, noncompliance with the **statute of frauds**, and the absence of mutual assent or consideration to support his obligation. **Fraud** or **duress** practiced by the creditor upon the surety also is a defense. Although, as a general rule, nondisclosure of material facts by the creditor to the surety is not fraud, there are two important exceptions. First, if a prospective surety requests information, the creditor must disclose it; and the concealment of material

◆ **FIGURE 38-8: Defenses of Surety and Principal Debtor**

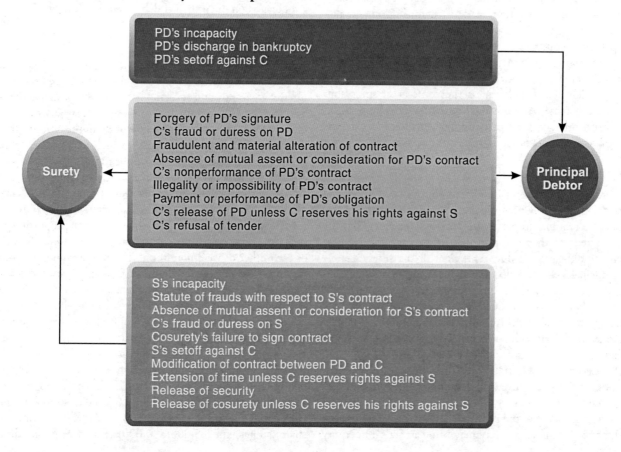

facts will constitute fraud. Second, if the creditor knows, or should know, that the surety is being deceived, the creditor is under a duty to disclose this information; and nondisclosure is considered fraud on the surety. Fraud on the part of the principal debtor may not be asserted against the creditor if the creditor is unaware of such fraud. Similarly, duress exerted by the principal debtor upon the surety is not a defense against the creditor.

A surety is not liable if an intended cosurety, as named in the contract instrument, does not sign. Furthermore, a surety may **set off** his claims against a solvent creditor. Against an insolvent creditor, however, the surety may use his claim only if the principal debtor is also insolvent.

If the principal debtor and the creditor enter into a binding **modification** of their contract, the surety may be discharged unless he assents to the modification. The courts vary in their approach to modifications made without the surety's assent. Often, the courts will discharge an uncompensated surety (an **accommodation surety**) for any material modification, even one that does not prejudice his rights. In contrast, when contemplating the discharge of a compensated surety, a number of courts require the alteration to be both material and prejudicial to the interests of the surety.

Such modifications include valid and binding extensions of the time of payment unless the creditor expressly reserves his rights against the surety. An extension of time with reservation is construed only as an agreement by the creditor not to sue the principal debtor for the period of the extension. Accordingly, the surety's rights of exoneration, reimbursement, and subrogation are not postponed. Thus, the surety's risk is not changed, and he is not discharged.

If the creditor releases or impairs the value of the security, the surety is discharged to the extent of the value of the security released or impaired. Similarly, if the creditor releases a cosurety, the other cosureties are discharged to the extent of the contributive share of the surety released. If the creditor reserves his rights against the remaining cosureties, however, the release is considered a promise not to sue. As a result, the remaining cosureties are not discharged.

DEFENSES OF BOTH SURETY AND PRINCIPAL DEBTOR

A number of defenses are available to both the surety and the principal debtor. If the principal debtor's signature on an instrument is **forged** or if the creditor has exerted **fraud** or **duress** upon the principal debtor, neither the principal debtor nor the surety is liable. Likewise, if the creditor has fraudulently and **materially altered** the contract instrument, both the principal debtor and the surety are discharged.

The absence of mutual assent or consideration to support the principal debtor's obligation is a defense for both the principal debtor and the surety. In addition, both may assert as defenses the **illegality** and **impossibility** of performance of the principal debtor's contract.

Payment or **performance** of the principal debtor's obligation discharges both the principal debtor and the surety. If the principal debtor owes several debts to the creditor and makes a payment to the creditor without specifying the debt to which the payment should apply, the creditor is free to apply it to any one of them. For example, Pam owes Charles two debts, one for $5,000 and another for $10,000. Susan is a surety on the $10,000 debt. Pam sends Charles a payment in the amount of $3,500. If Pam directs Charles to apply the payment to the $10,000 debt, Charles must apply it accordingly. Otherwise, Charles may, if he pleases, apply the payment to the $5,000 debt.

If the creditor **releases** the principal debtor, then the surety is also discharged unless the surety consents to the release. If the creditor reserves his rights against the surety, however, the surety is not discharged, as the release with reservation is construed as a promise not to sue, which leaves the surety's rights against the principal debtor unimpaired.

The creditor's refusal to accept **tender** of payment or performance by either the principal debtor or the surety completely discharges the surety. The creditor's refusal of tender of payment by the principal debtor does not, however, discharge the principal debtor. Rather, such refusal stops further accrual of interest on the debt and deprives the creditor of court costs on a subsequent suit by him to recover the amount due.

CHAPTER SUMMARY

SECURED TRANSACTIONS IN PERSONAL PROPERTY

ESSENTIALS OF SECURED TRANSACTIONS	**Definition of Secured Transaction** an agreement by which one party obtains a security interest in the personal property of another to secure the payment of a debt • *Debtor* person who has an interest in the collateral other than a security interest; typically is the person obligated on the debt secured by the security interest • *Secured Party* person in whose favor a security interest in the collateral is created or provided for under the security agreement • *Collateral* property subject to a security interest

- *Security Agreement* agreement that creates or provides for a security interest
- *Security Interest* right in personal property that secures payment or performance of an obligation
- *Purchase Money Security Interest* security interest in goods purchased; interest is retained either by the seller of the goods or by a lender who advances the purchase price

Fundamental Rights of Debtor
- To redeem collateral by payment of the debt
- To possess general rights of ownership

Fundamental Rights of Secured Party
- To recover amount of debt
- To have collateral applied to payment of debt upon default

CLASSIFICATION OF COLLATERAL

Goods things that are movable when a security interest attaches
- *Consumer Goods* goods bought or used primarily for personal, family, or household purposes
- *Farm Products* goods that are part of a farming operation, including crops, livestock, or supplies used or produced in farming
- *Inventory* includes nonfarm product goods (1) held for sale, lease, or to be furnished under a service contract, or (2) consisting of raw materials, work in process, or materials used or consumed in a business
- *Equipment* goods not included in the definition of consumer goods, inventory, or farm products
- *Fixtures* goods that are so related to real property that they are considered part of the real estate
- *Accession* goods installed in or firmly affixed to personal property

Indispensable Paper
- *Chattel Paper* tangible or electronic record that evidences both a debt and a security interest in specific goods
- *Instruments* negotiable instruments or any other writing that evidences a right to payment of money that is transferable by delivery with any necessary indorsement
- *Documents* documents of title
- *Investment Property* investment security (stocks and bonds), security accounts, commodity contracts, and commodity accounts

Intangibles
- *Account* right to payment for (1) goods sold, leased, licensed, or otherwise disposed of or (2) services rendered
- *General Intangibles* catchall category of collateral not otherwise covered; includes software, goodwill, literary rights, and interests in patents, trademarks, and copyrights

Other Types of Collateral
- *Proceeds* whatever is received upon sale, lease, license, exchange, or other disposition of collateral; the secured party, unless the security agreement states otherwise, has rights to the proceeds
- *Deposit Accounts* a demand, savings, time, or similar account maintained with a bank

ATTACHMENT

Definition security interest that is enforceable against the debtor
Value consideration under contract law, a binding commitment to extend credit, or an antecedent debt
Debtor's Rights in Collateral a debtor is deemed to have rights in personal property the debtor owns, possesses, is in the process of acquiring, or has the power to transfer rights to a secured party

Security Agreement agreement between debtor and creditor creating a security interest; must be in a record authenticated by the debtor, unless, in the case of most types of collateral, the secured party has possession of the collateral, and must contain a reasonable description of the collateral
- *Consumer Goods* Federal regulation prohibits a credit seller or lender from obtaining a consumer's grant of a nonpossessory security interest in household goods
- *After-Acquired Property* a security agreement may cover property the debtor may acquire in the future
- *Future Advances* a security agreement may include future advances

PERFECTION

Definition attachment plus any steps required for perfection
Effect enforceable against most third parties

METHODS OF PERFECTING

Filing a Financing Statement may be used for all collateral except deposit accounts, letter-of-credit rights, and money
- *Financing Statement* document filed to provide notice of a security interest
- *Duration* filing is effective for five years but may be continued by filing a continuation statement
- *Place of Filing* statements, except for real-estate-related collateral, must be filed in a central location designated by the State.
- *Subsequent Change of Debtor's Location*

Possession by the secured party (a pledge); may be used for goods, instruments, money, negotiable documents, tangible chattel paper, or certificated securities
Automatic Perfection perfection upon attachment; applies to a purchase money security interest in consumer goods and isolated assignments of accounts
Temporary Perfection a security interest in certificated securities, instruments, and negotiable documents is automatically perfected for twenty days
Control may be used to perfect a security interest in electronic chattel paper, investment property, nonconsumer deposit accounts, and letter-of-credit rights

PRIORITIES AMONG COMPETING INTERESTS

See *Figure 38-5* for a summary of the priority rules

DEFAULT

Repossession of Collateral the secured party may take possession of the collateral on default without judicial process if it can be done without a breach of the peace
Sale of Collateral the secured party may sell, lease, license, or otherwise dispose of any collateral
Acceptance of Collateral the secured party, unless the debtor objects, may retain the collateral in full or partial satisfaction of the obligation (with the exception of the compulsory disposition of some consumer goods)

SURETYSHIP

NATURE AND FORMATION

Definition of Surety a person who promises to answer for the payment of a debt or the performance of a duty owed to the creditor by the principal debtor, upon the principal debtor's failure to perform
- *Principal Debtor* the party primarily liable on the obligation
- *Cosurety* each of two or more sureties who are liable for the same debt of the principal debtor
- *Absolute Surety* surety liable to a creditor immediately upon the default of a principal debtor

- *Conditional Guarantor of Collection* surety liable to a creditor only after the creditor has exhausted the legal remedies against the principal debtor

Types of Sureties
- *Party Assuming a Mortgage*
- *Fidelity Bonds*
- *Performance Bonds*
- *Official Bonds*
- *Judicial Bonds*

Formation the promise of the surety must satisfy all the elements of a contract and must also be in writing

---

RIGHTS OF SURETY

Exoneration the right of a surety to be relieved of his obligation to the creditor by having the principal debtor perform the obligation

Reimbursement the right of a surety who has paid the creditor to be repaid by the principal debtor

Subrogation the right of a surety who has paid the creditor to assume all the rights the creditor has against the principal debtor

Contribution the right to payment from each cosurety of his proportionate share of the amount paid to the creditor

---

DEFENSES OF SURETY AND PRINCIPAL DEBTOR

Personal Defenses of Principal Debtor defenses available only to the principal debtor, including her incapacity, discharge in bankruptcy, and setoff

Personal Defenses of Surety defenses available only to the surety, including her own incapacity, the statute of frauds, contract defenses to her suretyship undertaking, setoff, modification of the contract between the creditor and the principal debtor, and the creditor's release of security or a cosurety

Defenses of Both Surety and Principal Debtor include contract defenses to the contract between the creditor and the principal debtor

Bankruptcy

A debt is an obligation to pay money owed by a debtor to a creditor. Debts are created daily by countless purchasers of goods at the consumer level; by retailers of goods in buying merchandise from a manufacturer, wholesaler, or distributor; by borrowers of funds from various lending institutions; and through the issuance and sale of bonds and other types of debt securities. Multitudes of business transactions are entered into daily on a credit basis. Commercial activity would be restricted greatly if credit were not readily obtainable or if needed funds were unavailable for lending.

Fortunately, most debts are paid when due, thus justifying the extension of credit and encouraging its continuation. Although defaults may create credit and collection problems, the total amount in default normally represents a very small percentage of the total amount of outstanding indebtedness. Nevertheless, financial crises and business misfortune confront both individuals and businesses. Both may accumulate debts that exceed their total assets. Conversely, their assets may exceed their total indebtedness but be in such non-liquid form that these debtors are unable to pay their debts as they become due. For businesses as well as individuals, relief from overly burdensome debt and from the threat of impending lawsuits by creditors is frequently necessary for economic survival.

The conflict between creditor rights and debtor relief has engendered various solutions, such as voluntary adjustments and compromises requiring installment payments to creditors over a period of time during which they agree to withhold legal action. Other voluntary methods include compositions and assignments of assets by a debtor to a trustee or assignee for the benefit of creditors, who sometimes also file for equity receiverships or insolvency proceedings in a State court, pursuant to statute. Nonetheless, the most adaptable and frequently employed method of debtor relief—one that also affords protection to creditors—is a proceeding in a Federal court under Federal bankruptcy law.

FEDERAL BANKRUPTCY LAW

The most important method of protecting creditor rights and granting debtor relief is Federal bankruptcy law, which is largely statutory and involves court supervision. U.S. bankruptcy law serves a dual purpose: (1) to effect a quick, equitable distribution of the debtor's property among her creditors, and (2) to discharge the debtor from her debts, enabling her to rehabilitate herself and start afresh. Other purposes are to provide uniform treatment of similarly situated creditors, preserve existing business relations, and stabilize commercial usages.

The Constitution of the United States provides that "the Congress shall have power … to establish … uniform Laws on the subject of Bankruptcies throughout the United States." Article I, Section 8, clause 4. Federal bankruptcy law has generally superseded State insolvency laws.

The U.S. Bankruptcy Abuse Prevention and Consumer Protection Act of 2005 (2005 Act) contains the most extensive amendments to Federal bankruptcy law since 1978. The U.S. Bankruptcy Code consists of eight odd-numbered chapters and one even-numbered chapter. Chapters 7, 9, 11, 12, and 13 provide five different types of proceedings; Chapters 1, 3, and 5 apply to all of those proceedings unless otherwise specified. **Straight**, or ordinary, **bankruptcy** (Chapter 7) provides for the liquidation of the debtor's property, whereas the other proceedings provide for the **reorganization** and adjustment of the debtor's debts and, in the case of a business debtor, the continuance of the debtor's business. In reorganization cases the creditors usually look to the debtor's future earnings, whereas in liquidation cases the creditors look to the debtor's property at the commencement of the bankruptcy proceeding. Chapters 7, 11, 12, and 13 have provisions governing conversion of a case under that chapter to another chapter. The 2005 Act added Chapter 15 to the Bankruptcy Code for cross-border insolvency cases. Chapter 1 and certain sections of Chapters 3 and 5 apply to proceedings under Chapter 15.

1. Chapter 7 applies to *all* debtors, with the exception of railroads, insurance companies, banks, savings and loan associations, homestead associations, licensed small business investment companies, and credit unions. (In the past several years, 60 to 75 percent of bankruptcies have been filed under Chapter 7.) Moreover, Chapter 7 has special provisions for liquidating the estates of stockbrokers and commodity brokers.

2. Chapter 11 applies to railroads and any person who may be a debtor under Chapter 7 (except a stockbroker or a commodity broker). (Less than 1 percent of bankruptcies are filed under Chapter 11.)

3. Chapter 9 applies only to municipalities that are generally authorized to be debtors under that chapter, that are insolvent, and that desire to effect plans to adjust their debts.

4. Chapter 12 applies to individuals, or individuals and their spouses, who are engaged in farming if 50 percent of their gross income is from farming, their aggregate debts do not exceed $3,792,650, and at least 50 percent of their debts arise out of farming operations. (Less than one-tenth of 1 percent of bankruptcies are filed under Chapter 12.) Corporations or partnerships also may qualify for Chapter 12. The 2005 Act made Chapter 12 permanent and extended its coverage to certain family fishermen if 50 percent of their gross income is from commercial fishing, their aggregate debts do not exceed $1,757,475, and at least 80 percent of their debts arise out of commercial fishing operations.

5. Chapter 13 applies to individuals with regular income who owe liquidated unsecured debts of less than $360,475 and secured debts of less than $1,081,400. (In the past several years, 25 to 39 percent of bankruptcies have been filed under Chapter 13.)

6. Chapter 15 covers cross-border (transnational) insolvencies and incorporates the Model Law on Cross-Border Insolvency, promulgated by the United Nations Commission on International Trade Law (UNCITRAL). These changes are intended to make cross-border filings easier to accomplish and provide greater predictability. Chapter 15 encourages cooperation between the United States and foreign countries with respect to transnational insolvency cases.

This text will not further cover Chapters 9, 12, and 15.

The 1994 amendments to the Bankruptcy Code require that every three years, beginning in 1998, the U.S. Judicial Conference adjust for inflation the dollar amounts of certain provisions, including eligibility for Chapters 12 and 13, requirements for filing involuntary cases, priorities, exemptions, and exceptions to discharge. Section 104.

The Bankruptcy Code grants to U.S. district courts original and exclusive jurisdiction over all bankruptcy cases and original, but not exclusive, jurisdiction over civil proceedings arising under bankruptcy cases. The district court must, however, abstain from related matters that, except for their relationship to a bankruptcy, could not have been brought in a Federal court. The district court in which a bankruptcy case is commenced has exclusive jurisdiction over all of the debtor's property. In addition, within each Federal district court the Bankruptcy Code establishes a bankruptcy court staffed by bankruptcy judges. Bankruptcy courts are authorized to hear certain matters specified by the Bankruptcy Code and to enter appropriate orders and judgments subject to review by the district court or, where established, by a panel of three bankruptcy judges. The Federal Circuit Court of Appeals has jurisdiction over appeals from the district court or panel. In all other matters, unless the parties agree otherwise, only the district court may issue final order or judgment based upon proposed findings of fact and conclusions of law submitted to the court by the bankruptcy judge.

The U.S. trustees are government officials appointed by the U.S. Attorney General with administrative responsibilities in bankruptcy cases in almost all of the districts. For example, the U.S. trustee selects bankruptcy trustees and, in Chapter 11 proceedings, appoints the members of the unsecured creditors' committee. The 2005 Act gives the U.S. trustees added responsibilities in a number of areas.

CASE ADMINISTRATION—CHAPTER 3

Chapter 3 of the Bankruptcy Code contains provisions dealing with the commencement of a case in bankruptcy, the meetings of creditors, the officers who administer the case, and the administrative powers of those officers.

COMMENCEMENT OF THE CASE

The filing of a voluntary or involuntary petition commences a bankruptcy case, thereby beginning the jurisdiction of the bankruptcy court and the operation of the bankruptcy laws.

VOLUNTARY PETITIONS More than 99 percent of all bankruptcy petitions are filed voluntarily. Any person eligible to be a debtor under a given bankruptcy proceeding may file a voluntary petition under that chapter and need *not* be insolvent to do so. Commencing a voluntary case by filing a petition constitutes an automatic **order for relief**. The petition must include a list of all creditors (secured and unsecured), a list of all property the debtor owns, a list of property that the debtor claims to be exempt, and a statement of the debtor's affairs.

The 2005 Act added a requirement that all individual debtors receive credit counseling from an approved non-profit budget and credit counseling agency within the 180-day period *before* filing the petition. This requirement does not apply to a debtor who (1) is exempted by the court, or (2) resides in a district for which the U.S. trustee or the bankruptcy administrator determines that approved non-profit budget and credit counseling agencies are not reasonably able to provide adequate services to the additional individuals who would seek required credit counseling. The role of the credit counseling agencies is to analyze the client's current financial condition, the factors that caused the financial distress, and how the client can develop a plan to respond to these problems. Section 109(h).

INVOLUNTARY PETITIONS An involuntary petition in bankruptcy may be filed only under Chapter 7 (liquidation) or Chapter 11 (reorganization). It may be filed (1) by three or more creditors who have undisputed unsecured claims that total $14,425 or more, or (2) if the debtor has fewer than twelve creditors, by one or more creditors whose total unsecured claims equal $14,425 or more. Section 303(b). An involuntary petition may not be filed against a farmer or against a banking, insurance, or nonprofit corporation. Section 303(a).

Like a voluntary petition, the filing of an involuntary petition commences a case, but unlike a voluntary petition, it does *not* operate as an order for relief. The debtor has the right to answer. If the debtor does not timely contest the involuntary petition, the court will enter an order for relief against the debtor. If the debtor timely opposes the petition, however, the court may enter an order of relief only (1) if the debtor is generally not paying his undisputed debts as they become due, or (2) if, within 120 days before the filing of the petition, a custodian assignee or general receiver was appointed or took possession of substantially all of the debtor's property. Section 303(h).

If an involuntary petition is contested successfully by the debtor and dismissed by the court, Section 303(i) empowers the court to grant a judgment in favor of the debtor against the petitioning creditors for (1) costs, (2) reasonable attorneys' fees, and (3) damages proximately caused by the trustee's taking possession of the debtor's property. Moreover, if the petition was filed in bad faith, the court may award damages proximately caused by the filing or punitive damages.

If the court orders relief, the debtor must provide the court with schedules the same as those provided by a voluntary petitioner.

DISMISSAL

The court may dismiss a Chapter 7 case for cause after notice and a hearing. Section 707(a). In a case filed by an individual debtor whose debts are primarily consumer debts, the court may dismiss the case, or with the debtor's consent, convert the case to one under Chapter 11 or 13, if the court finds that granting relief would be an abuse of the provisions of Chapter 7. Section 707(b). A court can find abuse in one of two ways: (1) on general grounds based on whether the debtor filed the petition in bad faith or the totality of the circumstances of the debtor's financial situation demonstrates abuse, or (2) on an unrebutted presumption of abuse based on the means test established by the 2005 Act. The means test will be discussed later in this chapter.

Under Chapter 11, the court may dismiss a case for cause after notice and a hearing. Section 1112(b). Under Chapter 13, the debtor has an absolute right to have his case dismissed. Under Chapter 13, if a motion to dismiss is filed by an interested party other than the debtor, the court may dismiss the case only for cause after notice and a hearing.

AUTOMATIC STAYS

The filing of a voluntary or involuntary petition operates as a **stay** (i.e., restraint against) all creditors beginning or continuing to recover claims against the debtor, or creating, perfecting, or enforcing liens against property of the debtor. Section 362. This stay applies to both secured and unsecured creditors, although a secured creditor may petition the court to terminate the stay as to her security upon showing that she lacks adequate protection in the secured property. An automatic stay ends when the bankruptcy case is closed or dismissed or when the debtor receives a discharge.

TRUSTEES

In a bankruptcy proceeding, the trustee represents the debtor's estate and has the capacity to sue and be sued on behalf of the estate. In proceedings under Chapter 7, trustees are selected by a vote of the creditors. The 1994 amendments allow the creditors to elect a trustee in a Chapter 11 proceeding if the court orders the appointment of a trustee for cause. In Chapter 13, the trustee is appointed. Under Chapter 7, the trustee is responsible for collecting, liquidating, and distributing the debtor's estate. Her duties and powers in fulfilling these responsibilities include the following: (1) to collect the property of the estate; (2) to challenge certain transfers of property of the estate; (3) to use, sell, or lease property of the estate; (4) to deposit or invest money of the estate; (5) to employ attorneys, accountants, appraisers, or auctioneers; (6) to assume or reject any executory contract or unexpired lease of the debtor; (7) to object to creditors' claims that are improper; and (8) to oppose, if advisable, the debtor's discharge. Trustees under Chapters 11 and 13 perform some but not all of the duties of a Chapter 7 trustee.

MEETINGS OF CREDITORS

Within a reasonable time after relief is ordered, a meeting of creditors must be held. The court may not attend this meeting. The debtor must appear and submit to an examination by creditors and the trustee with respect to his financial situation. In a proceeding under Chapter 7, qualified creditors at this meeting elect a permanent trustee.

CREDITORS, THE DEBTOR, AND THE ESTATE—CHAPTER 5

CREDITORS

The Bankruptcy Code defines a **creditor** as any entity having a claim against the debtor that arose at the time of or before the order for relief. A **claim** means a "right to payment whether or not such right is reduced to judgment, liquidated, unliquidated, fixed, contingent, matured, unmatured, disputed, undisputed, legal, equitable, secured, or unsecured." Section 101(5).

PROOF OF CLAIMS Creditors wishing to participate in the distribution of the debtor's estate may file a proof of claim. If a creditor does not do so in a timely manner, then the debtor or trustee may file a proof of such claim. Section 501. The debtor thereby may prevent a claim from becoming nondischargeable. Filed claims are allowed unless a party in interest objects. If an objection is made, the court determines, after a hearing, the amount and validity of the claim. The court may not allow any claim that (1) is unenforceable against the debtor or his property, (2) is for unmatured interest, or (3) is for insider or attorney services in excess of the reasonable value of such services. Section 502. An **insider** includes a relative or general partner of a debtor as well as a partnership in which the debtor is a general partner or a corporation of which the debtor is a director, officer, or person in control. Section 101(31).

SECURED AND UNSECURED CLAIMS A **lien** is a charge or interest in property to secure payment of a debt or performance of an obligation and must be satisfied before the property is available to satisfy the claims of unsecured creditors. An allowed claim of a creditor who has a lien on property of the estate is a *secured* claim to the extent of the value of the creditor's interest in the property. The creditor's claim is *unsecured* to the extent of the difference between the value of his secured interest and the allowed amount of his claim. Thus, if Andrew has an allowed claim of $5,000 against the estate of debtor Barbara and has a security interest in property of the estate that is valued at $3,000, Andrew has a secured claim in the amount of $3,000 and an unsecured claim for $2,000.

A lien or secured claim can arise by agreement, judicial proceeding, common law, or statute. Consensual security interests in personal property are governed by Article 9 of the Uniform Commercial Code (UCC) and are discussed in *Chapter 38*. Consensual security interests in real property, called mortgages or deeds of trust, are covered in *Chapter 50*. A **judicial lien** is obtained by a judgment, a levy, or some other legal or equitable process. The common law grants to certain creditors, including innkeepers and common carriers, a possessory lien on property of their debtors that is in the creditor's possession or on the creditor's premises. Finally, a number of Federal and State statutes grant liens to specified creditors.

PRIORITY OF CLAIMS After secured claims have been satisfied, the remaining assets are distributed among creditors with unsecured claims. Certain classes of unsecured claims, however, have a **priority**, which means that they must be paid in full before any distribution is made to claims of lesser rank. Each claimant within a priority class shares *pro rata* if the assets are not sufficient to satisfy all claims in that class. The claims having a priority and the order of their priority, as provided in Section 507, are as follows:

1. *Domestic support obligations* (debts owed to a spouse, former spouse, or child of the debtor in the nature of alimony, maintenance, or support) subject to the expenses of a trustee in administering assets that otherwise can be used to pay support obligation.
2. *Expenses of administration* of the debtor's estate, including the filing fees paid by creditors in involuntary cases; the expenses of creditors in recovering concealed assets for the benefit of the bankrupt's estate; the trustee's necessary expenses; and reasonable compensation to receivers, trustees, and their attorneys, as allowed by the court.
3. Unsecured claims of *"gap"* creditors. These are claims in an involuntary case arising in the ordinary course of the debtor's business after the commencement of the case but before the earlier of either the appointment of the trustee or the entering of the order for relief.
4. Allowed, unsecured claims up to $11,725 for *wages, salaries, or commissions* earned within 180 days before the filing of the petition or before the date on which the debtor's business ceases, whichever comes first.
5. Allowed, unsecured claims for contributions to *employee benefit plans* arising from services rendered within 180 days before the filing of the petition or the cessation of the debtor's business, whichever occurs first, but limited to $11,725 multiplied by the number of employees covered by the plan, less the aggregate amount paid to such employees under number 3 above.
6. Allowed, unsecured claims up to $5,775 for *grain* or *fish producers* against a storage facility.
7. Allowed, unsecured claims up to $2,600 for *consumer deposits*; that is, moneys deposited in connection with the purchase, lease, or rental of property or the purchase of services for personal, family, or household use.
8. Specified income, property, employment, or excise *taxes* owed to governmental units.
9. Allowed claims for death or personal injuries resulting from the debtor's operation of a motor vehicle or vessel while legally intoxicated from using alcohol, a drug, or other substance.

After creditors with secured claims and creditors with claims having a priority have been satisfied, creditors with allowed, unsecured claims share proportionately in any remaining assets.

SUBORDINATION OF CLAIMS A subordination agreement is enforceable under the Bankruptcy Code to the same extent that it is enforceable under nonbankruptcy law. Section 510. In addition to statutory and contract priorities, the bankruptcy court can, at its discretion in proper cases, apply equitable priorities. Section 510. The court accomplishes this through the doctrine of subordination of claims, whereby, assuming two claims of equal statutory priority, the court declares that one claim must be paid in full before the other claim can be paid anything. Subordination is applied in cases in which allowing a claim in full would be unfair and inequitable to other creditors. (Allowing the inflated salary claims of officers in a closely held corporation would be an example.) In such cases, the court does not disallow the claim but merely orders that it be paid after all other claims are paid in full. For example, the claim of a parent corporation against its bankrupt subsidiary may be subordinated to the claims of other creditors of the subsidiary if the parent has so mismanaged the subsidiary to the detriment of its innocent creditors that this unconscionable conduct precludes the parent from seeking the aid of a bankruptcy court.

DEBTORS

As previously indicated, the purpose of the Bankruptcy Code is to bring about an equitable distribution of the debtor's assets and to provide him a discharge. Accordingly, the Code explicitly subjects the debtor to specified duties while exempting some of his property and discharging most of his debts.

DEBTOR'S DUTIES Under the Bankruptcy Code, the debtor must file a list of creditors, a schedule of assets and liabilities, a schedule of current income and expenditures, and a statement of her financial affairs. In any case in which a trustee is serving, the debtor must cooperate with the trustee and surrender to the trustee all property of the estate and all records relating to such property.

DEBTOR'S EXEMPTIONS Section 522 of the Bankruptcy Code exempts specified property of an individual debtor from bankruptcy proceedings, including the following:

1. up to $21,625 in equity in property used as a residence or burial plot;
2. up to $3,450 in equity in one motor vehicle;
3. up to $550 for any particular item, and not to exceed $11,525 in aggregate value, of household furnishings, household goods, wearing apparel, appliances, books,

animals, crops, or musical instruments that are primarily for personal, family, or household use;

4. up to $1,450 in jewelry;
5. any property up to $1,150 plus up to $10,825 of any unused amount of the first exemption;
6. up to $2,175 in implements, professional books, or tools of the debtor's trade;
7. unmatured life insurance contracts owned by the debtor, other than a credit life insurance contract;
8. professionally prescribed health aids;
9. social security, veteran's, and disability benefits;
10. unemployment compensation;
11. alimony and support payments, including child support;
12. payments from pension, profit-sharing, and annuity plans;
13. tax exempt retirement funds; and
14. payments from an award under a crime victim's reparation law, a wrongful death award, and up to $21,625, not including compensation for pain and suffering or for actual pecuniary loss, from a personal injury award.

In addition, the debtor may avoid judicial liens on any exempt property and nonpossessory, nonpurchase money security interests on certain household goods, tools of the trade, and professionally prescribed health aids.

The debtor has the option of using either the exemptions provided by the Bankruptcy Code or those available under State law. Nevertheless, a State may by specific legislative action limit its citizens to the exemptions provided by State law. More than three-quarters of the States have enacted such "opt out" legislation. The 2005 Act specifies that a debtor's exemption is governed by the law of the State where the debtor was domiciled for 730 days immediately before filing. If the debtor did not maintain a domicile in a single State for the 730-day period, then the governing law is of the State where the debtor was domiciled for 180 days immediately preceding the 730-day period (or for a longer portion of such 180-day period than in any other State).

Whether or not Federal or State exemptions apply, the 2005 Act provides that tax-exempt retirement accounts are exempt. Individual retirement accounts (IRAs) are subject to a $1,171,650 cap periodically adjusted for inflation. Nevertheless, the 2005 Act makes exempt property liable for nondischargeable domestic support obligations.

The 2005 Act also imposes limits on the use of State homestead exemptions. First, to the extent that the homestead was obtained through fraudulent conversion of nonexempt assets during the ten-year period before filing the petition, the exemption is reduced by that amount. Second, regardless of the level of the State exemption, a debtor may only exempt up to $146,450 of an interest in a homestead that was acquired during the 1,215-day period prior to the filing, but this limitation does not apply to any equity that has been transferred from the debtor's principal residence acquired more than 1,215 days before filing to the debtor's current principal residence if both residences are located in the same State. Third, a debtor may not exempt more than $146,450 if (1) the debtor has been convicted of a felony, which under the circumstances demonstrates that the filing of the case was an abuse of the Bankruptcy Code; or (2) the debtor owes a debt arising from (a) any violation of State or Federal securities laws; (b) fraud, deceit, or manipulation in a fiduciary capacity or in connection with the purchase or sale of securities registered under the Securities Exchange Act of 1934; or (c) any criminal act, intentional tort, or willful or reckless misconduct that caused serious physical injury or death to another individual in the preceding five years. The $146,450 limitation is to be adjusted periodically for inflation.

DISCHARGE Discharge relieves the debtor from liability for all her dischargeable debts. Certain debts, however, are nondischargeable under the Code. A discharge of a debt voids any judgment obtained at any time with respect to that debt and operates as an injunction against commencing or continuing any action to recover that debt. Section 524. A discharge does not, however, affect a secured creditor to the extent of his security.

No private employer may terminate the employment of, or discriminate with respect to employment against, an individual who is or has been a debtor under the Bankruptcy Code solely because such debtor (1) is or has been such a debtor; (2) has been insolvent before the commencement of a case or during the case; or (3) has not paid a debt that is dischargeable in a case under the Bankruptcy Code. Section 525(b).

A reaffirmation agreement between a debtor and a creditor permitting the creditor to enforce a discharged debt is enforceable to the extent State law permits but only if (1) the agreement was made before the discharge has been granted; (2) the debtor received the required disclosures, which must be written, clear, and conspicuous, at or before the time at which the debtor signed the agreement; (3) the agreement has been filed with the court, accompanied, if applicable, by a declaration or an affidavit of the attorney who represented the debtor during the course of negotiating the agreement, which states that such agreement represents a fully informed and voluntary agreement by the debtor and imposes no undue hardship on her; (4) the debtor has not rescinded the agreement at any time prior to discharge or within sixty days after the agreement is filed with the court, whichever occurs later; (5) the court has informed a debtor who is an individual that he is not required to enter into such an agreement and has explained the legal effect of the agreement; and (6) in a case concerning an individual who was not represented by an attorney during the course of negotiating the agreement, the court has approved such agreement as imposing no undue hardship on the debtor and being in her best interests. Section 524.

Section 523 provides that certain debts of an individual are not dischargeable in bankruptcy. This section applies to individuals receiving discharges under Chapters 7, 11, and, as discussed later in this chapter, the "hardship discharge" provision of Chapter 13. (The 2005 Act makes *most* of these apply to the standard discharge provision of Chapter 13.) The nondischargeable debts include the following:

1. certain taxes and customs duties and debt incurred to pay such taxes or customs duties;
2. legal liabilities for obtaining money, property, or services by false pretenses, false representations, or actual fraud;
3. legal liability for willful and malicious injuries to the person or property of another;
4. domestic support obligations and property settlements arising from divorce or separation proceedings;
5. debts not scheduled, unless the creditor knew of the bankruptcy;
6. debts the debtor created by fraud or defalcation while acting in a fiduciary capacity, embezzlement, or larceny;
7. student loans unless excluding the debt from discharge would impose undue hardship;
8. debts that were or could have been listed in a previous bankruptcy in which the debtor waived or was denied a discharge;
9. consumer debts for luxury goods or services in excess of $600 per creditor, if incurred by an individual debtor on or within ninety days before the order for relief, are presumed to be nondischargeable;
10. cash advances aggregating more than $875 obtained by an individual debtor under an open-ended credit plan within seventy days before the order for relief are presumed to be nondischargeable;
11. liability for death or personal injury based upon the debtor's operation of a motor vehicle, vessel, or aircraft while legally intoxicated;
12. fines, penalties, or forfeitures owed to a governmental entity; and
13. certain debts incurred for violations of securities fraud law. (This provision was added by the Sarbanes-Oxley Act.)

The following illustrates the operation of discharge: Donaldson files a petition in bankruptcy. Donaldson owes Anders $1,500, Boynton $2,500, and Conroy $3,000. Assume that Anders's claim is not dischargeable in bankruptcy, whereas Boynton's and Conroy's claims are. Anders receives $180 from the liquidation of Donaldson's bankruptcy estate, Boynton receives $300, and Conroy receives $360. If Donaldson receives a bankruptcy discharge, Boynton and Conroy will be precluded from pursuing Donaldson for the remainder of their claims ($2,200 and $2,640, respectively). Anders, on the other hand, because his debt is not dischargeable, may pursue Donaldson for the remaining $1,320, subject to the applicable statute of limitations. If Donaldson does not receive a discharge, Anders, Boynton, and Conroy may all pursue Donaldson for the unpaid portions of their claims.

THE ESTATE

The commencement of a bankruptcy case creates an estate, which is treated as a separate legal entity, distinct from the debtor. The estate consists of all legal and equitable interests of the debtor in nonexempt property at that time. The estate also includes property that the debtor acquires within 180 days after the filing of the petition by inheritance, by a property settlement, by a divorce decree, or as a beneficiary of a life insurance policy. In addition, the estate includes proceeds, rents, and profits from property of the estate and any interest in property that the estate acquires after the case commences. Section 541. The 2005 Act *excludes* from the estate savings for postsecondary education through education IRAs and 529 plans if certain criteria are met. Finally, the estate includes property that the trustee recovers under her powers (1) as a lien creditor, (2) to avoid voidable preferences, (3) to avoid fraudulent transfers, and (4) to avoid statutory liens. While in a Chapter 7 case the estate does not include earnings from services an *individual* debtor performs after the case commences, in a Chapter 13 case, it does include wages an *individual* debtor earns and property she acquires after the case commences.

TRUSTEE AS LIEN CREDITOR The trustee has, as of the commencement of the case, the rights and powers of any creditor with a judicial lien against the debtor or an execution that is returned unsatisfied, whether or not such a creditor exists. Section 544(a). The trustee is made an ideal creditor possessing every right and power that the State confers by law upon its most favored creditor who has acquired a lien through legal or equitable proceedings. By assuming the rights and powers of a purely hypothetical lien creditor, the trustee has no need to locate an actual existing lien creditor.

Thus, under the UCC and the Bankruptcy Code, the trustee, as a hypothetical lien creditor, has priority over a creditor with a security interest that was not perfected when the bankruptcy petition was filed. A creditor with a purchase money security interest who files within the grace period allowed under State law, which in most States is twenty days after the debtor receives the collateral, however, will defeat the trustee, even if the creditor gap-files the petition before perfecting and after the security interest is created. For example, Donald borrows $5,000 from Cathy on September 1 and gives her a security interest in the equipment he purchases with the borrowed funds. On October 3, before Cathy perfects her security interest, Donald files for bankruptcy. The trustee in bankruptcy can invalidate Cathy's security interest because it was unperfected when the bankruptcy petition was filed. Cathy would be able to assert a claim only as an unsecured creditor. If, however, Donald had filed for bankruptcy on September 18 and Cathy had perfected the security interest on September 19, Cathy would prevail because she perfected her purchase money security interest within twenty days after Donald received the equipment.

VOIDABLE PREFERENCES The Bankruptcy Code invalidates certain preferential transfers from the debtor to favored creditors before the date of bankruptcy. A creditor who has received a transfer invalidated as preferential still may make a claim for the unpaid debt, but the property he received under the preferential transfer becomes a part of the debtor's estate to be shared by all creditors. Under Section 547 the trustee may recover any transfer of the debtor's property:

1. to or for the benefit of a creditor;
2. for or on account of an antecedent debt the debtor owed before such transfer was made;
3. made while the debtor was insolvent;
4. made on or within ninety days before the date of the filing of the petition or, if the creditor was an "insider" (as previously defined), made within one year of the date of the filing of the petition; *and*
5. that enables such creditor to receive more than he would have received under Chapter 7.

A **transfer** is any mode, direct or indirect, voluntary or involuntary, of disposing of property or an interest in property, including the retention of title as a security interest. Section 101(54). The debtor is presumed to have been insolvent on and during the ninety days immediately preceding the date on which the petition was filed. **Insolvency** is a financial condition of a debtor such that the sum of her debts exceeds the sum of all her property at fair valuation.

The policy behind the voidable preference provision is explained by the House of Representatives report as follows:

The purpose of the preference section is two-fold. First, by permitting the trustee to avoid prebankruptcy transfers that occur within a short period before bankruptcy, creditors are discouraged from racing to the courthouse to dismember the debtor during his slide into bankruptcy. The protection thus afforded the debtor often enables him to work his way out of a difficult financial situation through cooperation with all of his creditors. Second, and more important, the preference provisions facilitate the prime bankruptcy policy of equality of distribution among creditors of the debtor. Any creditor that received a greater payment than others of his class is required to disgorge so that all may share equally. *House of Representatives Report* 95–595 at 177–78 (1977).

For example, on March 3, David borrows $15,000 from Carla, promising to repay the loan on April 3. David repays Carla on April 3 as he promised. Then, on June 1, David files a petition in bankruptcy. His assets are sufficient to pay general creditors only forty cents on the dollar. David's repayment of the loan is a voidable preference, which the trustee may recover from Carla. The transfer (repayment) on April 3 (1) was to a creditor (Carla); (2) was on account of an antecedent debt (the $15,000 loan made on March 3); (3) was made while the debtor was insolvent (a debtor is presumed insolvent for the ninety days preceding the filing of the bankruptcy petition—June 1); (4) was made within ninety days of bankruptcy (April 3 is less than ninety days before June 1); and (5) enabled the creditor to receive more than she would have received under Chapter 7 (Carla received $15,000; she would have received 0.40 × $15,000 = $6,000 in bankruptcy). After returning the property to the trustee, Carla would have an unsecured claim of $15,000 against David's estate in bankruptcy, for which she would receive $6,000.

To illustrate further, consider the following example. On May 1, Debra buys and receives merchandise from Stuart and gives him a security interest in the goods for the unpaid price of $20,000. On May 25, Stuart files a financing statement. On August 1, Debra files a petition for bankruptcy. The trustee in bankruptcy may avoid the perfected security interest as a preferential transfer because (1) the transfer of the perfected security interest on May 25 was to benefit a creditor (Stuart); (2) it was on account of an antecedent debt (the $20,000 owed from the sale of the merchandise); (3) the debtor was insolvent at the time (the debtor's insolvency is presumed for the ninety days preceding the filing of the bankruptcy petition—August 1); (4) the transfer was made within ninety days of bankruptcy (May 25 is less than ninety days before August 1); and (5) the transfer enabled the creditor to receive more than he would have received in bankruptcy (on his secured claim, Stuart would recover more than he would on an unsecured claim).

Nevertheless, not all transfers made within ninety days of bankruptcy are voidable. The Bankruptcy Code makes exceptions for certain prebankruptcy transfers, including the following:

1. *Exchanges for new value.* If, for example, within ninety days before the petition is filed, the debtor purchases an automobile for $9,000, this transfer of property (i.e., the $9,000) is not voidable because it was not made for an antecedent debt but rather as a substantially contemporaneous exchange for new value.
2. *Enabling security interests.* If the creditor gives the debtor new value which the debtor uses to acquire property in which he grants the creditor a security interest, the security interest is not voidable if the creditor perfects it within thirty days after the debtor receives possession of the property. For example, if within ninety days of the filing of the petition, the debtor purchases a refrigerator on credit and grants the seller or lender a security interest in the refrigerator, the transfer of that interest is not voidable if the secured party perfects within thirty days after the debtor receives possession of the property.
3. *Payments in ordinary course.* The trustee may *not* avoid a transfer in payment of a debt incurred in the ordinary course of business or financial affairs of the debtor and the transferee and either (a) made in the ordinary course of business or financial affairs of the debtor and transferee, or (b) made according to ordinary business terms.
4. *Consumer debts.* This exception provides that if the debtor is an individual whose debts are primarily consumer debts, the trustee may not avoid any transfer of property valued at less than $600.
5. *Nonconsumer debts.* In a case filed by a debtor whose debts are not primarily consumer debts, the trustee may not avoid any transfer of property valued at less than $5,850.
6. *Domestic support obligations.* The trustee may not avoid any transfer that is a *bona fide* payment of a debt for a domestic support obligation. Section 547(c).

FRAUDULENT TRANSFERS The trustee may avoid fraudulent transfers made on or within two years before the date of the filing of the petition. Section 548. One type of fraudulent transfer consists of the debtor's transferring property with the actual intent to hinder, delay, or defraud any of her creditors. Another type of fraudulent transfer involves the debtor's transfer of property for less than a reasonably equivalent consideration when she is insolvent or when the transfer would render her so. For example, Dale, who is in debt, transfers title to her house to Tony, her father, without any payment by Tony to Dale and with the understanding that when the house is no longer in danger of seizure by creditors, Tony will reconvey it to Dale. The transfer of the house by Dale to Tony is a fraudulent transfer. The 2005 Act specifies that a fraudulent transfer includes a payment to an insider under an employment contract that is not in the ordinary course of business. A 1998 amendment to the Bankruptcy Code provides that a transfer of a charitable contribution to a qualified religious or charitable entity or organization will not be considered a fraudulent transfer if the amount of that contribution does not exceed 15 percent of the gross annual income of the debtor for the year in which the transfer is made. Transfers that exceed 15 percent are protected if they are "consistent with the practices of the debtor in making charitable contributions."

In addition, the trustee may avoid transfers of the debtor's property if the transfer is voidable under State law by a creditor with an allowable, unsecured claim. Section 544(b). This section empowers a trustee to avoid transfers that violate State fraudulent conveyance statutes, which make it illegal to transfer property to another party in order to defer, hinder, or defraud creditors. These statutes generally provide a three- to six-year limitations period, which the trustee can utilize under Section 544(b). At least forty-three States have adopted the Uniform Fraudulent Transfer Act, which has a four-year statute of limitations.

STATUTORY LIENS A **statutory lien** arises solely by force of a statute and does not include a security interest or judicial lien. Section 101(53). The trustee may avoid a statutory lien on property of the debtor if the lien (1) first becomes effective when the debtor becomes insolvent, (2) is not perfected or enforceable on the date of the commencement of the case against a *bona fide* purchaser, or (3) is for rent. Section 545.

LIQUIDATION—CHAPTER 7

To accomplish its dual goals of equitably distributing the debtor's property and providing the debtor with a fresh start, the Bankruptcy Code has established two approaches: liquidation and adjustment of debts. Chapter 7 uses liquidation, whereas Chapters 11 and 13, discussed below, take the second approach, that of adjusting debts. Liquidation involves terminating the business of the debtor, distributing his nonexempt assets, and, usually, discharging all of his dischargeable debts.

PROCEEDINGS

Proceedings under Chapter 7 apply to all debtors except railroads, insurance companies, banks, savings and loan associations, homestead associations, and credit unions. A petition commencing a case under Chapter 7 may be either voluntary or involuntary. After the order for relief, an interim trustee is appointed to serve until the creditors select a permanent trustee. If the creditors do not elect a trustee, the interim trustee becomes the permanent trustee. Under Chapter 7, the trustee collects and reduces to money the property of the estate; accounts for all property received; investigates the financial affairs of the debtor; examines and, if appropriate, challenges proofs of claims; opposes, if advisable, the discharge of the debtor; and makes a final report of the administration of the estate.

The creditors may also elect a committee of not fewer than three and not more than eleven unsecured creditors to consult with the trustee, to make recommendations to him, and to submit questions to the court.

CONVERSION

The debtor may convert a case under Chapter 7 to Chapter 11 or 13; however, any waiver of this right is unenforceable.

Moreover, on request of a party in interest and after notice and a hearing, the court may convert a case under Chapter 7 to Chapter 11. The court may also convert a case under Chapter 7 to Chapter 13, but this can occur only upon the debtor's request. Any conversion to another chapter can only occur if the debtor may also be a debtor under that chapter. Section 706.

DISMISSAL

The court may dismiss a Chapter 7 case for cause after notice and a hearing. In a case filed by an individual debtor whose debts are primarily consumer debts, the court may dismiss a case or, with the debtor's consent, convert the case to one under Chapter 11 or 13, if the court finds that granting relief would be an abuse of the provisions of Chapter 7. A court can find abuse (1) on general grounds based on whether the debtor filed the petition in bad faith or the totality of the circumstances of the debtor's financial situation demonstrates abuse, *or* (2) on an unrebutted presumption of abuse based on a new means test established by the 2005 Act.

Under the **means test** abuse is presumed (i.e., the debtor is not eligible for Chapter 7 unless the debtor can prove special circumstances) for an individual debtor whose net current monthly income is greater than the State median income *and* if either (1) the debtor has available net income (income after deducting allowed expenses) for repayment to creditors over five years totaling at least $11,725, or (2) the available net income for repayment to creditors over five years is between $7,025 and $11,725 and such available net income is at least 25 percent of nonpriority unsecured claims. Section 707. The means test can be explained by the following scenarios:

1. If the debtor's net current monthly income is less than or equal to the State median income, no presumption of abuse arises.

2. If the debtor's net current monthly income is greater than the State median income *and* the debtor's current monthly income less allowed expenses is less than $117.08 per month, no presumption of abuse arises.

3. If the debtor's net current monthly income is greater than the State median income *and* the debtor's current monthly income less allowed expenses is at least $117.08 per month, a presumption of abuse arises *if* the current monthly income less allowed expenses is sufficient to pay 25 percent of the debtor's nonpriority unsecured claims over sixty months.

4. If the debtor's net current monthly income is greater than the State median income *and* the debtor's current monthly income less allowed expenses is at least $195.42 per month, a presumption of abuse arises without regard to the amount of nonpriority unsecured claims.

For example, Debra's net current monthly income is greater than the State median income. After deducting allowed expenses her monthly income is $150, which places her in the third situation. If her nonpriority unsecured claims are $35,000, a presumption of abuse will arise because $150 multiplied by sixty equals $9,000, which is greater than 25 percent of $35,000, which equals $8,750. On the other hand, Debra would be eligible to file under Chapter 7 if her nonpriority unsecured claims are $36,100, because $150 multiplied by sixty equals $9,000, which is less than 25 percent of $36,100, which equals $9,025.

DISTRIBUTION OF THE ESTATE

After the trustee has collected all the assets of the debtor's estate, she distributes them to the creditors and, if any assets remain, to the debtor, in the following order:

1. Secured creditors are paid on their security interests.
2. Creditors entitled to a priority are paid in the order provided.
3. Unsecured creditors who filed their claims on time (or tardily, if they did not have notice or actual knowledge of the bankruptcy) are paid.
4. Unsecured creditors who filed their claims late are paid.
5. Claims for fines and multiple, exemplary, or punitive damages are paid.
6. Interest at the legal rate from the date of the filing of the petition is paid to all of the above claimants.
7. Whatever property remains is distributed to the debtor.

Claims of the same rank are paid *pro rata*. For example: Donley has filed a petition for a Chapter 7 proceeding. The total value of Donley's estate after paying the expenses of administration is $25,000. Evans, who is owed $15,000, has a security interest in property valued at $10,000. Fishel has an unsecured claim of $6,000, which is entitled to a priority of $2,000. The United States has a claim for income taxes of $4,000. Green has an unsecured claim of $9,000 that was filed on time. Hiller has an unsecured claim of $12,000 that was filed on time. Jerdee has a claim of $8,000 that was filed late. The distribution would be as follows:

1. Evans receives $11,500
2. Fishel receives $3,200
3. United States receives $4,000
4. Green receives $2,700
5. Hiller receives $3,600
6. Jerdee receives $0

To analyze this distribution: Evans receives $10,000 as a secured creditor and has an unsecured claim of $5,000. Fishel receives $2,000 on the portion of his claim entitled to a priority and has an unsecured claim of $4,000. The United States has a priority of $4,000. After paying $10,000 to Evans, $2,000 to Fishel, and $4,000 to the United States,

there remains $9,000 ($25,000 − $10,000 − $2,000 − $4,000) to be distributed *pro rata* to unsecured creditors who filed on time. Their claims total $30,000 (Evans = $5,000, Fishel = $4,000, Green = $9,000, and Hiller = $12,000). Therefore, each will receive $9,000/$30,000, or thirty cents on the dollar. Accordingly, Evans receives an additional $1,500, Fishel receives an additional $1,200, Green receives $2,700, and Hiller receives $3,600. Because the assets were insufficient to pay all unsecured claimants who filed on time, Jerdee, who filed tardily, receives nothing. If, however, Jerdee's late filing resulted from Donley's failure to schedule Jerdee's claim, then Donley's debts to Jerdee would not be discharged unless Jerdee knew or had notice of the bankruptcy.

◆ SEE FIGURE 39-1: **Collection and Distribution of the Debtor's Estate**

DISCHARGE

A discharge under Chapter 7 relieves the debtor of all dischargeable debts that arose before the date of the order for relief. The discharge does not include those debts that are not dischargeable. After distribution of the estate, the court will grant the debtor a discharge unless the debtor:

1. is not an individual (partnerships and corporations may not receive a discharge under Chapter 7);
2. has destroyed, falsified, concealed, or failed to keep records and account books;
3. has knowingly and fraudulently made a false oath or account, presented or used a false claim, or given or received bribes;
4. has transferred, removed, destroyed, or concealed any (a) of his property with intent to hinder, delay, or defraud his creditors within twelve months preceding the filing of the bankruptcy petition, or (b) property of the estate after the date of filing of the petition;
5. has within eight years prior to bankruptcy been granted a discharge under Chapter 7 or 11. A debtor also will be denied a discharge under Chapter 7 if she received a discharge under Chapter 13 within the past six years, unless payments under that chapter's plan totaled at least (1) 100 percent of the allowed unsecured claims or (2) 70 percent of such claims and the plan was the debtor's best effort;
6. refused to obey any lawful order of the court or to answer any question approved by the court;
7. has failed to explain satisfactorily, in terms of meeting his liabilities, any loss or deficiency of assets; or
8. has executed a written waiver of discharge approved by the court. Section 727.

The 2005 Act denies a discharge to an individual debtor who fails to complete a personal financial management course. This provision, however, does not apply if the debtor resides in a district for which the U.S. trustee or the

◆ **FIGURE 39-1: Collection and Distribution of the Debtor's Estate**

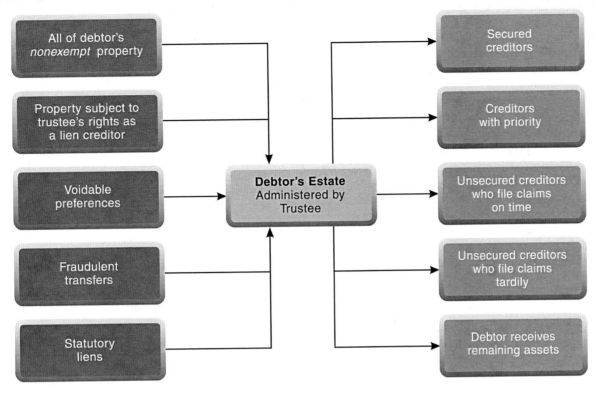

bankruptcy administrator has determined that the approved instructional courses are not adequate to service the additional individuals who would be required to complete these instructional courses.

On the request of the trustee or a creditor and after notice and a hearing, the court may revoke within one year a discharge the debtor obtained through fraud.

REORGANIZATION—CHAPTER 11

Reorganization is the process of correcting or eliminating factors responsible for the distress of a business enterprise, thereby preserving both the enterprise and its value as a going concern. Chapter 11 of the Bankruptcy Code governs reorganization of eligible debtors, including individuals, partnerships, and corporations, and permits the restructuring of their finances. A number of large corporations have made use of Chapter 11, including WorldCom, Enron, Kmart, Texaco, AH Robins, Johns-Manville, Allied Stores, Global Crossing, Pacific Gas and Electric, CIT, Conseco, Lehman Brothers, General Motors, and Chrysler. The main objective of a reorganization proceeding is to develop and carry out a fair, equitable, and feasible plan of reorganization.

After a plan has been prepared and filed, a hearing held before the court determines whether or not it will be con-

firmed. Chapter 11 permits but does not require a sale of assets. Rather, it contemplates that the debtor will keep its assets and use them to generate earnings that will pay creditors under the terms of the plan confirmed by the court.

The 1994 and 2005 amendments provide for streamlined and more flexible procedures in a small business case, which is any case under Chapter 11 filed by a small business. The amendments define *small business* to include (1) persons engaged in commercial or business activities whose aggregate, noncontingent, liquidated debts do not exceed $2,343,300 (subject to periodic adjustments for inflation); and (2) cases in which the U.S. trustee has not appointed a committee of unsecured creditors or the court has determined that the committee of unsecured creditors is not sufficiently active and representative to provide effective oversight of the debtor. Under a small business case, the U.S. trustee has additional oversight duties and the debtor has additional reporting requirements, while the plan process can be simpler and the time periods and deadlines are different.

PROCEEDINGS

Any person who may be a debtor under Chapter 7 (except stockbrokers and commodity brokers) and railroads may be a debtor under Chapter 11. Petitions may be voluntary or involuntary.

As soon as practicable after the order for relief, a committee of unsecured creditors is appointed. This committee usually consists of persons holding the seven largest unsecured claims against the debtor. In addition, the court may order the appointment of additional committees of creditors or of equity security holders, if necessary, to ensure adequate representation. Section 1102. The committee may, with the court's approval, employ attorneys, accountants, and other agents to represent or perform services for the committee. The committee may consult with the debtor or trustee concerning the administration of the case and may investigate the debtor's affairs and participate in formulating a reorganization plan. Section 1103.

The debtor will manage and remain in possession of the property of the estate unless the court orders the appointment of a trustee, who may then operate the debtor's business. The court will order the appointment of a trustee *only for cause* (including fraud, dishonesty, incompetence, or gross mismanagement of the debtor's affairs) or if the appointment is in the interests of creditors or equity security holders. Section 1104. The 1994 amendments allow the creditors to elect the trustee. If the court does not order the appointment of a trustee upon the request of a party in interest, the court will order the appointment of an examiner to investigate allegations of fraud, dishonesty, incompetence, misconduct, or mismanagement if (1) such appointment is in the interests of creditors or equity security holders or (2) the debtor's fixed, liquidated, unsecured debts exceed $5 million.

The duties of a trustee in a case under Chapter 11 include the following:

1. to be accountable for all property received;
2. to examine proofs of claims;
3. to furnish information to all parties in interest;
4. to provide the court and taxing authorities with financial reports of the debtor's business operations;
5. to make a final report and account of the administration of the estate;
6. to investigate the financial condition of the debtor and determine the desirability of continuing the debtor's business; and
7. to file a plan, to file a report explaining why there will be no plan, or to recommend that the case be converted to Chapter 7.

At any time before confirmation of a plan, the court may terminate the trustee's appointment and restore the debtor to possession and management of the property of the estate and operation of the debtor's business. Section 1105.

When a trustee has not been appointed, which is usually the case, the debtor in possession performs many of the functions and duties of a trustee, with the principal exception of investigating the debtor. Section 1107.

The Bankruptcy Code (Section 1113) deals with the rejection of collective bargaining agreements. Subsection (b)(1) provides that subsequent to filing and prior to seeking such rejection, the trustee or debtor-in-possession must propose the labor contract modifications that are necessary to enable the debtor to reorganize and that will provide for the fair and equitable treatment of all parties concerned. Subsection (b)(2) requires that good faith meetings to reach a mutually satisfactory agreement be held between management and the union. Subsection (c) authorizes the court to approve rejection of the collective bargaining agreement only if the court finds that the proposal for rejection was made in accordance with these conditions, that the union refused the proposal without good cause, and that the balance of equities clearly favors rejection.

◆ SEE FIGURE 39-2: **Comparison of Bankruptcy Proceedings**

◆ FIGURE 39-2: **Comparison of Bankruptcy Proceedings**

	Chapter 7	Chapter 11	Chapter 12	Chapter 13
Objective	Liquidation	Reorganization	Adjustment	Adjustment
Eligible Debtors	Most debtors	Most debtors, including railroads	Family farmer who meets certain debt limitations	Individual with regular income who meets certain debt limitations
Type of Petition	Voluntary or involuntary	Voluntary or involuntary	Voluntary	Voluntary
Trustee	Usually selected by creditors; otherwise appointed	Only if court orders appointment for cause; creditors then may select trustee	Appointed	Appointed

PLAN OF REORGANIZATION

The debtor may file a plan at any time and has the exclusive right to file a plan during the 120 days after the order for relief, unless a trustee has been appointed. If the debtor has not filed a plan within 120 days or the plan has not been accepted within 180 days, then other parties in interest, including an appointed trustee or a creditors' committee, may file a plan. Section 1121. On request of an interested party and after notice and a hearing, the court may for cause reduce or increase the 120-day or 180-day periods. The 2005 Act provides, however, that the 120-day period may not be extended beyond eighteen months and the 180-day period may not be extended beyond twenty months.

A plan of reorganization must divide creditors' claims and shareholders' interests into classes, specify how each class will be treated, deal with claims within each class equally, and provide adequate means for implementing the plan. After a plan has been filed, the plan and a written disclosure statement approved by the court as containing adequate information must be transmitted to each holder of a claim before seeking acceptance or rejection of the plan. **Adequate information** is that which would enable a hypothetical, reasonable investor to make an informed judgment about the plan. Section 1125.

ACCEPTANCE OF PLAN

Each class of claims and interests has the opportunity to accept or reject the proposed plan. To be accepted by a **class of claims**, a plan must be accepted by creditors that hold at least two-thirds in amount and more than one-half in number of the allowed claims of such class that actually voted on the plan. Acceptance of a plan by a **class of interests**, such as shareholders, requires acceptance by holders of at least two-thirds in amount of the allowed interests of such class that actually voted on the plan.

A class that is not impaired under a plan is conclusively presumed to have accepted the plan. Basically, a class is unimpaired if the plan leaves unaltered the legal, equitable, and contractual rights to which the holder of such claim or interest is entitled. Section 1124. A class that will receive no distribution under a plan is deemed not to have accepted the plan.

CONFIRMATION OF PLAN

Before a plan is binding on any parties, the court, after notice and a hearing, must confirm such plan. To be confirmed, the plan must meet all the requirements of Section 1129 of the Bankruptcy Code. The most important of these requirements are the following.

GOOD FAITH The plan must have been proposed in good faith and not by any means forbidden by law. Section 1129(a)(3).

FEASIBILITY The court must find that confirmation of the plan is not likely to be followed by the debtor's liquidation or by its need for further financial reorganization. Section 1129(a)(11).

CASH PAYMENTS Unless the claim holder agrees otherwise, certain priority creditors must have their allowed claims paid in full in cash immediately or, in some instances, on a deferred basis. Section 1129(a)(9). These priority claims include the expenses of administration, gap creditors, claims for wages and salaries, and employee benefits and consumer deposits.

In the case of a debtor who is an individual, the 2005 Act requires that the plan provide for payments to be made out of the debtor's future earnings from personal services or other future income. It also imposes an additional requirement for confirmation if an unsecured creditor objects to confirmation of the plan: the value of property distributed on account of that claim must not be less than (1) the amount of that claim, or (2) the debtor's projected disposable income to be received during the longer of (a) the five-year period beginning on the first payment due date, or (b) the plan's term. Section 1129(a)(15).

ACCEPTANCE BY CREDITORS To be confirmed, the plan must be accepted by at least *one* class of claims, and with respect to *each* class, each holder must either accept the plan *or* receive not less than the amount he would have received under Chapter 7. In addition, each class must accept the plan or be unimpaired by it. Nonetheless, under certain circumstances, the court may confirm a plan that is not accepted by all impaired classes, upon determining that the plan does not discriminate unfairly and that it is fair and equitable. Section 1129(b)(1). Under these circumstances, a class of claims or interests may, despite objections by that class, be subjected to the provisions of a plan.

"Fair and equitable" with respect to secured creditors requires that (1) they either retain their security interest and receive deferred cash payments, the present value of which is at least equal to their claims, or (2) they realize the "indubitable equivalent" of their claims. Fair and equitable with respect to unsecured creditors means that such creditors are to receive property of value equivalent to the full amount of their claim or that no junior claim or interest is to receive anything. With respect to a class of interests, a plan is fair and equitable if the holders receive full value or if no junior interest receives anything at all.

EFFECT OF CONFIRMATION

Once confirmed, the plan governs the debtor's performance obligations. The plan binds the debtor and any creditor, equity security holder, or general partner of the debtor. Upon the entry of a final decree closing the proceedings, a debtor that is *not* an individual is discharged from all of its debts and liabilities that arose before the date the plan was confirmed, except as otherwise provided in the plan, the order of confirmation, or the Bankruptcy Code. Section 1141. Unlike under Chapter 7, under Chapter 11, partnerships and corporations may receive a discharge unless the plan calls for the liquidation of the business entity's property and termination of its business. The 2005 Act excepts from the discharge of any corporate debtor any debt (1) owed to the government as a result of fraud, or (2) arising from a fraudulent tax return or willful evasion of taxes.

An *individual* debtor is not discharged until all plan payments have been made. However, if the debtor fails to make all payments, the court may, after a hearing, grant a "hardship discharge" if the value of property actually distributed is not less than what the creditors would have received under Chapter 7 and modification of the plan is not practicable. A discharge under Chapter 11 does not discharge an *individual* debtor from debts that are not dischargeable under Section 523.

ADJUSTMENTS OF DEBTS OF INDIVIDUALS—CHAPTER 13

To encourage debtors to pay their debts wherever possible, Congress enacted Chapter 13 of the Bankruptcy Code. This chapter permits an individual debtor to file a repayment plan which, if confirmed by the court, will discharge him from almost all of his debts when he completes his payments under the plan. If, as occurs in many cases, the debtor does not make the required payments under the plan, the case will be converted to Chapter 7 or dismissed.

PROCEEDINGS

Chapter 13 provides a procedure for adjusting the debts of an individual with regular income who owes liquidated, unsecured debts of less than $360,475 and secured debts of less than $1,081,400. Sole proprietorships meeting these debt limitations are also eligible; partnerships and corporations are not eligible. Only a voluntary petition may initiate a case under Chapter 13, and a trustee is appointed in every Chapter 13 case. Property of the estate in Chapter 13 includes wages earned and other property acquired by the debtor after the Chapter 13 filing. Section 1306.

CONVERSION OR DISMISSAL

The debtor may convert a case under Chapter 13 to Chapter 7. On request of the debtor, if the case has not been previously converted from Chapter 7 or 11, the court shall dismiss a case under Chapter 13. On request of a party in interest or the U.S. trustee, and after notice and a hearing,

the court may convert a case under Chapter 13 to Chapter 7 *or* may dismiss a case under Chapter 13, whichever is in the best interests of creditors and the estate, for cause, including (1) unreasonable delay by the debtor; (2) failure of the debtor to file a plan timely; (3) denial of confirmation of a plan; or (4) material default by the debtor with respect to a term of a confirmed plan. Before the confirmation of a plan, on request of a party in interest or the U.S. trustee and after notice and a hearing, the court may convert a case under Chapter 13 to Chapter 11. Nonetheless, a case may *not* be converted to another chapter unless the debtor may be a debtor under that chapter. Section 1307.

THE PLAN

The debtor files the plan and may modify it at any time before confirmation. The plan must meet three requirements under Section 1322:

1. It must require the debtor to submit all or any portion of her future earnings or income, as is necessary for the execution of the plan, to the trustee's supervision and control.
2. It must provide for full payment on a deferred basis of all claims entitled to a priority unless a holder of a claim agrees to a different treatment of such claim.
3. If the plan classifies claims, it must provide the same treatment for each claim in the same class.

In addition, the plan may modify the rights of unsecured and secured creditors, except those secured only by a security interest in the debtor's principal residence. The plan also may provide for payments on any unsecured claim to be made concurrently with payments on any secured claim. If the debtor's net current monthly income is equal to or greater than the State median income, the plan may not provide for payments over a period longer than five years. If the debtor's net current monthly income is less than the State median income, the plan may not provide for payments over a period longer than three years, unless the court approves, for cause, a longer period not to exceed five years.

CONFIRMATION

To be confirmed by the court, the plan must meet certain requirements. Section 1325. First, the filing of the case must have been in good faith, and the plan must comply with applicable law and be proposed in good faith. Second, the present value of the property to be distributed to unsecured creditors must be not less than the amount they would receive under Chapter 7. Third, either the secured creditors must accept the plan, the plan must provide that the debtor will surrender the collateral to the secured creditors, *or* the plan must permit the secured creditors to retain their security interest and the present value of the property to be distributed to them is not less than the allowed amount of their claim. Fourth, the debtor must be able to make all payments and comply with the plan. Fifth, if the trustee or the holder of an unsecured claim objects to the plan's confirmation, then the plan must either provide for payments the present value of which is not less than the amount of that claim or provide that all of the debtor's disposable income for three years be paid to unsecured creditors under the plan. If, however, the debtor's net current monthly income is equal to or greater than the State median income, the debtor's disposable income for not less than five years must be committed to pay unsecured creditors. For purposes of this provision, *disposable income* means current monthly income received by the debtor that is not reasonably necessary for the maintenance or support of the debtor or a dependent of the debtor, for domestic support obligations, or, if the debtor is engaged in business, for the payment of expenditures necessary for continuing, preserving, and operating the business. Sixth, if a debtor is required by judicial or administrative order or statute to pay a domestic support obligation, then the debtor must pay all such obligations that became payable after the filing.

EFFECT OF CONFIRMATION

The provisions of a confirmed plan bind the debtor and all of her creditors. The confirmation of a plan vests in the debtor all property of the estate free and clear of any creditor's claim or interest for which the plan provides, except as otherwise provided in the plan or in the order confirming the plan. Section 1327. A plan may be modified after confirmation at the request of the debtor, the trustee, or a holder of an unsecured claim. The modification may increase or decrease the amount of payments on claims of a particular class or extend or reduce the time for such payments. Section 1329.

DISCHARGE

Before the 2005 Act, the discharge under Chapter 13 was considerably more extensive than that granted under Chapter 7. The 2005 Act, however, made the discharge of debts under Chapter 13 less extensive than it was previously. As a result, Chapter 13 discharges only a few types of debts that are not also discharged under Chapter 7.

After a debtor completes all payments under the plan and of certain postpetition domestic support obligations, the court will grant him a discharge of all debts provided for by the plan, with the exception of nondischargeable debts for (1) unfiled, late-filed, and fraudulent tax returns; (2) legal liabilities resulting from obtaining money, property, or services by false pretenses, false representations, or actual fraud;

(3) legal liability for willful *or* malicious conduct that caused personal injury to an individual; (4) domestic support obligations; (5) debts not scheduled unless the creditor knew of the bankruptcy; (6) debts the debtor created by fraud or embezzlement while acting in a fiduciary capacity; (7) most student loans; (8) consumer debts for luxury goods or services in excess of $600 per creditor if incurred by an individual debtor on or within ninety days before the order for relief; (9) cash advances aggregating more than $875 obtained by an individual debtor under an open-ended credit plan within seventy days before the order for relief; (10) liability for death or personal injury based upon the debtor's operation of a motor vehicle, vessel, or aircraft while legally intoxicated; (11) restitution or criminal fine included in a sentence for a criminal conviction; and (12) certain long-term obligations on which payments extend beyond the term of the plan.

Even if the debtor fails to make all payments, the court may, after a hearing, grant a "hardship discharge" if the debtor's failure is due to circumstances for which the debtor is not justly accountable, the value of property actually distributed is not less than what the creditors would have received under Chapter 7, and modification of the plan is impracticable. Section 1328(b). This discharge is subject, however, to the same exceptions for nondischargeable debts as a discharge under Chapter 7.

The 2005 Act denies a discharge under Chapter 13 to a debtor who has received a discharge (1) in a prior Chapter 7 or 11 case filed during the four-year period preceding the filing of the Chapter 13 case, or (2) in a prior Chapter 13 case filed during the two-year period preceding the date of filing the subsequent Chapter 13 case. It also denies a discharge to a debtor who fails to complete a personal financial management course. This provision, however, does not apply if the debtor resides in a district for which the U.S. trustee or the bankruptcy administrator has determined that the approved instructional courses are not adequate to service the additional individuals who would be required to complete these required instructional courses. Sections 1328(f), (g).

◆ **SEE FIGURE 39-2: Comparison of Bankruptcy Proceedings**

CREDITORS' RIGHTS AND DEBTOR'S RELIEF OUTSIDE OF BANKRUPTCY

The rights and remedies of debtors and creditors outside of bankruptcy are governed mainly by State law. Because of the expense and notoriety associated with bankruptcy, resolving claims outside of a bankruptcy proceeding is often in the best interests of both debtor and creditor. Accordingly, bankruptcy usually is considered a last resort.

The rights and remedies of creditors outside of bankruptcy are varied. The first part of this section examines the basic right of all creditors to pursue their overdue claims to judgment and to satisfy that judgment out of property belonging to the debtor. Other rights and remedies are discussed elsewhere in this book. The rights under Article 2 of the UCC of an unpaid credit seller to reclaim the goods sold are covered in *Chapter 25*. The right of a secured creditor to enforce a security interest in personal property is the subject of *Chapter 38*. Likewise, the right of a creditor to foreclose a mortgage on real property is discussed in *Chapter 50*. In addition, the right of a creditor to proceed against a surety on the debt is addressed in *Chapter 38*.

At the same time, the law attempts to protect debtors against overreaching by creditors. This goal has been pursued by a number of means. States have enacted usury laws, as discussed in *Chapter 13*. The Federal Trade Commission has limited the rights of a holder in due course against consumer debtors, as explained in *Chapter 28*. Congress has prohibited abusive, deceptive, and unfair debt collection practices employed by debt collection agencies, as discussed in *Chapter 42*. That chapter also covers other legal protection offered to *consumer* debtors. The second part of this section describes the various forms of nonbankruptcy compromises that provide relief to debtors who have become overextended and who are unable to pay all of their creditors.

CREDITORS' RIGHTS

When a debtor fails to pay a debt, the creditor may file suit to collect the debt owed. The objective is to obtain a judgment against the debtor and ultimately to collect on that judgment.

PREJUDGMENT REMEDIES

Because litigation takes time, a creditor attempting to collect on a claim through the judicial process will almost always experience delay in obtaining judgment. To prevent the debtor from meanwhile disposing of his assets, the creditor may use, when available, certain prejudgment remedies. The most important of these is **attachment**, the process of seizing property, by virtue of a writ, summons, or other judicial order, and bringing the property into the custody of the court to secure satisfaction of the judgment ultimately to be entered in the action. At common law, the main objective of attachment was to coerce the defendant debtor into appearing in court; today the writ of attachment is statutory and is used primarily to seize the debtor's property in the event a judgment is rendered. Most States limit attachment to specified grounds and provide the debtor an opportunity for a hearing before a judge prior to the issuance of a writ of execution. Generally, attachment is limited to situations in which (1) the defendant cannot be personally served; (2) the claim is based upon fraud or

the equivalent; or (3) the defendant has or is likely to transfer his property. In addition, the plaintiff generally must post a bond to compensate the defendant for loss should the plaintiff not prevail in the cause of action.

Similar in purpose is the remedy of prejudgment **garnishment**, which is a statutory proceeding directed at a third person who owes a debt to the debtor or who has property belonging to the debtor. Garnishment is most commonly used against the employer of the debtor and the bank in which the debtor has a savings or checking account. Property garnished remains in the hands of the third party pending the outcome of the suit. For example, Calvin brings an action against Daisy to collect a debt that is past due. Alvin has property belonging to Daisy. Calvin might garnish this property so that if he is successful in his action against Daisy, his judgment could be satisfied out of that property held by Alvin. If Alvin no longer had the property when Calvin obtained judgment, Calvin could recover from Alvin.

POSTJUDGMENT REMEDIES

If the debtor still has not paid the claim, the creditor may proceed to trial and try to obtain a court judgment against the debtor. Though necessary, obtaining a judgment is, nevertheless, only the first step in collecting the debt. If the debtor does not voluntarily pay the judgment, the creditor will have to take additional steps to collect on it. These steps are called "postjudgment remedies."

First, the judgment creditor will have the court clerk issue a **writ of execution** demanding payment of the judgment, which is served by the sheriff upon the defendant/debtor. Upon return of the writ "unsatisfied," the judgment creditor may post bond or other security and order a levy on and sale of specified nonexempt property belonging to the defendant/debtor, which is then seized by the sheriff, advertised for sale, and sold at public sale under the writ of execution.

The writ of execution is limited to nonexempt property of the debtor. All States restrict creditors from recourse to certain property, the type and amount of which varies greatly from State to State.

If the proceeds of the sale do not produce funds sufficient to pay the judgment, the creditor may institute a **supplementary proceeding** in an attempt to locate money or other property belonging to the defendant. He also may proceed by **garnishment** against the debtor's employer or against a bank in which the debtor has an account. As discussed in Chapter 42, State and Federal statutes contain exemption provisions which limit the amount of wages subject to garnishment.

DEBTOR'S RELIEF

The creditor's pursuit of a judgment on which she can collect and the debtor's quest for relief inherently give rise to conflicts among (1) the right of diligent creditors to pursue their claims to judgment and to satisfy their judgments by sale of property of the debtor; (2) the right of unsecured creditors who have refrained from suing the debtor; and (3) the social policy of affording relief to a debtor who has contracted debts beyond his ability to pay and who therefore may bear a lifetime burden.

Various nonbankruptcy compromises provide relief to debtors. Certain compromises, such as those offered by credit agencies and adjustment bureaus, are relatively informal. Some, such as compositions and assignments, are founded in common law and involve simple contract and trust principles; others, such as statutory assignments, are statutory. Some, such as equity receiverships, involve the intervention of a court and its officers, while others do not.

COMPOSITIONS

A common law or nonstatutory **composition** (or "workout") is an ordinary contract or agreement between the debtor and two or more of her creditors, under which the creditors receive *pro rata* a part of their claims and the debtor is discharged from the balance of the claims. A composition is the State law analogue of Chapter 11 of the Bankruptcy Act. As a contract, it requires contractual formalities, such as offer, acceptance, and consideration. For example, debtor D, owing debts of $5,000 to A, $2,000 to B, and $1,000 to C, offers to settle these claims by paying a total of $4,000 to A, B, and C. If A, B, and C accept the offer, a composition results, with A receiving $2,500, B $1,000, and C $500. The consideration for the promise of A to forgive the balance of his claim consists of the promises of B and C to forgive the balance of their claims. By avoiding a race among themselves to obtain the debtor's limited assets, all the creditors benefit.

It should be noted, however, that the debtor in a composition is discharged from liability only regarding the claims of those creditors who voluntarily consent to the composition. If, in the illustration above, C had refused to accept the offer of composition and had refused to take the $500, he could attempt to collect his full $1,000 claim. Likewise, if D owed additional debts to X, Y, and Z, these creditors would not be bound by the agreement between D and A, B, and C. Another disadvantage of the composition is the fact that any creditor can attach the assets of the debtor during the negotiation period that usually precedes the execution of the composition agreement. For instance, once D advised A, B, and C that he was offering to compose the claims, any one of the creditors could seize D's property.

A variation of the composition is an extension agreement, developed by the debtor and two or more of her creditors, that provides an extended period of time for payment of her debts either in full or proportionately reduced.

ASSIGNMENTS FOR BENEFIT OF CREDITORS

A common law or nonstatutory assignment for the benefit of creditors, sometimes called a general assignment, is a voluntary transfer by the debtor of his property to a trustee who applies the property to the payment of all the debtor's debts. For instance, debtor D transfers title to his property to trustee T, who converts the property into money and pays it to all of the creditors on a *pro rata* basis. An assignment for the benefit of creditors is a State law analogue of Chapter 7 of the Bankruptcy Act.

In most States, statutes now govern assignments for the benefit of creditors. These statutes typically require recording of the assignment, filing schedules of assets and liabilities, and providing notice to the creditors. Almost all of the statutes require that all creditors be treated equally except those with liens or statutorily created priorities.

The advantages of an assignment over a composition are that it protects the debtor's assets from attachment and execution and that it halts diligent creditors in their race to attach. An assignment does not require the creditors' consent, and payment by the trustee of part of the claims does not discharge the debtor from the balance of them. Thus, in the previous example, even after T pays A $2,500, B $1,000, and C $500 (and makes appropriate payments to all other creditors), A, B, and C and the other creditors still may attempt to collect the balance of their claims. Moreover, an assignment for the benefit of creditors is a ground for sustaining an involuntary petition for bankruptcy.

Because assignments benefit creditors by protecting the debtor's assets from attachment, some statutory enactments have endeavored to combine the idea of the assignment with a corresponding benefit that would discharge the debtor from the balance of his debts. But because the U.S. Constitution prohibits a State from impairing the contractual obligation between private citizens, it is impossible for a State to force all creditors to discharge a debtor upon a *pro rata* distribution of assets, although, as previously discussed, the Federal government *does* have such power and exercises it in the Bankruptcy Code. Accordingly, the States generally have enacted assignment statutes permitting the debtor to obtain *voluntary* releases of the balance of claims from creditors who accept partial payments, thus combining the advantages of common law compositions and assignments.

EQUITY RECEIVERSHIPS

One of the oldest remedies in equity is the appointment of a receiver by the court. The receiver is a disinterested person who collects and preserves the debtor's assets and income and disposes of them at the direction of the court which appointed her. The court may instruct her (1) to liquidate the assets by public or private sale; (2) to operate the business as a going concern temporarily; or (3) to conserve the assets until final disposition of the matter before the court.

The court will appoint a receiver upon the petition (1) of a secured creditor seeking foreclosure of his security; (2) of a judgment creditor who has exhausted legal remedies to satisfy the judgment; or (3) of a shareholder of a corporate debtor whose assets will likely be dissipated by fraud or mismanagement. The appointment of a receiver always rests within the sound discretion of the court. Insolvency, in the equity sense of inability by the debtor to pay his debts as they mature, is one of the factors the court considers in appointing a receiver.

CHAPTER SUMMARY

FEDERAL BANKRUPTCY LAW

CASE ADMINISTRATION— CHAPTER 3	**Commencement of the Case** the filing of a voluntary or involuntary petition begins jurisdiction of the bankruptcy court • *Voluntary Petitions* available to any eligible debtor even if solvent • *Involuntary Petitions* may be filed only under Chapter 7 or 11 if the debtor is generally not paying his debts as they become due **Dismissal** the court may dismiss a case for cause after notice and a hearing; under Chapter 13 the debtor has an absolute right to have his case dismissed **Automatic Stay** prevents attempts by creditors to recover claims against the debtor **Trustee** responsible for collecting, liquidating, and distributing the debtor's estate **Meeting of Creditors** debtor must appear and submit to an examination of her financial situation
CREDITORS, THE DEBTOR, AND THE ESTATE— CHAPTER 5	**Creditor** any entity that has a claim against the debtor • *Claim* a right to payment • *Lien* charge or interest in property to secure payment of a debt or performance of an obligation • *Secured Claim* claim with a lien on property of the debtor • *Unsecured Claim* portion of a claim that exceeds the value of any property securing that claim • *Priority of Claims* the right of certain claims to be paid before claims of lesser rank **Debtors** • *Debtor's Duties* the debtor must file specified information, cooperate with the trustee, and surrender all property of the estate • *Debtor's Exemptions* determined by State or Federal law, depending upon the State • *Discharge* relief from liability for all debts except those the Bankruptcy Code specifies as not dischargeable **The Estate** all legal and equitable interests of the debtor in nonexempt property • *Trustee as Lien Creditor* trustee gains the rights and powers of creditor with judicial lien (an interest in property, obtained by court action, to secure payment of a debt) • *Voidable Preferences* Bankruptcy Code invalidates certain preferential transfers made before the date of bankruptcy from the debtor to favored creditors • *Fraudulent Transfers* trustee may avoid fraudulent transfers made on or within two years before the date of bankruptcy • *Statutory Liens* trustee may avoid statutory liens which first become effective on insolvency, are not perfected at commencement of case, or are for rent
LIQUIDATION—CHAPTER 7	**Purpose** to distribute equitably the debtor's nonexempt assets and usually to discharge all dischargeable debts of the debtor

Proceedings apply to most debtors

Conversion a case may be voluntarily converted to Chapter 11 or Chapter 13; it may be involuntarily converted by the court to Chapter 11

Dismissal the court may dismiss a case on general grounds *and* in a case filed by an individual debtor based on a means test

Distribution of the Estate in the following order: (1) secured creditors, (2) creditors entitled to a priority, (3) unsecured creditors, and (4) the debtor

Discharge granted by the court unless the debtor has committed an offense under the Bankruptcy Code or has received a discharge (1) within eight years under Chapter 7 or 11, or (2) subject to exceptions within six years under Chapter 13

REORGANIZATION— CHAPTER 11	**Purpose** to preserve a distressed entity and its value as a going concern **Proceedings** debtor usually remains in possession of the property of the estate **Acceptance of Plan** requires a specified proportion of creditors to approve the plan **Confirmation of Plan** requires (1) good faith, (2) feasibility, (3) cash payments to certain priority creditors, and (4) usually acceptance by creditors **Effect of Confirmation** binds the debtor and creditors and discharges the debtor
ADJUSTMENT OF DEBTS OF INDIVIDUALS—CHAPTER 13	**Purpose** to permit an individual debtor to file a repayment plan that will discharge her from most debts **Conversion or Dismissal** a Chapter 13 case may be voluntarily or involuntarily dismissed or converted to Chapter 7 or 11 **Confirmation of Plan** requires (1) good faith, (2) that the present value of property distributed to unsecured creditors be not less than the amount that would be paid them under Chapter 7, (3) that secured creditors accept the plan, keep their collateral, or retain their security interest and the present value of the property to be distributed to them is not less than the allowed amount of their claim, and (4) that the debtor be able to make all payments and comply with the plan **Discharge** after a debtor completes all payments under the plan

CREDITORS' RIGHTS AND DEBTOR'S RELIEF OUTSIDE OF BANKRUPTCY

CREDITORS' RIGHTS	**Prejudgment Remedies** include attachment and garnishment **Postjudgment Remedies** include writ of execution and garnishment
DEBTOR'S RELIEF	**Compositions** agreement between debtor and two or more of her creditors that each will take a portion of his claim as full payment **Assignment for Benefit of Creditors** voluntary transfer by the debtor of his property to a trustee, who applies the property to the payment of all the debtor's debts **Equity Receivership** receiver is a disinterested person appointed by the court to collect and preserve the debtor's assets and income and to dispose of them at the direction of the court

PART 9
Regulation of Business

Protection of Intellectual Property

The economic system in the United States is based upon free and fair competition. The law prevents businesses from taking unfair advantage of their competitors. Essential to this legal prevention is the protection of intellectual property, which includes trade secrets, trade symbols, copyrights, and patents. These interests are protected from infringement, or unauthorized use, by others. Such protection is essential to the conduct of business. For example, a business would be far less willing to invest considerable resources in research and development if the resulting discoveries, inventions, and processes were not protected by patents and trade secrets. Similarly, a company would not be secure in devoting time and money to marketing its products and services without laws that protect its trade symbols and trade names. Moreover, without copyright protection, the publishing, entertainment, and computer software industries would be vulnerable to piracy, both by corporate competitors and by the general public. This chapter will discuss the law protecting (1) trade secrets; (2) trade symbols, including trademarks, service marks, certification marks, collective marks, and trade names; (3) copyrights; and (4) patents.

TRADE SECRETS

Every business has secret information. Such information may include customer lists or contracts with suppliers and customers; it also may comprise formulas, processes, and production methods that are vital to the successful operation of the business. A business may disclose a trade secret in confidence to an employee with the understanding that the employee will not reveal the information to others. To the extent the owner of the information obtains a patent on it, it is no longer a trade secret but is protected by patent law. Some businesses, however, choose not to obtain a patent because it provides protection for only a limited time, whereas State trade secret law protects a trade secret as long as it is kept secret. Moreover, if the courts invalidate a pat-

ent, the information will have been disclosed to competitors without the owner of the information obtaining any benefit. The Uniform Trade Secrets Act, promulgated in 1979 and amended in 1985, has been adopted by almost all of the States.

DEFINITION

A **trade secret** is commercially valuable information that is guarded from disclosure and is not general knowledge. The Uniform Trade Secrets Act defines a trade secret as

> information, including a formula, pattern, compilation, program, device, method, technique, or process, that:
> (i) derives independent economic value, actual or potential, from not being generally known to, and not being readily ascertainable by proper means by, other persons who can obtain economic value from its disclosure or use, and
> (ii) is the subject of efforts that are reasonable under the circumstances to maintain its secrecy.

A famous example of a trade secret is the formula for Coca-Cola.

MISAPPROPRIATION

Misappropriation of a trade secret is the wrongful use of a trade secret. A person misappropriates a trade secret of another (1) by knowingly acquiring it through improper means or (2) by disclosing or using it without consent, if her knowledge of the trade secret came under circumstances giving rise to a duty to maintain secrecy or came from a person who used improper means or who owed the owner of the trade secret a duty to maintain secrecy. Trade secrets are most frequently misappropriated in two ways: (1) an employee wrongfully uses or discloses such information, or (2) a competitor wrongfully obtains it.

An employee is under a duty of loyalty to his employer, which, among other responsibilities, obligates the employee not to disclose trade secrets to competitors. It is wrongful, in turn, for a competitor to obtain vital secret trade information from an employee through bribery or other means. Besides breaching the duty of loyalty, the faithless employee who divulges secret trade information also commits a tort. In the absence of a contract restriction, an employee is under no duty upon termination of his employment to refrain either from competing with a former employer or from working for a competitor of that employer; however, he may not use trade secrets or disclose them to third persons. The employee is entitled, nevertheless, to use the skill, knowledge, and general information he acquired during the previous employment relationship.

Another improper method of acquiring trade secrets is industrial espionage conducted through methods such as electronic surveillance or spying. Improper means of acquiring another person's trade secrets also include theft, bribery, fraud, unauthorized interception of communications, and inducement or knowing participation in a breach of confidence. In the broadest sense, discovering another's trade secrets by any means other than independent research or personal inspection of the publicly available finished product is improper unless the other party voluntarily discloses the secret or fails to take reasonable precautions to protect its secrecy.

REMEDIES

Remedies for misappropriation of trade secrets are damages and, where appropriate, injunctive relief. Damages are awarded in the amount of either the pecuniary loss to the plaintiff caused by the misappropriation or the pecuniary gain to the defendant, whichever is greater. A court will grant an injunction to prevent a continuing or threatened misappropriation of a trade secret for as long as is necessary to protect the plaintiff from any harm attributable to the misappropriation and to deprive the defendant of any economic advantage attributable to the misappropriation.

CRIMINAL PENALTIES

In 1996 Congress enacted the Economic Espionage Act of 1996 prohibiting the theft of trade secrets and providing criminal penalties for violations. (The statute does not provide any civil remedies.) The statute defines trade secrets to mean

> all forms and types of financial, business, scientific, technical, economic, or engineering information, including patterns, plans, compilations, program devices, formulas, designs, prototypes, methods, techniques, processes, procedures, programs, or codes, whether tangible or intangible, and whether or how stored, compiled, or memorialized physically, electron-

ically, graphically, photographically, or in writing if (A) the owner thereof has taken reasonable measures to keep such information secret; and (B) the information derives independent economic value, actual or potential, from not being generally known to, and not being readily ascertainable through proper means by, the public.

The Act broadly defines theft to include all types of conversion of trade secrets, including the following:

1. stealing, obtaining by fraud, or concealing such information;
2. without authorization copying, duplicating, sketching, drawing, photographing, downloading, uploading, photocopying, mailing, or conveying such information; and
3. purchasing or possessing a trade secret with knowledge that it had been stolen.

The Act punishes thefts of trade secrets, as well as attempts and conspiracies to steal secrets, with fines, imprisonment for up to 10 years, or both. Organizations that violate the Act are subject to fines of up to $5 million.

TRADE SYMBOLS

One of the earliest forms of unfair competition was the fraudulent marketing of one person's goods as those of another. Still common, this unlawful practice is sometimes referred to as "passing off" or "palming off." Basically the process of "cashing in" on the goodwill, good name, and reputation of a competitor and of his products, this fraudulent marketing deceives the public and deprives honest businesses of trade. Section 43(a) of the Federal Trademark Act (the Lanham Act) prohibits a person from using a false designation of origin in connection with any goods or services in interstate commerce. This section also prohibits a person from making a false or misleading description or representation of fact which misrepresents the nature, characteristics, qualities, or geographic origin of her own goods, services, or commercial activities. In 1988, this section was amended to prohibit misrepresentations of *another* person's goods, services, or commercial activities. As a result, Section 43(a) also forbids "reverse palming off," by which a producer misrepresents someone else's goods as his own. Accordingly, James would violate Section 43(a) by passing off his product as Sally's or by reverse passing off Sally's product as his. A violator of Section 43(a) is liable in a civil action to any person who is, or is likely to be, injured by the violation. The remedies are (1) injunctive relief, (2) an accounting for profits, (3) damages, (4) destruction of infringing articles, (5) costs, and (6) attorneys' fees in exceptional cases.

The Lanham Act also established Federal registration of trade symbols and protection against misuse or infringement by injunctive relief and a right of action for damages against the infringer. A form of passing off one's goods or services as those of the owner of the mark, an infringement deceives the public and constitutes unfair competition. Thus, trade symbol infringement law protects both consumers from being misled by the use of infringing trade symbols as well as producers from unfair practices by competitors.

TYPES OF TRADE SYMBOLS

The Lanham Act recognizes four types of trade symbols or **marks**. A **trademark** is a distinctive symbol, word, name, device, letter, number, design, picture, or combination in any arrangement that a person adopts or uses to identify goods that he manufactures or sells and to distinguish them from those manufactured or sold by others. Examples of trademarks include Kodak, Xerox, and the rainbow apple logo on Apple computers. A trademark can also consist of goods' "trade dress," which is the appearance or image of goods as presented to prospective purchasers. Trade dress would include the distinctive but nonfunctional design of packaging, labels, containers, and the product itself or its features. Examples include the Campbell Soup label and the shape of the Coca-Cola bottle. Internet domain names that are used to identify and distinguish the goods or services of one person from the goods or services of others and to indicate the source of the goods and services may be registered as trademarks. To qualify, an applicant must show that it offers services via the Internet and that it uses the Internet domain name as a source identifier.

Some trademarks are embodied in sounds, scents, and other formats that cannot be represented by a drawing. Examples of distinctive sound marks are MGM's lion's roar, NBC's chimes, the Harlem Globetrotters' theme song "Sweet Georgia Brown," Intel's chimes, and Lucasfilm's THX logo theme.

Similar in function to the trademark, which identifies tangible goods and products, a **service mark** is used to identify and distinguish one person's services from those of others. For example, the titles, character names, and other distinctive features of radio and television shows may be registered as service marks. Service marks may also consist of trade dress such as the décor or shape of buildings in which services are provided. Examples include the Hard Rock Cafe and Howard Johnson's orange roof.

A **certification mark** is used upon or in connection with goods or services to certify their regional or other origin, composition, mode of manufacture, quality, accuracy, or other characteristics or to certify that members of a union or other organization performed the work or labor in such goods or services. The marks "Good Housekeeping Seal of Approval" and "Underwriter's Laboratory" are examples of certification marks. The owner of the certification mark does *not* produce or provide the goods or services with which the mark is used.

A **collective mark** is a distinctive mark or symbol used to indicate either that the producer or provider is a member of a trade union, trade association, fraternal society, or other organization or that members of a collective group produce the goods or services. As in the case of a certification mark, the owner of a collective mark is not the producer or provider but rather is the group of which the producer or provider is a member. An example of a collective mark is the union mark attached to a product to indicate its manufacture by a unionized company.

REGISTRATION

To be protected by the Lanham Act, a mark must be distinctive enough to identify clearly the origin of goods or services. A trade symbol may satisfy the distinctiveness requirement in either of two ways. First, it may be **inherently distinctive** if prospective purchasers are likely to associate it with the product or service it designates because of the nature of the designation and the context in which it is used. Fanciful, arbitrary, or suggestive marks satisfy the distinctiveness requirement. In contrast, a descriptive or geographic designation is *not* inherently distinctive. Such a designation is one that is likely to be perceived by prospective purchasers as merely descriptive of the nature, qualities, or other characteristics of the goods or service with which it is used. Thus, the word *Apple* cannot be a trademark for apples, although it may be a trademark for computers.

Descriptive or geographic designations may, however, satisfy the distinctiveness requirement through the second method: acquiring distinctiveness through a "**secondary meaning**." A designation acquires a secondary meaning when a substantial number of prospective purchasers associate the designation with the product or service it identifies. The trademark office may accept proof of substantially exclusive and continuous use of a mark for five years as *prima facie* evidence of secondary meaning.

A **generic name** is one that is understood by prospective purchasers to denominate the general category, type, or class of goods or services with which it is used. A user cannot acquire rights in a generic name as a trade symbol. Moreover, a trade symbol will lose its eligibility for protection if prospective purchasers come to perceive a trade symbol primarily as a generic name for the category, type, or class of goods or services with which it is used. Under the Lanham Act, the test for when this has occurred is "the primary significance of the registered mark to the relevant public rather than purchaser motivation." Examples of marks that have lost protection because they became generic include "aspirin," "thermos," and "cellophane."

For example in *Zobmondo Entertainment v. Falls Media* (2010), two manufacturers of board games used the phrase

"WOULD YOU RATHER" to identify board games and books that incorporate questions posing humorous, bizarre, or undesirable choices. Falls Media sued Zobmondo for trademark infringement arising from Zobmondo's use of Falls Media's Federally registered trademark, "WOULD YOU RATHER... ?". On summary judgment the district court held that "WOULD YOU RATHER... ?" is not entitled to Federal trademark protection because the mark is "merely descriptive" and lacks secondary meaning; accordingly the court ordered the mark cancelled from the Federal trademark registry. The U.S. Court of Appeals for the 9th Circuit reversed and sent the case back for trial, noting that the presumption of validity and distinctiveness that comes with Federal registration is strong. The court stated that

> Marks are generally classified in one of five categories of increasing distinctiveness: (1) generic, (2) descriptive, (3) suggestive, (4) arbitrary, or (5) fanciful. Which category a mark belongs in is a question of fact. * * * Suggestive, arbitrary, and fanciful marks are considered "inherently distinctive" and are automatically entitled to federal trademark protection because "their intrinsic nature serves to identify a particular source of a product."

The court examined two main tests used to distinguish suggestive from descriptive marks. The first test—the "imagination" test—attempts to determine whether an imaginative leap is required by the ordinary consumer to understand the nature of the product being referenced. Here, the court found the imagination test to be inconclusive by itself because while "WOULD YOU RATHER ... ?" has no literal meaning to tell someone that the game would serve up a bizarre or humorous choice, someone familiar with the game might not think the phrase very suggestive. Without consumer surveys it was unclear what consumers would understand the phrase to mean. The second test—the "competitors' needs" test—assesses whether competitors need to use the mark to identify their own goods and services, in which case the mark is more likely to be descriptive. In sending the case back for trial, the appellate court concluded "that there is a genuine issue of material fact whether 'WOULD YOU RATHER ... ?' is suggestive or merely descriptive as a mark for a boardgame. The issue of descriptiveness or suggestiveness in this case cannot correctly be resolved by summary judgment."

Federal registration is denied to marks that are immoral, deceptive, or scandalous. Marks may not be registered if they disparage or falsely suggest a connection with persons, living or dead; institutions; beliefs; or national symbols. In addition, a trademark may not consist of the flag, coat of arms, or other insignia of the United States or of any State, municipality, or foreign nation. Moreover, a mark will not be registered if it so resembles a registered or previously used mark such that it would be likely to cause confusion, mistake, or deceit.

To obtain Federal protection, which has a ten-year term with unlimited ten-year renewals, the mark must be registered with the U.S. Patent and Trademark Office. An applicant must either (1) have actually used the mark in commerce or (2) demonstrate a *bona fide* intent to use the mark in commerce and actually use it within six months, which period may be extended.

Federal registration is not required to establish rights in a mark, nor is it required to begin using a mark. Registration, however, provides numerous advantages. It gives nationwide constructive notice of the mark to all later users. It permits the registrant to use the Federal courts to enforce the mark and constitutes *prima facie* evidence of the registrant's exclusive right to use the mark. This right becomes incontestable, subject to certain specified limitations, after five years. Finally, registration provides the registrant with Customs Bureau protection against imports that threaten to infringe upon the mark. A U.S. trade symbol registration provides protection only in the United States. However, in 2002 Congress enacted legislation implementing the Madrid Protocol, a procedural agreement allowing U.S. trademark owners to file for registration in more than eighty member countries by filing a single application.

To retain trademark protection, the owner of a mark must not abandon it by failing to make *bona fide* use of it in the ordinary course of trade. Abandonment occurs when an owner does not use a mark and no longer intends to use it. Three years of nonuse raises a presumption of abandonment, which the owner may rebut by proving her intent to resume use.

Anyone who claims rights in a mark may use the ™ (trademark) or ˢᴹ (service mark) designation, even if the mark is not registered. Only owners of registered marks may use the symbol ®.

INFRINGEMENT

Infringement of a mark occurs when a person without authorization uses an identical or substantially indistinguishable mark that is *likely* to cause confusion, to cause mistake, or to deceive. The intent to confuse is not required, nor is proof of actual confusion, although likelihood of confusion may be inferred from either. In a case involving consumer confusion, infringement occurs if an appreciable number of ordinarily prudent purchasers are *likely* to be misled or confused as to the source of the goods or services. In deciding whether infringement has occurred, the courts consider various factors, including the strength of the mark, the intent of the unauthorized user, the degree of similarity between the two marks, the relation between the two products or services the marks identify, and the marketing channels through which the goods or services are purchased.

The Federal Trademark Dilution Act of 1995 amended the Lanham Act to protect famous marks from dilution of their distinctive quality. The term *dilution* means the lessening of the capacity of a famous mark to identify and distinguish goods or services even if (1) there is no competition between the owner of the famous mark and the other party using the mark, or (2) the other party's use of the mark does not result in the likelihood of confusion, mistake, or deception. Examples of dilution would include DuPont shoes, Toyota aspirin, and Rolex cameras. In determining whether a mark is distinctive and famous, a court may consider factors such as (1) the degree of inherent or acquired distinctiveness of the mark; (2) the degree of recognition of the mark; (3) the duration and extent of the use, advertising, and publicity of the mark; (4) the geographical extent of the trading area in which the mark is used; and (5) the channels of trade for the goods or services with which the mark is used. The amendment exempts fair use of a famous mark in comparative commercial advertising, noncommercial use of a mark, and mention of a famous mark in news reporting.

The Trademark Cyberpiracy Prevention Act of 1999 amended the Lanham Act to protect the owner of a trademark or service mark from any person who, with a bad faith intent to profit from the mark, registers, traffics in, or uses a domain name which, at the time of its registration, is (1) identical or confusingly similar to a distinctive mark; or (2) dilutive of a famous mark; or (3) is a protected trademark, word, or name. The Act specifies factors a court may consider in determining bad faith intent but prohibits such a determination if the defendant believed, with reasonable grounds, that the use of the domain name was fair or otherwise lawful. It further authorizes a court to order cancellation of the domain name or its transfer to the owner of the mark. In addition to injunctive relief, the Act makes available remedies that include recovery of the defendant's profits, actual damages, attorneys' fees, and court costs. It also provides for statutory damages in an amount of at least $1,000 and up to $100,000 per domain name. The Act shields a registrar, registry, or other registration authority from liability for damages for the registration or maintenance of a domain name for another, unless there is a showing of bad faith intent to profit from such registration or maintenance of the domain name registration.

REMEDIES

The Lanham Act provides several remedies for infringement: (1) injunctive relief, (2) an accounting for profits, (3) damages, (4) destruction of infringing articles, (5) attorneys' fees in exceptional cases, and (6) costs. In assessing profits, the plaintiff has to prove only the gross sales made by the defendant; the defendant has the burden of proving any costs to be deducted in determining profits. If the court finds that the amount of recovery based on profits is either inadequate or excessive, the court may, in its discretion, award an amount it determines to be just. In assessing damages, the court may award up to three times the actual damages, according to the circumstances of the case. When an infringement is knowing and intentional, the court in the absence of extenuating circumstances shall award attorneys' fees plus the greater of treble profits or treble damages. In an action brought under the Federal Trademark Dilution Act of 1995, the owner of the famous mark can obtain only injunctive relief unless the person against whom the injunction is sought willfully intended to trade on the owner's reputation or to cause dilution of the famous mark. If willful intent is proven, the owner of the famous mark may also obtain the other remedies discussed.

When a person intentionally traffics in goods or services known to bear a counterfeit mark, both civil and criminal remedies are available. In addition, goods bearing the counterfeit mark may be seized and destroyed. A **counterfeit mark** is a spurious mark that is identical with, or substantially indistinguishable from, a registered mark and the use of which is likely to cause confusion, to cause mistake, or to deceive. In assessing damages for trademark counterfeiting, the court shall, unless it finds extenuating circumstances, enter judgment for three times the defendant's profits or the plaintiff's damages, whichever is greater, plus reasonable attorneys' fees. Instead of actual damages and profits, the plaintiff may elect to receive an award of statutory damages, in an amount the court considers just, between $500 and $100,000 per counterfeit mark or, if the use of the counterfeit mark was willful, not more than $1 million per counterfeit mark. Criminal sanctions include a fine of up to $2 million, imprisonment of up to ten years, or both. For a repeat offense, the limits are $5 million and twenty years, respectively. For a nonindividual offender, such as a corporation, the fine may be up to $5 million for a first offense and up to $15 million for a repeat offense.

TRADE NAMES

A **trade name** is any name used to identify a business, vocation, or occupation. Descriptive and generic words, and personal and generic names, although not proper trademarks, may become protected as trade names upon acquiring a special significance in the trade. A name acquires such significance, frequently referred to as a "secondary meaning," through its continuing and extended use in connection with specific goods or services, whereby the acquired meaning eclipses the primary meaning of the name in the minds of a substantial number of purchasers or users of the goods or services. Although they are not eligible for Federal registration under the Lanham Act, trade names are protected, and a person who palms off her goods or services by using the trade name of another is liable in damages and also may be enjoined from doing so.

COPYRIGHTS

Copyright is a form of protection provided by Federal law to authors of original works, which, under Section 102 of the Copyright Act, include literary, musical, and dramatic works; pantomimes; choreographic works; pictorial, graphic, and sculptural works; motion picture and other audiovisual works; sound recordings; and architectural works. This listing is illustrative, not exhaustive, as the Act extends copyright protection to "original works of authorship in any tangible medium of expression, now known or later developed." Section 102(a). Moreover, in 1980, the Copyright Act was amended to extend copyright protection to computer programs. Furthermore, the Semiconductor Chip Protection Act of 1984 extended protection for ten years to safeguard mask works embodied in a semiconductor chip product.

On March 1, 1989, the United States joined the Berne Convention, an international treaty protecting copyrighted works. In 1998 Congress enacted the Digital Millennium Copyright Act (DMCA), which amended the Copyright Act to implement the World Intellectual Property Organization (WIPO) Copyright Treaty and the WIPO Performances and Phonograms Treaty of 1996 by extending U.S. copyright protection to works required to be protected under these two treaties. The WIPO treaty called for adequate legal protection and effective legal remedies against the circumvention of effective technological measures that are used by copyright owners to prevent unauthorized exercise of their copyrights. The DMCA contains three principal anticircumvention provisions.

The first provision prohibits the act of circumventing a technological protection measure put in place by a copyright owner to control *access* to a copyrighted work. Under the DMCA, "to circumvent a technological measure" means "to descramble a scrambled work, to decrypt an encrypted work, or otherwise to avoid, bypass, remove, deactivate, or impair a technological measure, without the authority of the copyright owner." The second provision prohibits creating or making available technologies developed or advertised to defeat technological protections against unauthorized *access* to a copyrighted work. The third provision prohibits creating or making available technologies developed or advertised to defeat technological protections against unauthorized copying or other infringements of the exclusive rights of the copyright owner in a copyrighted work. Thus, the first two prohibitions deal with access controls while the third prohibition deals with copy controls. They make it illegal, for example, to create or distribute a computer program that can break the access or copy protection security code on an electronic book or a DVD movie.

In no case does the copyright protection accorded an original work of authorship extend to any idea, procedure, process, system, method of operation, concept, principle, or discovery, regardless of the form in which it is described, explained, illustrated, or embodied in such work. Section 102(b). Copyright protection encompasses only an *original expression* of an idea. For example, the idea of interfamily feuding cannot be copyrighted, but a particular expression of that idea in the form of a novel, drama, movie, or opera may be copyrighted.

PROCEDURE

Copyright applications are filed with the Register of Copyrights in Washington, D.C. Although copyright registration is not required, because copyright protection begins automatically as soon as the work is fixed in a tangible medium, registration is advisable, nonetheless, because it is a condition of certain remedies (statutory damages and attorneys' fees) for copyright infringement. When a work is published, it is advisable, though no longer required, to place a copyright notice on all publicly distributed copies so as to notify users about the copyright claim. If proper notice appears on the published copies to which a defendant in a copyright infringement case had access, then the defendant will be unable to mitigate actual or statutory damages by asserting a defense of innocent infringement. Section 401. Innocent infringement occurs when the infringer did not realize that the work was protected. Notice consists of (1) the symbol © or the word "Copyright" or the abbreviation "Copr."; (2) the year of first publication; and (3) the name of the owner of the copyright.

RIGHTS

As amended in 1998 by the Sonny Bono Copyright Extension Act, in most instances, copyright protection subsists for the duration of the author's life plus an additional seventy years. Section 106 of the Copyright Act gives the owner of the copyright the exclusive right to—

1. reproduce the copyrighted work in copies or recordings;
2. prepare derivative works based upon the copyrighted work;
3. distribute copies or recordings of the copyrighted work to the public by sale or other transfer of ownership or by rental, lease, or lending;
4. perform the copyrighted work publicly, in the case of literary, musical, dramatic, choreographic, pantomime, motion picture, and other audiovisual works; and
5. display the copyrighted work publicly, in the case of literary, musical, dramatic, and choreographic works, pantomimes, and pictorial, graphic, or sculptural works, including the individual images of a motion picture or other audiovisual work.

These broad rights are subject, however, to several limitations, the most important of which are "compulsory licenses" and "fair use." **Compulsory licenses** permit certain limited uses of copyrighted material upon the payment of specified royalties and compliance with statutory conditions. Section 107 codifies the common law doctrine of fair use by providing that the fair use of a copyrighted work for purposes such as criticism, comment, news reporting, teaching (including multiple copies for classroom use), scholarship, or research is not an infringement of copyright. In determining whether the use made of a work in any particular case is fair, the courts consider the following factors: (1) the purpose and character of the use, including whether such use is of a commercial nature or is for nonprofit educational purposes; (2) the nature of the copyrighted work; (3) the amount and substantiality of the portion used in relation to the copyrighted work as a whole; and (4) the effect of the use upon the potential market for or value of the copyrighted work.

OWNERSHIP

The author of a creative work owns the entire copyright. Although the actual creator of a work is usually the author, in two situations under the doctrine of **works for hire**, she is not considered the author. Section 101. First, if an employee prepares a work within the scope of her employment, her employer is considered to be the author of the work. Second, if a work is specially ordered or commissioned for certain purposes specified in the copyright statute *and* the parties expressly agree in writing that the work shall be considered a work for hire, the person commissioning the work is deemed to be the author. The kinds of works subject to becoming works for hire by commission include contributions to collective works; parts of motion pictures or other audiovisual works; translations; supplementary works such as prefaces, illustrations, or afterwords; compilations; instructional texts; and tests. In a work made for hire the copyright lasts for a term of 95 years from the year of its first publication, or a term of 120 years from the year of its creation, whichever expires first.

The ownership of a copyright may be transferred in whole or in part by conveyance, will, or intestate succession. Section 201. A transfer of copyright ownership, other than by operation of law, is not valid, however, unless it is memorialized in a note or memorandum signed by the owner of the rights conveyed or by the owner's duly authorized agent. Section 204. An author may terminate any transfer of copyright ownership, other than that of a work for hire, during the five-year period beginning thirty-five years after the transfer was granted. Section 203.

Ownership of a copyright or of any of the exclusive rights under a copyright is distinct from the ownership of any material object that embodies the work. Transferring the ownership of any material object, including the copy or recording in which the work was first fixed, does not in itself convey any rights in the copyrighted work embodied in the object; nor, in the absence of an agreement, does the transfer of copyright ownership or of any exclusive rights under a copyright convey property rights in any material object. Section 202. Thus, the purchase of this textbook neither affects the publisher's copyright nor authorizes the purchaser to make and sell copies of the book. The purchaser may, however, rent, lend, or resell the book.

INFRINGEMENT AND REMEDIES

Infringement occurs whenever somebody exercises, without authorization, the rights exclusively reserved for the copyright owner. Infringement need not be intentional. To prove infringement, the plaintiff need only establish that he owns the copyright and that the defendant violated one or more of the plaintiff's exclusive rights under the copyright. Proof of infringement usually consists of showing that the allegedly infringing work is substantially similar to the copyrighted work and that the alleged infringer had access to the copyrighted work. The DMCA amended the Copyright Act to create limitations on the liability of online providers for copyright infringement when engaging in certain activities.

To be the subject of a suit for infringement, the copyright must be registered with the Copyright Office, unless the work is a Berne Convention work whose country of origin is not the United States. For an infringement occurring after registration, the following remedies are available: (1) injunction; (2) the impoundment and, possibly, destruction of infringing articles; (3) actual damages, plus profits made by the infringer that are additional to those damages, *or* statutory damages of at least $750 but no more than $30,000 ($150,000 if the infringement is willful), according to what the court determines to be just; (4) in the court's discretion, costs including reasonable attorneys' fees to the prevailing party; and (5) criminal penalties of a fine and/or up to one year's imprisonment for willful infringement for purposes of commercial advantage or private financial gain.

In 1997 Congress enacted the No Electronic Theft Act (NET Act) to close a loophole in the Copyright Act, which permitted infringers to pirate copyrighted works willfully and knowingly, so long as they did not do so for profit. The NET Act amended Federal copyright law to define "financial gain" to include the receipt of anything of value, including the receipt of other copyrighted works. The NET Act also clarified that when Internet users or any other individuals distribute copyrighted works broadly, even if they do not intend to profit personally, they have violated the Copyright Act. The Act accomplished this by imposing penalties for willfully infringing a copyright (1) for purposes of commercial advantage or private financial gain, or (2) by reproducing or distributing, including by electronic means, during any 180-day period, one or more copies of one or more copyrighted works with a total retail value of more than $1,000. It also extended the statute of limitations for criminal copyright infringement from three to five years. Finally, it increased criminal penalties for certain copyright violations. Imprisonment for up to five years (ten years for subsequent offenses) may be imposed for willful infringement if at least ten copies with a total retail value of more than $2,500 in a 180-day period are reproduced or distributed.

The Family Entertainment and Copyright Act of 2005 established criminal penalties for willful copyright infringement by the distribution of a computer program, musical work, motion picture or other audiovisual work, or sound recording being prepared for commercial distribution by making it available on a computer network accessible to members of the public, if the person knew or should have known that the work was intended for commercial distribution. In essence, it prohibits (1) bootlegging of copyrighted audio and video material, or (2) recording a cinema-released film on videotape from the audience (the primary way bootleggers make illegal copies of recently released movies). The bill does, however, allow for the sale and use of technology that can skip content of films in order to edit out language, violence, or sex. The criminal penalties are a fine and/or imprisonment for up to three years (six years for subsequent offenses), but if the infringement was for purposes of commercial advantage or private financial gain, then imprisonment may be imposed for up to five years (ten years for subsequent offenses).

The Anti-counterfeiting Amendments Act of 2004 prohibits knowingly trafficking in (1) a counterfeit or illicit label of a copy of a computer program, motion picture (or other audiovisual work), literary work, or pictorial, graphic, or sculptural work, a phonorecord, a work of visual art, or documentation or packaging; or (2) counterfeit documentation or packaging. Violators are subject to fines and/or imprisonment of up to five years. In addition, a copyright owner who is injured, or threatened with injury, may bring a civil action to obtain (1) an injunction; (2) impoundment and possible destruction of infringing articles; (3) reasonable attorneys' fees and costs; and (4) actual damages and any additional profits of the violator or statutory damages of at least $2,500 but no more than $25,000. Moreover, the court may increase an award of damages by three times the amount that would otherwise be awarded for a violation occurring within three years after a final judgment was entered for a previous violation.

PATENTS

Through a **patent**, the Federal government grants an inventor a monopolistic right to make, use, or sell an invention to the absolute exclusion of others for the period of the patent. The patent owner may also profit by selling the patent or by licensing others to use the patent on a royalty basis. The patent may not be renewed, however: upon expiration, the invention enters the "public domain," and anyone may use it.

PATENTABILITY

The Patent Act specifies those inventions that may be patented as **utility patents**. Section 101 provides:

> Whoever invents or discovers any new and useful process, machine, manufacture, or composition of matter, or any new and useful improvement thereof, may obtain a patent therefor, subject to the conditions and requirements of this title.

Thus, naturally occurring substances are not patentable, as the invention must be made or modified by humans. For example, the discovery of a bacterium with useful properties is not patentable, whereas the manufacture of a genetically engineered bacterium is. By the same token, laws of nature, principles, bookkeeping systems, fundamental truths, methods of calculation, and ideas are not patentable. Accordingly, as Chief Justice Burger noted in *Diamond, Commissioner of Patents and Trademarks v. Chakrabarty*, "Einstein could not patent his law that $E = mc^2$, nor could Newton have patented the law of gravity." Similarly, isolated computer programs are not patentable, although, as mentioned above, they may be copyrighted.

To be patentable as a utility patent, the process, machine, manufacture, or composition of matter must meet three criteria:

1. *Novelty.* The invention must not conflict with a prior pending application or a previously issued patent;
2. *Utility.* The invention must possess specific and substantial usefulness, which must be affirmatively disclosed by the application; and
3. *Nonobviousness.* The invention, in light of the prior art, must not be obvious to a person skilled in such prior art.

In addition to utility patents, the Patent Act provides for plant patents and design patents. A **plant patent** protects the exclusive right to reproduce a new and distinctive variety of asexually reproducing plant. Asexually propagated plants are those that are reproduced by means other than from seeds, such as by the rooting of cuttings as well as by layering, budding, or grafting. Plant patents require (1) novelty, (2) distinctiveness, and (3) nonobviousness. A **design patent** protects a new, original, ornamental design for an article of manufacture. A design patent protects only the appearance of an article—not its structural or functional features. Design patents require (1) novelty, (2) ornamentality, and (3) nonobviousness.

Utility and plant patents have a term that begins on the date of the patent's grant and ends twenty years from the date of application, subject to extensions for statutorily specified delays. Design patents have a term of fourteen years from the date of grant.

PROCEDURE

The U.S. Patent and Trademark Office issues a patent upon the basis of a patent application containing a *specification*, which describes how the invention works, and *claims*, which describe the features that make the invention patentable. The applicant must be the inventor. Before granting a patent, the Patent Office thoroughly examines the prior art and determines whether the submitted invention is nonobvious and has novelty and utility (or distinctiveness or ornamentality, in the case of plant or design patents). An application for a patent is confidential, and the Patent Office will not divulge its contents. This confidentiality ends, however, upon the granting of the patent. Unlike rights under a copyright, no monopoly rights arise until the Patent Office actually issues a patent. Therefore, anyone is free to make, use, and sell an invention for which a patent application is filed until the patent has been granted.

The rights granted by a U.S. patent extend only to the United States. A person desiring a patent in another country must apply for a patent in that country. The Patent Cooperation Treaty, adhered to by the United States and more than 140 other countries, facilitates the filing of applications for patents on the same invention in member countries by providing for centralized filing procedures and a standardized application format.

Congress amended the Patent Act to require the publication of certain utility and plant patent applications eighteen months after filing even if the patent has not yet been granted. This requirement applies only to those patent applications that are filed in other countries that require publication after eighteen months or under the Patent Cooperation Treaty. An applicant may obtain a reasonable royalty from a third party who between publication and issuance of the patent infringes it, provided the third party had actual notice of the published application. An applicant whose application is rejected may apply for reexamination. If the application is again rejected, the applicant may appeal to the Patent and Trademark Office's Board of Appeals and from there to the Federal courts.

INFRINGEMENT

Anyone who, without permission, makes, uses, or sells a patented invention is a **direct infringer**, whereas a person who actively encourages another to make, use, offer to sell, or sell a patented invention without permission is an **indirect infringer**. A **contributory infringer** is one who knowingly sells or offers to sell a part or component of a patented invention, unless the component is a staple or commodity or is suitable for a substantial noninfringing use.

◆ FIGURE 40-1: **Intellectual Property**

	Trade Secrets	Trade Symbols	Copyrights	Patents
What Is Protected	Information	Mark	Work of authorship	Invention
Rights Protected	Use or sell	Use or sell	Reproduce, prepare derivative works, distribute, perform, or display	Make, use, or sell
Duration	Until disclosed	Until abandoned	Usually author's life plus seventy years	For utility and plant patents, twenty years from application; For design patents, fourteen years from grant
Federally Protected	No	Yes	Yes	Yes
Requirements for Protection	Valuable secret	Distinctive	Original and fixed	Novel, useful, and nonobvious

While good faith and ignorance are defenses to contributory infringement, they are not defenses to direct infringement. To recover damages a patent owner must mark a patented article with the word "Patent" and the number of the patent or give actual notice to an infringer.

The rights under a patent do not extend beyond the first sale; that is, the purchaser of a patented item is permitted to use or resell that item. The right to use a purchased item includes the right to repair it so long as the repair does not constitute reconstruction, which would infringe upon the patent holder's exclusive right to make the invention.

REMEDIES

If a patent is infringed, the patent owner may sue for relief in Federal court. The remedies for infringement under the Patent Act are (1) injunctive relief; (2) damages adequate to compensate the plaintiff but "in no event less than a reasonable royalty for the use made of the invention by the infringer"; (3) treble damages, when appropriate; (4) attorneys' fees in exceptional cases, such as those that involve knowing infringement; and (5) costs.

◆ **SEE FIGURE 40-1: Intellectual Property**

CHAPTER SUMMARY

TRADE SECRETS
Definition commercially valuable, secret information
Protection owner of a trade secret may obtain damages or injunctive relief when the secret is misappropriated (wrongfully used) by an employee or a competitor

TRADE SYMBOLS
Types of Trade Symbols
* *Trademark* distinctive symbol, word, or design that is used to identify the manufacturer
* *Service Mark* distinctive symbol, word, or design that is used to identify a provider's services
* *Certification Mark* distinctive symbol, word, or design used with goods or services to certify specific characteristics
* *Collective Mark* distinctive symbol used to indicate membership in an organization

Registration to be registered and thus protected by the Lanham Act, a mark must be distinctive and not immoral, deceptive, or scandalous
Infringement occurs when a person without authorization uses a substantially indistinguishable mark that is likely to cause confusion, mistake, or deception
Remedies the Lanham Act provides the following remedies for infringement: injunctive relief, profits, damages, destruction of infringing articles, costs, and, in exceptional cases, attorneys' fees

TRADE NAMES
Definition any name used to identify a business, vocation, or occupation
Protection may not be registered under the Lanham Act, but infringement is prohibited
Remedies damages and injunctions are available if infringement occurs

COPYRIGHTS
Definition exclusive right, usually for the author's life plus seventy years, to original works of authorship
Procedure registration is not required but provides additional remedies for infringement
Rights copyright protection provides the exclusive right to (1) reproduce the copyrighted work, (2) prepare derivative works based on the work, (3) distribute copies of the work, and (4) perform or display the work publicly
Ownership the author of the copyrighted work is usually the owner of the copyright, which may be transferred in whole or in part
Infringement occurs when someone exercises the copyright owner's rights without authorization

Remedies if infringement occurs after registration, the following remedies are available: (1) injunction, (2) impoundment and possible destruction of infringing articles, (3) actual damages plus profits or statutory damages, (4) costs, and (5) criminal penalties

---

PATENTS **Definition** the exclusive right to an invention for twenty years from the date of application for utility and plant patents; fourteen years from grant for design patents
Patentability to be patentable, the invention must be (1) novel, (2) useful, and (3) not obvious
Procedure patents are issued upon application to and after examination by the U.S. Patent and Trademark Office
Infringement occurs when anyone without permission makes, uses, or sells a patented invention
Remedies for infringement of a patent are (1) injunctive relief; (2) damages; (3) treble damages, where appropriate; (4) attorneys' fees; and (5) costs

CHAPTER 41
Antitrust

The economic community is best served by free competition in trade and industry. It is in the public interest that quality, price, and service in an open, competitive market for goods and services be determining factors in the business rivalry for the customer's dollar. Nevertheless, in lieu of competing, businesses would prefer to eliminate their rivals and consequently gain a position from which they could dictate both the price of their goods and the quantity they produce. Although to eliminate competition by producing a better product is the goal of a business, some businesses try to effect this elimination through illegitimate means, such as fixing prices and allocating exclusive territories to certain competitors within an industry. The law of antitrust prohibits such activities and attempts to ensure free and fair competition in the marketplace.

The common law has traditionally favored competition and has held agreements and contracts in restraint of trade illegal and unenforceable. In addition, several States enacted antitrust statutes during the 1800s. The latter half of the nineteenth century, however, disclosed concentrations of economic power in the form of "trusts" and "combinations" that were too powerful and widespread to be effectively curbed by State action. In 1890, this awesome growth of corporate power prompted Congress to enact the Sherman Antitrust Act, which was the first Federal statute in this field. Since then, Congress has enacted other antitrust statutes, including the Clayton Act, the Robinson-Patman Act, and the Federal Trade Commission Act. These statutes prohibit anticompetitive practices and seek to prevent unreasonable concentrations of economic power that stifle or weaken competition.

SHERMAN ACT

Section 1 of the Sherman Act prohibits contracts, combinations, and conspiracies that restrain trade, while Section 2 prohibits monopolies and attempts to monopolize. Failure to comply with either section is a criminal felony and subjects the offender to fine or imprisonment, or both. As amended by the Antitrust Criminal Penalty Enhancement and Reform Act of 2004, the Act subjects individual offenders to imprisonment of up to ten years and fines up to $1 million, while corporate offenders are subject to fines of up to $100 million per violation. Moreover, the Sherman Act empowers the Federal district courts to issue injunctions restraining violations, and anyone injured by a violation is entitled to recover in a civil action **treble damages**, that is, three times the amount of the actual loss sustained. In addition, State Attorneys General may bring suit for treble damages on behalf of citizens of their States. The U.S. Justice Department and the Federal Trade Commission (FTC) have the duty to institute appropriate enforcement proceedings other than treble damage actions.

Moreover, the Justice Department has expanded its policy of enforcement regarding the Sherman Act to cover conduct by foreign companies that harms U.S. exports. Under this policy, the department examines conduct to determine whether it would violate the law if it occurred within the borders of the United States. The department has indicated that it will focus primarily on boycotts and cartels that injure the export of U.S. products and services.

RESTRAINT OF TRADE

Section 1 of the Sherman Act provides that "[e]very contract, combination in the form of trust or otherwise, or conspiracy, in restraint of trade or commerce among the several states, or with foreign nations is hereby declared to be illegal." Because the language of the section is so broad, judicial interpretation has played a significant role in establishing the elements that constitute a violation.

STANDARDS As noted, Section 1 prohibits every contract, combination, or conspiracy in restraint of trade. Taken literally, this prohibition would invalidate every unperformed contract. For example, under a strict interpretation of the section, a contract in which a seller agrees to supply a buyer with one thousand pounds of grapes, no one but the seller would be permitted to fulfill the buyer's need for those one

COLUMN: © PHOTOGRAPHEROLYMPUS   CLOUDS: © KERTLIS

thousand pounds of grapes, and the seller would not be allowed to sell those grapes to any other buyer. This agreement would therefore restrain trade. To avoid such a broad and impractical application, the courts have interpreted this section to invalidate only *unreasonable* restraints of trade:

> The true test of legality is whether the restraint imposed is such as merely regulates and perhaps thereby promotes competition or whether it is such as may suppress or even destroy competition. To determine that question the courts must ordinarily consider the facts peculiar to the business to which the restraint is applied; its condition before and after the restraint was imposed; the nature of the restraint and its effect, actual or probable. The history of the restraint, the evil believed to exist, the reason for adopting the particular remedy, the purpose or end sought to be attained, are all relevant facts. This is not because a good intention will save an otherwise objectionable regulation or the reverse; but because knowledge of intent may help the court to interpret facts and to predict consequences. *Chicago Board of Trade v. United States*, 246 U.S. 231 (1918).

This flexible standard, known as the **rule of reason test**, requires the courts, in determining whether a challenged practice unreasonably restricts competition, to consider a variety of factors, including the makeup of the relevant industry, the defendants' positions within that industry, the ability of the defendants' competitors to respond to the challenged practice, and the defendants' purpose in adopting the restraint. After reviewing the various factors, a court determines whether the challenged restraint unreasonably restricts competition. By requiring courts to balance the anticompetitive effects of every questioned restraint against its procompetitive effects, this standard places a substantial burden upon the judicial system. The U.S. Supreme Court addressed this problem by declaring certain categories of restraints to be unreasonable by their very nature, that is, **illegal** *per se*:

> [T]here are certain agreements or practices which because of their pernicious effect on competition and lack of any redeeming virtue are conclusively presumed to be unreasonable and therefore illegal without elaborate inquiry as to the precise harm they have caused or the business excuse for their use. This principle of *per se* unreasonableness not only makes the type of restraints which are proscribed by the Sherman Act more certain to the benefit of everyone concerned, but it also avoids the necessity for an incredibly complicated and prolonged economic investigation into the entire history of the industry involved, as well as related industries, in an effort to determine at large

whether a particular restraint has been unreasonable—an inquiry so often wholly fruitless when undertaken. *Northern Pacific Railway Co. v. United States*, 356 U.S.1 (1958).

Characterizing a type of restraint as *per se* illegal therefore has a significant effect on the prosecution of an antitrust suit. In such a case, the plaintiff need only show that the type of restraint occurred; she does not need to prove that the restraint limited competition. Furthermore, the defendants may not defend on the basis that the restraint is reasonable. Additionally, as noted in *Northern Pacific Railway*, the court is not required to conduct extensive, and often difficult, economic analysis. Not surprisingly, the ease of applying the *per se* rule has helped to deter those restraints subject to the rule.

More recently a third, intermediate test has been frequently used when the *per se* approach is not appropriate for the situation but the challenged conduct has obvious anticompetitive effects. Under this "quick look" rule of reason analysis, the courts will apply an **abbreviated rule of reason standard** rather than using the extensive analysis required by a full-blown rule of reason test. However, the extensiveness of the legal analysis required under the quick look test will vary based upon the circumstances, details, and logic of the restraint being reviewed.

Horizontal and Vertical Restraints A restraint of trade may be classified as either horizontal or vertical. A **horizontal restraint** involves collaboration among competitors at the same level in the chain of distribution. For example, an agreement among manufacturers, among wholesalers, or among retailers would be horizontal.

On the other hand, an agreement made by parties that are not in direct competition at the same level of distribution is a **vertical restraint**. Thus, an agreement between a manufacturer and a wholesaler is vertical.

Although the distinction between horizontal and vertical restraints can become blurred, it often determines whether a restraint is illegal *per se* or should be judged by the rule of reason test. For instance, horizontal market allocations are illegal *per se*, whereas vertical market allocations are subject to the rule of reason test.

Concerted Action Section 1 does not prohibit unilateral conduct; rather, it forbids **concerted action**. Thus, one person or business by itself cannot violate the section. An organization has the "right to deal, or refuse to deal, with whomever it likes, as long as it does so independently." *Monsanto Co. v. Spray-Rite Service Corporation*, 465 U.S. 752 (1984). For example, if a manufacturer announces its resale prices in advance and refuses to deal with those who disagree with the pricing, there is no violation of Section 1 because the manufacturer has acted alone. On the other hand, if a manufacturer and its retailers together agree that the manufacturer will sell only to those retailers who agree to sell at a specified price, there may be a violation of Section 1.

For purposes of the concerted action requirement, a firm and its employees are viewed as one entity. The same rule is also true for a corporation and its wholly owned subsidiaries; thus, the Sherman Act is not violated when a parent and its wholly owned subsidiary agree to a restraint in trade. *Copperwald Corp. v. Independence Tube Corp.*, 467 U.S. 752 (1984). The Supreme Court has yet to decide, however, whether a parent and its partially owned subsidiary may violate Section 1.

The concerted action requirement may be established by an express agreement. Not surprisingly, however, an express agreement often is nonexistent, leaving the court to infer an agreement between the parties from circumstantial evidence:

No formal agreement is necessary to constitute an unlawful conspiracy. Often crimes are a matter of inference deduced from the acts of the person accused and done in pursuance of a criminal purpose. Where the conspiracy is proved, as here, from the evidence of the action taken in concert by the parties to it, it is all the more convincing proof of an intent to exercise the power of exclusion acquired through the conspiracy. The essential combination or conspiracy in violation of the Sherman Act may be found in a course of dealings or other circumstances as well as in any exchange of words.... Where the circumstances are such as to warrant a jury in finding that the conspirators had a unity of purpose or a common design and understanding, or a meeting of minds in an unlawful arrangement, the conclusion that a conspiracy is established is justified. *American Tobacco Co. v. United States*, 328 U.S. 781 (1946).

Nonetheless, similar patterns of conduct among competitors, called **conscious parallelism**, are not sufficient in themselves to suggest a conspiracy in violation of Section 1. Actual conspiracy requires an additional factor, such as complex action that, to benefit the competitors, requires the participation of each or indications of a traditional conspiracy, such as identical sealed bids from each competitor.

Joint ventures, which are discussed in *Chapter 31*, are a form of business association organized to carry out a particular business enterprise. Competitors frequently will pool their resources to share costs and to eliminate wasteful redundancy.

The validity under antitrust law of a joint venture generally depends on the competitors' primary purpose in forming it. A joint venture that was not formed to fix prices or divide markets will be judged under the rule of reason. However, because uncertainty about the legality of joint ventures seemed to discourage their use for joint research and development, Congress passed the National Cooperative Research Act to facilitate such applications. The Act provides that joint ventures in the research and development of new technology are to be judged under the rule of reason test and that treble damages do not apply to ventures formed in violation of Section 1 if those forming the venture have notified the Justice Department and the FTC of their intent to form the joint venture.

PRICE FIXING Price fixing is an agreement with the purpose or effect of inhibiting price competition; such an agreement may attempt to raise, depress, fix, peg, or stabilize prices. Price fixing is the primary and most serious example of a *per se* violation under the Sherman Act. As held in *United States v. Socony-Vacuum Oil Co.*, 310 U.S. 150 (1940), all **horizontal** price-fixing agreements are illegal *per se*. This prohibition not only covers any agreement between sellers to establish the *maximum* prices at which certain commodities or services will be offered for sale but encompasses agreements establishing *minimum* prices as well.

The U.S. Supreme Court has condemned not only agreements among horizontal competitors that directly fix prices but also agreements whose effect on price is indirect. For example, in *Catalano, Inc. v. Target Sales, Inc.*, 446 U.S. 643 (1980), the Court held that an agreement among beer wholesalers to eliminate interest-free short-term credit on sales to beer retailers was illegal *per se*. The Court viewed the credit terms "as an inseparable part of price" and concluded that the agreement to eliminate interest-free short-term credit was equivalent to an agreement to eliminate discounts and was thus an agreement to fix prices.

In a 2007 case, *Leegin Creative Leather Products, Inc v. PSKS, Inc.*, 551 U.S 877, 127 S.Ct. 2705, 168 L.Ed.2d 623, the U.S. Supreme Court ruled that vertical price restraints are to be judged by the rule of reason. This decision overruled a 1911 U.S. Supreme Court decision that established the rule that it is *per se* illegal under Section 1 of the Sherman Act for a manufacturer to agree with its retailers to set the minimum price the retailer can charge for the manufacturer's goods.

MARKET ALLOCATIONS Direct price fixing is not the only way to control prices. Another method involves **market allocation**, whereby competitors agree not to compete with each other in specific markets, which may be defined by geographic area, customer type, or product class. All **horizontal** agreements to divide markets have been declared illegal *per se*, because they confer upon the firm remaining in the market a monopolistic control over price. Thus, if Suny and

RGE, both manufacturers of televisions, agree that Suny shall have the exclusive right to sell televisions in Illinois and Iowa and that RGE shall have the exclusive right in Minnesota and Wisconsin, Suny and RGE have committed a *per se* violation of Section 1 of the Sherman Act. Likewise, if Suny and RGE agree that Suny shall have the exclusive right to sell televisions to Walmart and that RGE shall sell exclusively to Target, or that Suny shall have the exclusive right to manufacture nineteen-inch televisions while RGE alone manufactures twenty-six-inch sets, they are also in *per se* violation of Section 1 of the Sherman Antitrust Act. Horizontal market allocations may be found not only on the manufacturing level but also on the wholesale or retail level.

No longer illegal *per se*, **vertical** territorial and customer restrictions are now judged by the rule of reason. This change in approach resulted from a U.S. Supreme Court decision that mandated the lower Federal courts to balance the positive effect of vertical market restrictions upon interbrand competition against the negative effects upon intrabrand competition. Consequently, in some situations, vertical market restrictions will be found legitimate if, on balance, they do not inhibit competition in the relevant market.

The U.S. Department of Justice has issued a "market structure screen," under which the Justice Department will not challenge restraints by a firm having less than 10 percent of the relevant market or a "Vertical Restraint Index" (a measure of relative market share) indicating that neither collusion nor exclusion is possible. The concept of relevant market is discussed later, in the section on monopolization.

BOYCOTTS As noted, Section 1 of the Sherman Act applies not to unilateral action but only to agreements or combinations. Accordingly, a seller's refusal to deal with any particular buyer does not violate the Act, and a manufacturer thus can refuse to sell to a retailer who persists in selling below the manufacturer's suggested retail price. On the other hand, when two or more firms agree not to deal with a third party, their agreement constitutes a **concerted refusal to deal**, or a group boycott, which may violate Section 1 of the Sherman Act. Such a boycott may be clearly anticompetitive, eliminating competition or reducing market entry.

Some group boycotts are illegal *per se*, while others are subject to the rule of reason. Group boycotts designed to eliminate a competitor or to force that competitor to meet a group standard are illegal *per se* if the group has market power. On the other hand, cooperative arrangements "designed to increase economic efficiency and render markets more, rather than less, competitive" are subject to the rule of reason.

Finally, most courts hold that the *per se* rule of illegality for concerted refusals to deal extends only to horizontal boycotts, not to vertical refusals to deal. Most courts have held that a rule of reason test should govern all nonprice vertical restraints, including concerted refusals to deal.

TYING ARRANGEMENTS A tying arrangement occurs when the seller of a product, service, or intangible (the "tying" product) conditions its sale on the buyer's purchasing a second product, service, or intangible (the "tied" product) from the seller. For example, assume that Xerox, a major manufacturer of photocopying equipment, were to require that all purchasers of its photocopiers also purchase from Xerox all of the paper they would use with the copiers. Xerox thereby would tie the sale of its photocopier—the *tying* product—to the sale of paper—the *tied* product.

Because tying arrangements limit buyers' freedom of choice and may exclude competitors, the law closely scrutinizes such agreements. A tying arrangement exists in situations in which a seller exploits its economic power in one market to expand its empire into another market. When the seller has considerable economic power in the tying product and more than an insubstantial amount of interstate commerce is affected in the tied product, the tying arrangement will be *per se* illegal. The courts may establish a seller's economic power by showing that (1) the seller occupied a dominant position in the tying market, (2) the seller's product enjoys an advantage not shared by its competitors in the tying market, or (3) a substantial number of customers have accepted the tying arrangement, and the sole explanation for their willingness to comply is the seller's economic power in the tying market. If the seller lacks economic power, the tying arrangement is judged by the rule of reason test.

◆ SEE FIGURE 41-1: **Restraints of Trade under Sherman Act**

MONOPOLIES

Economic analysis indicates that a monopolist will use its power to limit production and increase prices. Accordingly, a monopolistic market will produce fewer goods than a competitive market would and will sell those goods at higher prices. To address the problem of monopolization, Section 2 of the Sherman Act prohibits monopolies and all attempts or conspiracies to monopolize. Thus, Section 2 prohibits both agreements among businesses and, unlike Section 1, unilateral conduct by one firm.

MONOPOLIZATION Although the language of Section 2 appears to prohibit without exception *all* monopolization, the courts have required that in addition to merely possessing market power, a firm must have either attained the monopoly power unfairly or abused that power, once attained. Possession of monopoly power is not in itself considered a violation of Section 2 because a firm may have obtained such power through its skills in developing, marketing, and selling products; that is, through the very

◆ FIGURE 41-1: **Restraints of Trade under Sherman Act**

Type of Restraint	Standard	
	Per Se Illegal	Rule of Reason
Price fixing	Horizontal	Vertical
Market allocations	Horizontal	Vertical
Group boycotts or refusals to deal	Horizontal Vertical (Minority)	Vertical (Majority)
Tying arrangements	If seller has economic power in tying product and affects a substantial amount of interstate commerce in the tied product	If seller lacks economic power in tying product

competitive conduct that the antitrust laws are designed to promote.

Because it is extremely rare to find an unregulated industry with only one firm, determining the presence of monopoly power involves defining the degree of market dominance that constitutes such power. Monopoly power is the ability to control prices or to exclude competitors from the marketplace. In grappling with this question of power, the courts have developed a number of criteria, but the prevalent test is market share. A market share greater than 75 percent generally indicates monopoly power, whereas a share less than 50 percent does not. A share between 50 percent and 75 percent share is inconclusive.

Market share is a firm's fractional share of the total relevant product and geographic markets, but defining these relevant markets is often a difficult and subjective task for the courts. The relevant *product market* includes products that are substitutable for the firm's product on the basis of price, quality, and elasticity. For example, although brick and wood siding are both used on building exteriors, they would not likely be considered part of the same product market. On the other hand, Coca-Cola and Pepsi are both soft drinks and would be considered part of the same product market.

The relevant *geographic market* is that territory in which the firm makes sales of its products or services. This may be at the local, regional, or national level. For instance, the relevant geographic market for the manufacture and sale of aluminum might be national, whereas that of a taxicab operating company would be local. The scope of a geographic market depends upon factors such as transportation costs, the type of product or services, and the location of competitors and customers.

If sufficient monopoly power has been proved, the law then must show that the firm has engaged in **unfair conduct**. The courts, however, have yet to agree upon what

constitutes such conduct. One judicial approach is to place upon a firm possessing monopoly power the burden of proving that it acquired such power passively or that the power was "thrust" upon it. An alternative view is that monopoly power, when coupled with conduct designed to exclude competitors, violates Section 2. A third approach requires monopoly power plus some type of predatory practice, such as pricing below marginal costs. For example, one case that adopted the third approach held that a firm does not violate Section 2 of the Sherman Act if it attained its market share through either (1) research, technical innovation, or a superior product, or (2) ordinary marketing methods available to all. *Telex Corp. v. IBM*, 510 F.2d 894 (10th Cir. 1975).

The U.S. Supreme Court decision in *Aspen Skiing Co. v. Aspen Highlands Skiing Corp.*, 472 U.S. 585 (1985), appears to combine these approaches. The Court held that "[i]f a firm has been attempting to exclude rivals on some basis other than efficiency, it is fair to characterize its behavior as predatory."

To date, however, the U.S. Supreme Court has yet to define the exact conduct, beyond the mere possession of monopoly power, that violates Section 2. To do so, the Court must resolve the complex and conflicting policies this most basic question regarding monopolies involves. On the one hand, condemning fairly acquired monopoly power—that acquired "merely by virtue of superior skill, foresight, and industry"—penalizes firms that compete effectively. On the other hand, permitting firms with monopoly power to continue provides them the opportunity to lower output and raise prices, thereby injuring consumers.

ATTEMPTS TO MONOPOLIZE Section 2 also prohibits attempts to monopolize. As with monopolization, the courts have had difficulty developing a standard that distinguishes undesirable conduct likely to engender a monopoly from healthy competitive conduct. The standard test applied by the courts requires proof of a specific intent to monopolize plus a dangerous probability of success; however, this test neither defines an "intent" nor provides a standard of power by which to measure "success." Recent cases suggest that the greater the measure of market power a firm acquires, the less flagrant must its conduct be to constitute an attempt. These cases do not, however, specify any threshold level of market power.

CONSPIRACIES TO MONOPOLIZE Section 2 also condemns conspiracies to monopolize. Few cases involve this offense alone, as any conspiracy to monopolize would also constitute a combination in restraint of trade in violation of Section 1. Because of the overlap between these two provisions, some scholars have stated that the offense of conspiracy to monopolize is "redundant."

CLAYTON ACT

In 1914, Congress strengthened the Sherman Act by adopting the Clayton Act, which was expressly designed "to supplement existing laws against unlawful restraints and monopolies." The Act is intended to stop trade practices before they become restraints of trade or monopolies forbidden by the Sherman Act. The Clayton Act provides only for civil actions, not for criminal penalties. Private parties may bring civil actions in Federal court for treble damages and attorneys' fees. In addition, the Justice Department and the FTC are authorized to bring civil actions, including proceedings in equity, to prevent and restrict violations of the Act.

The substantive provisions of the Clayton Act deal with price discrimination, tying contracts, exclusive dealing, mergers, and interlocking directorates. Section 2, which deals with price discrimination, was amended and rewritten by the Robinson-Patman Act, discussed later. In addition, the Clayton Act exempts labor, agricultural, and horticultural organizations from all antitrust laws.

TYING CONTRACTS AND EXCLUSIVE DEALING

Section 3 of the Clayton Act prohibits tying arrangements and exclusive dealing, selling, or leasing arrangements that prevent purchasers from dealing with the seller's competitors and which *may* substantially lessen competition or *tend* to create a monopoly. This section is intended to attack incipient anticompetitive practices before they ripen into violations of Section 1 or 2 of the Sherman Act. Unlike the Sherman Act, however, Section 3 applies only to practices involving commodities, not to those that involve services, intangibles, or land.

Tying arrangements, which were discussed in the sections covering the Sherman Act, have been labeled by the Supreme Court as serving "hardly any purpose beyond the suppression of competition." Although the Court at one time indicated that different standards applied under the Sherman Act and the Clayton Act, recent lower court cases suggest that the same rules now govern both types of actions.

Exclusive dealing arrangements are agreements by which the seller or lessor of a product conditions the agreement upon the buyer's or lessor's promise not to deal in the goods of a competitor. For example, a manufacturer of razors might require retailers wishing to sell its line of shaving equipment to agree not to carry competing merchandise. Such conduct, although treated more leniently than tying arrangements, violates Section 3 if it tends to create a monopoly or may substantially lessen competition. The courts regard exclusive dealing arrangements more tolerantly because such arrangements may be procompetitive to the extent that they benefit buyers, and thus, indirectly, ultimate consumers, by ensuring supplies, deterring price increases, and enabling long-term planning on the basis of known costs.

MERGERS

In the United States, corporate mergers have played a significant role in reshaping both the structure of corporations and our economic system. Mergers are horizontal, vertical, or conglomerate, depending upon the relationship between the acquirer and the acquired company. A **horizontal merger** involves the acquisition by a company of all or part of the stock or assets of a competing company. For example, if IBM were to acquire Apple, this would be a horizontal merger. A **vertical** merger is a company's acquisition of one of its customers or suppliers. A vertical merger is a *forward* merger if the acquiring company purchases a customer, such as the purchase of Revco Discount Drug Stores by Procter & Gamble. A vertical merger is a *backward* merger if the acquiring company purchases a supplier, for example, Circuit City's purchase of Maytag Appliance. The third type of merger, the **conglomerate merger**, is a catchall category that covers all acquisitions not involving a competitor, customer, or supplier.

Section 7 of the Clayton Act prohibits a corporation from merging or acquiring stock or assets of another corporation where such action would lessen competition substantially or would tend to create a monopoly.

Section 7 of the Clayton Act was intended to arrest the anticompetitive effects of market power in their incipiency. The core question is whether a merger may substantially lessen competition, and necessarily requires a prediction of the merger's impact on competition, present and future. The section can deal only with probabilities, not with certainties. And there is certainly no requirement that the anticompetitive power manifest itself in anticompetitive action before §7 can be called into play. If the enforcement of §7 turned on the existence of actual anticompetitive practices, the congressional policy of thwarting such practices in their incipiency would be frustrated. *F.T.C. v. Procter & Gamble Co.*, 386 U.S. 568 (1967).

The principal objective of the antitrust law governing mergers is to maintain competition. Accordingly, horizontal mergers are scrutinized most stringently. Factors that the courts consider in reviewing the legality of a horizontal merger include the market share of each of the merging firms, the degree of industry concentration, the number of firms in the industry, entry barriers, market trends, the strength of other competitors in the industry, the character and history of the merging firms, market demand, and the extent of industry price competition. The leading Supreme Court cases on horizontal mergers date from the 1960s and early 1970s. Since then, lower Federal courts, the Department of Justice, and the FTC have emphasized antitrust's goal of promoting economic efficiency. Accordingly, while the Supreme Court cases remain the law of the land, recent lower court decisions reflect a greater willingness to tolerate industry concentrations. Nevertheless, the government continues to prosecute, and the courts continue to condemn, horizontal mergers that are likely to hurt consumers.

Though vertical mergers are far less likely to be challenged, the Justice Department and the FTC have attacked vertical mergers that threatened to raise entry barriers in the industry or to foreclose other firms in the acquiring firm's industry from competitively significant customers or suppliers. While the Supreme Court has not decided a vertical merger case since 1972, recent decisions indicate that at least some lower courts have been willing to condemn only those vertical mergers that clearly show anticompetitive effects.

Finally, conglomerate mergers have been challenged only (1) where one of the merging firms would be highly likely to enter the market of the other firm or (2) where the merged company would be disproportionately large as compared with the largest competitors in its industry.

The Justice Department and the FTC have both indicated that they will be primarily concerned with horizontal mergers in highly or moderately concentrated industries and that they question the benefits of challenging vertical and conglomerate mergers. Both the Justice Department and the FTC have justified this policy on the basis that the latter two types of mergers are necessary to transfer assets to their most productive use and that any challenge to such mergers would impose costs on consumers without corresponding benefits.

Antitrust law, as currently applied, focuses on the size of the merged firm in relation to the relevant market, not on the resulting entity's absolute size. In 1992 (subsequently revised in 1997 and 2010), the Justice Department and the FTC jointly issued new Horizontal Merger Guidelines to replace their earlier and separate guidelines (originally issued in 1968). In doing so, the two agencies sought to prevent market power that results in "a transfer of wealth from buyers to sellers or a misallocation of resources." The guidelines are designed to provide an analytical framework to judge the impact of potential mergers:

The 2010 guidelines are intended to identify harmful mergers while avoiding unnecessary interference with those mergers that are economically beneficial or likely will have no competitive effect on the market. "These guidelines are intended to assist the business community ... by increasing the transparency of the analytical process." The 2010 guidelines clarify that "merger analysis does not use a single methodology but rather is a fact-specific process through which the agencies employ a variety of tools to analyze the evidence to determine whether a merger may substantially lessen competition." In addition, the 2010 rules explain (1) what sources of evidence and categories of evidence the agencies have found to be informative; (2) that market definition is not an end in itself or a necessary starting point of merger analysis; and (3) that market concentration is a useful tool to the extent it illuminates the merger's likely competitive effects. The 2010 guidelines add a new section dealing with mergers of powerful buyers and mergers between competing buyers.

The 1992, 1997, and 2010 guidelines, like their earlier counterparts, quantify market concentration through the Herfindahl-Hirschman Index (HHI) and measure a horizontal merger's impact on the index. This concentration index is calculated by summing the squares of the individual market shares of all firms in the market. An industry with only one firm would have an HHI of 10,000 (100^2). With two firms of equal size, the index would be 5,000 ($50^2 + 50^2$); with five firms of equal size, the result would be 2,000 ($20^2 + 20^2 + 20^2 + 20^2 + 20^2$). The increase a merger would cause in the index is calculated by doubling the product of the merging firms' market shares. For example, the merger of two firms with market shares of 5 percent and 10 percent, respectively, would increase the index by 100 ($5 \times 10 \times 2 = 100$).

The 2010 guidelines classify an HHI of less than 1,500 as an unconcentrated market, an HHI between 1,500 and 2,500 as a moderately concentrated market, and an HHI above 2,500 as a highly concentrated market. The 2010 guidelines indicate that the FTC and Department of Justice employ the following general standards for the relevant markets they have defined:

Small Change in Concentration: Mergers involving an increase in the HHI of less than 100 points are unlikely to have adverse competitive effects and ordinarily require no further analysis.

Unconcentrated Markets: Mergers resulting in unconcentrated markets are unlikely to have adverse competitive effects and ordinarily require no further analysis.

Moderately Concentrated Markets: Mergers resulting in moderately concentrated markets that involve an increase in the HHI of more than 100 points potentially raise significant competitive concerns and often warrant scrutiny.

Highly Concentrated Markets: Mergers resulting in highly concentrated markets that involve an increase in the HHI of between 100 points and 200 points potentially raise significant competitive concerns and often warrant scrutiny. Mergers resulting in highly concentrated markets that involve an increase in the HHI of more than 200 points will be presumed to be likely to enhance market power. The presumption may be rebutted by persuasive evidence showing that the merger is unlikely to enhance market power.

The 2010 guidelines explain that the purpose of these thresholds is to

provide one way to identify some mergers unlikely to raise competitive concerns and some others for which it is particularly important to examine whether other competitive factors confirm, reinforce, or counteract the potentially harmful effects of increased concentration. The higher the post-merger HHI and the increase in the HHI, the greater are the Agencies' potential competitive concerns and the greater is the likelihood that the Agencies will request additional information to conduct their analysis.

In 1987, the National Association of Attorneys General, composed of the Attorneys General of the fifty States and five U.S. territories and protectorates, promulgated its own set of guidelines for horizontal mergers. Intended to apply to enforcement actions brought by the State Attorneys General under Federal and State antitrust statutes, the State guidelines place a greater emphasis on preventing transfers of wealth from consumers to producers than do the Federal guidelines. Accordingly, the State Attorneys General would be more likely to challenge certain mergers than would the Federal government.

ROBINSON-PATMAN ACT

Section 2 of the Clayton Act originally prohibited only sellers from differentially pricing their products to injure local or regional competitors. In 1936, in an attempt to limit the power of large purchasers, Congress amended Section 2 of the Clayton Act by adopting the Robinson-Patman Act, which further prohibited **price discrimination** in interstate commerce involving commodities of like grade and quality. Thus, the Act prohibits buyers from inducing and sellers from granting discrimination in prices. To constitute a vio-

lation, the price discrimination must substantially lessen competition or tend to create a monopoly.

Under this Act, a seller of goods may not grant discounts to buyers, including allowances for advertisements, counter displays, and samples, unless the seller offers the same discounts to all other purchasers on proportionately equal terms. The Act also prohibits other types of discounts, rebates, and allowances and makes it unlawful to sell goods at unreasonably low prices for the purpose of destroying competition or eliminating a competitor. Furthermore, the Act makes it unlawful for a person knowingly to "induce or receive" an illegal discrimination in price, thus imposing liability on the buyer as well as the seller. Violation of the Robinson-Patman Act, with limited exceptions, is civil, not criminal, in nature. The Act does permit price differentials that are justified by proof of either a cost savings to the seller or a good-faith price reduction to meet the lawful price of a competitor.

PRIMARY-LINE INJURY

In enacting Section 2 of the Clayton Act in 1914, Congress was concerned with sellers who sought to harm or eliminate their competitors through price discrimination. Injuries accruing to a seller's competitors are called "primary-line" injuries. Because the Act forbids price discrimination only where such discrimination may substantially lessen competition or tend to create a monopoly, the plaintiff in a Robinson-Patman primary-line injury case must either show that the defendant, with the intent to harm competition, has engaged in predatory pricing or present a detailed market analysis that demonstrates how the defendant's price discrimination actually harmed competition. To prove predatory intent, a plaintiff may rely either on direct evidence of such intent or, more commonly, on inferences drawn from the defendant's conduct, such as a significant period of below-cost or unprofitable pricing. A predatory pricing scheme also may be challenged under the Sherman Act.

SECONDARY- AND TERTIARY-LINE INJURY

In amending Section 2 of the Clayton Act in 1936 through the adoption of the Robinson-Patman Act, Congress was concerned primarily with small buyers, who were harmed by the discounts that sellers granted to large buyers. Injuries accruing to some buyers because of the lower prices granted to other buyers are called "secondary-line" injuries. To prove the required harm to competition, a plaintiff in a secondary-line injury case must either show substantial and sustained price differentials in a market or offer a detailed market analysis that demonstrates actual harm to competition. Because courts have been willing in secondary-line injury cases to infer harm to competition from a sustained and substantial price differential, proving a secondary-line injury generally is easier than proving a primary-line injury.

Tertiary-line injury occurs when the recipient of a favored price passes the benefits of the lower price on to the next level of distribution. Purchasers from other secondary-line sellers are injured in that they do not receive the benefits of the lower price; these purchasers may recover damages from the original discriminating seller.

COST JUSTIFICATION

If a seller can show that it costs less to sell a product to a particular buyer, the seller may lawfully pass along the cost savings. Section 2(a) provides that the Act does not "prevent differentials which make only due allowance for differences in the cost of manufacture, sale, or delivery resulting from the differing methods or quantities in which … commodities are … sold or delivered." For example, if Retailer A orders goods from Seller X by the carload, whereas Retailer B orders in small quantities, Seller X, who delivers F.O.B. (free on board) buyer's warehouse, may pass along the transportation savings to Retailer A. Nonetheless, although it is possible to pass along transportation savings, it is extremely difficult to pass along alleged savings in manufacturing or distribution because of the complexity involved in calculating and proving such savings. Therefore, sellers rarely rely upon the defense of cost justification.

MEETING COMPETITION

A seller may lower his price in a good faith attempt to meet competition. To illustrate:

1. Manufacturer X sells its motor oil to retail outlets for $0.65 per can. Manufacturer Y approaches A, one of Manufacturer X's customers, and offers to sell a comparable type of motor oil for $0.60 per can. Manufacturer X will be permitted to lower its price to A to $0.60 per can and need not lower its price to its other retail customers—B, C, and D. Manufacturer X, however, may not lower its price to A to $0.55 unless it also offers this lower price to B, C, and D.
2. To allow A to meet the lower price that A's competitor, N, charges when selling Manufacturer Y's oil, Manufacturer X will not be permitted to lower its price to A without also lowering its price to B, C, and D.

A seller may beat its competitor's price, however, if it does not know the competitor's price, cannot reasonably determine the competitor's price, and acts reasonably in setting its own price.

◆ **SEE FIGURE 41-2: Meeting Competition Defense**

◆ **FIGURE 41-2: Meeting Competition Defense**

Illustration One

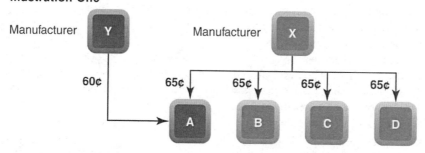

Result: Manufacturer **X** may lower its price to A to 60¢ without lowering its price to B, C, and D.

Illustration Two

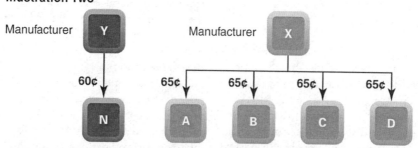

Result: Manufacturer **X** may *not* lower its price to A to 60¢ without lowering its price to B, C, and D.

FEDERAL TRADE COMMISSION ACT

In 1914, through the enactment of the Federal Trade Commission Act, Congress created the FTC and charged it with the duty to prevent "unfair methods of competition in commerce, and unfair or deceptive acts or practices in commerce." To this end, the five-member commission is empowered to conduct appropriate investigations and hearings and to issue against violators "cease-and-desist" orders enforceable in the Federal courts. Its broad power has been described by the U.S. Supreme Court:

> The "unfair methods of competition," which are condemned by … the Act, are not confined to those that were illegal at common law or that were condemned by the Sherman Act.… It is also clear that the Federal Trade Commission Act was designed to supplement and bolster the Sherman Act and the Clayton Act … *to stop in their incipiency acts and practices which, when full blown, would violate those Acts. F.T.C. v. Motion Picture Advertising Service Co.*, 344 U.S. 392 (1953). (Emphasis supplied.)

Complaints may be instituted by the commission, which, after a hearing, "has wide latitude for judgment and the courts will not interfere except where the remedy selected has no reasonable relation to the unlawful practices found to exist." Although the commission most frequently enters a cease-and-desist order having the effect of an injunction, it may order other relief, such as affirmative disclosure, corrective advertising, and the granting of patent licenses on a reasonable royalty basis. Appeals may be taken from orders of the commission to the U.S. Courts of Appeals, which have exclusive jurisdiction to enforce, set aside, or modify orders of the commission.

In performing its duties, the FTC investigates not only possible violations of the antitrust laws but also unfair methods of competition, such as false and misleading advertisements, false or inadequate product labeling, the passing or palming off of goods as those of a competitor, lotteries, gambling schemes, discriminatory rebate or discount offers, false disparagement of a competitor's goods, false or misleading descriptive names of products, the use of false testimonials, and other unfair trade practices. For a more detailed discussion of the FTC and its powers, see *Chapter 42*.

CHAPTER SUMMARY

SHERMAN ANTITRUST ACT

Restraint of Trade Section 1 prohibits contracts, combinations, and conspiracies that restrain trade
- *Rule of Reason* standard that balances the anticompetitive effects against the procompetitive effects of the restraint
- **Per se** *Violations* conclusively presumed unreasonable and therefore illegal
- *Quick Look Standard* a modified or abbreviated rule of reason standard
- *Horizontal Restraints* agreements among competitors
- *Vertical Restraints* agreements among parties at different levels in the chain of distribution

Application of Section 1
- *Price Fixing* an agreement with the purpose or effect of inhibiting price competition; horizontal agreements are *per se* illegal, while vertical price fixing is judged by the rule of reason
- *Market Allocation* division of markets by customer type, geography, or products; horizontal agreements are *per se* illegal, while vertical agreements are judged by the rule of reason standard
- *Boycott* agreement among competitors not to deal with a supplier or customer; *per se* illegal
- *Tying Arrangement* conditioning a sale of a desired product (tying product) on the buyer's purchasing a second product (tied product); *per se* illegal if the seller has considerable power in the tying product or affects a not-insubstantial amount of interstate commerce in the tied product

Monopolies Section 2 prohibits monopolization, attempts to monopolize, and conspiracies to monopolize
- *Monopolization* requires market power (ability to control price or exclude others from the marketplace) plus either the unfair attainment of the power or the abuse of such power

- *Attempt to Monopolize* specific intent to monopolize, plus a dangerous probability of success
- *Conspiracies to Monopolize*

Sanctions
- *Treble Damages* three times actual loss
- *Criminal Penalties*

CLAYTON ACT

Tying Arrangement prohibited if it tends to create a monopoly or may substantially lessen competition

Exclusive Dealing arrangement by which a party has sole right to a market; prohibited if it tends to create a monopoly or may substantially lessen competition

Merger prohibited if it tends to create a monopoly or may substantially lessen competition
- *Horizontal Merger* one company's acquisition of a competing company
- *Vertical Merger* a company's acquisition of one of its suppliers or customers
- *Conglomerate Merger* the acquisition of a company that is not a competitor, customer, or supplier

Sanctions treble damages

ROBINSON-PATMAN ACT

Price Discrimination the Act prohibits buyers from inducing or sellers from giving different prices to buyers of commodities of similar grade and quality

Injury plaintiff may prove injury to competitors of the seller (primary-line injury), to competitors of other buyers (secondary-line injury), or to purchasers from other secondary-line sellers (tertiary-line injury)

Defenses (1) cost justification, (2) meeting competition, and (3) functional discounts

Sanctions civil (treble damages); criminal in limited situations

---

FEDERAL TRADE COMMISSION ACT

Purpose to prevent unfair methods of competition and unfair or deceptive practices

Sanctions actions may be brought by the Federal Trade Commission, not by private individuals

Securities Regulation

The primary purpose of Federal securities regulation is to foster public confidence in the securities market by preventing fraudulent practices in the sale of securities. Federal securities law consists principally of two statutes: the Securities Act of 1933, which focuses on the issuance of securities, and the Securities Exchange Act of 1934, which deals mainly with trading in issued securities. These "secondary" transactions greatly exceed in number and dollar value the original offerings by issuers.

Both statutes are administered by the Securities and Exchange Commission (SEC), an independent, quasi-judicial agency consisting of five commissioners. The responsibilities of the SEC include interpreting Federal securities laws; issuing new rules and amending existing rules; and coordinating U.S. securities regulation with Federal, State, and foreign authorities. In 1996 Congress enacted legislation requiring the SEC, when making rules under either of the securities statutes, to consider, in addition to the protection of investors, whether its action will promote efficiency, competition, and capital formation.

In July 2010, President Obama signed into law the Dodd-Frank Wall Street Reform and Consumer Protection Act (CFPA), the most significant change to U.S. financial regulation since the New Deal. One of the many stand-alone statutes included in the CFPA is the Investor Protection and Securities Reform Act of 2010, which imposes new corporate governance and investor protection rules on publicly held companies. Corporate governance and investor protection provisions of the CFPA are discussed in this chapter as well as in *Chapters 36, 37,* and *47.*

The SEC has the power to seek, in a Federal district court, civil injunctions against violations of the statutes; to recommend that the Justice Department bring criminal prosecutions; and to issue orders censuring, suspending, or expelling broker-dealers, investment advisers, and investment companies. The Securities Enforcement Remedies and Penny Stock Reform Act of 1990 granted the SEC the power to issue cease-and-desist orders and to impose administrative, civil penalties up to the current inflation-adjusted amount of $725,000. Congress enacted the Private Securities Litigation Reform Act of 1995 (Reform Act), which amends both the 1933 Act and the 1934 Act. One of its provisions grants authority to the SEC to bring civil actions for specified violations of the 1934 Act against aiders and abettors (those who knowingly provide substantial assistance to a person who violates the statute). The CFPA has extended this authority in two ways: (1) the CFPA empowers the SEC to bring enforcement actions under the 1933 Act against aiders and abettors and (2) the CFPA amends the 1933 and 1934 Acts to allow *recklessness* as well as knowledge to satisfy the mental state required for the SEC to bring aiding and abetting cases.

The Reform Act sought to prevent abuses in private securities fraud lawsuits. To prevent certain State private securities class action lawsuits alleging fraud from being used to frustrate the objectives of the Reform Act, Congress enacted the Securities Litigation Uniform Standards Act of 1998. The Act sets national standards for securities class action lawsuits involving nationally traded securities, while preserving the appropriate enforcement powers of State securities regulators and leaving unchanged the current treatment of individual lawsuits. The Act amends both the 1933 Act and the 1934 Act by prohibiting any private class action suit in State or Federal court by any private party based upon State statutory or common law alleging: (1) an untrue statement or omission in connection with the purchase or sale of a covered security; or (2) that the defendant used any manipulative or deceptive device in connection with such a transaction.

In response to the business scandals involving companies such as Enron, WorldCom, Global Crossing, Adelphia, and Arthur Andersen, in 2002 Congress passed the Sarbanes-Oxley Act, which amends the securities acts in a number of significant respects. The Act allows the SEC to add civil penalties to a disgorgement fund for the benefit of victims of violations of the 1933 Act or the 1934 Act. Other provisions of the Act are discussed later in this chapter, as well as in *Chapters 6, 36,* and *45.* In addition, the CFPA requires the SEC to make an award to whistleblowers who voluntarily provide original information that leads to a successful enforcement action in which the SEC imposes monetary sanctions in excess of $1 million. The amount of the award must be between 10 percent and 30 percent of funds collected as monetary sanctions, as determined by the SEC.

The 1933 Act has two basic objectives: (1) to provide investors with material information concerning securities offered for sale to the public and (2) to prohibit misrepresentation, deceit, and other fraudulent acts and unfair practices in the sale of securities generally, whether or not they are required to be registered.

The 1934 Act extends protection to investors trading in securities that are already issued and outstanding. The 1934 Act also imposes disclosure requirements on publicly held corporations and regulates tender offers and proxy solicitations.

The SEC has recognized that the "use of electronic media also enhances the efficiency of the securities markets by allowing for the rapid dissemination of information to investors and financial markets in a more cost-efficient, widespread, and equitable manner than traditional paper-based methods." The SEC has provided interpretative guidance for the use of electronic media for the delivery of information required by the Federal securities laws. The SEC defined *electronic media* to include audiotapes, videotapes, facsimiles, CD-ROM, electronic mail, bulletin boards, Internet Web sites, and computer networks. Basically, electronic delivery must provide notice, access, and evidence of delivery comparable to that provided by paper delivery.

The SEC has established the EDGAR (Electronic Data Gathering, Analysis, and Retrieval) computer system, which performs automated collection, validation, indexing, acceptance, and dissemination of reports required to be filed with the SEC. Its primary purpose is to increase the efficiency and fairness of the securities market for the benefit of investors, corporations, and the economy by speeding up the receipt, acceptance, dissemination, and analysis of corporate information filed with the SEC. The SEC now requires all public domestic companies to make their filings on EDGAR, except filings exempted for hardship. EDGAR filings are posted at the SEC's Web site twenty-four hours after the date of filing.

In addition to the Federal laws regulating the sale of securities, each State has its own laws regulating such sales within its borders. Commonly called **blue sky laws**, these statutes all contain provisions prohibiting fraud in the sale of securities. In addition, most States require the registration of securities and also regulate brokers and dealers. The Uniform Securities Act of 1956 has been adopted at one time or another, in whole or in part, by thirty-seven jurisdictions, whereas the Revised Uniform Securities Act of 1985 has been adopted in only a few States. Both Acts, however, have been preempted in part by the National Securities Markets Improvement Act of 1996 and the Securities Litigation Uniform Standards Act of 1998. In 2002 the National Conference of Commissioners on Uniform State Laws promulgated a new Uniform Securities Act, which has been adopted by at least seventeen States. The 2002 Uniform Securities Act seeks to give States regulatory and enforcement authority that minimizes duplication of regulatory resources and that blends with Federal regulation and enforcement.

Any person who sells securities must comply with the Federal securities laws as well as with the securities laws of each State in which he intends to offer his securities. However, in 1996 Congress enacted the National Securities Markets Improvements Act, preempting State regulation of many offerings of securities. Because the State securities laws vary greatly, this chapter will discuss only the 1933 Act and the 1934 Act.

SECURITIES ACT OF 1933

The 1933 Act, also called the "Truth in Securities Act," requires that a registration statement be filed with the SEC and that it become effective before any securities may be offered for sale to the public, unless either the securities or the transaction in which they are offered is exempt from registration. The purpose of registration is to disclose financial and other information about the issuer and those who control it, so that potential investors may appraise the merits of the securities. The 1933 Act also requires that potential investors be furnished with a **prospectus** (a document offering the securities for sale) containing the important data set forth in the registration statement. The 1933 Act prohibits fraud in all sales of securities involving interstate commerce or the mails, even if the securities are exempt from the registration and disclosure requirements of the 1933 Act. Civil and criminal liability may be imposed for violations of the 1933 Act.

The National Securities Markets Improvements Act of 1996 broadly authorized the SEC to issue regulations or rules exempting any person, security, or transaction from any of the provisions of the 1933 Act or the SEC's rules promulgated under that Act. This authorization extends so far as such exemption is necessary or appropriate in the public interest and is consistent with the protection of investors.

DEFINITION OF A SECURITY

Section 2(1) of the 1933 Act defines a security as

any note, stock, treasury stock, bond, debenture, evidence of indebtedness, certificate of interest or participation in any profit-sharing agreement, collateral-trust certificate, preorganization certificate or subscription, transferable share, investment contract, voting-trust certificate, certificate of deposit for a security, fractional undivided interest in oil, gas, or other mineral rights, any put, call, straddle, option, or privilege on any security … or, in general, any interest or instrument commonly known as a "security," or any certificate of interest or participation in, temporary or interim certificate for, receipt for, guarantee of, or warrant or right to subscribe to or purchase, any of the foregoing.

This definition broadly incorporates the many types of instruments that fall within the concept of a security. Furthermore, the courts generally have interpreted the statutory definition to include nontraditional forms of investments. In *Landreth Timber Co. v. Landreth*, 471 U.S. 681 (1985), the Supreme Court adopted a two-tier analysis of what constitutes a security. Under this analysis, the Court will presumptively treat as a security a financial instrument designated as a note, stock, bond, or other instrument specifically named in the Act.

On the other hand, if a financial transaction lacks the traditional characteristics of an instrument specifically named in the statute, the Court has used a three-part test, derived from *Securities and Exchange Commission v. W.J. Howey Co.*, 328 U.S. 293 (1946), to determine whether that financial transaction constitutes an investment contract and thus a security. Under the *Howey* test, a financial instrument or transaction that involves (1) an investment in a common venture (2) premised on a reasonable expectation of profit (3) to be derived from the entrepreneurial or managerial efforts of others constitutes an investment contract. Thus, limited partnership interests are usually considered securities because limited partners may not participate in management or control of the limited partnership. On the other hand, general partnership interests are usually held not to be securities because general partners have the right to participate in management of the general partnership. Similarly, interests in limited liability companies (LLCs) are considered securities when the members do not take part in management (manager-managed LLCs) but are not deemed securities when the members exercise control of the company (member-managed LLCs). In certain circumstances, investments in citrus groves, whiskey warehouse receipts, real estate condominiums, cattle, franchises, and pyramid schemes have been held to be securities under the *Howey* test.

REGISTRATION OF SECURITIES

The 1933 Act prohibits the offer or sale of any security through the use of the mails or any means of interstate commerce unless a registration statement for the securities being offered is in effect or the issuer secures an exemption from registration. Section 5. The purpose of registration is to adequately and accurately disclose financial and other information upon which investors may appraise the merits of the securities. Registration does not, however, insure investors against loss—the SEC does not judge the financial merits of any security. Moreover, the SEC does not guarantee the accuracy of the information presented in a registration statement.

DISCLOSURE REQUIREMENTS

In general, registration (Form S–1) calls for disclosure of such information as (1) a description of the registrant's properties, business, and competition; (2) a description of the significant provisions of the security to be offered for sale and its relationship to the registrant's other capital securities; (3) information about the management of the registrant; and (4) financial statements certified by independent public accountants. In 1992, the SEC imposed new disclosure requirements regarding compensation paid to senior executives and directors. In 2006 the SEC amended these rules to mandate clearer and more complete disclosure of compensation paid to directors, the chief executive officer (CEO), the chief financial officer (CFO), and the three other highest-paid executive officers. The registration statement must be signed by the issuer, its CEO, its CFO, its chief accounting officer, and a majority of its board of directors.

A registration statement and the prospectus become public immediately on filing with the SEC, and investors can access them using EDGAR. The effective date of a registration statement is the twentieth day after filing, although the commission, at its discretion, may advance the effective date or require an amendment to the filing, which will begin a new twenty-day period. After the effective date, the issuer may make sales, provided the purchaser has received a final prospectus. The SEC has also adopted rules to provide for an "access equals delivery" prospectus delivery model: the final prospectus delivery obligations are satisfied without printing and actually delivering final prospectuses if the issuer timely filed a final prospectus with the SEC.

In 1998 the SEC issued a rule requiring issuers to write and design the cover page, summary, and risk factors section of their prospectuses in plain English. In these sections issuers must use short sentences; definite, concrete, everyday language; tabular presentation of complex information; no legal or business jargon; and no multiple negatives. Issuers will also have to design these sections to make them inviting to the reader and free from legalese and repetition that blur important information.

INTEGRATED DISCLOSURE

The disclosure system under the 1933 Act developed independently of that required by the 1934 Act, which is discussed later in this chapter. As a result, issuers subject to both statutes were compelled to provide duplicative or over-lapping disclosure. In an effort to reduce or eliminate unnecessary duplication of corporate reporting, the SEC in 1982 adopted an integrated system that provides for different levels of disclosure, depending on the issuer's reporting history and market following. All issuers may use the detailed form (S–1) described previously. The SEC has amended these rules to recognize four categories of issuers: nonreporting issuers, unseasoned issuers, seasoned issuers, and well-known seasoned issuers.

1. A nonreporting issuer is an issuer that is not required to file reports under the 1934 Act. Such an issuer must use Form S–1.
2. An unseasoned issuer is an issuer that has reported continuously under the 1934 Act for at least three years. Such an issuer must use Form S–1, but is permitted to disclose less detailed information and to incorporate some information by reference to reports filed under the 1934 Act.
3. A seasoned issuer is an issuer that has filed continuously under the 1934 Act for at least one year and has a minimum market value of publicly held voting and nonvoting stock of $75 million. Such an issuer is permitted to use Form S–3, thus disclosing even less detail in the 1933 Act registration and incorporating even more information by reference to 1934 Act reports. An issuer that does not meet the $75 million "public float" requirement can use Form S-3 if it (a) has a class of common equity securities listed and registered on a national securities exchange, (b) has a class of securities registered under the 1934 Act, (c) has filed continuously under the 1934 Act for at least one year, and (d) does not sell more than the equivalent of one-third of its public float in primary offerings over any period of twelve calendar months. "Public float" means the value of a company's outstanding shares that is in the hands of public investors, as opposed to company officers, directors, or controlling-interest investors.
4. A well-known seasoned issuer is an issuer that has filed continuously under the 1934 Act for at least one year and has either (a) a minimum worldwide market value of its outstanding publicly held voting and nonvoting stock of $700 million, or (b) $1 billion of nonconvertible debt or preferred stock that has been issued for cash in a registered offering within the preceding three years. A well-known seasoned issuer is also eligible to use Form S–3.

In 1992, the SEC established an integrated registration and reporting system for small business issuers. These rules are intended to facilitate access to the public financial markets for start-up and developing companies and to reduce costs for small business issuers wishing to have their securities traded in public markets. As amended in 2008, the rules define a small business issuer as a noninvestment company with less than $75 million in public float. When a company is unable to calculate public float, however, the standard is less than $50 million in revenue in the last fiscal year. Small business issuers may use Form SB–2, which has no dollar limit, or Form SB–1, which permits sales of up to $10 million of securities in any twelve-month period. Form SB–1 is a streamlined disclosure document permitting either a narrative or a question-and-answer format.

SHELF REGISTRATIONS

As amended in 2005, shelf registrations permit seasoned and well-known seasoned issuers to register unlimited amounts of securities that are to be offered and sold "off the shelf" on a delayed or continuous basis in the future. This is a departure from the requirement that an issuer must file a registration for *every* new distribution of nonexempt securities. The information in the original registration must be kept accurate and current, and the issuer must reasonably expect that the securities will be sold within three years of the effective date of the registration. Well-known seasoned issuers are eligible for a more streamlined shelf-registration process and automatic effectiveness of shelf-registration statements upon filing. Shelf registrations allow issuers to respond more quickly to market conditions such as changes in stock prices and interest rates.

COMMUNICATIONS

The SEC's 2005 revisions greatly liberalize the rules regarding written communications before and during registered securities offerings. These rules create a new type of written communication, called a "free-writing prospectus," which is any written offer, including electronic communications, other than a statutory prospectus. The flexibility provided under the new rules depends upon the characteristics of the issuer, including the type of issuer, the issuer's history of reporting, and the issuer's market capitalization.

1. Well-known seasoned issuers may engage at any time in oral and written communications, including a free-writing prospectus, subject to certain conditions.
2. All reporting issuers (unseasoned issuers, seasoned issuers, and well-known seasoned issuers) may at any time continue to publish regularly released factual business information and forward-looking information (predictions).
3. Nonreporting issuers may at any time continue to publish factual business information that is regularly released and intended for use by persons other than in their capacity as investors or potential investors.
4. Communications by issuers more than thirty days before filing a registration statement are permitted so long as they do not refer to a securities offering that is the subject of a registration statement.
5. All issuers may use a free-writing prospectus after the filing of the registration statement, subject to certain conditions.

EXEMPT SECURITIES

The 1933 Act exempts a number of specific securities from its registration requirements. Because these exemptions apply to the securities themselves, the securities also may be resold without registration.

SHORT-TERM COMMERCIAL PAPER

The Act exempts any note, draft, or bankers' acceptance (a draft accepted by a bank) issued for working capital that has a maturity of not more than nine months when issued. Section 3(a)(3). This exemption is not available, however, if the proceeds are to be used for permanent purposes, such as the acquisition of a plant, or if the paper is of a type not ordinarily purchased by the general public.

OTHER EXEMPT SECURITIES

The 1933 Act also exempts the following kinds of securities from registration:

1. securities issued or guaranteed by domestic governmental organizations, such as municipal bonds;
2. securities of domestic banks and savings and loan associations;
3. securities of not-for-profit, charitable organizations;
4. certain securities issued by Federally regulated common carriers; and
5. insurance policies and annuity contracts issued by State-regulated insurance companies.

EXEMPT TRANSACTIONS FOR ISSUERS

In addition to exempting specific types of securities, the 1933 Act also exempts *issuers* from the registration requirements for certain kinds of transactions. These exempt transactions include (1) private placements (Rule 506), (2) limited offers not exceeding $5 million (Rule 505), (3) limited offers not exceeding $1 million (Rule 504), and (4) limited offers solely to accredited investors (Section 4(6)). Except for some issuances under Rule 504, these exemptions from registration apply only to the transaction in which the securities are issued; therefore, any resale must be made by registration, unless the resale qualifies as an exempt transaction.

In addition, the 1933 Act provides a number of securities exemptions that are in effect transaction exemptions. These include intrastate issues, exchanges between an issuer and its security holders, and reorganization securities issued and exchanged with court or other governmental approval. Moreover, the Bankruptcy Act exempts securities issued by a debtor if they are offered under a reorganization plan in exchange for a claim or interest in the debtor. Bankruptcy

Act, Section 1145(a). These exemptions apply only to the original issuance; resales may be made only by registration unless the resale qualifies as an exempt transaction.

Another transaction exemption is Regulation A, which permits an issuer to sell a limited amount of securities in an unregistered public offering if certain conditions are met. Unlike other transaction exemptions, Regulation A places no restrictions upon the resale of securities issued pursuant to it.

◆ SEE FIGURE 44-1: **Registration and Exemptions under the 1933 Act**

LIMITED OFFERS

The 1933 Act exempts, or authorizes the SEC to exempt, transactions that do not require the protection of registration because they either involve a small amount of money or are made in a limited manner. Sections 3(b) and 4(2). Promulgated in 1982 to simplify and clarify the transaction exemptions relating to small issues and small issuers, Regulation D contains three separate exemptions (Rules 504, 505, and 506), each involving limited offers. Section 4(6), also aimed at small issues, is a companion section to the exemptions under Regulation D. Each of these exemptions requires the issuer to file a Form D with the SEC online within fifteen days after the first sale of securities in the offering. Moreover, the CFPA requires the SEC to issue rules disqualifying offerings and sales of securities made under Regulation D when the person offering the securities has been convicted of any felony or misdemeanor (1) in connection with the purchase or sale of any security or (2) involving the making of any false filing with the SEC.

Securities sold pursuant to these exemptions (with the exception of some sold pursuant to Rule 504) are considered **restricted securities** and may be resold only by registration or in another transaction exempt from registration. An issuer who uses these exemptions must take reasonable care to prevent nonexempt, unregistered resales of restricted securities. Reasonable care includes, but is not limited to, the following: (1) making a reasonable inquiry to determine whether the purchaser is acquiring the securities for herself or for other persons; (2) providing written disclosure prior to the sale to each purchaser that the securities have not been registered and therefore cannot be resold unless they are registered or unless an exemption from registration is available; and (3) placing a legend on the securities certificate stating that the securities have not been registered and that they are restricted securities.

PRIVATE PLACEMENTS The most important transaction exemption for issuers is the so-called private placement provision of the Act, which exempts "transactions by an issuer not involving any public offering." Section 4(2). SEC **Rule**

◆ **FIGURE 44-1:** **Registration and Exemptions under the 1933 Act**

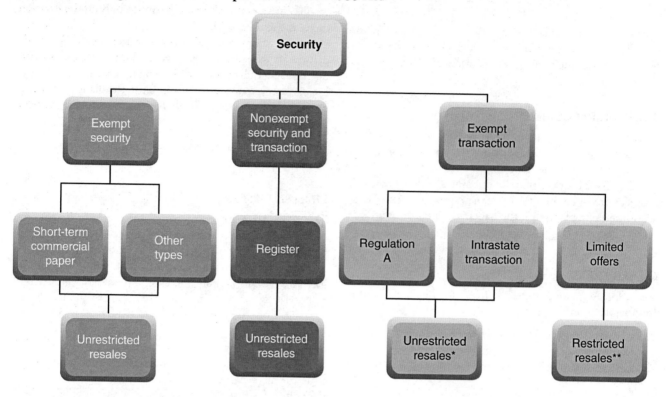

* Under intrastate exemption, resales to nonresidents may only be made nine months after the last sale in the initial issuance.
** Except some issuances under Rule 504.

506 establishes for all issuers a nonexclusive safe harbor for limited offers and sales without regard to the dollar amount of the offering. While compliance with the rule ensures the exemption, the exemption is not presumed to be unavailable for noncomplying transactions.

Securities sold under this exemption are restricted securities and may be resold only by registration or in a transaction exempt from registration. General advertising or general solicitation is not permitted. The issue may be purchased by an unlimited number of "accredited investors" and by no more than thirty-five other purchasers. **Accredited investors** include banks, insurance companies, investment companies, executive officers or directors of the issuer, savings and loan associations, registered broker-dealers, certain employee benefit plans with total assets in excess of $5 million, any person whose net worth exceeds $1 million, and any person whose income exceeded $200,000 in each of the two preceding years and who reasonably expects an income in excess of $200,000 in the current year. Before a sale involving any nonaccredited investors, such purchasers must receive specified material information about the issuer, its business, and the securities being offered. If the sale involves only accredited investors, such disclosure is not mandatory. The issuer

must reasonably believe that each purchaser who is not an accredited investor has sufficient knowledge regarding and experience in financial and business matters to evaluate capably the merits and risks of the investment or has the services of a representative possessing such knowledge and experience. The issuer must notify the SEC of sales made under the exemption and must take precautions against non-exempt, unregistered resales.

LIMITED OFFERS NOT EXCEEDING $5 MILLION SEC **Rule 505** exempts from registration those offerings by noninvestment company issuers that do not exceed $5 million over twelve months. Securities sold under this exemption are restricted securities and may be resold only by registration or in a transaction exempt from registration. General advertising or general solicitation is not permitted. The issue may be purchased by an unlimited number of accredited investors and by no more than thirty-five other purchasers. Before a sale involving any nonaccredited investors, such purchasers must receive specified material information about the issuer, its business, and the securities being offered; in the absence of nonaccredited investors, such disclosure is unnecessary. Unlike the issuer under Rule 506, however, the issuer under

Rule 505 is *not* required to believe reasonably that each nonaccredited investor, either alone or with his representative, has sufficient knowledge and experience regarding financial matters to be capable of evaluating the merits and risks of the investment. Like its counterpart under Rule 506, the issuer must take precautions against nonexempt, unregistered resales and must notify the SEC of sales made under the exemption.

LIMITED OFFERS NOT EXCEEDING $1 MILLION As amended in 1999, SEC **Rule 504** provides private, noninvestment company issuers with an exemption from registration for issues not exceeding $1 million within twelve months. Issuers required to report under the 1934 Act and investment companies may not use Rule 504. The issuer is to notify the SEC of sales under the rule, which permits sales to an unlimited number of investors and does not require the issuer to furnish any information to them.

If the issuance meets certain conditions, Rule 504 permits general solicitations, and acquired shares are freely transferable. The conditions are that the issuance is either (1) registered under State law requiring public filing and delivery of a disclosure document to investors before sale or (2) exempted under State law permitting general solicitation and advertising so long as sales are made only to accredited investors.

If the issuance does not meet these conditions, general solicitation and advertising is not permitted. Moreover, the securities issued are restricted, and the issuer must take precautions against nonexempt, unregistered resales.

LIMITED OFFERS SOLELY TO ACCREDITED INVESTORS In 1980, Congress added **Section 4(6)**, which provides an exemption for offers and sales of $5 million made by an issuer solely to accredited investors. General advertising or public solicitation is not permitted. As with Rules 505 and 506, an unlimited number of accredited investors may purchase the issue; however, unlike these rules, Section 4(6) allows no unaccredited investors to purchase. No information is required to be furnished to the purchasers. Securities sold under this exemption are restricted securities and may be resold only by registration or in a transaction exempt from registration. The issuer must notify the SEC of sales made under the exemption and must take precautions against nonexempt, unregistered resales.

REGULATION A

As amended in 1992, Regulation A permits an issuer to offer up to $5 million of securities in any twelve-month period without registering them, provided that the issuer files an offering statement with the SEC prior to the sale of the securities. An offering circular must also be provided to offerees and purchasers. The issuer may make offers upon filing the offering statement but may make sales only after the SEC has qualified it. Issuers required to report under the 1934 Act and investment companies may not use Regula-

tion A. Regulation A filings are less detailed and time-consuming than full registration statements, and the required financial statements are simpler and need not be audited unless the issuer has audited financial statements prepared for other purposes. Issuers now may use an optional, simplified question-and-answer disclosure document.

Regulation A sets no restrictions regarding the number or qualifications of investors who may purchase securities under its provisions. Furthermore, securities sold under Regulation A may be resold freely after they are issued.

INTRASTATE ISSUES

The 1933 Act also exempts from registration any security that is part of an issue offered and sold only to persons resident within a single State where the issuer of such security is resident and doing business. Section 3(a)(11). This exemption is intended to apply to local issues representing local financing carried out by local persons through local investments. The exemption does not apply if *any* offeree, who need not become a purchaser, is not a resident of the State in which the issuer is resident.

The courts and the SEC have interpreted the exemption narrowly. **Rule 147**, promulgated by the SEC, provides a nonexclusive safe harbor for securing the intrastate exemption. While compliance with the rule ensures the exemption, the exemption is not presumed to be unavailable for noncomplying transactions. Rule 147 requires that

1. the issuer be incorporated or organized in the State in which the issuance occurs;
2. the issuer be principally doing business in that State, which means that the issuer must derive 80 percent of its gross revenues from that State, 80 percent of its assets must be located in that State, and 80 percent of its net proceeds from the issue must be used in that State;
3. all of the *offerees* and purchasers be residents of that State;
4. no resales to nonresidents be made during the period of sale and for nine months after the last sale; and
5. the issuer take precautions against interstate distributions. Such precautions include (a) placing on the security certificate a legend stating that the securities have not been registered and that resales can be made only to residents of the State and (b) obtaining a written statement of residence from each purchaser.

◆ **SEE FIGURE 44-2: Exempt Transactions for Issuers under the 1933 Act**

EXEMPT TRANSACTIONS FOR NONISSUERS

The 1933 Act requires registration for any sale by any person (including nonissuers) of any nonexempt security unless a statutory exemption can be found for the transaction. The

◆ **FIGURE 44-2: Exempt Transactions for Issuers under the 1933 Act**

Exemption	Price Limitation	Information Required	Limitations on Purchasers	Resales
Regulation A	$5 million	Offering circular	None	Unrestricted
Intrastate Rule 147	None	None	Intrastate only	Only to residents before nine months
Rule 506	None	Material information to unaccredited purchasers	Unlimited accredited; 35 unaccredited	Restricted
Rule 505	$5 million	Material information to unaccredited purchasers	Unlimited accredited; 35 unaccredited	Restricted
Rule 504	$1 million	None	None	Restricted*
Section 4(6)	$5 million	None	Only accredited	Restricted

* Unrestricted if under State law the issuance is either (1) registered or (2) exempted with sales only to accredited investors.

Act, however, provides a transaction exemption for any person other than an issuer, underwriter, or dealer. Section 4(1). In addition, the Act exempts most transactions by dealers and brokers. Sections 4(3) and 4(4). These three provisions exempt from the registration requirements of the 1933 Act most secondary transactions; that is, the numerous resales that occur on an exchange or in the over-the-counter market. Nevertheless, these exemptions do not extend to some situations involving resales by nonissuers, in particular to (1) resales of restricted securities acquired under Regulation D (Rules 506, 505, or 504) or Sections 4(6) and (2) sales of restricted or nonrestricted securities by affiliates. Such sales must be made pursuant to registration, Rule 144, or Regulation A, subject to the limited exception provided to some issuances by Rule 504. An **affiliate** is a person who controls, is controlled by, or is under common control with the issuer. **Control** is the direct or indirect possession of the power to direct the management and policies of a person through ownership of securities, by contract, or otherwise. Rule 405.

RULE 144

Rule 144 of the SEC sets forth conditions that, if met by an affiliate or any person selling restricted securities, exempt her from registering those securities. As amended in 2008, the rule imposes less strict requirements on resales of securities of issuers that are subject to the reporting requirements of the 1934 Act than on resales of securities of nonreporting issuers.

NONREPORTING ISSUERS Amended Rule 144 requires for an affiliate selling *restricted* securities that there be adequate current public information about the issuer, that the affiliate

selling under the rule have owned the restricted securities for at least one year, that she sell them only in limited amounts in unsolicited brokers' transactions, and that notice of the sale be provided to the SEC. An affiliate selling *nonrestricted* securities is subject to the same require-ments except that the one-year holding period does not apply.

A person who is not an affiliate of the issuer when the restricted securities are sold and who has owned the restricted securities for at least one year may sell them in unlimited amounts and is not subject to any of the other requirements of Rule 144.

REPORTING ISSUERS Amended Rule 144 requires for an affiliate selling *restricted* securities that there be adequate current public information about the issuer, that the affiliate selling under the rule have owned the restricted securities for at least six months, that she sell them only in limited amounts in unsolicited brokers' transactions, and that notice of the sale be provided to the SEC. An affiliate selling *nonrestricted* securities is subject to the same requirements except for the one-year holding period.

If there is adequate current public information about the issuer, a person who is *not* an affiliate of the issuer when the *restricted* securities are sold and has owned the restricted securities for at least six months may sell them in unlimited amounts and is not subject to any of the other requirements of Rule 144. After one year, the nonaffiliate selling *restricted* securities need not comply with the current information requirement of Rule 144.

RULE 144A

While Rule 144 permits sales of restricted securities, the requirements of the rule have hampered the liquidity of privately placed securities. To improve the liquidity of such securities, in 1990 the SEC adopted Rule 144A, which provides an additional, nonexclusive safe harbor from registration for resales of restricted securities. Only securities that at the time of issue are not of the same class as securities listed on a national securities exchange or quoted in a U.S. automated interdealer quotation system ("nonfungible securities") may be sold under Rule 144A. Such nonfungible securities may be sold only to a qualified institutional buyer, defined generally as an institution that in the aggregate owns and invests on a discretionary basis at least $100 million in securities. Rule 144A also requires the seller of the nonfungible securities to take reasonable steps to ensure that the buyer knows that the seller is relying on Rule 144A. In addition, special requirements apply to securities issued by foreign companies. Securities acquired pursuant to Rule 144A are restricted securities.

REGULATION A

In addition to providing issuers an exemption from registration for securities up to $5 million, Regulation A provides an exemption for nonissuers. Use of this exemption, which places a $1.5 million limit on the total amount of securities sold in any twelve-month period by all nonissuers, requires compliance with all of the conditions Regulation A imposes upon issuers, as discussed above.

LIABILITY

To implement the statutory objectives of providing full disclosure and preventing fraud in the sale of securities, the 1933 Act imposes a number of sanctions for noncompliance with its requirements. These sanctions include administrative remedies by the SEC, civil liability to injured investors, and criminal penalties.

The Reform Act provides "forward-looking" statements (predictions) a "safe harbor" under the 1933 Act from civil liability based on an untrue statement of material fact or an omission of a material fact necessary to make the statement not misleading. The safe harbor applies only to issuers required to report under the 1934 Act. The safe harbor eliminates civil liability if a forward-looking statement is (1) immaterial, (2) made without actual knowledge that it was false or misleading, or (3) identified as a forward-looking statement and is accompanied by meaningful cautionary statements identifying important factors that could cause actual results to differ materially from those predicted. "Forward-looking statements" include projections of revenues, income, earnings per share, capital expenditures, dividends, or capital structure; management's plans and objectives for future operations; and statements of future economic per-

formance. The safe harbor provision, however, does not cover statements made in connection with an initial public offering, a tender offer, a going private transaction, or offerings by a partnership or an LLC.

UNREGISTERED SALES

The Act imposes express civil liability for the sale of an unregistered security that is required to be registered, the sale of a registered security without delivery of a prospectus, the sale of a security by use of an outdated prospectus, or the offer of a sale prior to the filing of the registration statement. **Section 12(a)(1).** Liability is strict or absolute because there are no defenses. The person who purchases a security sold in violation of this provision has the right to tender it back to the seller and recover the purchase price. If the purchaser no longer owns the security, he may recover monetary damages from the seller.

FALSE REGISTRATION STATEMENTS

When securities have been sold subject to a registration statement, **Section 11** of the Act imposes express liability upon those who have included any untrue statement in the registration statement or who omit from the statement any material fact. **Material** matters are those to which a reasonable investor would be substantially likely to attach importance in determining whether to purchase the security registered. SEC Rule 405. Usually, proof of reliance upon the misstatement or omission is not required. The section imposes liability upon (1) the issuer; (2) all persons who signed the registration statement, including the principal executive officer, principal financial officer, and principal accounting officer; (3) every person who was a director or partner; (4) every accountant, engineer, appraiser, or expert who prepared or certified any part of the registration statement; and (5) all underwriters. These persons generally are jointly and severally liable for the amount paid for the security, less either its value at the time of suit or the price for which it was sold, to any person who acquires the security without knowledge of the untruth or omission. A defendant is not liable for any or the entire amount otherwise recoverable under Section 11 that the defendant proves was caused by something other than the defective disclosure. The court may award attorneys' fees against any party who brings suit or asserts a defense without merit.

An expert is liable only for misstatements or omissions in the portion of the registration that he prepared or certified. Moreover, any defendant, other than the issuer (who has strict liability), may assert the affirmative defense of due diligence. This **due diligence** defense generally requires the defendant to show that she had reasonable grounds to believe, and did believe, that there were no untrue statements or material omissions. In some instances, due diligence requires a reasonable investigation to determine grounds for belief. The standard of reasonableness for such investigation and such grounds is that required of a prudent person in the management of his own property. Section 11(c).

ANTIFRAUD PROVISIONS

The 1933 Act also contains two antifraud provisions: Section 12(a)(2) and Section 17(a). In addition, Rule 10b–5 of the 1934 Act applies to the issuance or sale of all securities, even those exempted by the 1933 Act. Rule 10b–5 is discussed later in this chapter.

Section 12(a)(2) Section 12(a)(2) imposes express liability upon any person who offers or sells a security by means of a prospectus or oral communication that contains an untrue statement of material fact or omits a material fact. That liability extends only to the immediate purchaser, provided she did not know of the untruth or omission. The seller may avoid liability by proving that he did not know and in the exercise of reasonable care could not have known of the untrue statement or omission. The seller is liable to the purchaser for the amount paid upon tender of the security. If the purchaser no longer owns the security, she may recover damages from the seller. A defendant is not liable for any portion of or the entire amount otherwise recoverable under Section 12(a)(2) that the defendant proves was caused by something other than the defective disclosure.

Section 17(a) Section 17(a) makes it unlawful for any person in the offer or sale of any securities, whether registered or not, to do any of the following when using any means of transportation or communication in interstate commerce or the mails:

1. employ any device, scheme, or artifice to defraud;
2. obtain money or property by means of any untrue statement of a material fact or any statement that omits a material fact, without which the information is misleading; or
3. engage in any transaction, practice, or course of business that operates or would operate as a fraud or deceit upon the purchaser.

There is considerable doubt whether the courts may imply a private right of action for persons injured by violations of

◆ **FIGURE 44-3: Registration and Liability Provisions of the 1933 Act**

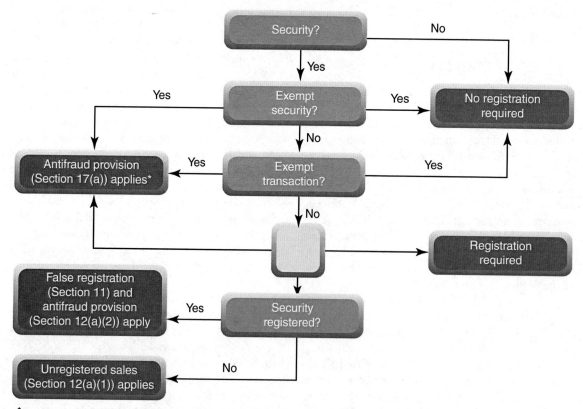

*Section 12 (a)(2) *may* apply to some of these issuances.

this section. The Supreme Court has reserved this question, and most lower courts have denied the existence of a private remedy. The SEC may, however, bring enforcement actions under Section 17(a).

CRIMINAL SANCTIONS

The 1933 Act imposes criminal sanctions upon any person who willfully violates any of its provisions or the rules and regulations the SEC promulgates pursuant to the Act. Section 24. Conviction may carry a fine of not more than $10,000 or imprisonment of not more than five years, or both.

◆ **SEE FIGURE 44-3: Registration and Liability Provisions of the 1933 Act**

SECURITIES EXCHANGE ACT OF 1934

The Securities Exchange Act of 1934 deals principally with the secondary distribution (resale) of securities. The definition of a security in the 1934 Act is substantially the same as the definition in the 1933 Act. The 1934 Act seeks to ensure fair and orderly securities markets by prohibiting fraudulent and manipulative practices and by establishing rules for market operations. It provides protection for holders of all securities listed on national exchanges, as well as for those holders of equity securities of companies traded over the counter whose corporate assets exceed $10 million and whose equity securities include a class with five hundred or more shareholders. Companies must register such securities and are also subject to the 1934 Act's periodic reporting

requirements, short-swing profits provision, tender offer provisions, and proxy solicitation provisions, as well as the internal control and recordkeeping requirements of the Foreign Corrupt Practices Act. An over-the-counter issuer may terminate its registration when the holders of its registered equity securities number fewer than three hundred or when the issuer has had fewer than five hundred shareholders *and* assets totaling less than $10 million on the last day of each of the past three years. In addition, issuers of securities, whether registered under the 1934 Act or not, must comply with the antifraud and antibribery provisions of the Act.

◆ **SEE FIGURE 44-4: Applicability of the 1934 Act**

The National Securities Markets Improvements Act of 1996 broadly authorized the SEC to issue regulations, rules, or orders exempting any person, security, or transaction from any of the provisions of the 1934 Act or the SEC's rules promulgated under that Act. This authorization extends so far as such exemption is necessary or appropriate in the public interest and is consistent with the protection of investors. This exemptive authority does not, however, extend to the regulation of government securities broker-dealers.

DISCLOSURE

The 1934 Act imposes significant disclosure requirements upon reporting companies. These include the filing of

◆ **FIGURE 44-4: Applicability of the 1934 Act**

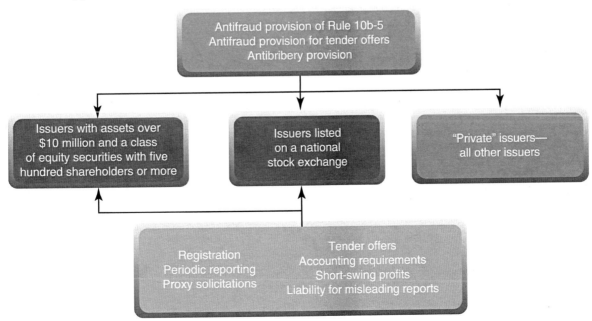

securities registrations, periodic reports, disclosure statements for proxy solicitations, and disclosure statements for tender offers, as well as compliance with the accounting requirements imposed by the Foreign Corrupt Practices Act. As part of its integrated registration and reporting system for small business issuers, in 1992 the SEC developed a new series of forms for qualifying issuers to use for registration and periodic reporting under the 1934 Act. Also in 1992, the SEC imposed new disclosure requirements for registration statements, periodic reports, and proxy statements that contain information regarding the compensation paid to senior executives and directors. As previously noted, in 2006 the SEC amended these rules to mandate clearer and more complete disclosure of compensation paid to directors, the

CEO, the CFO, and the three other highest-paid executive officers. The issuer must disclose executive compensation over the past three years including salary, bonus, a dollar value for stock and option awards, amount of compensation under nonequity incentive plans, annual change in present value of accumulated pension benefits and above-market earnings on nonqualified deferred compensation, and all other compensation including perquisites. Similar disclosure is required for director compensation for the last fiscal year. Effective in 2000, a plain English summary term sheet is required in all tender offers, mergers, and going private transactions.

◆ **SEE FIGURE 44-5: Disclosure under the 1934 Act**

◆ **FIGURE 44-5: Disclosure under the 1934 Act**

	Initial Registration	Periodic Reporting	Insider Reporting	Proxy Statement	Tender Offer
Registrant	Issuer if regulated, publicly held company	Issuer if regulated, publicly held company	Statutory insiders (directors, officers, and principal stockholders)	Issuer and other persons soliciting proxies	5 percent stockholder, tender offeror, or issuer
Information	Nature of business; Financial structure; Directors and executive officers; Financial statements	Annual, quarterly, or current report updating information in initial registration	Initial statement of beneficial ownership of equity securities; Changes in beneficial ownership	Details of solicitation; Legal terms of proxy; Annual report (if directors to be elected)	Identity and background; Terms of transaction; Source of funds; Intentions
Filing Date	Within 120 days after becoming a reporting company	Annual: within 90 days* after year's end; Quarterly: within 45 days** after quarter's end; Current: within 15 days after any material change	Within 10 days of becoming a statutory insider; Within 2 days after a change in ownership takes place	10 days before final proxy statement is distributed	5 percent stockholder: within 10 days after acquiring more than 5 percent of a class of registered securities; Tender offeror: before tender offer is made; Issuer: before offer to repurchase
Purpose of Disclosure	Adequate and accurate disclosure of material facts regarding securities listed on a national exchange or traded publicly over the counter	Update information contained in initial registration	Prevent unfair use of information that may have been obtained by a statutory insider	Full disclosure of material information; Facilitation of shareholder proposals	Adequate and accurate disclosure of material facts; Opportunity to reach uncoerced decision

*Certain issuers must file within sixty or seventy-five days.
**Certain issuers must file within forty days.

REGISTRATION REQUIREMENTS FOR SECURITIES

The 1934 Act requires all regulated publicly held companies to register with the SEC. Section 12. These one-time registrations apply to an entire class of securities. Thus, they differ from registrations under the Securities Act of 1933, which relate only to the securities involved in a specific offering. Registration requires disclosure of information such as the organization, financial structure, and nature of the business; the terms, positions, rights, and privileges of the different classes of outstanding securities; the names of the directors, officers, and underwriters and of each security holder owning more than 10 percent of any class of non-exempt equity security; bonus and profit-sharing arrangements; and balance sheets and profit-and-loss statements for the three preceding fiscal years.

PERIODIC REPORTING REQUIREMENTS

Following registration, an issuer must file specified annual (10–K) and periodic (10–Q and 8–K) reports to update the information contained in the original registration. Also subject to the periodic reporting requirements are issuers who have filed a 1933 Act registration statement with respect to any security. Section 15. This duty is suspended, however, in any subsequent year during which the securities registered under the 1933 Act are held by fewer than three hundred persons.

Effective in early 2010, the SEC adopted new requirements to improve the disclosure shareholders of public companies receive regarding compensation and corporate governance. These new rules require disclosure of (1) the qualifications of directors and nominees for director, and the reasons why that person should serve as a director of the issuer; (2) any directorships held by each director and nominee at any time during the past five years at any public company or registered investment company; (3) the consideration of diversity in the process by which candidates for director are considered for nomination by an issuer's nominating committee; (4) an issuer's board leadership structure and the board's role in the oversight of risk; (5) the aggregate grant date fair value of stock awards and option awards granted in the fiscal year computed in accordance with Financial Accounting Standards Board Accounting Standards; and (6) to the extent that risks arising from an issuer's compensation policies and practices for employees are reasonably likely to have a material adverse effect on the issuer, discussion of the issuer's compensation policies or practices as they relate to risk management and risk-taking incentives that can affect the issuer's risk and management of that risk.

The SEC has adopted rules under the Sarbanes-Oxley Act requiring an issuer's CEO and CFO to *certify* the financial and other information contained in the issuer's annual and quarterly reports. Moreover, the Act requires that each periodic report shall be *accompanied* by a written statement by the CEO and CFO of the issuer certifying that the periodic report fully complies with the requirements of the 1934 Act and that information contained in the periodic report fairly presents, in all material respects, the financial condition and results of operations of the issuer. A CEO or CFO who certifies while *knowing* that the report does not comply with the Act is subject to a fine of not more than $1 million or imprisonment of not more than ten years, or both. A CEO or CFO who *willfully* certifies a statement knowing it does not comply with the Act shall be fined not more than $5 million or imprisoned not more than twenty years, or both.

The Sarbanes-Oxley Act requires that issuers disclose in plain English to the public on a rapid and current basis such additional information concerning material changes in the financial condition or operations of the issuer as the SEC determines is necessary or useful for the protection of investors and in the public interest.

The Act, as amended by the CFPA, requires that each director, each officer, and any person who owns more than 10 percent of a registered equity security file reports with the SEC within ten days after he or she becomes such beneficial owner, director, or officer, or within such shorter time as the SEC may establish by rule. The 1934 Act also requires that each director, each officer, and any person who owns more than 10 percent of a registered equity security file reports with the SEC for any month during which changes in his ownership of such equity securities have occurred. Previously, such changes in ownership were required to be reported within ten days after the end of that month. The Sarbanes-Oxley Act requires that these reports be filed before the end of the second business day following the day on which the transaction was executed, unless the SEC establishes a different deadline. The 1934 Act also requires that these filings reporting changes in ownership be made electronically on EDGAR, that the SEC make them publicly available on its Internet site, and that the issuers make them available on their corporate Web sites, if they maintain one.

PROXY SOLICITATIONS

A **proxy** is a writing signed by a shareholder authorizing a named person to vote his shares of stock at a specified shareholders' meeting. To ensure that shareholders have adequate information with which to vote and an opportunity to participate effectively at shareholder meetings, the 1934 Act regulates the proxy solicitation process. The Act makes it unlawful for any person to solicit any proxy with respect to any registered security "in contravention of such rules and regulations as the Commission may prescribe." Section 14. **Solicitation** includes any request for a proxy, any request not to execute a proxy, or any request to revoke a proxy. The SEC has issued comprehensive and detailed rules prescribing the solicitation process and the disclosure of information about the issuer.

PROXY STATEMENTS Rule 14a–3 prohibits the solicitation of a proxy unless each person solicited has been furnished with a written proxy statement containing specified information. An issuer making solicitations must furnish security holders with a *proxy statement* describing all material facts concerning the matters being submitted to their vote, together with a *proxy form* on which the security holders can indicate their approval or disapproval of each proposal to be presented. Even a company that submits a matter to a shareholder vote rather than solicits proxies must provide its shareholders with information substantially equivalent to what would appear in a proxy statement. With few exceptions, the issuer must file preliminary copies of a proxy statement and proxy form with the SEC at least ten days prior to the first date they are to be sent. In addition, in an election of directors, solicitations of proxies by a person other than the issuer are subject to similar disclosure requirements. The issuer in such an election also must include an annual report with the proxy statement. Effective in early 2010, the SEC requires in proxy materials relating to election of directors that the issuer disclose the qualifications of nominees for director, and the reasons why that person should serve as a director of the issuer. The same information is required in the proxy materials prepared with respect to nominees for director nominated by others. Moreover, the CFPA authorizes the SEC to issue rules requiring that an issuer's proxy solicitation include nominations for the board of directors submitted by shareholders. Under the CFPA, the SEC must issue rules requiring issuers to disclose in annual proxy statements the reasons why the issuer has chosen to separate or combine the positions of chairman of the board of directors and CEO.

The CFPA contains several provisions regarding executive compensation. First, at least once every three years, issuers must include a provision in certain proxy statements for a nonbinding shareholder vote on the compensation of executives. In a separate resolution, shareholders determine whether this "say on pay" vote should be held every one, two, or three years. Second, the SEC must issue rules requiring issuers to describe clearly in annual proxy statements information that shows the relationship between executive compensation actually paid and the financial performance of the issuer, taking into account any change in the value of the shares of stock and dividends of the issuer and any distributions. Third, the SEC must issue rules requiring the disclosure of (1) the median of the annual total compensation of all issuer's employees except the CEO, (2) the annual total compensation of the CEO, and (3) the ratio of the amount described in (1) to the amount described in (2).

Effective March 30, 2007, the SEC amended its proxy rules to provide an alternative method for issuers and other persons to furnish proxy materials to shareholders: posting them on an Internet Web site and providing shareholders with notice of the availability of the proxy materials. Issuers must make paper or e-mail copies of the proxy materials available without charge to shareholders on request.

SHAREHOLDER PROPOSALS Where management makes a solicitation, any security holder entitled to vote has the opportunity to communicate with other security holders. Upon written request, the corporation must mail the communication at the security holder's expense or, at its option, promptly furnish to that security holder a current list of security holders.

If an eligible security holder entitled to vote submits a timely and appropriate proposal for action at a forthcoming meeting, management must include the proposal in its proxy statement and provide security holders with an opportunity to vote for or against it. To be eligible, the holder must own the lesser of 1 percent or $2,000 in market value of the security for at least one year prior to submitting the proposal. If management opposes the proposal, it must include in its proxy materials a statement by the security holder in support of the proposal. The aggregate length of the proposal and the supporting statement may not exceed five hundred words. A security holder is limited to submitting one proposal to an issuer each year.

Management may omit a proposal if, among other things, (1) under State law it is not a proper subject for shareholder action, (2) it would require the company to violate any law, (3) it is beyond the issuer's power or authority to effectuate, (4) it relates to the conduct of the ordinary business operations of the issuer, or (5) it relates to a nomination or an election for membership on the issuer's board of directors or to a procedure for such nomination or election. However, in 2010, the SEC amended the last exclusion by providing shareholders, under certain circumstances, the power to include in an issuer's proxy materials a shareholder proposal to establish in the issuer's governing documents a procedure for the inclusion in the proxy materials of director nominees selected by a shareholder or group of shareholders. Such a proposal must be consistent with the following new rule.

Under a new SEC rule issued in 2010, an issuer will be required at its own expense to include (1) on the issuer's proxy card, director nominees selected by a shareholder or a group of shareholders that meet certain eligibility requirements; and (2) in the issuer's proxy statement, information about such nominees. To use the new rule, a nominating shareholder or group of shareholders must have continuously owned for at least three years at least 3 percent of the voting power of the issuer's securities entitled to be voted at the meeting. Under the new rule, an issuer will not be required to include more than the greater of one shareholder nominee or the number of nominees that represents up to 25 percent of the issuer's board of directors. (When an issuer has a classified or staggered board, the 25 percent limit is based on the total number of directors on the board.) If more than one nominating shareholder or group of shareholders is eligible, the nominating shareholder or group with the highest percentage of the issuer's voting power will have its nominees included in the issuer's proxy materials. For smaller reporting issuers—generally, those with market capitalization of less than $75 million—the effectiveness of the new rule is deferred for three years.

TENDER OFFERS

A **tender offer** is a general invitation by a buyer (bidder) to the shareholders of a target company to tender their shares for sale at a specified price for a specified time. In 1968, Congress enacted the Williams Act, which amended the 1934 Act to extend reporting and disclosure requirements to tender offers and other block acquisitions. The purpose of the Williams Act is to provide public shareholders with full disclosure by both the bidder and the target company, so that the shareholders may make an informed decision.

DISCLOSURE REQUIREMENTS The 1934 Act imposes disclosure requirements in three situations: (1) when a person or group acquires more than 5 percent of a class of voting securities registered under the 1934 Act, (2) when a person makes a tender offer for more than 5 percent of a class of registered equity securities, or (3) when the issuer makes an offer to repurchase its own registered shares. Although each situation is governed by different rules, the disclosure required is substantially the same. A statement must be filed with the SEC containing (1) the acquisitor's background; (2) the source of the funds used to acquire the securities; (3) the purpose of the acquisition, including any plans to liquidate the company or to make major changes in the corporate structure; (4) the number of shares owned; (5) the terms of the transaction; and (6) any relevant contracts, arrangements, or understandings. Sections 13(d) and 14(d). This disclosure is also required of anyone soliciting shareholders to accept or reject a tender offer. A copy of the statement must be furnished to each offeree and sent to the issuer. The target company has ten days in which to respond to the bidder's tender offer by (1) recommending acceptance or rejection, (2) expressing no opinion and remaining neutral, or (3) stating that it is unable to take a position. The target company's response must include the reasons for the position taken.

REQUIRED PRACTICES A tender offer by either a third party or the issuer is subject to the following rules. The initial tender offer must be kept open for at least twenty business days

and for at least ten days after any change in terms. Shareholders who tender their shares may withdraw them at any time during the offering period. The tender offer must be open to all holders of the class of shares subject to the offer, and all shares tendered must be purchased for the same price; thus, if an offering price is increased, both those who have tendered and those who have yet to tender will receive the benefit of the increase. A tender offeror who offers to purchase less than all of the outstanding securities of the target must accept, on a *pro rata* basis, securities tendered during the offer. During the tender offer, the bidder may buy shares of the target only through that tender offer. Effective in 2000, in a tender offer for all outstanding shares of a class, a tender offeror may provide a subsequent offering period of three to twenty days after completion of a tender offer, during which time security holders can tender shares without withdrawal rights.

DEFENSIVE TACTICS When confronted by an uninvited takeover bid—or by a potential, uninvited bid—management of the target company may decide either to oppose the bid or seek to prevent it. The defensive tactics management employs to prevent or defend against undesired tender offers have developed (and are still evolving) into a highly ingenious, and metaphorically named, set of maneuvers, some of which require considerable planning and several of which are of questionable legality.

STATE REGULATION More than forty States have enacted statutes regulating tender offers. Although they vary greatly, most of these statutes tend to protect a target company from an unwanted tender offer. Some empower the State to review the merits of an offer or the adequacy of disclosure. Many impose waiting periods before the tender offer becomes effective. The State statutes generally require disclosures more detailed than those the Williams Act requires, and many of them exempt tender offers supported by the target company's management. A number of States have adopted fair price statutes, which require the acquisitor to pay to all shareholders the highest price paid to any shareholder. Some States have enacted business combination statutes prohibiting transactions with an acquisitor for a specified time after change in control, unless disinterested shareholders approve.

FOREIGN CORRUPT PRACTICES ACT

In 1977, Congress enacted the Foreign Corrupt Practices Act (FCPA) as an amendment to the 1934 Act. Amended in 1988, the Act imposes internal control requirements upon companies with securities registered under the 1934 Act and, as discussed later in this chapter, prohibits all domestic concerns from bribing foreign governmental or political officials.

The accounting requirements of the FCPA reflect the ideas that accurate recordkeeping is essential to managerial responsibility and that investors should be able to rely on the financial reports they receive. Accordingly, the accounting requirements were enacted (1) to assure that an issuer's books accurately reflect financial transactions, (2) to protect the integrity of independent audits of financial statements, and (3) to promote the reliability of financial information required by the 1934 Act.

The FCPA requires every issuer that has a class of registered securities to

1. make and keep books, records, and accounts which, in reasonable detail, accurately and fairly reflect the transactions and disposition of the assets of the issuer; and
2. devise and maintain a system of internal controls to assure that transactions are executed as authorized and recorded in conformity with generally accepted accounting principles, thereby establishing accountability with regard to assets and assuring that access to those assets is permitted only with management's authorization. Section 13(b).

LIABILITY

To implement its objectives, the 1934 Act imposes a number of sanctions for noncompliance with its disclosure and antifraud requirements. These sanctions include civil liability to injured investors and issuers, civil penalties, and criminal penalties.

The Reform Act contains several provisions that affect civil liability under the 1934 Act. First, the Reform Act imposes on a plaintiff in any private action under the 1934 Act the burden of proving that the defendant's alleged violation of the 1934 Act caused the loss for which the plaintiff seeks to recover damages. Second, the Reform Act imposes a limit on the amount of damages a plaintiff can recover in any private action under the 1934 Act based on a material misstatement or omission in which she seeks to establish damages by reference to the market price of a security. The plaintiff may not recover damages in excess of the difference between the purchase or sale price she paid or received for the security and the mean trading price of that security during the ninety-day period beginning on the date when the information correcting the misstatement or omission is disseminated to the market. Third, the Reform Act provides a "safe harbor" under the 1934 Act from civil liability based on an untrue statement of material fact or an omission of a material fact necessary to make the statement not misleading. The safe harbor applies to issuers required to report under the 1934 Act and who make "forward-looking" statements (predictions) if the statements meet specified requirements. The requirements of the safe harbor and the transactions to which it does not apply were discussed earlier in this chapter.

MISLEADING STATEMENTS IN REPORTS

Section 18 imposes express civil liability upon any person who makes or causes to be made any false or misleading statement with respect to any material fact in any application, report, document, or registration filed with the SEC under the 1934 Act. Any person who purchased or sold a security in reliance upon a false or misleading statement without knowing that it was false or misleading may recover under Section 18. Nevertheless, a person who made such a statement or who caused one to be made is not liable if she proves that she acted in good faith and had no knowledge that such statement was false or misleading. The court may award attorneys' fees against either the plaintiff or the defendant.

SHORT-SWING PROFITS

Section 16(b) of the 1934 Act imposes express liability upon insiders—directors, officers, and any person owning more than 10 percent of the stock of a corporation listed on a national stock exchange or registered with the SEC—for all profits resulting from their "short-swing" trading in such stock. If any insider sells such stock within six months from the date of its purchase or purchases such stock within six months from the date of a sale of the stock, the corporation is entitled to recover any and all profit the insider realizes from these transactions. The "profit" recoverable is calculated by matching the highest sale price against the lowest purchase price within the relevant six-month period. Losses cannot be offset against profits. Suit to recover such profit may be brought by the issuer or by the owner of any security of the issuer in the name and on behalf of the issuer if the issuer fails or refuses to bring such suit within sixty days of the owner's request.

ANTIFRAUD PROVISION

Section 10(b) of the 1934 Act and SEC **Rule 10b–5** make it unlawful for any person to do any of the following when using the mails or facilities of interstate commerce in connection with the purchase or sale of any security

1. employ any device, scheme, or artifice to defraud;
2. make any untrue statement of a material fact;
3. omit to state a material fact necessary to make the statements made not misleading; or
4. engage in any act, practice, or course of business that operates or would operate as a fraud or deceit upon any person.

Rule 10b–5 applies to any purchase or sale of any security, whether it is registered under the 1934 Act or not, whether it is publicly traded or closely held, whether it is listed on an exchange or sold over the counter, or whether it is part of an initial issuance or a secondary distribution.

There are *no* exemptions. The implied liability under Rule 10b–5 applies to purchaser as well as seller misconduct and allows both defrauded sellers and buyers to recover.

REQUISITES OF RULE 10B–5 Recovery of damages under Rule 10b–5 requires proof of (1) a misstatement or omission (2) that is material, (3) made with *scienter*, and (4) relied upon (5) in connection with the purchase or sale of a security, and (6) that causes economic loss. This rule differs from common law fraud in that Rule 10b–5 imposes an affirmative duty of disclosure. A misstatement or omission is **material** if there is a substantial likelihood that a reasonable investor would consider it important in deciding whether to purchase or sell the security. Examples of material facts include substantial changes in dividends or earnings, significant misstatements of asset value, and the fact that the issuer is about to become a target of a tender offer. In an action for damages under Rule 10b–5, it must be shown that the violation was committed with **scienter**, or intentional misconduct. Negligence is not sufficient. Although the Supreme Court has yet to decide whether reckless conduct is sufficient to satisfy the requirement of *scienter*, the vast majority of circuit and district courts have held recklessness to be sufficient.

Direct reliance may be difficult to prove in a 10b–5 action because the buyer and seller usually do not negotiate their deal face to face. Recognizing the special nature of securities market transactions, the Supreme Court adopted the fraud-on-the-market theory, which establishes a rebuttable presumption of reliance based on the premise that the market price of a stock reflects any misstatement or omission and that the fraudulently affected market price has injured the plaintiff.

Remedies for violations of Rule 10b–5 include rescission, damages, and injunctions. The courts are divided over the measure of damages to impose.

INSIDER TRADING Rule 10b–5 applies to sales or purchases of securities made by an "insider" who possesses material information that is not available to the general public. An insider who fails to disclose the material, nonpublic information before trading on the information will be liable under Rule 10b–5 unless he waits for the information to become public. Under SEC Rule 10b5-1, a purchase or sale of an issuer's security is based on material nonpublic information about that security or issuer if the person making the purchase or sale was *aware* of the information when the person entered into the transaction. **Insiders**, for the purpose of Rule 10b–5, include directors, officers, employees, and agents of the security issuer, as well as those with whom the issuer has entrusted information solely for corporate purposes, such as underwriters, accountants, lawyers, and consultants. In some instances, the rule also precludes persons who receive material, nonpublic information from insiders—tippees—from trading on that information. A tippee who knows or should know that an insider has breached his fiduciary duty to the shareholders by disclosing inside information to the tippee is under a duty not to trade on such information.

◆ **SEE FIGURE 44-6: Parties Forbidden to Trade on Inside Information**

The U.S. Supreme Court has upheld the misappropriation theory as an additional and complementary basis for

◆ **FIGURE 44-6: Parties Forbidden to Trade on Inside Information**

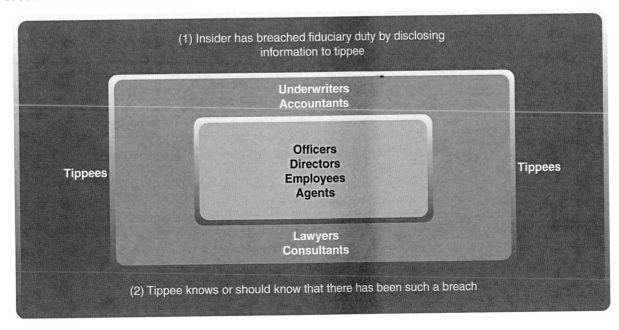

(1) Insider has breached fiduciary duty by disclosing information to tippee

Underwriters
Accountants

Tippees

Officers
Directors
Employees
Agents

Tippees

Lawyers
Consultants

(2) Tippee knows or should know that there has been such a breach

imposing liability for insider trading. Under this theory, a person may be held liable for insider trading under Rule 10b–5 if she trades in securities for personal profit using confidential information misappropriated in breach of a fiduciary duty to the source of the information. This liability applies even though the source of information is not the issuer of the securities that were traded. SEC Rule 10b5-2 adopts the misappropriation theory of liability: A violation of Section 10(b) includes the purchase or sale of a security of an issuer on the basis of material nonpublic information about that security or issuer in breach of trust or confidence that is owed to the issuer, the shareholders of that issuer, *or any other person who is the source of the material nonpublic information.* Under SEC Rule 10b5-2, a person has a duty of trust or confidence for purposes of the misappropriation theory of liability when (1) a person agrees to maintain information in confidence; (2) two people have a history, pattern, or practice of sharing confidences such that the recipient of the information knows or reasonably should know that the person communicating the material nonpublic information expects that the recipient will maintain its confidentiality; *or* (3) a person receives or obtains material nonpublic information from his or her spouse, parent, child, or sibling.

Under SEC Regulation FD (for "fair disclosure"), regulated issuers who disclose material nonpublic information to specified persons (primarily securities market professionals such as analysts and mutual fund managers) must make public disclosure of that information. If the selective disclosure was intentional or reckless, the issuer must make public disclosure simultaneously; for a nonintentional disclosure, the issuer must make public disclosure promptly, usually within twenty-four hours. With a few exceptions, Regulation FD does not apply to disclosures made in connection with a securities offering registered under the 1933 Act. The SEC can enforce this rule by bringing an administrative action seeking a cease-and-desist order or a civil action seeking an injunction and/or civil money penalties.

Although both Section 16(b) and Rule 10b–5 address the problem of insider trading and both may apply to the same transaction, they differ in several respects. First, Section 16(b) applies only to transactions involving registered equity securities; Rule 10b–5 applies to all securities. Second, the definition of *insider* under Rule 10b–5 extends beyond directors, officers, and owners of more than 10 percent of a company's stock, whereas the definition under Section 16(b) is limited to these persons. Third, Section 16(b) does not require that the insider possess material, nonpublic information; liability is strict. Rule 10b–5 applies to insider trading only where such information is not disclosed.

Fourth, Section 16(b) applies only to transactions occurring within six months of each other; Rule 10b–5 has no such limitation. Fifth, under Rule 10b–5, injured investors may recover damages on their own behalf; under Section 16(b), although shareholders may bring suit, any recovery is on behalf of the corporation.

EXPRESS INSIDER TRADING LIABILITY

In 1988, Congress amended the 1934 Act by adding **Section 20A**, which imposes express civil liability upon any person who violates the Act by purchasing or selling a security while in possession of material, nonpublic information. Any person who contemporaneously sold or purchased securities of the same class as those improperly traded may bring a private action against the traders to recover damages for the violation. The total amount of damages may not exceed the profit gained or loss avoided by the violation, diminished by any amount the violator disgorges to the SEC pursuant to a court order. The action must be brought within five years after the date of the last transaction that is the subject of the violation. Tippers are jointly and severally liable with tippees who commit a violation by trading on the inside information.

CIVIL PENALTIES FOR INSIDER TRADING

In addition to the remedies discussed above, the SEC is authorized by legislation enacted in 1984 and 1988 to bring an action in a U.S. district court to have a civil penalty imposed upon any person who purchases or sells a security while in possession of material, nonpublic information. Liability also extends to any person who by communicating material, nonpublic information aids and abets another in committing such a violation. Liability may also be imposed on any person who directly or indirectly controlled a person who ultimately committed a violation if the controlling person knew or recklessly disregarded the fact that the controlled person was likely to commit a violation and consequently failed to take appropriate steps to prevent the transgression. Under this provision law firms, accounting firms, issuers, financial printers, news media, and others must implement policies to prevent insider trading. The violating transaction must be on or through the facilities of a national securities exchange or from or through a broker or dealer. Purchases that are part of a public offering by an issuer of securities are not subject to this provision.

The civil penalty for a person who trades on inside information is determined by the court in light of the facts and circumstances but may not exceed three times the profit gained or loss avoided as a result of the unlawful purchase or sale. The maximum amount that may be imposed upon a controlling person is the greater of $1,425,000 or three times the profit gained or loss avoided as a result of the controlled person's violation. If that violation consists of tipping inside information, the court measures the controller's liability by the profit gained or loss avoided by the person to whom the controlled person directed the tip. For the purpose of this provision, "profit gained" or "loss avoided" is "the difference between the purchase or sale price of the security and the value of that security as measured by the trading price of the security a reasonable period after public dissemination of the nonpublic information."

Civil penalties for insider trading are payable into the U.S. Treasury. An action to recover a penalty must be brought within five years after the date of the purchase or sale. The SEC is authorized to award bounties of up to 10 percent of a recovered penalty to informants who provide information leading to the imposition of the penalty. However, the CFPA has expanded whistleblower awards: the SEC now must award whistleblowers who voluntarily provide original information that leads to *any* successful enforcement action in which the SEC imposes monetary sanctions in excess of $1 million. The amount of the award must be between 10 percent and 30 percent of funds collected as monetary sanctions, as determined by the SEC.

MISLEADING PROXY STATEMENTS

Any person who distributes a materially false or misleading proxy statement may be liable to a shareholder who relies upon the statement in purchasing or selling a security and thereby suffers a loss. In this context, a misstatement or omission is material if there is a substantial likelihood that a reasonable shareholder would consider it important in deciding how to vote. A number of courts have held that negligence is sufficient for an action under the proxy rule's antifraud provisions. In addition, when the proxy disclosure or filing requirement has been violated, a court may, if appropriate, enjoin a shareholder meeting or any action taken at that meeting. Other remedies are rescission, damages, and attorneys' fees. Since a proxy statement is filed with the SEC, a materially false or misleading proxy statement may also give rise to liability under Section 18, discussed above.

In addition, Rule 10b–5 also applies to misstatements in proxy statements. Moreover, most proxy statements used with mergers and sales of assets are also considered 1933 registration statements subject to civil liability under Section 11 of the 1933 Act.

FRAUDULENT TENDER OFFERS

It is unlawful for any person to make any untrue statement of material fact, to omit to state any material fact, or to engage in any fraudulent, deceptive, or manipulative practices in connection with any tender offer. Section 14(e). This provision applies even if the target company is not subject to the 1934 Act's reporting requirements. Insider trading during a tender offer is prohibited by Rule 14e–3, which has been upheld by the U.S. Supreme Court in *United States v. O'Hagan*.

Some courts have implied civil liability for violations of Section 14(e). Because relatively few cases have involved such violations, however, the requirements for such an action are not entirely clear. At present, a target company may seek an injunction, and a shareholder of the target may be able to recover damages or obtain rescission. Furthermore, it appears likely that the courts will require *scienter*.

◆ **SEE FIGURE 44-7: Civil Liability under the 1933 and 1934 Acts**

ANTIBRIBERY PROVISION OF FCPA

The FCPA makes it unlawful for any domestic concern or any of its officers, directors, employees, or agents to offer or give anything of value directly or indirectly to any foreign official, political party, or political official for the purpose of (1) influencing any act or decision of that person or party in his or its official capacity, (2) inducing an act or omission in violation of his or its lawful duty, or (3) inducing such person or party to use his or its influence to affect a decision of a foreign government in order to assist the domestic concern in obtaining or retaining business. An offer or promise to make a prohibited payment is a violation even if the offer is not accepted or the promise is not performed. The 1988 amendments to the Act explicitly excluded routine governmental actions not involving the official's discretion, such as obtaining permits or processing applications. They also added an affirmative defense for payments that are lawful under the written laws or regulations of the foreign official's country.

Violations can result in fines of up to $2 million for companies; individuals may be fined a maximum of $100,000 or be imprisoned for up to five years, or both. Section 32(c). Fines imposed upon individuals may not be paid directly or indirectly by the domestic concern on whose behalf they acted. In addition, the courts may impose civil penalties of up to $16,000.

In 1997 the United States and thirty-three other nations signed the Organisation for Economic Co-operation and Development Convention on Combating Bribery of Foreign Public Officials in International Business Transactions (OECD Convention). Since then, four additional nations have signed the treaty. In 1998 Congress enacted the International Anti-Bribery and Fair Competition Act of 1998 to conform the FCPA to the Convention. The 1998 Act expands the FCPA to include (1) payments made to "secure any improper advantage" from foreign officials, (2) all

◆ FIGURE 44-7: **Civil Liability under the 1933 and 1934 Acts**

Provision	Conduct	Plaintiffs	Defendants	Standard of Culpability	Reliance Required	Type of Liability	Remedies
Section 12(a)(1) 1933 Act	Unregistered sale or sale without prospectus	Purchasers from a violator	Sellers in violation	Strict liability	No	Express	Rescission Damages
Section 11 1933 Act	Registration statement containing material misstatement or omission	Purchasers of registered security	Issuer; Directors; Signers; Underwriters; Experts	Strict liability for issuer; Negligence for others	No	Express	Damages Attorneys' fees
Section 12(a)(2) 1933 Act	Material misstatement or omission	Purchasers from a violator	Sellers in violation	Negligence	No	Express	Rescission Damages
Section 18 1934 Act	False or misleading statements in a document filed with SEC	Purchasers or sellers	Persons making filing in violation	Knowledge or bad faith	Yes	Express	Damages Attorneys' fees
Section 16(b) 1934 Act	Short-swing profit by insider	Issuer; Shareholder of issuer	Directors; Officers; 10 percent shareholders	Strict liability	No	Express	Damages
Rule 10b–5 1934 Act	Deception or material misstatement or omission	Purchasers or sellers	Purchasers or sellers in violation	*Scienter*	Yes	Implied	Rescission Damages Injunction
Section 20A 1934 Act	Insider trading	Contemporaneous purchasers or sellers	Inside traders	*Scienter*	No	Express	Damages
Section 14(a) 1934 Act	Materially false or misleading proxy solicitation	Shareholders	Persons making proxy solicitation in violation	Negligence (probably)	Probably	Implied	Rescission Damages Injunction Attorneys' fees
Section 14(e) 1934 Act	Tender offer with deception or manipulation or material misstatement or material omission	Target company; Shareholders of target	Persons making tender offer in violation	*Scienter* (probably)	Probably	Implied	Rescission Damages Injunction

Note: SEC = Securities and Exchange Commission.

foreign persons who commit an act in furtherance of a foreign bribe while in the United States, and (3) officials of public international organizations within the definition of a "foreign official." A public international organization is defined as either an organization designated by executive order pursuant to the International Organizations Immunities Act, or any other international organization designated by executive order of the president.

(except the antibribery provision) or the rules and regulations the SEC promulgates pursuant to the Act. As amended by the Sarbanes-Oxley Act, for individuals, conviction may carry a fine of not more than $5 million or imprisonment for not more than twenty years, or both, with one exception: a person who proves she had no knowledge of the rule or regulation is not subject to imprisonment. If the person, however, is not a natural person (e.g., a corporation), a fine not exceeding $25 million may be imposed.

CRIMINAL SANCTIONS

Section 32 of the 1934 Act imposes criminal sanctions on any person who willfully violates any provision of the Act

---

CHAPTER SUMMARY

SECURITIES ACT OF 1933

DEFINITION OF A SECURITY	**Security** includes any note, stock, bond, preorganization subscription, and investment contract **Investment Contract** any investment of money or property made in expectation of receiving a financial return solely from the efforts of others
REGISTRATION OF SECURITIES	**Disclosure Requirements** disclosure of accurate material information required in all public offerings of nonexempt securities unless offering is an exempt transaction **Integrated Disclosure and Shelf Registrations** permitted for certain qualified issuers
EXEMPT SECURITIES	**Definition** securities not subject to the registration requirements of the 1933 Act **Types** exempt securities include short-term commercial paper, municipal bonds, and certain insurance policies and annuity contracts
EXEMPT TRANSACTIONS FOR ISSUERS	**Definition** issuance of securities not subject to the registration requirements of the 1933 Act **Types** exempt transactions include limited offers under Regulation D and Section 4(6), Regulation A, and intrastate issues
EXEMPT TRANSACTIONS FOR NONISSUERS	**Definition** resales by persons other than the issuer that are exempted from the registration requirements of the 1933 Act **Types** exempt transactions include Rule 144 for reporting and nonreporting issuers, Regulation A, and Rule 144A
LIABILITY	**Unregistered Sales** Section 12(a)(1) imposes absolute civil liability as there are no defenses **False Registration Statements** Section 11 imposes liability on the issuer, all persons who signed the statement, every director or partner, experts who prepared or certified any part of the statement, and all underwriters; defendants other than issuer may assert the defense of due diligence **Antifraud Provisions** Section 12(a)(2) imposes liability upon the seller to the immediate purchaser, provided the purchaser did not know of the untruth or omission, but the seller is not liable if he did not know and, in the exercise of

reasonable care could not have known, of the untrue statement or omission; Section 17(a) broadly prohibits fraud in the sale of securities

Criminal Sanctions willful violations are subject to a fine of not more than $10,000 and/or imprisonment of not more than five years

---

SECURITIES EXCHANGE ACT OF 1934

DISCLOSURE
Registration and Periodic Reporting Requirements apply to all regulated publicly held companies and include one-time registration as well as annual, quarterly, and monthly reports

Proxy Solicitations
- *Definition of a Proxy* a signed writing by a shareholder authorizing a named person to vote her stock at a specified meeting of shareholders
- *Proxy Statements* proxy disclosure statements are required when proxies are solicited or an issuer submits a matter to a shareholder vote

Tender Offers
- *Definition of a Tender Offer* a general invitation to shareholders to purchase their shares at a specified price for a specified time
- *Disclosure Requirements* a statement disclosing specified information must be filed with the Securities and Exchange Commission and furnished to each offeree

Foreign Corrupt Practices Act imposes internal control requirements on companies with securities registered under the 1934 Act

LIABILITY
Misleading Statements in Reports Section 18 imposes civil liability for any false or misleading statement made in a registration or report filed with the Securities and Exchange Commission

Short-Swing Profits Section 16(b) imposes liability on certain insiders (directors, officers, and shareholders owning more than 10 percent of the stock of a corporation) for all profits made on sales and purchases within six months of each other, with any recovery going to the issuer

Antifraud Provision Rule 10b–5 makes it unlawful to (1) employ any device, scheme, or artifice to defraud; (2) make any untrue statement of a material fact; (3) omit to state a material fact; or (4) engage in any act that operates as a fraud
- *Requisites of Rule 10b–5* recovery requires (1) a misstatement or omission, (2) materiality, (3) *scienter* (intentional and knowing conduct), (4) reliance, and (5) connection with the purchase or sale of a security
- *Insider Trading* "insiders" are liable under Rule 10b–5 for failing to disclose material, nonpublic information before trading on the information

Express Insider Trading Liability is imposed on any person who sells or buys a security while in possession of inside information

Civil Penalties for Inside Trading may be imposed on inside traders in an amount up to three times the gains they made or losses they avoided

Misleading Proxy Statements any person who distributes a false or misleading proxy statement is liable to injured investors

Fraudulent Tender Offers Section 14(e) imposes civil liability for false and material statements or omissions or fraudulent, deceptive, or manipulative practices in connection with any tender offer

Antibribery Provision of FCPA prohibited bribery can result in fines and imprisonment

Criminal Sanctions individuals who willfully violate the 1934 Act are subject to a fine of not more than $5 million and/or imprisonment of not more than twenty years

Accountants' Legal Liability

Accountants perform a number of important roles in our business society. One such role is to provide reliable financial information to facilitate the effective and efficient allocation of resources in the economy. As Harold M. Williams, former chair of the Securities and Exchange Commission (SEC), has observed, "Obviously, if users of financial data, who often may have little or no contact with the business in question, could not trust in its financial statements, capital formation and lending could not be carried on as they are today."

An accountant is subject to potential civil liability arising from the professional services he provides to his clients and third parties. This legal liability is imposed both by the common law at the State level and by securities laws at the Federal level. In addition, an accountant may violate Federal or State criminal law through the performance of his professional activities. This chapter will deal with accountants' legal liability under both State and Federal law.

COMMON LAW

An accountant's legal responsibility under State law may be based upon (1) contract law, (2) tort law, or (3) criminal law. In addition, the common law provides accountants with certain rights and privileges: in particular, the ownership of their working papers and, in some States, a limited accountant–client privilege.

CONTRACT LIABILITY

The employment contract between an accountant and her client is subject to the general principles of contract law. For the contract to be binding, therefore, it must meet all of the requirements of a common law contract, including offer and acceptance, capacity, consideration, legality, and a writing if, as is often the case, the agreement falls within the one-year provision of the statute of frauds.

Upon entering into a contract (frequently referred to as an *engagement* letter), the accountant is bound to perform all the duties she **explicitly** agrees to provide under the contract. For example, if an accountant agrees to complete her audit of a client by October 15 so that the client may release its annual report on time, the accountant is under a contractual obligation to do so. Likewise, an accountant who contractually promises to conduct an audit to detect possible embezzlement is under a contractual obligation to provide for her client an expanded audit *beyond* Generally Accepted Auditing Standards (GAAS).

By entering into a contract, an accountant also **implicitly** agrees to perform the contract in a competent and professional manner. His agreement to render professional services holds an accountant to those standards that are generally accepted by the accounting profession, such as GAAS and Generally Accepted Accounting Practices (GAAP). Although accountants need not ensure the absolute accuracy of their work, they must exercise the care of reasonably skilled professionals.

An accountant who breaches his contract incurs liability not only to his client but also to certain third-party contract beneficiaries. A **third-party beneficiary** is a noncontracting party whom the contracting parties *intend* to receive the primary benefit under the contract. For example, Otis Manufacturing Co. hires Adler, an accountant, to prepare a financial statement for Otis to use in obtaining a loan from Chemical Bank. Chemical Bank is a third-party beneficiary of the contract between Otis and Adler. Another example of a potential third party is an investor considering the purchase of part or all of a particular company. For a more detailed discussion of third-party beneficiaries, see *Chapter 16*.

Pursuant to general contract principles, an accountant who *materially breaches* his contract is entitled to no compensation (i.e., the client is discharged from his obligations under the contract because of the material breach). Thus, if an accountant does not perform an audit on time when time is of the essence, or completes only 60 percent of the audit, she has committed a material breach. On the other hand, an accountant who *substantially performs* his contractual duties

COLUMN: © PHOTOGRAPHEROLYMPUS   CLOUDS: © KERTLIS

is generally entitled to be compensated for the contractually agreed-upon fee, less any damages or loss his nonmaterial breach has caused the client. (See *Chapter 18.*)

TORT LIABILITY In performing his professional services, an accountant may incur tort liability to his client or third parties for negligence or fraud. A tort, as discussed in *Chapter 7* (intentional torts, including fraud) and *Chapter 8* (negligence), is a private or civil wrong or injury, other than a breach of contract, for which the courts will provide a remedy in the form of an action for damages.

NEGLIGENCE An accountant is negligent if she does not exercise the degree of care a reasonably competent accountant would exercise under the circumstances. For example, Arthur, an accountant, is engaged to audit the books of Zebra Corporation. During the course of Arthur's investigation, Olivia, an officer of Zebra, notifies Arthur that she suspects that Terrence, Zebra's treasurer, is engaged in a scheme to embezzle from the corporation. Previously informed that Olivia and Terrence are on bad terms with each other, Arthur does not pursue the matter. Terrence is, in fact, engaged in a common embezzlement scheme. Arthur is negligent for failing to conduct a reasonable investigation of the alleged defalcation. Nonetheless, an accountant is *not* liable for honest inaccuracies or errors of judgment so long as she exercised reasonable care in performing her duties. Moreover, as previously mentioned, an accountant need *not* guarantee the accuracy of her reports, provided she acted in a reasonably competent and professional manner.

Most courts do not permit an accountant to raise the defense of the plaintiff's contributory (or comparative) negligence. Nevertheless, a few courts do permit the defense of contributory or comparative negligence despite the fact that they recognize "that professional malpractice actions pose peculiar problems and that the comparison of fault between a layperson and a professional should be approached with caution." *Halla Nursery, Inc. v. Baumann-Furrie & Co.*, 454 N.W.2d 905 (Minn. 1990).

Historically, an accountant's liability for negligence extended only to the client and to third-party beneficiaries. Under this view, **privity** of contract was a requirement for a cause of action based upon negligence. This approach was established by the landmark case *Ultramares Corporation v. Touche*, 255 N.Y. 170, 170 N.E. 441 (1931):

The defendants owed to their employer a duty imposed by law to make their certificate without fraud, and a duty growing out of contract to make it with the care and caution proper to their calling. Fraud includes the pretense of knowledge when knowledge there is none. To creditors and investors to whom the employer exhibited the certificate, the defendants owed a like duty to make it without fraud,

since there was notice in the circumstances of its making that the employer did not intend to keep it to himself. [Citations.] A different question develops when we ask whether they owed a duty to these to make it without negligence. If liability for negligence exists, a thoughtless slip or blunder, the failure to detect a theft or forgery beneath the cover of deceptive entries, may expose accountants to a liability in an indeterminate amount for an indeterminate time to an indeterminate class. The hazards of a business conducted on these terms are so extreme as to enkindle doubt whether a flaw may not exist in the implication of a duty that exposes to these consequences.

* * *

Our holding does not emancipate accountants from the consequences of fraud. It does not relieve them if their audit has been so negligent as to justify a finding that they had no genuine belief in its adequacy, for this again is fraud. It does no more than say that, if less than this is proved, if there has been neither reckless misstatement nor insincere profession of an opinion, but only honest blunder, the ensuing liability for negligence is one that is bounded by the contract and is to be enforced between the parties by whom the contract has been made. We doubt whether the average business man receiving a certificate without paying for it, and receiving it merely as one among a multitude of possible investors, would look for anything more.

Today, the courts apply three different tests to determine accountants' liability for negligence to third parties. Several States follow the *Ultramares* test, which has evolved into a **primary-benefit test**, explained in *Credit Alliance Corp. v. Arthur Andersen & Co.*, 65 N.Y.2d 536 (1985), as follows:

Before accountants may be held liable in negligence to noncontractual parties who rely to their detriment on inaccurate financial reports, certain prerequisites must be satisfied: (1) the accountants must have been aware that the financial reports were to be used for a particular purpose or purposes; (2) in the furtherance of which a known party or parties was intended to rely; and (3) there must have been some conduct on the part of the accountants linking them to that party or parties, which evinces the accountants' understanding of that party or parties' reliance.

In recent years, a majority of the States has adopted a **foreseen users** or **foreseen class of users** test. This test expands the class of protected individuals to include those whom the accountant knew would use the work product *or* those who use the accountant's work for a purpose for which the accountant knew the work would be used. For instance, an accountant knows that her client will use a work product to try to obtain a loan from a particular bank. Even if the client uses the audited financial statements to obtain a loan from a different bank, the auditor would be liable to that second bank for any negligent misrepresentations in the financial statements. This class of protected individuals does not, however, include potential investors and the general public.

This approach has also been adopted by the Second Restatement of Torts. Section 552 provides:

(1) One who, in the course of his business, profession or employment, or in any other transaction in which he has a pecuniary interest, supplies false information for the guidance of others in their business transactions, is subject to liability for pecuniary loss caused to them by their justifiable reliance upon the information, if he fails to exercise reasonable care or competence in obtaining or communicating the information.

(2) Except as stated in Subsection (3), the liability stated in Subsection (1) is limited to loss suffered

(a) by the person or one of a limited group of persons for whose benefit and guidance he intends to supply the information or knows that the recipient intends to supply it; and

(b) through reliance upon it in a transaction that he intends the information to influence or knows that the recipient so intends or in a substantially similar transaction.

(3) The liability of one who is under a public duty to give the information extends to loss suffered by any of the class of persons for whose benefit the duty is created, in any of the transactions in which it is intended to protect them.

Some courts have extended liability to benefit an even broader group: reasonably **foreseeable plaintiffs**, including those who are neither known to the accountant nor are members of a class of intended recipients. A few States have adopted this test, which requires only that the accountant reasonably foresee that such individuals might use the financial statements. The rationale behind the foreseeability standard of the law of negligence is that a tortfeasor should be fully liable for all reasonably foreseeable consequences of her conduct.

◆ **SEE FIGURE 45-1: Accountants' Liability to Third Parties for Negligent Misrepresentation**

FRAUD An accountant who commits a fraudulent act is liable to any person whom the accountant reasonably should have foreseen would be injured through justifiable reliance on the misrepresentation. The requisite elements of fraud, which are more fully discussed in *Chapter 11*, are (1) a false representation (2) of fact (3) that is material and (4) is made with knowledge of its falsity and with the intention to deceive, (5) is justifiably relied upon, and (6) causes injury to the

◆ **FIGURE 45-1: Accountants' Liability to Third Parties for Negligent Misrepresentation**

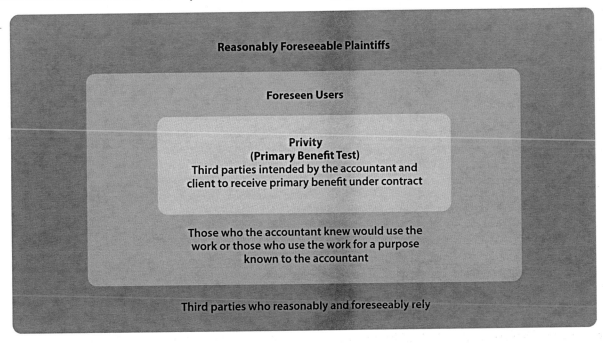

Reasonably Foreseeable Plaintiffs

Foreseen Users

**Privity
(Primary Benefit Test)**
Third parties intended by the accountant and client to receive primary benefit under contract

Those who the accountant knew would use the work or those who use the work for a purpose known to the accountant

Third parties who reasonably and foreseeably rely

plaintiff. An accountant who commits fraud may be held liable for both compensatory and punitive damages.

In recent years, accountants also have been subject to a number of civil lawsuits based on the Racketeer Influenced and Corrupt Organizations Act (RICO). For a discussion of this Act, see *Chapter 6*.

CRIMINAL LIABILITY

An accountant's potential criminal liability in rendering professional services is based primarily on the Federal law of securities regulation (discussed later) and taxation. Nonetheless, an accountant would violate State criminal law if she knowingly and willfully certified false documents, altered or tampered with accounting records, used false financial reports, gave false testimony under oath, or committed forgery.

Criminal sanctions may be imposed under the Internal Revenue Code for knowingly preparing false or fraudulent tax returns or documents used in connection with a tax return. Such liability also extends to willfully assisting or advising a client or others to prepare a false return. Penalties for tax fraud may be a fine not to exceed $250,000 ($500,000 for a corporation) or three years' imprisonment, or both.

CLIENT INFORMATION

In providing services for his client, an accountant necessarily obtains information concerning the client's business affairs. Two legal issues concerning this client information involve (1) the ownership of the working papers generated by the accountant and (2) the question of whether or not client information is privileged.

WORKING PAPERS Audit working papers include an auditor's records of the procedures she followed, the tests she performed, the information she obtained, and the conclusions she reached in connection with an audit. All relevant information pertaining to the examination should be included in the working papers. Because an accountant is held to be the owner of his working papers, he need not surrender them to his client. Nevertheless, the accountant may not disclose the contents of these papers unless either (1) the client consents or (2) a court orders the disclosure.

ACCOUNTANT–CLIENT PRIVILEGE Because information considered to be privileged may not be admitted into evidence over the objection of the person possessing the privilege, an accountant must endeavor to maintain confidentiality regarding her communications with her client. The question of a possible accountant-client privilege frequently arises in tax disputes, criminal prosecution, and civil litigation.

Neither the common law nor Federal law recognizes a general privilege. Nevertheless, a number of States have adopted statutes granting some form of accountant-client privilege. Most of these statutes grant the privilege to the client, although a few extend the privilege to the accountant. In addition, the Internal Revenue Service (IRS) Restructuring and Reform Act grants accountants, who are authorized under Federal law to practice before the IRS, the privilege of confidentiality for tax advice given to their client-taxpayers with respect to Internal Revenue Code matters. Regardless of whether or not the privilege exists, it is generally considered to be professionally unethical for an accountant to disclose confidential communications from a client unless the disclosure is in accordance with (1) American Institute of Certified Public Accountants (AICPA) or GAAS requirements, (2) a court order, or (3) the client's request.

FEDERAL SECURITIES LAW

Accountants may be both civilly and criminally liable under provisions of the Securities Act of 1933 and the Securities Exchange Act of 1934. (*Chapter 44* contains a fuller discussion of the securities laws.) This liability is more extensive and has fewer limitations than liability under the common law. SEC regulations require that auditors are qualified and independent of their audit clients both in fact and in appearance. Accordingly, Rule 2–01 of SEC Regulation S-X imposes restrictions on financial, employment, and business relationships between an accountant and an audit client and restrictions on an accountant providing certain nonaudit services to an audit client.

SECURITIES ACT OF 1933

Accountants are subject to express civil liability under Section 11 if the financial statements they prepare or certify for inclusion in a registration statement contain any untrue statement or omit any material fact. This liability extends to anyone who acquires the security without knowledge of the untruth or omission. Not only does such liability require no proof of privity between the accountant and the purchasers, but proof of reliance upon the financial statements is also usually not required under Section 11. An accountant will not be liable, however, if he can prove his "due diligence defense." **Due diligence** requires that the accountant had, after reasonable investigation, reasonable ground to believe and did believe, at the time the registration statement became effective, that the financial statements were true, complete, and accurate. The standard of reasonableness is that required of a prudent person in the management of her own property. Thus, Section 11 imposes liability upon accountants for negligence in the conduct of an audit or in the presentation of information in financial statements. In addition, an accountant is not liable for any or the entire amount otherwise recoverable under Section 11 that the defendant proves was caused by something other than the defective disclosure. Moreover, an accountant who *willfully* violates this section may be held criminally liable for a fine of not more than $10,000 or imprisonment of not more than five years, or both. Section 24.

SECURITIES EXCHANGE ACT OF 1934

CIVIL LIABILITY Section 18 imposes express civil liability upon an accountant who makes or causes to be made any false or misleading statement with respect to any material fact in any application, report, document, or registration filed with the SEC under the 1934 Act. Liability extends to any person who purchased or sold a security in reliance upon that statement without knowing that it was false or misleading. An accountant is not liable, however, if she proves that she acted in good faith and had no knowledge that such statement was false or misleading. Thus, an accountant is not liable for false or misleading statements resulting from good faith negligence.

Accountants also may be held civilly liable for violations of **Rule 10b–5**. Rule 10b–5, as discussed in *Chapter 44*, is extremely broad in that it applies to both oral and written misstatements or omissions of material fact and to all securities. An accountant may be liable for a violation of the rule to those who rely upon the misstatement or omission of material fact when purchasing or selling a security. Nevertheless, liability is imposed only if the accountant acted with scienter, or intentional or knowing conduct. Therefore, accountants are not liable under Rule 10b–5 for mere negligence, although most courts have held that reckless disregard of the truth is sufficient.

◆ SEE FIGURE 45-2: **Accountants' Liability under Federal Securities Law**

CRIMINAL LIABILITY Accountants may also be held criminally liable for any willful violation of Section 18 or Rule 10b–5. As amended by the Sarbanes-Oxley Act, conviction may carry a fine of not more than $5 million or imprisonment for not more than twenty years, or both. An accounting firm may be fined up to $25 million. Section 32.

AUDIT REQUIREMENTS The **Private Securities Litigation Reform Act of 1995** (Reform Act) imposed a significant set of obligations upon independent public accountants who audit financial statements required by the 1934 Act. The Reform Act authorizes the SEC to adopt rules that modify or supplement the practices or procedures followed by auditors in the conduct of an audit. Moreover, the Act requires auditors to establish procedures capable of detecting material illegal acts, identifying material related to party transactions, and evaluating whether there is a substantial doubt about the issuer's ability to continue as a going concern during the next fiscal year.

If the auditor becomes aware of information indicating an illegal act, the auditor must determine whether an illegal act occurred and the illegal act's possible effect on the issuer's financial statements. Then the auditor must inform the issuer's management about any illegal activity and make sure that the audit committee or the board of directors is adequately informed. If the auditor concludes that (1) the illegal act has a material effect on the issuer's financial statements, (2) neither senior management nor the board has taken timely and appropriate remedial actions, *and* (3) the failure to take remedial action is reasonably expected to warrant departure from a standard auditor report or warrant resignation from the auditor's engagement, then the auditor promptly must report these conclusions to the issuer's

◆ FIGURE 45-2: **Accountants' Liability under Federal Securities Law**

	Section 11 (1933 Act)	Section 18 (1934 Act)	Rule 10b–5 (1934 Act)
Conduct	Registration statement containing material misstatement or omission	False or misleading statements in a document filed with SEC	Deception or material misstatement or opinion
Fault	Negligence	Knowledge or bad faith	*Scienter*
Plaintiff's knowledge is a defense	Yes	Yes	Yes
Reliance required	No	Yes	Yes
Privity required	No	No	No

Note: SEC = Securities and Exchange Commission.

board. Within one day of receiving such report, the issuer must notify the SEC and furnish the auditor with a copy of that notice. If the auditor does not receive such notice, then the auditor must either resign or furnish the SEC with the auditor's report to the board. If the auditor resigns, the auditor must furnish the SEC with a copy of the auditor's report.

The Reform Act provides that an auditor shall not be held liable in a private action for any finding, conclusion, or statement expressed in the report the Act requires the auditor to make to the SEC. The SEC can impose civil penalties against an auditor who willfully violates the Reform Act by failing to resign or to furnish a report to the SEC.

SARBANES-OXLEY ACT In response to the business scandals involving companies such as Enron, WorldCom, Global Crossing, and the accounting firm of Arthur Andersen, in 2002 Congress passed the Sarbanes-Oxley Act, which amends the securities acts in a number of significant respects to protect investors by improving the accuracy and reliability of corporate disclosures. The Act provides for the establishment of the five-member Public Company Accounting Oversight Board (the Board) to oversee the audit of public companies to further the public interest in the preparation of informative, accurate, and independent audit reports for public companies. The SEC has oversight and enforcement authority over the Board. The Board enforces the Sarbanes-Oxley Act, the Federal securities laws, the SEC's rules, the Board's rules, and professional accounting standards. The duties of the Board include (1) registering public accounting firms that prepare audit reports for issuers; (2) overseeing the audit of public companies; (3) establishing audit report standards and rules; and (4) inspecting, investigating, and enforcing compliance on the part of registered public accounting firms and their associated persons. The Act

directs the Board to establish or modify the auditing and related attestation standards, quality control standards, and ethics standards used by registered public accounting firms to prepare and issue audit reports. The willful violation of any Board rule is treated as a willful violation of the 1934 Act. Moreover, the Board can impose sanctions in its disciplinary proceedings, including the permanent revocation of an accounting firm's registration, a permanent ban on a person's associating with any registered firm, and monetary penalties of $15 million for an accounting firm and $750,000 for a natural person.

To make auditors more independent from their clients, the Act prohibits accounting firms from performing eight specified nonaudit services for audit clients, including bookkeeping or other services related to the accounting records or financial statements; financial information systems design and implementation; appraisal or valuation services; fairness opinions; management functions or human resources; and actuarial services. Accounting firms may perform other nonaudit services not expressly forbidden by the Act if the company's audit committee grants prior approval and the approval by the audit committee is disclosed to investors in periodic reports. The lead audit partner having primary responsibility for the audit and the audit partner responsible for reviewing the audit must rotate at least every five years.

Auditors must report directly to the company's audit committee and make timely disclosure of accounting issues concerning (1) critical accounting policies and practices used in the audit; (2) alternative treatments and their ramifications within generally accepted accounting principles that have been discussed with management officials and the treatment preferred by the auditor; and (3) other material written communications between the auditor and management.

CHAPTER SUMMARY

COMMON LAW   **Contract Liability** the employment contract between an accountant and her client is subject to the general principles of contract law
- *Explicit Duties* the accountant is bound to perform all the duties she expressly agrees to provide
- *Implicit Duties* the accountant impliedly agrees to perform the contract in a competent and professional manner
- *Beneficiaries* contract liability extends to the client or contracting party and to third-party beneficiaries (noncontracting parties intended by the contracting parties to receive the primary benefit under the contract)
- *Breach of Contract* general contract law principles apply

Tort Liability a tort is a private or civil wrong or injury other than a breach of contract
- *Negligence* an accountant is liable for failing to exercise the degree of care a reasonably competent accountant would exercise under the circumstances; most courts have extended an accountant's liability for negligence beyond the client and third-party beneficiaries to foreseen third parties
- *Fraud* an accountant who commits a fraudulent act is liable for both compensatory and punitive damages to any person who he should have reasonably foreseen would be injured; a fraudulent act is a false representation of fact that is material, is made with knowledge of its falsity and with the intention to deceive, and is justifiably relied on

Criminal Liability State law imposes criminal liability on accountants for willfully certifying false documents, altering or tampering with accounting records, using false financial reports, giving false testimony, and committing forgery

Client Information
- *Working Papers* an accountant is considered the owner of his working papers but may not disclose their contents unless the client agrees or a court orders the disclosure
- *Accountant-Client Privilege* not recognized generally by the common law or Federal law, although some States have adopted statutes granting some form of privilege; accountants authorized to practice before the Internal Revenue Service have privilege for tax advice given to their client-taxpayers with respect to Internal Revenue Code matters

FEDERAL SECURITIES LAW

1933 Act
- *Civil Liability* Section 11 imposes express civil liability upon accountants if the financial statements they prepare or certify for a registration statement contain any untrue statement or omit any material fact, unless the accountant proves her due diligence defense, which requires that the accountant had, after reasonable investigation, reasonable grounds to believe and did believe that the financial statements were true, complete, and accurate
- *Criminal Liability* a willful violator of Section 11 is subject to fines of not more than $10,000 and/or imprisonment of not more than five years

1934 Act
- *Section 18* imposes express civil liability on an accountant who knowingly makes any false or misleading statement about any material fact in any report, document, or registration filed with the Securities and Exchange Commission
- *Rule 10b–5* an accountant is civilly liable under this rule if he acts with *scienter* in making oral or written misstatements or omissions of material fact in connection with the purchase or sale of a security
- *Criminal Liability* a willful violator of either Section 18 or Rule 10b–5 is subject to fines of not more than $5 million and/or imprisonment of not more than twenty years
- *Audit Requirements* auditors must establish procedures capable of detecting material illegal acts, identifying material related to party transactions, and evaluating whether there is a substantial doubt about the issuer's ability to continue as a going concern during the next fiscal year
- *Sarbanes-Oxley Act* establishes a new regulatory body to oversee public company auditors, makes auditors more independent from their clients, and places direct responsibility for the audit relationship on audit committees

COLUMN: © PHOTOGRAPHEROLYMPUS   CLOUDS: © KERTLIS

Introduction to Property, Property Insurance, Bailments, and Documents of Title

I n our democratic and free enterprise society, the importance of the concept of property is second only to that of the idea of liberty. Although many of our rules of property stem directly from English law, in the United States property occupies a unique status because of the protection expressly granted it by the U.S. Constitution and by most State constitutions as well. The Fifth Amendment to the Federal Constitution provides that "No person shall be … deprived of life, liberty, or property, without due process of law; nor shall private property be taken for public use, without just compensation." The Fourteenth Amendment contains a similar requirement: "No State shall … deprive any person of life, liberty, or property, without due process of law." Under the police power, however, this protection afforded to property owners is subject to regulation for the public good.

In the first part of this chapter, we will provide a general introduction to the law governing real and personal property. The second part of this chapter deals specifically with personal property; the third part covers property insurance. The fourth part of the chapter covers bailments and the last part of the chapter discusses documents of title.

INTRODUCTION TO PROPERTY AND PERSONAL PROPERTY

Property is a legally protected interest or group of interests. It is valuable only because our law provides that certain consequences follow from the ownership of it. The right to use property, to sell it, and to control to whom it shall pass on the death of the owner are all included within the term *property*. Thus, a person who speaks of "owning property" may have one of two separate ideas in mind: (1) the *physical thing itself*, as when a homeowner says, "I just bought a piece of property in Oakland," meaning complete ownership of a physically identifiable parcel of land, or (2) a *right or interest* in a physical object (for example, with respect to land, a tenant under a lease has a property interest in the leased land, although he does not own the land).

KINDS OF PROPERTY

Property may be classified as (1) tangible or intangible and (2) real or personal, but these classifications are not mutually exclusive.

◆ **SEE FIGURE 48-1: Kinds of Property**

TANGIBLE AND INTANGIBLE

A forty-acre farm, a chair, and a household pet are tangible property. Each of these *physical* objects embodies the group of rights or interests known as "title" to or "ownership" of **tangible property**. **Intangible property**, in contrast, does not exist in a physical form. For example, the rights represented by a stock certificate, a promissory note, and a deed granting Jones a right-of-way over Smith's land are intangible property. Each represents certain rights that defy reduction to physical possession but have a legal reality in that the courts will protect them.

The same item may be the object of both tangible and intangible property rights. Suppose Ann purchases a book published by Brown & Sons. On the first page is the statement "Copyright 2011 by Brown & Sons." Ann owns the volume she has purchased. She has the right to exclusive physical possession and use of that particular copy. It is a tangible piece of property of which she is the owner. Brown & Sons, however, has the exclusive right to publish copies of the book, a right granted the publisher by the copyright laws. The courts will protect this intangible property of Brown & Sons, as well as Ann's right to her particular volume.

REAL AND PERSONAL

The most significant practical distinction between types of property is the classification into real and personal property. To define this distinction simply, land and all interests in it

◆ **FIGURE 48-1: Kinds of Property**

	Personal	Real
Tangible	Goods	Land Buildings Fixtures
Intangible	Negotiable instruments Stock certificates Contract rights Copyrights Patents	Leases Easements Mortgages

are **real property** (also called **realty**), and every other thing or interest identified as property is **personal property** (also called **chattel**). This easy description encompasses most property, with the exception of certain physical objects that are personal property under most circumstances but that may, because of their attachment to land or their use in connection with land, become a form of real property called fixtures.

FIXTURES

As we noted above, a **fixture** is an article or piece of property that was formerly treated as personal property but has been attached in such a manner to land or a building that it is now designated as real property even though it retains its original identity. The intent of the parties to convert the property to real property from personal property is usually shown by the permanent manner of affixation or the adaptation of the affixed object to the property. For example, building materials are clearly personal property; however, when worked into a building as its construction progresses, such materials become real property, as buildings are a part of the land they occupy. Thus, clay in its natural state is, of course, real property; when made into bricks, it becomes personal property; and if the bricks are then built into the wall of a house, the "clay" once again becomes real property.

Although doing so may be difficult, determining whether various items are personal property or real property may be the only way to settle certain conflicting ownership claims. Unless otherwise provided by agreement, personal property remains the property of the person who placed it on the real estate. On the other hand, property that has been affixed so as to become a fixture (an actual part of the real estate) becomes the property of the real estate owner.

In determining whether personal property has become a fixture, the intention of the parties, as expressed in their agreement, will control the settlement of conflicting claims. In the absence of an agreement, the following factors are relevant in determining whether any particular item is a fixture:

1. the physical relationship of the item to the land or building;
2. the intention of the person who attached the item to the land or building;
3. the purpose the item serves in relation to the land or building and in relation to the person who brought it there; and
4. the interest of that person in the land or building at the time of the item's attachment.

Although physical attachment is significant, a more important test is whether the item can be removed without causing material injury to the land or building on the land. If it *cannot* be so removed, the item is generally held to have become part of the realty.

By comparison, the test of purpose or use applies only if the item (1) is affixed to the realty in some way but (2) can be removed without material injury to the realty. In such a situation, if the use or purpose of the item is peculiar to a particular owner or occupant of the premises, the courts will tend to let him remove the item when he leaves. Accordingly, in the law of landlord and tenant, the tenant may remove trade fixtures (that is, items used in connection with a trade but not intended to become part of the realty), provided that she can accomplish this without material injury to the realty. On the other hand, doors may be removed without injury to the structure; yet, because they are necessary to the ordinary use of the building and are not peculiar to the use of the occupant, they are considered to be fixtures and thus part of the real property.

TRANSFER OF TITLE TO PERSONAL PROPERTY

The transfer of title to real property typically is a formal affair. In contrast, title to personal property may be acquired and transferred with relative ease and little formality. Such facility with regard to the transfer of personal property is essential within a society whose trade and industry are based principally on transactions in personal property. In a free economy, stocks, bonds, merchandise, and intellectual property must be sold with minimal delay. It is only natural that the law will reflect these needs.

Accordingly, the law concerning personal property has been largely codified. The Uniform Commercial Code (UCC or the Code) includes the law of sales of goods (Article 2), as well as the law governing the transfer and negotiation of negotiable instruments (Article 3) and of investment securities (Article 8). Nonetheless, the Code does not cover a number of issues (addressed in this chapter) involving the ownership and transfer of title to personal property. In addition, personal property may be, and often is, acquired by producing the item, rather than by selling or transferring it.

BY SALE

By definition, a **sale** of *tangible* personal property (goods) is transfer of title to specified existing goods for a consideration known as the price. Title passes when the parties intend it to pass, and transfer of possession is not required for a transfer of title. For a discussion of transfer of title, see *Chapter 21*.

Sales of *intangible* personal property also involve the transfer of title. Many of these sales also are governed by UCC provisions, while some, such as sales of copyrights and patents, are governed by specialized Federal legislation.

BY GIFT

A **gift** is a transfer of title to property from one person to another without consideration. This lack of consideration is the basic distinction between a gift and a sale. Because a gift involves no consideration or compensation, it must be completed by delivery of the gift to be effective. A gratuitous promise to make a gift is not binding. In addition, there must be intent on the part of the maker (the **donor**) of the gift to make a present transfer, and there must be acceptance by the recipient (the **donee**) of the gift.

DELIVERY Delivery is essential to a valid gift. The term *delivery* has a very special meaning that includes, but is not limited to, the manual transfer of the item to the donee. A donor may effect an irrevocable delivery by, for example, turning an item over to a third person with instructions to give it to the donee. Frequently, an item, because of its size, location, or intangibility, is incapable of immediate manual delivery. In such cases, an irrevocable gift may be effected through the delivery of something that symbolizes dominion over the item. This is referred to as **constructive delivery**. For example, if Joanne declares that she gives an antique desk and all its contents to Barry and hands Barry the key to the desk, in many states a valid gift has been made.

INTENT The law also provides clearly that the donor must intend to make a gift of the property. Thus, if Jack leaves a packet of stocks and bonds with Joan, her acquiring good title to them depends on whether Jack intended to make a gift of them or simply intended to place them in Joan's hands for safekeeping. A voluntary, uncompensated delivery made with the intent to give the recipient title constitutes a gift when the donee accepts the delivery. If these conditions are met, the donor has no further claim to the property.

Gifts, therefore, cannot be conditional. There is, however, one major exception to this rule: an engagement gift given in anticipation of marriage. If the marriage does not take place, the donor usually can recover the gift unless the donor broke the engagement without justification. But the courts will not apply the exception when a marriage is called off due to the death of one of the engaged parties.

ACCEPTANCE The final requirement of a valid gift is acceptance by the donee. In most instances, of course, the donee will accept the gift gratefully. Accordingly, the law usually presumes that the donee has accepted. But certain circumstances may render acceptance objectionable, such as when a gift would impose a burden upon the donee. In such cases, the law will not require the recipient to accept an unwanted gift. For example, a donee may prudently reject a gift of an elephant or a wrecked car in need of extensive repairs.

CLASSIFICATION Gifts may be either *inter vivos* or *causa mortis*. An *inter vivos* gift is a gift made by a donor during her lifetime. A gift *causa mortis* is a gift made by a donor in contemplation of her imminent death. A gift *causa mortis* is a conditional gift, contingent upon (1) the donor's death as she anticipated, (2) the donor's not revoking the gift prior to her death, and (3) the donee's surviving the donor.

BY WILL OR DESCENT

Title to personal property frequently is acquired by inheritance from a person who dies, either with or without a will. We will discuss this method of acquiring title in *Chapter 51*.

BY ACCESSION

Many of the practical problems surrounding the right to title to personal property stem from its principal characteristic—movability. The phrase "title by accession" denotes one general solution to the movability problem. **Accession**, in its strict sense, means the right of the owner of property to any increase in it, whether natural or human-made. For example, the owner of a cow acquires title by accession to any calves born to that cow.

BY CONFUSION

The basic problem of confusion is somewhat similar to problems involving title by accession. **Confusion** arises when identical goods belonging to different people become so *commingled* (mixed) that the owners cannot identify their own property. For example, Hereford cattle belonging to Benton become mixed with Hereford cattle belonging to Armstrong, and neither can specifically identify his herd as a result; or grain owned by Courts is combined inseparably with similar grain owned by Reichel. Confusion may result from accident, mistake, willful act, or agreement of the parties. If the goods can be apportioned, each owner who can prove his proportion of the whole is entitled to receive his share. If, however, the confusion results from the willful and wrongful act of one of the parties, he will lose his entire interest if unable to prove his share. Frequently, problems arise not because the owners cannot prove their original interests but because there is not enough left to distribute a full share to each. In such cases, if the confusion was due to mistake, accident, or agreement, each owner will bear the loss in proportion to his share. If the confusion resulted from an intentional and unauthorized act, the wrongdoer will first bear any loss.

BY POSSESSION

Sometimes a person may acquire title to movable personal property by taking possession of it. If the property has been intentionally **abandoned** (intentionally disposed of), a finder is entitled to the property. Moreover, under the general rule, a *finder* is entitled to **lost** (unintentionally left) **property** against everyone except the true *owner*. Suppose Zenner, the owner of an apartment complex, leases a kitchenette apartment to Terrell. One night, Waters, Terrell's mother-in-law, is invited to sleep in the convertible bed in the living room. In the course of preparing the bed, Waters finds an emerald ring caught on the springs under the mattress. She turns the ring over to the police, but diligent inquiry fails to ascertain the true owner. As the finder, Waters will be entitled to the ring.

A different rule applies when the lost property is in the ground. Here, the owner of the land has a claim superior to that of the finder. For example, Josephs employs Kasarda to excavate a lateral sewer. Kasarda uncovers ancient Native American artifacts. Josephs, not Kasarda, has the superior claim.

A further exception to the rule gives the finder first claim against all but the true owner. If property is intentionally placed somewhere by the owner, who then unintentionally leaves it, it becomes **mislaid property**. Most courts hold that if property has been mislaid, not lost, then the owner of the premises, not the finder, has first claim if the true owner is not discovered. This doctrine is frequently invoked in cases involving items found in restaurants or on trains, buses, or airplanes.

Another category of property is the **treasure trove**, which consists of coins or currency concealed by the owner. To be classified as treasure trove, the property must have been hidden or concealed for such a length of time that the owner is probably dead or undiscoverable. Treasure trove belongs to the finder as against all but the true owner.

Many States now have statutes that provide a means of vesting title to lost property in the finder where a prescribed search for the owner proves fruitless.

PROPERTY INSURANCE

Insurance covers a vast range of contracts, each of which distributes risk among a large number of members (the insureds) through an insurance company (the insurer). **Insurance** is a contractual undertaking by the insurer to pay a sum of money or give something of value to the insured or a beneficiary upon the happening of a contingency or fortuitous event that is beyond the control of the contracting parties.

Insurance coverage of one form or another affects every commercial activity. Through insurance, a business can safeguard its tangible assets against almost any form of damage or destruction, whether resulting from natural causes or from the accidental or improper actions of people. Insurance may also protect a business from tort liability, including assertions involving strict liability, negligence, or the intentional acts of its representatives. A business may procure credit insurance to guard against losses from poor credit risks and fidelity bonds to secure it against losses incurred through employee defalcations. If a business hires a famous pianist, it may insure the latter's hands; if it decides to present an outdoor concert, it may insure against the possibility of rain. A business may purchase life insurance on its key executives to reimburse it for financial losses arising from their deaths, or it may purchase such life insurance payable to the families of executives as part of their compensation. An additional, increasingly important use of insurance is to carry out pension commitments arising from agreements with employees. Nonetheless, the remaining sections of this chapter will focus on the insurance of property.

The McCarran-Ferguson Act, enacted by Congress in 1945, left insurance regulation to the States. Statutes in each State regulate domestic insurance companies and establish standards for foreign (out-of-state) insurance companies wishing to do business within the State. Most State legislation relates to the incorporation, licensing, supervision, and liquidation of insurers and to the licensing and supervision of agents and brokers.

Because the insurance relationship arises from a contract of insurance between the insurer and the insured, the law of insurance is a branch of contract law. For this reason, the doctrines of offer and acceptance, consideration, and other rules applicable to contracts in general are equally applicable to insurance contracts. Beyond that, however, insurance law, like the law of sales, bailments, negotiable instruments, or other specialized types of contracts, contains numerous modifications of fundamental contract law, which we will examine in the following sections.

FIRE AND PROPERTY INSURANCE

Fire and property insurance protects the owner (or another person with an insurable interest, such as a secured creditor or mortgagee) of real or personal property against loss resulting from damage to or destruction of the property by fire and certain related perils. Most fire insurance policies also cover damage caused by lightning, explosion, earthquake, water, wind, rain, collision, and riot.

Fire insurance policies are standardized in the United States, either by statute or by order of the State insurance departments, but their coverage is frequently enlarged through an "endorsement" or "rider" to include other perils or to benefit the insured in ways the provisions in the standard form do not. These policies normally are written for periods of one or three years.

TYPES OF FIRE

Fire insurance policies usually are held to cover damage from "hostile" fires, but they do not cover losses caused by "friendly" fires. A **friendly fire** is one contained in its intended location (for instance, a fire in a fireplace, furnace, or stove). A **hostile fire** is any other fire—all fires outside their intended or usual locales. Thus, a friendly fire becomes hostile if it escapes from its usual confines.

A standard insurance policy therefore will not cover heat or soot damage to a fireplace resulting from its continual use or damage done to personal property accidentally thrown into a stove. Damages caused by smoke, soot, water, and heat from a hostile fire are covered by the standard fire insurance policy, whereas such damages caused by a friendly fire generally are not. Moreover, most policies do not cover recovery for business interruption, unless they contain endorsements specifically covering such loss.

CO-INSURANCE CLAUSES

An arrangement common in property insurance, **co-insurance** is a means of sharing the risk between insurer and insured. For example, under the typical 80 percent co-insurance clause, the insured may recover the full amount of loss, not to exceed the face amount of the policy, provided the policy is for an amount not less than 80 percent of the property's insurable value. If the policy is for less than 80 percent, the insured recovers that pro-

portion of the loss that the amount of the policy bears, up to 80 percent of the insurable value. The formula for recovery is as follows:

$$\text{Recovery} = \frac{\text{Face Value of Policy}}{\text{Fair Market Value of Property} \times \text{Co-insurance \%}} \times \text{Loss}$$

Thus, if the co-insurance percentage is 80 percent, the value of the property is $100,000, and the policy is for $80,000 or more, the insured is fully protected against loss not to exceed the policy amount. If the policy amount is less than 80 percent of the property value, however, the insured receives only the proportion of the loss amount as determined in the formula above. Thus, in the above example, if the fire policy was for $60,000 and the property was 50 percent destroyed, the loss would be $50,000, of which the insurer would pay $37,500, which is $60,000/($100,000 × 80%) of $50,000. On a total loss, the recovery could not, of course, exceed the face amount of the policy. Some States do not favor co-insurance clauses and strictly construe the applicable statute against their validity. In addition, property insurance is not held to be co-insurance unless the policy specifically so provides.

OTHER INSURANCE CLAUSES

Recovery under property insurance policies typically is also limited by **other insurance clauses**, which generally require that liability be distributed *pro rata* among the various insurers. For example, Alexander insures his $120,000 building with Hamilton Insurance Co. for $60,000 and Jefferson Insurance Co. for $90,000. Alexander's building is partially destroyed by fire, causing Alexander $20,000 in damages. Alexander will collect two-fifths ($60,000/$150,000) of his damages from Hamilton ($8,000) and three-fifths ($90,000/$150,000) from Jefferson ($12,000).

TYPES OF POLICIES

Property insurance may be either a valued policy or an open policy. A **valued policy** is one providing for the full value of the property, upon which value the insured and the insurer specifically agree at the time the policy is issued. Should total loss occur, the insurer must pay this amount, not the actual or fair market value of the property. By comparison, no agreement in an **open policy** specifies the property's value; instead, the insurer pays the fair market value of the property calculated immediately prior to its loss. Thus, if Latrisha insures her building for $650,000 and at the time of its loss the property is valued at $600,000, under an open policy Latrisha would recover $600,000, while under a valued policy she would recover $650,000. If she insured the building for $700,000, and it was valued at that amount just prior to being blown apart by a tornado, under both types of policies Latrisha would recover $700,000. Insurance of property under a marine policy (insurance covering marine vessels and cargo) is generally considered to be valued, whereas nonmarine property insurance is presumed to be unvalued or open.

NATURE OF INSURANCE CONTRACTS

The basic principles of **contract** law apply to insurance policies. Furthermore, because insurance companies engage in a large volume of business over wide areas, they tend to standardize their policies. In some States, standardization is required by statute. This usually means that the insured must accept a given policy or do without the desired insurance.

OFFER AND ACCEPTANCE

No matter how many stories tell of insurance agents aggressively soliciting would-be insureds to take out policies, the applicant usually makes the offer, and the contract is created when the insurance company accepts that offer. The company may condition its acceptance—upon payment of the premium, for instance. It also may write a policy that differs from the application, thereby making a counteroffer that the applicant may or may not choose to accept.

In fire and casualty insurance, agents often have authority to make the insurance effective immediately, when needed, by means of a **binder**. Should a loss occur before the company actually issues a policy, the binder will be effective on the same terms and conditions the policy would have had if it had been issued.

In general, insurance contracts have not been held to be subject to the statute of frauds; thus, courts have held oral contracts for insurance to be enforceable. As a practical matter, however, oral contracts for insurance are very infrequent.

INSURABLE INTEREST

The concept of insurable interest has been developed over many years, primarily to eliminate gambling and to lessen the moral hazard. If a person could obtain an enforceable fire insurance policy on property that he did not own or in which he had no interest, he would be in a position to profit unfairly by the destruction of such property. An **insurable interest** is a relationship a person has with respect to certain property such that the happening of a possible, specific, damage-causing contingency would result in direct loss or injury to her. The purpose of insurance is protection against the risk of loss that would result from such a happening, not the realization of gain or profit.

Whether sole or concurrent, ownership obviously creates an insurable interest in property. Moreover, a right deriving from a contract concerning the property also gives rise to an insurable interest. For instance, shareholders in a closely held corporation have been held to have an insurable interest in the corporation's property to the extent of their interest. Likewise, lessees of property have insurable interests, as do holders of security interests, such as mortgagees or sellers with a purchase money security interest. Most courts have gone beyond the requirement of a legally recognized interest and apply a factual expectancy test. Under this test, the determinative question is whether the insured will obtain a benefit from the continued existence of the property or suffer a loss from its destruction. Thus, an individual who buys and insures a stolen automobile without knowledge that the automobile is stolen has an insurable interest in the automobile.

The insurable interest must exist at the time the property *loss* occurs, although some courts speak in terms of having the insurable interest at the time of insuring *and* at the time of loss. Property insurance policies are freely assignable after, but not before, a loss occurs.

PREMIUMS

Premiums are the consideration paid for an insurance policy. Property insurance policies are written only for periods lasting a few years at most. Long, continued liability on this type of policy is the exception rather than the rule. State law regulates the rates that may be charged for fire and various kinds of casualty insurance. The regulatory authorities are under a duty to require that the companies' rates be reasonable, not unfairly discriminatory, and neither excessively high nor inordinately low.

DEFENSES OF THE INSURER

An insurer may assert the ordinary defenses available to any contract. In addition, the terms of the insurance contract may provide specific defenses, such as the subject matter of the policy, types of perils covered, amount of coverage, and period of coverage. Moreover, the insurer may assert the closely related defenses of misrepresentation, breach of warranty, and concealment.

MISREPRESENTATION A representation is a statement made by or on behalf of an applicant for insurance to induce an insurer to enter into a contract. The representation is not a part of the insurance contract, but if the application containing the representation is incorporated by reference into the contract, the representation becomes a warranty. For a **misrepresentation** to have legal consequences, it must be material, the insurer must have relied on it as an inducement to enter into the contract, and it must either have been substantially false when the insured made it or have become so, to the insured's knowledge, before the contract was created. The principal remedy of the insurer on discovery of the material misrepresentation is rescission of the contract. To rescind the contract, the insurer must tender to the insured all premiums that have been paid, unless the misrepresentation was fraudulent. To be effective, rescission must be made as soon as possible after discovery of the misrepresentation.

BREACH OF WARRANTY Warranties are of great importance in insurance contracts because they operate as conditions that must exist before the contract is effective or before the insurer's promise to pay is enforceable. If such is the case, the insurer does not merely have a defense against payment of the policy but can void the policy.

Failure of the condition to exist or to occur relieves the insurer from any obligation to perform its promise. Broadly speaking, a condition is simply an event whose happening or failure to happen either precedes the existence of a legal relationship or terminates one previously existing. Conditions are either precedent or subsequent. For example, payment of the premium is a condition precedent to the enforcement of the insurer's promise, as is the happening of the insured event. A condition subsequent is an operative event the happening of which terminates an existing, matured legal obligation. A provision in a policy to the effect that the insured shall not be liable unless suit is brought within twelve months from the date on which the loss occurs is an example of a condition subsequent.

To be a warranty, the provision must be expressly included in the insurance contract or clearly incorporated by reference. Usually, the policy statements that the insurer considers to be express warranties are characterized by words such as *warrant*, *on condition that*, *provided that*, or words of similar import. Other statements important to the risk assumed, such as the address of a building in a case in which personal property at a particular location is insured against fire, are sometimes held to be informal warranties.

Generally, it is becoming more difficult for an insurer to avoid liability on a policy when an insured breaches a warranty. For example, a number of States now require a breach to be material before the insurer may avoid liability.

CONCEALMENT **Concealment** is the failure of an applicant for insurance to disclose material facts that the insurer does not know. The nondisclosure normally must be fraudulent as well as material to invalidate the policy; the applicant must have had reason to believe the fact was material; and its disclosure must have affected the insurer's acceptance of the risk.

WAIVER AND ESTOPPEL

In certain instances, an insurer who normally would be entitled to deny liability under a policy because of a misrepresentation, breach of condition, or concealment is "estopped"

from taking advantage of the defense or else is said to have "waived" the right to rely on it because of other facts.

The terms *waiver* and *estoppel* are used interchangeably, although by definition they are not synonymous. As generally defined, **waiver** is the intentional relinquishment of a known right; and **estoppel** means that a person is prevented by his own conduct from asserting a position inconsistent with such conduct, on which another person has justifiably relied.

Because a corporation such as an insurance company can act only through agents, situations involving waiver invariably are based on an agent's conduct. The higher the agent's position in the company's organization, the more likely his conduct is to bind the company, as an agent acting within the scope of his authority binds his principal. Insureds have the right to rely on representations made by the insurer's employees, and when such representations reasonably induce or cause the insured to change her position or prevent her from causing a condition to occur, the insurer may not assert as a defense the condition's failure to occur, whether the term applied to her situation be waiver or estoppel. Companies have tried with little success to limit the authority of local selling agents to bind the company through waiver or estoppel.

TERMINATION

Most insurance contracts are performed according to their terms, and due **performance** terminates the insurer's obligation. Normally, the insurer pays the principal sum due and the contract is thereby performed and discharged.

Cancellation by mutual consent is another way of terminating an insurance contract. Cancellation by the insurer alone means that the insurer remains liable, according to the terms of the policy, until such time as the cancellation is effective. To cancel a policy, the insurer must tender the unearned portion of the premium to the insured.

BAILMENTS AND DOCUMENTS OF TITLE

BAILMENTS

A **bailment** is the relationship created when one person (the bailor) transfers the possession of personal property by delivery, without transfer of title, to another (the **bailee**) for the accomplishment of a certain purpose, after which the bailee is to return the property to the bailor or dispose of it according to the bailor's directions. One of the most common occurrences in everyday life, bailments are of great commercial importance. Bailments include the transportation, storage, repair, and rental of goods, which together involve billions of dollars in transactions each year. The following are common examples of bailments: keeping a car in a public garage; leaving a car, a watch, or any other article to be repaired; renting a car or truck; checking a hat or coat at a theater or restaurant; leaving clothes to be laundered; delivering jewelry, stocks, bonds, or other valuables to secure the payment of a debt; storing goods in a warehouse; and shipping goods by public or private transportation. The benefit of a bailment may, by its terms, accrue solely to the bailor, solely to the bailee, or to both parties. A bailment may be with or without compensation. On these bases, bailments are classified as follows:

1. *Bailments for the bailor's sole benefit* include the gratuitous custody of personal property and the gratuitous services that involve custody of personal property, such as repairs or transportation. For example, if Sherry stores, repairs, or transports Tim's goods without compensation, this is a bailment for the sole benefit of the bailor, Tim.
2. *Bailments for the bailee's sole benefit* are usually limited to the gratuitous loan of personal property for use by the bailee, as where Tim, without compensation, lends his car, lawn mower, or book to Sherry for her use.
3. *Bailments for the mutual benefit* of both parties include ordinary commercial bailments, such as the delivery of goods to a person for repair, jewels to a pawnbroker, or an automobile to a parking lot attendant.

ESSENTIAL ELEMENTS OF A BAILMENT

The basic elements of a bailment are (1) the delivery of possession from a bailor to a bailee; (2) the delivery of personal property, not real property; (3) possession without ownership by the bailee for a determinable period; and (4) an absolute duty on the bailee to return the property to the bailor or to dispose of it according to the bailor's directions.

In most cases, two simple elements determine the existence of a bailment: (1) a separation of ownership and possession of the property (possession without ownership) and (2) a duty on the party in possession to redeliver the identical property to the owner or to dispose of it according to the owner's directions. Since a bailment need not be a contract, consideration is not required. A bailment may be created by operation of law from the facts of a particular situation; thus, a bailment may be **implied** or **constructive**.

DELIVERY OF POSSESSION Possession by a bailee involves (1) the bailee's power to control the personal property and (2) either the bailee's intention to control the property or her awareness that the rightful possessor has given up physical control of it. Thus, for example, when a restaurant customer hangs his hat or coat on a hook furnished for that purpose, the hat or coat is within an area under the restaurant owner's physical control. But the restaurant owner is not a bailee of the hat or coat unless he clearly signifies an intention to exercise control over the hat or coat. On the other hand, when a clerk in a store helps a customer to remove his coat to try on a new one, the owner of the store usually is held to have become a bailee of the old coat through the clerk, her employee. Here, the clerk has signified an intention to control the coat by taking it from the customer, and a bailment results.

PERSONAL PROPERTY The bailment relationship can exist only with respect to personal property. The delivery of possession of real property by the owner to another is covered by real property law. Bailed property need not be tangible. Intangible property, such as the rights represented by promissory notes, corporate bonds, shares of stock, documents of title, and life insurance policies that are evidenced by written instruments and are thus capable of delivery, may be and frequently are the subject matter of bailments.

POSSESSION FOR A DETERMINABLE TIME To establish a bailment relationship, the person receiving possession must be under a duty to return the personal property and must not obtain title to it. If the identical property transferred is to be returned, even in an altered form, the transaction is a bailment; however, if other property of equal value or the money value of the original property may be returned, a transfer of title has occurred, and the transaction is a sale.

RESTORATION OF POSSESSION TO THE BAILOR The bailee is legally obligated to restore the property to the bailor's possession when the bailment period ends. Normally, the bailee is required to return the identical goods bailed, although their condition may be changed because of the work that the bailee was required to perform on them. An exception to this rule concerns **fungible goods**, such as grain, which, for all practical purposes, consist of particles that are the equivalent of every other particle and are expected to be mingled with other like goods during a bailment. Given such goods, a bailee obviously cannot be required to return the identical goods bailed. His obligation is simply to return goods of the same quality and quantity.

A bailee has a duty to return the property to the right person. Her mistake in delivering property to the wrong person does not excuse her, even when the bailor's negligence induces the mistake. A bailee who, through mistake or intention, misdelivers the property to a third person who has no right to its possession is guilty of conversion and is liable to the bailor.

RIGHTS AND DUTIES OF BAILOR AND BAILEE

The bailment relationship creates rights and duties on the part of the bailor and the bailee. The bailee is under a duty to exercise due care for the safety of the property and to return it to the right person; conversely, the bailee has the exclusive right to possess the property for the term of the bailment. In addition, depending on the nature of the transaction, a bailee may have the right to limit his liability, as well as to receive compensation and reimbursement of expenses. The bailor, in turn, has certain duties with respect to the condition of the bailed goods.

BAILEE'S DUTY TO EXERCISE DUE CARE The bailee must exercise due care not to permit injury to or destruction of the property by the bailee or by third parties. The degree of care depends on the nature of the bailment relationship and the character of the property. In the context of a **commercial bailment**, from which the parties derive a mutual benefit, the law requires the bailee to exercise the care that a reasonably prudent person would exercise under the same circumstances. When the bailment benefits the bailee alone (Tim's borrowing Michael's truck without payment would be an example), the law requires more-than-reasonable care of the bailee. On the other hand, where the bailee accepts the property for the bailor's sole benefit, the law requires a lesser degree of care. Nevertheless, the amount of care required to satisfy any of the standards will vary with the character of the property.

When the property is lost, damaged, or destroyed while in the bailee's possession, it is often impossible for the bailor to obtain enough information to show that the loss or damage was due to the bailee's failure to exercise required care. The law aids the bailor in this respect by *presuming* that the bailee was at fault. The bailor is merely required to show that certain property was delivered by way of bailment and that the bailee either has failed to return it or has returned it in a damaged condition. The burden is then on the bailee to prove that he exercised the degree of care required.

◆ **SEE FIGURE 48-2: Duties in a Bailment**

BAILEE'S ABSOLUTE LIABILITY TO RETURN PROPERTY As discussed, the bailee is free from liability if she exercised the degree of care required of her under the particular bailment while the property was within her control. This general rule has certain important exceptions that impose an absolute duty on the bailee to return the property undamaged to the proper person.

When the bailee has an obligation by express agreement with the bailor or by custom to insure the property against certain risks but fails to do so, and the property is destroyed or damaged through such risks, she is liable for the damage or nondelivery, even if she has exercised due care.

When the bailee uses the bailed property in a manner not authorized by the bailor or by the character of the bailment, and during the course of such use the property is damaged or destroyed, without fault on the bailee's part, the bailee is nonetheless absolutely (strictly) liable for the damage or destruction. The wrongful use by the bailee automatically terminates her lawful possession: she becomes a trespasser as to the property and, as such, is absolutely liable for whatever harm befalls it.

BAILEE'S RIGHT TO LIMIT LIABILITY Certain bailees—namely, common carriers, public warehousers, and innkeepers—may limit their liability for breach of their duties to the bailor only as provided by statute. Other bailees, however, may vary their duties and liabilities by contract with the bailor. When liability may be limited by contract, the law requires that any such limitation be properly brought to the bailor's attention before he bails the property. This is especially true in the case of "professional bailees," such as repair garages, who make it their business to act as bailees and who deal with the public on a uniform, rather than on an individual, basis. Thus, a variation or limitation in writing, contained, for example, in a claim check or stub given to the bailor or posted on the walls of the bailee's place of business, ordinarily will *not* bind the bailor unless (1) the bailee draws the bailor's attention to the writing, (2) the bailee informs the bailor that it contains a limitation or variation of liability, and (3) the limitation is not the result of unequal bargaining power. Some States do not permit professional bailees (who

◆ **FIGURE 48-2: Duties in a Bailment**

Type of Bailment	Bailor's Duty	Bailee's Duty of Care
For sole benefit of bailor	Slight care	To warn of defects of which she knew or should have known
For sole benefit of bailee	Utmost care	To warn of known defects
For mutual benefit	Ordinary care	To warn of defects of which she knew or should have known

commonly include warehousers, garagers, and parking lot owners) to disclaim liability for their own negligence.

BAILEE'S RIGHT TO COMPENSATION A bailee who by express or implied agreement undertakes to perform work on or render services in connection with the bailed goods is entitled to reasonable compensation for those services or that work. In most cases, the agreement between bailor and bailee fixes the amount of compensation and provides how it shall be paid. In the absence of a contrary agreement, the compensation is payable when the bailee completes the work or performs the services. If, after such completion or performance but before the redelivery of the goods to the bailor, the goods are lost or damaged through no fault of the bailee, the bailee is still entitled to compensation for his work and services.

Most bailees who are entitled to compensation for work and services performed in connection with bailed goods acquire a possessory lien on the goods to secure the payment of such compensation. In most jurisdictions, the bailee has a statutory right to obtain a judicial foreclosure of his lien and a sale of the goods. Many statutes also provide that the bailee does not lose his lien on redelivery of the goods to the bailor, as was the case at common law. Instead, the lien will continue for a specified period after redelivery, if the bailee timely records with the proper authorities an instrument claiming such a lien.

BAILOR'S DUTIES In a bailment for the sole benefit of the bailee, the bailor warrants that she is unaware of any defects in the bailed property. In all other instances, the bailor has a duty to warn the bailee of all defects she knows of or should have discovered upon a reasonable inspection of the bailed property. A number of courts have extended strict liability in tort and the implied warranties under Article 2 of the UCC to leases and bailments. Article 2A imposes implied warranties on the lease of goods.

SPECIAL TYPES OF BAILMENTS

Although the general principles that apply to all bailees govern pledgees, warehousers, and safe deposit companies, certain special features about the transactions in which they respectively engage subject them to extraordinary duties of care and liability. Innkeepers and common carriers may also be said to be *extraordinary* bailees, whereas all other bailees are *ordinary* bailees. This distinction is based on the character and extent of the liability of these two classes of bailees for the loss of or injury to bailed goods. As we have seen, an **ordinary bailee** is liable only for the loss or injury that results from his failure to exercise ordinary or reasonable care. The liability of the **extraordinary bailee**, on the other hand, is, in general, *absolute*. Just as an insurer, in general, becomes automatically liable to the insured on the happening

of the hazard insured against, regardless of the cause, the extraordinary bailee becomes liable to the bailor for any loss or injury to the goods, regardless of the cause and without regard to the question of his care or negligence. Thus, he insures the safety of the goods.

PLEDGES A **pledge** is a bailment for security in which the owner gives possession of her personal property to another (the secured party) to secure a debt or the performance of some obligation. The secured party does not have title to the property involved but merely a possessory security interest. Pledges of most types of personal property for security purposes are governed by Article 9 of the UCC, which we discussed in *Chapter 38*. In most respects, the secured party's duties and liabilities are the same as those of a bailee for compensation.

WAREHOUSING A **warehouser** is a bailee who, for compensation, receives goods to be stored in a warehouse. Under the common law, his duties and liabilities were identical to those of the ordinary bailee for compensation. Today, because a strong public interest affects their activities, warehousers are subject to extensive State and Federal regulation. Warehousers also must be distinguished from ordinary bailees in that the receipts they issue for storage have acquired a special status in commerce. Regarded as documents of title, these receipts are governed by Article 7 of the UCC. (We will discuss documents of title later in this chapter.)

SAFE DEPOSIT BOXES A majority of States hold that a person who rents a safe deposit box from a bank enters into a bailment relationship. As this constitutes a bailment for the parties' mutual benefit, the bailee bank owes the customer the duty to act with ordinary due care and is liable only if negligent.

CARRIERS OF GOODS In the broadest sense, anyone who transports goods from one place to another, either gratuitously or for compensation, is a **carrier**. Carriers are classified primarily as common carriers and private carriers. A **common carrier** offers its services and facilities to the public on terms and under circumstances indicating that the offering is made to all persons. Stated somewhat differently, the criteria that define common carriers are as follows: (1) the carriage must be part of its business; (2) the carriage must be for remuneration; and (3) the carrier must represent to the general public that it is willing to serve the public in the transportation of property. Common carriers of goods include railroad, steamship, aircraft, public trucking, and pipeline companies. In contrast, a **private** or **contract carrier** is one who carries the goods of another on isolated occasions or who serves a limited number of customers under individual contracts without offering the same or similar contracts to the public at large.

The person who delivers goods to a carrier for shipment is known as the **consignor** or shipper. The person to whom the carrier is to deliver the goods is known as the **consignee**. The instrument containing the terms of the contract of transportation, which the carrier issues to the shipper, is called a **bill of lading** (discussed later in this chapter).

A common carrier is under a duty to serve the public to the limits of its capacity and, within those limits, to accept for carriage goods of the kind that it normally transports. A private carrier, by comparison, has no duty to accept goods for carriage, except where it agrees by contract to do so. Whether common or private, the carrier is under an absolute duty to deliver the goods to the person to whom the shipper has consigned them.

A private carrier, in the absence of special contract terms, is liable as a bailee for the goods it undertakes to carry. The liability of a common carrier, on the other hand, approaches that of an insurer of the safety of the goods, except when loss or damage is caused by an act of God, an act of a public enemy, the acts or fault of the shipper, the inherent nature of or a defect in the goods, or an act of public authority. The carrier, however, is permitted, through its contract with the shipper, to limit its liability, provided the carrier gives the shipper notice of this limitation and the opportunity to declare a higher value for the goods.

INNKEEPERS At common law, **innkeepers** (better known as hotel and motel owners or operators) are held to the same **strict** or **absolute liability** for their guests' belongings as are common carriers for the goods they carry. This rule of strict liability applies only to those who furnish lodging to the public for compensation as a regular business and extends only to the belongings of lodgers who are guests. In almost all jurisdictions, case law and statute have substantially modified the innkeeper's strict liability under common law.

DOCUMENTS OF TITLE

A **document of title**, which includes warehouse receipts and bills of lading, is a record evidencing a right to receive, control, hold, and dispose of the record *and* the goods it covers. Documents of title thus represent title to goods. To be a document of title, a document must be issued by or addressed to a bailee and must cover goods in the bailee's possession that are either identified or are fungible portions of an identified mass.

Briefly, a document of title symbolizes ownership of the goods it describes. Because of the document's legal characteristics, its ownership is equivalent to the ownership or control of the goods it represents, without the necessity of actual or physical possession of the goods. Likewise, it transfers the ownership or control of the goods without necessitating the physical transfer of the goods themselves. For these reasons, documents of title are a convenient means of handling the billions of dollars' worth of goods that are transported by carriers or are stored with warehousers. Documents of title also facilitate the transfer of title to goods and the creation of a security interest in goods. Article 7 of the UCC governs documents of title. In 2003 a revision of UCC Article 7 was promulgated to update the original Article 7 and provide a framework for the further development of electronic documents of title. At least thirty-nine States have adopted Revised Article 7. This chapter will cover both original Article 7 and Revised Article 7.

TYPES OF DOCUMENTS OF TITLE

To facilitate electronic documents of title, several definitions in Article 1 have been revised, including "bearer," "bill of lading," "delivery," "document of title," "holder," and "warehouse receipt." The term "electronic document of title" means "a document of title evidenced by a record consisting of information stored in an electronic medium." Revised Section 1–201(b)(16). The term "tangible document of title" means "a document of title evidenced by a record consisting of information that is inscribed in a tangible medium." Revised Section 1–201(b)(16). "Record" means "information that is inscribed on a tangible medium or that is stored in an electronic or other medium and is retrievable in perceivable form." Revised Article 7–102(10). The concept of an electronic document of title allows for commercial practice to determine whether records issued by bailees are "in the regular course of business or financing" and are "treated as adequately evidencing that the person in possession or control of the record is entitled to receive, control, hold, and dispose of the record and the goods the record covers." Preface to Revised Article 7.

WAREHOUSE RECEIPTS A warehouse receipt is a document of title issued by a person engaged in the business of storing goods for hire. A warehouser is liable for damages for loss or injury to the goods caused by his failure to exercise such care in regard to them as a reasonably careful person would exercise under the circumstances. The warehouser must deliver the goods to the person entitled to receive them under the terms of the warehouse receipt. Though a warehouser may limit his liability through a provision in the warehouse receipt fixing a specific maximum liability per article or item or unit of weight, this limitation does not apply when a warehouser converts goods to his own use.

To enforce the payment of her charges and necessary expenses in connection with keeping and handling the goods, a warehouser has a lien on the goods that enables her to sell them at public or private sale after notice and to apply the net proceeds of the sale to the amount of her charges. The Code, moreover, provides the warehouser a definite procedure for enforcing her lien against the goods stored and in her possession.

BILLS OF LADING A **bill of lading** is a document of title evidencing the receipt of goods issued by a person engaged in the business of directly or indirectly transporting or forwarding goods. It serves a threefold function: (1) as a receipt for the goods, (2) as evidence of the contract of carriage, and (3) as a document of title. A bill of lading is negotiable if, by its terms, the goods are deliverable to bearer or to the order of a named person. Any other document is nonnegotiable.

Under the Code, bills of lading may be issued not only by common carriers but also by contract carriers, freight forwarders, or any person engaged in the business of transporting or forwarding goods.

The carrier must deliver the goods to the person entitled to receive them under the terms of the bill of lading. Common carriers are extraordinary bailees under the law and are subject to greater liability than are ordinary bailees, such as warehousers.

The Code allows a carrier to limit its liability by contract in all cases in which its rates depend on the value of the goods and the carrier allows the shipper an opportunity to declare a higher value. The limitation does not apply, however, when the carrier converts goods to its own use.

On goods in its possession that are covered by a bill of lading, the carrier has a lien for the charges and expenses necessary for its preservation of such goods. Against a purchaser for value of a negotiable bill of lading, this lien is limited to charges stated in the bill or in the applicable published tariff or, if no charges are so stated, to a reasonable charge.

The carrier may enforce its lien by public or private sale of the goods after notice to all persons known by the carrier to claim an interest in them. The sale must be on terms that are "commercially reasonable," and the carrier must conduct it in a "commercially reasonable manner."

A purchaser in good faith of goods sold to enforce the lien takes those goods free of any rights of persons against whom the lien was valid, even if the enforcement of the lien does not comply with Code requirements. This rule applies both to carrier's and to warehouser's liens. Good faith, as indicated in previous chapters, has been revised to mean "honesty in fact and the observance of reasonable commercial standards of fair dealing." Revised Section 7–102(6); Revised Section 1–201(b)(20).

NEGOTIABILITY OF DOCUMENTS OF TITLE

The concept of negotiability has long been established in law. It is important not only in connection with documents of title but also in connection with commercial paper and investment securities, topics treated in other chapters of this book.

The Code provides that a warehouse receipt, bill of lading, or other document of title is negotiable if, by its terms, the goods are to be delivered to bearer or to the order of a named person or in situations, in overseas trade, in which the document runs to a named person or assigns. Revised Article 7 provides that a document of title is negotiable if, by its terms, the goods are to be delivered to bearer or to the order of a named person. Revised Section 7–104(a). Any other document is nonnegotiable. The negotiability of a document is determined at its time of issue. Revised Section 7–104, Comment 2. Revised Article 7 provides for the integration of electronic documents of title and, to the extent possible, applies the same rules for electronic and tangible documents of title.

A nonnegotiable document, such as a straight bill of lading or a warehouse receipt under which the goods are deliverable only to a person named in the bill, not to the order of any person or to bearer, may be transferred by assignment but may not be negotiated. Only a negotiable document or instrument may be negotiated.

An individual has "control" of an **electronic document of title** "if a system employed for evidencing the transfer of interests in the electronic document reliably establishes that person as the person to which the electronic document was issued or transferred." Revised Section 7–106(a). Control of an electronic document of title replaces the concept of possession and indorsement applicable to a tangible document of title. Thus, a person with a tangible document of title delivers the document by voluntarily transferring *possession* while a person with an electronic document of title delivers the document by voluntarily transferring *control*. Revised Section 7–106, Comment 2. The key to having a system of control under Revised Article 7 is the ability to show at any point in time the one person entitled to the goods under the electronic document. Revised Section 7–106, Comment 3. Revised Article 7 leaves to the marketplace the creation of systems that meet this standard.

DUE NEGOTIATION

The Code sets forth the manner in which a negotiable document of title may be negotiated and the requirements of due negotiation. An order form negotiable *tangible* document of title running to the order of a named person is negotiated by her indorsement and delivery. Revised Section 7–501(a). Delivery of a tangible document of title means voluntary transfer of possession. Revised Article 1–201(b)(15). After such indorsement in blank or to bearer, the document may be negotiated by delivery alone. A special indorsement, by which the document is indorsed over to a specified person, requires the indorsement of the special indorsee as well as delivery to accomplish a further negotiation.

A negotiable *electronic* document of title running to the order of a named person *or* to bearer is negotiated by delivery. Indorsement by the named person is not required to negotiate an electronic document of title. Revised Section 7–501(b). Delivery of an electronic document of title means voluntary transfer of control. Revised Article 1–201(b)(15).

Due negotiation, a term peculiar to Article 7, requires not only that the purchaser of the negotiable document take it in good faith, without notice of any adverse claim or defense, and pay value, but also that she take it in the regular course of business or financing, not in settlement or payment of a money obligation (in essence, a holder by due negotiation). Thus, a transfer for value of a negotiable document of title to a nonbanker or to a person not in business, such as a college professor or student, would not be a due negotiation.

Due negotiation creates new rights in the holder of the document. The transferee does not stand in the shoes of his transferor; in other words, the defects and defenses available against the transferor are not available against the new holder. Newly created by the negotiation, his rights are free of such defects and defenses. This enables bankers and businesspersons to extend credit on documents of title without concern about possible adverse claims or the rights of third parties.

The rights of a holder of a negotiable document of title to whom it has been duly negotiated include (1) title to the document; (2) title to the goods; (3) all rights accruing under the law of agency or estoppel, including rights to goods delivered to the bailee after the document was issued; and (4) the issuer's direct obligation to hold or deliver the goods according to the document's terms.

WARRANTIES

A person, other than a collecting bank or other intermediary, who either negotiates or delivers a document of title for value incurs certain warranty obligations, unless otherwise agreed. Such transferor warrants to her immediate purchaser (1) that the document is genuine, (2) that she had no knowledge of any fact that would impair its validity or worth, and (3) that her negotiation or delivery is rightful and fully effective with respect to the title to the document and the goods it represents. Revised Article 7 makes it clear that these warranties only arise in the case of voluntary transfer of possession or control for value. Revised Section 7–507.

INEFFECTIVE DOCUMENTS OF TITLE

For a person to obtain title to goods through the negotiation of a document to him, the goods must have been delivered to the document's issuer by their owner or by either one to whom the owner has delivered the goods or one whom the owner has entrusted with actual or apparent authority to ship, store, or sell them. A warehouser or carrier, however, may deliver goods according to the terms of the document that it has issued or otherwise dispose of the goods as provided in the Code without incurring liability, even if the document did not represent title to the goods. The warehouser or carrier need only have acted in good faith and complied with reasonable commercial standards in both the receipt and delivery or other disposition of the goods. Such a bailee has no liability even though the person from whom the bailee received the goods had no authority to obtain the issuance of the document or to dispose of the goods, and the person to whom it delivered the goods had no authority to receive them.

Thus, a carrier or warehouser who receives goods from a thief or finder and later delivers them to a person to whom the thief or finder ordered them to be delivered is not liable to the true owner of the goods. Even a sale of the goods by the carrier or warehouser to enforce a lien for transportation or storage charges and expenses would not subject it to liability.

CHAPTER SUMMARY

INTRODUCTION TO PROPERTY AND PERSONAL PROPERTY

KINDS OF PROPERTY
Definition interest, or group of interests, that is legally protected
Tangible Property physical objects
Intangible Property property that does not exist in a physical form
Real Property land and interests in land
Personal Property all property that is not real property
Fixture personal property so firmly attached to real property that an interest in it arises under real property law

TRANSFER OF TITLE TO PERSONAL PROPERTY	**Sale** transfer of property for consideration (price) **Gift** transfer of property without consideration • *Delivery* includes both manual transfer of the item and constructive delivery (delivery of something that symbolizes control over the item) • *Intent* • *Acceptance* • *Classification* **Will** right to property acquired upon death of the owner **Accession** right of a property owner to any increase in such property **Confusion** intermixing of goods belonging to two or more owners such that they can identify their individual property only as part of a mass of like goods • If due to mistake, accident, or agreement, loss shared proportionately • If caused by an intentional or unauthorized act, wrongdoer bears loss **Possession** a person may acquire title by taking possession of property • *Abandoned Property* intentionally disposed of by the owner; the finder is entitled to the property • *Lost Property* unintentionally left by the owner; the finder is generally entitled to the property • *Mislaid Property* intentionally placed by the owner but unintentionally left; the owner of the premises is generally entitled to the property • *Treasure Trove* coins or currency concealed by the owner for such a length of time that the owner is probably dead or undiscoverable; the finder is entitled to the property

PROPERTY INSURANCE

FIRE AND PROPERTY INSURANCE	**General Definition of Insurance** contractual arrangement that distributes risk of loss among a large number of members (the insureds) through an insurance company (the insurer) **Coverage** of fire and property insurance provides protection against loss due to fire or related perils **Types of Fire** • *Friendly Fire* fire contained in its intended location • *Hostile Fire* any fire outside its intended or usual location **Co-insurance** insurance in which a person insures property for less than its full or stated value and agrees to share the risk of loss **Other Insurance Clauses** if multiple insurers are involved, liability is distributed *pro rata* **Types of Policies** • *Valued Policy* covers full value of property as agreed upon by the parties at the time the policy is issued • *Open Policy* covers fair market value of property as calculated immediately prior to the loss
NATURE OF INSURANCE CONTRACTS	**General Contract Law** basic principles of contract law apply **Insurable Interest** a financial interest or a factual expectancy in someone's property that justifies insuring the property; the interest must exist at the time the property loss occurs **Premiums** amount to be paid for an insurance policy

Defenses of the Insurer

- *Misrepresentation* false representation of a material fact made by the insured that is justifiably relied upon by the insurer; enables the insurer to rescind the contract within a specified time
- *Breach of Warranty* the failure of a required condition; generally an insurer may avoid liability for a breach of warranty only if the breach is material
- *Concealment* fraudulent failure of an applicant for insurance to disclose material facts that the insurer does not know; allows the insurer to rescind the contract
- *Waiver* an insurer intentionally relinquishes the right to deny liability
- *Estoppel* an insurer is prevented by its own conduct from asserting a defense

Termination an insurance contract may be terminated by due performance or cancellation

BAILMENTS AND DOCUMENTS OF TITLE

BAILMENTS   **Definition** the temporary transfer of personal property by one party (the bailor) to another (the bailee)

Classification of Bailments
- *For the Bailor's Sole Benefit*
- *For the Bailee's Sole Benefit*
- *For Mutual Benefit* includes ordinary commercial bailments

Essential Elements
- *Delivery of Possession*
- *Personal Property*
- *Possession, but Not Ownership, for a Determinable Time*
- *Restoration of Possession to the Bailor*

Rights and Duties
- *Bailee's Duty to Exercise Due Care* the bailee must exercise reasonable care to protect the safety of the property and to return it to the proper person
- *Bailee's Absolute Liability* occurs when (1) the parties so agree; (2) the custom of the industry requires the bailee to insure the property against the risk in question, but he fails to do so; or (3) the bailee uses the bailed property in an unauthorized manner
- *Bailee's Right to Limit Liability* certain bailees are not permitted to limit their liability for breach of their duties, except as provided by statute
- *Bailee's Right to Compensation* entitled to reasonable compensation for work or services performed on the bailed goods
- *Bailor's Duties* in bailment for sole benefit of bailee, the bailor warrants that she is unaware of any defects; in all other bailments, the bailor has a duty to warn of all known defects and all defects she should discover upon a reasonable inspection

Special Types
- *Pledge* security interest by possession
- *Warehouser* storer of goods for compensation; warehouser must exercise reasonable care to protect the safety of the stored goods and to deliver them to the proper person
- *Carrier of Goods* transporter of goods; a common carrier is an extraordinary bailee, and a private carrier is an ordinary bailee
- *Innkeeper* hotel or motel operator; is an extraordinary bailee except as limited by statute or case law

DOCUMENTS OF TITLE

Definition an instrument evidencing ownership of the record and the goods it covers

Types
- *Warehouse Receipt* receipt issued by person storing goods
- *Bill of Lading* document issued to the shipper by the carrier (1) as a receipt for the goods, (2) as evidence of their carriage contract, and (3) as a document of title

Negotiability a document of title is negotiable if, by its terms, the goods are to be delivered to bearer or to the order of a named person

Due Negotiation delivery of a negotiable document in the regular course of business to a holder, who takes in good faith, for value, and without notice of any defense or claim

Warranties a person who negotiates or delivers a document of title for value, other than a collecting bank or other intermediary, incurs certain warranty obligations unless otherwise agreed

Ineffective Documents for a person to obtain title to goods by negotiation of a document, the goods must have been delivered to the issuer of the document by their owner or by one to whom the owner has entrusted actual or apparent authority

CHAPTER 49

Interests in Real Property

Interests in real property may be classified as possessory or nonpossessory interests. Possessory interests in real property, called estates, are classified to indicate the quantity, nature, and extent of the rights they involve. The two major categories are freehold estates (those existing for an indefinite time or for the life of a person) and estates less than freehold (those that exist for a predetermined time), called leasehold estates. Both freehold estates and leasehold estates are regarded as possessory interests in property. In addition, there are several nonpossessory interests in property, including easements and *profits à prendre*. In addition, a person may have a privilege or a license to go on the property for a certain purpose. The ownership of an interest in property may be held by one individual or concurrently by two or more persons, each of whom is entitled to an undivided interest in the entire property. This chapter will consider these topics.

FREEHOLD ESTATES

As stated above, a freehold estate is a right of ownership of real property for an indefinite time or for the life of a person. Of all the estates in real property, the most valuable usually are those estates that combine the enjoyment of immediate possession with ownership at least for life. These estates are either some form of fee estates or estates for life. In addition, either type of estate may be created without immediate right to possession; such an estate is known as a future interest. Estates are classified according to their duration.

FEE ESTATES

Fee estates include the right to immediate possession for an indefinite time and the right to transfer the interest by deed or will. Fee estates include both fee simple and qualified fee estates.

FEE SIMPLE When a person says that he has "bought" a house or a corporation informs its shareholders that it has

"purchased" an industrial site, the property generally is held in fee simple. **Fee simple** means that the property is owned absolutely and can be sold or passed on at will; this estate provides the greatest possible ownership interest. The absolute rights to transfer ownership and to transmit that ownership through inheritance are basic characteristics of a fee simple estate. The estate signifies full control over the property, which can be sold or disposed of as desired. Fee simple is the most extensive and comprehensive estate in land; all other estates are derived from it.

A fee simple is created by any words that indicate an intent to convey absolute ownership. "To B in fee simple" will accomplish this, as will "To B forever." The general presumption is that a conveyance is intended to convey full and absolute title in the absence of a clear intent to the contrary. The grantor must possess, or have the right to transfer, a fee simple interest to transfer such an interest.

QUALIFIED OR BASE FEE It is possible to convey or will property to a person to enjoy absolutely, subject to its being taken away at a later date should a certain event occur. The estate thus created is known as a **qualified fee**, base fee, conditional fee, or fee simple defeasible. For example, Abe may provide in his will that his daughter is to have his house and lot in "fee simple forever so long as she does not use it to sell alcoholic beverages, in which case the house shall revert to Abe's estate." If his daughter dies without using the house to sell alcoholic beverages, the property is transferred to her heirs as though she owned it absolutely. If, however, Abe's daughter uses the house to sell alcoholic beverages, the daughter would lose her title to the land, and it would revert to Abe's heirs.

The holder of a qualified fee interest may transfer the property by deed or will, and the property will pass by intestate succession. All transferees, however, take the property subject to the initial condition imposed upon the interest.

LIFE ESTATES

A grant or a devise (grant by will) "to Alex for life" creates in Alex an estate that terminates on his death. Such a provision

COLUMN: © PHOTOGRAPHEROLYMPUS CLOUDS: © KERTLIS

may stand alone, in which case the property will revert to the grantor and his heirs; or, as is more likely, it will be followed by a subsequent grant to another party, such as "to Alex for life and then to Benjamin and his heirs." Alex is the life tenant, and Benjamin is generally described as the remainderman. Alex's life, however, need not be the measure of his life estate, as where an estate is granted "to Alex for the life of Dale." Upon Dale's death, Alex's interest terminates; if Alex dies before Dale, Alex's interest passes to his heirs or as he directs in his will for the remainder of Dale's life. Thus, a life estate is an ownership right in property for the life of a designated individual, while a remainder is the ownership estate that takes effect when a prior life estate terminates.

No particular words are necessary to create a life estate, so long as the words chosen clearly reflect the intent of the grantor. Life estates arise most frequently in connection with the creation of trusts, a subject considered in *Chapter 51*.

Generally, a life tenant may make reasonable use of the property as long as he does not commit "waste." Any act or omission that permanently injures the realty or unreasonably changes its characteristics or value constitutes **waste**. For example, failing to repair a building, cutting timber excessively without replanting, or neglecting to observe adequate conservation techniques may subject the life tenant to an action by the remainderman to recover damages for waste.

A conveyance by the life tenant passes only her interest. The life tenant and the remainderman may, however, join in a conveyance to pass the entire fee to the property, or the life tenant may terminate her interest by conveying it to the remainderman.

FUTURE INTERESTS

Not every interest in property carries the right to immediate possession, even though the right and title to the interest are absolute. Thus, where property is conveyed or devised by will "to Anderson during his life and then to Brown and her heirs," Brown has a definite presently existing *interest* in the property, but she is not entitled to immediate *possession*. This right and similar rights, generically referred to as **future interests**, are of two principal types: reversions and remainders.

REVERSIONS If Anderson conveys property "to Brown for life" and makes no disposition of the remainder of the estate, Anderson holds the **reversion**—the grantor's right to the property upon the death of the life tenant. Thus, Anderson would regain ownership to the property when Brown dies. Furthermore, because the grantor has only to allow his grantee's estate to expire before he may regain ownership, a reversion in Anderson also is created if he conveys property "to Caldwell for ten years." Reversions may be transferred by deed or will and pass by intestate succession.

A **possibility of reverter**, or a conditional reversionary interest, exists where property *may* return to the grantor or his successor in interest because an event upon which a fee simple estate was to terminate has occurred. This potential for reversion is present in the grant of a base or qualified fee, previously discussed in this chapter. Thus, Ellen has a possibility of reverter if she dedicates property to a public use "so long as it is used as a park" and indicates that if it is not so used it will revert to her heirs. If, in one hundred years, the city ceases to use the property for a park, Ellen's heirs would be entitled to the property. A possibility of a reverter may pass by will or intestate succession. In some States, it may be transferred by deed.

REMAINDERS A remainder, as discussed, is an estate in property that, like a reversion, will take effect in possession, if at all, upon the termination of a prior estate created by the *same instrument*. Unlike a reversion, a remainder is held by a person other than the grantor or his successors. A grant from Gwen to "William for his life and then to Charles and his heirs" creates a remainder in Charles. Upon the termination of the life estate, Charles will be entitled to possession as remainderman, taking his title not from William but from the original grantor, Gwen. Remainders are of two kinds: vested remainders and contingent remainders.

A **vested remainder** is one in which the only contingency to possession by the remainderman is the termination of all preceding estates created by the transferor. When Jalen has a remainder in fee, subject only to a life estate in Carol, the only obstacle to the right of immediate possession by Jalen or his heirs is Carol's life. Carol's death is sufficient and necessary to place Jalen in possession. The law considers this unconditional or vested remainder as a fixed, present interest to be enjoyed in the future. Such an interest in property is just as transferable as the life estate that precedes it, and it is characteristic of a vested remainder that the owner of the preceding estate can do nothing to defeat the remainder.

A **contingent remainder**, by comparison, is one in which the right to possession is dependent or conditional on the happening of some event in addition to the termination of the preceding estates. The contingent remainder may be conditioned on the existence of some person not yet born or on the happening of an event that may never occur. A provision in a will "to Sandy for life and then to her children, but if she has no children then to Douglas" creates contingent remainders both as to the children and as to Douglas. If Sandy marries and has a child, the remainder then vests in that child, and Douglas's expectancy is closed out. If Sandy dies without having had a child, then and only then will an estate vest in Douglas. It is, of course, possible for a contingent remainder to become vested while possession is still in the preceding life estate, as evidenced by the birth of a child to Sandy in the above example. In most States, a contingent

◆ **FIGURE 49-1: Freehold Estates**

Interest	Complementary Estate	Duration	Transfer by Deed	Transfer by Will or Intestacy
Fee Simple	None	Perpetual	Yes	Yes
Qualified Fee	Possibility of reverter	Until contingency occurs	Yes	Yes
Life Estate	Reversion or remainder	Life of indicated person	Yes	No, unless measuring life is not life tenant's
Reversion	Life estate	Perpetual	Yes	Yes
Possibility of Reverter	Qualified fee	Perpetual if contingency occurs	In some States	Yes
Vested Remainder	Life estate	Perpetual	Yes	Yes
Contingent Remainder	Life estate	Perpetual if contingency occurs	In most States	Yes, unless it is limited such that it terminates before the death of the remainderman

remainder is transferable by deed. It also is inheritable, unless by limitation it terminates before the death of the remainderman.

◆ **SEE FIGURE 49-1: Freehold Estates**

LEASEHOLD ESTATES

A **lease** is both a contract and a conveyance of an estate in land. It is a contract, express or implied, by which the owner of the land, the **landlord (lessor)**, grants to another, the **tenant (lessee)**, an exclusive right to use and possession of the land for a definite or ascertainable time, or term. The possessory term thus granted is an estate in land called a **leasehold**, which is a nonfreehold estate. The landlord retains an interest in the property, called a *reversion*. A leasehold estate has two principal characteristics: it continues for a definite or ascertainable term and carries with it the tenant's obligation to pay rent to the landlord. Thus, if Linda, the owner of a house and lot, rents both to Ted for a year, Linda, of course, retains the title to the property, but she has sold to Ted the right to occupy it. During the term of the lease, Ted's right to occupy the property is superior to that of Linda, and as long as he occupies in accordance with the lease contract, he has, as a practical matter, exclusive possession against all the world as though he were the actual owner.

The law of leasehold estates has changed considerably over the past few decades. Traditionally, the common law viewed a leasehold estate less as a contract than as a conveyance of the use of land. In the twenty-first century, the landlord-tenant relationship is primarily viewed as a contract and therefore subject to the contract doctrines of unconscionability, implied warranties, and constructive conditions.

Moreover, numerous ordinances and statutes, such as the Uniform Residential Landlord and Tenant Act enacted by more than twenty States, now protect tenants' rights, thereby further modifying the landlord-tenant relationship. The Uniform Residential Landlord and Tenant Act, which was promulgated by the Commission on Uniform State Laws, provides a comprehensive system for regulating the relationship between landlords and tenants and governs most persons who reside in rental housing. The Act does not apply to commercial or industrial properties, the occupancy of hotels or motels, mobile home park tenants, and recreational vehicle long-term tenants. The Act contains detailed requirements regarding the landlord's obligations (restrictions on security deposits and methods for providing notices to tenants and prohibitions on certain provisions in rental agreements); the landlord's rights (collection of rent, eviction, entering the premises, and termination of the lease); the tenant's obligations (payment of rent and compliance with rules), and the tenant's rights (possession, termination of the lease, receipt of essential services, and avoidance of unlawful eviction). Finally, the Act provides remedies for noncompliance by either the landlord or tenant.

CREATION AND DURATION

Because they are created by contract, the usual requirements for contract formation apply to leaseholds. In most jurisdictions, leases for a term longer than a statutorily specified period, generally fixed at either one or three years, must be in writing. A few States require that all leases be in writing. Leasehold interests have historically been divided into four categories: (1) definite term, (2) periodic tenancy, (3) tenancy at will, and (4) tenancy at sufferance. These tenancies most significantly vary in their duration and their manner of termination.

DEFINITE TERM A lease for a definite term automatically expires at the end of the term. Such a lease is frequently termed a tenancy for years, even though its duration may be one year or less. It is created by express agreement, oral or written. No notice to terminate is required since the lease established its termination date.

PERIODIC TENANCY A **periodic tenancy** is a lease of indefinite duration that continues for successive periods unless one party terminates it by notice to the other. For example, a lease to Ted "from month to month" or "from year to year" creates a periodic tenancy. Periodic tenancies are generally express, oral, or written, but also arise by implication. If Laura leases to Ted without stating any term in the lease, this creates a tenancy at will. If, moreover, Ted pays rent to Laura at the beginning of each month (or some other regular time) and Laura accepts such payments, most courts would hold that the tenancy at will has been transformed into a tenancy from month to month.

Either party may terminate a periodic tenancy at the expiration of any one period, but only upon adequate notice to the other party. In the absence of an express agreement in the lease, the common law requires six months' notice in tenancies from year to year. In most jurisdictions, this period has been shortened by statute to periods ranging between thirty and ninety days. In periodic tenancies involving periods of less than one year, the notice required at common law is one full period in advance, but, again, this requirement may be subject to statutory regulation.

TENANCY AT WILL A lease containing a provision that either party may terminate at any time creates a tenancy at will. A lease that does not specify duration likewise creates a tenancy at will. At common law, such tenancies were terminable without any prior notice, but many jurisdictions now have statutes requiring a period of notice before termination, usually ten to ninety days.

TENANCY AT SUFFERANCE A **tenancy at sufferance** arises when a tenant fails to vacate the premises at the expiration of the lease and thereby becomes a holdover tenant. The common law gives the landlord the right to elect either to dispossess such tenant or to hold her for another term. Until the landlord makes this election, a tenancy at sufferance exists.

TRANSFER OF INTERESTS

Both the tenant's possessory interest in the leasehold and the landlord's reversionary interest in the property may be freely transferred in the absence of contractual or statutory prohibition. This general rule is subject to one major exception: the tenancy at will. Any attempt by either party to transfer her interest is usually considered an expression of the intent (will) to terminate the tenancy.

TRANSFERS BY LANDLORD After conveying the leasehold interest, a landlord is left with a reversionary interest in the property plus the right to rent and other benefits acquired under the lease. The landlord may transfer either or both of these interests. The party to whom the reversion is transferred takes the property subject to the tenant's leasehold interest, if the transferee has actual *or* constructive notice of the lease. For example, Linda leases Whiteacre to Tina for five years, and Tina records the lease with the register of deeds. Linda then sells Whiteacre to Arthur. Tina's lease is still valid and enforceable against Arthur, whose right to possession of Whiteacre begins only after the lease expires.

TRANSFERS BY TENANT In the absence of a prohibitive lease or statutory provision, a tenant, except for a tenant at will, may dispose of his interest either by (1) assignment or (2) sublease. As a result, most standard leases expressly require the consent of the landlord to an assignment or subletting of the premises. Under the majority view, a covenant against assignment of a lease does not prohibit the tenant from subleasing the premises. Conversely, a prohibition against subleasing is not considered a restriction upon the right to assign the lease.

If a tenant transfers *all* his interest in a leasehold, thereby forfeiting his reversionary rights, he has made an **assignment**. Many leases prohibit assignment without the landlord's written consent.

If the tenant assigns the lease without consent, the assignment is not void, but it may be avoided by the landlord. In other words, the prohibition of assignment in a lease is solely for the landlord's benefit; the assignor, therefore, cannot rely upon the prohibition in attempting to terminate an otherwise valid assignment on the ground that the landlord did not consent. If, however, the landlord accepts rent from the assignee, he will be held to have waived the restriction.

The tenant's agreement to pay rent and other contractual **covenants** (express promises) pass to and obligate the assignee of the lease as long as the assignee remains in possession of the leasehold estate. Although the assignee is thus bound to pay rent, the original tenant is not thereby relieved of his contractual obligation to do so. If the assignee fails to pay the stipulated rent, the original tenant will have to pay, though he will have a right to be reimbursed by the assignee. Thus, after an assignment of a tenant's interest, both the original tenant and the assignee are liable to the landlord for failure to pay rent.

A **sublease** differs from an assignment in that the tenant transfers *less* than all of her rights in the lease and thereby retains a reversion in the leasehold. For example, Mary is a tenant under a lease from Leon which is to terminate on December 31, 2011. If Mary leases the premises to Tony for a period shorter than that covered by her own lease, for example, until November 30, 2011, Mary has subleased the premises because she has transferred less than her whole interest in the lease.

The legal effects of a sublease are entirely different from those of an assignment. In a sublease, the sublessee (Tony, in this example) has no obligation to Mary's landlord, Leon. Tony's obligations run solely to Mary, the original tenant, and Mary is not relieved of any of her obligations under the lease. Thus, Leon has no right of action against Mary's sublessee, Tony, under any covenants contained in the original lease between him and Mary because that lease has not been assigned to Tony. Mary, of course, remains liable to Leon for the rent and for all other covenants in the original lease.

◆ **SEE FIGURE 49-2: Assignment Compared with Sublease**

TENANT'S OBLIGATIONS

While the leasehold estate carries with it only an implied obligation on the part of the tenant to pay reasonable rent, the lease contract almost always contains an express promise or covenant by the tenant to pay rent in specified amounts at specified times. In the absence of a specific covenant providing the amount of rental and the times for payment, the rent will be a *reasonable* amount *payable only at the end of the term.*

Most leases provide that if the tenant breaches any of the covenants in the lease, the landlord may declare the lease at an end and regain possession of the premises. The tenant's express undertaking to pay rent thus becomes one of the covenants upon which this provision can operate. Where the lease makes no such provision, at common law the tenant's failure to pay rent when due gives the landlord only the right to recover a judgment for the amount of such rent; it gives him no right to oust the tenant from the premises. In most jurisdictions, however, the common law rule has been changed by statute to entitle the landlord to dispossess the tenant for nonpayment of rent, even if the lease does not provide for such action.

Unless the lease contains express provisions to the contrary, a tenant is under no duty to make any repairs to the leased premises. He is not obliged to repair or restore substantial or extraordinary damage occurring without his fault, nor must he repair damage caused by ordinary wear and tear. The tenant is obliged, however, to use the premises in a manner that causes them no substantial injury. The law

◆ **FIGURE 49-2: Assignment Compared with Sublease**

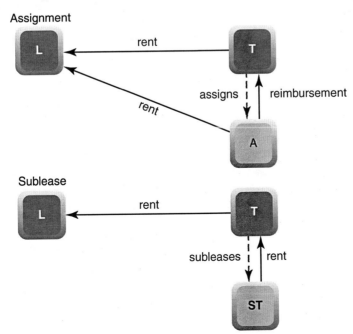

imposes this duty; it need not be expressly stipulated in the lease. For example, a tenant who overloads an electrical connection, thereby damaging a wiring system, is liable to the landlord.

DESTRUCTION OF THE PREMISES The dual character of a lease as a contract and as a grant of an estate in land is particularly evident with regard to the common law rule governing the destruction of premises by fire or other cause. Where the tenant leases land together with a building, and the building is destroyed by fire or some other adverse cause, the common law neither relieves him of his obligation to pay rent nor permits him to terminate the lease. In most States, however, the common law rule has been modified by statute to exclude tenants who occupy only a portion of a building and who have no interest in the building as a whole, such as apartment tenants. Most leases contain clauses covering the accidental destruction of the premises.

EVICTION When the tenant breaches one of the covenants in her lease, such as the covenant to pay rent, and the landlord evicts or dispossesses her pursuant to an express provision in the lease or under a statute authorizing her to do so, the lease is terminated. Because the breach of the covenant to pay rent does not involve any injury to the premises and because the landlord's action in evicting the tenant terminates the lease, the evicted tenant is not liable to the landlord for any future installments of rent. Most long-term leases, however, contain a survival clause providing that the eviction of the tenant for nonpayment of rent will not relieve her of liability for damages equal to the difference between the rent reserved in the lease and the rent the landlord is able to obtain when reletting the premises. The landlord generally can terminate the tenancy if a tenant repeatedly disturbs other tenants and neighbors, such as by throwing loud parties or selling drugs, or otherwise violates the lease or the law. If the landlord wrongfully evicts the tenant, the tenant's obligations under the lease are terminated, and, as discussed below, the landlord is liable for breach of the tenant's right of quiet enjoyment.

ABANDONMENT If the tenant wrongfully abandons the premises before the term of the lease expires, and the landlord reenters the premises or relets them to another, a majority of the courts hold that the tenant's obligation to pay rent after reentry terminates. The landlord, if he desires to hold the tenant to his obligation to pay rent, either must leave the premises vacant or must have in the lease another "survival clause" that covers this situation.

LANDLORD'S OBLIGATIONS

Under the Federal Fair Housing Act, a landlord cannot discriminate against a tenant with regard to race, color, sex, religion, national origin, disability, or familial status (except under the housing for older persons exception). Nevertheless, absent express provisions in the lease, the landlord, under the common law, has few obligations to her tenant. Under the majority (American) rule, at the beginning of the lease, she has only to give the tenant the right to possession. In a minority of States (the English rule), she has to give actual possession. Thus, in States following the American rule, if the previous tenant refuses to move out when his lease terminates, the landlord must bring dispossession proceedings to oust him; she is not responsible to the new tenant for the delay thus brought about, and the new tenant is not relieved of the obligation to pay rent from the starting date of the lease.

QUIET ENJOYMENT The landlord may not interfere with the tenant's right to physical possession, use, and enjoyment of the premises. Rather, the landlord is bound to provide the tenant with quiet and peaceful enjoyment, a duty known as the covenant of **quiet enjoyment**. The landlord breaches this covenant, which arises by implication, whenever he wrongfully evicts the tenant. He is also regarded as having breached this covenant if someone having better title to the property than the landlord evicts the tenant. The landlord is not responsible, however, for the wrongful acts of third parties unless they are done with his assent and under his direction.

Eviction need not be actual. Under the doctrine of **constructive eviction**, a failure by the landlord in any of her undertakings under the lease that causes a substantial and lasting injury to the tenant's beneficial enjoyment of the premises is regarded as being, in effect, an eviction of the tenant. Under such circumstances, the courts permit the tenant to abandon the premises and terminate the lease. The tenant must abandon possession within a reasonable time, however, to claim that a constructive eviction occurred.

FITNESS FOR USE Historically, as the primary value of the lease to the tenant was the land, the landlord, under the common law, is under no obligation to provide or maintain the premises in a tenantable (livable) condition or to make them fit for any purpose, unless there is a specific provision in the lease. Most States, however, have abandoned this rule in residential leases by imposing an **implied warranty of habitability** that requires the leased premises to be fit for ordinary residential purposes, having adequate weatherproofing; heat, water, and electricity; as well as clean, sanitary, and structurally safe premises. These courts also have held that the covenant to pay rent is conditioned upon the landlord's performance of this implied warranty of habitability. Courts reaching these results have emphasized that the tenant's interest is in a place to live, not merely in land. The common law assumption that the value of the leasehold is the land may have been valid in an agricultural society and may continue to be valid with regard to certain farm leases, but it is not applicable in the case of a modern apartment rental.

A number of States have statutes requiring landlords to keep residential premises fit for occupation. Zoning ordinances, health and safety regulations, and building and housing codes may also impose certain duties upon the landlord.

If the landlord violates the warranty of habitability, the tenant may terminate the lease and avoid further liability for rent and in some States withhold rent and sue for damages.

REPAIR Under the common law, in the absence of an express provision in the lease or a statutory duty to do so, the landlord has no obligation to repair or restore the premises. The landlord does, however, have a duty to maintain, repair, and keep in safe condition those portions of the premises that remain under her control. For example, an apartment house owner who controls the lobbies, stairways, elevators, and other common areas of the building is liable for their maintenance and repair and is responsible for injuries that occur as a result of her failure to do so. With respect to apartment buildings, the courts presume that any portion of the premises that is not expressly leased to the tenants remains under the landlord's control. Thus, the landlord, in such cases, is liable to make external repairs, including repairs to the roof.

While at common law in a number of States the landlord is under no duty to repair, restore, or keep the premises in a tenantable condition, she may and often does assume those duties in the lease. Her breach of any such undertakings does not, however, entitle the tenant to abandon the premises and refuse to pay rent. Unless an express provision in the lease gives the tenant this right, the common law allows him only an action for damages. As mentioned above, a number of States now have statutes that require the landlord to keep residential premises fit for occupancy and accordingly have imposed upon the landlord a duty to repair those items.

LANDLORD'S LIABILITY FOR INJURY CAUSED BY THIRD PARTIES
Chapter 7 discusses the duties and tort liabilities of a landlord to a tenant for defects in common areas and for failure to disclose hidden defects in the rented premises of which the landlord knew or should have known. Under the common law, a landlord also was liable if he did not exercise reasonable care in repairing such defects. In the twenty-first century, by statute or judicial decision, many States are requiring landlords to maintain leased premises in good repair and are holding them liable for a negligent failure to do so.

Some States hold landlords liable for injuries their tenants and others suffer as a result of the foreseeable criminal conduct of third parties. Although landlords cannot be insurers of their tenants' safety, courts have held landlords liable for

failure "to take minimal precautions to protect members of the public from the reasonably foreseeable criminal acts of third persons." *Ianelli v. Powers*, 498 N.Y.S.2d 377 (N.Y. App. Div. 1986).

CONCURRENT OWNERSHIP

Property may be owned by one individual or by two or more persons concurrently. Two or more persons who hold title concurrently are generally referred to as **co-tenants**. Each is entitled to an undivided interest in the entire property, and neither has a claim to any specific portion of it. Each may have equal undivided interests, or one may have a larger undivided share than the other. Regardless of the particular relationships between the co-tenants, this form of ownership is distinct from the separate ownership of specific parts of property by different persons. Thus, Anne, Barbara, and Carol each may own separate parts of Blackstone Manor, or each may own, as a co-tenant, an undivided one-third interest in all of Blackstone Manor. Their being co-tenants or the owners of specific portions depends on the manner and form in which they acquired their interests.

The two major types of concurrent ownership are tenancy in common and joint tenancy. Both provide an undivided interest in the whole, the right of both tenants to possession, and the right of either to sell his interest during life and thus terminate the original relationship. Other forms of co-ownership of real estate are tenancy by the entireties, community property, condominiums, and cooperatives.

TENANCY IN COMMON

Under a **tenancy in common**, the most frequently used form of concurrent ownership, each co-owner has both an undivided interest in the property and the right to possession and use, but none claims any specific portion of the property. Tenants in common need not have acquired their interests at the same time or by the same instrument, and their interests may differ as to duration and scope. Because there is no right of survivorship, the interests of tenants in common may be devised by will or pass by intestate succession. By statute in all States, a transfer of title to two or more persons is presumed to create a tenancy in common. Tenants in common may terminate their tenancy either by transferring all of their co-interests to one person or by partitioning the property among themselves. Partition is the act of physically dividing the property and thereby changing undivided interests into smaller parcels that each person owns individually. The size of an individual parcel is based upon the size of the owner's prior share of the undivided interest. If physical division of the property (e.g., a house) is not practicable, the property will be sold and the proceeds divided.

JOINT TENANCY

The most significant feature of joint tenancy is the right of *survivorship*: upon the death of a joint tenant, title to the entire property passes by operation of law to the survivor or survivors. Neither the heirs of the deceased joint tenant nor his general creditors have a claim to his interest after his death, and a joint tenant cannot transfer his interest by executing a will. Nevertheless, a joint tenant may sever the tenancy by conveying or mortgaging his interest to a third party. Further, the interest of either co-tenant is subject to levy and sale upon execution. To sever a joint tenancy is to forfeit the right of survivorship: following severance, the tenancy becomes a tenancy in common among the remaining joint tenants and the transferee. A joint tenancy may be terminated by partitioning the property among the tenants, making each the exclusive owner of a specific part of the entire property.

To sustain a **joint tenancy**, the common law requires the presence of what are known as the *four unities* of time, title, interest, and possession:

1. the unity of time means that the interests of all tenants must vest at the same time;
2. the unity of title means that all tenants must acquire title by the same instrument;
3. the unity of interest means that the tenants' interests must be identical in duration and scope; and
4. the unity of possession means that the tenants have identical rights of possession and enjoyment.

While the absence of any unity will prevent the creation of a joint tenancy, the presence of the fourth unity and any two of the others will result in the creation of a tenancy in common, because the only unity required of a tenancy in common is the unity of possession.

TENANCY BY THE ENTIRETIES

Tenancy by the entireties, which is recognized in some States, is created only by a conveyance to a *husband and wife*. It is distinguished from joint tenancy by the inability of either spouse to convey separately his or her interest during life and thus destroy the right of survivorship. Likewise, the interest of either spouse cannot be attached by creditors. By the nature of the tenancy, divorce would terminate the relationship, and partition would then be available as a method of creating separate interests in the property.

◆ **SEE FIGURE 49-3: Rights of Concurrent Owners**

COMMUNITY PROPERTY

In Arizona, California, Idaho, Louisiana, Nevada, New Mexico, Puerto Rico, Texas, Washington, and Wisconsin, one-half of any property acquired by either a husband or wife belongs to each spouse. Originating in the civil law of continental Europe, this system, known as **community property**, has been modified by United States common law and by statutes as well.

In most instances, the only property belonging separately to either spouse is that acquired prior to the marriage or acquired subsequent to it by gift or devise. Upon the death of either spouse, one-half of the community property belongs outright to the survivor, and the interest of the deceased spouse in the other half may go to the heirs of the decedent or as directed by will. Under certain conditions in a few jurisdictions, however, the surviving spouse may also claim an interest in the decedent's one-half share of the property.

CONDOMINIUMS

Condominiums embody a form of co-ownership now widely utilized in the United States. All States have enacted statutes authorizing this form of ownership. The purchaser of a condominium acquires separate ownership to the unit and becomes a tenant in common with respect to its common facilities, such as the land upon which the project is built, recreational facilities, hallways, parking areas, and spaces between the units. A condominium association, funded by assessments levied on each unit, maintains the common elements. The transfer of a condominium conveys both the separate ownership of the unit and the share in the common elements.

◆ **FIGURE 49-3: Rights of Concurrent Owners**

	Undivided Interest	Right to Possession	Right to Sell	Right to Mortgage	Levy by Creditors	Right to Will	Right of Survivorship
Joint Tenancy	Yes	Yes	Yes	Yes	Yes	No	Yes
Tenancy in Common	Yes	Yes	Yes	Yes	Yes	Yes	No
Tenancy by Entireties	Yes	Yes	No	No	No	No	Yes

COOPERATIVES

Cooperatives involve an indirect form of common ownership. A cooperative, usually a corporation, purchases or constructs the dwelling units and then leases the units to its shareholders as tenants, who acquire the right to use and occupy their units.

NONPOSSESSORY INTERESTS

Although a nonpossessory interest in land entitles the holder to use the land or to take something from it, the interest does not give him the right to possess the land. Nonpossessory interests include easements, *profits à prendre*, and licenses, all of which differ from a tenancy because the tenant has an exclusive *possessory* interest.

DEFINITION OF EASEMENTS

An **easement** is a limited right to use the land of another in a manner specified by the acts of the parties or by operation of law and possessing all the attributes of an estate in the land itself. The easement can involve all or a specific portion of the property. For example, a typical easement exists where Liz sells part of her land to Neal and expressly provides in the same or a separate document that Neal, as the adjoining landowner, shall have a right-of-way over a strip of Liz's remaining parcel of land. Neal's land is said to be the **dominant** parcel (land whose owner has rights in other land), and Liz's land, which is subject to the easement, is the **servient** parcel. Easements may, of course, involve a multitude of different uses, as, for example, a right to run a ditch across another's land, to lay pipe under the surface, to erect power lines, or, in the case of adjacent buildings, to use a stairway or a common or "party" wall.

Because the owner of the entire servient tract retains the title to the servient parcel, she may make any use of or allow others the use of the tract as long as this use does not interfere with the easement. Thus, crops may be grown over an easement for a pipeline, but livestock cannot be pastured on an easement for a driveway. Although the owner of the servient parcel is under a duty not to interfere with the use of the easement, the owner of the dominant parcel generally is responsible for maintaining the easement and keeping it in repair.

TYPES OF EASEMENTS

Easements fall into two classes: appurtenant easements and easements in gross. **Appurtenant** easements are by far the more common type; the rights and duties they create pertain to the land itself, not to the individuals who have created such easements. Therefore, the easement usually stays with the land when it is sold. For example, if Liz (from the previous example) sells her servient parcel to Kyle, who has actual notice of the easement for the benefit of Neal's land or constructive notice by means of the local recording act, Kyle takes the parcel subject to the easement. Likewise, if Neal conveys his dominant parcel to Daniel, the deed from Neal to Daniel need contain no specific reference to the easement to give to Daniel, as the dominant parcel's new owner, the right to use the right-of-way over the servient parcel. As Neal does not then own the dominant parcel, he has no further right to use the right-of-way. Neal could not, however, transfer the benefit of the easement to a party who did not acquire an interest in the dominant parcel of land. Most frequently, a deed conveying certain land "together with all appurtenances" is sufficient to transfer an easement. This characteristic of an appurtenant easement is described by the statement that both the burden and the benefit of an appurtenant easement pass with the land.

The second type of easement is an **easement in gross**, which is personal to the particular individual who receives the right. It, in effect, amounts to little more than an irrevocable personal right to use.

CREATION OF EASEMENTS

Easements may be created by (1) express grant or reservation, (2) implied grant or reservation, (3) necessity, (4) dedication, and (5) prescription.

EXPRESS GRANT OR RESERVATION The most common way to create an easement is to convey it by deed. For example, when Amy conveys part of her land to Robert, she may, in the same deed, expressly grant him an easement over her remaining property. Alternatively, Amy may grant an easement to Robert in a separate document. This document must comply with all the formalities of a deed. An easement is an interest in land subject to the statute of frauds. In other instances, when an owner transfers land, she may wish to retain certain rights in it. In the example given, Amy may want to "reserve" over the land she grants to Robert an easement in favor of the land she retains. Amy may reserve this right by express words in the deed of conveyance to Robert.

IMPLIED GRANT OR RESERVATION Easements by implied grant or implied reservation arise whenever an owner of adjacent properties establishes an *apparent* and *permanent* use in the nature of an easement and then conveys one of the properties without mention of any easement. For example, suppose that Andrew owns two adjacent lots, Nos. 1 and 2. There is a house on each lot. Behind each house is a garage. Andrew has constructed a driveway along the boundary between the two lots, partly on lot 1 and partly on lot 2, which leads from the street in front of the houses to the two garages in the rear. Andrew conveys lot 2 to Michael without any mention of the driveway. Andrew is held to have *impliedly granted* an easement to Michael over the portion of the driveway that lies on Andrew's lot 1, and he is held to have *impliedly reserved* an easement over the portion of the driveway that lies on Michael's lot 2.

NECESSITY If Sharon conveys part of her land to Terry, and the part conveyed to Terry is so situated that he would have no access to it except across Sharon's remaining land, the law implies a grant by Sharon to Terry of an easement by necessity across her remaining land. An easement by necessity usually will not arise if an alternative, albeit circuitous, approach to the land is available.

An easement by necessity may also arise by implied reservation. This would be the case in a situation in which Sharon conveys part of her land to Terry, and her remaining property would be wholly landlocked unless she were given a right-of-way across the land conveyed to Terry.

DEDICATION When an owner of land subdivides it into lots and records the plan or plat of the subdivision, she is held, both by common law and now more frequently by statute, to have dedicated *to the public* all of the streets, alleys, parks, playgrounds, and beaches shown on the plat. In addition, when the subdivider sells the lots by reference to the plat, it is now generally recognized that the purchasers acquire easements by implication over the areas shown to be dedicated to the public.

PRESCRIPTION An easement may arise by prescription in most States if certain required conditions are met. To obtain an easement by prescription, a person must use a portion of land owned by another in a way (1) that is adverse to the rightful owner's use, (2) that is open and notorious, and (3) that continues, uninterrupted, for a specific period that varies from State to State. The claimant acquires no easement by prescription, however, if given the owner's permission to use the land.

PROFITS À PRENDRE

The French phrase **profit à prendre** describes the right to remove the natural resources such as petroleum, minerals, timber, and wild game from the land of another. An example would be the grant by Jack to Roger, an adjoining landowner, of the right to remove coal, fish, or timber from Jack's land or to graze his cattle on Jack's land. Like an easement, a *profit à prendre* may arise by prescription, but if it comes about through an act of the parties, it must be created with all the formalities accorded the grant of an estate in real property. Unless the right is clearly designated as exclusive, the owner of the land is entitled to exercise it as well. Furthermore, even one who does not own adjacent land may hold the right to take profits. Thus, Norman may have a right to remove crushed gravel from John's acreage even though Norman lives in another part of the county.

LICENSES

Real interests in property such as easements or *profits à prendre* are considered interests in land. On the other hand, a license, which is created by a contract granting permission to make use of an owner's land, does not create an interest in the property. A license is usually exercised only at the will of the owner and subject to revocation by him at any time. For example, if Carter tells Karen she may cut across Carter's land to pick hickory nuts, Karen has nothing but a license subject to revocation at any time. It is possible that, upon the basis of a license, Karen may expend funds to exercise the right, and the courts may prevent Carter from revoking the license simply because it would be unfair to penalize Karen under the circumstances. In such a case, Karen's interest is practicably indistinguishable from an easement.

A common example of a license is a theater ticket or the use of a hotel room. No interest is acquired in the premises; there is simply a right of use for a given length of time, subject to good behavior. No formality is required to create a license; a shopkeeper licenses persons to enter his establishment merely by being open for business.

CHAPTER SUMMARY

FREEHOLD ESTATES **Fee Estates** right to immediate possession of real property for an indefinite time
- *Fee Simple* absolute ownership of property
- *Qualified Fee* ownership subject to its being taken away upon the happening of an event

Life Estates ownership right in property for the life of a designated person, while the remainder is the ownership estate that takes effect when the prior estate terminates

Future Interests
- *Reversion* grantor's right to property upon termination of another estate
- *Remainders* are of two kinds: vested remainders (unconditional remainder that is a fixed, present interest to be enjoyed in the future) and contingent remainders (remainder interest conditional upon the happening of an event in addition to the termination of the preceding estate)

LEASEHOLD ESTATES   **Lease** both (1) a contract for use and possession of land and (2) a grant of an estate in land
- *Landlord* owner of land who grants a leasehold interest to another while retaining a reversionary interest in the property
- *Tenant* possessor of the leasehold interest in the land

Duration of Leases
- *Definite Term* lease that automatically expires at the end of the term
- *Periodic Tenancy* lease consisting of specific terms that continue in indefinite succession
- *Tenancy at Will* lease that is terminable at any time
- *Tenancy at Sufferance* possession of real property without a lease

Transfer of Tenant's Interest
- *Assignment* transfer of all of the tenant's interest in the leasehold
- *Sublease* transfer of less than all of the tenant's interest in the leasehold

Tenant's Obligations the tenant has an obligation to pay a specified rent at specified times or, if none is specified, to pay a reasonable amount at the end of the term
- *Destruction of the Premises* under the common law, if the premises are destroyed the tenant is not relieved of his obligation to pay rent and cannot terminate the lease
- *Eviction* if the tenant breaches one of the covenants of her lease, the landlord may terminate the lease and evict (remove) her from the premises
- *Abandonment* if tenant abandons property and the landlord reenters or relets it, tenant's obligation to pay rent terminates

Landlord's Obligations
- *Quiet Enjoyment* the right of the tenant to have physical possession of the premises free of landlord interference
- *Fitness for Use* most courts impose for residential leases an implied warranty of habitability that the leased premises are fit for ordinary residential purposes
- *Repair* unless there is a statute or a specific provision in the lease, the landlord has no duty to repair or restore the premises

CONCURRENT OWNERSHIP   **Tenancy in Common** co-ownership in which each tenant holds an undivided interest with no right of survivorship

Joint Tenancy co-ownership with the right of survivorship; requires the presence of the four unities (time, title, interest, and possession)

Tenancy by the Entireties co-ownership by spouses in which neither may convey his or her interest during life

Community Property spouses' rights in property acquired by the other during their marriage

Condominium separate ownership of an individual unit with tenancy in common with respect to common areas

Cooperative the corporate owner of the property leases units to its shareholders as tenants

NONPOSSESSORY INTERESTS   **Easement** limited right to use the land of another in a specified manner
- *Appurtenant* rights and duties created by the easement pertain to and run with the land of the owner of the easement (dominant parcel) and the land subject to the easement (servient parcel)

- *In Gross* rights and duties created by the easement are personal to the individual who received the right
- *Creation of Easements* easements may be created by (1) express grant or reservation, (2) implied grant or reservation, (3) necessity, (4) dedication, and (5) prescription (adverse use)

Profits à Prendre right to remove natural resources from the land of another

Licenses permission to use the land of another

Transfer and Control of Real Property

The law has always been, and still is, extremely cautious about the transfer of title to real estate. Personal property may, for the most part, be passed from owner to owner easily and informally, but real property can be transferred only through compliance with a variety of formalities. Such protocol is apparent in the transfer of property at death, where strict formalities are relaxed only with respect to personal property; it is most evident in a transfer of land during the owner's lifetime.

Title to land may be transferred in three principal ways: (1) by deed; (2) by will or by the law of descent upon the death of the owner; and (3) by open, continuous, and adverse possession by a nonowner for a statutorily prescribed period of years. This chapter will discuss the first and third methods of transfer—transfer by deed and adverse possession. The second method is covered in *Chapter 51*.

In addition to the legal restrictions placed on the transfer of real property, a number of other controls apply to the use of privately owned property. Government units impose some of these, including zoning and the taking of property by eminent domain. Private parties through restrictive covenants impose others. These three controls are considered in the second part of this chapter.

TRANSFER OF REAL PROPERTY

The most common way in which real property is transferred is by deed. Such transfers usually involve a contract for the sale of the land, the subsequent delivery of the deed, and payment of the agreed consideration. The transfer of real estate by deed, however, does not require consideration to be valid; it may be made as a gift. In most cases, the real estate purchaser must borrow part of the purchase price, using the real property as security. A far less usual method of transferring title, called *adverse possession*, requires no contract, deed, or other formality.

CONTRACT OF SALE

As indicated in the chapter on contracts, general contract law governs the sale of real property. In general, the seller agrees to convey the land and the buyer to pay for it. In addition, the Federal Fair Housing Act (Title VIII of the Civil Rights Act, as amended) prohibits discrimination in the real estate market on the basis of race, color, religion, sex, national origin, disability, or familial status. The Act exempts the sale or rental of a single-family house owned by a private individual who owns fewer than four houses, provided that the owner does not use a broker or discriminatory advertising. Nevertheless, these exemptions do not apply to discrimination based on race or color; in the sale or rental of property, the Act prohibits all discrimination based on these factors.

FORMATION

Because an oral agreement for the sale of an interest in land is not enforceable under the statute of frauds, the buyer and seller must reduce the agreement to writing and have it signed by the other party to be able to enforce the agreement against that party. The simplest agreement should contain (1) the names and addresses of the parties, (2) a description of the property to be conveyed, (3) the time for the conveyance (called the *closing*), (4) the type of deed to be given, and (5) the price and manner of payment. To avoid dispute and to protect the rights of both parties, a properly drawn contract for the sale of land will cover many other points as well.

A majority of jurisdictions adhere to the common law rule that the risk of loss or destruction of the property, not caused through the fault of the seller, rests with the purchaser after the contract is formed. The contract of sale may, of course, provide that such risk shall remain with the seller until she conveys the deed to the purchaser, that the seller must obtain insurance for the benefit of the purchaser, or that the risk is allocated in some other manner on which the parties have agreed.

MARKETABLE TITLE

The law of conveyancing has firmly established that a contract for the sale of land carries with it an implied obligation on the part of the seller to transfer marketable title. Marketable title means that the title is free from (1) encumbrances (such as mortgages, easements, liens, leases, and restrictive covenants); (2) defects in the chain of title appearing in the land records (such as a prior recorded conveyance of the same property by the seller); and (3) events depriving the seller of title, such as adverse possession or eminent domain. The seller's obligation to convey marketable title is significant, for if a title search reveals any flaw not specifically excepted in the contract, the seller has materially breached the contract. The buyer's remedies for breach include specific performance with a price reduction, rescission and restitution, or damages for loss of bargain. There are two important exceptions to this rule. First, most courts hold that the seller's implied or express obligation to convey marketable title does not include the obligation to convey title free from existing zoning restrictions. Second, some courts also hold that the seller's implied or express obligation to convey marketable title does not require him to convey title free from open and visible public rights-of-way or easements, such as public roads and sewers.

Before title to the property passes, the buyer should ensure that she is receiving good title by having the title searched. A title search involves examining prior transfers of and encumbrances to the property. Such an examination does not guarantee rightful ownership, however; consequently, most buyers purchase **title insurance** as well. Issued in the amount of the purchase price of the property, title insurance indemnifies the owner against any loss due to defects in the title to the property or due to liens or encumbrances, except for those stated in the policy as existing at the time the policy is issued. Such policies also may be issued to protect the interests of mortgagees or tenants of property.

IMPLIED WARRANTY OF HABITABILITY

Because the obligation of marketable title involves only the title to the property conveyed, such an obligation does not apply to the quality of any improvements to the land. The traditional common law rule is *caveat emptor*—let the buyer beware. Under this rigid maxim, the buyer must inspect the property thoroughly before completing the sale, as any defect discovered only after the transaction is complete would not be the seller's responsibility. The seller is liable only for any misrepresentation or express warranty he may have made about the property.

A majority of States have relaxed the harshness of the common law in sales made by one who builds and then sells residential dwellings. In such a sale, the builder-seller impliedly warrants a newly constructed house to be free of latent defects, that is, those defects not apparent upon a reasonable inspection of the house at the time of sale. In some States, this implied warranty of habitability benefits only the original purchaser. In other States, the warranty has been extended to subsequent purchasers for a reasonable time. In addition, many jurisdictions now require *all* sellers to disclose hidden defects that materially affect the property's value and that would remain undetected following a reasonable examination. See *Chapter 11* for a discussion of misrepresentation.

DEEDS

A **deed** is a formal document transferring any interest in land upon delivery and acceptance. The party who transfers property by a deed is called the **grantor**; the transferee of the property is the **grantee**.

TYPES OF DEEDS

The rights conveyed by a deed vary, depending on the type of deed used. Deeds are of three basic types: warranty, special warranty, and quitclaim.

WARRANTY By a warranty deed (also called a general warranty deed), the grantor promises the grantee that the grantor has a valid title to the property. In addition, under a warranty deed, the grantor, either expressly or impliedly, obliges herself to make the grantee whole for any damage the grantee might suffer should the grantor's title prove to be defective. Aside from rendering the grantor liable for any defects in her title, the general warranty deed is distinct in that it will convey after-acquired title. For example, on January 30, Andrea conveys Blackacre by warranty deed to Bob. On January 30, Andrea's title to Blackacre is defective, but by February 14, Andrea has acquired a good title. Without more, Bob has acquired Andrea's good title under the January 30 warranty deed.

SPECIAL WARRANTY Whereas a warranty deed contains a general warranty of title, a special warranty deed warrants only that the title has not been impaired, encumbered, or rendered defective because of any act or omission of the grantor. The grantor merely warrants the title so far as his acts or omissions are concerned. He does not warrant the title to be free of defects caused by the acts or omissions of others.

QUITCLAIM By a quitclaim deed, the grantor, in effect, says no more than "I make no promise as to what interest I have in this land, but whatever it is I convey it to you." Quitclaim deeds most commonly are used as a means for persons apparently having an interest in land to release their interest.

FORMAL REQUIREMENTS

As previously noted, any transfer of an interest in land that is of more than a limited duration falls within the statute of frauds and must therefore be in writing. The wording of nearly all deeds, whatever the type, follows substantially the same pattern, though the words used will vary, depending upon whether the instrument is a warranty deed, a special warranty deed, or a quitclaim deed. Moreover, statutes in most States suggest that certain words of conveyance be used to make the deed effective. A common phrase for a warranty deed is "convey and warrant," although in a number of States the phrase "grant, bargain, and sell" is used together with a covenant by the seller later in the deed that she will "warrant and defend the title." A quitclaim deed generally will provide that the grantor "conveys and quitclaims" or, more simply, "quitclaims all interest" in the property.

DESCRIPTION OF THE LAND The description must be sufficiently clear to permit identification of the property conveyed. A common test of clarity is to ask whether a subsequent purchaser or a surveyor employed by him could mark off the land using the description.

QUANTITY OF THE ESTATE After describing the property, the deed usually will describe the quantity of estate conveyed to the grantee. Thus, either "to have and to hold to himself and his heirs forever" or "to have and to hold in fee simple" would vest the grantee with absolute title to the land. A deed conveying title to "George for life and to Elliott upon George's death," by comparison, would grant a life estate to George and a remainder interest to Elliott.

COVENANTS OF TITLE Customarily, in making a deed, the grantor makes certain promises concerning her title to the land. Such promises or covenants, the most usual of which are title (*seisen*), **against encumbrances**, **quiet enjoyment**, and **warranty**, ensure that the grantee will have undisturbed possession of the land and will, in turn, be able to transfer it free of the adverse claims of third parties. For the grantor's breach of covenant, the grantee is, moreover, entitled to be indemnified. In many States, all or many of these covenants are implied from the words of conveyance themselves—for example, "warrants" or "grant, bargain, and sell."

EXECUTION Deeds generally end with the signature of the grantor, a seal, and an acknowledgment before a notary public or other official authorized to attest to the authenticity of documents. The grantor's signature can be made by an agent having written authority from the grantor in a form required by law. Today the seal has lost most of its former significance, and in those few jurisdictions in which it is required, the seal is sufficient if the word *Seal* or the letters *L.S.* appear next to the signature.

DELIVERY OF DEEDS

A deed does not transfer title to land until it is delivered. Delivery consists of the grantor's *intent* that the deed shall take effect, as evidenced by his acts or statements. Indispensable to delivery is the grantor's parting with control of the deed with the intention that it immediately will become operative to convey the estate it describes. Physical transfer of the deed is usually the best evidence of this intent, but it is not necessary. For example, the act of the grantor in placing a deed in a safe deposit box may or may not constitute delivery, depending on such facts as whether the grantee did or did not have access to the box and whether the grantor acts as if the property were the grantee's. A deed conceivably may be "delivered" even when kept in the grantor's possession; just as conceivably, physical delivery of a deed to a grantee may fail to transfer title. Frequently, in a transfer known as an escrow, a grantor will turn a deed over to a third party, the escrow agent, to hold until the grantee performs certain conditions. Upon the performance of the condition, the escrow agent must turn the deed over to the grantee.

RECORDATION

In almost all States, recording a deed is not necessary to pass title from grantor to grantee. Unless the grantee has the deed recorded, however, a subsequent good faith purchaser for value of the property will acquire title superior to that of the grantee. Recordation consists of delivering a duly executed and acknowledged deed to the recorder's office in the county where the property is located. There, a copy of the instrument is inserted in the current deed book and indexed.

In some States, called **notice** States, unrecorded instruments are invalid against any subsequent purchaser without notice. In **notice-race** States, an unrecorded deed is invalid against any subsequent purchaser without notice who records first. Finally, in a few States, known as race States, an unrecorded deed is invalid against any deed recorded before it.

More than twenty States have adopted the Uniform Real Property Electronic Recording Act. This Act permits the electronic filing of real property instruments as well as systems for searching for and retrieving these land records.

SECURED TRANSACTIONS

The purchase of real estate usually involves a relatively large outlay of money, and few people pay cash for a house or business real estate. Most people must borrow part of the purchase price or defer payment over time. In these cases, the real estate itself is used to secure the obligation, which is evidenced by a note and either a mortgage or a deed of trust. The debtor is referred to as the **mortgagor** and the creditor as the **mortgagee**.

A secured transaction includes two elements: (1) a debt or obligation to pay money and (2) the creditor's interest in specific property that secures performance of the obligation. A security interest in property cannot exist apart from the debt it secures; consequently, discharging the debt in any manner terminates the interest. Transactions involving the use of real estate as security for a debt are subject to real estate law, which consists of statutes and rules developed by the common law of mortgages and trust deeds. The Uniform Commercial Code (UCC) does *not* apply to real estate mortgages or deeds of trust.

FORM OF MORTGAGES

The instrument creating a mortgage is in the form of a conveyance from the mortgagor to the mortgagee and must meet all the requirements for such documents: it must be in writing, it must contain an adequate description of the property, and it must be executed and delivered. The usual mortgage, however, differs from an outright conveyance of property by providing, in a condition referred to as a "defeasance," that, upon the performance of the promise by the mortgagor, the conveyance is void and of no effect. Although the defeasance normally appears on the face of the mortgage, it may be in a separate document.

The concept of a **mortgage** as a lien upon real property for the payment of a debt applies with equal force to transactions having the same purpose but possessing a different name and form. A **deed of trust** is fundamentally identical to a mortgage, the most striking difference being that, under a deed of trust, the property is conveyed not to the creditor as security but to a third person who acts as trustee for the creditor's benefit. The deed of trust creates rights substantially similar to those created by a mortgage. In some States, it is customary to use a deed of trust in lieu of the ordinary form of mortgage.

As with all interests in realty, the mortgage or deed of trust should be promptly recorded to protect the mortgagee's rights against third persons who acquire an interest in the mortgaged property without knowledge of the mortgage.

RIGHTS AND DUTIES

The rights and duties of the parties to a mortgage may depend upon whether it is viewed as creating a lien or as transferring legal title to the mortgagee. Most States have adopted the **lien** theory. The mortgagor retains title and, even in the absence of any stipulation in the mortgage, is entitled to possession of the premises to the exclusion of the mortgagee, even if the mortgagor defaults. Only through foreclosure or sale or through the court appointment of a receiver can the right of possession be taken from the mortgagor. A minority of States have adopted the common law **title** theory, which gives the mortgagee the right of ownership and possession. In most cases, as a practical matter, the mortgagor retains possession simply because the mortgagee has little interest in possession unless the mortgagor defaults.

Even though the mortgagor is generally entitled to possession and to many of the advantages of unrestricted ownership, he has a responsibility to deal with the property in a manner that will not impair the security. In most instances, *waste* (impairment of the security) results from the mortgagor's failure to prevent the actual or threatened action of third parties against the land. Thus, the debtor's failure to pay taxes or to discharge a prior lien may seriously impair the security of the mortgagee. In such cases, the courts generally permit the mortgagee to pay the obligation and add it to his claim against the mortgagor.

The mortgagor has the right to relieve his mortgaged property from the lien of a mortgage by paying the debt that it secures. Characteristic of a mortgage, this right of **redemption** can be extinguished only by operation of law. The right to redeem carries with it the obligation to pay the debt, and payment in full, with interest, is prerequisite to redemption.

MORTGAGE REGULATION

In July 2010, President Obama signed into law the Dodd-Frank Wall Street Reform and Consumer Protection Act (CFPA), the most significant change to U.S. financial regulation since the New Deal. One of the many stand-alone statutes included in the CFPA is the Mortgage Reform and Anti-Predatory Lending Act of 2010, which modifies the Truth-in-Lending Act to make mortgage brokers and lenders more accountable for the loans that they make. The CFPA requires that lenders ensure a borrower's reasonable ability to repay the loan; prohibits unfair and deceptive lending practices (especially with respect to subprime mortgages); expands protection for borrowers of high-cost loans; and requires lenders to disclose the maximum amount a consumer could pay on a variable rate mortgage, with a warning that payments will vary based on interest rate changes.

◆ **SEE FIGURE 50-1: Fundamental Rights of Mortgagor and Mortgagee**

TRANSFER OF MORTGAGE INTERESTS

The original mortgagor and mortgagee can transfer their interests to assignees whose rights and obligations will depend primarily upon (1) the agreement of the parties to the assignment and (2) the legal rules protecting the interest of one who is party to the mortgage but not to the transfer.

◆ FIGURE 50-1: Fundamental Rights of Mortgagor and Mortgagee

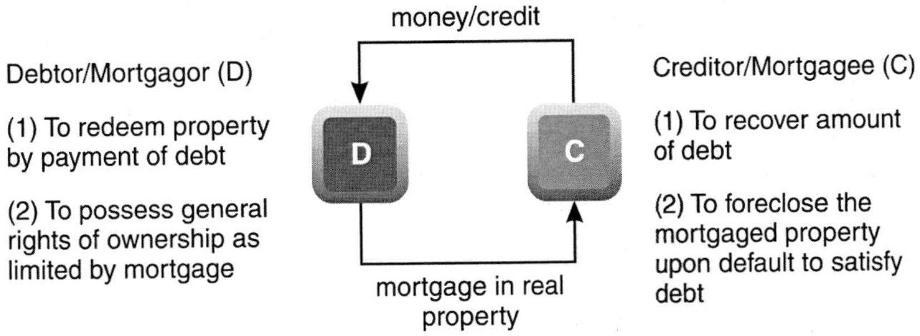

money/credit

Debtor/Mortgagor (D)

(1) To redeem property by payment of debt

(2) To possess general rights of ownership as limited by mortgage

Creditor/Mortgagee (C)

(1) To recover amount of debt

(2) To foreclose the mortgaged property upon default to satisfy debt

mortgage in real property

BY MORTGAGOR If the mortgagor conveys the land, the purchaser is not personally liable for the mortgage debt unless she expressly assumes the mortgage. If she **assumes the mortgage**, she is personally obligated to pay the debt the mortgagor owes to the mortgagee, who can also hold the mortgagor on his promise to pay. A transfer of mortgaged property **subject to the mortgage** does not personally obligate the transferee to pay the mortgage debt. In such a case, the transferee's risk of loss is limited to the realty.

BY MORTGAGEE A mortgagee has the right to assign the mortgage to another person without the consent of the mortgagor. An assignee of a mortgage is well advised to protect her rights against persons who subsequently acquire an interest in the mortgaged property without knowledge of the assignment by obtaining the assignment in a writing duly executed by the mortgagee and recording it promptly with the proper public official. Failure to record an assignment may cause an assignee of a mortgage note to lose her security. For example, Dylan buys land from Owen, relying upon a release executed and recorded by the mortgagee, Kristi. Kristi, however, had previously assigned the mortgage to Ali, who failed to have her assignment recorded. In the absence of Dylan's actual knowledge of the assignment by Kristi, Ali has no claim against the property.

FORECLOSURE

The right to foreclose usually arises upon default by the mortgagor. Foreclosure is an action through which the mortgage holder takes the property from the mortgagor, ends the mortgagor's rights in the property, and sells the property to pay the mortgage debt. The mortgagor's failure to perform other promises in the mortgage also may give the mortgagee this right. Thus, a mortgage may provide that the mortgagor's failure to pay taxes constitutes a default that permits foreclosure. Mortgages also commonly provide that default in the payment of an installment makes the entire unpaid balance of the debt immediately due and payable, permitting foreclosure for the entire amount.

Whether foreclosure is by sale under judicial proceeding or by grant of power in the mortgage itself, the transaction is still a procedure to obtain satisfaction of a debt. If the proceeds are insufficient to satisfy the debt in full, the debtor-mortgagor remains liable for paying the balance. Generally, the mortgagee will obtain a *deficiency judgment* for any unsatisfied balance of the debt and may proceed to enforce the payment of this amount out of the mortgagor's other assets.

ADVERSE POSSESSION

It is possible, although very rare, for title to land to be transferred **involuntarily**, without deed or other formality, by "adverse possession." In most States, a person who openly and continuously occupies the land of another for a statutorily prescribed time, typically five to twenty years, will gain title to the land. The possession must be actual, not merely constructive. Courts have held that living on land, farming it, building on it, or maintaining structures on it are sufficient to constitute possession. Possession, however, must be adverse. This means that any act of dominion by the true owner, such as her entry on the land or assertion of ownership, will stop the period from running. In such event, the period will commence anew from the point at which the owner interrupted it.

By statute, some jurisdictions have established shorter periods of adverse possession where possession is accompanied by some other claim, such as the payment of taxes or an apparent, even if invalid, claim of title.

PUBLIC AND PRIVATE CONTROLS

As discussed in *Chapter 7*, the law of nuisance imposes controls upon a landowner's use of her property. In exercising its police power for the benefit of the community, the State also can and does place controls upon the use of privately owned land. Moreover, the State does not compensate an owner for loss or damage he sustains by reason of such legitimate controls. The enforcement of zoning laws, which is a proper exercise of the police power, is not a taking of property but a regulation of its use. The taking of private property for a public use or purpose under the State's power of eminent domain is not, however, an exercise of the police power; and the owners of the property so taken are entitled to be paid its fair and reasonable value. In addition, private owners are entitled to control the use of privately owned property by means of restrictive covenants. This section will address these various methods of State and private control of property.

ZONING

Zoning is the principal method of public control over land use. The validity of zoning is rooted in the police power of the State, the inherent power of government to provide for the public health, safety, morals, and welfare. Police power can be used only to regulate private property, never to "take" it. It is firmly established that regulation which has no reasonable relation to public health, safety, morals, or welfare is unconstitutional as a denial of due process of law.

ENABLING ACTS AND ZONING ORDINANCES

The power to zone is generally delegated to local authorities by statutes known as enabling statutes. A typical enabling statute grants municipalities the following powers: (1) to regulate and limit the height and bulk of buildings to be erected; (2) to establish, regulate, and limit the building or setback lines on or along any street, traffic way, drive, or parkway; (3) to regulate and limit the intensity of the use of lot areas and to regulate and determine the area of open spaces within and around buildings; (4) to classify, regulate, and restrict the location of trades and industries and the location of buildings designated for specified industrial, business, residential, and other uses; (5) to divide the entire municipality into districts of such number, shape, area, and class (or classes) as may be deemed best suited to carry out the purposes of the statute; and (6) to fix standards to which buildings or structures must conform.

Under these powers, the local authorities may enact zoning ordinances consisting of a map and correlating descriptive text. The map divides the municipality into districts, which are designated principally as industrial, commercial, or residential, with possible subclassifications. A well-drafted zoning ordinance will carefully define the uses permitted in each area.

VARIANCE

Enabling statutes empower zoning authorities to grant variances where the application of a zoning ordinance to specific property would cause its owner "particular hardship" unique or peculiar to the property. A **variance** permits a deviation from the zoning ordinance. Special circumstances applicable to particular property might include its unusual shape, topography, size, location, or surroundings. A variance is not available, however, if the hardship is caused by conditions general to the neighborhood or by the actions of the property owner. It must affirmatively appear that the property as presently zoned cannot yield a reasonable return upon the owner's investment.

NONCONFORMING USES

A zoning ordinance may not immediately terminate a lawful use that existed before it was enacted. Rather, such a nonconforming use must be permitted to continue—at least for a reasonable time. Most ordinances provide that nonconforming use may be eliminated (1) when the use is discontinued, (2) when a nonconforming structure is destroyed or substantially damaged, or (3) when a nonconforming structure has been permitted to exist for the period of its useful life as fixed by municipal authorities.

JUDICIAL REVIEW OF ZONING

Although the zoning process is traditionally viewed as legislative, it is subject to judicial review on a number of grounds, including claims that the zoning ordinance is invalid or amounts to a taking of property.

INVALIDITY OF ZONING ORDINANCE A zoning ordinance may be invalid as a whole either because it bears no reasonable relation to public health, safety, morals, or welfare; because it involves the exercise of powers not granted to the municipality by the enabling act; or because it violates the State or U.S. Constitution.

ZONING AMOUNTS TO A TAKING Another form of attack is to show that zoning restrictions amount to confiscation or a "taking." It is not sufficient that the property owner will sustain a financial loss if the restrictions are not lifted. But when the owner can show that the restrictions make it impracticable for him to use the property for *any* beneficial purpose, he should prevail. Deprivation of all beneficial use is confiscation.

SUBDIVISION MASTER PLANS

A growing municipality has a special interest in regulating new housing developments so that they will harmonize with the rest of the community; so that streets within the development are integrated with existing streets or planned roads; and so that adequate provision is made for water, drainage, and sanitary facilities, as well as for traffic, recreation, light, and air. Accordingly, most States have legislation enabling local authorities to require municipal approval of every land subdivision plat. These enabling statutes provide penalties for failure to secure such approval where required by local ordinance. Some statutes provide that selling lots by reference to unrecorded plats is a criminal offense and provide further that such plats may not be recorded unless approved by the local planning board. Other statutes provide that building permits will not be issued unless the plat is approved and recorded.

EMINENT DOMAIN

The power to take private property for public use, known as the power of **eminent domain**, is recognized as one of the inherent powers of government both in the U.S. Constitution and in the constitutions of the States. At the same time, however, the power is carefully circumscribed and controlled. The Fifth Amendment to the U.S. Constitution provides, "[N]or shall private property be taken for public use, without just compensation." Similar or identical provisions are found in the constitutions of the States. There is, therefore, a direct constitutional prohibition against taking private property without just compensation and an implicit prohibition against taking private property for other than public use. Moreover, under both Federal and State constitutions, the individual from whom property is to be taken is entitled to due process of law.

PUBLIC USE

As noted, there is an implicit constitutional prohibition against taking private property for other than public use.

Most States interpret public use to mean "public advantage." Thus, the power of eminent domain may be delegated to railroad and public utility companies. Because it enables such companies to offer continued and improved service to the public, the reasonable exercise of this power is upheld as being for a public advantage. As society grows more complex, other public purposes become legitimate grounds for exercising the power of eminent domain. One such use is in the area of urban renewal. Most States have legislation permitting the establishment of housing authorities with the power to condemn slum, blighted, and vacant areas and to finance, construct, and maintain housing projects. Some States recently have gone further by permitting private companies to exercise the power of eminent domain, provided the use is primarily for a public benefit, such as the alleviation of unemployment or economic decay within the community.

JUST COMPENSATION When the power of eminent domain is exercised, just compensation must be made to the owners of the property taken. The measure of compensation is the fair market value of the property as of the time of taking. The compensation goes to holders of vested interests in the condemned property.

◆   **SEE FIGURE 50-2: Eminent Domain**

◆ **FIGURE 50-2: Eminent Domain**

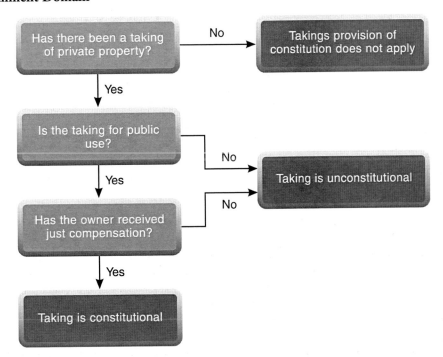

PRIVATE RESTRICTIONS UPON LAND USE

Owners of real property may impose private restrictions, called **restrictive covenants** (or negative covenants), on the use of land. Historically, two types of private restrictions developed—real covenants and equitable servitudes. The two had different, although overlapping, requirements. In the twenty-first century, equitable servitudes have nearly replaced real covenants. Accordingly, this section will cover only equitable servitudes, which will be referred to by the more general term *restrictive covenant*.

COVENANTS RUNNING WITH THE LAND

If certain conditions are satisfied, a restrictive covenant will bind not only the original parties to it but also remote parties who subsequently acquire the property. A restrictive covenant that binds remote parties is said to "run with the land." To run with the land, the restrictive covenant must involve promises that are enforceable under the law of contracts. A majority of courts hold that the covenant must be in writing. The parties who agree to the restrictive covenant must intend that the covenant will bind their successors. Moreover, the covenant must "touch and concern" the land by affecting its use, utility, or value. Finally, a restrictive covenant will bind only those successors who have actual or constructive notice of the covenant.

RESTRICTIVE COVENANTS IN SUBDIVISIONS

Restrictive covenants are widely used in subdivisions. The owners of lots are subject to restrictive covenants which, if actually brought to the attention of subsequent purchasers or recorded either by original deed or by means of a recorded plat or separate agreement, bind purchasers of lots in the subdivision as though the restrictions had been inserted in their own deeds. If the entire subdivision has been subjected to a general building plan designed to benefit all of the lots, any lot owner in the subdivision has the right to enforce the restriction against a purchaser whose title descends from a common grantor. If a restriction clearly is intended to benefit an entire tract, the covenant will be enforced against a subsequent purchaser of one of the lots in the tract if (1) the restriction apparently was intended to benefit the purchaser of any lot in the tract and (2) the restriction appears somewhere in the chain of title to which the lot is subject.

Subdivisions may involve many types of restrictive covenants. The more common ones limit the use of property to residential purposes, restrict the area of the lot on which a structure can be built, or provide for a special type of architecture. Frequently a subdivider will specify a minimum size for each house in an attempt to maintain structural unity in a neighborhood.

TERMINATION OF RESTRICTIVE COVENANTS

A restrictive covenant may end by the terms of the original agreement. For example, the developer of a subdivision may provide that the restrictive covenant will terminate after thirty-five years unless a specified majority of the property owners reaffirm the covenant. In addition, a court will not enforce a restrictive covenant if changed circumstances make enforcement inequitable and oppressive. Evidence of changed conditions may be found either within the tract covered by the original covenant or within the area adjacent to or surrounding the tract.

VALIDITY OF RESTRICTIVE COVENANTS

Although restrictions upon land use have never been popular in the law, the courts will enforce a restriction that apparently will operate to the general benefit of the owners of all the land the restriction is intended to affect. The usual method of enforcing such agreements is by an injunction restraining violation.

The law for many years has held, however, that under the Fourteenth Amendment to the U.S. Constitution, a State or municipality cannot impose any racial restrictions by statute or ordinance. In 1947, the U.S. Supreme Court held that because State courts are an arm of State government, such courts cannot enforce private racial restrictive covenants. This effectively invalidated private racial restrictive covenants.

CHAPTER SUMMARY

TRANSFER OF REAL PROPERTY

CONTRACT OF SALE **Formation** a contract to transfer any interest in land must be in writing to be enforceable

Marketable Title the seller must transfer marketable title, which is a title free from any defects or encumbrances

Quality of Improvements
- *Common Law Rule* under *caveat emptor* ("let the buyer beware") the seller is not liable for any undiscovered defects
- *Implied Warranty of Habitability* in a number of States, the builder-seller of a dwelling impliedly warrants that a newly constructed house is free from latent defects

DEEDS	**Definition** a formal document transferring any type of interest in land

DEEDS   **Definition** a formal document transferring any type of interest in land

Types
- *Warranty Deed* the grantor (seller) promises the grantee (buyer) that she has valid title to the property without defect
- *Special Warranty Deed* the seller promises that he has not impaired the title
- *Quitclaim Deed* the seller transfers whatever interest she has in the property

Requirements the deed must (1) be written, (2) contain certain words of conveyance and a description of the property, (3) end with the signature of the grantor, a seal, and an acknowledgment before a notary public, and (4) be delivered

Delivery intent that the deed take effect, as evidenced by acts or statements of the grantor

Recordation required to protect the buyer's interest against third parties; consists of delivery of a duly executed and acknowledged deed to the appropriate recorder's office

SECURED TRANSACTIONS   **Elements** a secured transaction involves (1) a debt or obligation to pay money, (2) an interest of the creditor in specific property that secures performance, and (3) the debtor's right to redeem the property (remove the security interest) by paying the debt

Mortgage interest in land created by a written document that provides security to the mortgagee (secured party) for payment of the mortgagor's debt

Deed of Trust an interest in real property which is conveyed to a third person as trustee for the benefit of the creditor

Transfer of Mortgage Interests
- *Assumes the Mortgage* the purchaser of mortgaged property becomes personally liable to pay the debt
- *Subject to the Mortgage* purchaser is not personally liable to pay the debt, but the property remains subject to the mortgage

Foreclosure upon default, sale of the mortgaged property to satisfy the debt

ADVERSE POSSESSION   **Definition** acquisition of title to land by open, continuous, and adverse occupancy for a statutorily prescribed period

Possession must be actual and without intervening domination by true owner

PUBLIC AND PRIVATE CONTROLS

ZONING   **Definition** principal method of public control over private land use; involves regulation of land but may not constitute a taking of the property

Authority the power to zone is generally delegated to local authorities by statutes known as *enabling acts*

Variance a use differing from that provided in the zoning ordinance and granted to avoid undue hardship

Nonconforming Use a use not in accordance with, but existing prior to, a zoning ordinance; permitted to continue for at least a reasonable time

Judicial Review zoning ordinances may be reviewed to determine if they are invalid or a confiscation of property

EMINENT DOMAIN	**Definition** the power of a government to take (buy) private land for public use
	Public Use public advantage
	Just Compensation the owner of the property taken by eminent domain must be paid the fair market value of the property

PRIVATE RESTRICTIONS UPON LAND USE	**Definition** private restrictions on property contained in a conveyance
	Covenants Running with the Land covenants that bind not only the original parties but also subsequent owners of the property
	Covenants in Subdivision bind purchasers of lots in the subdivision as if the restrictions had been inserted in their own deeds

Trusts and Decedents' Estates

I n previous chapters, we have seen that real and personal property may be transferred in a number of ways, including by sale and by gift. Another important way in which a person may convey property or allow others to use or benefit from it is through trusts and wills. Trusts may take effect during the transferor's lifetime or, when used in a will, they may become effective upon his death. Wills enable individuals to control the transfer of their property at their death. Upon a person's death, his or her property must pass to someone, and individuals are well advised to decide how their property should be distributed. Except for statutory or common law rights of spouses, the law permits individuals to make such distributions by sale, gift, trust, and will. If, however, an individual dies without a will—that is, intestate— State law prescribes who shall be entitled to the property that individual owned at death. This chapter will examine trusts and wills, as well as the manner in which property descends when a person dies without leaving a will.

TRUSTS

A **trust** is a *fiduciary relationship* in which one or more persons hold *legal title* to property while its use, enjoyment, and benefit (*equitable title*) belong to another. A trust may be created for any purpose that is not against the law or public policy and may be established by agreement of the parties, by bequest in a will, or by a court decree. However created, the relationship is known as a trust. The party creating the trust is the creator or settlor, the party holding the legal title to the property is the trustee of the trust, and the person who receives the benefit of the trust is the beneficiary.

◆ **SEE FIGURE 51-1: Trusts**

TYPES OF TRUSTS

Although they are of many varieties, all trusts may be divided into two major groups: express and implied. Implied trusts, which are imposed upon property by court order, are categorized as either "constructive" or "resulting" trusts.

EXPRESS TRUSTS

An **express trust** is, as the name indicates, a trust established by voluntary action and is represented by a written document, an oral statement, or conduct of the settlor. In a majority of jurisdictions, an express trust of real property must be in writing to meet the requirements of the statute of frauds. Trusts of personal property and implied trusts do not fall within the requirements of the statute of frauds.

No particular words are necessary to create a trust, provided that the intent of the settlor to establish a trust is unmistakable. Sometimes a settlor will offer a gift accompanied by words of request or recommendation implying or expressing the settlor's hope that the gift should or will be used for a particular purpose. Thus, instead of clearly creating a trust by leaving property "to X for the benefit and use of Y," a settlor may leave property to X "in full confidence and with hope that he will care for Y." Such a "**precatory expression**" (words of request) may be so definite as to impose a trust upon the property for the benefit of Y. Whether it creates a trust or is considered nothing more than a gratuitous wish depends on whether the court concludes from all the facts that the settlor genuinely intended a trust. Generally, courts hold that words such as *request*, *hope*, and *rely* place no legal obligation upon the recipient of a gift and therefore do not create a trust.

TESTAMENTARY TRUST Trusts employed in wills are known as **testamentary trusts** because they become effective after the settlor's death.

***INTER VIVOS* TRUST** A trust established during the settlor's lifetime is referred to as an *inter vivos* or "between the living" trust.

CHARITABLE TRUSTS Almost any trust that has for its purpose a benefit for the public or a sizeable segment of the public is

◆ **FIGURE 51-1: Trusts**

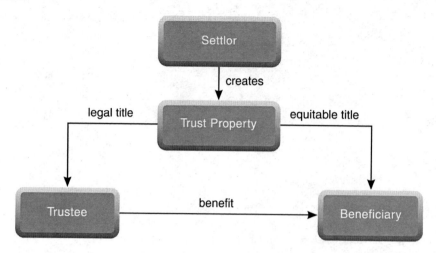

classified as a **charitable trust**, unless it is so vague that it cannot be enforced. Gifts for public museums, for park maintenance, and for the dissemination of a particular political doctrine or religious belief have been upheld as charitable.

SPENDTHRIFT TRUSTS Often, believing that a beneficiary cannot be relied on to preserve even the limited rights granted her as beneficiary, a settlor may provide in the trust instrument that the beneficiary cannot, by assignment or otherwise, impair her rights to receive principal or income in the future and that creditors of the beneficiary cannot attach the fund or the income. The term *spendthrift*, as used in connection with the relationship known as a **spendthrift trust**, refers to a provision in a trust instrument under which the trust estate is removed both from the beneficiary's control and disposition and from liability for her individual debts. Spendthrift provisions are valid in most States. Once the beneficiary actually receives income from the trust, however, creditors may seize the income or the beneficiary may use it as she pleases.

TOTTEN TRUSTS A **totten trust** or **savings account trust** involves a bank account opened by the settlor of the trust. For example, Joanne deposits a sum of money into a savings account in the name of "Joanne, in trust for Justin." The settlor, Joanne, may make additional deposits in the account from time to time and may withdraw money from it whenever she pleases. Because the settlor may revoke the totten trust by withdrawing the funds or by changing the form of the account, the courts have held such a trust to be tentative. Usually the transfer of ownership becomes complete only upon the depositor's death, when the beneficiary is entitled to the balance of the account.

IMPLIED TRUSTS

In some cases, the courts, in the absence of any express intent to create a trust, will impose a trust upon property because the acts of the parties appear to warrant such a construction. An implied trust owes its existence to the law. As previously stated, implied trusts generally are divided into two classes: constructive trusts and resulting trusts.

CONSTRUCTIVE TRUSTS A court of equity creates a **constructive trust** to rectify misconduct, to prevent unjust enrichment, or to undo a morally wrong situation. Misconduct includes abuse of a confidential relationship, actual fraud, undue influence, and duress. Justice Cardozo referred to a constructive trust as "the formula through which the conscience of equity finds expression. When property has been acquired in such circumstances that the holder of the legal title may not in good conscience retain the beneficial interest, equity converts him into a trustee." *Beatty v. Guggenheim Exploration Co.*, 225 N.Y. 380, 122 N.E. 378 (1919). Rather than reflect the intent of the parties, a constructive trust represents a court's attempt to achieve an equitable and just result.

Business and personal affairs provide many examples of constructive trusts. A director of a corporation who takes advantage of a "corporate opportunity" or who makes an undisclosed profit in a deal with the corporation will be treated as a trustee for the corporation with respect to the property or profits he acquires. Likewise, a trustee under an express trust who permits a lease held by the trust to expire and then acquires a new lease of the property in his individual capacity will be required to hold the new lease in trust for the beneficiary. If an agent who is given money by his principal to purchase property in the name of the principal instead uses the funds to acquire title in himself, courts will treat him as a trustee for the principal.

As previously indicated, the courts also invoke constructive trusts in situations involving those who use positions of friendship or marriage to their unjust advantage.

RESULTING TRUSTS A **resulting trust** serves to effect the inferred or presumed intent of parties who have inadequately expressed their actual wishes. A resulting trust does not depend on contract or agreement and, as it is created by implication and by operation of law, it does not need to be evidenced in writing. The essence of a resulting trust is the presumption made by the law that the holder of legal title does not hold the property personally but as a trustee for another party. The most common example of a resulting trust is where Joel pays the purchase price for property and takes title in the name of Ann. The presumption here is that the parties intended Ann to hold the property for Joel's benefit, and Ann will be treated as a trustee. The presumption, however, may be rebutted by evidence that Joel intended to make a gift to Ann. A second example of a resulting trust occurs when an express trust fails; then the trustee holds the property in trust for the settlor, to whom the property reverts.

CREATION OF TRUSTS

Each trust has (1) a creator or settlor, (2) a "corpus" or trust property, (3) a trustee, and (4) a beneficiary. As previously mentioned, no particular words are necessary to create a trust, provided that the settlor's intent to establish a trust is unmistakable. Consideration is not essential to an enforceable trust.

SETTLOR

Any person legally capable of making a contract may create a trust. But if the settlor's contract would be voidable or void because of infancy, incompetency, or some other reason, her declaration of trust is also voidable or void.

TRUST CORPUS OR PROPERTY

One essential characteristic of a trust is a trust corpus or *res* consisting of definite and specific property. The *res* may be any type of property that exists and is assignable. A trust cannot be effective immediately for property not yet in existence or yet to be acquired.

TRUSTEE

Anyone legally capable of holding title to the trust property may be a trustee. Furthermore, the lack of a trustee will not destroy a trust. If the settlor neglects to appoint one, if the named trustee does not qualify, or if the named trustee declines to serve, the court will appoint an individual or institution to act as trustee. A trustee can, of course, decline to serve, and before the property will vest in her it is necessary that she accept the trust.

DUTIES OF THE TRUSTEE A trustee has three primary duties:

1. to carry out the purposes of the trust,
2. to act with prudence and care in the administration of the trust, and
3. to exercise a high degree of loyalty toward the beneficiary.

Under ordinary circumstances, no special skills are required of a trustee, who is required simply to act with the same degree of care that a **prudent person** would exercise with respect to his personal affairs. The trustee has a duty to make the trust property productive and thus to invest it in income-producing assets. Given the myriad circumstances that may affect any particular case, what constitutes the care of a "prudent person" is, of course, not easy to generalize.

The duty of loyalty arises from and illustrates the fiduciary character of the relationship between the trustee and the beneficiary. In all his dealings with the trust property, the beneficiary, and third parties, the trustee must act exclusively in the interest of the beneficiary. A failure to so act may arise from obvious self-dealing, or it may be entirely innocent; in either event, the trustee can be charged with lack of loyalty.

POWERS OF THE TRUSTEE The **powers** of a trustee are determined by (1) the authority granted him by the settlor in the instrument creating the trust and (2) the rules of law in the jurisdiction in which the trust is established. State laws affecting the powers of trustees have their greatest impact upon the investments a trustee may make with trust funds. Most States have adopted a prudent investor rule. Some States, however, still follow the historical test, which prescribes a list of types of securities qualified for trust investment. In some jurisdictions, this list is permissive; in others, it is mandatory. If the list is permissive, the trustee may invest in types of securities not listed but carries the burden of showing that he made a prudent choice. The trust instrument may give the trustee wide discretion as to investments; in such an event, the trustee need not adhere to the list deemed advisable under the statute.

ALLOCATION OF PRINCIPAL AND INCOME Trusts often settle a life estate in the trust corpus on one beneficiary and a remainder interest on another beneficiary. For example, on his death, a man leaves his property to a trustee who is instructed to pay the income from the property to his widow during her life and to distribute the property to his children upon her death. In these instances, the trustee must distribute the principal to one party (the remainderman) and the income to another (the life tenant or income beneficiary). The trustee also must allocate receipts and charge expenses between the income beneficiary and the remainderman. If the trust agreement does not specify how the funds should be allocated, the trustee is provided statutory guidance, derived in more than forty States from the **Uniform Principal and Income Act**. The Act was amended and updated in 2008 to implement technical changes related to developments and interpretations relating to tax matters. At least twenty States have adopted the 2008 amendments.

A trustee who fails to comply with the trust agreement or the statute is personally liable for any loss. The general rule in allocating benefits and burdens between income beneficiaries and remaindermen is that *ordinary* or current receipts and expenses are chargeable to the income beneficiary, whereas *extraordinary* receipts and expenses are allocated to the remainderman. Ordinary income is money paid for the use of trust property and any gain from the use of the trust property, while property received as a substitute for or a change in the form of the trust *res* is allocated to the trust principal.

◆ **SEE FIGURE 51-2: Allocation of Principal and Income**

BENEFICIARY

There are very few restrictions on who (or what) may be a beneficiary. Charitable uses are a common purpose of trusts, and if the settlor's object does not outrage public policy or morals, the courts will uphold almost any purpose that happens to strike a settlor's fancy.

A person named as a beneficiary of a trust may accept or reject the trust. In the absence of restrictive provisions in the trust instrument, such as a spendthrift clause, a beneficiary's interest may be reached by his creditors, or the beneficiary may sell or dispose of his interest. Upon his death, if the beneficiary held more than a life estate in the trust, the beneficiary's interest, unless disposed of by his will, passes to his heirs or personal representatives.

TERMINATION OF A TRUST

Unless the settlor reserves a power of revocation, the general rule is that a trust, once validly created, is irrevocable. If subject to such reservation, the trust may be terminated at the settlor's discretion.

Normally, the instrument creating a trust establishes the date on which the trust will terminate. The instrument may specify a period of years for which the trust is to endure, or the settlor may provide that the trust shall continue during the life of a named individual. The death of the trustee or beneficiary does not terminate the trust if neither of their lives delimits the duration of the trust.

If the purpose for which a trust has been established is fulfilled before the specified termination date, a court may decree the trust terminated. Most courts will not order the termination of a trust, even at the request of all the beneficiaries, if any of its purposes remain unfulfilled. The purposes the settlor set forth in the trust instrument, not the beneficiaries' wishes, will govern the court's actions. If the trustee acquires both the equitable and legal title to the trust *res*, the *merger doctrine* applies, and the trust terminates as the trustee and beneficiary must be different persons for a trust to exist.

DECEDENTS' ESTATES

When a person dies, the title to his property must pass to someone. If the decedent leaves a valid will, his property will pass as he directs, subject only to certain limitations imposed by the State. If, however, no valid will has been executed, the decedent is said to have died "intestate," and the State prescribes who shall be entitled to the property. If a decedent dies leaving a valid will that disposes of less than all of her net probate estate, intestacy laws govern the portion not effectively devised by the will. If a person dies without a will and leaves

◆ **FIGURE 51-2: Allocation of Principal and Income**

	Receipts	Expenses
Ordinary—Income Beneficiary	Rents Royalties Cash dividends (regular and extraordinary) Interest	Interest payments Insurance Ordinary taxes Ordinary repairs Depreciation
Extraordinary—Remainderman	Stock dividends Stock splits Proceeds from sale or exchange of corpus Settlement of claims for injury to corpus	Extraordinary repairs Long-term improvements Principal amortization Costs incurred in the sale or purchase of corpus Business losses

no heirs or next of kin, her property escheats (reverts) to the State. Nonetheless, not all of a decedent's property will pass through the probate estate (the distribution of a decedent's estate to her successors). Certain property will pass outside of the estate, through arrangements unaffected by the distribution of the decedent's estate. For instance, a decedent's life insurance policy or pension plan will pass to the beneficiary of the policy or plan, property the decedent jointly owned with a right of survivorship will pass to the survivor, and property subject to a trust will be governed by the trust instrument.

WILLS

A **will** is a written instrument, executed according to statutorily imposed formalities, whereby a person makes a disposition of his property which is to take effect after his death. A will is also called a **testament**; the maker of the will is called a testator; and gifts made in a will are called devises or bequests. A **bequest** or **legacy** is a gift by will of personal property; a devise is a gift by will of real property.

One major characteristic of a will sets it apart from other transactions such as deeds and contracts: a will is revocable at any time during life. There is no such thing as an irrevocable will. A document binding during life (such as a promise to make a will) may be a contract or a deed (conveying, for instance, a vested remainder after a life estate in the grantor), but it is not a will. Even a testator who, by executing a joint or mutual will, contractually promises not to revoke her will retains the power to revoke. Nonetheless, such a testator may be liable for breach of contract, and the courts may impose a constructive trust upon the beneficiaries of her estate. A will takes effect only on the death of the testator.

In 1969, the National Conference of Commissioners on Uniform State Laws and the American Bar Association approved the Uniform Probate Code (UPC), an attempt to encourage throughout the United States the adoption of a uniform, flexible, speedy, efficient, and, in most cases, less expensive system of settling a decedent's estate. Approximately twenty States have adopted the UPC. The UPC, which has been updated a number of times, is based on the major premise that the probate court's appropriate role in the settlement of an estate is to offer assistance as requested or required, not to impose supervision or pointlessly detailed formality upon completely noncontentious settlements. The following discussion summarizes the general principles and procedures applicable to decedents' estates and notes the parallel principles and procedures under the UPC.

MENTAL CAPACITY

To make a valid will, the testator must have both the "power" and the "capacity" to do so. The requisite testamentary intent must always be present to create a valid will.

TESTAMENTARY POWER AND CAPACITY The State grants the *power* to make a will to persons who are of a class believed generally able to handle their affairs without regard to the personal limitations of individual members of that class. Thus, in most States, children under a certain age cannot make valid wills.

The *capacity* to make a will refers to the measures by which the courts determine whether a particular person in the class generally granted the power to make wills is, in fact, mentally capable of doing so. Testamentary capacity generally requires that the testator be of sound mind and that she know the nature and extent of her property and the objects of her bounty. Underlying the notion of capacity is the premise that, for a will to be valid, a testator must *intend* a document to be his will. This requisite intent is considered absent if the testator is mentally incompetent or suffers from delusions. Nevertheless, because capacity is an individual matter, devising a universal test to measure this qualification is not easy. A person adjudicated incompetent can, in a lucid period, make a valid will. An aged and enfeebled octogenarian may have the capacity to execute a will. Meeting the test of capacity to make a will takes less in the way of mental ability than does independently managing one's affairs during her lifetime.

Under the UPC, any person eighteen or more years of age who is of sound mind may make a will. Section 2–501.

CONDUCT INVALIDATING A WILL Any document that purports to be a will but has been induced by misconduct negating the testator's voluntary intent is not a valid will. This is the basis for the rule that a will resulting from *duress, undue influence,* or *fraud* is no will at all.

Undue influence is influence that destroys the testator's free will and substitutes another person's will for that of the testator. A general influence over the testator is not sufficient to prove improper pressure. The influence must be directed specifically to the act of making the will. A wife urges her husband to leave all his property to her; this influence is not "undue." Most frequently, the charge of undue influence arises when a testator leaves her property to one who is not a blood relative, such as a friend who took care of the testator in her last illness or during her last years. Evidence demonstrating that the beneficiary under the will was in close contact with the testator and that the natural objects of the testator's bounty are ignored in the will may imply undue influence.

Fraud is a misrepresentation of material fact that is made by a beneficiary of a will with the intent to deceive the decedent and that causes the decedent to write or change her will in reliance upon it. The charge of fraud can also be used to invalidate a will. For example, Brian dies, leaving all his property to Mark upon Mark's representation that he is Brian's long-lost son. Mark in fact is not Brian's son. In such a case, the will may be set aside because the misrepresentation was made with the intent to deceive, and Brian justifiably relied upon it.

See *Chapter 11* for a more complete discussion of duress, undue influence, and fraud.

FORMAL REQUIREMENTS OF A WILL

By statute in all jurisdictions, a will must comply with certain formalities to be valid. These formalities are intended both to ensure that the testator understood what she was doing and to help prevent fraud. As discussed later, some States permit specific types of wills that do not meet all of these requirements to be enforced with respect to testamentary dispositions of certain property.

WRITING A basic requirement of a valid will is that it be in writing. UPC, Section 2–502. The writing may be informal, as long as it substantially meets the basic statutory requirements. Pencil, ink, typewriting, and photocopy are equally valid media, and valid wills have been made on scratch paper and on an envelope.

It is also valid to incorporate into a will by reference another document which in itself is not a will for lack of proper execution. For a memorandum to be thus incorporated, the following four conditions must exist: (1) the memorandum must be in writing; (2) it must be in existence when the will is executed; (3) it must be adequately described in the will; and (4) in some States it must be described in the will as being in existence. UPC, Section 2–510.

SIGNATURE A will must be signed by the testator or in the testator's name by some other individual in the testator's presence and at the testator's direction. UPC, Section 2–502. A fundamental requirement in almost all jurisdictions, the signature verifies that the will has been executed. The testator's initials, a single word, such as "father," or a mark at the end of a will in the testator's handwriting are adequate if intended as an execution.

Most statutes require the signature to be at the end of the will. Even in jurisdictions that do not so require, placing the signature at the end will preclude the charge that the portions of a will that follow the signature were written subsequent to its execution and are therefore invalid.

ATTESTATION A written will must be attested (witnessed or certified) by witnesses, who serve to acknowledge that the testator did execute the will and that she had the requisite intent and capacity. The number and qualifications of witnesses and the manner of attestation are generally specified by statute. Usually two or three witnesses are required. Section 2–502 of the UPC requires that at least two persons, each of whom witnessed either the signing or the testator's acknowledgment of the will, act as witnesses to the will.

The most common restriction on the ability to act as a witness is that a witness must not have any interest under the will. This requirement takes at least two forms under statutes. One type of statute disqualifies a witness who is also a beneficiary under the will. The other type voids the bequest or devise to the interested witness, thus making him a disinterested and thereby qualified witness. Defining what constitutes an "interest" sufficient to disqualify a witness is not always easy. The spouse of a beneficiary under a will has been held to be "interested" and thus not qualified. Usually, though, the courts will not disqualify a person simply because he is named as executor in the will. The attorney who drafts the will generally is a qualified witness. Under the UPC, attestation by an interested witness does not invalidate a will or any provision thereof. Section 2–505(b).

REVOCATION OF A WILL

A will is revocable by the testator, and, under certain circumstances, a will may be revoked by operation of law. Most jurisdictions specify by statute the methods by which a will may be revoked. The five generally accepted methods for revoking a will are as follows:

DESTRUCTION OR ALTERATION Tearing, burning, or otherwise destroying a will is an effective way of revoking a will, unless such destruction is shown to be inadvertent or without intent. UPC, Section 2–507. In some States, partial revocation may be accomplished by erasing or obliterating a part of the will. In no case, however, will a substituted or additional bequest by interlineation be effective without reexecution and reattestation.

Courts occasionally face the difficult question of determining whether a will was revoked by destruction or simply mislaid.

SUBSEQUENT WILL The execution of a second will does not in itself constitute a revocation of an earlier will. The first will is revoked to the extent that the second will is inconsistent with the first. UPC, Section 2–507. The most certain manner of revocation is the execution of a later will containing a declaration that all former wills are revoked. In some but not all jurisdictions, a testator may revoke a will by a written declaration to this effect in a subsequent document, such as a letter, even though the document does not meet the formal requirements of a will.

OPERATION OF LAW A *marriage* generally revokes a will executed prior to the marriage. Divorce, on the other hand, under the general rule, does not revoke a provision in the will of one party for the benefit of the other. Section 2–508 of the UPC takes a different position by providing that a divorce or annulment occurring after the execution of a will revokes any disposition of property the will made to the former spouse.

No change of circumstances, however, other than divorce, annulment, or the testator's homicide by a devisee, revokes a will. Thus, a subsequent marriage does not revoke a will. Nonetheless, a spouse who marries the testator after the execution of the will is entitled only to the share she would receive if the testator were to die without a will. UPC, Section 2–301.

The *birth* of a child after execution of a will may revoke a will at least as far as that child is concerned if it appears that the testator omitted to make a provision for the child. In some jurisdictions and under the UPC, the subsequent birth of a child will not revoke the will; rather, unless it appears from the will that the omission was intentional, the child is entitled to a share the same as the one he would receive were the testator to die without a will. Section 2–302.

EFFECTIVENESS OF TESTAMENTARY PROVISIONS

RENUNCIATION BY THE SURVIVING SPOUSE Statutes generally provide a surviving spouse the right to renounce a will and set forth the method by which the spouse may do so. Such statutory provisions enable the spouse to decide which method of taking—under the will or under intestate succession—would be most advantageous. Only those whom the statute designates may exercise the right to renounce a will, and the right conferred on the surviving spouse is personal. Upon renunciation of the will, the law of intestate succession determines the share of the estate taken by the surviving spouse.

ABATEMENT AND ADEMPTION OF A BEQUEST Abatement is the reduction or elimination of gifts by category upon the reduction in the value of the estate of the testator after the execution of his will. It can have serious implications. The first items to abate in a will are the **residue**, or those items remaining after provisions for specific and general gifts. **Specific gifts**, which must be satisfied first, involve particular or uniquely identifiable items; **general gifts** do not. For example, if John, a widower, after making specific gifts, leaves "all the rest, residue, and remainder of my estate to my daughter, Mary," Mary may receive a great deal less than her deceased father intended. Suppose at the time John executes his will he estimates his worth at $150,000. He leaves $20,000 to his church, $10,000 to the Salvation Army, and his car, worth $10,000, to his business partner, and he assumes that Mary will receive approximately $110,000. Having suffered substantial business and market reverses, John dies five years later without having changed his will. His executor reports that there is only $50,000 in the estate. Mary will receive only $10,000 because the specific devise of the car and the general devises of the $20,000 and $10,000 will abate only after the residue is depleted.

Ademption, or the removal or extinction of a gift by act of the testator, occurs when a testator neglects to change his will after changed circumstances have made the performance of a provision in the will impossible. For example, Hope buys a farm, Blackacre, wishing it to go on her death to a favorite nephew who is studying agriculture at college. After so providing in her will, she sells Blackacre and uses the money to buy Greenacre. The general rule is that the nephew will not be entitled to Greenacre. Nonetheless, the courts sometimes have modified this doctrine to reflect the perceived intent of the decedent. Under the "modified intention theory," through which a court attempts to effectuate the decedent's presumed intent, no ademption occurs where the property in question is missing from the estate because of some involuntary act of the decedent or some event over which he had no control.

SPECIAL TYPES OF WILLS

There are a number of special types of wills, including nuncupative wills, holographic wills, soldiers' and sailors' wills, conditional wills, joint and reciprocal wills, and living wills.

NUNCUPATIVE WILLS A nuncupative will is an unwritten oral declaration made before witnesses. In the few jurisdictions that authorize them, such declarations usually can be made only when the testator is in his last illness. Under most statutes permitting nuncupative wills, only limited amounts of personal property, generally under $1,000, may be passed by such wills. Under the UPC, all wills must be in writing. Section 2–502.

HOLOGRAPHIC WILLS In approximately one-half of the jurisdictions, a signed will *entirely* in the handwriting of the testator is a valid testamentary document even if the will is not witnessed. Under the UPC, Section 2–503, the signature and *material* provisions must be in the testator's handwriting. Such an instrument, referred to as a **holographic will**, must comply strictly with the statutory requirements for such wills.

SOLDIERS' AND SAILORS' WILLS For soldiers on active duty and sailors at sea, most statutes relax the formal requirements for a will and permit a testamentary disposition to be valid regardless of the informality of the document. In most jurisdictions, however, such a will cannot pass title to real estate.

CONDITIONAL WILLS A contingent or conditional will is one that takes effect only on the happening of a specified contingency, which is a condition precedent to the operation of the will.

JOINT AND MUTUAL OR RECIPROCAL WILLS A joint will consists of a single instrument that is made the will of two or more persons and is signed by them jointly. By comparison, in making mutual or reciprocal wills, two or more persons execute separate instruments with reciprocal terms in which each testator makes a testamentary disposition in favor of the other.

LIVING WILLS Almost all States have adopted statutes that permit an individual to execute a living will. A **living will** is

◆ **FIGURE 51-3:** *Per Stirpes* **and** *Per Capita*

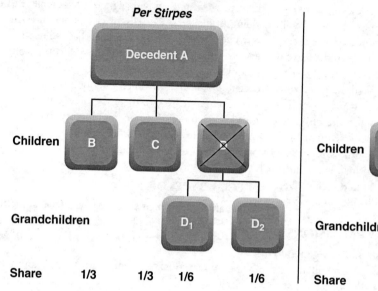
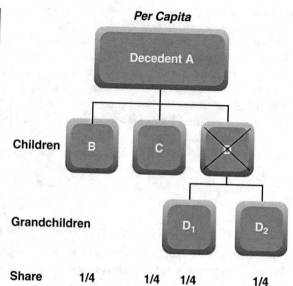

testator likely has named her executor in it. If there is no will or if a will exists but fails to name an executor, the court will, upon petition, appoint an administrator. The closest adult relative who is a resident of the State is entitled to such appointment.

Once approved or appointed by the court, the **executor** or **administrator** holds title to all the personal property of the deceased and is accountable to the creditors and the beneficiaries. The estate is his responsibility.

If there is a will, the witnesses must prove it before the court by testifying to the signing of the will by all signatories and by confirming the mental condition of the testator at the time she executed the will. If the witnesses are dead, proof of their handwriting is necessary. If satisfied that the will is proved, the court will enter a formal decree admitting the will to probate.

Soon after the admission of the will to probate, the decedent's personal representative—the executor or administrator—must file an inventory of the estate. The personal representative will then commence her duties of collecting the assets, paying the debts, and disbursing the remainder. The executor or administrator occupies a fiduciary position not unlike that of a trustee, and his responsibility for investing proceeds and otherwise managing the estate is equally demanding.

The administration of every estate involves probate expenses as well as fees to be paid to the executor or administrator and to the attorney who handles the estate. In addition, taxes are imposed at death by both the Federal and State governments. The Federal government imposes an **estate tax** on the transfer of property at death, while most State governments impose an **inheritance tax** on the privilege of an heir or beneficiary to receive the property. These taxes are separate from the basic income tax that the estate must pay on income received during estate administration.

CHAPTER SUMMARY

TRUSTS

	Definition a trust is a fiduciary relationship in which legal title to property (trust corpus) is held by one or more parties (the trustee) for the use, enjoyment, and benefit of another (the beneficiary)
TYPES OF TRUSTS	**Express Trust** a trust established by voluntary action by the creator (settlor); usually in writing, although it may be oral
	• *Testamentary Trust* a trust employed in a will; it becomes effective after the creator's death

- **Inter Vivos *Trust*** a trust established during the settlor's lifetime
- ***Charitable Trust*** a trust that has as its purpose the benefit of humankind
- ***Spendthrift Trust*** a trust designed to remove the trust estate from the beneficiary's control and from liability for his individual debts
- ***Totten Trust*** a tentative trust consisting of a joint bank account opened by the settlor (creator of the trust)

Implied Trust a trust created by operation of law
- ***Constructive Trust*** an implied trust imposed to rectify fraud or to prevent unjust enrichment
- ***Resulting Trust*** an implied trust imposed to fulfill the presumed intent of the settlor

Trustee anyone legally capable of holding title to and dealing with property may be a trustee
- ***Duties*** the three primary duties of a trustee are to (1) carry out the purposes of the trust, (2) act prudently, and (3) act with utmost loyalty
- ***Powers*** generally established by the trust instrument and State law
- ***Allocation of Principal and Income*** see *Figure 51-2*

Termination the general rule is that the trust is irrevocable unless a power of revocation is reserved in the trust instrument

DECEDENTS' ESTATES

WILLS   **Definition** a will (or testament) is a written instrument, executed with the formalities required by statute, whereby a person makes a disposition of his property to take effect after his death

Mental Capacity
- ***Testamentary Capacity*** for a will to be valid the testator must be sufficiently competent to intend the document to be her will
- ***Conduct Invalidating a Will*** a will that is the product of duress, undue influence, or fraud is invalid and of no effect

Formal Requirements a will must be (1) in writing, (2) signed, and (3) attested to by witnesses

Revocation a will is revocable by the testator and under certain circumstances may be revoked by operation of law
- ***Destruction or Alteration*** revokes a will
- ***Subsequent Will*** revokes prior wills to the extent they are inconsistent
- ***Codicil*** an addition to or revision of a will executed with all the formalities of a will
- ***Marriage*** generally revokes a will executed before the marriage
- ***Birth of a Child*** may revoke a will at least as far as that child is concerned
- ***Renunciation by Surviving Spouse*** surviving spouse may elect to take under laws of descent

Special Types of Wills generally binding only in specific situations and may have limitations upon their use

INTESTATE SUCCESSION   **Intestate** condition of person who dies without a valid will

Course of Descent each State prescribes rules for the passage of property not governed by a valid will; as a general rule the property passes in equal shares to each child after the widow's statutory or dower rights have been settled

ADMINISTRATION OF ESTATES   **Probate** the court's supervision of the management and distribution of the estate

Executor or Administrator a person who is responsible for collecting the assets, paying the debts, and disbursing the remainder according to the will or intestate statute
- ***Executor*** the person named in the will and appointed by the court to administer the will
- ***Administrator*** a person appointed by the court to administer the estate when there is no will or when the person named in the will fails to qualify

a document by which an individual states that she does not wish to receive extraordinary medical treatment to preserve her life. Such a document, which must comply with applicable statutory requirements, allows an individual to reject the use of life-prolonging procedures that artificially delay the dying process and to die naturally should she suffer an incurable illness or injury.

CODICILS

A **codicil** is a subsequent will, executed with all the formal requirements of a will, that augments or revises a prior will. The most frequent problem such an instrument raises involves the extent to which its terms, if not absolutely clear, revoke or alter provisions in the will. For the purpose of determining the testator's intent, the codicil and the will are regarded as a single instrument.

INTESTATE SUCCESSION

Property not effectively disposed of before death or by will passes in accordance with the law of intestate succession. The rules set forth in statutes for determining, in case of intestacy, to whom the decedent's property shall be distributed not only ensure an orderly transfer of title to property but also purport to effect what would probably be the wishes of the decedent. Nonetheless, the intestacy statute will govern the distribution of the estate even if such distribution is contrary to the clear intention of the decedent.

The rules of descent vary widely from State to State, but as a general rule and except for the specific statutory or dower rights of the widow, the intestate property passes in equal shares to each child of the decedent living at the time of his death, with the share of any predeceased child to be divided equally among the children of such predeceased child. For example, if Arthur dies intestate leaving a widow and children, his widow generally will receive one-third of his real estate and personal property, and the remainder will pass to his children in the manner stated above. If his wife does not survive Arthur, his entire estate passes to their children. If Arthur dies leaving two surviving children, Belinda and Carl, and two grandchildren, Donna and David, the children of a predeceased child Darwin, the estate will go one-third to Belinda, one-third to Carl, and one-sixth each to Donna and David, the grandchildren, who divide equally their parent's one-third share. This result is described legally by the statement that *lineal descendants* of predeceased children take **per stirpes**, or by representation of their parent. If Arthur had executed a will, he may have provided that all his lineal descendants, regardless of generation, would share equally. In that case, Arthur's estate would be divided into four equal parts, and his descendants would be said to take **per capita**.

If only the widow and relatives other than his children survive the decedent, a larger share is generally allotted the widow. She may receive all the decedent's personal property and one-half his real estate or, in some States, his entire estate.

At common law, property could not ascend lineally; parents of an intestate decedent did not share in his estate. Today, in many States, if a decedent has no lineal descendants or a surviving spouse, the statute provides that parents are the next to share.

Most statutes make some provision for brothers and sisters in the event no spouse, parents, or children survive the decedent. Brothers and sisters, together with nieces, nephews, aunts, and uncles, are termed *collateral heirs*. Beyond these limits, most statutes provide that, if there are no survivors in the named classes, the property shall be distributed equally among the next of kin in equal degree.

The common law did not consider a stepchild as an heir or next of kin, that is, as one to whom property would descend by operation of law, and this rule prevails. Legally adopted children are, however, recognized as lawful heirs of their adoptive parents.

These generalities should be accepted as such; few fields of the law of property are so strictly a matter of statute, and the rights of heirs cannot reasonably be predicted without a knowledge of the exact terms of the applicable statute.

Under the UPC, if the decedent dies without a will, (1) if there is no descendant and no parent surviving or if all surviving children are children of the decedent and the spouse, the surviving spouse is entitled to the entire estate; (2) if there is a parent surviving but no descendants, the spouse is entitled to the first $200,000 plus three-quarters of the remaining estate; (3) if the decedent is survived by one or more descendants who are also descendants of the surviving spouse and also by descendants who are not descendants of the surviving spouse, the spouse is entitled to the first $150,000 plus one-half of the remaining estate; and (4) if the decedent is survived by descendants who are not also descendants of the surviving spouse, the spouse is entitled to the first $100,000 plus one-half of the remaining estate.

◆ **SEE FIGURE 51-3:** *Per Stirpes* **and** *Per Capita*

ADMINISTRATION OF ESTATES

Because they are statutory, the rules and procedures controlling the management of a decedent's estate vary somewhat from State to State. In all jurisdictions, the estate is managed and finally disbursed under the supervision of a court. The procedure for managing the distribution of decedents' estates is known as **probate**, and the court that supervises the procedure is often designated the probate court.

The first legal step after death is usually to determine whether or not the deceased left a will. If a will exists, the

APPENDICES

The Constitution of the United States of America

We the People of the United States, in Order to form a more perfect Union, establish Justice, insure domestic Tranquility, provide for the common defense, promote the general Welfare, and secure the Blessings of Liberty to ourselves and our Posterity, do ordain and establish this Constitution for the United States of America.

ARTICLE I

Section 1

All legislative Powers herein granted shall be vested in a Congress of the United States, which shall consist of a Senate and House of Representatives.

Section 2

The House of Representatives shall be composed of Members chosen every second Year by the People of the several States, and the Electors in each State shall have the Qualifications requisite for Electors of the most numerous Branch of the State Legislature.

No Person shall be a Representative who shall not have attained to the Age of twenty five Years, and been seven Years a Citizen of the United States, and who shall not, when elected, be an Inhabitant of that State in which he shall be chosen.

Representatives and direct Taxes shall be apportioned among the several States which may be included within this Union, according to their respective Numbers, which shall be determined by adding to the whole Number of free Persons, including those bound to Service for a Term of Years, and excluding Indians not taxed, three fifths of all other Persons. The actual Enumeration shall be made within three Years after the first Meeting of the Congress of the United States, and within every subsequent Term of ten Years, in such Manner as they shall by Law direct. The number of Representatives shall not exceed one for every thirty Thousand, but each State shall have at Least one Representative; and until such enumeration shall be made, the State of New Hampshire shall be entitled to chuse three, Massachusetts eight, Rhode Island and Providence Plantations one, Connecticut five, New-York six, New Jersey four, Pennsylvania eight, Delaware one, Maryland six, Virginia ten, North Carolina five, South Carolina five, and Georgia three.

When vacancies happen in the Representation from any State, the Executive Authority thereof shall issue Writs of Election to fill such vacancies.

The House of Representatives shall chuse their Speaker and other Officers; and shall have the sole Power of Impeachment.

Section 3

The Senate of the United States shall be composed of two Senators from each State, chosen by the Legislature thereof, for six Years; and each Senator shall have one Vote.

Immediately after they shall be assembled in Consequence of the first Election, they shall be divided as equally as may be into three Classes. The Seats of the Senators of the first Class shall be vacated at the Expiration of the second Year, of the second Class at the Expiration of the fourth Year, and of the third Class at the Expiration of the sixth Year, so that one third may be chosen every second Year; and if Vacancies happen by Resignation or otherwise, during the Recess of the Legislature of any State, the Executive thereof may make temporary Appointments until the next Meeting of the Legislature, which shall then fill such Vacancies.

No Person shall be a Senator who shall not have attained to the Age of thirty Years, and been nine Years a Citizen of the United States, and who shall not, when elected, be an Inhabitant of that State for which he shall be chosen.

The Vice President of the United States shall be President of the Senate, but shall have no Vote, unless they be equally divided.

The Senate shall chuse their other Officers, and also a President pro tempore, in the Absence of the Vice President, or when he shall exercise the Office of President of the United States.

The Senate shall have the sole power to try all Impeachments. When sitting for that Purpose, they shall be an Oath or Affirmation. When the President of the United States is tried, the Chief Justice shall preside: And no Person shall be convicted without the Concurrence of two thirds of the Members present.

Judgment in Cases of Impeachment shall not extend further than to removal from Office, and disqualification to hold and enjoy any Office of honor, Trust or Profit under the United States: but the Party convicted shall nevertheless be liable and subject to Indictment, Trial, Judgment and Punishment, according to Law.

Section 4

The Times, Places and Manner of holding Elections for Senators and Representatives, shall be prescribed in each State by the Legislature thereof: but the Congress may at any time by Law make or alter such Regulations, except as to the Places of chusing Senators.

The Congress shall assemble at least once in every Year, and such Meeting shall be on the first Monday in December, unless they shall by Law appoint a different Day.

Section 5

Each House shall be the Judge of the Elections, Returns and Qualifications of its own Members, and a Majority of each shall constitute a Quorum to do Business; but a smaller Number may adjourn from day to day, and may be authorized to compel the Attendance of absent Members, in such Manner, and under such Penalties as each House may provide.

Each House may determine the Rules of its Proceedings, punish its Members for disorderly Behaviour, and, with the Concurrence of two thirds, expel a Member.

Each House shall keep a Journal of its Proceedings, and from time to time publish the same, excepting such Parts as may in their Judgment require Secrecy; and the Yeas and Nays of the Members of either House on any question shall, at the Desire of one fifth of those Present, be entered on the Journal.

Neither House, during the Session of Congress, shall, without the Consent of the other, adjourn for more than three days, nor to any other Place than that in which the two Houses shall be sitting.

Section 6

The Senators and Representatives shall receive a Compensation for their Services, to be ascertained by Law, and paid out of the Treasury of the United States. They shall in all Cases, except Treason, Felony and Breach of the Peace, be privileged from Arrest and Breach of the Peace, be privileged from Arrest during their Attendance at the Session of their respective Houses, and in going to and returning from the same; and for any Speech or Debate in either House, they shall not be questioned in any other Place.

No Senator or Representative shall, during the Time for which he was elected, be appointed to any civil Office under the Authority of the United States, which shall have been created, or the Emoluments whereof shall have been encreased during such time; and no Person holding any Office under the United States, shall be a Member of either House during his Continuance in Office.

Section 7

All Bills for raising Revenue shall originate in the House of Representatives; but the Senate may propose or concur with Amendments as on other Bills.

Every Bill which shall have passed the House of Representatives and the Senate, shall, before it become a Law, be presented to the President of the United States; If he approve he shall sign it, but if not he shall return it, with his Objections to that House in which it shall have originated, who shall enter the Objections at large on their Journal, and proceed to reconsider it. If after such Reconsideration two thirds of that House shall agree to pass the Bill, it shall be sent, together with the Objections, to the other House, by which it shall likewise be reconsidered, and if approved by two thirds of that House, it shall become a Law. But in all such Cases the Votes of both Houses shall be determined by Yeas and Nays, and the Names of the Persons voting for and against the Bill shall be entered on the Journal of each House respectively. If any Bill shall not be returned by the President within ten Days (Sundays excepted) after it shall have been presented to him, the Same shall be a Law, in like Manner as if he had signed it, unless the Congress by their Adjournment prevent its Return, in which Case it shall not be a Law.

Every Order, Resolution, or Vote to which the Concurrence of the Senate and House of Representatives may be necessary (except on a question of Adjournment) shall be presented to the President of the United States; and before the Same shall take Effect, shall be approved by him, or being disapproved by him, shall be repassed by two thirds of the Senate and House of Representatives, according to the Rules and Limitations prescribed in the Case of a Bill.

Section 8

The Congress shall have Power to lay and collect Taxes, Duties, Imposts and Excises, to pay the Debts and provide for the common Defense and general Welfare of the United States; but all Duties, Imposts and Excises shall be uniform throughout the United States;

To borrow Money on the credit of the United States;

To regulate Commerce with foreign Nations, and among the several States, and with the Indian Tribes;

To establish an uniform Rule of Naturalization, and uniform Laws on the subject of Bankruptcies throughout the United States;

To coin Money, regulate the Value thereof, and of foreign Coin, and fix the Standard of Weights and Measures;

To provide for the Punishment of counterfeiting the Securities and current Coin of the United States;

To establish Post Offices and post Roads;

To promote the Progress of Science and useful Arts, by securing for limited Times to Authors and Inventors the exclusive Right to their respective Writings and Discoveries;

To constitute Tribunals inferior to the supreme Court;

To define and punish Piracies and Felonies committed on the high Seas, and Offenses against the Law of Nations;

To declare War, grant Letters of Marque and Reprisal, and make Rules concerning Captures on Land and Water;

To raise and support Armies, but no Appropriation of Money to that Use shall be for a longer Term than two Years;

To provide and maintain a Navy;

To make Rules for the Government and Regulation of the land and naval Forces;

To provide for calling forth the Militia to execute the Laws of the Union, suppress Insurrections and repel Invasions;

To provide for organizing, arming, and disciplining, the Militia, and for governing such Part of them as may be employed in the Service of the United States, reserving to the States respectively, the Appointment of the Officers, and the Authority of training the Militia according to the discipline described by Congress;

To exercise exclusive Legislation in all Cases whatsoever, over such District (not exceeding ten Miles square) as may, by Cession of particular States, and the Acceptance of Congress, become the Seat of the Government of the United States, and to exercise like Authority over all Places purchased by the Consent of the Legislature of the State in which the Same shall be, for the Erection of Forts, Magazines, Arsenals, dock-Yards, and other needful Buildings;—And

To make all Laws which shall be necessary and proper for carrying into Execution the foregoing Powers, and all other Powers vested by this Constitution in the Government of the United States, or in any Department or Officer thereof.

Section 9

The Migration or Importation of such Persons as any of the States now existing shall think proper to admit, shall not be prohibited by the Congress prior to the Year one thousand eight hundred and eight, but a Tax of Duty may be imposed on such Importation, not exceeding ten dollars for each Person.

The Privilege of the Writ of Habeas Corpus shall not be suspended, unless when in Cases of Rebellion or Invasion the public Safety may require it.

No Bill of Attainder or ex post facto Law shall be passed.

No Capitation, or other direct, Tax shall be laid, unless in Proportion to the Census or Enumeration herein before directed to be taken.

No Tax or Duty shall be laid on Articles exported from any State.

No Preference shall be given by any Regulation of Commerce or Revenue to the Ports of one State over those of another; nor shall Vessels bound to, or from, one State, be obliged to enter, clear, or pay Duties in another.

No Money shall be drawn from the Treasury, but in Consequence of Appropriations made by Laws; and a regular Statement and Account of the Receipts and Expenditures of all public Money shall be published from time to time.

No Title of Nobility shall be granted by the United States: And no Person holding any Office of Profit or Trust under them, shall, without the Consent of the Congress, accept of any present, Emolument, Office, or Title, of any kind whatever, from any King, Prince, or foreign State.

Section 10

No State shall enter into any Treaty, Alliance, or Confederation; grant Letters of Marque and Reprisal; coin Money; emit Bills of Credit; make any Thing but gold and silver Coin a Tender in Payment of Debts; pass any Bill of Attainder, ex post facto Law, or Law impairing the Obligation of Contracts, or grant any Title of Nobility.

No State shall, without the Consent of the Congress, lay any Imposts or Duties on Imports or Exports, except what may be absolutely necessary for executing its inspection Laws: and the net Produce of all Duties and Imposts, laid by any State on Imports or Exports, shall be for the Use of the Treasury of the United States; and all such Laws shall be subject to the Revision and Controul of the Congress.

No State shall, without the Consent of Congress, lay any Duty of Tonnage, keep Troops, or Ships of War in time of Peace, enter into any Agreement or Compact with another State, or with a foreign Power, or engage in War, unless actually invaded, or in such imminent Danger as will not admit of delay.

ARTICLE II

Section 1

The executive Power shall be vested in a President of the United States of America. He shall hold his Office during the Term of four Years, and, together with the Vice President, chosen for the same Term, be elected, as follows:

Each State shall appoint, in such Manner as the Legislature thereof may direct, a Number of Electors, equal to the whole Number of Senators and Representatives to which the State may be entitled in the Congress: but no Senator or Representative, or Person holding an Office of Trust or Profit under the United States, shall be appointed an Elector.

The Electors shall meet in their respective States, and vote by Ballot for two Persons, of whom one at least shall not be an Inhabitant of the same State with themselves. And they shall make a list of all the Persons voted for, and of the Number of Votes for each; which List they shall sign and certify, and transmit sealed to the Seat of the Government of the United States, directed to the President of the Senate. The President of the Senate shall, in the presence of the Senate and House of Representatives, open all the Certificates, and the Votes shall be counted. The Person having the greatest Number of Votes shall be the President, if such Number be a Majority of the whole Number of Electors appointed; and if there be more than one who have such Majority, and have an equal Number of Votes, then the House of Representatives shall immediately chuse by Ballot one of them for President; and if no Person have a Majority, then from the five highest on the List the said House shall in like Manner chuse the President. But in chusing the President, the Votes shall be taken by States, the Representation from each State having one Vote; A quorum for this Purpose shall consist of a Member or Members from two thirds of the States, and a Majority of all the States shall be necessary to a Choice. In every Case, after the Choice of the President, the Person having the Greatest Number of Votes of the Electors shall be the Vice President. But if there should remain two or more who have equal Votes, the Senate shall chuse from them by Ballot the Vice President.

The Congress may determine the Time of Chusing the Electors, and the Day on which they shall give their Votes; which Day shall be the same throughout the United States.

No Person except a natural born Citizen, or a Citizen of the United States, at the time of the Adoption of this Constitution, shall be eligible to the Office of President; neither shall any Person be eligible to that Office who shall not have attained to the Age of thirty five Years, and been fourteen Years a Resident within the United States.

In Case of the Removal of the President from Office, or of his Death, Resignation, or Inability to discharge the Powers and Duties of the said Office, the Same shall devolve on the Vice President, and the Congress may by Law provide for the Case of Removal, Death, Resignation or Inability, both of the President and Vice President, declaring what Officer shall then act as President, and such Officer shall act accordingly, until the Disability be removed, or a President shall be elected.

The President shall, at stated Times, receive for his Services, a Compensation, which shall neither be encreased nor diminished during the Period for which he shall have been elected, and he shall not receive within that Period any other Emolument from the United States, or any of them.

Before he enter on the Execution of his Office, he shall take the following Oath or Affirmation:—"I do solemnly swear (or affirm) that I will faithfully execute the Office of President of the United States, and will to the best of my Ability, preserve, protect and defend the Constitution of the United States."

Section 2

The President shall be Commander in Chief of the Army and Navy of the United States, and of the Militia of the several States, when called into the actual Service of the United States; he may require the Opinion, in writing, of the principal Officer in each of the executive Departments, upon any Subject relating to the Duties of their respective Offices, and he shall have Power to grant Reprieves and Pardons for Offences against the United States, except in Cases of Impeachment.

He shall have Power, by and with the Advice and Consent of the Senate, to make Treaties, providing two thirds of the Senators present concur; and he shall nominate, and by and with the Advice and Consent of the Senate, shall appoint Ambassadors, other public Ministers and Consuls, Judges of the supreme Court, and all other Officers of the United States, whose Appointments are not herein otherwise provided for, and which shall be established by Law: but the Congress may by Law vest the Appointment of such inferior Officers, as they think proper, in the President alone, in the Courts of Law, or in the Heads of Departments.

The President shall have Power to fill up all Vacancies that may happen during the Recess of the Senate, by granting Commissions which shall expire at the End of their next Session.

Section 3

He shall from time to time give to the Congress Information of the State of the Union, and recommend to their Consideration such Measures as he shall judge necessary and expedient; he may, on extraordinary Occasions, convene both Houses, or either of them, and in Case of Disagreement between them, with Respect to the Time of Adjournment, he may adjourn them to such Time as he shall think proper, he shall receive Ambassadors and other public Ministers; he shall take Care that the Laws be faithfully executed, and shall Commission all the Offices of the United States.

Section 4

The President, Vice President and all civil Officers of the United States, shall be removed from Office on Impeachment for, and Conviction of, Treason, Bribery, or other high Crimes and Misdemeanors.

ARTICLE III

Section 1

The judicial Power of the United States, shall be vested in one supreme Court, and in such inferior Courts as the Congress may from time to time ordain and establish. The Judges, both of the supreme and inferior Courts, shall hold their Offices during good Behaviour, and shall, at Times, receive for their Services, a Compensation, which shall not be diminished during their Continuance in Office.

Section 2

The judicial Power shall extend to all Cases, in Law and Equity, arising under this Constitution, the Laws of the United States, and Treaties made, or which shall be made, under their Authority;—to all Cases affecting Ambassadors, other public Ministers and Consuls;—to all Cases of admiralty and maritime Jurisdiction;—to Controversies to which the United States shall be a Party;—to controversies between two or more States;— between a State and Citizens of another State;— between Citizens of different States;—between Citizens of the same State claiming Lands under Grants of different States; and between a State, or the Citizens thereof, and foreign States, Citizens or Subjects.

In all Cases affecting Ambassadors, other public Ministers and Consuls, and those in which a State shall be Party, the supreme Court shall have original Jurisdiction. In all the other Cases before mentioned, the supreme Court shall have appellate Jurisdiction, both as to Law and Fact, with such Exceptions, and under such Regulations as the Congress shall make.

The Trial of all Crimes, except in Cases of Impeachment, shall be by Jury; and such Trial shall be held in the State where the said Crimes shall have been committed; but when not committed within any State, the Trial shall be at such Place or Places as the Congress may by Law have directed.

Section 3

Treason against the United States, shall consist only in levying War against them, or in adhering to their Enemies, giving them Aid and Comfort. No Person shall be convicted of Treason unless on the Testimony of two Witnesses to the same overt Act, or on Confession in open Court.

The Congress shall have Power to declare the Punishment of Treason, but no Attainder of Treason shall work Corruption of Blood, or Forfeiture except during the Life of the Person attainted.

ARTICLE IV

Section 1

Full Faith and Credit shall be given in each State to the public Acts, Records, and judicial Proceedings of every other State. And the Congress may by general Laws prescribe the Manner in which such Arts, Records and Proceedings shall be proved, and the Effect thereof.

Section 2

The Citizens of each State shall be entitled to all Privileges and Immunities of Citizens in the several States.

A Person charged in any State with Treason, Felony, or other Crime, who shall flee from Justice, and be found in another State, shall on Demand of the executive Authority of the State from which he fled, be delivered up, to be removed to the State having Jurisdiction of the Crime.

No Person held to Service or Labour in one State, under the Laws thereof, escaping into another, shall, in Consequence of any Law or Regulation therein, be discharged from such Service or Labour, but shall be delivered up on Claim of the Party to whom such Service or Labour may be due.

Section 3

New States may be admitted by the Congress into this Union; but no new State shall be formed or erected within the Jurisdiction of any other State; nor any State be formed by the Junction of two or more States, or Parts of States, without the Consent of the Legislatures of the States concerned as well as the Congress.

The Congress shall have Power to dispose of and make all needful Rules and Regulations respecting the Territory or other Property belonging to the United States; and nothing in this Constitution shall be so construed as to Prejudice any Claims of the United States, or of any particular State.

Section 4

The United States shall guarantee to every State in this Union a Republican Form of Government, and shall protect each of them against Invasion; and on Application of the Legislature, or of the Executive (when the Legislature cannot be convened) against domestic Violence.

ARTICLE V

The Congress, whenever two thirds of both Houses shall deem it necessary, shall propose Amendments to this Constitution, or, on the Application of the Legislatures of two thirds of the several States, shall call a Convention for proposing Amendments, which, in either Case, shall be valid to all Intents and Purposes, as Part of this Constitution, when ratified by the Legislatures of three fourths of the several States, or by Conventions in three fourths thereof, as the one or the other Mode of Ratification may be proposed by the Congress; Provided that no Amendment which may be made prior to the Year One thousand eight hundred and eight shall in any Manner affect the first and fourth Clauses in the Ninth Section of the first Article; and that no State, without its Consent, shall be deprived of its equal Suffrage in the Senate.

ARTICLE VI

All Debts contracted and Engagements entered into, before the Adoption of this Constitution, shall be as valid against the United States under this Constitution, as under the Confederation.

This Constitution, and the Laws of the United States which shall be made in Pursuance thereof; and all Treaties made, or which shall be made, under the Authority of the United States, shall be the supreme Law of the Land; and the Judges in every State shall be bound thereby, any Thing in the Constitution or Laws of any State to the Contrary notwithstanding.

The Senators and Representatives before mentioned, and the Members of the several State Legislatures, and all executive and judicial Officers, both of the United States and of the Several States, shall be bound by Oath or Affirmation, to support this Constitution; but no religious Test shall ever be required as a Qualification to any Office or public Trust under the United States.

ARTICLE VII

The Ratification of the Conventions of nine States, shall be sufficient for the Establishment of this Constitution between the States so ratifying the Same.

Amendment I [1791]

Congress shall make no law respecting an establishment of religion, or prohibiting the free exercise thereof; or abridging the freedom of speech, or the press; or the right of the people peaceably to assemble, and to petition the Government for a redress of grievances.

Amendment II [1791]

A well regulated Militia, being necessary to the security for a free State, the right of the people to keep and bear Arms, shall not be infringed.

Amendment III [1791]

No Soldier shall, in time of peace be quartered in any house, without the consent of the Owner, nor in time of war, but in a manner to be prescribed by law.

Amendment IV [1791]

The right of the people to be secure in their persons, houses, papers, and effects, against unreasonable searches and seizures, shall not be violated, and no Warrants shall issue, but upon probable cause, supported by Oath or Affirmation, and particularly describing the place to be searched, and the persons or things to be seized.

Amendment V [1791]

No person shall be held to answer for a capital, or otherwise infamous crime, unless on a presentment or indictment of a Grand Jury, except in cases arising in the land or naval forces, or in the Militia, when in actual service in time of War or public danger; nor shall any person be subject for the same offense to be twice put in jeopardy of life or limb; nor shall be compelled in any criminal case to be a witness against himself, nor be deprived of life, liberty, or property, without due process of law; nor shall private property be taken for public use, without just compensation.

Amendment VI [1791]

In all criminal prosecutions, the accused shall enjoy the right to a speedy and public trial, by an impartial jury of the State and district wherein the crime shall have been committed, which district shall have been previously ascertained by law, and to be informed of the nature and cause of the accusation; to be confronted with the Witnesses against him; to have compulsory process for obtaining witnesses in his favor, and to have the Assistance of counsel for his defense.

Amendment VII [1791]

In suits at common law, where the value in controversy shall exceed twenty dollars, the right of trial by jury shall be preserved, and no fact tried by a jury, shall be otherwise re-examined in any Court of the United States, than according to the rules of the common law.

Amendment VIII [1791]

Excessive bail shall not be required, no excessive fines imposed, nor cruel and unusual punishments inflicted.

Amendment IX [1791]

The enumeration in the Constitution, of certain rights, shall not be construed to deny or disparage others retained by the people.

Amendment X [1791]

The powers not delegated to the United States by the Constitution, nor prohibited by it to the States, are reserved to the States respectively, or to the people.

Amendment XI [1798]

The judicial power of the United States shall not be construed to extend to any suit in law or equity, commenced or prosecuted against one of the United States by Citizens of another State, or by Citizens or Subjects of any Foreign State.

Amendment XII [1804]

The Electors shall meet in their respective states and vote by ballot for President and Vice-President, one of whom, at least, shall not be an inhabitant of the same state with themselves; they shall name in their ballots the person voted for as President, and in distinct ballots the person voted for as Vice-President, and they shall make distinct lists of all persons voted for as President, and of all persons voted for as Vice-President, and of the number of votes for each, which lists they shall sign and certify, and transmit sealed to the seat of the government of the United States, directed to the President of the Senate;—The President of the Senate shall, in the presence of the Senate and House of Representatives, open all the certificates and the votes shall then be counted;—The person having the greatest number of votes for President, shall be the President, if such a number be a majority of the whole number of Electors appointed; and if no person have such majority, then from the persons having the highest numbers not exceeding three on the list of those voted for as President, the House of Representatives shall choose immediately, by ballot, the President. But in choosing the President, the votes shall be taken by states, the representation from each state having one vote; a quorum for this purpose shall consist of a member or members from two-thirds of the states, and a majority of all the states shall be necessary to a choice. And if the House of Representatives shall not choose a President whenever the right of choice shall devolve upon them, before the fourth day of March next following, then the Vice-President shall act as President, as in the case of the death or other constitutional disability of the President. The person having the greatest number of votes as Vice-President, shall be the Vice-President, if such number be a majority of the whole number of Electors appointed, and if no person have a majority, then from the two highest numbers on the list, the Senate shall choose the Vice-President; a quorum for the purpose shall consist of two-thirds of the whole number of Senators, and a majority of the whole number shall be necessary to a choice. But no person constitutionally ineligible to the office of President shall be eligible to that of the Vice-President of the United States.

Amendment XIII [1865]

Section 1. Neither slavery nor involuntary servitude, except as a punishment for crime whereof the party shall have been duly convicted, shall exist within the United States, or any place subject to their jurisdiction.

Section 2. Congress shall have power to enforce this article by appropriate legislation.

Amendment XIV [1868]

Section 1. All persons born or naturalized in the United States, and subject to the jurisdiction thereof, are citizens of the United States and of the State wherein they reside. No State shall make or enforce any law which shall abridge the privileges or immunities of citizens of the United States; nor shall any State deprive any person of life, liberty, or property, without due process of law; nor deny to any person within its jurisdiction the equal protection of the laws.

Section 2. Representatives shall be appointed among the several States according to their respective numbers, counting the whole number of persons in each State, excluding Indians not taxed. But when the right to vote at any election for the choice of electors for President and Vice President of the United States, Representatives in Congress, the Executive and Judicial officers of a State, or the members of the Legislature thereof, is denied to any of the male inhabitants of such State, being twenty-one years of age, and citizens of the United States, or in any way abridged, except for participation in rebellion, or other crime, the basis of representation therein shall be reduced in the proportion which the number of such male citizens shall bear the whole number of male citizens twenty-one years of age in such State.

Section 3. No person shall be a Senator or Representative in Congress, or elector of President and Vice President, or hold any office, civil or military, under the United States, or under any State, who, having previously taken an oath, as a member of Congress, or as an officer of the United States, or as a member of any State legislature, or as an executive or judicial officer of any State, to support the Constitution of the United States, shall have engaged in insurrection or rebellion against the same, or given aid or comfort to the enemies thereof. But Congress may by a vote of two-thirds of each House, remove such disability.

Section 4. The validity of the public debt of the United States, authorized by law, including debts incurred for payment of pensions and bounties for services in suppressing insurrection or rebellion, shall not be questioned. But neither the United States nor any State shall assume or pay any debt or obligation incurred in aid of insurrection of rebellion against the United States, or any claim for the loss or emancipation of any slave; but all such debts, obligations and claims shall be held illegal and void.

Section 5. The Congress shall have power to enforce, by appropriate legislation, the provisions of this article.

Amendment XV [1870]

Section 1. The right of citizens of the United States to vote shall not be denied or abridged by the United States or by any State on account of race, color, or previous condition of servitude.

Section 2. The Congress shall have power to enforce this article by appropriate legislation.

Amendment XVI [1913]

The Congress shall have power to lay and collect taxes on incomes, from whatever source derived, without apportionment among the several States, and without regard to any census or enumeration.

Amendment XVII [1913]

The Senate of the United States shall be composed of two Senators from each State, elected by the people thereof, for six years; and each Senator shall have one vote. The electors in each State shall have the qualifications requisite for electors of the most numerous branch of the State legislatures.

When vacancies happen in the representation of any State in the Senate, the executive authority of each State shall issue writs of election to fill such vacancies; Provided, That the legislature of any State may empower the executive thereof to make temporary appointments until the people fill the vacancies by election as the legislature may direct.

This amendment shall not be construed as to affect the election or term of any Senator chosen before it becomes valid as part of the Constitution.

Amendment XVIII [1919]

Section 1. After one year from the ratification of this article the manufacture, sale, or transportation of intoxicating liquors within, the importation thereof into, or the exportation thereof from the United States and all territory subject to the jurisdiction thereof for beverage purposes is hereby prohibited.

Section 2. The Congress and the several States shall have concurrent power to enforce this article by appropriate legislation.

Section 3. This article shall be inoperative unless it shall have been ratified as an amendment to the Constitution by the legislatures of the several States, as provided in the Constitution, within seven years from the date of the submission hereof to the States by the Congress.

Amendment XIX [1920]

The right of citizens of the United States to vote shall not be denied or abridged by the United States or by any State on account of sex.

Congress shall have power to enforce this article by appropriate legislation.

Amendment XX [1933]

Section 1. The terms of the President and Vice President shall end at noon on the 20th day of January, and the terms of Senators and Representatives at noon on the 3d day of January, of the years in which such terms would have ended if this article had not been ratified; and the terms of their successors shall then begin.

Section 2. The Congress shall assemble at least once in every year, and such meeting shall begin at noon on the 3d day of January, unless they shall by law appoint a different day.

Section 3. If, at the time fixed for the beginning of the term of the President, the President elect shall have died, the Vice President elect shall become President. If a President shall not have been chosen before the time fixed for the beginning of his term, or if the President elect shall have failed to qualify, then the Vice President elect shall act as President until a President shall have qualified; and the Congress may by law provide for the case wherein neither a President elect nor a Vice President elect shall have qualified, declaring who shall then act as President, or the manner in which one who is to act shall be selected, and such person shall act accordingly until a President or Vice President shall have qualified.

Section 4. The Congress may by law provide for the case of the death of any of the persons from whom the House of Representatives may choose a President whenever the right of choice shall have devolved upon them, and for the case of the death of any of the persons from whom the Senate may choose a Vice President whenever the right of choice shall have devolved upon them.

Section 5. Sections 1 and 2 shall take effect on the 15th day of October following the ratification of this article.

Section 6. This article shall be inoperative unless it shall have been ratified as an amendment to the Constitution by the legislatures of three-fourths of the several States within seven years from the date of its submission.

Amendment XXI [1933]

Section 1. The eighteenth article of amendment to the Constitution of the United States is hereby repealed.

Section 2. The transportation or importation into any State, Territory, or possession of the United States for delivery or use therein of intoxicating liquors, in violation of the laws thereof, is hereby prohibited.

Section 3. This article shall be inoperative unless it shall have been ratified as an amendment to the Constitution by conventions in the several States, as provided in the Constitution, within seven years from the date of the submission hereof to the States by the Congress.

Amendment XXII [1951]

Section 1. No person shall be elected to the office of the President more than twice, and no person who has held the office of President, or acted as President, for more than two years of a term to which some other person was elected President shall be elected to the office of the President more than once. But this Article shall not apply to any person holding the office of President when this Article was proposed by the Congress, and shall not prevent any person who may be holding the office of President, or acting as President, during the term within which this Article becomes operative from holding the office of President, or acting as President during the remainder of such term.

Section 2. This article shall be inoperative unless it shall have been ratified as an amendment to the Constitution by the legislatures of three-fourths of the several States within seven years from the date of its submission to the States by the Congress.

Amendment XXIII [1961]

Section 1. The District constituting the seat of Government of the United States shall appoint in such manner as the Congress may direct:

A number of electors of President and Vice President equal to the whole number of Senators and Representatives in Congress to which the District would be entitled if it were a State, but in no event more than the least populous State; they shall be in addition to those appointed by the States, but they shall be considered, for the purposes of the election of President and Vice President, to be electors appointed by a State; and they shall meet in the District and perform such duties as provided by the twelfth article of amendment.

Section 2. The Congress shall have power to enforce this article by appropriate legislation.

Amendment XXIV [1964]

Section 1. The right of citizens of the United States to vote in any primary or other election for President or Vice President, for electors for President or Vice President or for Senator or Representative in Congress, shall not be denied or abridged by the United States or any State by reason of failure to pay any poll tax or other tax.

Section 2. The Congress shall have power to enforce this article by appropriate legislation.

Amendment XXV [1967]

Section 1. In case of the removal of the President from office or of his death or resignation, the Vice President shall become President.

Section 2. Whenever there is a vacancy in the office of the Vice President, the President shall nominate a Vice President who shall take office upon confirmation by a majority vote of both Houses of Congress.

Section 3. Whenever the President transmits to the President pro tempore of the Senate and the Speaker of the House of Representatives his written declaration that he is unable to discharge the powers and duties of his office, and until he transmits to them a written declaration to the contrary, such powers and duties shall be discharged by the Vice President as Acting President.

Section 4. Whenever the Vice President and a majority of either the principal officers of the executive departments or of such other body as Congress may by law provide, transmit to the President pro tempore of the Senate and the Speaker of the House of Representatives their written declaration that the President is unable to discharge the powers and duties of his office, the Vice President shall immediately assume the powers and duties of the office as Acting President.

Thereafter, when the President transmits to the President pro tempore of the Senate and the Speaker of the House of Representatives his written declaration that no inability exists, he shall resume the powers and duties of his office unless the Vice President and a majority of either the principal officers of the executive department or of such other body as Congress may by law provide, transmit within four days to the President pro tempore of the Senate and the Speaker of the House of Representatives their written declaration that the President is unable to discharge the powers and duties of his office. Thereupon Congress shall decide the issue, assembling within forty-eight hours for that purpose if not in session. If the Congress, within twenty-one days after receipt of the latter written declaration, or, if Congress is not in session, within twenty-one days after Congress is required to assemble, determines by two-thirds vote of both Houses that the President is unable to discharge the powers and duties of his office, the Vice President shall continue to discharge the same as Acting President; otherwise, the President shall resume the powers and duties of his office.

Amendment XXVI [1971]

Section 1. The right of citizens of the United States, who are eighteen years of age or older, to vote shall not be denied or abridged by the United States or by any State on account of age.

Section 2. The Congress shall have power to enforce this article by appropriate legislation.

Amendment XXVII [1992]

No law, varying the compensation for the services of the Senators and Representatives, shall take effect, until an election of Representatives shall have intervened.

The Code consists of the following Articles:

1. General Provisions
2. Sales
2A. Leases
3. Negotiable Instruments
4. Bank Deposits and Collections
4A. Funds Transfers
5. Letters of Credit
6. Bulk Transfers
7. Warehouse Receipts, Bills of Lading and Other Documents of Title
8. Investment Securities
9. Secured Transactions
10. Effective Date and Repealer
11. Effective Date and Transition Provisions

REVISION OF UNIFORM COMMERCIAL CODE
ARTICLE 1—GENERAL PROVISIONS
Part 1—General Provisions

§1-101. Short Titles.
(a) This [Act] may be cited as the Uniform Commercial Code.
(b) This article may be cited as Uniform Commercial Code—General Provisions.

§1-102. Scope of Article.
This article applies to a transaction to the extent that it is governed by another article of [the Uniform Commercial Code].

§1-103. Construction of [Uniform Commercial Code] to Promote Its Purposes and Policies; Applicability of Supplemental Principles of Law.
(a) [The Uniform Commercial Code] must be liberally construed and applied to promote its underlying purposes and policies, which are:
  (1) to simplify, clarify, and modernize the law governing commercial transactions;
  (2) to permit the continued expansion of commercial practices through custom, usage, and agreement of the parties; and
  (3) to make uniform the law among the various jurisdictions.
(b) Unless displaced by the particular provisions of [the Uniform Commercial Code], the principles of law and equity, including the law merchant and the law relative to capacity to contract, principal and agent, estoppel, fraud, misrepresentation, duress, coercion, mistake, bankruptcy, and other validating or invalidating cause supplement its provisions.

§1-104. Construction Against Implied Repeal.
[The Uniform Commercial Code] being a general act intended as a unified coverage of its subject matter, no part of it shall be deemed to be impliedly repealed by subsequent legislation if such construction can reasonably be avoided.

§1-105. Severability.
If any provision or clause of [the Uniform Commercial Code] or its application to any person or circumstance is held invalid, the invalidity does not affect other provisions or applications of [the Uniform Commercial Code] which can be given effect without the invalid provision or application, and to this end the provisions of [the Uniform Commercial Code] are severable.

§1-106. Use of Singular and Plural; Gender.
In [the Uniform Commercial Code], unless the statutory context otherwise requires:
(1) words in the singular number include the plural, and those in the plural include the singular; and
(2) words of any gender also refer to any other gender.

§1-107. Section Captions.
Section captions are part of [the Uniform Commercial Code].

§1-108. Relation to Electronic Signatures in Global and National Commerce Act.
This article modifies, limits, and supersedes the federal Electronic Signatures in Global and National Commerce Act, 15 U.S.C. Section 7001 *et seq.*, except that nothing in this article modifies, limits, or supersedes Section 7001(c) of that Act or authorizes electronic delivery of any of the notices described in Section 7003(b) of that Act.

Part 2—General Definitions and Principles of Interpretation
§1-201. General Definitions.
(a) Unless the context otherwise requires, words or phrases defined in this section, or in the additional definitions contained in other articles of [the Uniform Commercial Code] that apply to particular articles or parts thereof, have the meanings stated.
(b) Subject to definitions contained in other articles of [the Uniform Commercial Code] that apply to particular articles or parts thereof:
  (1) "Action", in the sense of a judicial proceeding, includes recoupment, counterclaim, set-off, suit in equity, and any other proceeding in which rights are determined.
  (2) "Aggrieved party" means a party entitled to pursue a remedy.
  (3) "Agreement", as distinguished from "contract", means the bargain of the parties in fact, as found in their language or inferred from other circumstances, including course of performance, course of dealing, or usage of trade as provided in Section 1-303.

(4) "Bank" means a person engaged in the business of banking and includes a savings bank, savings and loan association, credit union, and trust company.

(5) "Bearer" means a person in possession of a negotiable instrument, document of title, or certificated security that is payable to bearer or indorsed in blank.

(6) "Bill of lading" means a document evidencing the receipt of goods for shipment issued by a person engaged in the business of transporting or forwarding goods.

(7) "Branch" includes a separately incorporated foreign branch of a bank.

(8) "Burden of establishing" a fact means the burden of persuading the trier of fact that the existence of the fact is more probable than its non-existence.

(9) "Buyer in ordinary course of business" means a person that buys goods in good faith, without knowledge that the sale violates the rights of another person in the goods, and in the ordinary course from a person, other than a pawnbroker, in the business of selling goods of that kind. A person buys goods in the ordinary course if the sale to the person comports with the usual or customary practices in the kind of business in which the seller is engaged or with the seller's own usual or customary practices. A person that sells oil, gas, or other minerals at the wellhead or minehead is a person in the business of selling goods of that kind. A buyer in ordinary course of business may buy for cash, by exchange of other property, or on secured or unsecured credit, and may acquire goods or documents of title under a preexisting contract for sale. Only a buyer that takes possession of the goods or has a right to recover the goods from the seller under Article 2 may be a buyer in ordinary course of business. "Buyer in ordinary course of business" does not include a person that acquires goods in a transfer in bulk or as security for or in total or partial satisfaction of a money debt.

(10) "Conspicuous", with reference to a term, means so written, displayed, or presented that a reasonable person against which it is to operate ought to have noticed it. Whether a term is "conspicuous" or not is a decision for the court. Conspicuous terms include the following:

(A) a heading in capitals equal to or greater in size than the surrounding text, or in contrasting type, font, or color to the surrounding text of the same or lesser size; and

(B) language in the body of a record or display in larger type than the surrounding text, or in contrasting type, font, or color to the surrounding text of the same size, or set off from surrounding text of the same size by symbols or other marks that call attention to the language.

(11) "Consumer" means an individual who enters into a transaction primarily for personal, family, or household purposes.

(12) "Contract", as distinguished from "agreement", means the total legal obligation that results from the parties' agreement as determined by [the Uniform Commercial Code] as supplemented by any other applicable laws.

(13) "Creditor" includes a general creditor, a secured creditor, a lien creditor, and any representative of creditors, including an assignee for the benefit of creditors, a trustee in bankruptcy, a receiver in equity, and an executor or administrator of an insolvent debtor's or assignor's estate.

(14) "Defendant" includes a person in the position of defendant in a counterclaim, cross-claim, or third-party claim.

(15) "Delivery", with respect to an instrument, document of title, or chattel paper, means voluntary transfer of possession.

(16) "Document of title" includes bill of lading, dock warrant, dock receipt, warehouse receipt or order for the delivery of goods, and also any other document which in the regular course of business or financ-ing is treated as adequately evidencing that the person in possession of it is entitled to receive, hold, and dispose of the document and the goods it covers. To be a document of title, a document must purport to be issued by or addressed to a bailee and purport to cover goods in the bailee's possession which are either identified or are fungible portions of an identified mass.

(17) "Fault" means a default, breach, or wrongful act or omission.

(18) "Fungible goods" means:

(A) goods of which any unit, by nature or usage of trade, is the equivalent of any other like unit; or

(B) goods that by agreement are treated as equivalent.

(19) "Genuine" means free of forgery or counterfeiting.

(20) "Good faith," except as otherwise provided in Article 5, means honesty in fact and the observance of reasonable commercial standards of fair dealing.

(21) "Holder" means:

(A) the person in possession of a negotiable instrument that is payable either to bearer or to an identified person that is the person in possession; or

(B) the person in possession of a document of title if the goods are deliverable either to bearer or to the order of the person in possession.

(22) "Insolvency proceeding" includes an assignment for the benefit of creditors or other proceeding intended to liquidate or rehabilitate the estate of the person involved.

(23) "Insolvent" means:

(A) having generally ceased to pay debts in the ordinary course of business other than as a result of bona fide dispute;

(B) being unable to pay debts as they become due; or

(C) being insolvent within the meaning of federal bankruptcy law.

(24) "Money" means a medium of exchange currently authorized or adopted by a domestic or foreign government. The term includes a monetary unit of account established by an intergovernmental organization or by agreement between two or more countries.

(25) "Organization" means a person other than an individual.

(26) "Party", as distinguished from "third party", means a person that has engaged in a transaction or made an agreement subject to [the Uniform Commercial Code].

(27) "Person" means an individual, corporation, business trust, estate, trust, partnership, limited liability company, association, joint venture, government, governmental subdivision, agency, or instrumentality, public corporation, or any other legal or commercial entity.

(28) "Present value" means the amount as of a date certain of one or more sums payable in the future, discounted to the date certain by use of either an interest rate specified by the parties if that rate is not manifestly unreasonable at the time the transaction is entered into or, if an interest rate is not so specified, a commercially reasonable rate that takes into account the facts and circumstances at the time the transaction is entered into.

(29) "Purchase" means taking by sale, lease, discount, negotiation, mortgage, pledge, lien, security interest, issue or reissue, gift, or any other voluntary transaction creating an interest in property.

(30) "Purchaser" means a person that takes by purchase.

(31) "Record" means information that is inscribed on a tangible medium or that is stored in an electronic or other medium and is retrievable in perceivable form.

(32) "Remedy" means any remedial right to which an aggrieved party is entitled with or without resort to a tribunal.

(33) "Representative" means a person empowered to act for another, including an agent, an officer of a corporation or association, and a trustee, executor, or administrator of an estate.

(34) "Right" includes remedy.

(35) "Security interest" means an interest in personal property or fixtures which secures payment or performance of an obligation. "Security interest" includes any interest of a consignor and a buyer of accounts, chattel paper, a payment intangible, or a promissory note in a transaction that is subject to Article 9. "Security interest" does not include the special property interest of a buyer of goods on identification of those goods to a contract for sale under Section 2-401, but a buyer may also acquire a "security interest" by complying with Article 9. Except as otherwise provided in Section 2-505, the right of a seller or lessor of goods under Article 2 or 2A to retain or acquire possession of the goods is not a "security interest", but a seller or lessor may also acquire a "security interest" by complying with Article 9. The retention or reservation of title by a seller of goods notwithstanding shipment or delivery to the buyer under Section 2-401 is limited in effect to a reservation of a "security interest." Whether a transaction in the form of a lease creates a "security interest" is determined pursuant to Section 1-203.

(36) "Send" in connection with a writing, record, or notice means:

(A) to deposit in the mail or deliver for transmission by any other usual means of communication with postage or cost of transmission provided for and properly addressed and, in the case of an instrument, to an address specified thereon or otherwise agreed, or if there be none to any address reasonable under the circumstances; or

(B) in any other way to cause to be received any record or notice within the time it would have arrived if properly sent.

(37) "Signed" includes using any symbol executed or adopted with present intention to adopt or accept a writing.

(38) "State" means a State of the United States, the District of Columbia, Puerto Rico, the United States Virgin Islands, or any territory or insular possession subject to the jurisdiction of the United States.

(39) "Surety" includes a guarantor or other secondary obligor.

(40) "Term" means a portion of an agreement that relates to a particular matter.

(41) "Unauthorized signature" means a signature made without actual, implied, or apparent authority. The term includes a forgery.

(42) "Warehouse receipt" means a receipt issued by a person engaged in the business of storing goods for hire.

(43) "Writing" includes printing, typewriting, or any other intentional reduction to tangible form. "Written" has a corresponding meaning.

§1-202. Notice; Knowledge.

(a) Subject to subsection (f), a person has "notice" of a fact if the person:

(1) has actual knowledge of it;

(2) has received a notice or notification of it; or

(3) from all the facts and circumstances known to the person at the time in question, has reason to know that it exists.

(b) "Knowledge" means actual knowledge. "Knows" has a corresponding meaning.

(c) "Discover", "learn", or words of similar import refer to knowledge rather than to reason to know.

(d) A person "notifies" or "gives" a notice or notification to another person by taking such steps as may be reasonably required to inform the other person in ordinary course, whether or not the other person actually comes to know of it.

(e) Subject to subsection (f), a person "receives" a notice or notification when:

(1) it comes to that person's attention; or

(2) it is duly delivered in a form reasonable under the circumstances at the place of business through which the contract was made or at another location held out by that person as the place for receipt of such communications.

(f) Notice, knowledge, or a notice or notification received by an organization is effective for a particular transaction from the time it is brought to the attention of the individual conducting that transaction and, in any event, from the time it would have been brought to the individual's attention if the organization had exercised due diligence. An organization exercises due diligence if it maintains reasonable routines for communicating significant information to the person conducting the transaction and there is reasonable compliance with the routines. Due diligence does not require an individual acting for the organization to communicate information unless the communication is part of the individual's regular duties or the individual has reason to know of the transaction and that the transaction would be materially affected by the information.

§1-203. Lease Distinguished from Security Interest.

(a) Whether a transaction in the form of a lease creates a lease or security interest is determined by the facts of each case.

(b) A transaction in the form of a lease creates a security interest if the consideration that the lessee is to pay the lessor for the right to possession and use of the goods is an obligation for the term of the lease and is not subject to termination by the lessee, and:

(1) the original term of the lease is equal to or greater than the remaining economic life of the goods;

(2) the lessee is bound to renew the lease for the remaining economic life of the goods or is bound to become the owner of the goods;

(3) the lessee has an option to renew the lease for the remaining economic life of the goods for no additional consideration or for nominal additional consideration upon compliance with the lease agreement; or

(4) the lessee has an option to become the owner of the goods for no additional consideration or for nominal additional consideration upon compliance with the lease agreement.

(c) A transaction in the form of a lease does not create a security interest merely because:

(1) the present value of the consideration the lessee is obligated to pay the lessor for the right to possession and use of the goods is substantially equal to or is greater than the fair market value of the goods at the time the lease is entered into;

(2) the lessee assumes risk of loss of the goods;

(3) the lessee agrees to pay, with respect to the goods, taxes, insurance, filing, recording, or registration fees, or service or maintenance costs;

(4) the lessee has an option to renew the lease or to become the owner of the goods;

(5) the lessee has an option to renew the lease for a fixed rent that is equal to or greater than the reasonably predictable fair market rent for the use of the goods for the term of the renewal at the time the option is to be performed; or

(6) the lessee has an option to become the owner of the goods for a fixed price that is equal to or greater than the reasonably predictable fair market value of the goods at the time the option is to be performed.

(d) Additional consideration is nominal if it is less than the lessee's reasonably predictable cost of performing under the lease agreement if the option is not exercised. Additional consideration is not nominal if:

(1) when the option to renew the lease is granted to the lessee, the rent is stated to be the fair market rent for the use of the goods for the term of the renewal determined at the time the option is to be performed; or

(2) when the option to become the owner of the goods is granted to the lessee, the price is stated to be the fair market value of the goods determined at the time the option is to be performed.

(e) The "remaining economic life of the goods" and "reasonably predictable" fair market rent, fair market value, or cost of performing under the lease agreement must be determined with reference to the facts and circumstances at the time the transaction is entered into.

§1-204. Value.

Except as otherwise provided in Articles 3, 4, [and] 5, [and 6], a person gives value for rights if the person acquires them:

(1) in return for a binding commitment to extend credit or for the extension of immediately available credit, whether or not drawn upon and whether or not a charge-back is provided for in the event of difficulties in collection;

(2) as security for, or in total or partial satisfaction of, a preexisting claim;

(3) by accepting delivery under a preexisting contract for purchase; or

(4) in return for any consideration sufficient to support a simple contract.

§1-205. Reasonable Time; Seasonableness.

(a) Whether a time for taking an action required by [the Uniform Commercial Code] is reasonable depends on the nature, purpose, and circumstances of the action.

(b) An action is taken seasonally if it is taken at or within the time agreed or, if no time is agreed, at or within a reasonable time.

§1-206. Presumptions.

Whenever [the Uniform Commercial Code] creates a "presumption" with respect to a fact, or provides that a fact is "presumed," the trier of fact must find the existence of the fact unless and until evidence is introduced that supports a finding of its nonexistence.

Part 3—Territorial Applicability and General Rules

§1-301. Territorial Applicability; Parties' Power to Choose Applicable Law.

(a) In this section:

(1) "Domestic transaction" means a transaction other than an international transaction.

(2) "International transaction" means a transaction that bears a reasonable relation to a country other than the United States.

(b) This section applies to a transaction to the extent that it is governed by another article of the [Uniform Commercial Code].

(c) Except as otherwise provided in this section:

(1) an agreement by parties to a domestic transaction that any or all of their rights and obligations are to be determined by the law of this State or of another State is effective, whether or not the transaction bears a relation to the State designated; and

(2) an agreement by parties to an international transaction that any or all of their rights and obligations are to be determined by the law of this State or of another State or country is effective, whether or not the transaction bears a relation to the State or country designated.

(d) In the absence of an agreement effective under subsection (c), and except as provided in subsections (e) and (g), the rights and obligations of the parties are determined by the law that would be selected by application of this State's conflict of laws principles.

(e) If one of the parties to a transaction is a consumer, the following rules apply:

(1) An agreement referred to in subsection (c) is not effective unless the transaction bears a reasonable relation to the State or country designated.

(2) Application of the law of the State or country determined pursuant to subsection (c) or (d) may not deprive the consumer of the protection of any rule of law governing a matter within the scope of this section, which both is protective of consumers and may not be varied by agreement:

(A) of the State or country in which the consumer principally resides, unless subparagraph (B) applies; or

(B) if the transaction is a sale of goods, of the State or country in which the consumer both makes the contract and takes delivery of those goods, if such State or country is not the State or country in which the consumer principally resides.

(f) An agreement otherwise effective under subsection (c) is not effective to the extent that application of the law of the State or country designated would be contrary to a fundamental policy of the State or country whose law would govern in the absence of agreement under subsection (d).

(g) To the extent that [the Uniform Commercial Code] governs a transaction, if one of the following provisions of [the Uniform Commercial Code] specifies the applicable law, that provision governs and a contrary agreement is effective only to the extent permitted by the law so specified:

(1) Section 2-402;

(2) Sections 2A-105 and 2A-106;

(3) Section 4-102;

(4) Section 4A-507;

(5) Section 5-116;

[(6) Section 6-103;]

(7) Section 8-110;

(8) Sections 9-301 through 9-307.

§1-302. Variation by Agreement.

(a) Except as otherwise provided in subsection (b) or elsewhere in [the Uniform Commercial Code], the effect of provisions of [the Uniform Commercial Code] may be varied by agreement.

(b) The obligations of good faith, diligence, reasonableness, and care prescribed by [the Uniform Commercial Code] may not be disclaimed by agreement. The parties, by agreement, may determine the standards by which the performance of those obligations is to be measured if those standards are not manifestly unreasonable. Whenever [the Uniform Commercial Code] requires an action to be taken within a reasonable time, a time that is not manifestly unreasonable may be fixed by agreement.

(c) The presence in certain provisions of [the Uniform Commercial Code] of the phrase "unless otherwise agreed", or words of similar import, does not imply that the effect of other provisions may not be varied by agreement under this section.

§1-303. Course of Performance, Course of Dealing, and Usage of Trade.

(a) A "course of performance" is a sequence of conduct between the parties to a particular transaction that exists if:

(1) the agreement of the parties with respect to the transaction involves repeated occasions for performance by a party; and

(2) the other party, with knowledge of the nature of the performance and opportunity for objection to it, accepts the performance or acquiesces in it without objection.

(b) A "course of dealing" is a sequence of conduct concerning previous transactions between the parties to a particular transaction that is fairly to be regarded as establishing a common basis of understanding for interpreting their expressions and other conduct.

(c) A "usage of trade" is any practice or method of dealing having such regularity of observance in a place, vocation, or trade as to justify an expectation that it will be observed with respect to the transaction in question. The existence and scope of such a usage must be proved as facts. If it is established that such a usage is embodied in a trade code or similar record, the interpretation of the record is a question of law.

(d) A course of performance or course of dealing between the parties or usage of trade in the vocation or trade in which they are engaged or of which they are or should be aware is relevant in ascertaining the meaning of the parties' agreement, may give particular meaning to specific terms of the agreement, and may supplement or qualify the terms of the agreement. A usage of trade applicable in the place in which part of the performance under the agreement is to occur may be so utilized as to that part of the performance.

(e) Except as otherwise provided in subsection (f), the express terms of an agreement and any applicable course of performance, course of dealing, or usage of trade must be construed whenever reasonable as consistent with each other. If such a construction is unreasonable:

(1) express terms prevail over course of performance, course of dealing, and usage of trade;

(2) course of performance prevails over course of dealing and usage of trade; and

(3) course of dealing prevails over usage of trade.

(f) Subject to Section 2-209, a course of performance is relevant to show a waiver or modification of any term inconsistent with the course of performance.

(g) Evidence of a relevant usage of trade offered by one party is not admissible unless that party has given the other party notice that the court finds sufficient to prevent unfair surprise to the other party.

§1-304. Obligation of Good Faith.

Every contract or duty within [the Uniform Commercial Code] imposes an obligation of good faith in its performance and enforcement.

§1-305. Remedies to be Liberally Administered.

(a) The remedies provided by [the Uniform Commercial Code] must be liberally administered to the end that the aggrieved party may be put in as good a position as if the other party had fully performed but neither consequential or special damages nor penal damages may be had except as specifically provided in [the Uniform Commercial Code] or by other rule of law.

(b) Any right or obligation declared by [the Uniform Commercial Code] is enforceable by action unless the provision declaring it specifies a different and limited effect.

§1-306. Waiver or Renunciation of Claim or Right After Breach.

A claim or right arising out of an alleged breach may be discharged in whole or in part without consideration by agreement of the aggrieved party in an authenticated record.

§1-307. Prima Facie Evidence by Third-party Documents.

A document in due form purporting to be a bill of lading, policy or certificate of insurance, official weigher's or inspector's certificate, consular invoice, or any other document authorized or required by the contract to be issued by a third party is prima facie evidence of its own authenticity and genuineness and of the facts stated in the document by the third party.

§1-308. Performance or Acceptance Under Reservation of Rights.

(a) A party that with explicit reservation of rights performs or promises performance or assents to performance in a manner demanded or offered by the other party does not thereby prejudice the rights reserved. Such words as "without prejudice," "under protest," or the like are sufficient.

(b) Subsection (a) does not apply to an accord and satisfaction.

§1-309. Option to Accelerate at Will.

A term providing that one party or that party's successor in interest may accelerate payment or performance or require collateral or additional collateral "at will" or when the party "deems itself insecure," or words of similar import, means that the party has power to do so only if that party in good faith believes that the prospect of payment or performance is impaired. The burden of establishing lack of good faith is on the party against which the power has been exercised.

§1-310. Subordinated Obligations.

An obligation may be issued as subordinated to performance of another obligation of the person obligated, or a creditor may subordinate its right to performance of an obligation by agreement with either the person obligated or another creditor of the person obligated. Subordination does not create a security interest as against either the common debtor or a subordinated creditor.

ARTICLE 1: GENERAL PROVISIONS

Part 1—Short Title, Construction, Application and Subject Matter of the Act

§1-101. Short Title.

This Act shall be known and may be cited as Uniform Commercial Code.

§1-102. Purposes; Rules of Construction; Variation by Agreement.

(1) This Act shall be liberally construed and applied to promote its underlying purposes and policies.

(2) Underlying purposes and policies of this Act are

(a) to simplify, clarify and modernize the law governing commercial transactions;

(b) to permit the continued expansion of commercial practices through custom, usage and agreement of the parties;

(c) to make uniform the law among the various jurisdictions.

(3) The effect of provisions of this Act may be varied by agreement, except as otherwise provided in this Act and except that the obligations of good faith, diligence, reasonableness and care prescribed by this Act may not be disclaimed by agreement but the parties may by agreement determine the standards by which the performance of such obligations is to be measured if such standards are not manifestly unreasonable.

(4) The presence in certain provisions of this Act of the words "unless otherwise agreed" or words of similar import does not imply that the effect of other provisions may not be varied by agreement under subsection (3).

(5) In this Act unless the context otherwise requires

(a) words in the singular number include the plural, and in the plural include the singular;

(b) words of the masculine gender include the feminine and the neuter, and when the sense so indicates words of the neuter gender may refer to any gender.

§1-103. Supplementary General Principles of Law Applicable.

Unless displaced by the particular provisions of this Act, the principles of law and equity, including the law merchant and the law relative to capacity to contract, principal and agent, estoppel, fraud, misrepresentation, duress, coercion, mistake, bankruptcy, or other validating or invalidating cause shall supplement its provisions.

§1-104. Construction Against Implicit Repeal.

This Act being a general act intended as a unified coverage of its subject matter, no part of it shall be deemed to be impliedly repealed by subsequent legislation if such construction can reasonably be avoided.

§1-105. Territorial Application of the Act; Parties' Power to Choose Applicable Law.

(1) Except as provided hereafter in this section, when a transaction bears a reasonable relation to this state and also to another state or nation the parties may agree that the law either of this state or of such other state or nation shall govern their rights and duties. Failing such agreement this Act applies to transactions bearing an appropriate relation to this state.

(2) Where one of the following provisions of this Act specifies the applicable law, that provision governs and a contrary agreement is effective only to the extent permitted by the law (including the conflict of laws rules) so specified:

Rights of creditors against sold goods. Section 2-402.

Applicability of the Article on Bank Deposits and Collections. Section 4-102.

Bulk transfers subject to the Article on Bulk Transfers. Section 6-102.

Applicability of the Article on Investment Securities. Section 8-106.

Perfection provisions of the Article on Secured Transactions. Section 9-103.

§1-106. Remedies to Be Liberally Administered.

(1) The remedies provided by this Act shall be liberally administered to the end that the aggrieved party may be put in as good a position as if the other party had fully performed but neither consequential or special nor penal damages may be had except as specifically provided in this Act or by other rule of law.

(2) Any right or obligation declared by this Act is enforceable by action unless the provision declaring it specifies a different and limited effect.

§1-107. Waiver or Renunciation of Claim or Right After Breach.

Any claim or right arising out of an alleged breach can be discharged in whole or in part without consideration by a written waiver or renunciation signed and delivered by the aggrieved party.

§1-108. Severability.

If any provision or clause of this Act or application thereof to any person or circumstances is held invalid, such invalidity shall not affect other provisions or applications of the Act which can be given effect without the invalid provision or application, and to this end the provisions of this Act are declared to be severable.

§1-109. Section Captions.

Section captions are parts of this Act.

Part 2—General Definitions and Principles of Interpretation

§1-201. General Definitions.

Subject to additional definitions contained in the subsequent Articles of this Act which are applicable to specific Articles or Parts thereof, and unless the context otherwise requires, in this Act:

(1) "Action" in the sense of a judicial proceeding includes recoupment, counterclaim, set-off, suit in equity and any other proceedings in which rights are determined.

(2) "Aggrieved party" means a party entitled to resort to a remedy.

(3) "Agreement" means the bargain of the parties in fact as found in their language or by implication from other circumstances including course of dealing or usage of trade or course of performance as provided in this Act (Sections 1-205 and 2-208). Whether an agreement has legal consequences is determined by the provisions of this Act, if applicable; otherwise by the law of contracts (Section 1-103). (Compare "Contract".)

(4) "Bank" means any person engaged in the business of banking.

(5) "Bearer" means the person in possession of an instrument, document of title, or certificated security payable to bearer or indorsed in blank.

(6) "Bill of lading" means a document evidencing the receipt of goods for shipment issued by a person engaged in the business of transporting or forwarding goods, and includes an airbill. "Airbill" means a document serving for air transportation as a bill of lading does for marine or rail transportation, and includes an air consignment note or air waybill.

(7) "Branch" includes a separately incorporated foreign branch of a bank.

(8) "Burden of establishing" a fact means the burden of persuading the triers of fact that the existence of the fact is more probable than its non-existence.

(9) "Buyer in ordinary course of business" means a person who in good faith and without knowledge that the sale to him is in violation of the ownership rights or security interest of a third party in the goods buys in ordinary course from a person in the business of selling goods of that kind but does not include a pawnbroker. All persons who sell minerals or the like (including oil and gas) at wellhead or minehead shall be deemed to be persons in the business of selling goods of that kind. "Buying" may be for cash or by exchange of other property or on secured or unsecured credit and includes receiving goods or documents of title under a pre-existing contract for sale but does not include a transfer in bulk or as security for or in total or partial satisfaction of a money debt.

(10) "Conspicuous": A term or clause is conspicuous when it is so written that a reasonable person against whom it is to operate ought to have noticed it. A printed heading in capitals (as: NON-NEGOTIABLE BILL OF LADING) is conspicuous. Language in the body of a form is "conspicuous" if it is in larger or other contrasting type or color. But in a telegram any stated term is "conspicuous". Whether a term or clause is "conspicuous" or not is for decision by the court.

(11) "Contract" means the total legal obligation which results from the parties' agreement as affected by this Act and any other applicable rules of law. (Compare "Agreement".)

(12) "Creditor" includes a general creditor, a secured creditor, a lien creditor and any representative of creditors, including an assignee for the benefit of creditors, a trustee in bankruptcy, a receiver in equity and an executor or administrator of an insolvent debtor's or assignor's estate.

(13) "Defendant" includes a person in the position of defendant in a cross-action or counterclaim.

(14) "Delivery" with respect to instruments, documents of title, chattel paper, or certificated securities means voluntary transfer of possession.

(15) "Document of title" includes bill of lading, dock warrant, dock receipt, warehouse receipt or order for the delivery of goods, and also any other document which in the regular course of business or financing is treated as adequately evidencing that the person in possession of it is entitled to receive, hold and dispose of the document and the goods it covers. To be a document of title a document must purport to be issued by or addressed to a bailee and purport to cover goods in the bailee's possession which are either identified or are fungible portions of an identified mass.

(16) "Fault" means wrongful act, omission or breach.

(17) "Fungible" with respect to goods or securities means goods or securities of which any unit is, by nature or usage of trade, the equivalent of any other like unit. Goods which are not fungible shall be deemed fungible for the purposes of this Act to the extent that under a particular agreement or document unlike units are treated as equivalents.

(18) "Genuine" means free of forgery or counterfeiting.

(19) "Good faith" means honesty in fact in the conduct or transaction concerned.

(20) "Holder" means a person who is in possession of a document of title or an instrument or a certificated investment security drawn, issued, or indorsed to him or his order or to bearer or in blank.

(21) To "honor" is to pay or to accept and pay, or where a credit so engages to purchase or discount a draft complying with the terms of the credit.

(22) "Insolvency proceedings" includes any assignment for the benefit of creditors or other proceedings intended to liquidate or rehabilitate the estate of the person involved.

(23) A person is "insolvent" who either has ceased to pay his debts in the ordinary course of business or cannot pay his debts as they become due or is insolvent within the meaning of the federal bankruptcy law.

(24) "Money" means a medium of exchange authorized or adopted by a domestic or foreign government as a part of its currency.

(25) A person has "notice" of a fact when

    (a) he has actual knowledge of it; or

    (b) he has received a notice or notification of it; or

    (c) from all the facts and circumstances known to him at the time in question he has reason to know that it exists.

A person "knows" or has "knowledge" of a fact when he has actual knowledge of it. "Discover" or "learn" or a word or phrase of similar import refers to knowledge rather than to reason to know. The time and circumstances under which a notice or notification may cease to be effective are not determined by this Act.

(26) A person "notifies" or "gives" a notice or notification to another by taking such steps as may be reasonably required to inform the other in ordinary course whether or not such other actually comes to know of it. A person "receives" a notice or notification when

    (a) it comes to his attention; or

(b) it is duly delivered at the place of business through which the contract was made or at any other place held out by him as the place for receipt of such communications.

(27) Notice, knowledge or a notice or notification received by an organization is effective for a particular transaction from the time when it is brought to the attention of the individual conducting that transaction, and in any event from the time when it would have been brought to his attention if the organization had exercised due diligence. An organization exercises due diligence if it maintains reasonable routines for communicating significant information to the person conducting the transaction and there is reasonable compliance with the routines. Due diligence does not require an individual acting for the organization to communicate information unless such communication is part of his regular duties or unless he has reason to know of the transaction and that the transaction would be materially affected by the information.

(28) "Organization" includes a corporation, government or governmental subdivision or agency, business trust, estate, trust, partnership or association, two or more persons having a joint or common interest, or any other legal or commercial entity.

(29) "Party", as distinct from "third party", means a person who has engaged in a transaction or made an agreement within this Act.

(30) "Person" includes an individual or an organization (See Section 1-102).

(31) "Presumption" or "presumed" means that the trier of fact must find the existence of the fact presumed unless and until evidence is introduced which would support a finding of its non-existence.

(32) "Purchase" includes taking by sale, discount, negotiation, mortgage, pledge, lien, or re-issue, gift or any other voluntary transaction creating an interest in property.

(33) "Purchaser" means a person who takes by purchase.

(34) "Remedy" means any remedial right to which an aggrieved party is entitled with or without resort to a tribunal.

(35) "Representative" includes an agent, an officer of a corporation or association, and a trustee, executor or administrator of an estate, or any other person empowered to act for another.

(36) "Rights" includes remedies.

(37) "Security interest" means an interest in personal property or fixtures which secures payment or performance of an obligation. The retention or reservation of title by a seller of goods notwithstanding shipment or delivery to the buyer (Section 2-401) is limited in effect to a reservation of a "security interest". The term also includes any interest of a buyer of accounts or chattel paper which is subject to Article 9. The special property interest of a buyer of goods on identification of such goods to a contract for sale under Section 2-401 is not a "security interest", but a buyer may also acquire a "security interest" by complying with Article 9. Unless a lease or consignment is intended as security, reservation of title thereunder is not a "security interest" but a consignment is in any event subject to the provisions on consignment sales (Section 2-326). Whether a lease is intended as security is to be determined by the facts of each case; however, (a) the inclusion of an option to purchase does not of itself make the lease one intended for security, and (b) an agreement that upon compliance with the terms of the lease the leasee shall become or has the option to become the owner of the property for no additional consideration or for a nominal consideration does make the lease one intended for security.

(38) "Send" in connection with any writing or notice means to deposit in the mail or delivery for transmission by any other usual means of communication with postage or cost of transmission provided for and properly addressed and in the case of an instrument to an address specified thereon or otherwise agreed, or if there be none to any address reasonable under the circumstances. The receipt of any writing or notice within the time at which it would have arrived if properly sent has the effect of a proper sending.

(39) "Signed" includes any symbol executed or adopted by a party with present intention to authenticate a writing.

(40) "Surety" includes guarantor.

(41) "Telegram" includes a message transmitted by radio, teletype, cable, any mechanical method of transmission, or the like.

(42) "Term" means that portion of an agreement which relates to a particular matter.

(43) "Unauthorized" signature or indorsement means one made without actual, implied or apparent authority and includes a forgery.

(44) "Value". Except as otherwise provided with respect to negotiable instruments and bank collections (Sections 3-303, 4-208 and 4-209) a person gives "value" for rights if he acquires them

(a) in return for a binding commitment to extend credit or for the extension of immediately available credit whether or not drawn upon or whether or not a chargeback is provided for in the event of difficulties in collection; or

(b) as security for or in total or partial satisfaction of a pre-existing claim; or

(c) by accepting delivery pursuant to a pre-existing contract for purchase; or

(d) generally, in return for any consideration sufficient to support a simple contract.

(45) "Warehouse receipt" means a receipt issued by a person engaged in the business of storing goods for hire.

(46) "Written" or "writing" includes printing, typewriting or any other intentional reduction to tangible form. Amended in 1962, 1972 and 1977.

§1-202. Prima Facie Evidence by Third Party Documents.
A document in due form purporting to be a bill of lading, policy or certificate of insurance, official weigher's or inspector's certificate, consular invoice, or any other document authorized or required by the contract to be issued by a third party shall be prima facie evidence of its own authenticity and genuineness and of the facts stated in the document by the third party.

§1-203. Obligation of Good Faith.
Every contract or duty within this Act imposes an obligation of good faith in its performance or enforcement.

§1-204. Time; Reasonable Time; "Seasonably".
(1) Whenever this Act requires any action to be taken within a reasonable time, any time which is not manifestly unreasonable may be fixed by agreement.

(2) What is a reasonable time for taking any action depends on the nature, purpose and circumstances of such action.

(3) An action is taken "seasonably" when it is taken at or within the time agreed or if no time is agreed at or within a reasonable time.

§1-205. Course of Dealing and Usage of Trade.
(1) A course of dealing is a sequence of previous conduct between the parties to a particular transaction which is fairly to be regarded as establishing a common basis of understanding for interpreting their expressions and other conduct.

(2) A usage of trade is any practice or method of dealing having such regularity of observance in a place, vocation or trade as to justify an expectation that it will be observed with respect to the transaction in question. The existence and scope of such a usage are to be proved as facts. If it is established that such a usage is embodied in a written trade code or similar writing the interpretation of the writing is for the court.

(3) A course of dealing between parties and any usage of trade in the vocation or trade in which they are engaged or of which they are or should be aware give particular meaning to and supplement or qualify terms of an agreement.

(4) The express terms of an agreement and an applicable course of dealing or usage of trade shall be construed wherever reasonable as consistent with each other, but when such construction is unreasonable express terms

control both course of dealing and usage of trade and course of dealing controls usage of trade.

(5) An applicable usage of trade in the place where any part of performance is to occur shall be used in interpreting the agreement as to that part of the performance.

(6) Evidence of a relevant usage of trade offered by one party is not admissible unless and until he has given the other party such notice as the court finds sufficient to prevent unfair surprise to the latter.

§1-206. Statute of Frauds for Kinds of Personal Property Not Otherwise Covered.

(1) Except in the cases described in subsection (2) of this section a contract for the sale of personal property is not enforceable by way of action or defense beyond five thousand dollars in amount or value of remedy unless there is some writing which indicates that a contract for sale has been made between the parties at a defined or stated price, reasonably identifies the subject matter, and is signed by the party against whom enforcement is sought or by his authorized agent.

(2) Subsection (1) of this section does not apply to contracts for the sale of goods (Section 2-201) nor of securities (Section 8-319) nor to security agreements (Section 9-203).

§1-207. Performance or Acceptance Under Reservation of Rights.

A party who with explicit reservation of rights performs or promises performance or assents to performance in a manner demanded or offered by the other party does not thereby prejudice the rights reserved. Such words as "without prejudice", "under protest" or the like are sufficient.

§1-208. Option to Accelerate at Will.

A term providing that one party or his successor in interest may accelerate payment or performance or require collateral or additional collateral "at will" or "when he deems himself insecure" or in words of similar import shall be construed to mean that he shall have power to do so only if he in good faith believes that the prospect of payment or performance is impaired. The burden of establishing lack of good faith is on the party against whom the power has been exercised.

§1-209. Subordinated Obligations.

An obligation may be issued as subordinated to payment of another obligation of the person obligated, or a creditor may subordinate his right to payment of an obligation by agreement with either the person obligated or another creditor of the person obligated. Such a subordination does not create a security interest as against either the common debtor or a subordinated creditor. This section shall be construed as declaring the law as it existed prior to the enactment of this section and not as modifying it. Added 1966.

Note: *This new section is proposed as an optional provision to make it clear that a subordination agreement does not create a security interest unless so intended.*

ARTICLE 2: SALES

Part 1—Short Title, Construction and Subject Matter

§2-101. Short Title.

This Article shall be known and may be cited as Uniform Commercial Code—Sales.

§2-102. Scope; Certain Security and Other Transactions Excluded From This Article.

Unless the context otherwise requires, this Article applies to transactions in goods; it does not apply to any transaction which although in the form of an unconditional contract to sell or present sale is intended to operate only as a security transaction nor does this Article impair or repeal any statute regulating sales to consumers, farmers or other specified classes of buyers.

§2-103. Definitions and Index of Definitions.

(1) In this Article unless the context otherwise requires

   (a) "Buyer" means a person who buys or contracts to buy goods.

   (b) "Good faith" in the case of a merchant means honesty in fact and the observance of reasonable commercial standards of fair dealing in the trade.

   (c) "Receipt" of goods means taking physical possession of them.

   (d) "Seller" means a person who sells or contracts to sell goods.

(2) Other definitions applying to this Article or to specified Parts thereof, and the sections in which they appear are:

   "Acceptance". Section 2-606.
   "Banker's credit". Section 2-325.
   "Between merchants". Section 2-104.
   "Cancellation". Section 2-106(4).
   "Commercial unit". Section 2-105.
   "Confirmed credit". Section 2-325.
   "Conforming to contract". Section 2-106.
   "Contract for sale". Section 2-106.
   "Cover". Section 2-712.
   "Entrusting". Section 2-403.
   "Financing agency". Section 2-104.
   "Future goods". Section 2-105.
   "Goods". Section 2-105.
   "Identification". Section 2-501.
   "Installment contract". Section 2-612.
   "Letter of Credit". Section 2-325.
   "Lot". Section 2-105.
   "Merchant". Section 2-104.
   "Overseas". Section 2-323.
   "Person in position of seller". Section 2-707.
   "Present sale". Section 2-106.
   "Sale". Section 2-106.
   "Sale on approval". Section 2-326.
   "Sale or return". Section 2-326.
   "Termination". Section 2-106.

(3) The following definitions in other Articles apply to this Article:

   "Check". Section 3-104.
   "Consignee". Section 7-102.
   "Consignor". Section 7-102.
   "Consumer goods". Section 9-109.
   "Dishonor". Section 3-507. "Draft". Section 3-104.

(4) In addition Article 1 contains general definitions and principles of construction and interpretation applicable throughout this Article.

§2-104. Definitions: "Merchant"; "Between Merchants"; "Financing Agency".

(1) "Merchant" means a person who deals in goods of the kind or otherwise by his occupation holds himself out as having knowledge or skill peculiar to the practices or goods involved in the transaction or to whom such knowledge or skill may be attributed by his employment of an agent or broker or other intermediary who by his occupation holds himself out as having such knowledge or skill.

(2) "Financing agency" means a bank, finance company or other person who in the ordinary course of business makes advances against goods or documents of title or who by arrangement with either the seller or the buyer intervenes in ordinary course to make or collect payment due or claimed under the contract for sale, as by purchasing or paying the seller's draft or making advances against it or by merely taking it for collection whether or not documents of title accompany the draft. "Financing agency" includes also a bank or other person who similarly intervenes

between persons who are in the position of seller and buyer in respect to the goods (Section 2-707).

(3) Between merchants" means in any transaction with respect to which both parties are chargeable with the knowledge or skill of merchants.

§2-105. Definitions: Transferability; "Goods"; "Future" Goods; "Lot"; "Commercial Unit".

(1) "Goods" means all things (including specially manufactured goods) which are movable at the time of identification to the contract for sale other than the money in which the price is to be paid, investment securities (Article 8) and things in action. "Goods" also includes the unborn young of animals and growing crops and other identified things attached to realty as described in the section on goods to be severed from realty (Section 2-107).

(2) Goods must be both existing and identified before any interest in them can pass. Goods which are not both existing and identified are "future" goods. A purported present sale of future goods or of any interest therein operates as a contract to sell.

(3) There may be a sale of a part interest in existing identified goods.

(4) An undivided share in an identified bulk of fungible goods is sufficiently identified to be sold although the quantity of the bulk is not determined. Any agreed proportion of such a bulk or any quantity thereof agreed upon by number, weight or other measure may to the extent of the seller's interest in the bulk be sold to the buyer who then becomes an owner in common.

(5) "Lot" means a parcel or a single article which is the subject matter of a separate sale or delivery, whether or not it is sufficient to perform the contract.

(6) "Commercial unit" means such a unit of goods as by commercial usage is a single whole for purposes of sale and division of which materially impairs its character or value on the market or in use. A commercial unit may be a single article (as a machine) or a set of articles (as a suite of furniture or an assortment of sizes) or a quantity (as a bale, gross, or carload) or any other unit treated in use or in the relevant market as a single whole.

§2-106. Definitions: "Contract"; "Agreement"; "Contract for Sale"; "Sale"; "Present Sale"; "Conforming" to Contract; "Termination"; "Cancellation".

(1) In this Article unless the context otherwise requires "contract" and "agreement" are limited to those relating to the present or future sale of goods. "Contract for sale" includes both a present sale of goods and a contract to sell goods at a future time. A "sale" consists in the passing of title from the seller to the buyer for a price (Section 2-401). A "present sale" means a sale which is accomplished by the making of the contract.

(2) Goods or conduct including any part of a performance are "conforming" or conform to the contract when they are in accordance with the obligations under the contract.

(3) "Termination" occurs when either party pursuant to a power created by agreement or law puts an end to the contract otherwise than for its breach. On "termination" all obligations which are still executory on both sides are discharged but any right based on prior breach or performance survives.

(4) "Cancellation" occurs when either party puts an end to the contract for breach by the other and its effect is the same as that of "termination" except that the cancelling party also retains any remedy for breach of the whole contract or any unperformed balance.

§2-107. Goods to Be Severed From Realty: Recording.

(1) A contract for the sale of minerals or the like (including oil and gas) or a structure or its materials to be removed from realty is a contract for the sale of goods within this Article if they are to be severed by the seller but

until severance a purported present sale thereof which is not effective as a transfer of an interest in land is effective only as a contract to sell.

(2) A contract for the sale apart from the land of growing crops or other things attached to realty and capable of severance without material harm thereto but not described in subsection (1) or of timber to be cut is a contract for the sale of goods within this Article whether the subject matter is to be severed by the buyer or by the seller even though it forms part of the realty at the time of contracting, and the parties can by identification effect a present sale before severance.

(3) The provisions of this section are subject to any third party rights provided by the law relating to realty records, and the contract for sale may be executed and recorded as a document transferring an interest in land and shall then constitute notice to third parties of the buyer's rights under the contract for sale.

Part 2—Form, Formation and Readjustment of Contract

§2-201. Formal Requirements; Statute of Frauds.

(1) Except as otherwise provided in this section a contract for the sale of goods for the price of $500 or more is not enforceable by way of action or defense unless there is some writing sufficient to indicate that a contract for sale has been made between the parties and signed by the party against whom enforcement is sought or by his authorized agent or broker. A writing is not insufficient because it omits or incorrectly states a term agreed upon but the contract is not enforceable under this paragraph beyond the quantity of goods shown in such writing.

(2) Between merchants if within a reasonable time a writing in confirmation of the contract and sufficient against the sender is received and the party receiving it has reason to know its contents, it satisfies the requirements of subsection (1) against such party unless written notice of objection to its contents is given within ten days after it is received.

(3) A contract which does not satisfy the requirements of subsection (1) but which is valid in other respects is enforceable

    (a) if the goods are to be specially manufactured for the buyer and are not suitable for sale to others in the ordinary course of the seller's business and the seller, before notice of repudiation is received and under circumstances which reasonably indicate that the goods are for the buyer, has made either a substantial beginning of their manufacture or commitments for their procurement; or

    (b) if the party against whom enforcement is sought admits in his pleading, testimony or otherwise in court that a contract for sale was made, but the contract is not enforceable under this provision beyond the quantity of goods admitted; or

    (c) with respect to goods for which payment has been made and accepted or which have been received and accepted (Sec. 2-606).

§2-202. Final Written Expression: Parol or Extrinsic Evidence.

Terms with respect to which the confirmatory memoranda of the parties agree or which are otherwise set forth in a writing intended by the parties as a final expression of their agreement with respect to such terms as are included therein may not be contradicted by evidence of any prior agreement or of a contemporaneous oral agreement but may be explained or supplemented

    (a) by course of dealing or usage of trade (Section 1-205) or by course of performance (Section 2-208); and

    (b) by evidence of consistent additional terms unless the court finds the writing to have been intended also as a complete and exclusive statement of the terms of the agreement.

§2-203. Seals Inoperative.

The affixing of a seal to a writing evidencing a contract for sale or an offer to buy or sell goods does not constitute the writing a sealed instrument and the law with respect to sealed instruments does not apply to such a contract or offer.

§2-204. Formation in General.

(1) A contract for sale of goods may be made in any manner sufficient to show agreement, including conduct by both parties which recognizes the existence of such a contract.

(2) An agreement sufficient to constitute a contract for sale may be found even though the moment of its making is undetermined.

(3) Even though one or more terms are left open a contract for sale does not fail for indefiniteness if the parties have intended to make a contract and there is a reasonably certain basis for giving an appropriate remedy.

§2-205. Firm Offers.

An offer by a merchant to buy or sell goods in a signed writing which by its terms gives assurance that it will be held open is not revocable, for lack of consideration, during the time stated or if no time is stated for reasonable time, but in no event may such period of irrevocability exceed three months; but any such term of assurance on a form supplied by the offeree must be separately signed by the offeror.

§2-206. Offer and Acceptance in Formation of Contract.

(1) Unless other unambiguously indicated by the language or circumstances

    (a) an offer to make a contract shall be construed as inviting acceptance in any manner and by any medium reasonable in the circumstances;

    (b) an order or other offer to buy goods for prompt or current shipment shall be construed as inviting acceptance either by a prompt promise to ship or by the prompt or current shipment of conforming or nonconforming goods, but such a shipment of nonconforming goods does not constitute an acceptance if the seller seasonably notifies the buyer that the shipment is offered only as an accommodation to the buyer.

(2) Where the beginning of a requested performance is a reasonable mode of acceptance an offeror who is not notified of acceptance within a reasonable time may treat the offer as having lapsed before acceptance.

§2-207. Additional Terms in Acceptance or Confirmation.

(1) A definite and seasonable expression of acceptance or a written confirmation which is sent within a reasonable time operates as an acceptance even though it states terms additional to or different from those offered or agreed upon, unless acceptance is expressly made conditional on assent to the additional or different terms.

(2) The additional terms are to be construed as proposals for addition to the contract. Between merchants such terms become part of the contract unless:

    (a) the offer expressly limits acceptance to the terms of the offer;

    (b) they materially alter it; or

    (c) notification of objection to them has already been given or is given within a reasonable time after notice of them is received.

(3) Conduct by both parties which recognizes the existence of a contract is sufficient to establish a contract for sale although the writings of the parties do not otherwise establish a contract. In such case the terms of the particular contract consist of those terms on which the writings of the parties agree, together with any supplementary terms incorporated under any other provisions of this Act.

§2-208. Course of Performance or Practical Construction.

(1) Where the contract for sale involves repeated occasions for performance by either party with knowledge of the nature of the performance and opportunity for objection to it by the other, any course of performance accepted or acquiesced in without objection shall be relevant to determine the meaning of the agreement.

(2) The express terms of the agreement and any such course of performance, as well as any course of dealing and usage of trade, shall be construed whenever reasonable as consistent with each other; but when such construction is unreasonable, express terms shall control course of performance and course of performance shall control both course of dealing and usage of trade (Section 1-205).

(3) Subject to the provisions of the next section on modification and waiver, such course of performance shall be relevant to show a waiver or modification of any term inconsistent with such course of performance.

§2-209. Modification, Rescission and Waiver.

(1) An agreement modifying a contract within this Article needs no consideration to be binding.

(2) A signed agreement which excludes modification or rescission except by a signed writing cannot be otherwise modified or rescinded, but except as between merchants such a requirement on a form supplied by the merchant must be separately signed by the other party.

(3) The requirements of the statute of frauds section of this Article (Section 2-201) must be satisfied if the contract as modified is within its provisions.

(4) Although an attempt at modification or rescission does not satisfy the requirements of subsection (2) or (3) it can operate as a waiver.

(5) A party who has made a waiver affecting an executory portion of the contract may retract the waiver by reasonable notification received by the other party that strict performance will be required of any term waived, unless the retraction would be unjust in view of a material change of position in reliance on the waiver.

§2-210. Delegation of Performance; Assignment of Rights.

(1) A party may perform his duty through a delegate unless otherwise agreed or unless the other party has a substantial interest in having his original promisor perform or control the acts required by the contract. No delegation of performance relieves the party delegating of any duty to perform or any liability for breach.

(2) Unless otherwise agreed all rights of either seller or buyer can be assigned except where the assignment would materially change the duty of the other party, or increase materially the burden or risk imposed on him by his contract, or impair materially his chance of obtaining return performance. A right to damages for breach of the whole contract or a right arising out of the assignor's due performance of his entire obligation can be assigned despite agreement otherwise.

(3) Unless the circumstances indicate the contrary a prohibition of assignment of "the contract" is to be construed as barring only the delegation to the assignee of the assignor's performance.

(4) An assignment of "the contract" or of "all my rights under the contract" or an assignment in similar general terms is an assignment of rights and unless the language or the circumstances (as in an assignment for security) indicate the contrary, it is a delegation of performance of the duties of the assignor and its acceptance by the assignee constitutes a promise by him to perform those duties. This promise is enforceable by either the assignor or the other party to the original contract.

(5) The other party may treat any assignment which delegates performance as creating reasonable grounds for insecurity and may without prejudice to his rights against the assignor demand assurances from the assignee (Section 2-609).

Part 3—General Obligation and Construction of Contract

§2-301. General Obligations of Parties.

The obligation of the seller is to transfer and deliver and that of the buyer is to accept and pay in accordance with the contract.

§2-302. Unconscionable Contract or Clause.

(1) If the court as a matter of law finds the contract or any clause of the contract to have been unconscionable at the time it was made the court may refuse to enforce the contract, or it may enforce the remainder of the contract without the unconscionable clause, or it may so limit the application of any unconscionable clause as to avoid any unconscionable result.

(2) When it is claimed or appears to the court that the contract or any clause thereof may be unconscionable the parties shall be afforded a reasonable opportunity to present evidence as to its commercial setting, purpose and effect to aid the court in making the determination.

§2-303. Allocation or Division of Risks.

Where this Article allocates a risk or a burden as between the parties "unless otherwise agreed", the agreement may not only shift the allocation, but may also divide the risk or burden.

§2-304. Price Payable in Money, Goods, Realty, or Otherwise.

(1) The price can be made payable in money or otherwise. If it is payable in whole or in part in goods each party is a seller of the goods which he is to transfer.

(2) Even though all or part of the price is payable in an interest in realty the transfer of the goods and the seller's obligations with reference to them are subject to this Article, but not the transfer of the interest in realty or the transferor's obligations in connection therewith.

§2-305. Open Price Term.

(1) The parties if they so intend can conclude a contract for sale even though the price is not settled. In such a case the price is a reasonable price at the time for delivery if

   (a) nothing is said as to price; or

   (b) the price is left to be agreed by the parties and they fail to agree; or

   (c) the price is to be fixed in terms of some agreed market or other standard as set or recorded by a third person or agency and it is not so set or recorded.

(2) A price to be fixed by the seller or by the buyer means a price for him to fix in good faith.

(3) When a price left to be fixed otherwise than by agreement of the parties fails to be fixed through fault of one party the other may at his option treat the contract as cancelled or himself fix a reasonable price.

(4) Where, however, the parties intend not to be bound unless the price be fixed or agreed and it is not fixed or agreed there is no contract. In such a case the buyer must return any goods already received or if unable so to do must pay their reasonable value at the time of delivery and the seller must return any portion of the price paid on account.

§2-306. Output, Requirements and Exclusive Dealings.

(1) A term which measures the quantity by the output of the seller or the requirements of the buyer means such actual output or requirements as may occur in good faith, except that no quantity unreasonably disproportionate to any stated estimate or in the absence of a stated estimate to any normal or otherwise comparable prior output or requirements may be tendered or demanded.

(2) A lawful agreement by either the seller or the buyer for exclusive dealing in the kind of goods concerned imposes unless otherwise agreed an obligation by the seller to use best efforts to supply the goods and by the buyer to use best efforts to promote their sale.

§2-307. Delivery in Single Lot or Several Lots.

Unless otherwise agreed all goods called for by a contract for sale must be tendered in a single delivery and payment is due only on such tender but where the circumstances give either party the right to make or demand delivery in lots the price if it can be apportioned may be demanded for each lot.

§2-308. Absence of Specified Place for Delivery.

Unless otherwise agreed

(a) the place for delivery of goods is the seller's place of business or if he has none his residence; but

(b) in a contract for sale of identified goods which to the knowledge of the parties at the time of contracting are in some other place, that place is the place for their delivery; and

(c) documents of title may be delivered through customary banking channels.

§2-309. Absence of Specific Time Provisions; Notice of Termination.

(1) The time for shipment or delivery or any other action under a contract if not provided in this Article or agreed upon shall be a reasonable time.

(2) Where the contract provides for successive performances but is indefinite in duration it is valid for a reasonable time but unless otherwise agreed may be terminated at any time by either party.

(3) Termination of a contract by one party except on the happening of an agreed event requires that reasonable notification be received by the other party and an agreement dispensing with notification is invalid if its operation would be unconscionable.

§2-310. Open Time for Payment or Running of Credit; Authority to Ship Under Reservation.

Unless otherwise agreed

(a) payment is due at the time and place at which the buyer is to receive the goods even though the place of shipment is the place of delivery; and

(b) if the seller is authorized to send the goods he may ship them under reservation, and may tender the documents of title, but the buyer may inspect the goods after their arrival before payment is due unless such inspection is inconsistent with the terms of the contract (Section 2-513); and

(c) if delivery is authorized and made by way of documents of title otherwise than by subsection (b) then payment is due at the time and place at which the buyer is to receive the documents regardless of where the goods are to be received; and

(d) where the seller is required or authorized to ship the goods on credit the credit period runs from the time of shipment but post-dating the invoice or delaying its dispatch will correspondingly delay the starting of the credit period.

§2-311. Options and Cooperation Respecting Performance.

(1) An agreement for sale which is otherwise sufficiently definite (subsection (3) of Section 2-204) to be a contract is not made invalid by the fact that it leaves particulars of performance to be specified by one of the parties. Any such specification must be made in good faith and within limits set by commercial reasonableness.

(2) Unless otherwise agreed specifications relating to assortment of the goods are at the buyer's option and except as otherwise provided in subsections (1)(c) and (3) of Section 2-319 specifications or arrangements relating to shipment are at the seller's option.

(3) Where such specification would materially affect the other party's performance but is not seasonably made or where one party's cooperation is necessary to the agreed performance of the other but is not seasonably forthcoming, the other party in addition to all other remedies

   (a) is excused for any resulting delay in his own performance; and

   (b) may also either proceed to perform in any reasonable manner or after the time for a material part of his own performance treat the failure to specify or to cooperate as a breach by failure to deliver or accept the goods.

§2-312. Warranty of Title and Against Infringement; Buyer's Obligation Against Infringement.

(1) Subject to subsection (2) there is in a contract for sale a warranty by the seller that

   (a) the title conveyed shall be good, and its transfer rightful; and

   (b) the goods shall be delivered free from any security interest or other lien or encumbrance of which the buyer at the time of contracting has no knowledge.

(2) A warranty under subsection (1) will be excluded or modified only by specific language or by circumstances which give the buyer reason to know that the person selling does not claim title in himself or that he is

purporting to sell only such right or title as he or a third person may have.

(3) Unless otherwise agreed a seller who is a merchant regularly dealing in goods of the kind warrants that the goods shall be delivered free of the rightful claim of any third person by way of infringement or the like but a buyer who furnishes specifications to the seller must hold the seller harmless against any such claim which arises out of compliance with the specifications.

§2-313. Express Warranties by Affirmation, Promise, Description, Sample.

(1) Express warranties by the seller are created as follows:

(a) Any affirmation of fact or promise made by the seller to the buyer which relates to the goods and becomes part of the basis of the bargain creates an express warranty that the goods shall conform to the affirmation or promise.

(b) Any description of the goods which is made part of the basis of the bargain creates an express warranty that the goods shall conform to the description.

(c) Any sample or model which is made part of the basis of the bargain creates an express warranty that the whole of the goods shall conform to the sample or model.

(2) It is not necessary to the creation of an express warranty that the seller use formal words such as "warrant" or "guarantee" or that he have a specific intention to make a warranty, but an affirmation merely of the value of the goods or a statement purporting to be merely the seller's opinion or commendation of the goods does not create a warranty.

§2-314. Implied Warranty: Merchantability; Usage of Trade.

(1) Unless excluded or modified (Section 2-316), a warranty that the goods shall be merchantable is implied in a contract for their sale if the seller is a merchant with respect to goods of that kind. Under this section the serving for value of food or drink to be consumed either on the premises or elsewhere is a sale.

(2) Goods to be merchantable must be at least such as

(a) pass without objection in the trade under the contract description; and

(b) in the case of fungible goods, are of fair average quality within the description; and

(c) are fit for the ordinary purpose for which such goods are used; and

(d) run, within the variations permitted by the agreement, of even kind, quality and quantity within each unit and among all units involved; and

(e) are adequately contained, packaged, and labeled as the agreement may require; and

(f) conform to the promises or affirmations of fact made on the container or label if any.

(3) Unless excluded or modified (Section 2-316) other implied warranties may arise from course of dealing or usage of trade.

§2-315. Implied Warranty: Fitness for Particular Purpose.

Where the seller at the time of contracting has reason to know any particular purpose for which the goods are required and that the buyer is relying on the seller's skill or judgment to select or furnish suitable goods, there is unless excluded or modified under the next section an implied warranty that the goods shall be fit for such purpose.

§2-316. Exclusion or Modification of Warranties.

(1) Words or conduct relevant to the creation of an express warranty and words or conduct tending to negate or limit warranty shall be construed wherever reasonable as consistent with each other, but subject to the provisions of this Article on parol or extrinsic evidence (Section 2-202) negation

or limitation is inoperative to the extent that such construction is unreasonable.

(2) Subject to subsection (3), to exclude or modify the implied warranty of merchantability or any part of it the language must mention merchantability and in case of a writing must be conspicuous, and to exclude or modify any implied warranty of fitness the exclusion must be by a writing and conspicuous. Language to exclude all implied warranties of fitness is sufficient if it states, for example, that "There are no warranties which extend beyond the description on the face hereof."

(3) Notwithstanding subsection (2)

(a) unless the circumstances indicate otherwise, all implied warranties are excluded by expressions like "as is", "with all faults" or other language which in common understanding calls the buyer's attention to the exclusion of warranties and makes plain that there is no implied warranty; and

(b) when the buyer before entering into the contract has examined the goods or the sample or model as fully as he desired or has refused to examine the goods there is no implied warranty with regard to defects which an examination ought in the circumstances to have revealed to him; and

(c) an implied warranty can also be excluded or modified by course of dealing or course of performance or usage of trade.

(4) Remedies for breach of warranty can be limited in accordance with the provisions of this Article on liquidation or limitation of damages and on contractual modification of remedy (Sections 2-718 and 2-719).

§2-317. Cumulation and Conflict of Warranties Express or Implied.

Warranties whether express or implied shall be construed as consistent with each other and as cumulative, but if such construction is unreasonable the intention of the parties shall determine which warranty is dominant. In ascertaining that intention the following rules apply:

(a) Exact or technical specifications displace an inconsistent sample or model or general language of description.

(b) A sample from an existing bulk displaces inconsistent general language of description.

(c) Express warranties displace inconsistent implied warranties other than an implied warranty of fitness for a particular purpose.

§2-318. Third Party Beneficiaries of Warranties Express or Implied.

Note: *If this Act is introduced in the Congress of the United States this section should be omitted. (States to select one alternative.)*

Alternative A A seller's warranty whether express or implied extends to any natural person who is in the family or household of his buyer or who is a guest in his home if it is reasonable to expect that such person may use, consume or be affected by the goods and who is injured in person by breach of the warranty. The seller may not exclude or limit the operation of this section.

Alternative B A seller's warranty whether express or implied extends to any natural person who may reasonably be expected to use, consume or be affected by the goods and who is injured in person by breach of the warranty. A seller may not exclude or limit the operation of this section.

Alternative C A seller's warranty whether express or implied extends to any person who may reasonably be expected to use, consume or be affected by the goods and who is injured by breach of the warranty. A seller may not exclude or limit the operation of this section with respect to injury to the person of an individual to whom the warranty extends. As amended 1966.

§2-319. F.O.B. and F.A.S. Terms.

(1) Unless otherwise agreed the term F.O.B. (which means "free on board") at a named place, even though used only in connection with the stated price, is a delivery term under which

(a) when the term is F.O.B. the place of shipment, the seller must at that place ship the goods in the manner provided in this Article (Section 2-504) and bear the expense and risk of putting them into the possession of the carrier; or

(b) when the term is F.O.B. the place of destination, the seller must at his own expense and risk transport the goods to that place and there tender delivery of them in the manner provided in this Article (Section 2-503);

(c) when under either (a) or (b) the term is also F.O.B. vessel, car or other vehicle, the seller must in addition at his own expense and risk load the goods on board. If the term is F.O.B. vessel the buyer must name the vessel and in an appropriate case the seller must comply with the provisions of this Article on the form of bill of lading (Section 2-323).

(2) Unless otherwise agreed the term F.A.S. vessel (which means "free alongside") at a named port, even though used only in connection with the stated price, is a delivery term under which the seller must

(a) at his own expense and risk deliver the goods alongside the vessel in the manner usual in that port or on a dock designated and provided by the buyer; and

(b) obtain and tender a receipt for the goods in exchange for which the carrier is under a duty to issue a bill of lading.

(3) Unless otherwise agreed in any case falling within subsection (1)(a) or (c) or subsection (2) the buyer must seasonably give any needed instructions for making delivery, including when the term is F.A.S. or F.O.B. the loading berth of the vessel and in an appropriate case its name and sailing date. The seller may treat the failure of needed instructions as a failure of cooperation under this Article (Section 2-311). He may also at his option move the goods in any reasonable manner preparatory to delivery or shipment.

(4) Under the term F.O.B. vessel or F.A.S. unless otherwise agreed the buyer must make payment against tender of the required documents and the seller may not tender nor the buyer demand delivery of the goods in substitution for the documents.

§2-320. C.I.F. and C. & F. Terms.

(1) The term C.I.F. means that the price includes in a lump sum the cost of the goods and the insurance and freight to the named destination. The term C. & F. or C.F. means that the price so includes cost and freight to the named destination.

(2) Unless otherwise agreed and even though used only in connection with the stated price and destination, the term C.I.F. destination or its equivalent requires the seller at his own expense and risk to

(a) put the goods into the possession of a carrier at the port for shipment and obtain a negotiable bill or bills of lading covering the entire transportation to the named destination; and

(b) load the goods and obtain a receipt from the carrier (which may be contained in the bill of lading) showing that the freight has been paid or provided for; and

(c) obtain a policy or certificate of insurance, including any war risk insurance, of a kind and on terms then current at the port of shipment in the usual amount, in the currency of the contract, shown to cover the same goods covered by the bill of lading and providing for payment of loss to the order of the buyer or for the account of whom it may concern; but the seller may add to the price the amount of premium for any such war risk insurance; and

(d) prepare an invoice of the goods and procure any other documents required to effect shipment or to comply with the contract; and

(e) forward and tender with commercial promptness all the documents in due form and with any indorsement necessary to perfect the buyer's rights.

(3) Unless otherwise agreed the term C. & F. or its equivalent has the same effect and imposes upon the seller the same obligations and risks as a C.I.F. term except the obligation as to insurance.

(4) Under the term C.I.F. or C. & F. unless otherwise agreed the buyer must make payment against tender of the required documents and the seller may not tender nor the buyer demand delivery of the goods in substitution for the documents.

§2-321. C.I.F. or C. & F.: "Net Landed Weights"; "Payment on Arrival"; Warranty of Condition on Arrival.

Under a contract containing a term C.I.F. or C. & F.

(1) Where the price is based on or is to be adjusted according to "net landed weights", "delivered weights", "out turn" quantity or quality or the like, unless otherwise agreed the seller must reasonably estimate the price. The payment due on tender of the documents called for by the contract is the amount so estimated, but after final adjustment of the price a settlement must be made with commercial promptness.

(2) An agreement described in subsection (1) or any warranty of quality or condition of the goods on arrival places upon the seller the risk of ordinary deterioration, shrinkage and the like in transportation but has no effect on the place or time of identification to the contract for sale or delivery or on the passing of the risk of loss.

(3) Unless otherwise agreed where the contract provides for payment on or after arrival of the goods the seller must before payment allow such preliminary inspection as is feasible; but if the goods are lost delivery of the documents and payment are due when the goods should have arrived.

§2-322. Delivery "Ex-Ship".

(1) Unless otherwise agreed a term for delivery of goods "ex-ship" (which means from the carrying vessel) or in equivalent language is not restricted to a particular ship and requires delivery from a ship which has reached a place at the named port of destination where goods of the kind are usually discharged.

(2) Under such a term unless otherwise agreed

(a) the seller must discharge all liens arising out of the carriage and furnish the buyer with a direction which puts the carrier under a duty to deliver the goods; and

(b) the risk of loss does not pass to the buyer until the goods leave the ship's tackle or are otherwise properly unloaded.

§2-323. Form of Bill of Lading Required in Overseas Shipment; "Overseas".

(1) Where the contract contemplates overseas shipment and contains a term C.I.F. or C. & F. or F.O.B. vessel, the seller unless otherwise agreed must obtain a negotiable bill of lading stating that the goods have been loaded on board or, in the case of a term C.I.F. or C. & F., received for shipment.

(2) Where in a case within subsection (1) a bill of lading has been issued in a set of parts, unless otherwise agreed if the documents are not to be sent from abroad the buyer may demand tender of the full set; otherwise only one part of the bill of lading need be tendered. Even if the agreement expressly requires a full set

(a) due tender of a single part is acceptable within the provisions of this Article on cure of improper delivery (subsection (1) of Section 2-508); and

(b) even though the full set is demanded, if the documents are sent from abroad the person tendering an incomplete set may nevertheless require payment upon furnishing an indemnity which the buyer in good faith deems adequate.

(3) A shipment by water or by air or a contract contemplating such shipment is "overseas" insofar as by usage of trade or agreement it is subject to the commercial, financing or shipping practices characteristic of international deep water commerce.

§2-324. "No Arrival, No Sale" Term.

Under a term "no arrival, no sale" or terms of like meaning, unless otherwise agreed,

(a) the seller must properly ship conforming goods and if they arrive by any means he must tender them on arrival but he assumes no obligation that the goods will arrive unless he has caused the non-arrival; and

(b) where without fault of the seller the goods are in part lost or have so deteriorated as no longer to conform to the contract or arrive after the contract time, the buyer may proceed as if there had been casualty to identified goods (Section 2-613).

§2-325. "Letter of Credit" Term; "Confirmed Credit".

(1) Failure of the buyer seasonably to furnish an agreed letter of credit is a breach of the contract for sale.

(2) The delivery to seller of a proper letter of credit suspends the buyer's obligation to pay. If the letter of credit is dishonored, the seller may on seasonable notification to the buyer require payment directly from him.

(3) Unless otherwise agreed the term "letter of credit" or "banker's credit" in a contract for sale means an irrevocable credit issued by a financing agency of good repute and, where the shipment is overseas, of good international repute. The term "confirmed credit" means that the credit must also carry the direct obligation of such an agency which does business in the seller's financial market.

§2-326. Sale on Approval and Sale or Return; Consignment Sales and Rights of Creditors.

(1) Unless otherwise agreed, if delivered goods may be returned by the buyer even though they conform to the contract, the transaction is

(a) a "sale on approval" if the goods are delivered primarily for use, and

(b) a "sale or return" if the goods are delivered primarily for resale.

(2) Except as provided in subsection (3), goods held on approval are not subject to the claims of the buyer's creditors until acceptance; goods held on sale or return are subject to such claims while in the buyer's possession.

(3) Where goods are delivered to a person for sale and such person maintains a place of business at which he deals in goods of the kind involved, under a name other than the name of the person making delivery, then with respect to claims of creditors of the person conducting the business the goods are deemed to be on sale or return. The provisions of this subsection are applicable even though an agreement purports to reserve title to the person making delivery until payment or resale or uses such words as "on consignment" or "on memorandum". However, this subsection is not applicable if the person making delivery

(a) complies with an applicable law providing for a consignor's interest or the like to be evidenced by a sign, or

(b) establishes that the person conducting the business is generally known by his creditors to be substantially engaged in selling the goods of others, or

(c) complies with the filing provisions of the Article on Secured Transactions (Article 9).

(4) Any "or return" term of a contract for sale is to be treated as a separate contract for sale within the statute of frauds section of this Article (Section 2-201) and as contradicting the sale aspect of the contract within the provisions of this Article on parol or extrinsic evidence (Section 2-202).

§2-327. Special Incidents of Sale on Approval and Sale or Return.

(1) Under a sale on approval unless otherwise agreed

(a) although the goods are identified to the contract the risk of loss and the title do not pass to the buyer until acceptance; and

(b) use of the goods consistent with the purpose of trial is not acceptance but failure seasonably to notify the seller of election to return the goods is acceptance, and if the goods conform to the contract acceptance of any part is acceptance of the whole; and

(c) after due notification of election to return, the return is at the seller's risk and expense but a merchant buyer must follow any reasonable instructions.

(2) Under a sale or return unless otherwise agreed

(a) the option to return extends to the whole or any commercial unit of the goods while in substantially their original condition, but must be exercised seasonally; and

(b) the return is at the buyer's risk and expense.

§2-328. Sale by Auction.

(1) In a sale by auction if goods are put up in lots each lot is the subject of a separate sale.

(2) A sale by auction is complete when the auctioneer so announces by the fall of the hammer or in other customary manner. Where a bid is made while the hammer is falling in acceptance of a prior bid the auctioneer may in his discretion reopen the bidding or declare the goods sold under the bid on which the hammer was falling.

(3) Such a sale is with reserve unless the goods are in explicit terms put up without reserve. In an auction with reserve the auctioneer may withdraw the goods at any time until he announces completion of the sale. In an auction without reserve, after the auctioneer calls for bids on an article or lot, that article or lot cannot be withdrawn unless no bid is made within a reasonable time. In either case a bidder may retract his bid until the auctioneer's announcement of completion of the sale, but a bidder's retraction does not revive any previous bid.

(4) If the auctioneer knowingly receives a bid on the seller's behalf or the seller makes or procures such a bid, and notice has not been given that liberty for such bidding is reserved, the buyer may at his option avoid the sale or take the goods at the price of the last good faith bid prior to the completion of the sale. This subsection shall not apply to any bid at a forced sale.

Part 4—Title, Creditors and Good Faith Purchasers

§2-401. Passing of Title; Reservation for Security; Limited Application of This Section.

Each provision of this Article with regard to the rights, obligations and remedies of the seller, the buyer, purchasers or other third parties applies irrespective of title to the goods except where the provision refers to such title. Insofar as situations are not covered by the other provisions of this Article and matters concerning title became material the following rules apply:

(1) Title to goods cannot pass under a contract for sale prior to their identification to the contract (Section 2-501), and unless otherwise explicitly agreed the buyer acquires by their identification a special property as limited by this Act. Any retention or reservation by the seller of the title (property) in goods shipped or delivered to the buyer is limited in effect to a reservation of a security interest. Subject to these provisions and to the provisions of the Article on Secured Transactions (Article 9), title to goods passes from the seller to the buyer in any manner and on any conditions explicitly agreed on by the parties.

(2) Unless otherwise explicitly agreed title passes to the buyer at the time and place at which the seller completes his performance with reference to the physical delivery of the goods, despite any reservation of a security interest and even though a document of title is to be delivered at a different time or place; and in particular and despite any reservation of a security interest by the bill of lading

(a) if the contract requires or authorizes the seller to send the goods to the buyer but does not require him to deliver them at destination, title passes to the buyer at the time and place of shipment; but

(b) if the contract requires delivery at destination, title passes on tender there.

(3) Unless otherwise explicitly agreed where delivery is to be made without moving the goods,

(a) if the seller is to deliver a document of title, title passes at the time when and the place where he delivers such documents; or

(b) if the goods are at the time of contracting already identified and no documents are to be delivered, title passes at the time and place of contracting.

(4) A rejection or other refusal by the buyer to receive or retain the goods, whether or not justified, or a justified revocation of acceptance revests title to the goods in the seller. Such revesting occurs by operation of law and is not a "sale".

§2-402. Rights of Seller's Creditors Against Sold Goods.

(1) Except as provided in subsections (2) and (3), rights of unsecured creditors of the seller with respect to goods which have been identified to a contract for sale are subject to the buyer's rights to recover the goods under this Article (Sections 2-502 and 2-716).

(2) A creditor of the seller may treat a sale or an identification of goods to a contract for sale as void if as against him a retention of possession by the seller is fraudulent under any rule of law of the state where the goods are situated, except that retention of possession in good faith and current course of trade by a merchant-seller for a commercially reasonable time after a sale or identification is not fraudulent.

(3) Nothing in this Article shall be deemed to impair the rights of creditors of the seller

(a) under the provisions of the Article on Secured Transactions (Article 9); or

(b) where identification to the contract or delivery is made not in current course of trade but in satisfaction of or as security for a pre-existing claim for money, security or the like and is made under circumstances which under any rule of law of the state where the goods are situated would apart from this Article constitute the transaction a fraudulent transfer or voidable preference.

§2-403. Power to Transfer; Good Faith Purchase of Goods; "Entrusting".

(1) A purchaser of goods acquires all title which his transferor had or had power to transfer except that a purchaser of a limited interest acquires rights only to the extent of the interest purchased. A person with voidable title has power to transfer a good title to a good faith purchaser for value. When goods have been delivered under a transaction of purchase the purchaser has such power even though

(a) the transferor was deceived as to the identity of the purchaser, or

(b) the delivery was in exchange for a check which is later dishonored, or

(c) it was agreed that the transaction was to be a "cash sale", or

(d) the delivery was procured through fraud punishable as larcenous under the criminal law.

(2) Any entrusting of possession of goods to a merchant who deals in goods of that kind gives him power to transfer all rights of the entruster to a buyer in ordinary course of business.

(3) "Entrusting" includes any delivery and any acquiescence in retention of possession regardless of any condition expressed between the parties to the delivery or acquiescence and regardless of whether the procurement of the entrusting or the possessor's disposition of the goods have been such as to be larcenous under the criminal law.

(4) The rights of other purchasers of goods and of lien creditors are governed by the Articles on Secured Transactions (Article 9), Bulk Transfers (Article 6) and Documents of Title (Article 7).

Part 5—Performance

§2-501. Insurable Interest in Goods; Manner of Identification of Goods.

(1) The buyer obtains a special property and an insurable interest in goods by identification of existing goods as goods to which the contract refers even though the goods so identified are nonconforming and he has an option to return or reject them. Such identification can be made at any time and in any manner explicitly agreed to by the parties. In the absence of explicit agreement identification occurs

(a) when the contract is made if it is for the sale of goods already existing and identified;

(b) if the contract is for the sale of future goods other than those described in paragraph (c), when goods are shipped, marked or otherwise designated by the seller as goods to which the contract refers;

(c) when the crops are planted or otherwise become growing crops or the young are conceived if the contract is for the sale of unborn young to be born within twelve months after contracting or for the sale of crops to be harvested within twelve months or the next normal harvest season after contracting whichever is longer.

(2) The seller retains an insurable interest in goods so long as title to or any security interest in the goods remains in him and where the identification is by the seller alone he may until default or insolvency or notification to the buyer that the identification is final substitute other goods for those identified.

(3) Nothing in this section impairs any insurable interest recognized under any other statute or rule of law.

§2-502. Buyer's Right to Goods on Seller's Insolvency.

(1) Subject to subsection (2) and even though the goods have not been shipped a buyer who has paid a part or all of the price of goods in which he has a special property under the provisions of the immediately preceding section may on making and keeping good a tender of any unpaid portion of their price recover them from the seller if the seller becomes insolvent within ten days after receipt of the first installment on their price.

(2) If the identification creating his special property has been made by the buyer he acquires the right to recover the goods only if they conform to the contract for sale.

§2-503. Manner of Seller's Tender of Delivery.

(1) Tender of delivery requires that the seller put and hold conforming goods at the buyer's disposition and give the buyer any notification reasonably necessary to enable him to take delivery. The manner, time and place for tender are determined by the agreement and this Article, and in particular

(a) tender must be at a reasonable hour, and if it is of goods they must be kept available for the period reasonably necessary to enable the buyer to take possession; but

(b) unless otherwise agreed the buyer must furnish facilities reasonably suited to the receipt of the goods.

(2) Where the case is within the next section respecting shipment tender requires that the seller comply with its provisions.

(3) Where the seller is required to deliver at a particular destination tender requires that he comply with subsection (1) and also in any appropriate case tender documents as described in subsections (4) and (5) of this section.

(4) Where goods are in the possession of a bailee and are to be delivered without being moved

(a) tender requires that the seller either tender a negotiable document of title covering such goods or procure acknowledgment by the bailee of the buyer's right to possession of the goods; but

(b) tender to the buyer of a non-negotiable document of title or of a written direction to the bailee to deliver is sufficient tender unless the buyer seasonably objects, and receipt by the bailee of notification of the buyer's rights fixes those rights as against the bailee and all third persons; but risk of loss of the goods and of any failure by the bailee to honor the non-negotiable document of title or to obey the direction remains on the seller until the buyer has had a reasonable time to present the document or direction, and a refusal by the bailee to honor the document or to obey the direction defeats the tender.

(5) Where the contract requires the seller to deliver documents

(a) he must tender all such documents in correct form, except as provided in this Article with respect to bills of lading in a set (subsection (2) of Section 2-323); and

(b) tender through customary banking channels is sufficient and dishonor of a draft accompanying the documents constitutes non-acceptance or rejection.

§2-504. Shipment by Seller.

Where the seller is required or authorized to send the goods to the buyer and the contract does not require him to deliver them at a particular destination, then unless otherwise agreed he must

(a) put the goods in the possession of such a carrier and make such a contract for their transportation as may be reasonable having regard to the nature of the goods and other circumstances of the case; and

(b) obtain and promptly deliver or tender in due form any document necessary to enable the buyer to obtain possession of the goods or otherwise required by the agreement or by usage of trade; and

(c) promptly notify the buyer of the shipment.

Failure to notify the buyer under paragraph (c) or to make a proper contract under paragraph (a) is a ground for rejection only if material delay or loss ensues.

§2-505. Seller's Shipment Under Reservation.

(1) Where the seller has identified goods to the contract by or before shipment:

(a) his procurement of a negotiable bill of lading to his own order or otherwise reserves in him a security interest in the goods. His procurement of the bill to the order of a financing agency or of the buyer indicates in addition only the seller's expectation of transferring that interest to the person named.

(b) a non-negotiable bill of lading to himself or his nominee reserves possession of the goods as security but except in a case of conditional delivery (subsection (2) of Section 2-507) a non-negotiable bill of lading naming the buyer as consignee reserves no security interest even though the seller retains possession of the bill of lading.

(2) When shipment by the seller with reservation of a security interest is in violation of the contract for sale it constitutes an improper contract for transportation within the preceding section but impairs neither the rights given to the buyer by shipment and identification of the goods to the contract nor the seller's powers as a holder of a negotiable document.

§2-506. Rights of Financing Agency.

(1) A financing agency by paying or purchasing for value a draft which relates to a shipment of goods acquires to the extent of the payment or purchase and in addition to its own rights under the draft and any document of title securing it any rights of the shipper in the goods including the right to stop delivery and the shipper's right to have the draft honored by the buyer.

(2) The right to reimbursement of a financing agency which has in good faith honored or purchased the draft under commitment to or authority from the buyer is not impaired by subsequent discovery of defects with reference to any relevant document which was apparently regular on its face.

§2-507. Effect of Seller's Tender; Delivery on Condition.

(1) Tender of delivery is a condition to the buyer's duty to accept the goods and, unless otherwise agreed, to his duty to pay for them. Tender entitles the seller to acceptance of the goods and to payment according to the contract.

(2) Where payment is due and demanded on the delivery to the buyer of goods or documents of title, his right as against the seller to retain or dispose of them is conditional upon his making the payment due.

§2-508. Cure by Seller of Improper Tender or Delivery; Replacement.

(1) Where any tender or delivery by the seller is rejected because nonconforming and the time for performance has not yet expired, the seller may seasonably notify the buyer of his intention to cure and may then within the contract time make a conforming delivery.

(2) Where the buyer rejects a non-conforming tender which the seller had reasonable grounds to believe would be acceptable with or without money allowance the seller may if he seasonably notifies the buyer have a further reasonable time to substitute a conforming tender.

§2-509. Risk of Loss in the Absence of Breach.

(1) Where the contract requires or authorizes the seller to ship the goods by carrier

(a) if it does not require him to deliver them at a particular destination, the risk of loss passes to the buyer when the goods are duly delivered to the carrier even though the shipment is under reservation (Section 2-505); but

(b) if it does require him to deliver them at a particular destination and the goods are there duly tendered while in the possession of the carrier, the risk of loss passes to the buyer when the goods are there duly so tendered as to enable the buyer to take delivery.

(2) Where the goods are held by a bailee to be delivered without being moved, the risk of loss passes to the buyer

(a) on his receipt of a negotiable document of title covering the goods; or

(b) on acknowledgment by the bailee of the buyer's right to possession of the goods; or

(c) after his receipt of a non-negotiable document of title or other written direction to deliver, as provided in subsection (4)(b) of Section 2-503.

(3) In any case not within subsection (1) or (2), the risk of loss passes to the buyer on his receipt of the goods if the seller is a merchant; otherwise, the risk passes to the buyer on tender of delivery.

(4) The provisions of this section are subject to contrary agreement of the parties and to the provisions of this Article on sale on approval (Section 2-327) and on effect of breach on risk of loss (Section 2-510).

§2-510. Effect of Breach on Risk of Loss.

(1) Where a tender or delivery of goods so fails to conform to the contract as to give a right of rejection the risk of their loss remains on the seller until cure or acceptance.

(2) Where the buyer rightfully revokes acceptance he may to the extent of any deficiency in his effective insurance coverage treat the risk of loss as having rested on the seller from the beginning.

(3) Where the buyer as to conforming goods already identified to the contract for sale repudiates or is otherwise in breach before risk of their loss has passed to him, the seller may to the extent of any deficiency in his effective insurance coverage treat the risk of loss as resting on the buyer for a commercially reasonable time.

§2-511. Tender of Payment by Buyer; Payment by Check.

(1) Unless otherwise agreed tender of payment is a condition to the seller's duty to tender and complete any delivery.

(2) Tender of payment is sufficient when made by any means or in any manner current in the ordinary course of business unless the seller demands payment in legal tender and gives any extension of time reasonably necessary to procure it.

(3) Subject to the provisions of this Act on the effect of an instrument on an obligation (Section 3-802), payment by check is conditional and is defeated as between the parties by dishonor of the check on due presentment.

§2-512. Payment by Buyer Before Inspection.

(1) Where the contract requires payment before inspection non-conformity of the goods does not excuse the buyer from so making payment unless

(a) the non-conformity appears without inspection; or

(b) despite tender of the required documents the circumstances would justify injunction against honor under the provisions of this Act (Section 5-114).

(2) Payment pursuant to subsection (1) does not constitute an acceptance of goods or impair the buyer's right to inspect or any of his remedies.

§2-513. Buyer's Right to Inspection of Goods.

(1) Unless otherwise agreed and subject to subsection (3), where goods are tendered or delivered or identified to the contract for sale, the buyer has a right before payment or acceptance to inspect them at any reasonable place and time and in any reasonable manner. When the seller is required or authorized to send the goods to the buyer, the inspection may be after their arrival.

(2) Expenses of inspection must be borne by the buyer but may be recovered from the seller if the goods do not conform and are rejected.

(3) Unless otherwise agreed and subject to the provisions of this Article on C.I.F. contracts (subsection (3) of Section 2-321), the buyer is not entitled to inspect the goods before payment of the price when the contract provides

(a) for delivery "C.O.D." or on other like terms; or

(b) for payment against documents of title, except where such payment is due only after the goods are to become available for inspection.

(4) A place or method of inspection fixed by the parties is presumed to be exclusive but unless otherwise expressly agreed it does not postpone identification or shift the place for delivery or for passing the risk of loss. If compliance becomes impossible, inspection shall be as provided in this section unless the place or method fixed was clearly intended as an indispensable condition failure of which avoids the contract.

§2-514. When Documents Deliverable on Acceptance; When on Payment.

Unless otherwise agreed documents against which a draft is drawn are to be delivered to the drawee on acceptance of the draft if it is payable more than three days after presentment; otherwise, only on payment.

§2-515. Preserving Evidence of Goods in Dispute.

In furtherance of the adjustment of any claim or dispute

(a) either party on reasonable notification to the other and for the purpose of ascertaining the facts and preserving evidence has the right to inspect, test and sample the goods including such of them as may be in the possession or control of the other; and

(b) the parties may agree to a third party inspection or survey to determine the conformity or condition of the goods and may agree that the findings shall be binding upon them in any subsequent litigation or adjustment.

Part 6—Breach, Repudiation and Excuse

§2-601. Buyer's Rights on Improper Delivery.

Subject to the provisions of this Article on breach in installment contracts (Section 2-612) and unless otherwise agreed under the sections on contractual limitations of remedy (Sections 2-718 and 2-719), if the goods or the tender of delivery fail in any respect to conform to the contract, the buyer may

(a) reject the whole; or

(b) accept the whole; or

(c) accept any commercial unit or units and reject the rest.

§2-602. Manner and Effect of Rightful Rejection.

(1) Rejection of goods must be within a reasonable time after their delivery or tender. It is ineffective unless the buyer seasonably notifies the seller.

(2) Subject to the provisions of the two following sections on rejected goods (Sections 2-603 and 2-604),

(a) after rejection any exercise of ownership by the buyer with respect to any commercial unit is wrongful as against the seller; and

(b) if the buyer has before rejection taken physical possession of goods in which he does not have a security interest under the provisions of this Article (subsection (3) of Section 2-711), he is under a duty after

rejection to hold them with reasonable care at the seller's disposition for a time sufficient to permit the seller to remove them; but

(c) the buyer has no further obligations with regard to goods rightfully rejected.

(3) The seller's rights with respect to goods wrongfully rejected are governed by the provisions of this Article on seller's remedies in general (Section 2-703).

§2-603. Merchant Buyer's Duties as to Rightfully Rejected Goods.

(1) Subject to any security interest in the buyer (subsection (3) of Section 2-711), when the seller has no agent or place of business at the market of rejection a merchant buyer is under a duty after rejection of goods in his possession or control to follow any reasonable instructions received from the seller with respect to the goods and in the absence of such instructions to make reasonable efforts to sell them for the seller's account if they are perishable or threaten to decline in value speedily. Instructions are not reasonable if on demand indemnity for expenses is not forthcoming.

(2) When the buyer sells goods under subsection (1), he is entitled to reimbursement from the seller or out of the proceeds for reasonable expenses of caring for and selling them, and if the expenses include no selling commission then to such commission as is usual in the trade or if there is none to a reasonable sum not exceeding ten per cent on the gross proceeds.

(3) In complying with this section the buyer is held only to good faith and good faith conduct hereunder is neither acceptance nor conversion nor the basis of an action for damages.

§2-604. Buyer's Options as to Salvage of Rightfully Rejected Goods.

Subject to the provisions of the immediately preceding section on perishables if the seller gives no instructions within a reasonable time after notification of rejection the buyer may store the rejected goods for the seller's account or reship them to him or resell them for the seller's account with reimbursement as provided in the preceding section. Such action is not acceptance or conversion.

§2-605. Waiver of Buyer's Objections by Failure to Particularize.

(1) The buyer's failure to state in connection with rejection a particular defect which is ascertainable by reasonable inspection precludes him from relying on the unstated defect to justify rejection or to establish breach

(a) where the seller could have cured it if stated seasonably; or

(b) between merchants when the seller has after rejection made a request in writing for a full and final written statement of all defects on which the buyer proposes to rely.

(2) Payment against documents made without reservation of rights precludes recovery of the payment for defects apparent on the face of the documents.

§2-606. What Constitutes Acceptance of Goods.

(1) Acceptance of goods occurs when the buyer

(a) after a reasonable opportunity to inspect the goods signifies to the seller that the goods are conforming or that he will take or retain them in spite of their nonconformity; or

(b) fails to make an effective rejection (subsection (1) of Section 2-602), but such acceptance does not occur until the buyer has had a reasonable opportunity to inspect them; or

(c) does any act inconsistent with the seller's ownership; but if such act is wrongful as against the seller it is an acceptance only if ratified by him.

(2) Acceptance of a part of any commercial unit is acceptance of that entire unit.

§2-607. Effect of Acceptance; Notice of Breach; Burden of Establishing Breach After Acceptance; Notice of Claim or Litigation to Person Answerable Over.

(1) The buyer must pay at the contract rate for any goods accepted.

(2) Acceptance of goods by the buyer precludes rejection of the goods accepted and if made with knowledge of a non-conformity cannot be

revoked because of it unless the acceptance was on the reasonable assumption that the non-conformity would be seasonably cured but acceptance does not of itself impair any other remedy provided by this Article for non-conformity.

(3) Where a tender has been accepted

(a) the buyer must within a reasonable time after he discovers or should have discovered any breach notify the seller of breach or be barred from any remedy; and

(b) if the claim is one for infringement or the like (subsection (3) of Section 2-312) and the buyer is sued as a result of such a breach he must so notify the seller within a reasonable time after he receives notice of the litigation or be barred from any remedy over for liability established by the litigation.

(4) The burden is on the buyer to establish any breach with respect to the goods accepted.

(5) Where the buyer is sued for breach of a warranty or other obligation for which his seller is answerable over

(a) he may give his seller written notice of the litigation. If the notice states that the seller may come in and defend and that if the seller does not do so he will be bound in any action against him by his buyer by any determination of fact common to the two litigations, then unless the seller after seasonable receipt of the notice does come in and defend he is so bound.

(b) if the claim is one for infringement or the like (subsection (3) of Section 2-312) the original seller may demand in writing that his buyer turn over to him control of the litigation including settlement or else be barred from any remedy over and if he also agrees to bear all expense and to satisfy any adverse judgment, then unless the buyer after seasonable receipt of the demand does turn over control the buyer is so barred.

(6) The provisions of subsections (3), (4) and (5) apply to any obligation of a buyer to hold the seller harmless against infringement or the like (subsection (3) of Section 2-312).

§2-608. Revocation of Acceptance in Whole or in Part.

(1) The buyer may revoke his acceptance of a lot or commercial unit whose non-conformity substantially impairs its value to him if he has accepted it

(a) on the reasonable assumption that its non-conformity would be cured and it has not been seasonably cured; or

(b) without discovery of such non-conformity if his acceptance was reasonably induced either by the difficulty of discovery before acceptance or by the seller's assurances.

(2) Revocation of acceptance must occur within a reasonable time after the buyer discovers or should have discovered the ground for it and before any substantial change in condition of the goods which is not caused by their own defects. It is not effective until the buyer notifies the seller of it.

(3) A buyer who so revokes has the same rights and duties with regard to the goods involved as if he had rejected them.

§2-609. Right to Adequate Assurance of Performance.

(1) A contract for sale imposes an obligation on each party that the other's expectation of receiving due performance will not be impaired. When reasonable grounds for insecurity arise with respect to the performance of either party the other may in writing demand adequate assurance of due performance and until he receives such assurance may if commercially reasonable suspend any performance for which he has not already received the agreed return.

(2) Between merchants the reasonableness of grounds for insecurity and the adequacy of any assurance offered shall be determined according to commercial standards.

(3) Acceptance of any improper delivery or payment does not prejudice the aggrieved party's right to demand adequate assurance of future performance.

(4) After receipt of a justified demand failure to provide within a reasonable time not exceeding thirty days such assurance of due performance as is adequate under the circumstances of the particular case is a repudiation of the contract.

§2-610. Anticipatory Repudiation.

When either party repudiates the contract with respect to a performance not yet due the loss of which will substantially impair the value of the contract to the other, the aggrieved party may

(a) for a commercially reasonable time await performance by the repudiating party; or

(b) resort to any remedy for breach (Section 2-703 or Section 2-711), even though he has notified the repudiating party that he would await the latter's performance and has urged retraction; and

(c) in either case suspend his own performance or proceed in accordance with the provisions of this Article on the seller's right to identify goods to the contract notwithstanding breach or to salvage unfinished goods (Section 2-704).

§2-611. Retraction of Anticipatory Repudiation.

(1) Until the repudiating party's next performance is due he can retract his repudiation unless the aggrieved party has since the repudiation cancelled or materially changed his position or otherwise indicated that he considers the repudiation final.

(2) Retraction may be by any method which clearly indicates to the aggrieved party that the repudiating party intends to perform, but must include any assurance justifiably demanded under the provisions of this Article (Section 2-609).

(3) Retraction reinstates the repudiating party's rights under the contract with due excuse and allowance to the aggrieved party for any delay occasioned by the repudiation.

§2-612. "Installment Contract"; Breach.

(1) An "installment contract" is one which requires or authorizes the delivery of goods in separate lots to be separately accepted, even though the contract contains a clause "each delivery is a separate contract" or its equivalent.

(2) The buyer may reject any installment which is non-conforming if the non-conformity substantially impairs the value of that installment and cannot be cured or if the non-conformity is a defect in the required documents; but if the non-conformity does not fall within subsection (3) and the seller gives adequate assurance of its cure the buyer must accept that installment.

(3) Whenever non-conformity or default with respect to one or more installments substantially impairs the value of the whole contract there is a breach of the whole. But the aggrieved party reinstates the contract if he accepts a non-conforming installment without seasonably notifying of cancellation or if he brings an action with respect only to past installments or demands performance as to future installments.

§2-613. Casualty to Identified Goods.

Where the contract requires for its performance goods identified when the contract is made, and the goods suffer casualty without fault of either party before the risk of loss passes to the buyer, or in a proper case under a "no arrival, no sale" term (Section 2-324) then

(a) if the loss is total the contract is avoided; and

(b) if the loss is partial or the goods have so deteriorated as no longer to conform to the contract the buyer may nevertheless demand inspection and at his option either treat the contract as avoided or accept the goods with due allowance from the contract price for the deterioration or the deficiency in quantity but without further right against the seller.

§2-614. Substituted Performance.

(1) Where without fault of either party the agreed berthing, loading, or unloading facilities fail or an agreed type of carrier becomes unavailable or the agreed manner of delivery otherwise becomes commercially

impracticable but a commercially reasonable substitute is available, such substitute performance must be tendered and accepted.

(2) If the agreed means or manner of payment fails because of domestic or foreign governmental regulation, the seller may withhold or stop delivery unless the buyer provides a means or manner of payment which is commercially a substantial equivalent. If delivery has already been taken, payment by the means or in the manner provided by the regulation discharges the buyer's obligation unless the regulation is discriminatory, oppressive or predatory.

§2-615. Excuse by Failure of Presupposed Conditions.

Except so far as a seller may have assumed a greater obligation and subject to the preceding section on substituted performance:

(a) Delay in delivery or non-delivery in whole or in part by a seller who complies with paragraphs (b) and (c) is not a breach of his duty under a contract for sale if performance as agreed has been made impracticable by the occurrence of a contingency the non-occurrence of which was a basic assumption on which the contract was made or by compliance in good faith with any applicable foreign or domestic governmental regulation or order whether or not it later proves to be invalid.

(b) Where the causes mentioned in paragraph (a) affect only a part of the seller's capacity to perform, he must allocate production and deliveries among his customers but may at his option include regular customers not then under contract as well as his own requirements for further manufacture. He may so allocate in any manner which is fair and reasonable.

(c) The seller must notify the buyer seasonably that there will be delay or non-delivery and, when allocation is required under paragraph (b), of the estimated quota thus made available for the buyer.

§2-616. Procedure on Notice Claiming Excuse.

(1) Where the buyer receives notification of a material or indefinite delay or an allocation justified under the preceding section he may by written notification to the seller as to any delivery concerned, and where the prospective deficiency substantially impairs the value of the whole contract under the provisions of this Article relating to breach of installment contracts (Section 2-612), then also as to the whole,

(a) terminate and thereby discharge any unexecuted portion of the contract; or

(b) modify the contract by agreeing to take his available quota in substitution.

(2) If after receipt of such notification from the seller the buyer fails so to modify the contract within a reasonable time not exceeding thirty days the contract lapses with respect to any deliveries affected.

(3) The provisions of this section may not be negated by agreement except in so far as the seller has assumed a greater obligation under the preceding section.

Part 7—Remedies

§2-701. Remedies for Breach of Collateral Contracts Not Impaired.

Remedies for breach of any obligation or promise collateral or ancillary to a contract for sale are not impaired by the provisions of this Article.

§2-702. Seller's Remedies on Discovery of Buyer's Insolvency.

(1) Where the seller discovers the buyer to be insolvent he may refuse delivery except for cash including payment for all goods theretofore delivered under the contract, and stop delivery under this Article (Section 2-705).

(2) Where the seller discovers that the buyer has received goods on credit while insolvent he may reclaim the goods upon demand made within ten days after the receipt, but if misrepresentation of solvency has been made to the particular seller in writing within three months before delivery the ten day limitation does not apply. Except as provided in this subsection the seller may not base a right to reclaim goods on the buyer's fraudulent or innocent misrepresentation of solvency or of intent to pay.

(3) The seller's right to reclaim under subsection (2) is subject to the rights of a buyer in ordinary course or other good faith purchaser under this Article (Section 2-403). Successful reclamation of goods excludes all other remedies with respect to them.

§2-703. Seller's Remedies in General.

Where the buyer wrongfully rejects or revokes acceptance of goods or fails to make a payment due on or before delivery or repudiates with respect to a part or the whole, then with respect to any goods directly affected and, if the breach is of the whole contract (Section 2-612), then also with respect to the whole undelivered balance, the aggrieved seller may

(a) withhold delivery of such goods;

(b) stop delivery by any bailee as hereafter provided (Section 2-705);

(c) proceed under the next section respecting goods still unidentified to the contract;

(d) resell and recover damages as hereafter provided (Section 2-706);

(e) recover damages for non-acceptance (Section 2-708) or in a proper case the price (Section 2-709);

(f) cancel.

§2-704. Seller's Right to Identify Goods to the Contract Notwithstanding Breach or to Salvage Unfinished Goods.

(1) An aggrieved seller under the preceding section may

(a) identify to the contract conforming goods not already identified if at the time he learned of the breach they are in his possession or control;

(b) treat as the subject of resale goods which have demonstrably been intended for the particular contract even though those goods are unfinished.

(2) Where the goods are unfinished an aggrieved seller may in the exercise of reasonable commercial judgment for the purposes of avoiding loss and of effective realization either complete the manufacture and wholly identify the goods to the contract or cease manufacture and resell for scrap or salvage value or proceed in any other reasonable manner.

§2-705. Seller's Stoppage of Delivery in Transit or Otherwise.

(1) The seller may stop delivery of goods in the possession of a carrier or other bailee when he discovers the buyer to be insolvent (Section 2-702) and may stop delivery of carload, truckload, planeload or larger shipments of express or freight when the buyer repudiates or fails to make a payment due before delivery or if for any other reason the seller has a right to withhold or reclaim the goods.

(2) As against such buyer the seller may stop delivery until

(a) receipt of the goods by the buyer; or

(b) acknowledgment to the buyer by any bailee of the goods except a carrier that the bailee holds the goods for the buyer; or

(c) such acknowledgment to the buyer by a carrier by reshipment or as warehouseman; or

(d) negotiation to the buyer of any negotiable document of title covering the goods.

(3) (a) To stop delivery the seller must so notify as to enable the bailee by reasonable diligence to prevent delivery of the goods.

(b) After such notification the bailee must hold and deliver the goods according to the directions of the seller but the seller is liable to the bailee for any ensuing charges or damages.

(c) If a negotiable document of title has been issued for goods the bailee is not obliged to obey a notification to stop until surrender of the document.

(d) A carrier who has issued a non-negotiable bill of lading is not obliged to obey a notification to stop received from a person other than the consignor.

§2-706. Seller's Resale Including Contract for Resale.

(1) Under the conditions stated in Section 2-703 on seller's remedies, the seller may resell the goods concerned or the undelivered balance thereof.

Where the resale is made in good faith and in a commercially reasonable manner the seller may recover the difference between the resale price and the contract price together with any incidental damages allowed under the provisions of this Article (Section 2-710), but less expenses saved in consequence of the buyer's breach.

(2) Except as otherwise provided in subsection (3) or unless otherwise agreed resale may be at public or private sale including sale by way of one or more contracts to sell or of identification to an existing contract of the seller. Sale may be as a unit or in parcels and at any time and place and on any terms but every aspect of the sale including the method, manner, time, place and terms must be commercially reasonable. The resale must be reasonably identified as referring to the broken contract, but it is not necessary that the goods be in existence or that any or all of them have been identified to the contract before the breach.

(3) Where the resale is at private sale the seller must give the buyer reasonable notification of his intention to resell.

(4) Where the resale is at public sale

(a) only identified goods can be sold except where there is a recognized market for a public sale of futures in goods of the kind; and

(b) it must be made at a usual place or market for public sale if one is reasonably available and except in the case of goods which are perishable or threaten to decline in value speedily the seller must give the buyer reasonable notice of the time and place of the resale; and

(c) if the goods are not to be within the view of those attending the sale the notification of sale must state the place where the goods are located and provide for their reasonable inspection by prospective bidders; and

(d) the seller may buy.

(5) A purchaser who buys in good faith at a resale takes the goods free of any rights of the original buyer even though the seller fails to comply with one or more of the requirements of this section.

(6) The seller is not accountable to the buyer for any profit made on any resale. A person in the position of a seller (Section 2-707) or a buyer who has rightfully rejected or justifiably revoked acceptance must account for any excess over the amount of his security interest, as hereinafter defined (subsection (3) of Section 2-711).

§2-707. "Person in the Position of a Seller".

(1) A "person in the position of a seller" includes as against a principal an agent who has paid or become responsible for the price of goods on behalf of his principal or anyone who otherwise holds a security interest or other right in goods similar to that of a seller.

(2) A person in the position of a seller may as provided in this Article withhold or stop delivery (Section 2-705) and resell (Section 2-706) and recover incidental damages (Section 2-710).

§2-708. Seller's Damages for Non-Acceptance or Repudiation.

(1) Subject to subsection (2) and to the provisions of this Article with respect to proof of market price (Section 2-723), the measure of damages for non-acceptance or repudiation by the buyer is the difference between the market price at the time and place for tender and the unpaid contract price together with any incidental damages provided in this Article (Section 2-710), but less expenses saved in consequence of the buyer's breach.

(2) If the measure of damages provided in subsection (1) is inadequate to put the seller in as good a position as performance would have done then the measure of damages is the profit (including reasonable overhead) which the seller would have made from full performance by the buyer, together with any incidental damages provided in this Article (Section 2-710), due allowance for costs reasonably incurred and due credit for payments or proceeds of resale.

§2-709. Action for the Price.

(1) When the buyer fails to pay the price as it becomes due the seller may recover, together with any incidental damages under the next section, the price

(a) of goods accepted or of conforming goods lost or damaged within a commercially reasonable time after risk of their loss has passed to the buyer; and

(b) of goods identified to the contract if the seller is unable after reasonable effort to resell them at a reasonable price or the circumstances reasonably indicate that such effort will be unavailing.

(2) Where the seller sues for the price he must hold for the buyer any goods which have been identified to the contract and are still in his control except that if resale becomes possible he may resell them at any time prior to the collection of the judgment. The net proceeds of any such resale must be credited to the buyer and payment of the judgment entitles him to any goods not resold.

(3) After the buyer has wrongfully rejected or revoked acceptance of the goods or has failed to make a payment due or has repudiated (Section 2-610), a seller who is held not entitled to the price under this section shall nevertheless be awarded damages for non-acceptance under the preceding section.

§2-710. Seller's Incidental Damages.

Incidental damages to an aggrieved seller include any commercially reasonable charges, expenses or commissions incurred in stopping delivery, in the transportation, care and custody of goods after the buyer's breach, in connection with return or resale of the goods or otherwise resulting from the breach.

§2-711. Buyer's Remedies in General; Buyer's Security Interest in Rejected Goods.

(1) Where the seller fails to make delivery or repudiates or the buyer rightfully rejects or justifiably revokes acceptance then with respect to any goods involved, and with respect to the whole if the breach goes to the whole contract (Section 2-612), the buyer may cancel and whether or not he has done so may in addition to recovering so much of the price as has been paid

(a) "cover" and have damages under the next section as to all the goods affected whether or not they have been identified to the contract; or

(b) recover damages for non-delivery as provided in this Article (Section 2-713).

(2) Where the seller fails to deliver or repudiates the buyer may also

(a) if the goods have been identified recover them as provided in this Article (Section 2-502); or

(b) in a proper case obtain specific performance or replevy the goods as provided in this Article (Section 2-716).

(3) On rightful rejection or justifiable revocation of acceptance a buyer has a security interest in goods in his possession or control for any payments made on their price and any expenses reasonably incurred in their inspection, receipt, transportation, care and custody and may hold such goods and resell them in like manner as an aggrieved seller (Section 2-706).

§2-712. "Cover"; Buyer's Procurement of Substitute Goods.

(1) After a breach within the preceding section the buyer may "cover" by making in good faith and without unreasonable delay any reasonable purchase of or contract to purchase goods in substitution for those due from the seller.

(2) The buyer may recover from the seller as damages the difference between the cost of cover and the contract price together with any incidental or consequential damages as hereinafter defined (Section 2-715), but less expenses saved in consequence of the seller's breach.

(3) Failure of the buyer to effect cover within this section does not bar him from any other remedy.

§2-713. Buyer's Damages for Non-Delivery or Repudiation.

(1) Subject to provisions of this Article with respect to the proof of market price (Section 2-723), the measure of damages for non-delivery or repudiation by the seller is the difference between the market price at the time when the buyer learned of the breach and the contract price together with any incidental and consequential damages provided in this Article (Section 2-715), but less expenses saved in consequence of the seller's breach.

(2) Market price is to be determined as of the place for tender or, in cases of rejection after arrival or revocation of acceptance, as of the place of arrival.

§2-714. Buyer's Damages for Breach in Regard to Accepted Goods.

(1) Where the buyer has accepted goods and given notification (subsection (3) of Section 2-607) he may recover as damages for any non-conformity of tender the loss resulting in the ordinary course of events from the seller's breach as determined in any manner which is reasonable.

(2) The measure of damages for breach of warranty is the difference at the time and place of acceptance between the value of the goods accepted and the value they would have had if they had been as warranted, unless special circumstances show proximate damages of a different amount.

(3) In a proper case any incidental and consequential damages under the next section may be recovered.

§2-715. Buyer's Incidental and Consequential Damages.

(1) Incidental damages resulting from the seller's breach include expenses reasonably incurred in inspection, receipt, transportation and care and custody of goods rightfully rejected, any commercially reasonable charges, expenses or commissions in connection with effecting cover and any other reasonable expense incident to the delay or other breach.

(2) Consequential damages resulting from the seller's breach include
   (a) any loss resulting from general or particular requirements and needs of which the seller at the time of contracting had reason to know and which could not reasonably be prevented by cover or otherwise; and
   (b) injury to person or property proximately resulting from any breach of warranty.

§2-716. Buyer's Right to Specific Performance or Replevin.

(1) Specific performance may be decreed where the goods are unique or in other proper circumstances.

(2) The decree for specific performance may include such terms and conditions as to payment of the price, damages, or other relief as the court may deem just.

(3) The buyer has a right of replevin for goods identified to the contract if after reasonable effort he is unable to effect cover for such goods or the circumstances reasonably indicate that such effort will be unavailing or if the goods have been shipped under reservation and satisfaction of the security interest in them has been made or tendered.

§2-717. Deduction of Damages From the Price.

The buyer on notifying the seller of his intention to do so may deduct all or any part of the damages resulting from any breach of the contract from any part of the price still due under the same contract.

§2-718. Liquidation or Limitation of Damages; Deposits.

(1) Damages for breach by either party may be liquidated in the agreement but only at an amount which is reasonable in the light of the anticipated or actual harm caused by the breach, the difficulties of proof of loss, and the inconvenience or nonfeasibility of otherwise obtaining an adequate remedy. A term fixing unreasonably large liquidated damages is void as a penalty.

(2) Where the seller justifiably withholds delivery of goods because of the buyer's breach, the buyer is entitled to restitution of any amount by which the sum of his payments exceeds

(a) the amount to which the seller is entitled by virtue of terms liquidating the seller's damages in accordance with subsection (1), or
(b) in the absence of such terms, twenty per cent of the value of the total performance for which the buyer is obligated under the contract or $500, whichever is smaller.

(3) The buyer's right to restitution under subsection (2) is subject to offset to the extent that the seller establishes
   (a) a right to recover damages under the provisions of this Article other than subsection (1), and
   (b) the amount or value of any benefits received by the buyer directly or indirectly by reason of the contract.

(4) Where a seller has received payment in goods their reasonable value or the proceeds of their resale shall be treated as payments for the purposes of subsection (2); but if the seller has notice of the buyer's breach before reselling goods received in part performance, his resale is subject to the conditions laid down in this Article on resale by an aggrieved seller (Section 2-706).

§2-719. Contractual Modification or Limitation of Remedy.

(1) Subject to the provisions of subsection (2) and (3) of this section and of the preceding section on liquidation and limitation of damages,
   (a) the agreement may provide for remedies in addition to or in substitution for those provided in this Article and may limit or alter the measure of damages recoverable under this Article, as by limiting the buyer's remedies to return of the goods and repayment of the price or to repair and replacement of non-conforming goods or parts; and
   (b) resort to a remedy as provided is optional unless the remedy is expressly agreed to be exclusive, in which case it is the sole remedy.

(2) Where circumstances cause an exclusive or limited remedy to fail of its essential purpose, remedy may be had as provided in this Act.

(3) Consequential damages may be limited or excluded unless the limitation or exclusion is unconscionable. Limitation of consequential damages for injury to the person in the case of consumer goods is prima facie unconscionable but limitation of damages where the loss is commercial is not.

§2-720. Effect of "Cancellation" or "Rescission" on Claims for Antecedent Breach.

Unless the contrary intention clearly appears, expressions of "cancellation" or "rescission" of the contract or the like shall not be construed as a renunciation or discharge of any claim in damages for an antecedent breach.

§2-721. Remedies for Fraud.

Remedies for material misrepresentation or fraud include all remedies available under this Article for non-fraudulent breach. Neither rescission or a claim for rescission of the contract for sale nor rejection or return of the goods shall bar or be deemed inconsistent with a claim for damages or other remedy.

§2-722. Who Can Sue Third Parties for Injury to Goods.

Where a third party so deals with goods which have been identified to a contract for sale as to cause actionable injury to a party to that contract
(a) a right of action against the third party is in either party to the contract for sale who has title to or a security interest or a special property or an insurable interest in the goods; and if the goods have been destroyed or converted a right of action is also in the party who either bore the risk of loss under the contract for sale or has since the injury assumed that risk as against the other;
(b) if at the time of the injury the party plaintiff did not bear the risk of loss as against the other party to the contract for sale and there is no arrangement between them for disposition of the recovery, his suit or settlement is subject to his own interest, as a fiduciary for the other party to the contract;

(c) either party may with the consent of the other sue for the benefit of whom it may concern.

§2-723. Proof of Market Price: Time and Place.

(1) If an action based on anticipatory repudiation comes to trial before the time for performance with respect to some or all of the goods, any damages based on market price (Section 2-708 or Section 2-713) shall be determined according to the price of such goods prevailing at the time when the aggrieved party learned of the repudiation.

(2) If evidence of a price prevailing at the times or places described in this Article is not readily available the price prevailing within any reasonable time before or after the time described or at any other place which in commercial judgment or under usage of trade would serve as a reasonable substitute for the one described may be used, making any proper allowance for the cost of transporting the goods to or from such other place.

(3) Evidence of a relevant price prevailing at a time or place other than the one described in this Article offered by one party is not admissible unless and until he has given the other party such notice as the court finds sufficient to prevent unfair surprise.

§2-724. Admissibility of Market Quotations.

Whenever the prevailing price or value of any goods regularly bought and sold in any established commodity market is in issue, reports in official publications or trade journals or in newspapers or periodicals of general circulation published as the reports of such market shall be admissible in evidence. The circumstances of the preparation of such a report may be shown to affect its weight but not its admissibility.

§2-725. Statute of Limitations in Contracts for Sale.

(1) An action for breach of any contract for sale must be commenced within four years after the cause of action has accrued. By the original agreement the parties may reduce the period of limitation to not less than one year but may not extend it.

(2) A cause of action occurs when the breach occurs, regardless of the aggrieved party's lack of knowledge of the breach. A breach of warranty occurs when tender of delivery is made, except that where a warranty explicitly extends to future performance of the goods and discovery of the breach must await the time of such performance the cause of action accrues when the breach is or should have been discovered.

(3) Where an action commenced within the time limited by subsection (1) is so terminated as to leave available a remedy by another action for the same breach such other action may be commenced after the expiration of the time limited and within six months after the termination of the first action unless the termination resulted from voluntary discontinuance or from dismissal for failure or neglect to prosecute.

(4) This section does not alter the law on tolling of the statute of limitations nor does it apply to causes of action which have accrued before this Act becomes effective.

ARTICLE 2A: LEASES

Part 1—General Provisions

§2A-101. Short Title.

This Article shall be known and may be cited as the Uniform Commercial Code—Leases.

§2A-102. Scope.

This Article applies to any transaction, regardless of form, that creates a lease.

§2A-103. Definitions and Index of Definitions.

(1) In this Article unless the context otherwise requires:

(a) "Buyer in ordinary course of business" means a person who in good faith and without knowledge that the sale to him [or her] is in violation of the ownership rights or security interest or leasehold interest of a third party in the goods buys in ordinary course from a person in the business of selling goods of that kind but does not include a pawnbroker. "Buying" may be for cash or by exchange of other property or on secured or unsecured credit and includes receiving goods or documents of title under a pre-existing contract for sale but does not include a transfer in bulk or as security for or in total or partial satisfaction of a money debt.

(b) "Cancellation" occurs when either party puts an end to the lease contract for default by the other party.

(c) "Commercial unit" means such a unit of goods as by commercial usage is a single whole for purposes of lease and division of which materially impairs its character or value on the market or in use. A commercial unit may be a single article, as a machine, or a set of articles, as a suite of furniture or a line of machinery, or a quantity, as a gross or carload, or any other unit treated in use or in the relevant market as a single whole.

(d) "Conforming" goods or performance under a lease contract means goods or performance that are in accordance with the obligations under the lease contract.

(e) "Consumer lease" means a lease that a lessor regularly engaged in the business of leasing or selling makes to a lessee who is an individual and who takes under the lease primarily for a personal, family, or household purpose [, if the total payments to be made under the lease contract, excluding payments for options to renew or buy, do not exceed $_____].

(f) "Fault" means wrongful act, omission, breach, or default.

(g) "Finance lease" means a lease with respect to which:

(i) the lessor does not select, manufacture, or supply the goods;

(ii) the lessor acquires the goods or the right to possession and use of the goods in connection with the lease; and

(iii) one of the following occurs:

(A) the lessee receives a copy of the contract by which the lessor acquired the goods or the right to possession and use of the goods before signing the lease contract;

(B) the lessee's approval of the contract by which the lessor acquired the goods or the right to possession and use of the goods is a condition to effectiveness of the lease contract;

(C) the lessee, before signing the lease contract, receives an accurate and complete statement designating the promises and warranties, and any disclaimers of warranties, limitations or modifications of remedies, or liquidated damages, including those of a third party, such as the manufacturer of the goods, provided to the lessor by the person supplying the goods in connection with or as part of the contract by which the lessor acquired the goods or the right to possession and use of the goods; or

(D) if the lease is not a consumer lease, the lessor, before the lessee signs the lease contract, informs the lessee in writing (a) of the identity of the person supplying the goods to the lessor, unless the lessee has selected that person and directed the lessor to acquire the goods or the right to possession and use of the goods from that person, (b) that the lessee is entitled under this Article to the promises and warranties, including those of any third party, provided to the lessor by the person supplying the goods in connection with or as part of the contract by which the lessor acquired the goods or the right to possession and use of the goods, and (c) that the lessee may communicate with the person supplying the goods to the lessor and receive an accurate and complete statement of those promises and warranties, including any disclaimers and limitations of them or of remedies.

(h) "Goods" means all things that are movable at the time of identification to the lease contract, or are fixtures (Section 2A-309), but the term does not include money, documents, instruments, accounts, chattel paper, general intangibles, or minerals or the like, including oil and gas, before extraction. The term also includes the unborn young of animals.

(i) "Installment lease contract" means a lease contract that authorizes or requires the delivery of goods in separate lots to be separately accepted, even though the lease contract contains a clause "each delivery is a separate lease" or its equivalent.

(j) "Lease" means a transfer of the right to possession and use of goods for a term in return for consideration, but a sale, including a sale on approval or a sale or return, or retention or creation of a security interest is not a lease. Unless the context clearly indicates otherwise, the term includes a sublease.

(k) "Lease agreement" means the bargain, with respect to the lease, of the lessor and the lessee in fact as found in their language or by implication from other circumstances including course of dealing or usage of trade or course of performance as provided in this Article. Unless the context clearly indicates otherwise, the term includes a sublease agreement.

(l) "Lease contract" means the total legal obligation that results from the lease agreement as affected by this Article and any other applicable rules of law. Unless the context clearly indicates otherwise, the term includes a sublease contract.

(m) "Leasehold interest" means the interest of the lessor or the lessee under a lease contract.

(n) "Lessee" means a person who acquires the right to possession and use of goods under a lease. Unless the context clearly indicates otherwise, the term includes a sublessee.

(o) "Lessee in ordinary course of business" means a person who in good faith and without knowledge that the lease to him [or her] is in violation of the ownership rights or security interest or leasehold interest of a third party in the goods, leases in ordinary course from a person in the business of selling or leasing goods of that kind but does not include a pawnbroker. "Leasing" may be for cash or by exchange of other property or on secured or unsecured credit and includes receiving goods or documents of title under a pre-existing lease contract but does not include a transfer in bulk or as security for or in total or partial satisfaction of a money debt.

(p) "Lessor" means a person who transfers the right to possession and use of goods under a lease. Unless the context clearly indicates otherwise, the term includes a sublessor.

(q) "Lessor's residual interest" means the lessor's interest in the goods after expiration, termination, or cancellation of the lease contract.

(r) "Lien" means a charge against or interest in goods to secure payment of a debt or performance of an obligation, but the term does not include a security interest.

(s) "Lot" means a parcel or a single article that is the subject matter of a separate lease or delivery, whether or not it is sufficient to perform the lease contract.

(t) "Merchant lessee" means a lessee that is a merchant with respect to goods of the kind subject to the lease.

(u) "Present value" means the amount as of a date certain of one or more sums payable in the future, discounted to the date certain. The discount is determined by the interest rate specified by the parties if the rate was not manifestly unreasonable at the time the transaction was entered into; otherwise, the discount is determined by a commercially reasonable rate that takes into account the facts and circumstances of each case at the time the transaction was entered into.

(v) "Purchase" includes taking by sale, lease, mortgage, security interest, pledge, gift, or any other voluntary transaction creating an interest in goods.

(w) "Sublease" means a lease of goods the right to possession and use of which was acquired by the lessor as a lessee under an existing lease.

(x) "Supplier" means a person from whom a lessor buys or leases goods to be leased under a finance lease.

(y) "Supply contract" means a contract under which a lessor buys or leases goods to be leased.

(z) "Termination" occurs when either party pursuant to a power created by agreement or law puts an end to the lease contract otherwise than for default.

(2) Other definitions applying to this Article and the sections in which they appear are:

"Accessions". Section 2A-310(1).
"Construction mortgage". Section 2A-309(1)(d).
"Encumbrance". Section 2A-309(1)(e).
"Fixtures". Section 2A-309(1)(a).
"Fixture filing". Section 2A-309(1)(b).
"Purchase money lease". Section 2A-309(1)(c).

(3) The following definitions in other Articles apply to this Article:

"Account". Section 9-106.
"Between merchants". Section 2-104(3).
"Buyer". Section 2-103(1)(a).
"Chattel paper". Section 9-105(1)(b).
"Consumer goods". Section 9-109(1).
"Document". Section 9-105(1)(f).
"Entrusting". Section 2-403(3).
"General intangibles". Section 9-106.
"Good faith". Section 2-103(1)(b).
"Instrument". Section 9-105(1)(i).
"Merchant". Section 2-104(1).
"Mortgage". Section 9-105(1)(j).
"Pursuant to commitment". Section 9-105(1)(k).
"Receipt". Section 2-103(1)(c).
"Sale". Section 2-106(1).
"Sale on approval". Section 2-326.
"Sale or return". Section 2-326.
"Seller". Section 2-103(1)(d).

(4) In addition Article 1 contains general definitions and principles of construction and interpretation applicable throughout this Article.

As amended in 1990.

§2A-104. Leases Subject to Other Law.

(1) A lease, although subject to this Article, is also subject to any applicable:

(a) certificate of title statute of this State: (list any certificate of title statutes covering automobiles, trailers, mobile homes, boats, farm tractors, and the like);

(b) certificate of title statute of another jurisdiction (Section 2A-105); or

(c) consumer protection statute of this State, or final consumer protection decision of a court of this State existing on the effective date of this Article.

(2) In case of conflict between this Article, other than Sections 2A-105, 2A-304(3), and 2A-305(3), and a statute or decision referred to in subsection (1), the statute or decision controls.

(3) Failure to comply with an applicable law has only the effect specified therein.

As amended in 1990.

§2A-108. Unconscionability.

(1) If the court as a matter of law finds a lease contract or any clause of a lease contract to have been unconscionable at the time it was made the court may refuse to enforce the lease contract, or it may enforce the remainder of the lease contract without the unconscionable clause, or it may so limit the application of any unconscionable clause as to avoid any unconscionable result.

(2) With respect to a consumer lease, if the court as a matter of law finds that a lease contract or any clause of a lease contract has been induced by unconscionable conduct or that unconscionable conduct has occurred in the collection of a claim arising from a lease contract, the court may grant appropriate relief.

(3) Before making a finding of unconscionability under subsection (1) or (2), the court, on its own motion or that of a party, shall afford the parties a reasonable opportunity to present evidence as to the setting, purpose, and effect of the lease contract or clause thereof, or of the conduct.

(4) In an action in which the lessee claims unconscionability with respect to a consumer lease:

(a) If the court finds unconscionability under subsection (1) or (2), the court shall award reasonable attorney's fees to the lessee.

(b) If the court does not find unconscionability and the lessee claiming unconscionability has brought or maintained an action he [or she] knew to be groundless, the court shall award reasonable attorney's fees to the party against whom the claim is made.

(c) In determining attorney's fees, the amount of the recovery on behalf of the claimant under subsections (1) and (2) is not controlling.

Part 2—Formation and Construction of Lease Contract

§2A-201. Statute of Frauds.

(1) A lease contract is not enforceable by way of action or defense unless:

(a) the total payments to be made under the lease contract, excluding payments for options to renew or buy, are less than $1,000; or

(b) there is a writing, signed by the party against whom enforcement is sought or by that party's authorized agent, sufficient to indicate that a lease contract has been made between the parties and to describe the goods leased and the lease term.

(2) Any description of leased goods or of the lease term is sufficient and satisfies subsection (1)(b), whether or not it is specific, if it reasonably identifies what is described.

(3) A writing is not insufficient because it omits or incorrectly states a term agreed upon, but the lease contract is not enforceable under subsection (1)(b) beyond the lease term and the quantity of goods shown in the writing.

(4) A lease contract that does not satisfy the requirements of subsection (1), but which is valid in other respects, is enforceable:

(a) if the goods are to be specially manufactured or obtained for the lessee and are not suitable for lease or sale to others in the ordinary course of the lessor's business, and the lessor, before notice of repudiation is received and under circumstances that reasonably indicate that the goods are for the lessee, has made either a substantial beginning of their manufacture or commitments for their procurement;

(b) if the party against whom enforcement is sought admits in that party's pleading, testimony or otherwise in court that a lease contract was made, but the lease contract is not enforceable under this provision beyond the quantity of goods admitted; or

(c) with respect to goods that have been received and accepted by the lessee.

(5) The lease term under a lease contract referred to in subsection (4) is:

(a) if there is a writing signed by the party against whom enforcement is sought or by that party's authorized agent specifying the lease term, the term so specified;

(b) if the party against whom enforcement is sought admits in that party's pleading, testimony, or otherwise in court a lease term, the term so admitted; or

(c) a reasonable lease term.

§2A-202. Final Written Expression: Parol or Extrinsic Evidence.

Terms with respect to which the confirmatory memoranda of the parties agree or which are otherwise set forth in a writing intended by the parties as a final expression of their agreement with respect to such terms as are included therein may not be contradicted by evidence of any prior agreement or of a contemporaneous oral agreement but may be explained or supplemented:

(a) by course of dealing or usage of trade or by course of performance; and

(b) by evidence of consistent additional terms unless the court finds the writing to have been intended also as a complete and exclusive statement of the terms of the agreement.

§2A-204. Formation in General.

(1) A lease contract may be made in any manner sufficient to show agreement, including conduct by both parties which recognizes the existence of a lease contract.

(2) An agreement sufficient to constitute a lease contract may be found although the moment of its making is undetermined.

(3) Although one or more terms are left open, a lease contract does not fail for indefiniteness if the parties have intended to make a lease contract and there is a reasonably certain basis for giving an appropriate remedy.

§2A-205. Firm Offers.

An offer by a merchant to lease goods to or from another person in a signed writing that by its terms gives assurance it will be held open is not revocable, for lack of consideration, during the time stated or, if no time is stated, for a reasonable time, but in no event may the period of irrevocability exceed 3 months. Any such term of assurance on a form supplied by the offeree must be separately signed by the offeror.

§2A-206. Offer and Acceptance in Formation of Lease Contract.

(1) Unless otherwise unambiguously indicated by the language or circumstances, an offer to make a lease contract must be construed as inviting acceptance in any manner and by any medium reasonable in the circumstances.

(2) If the beginning of a requested performance is a reasonable mode of acceptance, an offeror who is not notified of acceptance within a reasonable time may treat the offer as having lapsed before acceptance.

§2A-207. Course of Performance or Practical Construction.

(1) If a lease contract involves repeated occasions for performance by either party with knowledge of the nature of the performance and opportunity for objection to it by the other, any course of performance accepted or acquiesced in without objection is relevant to determine the meaning of the lease agreement.

(2) The express terms of a lease agreement and any course of performance, as well as any course of dealing and usage of trade, must be construed whenever reasonable as consistent with each other; but if that construction is unreasonable, express terms control course of performance, course of performance controls both course of dealing and usage of trade, and course of dealing controls usage of trade.

(3) Subject to the provisions of Section 2A-208 on modification and waiver, course of performance is relevant to show a waiver or modification of any term inconsistent with the course of performance.

§2A-208. Modification, Rescission and Waiver.

(1) An agreement modifying a lease contract needs no consideration to be binding.

(2) A signed lease agreement that excludes modification or rescission except by a signed writing may not be otherwise modified or rescinded, but, except as between merchants, such a requirement on a form supplied by a merchant must be separately signed by the other party.

(3) Although an attempt at modification or rescission does not satisfy the requirements of subsection (2), it may operate as a waiver.

(4) A party who has made a waiver affecting an executory portion of a lease contract may retract the waiver by reasonable notification received by the other party that strict performance will be required of any term waived, unless the retraction would be unjust in view of a material change of position in reliance on the waiver.

§2A-209. Lessee Under Finance Lease as Beneficiary of Supply Contract.

(1) The benefit of a supplier's promises to the lessor under the supply contract and of all warranties, whether express or implied, including those of any third party provided in connection with or as part of the supply contract, extends to the lessee to the extent of the lessee's leasehold interest under a finance lease related to the supply contract, but is subject to the terms of the warranty and of the supply contract and all defenses or claims arising therefrom.

(2) The extension of the benefit of a supplier's promises and of warranties to the lessee (Section 2A-209(1)) does not: (i) modify the rights and obligations of the parties to the supply contract, whether arising therefrom or otherwise, or (ii) impose any duty or liability under the supply contract on the lessee.

(3) Any modification or rescission of the supply contract by the supplier and the lessor is effective between the supplier and the lessee unless, before the modification or rescission, the supplier has received notice that the lessee has entered into a finance lease related to the supply contract. If the modification or rescission is effective between the supplier and the lessee, the lessor is deemed to have assumed, in addition to the obligations of the lessor to the lessee under the lease contract, promises of the supplier to the lessor and warranties that were so modified or rescinded as they existed and were available to the lessee before modification or rescission.

(4) In addition to the extension of the benefit of the supplier's promises and of warranties to the lessee under subsection (1), the lessee retains all rights that the lessee may have against the supplier which arise from an agreement between the lessee and the supplier or under other law.

As amended in 1990.

§2A-210. Express Warranties.

(1) Express warranties by the lessor are created as follows:

(a) Any affirmation of fact or promise made by the lessor to the lessee which relates to the goods and becomes part of the basis of the bargain creates an express warranty that the goods will conform to the affirmation or promise.

(b) Any description of the goods which is made part of the basis of the bargain creates an express warranty that the goods will conform to the description.

(c) Any sample or model that is made part of the basis of the bargain creates an express warranty that the whole of the goods will conform to the sample or model.

(2) It is not necessary to the creation of an express warranty that the lessor use formal words, such as "warrant" or "guarantee," or that the lessor have a specific intention to make a warranty, but an affirmation merely of the value of the goods or a statement purporting to be merely the lessor's opinion or commendation of the goods does not create a warranty.

§2A-211. Warranties Against Interference and Against Infringement; Lessee's Obligation Against Infringement.

(1) There is in a lease contract a warranty that for the lease term no person holds a claim to or interest in the goods that arose from an act or omission of the lessor, other than a claim by way of infringement or the like, which will interfere with the lessee's enjoyment of its leasehold interest.

(2) Except in a finance lease there is in a lease contract by a lessor who is a merchant regularly dealing in goods of the kind a warranty that the goods are delivered free of the rightful claim of any person by way of infringement or the like.

(3) A lessee who furnishes specifications to a lessor or a supplier shall hold the lessor and the supplier harmless against any claim by way of infringement or the like that arises out of compliance with the specifications.

§2A-212. Implied Warranty of Merchantability.

(1) Except in a finance lease, a warranty that the goods will be merchantable is implied in a lease contract if the lessor is a merchant with respect to goods of that kind.

(2) Goods to be merchantable must be at least such as

(a) pass without objection in the trade under the description in the lease agreement;

(b) in the case of fungible goods, are of fair average quality within the description;

(c) are fit for the ordinary purposes for which goods of that type are used;

(d) run, within the variation permitted by the lease agreement, of even kind, quality, and quantity within each unit and among all units involved;

(e) are adequately contained, packaged, and labeled as the lease agreement may require; and

(f) conform to any promises or affirmations of fact made on the container or label.

(3) Other implied warranties may arise from course of dealing or usage of trade.

§2A-213. Implied Warranty of Fitness for Particular Purpose.

Except in a finance lease, if the lessor at the time the lease contract is made has reason to know of any particular purpose for which the goods are required and that the lessee is relying on the lessor's skill or judgment to select or furnish suitable goods, there is in the lease contract an implied warranty that the goods will be fit for that purpose.

§2A-214. Exclusion or Modification of Warranties.

(1) Words or conduct relevant to the creation of an express warranty and words or conduct tending to negate or limit a warranty must be construed wherever reasonable as consistent with each other; but, subject to the provisions of Section 2A-202 on parol or extrinsic evidence, negation or limitation is inoperative to the extent that the construction is unreasonable.

(2) Subject to subsection (3), to exclude or modify the implied warranty of merchantability or any part of it the language must mention "merchantability", be by a writing, and be conspicuous. Subject to subsection (3), to exclude or modify any implied warranty of fitness the exclusion must be by a writing and be conspicuous. Language to exclude all implied warranties of fitness is sufficient if it is in writing, is conspicuous and states, for example, "There is no warranty that the goods will be fit for a particular purpose".

(3) Notwithstanding subsection (2), but subject to subsection (4),

(a) unless the circumstances indicate otherwise, all implied warranties are excluded by expressions like "as is," or "with all faults," or by other language that in common understanding calls the lessee's attention to the exclusion of warranties and makes plain that there is no implied warranty, if in writing and conspicuous;

(b) if the lessee before entering into the lease contract has examined the goods or the sample or model as fully as desired or has refused to examine the goods, there is no implied warranty with regard to defects that an examination ought in the circumstances to have revealed; and

(c) an implied warranty may also be excluded or modified by course of dealing, course of performance, or usage of trade.

(4) To exclude or modify a warranty against interference or against infringement (Section 2A-211) or any part of it, the language must be specific, be by a writing, and be conspicuous, unless the circumstances, including course of performance, course of dealing, or usage of trade, give the lessee reason to know that the goods are being leased subject to a claim or interest of any person.

§2A-215. Cumulation and Conflict of Warranties Express or Implied.

Warranties, whether express or implied, must be construed as consistent with each other and as cumulative, but if that construction is unreasonable, the intention of the parties determines which warranty is dominant. In ascertaining that intention the following rules apply:

(a) Exact or technical specifications displace an inconsistent sample or model or general language of description.

(b) A sample from an existing bulk displaces inconsistent general language of description.

(c) Express warranties displace inconsistent implied warranties other than an implied warranty of fitness for a particular purpose.

§2A-216. Third-Party Beneficiaries of Express and Implied Warranties.

Alternative A A warranty to or for the benefit of a lessee under this Article, whether express or implied, extends to any natural person who is in the family or household of the lessee or who is a guest in the lessee's home if it is reasonable to expect that such person may use, consume, or be affected by the goods and who is injured in person by breach of the warranty. This section does not displace principles of law and equity that extend a warranty to or for the benefit of a lessee to other persons. The operation of this section may not be excluded, modified, or limited, but an exclusion, modification, or limitation of the warranty, including any with respect to rights and remedies, effective against the lessee is also effective against any beneficiary designated under this section.

Alternative B A warranty to or for the benefit of a lessee under this Article, whether express or implied, extends to any natural person who may reasonably be expected to use, consume, or be affected by the goods and who is injured in person by breach of the warranty. This section does not displace principles of law and equity that extend a warranty to or for the benefit of a lessee to other persons. The operation of this section may not be excluded, modified, or limited, but an exclusion, modification, or limitation of the warranty, including any with respect to rights and remedies, effective against the lessee is also effective against the beneficiary designated under this section.

Alternative C A warranty to or for the benefit of a lessee under this Article, whether express or implied, extends to any person who may reasonably be expected to use, consume, or be affected by the goods and who is injured by breach of the warranty. The operation of this section may not be excluded, modified, or limited with respect to injury to the person of an individual to whom the warranty extends, but an exclusion, modification, or limitation of the warranty, including any with respect to rights and remedies, effective against the lessee is also effective against the beneficiary designated under this section.

§2A-219. Risk of Loss.

(1) Except in the case of a finance lease, risk of loss is retained by the lessor and does not pass to the lessee. In the case of a finance lease, risk of loss passes to the lessee.

(2) Subject to the provisions of this Article on the effect of default on risk of loss (Section 2A-220), if risk of loss is to pass to the lessee and the time of passage is not stated, the following rules apply:

(a) If the lease contract requires or authorizes the goods to be shipped by carrier

(i) and it does not require delivery at a particular destination, the risk of loss passes to the lessee when the goods are duly delivered to the carrier; but

(ii) if it does require delivery at a particular destination and the goods are there duly tendered while in the possession of the carrier, the risk of loss passes to the lessee when the goods are there duly so tendered as to enable the lessee to take delivery.

(b) If the goods are held by a bailee to be delivered without being moved, the risk of loss passes to the lessee on acknowledgment by the bailee of the lessee's right to possession of the goods.

(c) In any case not within subsection (a) or (b), the risk of loss passes to the lessee on the lessee's receipt of the goods if the lessor, or, in the case of a finance lease, the supplier, is a merchant; otherwise the risk passes to the lessee on tender of delivery.

Part 3—Effect of Lease Contract

§2A-302. Title to and Possession of Goods.

Except as otherwise provided in this Article, each provision of this Article applies whether the lessor or a third party has title to the goods, and whether the lessor, the lessee, or a third party has possession of the goods, notwithstanding any statute or rule of law that possession or the absence of possession is fraudulent.

§2A-303. Alienability of Party's Interest Under Lease Contract or of Lessor's Residual Interest in Goods; Delegation of Performance; Transfer of Rights.

(1) As used in this section, "creation of a security interest" includes the sale of a lease contract that is subject to Article 9, Secured Transactions, by reason of Section 9-102(1)(b).

(2) Except as provided in subsections (3) and (4), a provision in a lease agreement which (i) prohibits the voluntary or involuntary transfer, including a transfer by sale, sublease, creation or enforcement of a security interest, or attachment, levy, or other judicial process, of an interest of a party under the lease contract or of the lessor's residual interest in the goods, or (ii) makes such a transfer an event of default, gives rise to the rights and remedies provided in subsection (5), but a transfer that is prohibited or is an event of default under the lease agreement is otherwise effective.

(3) A provision in a lease agreement which (i) prohibits the creation or enforcement of a security interest in an interest of a party under the lease contract or in the lessor's residual interest in the goods, or (ii) makes such a transfer an event of default, is not enforceable unless, and then only to the extent that, there is an actual transfer by the lessee of the lessee's right of possession or use of the goods in violation of the provision or an actual delegation of a material performance of either party to the lease contract in violation of the provision. Neither the granting nor the enforcement of a security interest in (i) the lessor's interest under the lease contract or (ii) the lessor's residual interest in the goods is a transfer that materially impairs the prospect of obtaining return performance by, materially changes the duty of, or materially increases the burden or risk imposed on, the lessee within the purview of subsection (5) unless, and then only to the extent that, there is an actual delegation of a material performance of the lessor.

(4) A provision in a lease agreement which (i) prohibits a transfer of a right to damages for default with respect to the whole lease contract or of a right to payment arising out of the transferor's due performance of the transferor's entire obligation, or (ii) makes such a transfer an event of default, is not enforceable, and such a transfer is not a transfer that materially impairs the prospect of obtaining return performance by, materially changes the duty of, or materially increases the burden or risk imposed on, the other party to the lease contract within the purview of subsection

(5) Subject to subsections (3) and (4):

(a) if a transfer is made which is made an event of default under a lease agreement, the party to the lease contract not making the transfer, unless that party waives the default or otherwise agrees, has the rights and remedies described in Section 2A-501(2);

(b) if paragraph (a) is not applicable and if a transfer is made that (i) is prohibited under a lease agreement or (ii) materially impairs the prospect of obtaining return performance by, materially changes the duty of, or materially increases the burden or risk imposed on, the other party to the lease contract, unless the party not making the transfer agrees at any time to the transfer in the lease contract or otherwise, then, except as limited by contract, (i) the transferor is liable to the party not making the transfer for damages caused by the transfer to the extent that the damages could not reasonably be prevented by the party not making the transfer and (ii) a court having jurisdiction may grant other appropriate relief, including cancellation of the lease contract or an injunction against the transfer.

(6) A transfer of "the lease" or of "all my rights under the lease", or a transfer in similar general terms, is a transfer of rights and, unless the language or the circumstances, as in a transfer for security, indicate the contrary, the transfer is a delegation of duties by the transferor to the transferee. Acceptance by the transferee constitutes a promise by the transferee to perform those duties. The promise is enforceable by either the transferor or the other party to the lease contract.

(7) Unless otherwise agreed by the lessor and the lessee, a delegation of performance does not relieve the transferor as against the other party of any duty to perform or of any liability for default.

(8) In a consumer lease, to prohibit the transfer of an interest of a party under the lease contract or to make a transfer an event of default, the language must be specific, by a writing, and conspicuous.

As amended in 1990.

§2A-304. Subsequent Lease of Goods by Lessor.

(1) Subject to Section 2A-303, a subsequent lessee from a lessor of goods under an existing lease contract obtains, to the extent of the leasehold interest transferred, the leasehold interest in the goods that the lessor had or had power to transfer, and except as provided in subsection (2) and Section 2A-527(4), takes subject to the existing lease contract. A lessor with voidable title has power to transfer a good leasehold interest to a good faith subsequent lessee for value, but only to the extent set forth in the preceding sentence. If goods have been delivered under a transaction of purchase, the lessor has that power even though:

    (a) the lessor's transferor was deceived as to the identity of the lessor;

    (b) the delivery was in exchange for a check which is later dishonored;

    (c) it was agreed that the transaction was to be a "cash sale"; or

    (d) the delivery was procured through fraud punishable as larcenous under the criminal law.

(2) A subsequent lessee in the ordinary course of business from a lessor who is a merchant dealing in goods of that kind to whom the goods were entrusted by the existing lessee of that lessor before the interest of the subsequent lessee became enforceable against that lessor obtains, to the extent of the leasehold interest transferred, all of that lessor's and the existing lessee's rights to the goods, and takes free of the existing lease contract.

(3) A subsequent lessee from the lessor of goods that are subject to an existing lease contract and are covered by a certificate of title issued under a statute of this State or of another jurisdiction takes no greater rights than those provided both by this section and by the certificate of title statute.

As amended in 1990.

§2A-307. Priority of Liens Arising by Attachment or Levy on, Security Interests in, and Other Claims to Goods.

(1) Except as otherwise provided in Section 2A-306, a creditor of a lessee takes subject to the lease contract.

(2) Except as otherwise provided in subsections (3) and (4) and in Sections 2A-306 and 2A-308, a creditor of a lessor takes subject to the lease contract unless:

    (a) the creditor holds a lien that attached to the goods before the lease contract became enforceable;

    (b) the creditor holds a security interest in the goods and the lessee did not give value and receive delivery of the goods without knowledge of the security interest; or

    (c) the creditor holds a security interest in the goods which was perfected (Section 9-303) before the lease contract became enforceable.

(3) A lessee in the ordinary course of business takes the leasehold interest free of a security interest in the goods created by the lessor even though the security interest is perfected (Section 9-303) and the lessee knows of its existence.

(4) A lessee other than a lessee in the ordinary course of business takes the leasehold interest free of a security interest to the extent that it secures future advances made after the secured party acquires knowledge of the lease or more than 45 days after the lease contract becomes enforceable, whichever first occurs, unless the future advances are made pursuant to a commitment entered into without knowledge of the lease and before the expiration of the 45-day period.

As amended in 1990.

§2A-308. Special Rights of Creditors.

(1) A creditor of a lessor in possession of goods subject to a lease contract may treat the lease contract as void if as against the creditor retention of possession by the lessor is fraudulent under any statute or rule of law, but retention of possession in good faith and current course of trade by the lessor for a commercially reasonable time after the lease contract becomes enforceable is not fraudulent.

(2) Nothing in this Article impairs the rights of creditors of a lessor if the lease contract (a) becomes enforceable, not in current course of trade but in satisfaction of or as security for a pre-existing claim for money, security, or the like, and (b) is made under circumstances which under any statute or rule of law apart from this Article would constitute the transaction a fraudulent transfer or voidable preference.

(3) A creditor of a seller may treat a sale or an identification of goods to a contract for sale as void if as against the creditor retention of possession by the seller is fraudulent under any statute or rule of law, but retention of possession of the goods pursuant to a lease contract entered into by the seller as lessee and the buyer as lessor in connection with the sale or identification of the goods is not fraudulent if the buyer bought for value and in good faith.

Part 4—Performance of Lease Contract: Repudiated, Substituted and Excused

§2A-407. Irrevocable Promises: Finance Leases.

(1) In the case of a finance lease that is not a consumer lease the lessee's promises under the lease contract become irrevocable and independent upon the lessee's acceptance of the goods.

(2) A promise that has become irrevocable and independent under subsection (1):

    (a) is effective and enforceable between the parties, and by or against third parties including assignees of the parties; and

    (b) is not subject to cancellation, termination, modification, repudiation, excuse, or substitution without the consent of the party to whom the promise runs.

(3) This section does not affect the validity under any other law of a covenant in any lease contract making the lessee's promises irrevocable and independent upon the lessee's acceptance of the goods.

As amended in 1990.

Part 5—Default

A. IN GENERAL
§2A-503. Modification or Impairment of Rights and Remedies.

(1) Except as otherwise provided in this Article, the lease agreement may include rights and remedies for default in addition to or in substitution for those provided in this Article and may limit or alter the measure of damages recoverable under this Article.

(2) Resort to a remedy provided under this Article or in the lease agreement is optional unless the remedy is expressly agreed to be exclusive. If circumstances cause an exclusive or limited remedy to fail of its essential purpose, or provision for an exclusive remedy is unconscionable, remedy may be had as provided in this Article.

(3) Consequential damages may be liquidated under Section 2A-504, or may otherwise be limited, altered, or excluded unless the limitation, alteration, or exclusion is unconscionable. Limitation, alteration, or exclusion of consequential damages for injury to the person in the case of consumer goods is prima facie unconscionable but limitation, alteration, or exclusion of damages where the loss is commercial is not prima facie unconscionable.

(4) Rights and remedies on default by the lessor or the lessee with respect to any obligation or promise collateral or ancillary to the lease contract are not impaired by this Article.

As amended in 1990.

§2A-504. Liquidation of Damages.

(1) Damages payable by either party for default, or any other act or omission, including indemnity for loss or diminution of anticipated tax benefits or loss or damage to lessor's residual interest, may be liquidated in the lease agreement but only at an amount or by a formula that is reasonable in light of the then anticipated harm caused by the default or other act or omission.

(2) If the lease agreement provides for liquidation of damages, and such provision does not comply with subsection (1), or such provision is an exclusive or limited remedy that circumstances cause to fail of its essential purpose, remedy may be had as provided in this Article.

(3) If the lessor justifiably withholds or stops delivery of goods because of the lessee's default or insolvency (Section 2A-525 or 2A-526), the lessee is entitled to restitution of any amount by which the sum of his [or her] payments exceeds:

(a) the amount to which the lessor is entitled by virtue of terms liquidating the lessor's damages in accordance with subsection (1); or

(b) in the absence of those terms, 20 percent of the then present value of the total rent the lessee was obligated to pay for the balance of the lease term, or, in the case of a consumer lease, the lesser of such amount or $500.

(4) A lessee's right to restitution under subsection (3) is subject to offset to the extent the lessor establishes:

(a) a right to recover damages under the provisions of this Article other than subsection (1); and

(b) the amount or value of any benefits received by the lessee directly or indirectly by reason of the lease contract.

§2A-507. Proof of Market Rent: Time and Place.

(1) Damages based on market rent (Section 2A-519 or 2A-528) are determined according to the rent for the use of the goods concerned for a lease term identical to the remaining lease term of the original lease agreement and prevailing at the times specified in Sections 2A-519 and 2A-528.

(2) If evidence of rent for the use of the goods concerned for a lease term identical to the remaining lease term of the original lease agreement and prevailing at the times or places described in this Article is not readily available, the rent prevailing within any reasonable time before or after the time described or at any other place or for a different lease term which in commercial judgment or under usage of trade would serve as a reasonable substitute for the one described may be used, making any proper allowance for the difference, including the cost of transporting the goods to or from the other place.

(3) Evidence of a relevant rent prevailing at a time or place or for a lease term other than the one described in this Article offered by one party is not admissible unless and until he [or she] has given the other party notice the court finds sufficient to prevent unfair surprise.

(4) If the prevailing rent or value of any goods regularly leased in any established market is in issue, reports in official publications or trade journals or in newspapers or periodicals of general circulation published as the reports of that market are admissible in evidence. The circumstances of the preparation of the report may be shown to affect its weight but not its admissibility.

As amended in 1990.

B. Default by Lessor
§2A-508. Lessee's Remedies.

(1) If a lessor fails to deliver the goods in conformity to the lease contract (Section 2A-509) or repudiates the lease contract (Section 2A-402), or a lessee rightfully rejects the goods (Section 2A-509) or justifiably revokes acceptance of the goods (Section 2A-517), then with respect to any goods involved, and with respect to all of the goods if under an installment lease contract the value of the whole lease contract is substantially impaired (Section 2A-510), the lessor is in default under the lease contract and the lessee may:

(a) cancel the lease contract (Section 2A-505(1));

(b) recover so much of the rent and security as has been paid and is just under the circumstances;

(c) cover and recover damages as to all goods affected whether or not they have been identified to the lease contract (Sections 2A-518 and 2A-520), or recover damages for nondelivery (Sections 2A-519 and 2A-520);

(d) exercise any other rights or pursue any other remedies provided in the lease contract.

(2) If a lessor fails to deliver the goods in conformity to the lease contract or repudiates the lease contract, the lessee may also:

(a) if the goods have been identified, recover them (Section 2A-522); or

(b) in a proper case, obtain specific performance or replevy the goods (Section 2A-521).

(3) If a lessor is otherwise in default under a lease contract, the lessee may exercise the rights and pursue the remedies provided in the lease contract, which may include a right to cancel the lease, and in Section 2A-519(3).

(4) If a lessor has breached a warranty, whether express or implied, the lessee may recover damages (Section 2A-519(4)).

(5) On rightful rejection or justifiable revocation of acceptance, a lessee has a security interest in goods in the lessee's possession or control for any rent and security that has been paid and any expenses reasonably incurred in their inspection, receipt, transportation, and care and custody and may hold those goods and dispose of them in good faith and in a commercially reasonable manner, subject to Section 2A-527(5).

(6) Subject to the provisions of Section 2A-407, a lessee, on notifying the lessor of the lessee's intention to do so, may deduct all or any part of the damages resulting from any default under the lease contract from any part of the rent still due under the same lease contract.

As amended in 1990.

§2A-509. Lessee's Rights on Improper Delivery; Rightful Rejection.

(1) Subject to the provisions of Section 2A-510 on default in installment lease contracts, if the goods or the tender or delivery fail in any respect to conform to the lease contract, the lessee may reject or accept the goods or accept any commercial unit or units and reject the rest of the goods.

(2) Rejection of goods is ineffective unless it is within a reasonable time after tender or delivery of the goods and the lessee seasonably notifies the lessor.

§2A-510. Installment Lease Contracts: Rejection and Default.

(1) Under an installment lease contract a lessee may reject any delivery that is nonconforming if the nonconformity substantially impairs the value of that delivery and cannot be cured or the nonconformity is a defect in the required documents; but if the nonconformity does not fall within subsection (2) and the lessor or the supplier gives adequate assurance of its cure, the lessee must accept that delivery.

(2) Whenever nonconformity or default with respect to one or more deliveries substantially impairs the value of the installment lease contract as a whole there is a default with respect to the whole. But, the aggrieved party reinstates the installment lease contract as a whole if the aggrieved party accepts a nonconforming delivery without seasonably notifying of cancellation or brings an action with respect only to past deliveries or demands performance as to future deliveries.

§2A-511. Merchant Lessee's Duties as to Rightfully Rejected Goods.

(1) Subject to any security interest of a lessee (Section 2A-508(5)), if a lessor or a supplier has no agent or place of business at the market of

rejection, a merchant lessee, after rejection of goods in his [or her] possession or control, shall follow any reasonable instructions received from the lessor or the supplier with respect to the goods. In the absence of those instructions, a merchant lessee shall make reasonable efforts to sell, lease, or otherwise dispose of the goods for the lessor's account if they threaten to decline in value speedily. Instructions are not reasonable if on demand indemnity for expenses is not forthcoming.

(2) If a merchant lessee (subsection (1)) or any other lessee (Section 2A-512) disposes of goods, he [or she] is entitled to reimbursement either from the lessor or the supplier or out of the proceeds for reasonable expenses of caring for and disposing of the goods and, if the expenses include no disposition commission, to such commission as is usual in the trade, or if there is none, to a reasonable sum not exceeding 10 percent of the gross proceeds.

(3) In complying with this section or Section 2A-512, the lessee is held only to good faith. Good faith conduct hereunder is neither acceptance or conversion nor the basis of an action for damages.

(4) A purchaser who purchases in good faith from a lessee pursuant to this section or Section 2A-512 takes the goods free of any rights of the lessor and the supplier even though the lessee fails to comply with one or more of the requirements of this Article.

§2A-512. Lessee's Duties as to Rightfully Rejected Goods.

(1) Except as otherwise provided with respect to goods that threaten to decline in value speedily (Section 2A-511) and subject to any security interest of a lessee (Section 2A-508(5)):

(a) the lessee, after rejection of goods in the lessee's possession, shall hold them with reasonable care at the lessor's or the supplier's disposition for a reasonable time after the lessee's seasonable notification of rejection;

(b) if the lessor or the supplier gives no instructions within a reasonable time after notification of rejection, the lessee may store the rejected goods for the lessor's or the supplier's account or ship them to the lessor or the supplier or dispose of them for the lessor's or the supplier's account with reimbursement in the manner provided in Section 2A-511; but

(c) the lessee has no further obligations with regard to goods rightfully rejected.

(2) Action by the lessee pursuant to subsection (1) is not acceptance or conversion.

§2A-513. Cure by Lessor of Improper Tender or Delivery; Replacement.

(1) If any tender or delivery by the lessor or the supplier is rejected because nonconforming and the time for performance has not yet expired, the lessor or the supplier may seasonably notify the lessee of the lessor's or the supplier's intention to cure and may then make a conforming delivery within the time provided in the lease contract.

(2) If the lessee rejects a nonconforming tender that the lessor or the supplier had reasonable grounds to believe would be acceptable with or without money allowance, the lessor or the supplier may have a further reasonable time to substitute a conforming tender if he [or she] seasonably notifies the lessee.

§2A-515. Acceptance of Goods.

(1) Acceptance of goods occurs after the lessee has had a reasonable opportunity to inspect the goods and

(a) the lessee signifies or acts with respect to the goods in a manner that signifies to the lessor or the supplier that the goods are conforming or that the lessee will take or retain them in spite of their nonconformity; or

(b) the lessee fails to make an effective rejection of the goods (Section 2A-509(2)).

(2) Acceptance of a part of any commercial unit is acceptance of that entire unit.

§2A-517. Revocation of Acceptance of Goods.

(1) A lessee may revoke acceptance of a lot or commercial unit whose nonconformity substantially impairs its value to the lessee if the lessee has accepted it:

(a) except in the case of a finance lease, on the reasonable assumption that its nonconformity would be cured and it has not been seasonably cured; or

(b) without discovery of the nonconformity if the lessee's acceptance was reasonably induced either by the lessor's assurances or, except in the case of a finance lease, by the difficulty of discovery before acceptance.

(2) Except in the case of a finance lease that is not a consumer lease, a lessee may revoke acceptance of a lot or commercial unit if the lessor defaults under the lease contract and the default substantially impairs the value of that lot or commercial unit to the lessee.

(3) If the lease agreement so provides, the lessee may revoke acceptance of a lot or commercial unit because of other defaults by the lessor.

(4) Revocation of acceptance must occur within a reasonable time after the lessee discovers or should have discovered the ground for it and before any substantial change in condition of the goods which is not caused by the nonconformity. Revocation is not effective until the lessee notifies the lessor.

(5) A lessee who so revokes has the same rights and duties with regard to the goods involved as if the lessee had rejected them.

As amended in 1990.

§2A-518. Cover; Substitute Goods.

(1) After a default by a lessor under the lease contract of the type described in Section 2A-508(1), or, if agreed, after other default by the lessor, the lessee may cover by making any purchase or lease of or contract to purchase or lease goods in substitution for those due from the lessor.

(2) Except as otherwise provided with respect to damages liquidated in the lease agreement (Section 2A-504) or otherwise determined pursuant to agreement of the parties (Sections 1-102(3) and 2A-503), if a lessee's cover is by a lease agreement substantially similar to the original lease agreement and the new lease agreement is made in good faith and in a commercially reasonable manner, the lessee may recover from the lessor as damages (i) the present value, as of the date of the commencement of the term of the new lease agreement, of the rent under the new lease agreement applicable to that period of the new lease term which is comparable to the then remaining term of the original lease agreement minus the present value as of the same date of the total rent for the then remaining lease term of the original lease agreement, and (ii) any incidental or consequential damages, less expenses saved in consequence of the lessor's default.

(3) If a lessee's cover is by lease agreement that for any reason does not qualify for treatment under subsection (2), or is by purchase or otherwise, the lessee may recover from the lessor as if the lessee had elected not to cover and Section 2A-519 governs.

As amended in 1990.

§2A-519. Lessee's Damages for Non-delivery, Repudiation, Default, and Breach of Warranty in Regard to Accepted Goods.

(1) Except as otherwise provided with respect to damages liquidated in the lease agreement (Section 2A-504) or otherwise determined pursuant to agreement of the parties (Sections 1-102(3) and 2A-503), if a lessee elects not to cover or a lessee elects to cover and the cover is by lease agreement that for any reason does not qualify for treatment under Section 2A-518(2), or is by purchase or otherwise, the measure of damages for non-delivery or repudiation by the lessor or for rejection or revocation of acceptance by the lessee is the present value, as of the date of the default, of the then market rent minus the present value as of the same date of the original rent, computed for the remaining lease term of the original lease agreement, together with incidental and consequential damages, less expenses saved in consequence of the lessor's default.

(2) Market rent is to be determined as of the place for tender or, in cases of rejection after arrival or revocation of acceptance, as of the place of arrival.

(3) Except as otherwise agreed, if the lessee has accepted goods and given notification (Section 2A-516(3)), the measure of damages for nonconforming tender or delivery or other default by a lessor is the loss resulting in the ordinary course of events from the lessor's default as determined in any manner that is reasonable together with incidental and consequential damages, less expenses saved in consequence of the lessor's default.

(4) Except as otherwise agreed, the measure of damages for breach of warranty is the present value at the time and place of acceptance of the difference between the value of the use of the goods accepted and the value if they had been as warranted for the lease term, unless special circumstances show proximate damages of a different amount, together with incidental and consequential damages, less expenses saved in consequence of the lessor's default or breach of warranty.

As amended in 1990.

§2A-520. Lessee's Incidental and Consequential Damages.

(1) Incidental damages resulting from a lessor's default include expenses reasonably incurred in inspection, receipt, transportation, and care and custody of goods rightfully rejected or goods the acceptance of which is justifiably revoked, any commercially reasonable charges, expenses or commissions in connection with effecting cover, and any other reasonable expense incident to the default.

(2) Consequential damages resulting from a lessor's default include:

(a) any loss resulting from general or particular requirements and needs of which the lessor at the time of contracting had reason to know and which could not reasonably be prevented by cover or otherwise; and

(b) injury to person or property proximately resulting from any breach of warranty.

§2A-521. Lessee's Right to Specific Performance or Replevin.

(1) Specific performance may be decreed if the goods are unique or in other proper circumstances.

(2) A decree for specific performance may include any terms and conditions as to payment of the rent, damages, or other relief that the court deems just.

(3) A lessee has a right of replevin, detinue, sequestration, claim and delivery, or the like for goods identified to the lease contract if after reasonable effort the lessee is unable to effect cover for those goods or the circumstances reasonably indicate that the effort will be unavailing.

§2A-522. Lessee's Right to Goods on Lessor's Insolvency.

(1) Subject to subsection (2) and even though the goods have not been shipped, a lessee who has paid a part or all of the rent and security for goods identified to a lease contract (Section 2A-217) on making and keeping good a tender of any unpaid portion of the rent and security due under the lease contract may recover the goods identified from the lessor if the lessor becomes insolvent within 10 days after receipt of the first installment of rent and security.

(2) A lessee acquires the right to recover goods identified to a lease contract only if they conform to the lease contract.

C. Default by Lessee
§2A-523. Lessor's Remedies.

(1) If a lessee wrongfully rejects or revokes acceptance of goods or fails to make a payment when due or repudiates with respect to a part or the whole, then, with respect to any goods involved, and with respect to all of the goods if under an installment lease contract the value of the whole lease contract is substantially impaired (Section 2A-510), the lessee is in default under the lease contract and the lessor may:

(a) cancel the lease contract (Section 2A-505(1));

(b) proceed respecting goods not identified to the lease contract (Section 2A-524);

(c) withhold delivery of the goods and take possession of goods previously delivered (Section 2A-525);

(d) stop delivery of the goods by any bailee (Section 2A-526);

(e) dispose of the goods and recover damages (Section 2A-527), or retain the goods and recover damages (Section 2A-528), or in a proper case recover rent (Section 2A-529);

(f) exercise any other rights or pursue any other remedies provided in the lease contract.

(2) If a lessor does not fully exercise a right or obtain a remedy to which the lessor is entitled under subsection (1), the lessor may recover the loss resulting in the ordinary course of events from the lessee's default as determined in any reasonable manner, together with incidental damages, less expenses saved in consequence of the lessee's default.

(3) If a lessee is otherwise in default under a lease contract, the lessor may exercise the rights and pursue the remedies provided in the lease contract, which may include a right to cancel the lease. In addition, unless otherwise provided in the lease contract:

(a) if the default substantially impairs the value of the lease contract to the lessor, the lessor may exercise the rights and pursue the remedies provided in subsections (1) or (2); or

(b) if the default does not substantially impair the value of the lease contract to the lessor, the lessor may recover as provided in subsection (2).

As amended in 1990.

§2A-524. Lessor's Right to Identify Goods to Lease Contract.

(1) After default by the lessee under the lease contract of the type described in Section 2A-523(1) or 2A-523(3)(a) or, if agreed, after other default by the lessee, the lessor may:

(a) identify to the lease contract conforming goods not already identified if at the time the lessor learned of the default they were in the lessor's or the supplier's possession or control; and

(b) dispose of goods (Section 2A-527(1)) that demonstrably have been intended for the particular lease contract even though those goods are unfinished.

(2) If the goods are unfinished, in the exercise of reasonable commercial judgment for the purposes of avoiding loss and of effective realization, an aggrieved lessor or the supplier may either complete manufacture and wholly identify the goods to the lease contract or cease manufacture and lease, sell, or otherwise dispose of the goods for scrap or salvage value or proceed in any other reasonable manner.

As amended in 1990.

§2A-525. Lessor's Right to Possession of Goods.

(1) If a lessor discovers the lessee to be insolvent, the lessor may refuse to deliver the goods.

(2) After a default by the lessee under the lease contract of the type described in Section 2A-523(1) or 2A-523(3)(a) or, if agreed, after other default by the lessee, the lessor has the right to take possession of the goods. If the lease contract so provides, the lessor may require the lessee to assemble the goods and make them available to the lessor at a place to be designated by the lessor which is reasonably convenient to both parties. Without removal, the lessor may render unusable any goods employed in trade or business, and may dispose of goods on the lessee's premises (Section 2A-527).

(3) The lessor may proceed under subsection (2) without judicial process if it can be done without breach of the peace or the lessor may proceed by action.

As amended in 1990.

§2A-526. Lessor's Stoppage of Delivery in Transit or Otherwise.

(1) A lessor may stop delivery of goods in the possession of a carrier or other bailee if the lessor discovers the lessee to be insolvent and may stop delivery of carload, truckload, planeload, or larger shipments of express or freight if the lessee repudiates or fails to make a payment due before delivery, whether for

rent, security or otherwise under the lease contract, or for any other reason the lessor has a right to withhold or take possession of the goods.

(2) In pursuing its remedies under subsection (1), the lessor may stop delivery until

(a) receipt of the goods by the lessee;

(b) acknowledgment to the lessee by any bailee of the goods, except a carrier, that the bailee holds the goods for the lessee; or

(c) such an acknowledgment to the lessee by a carrier via reshipment or as warehouseman.

(3) (a) To stop delivery, a lessor shall so notify as to enable the bailee by reasonable diligence to prevent delivery of the goods.

(b) After notification, the bailee shall hold and deliver the goods according to the directions of the lessor, but the lessor is liable to the bailee for any ensuing charges or damages.

(c) A carrier who has issued a nonnegotiable bill of lading is not obliged to obey a notification to stop received from a person other than the consignor.

§2A-527. Lessor's Rights to Dispose of Goods.

(1) After a default by a lessee under the lease contract of the type described in Section 2A-523(1) or 2A-523(3)(a) or after the lessor refuses to deliver or takes possession of goods (Section 2A-525 or 2A-526), or, if agreed, after other default by a lessee, the lessor may dispose of the goods concerned or the undelivered balance thereof by lease, sale, or otherwise.

(2) Except as otherwise provided with respect to damages liquidated in the lease agreement (Section 2A-504) or otherwise determined pursuant to agreement of the parties (Sections 1-102(3) and 2A-503), if the disposition is by lease agreement substantially similar to the original lease agreement and the new lease agreement is made in good faith and in a commercially reasonable manner, the lessor may recover from the lessee as damages (i) accrued and unpaid rent as of the date of the commencement of the term of the new lease agreement, (ii) the present value, as of the same date, of the total rent for the then remaining lease term of the original lease agreement minus the present value, as of the same date, of the rent under the new lease agreement applicable to that period of the new lease term which is comparable to the then remaining term of the original lease agreement, and (iii) any incidental damages allowed under Section 2A-530, less expenses saved in consequence of the lessee's default.

(3) If the lessor's disposition is by lease agreement that for any reason does not qualify for treatment under subsection (2), or is by sale or otherwise, the lessor may recover from the lessee as if the lessor had elected not to dispose of the goods and Section 2A-528 governs.

(4) A subsequent buyer or lessee who buys or leases from the lessor in good faith for value as a result of a disposition under this section takes the goods free of the original lease contract and any rights of the original lessee even though the lessor fails to comply with one or more of the requirements of this Article.

(5) The lessor is not accountable to the lessee for any profit made on any disposition. A lessee who has rightfully rejected or justifiably revoked acceptance shall account to the lessor for any excess over the amount of the lessee's security interest (Section 2A-508(5)).

As amended in 1990.

§2A-528. Lessor's Damages for Non-acceptance, Failure to Pay, Repudiation, or Other Default.

(1) Except as otherwise provided with respect to damages liquidated in the lease agreement (Section 2A-504) or otherwise determined pursuant to agreement of the parties (Sections 1-102(3) and 2A-503), if a lessor elects to retain the goods or a lessor elects to dispose of the goods and the disposition is by lease agreement that for any reason does not qualify for treatment under Section 2A-527(2), or is by sale or otherwise, the lessor may recover from the lessee as damages for a default of the type described in Section 2A-523(1) or 2A-523(3)(a), or, if agreed, for other default of the

lessee, (i) accrued and unpaid rent as of the date of default if the lessee has never taken possession of the goods, or, if the lessee has taken possession of the goods, as of the date the lessor repossesses the goods or an earlier date on which the lessee makes a tender of the goods to the lessor, (ii) the present value as of the date determined under clause (i) of the total rent for the then remaining lease term of the original lease agreement minus the present value as of the same date of the market rent at the place where the goods are located computed for the same lease term, and (iii) any incidental damages allowed under Section 2A-530, less expenses saved in consequence of the lessee's default.

(2) If the measure of damages provided in subsection (1) is inadequate to put a lessor in as good a position as performance would have, the measure of damages is the present value of the profit, including reasonable overhead, the lessor would have made from full performance by the lessee, together with any incidental damages allowed under Section 2A-530, due allowance for costs reasonably incurred and due credit for payments or proceeds of disposition.

As amended in 1990.

§2A-529. Lessor's Action for the Rent.

(1) After default by the lessee under the lease contract of the type described in Section 2A-523(1) or 2A-523(3)(a) or, if agreed, after other default by the lessee, if the lessor complies with subsection (2), the lessor may recover from the lessee as damages:

(a) for goods accepted by the lessee and not repossessed by or tendered to the lessor, and for conforming goods lost or damaged within a commercially reasonable time after risk of loss passes to the lessee (Section 2A-219), (i) accrued and unpaid rent as of the date of entry of judgment in favor of the lessor, (ii) the present value as of the same date of the rent for the then remaining lease term of the lease agreement, and (iii) any incidental damages allowed under Section 2A-530, less expenses saved in consequence of the lessee's default; and

(b) for goods identified to the lease contract if the lessor is unable after reasonable effort to dispose of them at a reasonable price or the circumstances reasonably indicate that effort will be unavailing, (i) accrued and unpaid rent as of the date of entry of judgment in favor of the lessor, (ii) the present value as of the same date of the rent for the then remaining lease term of the lease agreement, and (iii) any incidental damages allowed under Section 2A-530, less expenses saved in consequence of the lessee's default.

(2) Except as provided in subsection (3), the lessor shall hold for the lessee for the remaining lease term of the lease agreement any goods that have been identified to the lease contract and are in the lessor's control.

(3) The lessor may dispose of the goods at any time before collection of the judgment for damages obtained pursuant to subsection (1). If the disposition is before the end of the remaining lease term of the lease agreement, the lessor's recovery against the lessee for damages is governed by Section 2A-527 or Section 2A-528, and the lessor will cause an appropriate credit to be provided against a judgment for damages to the extent that the amount of the judgment exceeds the recovery available pursuant to Section 2A-527 or 2A-528.

(4) Payment of the judgment for damages obtained pursuant to subsection (1) entitles the lessee to the use and possession of the goods not then disposed of for the remaining lease term of and in accordance with the lease agreement.

(5) After default by the lessee under the lease contract of the type described in Section 2A-523(1) or Section 2A-523(3)(a) or, if agreed, after other default by the lessee, a lessor who is held not entitled to rent under this section must nevertheless be awarded damages for non-acceptance under Section 2A-527 or Section 2A-528.

As amended in 1990.

§2A-530. Lessor's Incidental Damages.

Incidental damages to an aggrieved lessor include any commercially reasonable charges, expenses, or commissions incurred in stopping delivery, in the transportation, care and custody of goods after the lessee's default, in connection with return or disposition of the goods, or otherwise resulting from the default.

ARTICLE 3: NEGOTIABLE INSTRUMENTS
Part 1—General Provisions and Definitions
§3-101. Short Title.
This Article may be cited as Uniform Commercial Code—Negotiable Instruments.

§3-102. Subject Matter.
(a) This Article applies to negotiable instruments. It does not apply to money or to payment orders governed by Article 4A. A negotiable instrument that is also a certificated security under Section 8-102(1)(a) is subject to Article 8 and to this Article.

(b) In the event of conflict between the provisions of this Article and those of Article 4, Article 8, or Article 9, the provisions of Article 4, Article 8, and Article 9 prevail over those of this Article.

(c) Regulations of the Board of Governors of the Federal Reserve System and operating circulars of the Federal Reserve Banks supersede any inconsistent provision of this Article to the extent of the inconsistency.

§3-103. Definitions.
(a) In this Article:

(1) "Acceptor" means a drawee that has accepted a draft.

(2) "Drawee" means a person ordered in a draft to make payment.

(3) "Drawer" means a person that signs a draft as a person ordering payment.

(4) "Good faith" means honesty in fact and the observance of reasonable commercial standards of fair dealing.

(5) "Maker" means a person that signs a note as promisor of payment.

(6) "Order" means a written instruction to pay money signed by the person giving the instruction. The instruction may be addressed to any person, including the person giving the instruction, or to one or more persons jointly or in the alternative but not in succession. An authorization to pay is not an order unless the person authorized to pay is also instructed to pay.

(7) "Ordinary care" in the case of a person engaged in business means observance of reasonable commercial standards, prevailing in the area in which that person is located, with respect to the business in which that person is engaged. In the case of a bank that takes an instrument for processing for collection or payment by automated means, reasonable commercial standards do not require the bank to examine the instrument if the failure to examine does not violate the bank's prescribed procedures and the bank's procedures do not vary unreasonably from general banking usage not disapproved by this Article or Article 4.

(8) "Party" means party to an instrument.

(9) "Promise" means a written undertaking to pay money signed by the person undertaking to pay. An acknowledgment of an obligation by the obligor is not a promise unless the obligor also undertakes to pay the obligation.

(10) "Prove" with respect to a fact means to meet the burden of establishing the fact (Section 1-201(8)).

(11) "Remitter" means a person that purchases an instrument from its issuer if the instrument is payable to an identified person other than the purchaser.

(b) Other definitions applying to this Article and the sections in which they appear are:

"Acceptance" Section 3-409.
"Accommodated party" Section 3-419.
"Accommodation indorsement" Section 3-205.
"Accommodation party" Section 3-419.
"Alteration" Section 3-407.
"Blank indorsement" Section 3-205.
"Cashier's check" Section 3-104.
"Certificate of deposit" Section 3-104.
"Certified check" Section 3-409.
"Check" Section 3-104.
"Consideration" Section 3-303.
"Draft" Section 3-104.
"Fiduciary" Section 3-307.
"Guarantor" Section 3-417.
"Holder in due course" Section 3-302.
"Incomplete instrument" Section 3-115.
"Indorsement" Section 3-204.
"Indorser" Section 3-204.
"Instrument" Section 3-104.
"Issue" Section 3-105.
"Issuer" Section 3-105.
"Negotiable instrument" Section 3-104.
"Negotiation" Section 3-201.
"Note" Section 3-104.
"Payable at a definite time" Section 3-108.
"Payable on demand" Section 3-108.
"Payable to bearer" Section 3-109.
"Payable to order" Section 3-110.
"Payment" Section 3-603.
"Person entitled to enforce" Section 3-301.
"Presentment" Section 3-501.
"Reacquisition" Section 3-207.
"Represented person" Section 3-307.
"Special indorsement" Section 3-205.
"Teller's check" Section 3-104.
"Traveler's check" Section 3-104.
"Value" Section 3-303.

(c) The following definitions in other Articles apply to this Article:

"Bank" Section 4-105.
"Banking day" Section 4-104.
"Clearing house" Section 4-104.
"Collecting bank" Section 4-105.
"Customer" Section 4-104.
"Depositary bank" Section 4-105.
"Documentary draft" Section 4-104.
"Intermediary bank" Section 4-105.
"Item" Section 4-104.
"Midnight deadline" Section 4-104.
"Payor bank" Section 4-105.
"Suspends payments" Section 4-104.

(d) In addition, Article 1 contains general definitions and principles of construction and interpretation applicable throughout this Article.

§3-104. Negotiable Instrument.
(a) "Negotiable instrument" means an unconditional promise or order to pay a fixed amount of money, with or without interest or other charges described in the promise or order, if it:

(1) is payable to bearer or to order at the time it is issued or first comes into possession of a holder;

(2) is payable on demand or at a definite time; and

(3) does not state any other undertaking or instruction by the person promising or ordering payment to do any act in addition to the payment of money except that the promise or order may contain (i) an undertaking or power to give, maintain, or protect collateral to secure payment, (ii) an authorization or power to the holder to confess judgment or realize on or dispose of collateral, or (iii) a waiver of the benefit of any law intended for the advantage or protection of any obligor.

(b) "Instrument" means negotiable instrument.

(c) An order that meets all of the requirements of subsection (a) except subparagraph (1) and otherwise falls within the definition of "check" in subsection (f) is a negotiable instrument and a check.

(d) Notwithstanding subsection (a), a promise or order other than a check is not an instrument if, at the time it is issued or first comes into possession of a holder, it contains a conspicuous statement, however expressed, indicating that the writing is not an instrument governed by this Article.

(e) An instrument is a "note" if it is a promise, and is a "draft" if it is an order. If an instrument falls within the definition of both "note" and "draft," the person entitled to enforce the instrument may treat it as either.

(f) "Check" means (i) a draft, other than a documentary draft, payable on demand and drawn on a bank or (ii) a cashier's check or teller's check. An instrument may be a check even though it is described on its face by another term such as "money order."

(g) "Cashier's check" means a draft with respect to which the drawer and drawee are the same bank or branches of the same bank.

(h) "Teller's check" means a draft drawn by a bank (i) on another bank, or (ii) payable at or through a bank.

(i) "Traveler's check" means an instrument that (i) is payable on demand, (ii) is drawn on or payable at or through a bank, (iii) is designated by the term "traveler's check" or by a substantially similar term, and (iv) requires, as a condition to payment, a countersignature by a person whose specimen signature appears on the instrument.

(j) "Certificate of deposit" means an instrument containing an acknowledgment by a bank that a sum of money has been received by the bank, and a promise by the bank to repay the sum of money. A certificate of deposit is a note of the bank.

§3-105. Issue of Instrument.

(a) "Issue" means the first delivery of an instrument by the maker or drawer, whether to a holder or nonholder, for the purpose of giving rights on the instrument to any person.

(b) An unissued instrument, or an unissued incomplete instrument (Section 3-115) that is completed, is binding on the maker or drawer, but nonissuance is a defense. An instrument that is conditionally issued or is issued for a special purpose is binding on the maker or drawer, but failure of the condition or special purpose to be fulfilled is a defense.

(c) "Issuer" applies to issued and unissued instruments and means any person that signs an instrument as maker or drawer.

§3-106. Unconditional Promise or Order.

(a) Except as provided in subsections (b) and (c), for the purposes of Section 3-104(a), a promise or order is unconditional unless it states (i) an express condition to payment or (ii) that the promise or order is subject to or governed by another writing, or that rights or obligations with respect to the promise or order are stated in another writing; however, a mere reference to another writing does not make the promise or order conditional.

(b) A promise or order is not made conditional (i) by a reference to another writing for a statement of rights with respect to collateral, prepayment, or acceleration, or (ii) because payment is limited to resort to a particular fund or source.

(c) If a promise or order requires, as a condition to payment, a countersignature by a person whose specimen signature appears on the promise or order, the condition does not make the promise or order conditional for the purposes of Section 3-104(a). If the person whose specimen signature appears on an instrument fails to countersign the instrument, the failure to countersign is a defense to the obligation of the issuer, but the failure does not prevent a transferee of the instrument from becoming a holder of the instrument.

(d) If a promise or order at the time it is issued or first comes into possession of a holder contains a statement, required by applicable statutory or administrative law, to the effect that the rights of a holder or transferee are subject to claims or defenses that the issuer could assert against the original payee, the promise or order is not thereby made conditional for the pur-

poses of Section 3-104(a), but there cannot be a holder in due course of the promise or order.

§3-107. Instrument Payable in Foreign Money.

Unless the instrument otherwise provides, an instrument that states the amount payable in foreign money may be paid in the foreign money or in an equivalent amount in dollars calculated by using the current bank-offered spot rate at the place of payment for the purchase of dollars on the day on which the instrument is paid.

§3-108. Payable on Demand or at a Definite Time.

(a) A promise or order is "payable on demand" if (i) it states that it is payable on demand or at sight, or otherwise indicates that it is payable at the will of the holder, or (ii) it does not state any time of payment.

(b) A promise or order is "payable at a definite time" if it is payable on elapse of a definite period of time after sight or acceptance or at a fixed date or dates or at a time or times readily ascertainable at the time the promise or order is issued, subject to rights of (i) prepayment, (ii) acceleration, or (iii) extension at the option of the holder or (iv) extension to a further definite time at the option of the maker or acceptor or automatically upon or after a specified act or event.

(c) If an instrument, payable at a fixed date, is also payable upon demand made before the fixed date, the instrument is payable on demand until the fixed date and, if demand for payment is not made before that date, becomes payable at a definite time on the fixed date.

§3-109. Payable to Bearer or to Order.

(a) A promise or order is payable to bearer if it:

(1) states that it is payable to bearer or to the order of bearer or otherwise indicates that the person in possession of the promise or order is entitled to payment,

(2) does not state a payee, or

(3) states that it is payable to or to the order of cash or otherwise indicates that it is not payable to an identified person.

(b) A promise or order that is not payable to bearer is payable to order if it is payable (i) to the order of an identified person or (ii) to an identified person or order. A promise or order that is payable to order is payable to the identified person.

(c) An instrument payable to bearer may become payable to an identified person if it is specially indorsed as stated in Section 3-205(a). An instrument payable to an identified person may become payable to bearer if it is indorsed in blank as stated in Section 3-205(b).

§3-110. Identification of Person to Whom Instrument Is Payable.

(a) A person to whom an instrument is payable is determined by the intent of the person, whether or not authorized, signing as, or in the name or behalf of, the maker or drawer. The instrument is payable to the person intended by the signer even if that person is identified in the instrument by a name or other identification that is not that of the intended person. If more than one person signs in the name or behalf of the maker or drawer and all the signers do not intend the same person as payee, the instrument is payable to any person intended by one or more of the signers.

(b) If the signature of the maker or drawer of an instrument is made by automated means such as a check-writing machine, the payee of the instrument is determined by the intent of the person who supplied the name or identification of the payee, whether or not authorized to do so.

(c) A person to whom an instrument is payable may be identified in any way including by name, identifying number, office, or account number. For the purpose of determining the holder of an instrument, the following rules apply:

(1) If an instrument is payable to an account and the account is identified only by number, the instrument is payable to the person to whom the account is payable. If an instrument is payable to an account identified by number and by the name of a person, the instrument is payable

to the named person, whether or not that person is the owner of the account identified by number.

(2) If an instrument is payable to:

(i) a trust, estate, or a person described as trustee or representative of a trust or estate, the instrument is payable to the trustee, the representative, or a successor of either, whether or not the beneficiary or estate is also named;

(ii) a person described as agent or similar representative of a named or identified person, the instrument is payable either to the represented person, the representative, or a successor of the representative;

(iii) a fund or organization that is not a legal entity, the instrument is payable to a representative of the members of the fund or organization; or

(iv) an office or to a person described as holding an office, the instrument is payable to the named person, the incumbent of the office, or a successor to the incumbent.

(d) If an instrument is payable to two or more persons alternatively, it is payable to any of them and may be negotiated, discharged, or enforced by any of them in possession of the instrument. If an instrument is payable to two or more persons not alternatively, it is payable to all of them and may be negotiated, discharged, or enforced only by all of them. If an instrument payable to two or more persons is ambiguous as to whether it is payable to the persons alternatively, the instrument is payable to the persons alternatively.

§3-111. Place of Payment.

Except as otherwise provided for items in Article 4, an instrument is payable at the place of payment stated in the instrument. If no place of payment is stated, an instrument is payable at the address of the drawee or maker stated in the instrument. If no address is stated, the place of payment is the place of business of the drawee or maker. If a drawee or maker has more than one place of business, the place of payment is any place of business of the drawee or maker chosen by the person entitled to enforce the instrument. If the drawee or maker has no place of business, the place of payment is the residence of the drawee or maker.

§3-112. Interest.

(a) Unless otherwise provided in the instrument, (i) an instrument is not payable with interest, and (ii) interest on an interest-bearing instrument is payable from the date of the instrument.

(b) Interest may be stated in an instrument as a fixed or variable amount of money or it may be expressed as a fixed or variable rate or rates. The amount or rate of interest may be stated or described in the instrument in any manner and may require reference to information not contained in the instrument. If an instrument provides for interest but the amount of interest payable cannot be ascertained from the description, interest is payable at the judgment rate in effect at the place of payment of the instrument and at the time interest first accrues.

§3-113. Date of Instrument.

(a) An instrument may be antedated or postdated. The date stated determines the time of payment if the instrument is payable at a fixed period after date. Except as provided in Section 4-401(3), an instrument payable on demand is not payable before the date of the instrument.

(b) If an instrument is undated, its date is the date of its issue or, in the case of an unissued instrument, the date it first comes into possession of a holder.

§3-114. Contradictory Terms of Instrument.

If an instrument contains contradictory terms, typewritten terms prevail over printed terms, handwritten terms prevail over both, and words prevail over numbers.

§3-115. Incomplete Instrument.

(a) "Incomplete instrument" means a signed writing, whether or not issued by the signer, the contents of which show at the time of signing that it is incomplete but that the signer intended it to be completed by the addition of words or numbers.

(b) Subject to subsection (c), if an incomplete instrument is an instrument under Section 3-104, it may be enforced (i) according to its terms if it is not completed, or (ii) according to its terms as augmented by completion. If an incomplete instrument is not an instrument under Section 3-104 but, after completion, the requirements of Section 3-104 are met, the instrument may be enforced according to its terms as augmented by completion.

(c) If words or numbers are added to an incomplete instrument without authority of the signer, there is an alteration of the incomplete instrument governed by Section 3-407.

(d) The burden of establishing that words or numbers were added to an incomplete instrument without authority of the signer is on the person asserting the lack of authority.

§3-116. Joint and Several Liability; Contribution.

(a) Except as otherwise provided in the instrument, two or more persons who have the same liability on an instrument as makers, drawers, acceptors, indorsers who are indorsing joint payees, or anomalous indorsers, are jointly and severally liable in the capacity in which they sign.

(b) Except as provided in Section 3-417(e) or by agreement of the affected parties, a party with joint and several liability that pays the instrument is entitled to receive from any party with the same joint and several liability contribution in accordance with applicable law.

(c) Discharge of one party with joint and several liability by a person entitled to enforce the instrument does not affect the right under subsection (b) of a party with the same joint and several liability to receive contribution from the party discharged.

§3-117. Other Agreements Affecting an Instrument.

Subject to applicable law regarding exclusion of proof of contemporaneous or prior agreements, the obligation of a party to an instrument to pay the instrument may be modified, supplemented, or nullified by a separate agreement of the obligor and a person entitled to enforce the instrument if the instrument is issued or the obligation is incurred in reliance on the agreement or as part of the same transaction giving rise to the agreement. To the extent an obligation is modified, supplemented, or nullified by an agreement under this section, the agreement is a defense to the obligation.

§3-118. Statute of Limitations.

(a) Except as provided in subsection (e), an action to enforce the obligation of a party to pay a note payable at a definite time must be commenced within six years after the payment date or dates stated in the note or, if a payment date is accelerated, within six years after the accelerated payment date.

(b) Except as provided in subsection (d) or (e), if demand for payment is made to the maker of a note payable on demand, an action to enforce the obligation of a party to pay the note must be commenced within six years after the demand. If no demand for payment is made to the maker, an action to enforce the note is barred if neither principal nor interest on the note has been paid for a continuous period of 10 years.

(c) Except as provided in subsection (d), an action to enforce the obligation of a party to an unaccepted draft to pay the draft must be commenced within six years after dishonor of the draft or 10 years after the date of the draft, whichever period expires first.

(d) An action to enforce the obligation of the acceptor of a certified check or the issuer of a teller's check, cashier's check, or traveler's check must be commenced within six years after demand for payment is made to the acceptor or issuer, as the case may be.

(e) An action to enforce the obligation of a party to a certificate of deposit to pay the instrument must be commenced within six years after demand for payment is made to the maker, but if the instrument states a maturity date and the maker is not required to pay before that date, the six-year period begins when a demand for payment is in effect and the maturity date has passed.

(f) This subsection applies to an action to enforce the obligation of a party to pay an accepted draft, other than a certified check. If the obligation of the acceptor is payable at a definite time, the action must be commenced within six years after the payment date or dates stated in the draft or acceptance. If the obligation of the acceptor is payable on demand, the action must be commenced within six years after the date of the acceptance.

(g) Unless governed by other law regarding claims for indemnity or contribution, an action (i) for conversion of an instrument, for money had and received, or like action based on conversion, (ii) for breach of warranty, or (iii) to enforce an obligation, duty, or right arising under this Article and not governed by this section must be commenced within three years after the cause of action accrues.

§3-119. Notice of Right to Defend Action.

In an action for breach of an obligation for which a third person is answerable over pursuant to this Article or Article 4, the defendant may give the third person written notice of the litigation, and the person notified may then give similar notice to any other person who is answerable over. If the notice states (i) that the person notified may come in and defend and (ii) that failure to do so will bind the person notified in an action later brought by the person giving the notice as to any determination of fact common to the two litigations, the person notified is so bound unless after seasonable receipt of the notice the person notified does come in and defend.

Part 2—Negotiation, Transfer and Indorsement

§3-201. Negotiation.

(a) "Negotiation" means a transfer of possession, whether voluntary or involuntary, of an instrument to a person who thereby becomes its holder if possession is obtained from a person other than the issuer of the instrument.

(b) Except for a negotiation by a remitter, if an instrument is payable to an identified person, negotiation requires transfer of possession of the instrument and its indorsement by the holder. If an instrument is payable to bearer, it may be negotiated by transfer of possession alone.

§3-202. Negotiation Subject to Rescission.

(a) Negotiation is effective even if obtained (i) from an infant, a corporation exceeding its powers, or a person without capacity, or (ii) by fraud, duress, or mistake, or in breach of duty or as part of an illegal transaction.

(b) To the extent permitted by law, negotiation may be rescinded or may be subject to other remedies, but those remedies may not be asserted against a subsequent holder in due course or a person paying the instrument in good faith and without knowledge of facts that are a basis for rescission or other remedy.

§3-203. Rights Acquired by Transfer.

(a) An instrument is transferred when it is delivered by a person other than its issuer for the purpose of giving to the person receiving delivery the right to enforce the instrument.

(b) Transfer of an instrument, regardless of whether the transfer is a negotiation, vests in the transferee any right of the transferor to enforce the instrument, including any right as a holder in due course, but the transferee cannot acquire rights of a holder in due course by a transfer, directly or indirectly, from a holder in due course if the purchaser engaged in fraud or illegality affecting the instrument.

(c) Unless otherwise agreed, if an instrument is transferred for value and the transferee does not become a holder because of lack of indorsement by the transferor, the transferee has a specifically enforceable right to the unqualified indorsement of the transferor, but negotiation of the instrument does not occur until the indorsement is made.

(d) If a transferor purports to transfer less than the entire instrument, negotiation of the instrument does not occur. The transferee obtains no rights under this Article and has only the rights of a partial assignee.

§3-204. Indorsement.

(a) "Indorsement" means a signature, other than that of a maker, drawer, or acceptor, that alone or accompanied by other words, is made on an instrument for the purpose of (i) negotiating the instrument, (ii) restricting payment of the instrument, or (iii) incurring indorser's liability on the instrument, but regardless of the intent of the signer, a signature and its accompanying words is an indorsement unless the accompanying words, the terms of the instrument, the place of the signature, or other circumstances unambiguously indicate that the signature was made for a purpose other than indorsement. For the purpose of determining whether a signature is made on an instrument, a paper affixed to the instrument is a part of the instrument.

(b) "Indorser" means a person who makes an indorsement.

(c) For the purpose of determining whether the transferee of an instrument is a holder, an indorsement that transfers a security interest in the instrument is effective as an unqualified indorsement of the instrument.

(d) If an instrument is payable to a holder under a name that is not the name of the holder, indorsement may be made by the holder in the name stated in the instrument or in the holder's name or both, but signature in both names may be required by a person paying or taking the instrument for value or collection.

§3-205. Special Indorsement; Blank Indorsement; Anomalous Indorsement.

(a) If an indorsement is made by the holder of an instrument, whether payable to an identified person or payable to bearer, and the indorsement identifies a person to whom it makes the instrument payable, it is a "special indorsement." When specially indorsed, an instrument becomes payable to the identified person and may be negotiated only by the indorsement of that person. The principles stated in Section 3-110 apply to special indorsements.

(b) If an indorsement is made by the holder of an instrument and it is not a special indorsement, it is a "blank indorsement." When indorsed in blank, an instrument becomes payable to bearer and may be negotiated by transfer of possession alone until specially indorsed.

(c) The holder may convert a blank indorsement that consists only of a signature into a special indorsement by writing, above the signature of the indorser, words identifying the person to whom the instrument is made payable.

(d) "Anomalous indorsement" means an indorsement made by a person that is not the holder of the instrument. An anomalous indorsement does not affect the manner in which the instrument may be negotiated.

§3-206. Restrictive Indorsement.

(a) An indorsement limiting payment to a particular person or otherwise prohibiting further transfer or negotiation of the instrument is not effective to prevent further transfer or negotiation of the instrument.

(b) An indorsement stating a condition to the right of the indorsee to receive payment does not affect the right of the indorsee to enforce the instrument. A person paying the instrument or taking it for value or collection may disregard the condition, and the rights and liabilities of that person are not affected by whether the condition has been fulfilled.

(c) The following rules apply to an instrument bearing an indorsement (i) described in Section 4-201(2), or (ii) in blank or to a particular bank using the words "for deposit," "for collection," or other words indicating a purpose of having the instrument collected for the indorser or for a particular account:

(1) A person, other than a bank, that purchases the instrument when so indorsed converts the instrument unless the proceeds of the instrument are received by the indorser or are applied consistently with the indorsement.

(2) A depositary bank that purchases the instrument or takes it for collection when so indorsed converts the instrument unless the proceeds of the instrument are received by the indorser or applied consistently with the indorsement.

(3) A payor bank that is also the depositary bank or that takes the instrument for immediate payment over the counter from a person other than a collecting bank converts the instrument unless the proceeds of the instrument are received by the indorser or applied consistently with the indorsement.

(4) Except as otherwise provided in paragraph (3), a payor bank or intermediary bank may disregard the indorsement and is not liable if the proceeds of the instrument are not received by the indorser or applied consistently with the indorsement.

(d) Except for an indorsement covered by subsection (c), the following rules apply to an instrument bearing an indorsement using words to the effect that payment is to be made to the indorsee as agent, trustee, or other fiduciary for the benefit of the indorser or another person.

(1) Unless there is notice of breach of fiduciary duty as provided in Section 3-307, a person that purchases the instrument from the indorsee or takes the instrument from the indorsee for collection or payment may pay the proceeds of payment or the value given for the instrument to the indorsee without regard to whether the indorsee violates a fiduciary duty to the indorser.

(2) A later transferee of the instrument or person that pays the instrument is neither given notice nor otherwise affected by the restriction in the indorsement unless the transferee or payor knows that the fiduciary dealt with the instrument or its proceeds in breach of fiduciary duty.

(e) Purchase of an instrument bearing an indorsement to which this section applies does not prevent the purchaser from becoming a holder in due course of the instrument unless the purchaser is a converter under subsection (c).

(f) In an action to enforce the obligation of a party to pay the instrument, the obligor has a defense if payment would violate an indorsement to which this section applies and the payment is not permitted by this section.

§3-207. Reacquisition.

Reacquisition of an instrument occurs if it is transferred, by negotiation or otherwise, to a former holder. A former holder that reacquires the instrument may cancel indorsements made after the reacquirer first became a holder of the instrument. If the cancellation causes the instrument to be payable to the reacquirer or to bearer, the reacquirer may negotiate the instrument. An indorser whose indorsement is canceled is discharged, and the discharge is effective against any later holder.

Part 3—Enforcement of Instruments

§3-301. Person Entitled to Enforce Instrument.

"Person entitled to enforce" an instrument means (i) the holder of the instrument, (ii) a nonholder in possession of the instrument who has the rights of a holder, or (iii) a person not in possession of the instrument who is entitled to enforce the instrument pursuant to Section 3-309. A person may be a person entitled to enforce the instrument even though the person is not the owner of the instrument or is in wrongful possession of the instrument.

§3-302. Holder in Due Course.

(a) Subject to subsection (c) and Section 3-106(d), "holder in due course" means the holder of an instrument if:

(1) the instrument when issued or negotiated to the holder does not bear such apparent evidence of forgery or alteration or is not otherwise so irregular or incomplete as to call into question its authenticity, and

(2) the holder took the instrument (i) for value, (ii) in good faith, (iii) without notice that the instrument is overdue or has been dishonored or that there is an uncured default with respect to payment of another instrument issued as part of the same series, (iv) without notice that the instrument contains an unauthorized signature or has been altered, (v) without notice of any claim to the instrument stated in Section 3-306, and (vi) without notice that any party to the instrument has any defense or claim in recoupment stated in Section 3-305(a).

(b) Notice of discharge of a party to the instrument, other than discharge in an insolvency proceeding, is not notice of a defense under subsection (a), but discharge is effective against a person who became a holder in due course with notice of the discharge. Public filing or recording of a document does not of itself constitute notice of a defense, claim in recoupment, or claim to the instrument.

(c) Except to the extent a transferor or predecessor in interest has rights as a holder in due course, a person does not acquire rights of a holder in due course of an instrument taken (i) by legal process or by purchase at an execution, bankruptcy, or creditor's sale or similar proceeding, (ii) by purchase as part of a bulk transaction not in ordinary course of business of the transferor, or (iii) as the successor in interest to an estate or other organization.

(d) If, under Section 3-303(a)(1), the promise of performance that is the consideration for an instrument has been partially performed, the holder may assert rights as a holder in due course of the instrument only to the fraction of the amount payable under the instrument equal to the value of the partial performance divided by the value of the promised performance.

(e) If (i) the person entitled to enforce an instrument has only a security interest in the instrument and (ii) the person obliged to pay the instrument has a defense, claim in recoupment or claim to the instrument that may be asserted against the person who granted the security interest, the person entitled to enforce the instrument may assert rights as a holder in due course only to an amount payable under the instrument which, at the time of enforcement of the instrument, does not exceed the amount of the unpaid obligation secured.

(f) To be effective, notice must be received at such time and in such manner as to give a reasonable opportunity to act on it.

(g) This section is subject to any law limiting status as a holder in due course in particular classes of transactions.

§3-303. Value and Consideration.

(a) An instrument is issued or transferred for value if:

(1) the instrument is issued or transferred for a promise of performance, to the extent the promise has been performed;

(2) the transferee acquires a security interest or other lien in the instrument other than a lien obtained by judicial proceedings;

(3) the instrument is issued or transferred as payment of, or as security for, an existing obligation of any person, whether or not the obligation is due;

(4) the instrument is issued or transferred in exchange for a negotiable instrument; or

(5) the instrument is issued or transferred in exchange for the incurring of an irrevocable obligation to a third party by the person taking the instrument.

(b) "Consideration" means any consideration sufficient to support a simple contract. The drawer or maker of an instrument has a defense if the instrument is issued without consideration. If an instrument is issued for a promise of performance, the drawer or maker has a defense to the extent performance of the promise is due and the promise has not been performed. If an instrument is issued for value as stated in subsection (a), the instrument is also issued for consideration.

§3-304. Overdue Instrument.

(a) An instrument payable on demand becomes overdue at the earliest of the following times:

(1) on the day after the day demand for payment is duly made;

(2) if the instrument is a check, 90 days after its date; or

(3) if the instrument is not a check, when the instrument has been outstanding for a period of time after its date which is unreasonably long under the circumstances of the particular case in light of the nature of the instrument and trade usage.

(b) With respect to an instrument payable at a definite time the following rules apply: (1) If the principal is payable in installments and a due date has not been accelerated, the instrument becomes overdue upon default under the instrument for nonpayment of an installment, and the instrument remains overdue until the default is cured. (2) If the principal is not payable in installments and the due date has not been accelerated, the instrument becomes overdue on the day after the due date. (3) If a due date with respect to principal has been accelerated, the instrument becomes overdue on the day after the accelerated due date.

(c) Unless the due date of principal has been accelerated, an instrument does not become overdue if there is default in payment of interest but no default in payment of principal.

§3-305. Defenses and Claims in Recoupment.

(a) Except as stated in subsection (b), the right to enforce the obligation of a party to pay the instrument is subject to the following:

(1) A defense of the obligor based on (i) infancy of the obligor to the extent it is a defense to a simple contract, (ii) duress, lack of legal capacity, or illegality of the transaction that nullifies the obligation of the obligor, (iii) fraud that induced the obligor to sign the instrument with neither knowledge nor reasonable opportunity to learn of its character or its essential terms, or (iv) discharge of the obligor in insolvency proceedings.

(2) A defense of the obligor stated in another section of this Article or a defense of the obligor that would be available if the person entitled to enforce the instrument were enforcing a right to payment under a simple contract.

(3) A claim in recoupment of the obligor against the original payee of the instrument if the claim arose from the transaction that gave rise to the instrument. The claim of the obligor may be asserted against a transferee of the instrument only to reduce the amount owing on the instrument at the time the action is brought.

(b) The right of a holder in due course to enforce the obligation of a party to pay the instrument is subject to defenses of the obligor stated in subsection (a)(1), but is not subject to defenses of the obligor stated in subsection (a)(2) or claims in recoupment stated in subsection (a)(3) against a person other than the holder.

(c) Except as stated in subsection (d), in an action to enforce the obligation of a party to pay the instrument, the obligor may not assert against the person entitled to enforce the instrument a defense, claim in recoupment, or claim to the instrument (Section 3-306) of another person, but the other person's claim to the instrument may be asserted by the obligor if the other person is joined in the action and personally asserts the claim against the person entitled to enforce the instrument. An obligor is not obliged to pay the instrument if the person seeking enforcement of the instrument does not have rights of a holder in due course and the obligor proves that the instrument is a lost or stolen instrument.

(d) In an action to enforce the obligation of an accommodation party to pay an instrument, the accommodation party may assert against the person entitled to enforce the instrument any defense or claim in recoupment under subsection (a) that the accommodated party could assert against the person entitled to enforce the instrument, except the defenses of discharge in insolvency proceedings, infancy, or lack of legal capacity.

§3-306. Claims to an Instrument.

A person taking an instrument, other than a person having rights of a holder in due course, is subject to a claim of a property or possessory right in the instrument or its proceeds, including a claim to rescind a negotiation and to recover the instrument or its proceeds. A person having rights of a holder in due course takes free of the claim to the instrument.

§3-307. Notice of Breach of Fiduciary Duty.

(a) This section applies if (i) an instrument is taken from a fiduciary for payment or collection or for value, (ii) the taker has knowledge of the fiduciary status of the fiduciary, and (iii) the represented person makes a claim to the instrument or its proceeds on the basis that the transaction of the fiduciary is a breach of fiduciary duty. Notice of breach of fiduciary duty by the fiduciary is notice of the claim of the represented person. "Fiduciary" means an agent, trustee, partner, corporation officer or director, or other representative owing a fiduciary duty with respect to the instrument. "Represented person" means the principal, beneficiary, partnership, corporation, or other person to whom the duty is owed.

(b) If the instrument is payable to the fiduciary, as such, or to the represented person, the taker has notice of the breach of fiduciary duty if the instrument is (i) taken in payment of or as security for a debt known by the taker to be the personal debt of the fiduciary, (ii) taken in a transaction known by the taker to be for the personal benefit of the fiduciary, or (iii) deposited to an account other than an account of the fiduciary, as such, or an account of the represented person.

(c) If the instrument is made or drawn by the fiduciary, as such, payable to the fiduciary personally, the taker does not have notice of the breach of fiduciary duty unless the taker knows of the breach of fiduciary duty.

(d) If the instrument is made or drawn by or on behalf of the represented person to the taker as payee, the taker has notice of the breach of fiduciary duty if the instrument is (i) taken in payment of or as security for a debt known by the taker to be the personal debt of the fiduciary, (ii) taken in a transaction known by the taker to be for the personal benefit of the fiduciary, or (iii) deposited to an account other than an account of the fiduciary, as such, or an account of the represented person.

§3-308. Proof of Signatures and Status as Holder in Due Course.

(a) In an action with respect to an instrument, the authenticity of, and authority to make, each signature on the instrument is admitted unless specifically denied in the pleadings. If the validity of a signature is denied in the pleadings, the burden of establishing validity is on the person claiming validity, but the signature is presumed to be authentic and authorized unless the action is to enforce the liability of the purported signer and the signer is dead or incompetent at the time of trial of the issue of validity of the signature. If an action to enforce the instrument is brought against a person as the undisclosed principal of a person who signed the instrument as a party to the instrument, the plaintiff has the burden of establishing that the defendant is liable on the instrument as a represented person pursuant to Section 3-402(a).

(b) If the validity of signatures is admitted or proved and there is compliance with subsection (a), a plaintiff producing the instrument is entitled to payment if the plaintiff proves entitlement to enforce the instrument under Section 3-301, unless the defendant proves a defense or claim in recoupment. If a defense or claim in recoupment is proved, the right to payment of the plaintiff is subject to the defense or claim except to the extent the plaintiff proves that the plaintiff has rights of a holder in due course which are not subject to the defense or claim.

§3-309. Enforcement of Lost, Destroyed, or Stolen Instrument.

(a) A person not in possession of an instrument is entitled to enforce the instrument if (i) that person was in rightful possession of the instrument and entitled to enforce it when loss of possession occurred, (ii) the loss of possession was not the result of a voluntary transfer by that person or a lawful seizure, and (iii) that person cannot reasonably obtain possession of the instrument because the instrument was destroyed, its whereabouts cannot be determined, or it is in the wrongful possession of an unknown person or a person that cannot be found or is not amenable to service of process.

(b) A person seeking enforcement of an instrument pursuant to subsection (a) must prove the terms of the instrument and the person's right to enforce the instrument. If that proof is made, Section 3-308 applies to the case as though the person seeking enforcement had produced the instrument. The court may not enter judgment in favor of the person seeking enforcement unless it finds that the person required to pay the instrument is adequately protected against loss that might occur by reason of a claim by another person to enforce the instrument. Adequate protection may be provided by any reasonable means.

§3-310. Effect of Instrument on Obligation for Which Taken.

(a) Unless otherwise agreed, if a certified check, cashier's check, or teller's check is taken for an obligation, the obligation is discharged to the same extent discharge would result if an amount of money equal to the amount of the instrument were taken in payment of the obligation. Discharge of the obligation does not affect any liability that the obligor may have as an indorser of the instrument.

(b) Unless otherwise agreed and except as provided in subsection (a), if a note or an uncertified check is taken for an obligation, the obligation is suspended to the same extent the obligation would be discharged if an amount of money equal to the amount of the instrument were taken.

(1) In the case of an uncertified check, suspension of the obligation continues until dishonor of the check or until it is paid or certified. Payment or certification of the check results in discharge of the obligation to the extent of the amount of the check.

(2) In the case of a note, suspension of the obligation continues until dishonor of the note or until it is paid. Payment of the note results in discharge of the obligation to the extent of the payment.

(3) If the check or note is dishonored and the obligee of the obligation for which the instrument was taken has possession of the instrument, the obligee may enforce either the instrument or the obligation. In the case of an instrument of a third person which is negotiated to the obligee by the obligor, discharge of the obligor on the instrument also discharges the obligation.

(4) If the person entitled to enforce the instrument taken for an obligation is a person other than the obligee, the obligee may not enforce the obligation to the extent the obligation is suspended. If the obligee is the person entitled to enforce the instrument but no longer has possession of it because it was lost, stolen, or destroyed, the obligation may not be enforced to the extent of the amount payable on the instrument, and to that extent the obligee's rights against the obligor are limited to enforcement of the instrument.

(c) If an instrument other than one described in subsection (a) or (b) is taken for an obligation, the effect is (i) that stated in subsection (a) if the instrument is one on which a bank is liable as maker or acceptor, or (ii) that stated in subsection (b) in any other case.

§3-311. Accord and Satisfaction by Use of Instrument.

(a) This section applies if a person against whom a claim is asserted proves that (i) that person in good faith tendered an instrument to the claimant as full satisfaction of the claim, (ii) the amount of the claim was unliquidated or subject to a bona fide dispute, and (iii) the claimant obtained payment of the instrument.

(b) Unless subsection (c) applies, the claim is discharged if the person against whom the claim is asserted proves that the instrument or an accompanying written communication contained a conspicuous statement to the effect that the instrument was tendered as full satisfaction of the claim.

(c) Subject to subsection (d), a claim is not discharged under subsection (b) if the claimant is an organization and proves that within a reasonable time before the tender, the claimant sent a conspicuous statement to the person against whom the claim is asserted that communications concerning disputed debts, including an instrument tendered as full satisfaction of a debt, are to be sent to a designated person, office or place, and the instrument or accompanying communication was not received by that designated person, office, or place.

(d) Notwithstanding subsection (c), a claim is discharged under subsection (b) if the person against whom the claim is asserted proves that within a reasonable time before collection of the instrument was initiated, an agent of the claimant having direct responsibility with respect to the disputed obligation knew that the instrument was tendered in full satisfaction of the claim, or received the instrument and any accompanying written communication.

Part 4—Liability of Parties

§3-401. Signature.

(a) A person is not liable on an instrument unless (i) the person signed the instrument, or (ii) the person is represented by an agent or representative who signed the instrument and the signature is binding on the represented person under Section 3-402.

(b) A signature may be made (i) manually or by means of a device or machine, and (ii) by the use of any name, including any trade or assumed name, or by any word, mark, or symbol executed or adopted by a person with present intention to authenticate a writing.

§3-402. Signature by Representative.

(a) If a person acting, or purporting to act, as a representative signs an instrument by signing either the name of the represented person or the name of the signer, the represented person is bound by the signature to the same extent the represented person would be bound if the signature were on a simple contract. If the represented person is bound, the signature of the representative is the "authorized signature of the represented person" and the represented person is liable on the instrument, whether or not identified in the instrument.

(b) If a representative signs the name of the representative to an instrument and that signature is an authorized signature of the represented person, the following rules apply:

(1) If the form of the signature shows unambiguously that the signature is made on behalf of the represented person who is identified in the instrument, the representative is not liable on the instrument.

(2) Subject to subsection (c), if (i) the form of the signature does not show unambiguously that the signature is made in a representative capacity or (ii) the represented person is not identified in the instrument, the representative is liable on the instrument to a holder in due course that took the instrument without notice that the representative was not intended to be liable on the instrument. With respect to any other person, the representative is liable on the instrument unless the representative proves that the original parties to the instrument did not intend the representative to be liable on the instrument.

(c) If a representative signs the name of the representative as drawer of a check without indication of the representative status and the check is payable from an account of the represented person who is identified on the check, the signer is not liable on the check if the signature is an authorized signature of the represented person.

§3-403. Unauthorized Signature.

(a) Except as otherwise provided in this Article, an unauthorized signature is ineffective except as the signature of the unauthorized signer in favor of a person who in good faith pays the instrument or takes it for value. An unauthorized signature may be ratified for all purposes of this Article.

(b) If the signature of more than one person is required to constitute the authorized signature of an organization, the signature of the organization is unauthorized if one of the required signatures is missing.

(c) The civil or criminal liability of a person who makes an unauthorized signature is not affected by any provision of this Article that makes the unauthorized signature effective for the purposes of this Article.

§3-404. Impostors; Fictitious Payees.

(a) If an impostor by use of the mails or otherwise induces the maker or drawer of an instrument to issue the instrument to the impostor, or to a person acting in concert with the impostor, by impersonating the payee of the instrument or a person authorized to act for the payee, an indorsement of the instrument by any person in the name of the payee is effective as the indorsement of the payee in favor of any person that in good faith pays the instrument or takes it for value or for collection.

(b) If (i) a person whose intent determines to whom an instrument is payable (Section 3-110(a) or (b)) does not intend the person identified as payee to have any interest in the instrument, or (ii) the person identified as payee of the instrument is a fictitious person, the following rules apply until the instrument is negotiated by special indorsement:

(1) Any person in possession of the instrument is its holder.

(2) An indorsement by any person in the name of the payee stated in the instrument is effective as the indorsement of the payee in favor of any person that in good faith pays the instrument or takes it for value or for collection.

(c) Under subsection (a) or (b) an indorsement is made in the name of a payee if (i) it is made in a name substantially similar to that of the payee or (ii) the instrument, whether or not indorsed, is deposited in a depositary bank to an account in a name substantially similar to that of the payee.

(d) With respect to an instrument to which subsection (a) or (b) applies, if a person paying the instrument or taking it for value or for collection fails to exercise ordinary care in paying or taking the instrument and that failure substantially contributes to loss resulting from payment of the instrument, the person bearing the loss may recover from the person failing to exercise ordinary care to the extent the failure to exercise ordinary care contributed to the loss.

§3-405. Employer Responsibility for Fraudulent Indorsement by Employee.

(a) This section applies to fraudulent indorsements of instruments with respect to which an employer has entrusted an employee with responsibility as part of the employee's duties. The following definitions apply to this section:

(1) "Employee" includes, in addition to an employee of an employer, an independent contractor and employee of an independent contractor retained by the employer.

(2) "Fraudulent indorsement" means (i) in the case of an instrument payable to the employer, a forged indorsement purporting to be that of the employer, or (ii) in the case of an instrument with respect to which the employer is drawer or maker, a forged indorsement purporting to be that of the person identified as payee.

(3) "Responsibility" with respect to instruments means authority (i) to sign or indorse instruments on behalf of the employer, (ii) to process instruments received by the employer for bookkeeping purposes, for deposit to an account, or for other disposition, (iii) to prepare or process instruments for issue in the name of the employer, (iv) to supply information determining the names or addresses of payees of instruments to be issued in the name of the employer, (v) to control the disposition of instruments to be issued in the name of the employer, or (vi) to otherwise act with respect to instruments in a responsible capacity. "Responsibility" does not include the assignment of duties that merely allow an employee to have access to instruments or blank or incomplete instrument forms that are being stored or transported or are part of incoming or outgoing mail, or similar access.

(b) For the purpose of determining the rights and liabilities of a person who, in good faith, pays an instrument or takes it for value or for collection, if an employee entrusted with responsibility with respect to the instrument or a person acting in concert with the employee makes a fraudulent indorsement to the instrument, the indorsement is effective as the indorsement of the person to whom the instrument is payable if it is made in the name of that person. If the person paying the instrument or taking it for value or for collection fails to exercise ordinary care in paying or taking the instrument and that failure substantially contributes to loss resulting from the fraud, the person bearing the loss may recover from the person failing to exercise ordinary care to the extent the failure to exercise ordinary care contributed to the loss.

(c) Under subsection (b) an indorsement is made in the name of the person to whom an instrument is payable if (i) it is made in a name substantially similar to the name of that person or (ii) the instrument, whether or not indorsed, is deposited in a depositary bank to an account in a name substantially similar to the name of that person.

§3-406. Negligence Contributing to Forged Signature or Alteration of Instrument.

(a) A person whose failure to exercise ordinary care substantially contributes to an alteration of an instrument or to the making of a forged signature on an instrument is precluded from asserting the alteration or the forgery against a person that, in good faith, pays the instrument or takes it for value.

(b) If the person asserting the preclusion fails to exercise ordinary care in paying or taking the instrument and that failure substantially contributes to loss, the loss is allocated between the person precluded and the person asserting the preclusion according to the extent to which the failure of each to exercise ordinary care contributed to the loss.

(c) Under subsection (a) the burden of proving failure to exercise ordinary care is on the person asserting the preclusion. Under subsection (b) the burden of proving failure to exercise ordinary care is on the person precluded.

§3-407. Alteration.

(a) "Alteration" means (i) an unauthorized change in an instrument that purports to modify in any respect the obligation of a party to the instrument, or (ii) an unauthorized addition of words or numbers or other change to an incomplete instrument relating to the obligation of any party to the instrument.

(b) Except as provided in subsection (c), an alteration fraudulently made by the holder discharges any party to whose obligation the alteration applies unless that party assents or is precluded from asserting the alteration. No other alteration discharges any party, and the instrument may be enforced according to its original terms.

(c) If an instrument that has been fraudulently altered is acquired by a person having rights of a holder in due course, it may be enforced by that person according to its original terms. If an incomplete instrument is completed and is then acquired by a person having rights of a holder in due course, it may be enforced by that person as completed, whether or not the completion is a fraudulent alteration.

§3-408. Drawee Not Liable on Unaccepted Draft.

A check or other draft does not of itself operate as an assignment of funds in the hands of the drawee available for its payment, and the drawee is not liable on the instrument until the drawee accepts it.

§3-409. Acceptance of Draft; Certified Check.

(a) "Acceptance" means the drawee's signed agreement to pay a draft as presented. It must be written on the draft and may consist of the drawee's signature alone. Acceptance may be made at any time and becomes effective when notification pursuant to instructions is given or the accepted draft is delivered for the purpose of giving rights on the acceptance to any person.

(b) A draft may be accepted although it has not been signed by the drawer, is otherwise incomplete, is overdue, or has been dishonored.

(c) If a draft is payable at a fixed period after sight and the acceptor fails to date the acceptance, the holder may complete the acceptance by supplying a date in good faith.

(d) "Certified check" means a check accepted by the bank on which it is drawn. Acceptance may be made as stated in subsection (a) or by a writing on the check which indicates that the check is certified. The drawee of a check has no obligation to certify the check, and refusal to certify is not dishonor of the check.

§3-410. Acceptance Varying Draft.

(a) If the terms of a drawee's acceptance vary from the terms of the draft as presented, the holder may refuse the acceptance and treat the draft as dishonored. In that case, the drawee may cancel the acceptance.

(b) The terms of a draft are not varied by an acceptance to pay at a particular bank or place in the United States, unless the acceptance states that the draft is to be paid only at that bank or place.

(c) If the holder assents to an acceptance varying the terms of a draft, the obligation of each drawer and indorser that does not expressly assent to the acceptance is discharged.

§3-411. Refusal to Pay Cashier's Checks, Teller's Checks, and Certified Checks.

(a) In this section, "obligated bank" means the acceptor of a certified check or the issuer of a cashier's check or teller's check bought from the issuer.

(b) If the obligated bank wrongfully (i) refuses to pay a cashier's check or certified check, (ii) stops payment of a teller's check, or (iii) refuses to pay a dishonored teller's check, the person asserting the right to enforce the check is entitled to compensation for expenses and loss of interest resulting from the nonpayment and may recover consequential damages if the obligated bank refused to pay after receiving notice of particular circumstances giving rise to the damages.

(c) Expenses or consequential damages under subsection (b) are not recoverable if the refusal of the obligated bank to pay occurs because (i) the bank suspends payments, (ii) the obligated bank is asserting a claim or defense of the bank that it has reasonable grounds to believe is available against the person entitled to enforce the instrument, (iii) the obligated bank has a reasonable doubt whether the person demanding payment is the person entitled to enforce the instrument, or (iv) payment is prohibited by law.

§3-412. Obligation of Maker.

A maker of a note is obliged to pay the note (i) according to its terms at the time it was issued or, if not issued, at the time it first came into possession of a holder, or (ii) if the maker signed an incomplete instrument, according to its terms when completed as stated in Sections 3-115 and 3-407. The obligation is owed to a person entitled to enforce the note or to an indorser that paid the note pursuant to Section 3-415.

§3-413. Obligation of Acceptor.

(a) An acceptor of a draft is obliged to pay the draft (i) according to its terms at the time it was accepted, even though the acceptance states that the draft is payable "as originally drawn" or equivalent terms, (ii) if the acceptance varies the terms of the draft, according to the terms of the draft as varied, or (iii) if the acceptance is of a draft that is an incomplete instrument, according to its terms when completed as stated in Sections 3-115 and 3-407. The obligation is owed to a person entitled to enforce the draft or to the drawer or an indorser that paid the draft pursuant to Section 3-414 or 3-415.

(b) If the certification of a check or other acceptance of a draft states the amount certified or accepted, the obligation of the acceptor is that amount. If (i) the certification or acceptance does not state an amount, (ii) the instrument is subsequently altered by raising its amount, and (iii) the instrument is then negotiated to a holder in due course, the obligation of the acceptor is the amount of the instrument at the time it was negotiated to the holder in due course.

§3-414. Obligation of Drawer.

(a) If an unaccepted draft is dishonored, the drawer is obliged to pay the draft (i) according to its terms at the time it was issued or, if not issued, at the time it first came into possession of a holder, or (ii) if the drawer signed an incomplete instrument, according to its terms when completed as stated in Sections 3-115 and 3-407. The obligation is owed to a person entitled to enforce the draft or to an indorser that paid the draft pursuant to Section 3-415.

(b) If a draft is accepted by a bank and the acceptor dishonors the draft, the drawer has no obligation to pay the draft because of the dishonor, regardless of when or by whom acceptance was obtained.

(c) If a draft is accepted and the acceptor is not a bank, the obligation of the drawer to pay the draft if the draft is dishonored by the acceptor is the same as the obligation of an indorser stated in Section 3-415(a) and (c).

(d) Words in a draft indicating that the draft is drawn without recourse are effective to disclaim all liability of the drawer to pay the draft if the draft is not a check or a teller's check, but they are not effective to disclaim the obligation stated in subsection (a) if the draft is a check or a teller's check.

(e) If (i) a check is not presented for payment or given to a depositary bank for collection within 30 days after its date, (ii) the drawee suspends payments after expiration of the 30-day period without paying the check, and (iii) because of the suspension of payments the drawer is deprived of funds maintained with the drawee to cover payment of the check, the drawer to the extent deprived of funds may discharge its obligation to pay the check by assigning to the person entitled to enforce the check the rights of the drawer against the drawee with respect to the funds.

§3-415. Obligation of Indorser.

(a) Subject to subsections (b), (c) and (d) and to Section 3-419(d), if an instrument is dishonored, an indorser is obliged to pay the amount due on the instrument (i) according to the terms of the instrument at the time it was indorsed, or (ii) if the indorser indorsed an incomplete instrument, according to its terms when completed as stated in Sections 3-115 and 3-407. The obligation of the indorser is owed to a person entitled to enforce the instrument or to a subsequent indorser that paid the instrument pursuant to this section.

(b) If an indorsement states that it is made "without recourse" or otherwise disclaims liability of the indorser, the indorser is not liable under subsection (a) to pay the instrument.

(c) If notice of dishonor of an instrument is required by Section 3-503 and notice of dishonor complying with that section is not given to an indorser, the liability of the indorser under subsection (a) is discharged.

(d) If a draft is accepted by a bank after an indorsement was made and the acceptor dishonors the draft, the indorser is not liable under subsection (a) to pay the instrument.

(e) If an indorser of a check is liable under subsection (a) and the check is not presented for payment, or given to a depositary bank for collection, within 30 days after the day the indorsement was made, the liability of the indorser under subsection (a) is discharged.

§3-416. Transfer Warranties.

(a) A person that transfers an instrument for consideration warrants to the transferee and, if the transfer is by indorsement, to any subsequent transferee that:

(1) the warrantor is a person entitled to enforce the instrument,

(2) all signatures on the instrument are authentic and authorized,

(3) the instrument has not been altered,

(4) the instrument is not subject to a defense or claim in recoupment stated in Section 3-305(a) of any party that can be asserted against the warrantor, and

(5) the warrantor has no knowledge of any insolvency proceeding commenced with respect to the maker or acceptor or, in the case of an unaccepted draft, the drawer.

(b) A person to whom the warranties under subsection (a) are made and who took the instrument in good faith may recover from the warrantor as damages for breach of warranty an amount equal to the loss suffered as a result of the breach, but not more than the amount of the instrument plus expenses and loss of interest incurred as a result of the breach.

(c) The warranties stated in subsection (a) cannot be disclaimed with respect to checks. Unless notice of a claim for breach of warranty is given to the warrantor within 30 days after the claimant has reason to know of the breach and the identity of the warrantor, the warrantor is discharged to the extent of any loss caused by the delay in giving notice of the claim.

(d) A cause of action for breach of warranty under this section accrues when the claimant has reason to know of the breach.

§3-417. Presentment Warranties.

(a) If an unaccepted draft is presented to the drawee for payment or acceptance and the drawee pays or accepts the draft, (i) the person obtaining payment or acceptance, at the time of presentment, and (ii) a previous transferor of the draft, at the time of transfer, warrant to the drawee making payment or accepting the draft in good faith that:

(1) the warrantor is or was, at the time the warrantor transferred the draft, a person entitled to enforce the draft or authorized to obtain

payment or acceptance of the draft on behalf of a person entitled to enforce the draft;

(2) the draft has not been altered; and

(3) the warrantor has no knowledge that the signature of the purported drawer of the draft is unauthorized.

(b) A drawee making payment may recover from any warrantor damages for breach of warranty equal to the amount paid by the drawee less the amount the drawee received or is entitled to receive from the drawer because of payment of the draft. In addition the drawee is entitled to compensation for expenses and loss of interest resulting from the breach. The right of the drawee to recover damages under this subsection is not affected by any failure of the drawee to exercise ordinary care in making payment. If the drawee accepts the draft (i) breach of warranty is a defense to the obligation of the acceptor, and (ii) if the acceptor makes payment with respect to the draft, the acceptor is entitled to recover from any warrantor for breach of warranty the amounts stated in the first two sentences of this subsection.

(c) If a drawee asserts a claim for breach of warranty under subsection (a) based on an unauthorized indorsement of the draft or an alteration of the draft, the warrantor may defend by proving that the indorsement is effective under Section 3-404 or 3-405 or the drawer is precluded under Section 3-406 or 4-406 from asserting against the drawee the unauthorized indorsement or alteration.

(d) This subsection applies if (i) a dishonored draft is presented for payment to the drawer or an indorser or (ii) any other instrument is presented for payment to a party obliged to pay the instrument, and payment is received. The person obtaining payment and a prior transferor of the instrument warrant to the person making payment in good faith that the warrantor is or was, at the time the warrantor transferred the instrument, a person entitled to enforce the instrument or authorized to obtain payment on behalf of a person entitled to enforce the instrument. The person making payment may recover from any warrantor for breach of warranty an amount equal to the amount paid plus expenses and loss of interest resulting from the breach.

(e) The warranties stated in subsections (a) and (d) cannot be disclaimed with respect to checks. Unless notice of a claim for breach of warranty is given to the warrantor within 30 days after the claimant has reason to know of the breach and the identity of the warrantor, the warrantor is discharged to the extent of any loss caused by the delay in giving notice of the claim.

(f) A cause of action for breach of warranty under this section accrues when the claimant has reason to know of the breach.

§3-418. Payment or Acceptance by Mistake.

(a) Except as provided in subsection (c), if the drawee of a draft pays or accepts the draft and the drawee acted on the mistaken belief that (i) payment of the draft had not been stopped under Section 4-403, (ii) the signature of the purported drawer of the draft was authorized, or (iii) the balance in the drawer's account with the drawee represented available funds, the drawee may recover the amount paid from the person to whom or for whose benefit payment was made or, in the case of acceptance, may revoke the acceptance. Rights of the drawee under this subsection are not affected by failure of the drawee to exercise ordinary care in paying or accepting the draft.

(b) Except as provided in subsection (c), if an instrument has been paid or accepted by mistake and the case is not covered by subsection (a), the person paying or accepting may recover the amount paid or revoke acceptance to the extent allowed by the law governing mistake and restitution.

(c) The remedies provided by subsection (a) or (b) may not be asserted against a person who took the instrument in good faith and for value. This subsection does not limit remedies provided by Section 3-417 for breach of warranty.

§3-419. Instruments Signed for Accommodation.

(a) If an instrument is issued for value given for the benefit of a party to the instrument ("accommodated party") and another party to the instrument ("accommodation party") signs the instrument for the purpose of incurring liability on the instrument without being a direct beneficiary of the value given for the instrument, the instrument is signed by the accommodation party "for accommodation."

(b) An accommodation party may sign the instrument as maker, drawer, acceptor, or indorser and, subject to subsection (d), is obliged to pay the instrument in the capacity in which the accommodation party signs. The obligation of an accommodation party may be enforced notwithstanding any statute of frauds and regardless of whether the accommodation party receives consideration for the accommodation.

(c) A person signing an instrument is presumed to be an accommodation party and there is notice that the instrument is signed for accommodation if the signature is an anomalous indorsement or is accompanied by words indicating that the signer is acting as surety or guarantor with respect to the obligation of another party to the instrument. Except as provided in Section 3-606, the obligation of an accommodation party to pay the instrument is not affected by the fact that the person enforcing the obligation had notice when the instrument was taken by that person that the accommodation party signed the instrument for accommodation.

(d) If the signature of a party to an instrument is accompanied by words indicating unambiguously that the party is guaranteeing collection rather than payment of the obligation of another party to the instrument, the signer is obliged to pay the amount due on the instrument to a person entitled to enforce the instrument only if (i) execution of judgment against the other party has been returned unsatisfied, (ii) the other party is insolvent or in an insolvency proceeding, (iii) the other party cannot be served with process, or (iv) it is otherwise apparent that payment cannot be obtained from the party whose obligation is guaranteed.

(e) An accommodation party that pays the instrument is entitled to reimbursement from the accommodated party and is entitled to enforce the instrument against the accommodated party. An accommodated party that pays the instrument has no right of recourse against, and is not entitled to contribution from, an accommodation party.

§3-420. Conversion of Instrument.

(a) The law applicable to conversion of personal property applies to instruments. An instrument is also converted if the instrument lacks an indorsement necessary for negotiation and it is purchased or taken for collection or the drawee takes the instrument and makes payment to a person not entitled to receive payment. An action for conversion of an instrument may not be brought by (i) the maker, drawer, or acceptor of the instrument or (ii) a payee or indorsee who did not receive delivery of the instrument either directly or through delivery to an agent or a co-payee.

(b) In an action under subsection (a), the measure of liability is presumed to be the amount payable on the instrument, but recovery may not exceed the amount of the plaintiff's interest in the instrument.

(c) A representative, other than a depositary bank, that has in good faith dealt with an instrument or its proceeds on behalf of one who was not the person entitled to enforce the instrument is not liable in conversion to that person beyond the amount of any proceeds that it has not paid out.

Part 5—Dishonor

§3-501. Presentment.

(a) "Presentment" means a demand (i) to pay an instrument made to the maker, drawee, or acceptor or, in the case of a note or accepted draft payable at a bank, to the bank, or (ii) to accept a draft made to the drawee, by a person entitled to enforce the instrument.

(b) Subject to Article 4, agreement of the parties, clearing house rules and the like,

(1) presentment may be made at the place of payment of the instrument and must be made at the place of payment if the instrument is payable at a bank in the United States; may be made by any commercially reasonable means, including an oral, written, or electronic communication; is effective when the demand for payment or acceptance is

received by the person to whom presentment is made; is effective if made to any one of two or more makers, acceptors, drawees or other payors; and (2) without dishonoring the instrument, the party to whom presentment is made may (i) treat presentment as occurring on the next business day after the day of presentment if the party to whom presentment is made has established a cut-off hour not earlier than 2 P.M. for the receipt and processing of instruments presented for payment or acceptance and presentment is made after the cut-off hour, (ii) require exhibition of the instrument, (iii) require reasonable identification of the person making presentment and evidence of authority to make it if made on behalf of another person, (iv) require a signed receipt on the instrument for any payment made or surrender of the instrument if full payment is made, (v) return the instrument for lack of a necessary indorsement, or (vi) refuse payment or acceptance for failure of the presentment to comply with the terms of the instrument, an agreement of the parties, or other law or applicable rule.

§3-502. Dishonor.

(a) Dishonor of a note is governed by the following rules:

(1) If the note is payable on demand, the note is dishonored if presentment is duly made and the note is not paid on the day of presentment.

(2) If the note is not payable on demand and is payable at or through a bank or the terms of the note require presentment, the note is dishonored if presentment is duly made and the note is not paid on the day it becomes payable or the day of presentment, whichever is later.

(3) If the note is not payable on demand and subparagraph (2) does not apply, the note is dishonored if it is not paid on the day it becomes payable.

(b) Dishonor of an unaccepted draft other than a documentary draft is governed by the following rules:

(1) If a check is presented for payment otherwise than for immediate payment over the counter, the check is dishonored if the payor bank makes timely return of the check or sends timely notice of dishonor or nonpayment under Section 4-301 or 4-302, or becomes accountable for the amount of the check under Section 4-302.

(2) If the draft is payable on demand and subparagraph (1) does not apply, the draft is dishonored if presentment for payment is duly made and the draft is not paid on the day of presentment.

(3) If the draft is payable on a date stated in the draft, the draft is dishonored if (i) presentment for payment is duly made and payment is not made on the day the draft becomes payable or the day of presentment, whichever is later, or (ii) presentment for acceptance is duly made before the day the draft becomes payable and the draft is not accepted on the day of presentment.

(4) If the draft is payable on elapse of a period of time after sight or acceptance, the draft is dishonored if presentment for acceptance is duly made and the draft is not accepted on the day of presentment.

(c) Dishonor of an unaccepted documentary draft occurs according to the rules stated in subparagraphs (2), (3), and (4) of subsection (b) except that payment or acceptance may be delayed without dishonor until no later than the close of the third business day of the drawee following the day on which payment or acceptance is required by those subparagraphs.

(d) Dishonor of an accepted draft is governed by the following rules:

(1) If the draft is payable on demand, the draft is dishonored if presentment for payment is duly made and the draft is not paid on the day of presentment.

(2) If the draft is not payable on demand, the draft is dishonored if presentment for payment is duly made and payment is not made on the day it becomes payable or the day of presentment, whichever is later.

(e) In any case in which presentment is otherwise required for dishonor under this section and presentment is excused under Section 3-504, dishonor occurs without presentment if the instrument is not duly accepted or paid.

(f) If a draft is dishonored because timely acceptance of the draft was not made and the person entitled to demand acceptance consents to a late

acceptance, from the time of acceptance the draft is treated as never having been dishonored.

§3-503. Notice of Dishonor.

(a) The obligation of an indorser stated in Section 3-415(a) and the obligation of a drawer stated in Section 3-414(c) may not be enforced unless (i) the indorser or drawer is given notice of dishonor of the instrument complying with this section or (ii) notice of dishonor is excused under Section 3-504(c).

(b) Notice of dishonor may be given by any person; may be given by any commercially reasonable means including an oral, written, or electronic communication; is sufficient if it reasonably identifies the instrument and indicates that the instrument has been dishonored or has not been paid or accepted. Return of an instrument given to a bank for collection is a sufficient notice of dishonor.

(c) Subject to Section 3-504(d), with respect to an instrument taken for collection by a collecting bank, notice of dishonor must be given (i) by the bank before midnight of the next banking day following the banking day on which the bank receives notice of dishonor of the instrument, and (ii) by any other person within 30 days following the day on which the person receives notice of dishonor. With respect to any other instrument, notice of dishonor must be given within 30 days following the day on which dishonor occurs.

§3-504. Excused Presentment and Notice of Dishonor.

(a) Presentment for payment or acceptance of an instrument is excused if (i) the person entitled to present the instrument cannot with reasonable diligence make presentment, (ii) the maker or acceptor has repudiated an obligation to pay the instrument or is dead or in insolvency proceedings, (iii) by the terms of the instrument presentment is not necessary to enforce the obligation of indorsers or the drawer, or (iv) the drawer or indorser whose obligation is being enforced waived presentment or otherwise had no reason to expect or right to require that the instrument be paid or accepted.

(b) Presentment for payment or acceptance of a draft is also excused if the drawer instructed the drawee not to pay or accept the draft or the drawee was not obligated to the drawer to pay the draft.

(c) Notice of dishonor is excused if (i) by the terms of the instrument notice of dishonor is not necessary to enforce the obligation of a party to pay the instrument, or (ii) the party whose obligation is being enforced waived notice of dishonor. A waiver of presentment is also a waiver of notice of dishonor.

(d) Delay in giving notice of dishonor is excused if the delay was caused by circumstances beyond the control of the person giving the notice and the person giving the notice exercised reasonable diligence after the cause of the delay ceased to operate.

§3-505. Evidence of Dishonor.

(a) The following are admissible as evidence and create a presumption of dishonor and of any notice of dishonor stated:

(1) a document regular in form as provided in subsection (b) which purports to be a protest;

(2) a purported stamp or writing of the drawee, payor bank, or presenting bank on or accompanying the instrument stating that acceptance or payment has been refused unless reasons for the refusal are stated and the reasons are not consistent with dishonor;

(3) a book or record of the drawee, payor bank, or collecting bank, kept in the usual course of business which shows dishonor, even if there is no evidence of who made the entry.

(b) A protest is a certificate of dishonor made by a United States consul or vice consul, or a notary public or other person authorized to administer oaths by the law of the place where dishonor occurs. It may be made upon information satisfactory to that person. The protest must identify the instrument and certify either that presentment has been made or, if not made, the reason why it was not made, and that the instrument has been dishonored by nonacceptance or nonpayment. The protest may also certify that notice of dishonor has been given to some or all parties.

Part 6—Discharge and Payment

§3-601. Discharge and Effect of Discharge.

(a) The obligation of a party to pay the instrument is discharged as stated in this Article or by an act or agreement with the party which would discharge an obligation to pay money under a simple contract.

(b) Discharge of the obligation of a party is not effective against a person acquiring rights of a holder in due course of the instrument without notice of the discharge.

§3-602. Payment.

(a) Subject to subsection (b), an instrument is paid to the extent payment is made (i) by or on behalf of a party obliged to pay the instrument, and (ii) to a person entitled to enforce the instrument. To the extent of the payment, the obligation of the party obliged to pay the instrument is discharged even though payment is made with knowledge of a claim to the instrument under Section 3-306 by another person.

(b) The obligation of a party to pay the instrument is not discharged under subsection (a) if:

(1) a claim to the instrument under Section 3-306 is enforceable against the party receiving payment and (i) payment is made with knowledge by the payor that payment is prohibited by injunction or similar process of a court of competent jurisdiction, or (ii) in the case of an instrument other than a cashier's check, teller's check, or certified check, the party making payment accepted, from the person having a claim to the instrument, indemnity against loss resulting from refusal to pay the person entitled to enforce the instrument, or

(2) the person making payment knows that the instrument is a stolen instrument and pays a person that it knows is in wrongful possession of the instrument.

§3-603. Tender of Payment.

(a) If tender of payment of an obligation of a party to an instrument is made to a person entitled to enforce the obligation, the effect of tender is governed by principles of law applicable to tender of payment of an obligation under a simple contract.

(b) If tender of payment of an obligation to pay the instrument is made to a person entitled to enforce the instrument and the tender is refused, there is discharge, to the extent of the amount of the tender, of the obligation of an indorser or accommodation party having a right of recourse against the obligor making the tender.

(c) If tender of payment of an amount due on an instrument is made by or on behalf of the obligor to the person entitled to enforce the instrument, the obligation of the obligor to pay interest after the due date on the amount tendered is discharged. If presentment is required with respect to an instrument and the obligor is able and ready to pay on the due date at every place of payment stated in the instrument, the obligor is deemed to have made tender of payment on the due date to the person entitled to enforce the instrument.

§3-604. Discharge by Cancellation or Renunciation.

(a) A person entitled to enforce an instrument may, with or without consideration, discharge the obligation of a party to pay the instrument (i) by an intentional voluntary act such as surrender of the instrument to the party, destruction, mutilation, or cancellation of the instrument, cancellation or striking out of the party's signature, or the addition of words to the instrument indicating discharge, or (ii) by agreeing not to sue or otherwise renouncing rights against the party by a signed writing.

(b) Cancellation or striking out of an indorsement pursuant to subsection (a) does not affect the status and rights of a party derived from the indorsement.

§3-605. Discharge of Indorsers and Accommodation Parties.

(a) For the purposes of this section, the term "indorser" includes a drawer having the obligation stated in Section 3-414(c).

(b) Discharge of the obligation of a party to the instrument under Section 3-605 does not discharge the obligation of an indorser or accommodation party having a right of recourse against the discharged party.

(c) If a person entitled to enforce an instrument agrees, with or without consideration, to a material modification of the obligation of a party to the instrument, including an extension of the due date, there is discharge of the obligation of an indorser or accommodation party having a right of recourse against the person whose obligation is modified to the extent the modification causes loss to the indorser or accommodation party with respect to the right of recourse. The indorser or accommodation party is deemed to have suffered loss as a result of the modification equal to the amount of the right of recourse unless the person enforcing the instrument proves that no loss was caused by the modification or that the loss caused by the modification was less than the amount of the right of recourse.

(d) If the obligation of a party to an instrument is secured by an interest in collateral and impairment of the value of the interest is caused by a person entitled to enforce the instrument, there is discharge of the obligation of an indorser or accommodation party having a right of recourse against the obligor to the extent of the impairment. The value of an interest in collateral is impaired to the extent (i) the value of the interest is reduced to an amount less than the amount of the right of recourse of the party asserting discharge, or (ii) the reduction in value of the interest causes an increase in the amount by which the amount of the right of recourse exceeds the value of the interest. The burden of proving impairment is on the party asserting discharge.

(e) If the obligation of a party to an instrument is secured by an interest in collateral not provided by an accommodation party and the value of the interest is impaired by a person entitled to enforce the instrument, the obligation of any party who is jointly and severally liable with respect to the secured obligation is discharged to the extent the impairment causes the party asserting discharge to pay more than that party would have been obliged to pay, taking into account rights of contribution, if impairment had not occurred. If the party asserting discharge is an accommodation party not entitled to discharge under subsection (d), the party is deemed to have a right to contribution based on joint and several liability rather than a right to reimbursement. The burden of proving impairment is on the party asserting discharge.

(f) Under subsection (d) or (e) causation of impairment includes (i) failure to obtain or maintain perfection or recordation of the interest in collateral, (ii) release of collateral without substitution of collateral of equal value, (iii) failure to perform a duty to preserve the value of collateral owed, under Article 9 or other law, to a debtor or surety or other person secondarily liable, or (iv) failure to comply with applicable law in disposing of collateral.

(g) An accommodation party is not discharged under subsection (c) or (d) unless the person agreeing to the modification or causing the impairment knows of the accommodation or has notice under Section 3-419(c) that the instrument was signed for accommodation. There is no discharge of any party under subsection (c), (d), or (e) if (i) the party asserting discharge consents to the event or conduct that is the basis of the discharge, or (ii) the instrument or a separate agreement of the party provides for waiver of discharge under this section either specifically or by general language indicating that parties to the instrument waive defenses based on suretyship or impairment of collateral.

ARTICLE 4: BANK DEPOSITS AND COLLECTIONS

Part 1—General Provisions and Definitions

§4-101. Short Title.

This Article shall be known and may be cited as Uniform Commercial Code—Bank Deposits and Collections.

§4-102. Applicability.

(1) To the extent that items within this Article are also within the scope of Articles 3 and 8, they are subject to the provisions of those Articles. In the

event of conflict the provisions of this Article govern those of Article 3 but the provisions of Article 8 govern those of this Article.

(2) The liability of a bank for action or non-action with respect to any item handled by it for purposes of presentment, payment or collection is governed by the law of the place where the bank is located. In the case of action or non-action by or at a branch or separate office of a bank, its liability is governed by the law of the place where the branch or separate office is located.

§4-103. Variation by Agreement; Measure of Damages; Certain Action Constituting Ordinary Care.

(1) The effect of the provisions of this Article may be varied by agreement except that no agreement can disclaim a bank's responsibility for its own lack of good faith or failure to exercise ordinary care or can limit the measure of damages for such lack or failure; but the parties may by agreement determine the standards by which such responsibility is to be measured if such standards are not manifestly unreasonable.

(2) Federal Reserve regulations and operating letters, clearing house rules, and the like, have the effect of agreements under subsection (1), whether or not specifically assented to by all parties interested in items handled.

(3) Action or non-action approved by this Article or pursuant to Federal Reserve regulations or operating letters constitutes the exercise of ordinary care and, in the absence of special instructions, action or non-action consistent with clearing house rules and the like or with a general banking usage not disapproved by this Article, prima facie constitutes the exercise of ordinary care.

(4) The specification or approval of certain procedures by this Article does not constitute disapproval of other procedures which may be reasonable under the circumstances.

(5) The measure of damages for failure to exercise ordinary care in handling an item is the amount of the item reduced by an amount which could not have been realized by the use of ordinary care, and where there is bad faith it includes other damages, if any, suffered by the party as a proximate consequence.

§4-104. Definitions and Index of Definitions.

(1) In this Article unless the context otherwise requires

(a) "Account" means any account with a bank and includes a checking, time, interest or savings account;

(b) "Afternoon" means the period of a day between noon and midnight;

(c) "Banking day" means that part of any day on which a bank is open to the public for carrying on substantially all of its banking functions;

(d) "Clearing house" means any association of banks or other payors regularly clearing items;

(e) "Customer" means any person having an account with a bank or for whom a bank has agreed to collect items and includes a bank carrying an account with another bank;

(f) "Documentary draft" means any negotiable or non-negotiable draft with accompanying documents, securities or other papers to be delivered against honor of the draft;

(g) "Item" means any instrument for the payment of money even though it is not negotiable but does not include money;

(h) "Midnight deadline" with respect to a bank is midnight on its next banking day following the banking day on which it receives the relevant item or notice or from which the time for taking action commences to run, whichever is later;

(i) "Properly payable" includes the availability of funds for payment at the time of decision to pay or dishonor;

(j) "Settle" means to pay in cash, by clearing house settlement, in a charge or credit or by remittance, or otherwise as instructed. A settlement may be either provisional or final;

(k) "Suspends payments" with respect to a bank means that it has been closed by order of the supervisory authorities, that a public officer has

been appointed to take it over or that it ceases or refuses to make payments in the ordinary course of business.

(2) Other definitions applying to this Article and the sections in which they appear are:

"Collecting bank" Section 4-105.
"Depositary bank" Section 4-105.
"Intermediary bank" Section 4-105.
"Payor bank" Section 4-105.
"Presenting bank" Section 4-105.
"Remitting bank" Section 4-105. (3)

(3) The following definitions in other Articles apply to this Article:

"Acceptance" Section 3-410.
"Certificate of deposit" Section 3-104.
"Certification" Section 3-411.
"Check" Section 3-104.
"Draft" Section 3-104.
"Holder in due course" Section 3-302.
"Notice of dishonor" Section 3-508.
"Presentment" Section 3-504.
"Protest" Section 3-509.
"Secondary party" Section 3-102.

(4) In addition Article 1 contains general definitions and principles of construction and interpretation applicable throughout this Article.

§4-105. "Depositary Bank"; "Intermediary Bank"; "Collecting Bank"; "Payor Bank"; "Presenting Bank"; "Remitting Bank".

In this Article unless the context otherwise requires:

(a) "Depositary bank" means the first bank to which an item is transferred for collection even though it is also the payor bank;

(b) "Payor bank" means a bank by which an item is payable as drawn or accepted;

(c) "Intermediary bank" means any bank to which an item is transferred in course of collection except the depositary or payor bank;

(d) "Collecting bank" means any bank handling the item for collection except the payor bank;

(e) "Presenting bank" means any bank presenting an item except a payor bank;

(f) "Remitting bank" means any payor or intermediary bank remitting for an item.

§4-106. Separate Office of a Bank.

A branch or separate office of a bank [maintaining its own deposit ledgers] is a separate bank for the purpose of computing the time within which and determining the place at or to which action may be taken or notices or orders shall be given under this Article and under Article 3.

Note: *The brackets are to make it optional with the several states whether to require a branch to maintain its own deposit ledgers in order to be considered to be a separate bank for certain purposes under Article 4. In some states "maintaining its own deposit ledgers" is a satisfactory test. In others branch banking practices are such that this test would not be suitable.*

§4-107. Time of Receipt of Items.

(1) For the purpose of allowing time to process items, prove balances and make the necessary entries on its books to determine its position for the day, a bank may fix an afternoon hour of two P.M. or later as a cut-off hour for the handling of money and items and the making of entries on its books.

(2) Any item or deposit of money received on any day after a cut-off hour so fixed or after the close of the banking day may be treated as being received at the opening of the next banking day.

§4-108. Delays.

(1) Unless otherwise instructed, a collecting bank in a good faith effort to secure payment may, in the case of specific items and with or without the approval of any person involved, waive, modify or extend time limits imposed or permitted by this Act for a period not in excess of an additional

banking day without discharge of secondary parties and without liability to its transferor or any prior party.

(2) Delay by a collecting bank or payor bank beyond time limits prescribed or permitted by this Act or by instructions is excused if caused by interruption of communication facilities, suspension of payments by another bank, war, emergency conditions or other circumstances beyond the control of the bank provided it exercises such diligence as the circumstances require.

§4-109. Process of Posting.

The "process of posting" means the usual procedure followed by a payor bank in determining to pay an item and in recording the payment including one or more of the following or other steps as determined by the bank:

(a) verification of any signature;

(b) ascertaining that sufficient funds are available;

(c) affixing a "paid" or other stamp;

(d) entering a charge or entry to a customer's account;

(e) correcting or reversing an entry or erroneous action with respect to the item.

Part 2—Collection of Items: Depositary and Collecting Banks

§4-201. Presumption and Duration of Agency Status of Collecting Banks and Provisional Status of Credits; Applicability of Article; Item Indorsed "Pay Any Bank".

(1) Unless a contrary intent clearly appears and prior to the time that a settlement given by a collecting bank for an item is or becomes final (subsection (3) of Section 4-211 and Sections 4-212 and 4-213) the bank is an agent or sub-agent of the owner of the item and any settlement given for the item is provisional. This provision applies regardless of the form of indorsement or lack of indorsement and even though credit given for the item is subject to immediate withdrawal as of right or is in fact withdrawn; but the continuance of ownership of an item by its owner and any rights of the owner to proceeds of the item are subject to rights of a collecting bank such as those resulting from outstanding advances on the item and valid rights of setoff. When an item is handled by banks for purposes of presentment, payment and collection, the relevant provisions of this Article apply even though action of parties clearly establishes that a particular bank has purchased the item and is the owner of it.

(2) After an item has been indorsed with the words "pay any bank" or the like, only a bank may acquire the rights of a holder

    (a) until the item has been returned to the customer initiating collection; or

    (b) until the item has been specially indorsed by a bank to a person who is not a bank.

§4-202. Responsibility for Collection; When Action Seasonable.

(1) A collecting bank must use ordinary care in

    (a) presenting an item or sending it for presentment; and

    (b) sending notice of dishonor or non-payment or returning an item other than a documentary draft to the bank's transferor [or directly to the depositary bank under subsection (2) of Section 4-212] (*see note to Section 4-212*) after learning that the item has not been paid or accepted as the case may be; and

    (c) settling for an item when the bank receives final settlement; and

    (d) making or providing for any necessary protest; and

    (e) notifying its transferor of any loss or delay in transit within a reasonable time after discovery thereof.

(2) A collecting bank taking proper action before its midnight deadline following receipt of an item, notice or payment acts seasonably; taking proper action within a reasonably longer time may be seasonable but the bank has the burden of so establishing.

(3) Subject to subsection (1)(a), a bank is not liable for the insolvency, neglect, misconduct, mistake or default of another bank or person or for loss or destruction of an item in transit or in the possession of others.

§4-203. Effect of Instructions.

Subject to the provisions of Article 3 concerning conversion of instruments (Section 3-419) and the provisions of both Article 3 and this Article concerning restrictive indorsements only a collecting bank's transferor can give instructions which affect the bank or constitute notice to it and a collecting bank is not liable to prior parties for any action taken pursuant to such instructions or in accordance with any agreement with its transferor.

§4-204. Methods of Sending and Presenting; Sending Direct to Payor Bank.

(1) A collecting bank must send items by reasonably prompt method taking into consideration any relevant instructions, the nature of the item, the number of such items on hand, and the cost of collection involved and the method generally used by it or others to present such items.

(2) A collecting bank may send

    (a) any item direct to the payor bank;

    (b) any item to any non-bank payor if authorized by its transferor; and

    (c) any item other than documentary drafts to any non-bank payor, if authorized by Federal Reserve regulation or operating letter, clearing house rule or the like.

(3) Presentment may be made by a presenting bank at a place where the payor bank has requested that presentment be made.

§4-205. Supplying Missing Indorsement; No Notice from Prior Indorsement.

(1) A depositary bank which has taken an item for collection may supply any indorsement of the customer which is necessary to title unless the item contains the words "payee's indorsement required" or the like. In the absence of such a requirement a statement placed on the item by the depositary bank to the effect that the item was deposited by a customer or credited to his account is effective as the customer's indorsement.

(2) An intermediary bank, or payor bank which is not a depositary bank, is neither given notice nor otherwise affected by a restrictive indorsement of any person except the bank's immediate transferor.

§4-206. Transfer Between Banks.

Any agreed method which identifies the transferor bank is sufficient for the item's further transfer to another bank.

§4-207. Warranties of Customer and Collecting Bank on Transfer or Presentment of Items; Time for Claims.

(1) Each customer or collecting bank who obtains payment or acceptance of an item and each prior customer and collecting bank warrants to the payor bank or other payor who in good faith pays or accepts the item that

    (a) he has a good title to the item or is authorized to obtain payment or acceptance on behalf of one who has a good title; and

    (b) he has no knowledge that the signature of the maker or drawer is unauthorized, except that this warranty is not given by any customer or collecting bank that is a holder in due course and acts in good faith

        (i) to a maker with respect to the maker's own signature; or

        (ii) to a drawer with respect to the drawer's own signature, whether or not the drawer is also the drawee; or

        (iii) to an acceptor of an item if the holder in due course took the item after the acceptance or obtained the acceptance without knowledge that the drawer's signature was unauthorized; and

    (c) the item has not been materially altered, except that this warranty is not given by any customer or collecting bank that is a holder in due course and acts in good faith

        (i) to the maker of a note; or

        (ii) to the drawer of a draft whether or not the drawer is also the drawee; or

        (iii) to the acceptor of an item with respect to an alteration made prior to the acceptance if the holder in due course took the item after the acceptance, even though the acceptance provided "payable as originally drawn" or equivalent terms; or

(iv) to the acceptor of an item with respect to an alteration made after the acceptance.

(2) Each customer and collecting bank who transfers an item and receives a settlement or other consideration for it warrants to his transferee and to any subsequent collecting bank who takes the item in good faith that

(a) he has a good title to the item or is authorized to obtain payment or acceptance on behalf of one who has a good title and the transfer is otherwise rightful; and

(b) all signatures are genuine or authorized; and

(c) the item has not been materially altered; and

(d) no defense of any party is good against him; and

(e) he has no knowledge of any insolvency proceeding instituted with respect to the maker or acceptor or the drawer of an unaccepted item.

In addition each customer and collecting bank so transferring an item and receiving a settlement or other consideration engages that upon dishonor and any necessary notice of dishonor and protest he will take up the item.

(3) The warranties and the engagement to honor set forth in the two preceding subsections arise notwithstanding the absence of indorsement or words of guaranty or warranty in the transfer or presentment and a collecting bank remains liable for their breach despite remittance to its transferor. Damages for breach of such warranties or engagement to honor shall not exceed the consideration received by the customer or collecting bank responsible plus finance charges and expenses related to the item, if any.

(4) Unless a claim for breach of warranty under this section is made within a reasonable time after the person claiming learns of the breach, the person liable is discharged to the extent of any loss caused by the delay in making claim.

§4-208. Security Interest of Collecting Bank in Items, Accompanying Documents and Proceeds.

(1) A bank has a security interest in an item and any accompanying documents or the proceeds of either

(a) in case of an item deposited in an account to the extent to which credit given for the item has been withdrawn or applied;

(b) in case of an item for which it has given credit available for withdrawal as of right, to the extent of the credit given whether or not the credit is drawn upon and whether or not there is a right of charge-back; or

(c) if it makes an advance on or against the item.

(2) When credit which has been given for several items received at one time or pursuant to a single agreement is withdrawn or applied in part the security interest remains upon all the items, any accompanying documents or the proceeds of either. For the purpose of this section, credits first given are first withdrawn.

(3) Receipt by a collecting bank of a final settlement for an item is a realization on its security interest in the item, accompanying documents and proceeds. To the extent and so long as the bank does not receive final settlement for the item or give up possession of the item or accompanying documents for purposes other than collection, the security interest continues and is subject to the provisions of Article 9 except that

(a) no security agreement is necessary to make the security interest enforceable (subsection (1)(b) of Section 9-203); and

(b) no filing is required to perfect the security interest; and

(c) the security interest has priority over conflicting perfected security interests in the item, accompanying documents or proceeds.

§4-209. When Bank Gives Value for Purposes of Holder in Due Course.

For purposes of determining its status as a holder in due course, the bank has given value to the extent that it has a security interest in an item provided that the bank otherwise complies with the requirements of Section 3-302 on what constitutes a holder in due course.

§4-210. Presentment by Notice of Item Not Payable by, Through or at a Bank; Liability of Secondary Parties.

(1) Unless otherwise instructed, a collecting bank may present an item not payable by, through or at a bank by sending to the party to accept or pay a written notice that the bank holds the item for acceptance or payment. The notice must be sent in time to be received on or before the day when presentment is due and the bank must meet any requirement of the party to accept or pay under Section 3-505 by the close of the bank's next banking day after it knows of the requirement.

(2) Where presentment is made by notice and neither honor nor request for compliance with a requirement under Section 3-505 is received by the close of business on the day after maturity or in the case of demand items by the close of business on the third banking day after notice was sent, the presenting bank may treat the item as dishonored and charge any secondary party by sending him notice of the facts.

§4-211. Media of Remittance; Provisional and Final Settlement in Remittance Cases.

(1) A collecting bank may take in settlement of an item

(a) a check of the remitting bank or of another bank on any bank except the remitting bank; or

(b) a cashier's check or similar primary obligation of a remitting bank which is a member of or clears through a member of the same clearing house or group as the collecting bank; or

(c) appropriate authority to charge an account of the remitting bank or of another bank with the collecting bank; or

(d) if the item is drawn upon or payable by a person other than a bank, a cashier's check, certified check or other bank check or obligation.

(2) If before its midnight deadline the collecting bank properly dishonors a remittance check or authorization to charge on itself or presents or forwards for collection a remittance instrument of or on another bank which is of a kind approved by subsection (1) or has not been authorized by it, the collecting bank is not liable to prior parties in the event of the dishonor of such check, instrument or authorization.

(3) A settlement for an item by means of a remittance instrument or authorization to charge is or becomes a final settlement as to both the person making and the person receiving the settlement

(a) if the remittance instrument or authorization to charge is of a kind approved by subsection (1) or has not been authorized by the person receiving the settlement and in either case the person receiving the settlement acts seasonably before its midnight deadline in presenting, forwarding for collection or paying the instrument or authorization,—at the time the remittance instrument or authorization is finally paid by the payor by which it is payable;

(b) if the person receiving the settlement has authorized remittance by a non-bank check or obligation or by a cashier's check or similar primary obligation of or a check upon the payor or other remitting bank which is not of a kind approved by subsection (1)(b),—at the time of the receipt of such remittance check or obligation; or

(c) if in a case not covered by sub-paragraphs (a) or (b) the person receiving the settlement fails to seasonably present, forward for collection, pay or return a remittance instrument or authorization to it to charge before its midnight deadline,—at such midnight deadline.

§4-212. Right of Charge-Back or Refund.

(1) If a collecting bank has made provisional settlement with its customer for an item and itself fails by reason of dishonor, suspension of payments by a bank or otherwise to receive a settlement for the item which is or becomes final, the bank may revoke the settlement given by it, charge-back the amount of any credit given for the item to its customer's account or obtain refund from its customer whether or not it is able to return the items if by its midnight deadline or within a longer reasonable time after it learns the facts it returns the item or sends notification of the facts. These rights to revoke, charge-back and obtain refund terminate if and when a settlement for the item received by the bank is or becomes final (subsection (3) of Section 4-211 and subsections (2) and (3) of Section 4-213).

[(2) Within the time and manner prescribed by this section and Section 4-301, an intermediary or payor bank, as the case may be, may return an unpaid item directly to the depositary bank and may send for collection a draft on the depositary bank and obtain reimbursement. In such case, if the depositary bank has received provisional settlement for the item, it must reimburse the bank drawing the draft and any provisional credits for the item between banks shall become and remain final.]

Note: *Direct returns is recognized as an innovation that is not yet established bank practice, and therefore, Paragraph 2 has been bracketed. Some lawyers have doubts whether it should be included in legislation or left to development by agreement.*

(3) A depositary bank which is also the payor may charge-back the amount of an item to its customer's account or obtain refund in accordance with the section governing return of an item received by a payor bank for credit on its books (Section 4-301).

(4) The right to charge-back is not affected by

(a) prior use of the credit given for the item; or

(b) failure by any bank to exercise ordinary care with respect to the item but any bank so failing remains liable.

(5) A failure to charge-back or claim refund does not affect other rights of the bank against the customer or any other party.

(6) If credit is given in dollars as the equivalent of the value of an item payable in a foreign currency the dollar amount of any charge-back or refund shall be calculated on the basis of the buying sight rate for the foreign currency prevailing on the day when the person entitled to the charge-back or refund learns that it will not receive payment in ordinary course.

§4-213. Final Payment of Item by Payor Bank; When Provisional Debits and Credits Become Final; When Certain Credits Become Available for Withdrawal.

(1) An item is finally paid by a payor bank when the bank has done any of the following, whichever happens first:

(a) paid the item in cash; or

(b) settled for the item without reserving a right to revoke the settlement and without having such right under statute, clearing house rule or agreement; or

(c) completed the process of posting the item to the indicated account of the drawer, maker or other person to be charged therewith; or

(d) made a provisional settlement for the item and failed to revoke the settlement in the time and manner permitted by statute, clearing house rule or agreement.

Upon a final payment under subparagraphs (b), (c), or (d) the payor bank shall be accountable for the amount of the item.

(2) If provisional settlement for an item between the presenting and payor banks is made through a clearing house or by debits or credits in an account between them, then to the extent that provisional debits or credits for the item are entered in accounts between the presenting and payor banks or between the presenting and successive prior collecting banks seriatim, they become final upon final payment of the item by the payor bank.

(3) If a collecting bank receives a settlement for an item which is or becomes final (subsection (3) of Section 4-211, subsection (2) of Section 4-213) the bank is accountable to its customer for the amount of the item and any provisional credit given for the item in an account with its customer becomes final.

(4) Subject to any right of the bank to apply the credit to an obligation of the customer, credit given by a bank for an item in an account with its customer becomes available for withdrawal as of right

(a) in any case where the bank has received a provisional settlement for the item,—when such settlement becomes final and the bank has had a reasonable time to learn that the settlement is final;

(b) in any case where the bank is both a depositary bank and a payor bank and the item is finally paid,—at the opening of the bank's second banking day following receipt of the item.

(5) A deposit of money in a bank is final when made but, subject to any right of the bank to apply the deposit to an obligation of the customer, the deposit becomes available for withdrawal as of right at the opening of the bank's next banking day following receipt of the deposit.

§4-214. Insolvency and Preference.

(1) Any item in or coming into the possession of a payor or collecting bank which suspends payment and which item is not finally paid shall be returned by the receiver, trustee or agent in charge of the closed bank to the presenting bank or the closed bank's customer.

(2) If a payor bank finally pays an item and suspends payments without making a settlement for the item with its customer or the presenting bank which settlement is or becomes final, the owner of the item has a preferred claim against the payor bank.

(3) If a payor bank gives or a collecting bank gives or receives a provisional settlement for an item and thereafter suspends payments, the suspension does not prevent or interfere with the settlement becoming final if such finality occurs automatically upon the lapse of certain time or the happening of certain events (subsection (3) of Section 4-211, subsections (1)(d), (2) and (3) of Section 4-213).

(4) If a collecting bank receives from subsequent parties settlement for an item which settlement is or becomes final and suspends payments without making a settlement for the item with its customer which is or becomes final, the owner of the item has a preferred claim against such collecting bank.

Part 3—Collection of Items: Payor Banks

§4-301. Deferred Posting; Recovery of Payment by Return of Items; Time of Dishonor.

(1) Where an authorized settlement for a demand item (other than a documentary draft) received by a payor bank otherwise than for immediate payment over the counter has been made before midnight of the banking day of receipt the payor bank may revoke the settlement and recover any payment if before it has made final payment (subsection (1) of Section 4-213) and before its midnight deadline it

(a) returns the item; or

(b) sends written notice of dishonor or nonpayment if the item is held for protest or is otherwise unavailable for return.

(2) If a demand item is received by a payor bank for credit on its books it may return such item or send notice of dishonor and may revoke any credit given or recover the amount thereof withdrawn by its customer, if it acts within the time limit and in the manner specified in the preceding subsection.

(3) Unless previous notice of dishonor has been sent an item is dishonored at the time when for purposes of dishonor it is returned or notice sent in accordance with this section.

(4) An item is returned:

(a) as to an item received through a clearing house when it is delivered to the presenting or last collecting bank or to the clearing house or is sent or delivered in accordance with its rules; or

(b) in all other cases, when it is sent or delivered to the bank's customer or transferor or pursuant to his instructions.

§4-302. Payor Bank's Responsibility for Late Return of Item.

In the absence of a valid defense such as breach of a presentment warranty (subsection (1) of Section 4-207), settlement effected or the like, if an item is presented on and received by a payor bank the bank is accountable for the amount of

(a) a demand item other than a documentary draft whether properly payable or not if the bank, in any case where it is not also the depositary bank, retains the item beyond midnight of the banking day of receipt without settling for it or, regardless of whether it is also the depositary bank, does not pay or return the item or send notice of dishonor until after its midnight deadline; or

(b) any other properly payable item unless within the time allowed for acceptance or payment of that item the bank either accepts or pays the item or returns it and accompanying documents.

§4-303. When Items Subject to Notice, Stop-Order, Legal Process or Setoff; Order in Which Items May Be Charged or Certified.

(1) Any knowledge, notice or stop-order received by, legal process served upon or setoff exercised by a payor bank, whether or not effective under other rules of law to terminate, suspend or modify the bank's right or duty to pay an item or to charge its customer's account for the item, comes too late to so terminate, suspend or modify such right or duty if the knowledge, notice, stop-order or legal process is received or served and a reasonable time for the bank to act thereon expires or the setoff is exercised after the bank has done any of the following:

(a) accepted or certified the item;

(b) paid the item in cash;

(c) settled for the item without reserving a right to revoke the settlement and without having such right under statute, clearing house rule or agreement;

(d) completed the process of posting the item to the indicated account of the drawer, maker, or other person to be charged therewith or otherwise has evidenced by examination of such indicated account and by action its decision to pay the item; or

(e) become accountable for the amount of the item under subsection (1)(d) of Section 4-213 and Section 4-302 dealing with the payor bank's responsibility for late return of items.

(2) Subject to the provisions of subsection (1) items may be accepted, paid, certified or charged to the indicated account of its customer in any order convenient to the bank.

Part 4—Relationship Between Payor Bank and its Customer

§4-401. When Bank May Charge Customer's Account.

(1) As against its customer, a bank may charge against his account any item which is otherwise properly payable from that account even though the charge creates an overdraft.

(2) A bank which in good faith makes payment to a holder may charge the indicated account of its customer according to

(a) the original tenor of his altered item; or

(b) the tenor of his completed item, even though the bank knows the item has been completed unless the bank has notice that the completion was improper.

§4-402. Bank's Liability to Customer for Wrongful Dishonor.

A payor bank is liable to its customer for damages proximately caused by the wrongful dishonor of an item. When the dishonor occurs through mistake liability is limited to actual damages proved. If so proximately caused and proved damages may include damages for an arrest or prosecution of the customer or other consequential damages. Whether any consequential damages are proximately caused by the wrongful dishonor is a question of fact to be determined in each case.

§4-403. Customer's Right to Stop Payment; Burden of Proof of Loss.

(1) A customer may by order to his bank stop payment of any item payable for his account but the order must be received at such time and in such manner as to afford the bank a reasonable opportunity to act on it prior to any action by the bank with respect to the item described in Section 4-303.

(2) An oral order is binding upon the bank only for fourteen calendar days unless confirmed in writing within that period. A written order is effective for only six months unless renewed in writing.

(3) The burden of establishing the fact and amount of loss resulting from the payment of an item contrary to a binding stop payment order is on the customer.

§4-404. Bank Not Obligated to Pay Check More Than Six Months Old.

A bank is under no obligation to a customer having a checking account to pay a check, other than a certified check, which is presented more than six months after its date, but it may charge its customer's account for a payment made thereafter in good faith.

§4-405. Death or Incompetence of Customer.

(1) A payor or collecting bank's authority to accept, pay or collect an item or to account for proceeds of its collection if otherwise effective is not rendered ineffective by incompetence of a customer of either bank existing at the time the item is issued or its collection is undertaken if the bank does not know of an adjudication of incompetence. Neither death nor incompetence of a customer revokes such authority to accept, pay, collect or account until the bank knows of the fact of death or of an adjudication of incompetence and has reasonable opportunity to act on it.

(2) Even with knowledge a bank may for ten days after the date of death pay or certify checks drawn on or prior to that date unless ordered to stop payment by a person claiming an interest in the account.

§4-406. Customer's Duty to Discover and Report Unauthorized Signature or Alteration.

(1) When a bank sends to its customer a statement of account accompanied by items paid in good faith in support of the debit entries or holds the statement and items pursuant to a request or instructions of its customer or otherwise in a reasonable manner makes the statement and items available to the customer, the customer must exercise reasonable care and promptness to examine the statement and items to discover his unauthorized signature or any alteration on an item and must notify the bank promptly after discovery thereof.

(2) If the bank establishes that the customer failed with respect to an item to comply with the duties imposed on the customer by subsection (1) the customer is precluded from asserting against the bank

(a) his unauthorized signature or any alteration on the item if the bank also establishes that it suffered a loss by reason of such failure; and

(b) an unauthorized signature or alteration by the same wrongdoer on any other item paid in good faith by the bank after the first item and statement was available to the customer for a reasonable period not exceeding fourteen calendar days and before the bank receives notification from the customer of any such unauthorized signature or alteration.

(3) The preclusion under subsection (2) does not apply if the customer establishes lack of ordinary care on the part of the bank in paying the item(s).

(4) Without regard to care or lack of care of either the customer or the bank a customer who does not within one year from the time the statement and items are made available to the customer (subsection (1)) discover and report his unauthorized signature or any alteration on the face or back of the item or does not within three years from that time discover and report any unauthorized indorsement is precluded from asserting against the bank such unauthorized signature or indorsement or such alteration.

(5) If under this section a payor bank has a valid defense against a claim of a customer upon or resulting from payment of an item and waives or fails upon request to assert the defense the bank may not assert against any collecting bank or other prior party presenting or transferring the item a claim based upon the unauthorized signature or alteration giving rise to the customer's claim.

§4-407. Payor Bank's Right to Subrogation on Improper Payment.

If a payor bank has paid an item over the stop payment order of the drawer or maker or otherwise under circumstances giving a basis for objection by the drawer or maker, to prevent unjust enrichment and only to the extent necessary to prevent loss to the bank by reason of its payment of the item, the payor bank shall be subrogated to the rights.

(a) of any holder in due course on the item against the drawer or maker; and

(b) of the payee or any other holder of the item against the drawer or maker either on the item or under the transaction out of which the item arose; and

(c) of the drawer or maker against the payee or any other holder of the item with respect to the transaction out of which the item arose.

Part 5—Collection of Documentary Drafts

§4-501. Handling of Documentary Drafts; Duty to Send for Presentment and to Notify Customer of Dishonor.

A bank which takes a documentary draft for collection must present or send the draft and accompanying documents for presentment and upon learning that the draft has not been paid or accepted in due course must seasonably notify its customer of such fact even though it may have discounted or bought the draft or extended credit available for withdrawal as of right.

§4-502. Presentment of "On Arrival" Drafts.

When a draft or the relevant instructions require presentment "on arrival", "when goods arrive" or the like, the collecting bank need not present until in its judgment a reasonable time for arrival of the goods has expired. Refusal to pay or accept because the goods have not arrived is not dishonor; the bank must notify its transferor of such refusal but need not present the draft again until it is instructed to do so or learns of the arrival of the goods.

§4-503. Responsibility of Presenting Bank for Documents and Goods; Report of Reasons for Dishonor; Referee in Case of Need.

Unless otherwise instructed and except as provided in Article 5 a bank presenting a documentary draft

(a) must deliver the documents to the drawee on acceptance of the draft if it is payable more than three days after presentment; otherwise, only on payment; and

(b) upon dishonor, either in the case of presentment for acceptance or presentment for payment, may seek and follow instructions from any referee in case of need designated in the draft or if the presenting bank does not choose to utilize his services it must use diligence and good faith to ascertain the reason for dishonor, must notify its transferor of the dishonor and of the results of its effort to ascertain the reasons therefor and must request instructions.

But the presenting bank is under no obligation with respect to goods represented by the documents except to follow any reasonable instructions seasonably received; it has a right to reimbursement for any expense incurred in following instructions and to prepayment of or indemnity for such expenses.

§4-504. Privilege of Presenting Bank to Deal With Goods; Security Interest for Expenses.

(1) A presenting bank which, following the dishonor of a documentary draft, has seasonably requested instructions but does not receive them within a reasonable time may store, sell, or otherwise deal with the goods in any reasonable manner.

(2) For its reasonable expenses incurred by action under subsection (1) the presenting bank has a lien upon the goods or their proceeds, which may be foreclosed in the same manner as an unpaid seller's lien.

ARTICLE 4A: FUNDS TRANSFERS

Part 1—Subject Matter and Definitions

§4A-101. Short Title.

This Article may be cited as Uniform Commercial Code—Funds Transfers.

§4A-102. Subject Matter.

Except as otherwise provided in Section 4A-108, this Article applies to funds transfers defined in Section 4A-104.

§4A-103. Payment Order—Definitions.

(a) In this Article:

(1) "Payment order" means an instruction of a sender to a receiving bank, transmitted orally, electronically, or in writing, to pay, or to cause another bank to pay, a fixed or determinable amount of money to a beneficiary if:

(i) the instruction does not state a condition to payment to the beneficiary other than time of payment,

(ii) the receiving bank is to be reimbursed by debiting an account of, or otherwise receiving payment from, the sender, and

(iii) the instruction is transmitted by the sender directly to the receiving bank or to an agent, funds-transfer system, or communication system for transmittal to the receiving bank.

(2) "Beneficiary" means the person to be paid by the beneficiary's bank.

(3) "Beneficiary's bank" means the bank identified in a payment order in which an account of the beneficiary is to be credited pursuant to the order or which otherwise is to make payment to the beneficiary if the order does not provide for payment to an account.

(4) "Receiving bank" means the bank to which the sender's instruction is addressed.

(5) "Sender" means the person giving the instruction to the receiving bank.

(b) If an instruction complying with subsection (a)(1) is to make more than one payment to a beneficiary, the instruction is a separate payment order with respect to each payment.

(c) A payment order is issued when it is sent to the receiving bank.

§4A-104. Funds Transfer—Definitions.

In this Article:

(a) "Funds transfer" means the series of transactions, beginning with the originator's payment order, made for the purpose of making payment to the beneficiary of the order. The term includes any payment order issued by the originator's bank or an intermediary bank intended to carry out the originator's payment order. A funds transfer is completed by acceptance by the beneficiary's bank of a payment order for the benefit of the beneficiary of the originator's payment order.

(b) "Intermediary bank" means a receiving bank other than the originator's bank or the beneficiary's bank.

(c) "Originator" means the sender of the first payment order in a funds transfer.

(d) "Originator's bank" means (i) the receiving bank to which the payment order of the originator is issued if the originator is not a bank, or (ii) the originator if the originator is a bank.

§4A-105. Other Definitions.

(a) In this Article:

(1) "Authorized account" means a deposit account of a customer in a bank designated by the customer as a source of payment of payment orders issued by the customer to the bank. If a customer does not so designate an account, any account of the customer is an authorized account if payment of a payment order from that account is not inconsistent with a restriction on the use of that account.

(2) "Bank" means a person engaged in the business of banking and includes a savings bank, savings and loan association, credit union, and trust company. A branch or separate office of a bank is a separate bank for purposes of this Article.

(3) "Customer" means a person, including a bank, having an account with a bank or from whom a bank has agreed to receive payment orders.

(4) "Funds-transfer business day" of a receiving bank means the part of a day during which the receiving bank is open for the receipt, processing, and transmittal of payment orders and cancellations and amendments of payment orders.

(5) "Funds-transfer system" means a wire transfer network, automated clearing house, or other communication system of a clearing house or other association of banks through which a payment order by a bank may be transmitted to the bank to which the order is addressed.

(6) "Good faith" means honesty in fact and the observance of reasonable commercial standards of fair dealing.

(7) "Prove" with respect to a fact means to meet the burden of establishing the fact (Section 1-201(8)).

(b) Other definitions applying to this Article and the sections in which they appear are:

"Acceptance" Section 4A-209
"Beneficiary" Section 4A-103
"Beneficiary's bank" Section 4A-103
"Executed" Section 4A-301
"Execution date" Section 4A-301
"Funds transfer" Section 4A-104
"Funds-transfer system rule" Section 4A-501
"Intermediary bank" Section 4A-104
"Originator" Section 4A-104
"Originator's bank" Section 4A-104
"Payment by beneficiary's bank to beneficiary" Section 4A-405
"Payment by originator to beneficiary" Section 4A-406
"Payment by sender to receiving bank" Section 4A-403
"Payment date" Section 4A-401
"Payment order" Section 4A-103
"Receiving bank" Section 4A-103
"Security procedure" Section 4A-201
"Sender" Section 4A-103

(c) The following definitions in Article 4 apply to this Article:

"Clearing house" Section 4-104
"Item" Section 4-104
"Suspends payments" Section 4-104

(d) In addition Article 1 contains general definitions and principles of construction and interpretation applicable throughout this Article.

§4A-106. Time Payment Order Is Received.

(a) The time of receipt of a payment order or communication cancelling or amending a payment order is determined by the rules applicable to receipt of a notice stated in Section 1-201(27). A receiving bank may fix a cut-off time or times on a funds-transfer business day for the receipt and processing of payment orders and communications cancelling or amending payment orders. Different cut-off times may apply to payment orders, cancellations, or amendments, or to different categories of payment orders, cancellations, or amendments. A cut-off time may apply to senders generally or different cut-off times may apply to different senders or categories of payment orders. If a payment order or communication cancelling or amending a payment order is received after the close of a funds-transfer business day or after the appropriate cut-off time on a funds-transfer business day, the receiving bank may treat the payment order or communication as received at the opening of the next funds-transfer business day.

(b) If this Article refers to an execution date or payment date or states a day on which a receiving bank is required to take action, and the date or day does not fall on a funds-transfer business day, the next day that is a funds-transfer business day is treated as the date or day stated, unless the contrary is stated in this Article.

§4A-107. Federal Reserve Regulations and Operating Circulars.

Regulations of the Board of Governors of the Federal Reserve System and operating circulars of the Federal Reserve Banks supersede any inconsistent provision of this Article to the extent of the inconsistency.

§4A-108. Exclusion of Consumer Transactions Governed by Federal Law.

This Article does not apply to a funds transfer any part of which is governed by the Electronic Fund Transfer Act of 1978 (Title XX, Public Law 95-630, 92 Stat. 3728, 15 U.S.C. §1693 et seq.) as amended from time to time.

Part 2—Issue and Acceptance of Payment Order

§4A-201. Security Procedure.

"Security procedure" means a procedure established by agreement of a customer and a receiving bank for the purpose of (i) verifying that a payment order or communication amending or cancelling a payment order is that of the customer, or (ii) detecting error in the transmission or the content of the payment order or communication. A security procedure may require the use of algorithms or other codes, identifying words or numbers, encryption, callback procedures, or similar security devices. Comparison of a signature on a payment order or communication with an authorized specimen signature of the customer is not by itself a security procedure.

§4A-202. Authorized and Verified Payment Orders.

(a) A payment order received by the receiving bank is the authorized order of the person identified as sender if that person authorized the order or is otherwise bound by it under the law of agency.

(b) If a bank and its customer have agreed that the authenticity of payment orders issued to the bank in the name of the customer as sender will be verified pursuant to a security procedure, a payment order received by the receiving bank is effective as the order of the customer, whether or not authorized, if (i) the security procedure is a commercially reasonable method of providing security against unauthorized payment orders, and (ii) the bank proves that it accepted the payment order in good faith and in compliance with the security procedure and any written agreement or instruction of the customer restricting acceptance of payment orders issued in the name of the customer. The bank is not required to follow an instruction that violates a written agreement with the customer or notice of which is not received at a time and in a manner affording the bank a reasonable opportunity to act on it before the payment order is accepted.

(c) Commercial reasonableness of a security procedure is a question of law to be determined by considering the wishes of the customer expressed to the bank, the circumstances of the customer known to the bank, including the size, type, and frequency of payment orders normally issued by the customer to the bank, alternative security procedures offered to the customer, and security procedures in general use by customers and receiving banks similarly situated. A security procedure is deemed to be commercially reasonable if (i) the security procedure was chosen by the customer after the bank offered, and the customer refused, a security procedure that was commercially reasonable for that customer, and (ii) the customer expressly agreed in writing to be bound by any payment order, whether or not authorized, issued in its name and accepted by the bank in compliance with the security procedure chosen by the customer.

(d) The term "sender" in this Article includes the customer in whose name a payment order is issued if the order is the authorized order of the customer under subsection (a), or it is effective as the order of the customer under subsection (b).

(e) This section applies to amendments and cancellations of payment orders to the same extent it applies to payment orders.

(f) Except as provided in this section and in Section 4A-203(a)(1), rights and obligations arising under this section or Section 4A-203 may not be varied by agreement.

§4A-203. Unenforceability of Certain Verified Payment Orders.

(a) If an accepted payment order is not, under Section 4A-202(a), an authorized order of a customer identified as sender, but is effective as an order of the customer pursuant to Section 4A-202(b), the following rules apply:

(1) By express written agreement, the receiving bank may limit the extent to which it is entitled to enforce or retain payment of the payment order.

(2) The receiving bank is not entitled to enforce or retain payment of the payment order if the customer proves that the order was not caused, directly or indirectly, by a person (i) entrusted at any time with duties to act for the customer with respect to payment orders or the security procedure, or (ii) who obtained access to transmitting facilities of the customer or who obtained, from a source controlled by the customer and without authority of the receiving bank, information facilitating breach of the security procedure, regardless of how the

information was obtained or whether the customer was at fault. Information includes any access device, computer software, or the like.

(b) This section applies to amendments of payment orders to the same extent it applies to payment orders.

§4A-204. Refund of Payment and Duty of Customer to Report with Respect to Unauthorized Payment Order.

(a) If a receiving bank accepts a payment order issued in the name of its customer as sender which is (i) not authorized and not effective as the order of the customer under Section 4A-202, or (ii) not enforceable, in whole or in part, against the customer under Section 4A-203, the bank shall refund any payment of the payment order received from the customer to the extent the bank is not entitled to enforce payment and shall pay interest on the refundable amount calculated from the date the bank received payment to the date of the refund. However, the customer is not entitled to interest from the bank on the amount to be refunded if the customer fails to exercise ordinary care to determine that the order was not authorized by the customer and to notify the bank of the relevant facts within a reasonable time not exceeding 90 days after the date the customer received notification from the bank that the order was accepted or that the customer's account was debited with respect to the order. The bank is not entitled to any recovery from the customer on account of a failure by the customer to give notification as stated in this section.

(b) Reasonable time under subsection (a) may be fixed by agreement as stated in Section 1-204(1), but the obligation of a receiving bank to refund payment as stated in subsection (a) may not otherwise be varied by agreement.

§4A-205. Erroneous Payment Orders.

(a) If an accepted payment order was transmitted pursuant to a security procedure for the detection of error and the payment order (i) erroneously instructed payment to a beneficiary not intended by the sender, (ii) erroneously instructed payment in an amount greater than the amount intended by the sender, or (iii) was an erroneously transmitted duplicate of a payment order previously sent by the sender, the following rules apply:

(1) If the sender proves that the sender or a person acting on behalf of the sender pursuant to Section 4A-206 complied with the security procedure and that the error would have been detected if the receiving bank had also complied, the sender is not obliged to pay the order to the extent stated in paragraphs (2) and (3).

(2) If the funds transfer is completed on the basis of an erroneous payment order described in clause (i) or (iii) of subsection (a), the sender is not obliged to pay the order and the receiving bank is entitled to recover from the beneficiary any amount paid to the beneficiary to the extent allowed by the law governing mistake and restitution.

(3) If the funds transfer is completed on the basis of a payment order described in clause (ii) of subsection (a), the sender is not obliged to pay the order to the extent the amount received by the beneficiary is greater than the amount intended by the sender. In that case, the receiving bank is entitled to recover from the beneficiary the excess amount received to the extent allowed by the law governing mistake and restitution.

(b) If (i) the sender of an erroneous payment order described in subsection (a) is not obliged to pay all or part of the order, and (ii) the sender receives notification from the receiving bank that the order was accepted by the bank or that the sender's account was debited with respect to the order, the sender has a duty to exercise ordinary care, on the basis of information available to the sender, to discover the error with respect to the order and to advise the bank of the relevant facts within a reasonable time, not exceeding 90 days, after the bank's notification was received by the sender. If the bank proves that the sender failed to perform that duty, the sender is liable to the bank for the loss the bank proves it incurred as a result of the failure, but the liability of the sender may not exceed the amount of the sender's order.

(c) This section applies to amendments to payment orders to the same extent it applies to payment orders.

§4A-209. Acceptance of Payment Order.

(a) Subject to subsection (d), a receiving bank other than the beneficiary's bank accepts a payment order when it executes the order.

(b) Subject to subsections (c) and (d), a beneficiary's bank accepts a payment order at the earliest of the following times:

(1) when the bank (i) pays the beneficiary as stated in Section 4A-405(a) or 4A-405(b), or (ii) notifies the beneficiary of receipt of the order or that the account of the beneficiary has been credited with respect to the order unless the notice indicates that the bank is rejecting the order or that funds with respect to the order may not be withdrawn or used until receipt of payment from the sender of the order;

(2) when the bank receives payment of the entire amount of the sender's order pursuant to Section 4A-403(a)(1) or 4A-403(a)(2); or

(3) the opening of the next funds-transfer business day of the bank following the payment date of the order if, at that time, the amount of the sender's order is fully covered by a withdrawable credit balance in an authorized account of the sender or the bank has otherwise received full payment from the sender, unless the order was rejected before that time or is rejected within (i) one hour after that time, or (ii) one hour after the opening of the next business day of the sender following the payment date if that time is later. If notice of rejection is received by the sender after the payment date and the authorized account of the sender does not bear interest, the bank is obliged to pay interest to the sender on the amount of the order for the number of days elapsing after the payment date to the day the sender receives notice or learns that the order was not accepted, counting that day as an elapsed day. If the withdrawable credit balance during that period falls below the amount of the order, the amount of interest payable is reduced accordingly.

(c) Acceptance of a payment order cannot occur before the order is received by the receiving bank. Acceptance does not occur under subsection (b)(2) or (b)(3) if the beneficiary of the payment order does not have an account with the receiving bank, the account has been closed, or the receiving bank is not permitted by law to receive credits for the beneficiary's account.

(d) A payment order issued to the originator's bank cannot be accepted until the payment date if the bank is the beneficiary's bank, or the execution date if the bank is not the beneficiary's bank. If the originator's bank executes the originator's payment order before the execution date or pays the beneficiary of the originator's payment order before the payment date and the payment order is subsequently canceled pursuant to Section 4A-211(b), the bank may recover from the beneficiary any payment received to the extent allowed by the law governing mistake and restitution.

Part 3—Execution of Sender's Payment Order by Receiving Bank

§4A-301. Execution and Execution Date.

(a) A payment order is "executed" by the receiving bank when it issues a payment order intended to carry out the payment order received by the bank. A payment order received by the beneficiary's bank can be accepted but cannot be executed.

(b) "Execution date" of a payment order means the day on which the receiving bank may properly issue a payment order in execution of the sender's order. The execution date may be determined by instruction of the sender but cannot be earlier than the day the order is received and, unless otherwise determined, is the day the order is received. If the sender's instruction states a payment date, the execution date is the payment date or an earlier date on which execution is reasonably necessary to allow payment to the beneficiary on the payment date.

§4A-302. Obligations of Receiving Bank in Execution of Payment Order.

(a) Except as provided in subsections (b) through (d), if the receiving bank accepts a payment order pursuant to Section 4A-209(a), the bank has the following obligations in executing the order:

(1) The receiving bank is obliged to issue, on the execution date, a payment order complying with the sender's order and to follow the sender's instructions concerning (i) any intermediary bank or funds-transfer system to be used in carrying out the funds transfer, or (ii) the means by which payment orders are to be transmitted in the funds transfer. If the originator's bank issues a payment order to an intermediary bank, the originator's bank is obliged to instruct the intermediary bank according to the instruction of the originator. An intermediary bank in the funds transfer is similarly bound by an instruction given to it by the sender of the payment order it accepts.

(2) If the sender's instruction states that the funds transfer is to be carried out telephonically or by wire transfer or otherwise indicates that the funds transfer is to be carried out by the most expeditious means, the receiving bank is obliged to transmit its payment order by the most expeditious available means, and to instruct any intermediary bank accordingly. If a sender's instruction states a payment date, the receiving bank is obliged to transmit its payment order at a time and by means reasonably necessary to allow payment to the beneficiary on the payment date or as soon thereafter as is feasible.

(b) Unless otherwise instructed, a receiving bank executing a payment order may (i) use any funds-transfer system if use of that system is reasonable in the circumstances, and (ii) issue a payment order to the beneficiary's bank or to an intermediary bank through which a payment order conforming to the sender's order can expeditiously be issued to the beneficiary's bank if the receiving bank exercises ordinary care in the selection of the intermediary bank. A receiving bank is not required to follow an instruction of the sender designating a funds-transfer system to be used in carrying out the funds transfer if the receiving bank, in good faith, determines that it is not feasible to follow the instruction or that following the instruction would unduly delay completion of the funds transfer.

(c) Unless subsection (a)(2) applies or the receiving bank is otherwise instructed, the bank may execute a payment order by transmitting its payment order by first class mail or by any means reasonable in the circumstances. If the receiving bank is instructed to execute the sender's order by transmitting its payment order by a particular means, the receiving bank may issue its payment order by the means stated or by any means as expeditious as the means stated.

(d) Unless instructed by the sender, (i) the receiving bank may not obtain payment of its charges for services and expenses in connection with the execution of the sender's order by issuing a payment order in an amount equal to the amount of the sender's order less the amount of the charges, and (ii) may not instruct a subsequent receiving bank to obtain payment of its charges in the same manner.

§4A-303. Erroneous Execution of Payment Order.

(a) A receiving bank that (i) executes the payment order of the sender by issuing a payment order in an amount greater than the amount of the sender's order, or (ii) issues a payment order in execution of the sender's order and then issues a duplicate order, is entitled to payment of the amount of the sender's order under Section 4A-402(c) if that subsection is otherwise satisfied. The bank is entitled to recover from the beneficiary of the erroneous order the excess payment received to the extent allowed by the law governing mistake and restitution.

(b) A receiving bank that executes the payment order of the sender by issuing a payment order in an amount less than the amount of the sender's order is entitled to payment of the amount of the sender's order under Section 4A-402(c) if (i) that subsection is otherwise satisfied and (ii) the bank corrects its mistake by issuing an additional payment order for the benefit of the beneficiary of the sender's order. If the error is not corrected, the

issuer of the erroneous order is entitled to receive or retain payment from the sender of the order it accepted only to the extent of the amount of the erroneous order. This subsection does not apply if the receiving bank executes the sender's payment order by issuing a payment order in an amount less than the amount of the sender's order for the purpose of obtaining payment of its charges for services and expenses pursuant to instruction of the sender.

(c) If a receiving bank executes the payment order of the sender by issuing a payment order to a beneficiary different from the beneficiary of the sender's order and the funds transfer is completed on the basis of that error, the sender of the payment order that was erroneously executed and all previous senders in the funds transfer are not obliged to pay the payment orders they issued. The issuer of the erroneous order is entitled to recover from the beneficiary of the order the payment received to the extent allowed by the law governing mistake and restitution.

§4A-304. Duty of Sender to Report Erroneously Executed Payment Order.

If the sender of a payment order that is erroneously executed as stated in Section 4A-303 receives notification from the receiving bank that the order was executed or that the sender's account was debited with respect to the order, the sender has a duty to exercise ordinary care to determine, on the basis of information available to the sender, that the order was erroneously executed and to notify the bank of the relevant facts within a reasonable time not exceeding 90 days after the notification from the bank was received by the sender. If the sender fails to perform that duty, the bank is not obliged to pay interest on any amount refundable to the sender under Section 4A-402(d) for the period before the bank learns of the execution error. The bank is not entitled to any recovery from the sender on account of a failure by the sender to perform the duty stated in this section.

§4A-305. Liability for Late or Improper Execution or Failure to Execute Payment Order.

(a) If a funds transfer is completed but execution of a payment order by the receiving bank in breach of Section 4A-302 results in delay in payment to the beneficiary, the bank is obliged to pay interest to either the originator or the beneficiary of the funds transfer for the period of delay caused by the improper execution. Except as provided in subsection (c), additional damages are not recoverable.

(b) If execution of a payment order by a receiving bank in breach of Section 4A-302 results in (i) noncompletion of the funds transfer, (ii) failure to use an intermediary bank designated by the originator, or (iii) issuance of a payment order that does not comply with the terms of the payment order of the originator, the bank is liable to the originator for its expenses in the funds transfer and for incidental expenses and interest losses, to the extent not covered by subsection (a), resulting from the improper execution. Except as provided in subsection (c), additional damages are not recoverable.

(c) In addition to the amounts payable under subsections (a) and (b), damages, including consequential damages, are recoverable to the extent provided in an express written agreement of the receiving bank.

(d) If a receiving bank fails to execute a payment order it was obliged by express agreement to execute, the receiving bank is liable to the sender for its expenses in the transaction and for incidental expenses and interest losses resulting from the failure to execute. Additional damages, including consequential damages, are recoverable to the extent provided in an express written agreement of the receiving bank, but are not otherwise recoverable.

(e) Reasonable attorney's fees are recoverable if demand for compensation under subsection (a) or (b) is made and refused before an action is brought on the claim. If a claim is made for breach of an agreement under subsection (d) and the agreement does not provide for damages, reasonable attorney's fees are recoverable if demand for compensation under subsection (d) is made and refused before an action is brought on the claim.

(f) Except as stated in this section, the liability of a receiving bank under subsections (a) and (b) may not be varied by agreement.

Part 4—Payment

§4A-401. Payment Date.

"Payment date" of a payment order means the day on which the amount of the order is payable to the beneficiary by the beneficiary's bank. The payment date may be determined by instruction of the sender but cannot be earlier than the day the order is received by the beneficiary's bank and, unless otherwise determined, is the day the order is received by the beneficiary's bank.

§4A-402. Obligation of Sender to Pay Receiving Bank.

(a) This section is subject to Sections 4A-205 and 4A-207.

(b) With respect to a payment order issued to the beneficiary's bank, acceptance of the order by the bank obliges the sender to pay the bank the amount of the order, but payment is not due until the payment date of the order.

(c) This subsection is subject to subsection (e) and to Section 4A-303. With respect to a payment order issued to a receiving bank other than the beneficiary's bank, acceptance of the order by the receiving bank obliges the sender to pay the bank the amount of the sender's order. Payment by the sender is not due until the execution date of the sender's order. The obligation of that sender to pay its payment order is excused if the funds transfer is not completed by acceptance by the beneficiary's bank of a payment order instructing payment to the beneficiary of that sender's payment order.

(d) If the sender of a payment order pays the order and was not obliged to pay all or part of the amount paid, the bank receiving payment is obliged to refund payment to the extent the sender was not obliged to pay. Except as provided in Sections 4A-204 and 4A-304, interest is payable on the refundable amount from the date of payment.

(e) If a funds transfer is not completed as stated in subsection (c) and an intermediary bank is obliged to refund payment as stated in subsection (d) but is unable to do so because not permitted by applicable law or because the bank suspends payments, a sender in the funds transfer that executed a payment order in compliance with an instruction, as stated in Section 4A-302(a)(1), to route the funds transfer through that intermediary bank is entitled to receive or retain payment from the sender of the payment order that it accepted. The first sender in the funds transfer that issued an instruction requiring routing through that intermediary bank is subrogated to the right of the bank that paid the intermediary bank to refund as stated in subsection (d).

(f) The right of the sender of a payment order to be excused from the obligation to pay the order as stated in subsection (c) or to receive refund under subsection (d) may not be varied by agreement.

§4A-403. Payment by Sender to Receiving Bank.

(a) Payment of the sender's obligation under Section 4A-402 to pay the receiving bank occurs as follows:

(1) If the sender is a bank, payment occurs when the receiving bank receives final settlement of the obligation through a Federal Reserve Bank or through a funds-transfer system.

(2) If the sender is a bank and the sender (i) credited an account of the receiving bank with the sender, or (ii) caused an account of the receiving bank in another bank to be credited, payment occurs when the credit is withdrawn or, if not withdrawn, at midnight of the day on which the credit is withdrawable and the receiving bank learns of that fact.

(3) If the receiving bank debits an account of the sender with the receiving bank, payment occurs when the debit is made to the extent the debit is covered by a withdrawable credit balance in the account.

(b) If the sender and receiving bank are members of a funds-transfer system that nets obligations multilaterally among participants, the receiving bank receives final settlement when settlement is complete in accordance with the rules of the system. The obligation of the sender to pay the amount of a payment order transmitted through the funds-transfer system

may be satisfied, to the extent permitted by the rules of the system, by setting off and applying against the sender's obligation the right of the sender to receive payment from the receiving bank of the amount of any other payment order transmitted to the sender by the receiving bank through the funds-transfer system. The aggregate balance of obligations owed by each sender to each receiving bank in the funds-transfer system may be satisfied, to the extent permitted by the rules of the system, by setting off and applying against that balance the aggregate balance of obligations owed to the sender by other members of the system. The aggregate balance is determined after the right of setoff stated in the second sentence of this subsection has been exercised.

(c) If two banks transmit payment orders to each other under an agreement that settlement of the obligations of each bank to the other under Section 4A-402 will be made at the end of the day or other period, the total amount owed with respect to all orders transmitted by one bank shall be set off against the total amount owed with respect to all orders transmitted by the other bank. To the extent of the setoff, each bank has made payment to the other.

(d) In a case not covered by subsection (a), the time when payment of the sender's obligation under Section 4A-402(b) or 4A-402(c) occurs is governed by applicable principles of law that determine when an obligation is satisfied.

§4A-404. Obligation of Beneficiary's Bank to Pay and Give Notice to Beneficiary.

(a) Subject to Sections 4A-211(e), 4A-405(d), and 4A-405(e), if a beneficiary's bank accepts a payment order, the bank is obliged to pay the amount of the order to the beneficiary of the order. Payment is due on the payment date of the order, but if acceptance occurs on the payment date after the close of the funds-transfer business day of the bank, payment is due on the next funds-transfer business day. If the bank refuses to pay after demand by the beneficiary and receipt of notice of particular circumstances that will give rise to consequential damages as a result of nonpayment, the beneficiary may recover damages resulting from the refusal to pay to the extent the bank had notice of the damages, unless the bank proves that it did not pay because of a reasonable doubt concerning the right of the beneficiary to payment.

(b) If a payment order accepted by the beneficiary's bank instructs payment to an account of the beneficiary, the bank is obliged to notify the beneficiary of receipt of the order before midnight of the next funds-transfer business day following the payment date. If the payment order does not instruct payment to an account of the beneficiary, the bank is required to notify the beneficiary only if notice is required by the order. Notice may be given by first class mail or any other means reasonable in the circumstances. If the bank fails to give the required notice, the bank is obliged to pay interest to the beneficiary on the amount of the payment order from the day notice should have been given until the day the beneficiary learned of receipt of the payment order by the bank. No other damages are recoverable. Reasonable attorney's fees are also recoverable if demand for interest is made and refused before an action is brought on the claim.

(c) The right of a beneficiary to receive payment and damages as stated in subsection (a) may not be varied by agreement or a funds-transfer system rule. The right of a beneficiary to be notified as stated in subsection (b) may be varied by agreement of the beneficiary or by a funds-transfer system rule if the beneficiary is notified of the rule before initiation of the funds transfer.

§4A-405. Payment by Beneficiary's Bank to Beneficiary.

(a) If the beneficiary's bank credits an account of the beneficiary of a payment order, payment of the bank's obligation under Section 4A-404(a) occurs when and to the extent (i) the beneficiary is notified of the right to withdraw the credit, (ii) the bank lawfully applies the credit to a debt of the beneficiary, or (iii) funds with respect to the order are otherwise made available to the beneficiary by the bank.

(b) If the beneficiary's bank does not credit an account of the beneficiary of a payment order, the time when payment of the bank's obligation under Section 4A-404(a) occurs is governed by principles of law that determine when an obligation is satisfied.

(c) Except as stated in subsections (d) and (e), if the beneficiary's bank pays the beneficiary of a payment order under a condition to payment or agreement of the beneficiary giving the bank the right to recover payment from the beneficiary if the bank does not receive payment of the order, the condition to payment or agreement is not enforceable.

(d) A funds-transfer system rule may provide that payments made to beneficiaries of funds transfers made through the system are provisional until receipt of payment by the beneficiary's bank of the payment order it accepted. A beneficiary's bank that makes a payment that is provisional under the rule is entitled to refund from the beneficiary if (i) the rule requires that both the beneficiary and the originator be given notice of the provisional nature of the payment before the funds transfer is initiated, (ii) the beneficiary, the beneficiary's bank and the originator's bank agreed to be bound by the rule, and (iii) the beneficiary's bank did not receive payment of the payment order that it accepted. If the beneficiary is obliged to refund payment to the beneficiary's bank, acceptance of the payment order by the beneficiary's bank is nullified and no payment by the originator of the funds transfer to the beneficiary occurs under Section 4A-406.

(e) This subsection applies to a funds transfer that includes a payment order transmitted over a funds-transfer system that (i) nets obligations multilaterally among participants, and (ii) has in effect a loss-sharing agreement among participants for the purpose of providing funds necessary to complete settlement of the obligations of one or more participants that do not meet their settlement obligations. If the beneficiary's bank in the funds transfer accepts a payment order and the system fails to complete settlement pursuant to its rules with respect to any payment order in the funds transfer, (i) the acceptance by the beneficiary's bank is nullified and no person has any right or obligation based on the acceptance, (ii) the beneficiary's bank is entitled to recover payment from the beneficiary, (iii) no payment by the originator to the beneficiary occurs under Section 4A-406, and (iv) subject to Section 4A-402(e), each sender in the funds transfer is excused from its obligation to pay its payment order under Section 4A-402 (c) because the funds transfer has not been completed.

§4A-406. Payment by Originator to Beneficiary; Discharge of Underlying Obligation.

(a) Subject to Sections 4A-211(e), 4A-405(d), and 4A-405(e), the originator of a funds transfer pays the beneficiary of the originator's payment order (i) at the time a payment order for the benefit of the beneficiary is accepted by the beneficiary's bank in the funds transfer and (ii) in an amount equal to the amount of the order accepted by the beneficiary's bank, but not more than the amount of the originator's order.

(b) If payment under subsection (a) is made to satisfy an obligation, the obligation is discharged to the same extent discharge would result from payment to the beneficiary of the same amount in money, unless (i) the payment under subsection (a) was made by a means prohibited by the contract of the beneficiary with respect to the obligation, (ii) the beneficiary, within a reasonable time after receiving notice of receipt of the order by the beneficiary's bank, notified the originator of the beneficiary's refusal of the payment, (iii) funds with respect to the order were not withdrawn by the beneficiary or applied to a debt of the beneficiary, and (iv) the beneficiary would suffer a loss that could reasonably have been avoided if payment had been made by a means complying with the contract. If payment by the originator does not result in discharge under this section, the originator is subrogated to the rights of the beneficiary to receive payment from the beneficiary's bank under Section 4A-404(a).

(c) For the purpose of determining whether discharge of an obligation occurs under subsection (b), if the beneficiary's bank accepts a payment order in an amount equal to the amount of the originator's payment order less charges of one or more receiving banks in the funds transfer, payment

to the beneficiary is deemed to be in the amount of the originator's order unless upon demand by the beneficiary the originator does not pay the beneficiary the amount of the deducted charges.

(d) Rights of the originator or of the beneficiary of a funds transfer under this section may be varied only by agreement of the originator and the beneficiary.

ARTICLE 7: WAREHOUSE RECEIPTS, BILLS OF LADING AND OTHER DOCUMENTS OF TITLE

Part 1—General

§7-101. Short Title.

This Article shall be known and may be cited as Uniform Commercial Code—Documents of Title.

§7-102. Definitions and Index of Definitions.

(1) In this Article, unless the context otherwise requires:

(a) "Bailee" means the person who by a warehouse receipt, bill of lading or other document of title acknowledges possession of goods and contracts to deliver them.

(b) "Consignee" means the person named in a bill to whom or to whose order the bill promises delivery.

(c) "Consignor" means the person named in a bill as the person from whom the goods have been received for shipment.

(d) "Delivery order" means a written order to deliver goods directed to a warehouseman, carrier or other person who in the ordinary course of business issues warehouse receipts or bills of lading.

(e) "Document" means document of title as defined in the general definitions in Article 1 (Section 1-201).

(f) "Goods" means all things which are treated as movable for the purposes of a contract of storage or transportation.

(g) "Issuer" means a bailee who issues a document except that in relation to an unaccepted delivery order it means the person who orders the possessor of goods to deliver. Issuer includes any person for whom an agent or employee purports to act in issuing a document if the agent or employee has real or apparent authority to issue documents, notwithstanding that the issuer received no goods or that the goods were misdescribed or that in any other respect the agent or employee violated his instructions.

(h) "Warehouseman" is a person engaged in the business of storing goods for hire.

(2) Other definitions applying to this Article or to specified Parts thereof, and the sections in which they appear are:

"Duly negotiate". Section 7-501.

"Person entitled under the document". Section 7- 403(4).

(3) Definitions in other Articles applying to this Article and the sections in which they appear are:

"Contract for sale". Section 2-106.

"Overseas". Section 2-323.

"Receipt" of goods. Section 2-103.

(4) In addition Article 1 contains general definitions and principles of construction and interpretation applicable throughout this Article.

§7-104. Negotiable and Non-Negotiable Warehouse Receipt, Bill of Lading or Other Document of Title.

(1) A warehouse receipt, bill of lading or other document of title is negotiable

(a) if by its terms the goods are to be delivered to bearer or to the order of a named person; or

(b) where recognized in overseas trade, if it runs to a named person or assigns.

(2) Any other document is non-negotiable. A bill of lading in which it is stated that the goods are consigned to a named person is not made negotiable by a provision that the goods are to be delivered only against a written order signed by the same or another named person.

Part 2—Warehouse Receipts: Special Provisions

§7-201. Who May Issue a Warehouse Receipt; Storage Under Government Bond.

(1) A warehouse receipt may be issued by any warehouseman.

(2) Where goods including distilled spirits and agricultural commodities are stored under a statute requiring a bond against withdrawal or a license for the issuance of receipts in the nature of warehouse receipts, a receipt issued for the goods has like effect as a warehouse receipt even though issued by a person who is the owner of the goods and is not a warehouseman.

§7-202. Form of Warehouse Receipt; Essential Terms; Optional Terms.

(1) A warehouse receipt need not be in any particular form.

(2) Unless a warehouse receipt embodies within its written or printed terms each of the following, the warehouseman is liable for damages caused by the omission to a person injured thereby:

(a) the location of the warehouse where the goods are stored;

(b) the date of issue of the receipt;

(c) the consecutive number of the receipt;

(d) a statement whether the goods received will be delivered to the bearer, to a specified person, or to a specified person or his order;

(e) the rate of storage and handling charges, except that where goods are stored under a field warehousing arrangement a statement of that fact is sufficient on a non-negotiable receipt;

(f) a description of the goods or of the packages containing them;

(g) the signature of the warehouseman, which may be made by his authorized agent;

(h) if the receipt is issued for goods of which the warehouseman is owner, either solely or jointly or in common with others, the fact of such ownership; and

(i) a statement of the amount of advances made and of liabilities incurred for which the warehouseman claims a lien or security interest (Section 7-209). If the precise amount of such advances made or of such liabilities incurred is, at the time of the issue of the receipt, unknown to the warehouseman or to his agent who issues it, a statement of the fact that advances have been made or liabilities incurred and the purpose thereof is sufficient.

(3) A warehouseman may insert in his receipt any other terms which are not contrary to the provisions of this Act and do not impair his obligation of delivery (Section 7-403) or his duty of care (Section 7-204). Any contrary provisions shall be ineffective.

§7-204. Duty of Care; Contractual Limitation of Warehouseman's Liability.

(1) A warehouseman is liable for damages for loss of or injury to the goods caused by his failure to exercise such care in regard to them as a reasonably careful man would exercise under like circumstances but unless otherwise agreed he is not liable for damages which could not have been avoided by the exercise of such care.

(2) Damages may be limited by a term in the warehouse receipt or storage agreement limiting the amount of liability in case of loss or damage, and setting forth a specific liability per article or item, or value per unit of weight, beyond which the warehouseman shall not be liable; provided, however, that such liability may on written request of the bailor at the time of signing such storage agreement or within a reasonable time after receipt of the warehouse receipt be increased on part or all of the goods thereunder, in which event increased rates may be charged based on such increased valuation, but that no such increase shall be permitted contrary to a lawful limitation of liability contained in the warehouseman's tariff, if any. No such limitation is effective with respect to the warehouseman's liability for conversion to his own use.

(3) Reasonable provisions as to the time and manner of presenting claims and instituting actions based on the bailment may be included in the warehouse receipt or tariff.

(4) This section does not impair or repeal …

Note: *Insert in subsection (4) a reference to any statute which imposes a higher responsibility upon the warehouseman or invalidates contractual limitations which would be permissible under this Article.*

§7-206. Termination of Storage at Warehouseman's Option.

(1) A warehouseman may on notifying the person on whose account the goods are held and any other person known to claim an interest in the goods require payment of any charges and removal of the goods from the warehouse at the termination of the period of storage fixed by the document, or, if no period is fixed, within a stated period not less than thirty days after the notification. If the goods are not removed before the date specified in the notification, the warehouseman may sell them in accordance with the provisions of the section on enforcement of a warehouseman's lien (Section 7-210).

(2) If a warehouseman in good faith believes that the goods are about to deteriorate or decline in value to less than the amount of his lien within the time prescribed in subsection (1) for notification, advertisement and sale, the warehouseman may specify in the notification any reasonable shorter time for removal of the goods and in case the goods are not removed, may sell them at public sale held not less than one week after a single advertisement or posting.

(3) If as a result of a quality or condition of the goods of which the warehouseman had no notice at the time of deposit the goods are a hazard to other property or to the warehouse or to persons, the warehouseman may sell the goods at public or private sale without advertisement on reasonable notification to all persons known to claim an interest in the goods. If the warehouseman after a reasonable effort is unable to sell the goods he may dispose of them in any lawful manner and shall incur no liability by reason of such disposition.

(4) The warehouseman must deliver the goods to any person entitled to them under this Article upon due demand made at any time prior to sale or other disposition under this section.

(5) The warehouseman may satisfy his lien from the proceeds of any sale or disposition under this section but must hold the balance for delivery on the demand of any person to whom he would have been bound to deliver the goods.

§7-207. Goods Must Be Kept Separate; Fungible Goods.

(1) Unless the warehouse receipt otherwise provides, a warehouseman must keep separate the goods covered by each receipt so as to permit at all times identification and delivery of those goods except that different lots of fungible goods may be commingled.

(2) Fungible goods so commingled are owned in common by the persons entitled thereto and the warehouseman is severally liable to each owner for that owner's share. Where because of overissue a mass of fungible goods is insufficient to meet all the receipts which the warehouseman has issued against it, the persons entitled include all holders to whom overissued receipts have been duly negotiated.

§7-209. Lien of Warehouseman.

(1) A warehouseman has a lien against the bailor on the goods covered by a warehouse receipt or on the proceeds thereof in his possession for charges for storage or transportation (including demurrage and terminal charges), insurance, labor, or charges present or future in relation to the goods, and for expenses necessary for preservation of the goods or reasonably incurred in their sale pursuant to law. If the person on whose account the goods are held is liable for like charges or expenses in relation to other goods whenever deposited and it is stated in the receipt that a lien is claimed for charges and expenses in relation to other goods, the warehouseman also has a lien against him for such charges and expenses whether or not the other goods have been delivered by the warehouseman. But against a person to whom a negotiable warehouse receipt is duly negotiated a warehouseman's lien is limited to charges in an amount or at a rate specified on

the receipt or if no charges are so specified then to a reasonable charge for storage of the goods covered by the receipt subsequent to the date of the receipt.

(2) The warehouseman may also reserve a security interest against the bailor for a maximum amount specified on the receipt for charges other than those specified in subsection (1), such as for money advanced and interest. Such a security interest is governed by the Article on Secured Transactions (Article 9).

(3) (a) A warehouseman's lien for charges and expenses under subsection (1) or a security interest under subsection (2) is also effective against any person who so entrusted the bailor with possession of the goods that a pledge of them by him to a good faith purchaser for value would have been valid but is not effective against a person as to whom the document confers no right in the goods covered by it under Section 7-503.

(b) A warehouseman's lien on household goods for charges and expenses in relation to the goods under subsection (1) is also effective against all persons if the depositor was a legal possessor of the goods at the time of deposit. "Household goods" means furniture, furnishings and personal effects used by the depositor in a dwelling.

(4) A warehouseman loses his lien on any goods which he voluntarily delivers or which he unjustifiably refuses to deliver.

Part 3—Bills of Lading: Special Provisions

§7-301. Liability for Non-Receipt or Misdescription; "Said to Contain"; "Shipper's Load and Count"; Improper Handling.

(1) A consignee of a non-negotiable bill who has given value in good faith or a holder to whom a negotiable bill has been duly negotiated relying in either case upon the description therein of the goods, or upon the date therein shown, may recover from the issuer damages caused by the misdating of the bill or the non-receipt or misdescription of the goods, except to the extent that the document indicates that the issuer does not know whether any part of all of the goods in fact were received or conform to the description, as where the description is in terms of marks or labels or kind, quantity, or condition or the receipt or description is qualified by "contents or condition of contents of packages unknown", "said to contain", "shipper's weight, load and count" or the like, if such indication be true.

(2) When goods are loaded by an issuer who is a common carrier, the issuer must count the packages of goods if package freight and ascertain the kind and quantity if bulk freight. In such cases "shipper's weight, load and count" or other words indicating that the description was made by the shipper are ineffective except as to freight concealed by packages.

(3) When bulk freight is loaded by a shipper who makes available to the issuer adequate facilities for weighing such freight, an issuer who is a common carrier must ascertain the kind and quantity within a reasonable time after receiving the written request of the shipper to do so. In such cases "shipper's weight" or other words of like purport are ineffective.

(4) The issuer may by inserting in the bill the words "shipper's weight, load and count" or other words of like purport indicate that the goods were loaded by the shipper; and if such statement be true the issuer shall not be liable for damages caused by the improper loading. But their omission does not imply liability for such damages.

(5) The shipper shall be deemed to have guaranteed to the issuer the accuracy at the time of shipment of the description, marks, labels, number, kind, quantity, condition and weight, as furnished by him; and the shipper shall indemnify the issuer against damage caused by inaccuracies in such particulars. The right of the issuer to such indemnity shall in no way limit his responsibility and liability under the contract of carriage to any person other than the shipper.

§7-302. Through Bills of Lading and Similar Documents.

(1) The issuer of a through bill of lading or other document embodying an undertaking to be performed in part by persons acting as its agents or by connecting carriers is liable to anyone entitled to recover on the document for any breach by such other persons or by a connecting carrier of its obligation under the document but to the extent that the bill covers an undertaking to be performed overseas or in territory not contiguous to the continental United States or an undertaking including matters other than transportation this liability may be varied by agreement of the parties.

(2) Where goods covered by a through bill of lading or other document embodying an undertaking to be performed in part by persons other than the issuer are received by any such person, he is subject with respect to his own performance while the goods are in his possession to the obligation of the issuer. His obligation is discharged by delivery of the goods to another such person pursuant to the document, and does not include liability for breach by any other such persons or by the issuer.

(3) The issuer of such through bill of lading or other document shall be entitled to recover from the connecting carrier or such other person in possession of the goods when the breach of the obligation under the document occurred, the amount it may be required to pay to anyone entitled to recover on the document therefor, as may be evidenced by any receipt, judgment, or transcript thereof, and the amount of any expense reasonably incurred by it in defending any action brought by anyone entitled to recover on the document therefor.

§7-307. Lien of Carrier.

(1) A carrier has a lien on the goods covered by a bill of lading for charges subsequent to the date of its receipt of the goods for storage or transportation (including demurrage and terminal charges) and for expenses necessary for preservation of the goods incident to their transportation or reasonably incurred in their sale pursuant to law. But against a purchaser for value of a negotiable bill of lading a carrier's lien is limited to charges stated in the bill or the applicable tariffs, or if no charges are stated then to a reasonable charge.

(2) A lien for charges and expenses under subsection (1) on goods which the carrier was required by law to receive for transportation is effective against the consignor or any person entitled to the goods unless the carrier had notice that the consignor lacked authority to subject the goods to such charges and expenses. Any other lien under subsection (1) is effective against the consignor and any person who permitted the bailor to have control or possession of the goods unless the carrier had notice that the bailor lacked such authority.

(3) A carrier loses his lien on any goods which he voluntarily delivers or which he unjustifiably refuses to deliver.

§7-308. Enforcement of Carrier's Lien.

(1) A carrier's lien may be enforced by public or private sale of the goods, in bloc or in parcels, at any time or place and on any terms which are commercially reasonable, after notifying all persons known to claim an interest in the goods. Such notification must include a statement of the amount due, the nature of the proposed sale and the time and place of any public sale. The fact that a better price could have been obtained by a sale at a different time or in a different method from that selected by the carrier is not of itself sufficient to establish that the sale was not made in a commercially reasonable manner. If the carrier either sells the goods in the usual manner in any recognized market therefor or if he sells at the price current in such market at the time of his sale or if he has otherwise sold in conformity with commercially reasonable practices among dealers in the type of goods sold he has sold in a commercially reasonable manner. A sale of more goods than apparently necessary to be offered to ensure satisfaction of the obligation is not commercially reasonable except in cases covered by the preceding sentence.

(2) Before any sale pursuant to this section any person claiming a right in the goods may pay the amount necessary to satisfy the lien and the reasonable expenses incurred under this section. In that event the goods must not be sold, but must be retained by the carrier subject to the terms of the bill and this Article.

(3) The carrier may buy at any public sale pursuant to this section.

(4) A purchaser in good faith of goods sold to enforce a carrier's lien takes the goods free of any rights of persons against whom the lien was valid, despite noncompliance by the carrier with the requirements of this section.

(5) The carrier may satisfy his lien from the proceeds of any sale pursuant to this section but must hold the balance, if any, for delivery on demand to any person to whom he would have been bound to deliver the goods.

(6) The rights provided by this section shall be in addition to all other rights allowed by law to a creditor against his debtor.

(7) A carrier's lien may be enforced in accordance with either subsection (1) or the procedure set forth in subsection (2) of Section 7-210.

(8) The carrier is liable for damages caused by failure to comply with the requirements for sale under this section and in case of willful violation is liable for conversion.

§7-309. Duty of Care; Contractual Limitation of Carrier's Liability.

(1) A carrier who issues a bill of lading whether negotiable or non-negotiable must exercise the degree of care in relation to the goods which a reasonably careful man would exercise under like circumstances. This subsection does not repeal or change any law or rule of law which imposes liability upon a common carrier for damages not caused by its negligence.

(2) Damages may be limited by a provision that the carrier's liability shall not exceed a value stated in the document if the carrier's rates are dependent upon value and the consignor by the carrier's tariff is afforded an opportunity to declare a higher value or a value as lawfully provided in the tariff, or where no tariff is filed he is otherwise advised of such opportunity; but no such limitation is effective with respect to the carrier's liability for conversion to its own use.

(3) Reasonable provisions as to the time and manner of presenting claims and instituting actions based on the shipment may be included in a bill of lading or tariff.

Part 4—Warehouse Receipts and Bills of Lading: General Obligations

§7-401. Irregularities in Issue of Receipt or Bill or Conduct of Issuer.

The obligations imposed by this Article on an issuer apply to a document of title regardless of the fact that

(a) the document may not comply with the requirements of this Article or of any other law or regulation regarding its issue, form or content; or

(b) the issuer may have violated laws regulating the conduct of his business; or

(c) the goods covered by the document were owned by the bailee at the time the document was issued; or

(d) the person issuing the document does not come within the definition of warehouseman if it purports to be a warehouse receipt.

§7-402. Duplicate Receipt or Bill; Overissue.

Neither a duplicate nor any other document of title purporting to cover goods already represented by an outstanding document of the same issuer confers any right in the goods, except as provided in the case of bills in a set, overissue of documents for fungible goods and substitutes for lost, stolen or destroyed documents. But the issuer is liable for damages caused by his overissue or failure to identify a duplicate document as such by conspicuous notation on its face.

§7-403. Obligation of Warehouseman or Carrier to Deliver; Excuse.

(1) The bailee must deliver the goods to a person entitled under the document who complies with subsections (2) and (3), unless and to the extent that the bailee establishes any of the following:

(a) delivery of the goods to a person whose receipt was rightful as against the claimant;

(b) damage to or delay, loss or destruction of the goods for which the bailee is not liable [, but the burden of establishing negligence in such cases is on the person entitled under the document];

Note: *The brackets in (1)(b) indicate that State enactments may differ on this point without serious damage to the principle of uniformity.*

(c) previous sale or other disposition of the goods in lawful enforcement of a lien or on warehouseman's lawful termination of storage;

(d) the exercise by a seller of his right to stop delivery pursuant to the provisions of the Article on Sales (Section 2-705);

(e) a diversion, reconsignment or other disposition pursuant to the provisions of this Article (Section 7-303) or tariff regulating such right;

(f) release, satisfaction or any other fact affording a personal defense against the claimant;

(g) any other lawful excuse.

(2) A person claiming goods covered by a document of title must satisfy the bailee's lien where the bailee so requests or where the bailee is prohibited by law from delivering the goods until the charges are paid.

(3) Unless the person claiming is one against whom the document confers no right under Sec. 7-503(1), he must surrender for cancellation or notation of partial deliveries any outstanding negotiable document covering the goods, and the bailee must cancel the document or conspicuously note the partial delivery thereon or be liable to any person to whom the document is duly negotiated.

(4) "Person entitled under the document" means holder in the case of a negotiable document, or the person to whom delivery is to be made by the terms of or pursuant to written instructions under a non-negotiable document.

§7-404. No Liability for Good Faith Delivery Pursuant to Receipt or Bill.

A bailee who in good faith including observance of reasonable commercial standards has received goods and delivered or otherwise disposed of them according to the terms of the document of title or pursuant to this Article is not liable therefor. This rule applies even though the person from whom he received the goods had no authority to procure the document or to dispose of the goods and even though the person to whom he delivered the goods had no authority to receive them.

Part 5—Warehouse Receipts and Bills of Lading: Negotiation and Transfer

§7-501. Form of Negotiation and Requirements of "Due Negotiation".

(1) A negotiable document of title running to the order of a named person is negotiated by his indorsement and delivery. After his indorsement in blank or to bearer any person can negotiate it by delivery alone.

(2) (a) A negotiable document of title is also negotiated by delivery alone when by its original terms it runs to bearer.

(b) When a document running to the order of a named person is delivered to him the effect is the same as if the document had been negotiated.

(3) Negotiation of a negotiable document of title after it has been indorsed to a specified person requires indorsement by the special indorsee as well as delivery.

(4) A negotiable document of title is "duly negotiated" when it is negotiated in the manner stated in this section to a holder who purchases it in good faith without notice of any defense against or claim to it on the part of any person and for value, unless it is established that the negotiation is not in the regular course of business or financing or involves receiving the document in settlement or payment of a money obligation.

(5) Indorsement of a non-negotiable document neither makes it negotiable nor adds to the transferee's rights.

(6) The naming in a negotiable bill of a person to be notified of the arrival of the goods does not limit the negotiability of the bill nor constitute notice to a purchaser thereof of any interest of such person in the goods.

§7-502. Rights Acquired by Due Negotiation.

(1) Subject to the following section and to the provisions of Section 7-205 on fungible goods, a holder to whom a negotiable document of title has been duly negotiated acquires thereby:

(a) title to the document;

(b) title to the goods;

(c) all rights accruing under the law of agency or estoppel, including rights to goods delivered to the bailee after the document was issued; and

(d) the direct obligation of the issuer to hold or deliver the goods according to the terms of the document free of any defense or claim by him except those arising under the terms of the document or under this Article. In the case of a delivery order the bailee's obligation accrues only upon acceptance and the obligation acquired by the holder is that the issuer and any indorser will procure the acceptance of the bailee.

(2) Subject to the following section, title and rights so acquired are not defeated by any stoppage of the goods represented by the document or by surrender of such goods by the bailee, and are not impaired even though the negotiation or any prior negotiation constituted a breach of duty or even though any person has been deprived of possession of the document by misrepresentation, fraud, accident, mistake, duress, loss, theft or conversion, or even though a previous sale or other transfer of the goods or document has been made to a third person.

§7-503. Document of Title to Goods Defeated in Certain Cases.

(1) A document of title confers no right in goods against a person who before issuance of the document had a legal interest or a perfected security interest in them and who neither

(a) delivered or entrusted them or any document of title covering them to the bailor or his nominee with actual or apparent authority to ship, store or sell or with power to obtain delivery under this Article (Section 7-403) or with power of disposition under this Act (Sections 2-403 and 9-307) or other statute or rule of law; nor

(b) acquiesced in the procurement by the bailor or his nominee of any document of title.

(2) Title to goods based upon an unaccepted delivery order is subject to the rights of anyone to whom a negotiable warehouse receipt or bill of lading covering the goods has been duly negotiated. Such a title may be defeated under the next section to the same extent as the rights of the issuer or a transferee from the issuer.

(3) Title to goods based upon a bill of lading issued to a freight forwarder is subject to the rights of anyone to whom a bill issued by the freight forwarder is duly negotiated; but delivery by the carrier in accordance with Part 4 of this Article pursuant to its own bill of lading discharges the carrier's obligation to deliver.

§7-504. Rights Acquired in the Absence of Due Negotiation; Effect of Diversion; Seller's Stoppage of Delivery.

(1) A transferee of a document, whether negotiable or non-negotiable, to whom the document has been delivered but not duly negotiated, acquires the title and rights which his transferor had or had actual authority to convey.

(2) In the case of a non-negotiable document, until but not after the bailee receives notification of the transfer, the rights of the transferee may be defeated

(a) by those creditors of the transferor who could treat the sale as void under Section 2-402; or

(b) by a buyer from the transferor in ordinary course of business if the bailee has delivered the goods to the buyer or received notification of his rights; or

(c) as against the bailee by good faith dealings of the bailee with the transferor.

(3) A diversion or other change of shipping instructions by the consignor in a non-negotiable bill of lading which causes the bailee not to deliver to the consignee defeats the consignee's title to the goods if they have been delivered to a buyer in ordinary course of business and in any event defeats the consignee's rights against the bailee.

(4) Delivery pursuant to a non-negotiable document may be stopped by a seller under Section 2-705, and subject to the requirement of due notification there provided. A bailee honoring the seller's instructions is entitled to be indemnified by the seller against any resulting loss or expense.

§7-505. Indorser Not a Guarantor for Other Parties.

The indorsement of a document of title issued by a bailee does not make the indorser liable for any default by the bailee or by previous indorsers.

§7-506. Delivery Without Indorsement: Right to Compel Indorsement.

The transferee of a negotiable document of title has a specifically enforceable right to have his transferor supply any necessary indorsement but the transfer becomes a negotiation only as of the time the indorsement is supplied.

§7-507. Warranties on Negotiation or Transfer of Receipt or Bill.

Where a person negotiates or transfers a document of title for value otherwise than as a mere intermediary under the next following section, then unless otherwise agreed he warrants to his immediate purchaser only in addition to any warranty made in selling the goods

(a) that the document is genuine; and

(b) that he has no knowledge of any fact which would impair its validity or worth; and

(c) that his negotiation or transfer is rightful and fully effective with respect to the title to the document and the goods it represents.

§7-508. Warranties of Collecting Bank as to Documents.

A collecting bank or other intermediary known to be entrusted with documents on behalf of another or with collection of a draft of other claim against delivery of documents warrants by such delivery of the documents only its own good faith and authority. This rule applies even though the intermediary has purchased or made advances against the claim or draft to be collected.

Part 6—Warehouse Receipts and Bills of Lading: Miscellaneous Provisions

§7-601. Lost and Missing Documents.

(1) If a document has been lost, stolen or destroyed, a court may order delivery of the goods or issuance of a substitute document and the bailee may without liability to any person comply with such order. If the document was negotiable the claimant must post security approved by the court to indemnify any person who may suffer loss as a result of non-surrender of the document. If the document was not negotiable, such security may be required at the discretion of the court. The court may also in its discretion order payment of the bailee's reasonable costs and counsel fees.

(2) A bailee who without court order delivers goods to a person claiming under a missing negotiable document is liable to any person injured thereby, and if the delivery is not in good faith becomes liable for conversion. Delivery in good faith is not conversion if made in accordance with a filed classification or tariff or, where no classification or tariff is filed, if the claimant posts security with the bailee in an amount at least double the value of the goods at the time of posting to indemnify any person injured by the delivery who files a notice of claim within one year after the delivery.

REVISED ARTICLE 9: SECURED TRANSACTIONS

Part 1—General Provisions

§9-101. Short Title.

This article may be cited as Uniform Commercial Code—Secured Transactions.

§9-102. Definitions and Index of Definitions.

(a) [Article 9 definitions.] In this article:

(1) "Accession" means goods that are physically united with other goods in such a manner that the identity of the original goods is not lost.

(2) "Account", except as used in "account for", means a right to payment of a monetary obligation, whether or not earned by performance, (i) for property that has been or is to be sold, leased, licensed, assigned, or otherwise disposed of, (ii) for services rendered or to be rendered,

(iii) for a policy of insurance issued or to be issued, (iv) for a secondary obligation incurred or to be incurred, (v) for energy provided or to be provided, (vi) for the use or hire of a vessel under a charter or other contract, (vii) arising out of the use of a credit or charge card or information contained on or for use with the card, or (viii) as winnings in a lottery or other game of chance operated or sponsored by a State, governmental unit of a State, or person licensed or authorized to operate the game by a State or governmental unit of a State. The term includes health-care-insurance receivables. The term does not include (i) rights to payment evidenced by chattel paper or an instrument, (ii) commercial tort claims, (iii) deposit accounts, (iv) investment property, (v) letter-of-credit rights or letters of credit, or (vi) rights to payment for money or funds advanced or sold, other than rights arising out of the use of a credit or charge card or information contained on or for use with the card.

(3) "Account debtor" means a person obligated on an account, chattel paper, or general intangible. The term does not include persons obligated to pay a negotiable instrument, even if the instrument constitutes part of chattel paper.

(4) "Accounting", except as used in "accounting for", means a record:

(A) authenticated by a secured party;

(B) indicating the aggregate unpaid secured obligations as of a date not more than 35 days earlier or 35 days later than the date of the record; and

(C) identifying the components of the obligations in reasonable detail.

(5) "Agricultural lien" means an interest, other than a security interest, in farm products:

(A) which secures payment or performance of an obligation for:

(i) goods or services furnished in connection with a debtor's farming operation; or

(ii) rent on real property leased by a debtor in connection with its farming operation;

(B) which is created by statute in favor of a person that:

(i) in the ordinary course of its business furnished goods or services to a debtor in connection with a debtor's farming operation; or

(ii) leased real property to a debtor in connection with the debtor's farming operation; and

(C) whose effectiveness does not depend on the person's possession of the personal property.

(6) "As-extracted collateral" means:

(A) oil, gas, or other minerals that are subject to a security interest that:

(i) is created by a debtor having an interest in the minerals before extraction; and

(ii) attaches to the minerals as extracted; or

(B) accounts arising out of the sale at the wellhead or minehead of oil, gas, or other minerals in which the debtor had an interest before extraction.

(7) "Authenticate" means:

(A) to sign; or

(B) to execute or otherwise adopt a symbol, or encrypt or similarly process a record in whole or in part, with the present intent of the authenticating person to identify the person and adopt or accept a record.

(8) "Bank" means an organization that is engaged in the business of banking. The term includes savings banks, savings and loan associations, credit unions, and trust companies.

(9) "Cash proceeds" means proceeds that are money, checks, deposit accounts, or the like.

(10) "Certificate of title" means a certificate of title with respect to which a statute provides for the security interest in question to be indicated on the certificate as a condition or result of the security interest's obtaining priority over the rights of a lien creditor with respect to the collateral.

(11) "Chattel paper" means a record or records that evidence both a monetary obligation and a security interest in specific goods, a security interest in specific goods and software used in the goods, a security interest in specific goods and license of software used in the goods, a lease of specific goods, or a lease of specific goods and license of software used in the goods. In this paragraph, "monetary obligation" means a monetary obligation secured by the goods or owed under a lease of the goods and includes a monetary obligation with respect to software used in the goods. The term does not include (i) charters or other contracts involving the use or hire of a vessel or (ii) records that evidence a right to payment arising out of the use of a credit or charge card or information contained on or for use with the card. If a transaction is evidenced by records that include an instrument or series of instruments, the group of records taken together constitutes chattel paper.

(12) "Collateral" means the property subject to a security interest or agricultural lien. The term includes:

(A) proceeds to which a security interest attaches;

(B) accounts, chattel paper, payment intangibles, and promissory notes that have been sold; and

(C) goods that are the subject of a consignment.

(13) "Commercial tort claim" means a claim arising in tort with respect to which:

(A) the claimant is an organization; or

(B) the claimant is an individual and the claim:

(i) arose in the course of the claimant's business or profession; and

(ii) does not include damages arising out of personal injury to or the death of an individual.

(14) "Commodity account" means an account maintained by a commodity intermediary in which a commodity contract is carried for a commodity customer.

(15) "Commodity contract" means a commodity futures contract, an option on a commodity futures contract, a commodity option, or another contract if the contract or option is:

(A) traded on or subject to the rules of a board of trade that has been designated as a contract market for such a contract pursuant to federal commodities laws; or

(B) traded on a foreign commodity board of trade, exchange, or market, and is carried on the books of a commodity intermediary for a commodity customer.

(16) "Commodity customer" means a person for which a commodity intermediary carries a commodity contract on its books.

(17) "Commodity intermediary" means a person that:

(A) is registered as a futures commission merchant under federal commodities law; or

(B) in the ordinary course of its business provides clearance or settlement services for a board of trade that has been designated as a contract market pursuant to federal commodities law.

(18) "Communicate" means:

(A) to send a written or other tangible record;

(B) to transmit a record by any means agreed upon by the persons sending and receiving the record; or

(C) in the case of transmission of a record to or by a filing office, to transmit a record by any means prescribed by filing-office rule.

(19) "Consignee" means a merchant to which goods are delivered in a consignment.

(20) "Consignment" means a transaction, regardless of its form, in which a person delivers goods to a merchant for the purpose of sale and:

(A) the merchant:

(i) deals in goods of that kind under a name other than the name of the person making delivery;

(ii) is not an auctioneer; and

(iii) is not generally known by its creditors to be substantially engaged in selling the goods of others;

(B) with respect to each delivery, the aggregate value of the goods is $1,000 or more at the time of delivery;

(C) the goods are not consumer goods immediately before delivery; and

(D) the transaction does not create a security interest that secures an obligation.

(21) "Consignor" means a person that delivers goods to a consignee in a consignment.

(22) "Consumer debtor" means a debtor in a consumer transaction.

(23) "Consumer goods" means goods that are used or bought for use primarily for personal, family, or household purposes.

(24) "Consumer-goods transaction" means a consumer transaction in which:

(A) an individual incurs an obligation primarily for personal, family, or household purposes; and

(B) a security interest in consumer goods secures the obligation.

(25) "Consumer obligor" means an obligor who is an individual and who incurred the obligation as part of a transaction entered into primarily for personal, family, or household purposes.

(26) "Consumer transaction" means a transaction in which (i) an individual incurs an obligation primarily for personal, family, or household purposes, (ii) a security interest secures the obligation, and (iii) the collateral is held or acquired primarily for personal, family, or household purposes. The term includes consumer-goods transactions.

(27) "Continuation statement" means an amendment of a financing statement which:

(A) identifies, by its file number, the initial financing statement to which it relates; and

(B) indicates that it is a continuation statement for, or that it is filed to continue the effectiveness of, the identified financing statement.

(28) "Debtor" means:

(A) a person having an interest, other than a security interest or other lien, in the collateral, whether or not the person is an obligor;

(B) a seller of accounts, chattel paper, payment intangibles, or promissory notes; or

(C) a consignee.

(29) "Deposit account" means a demand, time, savings, passbook, or similar account maintained with a bank. The term does not include investment property or accounts evidenced by an instrument.

(30) "Document" means a document of title or a receipt of the type described in Section 7-201(2).

(31) "Electronic chattel paper" means chattel paper evidenced by a record or records consisting of information stored in an electronic medium.

(32) "Encumbrance" means a right, other than an ownership interest, in real property. The term includes mortgages and other liens on real property.

(33) "Equipment" means goods other than inventory, farm products, or consumer goods.

(34) "Farm products" means goods, other than standing timber, with respect to which the debtor is engaged in a farming operation and which are:

(A) crops grown, growing, or to be grown, including:

(i) crops produced on trees, vines, and bushes; and

(ii) aquatic goods produced in aquacultural operations;

(B) livestock, born or unborn, including aquatic goods produced in aquacultural operations;

(C) supplies used or produced in a farming operation; or

(D) products of crops or livestock in their unmanufactured states.

(35) "Farming operation" means raising, cultivating, propagating, fattening, grazing, or any other farming, livestock, or aquacultural operation.

(36) "File number" means the number assigned to an initial financing statement pursuant to Section 9-519(a).

(37) "Filing office" means an office designated in Section 9-501 as the place to file a financing statement.

(38) "Filing-office rule" means a rule adopted pursuant to Section 9-526.

(39) "Financing statement" means a record or records composed of an initial financing statement and any filed record relating to the initial financing statement.

(40) "Fixture filing" means the filing of a financing statement covering goods that are or are to become fixtures and satisfying Section 9-502(a) and (b). The term includes the filing of a financing statement covering goods of a transmitting utility which are or are to become fixtures.

(41) "Fixtures" means goods that have become so related to particular real property that an interest in them arises under real property law.

(42) "General intangible" means any personal property, including things in action, other than accounts, chattel paper, commercial tort claims, deposit accounts, documents, goods, instruments, investment property, letter-of-credit rights, letters of credit, money, and oil, gas, or other minerals before extraction. The term includes payment intangibles and software.

(43) "Good faith" means honesty in fact and the observance of reasonable commercial standards of fair dealing.

(44) "Goods" means all things that are movable when a security interest attaches. The term includes (i) fixtures, (ii) standing timber that is to be cut and removed under a conveyance or contract for sale, (iii) the unborn young of animals, (iv) crops grown, growing, or to be grown, even if the crops are produced on trees, vines, or bushes, and (v) manufactured homes. The term also includes a computer program embedded in goods and any supporting information provided in connection with a transaction relating to the program if (i) the program is associated with the goods in such a manner that it customarily is considered part of the goods, or (ii) by becoming the owner of the goods, a person acquires a right to use the program in connection with the goods. The term does not include a computer program embedded in goods that consist solely of the medium in which the program is embedded. The term also does not include accounts, chattel paper, commercial tort claims, deposit accounts, documents, general intangibles, instruments, investment property, letter-of-credit rights, letters of credit, money, or oil, gas, or other minerals before extraction.

(45) "Governmental unit" means a subdivision, agency, department, county, parish, municipality, or other unit of the government of the United States, a State, or a foreign country. The term includes an organization having a separate corporate existence if the organization is eligible to issue debt on which interest is exempt from income taxation under the laws of the United States.

(46) "Health-care-insurance receivable" means an interest in or claim under a policy of insurance which is a right to payment of a monetary obligation for health-care goods or services provided.

(47) "Instrument" means a negotiable instrument or any other writing that evidences a right to the payment of a monetary obligation, is not itself a security agreement or lease, and is of a type that in ordinary course of business is transferred by delivery with any necessary indorsement or assignment. The term does not include (i) investment property, (ii) letters of credit, or (iii) writings that evidence a right to payment arising out of the use of a credit or charge card or information contained on or for use with the card.

(48) "Inventory" means goods, other than farm products, which:

(A) are leased by a person as lessor;

(B) are held by a person for sale or lease or to be furnished under a contract of service;

(C) are furnished by a person under a contract of service; or

(D) consist of raw materials, work in process, or materials used or consumed in a business.

(49) "Investment property" means a security, whether certificated or uncertificated, security entitlement, securities account, commodity contract, or commodity account.

(50) "Jurisdiction of organization", with respect to a registered organization, means the jurisdiction under whose law the organization is organized.

(51) "Letter-of-credit right" means a right to payment or performance under a letter of credit, whether or not the beneficiary has demanded or is at the time entitled to demand payment or performance. The term does not include the right of a beneficiary to demand payment or performance under a letter of credit.

(52) "Lien creditor" means:

(A) a creditor that has acquired a lien on the property involved by attachment, levy, or the like;

(B) an assignee for benefit of creditors from the time of assignment;

(C) a trustee in bankruptcy from the date of the filing of the petition; or

(D) a receiver in equity from the time of appointment.

(53) "Manufactured home" means a structure, transportable in one or more sections, which, in the traveling mode, is eight body feet or more in width or 40 body feet or more in length, or, when erected on site, is 320 or more square feet, and which is built on a permanent chassis and designed to be used as a dwelling with or without a permanent foundation when connected to the required utilities, and includes the plumbing, heating, air-conditioning, and electrical systems contained therein. The term includes any structure that meets all of the requirements of this paragraph except the size requirements and with respect to which the manufacturer voluntarily files a certification required by the United States Secretary of Housing and Urban Development and complies with the standards established under Title 42 of the United States Code.

(54) "Manufactured-home transaction" means a secured transaction:

(A) that creates a purchase-money security interest in a manufactured home, other than a manufactured home held as inventory; or

(B) in which a manufactured home, other than a manufactured home held as inventory, is the primary collateral.

(55) "Mortgage" means a consensual interest in real property, including fixtures, which secures payment or performance of an obligation.

(56) "New debtor" means a person that becomes bound as debtor under Section 9-203(d) by a security agreement previously entered into by another person.

(57) "New value" means (i) money, (ii) money's worth in property, services, or new credit, or (iii) release by a transferee of an interest in property previously transferred to the transferee. The term does not include an obligation substituted for another obligation.

(58) "Noncash proceeds" means proceeds other than cash proceeds.

(59) "Obligor" means a person that, with respect to an obligation secured by a security interest in or an agricultural lien on the collateral, (i) owes payment or other performance of the obligation, (ii) has provided property other than the collateral to secure payment or other performance of the obligation, or (iii) is otherwise accountable in whole or in part for payment or other performance of the obligation. The term does not include issuers or nominated persons under a letter of credit.

(60) "Original debtor", except as used in Section 9-310(c), means a person that, as debtor, entered into a security agreement to which a new debtor has become bound under Section 9-203(d).

(61) "Payment intangible" means a general intangible under which the account debtor's principal obligation is a monetary obligation.

(62) "Person related to", with respect to an individual, means:

(A) the spouse of the individual;

(B) a brother, brother-in-law, sister, or sister-in-law of the individual;

(C) an ancestor or lineal descendant of the individual or the individual's spouse; or

(D) any other relative, by blood or marriage, of the individual or the individual's spouse who shares the same home with the individual.

(63) "Person related to", with respect to an organization, means:

(A) a person directly or indirectly controlling, controlled by, or under common control with the organization;

(B) an officer or director of, or a person performing similar functions with respect to, the organization;

(C) an officer or director of, or a person performing similar functions with respect to, a person described in subparagraph (A);

(D) the spouse of an individual described in subparagraph (A), (B), or (C); or

(E) an individual who is related by blood or marriage to an individual described in subparagraph (A), (B), (C), or (D) and shares the same home with the individual.

(64) "Proceeds", except as used in Section 9-609(b), means the following property:

(A) whatever is acquired upon the sale, lease, license, exchange, or other disposition of collateral;

(B) whatever is collected on, or distributed on account of, collateral;

(C) rights arising out of collateral;

(D) to the extent of the value of collateral, claims arising out of the loss, nonconformity, or interference with the use of, defects or infringement of rights in, or damage to, the collateral; or

(E) to the extent of the value of collateral and to the extent payable to the debtor or the secured party, insurance payable by reason of the loss or nonconformity of, defects or infringement of rights in, or damage to, the collateral.

(65) "Promissory note" means an instrument that evidences a promise to pay a monetary obligation, does not evidence an order to pay, and does not contain an acknowledgment by a bank that the bank has received for deposit a sum of money or funds.

(66) "Proposal" means a record authenticated by a secured party which includes the terms on which the secured party is willing to accept collateral in full or partial satisfaction of the obligation it secures pursuant to Sections 9-620, 9-621, and 9-622.

(67) "Public-finance transaction" means a secured transaction in connection with which:

(A) debt securities are issued;

(B) all or a portion of the securities issued have an initial stated maturity of at least 20 years; and

(C) the debtor, obligor, secured party, account debtor or other person obligated on collateral, assignor or assignee of a secured obligation, or assignor or assignee of a security interest is a State or a governmental unit of a State.

(68) "Pursuant to commitment", with respect to an advance made or other value given by a secured party, means pursuant to the secured party's obligation, whether or not a subsequent event of default or other event not within the secured party's control has relieved or may relieve the secured party from its obligation.

(69) "Record", except as used in "for record", "of record", "record or legal title", and "record owner", means information that is inscribed on a tangible medium or which is stored in an electronic or other medium and is retrievable in perceivable form.

(70) "Registered organization" means an organization organized solely under the law of a single State or the United States and as to which the State or the United States must maintain a public record showing the organization to have been organized.

(71) "Secondary obligor" means an obligor to the extent that:

(A) the obligor's obligation is secondary; or

(B) the obligor has a right of recourse with respect to an obligation secured by collateral against the debtor, another obligor, or property of either.

(72) "Secured party" means:

(A) a person in whose favor a security interest is created or provided for under a security agreement, whether or not any obligation to be secured is outstanding;

(B) a person that holds an agricultural lien;

(C) a consignor;

(D) a person to which accounts, chattel paper, payment intangibles, or promissory notes have been sold;

(E) a trustee, indenture trustee, agent, collateral agent, or other representative in whose favor a security interest or agricultural lien is created or provided for; or

(F) a person that holds a security interest arising under Section 2-401, 2-505, 2-711(3), 2A-508(5), 4-210, or 5-118.

(73) "Security agreement" means an agreement that creates or provides for a security interest.

(74) "Send", in connection with a record or notification, means:

(A) to deposit in the mail, deliver for transmission, or transmit by any other usual means of communication, with postage or cost of transmission provided for, addressed to any address reasonable under the circumstances; or

(B) to cause the record or notification to be received within the time that it would have been received if properly sent under subparagraph (A).

(75) "Software" means a computer program and any supporting information provided in connection with a transaction relating to the program. The term does not include a computer program that is included in the definition of goods.

(76) "State" means a State of the United States, the District of Columbia, Puerto Rico, the United States Virgin Islands, or any territory or insular possession subject to the jurisdiction of the United States.

(77) "Supporting obligation" means a letter-of-credit right or secondary obligation that supports the payment or performance of an account, chattel paper, a document, a general intangible, an instrument, or investment property.

(78) "Tangible chattel paper" means chattel paper evidenced by a record or records consisting of information that is inscribed on a tangible medium.

(79) "Termination statement" means an amendment of a financing statement which:

(A) identifies, by its file number, the initial financing statement to which it relates; and

(B) indicates either that it is a termination statement or that the identified financing statement is no longer effective.

(80) "Transmitting utility" means a person primarily engaged in the business of:

(A) operating a railroad, subway, street railway, or trolley bus;

(B) transmitting communications electrically, electromagnetically, or by light;

(C) transmitting goods by pipeline or sewer; or

(D) transmitting or producing and transmitting electricity, steam, gas, or water.

(b) **[Definitions in other articles.]** The following definitions in other articles apply to this article:

"Applicant" Section 5-102.

"Beneficiary" Section 5-102.

"Broker" Section 8-102.

"Certificated security" Section 8-102.

"Check" Section 3-104.

"Clearing corporation" Section 8-102.

"Contract for sale" Section 2-106.

"Customer" Section 4-104.

"Entitlement holder" Section 8-102.

"Financial asset" Section 8-102.

"Holder in due course" Section 3-302.

"Issuer" (with respect to a letter of credit or letter-of-credit right) Section 5-102.

"Issuer" (with respect to a security) Section 8-201.

"Lease" Section 2A-103.

"Lease agreement" Section 2A-103.

"Lease contract" Section 2A-103.

"Leasehold interest" Section 2A-103.

"Lessee" Section 2A-103.

"Lessee in ordinary course of business" Section 2A-103.

"Lessor" Section 2A-103.

"Lessor's residual interest" Section 2A-103.

"Letter of credit" Section 5-102.

"Merchant" Section 2-104.

"Negotiable instrument" Section 3-104.

"Nominated person" Section 5-102.

"Note" Section 3-104.

"Proceeds of a letter of credit" Section 5-114.

"Prove" Section 3-103.

"Sale" Section 2-106.

"Securities account" Section 8-501.

"Securities intermediary" Section 8-102.

"Security" Section 8-102.

"Security certificate" Section 8-102.

"Security entitlement" Section 8-102.

"Uncertificated security" Section 8-102.

(c) **[Article 1 definitions and principles.]** Article 1 contains general definitions and principles of construction and interpretation applicable throughout this article.

§9-103. Purchase-Money Security Interest; Application of Payments; Burden of Establishing.

(a) **[Definitions.]** In this section:

(1) "purchase-money collateral" means goods or software that secures a purchase-money obligation incurred with respect to that collateral; and

(2) "purchase-money obligation" means an obligation of an obligor incurred as all or part of the price of the collateral or for value given to enable the debtor to acquire rights in or the use of the collateral if the value is in fact so used.

(b) **[Purchase-money security interest in goods.]** A security interest in goods is a purchase-money security interest:

(1) to the extent that the goods are purchase-money collateral with respect to that security interest;

(2) if the security interest is in inventory that is or was purchase-money collateral, also to the extent that the security interest secures a purchase-money obligation incurred with respect to other inventory in which the secured party holds or held a purchase-money security interest; and

(3) also to the extent that the security interest secures a purchase-money obligation incurred with respect to software in which the secured party holds or held a purchase-money security interest.

(c) **[Purchase-money security interest in software.]** A security interest in software is a purchase-money security interest to the extent that the security interest also secures a purchase-money obligation incurred with respect to goods in which the secured party holds or held a purchase-money security interest if:

(1) the debtor acquired its interest in the software in an integrated transaction in which it acquired an interest in the goods; and

(2) the debtor acquired its interest in the software for the principal purpose of using the software in the goods.

(d) **[Consignor's inventory purchase-money security interest.]** The security interest of a consignor in goods that are the subject of a consignment is a purchase-money security interest in inventory.

(e) **[Application of payment in non-consumer-goods transaction.]** In a transaction other than a consumer-goods transaction, if the extent to which a security interest is a purchase-money security interest depends on the application of a payment to a particular obligation, the payment must be applied:

(1) in accordance with any reasonable method of application to which the parties agree;

(2) in the absence of the parties' agreement to a reasonable method, in accordance with any intention of the obligor manifested at or before the time of payment; or

(3) in the absence of an agreement to a reasonable method and a timely manifestation of the obligor's intention, in the following order:

(A) to obligations that are not secured; and

(B) if more than one obligation is secured, to obligations secured by purchase-money security interests in the order in which those obligations were incurred.

(f) **[No loss of status of purchase-money security interest in non-consumer-goods transaction.]** In a transaction other than a consumer-goods transaction, a purchase-money security interest does not lose its status as such, even if:

(1) the purchase-money collateral also secures an obligation that is not a purchase-money obligation;

(2) collateral that is not purchase-money collateral also secures the purchase-money obligation; or

(3) the purchase-money obligation has been renewed, refinanced, consolidated, or restructured.

(g) **[Burden of proof in non-consumer-goods transaction.]** In a transaction other than a consumer-goods transaction, a secured party claiming a purchase-money security interest has the burden of establishing the extent to which the security interest is a purchase-money security interest.

(h) **[Non-consumer-goods transactions; no inference.]** The limitation of the rules in subsections (e), (f), and (g) to transactions other than consumer-goods transactions is intended to leave to the court the determination of the proper rules in consumer-goods transactions. The court may not infer from that limitation the nature of the proper rule in consumer-goods transactions and may continue to apply established approaches.

§9-104. Control of Deposit Account.

(a) **[Requirements for control.]** A secured party has control of a deposit account if:

(1) the secured party is the bank with which the deposit account is maintained;

(2) the debtor, secured party, and bank have agreed in an authenticated record that the bank will comply with instructions originated by the secured party directing disposition of the funds in the deposit account without further consent by the debtor; or

(3) the secured party becomes the bank's customer with respect to the deposit account.

(b) **[Debtor's right to direct disposition.]** A secured party that has satisfied subsection (a) has control, even if the debtor retains the right to direct the disposition of funds from the deposit account.

§9-105. Control of Electronic Chattel Paper.

A secured party has control of electronic chattel paper if the record or records comprising the chattel paper are created, stored, and assigned in such a manner that:

(1) a single authoritative copy of the record or records exists which is unique, identifiable and, except as otherwise provided in paragraphs (4), (5), and (6), unalterable;

(2) the authoritative copy identifies the secured party as the assignee of the record or records;

(3) the authoritative copy is communicated to and maintained by the secured party or its designated custodian;

(4) copies or revisions that add or change an identified assignee of the authoritative copy can be made only with the participation of the secured party;

(5) each copy of the authoritative copy and any copy of a copy is readily identifiable as a copy that is not the authoritative copy; and

(6) any revision of the authoritative copy is readily identifiable as an authorized or unauthorized revision.

§9-106. Control of Investment Property.

(a) **[Control under Section 8-106.]** A person has control of a certificated security, uncertificated security, or security entitlement as provided in Section 8-106.

(b) **[Control of commodity contract.]** A secured party has control of a commodity contract if:

(1) the secured party is the commodity intermediary with which the commodity contract is carried; or

(2) the commodity customer, secured party, and commodity intermediary have agreed that the commodity intermediary will apply any value distributed on account of the commodity contract as directed by the secured party without further consent by the commodity customer.

(c) **[Effect of control of securities account or commodity account.]** A secured party having control of all security entitlements or commodity contracts carried in a securities account or commodity account has control over the securities account or commodity account.

§9-107. Control of Letter-of-Credit Right.

A secured party has control of a letter-of-credit right to the extent of any right to payment or performance by the issuer or any nominated person if the issuer or nominated person has consented to an assignment of proceeds of the letter of credit under Section 5-114(c) or otherwise applicable law or practice.

§9-108. Sufficiency of Description.

(a) **[Sufficiency of description.]** Except as otherwise provided in subsections (c), (d), and (e), a description of personal or real property is sufficient, whether or not it is specific, if it reasonably identifies what is described.

(b) **[Examples of reasonable identification.]** Except as otherwise provided in subsection (d), a description of collateral reasonably identifies the collateral if it identifies the collateral by:

(1) specific listing;

(2) category;

(3) except as otherwise provided in subsection (e), a type of collateral defined in [the Uniform Commercial Code];

(4) quantity;

(5) computational or allocational formula or procedure; or

(6) except as otherwise provided in subsection (c), any other method, if the identity of the collateral is objectively determinable.

(c) **[Supergeneric description not sufficient.]** A description of collateral as "all the debtor's assets" or "all the debtor's personal property" or using words of similar import does not reasonably identify the collateral.

(d) **[Investment property.]** Except as otherwise provided in subsection (e), a description of a security entitlement, securities account, or commodity account is sufficient if it describes:

(1) the collateral by those terms or as investment property; or

(2) the underlying financial asset or commodity contract.

(e) **[When description by type insufficient.]** A description only by type of collateral defined in [the Uniform Commercial Code] is an insufficient description of:

(1) a commercial tort claim; or

(2) in a consumer transaction, consumer goods, a security entitlement, a securities account, or a commodity account.

§9-109. Scope.

(a) **[General scope of article.]** Except as otherwise provided in subsections (c) and (d), this article applies to:

(1) a transaction, regardless of its form, that creates a security interest in personal property or fixtures by contract;

(2) an agricultural lien;

(3) a sale of accounts, chattel paper, payment intangibles, or promissory notes;

(4) a consignment;

(5) a security interest arising under Section 2-401, 2-505, 2-711(3), or 2A-508(5), as provided in Section 9-110; and

(6) a security interest arising under Section 4-210 or 5-118.

(b) **[Security interest in secured obligation.]** The application of this article to a security interest in a secured obligation is not affected by the fact that the obligation is itself secured by a transaction or interest to which this article does not apply.

(c) **[Extent to which article does not apply.]** This article does not apply to the extent that:

(1) a statute, regulation, or treaty of the United States preempts this article;

(2) another statute of this State expressly governs the creation, perfection, priority, or enforcement of a security interest created by this State or a governmental unit of this State;

(3) a statute of another State, a foreign country, or a governmental unit of another State or a foreign country, other than a statute generally applicable to security interests, expressly governs creation, perfection, priority, or enforcement of a security interest created by the State, country, or governmental unit; or

(4) the rights of a transferee beneficiary or nominated person under a letter of credit are independent and superior under Section 5-114.

(d) **[Inapplicability of article.]** This article does not apply to:

(1) a landlord's lien, other than an agricultural lien;

(2) a lien, other than an agricultural lien, given by statute or other rule of law for services or materials, but Section 9-333 applies with respect to priority of the lien;

(3) an assignment of a claim for wages, salary, or other compensation of an employee;

(4) a sale of accounts, chattel paper, payment intangibles, or promissory notes as part of a sale of the business out of which they arose;

(5) an assignment of accounts, chattel paper, payment intangibles, or promissory notes which is for the purpose of collection only;

(6) an assignment of a right to payment under a contract to an assignee that is also obligated to perform under the contract;

(7) an assignment of a single account, payment intangible, or promissory note to an assignee in full or partial satisfaction of a preexisting indebtedness;

(8) a transfer of an interest in or an assignment of a claim under a policy of insurance, other than an assignment by or to a health-care provider of a health-care-insurance receivable and any subsequent assignment of the right to payment, but Sections 9-315 and 9-322 apply with respect to proceeds and priorities in proceeds;

(9) an assignment of a right represented by a judgment, other than a judgment taken on a right to payment that was collateral;

(10) a right of recoupment or set-off, but:

(A) Section 9-340 applies with respect to the effectiveness of rights of recoupment or set-off against deposit accounts; and

(B) Section 9-404 applies with respect to defenses or claims of an account debtor;

(11) the creation or transfer of an interest in or lien on real property, including a lease or rents thereunder, except to the extent that provision is made for:

(A) liens on real property in Sections 9-203 and 9-308;

(B) fixtures in Section 9-334;

(C) fixture filings in Sections 9-501, 9-502, 9-512, 9-516, and 9-519; and

(D) security agreements covering personal and real property in Section 9-604;

(12) an assignment of a claim arising in tort, other than a commercial tort claim, but Sections 9-315 and 9-322 apply with respect to proceeds and priorities in proceeds; or

(13) an assignment of a deposit account in a consumer transaction, but Sections 9-315 and 9-322 apply with respect to proceeds and priorities in proceeds.

§9-110. Security Interests Arising under Article 2 or 2A.

A security interest arising under Section 2-401, 2-505, 2-711(3), or 2A-508(5) is subject to this article. However, until the debtor obtains possession of the goods:

(1) the security interest is enforceable, even if Section 9-203(b)(3) has not been satisfied;

(2) filing is not required to perfect the security interest;

(3) the rights of the secured party after default by the debtor are governed by Article 2 or 2A; and

(4) the security interest has priority over a conflicting security interest created by the debtor.

Part 2—Effectiveness of Security Agreement; Attachment of Security Interest; Rights of Parties to Security Agreement

§9-201. General Effectiveness of Security Agreement.

(a) **[General effectiveness.]** Except as otherwise provided in [the Uniform Commercial Code], a security agreement is effective according to its terms between the parties, against purchasers of the collateral, and against creditors.

(b) **[Applicable consumer laws and other law.]** A transaction subject to this article is subject to any applicable rule of law which establishes a different rule for consumers and [insert reference to (i) any other statute or regulation that regulates the rates, charges, agreements, and practices for loans, credit sales, or other extensions of credit and (ii) any consumer-protection statute or regulation].

(c) **[Other applicable law controls.]** In case of conflict between this article and a rule of law, statute, or regulation described in subsection (b), the rule of law, statute, or regulation controls. Failure to comply with a statute or regulation described in subsection (b) has only the effect the statute or regulation specifies.

(d) **[Further deference to other applicable law.]** This article does not:

(1) validate any rate, charge, agreement, or practice that violates a rule of law, statute, or regulation described in subsection (b); or

(2) extend the application of the rule of law, statute, or regulation to a transaction not otherwise subject to it.

§9-202. Title to Collateral Immaterial.

Except as otherwise provided with respect to consignments or sales of accounts, chattel paper, payment intangibles, or promissory notes, the provisions of this article with regard to rights and obligations apply whether title to collateral is in the secured party or the debtor.

§9-203. Attachment and Enforceability of Security Interest; Proceeds; Supporting Obligations; Formal Requisites.

(a) **[Attachment.]** A security interest attaches to collateral when it becomes enforceable against the debtor with respect to the collateral, unless an agreement expressly postpones the time of attachment.

(b) **[Enforceability.]** Except as otherwise provided in subsections (c) through (i), a security interest is enforceable against the debtor and third parties with respect to the collateral only if:

(1) value has been given;

(2) the debtor has rights in the collateral or the power to transfer rights in the collateral to a secured party; and

(3) one of the following conditions is met:

(A) the debtor has authenticated a security agreement that provides a description of the collateral and, if the security interest covers timber to be cut, a description of the land concerned;

(B) the collateral is not a certificated security and is in the possession of the secured party under Section 9-313 pursuant to the debtor's security agreement;

(C) the collateral is a certified security in registered form and the security certificate has been delivered to the secured party under Section 8-301 pursuant to the debtor's security agreement; or

(D) the collateral is deposit accounts, electronic chattel paper, investment property, or letter-of-credit rights, and the secured party has control under Section 9-104, 9-105, 9-106, or 9-107 pursuant to the debtor's security agreement.

(c) [**Other UCC provisions.**] Subsection (b) is subject to Section 4-210 on the security interest of a collecting bank, Section 5-118 on the security interest of a letter-of-credit issuer or nominated person, Section 9-110 on a security interest arising under Article 2 or 2A, and Section 9-206 on security interests in investment property.

(d) [**When person becomes bound by another person's security agreement.**] A person becomes bound as debtor by a security agreement entered into by another person if, by operation of law other than this article or by contract:

(1) the security agreement becomes effective to create a security interest in the person's property; or

(2) the person becomes generally obligated for the obligations of the other person, including the obligation secured under the security agreement, and acquires or succeeds to all or substantially all of the assets of the other person.

(e) [**Effect of new debtor becoming bound.**] If a new debtor becomes bound as debtor by a security agreement entered into by another person:

(1) the agreement satisfies subsection (b)(3) with respect to existing or after-acquired property of the new debtor to the extent the property is described in the agreement; and

(2) another agreement is not necessary to make a security interest in the property enforceable.

(f) [**Proceeds and supporting obligations.**] The attachment of a security interest in collateral gives the secured party the rights to proceeds provided by Section 9-315 and is also attachment of a security interest in a supporting obligation for the collateral.

(g) [**Lien securing right to payment.**] The attachment of a security interest in a right to payment or performance secured by a security interest or other lien on personal or real property is also attachment of a security interest in the security interest, mortgage, or other lien.

(h) [**Security entitlement carried in securities account.**] The attachment of a security interest in a securities account is also attachment of a security interest in the security entitlements carried in the securities account.

(i) [**Commodity contracts carried in commodity account.**] The attachment of a security interest in a commodity account is also attachment of a security interest in the commodity contracts carried in the commodity account.

§9-204. After-Acquired Property; Future Advances.

(a) [**After-acquired collateral.**] Except as otherwise provided in subsection (b), a security agreement may create or provide for a security interest in after-acquired collateral.

(b) [**When after-acquired property clause not effective.**] A security interest does not attach under a term constituting an after-acquired property clause to:

(1) consumer goods, other than an accession when given as additional security, unless the debtor acquires rights in them within 10 days after the secured party gives value; or

(2) a commercial tort claim.

(c) [**Future advances and other value.**] A security agreement may provide that collateral secures, or that accounts, chattel paper, payment intangibles, or promissory notes are sold in connection with, future advances or other value, whether or not the advances or value are given pursuant to commitment.

§9-205. Use or Disposition of Collateral Permissible.

(a) [**When security interest not invalid or fraudulent.**] A security interest is not invalid or fraudulent against creditors solely because:

(1) the debtor has the right or ability to:

(A) use, commingle, or dispose of all or part of the collateral, including returned or repossessed goods;

(B) collect, compromise, enforce, or otherwise deal with collateral;

(C) accept the return of collateral or make repossessions; or

(D) use, commingle, or dispose of proceeds; or

(2) the secured party fails to require the debtor to account for proceeds or replace collateral.

(b) [**Requirements of possession not relaxed.**] This section does not relax the requirements of possession if attachment, perfection, or enforcement of a security interest depends upon possession of the collateral by the secured party.

§9-206. Security Interest Arising in Purchase or Delivery of Financial Asset.

(a) [**Security interest when person buys through securities intermediary.**] A security interest in favor of a securities intermediary attaches to a person's security entitlement if:

(1) the person buys a financial asset through the securities intermediary in a transaction in which the person is obligated to pay the purchase price to the securities intermediary at the time of the purchase; and

(2) the securities intermediary credits the financial asset to the buyer's securities account before the buyer pays the securities intermediary.

(b) [**Security interest secures obligation to pay for financial asset.**] The security interest described in subsection (a) secures the person's obligation to pay for the financial asset.

(c) [**Security interest in payment against delivery transaction.**] A security interest in favor of a person that delivers a certificated security or other financial asset represented by a writing attaches to the security or other financial asset if:

(1) the security or other financial asset:

(A) in the ordinary course of business is transferred by delivery with any necessary indorsement or assignment; and

(B) is delivered under an agreement between persons in the business of dealing with such securities or financial assets; and

(2) the agreement calls for delivery against payment.

(d) [**Security interest secures obligation to pay for delivery.**] The security interest described in subsection (c) secures the obligation to make payment for the delivery.

§9-207. Rights and Duties of Secured Party Having Possession Or Control of Collateral.

(a) [**Duty of care when secured party in possession.**] Except as otherwise provided in subsection (d), a secured party shall use reasonable care in the custody and preservation of collateral in the secured party's possession. In the case of chattel paper or an instrument, reasonable care includes taking necessary steps to preserve rights against prior parties unless otherwise agreed.

(b) [**Expenses, risks, duties, and rights when secured party in possession.**] Except as otherwise provided in subsection (d), if a secured party has possession of collateral:

(1) reasonable expenses, including the cost of insurance and payment of taxes or other charges, incurred in the custody, preservation, use, or operation of the collateral are chargeable to the debtor and are secured by the collateral;

(2) the risk of accidental loss or damage is on the debtor to the extent of a deficiency in any effective insurance coverage;

(3) the secured party shall keep the collateral identifiable, but fungible collateral may be commingled; and

(4) the secured party may use or operate the collateral:

(A) for the purpose of preserving the collateral or its value;

(B) as permitted by an order of a court having competent jurisdiction; or

(C) except in the case of consumer goods, in the manner and to the extent agreed by the debtor.

(c) [**Duties and rights when secured party in possession or control.**] Except as otherwise provided in subsection (d), a secured party having possession of collateral or control of collateral under Section 9-104, 9-105, 9-106, or 9-107:

(1) may hold as additional security any proceeds, except money or funds, received from the collateral;

(2) shall apply money or funds received from the collateral to reduce the secured obligation, unless remitted to the debtor; and

(3) may create a security interest in the collateral.

(d) [**Buyer of certain rights to payment.**] If the secured party is a buyer of accounts, chattel paper, payment intangibles, or promissory notes or a consignor:

(1) subsection (a) does not apply unless the secured party is entitled under an agreement:

(A) to charge back uncollected collateral; or

(B) otherwise to full or limited recourse against the debtor or a secondary obligor based on the nonpayment or other default of an account debtor or other obligor on the collateral; and

(2) subsections (b) and (c) do not apply.

§9-208. Additional Duties of Secured Party Having Control of Collateral.

(a) [**Applicability of section.**] This section applies to cases in which there is no outstanding secured obligation and the secured party is not committed to make advances, incur obligations, or otherwise give value.

(b) [**Duties of secured party after receiving demand from debtor.**] Within 10 days after receiving an authenticated demand by the debtor:

(1) a secured party having control of a deposit account under Section 9-104(a)(2) shall send to the bank with which the deposit account is maintained an authenticated statement that releases the bank from any further obligation to comply with instructions originated by the secured party;

(2) a secured party having control of a deposit account under Section 9-104(a)(3) shall:

(A) pay the debtor the balance on deposit in the deposit account; or

(B) transfer the balance on deposit into a deposit account in the debtor's name;

(3) a secured party, other than a buyer, having control of electronic chattel paper under Section 9-105 shall:

(A) communicate the authoritative copy of the electronic chattel paper to the debtor or its designated custodian;

(B) if the debtor designates a custodian that is the designated custodian with which the authoritative copy of the electronic chattel paper is maintained for the secured party, communicate to the custodian an authenticated record releasing the designated custodian from any further obligation to comply with instructions originated by the secured party and instructing the custodian to comply with instructions originated by the debtor; and

(C) take appropriate action to enable the debtor or its designated custodian to make copies of or revisions to the authoritative copy which add or change an identified assignee of the authoritative copy without the consent of the secured party;

(4) a secured party having control of investment property under Section 8-106(d)(2) or 9-106(b) shall send to the securities intermediary or commodity intermediary with which the security entitlement or commodity contract is maintained an authenticated record that releases the securities intermediary or commodity intermediary from any further obligation to comply with entitlement orders or directions originated by the secured party; and

(5) a secured party having control of a letter-of-credit right under Section 9-107 shall send to each person having an unfulfilled obligation to pay or deliver proceeds of the letter of credit to the secured party an authenticated release from any further obligation to pay or deliver proceeds of the letter of credit to the secured party.

§9-209. Duties of Secured Party if Account Debtor Has Been Notified of Assignment.

(a) [**Applicability of section.**] Except as otherwise provided in subsection (c), this section applies if:

(1) there is no outstanding secured obligation; and

(2) the secured party is not committed to make advances, incur obligations, or otherwise give value.

(b) [**Duties of secured party after receiving demand from debtor.**] Within 10 days after receiving an authenticated demand by the debtor, a secured party shall send to an account debtor that has received notification of an assignment to the secured party as assignee under Section 9-406(a) an authenticated record that releases the account debtor from any further obligation to the secured party.

(c) [**Inapplicability to sales.**] This section does not apply to an assignment constituting the sale of an account, chattel paper, or payment intangible.

§9-210. Request for Accounting; Request Regarding List of Collateral or Statement of Account.

(a) [**Definitions.**] In this section:

(1) "Request" means a record of a type described in paragraph (2), (3), or (4).

(2) "Request for an accounting" means a record authenticated by a debtor requesting that the recipient provide an accounting of the unpaid obligations secured by collateral and reasonably identifying the transaction or relationship that is the subject of the request.

(3) "Request regarding a list of collateral" means a record authenticated by a debtor requesting that the recipient approve or correct a list of what the debtor believes to be the collateral securing an obligation and reasonably identifying the transaction or relationship that is the subject of the request.

(4) "Request regarding a statement of account" means a record authenticated by a debtor requesting that the recipient approve or correct a statement indicating what the debtor believes to be the aggregate amount of unpaid obligations secured by collateral as of a specified date and reasonably identifying the transaction or relationship that is the subject of the request.

(b) [**Duty to respond to requests.**] Subject to subsections (c), (d), (e), and (f), a secured party, other than a buyer of accounts, chattel paper, payment intangibles, or promissory notes or a consignor, shall comply with a request within 14 days after receipt:

(1) in the case of a request for an accounting, by authenticating and sending to the debtor an accounting; and

(2) in the case of a request regarding a list of collateral or a request regarding a statement of account, by authenticating and sending to the debtor an approval or correction.

(c) [**Request regarding list of collateral; statement concerning type of collateral.**] A secured party that claims a security interest in all of a particular type of collateral owned by the debtor may comply with a request regarding a list of collateral by sending to the debtor an authenticated record including a statement to that effect within 14 days after receipt.

(d) [**Request regarding list of collateral; no interest claimed.**] A person that receives a request regarding a list of collateral, claims no interest in the collateral when it receives the request, and claimed an interest in the collateral at an earlier time shall comply with the request within 14 days after receipt by sending to the debtor an authenticated record:

(1) disclaiming any interest in the collateral; and

(2) if known to the recipient, providing the name and mailing address of any assignee of or successor to the recipient's interest in the collateral.

(e) [**Request for accounting or regarding statement of account; no interest in obligation claimed.**] A person that receives a request for an accounting or a request regarding a statement of account, claims no interest in the obligations when it receives the request, and claimed an interest in the obligations at an earlier time shall comply with the request within 14 days after receipt by sending to the debtor an authenticated record:

(1) disclaiming any interest in the obligations; and

(2) if known to the recipient, providing the name and mailing address of any assignee of or successor to the recipient's interest in the obligations.

(f) **[Charges for responses.]** A debtor is entitled without charge to one response to a request under this section during any six-month period. The secured party may require payment of a charge not exceeding $25 for each additional response.

Part 3—Perfection and Priority

§9-301. Law Governing Perfection and Priority of Security Interests.

Except as otherwise provided in Sections 9-303 through 9-306, the following rules determine the law governing perfection, the effect of perfection or nonperfection, and the priority of a security interest in collateral:

(1) Except as otherwise provided in this section, while a debtor is located in a jurisdiction, the local law of that jurisdiction governs perfection, the effect of perfection or nonperfection, and the priority of a security interest in collateral.

(2) While collateral is located in a jurisdiction, the local law of that jurisdiction governs perfection, the effect of perfection or nonperfection, and the priority of a possessory security interest in that collateral.

(3) Except as otherwise provided in paragraph (4), while negotiable documents, goods, instruments, money, or tangible chattel paper is located in a jurisdiction, the local law of that jurisdiction governs:

(A) perfection of a security interest in the goods by filing a fixture filing;

(B) perfection of a security interest in timber to be cut; and

(C) the effect of perfection or nonperfection and the priority of a nonpossessory security interest in the collateral.

(4) The local law of the jurisdiction in which the wellhead or minehead is located governs perfection, the effect of perfection or nonperfection, and the priority of a security interest in as-extracted collateral.

§9-302. Law Governing Perfection and Priority of Agricultural Liens.

While farm products are located in a jurisdiction, the local law of that jurisdiction governs perfection, the effect of perfection or nonperfection, and the priority of an agricultural lien on the farm products.

§9-303. Law Governing Perfection and Priority of Security Interests in Goods Covered by a Certificate of Title.

(a) **[Applicability of section.]** This section applies to goods covered by a certificate of title, even if there is no other relationship between the jurisdiction under whose certificate of title the goods are covered and the goods or the debtor.

(b) **[When goods covered by certificate of title.]** Goods become covered by a certificate of title when a valid application for the certificate of title and the applicable fee are delivered to the appropriate authority. Goods cease to be covered by a certificate of title at the earlier of the time the certificate of title ceases to be effective under the law of the issuing jurisdiction or the time the goods become covered subsequently by a certificate of title issued by another jurisdiction.

(c) **[Applicable law.]** The local law of the jurisdiction under whose certificate of title the goods are covered governs perfection, the effect of perfection or nonperfection, and the priority of a security interest in goods covered by a certificate of title from the time the goods become covered by the certificate of title until the goods cease to be covered by the certificate of title.

§9-304. Law Governing Perfection and Priority of Security Interests in Deposit Accounts.

(a) **[Law of bank's jurisdiction governs.]** The local law of a bank's jurisdiction governs perfection, the effect of perfection or nonperfection, and the priority of a security interest in a deposit account maintained with that bank.

(b) **[Bank's jurisdiction.]** The following rules determine a bank's jurisdiction for purposes of this part:

(1) If an agreement between the bank and the debtor governing the deposit account expressly provides that a particular jurisdiction is the bank's jurisdiction for purposes of this part, this article, or [the Uniform Commercial Code], that jurisdiction is the bank's jurisdiction.

(2) If paragraph (1) does not apply and an agreement between the bank and its customer governing the deposit account expressly provides that the agreement is governed by the law of a particular jurisdiction, that jurisdiction is the bank's jurisdiction.

(3) If neither paragraph (1) nor paragraph (2) applies and an agreement between the bank and its customer governing the deposit account expressly provides that the deposit account is maintained at an office in a particular jurisdiction, that jurisdiction is the bank's jurisdiction.

(4) If none of the preceding paragraphs applies, the bank's jurisdiction is the jurisdiction in which the office identified in an account statement as the office serving the customer's account is located.

(5) If none of the preceding paragraphs applies, the bank's jurisdiction is the jurisdiction in which the chief executive office of the bank is located.

§9-305. Law Governing Perfection and Priority of Security Interests in Investment Property.

(a) **[Governing law: general rules.]** Except as otherwise provided in subsection (c), the following rules apply:

(1) While a security certificate is located in a jurisdiction, the local law of that jurisdiction governs perfection, the effect of perfection or nonperfection, and the priority of a security interest in the certificated security represented thereby.

(2) The local law of the issuer's jurisdiction as specified in Section 8-110(d) governs perfection, the effect of perfection or nonperfection, and the priority of a security interest in an uncertificated security.

(3) The local law of the securities intermediary's jurisdiction as specified in Section 8-110(e) governs perfection, the effect of perfection or nonperfection, and the priority of a security interest in a security entitlement or securities account.

(4) The local law of the commodity intermediary's jurisdiction governs perfection, the effect of perfection or nonperfection, and the priority of a security interest in a commodity contract or commodity account.

(b) **[Commodity intermediary's jurisdiction.]** The following rules determine a commodity intermediary's jurisdiction for purposes of this part:

(1) If an agreement between the commodity intermediary and commodity customer governing the commodity account expressly provides that a particular jurisdiction is the commodity intermediary's jurisdiction for purposes of this part, this article, or [the Uniform Commercial Code], that jurisdiction is the commodity intermediary's jurisdiction.

(2) If paragraph (1) does not apply and an agreement between the commodity intermediary and commodity customer governing the commodity account expressly provides that the agreement is governed by the law of a particular jurisdiction, that jurisdiction is the commodity intermediary's jurisdiction.

(3) If neither paragraph (1) nor paragraph (2) applies and an agreement between the commodity intermediary and commodity customer governing the commodity account expressly provides that the commodity account is maintained at an office in a particular jurisdiction, that jurisdiction is the commodity intermediary's jurisdiction.

(4) If none of the preceding paragraphs applies, the commodity intermediary's jurisdiction is the jurisdiction in which the office identified in an account statement as the office serving the commodity customer's account is located.

(5) If none of the preceding paragraphs applies, the commodity intermediary's jurisdiction is the jurisdiction in which the chief executive office of the commodity intermediary is located.

(c) [**When perfection governed by law of jurisdiction where debtor located.**] The local law of the jurisdiction in which the debtor is located governs:

(1) perfection of a security interest in investment property by filing;

(2) automatic perfection of a security interest in investment property created by a broker or securities intermediary; and

(3) automatic perfection of a security interest in a commodity contract or commodity account created by a commodity intermediary.

§9-306. Law Governing Perfection and Priority of Security Interests in Letter-of-Credit Rights.

(a) [**Governing law: issuer's or nominated person's jurisdiction.**] Subject to subsection (c), the local law of the issuer's jurisdiction or a nominated person's jurisdiction governs perfection, the effect of perfection or nonperfection, and the priority of a security interest in a letter-of-credit right if the issuer's jurisdiction or nominated person's jurisdiction is a State.

(b) [**Issuer's or nominated person's jurisdiction.**] For purposes of this part, an issuer's jurisdiction or nominated person's jurisdiction is the jurisdiction whose law governs the liability of the issuer or nominated person with respect to the letter-of-credit right as provided in Section 5-116.

(c) [**When section not applicable.**] This section does not apply to a security interest that is perfected only under Section 9-308(d).

§9-307. Location of Debtor.

(a) [**"Place of business."**] In this section, "place of business" means a place where a debtor conducts its affairs.

(b) [**Debtor's location: general rules.**] Except as otherwise provided in this section, the following rules determine a debtor's location:

(1) A debtor who is an individual is located at the individual's principal residence.

(2) A debtor that is an organization and has only one place of business is located at its place of business.

(3) A debtor that is an organization and has more than one place of business is located at its chief executive office.

(c) [**Limitation of applicability of subsection (b).**] Subsection (b) applies only if a debtor's residence, place of business, or chief executive office, as applicable, is located in a jurisdiction whose law generally requires information concerning the existence of a nonpossessory security interest to be made generally available in a filing, recording, or registration system as a condition or result of the security interest's obtaining priority over the rights of a lien creditor with respect to the collateral. If subsection (b) does not apply, the debtor is located in the District of Columbia.

(d) [**Continuation of location: cessation of existence, etc.**] A person that ceases to exist, have a residence, or have a place of business continues to be located in the jurisdiction specified by subsections (b) and (c).

(e) [**Location of registered organization organized under State law.**] A registered organization that is organized under the law of a State is located in that State.

(f) [**Location of registered organization organized under federal law; bank branches and agencies.**] Except as otherwise provided in subsection (i), a registered organization that is organized under the law of the United States and a branch or agency of a bank that is not organized under the law of the United States or a State are located:

(1) in the State that the law of the United States designates, if the law designates a State of location;

(2) in the State that the registered organization, branch, or agency designates, if the law of the United States authorizes the registered organization, branch, or agency to designate its State of location; or

(3) in the District of Columbia, if neither paragraph (1) nor paragraph (2) applies.

(g) [**Continuation of location: change in status of registered organization.**] A registered organization continues to be located in the jurisdiction specified by subsection (e) or (f) notwithstanding:

(1) the suspension, revocation, forfeiture, or lapse of the registered organization's status as such in its jurisdiction of organization; or

(2) the dissolution, winding up, or cancellation of the existence of the registered organization.

(h) [**Location of United States.**] The United States is located in the District of Columbia.

(i) [**Location of foreign bank branch or agency if licensed in only one state.**] A branch or agency of a bank that is not organized under the law of the United States or a State is located in the State in which the branch or agency is licensed, if all branches and agencies of the bank are licensed in only one State.

(j) [**Location of foreign air carrier.**] A foreign air carrier under the Federal Aviation Act of 1958, as amended, is located at the designated office of the agent upon which service of process may be made on behalf of the carrier.

(k) [**Section applies only to this part.**] This section applies only for purposes of this part.

§9-308. When Security Interest or Agricultural Lien Is Perfected; Continuity of Perfection.

(a) [**Perfection of security interest.**] Except as otherwise provided in this section and Section 9-309, a security interest is perfected if it has attached and all of the applicable requirements for perfection in Sections 9-310 through 9-316 have been satisfied. A security interest is perfected when it attaches if the applicable requirements are satisfied before the security interest attaches.

(b) [**Perfection of agricultural lien.**] An agricultural lien is perfected if it has become effective and all of the applicable requirements for perfection in Section 9-310 have been satisfied. An agricultural lien is perfected when it becomes effective if the applicable requirements are satisfied before the agricultural lien becomes effective.

(c) [**Continuous perfection; perfection by different methods.**] A security interest or agricultural lien is perfected continuously if it is originally perfected by one method under this article and is later perfected by another method under this article, without an intermediate period when it was unperfected.

(d) [**Supporting obligation.**] Perfection of a security interest in collateral also perfects a security interest in a supporting obligation for the collateral.

(e) [**Lien securing right to payment.**] Perfection of a security interest in a right to payment or performance also perfects a security interest in a security interest, mortgage, or other lien on personal or real property securing the right.

(f) [**Security entitlement carried in securities account.**] Perfection of a security interest in a securities account also perfects a security interest in the security entitlements carried in the securities account.

(g) [**Commodity contract carried in commodity account.**] Perfection of a security interest in a commodity account also perfects a security interest in the commodity contracts carried in the commodity account.

§9-309. Security Interest Perfected Upon Attachment.

The following security interests are perfected when they attach:

(1) a purchase-money security interest in consumer goods, except as otherwise provided in Section 9-311(b) with respect to consumer goods that are subject to a statute or treaty described in Section 9-311(a);

(2) an assignment of accounts or payment intangibles which does not by itself or in conjunction with other assignments to the same assignee transfer a significant part of the assignor's outstanding accounts or payment intangibles;

(3) a sale of a payment intangible;

(4) a sale of a promissory note;

(5) a security interest created by the assignment of a health-care-insurance receivable to the provider of the health-care goods or services;

(6) a security interest arising under Section 2-401, 2-505, 2-711(3), or 2A-508(5), until the debtor obtains possession of the collateral;

(7) a security interest of a collecting bank arising under Section 4-210;

(8) a security interest of an issuer or nominated person arising under Section 5-118;

(9) a security interest arising in the delivery of a financial asset under Section 9-206(c);

(10) a security interest in investment property created by a broker or securities intermediary;

(11) a security interest in a commodity contract or a commodity account created by a commodity intermediary;

(12) an assignment for the benefit of all creditors of the transferor and subsequent transfers by the assignee thereunder; and

(13) a security interest created by an assignment of a beneficial interest in a decedent's estate.

§9-310. When Filing Required to Perfect Security Interest or Agricultural Lien; Security Interests and Agricultural Liens to Which Filing Provisions Do Not Apply.

(a) **[General rule: perfection by filing.]** Except as otherwise provided in subsection (b) and Section 9-312(b), a financing statement must be filed to perfect all security interests and agricultural liens.

(b) **[Exceptions: filing not necessary.]** The filing of a financing statement is not necessary to perfect a security interest:

(1) that is perfected under Section 9-308(d), (e), (f), or (g);

(2) that is perfected under Section 9-309 when it attaches;

(3) in property subject to a statute, regulation, or treaty described in Section 9-311(a);

(4) in goods in possession of a bailee which is perfected under Section 9-312(d)(1) or (2);

(5) in certificated securities, documents, goods, or instruments which is perfected without filing or possession under Section 9-312(e), (f), or (g);

(6) in collateral in the secured party's possession under Section 9-313;

(7) in a certificated security which is perfected by delivery of the security certificate to the secured party under Section 9-313;

(8) in deposit accounts, electronic chattel paper, investment property, or letter-of-credit rights which is perfected by control under Section 9-314;

(9) in proceeds which is perfected under Section 9-315; or

(10) that is perfected under Section 9-316.

(c) **[Assignment of perfected security interest.]** If a secured party assigns a perfected security interest or agricultural lien, a filing under this article is not required to continue the perfected status of the security interest against creditors of and transferees from the original debtor.

§9-311. Perfection of Security Interests in Property Subject to Certain Statutes, Regulations, and Treaties.

(a) **[Security interest subject to other law.]** Except as otherwise provided in subsection (d), the filing of a financing statement is not necessary or effective to perfect a security interest in property subject to:

(1) a statute, regulation, or treaty of the United States whose requirements for a security interest's obtaining priority over the rights of a lien creditor with respect to the property preempt Section 9-310(a);

(2) [list any certificate-of-title statute covering automobiles, trailers, mobile homes, boats, farm tractors, or the like, which provides for a security interest to be indicated on the certificate as a condition or result of perfection, and any non-Uniform Commercial Code central filing statute]; or

(3) a certificate-of-title statute of another jurisdiction which provides for a security interest to be indicated on the certificate as a condition or result of the security interest's obtaining priority over the rights of a lien creditor with respect to the property.

(b) **[Compliance with other law.]** Compliance with the requirements of a statute, regulation, or treaty described in subsection (a) for obtaining priority over the rights of a lien creditor is equivalent to the filing of a financing statement under this article. Except as otherwise provided in subsection

(d) and Sections 9-313 and 9-316(d) and (e) for goods covered by a certificate of title, a security interest in property subject to a statute, regulation, or treaty described in subsection (a) may be perfected only by compliance with those requirements, and a security interest so perfected remains perfected notwithstanding a change in the use or transfer of possession of the collateral.

(c) **[Duration and renewal of perfection.]** Except as otherwise provided in subsection (d) and Section 9-316(d) and (e), duration and renewal of perfection of a security interest perfected by compliance with the requirements prescribed by a statute, regulation, or treaty described in subsection (a) are governed by the statute, regulation, or treaty. In other respects, the security interest is subject to this article.

(d) **[Inapplicability to certain inventory.]** During any period in which collateral subject to a statute specified in subsection (a)(2) is inventory held for sale or lease by a person or leased by that person as lessor and that person is in the business of selling goods of that kind, this section does not apply to a security interest in that collateral created by that person.

§9-312. Perfection of Security Interests in Chattel Paper, Deposit Accounts, Documents, Goods Covered by Documents, Instruments, Investment Property, Letter-of-Credit Rights, and Money; Perfection by Permissive Filing; Temporary Perfection Without Filing or Transfer of Possession.

(a) **[Perfection by filing permitted.]** A security interest in chattel paper, negotiable documents, instruments, or investment property may be perfected by filing.

(b) **[Control or possession of certain collateral.]** Except as otherwise provided in Section 9-315(c) and (d) for proceeds:

(1) a security interest in a deposit account may be perfected only by control under Section 9-314;

(2) and except as otherwise provided in Section 9-308(d), a security interest in a letter-of-credit right may be perfected only by control under Section 9-314; and

(3) a security interest in money may be perfected only by the secured party's taking possession under Section 9-313.

(c) **[Goods covered by negotiable document.]** While goods are in the possession of a bailee that has issued a negotiable document covering the goods:

(1) a security interest in the goods may be perfected by perfecting a security interest in the document; and

(2) a security interest perfected in the document has priority over any security interest that becomes perfected in the goods by another method during that time.

(d) **[Goods covered by nonnegotiable document.]** While goods are in the possession of a bailee that has issued a nonnegotiable document covering the goods, a security interest in the goods may be perfected by:

(1) issuance of a document in the name of the secured party;

(2) the bailee's receipt of notification of the secured party's interest; or

(3) filing as to the goods.

(e) **[Temporary perfection: new value.]** A security interest in certificated securities, negotiable documents, or instruments is perfected without filing or the taking of possession for a period of 20 days from the time it attaches to the extent that it arises for new value given under an authenticated security agreement.

(f) **[Temporary perfection: goods or documents made available to debtor.]** A perfected security interest in a negotiable document or goods in possession of a bailee, other than one that has issued a negotiable document for the goods, remains perfected for 20 days without filing if the secured party makes available to the debtor the goods or documents representing the goods for the purpose of:

(1) ultimate sale or exchange; or

(2) loading, unloading, storing, shipping, transshipping, manufacturing, processing, or otherwise dealing with them in a manner preliminary to their sale or exchange.

(g) [**Temporary perfection: delivery of security certificate or instrument to debtor.**] A perfected security interest in a certificated security or instrument remains perfected for 20 days without filing if the secured party delivers the security certificate or instrument to the debtor for the purpose of:

(1) ultimate sale or exchange; or

(2) presentation, collection, enforcement, renewal, or registration of transfer.

(h) [**Expiration of temporary perfection.**] After the 20-day period specified in subsection (e), (f), or (g) expires, perfection depends upon compliance with this article.

§9-313. When Possession by or Delivery to Secured Party Perfects Security Interest Without Filing.

(a) [**Perfection by possession or delivery.**] Except as otherwise provided in subsection (b), a secured party may perfect a security interest in negotiable documents, goods, instruments, money, or tangible chattel paper by taking possession of the collateral. A secured party may perfect a security interest in certificated securities by taking delivery of the certificated securities under Section 8-301.

(b) [**Goods covered by certificate of title.**] With respect to goods covered by a certificate of title issued by this State, a secured party may perfect a security interest in the goods by taking possession of the goods only in the circumstances described in Section 9-316(d).

(c) [**Collateral in possession of person other than debtor.**] With respect to collateral other than certificated securities and goods covered by a document, a secured party takes possession of collateral in the possession of a person other than the debtor, the secured party, or a lessee of the collateral from the debtor in the ordinary course of the debtor's business, when:

(1) the person in possession authenticates a record acknowledging that it holds possession of the collateral for the secured party's benefit; or

(2) the person takes possession of the collateral after having authenticated a record acknowledging that it will hold possession of collateral for the secured party's benefit.

(d) [**Time of perfection by possession; continuation of perfection.**] If perfection of a security interest depends upon possession of the collateral by a secured party, perfection occurs no earlier than the time the secured party takes possession and continues only while the secured party retains possession.

(e) [**Time of perfection by delivery; continuation of perfection.**] A security interest in a certificated security in registered form is perfected by delivery when delivery of the certificated security occurs under Section 8-301 and remains perfected by delivery until the debtor obtains possession of the security certificate.

(f) [**Acknowledgment not required.**] A person in possession of collateral is not required to acknowledge that it holds possession for a secured party's benefit.

(g) [**Effectiveness of acknowledgment; no duties or confirmation.**] If a person acknowledges that it holds possession for the secured party's benefit:

(1) the acknowledgment is effective under subsection (c) or Section 8-301(a), even if the acknowledgment violates the rights of a debtor; and

(2) unless the person otherwise agrees or law other than this article otherwise provides, the person does not owe any duty to the secured party and is not required to confirm the acknowledgment to another person.

(h) [**Secured party's delivery to person other than debtor.**] A secured party having possession of collateral does not relinquish possession by delivering the collateral to a person other than the debtor or a lessee of the collateral from the debtor in the ordinary course of the debtor's business if the person was instructed before the delivery or is instructed contemporaneously with the delivery:

(1) to hold possession of the collateral for the secured party's benefit; or

(2) to redeliver the collateral to the secured party.

(i) [**Effect of delivery under subsection (h); no duties or confirmation.**] A secured party does not relinquish possession, even if a delivery under subsection (h) violates the rights of a debtor. A person to which collateral is delivered under subsection (h) does not owe any duty to the secured party and is not required to confirm the delivery to another person unless the person otherwise agrees or law other than this article otherwise provides.

§9-314. Perfection by Control.

(a) [**Perfection by control.**] A security interest in investment property, deposit accounts, letter-of-credit rights, or electronic chattel paper may be perfected by control of the collateral under Section 9-104, 9-105, 9-106, or 9-107.

(b) [**Specified collateral: time of perfection by control; continuation of perfection.**] A security interest in deposit accounts, electronic chattel paper, or letter-of-credit rights is perfected by control under Section 9-104, 9-105, or 9-107 when the secured party obtains control and remains perfected by control only while the secured party retains control.

(c) [**Investment property: time of perfection by control; continuation of perfection.**] A security interest in investment property is perfected by control under Section 9-106 from the time the secured party obtains control and remains perfected by control until:

(1) the secured party does not have control; and

(2) one of the following occurs:

(A) if the collateral is a certificated security, the debtor has or acquires possession of the security certificate;

(B) if the collateral is an uncertificated security, the issuer has registered or registers the debtor as the registered owner; or

(C) if the collateral is a security entitlement, the debtor is or becomes the entitlement holder.

§9-315. Secured Party's Rights on Disposition of Collateral and in Proceeds.

(a) [**Disposition of collateral: continuation of security interest or agricultural lien; proceeds.**] Except as otherwise provided in this article and in Section 2-403(2):

(1) a security interest or agricultural lien continues in collateral notwithstanding sale, lease, license, exchange, or other disposition thereof unless the secured party authorized the disposition free of the security interest or agricultural lien; and

(2) a security interest attaches to any identifiable proceeds of collateral.

(b) [**When commingled proceeds identifiable.**] Proceeds that are commingled with other property are identifiable proceeds:

(1) if the proceeds are goods, to the extent provided by Section 9-336; and

(2) if the proceeds are not goods, to the extent that the secured party identifies the proceeds by a method of tracing, including application of equitable principles, that is permitted under law other than this article with respect to commingled property of the type involved.

(c) [**Perfection of security interest in proceeds.**] A security interest in proceeds is a perfected security interest if the security interest in the original collateral was perfected.

(d) [**Continuation of perfection.**] A perfected security interest in proceeds becomes unperfected on the 21st day after the security interest attaches to the proceeds unless:

(1) the following conditions are satisfied:

(A) a filed financing statement covers the original collateral;

(B) the proceeds are collateral in which a security interest may be perfected by filing in the office in which the financing statement has been filed; and

(C) the proceeds are not acquired with cash proceeds;

(2) the proceeds are identifiable cash proceeds; or

(3) the security interest in the proceeds is perfected other than under subsection (c) when the security interest attaches to the proceeds or within 20 days thereafter.

(e) [**When perfected security interest in proceeds becomes unperfected.**] If a filed financing statement covers the original collateral, a security interest in proceeds which remains perfected under subsection (d)(1) becomes unperfected at the later of:

> (1) when the effectiveness of the filed financing statement lapses under Section 9-515 or is terminated under Section 9-513; or
>
> (2) the 21st day after the security interest attaches to the proceeds.

§9-316. Continued Perfection of Security Interest Following Change in Governing Law.

(a) [**General rule: effect on perfection of change in governing law.**] A security interest perfected pursuant to the law of the jurisdiction designated in Section 9-301(1) or 9-305(c) remains perfected until the earliest of:

> (1) the time perfection would have ceased under the law of that jurisdiction;
>
> (2) the expiration of four months after a change of the debtor's location to another jurisdiction; or
>
> (3) the expiration of one year after a transfer of collateral to a person that thereby becomes a debtor and is located in another jurisdiction.

(b) [**Security interest perfected or unperfected under law of new jurisdiction.**] If a security interest described in subsection (a) becomes perfected under the law of the other jurisdiction before the earliest time or event described in that subsection, it remains perfected thereafter. If the security interest does not become perfected under the law of the other jurisdiction before the earliest time or event, it becomes unperfected and is deemed never to have been perfected as against a purchaser of the collateral for value.

(c) [**Possessory security interest in collateral moved to new jurisdiction.**] A possessory security interest in collateral, other than goods covered by a certificate of title and as-extracted collateral consisting of goods, remains continuously perfected if:

> (1) the collateral is located in one jurisdiction and subject to a security interest perfected under the law of that jurisdiction;
>
> (2) thereafter the collateral is brought into another jurisdiction; and
>
> (3) upon entry into the other jurisdiction, the security interest is perfected under the law of the other jurisdiction.

(d) [**Goods covered by certificate of title from this state.**] Except as otherwise provided in subsection (e), a security interest in goods covered by a certificate of title which is perfected by any method under the law of another jurisdiction when the goods become covered by a certificate of title from this State remains perfected until the security interest would have become unperfected under the law of the other jurisdiction had the goods not become so covered.

(e) [**When subsection (d) security interest becomes unperfected against purchasers.**] A security interest described in subsection (d) becomes unperfected as against a purchaser of the goods for value and is deemed never to have been perfected as against a purchaser of the goods for value if the applicable requirements for perfection under Section 9-311(b) or 9-313 are not satisfied before the earlier of:

> (1) the time the security interest would have become unperfected under the law of the other jurisdiction had the goods not become covered by a certificate of title from this State; or
>
> (2) the expiration of four months after the goods had become so covered.

(f) [**Change in jurisdiction of bank, issuer, nominated person, securities intermediary, or commodity intermediary.**] A security interest in deposit accounts, letter-of-credit rights, or investment property which is perfected under the law of the bank's jurisdiction, the issuer's jurisdiction, a nominated person's jurisdiction, the securities intermediary's jurisdiction, or the commodity intermediary's jurisdiction, as applicable, remains perfected until the earlier of:

> (1) the time the security interest would have become unperfected under the law of that jurisdiction; or
>
> (2) the expiration of four months after a change of the applicable jurisdiction to another jurisdiction.

(g) [**Subsection (f) security interest perfected or unperfected under law of new jurisdiction.**] If a security interest described in subsection (f) becomes perfected under the law of the other jurisdiction before the earlier

of the time or the end of the period described in that subsection, it remains perfected thereafter. If the security interest does not become perfected under the law of the other jurisdiction before the earlier of that time or the end of that period, it becomes unperfected and is deemed never to have been perfected as against a purchaser of the collateral for value.

§9-317. Interests That Take Priority over or Take Free of Security Interest or Agricultural Lien.

(a) [**Conflicting security interests and rights of lien creditors.**] A security interest or agricultural lien is subordinate to the rights of:

> (1) a person entitled to priority under Section 9-322; and
>
> (2) except as otherwise provided in subsection (e), a person that becomes a lien creditor before the earlier of the time:
>
> > (A) the security interest or agricultural lien is perfected; or
> >
> > (B) one of the conditions specified in Section 9-203(b)(3) is met and a financing statement covering the collateral is filed.

(b) [**Buyers that receive delivery.**] Except as otherwise provided in subsection (e), a buyer, other than a secured party, of tangible chattel paper, documents, goods, instruments, or a security certificate takes free of a security interest or agricultural lien if the buyer gives value and receives delivery of the collateral without knowledge of the security interest or agricultural lien and before it is perfected.

(c) [**Lessees that receive delivery.**] Except as otherwise provided in subsection (e), a lessee of goods takes free of a security interest or agricultural lien if the lessee gives value and receives delivery of the collateral without knowledge of the security interest or agricultural lien and before it is perfected.

(d) [**Licensees and buyers of certain collateral.**] A licensee of a general intangible or a buyer, other than a secured party, of accounts, electronic chattel paper, general intangibles, or investment property other than a certificated security takes free of a security interest if the licensee or buyer gives value without knowledge of the security interest and before it is perfected.

(e) [**Purchase-money security interest.**] Except as otherwise provided in Sections 9-320 and 9-321, if a person files a financing statement with respect to a purchase-money security interest before or within 20 days after the debtor receives delivery of the collateral, the security interest takes priority over the rights of a buyer, lessee, or lien creditor which arise between the time the security interest attaches and the time of filing.

§9-318. No Interest Retained in Right to Payment That Is Sold; Rights and Title of Seller of Account or Chattel Paper with Respect to Creditors and Purchasers.

(a) [**Seller retains no interest.**] A debtor that has sold an account, chattel paper, payment intangible, or promissory note does not retain a legal or equitable interest in the collateral sold.

(b) [**Deemed rights of debtor if buyer's security interest unperfected.**] For purposes of determining the rights of creditors of, and purchasers for value of an account or chattel paper from, a debtor that has sold an account or chattel paper, while the buyer's security interest is unperfected, the debtor is deemed to have rights and title to the account or chattel paper identical to those the debtor sold.

§9-319. Rights and Title of Consignee with Respect to Creditors and Purchasers.

(a) [**Consignee has consignor's rights.**] Except as otherwise provided in subsection (b), for purposes of determining the rights of creditors of, and purchasers for value of goods from, a consignee, while the goods are in the possession of the consignee, the consignee is deemed to have rights and title to the goods identical to those the consignor had or had power to transfer.

(b) [**Applicability of other law.**] For purposes of determining the rights of a creditor of a consignee, law other than this article determines the rights and title of a consignee while goods are in the consignee's possession if, under this part, a perfected security interest held by the consignor would have priority over the rights of the creditor.

§9-320. Buyer of Goods.

(a) **[Buyer in ordinary course of business.]** Except as otherwise provided in subsection (e), a buyer in ordinary course of business, other than a person buying farm products from a person engaged in farming operations, takes free of a security interest created by the buyer's seller, even if the security interest is perfected and the buyer knows of its existence.

(b) **[Buyer of consumer goods.]** Except as otherwise provided in subsection (e), a buyer of goods from a person who used or bought the goods for use primarily for personal, family, or household purposes takes free of a security interest, even if perfected, if the buyer buys:

(1) without knowledge of the security interest;

(2) for value;

(3) primarily for the buyer's personal, family, or household purposes; and

(4) before the filing of a financing statement covering the goods.

(c) **[Effectiveness of filing for subsection (b).]** To the extent that it affects the priority of a security interest over a buyer of goods under subsection (b), the period of effectiveness of a filing made in the jurisdiction in which the seller is located is governed by Section 9-316(a) and (b).

(d) **[Buyer in ordinary course of business at wellhead or minehead.]** A buyer in ordinary course of business buying oil, gas, or other minerals at the wellhead or minehead or after extraction takes free of an interest arising out of an encumbrance.

(e) **[Possessory security interest not affected.]** Subsections (a) and (b) do not affect a security interest in goods in the possession of the secured party under Section 9-313.

§9-321. Licensee of General Intangible and Lessee of Goods in Ordinary Course of Business.

(a) **["Licensee in ordinary course of business."]** In this section, "licensee in ordinary course of business" means a person that becomes a licensee of a general intangible in good faith, without knowledge that the license violates the rights of another person in the general intangible, and in the ordinary course from a person in the business of licensing general intangibles of that kind. A person becomes a licensee in the ordinary course if the license to the person comports with the usual or customary practices in the kind of business in which the licensor is engaged or with the licensor's own usual or customary practices.

(b) **[Rights of licensee in ordinary course of business.]** A licensee in ordinary course of business takes its rights under a nonexclusive license free of a security interest in the general intangible created by the licensor, even if the security interest is perfected and the licensee knows of its existence.

(c) **[Rights of lessee in ordinary course of business.]** A lessee in ordinary course of business takes its leasehold interest free of a security interest in the goods created by the lessor, even if the security interest is perfected and the lessee knows of its existence.

§9-322. Priorities among Conflicting Security Interests in and Agricultural Liens on Same Collateral.

(a) **[General priority rules.]** Except as otherwise provided in this section, priority among conflicting security interests and agricultural liens in the same collateral is determined according to the following rules:

(1) Conflicting perfected security interests and agricultural liens rank according to priority in time of filing or perfection. Priority dates from the earlier of the time a filing covering the collateral is first made or the security interest or agricultural lien is first perfected, if there is no period thereafter when there is neither filing nor perfection.

(2) A perfected security interest or agricultural lien has priority over a conflicting unperfected security interest or agricultural lien.

(3) The first security interest or agricultural lien to attach or become effective has priority if conflicting security interests and agricultural liens are unperfected.

(b) **[Time of perfection: proceeds and supporting obligations.]** For the purposes of subsection (a)(1):

(1) the time of filing or perfection as to a security interest in collateral is also the time of filing or perfection as to a security interest in proceeds; and

(2) the time of filing or perfection as to a security interest in collateral supported by a supporting obligation is also the time of filing or perfection as to a security interest in the supporting obligation.

(c) **[Special priority rules: proceeds and supporting obligations.]** Except as otherwise provided in subsection (f), a security interest in collateral which qualifies for priority over a conflicting security interest under Section 9-327, 9-328, 9-329, 9-330, or 9-331 also has priority over a conflicting security interest in:

(1) any supporting obligation for the collateral; and

(2) proceeds of the collateral if:

(A) the security interest in proceeds is perfected;

(B) the proceeds are cash proceeds or of the same type as the collateral; and

(C) in the case of proceeds that are proceeds of proceeds, all intervening proceeds are cash proceeds, proceeds of the same type as the collateral, or an account relating to the collateral.

(d) **[First-to-file priority rule for certain collateral.]** Subject to subsection (e) and except as otherwise provided in subsection (f), if a security interest in chattel paper, deposit accounts, negotiable documents, instruments, investment property, or letter-of-credit rights is perfected by a method other than filing, conflicting perfected security interests in proceeds of the collateral rank according to priority in time of filing.

(e) **[Applicability of subsection (d).]** Subsection (d) applies only if the proceeds of the collateral are not cash proceeds, chattel paper, negotiable documents, instruments, investment property, or letter-of-credit rights.

(f) **[Limitations on subsections (a) through (e).]** Subsections (a) through (e) are subject to:

(1) subsection (g) and the other provisions of this part;

(2) Section 4-210 with respect to a security interest of a collecting bank;

(3) Section 5-118 with respect to a security interest of an issuer or nominated person; and

(4) Section 9-110 with respect to a security interest arising under Article 2 or 2A.

(g) **[Priority under agricultural lien statute.]** A perfected agricultural lien on collateral has priority over a conflicting security interest in or agricultural lien on the same collateral if the statute creating the agricultural lien so provides.

§9-323. Future Advances.

(a) **[When priority based on time of advance.]** Except as otherwise provided in subsection (c), for purposes of determining the priority of a perfected security interest under Section 9-322(a)(1), perfection of the security interest dates from the time an advance is made to the extent that the security interest secures an advance that:

(1) is made while the security interest is perfected only:

(A) under Section 9-309 when it attaches; or

(B) temporarily under Section 9-312(e), (f), or (g); and

(2) is not made pursuant to a commitment entered into before or while the security interest is perfected by a method other than under Section 9-309 or 9-312(e), (f), or (g).

(b) **[Lien creditor.]** Except as otherwise provided in subsection (c), a security interest is subordinate to the rights of a person that becomes a lien creditor to the extent that the security interest secures an advance made more than 45 days after the person becomes a lien creditor unless the advance is made:

(1) without knowledge of the lien; or

(2) pursuant to a commitment entered into without knowledge of the lien.

(c) **[Buyer of receivables.]** Subsections (a) and (b) do not apply to a security interest held by a secured party that is a buyer of accounts, chattel paper, payment intangibles, or promissory notes or a consignor.

(d) **[Buyer of goods.]** Except as otherwise provided in subsection (e), a buyer of goods other than a buyer in ordinary course of business takes free of a security interest to the extent that it secures advances made after the earlier of:

(1) the time the secured party acquires knowledge of the buyer's purchase; or

(2) 45 days after the purchase.

(e) **[Advances made pursuant to commitment: priority of buyer of goods.]** Subsection (d) does not apply if the advance is made pursuant to a commitment entered into without knowledge of the buyer's purchase and before the expiration of the 45-day period.

(f) **[Lessee of goods.]** Except as otherwise provided in subsection (g), a lessee of goods, other than a lessee in ordinary course of business, takes the leasehold interest free of a security interest to the extent that it secures advances made after the earlier of:

(1) the time the secured party acquires knowledge of the lease; or

(2) 45 days after the lease contract becomes enforceable.

(g) **[Advances made pursuant to commitment: priority of lessee of goods.]** Subsection (f) does not apply if the advance is made pursuant to a commitment entered into without knowledge of the lease and before the expiration of the 45-day period.

§9-324. Priority of Purchase-Money Security Interests.

(a) **[General rule: purchase-money priority.]** Except as otherwise provided in subsection (g), a perfected purchase-money security interest in goods other than inventory or livestock has priority over a conflicting security interest in the same goods, and, except as otherwise provided in Section 9-327, a perfected security interest in its identifiable proceeds also has priority, if the purchase-money security interest is perfected when the debtor receives possession of the collateral or within 20 days thereafter.

(b) **[Inventory purchase-money priority.]** Subject to subsection (c) and except as otherwise provided in subsection (g), a perfected purchase-money security interest in inventory has priority over a conflicting security interest in the same inventory, has priority over a conflicting security interest in chattel paper or an instrument constituting proceeds of the inventory and in proceeds of the chattel paper, if so provided in Section 9-330, and, except as otherwise provided in Section 9-327, also has priority in identifiable cash proceeds of the inventory to the extent the identifiable cash proceeds are received on or before the delivery of the inventory to a buyer, if:

(1) the purchase-money security interest is perfected when the debtor receives possession of the inventory;

(2) the purchase-money secured party sends an authenticated notification to the holder of the conflicting security interest;

(3) the holder of the conflicting security interest receives the notification within five years before the debtor receives possession of the inventory; and

(4) the notification states that the person sending the notification has or expects to acquire a purchase-money security interest in inventory of the debtor and describes the inventory.

(c) **[Holders of conflicting inventory security interests to be notified.]** Subsections (b)(2) through (4) apply only if the holder of the conflicting security interest had filed a financing statement covering the same types of inventory:

(1) if the purchase-money security interest is perfected by filing, before the date of the filing; or

(2) if the purchase-money security interest is temporarily perfected without filing or possession under Section 9-312(f), before the beginning of the 20-day period thereunder.

(d) **[Livestock purchase-money priority.]** Subject to subsection (e) and except as otherwise provided in subsection (g), a perfected purchase-money security interest in livestock that are farm products has priority over a conflicting security interest in the same livestock, and, except as otherwise provided in Section 9-327, a perfected security interest in their identifiable proceeds and identifiable products in their unmanufactured states also has priority, if:

(1) the purchase-money security interest is perfected when the debtor receives possession of the livestock;

(2) the purchase-money secured party sends an authenticated notification to the holder of the conflicting security interest;

(3) the holder of the conflicting security interest receives the notification within six months before the debtor receives possession of the livestock; and

(4) the notification states that the person sending the notification has or expects to acquire a purchase-money security interest in livestock of the debtor and describes the livestock.

(e) **[Holders of conflicting livestock security interests to be notified.]** Subsections (d)(2) through (4) apply only if the holder of the conflicting security interest had filed a financing statement covering the same types of livestock:

(1) if the purchase-money security interest is perfected by filing, before the date of the filing; or

(2) if the purchase-money security interest is temporarily perfected without filing or possession under Section 9-312(f), before the beginning of the 20-day period thereunder.

(f) **[Software purchase-money priority.]** Except as otherwise provided in subsection (g), a perfected purchase-money security interest in software has priority over a conflicting security interest in the same collateral, and, except as otherwise provided in Section 9-327, a perfected security interest in its identifiable proceeds also has priority, to the extent that the purchase-money security interest in the goods in which the software was acquired for use has priority in the goods and proceeds of the goods under this section.

(g) **[Conflicting purchase-money security interests.]** If more than one security interest qualifies for priority in the same collateral under subsection (a), (b), (d), or (f):

(1) a security interest securing an obligation incurred as all or part of the price of the collateral has priority over a security interest securing an obligation incurred for value given to enable the debtor to acquire rights in or the use of collateral; and

(2) in all other cases, Section 9-322(a) applies to the qualifying security interests.

§9-325. Priority of Security Interests in Transferred Collateral.

(a) **[Subordination of security interest in transferred collateral.]** Except as otherwise provided in subsection (b), a security interest created by a debtor is subordinate to a security interest in the same collateral created by another person if:

(1) the debtor acquired the collateral subject to the security interest created by the other person;

(2) the security interest created by the other person was perfected when the debtor acquired the collateral; and

(3) there is no period thereafter when the security interest is unperfected.

(b) **[Limitation of subsection (a) subordination.]** Subsection (a) subordinates a security interest only if the security interest:

(1) otherwise would have priority solely under Section 9-322(a) or 9-324; or

(2) arose solely under Section 2-711(3) or 2A-508(5).

§9-326. Priority of Security Interests Created by New Debtor.

(a) **[Subordination of security interest created by new debtor.]** Subject to subsection (b), a security interest created by a new debtor which is perfected by a filed financing statement that is effective solely under Section 9-508 in collateral in which a new debtor has or acquires rights is subordinate to a security interest in the same collateral which is perfected other than by a filed financing statement that is effective solely under Section 9-508.

(b) **[Priority under other provisions; multiple original debtors.]** The other provisions of this part determine the priority among conflicting security interests in the same collateral perfected by filed financing statements that are effective solely under Section 9-508. However, if the security agreements to which a new debtor became bound as debtor were not entered into by the same original debtor, the conflicting security interests rank according to priority in time of the new debtor's having become bound.

§9-327. Priority of Security Interests in Deposit Account.

The following rules govern priority among conflicting security interests in the same deposit account:

(1) A security interest held by a secured party having control of the deposit account under Section 9-104 has priority over a conflicting security interest held by a secured party that does not have control.

(2) Except as otherwise provided in paragraphs (3) and (4), security interests perfected by control under Section 9-314 rank according to priority in time of obtaining control.

(3) Except as otherwise provided in paragraph (4), a security interest held by the bank with which the deposit account is maintained has priority over a conflicting security interest held by another secured party.

(4) A security interest perfected by control under Section 9-104(a)(3) has priority over a security interest held by the bank with which the deposit account is maintained.

§9-328. Priority of Security Interests in Investment Property.

The following rules govern priority among conflicting security interests in the same investment property:

(1) A security interest held by a secured party having control of investment property under Section 9-106 has priority over a security interest held by a secured party that does not have control of the investment property.

(2) Except as otherwise provided in paragraphs (3) and (4), conflicting security interests held by secured parties each of which has control under Section 9-106 rank according to priority in time of:

(A) if the collateral is a security, obtaining control;

(B) if the collateral is a security entitlement carried in a securities account and:

(i) if the secured party obtained control under Section 8-106(d)(1), the secured party's becoming the person for which the securities account is maintained;

(ii) if the secured party obtained control under Section 8-106(d)(2), the securities intermediary's agreement to comply with the secured party's entitlement orders with respect to security entitlements carried or to be carried in the securities account; or

(iii) if the secured party obtained control through another person under Section 8-106(d)(3), the time on which priority would be based under this paragraph if the other person were the secured party; or

(C) if the collateral is a commodity contract carried with a commodity intermediary, the satisfaction of the requirement for control specified in Section 9-106(b)(2) with respect to commodity contracts carried or to be carried with the commodity intermediary.

(3) A security interest held by a securities intermediary in a security entitlement or a securities account maintained with the securities intermediary has priority over a conflicting security interest held by another secured party.

(4) A security interest held by a commodity intermediary in a commodity contract or a commodity account maintained with the commodity intermediary has priority over a conflicting security interest held by another secured party.

(5) A security interest in a certificated security in registered form which is perfected by taking delivery under Section 9-313(a) and not by control under Section 9-314 has priority over a conflicting security interest perfected by a method other than control.

(6) Conflicting security interests created by a broker, securities intermediary, or commodity intermediary which are perfected without control under Section 9-106 rank equally.

(7) In all other cases, priority among conflicting security interests in investment property is governed by Sections 9-322 and 9-323.

§9-329. Priority of Security Interests in Letter-of-Credit Right.

The following rules govern priority among conflicting security interests in the same letter-of-credit right:

(1) A security interest held by a secured party having control of the letter-of-credit right under Section 9-107 has priority to the extent of its control over a conflicting security interest held by a secured party that does not have control.

(2) Security interests perfected by control under Section 9-314 rank according to priority in time of obtaining control.

§9-330. Priority of Purchaser of Chattel Paper or Instrument.

(a) **[Purchaser's priority: security interest claimed merely as proceeds.]** A purchaser of chattel paper has priority over a security interest in the chattel paper which is claimed merely as proceeds of inventory subject to a security interest if:

(1) in good faith and in the ordinary course of the purchaser's business, the purchaser gives new value and takes possession of the chattel paper or obtains control of the chattel paper under Section 9-105; and

(2) the chattel paper does not indicate that it has been assigned to an identified assignee other than the purchaser.

(b) **[Purchaser's priority: other security interests.]** A purchaser of chattel paper has priority over a security interest in the chattel paper which is claimed other than merely as proceeds of inventory subject to a security interest if the purchaser gives new value and takes possession of the chattel paper or obtains control of the chattel paper under Section 9-105 in good faith, in the ordinary course of the purchaser's business, and without knowledge that the purchase violates the rights of the secured party.

(c) **[Chattel paper purchaser's priority in proceeds.]** Except as otherwise provided in Section 9-327, a purchaser having priority in chattel paper under subsection (a) or (b) also has priority in proceeds of the chattel paper to the extent that:

(1) Section 9-322 provides for priority in the proceeds; or

(2) the proceeds consist of the specific goods covered by the chattel paper or cash proceeds of the specific goods, even if the purchaser's security interest in the proceeds is unperfected.

(d) **[Instrument purchaser's priority.]** Except as otherwise provided in Section 9-331(a), a purchaser of an instrument has priority over a security interest in the instrument perfected by a method other than possession if the purchaser gives value and takes possession of the instrument in good faith and without knowledge that the purchase violates the rights of the secured party.

(e) **[Holder of purchase-money security interest gives new value.]** For purposes of subsections (a) and (b), the holder of a purchase-money security interest in inventory gives new value for chattel paper constituting proceeds of the inventory.

(f) **[Indication of assignment gives knowledge.]** For purposes of subsections (b) and (d), if chattel paper or an instrument indicates that it has been assigned to an identified secured party other than the purchaser, a purchaser of the chattel paper or instrument has knowledge that the purchase violates the rights of the secured party.

§9-331. Priority of Rights of Purchasers of Instruments, Documents, and Securities under Other Articles; Priority of Interests in Financial Assets and Security Entitlements under Article 8.

(a) **[Rights under Articles 3, 7, and 8 not limited.]** This article does not limit the rights of a holder in due course of a negotiable instrument, a holder to which a negotiable document of title has been duly negotiated, or a protected purchaser of a security. These holders or purchasers take priority over an earlier security interest, even if perfected, to the extent provided in Articles 3, 7, and 8.

(b) **[Protection under Article 8.]** This article does not limit the rights of or impose liability on a person to the extent that the person is protected against the assertion of a claim under Article 8.

(c) **[Filing not notice.]** Filing under this article does not constitute notice of a claim or defense to the holders, or purchasers, or persons described in subsections (a) and (b).

§9-332. Transfer of Money; Transfer of Funds from Deposit Account.

(a) **[Transferee of money.]** A transferee of money takes the money free of a security interest unless the transferee acts in collusion with the debtor in violating the rights of the secured party.

(b) **[Transferee of funds from deposit account.]** A transferee of funds from a deposit account takes the funds free of a security interest in the deposit account unless the transferee acts in collusion with the debtor in violating the rights of the secured party.

§9-333. Priority of Certain Liens Arising by Operation of Law.

(a) **["Possessory lien."]** In this section, "possessory lien" means an interest, other than a security interest or an agricultural lien:

(1) which secures payment or performance of an obligation for services or materials furnished with respect to goods by a person in the ordinary course of the person's business;

(2) which is created by statute or rule of law in favor of the person; and

(3) whose effectiveness depends on the person's possession of the goods.

(b) **[Priority of possessory lien.]** A possessory lien on goods has priority over a security interest in the goods unless the lien is created by a statute that expressly provides otherwise.

§9-334. Priority of Security Interests in Fixtures and Crops.

(a) **[Security interest in fixtures under this article.]** A security interest under this article may be created in goods that are fixtures or may continue in goods that become fixtures. A security interest does not exist under this article in ordinary building materials incorporated into an improvement on land.

(b) **[Security interest in fixtures under real-property law.]** This article does not prevent creation of an encumbrance upon fixtures under real property law.

(c) **[General rule: subordination of security interest in fixtures.]** In cases not governed by subsections (d) through (h), a security interest in fixtures is subordinate to a conflicting interest of an encumbrancer or owner of the related real property other than the debtor.

(d) **[Fixtures purchase-money priority.]** Except as otherwise provided in subsection (h), a perfected security interest in fixtures has priority over a conflicting interest of an encumbrancer or owner of the real property if the debtor has an interest of record in or is in possession of the real property and:

(1) the security interest is a purchase-money security interest;

(2) the interest of the encumbrancer or owner arises before the goods become fixtures; and

(3) the security interest is perfected by a fixture filing before the goods become fixtures or within 20 days thereafter.

(e) **[Priority of security interest in fixtures over interests in real property.]** A perfected security interest in fixtures has priority over a conflicting interest of an encumbrancer or owner of the real property if:

(1) the debtor has an interest of record in the real property or is in possession of the real property and the security interest:

(A) is perfected by a fixture filing before the interest of the encumbrancer or owner is of record; and

(B) has priority over any conflicting interest of a predecessor in title of the encumbrancer or owner;

(2) before the goods become fixtures, the security interest is perfected by any method permitted by this article and the fixtures are readily removable:

(A) factory or office machines;

(B) equipment that is not primarily used or leased for use in the operation of the real property; or

(C) replacements of domestic appliances that are consumer goods;

(3) the conflicting interest is a lien on the real property obtained by legal or equitable proceedings after the security interest was perfected by any method permitted by this article; or

(4) the security interest is:

(A) created in a manufactured home in a manufactured-home transaction; and

(B) perfected pursuant to a statute described in Section 9-311(a)(2).

(f) **[Priority based on consent, disclaimer, or right to remove.]** A security interest in fixtures, whether or not perfected, has priority over a conflicting interest of an encumbrancer or owner of the real property if:

(1) the encumbrancer or owner has, in an authenticated record, consented to the security interest or disclaimed an interest in the goods as fixtures; or

(2) the debtor has a right to remove the goods as against the encumbrancer or owner.

(g) **[Continuation of paragraph (f)(2) priority.]** The priority of the security interest under paragraph (f)(2) continues for a reasonable time if the debtor's right to remove the goods as against the encumbrancer or owner terminates.

(h) **[Priority of construction mortgage.]** A mortgage is a construction mortgage to the extent that it secures an obligation incurred for the construction of an improvement on land, including the acquisition cost of the land, if a recorded record of the mortgage so indicates. Except as otherwise provided in subsections (e) and (f), a security interest in fixtures is subordinate to a construction mortgage if a record of the mortgage is recorded before the goods become fixtures and the goods become fixtures before the completion of the construction. A mortgage has this priority to the same extent as a construction mortgage to the extent that it is given to refinance a construction mortgage.

(i) **[Priority of security interest in crops.]** A perfected security interest in crops growing on real property has priority over a conflicting interest of an encumbrancer or owner of the real property if the debtor has an interest of record in or is in possession of the real property.

(j) **[Subsection (i) prevails.]** Subsection (i) prevails over any inconsistent provisions of the following statutes:

§9-335. Accessions.

(a) **[Creation of security interest in accession.]** A security interest may be created in an accession and continues in collateral that becomes an accession.

(b) **[Perfection of security interest.]** If a security interest is perfected when the collateral becomes an accession, the security interest remains perfected in the collateral.

(c) **[Priority of security interest.]** Except as otherwise provided in subsection (d), the other provisions of this part determine the priority of a security interest in an accession.

(d) **[Compliance with certificate-of-title statute.]** A security interest in an accession is subordinate to a security interest in the whole which is perfected by compliance with the requirements of a certificate-of-title statute under Section 9-311(b).

(e) **[Removal of accession after default.]** After default, subject to Part 6, a secured party may remove an accession from other goods if the security interest in the accession has priority over the claims of every person having an interest in the whole.

(f) **[Reimbursement following removal.]** A secured party that removes an accession from other goods under subsection (e) shall promptly reimburse any holder of a security interest or other lien on, or owner of, the whole or of the other goods, other than the debtor, for the cost of repair of any physical injury to the whole or the other goods. The secured party need not reimburse the holder or owner for any diminution in value of the whole or the other goods caused by the absence of the accession removed or by any necessity for replacing it. A person entitled to reimbursement may refuse permission to remove until the secured party gives adequate assurance for the performance of the obligation to reimburse.

§9-336. Commingled Goods.

(a) [**"Commingled goods."**] In this section, "commingled goods" means goods that are physically united with other goods in such a manner that their identity is lost in a product or mass.

(b) [**No security interest in commingled goods as such.**] A security interest does not exist in commingled goods as such. However, a security interest may attach to a product or mass that results when goods become commingled goods.

(c) [**Attachment of security interest to product or mass.**] If collateral becomes commingled goods, a security interest attaches to the product or mass.

(d) [**Perfection of security interest.**] If a security interest in collateral is perfected before the collateral becomes commingled goods, the security interest that attaches to the product or mass under subsection (c) is perfected.

(e) [**Priority of security interest.**] Except as otherwise provided in subsection (f), the other provisions of this part determine the priority of a security interest that attaches to the product or mass under subsection (c).

(f) [**Conflicting security interests in product or mass**] If more than one security interest attaches to the product or mass under subsection (c), the following rules determine priority:

(1) A security interest that is perfected under subsection (d) has priority over a security interest that is unperfected at the time the collateral becomes commingled goods.

(2) If more than one security interest is perfected under subsection (d), the security interests rank equally in proportion to the value of the collateral at the time it became commingled goods.

§9-337. Priority of Security Interests in Goods Covered by Certificate of Title.

If, while a security interest in goods is perfected by any method under the law of another jurisdiction, this State issues a certificate of title that does not show that the goods are subject to the security interest or contain a statement that they may be subject to security interests not shown on the certificate:

(1) a buyer of the goods, other than a person in the business of selling goods of that kind, takes free of the security interest if the buyer gives value and receives delivery of the goods after issuance of the certificate and without knowledge of the security interest; and

(2) the security interest is subordinate to a conflicting security interest in the goods that attaches, and is perfected under Section 9-311(b), after issuance of the certificate and without the conflicting secured party's knowledge of the security interest.

§9-338. Priority of Security Interest or Agricultural Lien Perfected by Filed Financing Statement Providing Certain Incorrect Information.

If a security interest or agricultural lien is perfected by a filed financing statement providing information described in Section 9-516(b)(5) which is incorrect at the time the financing statement is filed:

(1) the security interest or agricultural lien is subordinate to a conflicting perfected security interest in the collateral to the extent that the holder of the conflicting security interest gives value in reasonable reliance upon the incorrect information; and

(2) a purchaser, other than a secured party, of the collateral takes free of the security interest or agricultural lien to the extent that, in reasonable reliance upon the incorrect information, the purchaser gives value

and, in the case of chattel paper, documents, goods, instruments, or a security certificate, receives delivery of the collateral.

§9-339. Priority Subject to Subordination.

This article does not preclude subordination by agreement by a person entitled to priority.

§9-340. Effectiveness of Right of Recoupment or Set-Off Against Deposit Account.

(a) [**Exercise of recoupment or set-off.**] Except as otherwise provided in subsection (c), a bank with which a deposit account is maintained may exercise any right of recoupment or set-off against a secured party that holds a security interest in the deposit account.

(b) [**Recoupment or set-off not affected by security interest.**] Except as otherwise provided in subsection (c), the application of this article to a security interest in a deposit account does not affect a right of recoupment or set-off of the secured party as to a deposit account maintained with the secured party.

(c) [**When set-off ineffective.**] The exercise by a bank of a set-off against a deposit account is ineffective against a secured party that holds a security interest in the deposit account which is perfected by control under Section 9-104(a)(3), if the set-off is based on a claim against the debtor.

§9-341. Bank's Rights and Duties with Respect to Deposit Account.

Except as otherwise provided in Section 9-340(c), and unless the bank otherwise agrees in an authenticated record, a bank's rights and duties with respect to a deposit account maintained with the bank are not terminated, suspended, or modified by:

(1) the creation, attachment, or perfection of a security interest in the deposit account;

(2) the bank's knowledge of the security interest; or

(3) the bank's receipt of instructions from the secured party.

§9-342. Bank's Right to Refuse to Enter into or Disclose Existence of Control Agreement.

This article does not require a bank to enter into an agreement of the kind described in Section 9-104(a)(2), even if its customer so requests or directs. A bank that has entered into such an agreement is not required to confirm the existence of the agreement to another person unless requested to do so by its customer.

Part 4—Rights of Third Parties

§9-401. Alienability of Debtor's Rights.

(a) [**Other law governs alienability; exceptions.**] Except as otherwise provided in subsection (b) and Sections 9-406, 9-407, 9-408, and 9-409, whether a debtor's rights in collateral may be voluntarily or involuntarily transferred is governed by law other than this article.

(b) [**Agreement does not prevent transfer.**] An agreement between the debtor and secured party which prohibits a transfer of the debtor's rights in collateral or makes the transfer a default does not prevent the transfer from taking effect.

§9-402. Secured Party Not Obligated on Contract of Debtor or in Tort.

The existence of a security interest, agricultural lien, or authority given to a debtor to dispose of or use collateral, without more, does not subject a secured party to liability in contract or tort for the debtor's acts or omissions.

§9-403. Agreement Not to Assert Defenses Against Assignee.

(a) [**"Value."**] In this section, "value" has the meaning provided in Section 3-303(a).

(b) [**Agreement not to assert claim or defense.**] Except as otherwise provided in this section, an agreement between an account debtor and an assignor not to assert against an assignee any claim or defense that the account debtor may have against the assignor is enforceable by an assignee that takes an assignment:

(1) for value;

(2) in good faith;

(3) without notice of a claim of a property or possessory right to the property assigned; and

(4) without notice of a defense or claim in recoupment of the type that may be asserted against a person entitled to enforce a negotiable instrument under Section 3-305(a).

(c) **[When subsection (b) not applicable.]** Subsection (b) does not apply to defenses of a type that may be asserted against a holder in due course of a negotiable instrument under Section 3-305(b).

(d) **[Omission of required statement in consumer transaction.]** In a consumer transaction, if a record evidences the account debtor's obligation, law other than this article requires that the record include a statement to the effect that the rights of an assignee are subject to claims or defenses that the account debtor could assert against the original obligee, and the record does not include such a statement:

(1) the record has the same effect as if the record included such a statement; and

(2) the account debtor may assert against an assignee those claims and defenses that would have been available if the record included such a statement.

(e) **[Rule for individual under other law.]** This section is subject to law other than this article which establishes a different rule for an account debtor who is an individual and who incurred the obligation primarily for personal, family, or household purposes.

(f) **[Other law not displaced.]** Except as otherwise provided in subsection (d), this section does not displace law other than this article which gives effect to an agreement by an account debtor not to assert a claim or defense against an assignee.

§9-404. Rights Acquired by Assignee; Claims and Defenses Against Assignee.

(a) **[Assignee's rights subject to terms, claims, and defenses; exceptions.]** Unless an account debtor has made an enforceable agreement not to assert defenses or claims, and subject to subsections (b) through (e), the rights of an assignee are subject to:

(1) all terms of the agreement between the account debtor and assignor and any defense or claim in recoupment arising from the transaction that gave rise to the contract; and

(2) any other defense or claim of the account debtor against the assignor which accrues before the account debtor receives a notification of the assignment authenticated by the assignor or the assignee.

(b) **[Account debtor's claim reduces amount owed to assignee.]** Subject to subsection (c) and except as otherwise provided in subsection (d), the claim of an account debtor against an assignor may be asserted against an assignee under subsection (a) only to reduce the amount the account debtor owes.

(c) **[Rule for individual under other law.]** This section is subject to law other than this article which establishes a different rule for an account debtor who is an individual and who incurred the obligation primarily for personal, family, or household purposes.

(d) **[Omission of required statement in consumer transaction.]** In a consumer transaction, if a record evidences the account debtor's obligation, law other than this article requires that the record include a statement to the effect that the account debtor's recovery against an assignee with respect to claims and defenses against the assignor may not exceed amounts paid by the account debtor under the record, and the record does not include such a statement, the extent to which a claim of an account debtor against the assignor may be asserted against an assignee is determined as if the record included such a statement.

(e) **[Inapplicability to health-care-insurance receivable.]** This section does not apply to an assignment of a health-care-insurance receivable.

§9-405. Modification of Assigned Contract.

(a) **[Effect of modification on assignee.]** A modification of or substitution for an assigned contract is effective against an assignee if made in good faith. The assignee acquires corresponding rights under the modified or substituted contract. The assignment may provide that the modification or substitution is a breach of contract by the assignor. This subsection is subject to subsections (b) through (d).

(b) **[Applicability of subsection (a).]** Subsection (a) applies to the extent that:

(1) the right to payment or a part thereof under an assigned contract has not been fully earned by performance; or

(2) the right to payment or a part thereof has been fully earned by performance and the account debtor has not received notification of the assignment under Section 9-406(a).

(c) **[Rule for individual under other law.]** This section is subject to law other than this article which establishes a different rule for an account debtor who is an individual and who incurred the obligation primarily for personal, family, or household purposes.

(d) **[Inapplicability to health-care-insurance receivable.]** This section does not apply to an assignment of a health-care-insurance receivable.

§9-406. Discharge of Account Debtor; Notification of Assignment; Identification and Proof of Assignment; Restrictions on Assignment of Accounts, Chattel Paper, Payment Intangibles, and Promissory Notes Ineffective.

(a) **[Discharge of account debtor; effect of notification.]** Subject to subsections (b) through (i), an account debtor on an account, chattel paper, or a payment intangible may discharge its obligation by paying the assignor until, but not after, the account debtor receives a notification, authenticated by the assignor or the assignee, that the amount due or to become due has been assigned and that payment is to be made to the assignee. After receipt of the notification, the account debtor may discharge its obligation by paying the assignee and may not discharge the obligation by paying the assignor.

(b) **[When notification ineffective.]** Subject to subsection (h), notification is ineffective under subsection (a):

(1) if it does not reasonably identify the rights assigned;

(2) to the extent that an agreement between an account debtor and a seller of a payment intangible limits the account debtor's duty to pay a person other than the seller and the limitation is effective under law other than this article; or

(3) at the option of an account debtor, if the notification notifies the account debtor to make less than the full amount of any installment or other periodic payment to the assignee, even if:

(A) only a portion of the account, chattel paper, or payment intangible has been assigned to that assignee;

(B) a portion has been assigned to another assignee; or

(C) the account debtor knows that the assignment to that assignee is limited.

(c) **[Proof of assignment.]** Subject to subsection (h), if requested by the account debtor, an assignee shall seasonably furnish reasonable proof that the assignment has been made. Unless the assignee complies, the account debtor may discharge its obligation by paying the assignor, even if the account debtor has received a notification under subsection (a).

(d) **[Term restricting assignment generally ineffective.]** Except as otherwise provided in subsection (e) and Sections 2A-303 and 9-407, and subject to subsection (h), a term in an agreement between an account debtor and an assignor or in a promissory note is ineffective to the extent that it:

(1) prohibits, restricts, or requires the consent of the account debtor or person obligated on the promissory note to the assignment or transfer of, or the creation, attachment, perfection, or enforcement of a security interest in, the account, chattel paper, payment intangible, or promissory note; or

(2) provides that the assignment or transfer or the creation, attachment, perfection, or enforcement of the security interest may give rise to a

default, breach, right of recoupment, claim, defense, termination, right of termination, or remedy under the account, chattel paper, payment intangible, or promissory note.

(e) **[Inapplicability of subsection (d) to certain sales.]** Subsection (d) does not apply to the sale of a payment intangible or promissory note.

(f) **[Legal restrictions on assignment generally ineffective.]** Except as otherwise provided in Sections 2A-303 and 9-407 and subject to subsections (h) and (i), a rule of law, statute, or regulation that prohibits, restricts, or requires the consent of a government, governmental body or official, or account debtor to the assignment or transfer of, or creation of a security interest in, an account or chattel paper is ineffective to the extent that the rule of law, statute, or regulation:

(1) prohibits, restricts, or requires the consent of the government, governmental body or official, or account debtor to the assignment or transfer of, or the creation, attachment, perfection, or enforcement of a security interest in the account or chattel paper; or

(2) provides that the assignment or transfer or the creation, attachment, perfection, or enforcement of the security interest may give rise to a default, breach, right of recoupment, claim, defense, termination, right of termination, or remedy under the account or chattel paper.

(g) **[Subsection (b)(3) not waivable.]** Subject to subsection (h), an account debtor may not waive or vary its option under subsection (b)(3).

(h) **[Rule for individual under other law.]** This section is subject to law other than this article which establishes a different rule for an account debtor who is an individual and who incurred the obligation primarily for personal, family, or household purposes.

(i) **[Inapplicability to health-care-insurance receivable.]** This section does not apply to an assignment of a health-care-insurance receivable.

(j) **[Section prevails over specified inconsistent law.]** This section prevails over any inconsistent provisions of the following statutes, rules, and regulations:

§9-407. Restrictions on Creation or Enforcement of Security Interest in Leasehold Interest or in Lessor's Residual Interest.

(a) **[Term restricting assignment generally ineffective.]** Except as otherwise provided in subsection (b), a term in a lease agreement is ineffective to the extent that it:

(1) prohibits, restricts, or requires the consent of a party to the lease to the assignment or transfer of, or the creation, attachment, perfection, or enforcement of a security interest in, an interest of a party under the lease contract or in the lessor's residual interest in the goods; or

(2) provides that the assignment or transfer or the creation, attachment, perfection, or enforcement of the security interest may give rise to a default, breach, right of recoupment, claim, defense, termination, right of termination, or remedy under the lease.

(b) **[Effectiveness of certain terms.]** Except as otherwise provided in Section 2A-303(7), a term described in subsection (a)(2) is effective to the extent that there is:

(1) a transfer by the lessee of the lessee's right of possession or use of the goods in violation of the term; or

(2) a delegation of a material performance of either party to the lease contract in violation of the term.

(c) **[Security interest not material impairment.]** The creation, attachment, perfection, or enforcement of a security interest in the lessor's interest under the lease contract or the lessor's residual interest in the goods is not a transfer that materially impairs the lessee's prospect of obtaining return performance or materially changes the duty of or materially increases the burden or risk imposed on the lessee within the purview of Section 2A-303(4) unless, and then only to the extent that, enforcement actually results in a delegation of material performance of the lessor.

§9-408. Restrictions on Assignment of Promissory Notes, Health-Care-Insurance Receivables, and Certain General Intangibles Ineffective.

(a) **[Term restricting assignment generally ineffective.]** Except as otherwise provided in subsection (b), a term in a promissory note or in an

agreement between an account debtor and a debtor which relates to a health-care-insurance receivable or a general intangible, including a contract, permit, license, or franchise, and which term prohibits, restricts, or requires the consent of the person obligated on the promissory note or the account debtor to, the assignment or transfer of, or creation, attachment, or perfection of a security interest in, the promissory note, health-care-insurance receivable, or general intangible, is ineffective to the extent that the term:

(1) would impair the creation, attachment, or perfection of a security interest; or

(2) provides that the assignment or transfer or the creation, attachment, or perfection of the security interest may give rise to a default, breach, right of recoupment, claim, defense, termination, right of termination, or remedy under the promissory note, health-care-insurance receivable, or general intangible.

(b) **[Applicability of subsection (a) to sales of certain rights to payment.]** Subsection (a) applies to a security interest in a payment intangible or promissory note only if the security interest arises out of a sale of the payment intangible or promissory note.

(c) **[Legal restrictions on assignment generally ineffective.]** A rule of law, statute, or regulation that prohibits, restricts, or requires the consent of a government, governmental body or official, person obligated on a promissory note, or account debtor to the assignment or transfer of, or creation of a security interest in, a promissory note, health-care-insurance receivable, or general intangible, including a contract, permit, license, or franchise between an account debtor and a debtor, is ineffective to the extent that the rule of law, statute, or regulation:

(1) would impair the creation, attachment, or perfection of a security interest; or

(2) provides that the assignment or transfer or the creation, attachment, or perfection of the security interest may give rise to a default, breach, right of recoupment, claim, defense, termination, right of termination, or remedy under the promissory note, health-care-insurance receivable, or general intangible.

(d) **[Limitation on ineffectiveness under subsections (a) and (c).]** To the extent that a term in a promissory note or in an agreement between an account debtor and a debtor which relates to a health-care-insurance receivable or general intangible or a rule of law, statute, or regulation described in subsection (c) would be effective under law other than this article but is ineffective under subsection (a) or (c), the creation, attachment, or perfection of a security interest in the promissory note, health-care-insurance receivable, or general intangible:

(1) is not enforceable against the person obligated on the promissory note or the account debtor;

(2) does not impose a duty or obligation on the person obligated on the promissory note or the account debtor;

(3) does not require the person obligated on the promissory note or the account debtor to recognize the security interest, pay or render performance to the secured party, or accept payment or performance from the secured party;

(4) does not entitle the secured party to use or assign the debtor's rights under the promissory note, health-care-insurance receivable, or general intangible, including any related information or materials furnished to the debtor in the transaction giving rise to the promissory note, health-care-insurance receivable, or general intangible;

(5) does not entitle the secured party to use, assign, possess, or have access to any trade secrets or confidential information of the person obligated on the promissory note or the account debtor; and

(6) does not entitle the secured party to enforce the security interest in the promissory note, health-care-insurance receivable, or general intangible.

(e) **[Section prevails over specified inconsistent law.]** This section prevails over any inconsistent provisions of the following statutes, rules, and regulations:

§9-409. Restrictions on Assignment of Letter-of-Credit Rights Ineffective.

(a) **[Term or law restricting assignment generally ineffective.]** A term in a letter of credit or a rule of law, statute, regulation, custom, or practice applicable to the letter of credit which prohibits, restricts, or requires the consent of an applicant, issuer, or nominated person to a beneficiary's assignment of or creation of a security interest in a letter-of-credit right is ineffective to the extent that the term or rule of law, statute, regulation, custom, or practice:

(1) would impair the creation, attachment, or perfection of a security interest in the letter-of-credit right; or

(2) provides that the assignment or the creation, attachment, or perfection of the security interest may give rise to a default, breach, right of recoupment, claim, defense, termination, right of termination, or remedy under the letter-of-credit right.

(b) **[Limitation on ineffectiveness under subsection (a).]** To the extent that a term in a letter of credit is ineffective under subsection (a) but would be effective under law other than this article or a custom or practice applicable to the letter of credit, to the transfer of a right to draw or otherwise demand performance under the letter of credit, or to the assignment of a right to proceeds of the letter of credit, the creation, attachment, or perfection of a security interest in the letter-of-credit right:

(1) is not enforceable against the applicant, issuer, nominated person, or transferee beneficiary;

(2) imposes no duties or obligations on the applicant, issuer, nominated person, or transferee beneficiary; and

(3) does not require the applicant, issuer, nominated person, or transferee beneficiary to recognize the security interest, pay or render performance to the secured party, or accept payment or other performance from the secured party.

Part 5—Filing

§9-501. Filing Office.

(a) **[Filing offices.]** Except as otherwise provided in subsection (b), if the local law of this State governs perfection of a security interest or agricultural lien, the office in which to file a financing statement to perfect the security interest or agricultural lien is:

(1) the office designated for the filing or recording of a record of a mortgage on the related real property, if:

(A) the collateral is as-extracted collateral or timber to be cut; or

(B) the financing statement is filed as a fixture filing and the collateral is goods that are or are to become fixtures; or

(2) the office of [Ê] [or any office duly authorized by [Ê]], in all other cases, including a case in which the collateral is goods that are or are to become fixtures and the financing statement is not filed as a fixture filing.

(b) **[Filing office for transmitting utilities.]** The office in which to file a financing statement to perfect a security interest in collateral, including fixtures, of a transmitting utility is the office of [Ê]. The financing statement also constitutes a fixture filing as to the collateral indicated in the financing statement which is or is to become fixtures.

§9-502. Contents of Financing Statement; Record of Mortgage as Financing Statement; Time of Filing Financing Statement.

(a) **[Sufficiency of financing statement.]** Subject to subsection (b), a financing statement is sufficient only if it:

(1) provides the name of the debtor;

(2) provides the name of the secured party or a representative of the secured party; and

(3) indicates the collateral covered by the financing statement.

(b) **[Real-property-related financing statements.]** Except as otherwise provided in Section 9-501(b), to be sufficient, a financing statement that covers as-extracted collateral or timber to be cut, or which is filed as a fixture filing and covers goods that are or are to become fixtures, must satisfy subsection (a) and also:

(1) indicate that it covers this type of collateral;

(2) indicate that it is to be filed [for record] in the real property records;

(3) provide a description of the real property to which the collateral is related [sufficient to give constructive notice of a mortgage under the law of this State if the description were contained in a record of the mortgage of the real property]; and

(4) if the debtor does not have an interest of record in the real property, provide the name of a record owner.

(c) **[Record of mortgage as financing statement.]** A record of a mortgage is effective, from the date of recording, as a financing statement filed as a fixture filing or as a financing statement covering as-extracted collateral or timber to be cut only if:

(1) the record indicates the goods or accounts that it covers;

(2) the goods are or are to become fixtures related to the real property described in the record or the collateral is related to the real property described in the record and is as-extracted collateral or timber to be cut;

(3) the record satisfies the requirements for a financing statement in this section other than an indication that it is to be filed in the real property records; and

(4) the record is [duly] recorded.

(d) **[Filing before security agreement or attachment.]** A financing statement may be filed before a security agreement is made or a security interest otherwise attaches.

§9-503. Name of Debtor and Secured Party.

(a) **[Sufficiency of debtor's name.]** A financing statement sufficiently provides the name of the debtor:

(1) if the debtor is a registered organization, only if the financing statement provides the name of the debtor indicated on the public record of the debtor's jurisdiction of organization which shows the debtor to have been organized;

(2) if the debtor is a decedent's estate, only if the financing statement provides the name of the decedent and indicates that the debtor is an estate;

(3) if the debtor is a trust or a trustee acting with respect to property held in trust, only if the financing statement:

(A) provides the name specified for the trust in its organic documents or, if no name is specified, provides the name of the settlor and additional information sufficient to distinguish the debtor from other trusts having one or more of the same settlors; and

(B) indicates, in the debtor's name or otherwise, that the debtor is a trust or is a trustee acting with respect to property held in trust; and

(4) in other cases:

(A) if the debtor has a name, only if it provides the individual or organizational name of the debtor; and

(B) if the debtor does not have a name, only if it provides the names of the partners, members, associates, or other persons comprising the debtor.

(b) **[Additional debtor-related information.]** A financing statement that provides the name of the debtor in accordance with subsection (a) is not rendered ineffective by the absence of:

(1) a trade name or other name of the debtor; or

(2) unless required under subsection (a)(4)(B), names of partners, members, associates, or other persons comprising the debtor.

(c) **[Debtor's trade name insufficient.]** A financing statement that provides only the debtor's trade name does not sufficiently provide the name of the debtor.

(d) **[Representative capacity.]** Failure to indicate the representative capacity of a secured party or representative of a secured party does not affect the sufficiency of a financing statement.

(e) [**Multiple debtors and secured parties.**] A financing statement may provide the name of more than one debtor and the name of more than one secured party.

§9-504. Indication of Collateral.
A financing statement sufficiently indicates the collateral that it covers if the financing statement provides:

(1) a description of the collateral pursuant to Section 9-108; or

(2) an indication that the financing statement covers all assets or all personal property.

§9-505. Filing and Compliance with Other Statutes and Treaties for Consignments, Leases, Other Bailments, and Other Transactions.
(a) [**Use of terms other than "debtor" and "secured party."**] A consignor, lessor, or other bailor of goods, a licensor, or a buyer of a payment intangible or promissory note may file a financing statement, or may comply with a statute or treaty described in Section 9-311(a), using the terms "consignor", "consignee", "lessor", "lessee", "bailor", "bailee", "licensor", "licensee", "owner", "registered owner", "buyer", "seller", or words of similar import, instead of the terms "secured party" and "debtor".

(b) [**Effect of financing statement under subsection (a).**] This part applies to the filing of a financing statement under subsection (a) and, as appropriate, to compliance that is equivalent to filing a financing statement under Section 9-311(b), but the filing or compliance is not of itself a factor in determining whether the collateral secures an obligation. If it is determined for another reason that the collateral secures an obligation, a security interest held by the consignor, lessor, bailor, licensor, owner, or buyer which attaches to the collateral is perfected by the filing or compliance.

§9-506. Effect of Errors or Omissions.
(a) [**Minor errors and omissions.**] A financing statement substantially satisfying the requirements of this part is effective, even if it has minor errors or omissions, unless the errors or omissions make the financing statement seriously misleading.

(b) [**Financing statement seriously misleading.**] Except as otherwise provided in subsection (c), a financing statement that fails sufficiently to provide the name of the debtor in accordance with Section 9-503(a) is seriously misleading.

(c) [**Financing statement not seriously misleading.**] If a search of the records of the filing office under the debtor's correct name, using the filing office's standard search logic, if any, would disclose a financing statement that fails sufficiently to provide the name of the debtor in accordance with Section 9-503(a), the name provided does not make the financing statement seriously misleading.

(d) [**"Debtor's correct name."**] For purposes of Section 9-508(b), the "debtor's correct name" in subsection (c) means the correct name of the new debtor.

§9-507. Effect of Certain Events on Effectiveness of Financing Statement.
(a) [**Disposition.**] A filed financing statement remains effective with respect to collateral that is sold, exchanged, leased, licensed, or otherwise disposed of and in which a security interest or agricultural lien continues, even if the secured party knows of or consents to the disposition.

(b) [**Information becoming seriously misleading.**] Except as otherwise provided in subsection (c) and Section 9-508, a financing statement is not rendered ineffective if, after the financing statement is filed, the information provided in the financing statement becomes seriously misleading under Section 9-506.

(c) [**Change in debtor's name.**] If a debtor so changes its name that a filed financing statement becomes seriously misleading under Section 9-506:

(1) the financing statement is effective to perfect a security interest in collateral acquired by the debtor before, or within four months after, the change; and

(2) the financing statement is not effective to perfect a security interest in collateral acquired by the debtor more than four months after the change, unless an amendment to the financing statement which renders the financing statement not seriously misleading is filed within four months after the change.

§9-508. Effectiveness of Financing Statement if New Debtor Becomes Bound by Security Agreement.
(a) [**Financing statement naming original debtor.**] Except as otherwise provided in this section, a filed financing statement naming an original debtor is effective to perfect a security interest in collateral in which a new debtor has or acquires rights to the extent that the financing statement would have been effective had the original debtor acquired rights in the collateral.

(b) [**Financing statement becoming seriously misleading.**] If the difference between the name of the original debtor and that of the new debtor causes a filed financing statement that is effective under subsection (a) to be seriously misleading under Section 9-506:

(1) the financing statement is effective to perfect a security interest in collateral acquired by the new debtor before, and within four months after, the new debtor becomes bound under Section 9-203(d); and

(2) the financing statement is not effective to perfect a security interest in collateral acquired by the new debtor more than four months after the new debtor becomes bound under Section 9-203(d) unless an initial financing statement providing the name of the new debtor is filed before the expiration of that time.

(c) [**When section not applicable.**] This section does not apply to collateral as to which a filed financing statement remains effective against the new debtor under Section 9-507(a).

§9-509. Persons Entitled to File A Record.
(a) [**Person entitled to file record.**] A person may file an initial financing statement, amendment that adds collateral covered by a financing statement, or amendment that adds a debtor to a financing statement only if:

(1) the debtor authorizes the filing in an authenticated record or pursuant to subsection (b) or (c); or

(2) the person holds an agricultural lien that has become effective at the time of filing and the financing statement covers only collateral in which the person holds an agricultural lien.

(b) [**Security agreement as authorization.**] By authenticating or becoming bound as debtor by a security agreement, a debtor or new debtor authorizes the filing of an initial financing statement, and an amendment, covering:

(1) the collateral described in the security agreement; and

(2) property that becomes collateral under Section 9-315(a)(2), whether or not the security agreement expressly covers proceeds.

(c) [**Acquisition of collateral as authorization.**] By acquiring collateral in which a security interest or agricultural lien continues under Section 9-315(a)(1), a debtor authorizes the filing of an initial financing statement, and an amendment, covering the collateral and property that becomes collateral under Section 9-315(a)(2).

(d) [**Person entitled to file certain amendments.**] A person may file an amendment other than an amendment that adds collateral covered by a financing statement or an amendment that adds a debtor to a financing statement only if:

(1) the secured party of record authorizes the filing; or

(2) the amendment is a termination statement for a financing statement as to which the secured party of record has failed to file or send a termination statement as required by Section 9-513(a) or (c), the debtor authorizes the filing, and the termination statement indicates that the debtor authorized it to be filed.

(e) [**Multiple secured parties of record.**] If there is more than one secured party of record for a financing statement, each secured party of record may authorize the filing of an amendment under subsection (d).

9-510. Effectiveness of Filed Record.
(a) [**Filed record effective if authorized.**] A filed record is effective only to the extent that it was filed by a person that may file it under Section 9-509.

(b) [**Authorization by one secured party of record.**] A record authorized by one secured party of record does not affect the financing statement with respect to another secured party of record.

(c) [**Continuation statement not timely filed.**] A continuation statement that is not filed within the six-month period prescribed by Section 9-515(d) is ineffective.

§9-511. Secured Party of Record.

(a) [**Secured party of record.**] A secured party of record with respect to a financing statement is a person whose name is provided as the name of the secured party or a representative of the secured party in an initial financing statement that has been filed. If an initial financing statement is filed under Section 9-514(a), the assignee named in the initial financing statement is the secured party of record with respect to the financing statement.

(b) [**Amendment naming secured party of record.**] If an amendment of a financing statement which provides the name of a person as a secured party or a representative of a secured party is filed, the person named in the amendment is a secured party of record. If an amendment is filed under Section 9-514(b), the assignee named in the amendment is a secured party of record.

(c) [**Amendment deleting secured party of record.**] A person remains a secured party of record until the filing of an amendment of the financing statement which deletes the person.

§9-512. Amendment of Financing Statement.

[Alternative A]

(a) [**Amendment of information in financing statement.**] Subject to Section 9-509, a person may add or delete collateral covered by, continue or terminate the effectiveness of, or, subject to subsection (e), otherwise amend the information provided in, a financing statement by filing an amendment that:

(1) identifies, by its file number, the initial financing statement to which the amendment relates; and

(2) if the amendment relates to an initial financing statement filed [or recorded] in a filing office described in Section 9-501(a)(1), provides the information specified in Section 9-502(b).

[Alternative B]

(a) [**Amendment of information in financing statement.**] Subject to Section 9-509, a person may add or delete collateral covered by, continue or terminate the effectiveness of, or, subject to subsection (e), otherwise amend the information provided in, a financing statement by filing an amendment that:

(1) identifies, by its file number, the initial financing statement to which the amendment relates; and

(2) if the amendment relates to an initial financing statement filed [or recorded] in a filing office described in Section 9-501(a)(1), provides the date [and time] that the initial financing statement was filed [or recorded] and the information specified in Section 9-502(b).

[End of Alternatives]

(b) [**Period of effectiveness not affected.**] Except as otherwise provided in Section 9-515, the filing of an amendment does not extend the period of effectiveness of the financing statement.

(c) [**Effectiveness of amendment adding collateral.**] A financing statement that is amended by an amendment that adds collateral is effective as to the added collateral only from the date of the filing of the amendment.

(d) [**Effectiveness of amendment adding debtor.**] A financing statement that is amended by an amendment that adds a debtor is effective as to the added debtor only from the date of the filing of the amendment.

(e) [**Certain amendments ineffective.**] An amendment is ineffective to the extent it:

(1) purports to delete all debtors and fails to provide the name of a debtor to be covered by the financing statement; or

(2) purports to delete all secured parties of record and fails to provide the name of a new secured party of record.

§9-513. Termination Statement.

(a) [**Consumer goods.**] A secured party shall cause the secured party of record for a financing statement to file a termination statement for the financing statement if the financing statement covers consumer goods and:

(1) there is no obligation secured by the collateral covered by the financing statement and no commitment to make an advance, incur an obligation, or otherwise give value; or

(2) the debtor did not authorize the filing of the initial financing statement.

(b) [**Time for compliance with subsection (a).**] To comply with subsection (a), a secured party shall cause the secured party of record to file the termination statement:

(1) within one month after there is no obligation secured by the collateral covered by the financing statement and no commitment to make an advance, incur an obligation, or otherwise give value; or

(2) if earlier, within 20 days after the secured party receives an authenticated demand from a debtor.

(c) [**Other collateral.**] In cases not governed by subsection (a), within 20 days after a secured party receives an authenticated demand from a debtor, the secured party shall cause the secured party of record for a financing statement to send to the debtor a termination statement for the financing statement or file the termination statement in the filing office if:

(1) except in the case of a financing statement covering accounts or chattel paper that has been sold or goods that are the subject of a consignment, there is no obligation secured by the collateral covered by the financing statement and no commitment to make an advance, incur an obligation, or otherwise give value;

(2) the financing statement covers accounts or chattel paper that has been sold but as to which the account debtor or other person obligated has discharged its obligation;

(3) the financing statement covers goods that were the subject of a consignment to the debtor but are not in the debtor's possession; or

(4) the debtor did not authorize the filing of the initial financing statement.

(d) [**Effect of filing termination statement.**] Except as otherwise provided in Section 9-510, upon the filing of a termination statement with the filing office, the financing statement to which the termination statement relates ceases to be effective. Except as otherwise provided in Section 9-510, for purposes of Sections 9-519(g), 9-522(a), and 9-523(c), the filing with the filing office of a termination statement relating to a financing statement that indicates that the debtor is a transmitting utility also causes the effectiveness of the financing statement to lapse.

§9-514. Assignment of Powers of Secured Party of Record.

(a) [**Assignment reflected on initial financing statement.**] Except as otherwise provided in subsection (c), an initial financing statement may reflect an assignment of all of the secured party's power to authorize an amendment to the financing statement by providing the name and mailing address of the assignee as the name and address of the secured party.

(b) [**Assignment of filed financing statement.**] Except as otherwise provided in subsection (c), a secured party of record may assign of record all or part of its power to authorize an amendment to a financing statement by filing in the filing office an amendment of the financing statement which:

(1) identifies, by its file number, the initial financing statement to which it relates;

(2) provides the name of the assignor; and

(3) provides the name and mailing address of the assignee.

(c) [**Assignment of record of mortgage.**] An assignment of record of a security interest in a fixture covered by a record of a mortgage which is effective as a financing statement filed as a fixture filing under Section 9-502(c) may be made only by an assignment of record of the mortgage in the manner provided by law of this State other than [the Uniform Commercial Code].

§9-515. Duration and Effectiveness of Financing Statement; Effect of Lapsed Financing Statement.

(a) [**Five-year effectiveness.**] Except as otherwise provided in subsections (b), (e), (f), and (g), a filed financing statement is effective for a period of five years after the date of filing.

(b) [**Public-finance or manufactured-home transaction.**] Except as otherwise provided in subsections (e), (f), and (g), an initial financing statement filed in connection with a public-finance transaction or manufactured-home transaction is effective for a period of 30 years after the date of filing if it indicates that it is filed in connection with a public-finance transaction or manufactured-home transaction.

(c) [**Lapse and continuation of financing statement.**] The effectiveness of a filed financing statement lapses on the expiration of the period of its effectiveness unless before the lapse a continuation statement is filed pursuant to subsection (d). Upon lapse, a financing statement ceases to be effective and any security interest or agricultural lien that was perfected by the financing statement becomes unperfected, unless the security interest is perfected otherwise. If the security interest or agricultural lien becomes unperfected upon lapse, it is deemed never to have been perfected as against a purchaser of the collateral for value.

(d) [**When continuation statement may be filed.**] A continuation statement may be filed only within six months before the expiration of the five-year period specified in subsection (a) or the 30-year period specified in subsection (b), whichever is applicable.

(e) [**Effect of filing continuation statement.**] Except as otherwise provided in Section 9-510, upon timely filing of a continuation statement, the effectiveness of the initial financing statement continues for a period of five years commencing on the day on which the financing statement would have become ineffective in the absence of the filing. Upon the expiration of the five-year period, the financing statement lapses in the same manner as provided in subsection (c), unless, before the lapse, another continuation statement is filed pursuant to subsection (d). Succeeding continuation statements may be filed in the same manner to continue the effectiveness of the initial financing statement.

(f) [**Transmitting utility financing statement.**] If a debtor is a transmitting utility and a filed financing statement so indicates, the financing statement is effective until a termination statement is filed.

(g) [**Record of mortgage as financing statement.**] A record of a mortgage that is effective as a financing statement filed as a fixture filing under Section 9-502(c) remains effective as a financing statement filed as a fixture filing until the mortgage is released or satisfied of record or its effectiveness otherwise terminates as to the real property.

§9-516. What Constitutes Filing; Effectiveness of Filing.

(a) [**What constitutes filing.**] Except as otherwise provided in subsection (b), communication of a record to a filing office and tender of the filing fee or acceptance of the record by the filing office constitutes filing.

(b) [**Refusal to accept record; filing does not occur.**] Filing does not occur with respect to a record that a filing office refuses to accept because:

(1) the record is not communicated by a method or medium of communication authorized by the filing office;

(2) an amount equal to or greater than the applicable filing fee is not tendered;

(3) the filing office is unable to index the record because:

(A) in the case of an initial financing statement, the record does not provide a name for the debtor;

(B) in the case of an amendment or correction statement, the record:

(i) does not identify the initial financing statement as required by Section 9-512 or 9-518, as applicable; or

(ii) identifies an initial financing statement whose effectiveness has lapsed under Section 9-515;

(C) in the case of an initial financing statement that provides the name of a debtor identified as an individual or an amendment that

provides a name of a debtor identified as an individual which was not previously provided in the financing statement to which the record relates, the record does not identify the debtor's last name; or

(D) in the case of a record filed [or recorded] in the filing office described in Section 9-501(a)(1), the record does not provide a sufficient description of the real property to which it relates;

(4) in the case of an initial financing statement or an amendment that adds a secured party of record, the record does not provide a name and mailing address for the secured party of record;

(5) in the case of an initial financing statement or an amendment that provides a name of a debtor which was not previously provided in the financing statement to which the amendment relates, the record does not:

(A) provide a mailing address for the debtor;

(B) indicate whether the debtor is an individual or an organization; or

(C) if the financing statement indicates that the debtor is an organization, provide:

(i) a type of organization for the debtor;

(ii) a jurisdiction of organization for the debtor; or

(iii) an organizational identification number for the debtor or indicate that the debtor has none;

(6) in the case of an assignment reflected in an initial financing statement under Section 9-514(a) or an amendment filed under Section 9-514(b), the record does not provide a name and mailing address for the assignee; or

(7) in the case of a continuation statement, the record is not filed within the six-month period prescribed by Section 9-515(d).

(c) [**Rules applicable to subsection (b).**] For purposes of subsection (b):

(1) a record does not provide information if the filing office is unable to read or decipher the information; and

(2) a record that does not indicate that it is an amendment or identify an initial financing statement to which it relates, as required by Section 9-512, 9-514, or 9-518, is an initial financing statement.

(d) [**Refusal to accept record; record effective as filed record.**] A record that is communicated to the filing office with tender of the filing fee, but which the filing office refuses to accept for a reason other than one set forth in subsection (b), is effective as a filed record except as against a purchaser of the collateral which gives value in reasonable reliance upon the absence of the record from the files.

§9-517. Effect of Indexing Errors.

The failure of the filing office to index a record correctly does not affect the effectiveness of the filed record.

§9-518. Claim Concerning Inaccurate or Wrongfully Filed Record.

(a) [**Correction statement.**] A person may file in the filing office a correction statement with respect to a record indexed there under the person's name if the person believes that the record is inaccurate or was wrongfully filed.

[**Alternative A**]

(b) [**Sufficiency of correction statement.**] A correction statement must:

(1) identify the record to which it relates by the file number assigned to the initial financing statement to which the record relates;

(2) indicate that it is a correction statement; and

(3) provide the basis for the person's belief that the record is inaccurate and indicate the manner in which the person believes the record should be amended to cure any inaccuracy or provide the basis for the person's belief that the record was wrongfully filed.

[**Alternative B**]

(b) [**Sufficiency of correction statement.**] A correction statement must:

(1) identify the record to which it relates by:

(A) the file number assigned to the initial financing statement to which the record relates; and

(B) if the correction statement relates to a record filed [or recorded] in a filing office described in Section 9-501(a)(1), the date [and time] that the initial financing statement was filed [or recorded] and the information specified in Section 9-502(b);

(2) indicate that it is a correction statement; and

(3) provide the basis for the person's belief that the record is inaccurate and indicate the manner in which the person believes the record should be amended to cure any inaccuracy or provide the basis for the person's belief that the record was wrongfully filed.

[End of Alternatives]

(c) **[Record not affected by correction statement.]** The filing of a correction statement does not affect the effectiveness of an initial financing statement or other filed record.

§9-519. Numbering, Maintaining, and Indexing Records; Communicating Information Provided in Records.

(a) **[Filing office duties.]** For each record filed in a filing office, the filing office shall:

(1) assign a unique number to the filed record;

(2) create a record that bears the number assigned to the filed record and the date and time of filing;

(3) maintain the filed record for public inspection; and

(4) index the filed record in accordance with subsections (c), (d), and (e).

(b) **[File number.]** A file number [assigned after January 1, 2002,] must include a digit that:

(1) is mathematically derived from or related to the other digits of the file number; and

(2) aids the filing office in determining whether a number communicated as the file number includes a single-digit or transpositional error.

(c) **[Indexing: general.]** Except as otherwise provided in subsections (d) and (e), the filing office shall:

(1) index an initial financing statement according to the name of the debtor and index all filed records relating to the initial financing statement in a manner that associates with one another an initial financing statement and all filed records relating to the initial financing statement; and

(2) index a record that provides a name of a debtor which was not previously provided in the financing statement to which the record relates also according to the name that was not previously provided.

(d) **[Indexing: real-property-related financing statement.]** If a financing statement is filed as a fixture filing or covers as-extracted collateral or timber to be cut, [it must be filed for record and] the filing office shall index it:

(1) under the names of the debtor and of each owner of record shown on the financing statement as if they were the mortgagors under a mortgage of the real property described; and

(2) to the extent that the law of this State provides for indexing of records of mortgages under the name of the mortgagee, under the name of the secured party as if the secured party were the mortgagee thereunder, or, if indexing is by description, as if the financing statement were a record of a mortgage of the real property described.

(e) **[Indexing: real-property-related assignment.]** If a financing statement is filed as a fixture filing or covers as-extracted collateral or timber to be cut, the filing office shall index an assignment filed under Section 9-514(a) or an amendment filed under Section 9-514(b):

(1) under the name of the assignor as grantor; and

(2) to the extent that the law of this State provides for indexing a record of the assignment of a mortgage under the name of the assignee, under the name of the assignee.

[Alternative A]

(f) **[Retrieval and association capability.]** The filing office shall maintain a capability:

(1) to retrieve a record by the name of the debtor and by the file number assigned to the initial financing statement to which the record relates; and

(2) to associate and retrieve with one another an initial financing statement and each filed record relating to the initial financing statement.

[Alternative B]

(f) **[Retrieval and association capability.]** The filing office shall maintain a capability:

(1) to retrieve a record by the name of the debtor and:

(A) if the filing office is described in Section 9-501(a)(1), by the file number assigned to the initial financing statement to which the record relates and the date [and time] that the record was filed [or recorded]; or

(B) if the filing office is described in Section 9-501(a)(2), by the file number assigned to the initial financing statement to which the record relates; and

(2) to associate and retrieve with one another an initial financing statement and each filed record relating to the initial financing statement.

[End of Alternatives]

(g) **[Removal of debtor's name.]** The filing office may not remove a debtor's name from the index until one year after the effectiveness of a financing statement naming the debtor lapses under Section 9-515 with respect to all secured parties of record.

(h) **[Timeliness of filing office performance.]** The filing office shall perform the acts required by subsections (a) through (e) at the time and in the manner prescribed by filing-office rule, but not later than two business days after the filing office receives the record in question.

(i) **[Inapplicability to real-property-related filing office.]** Subsection[s] [(b)] [and] [(h)] do[es] not apply to a filing office described in Section 9-501(a)(1).]

§9-520. Acceptance and Refusal to Accept Record.

(a) **[Mandatory refusal to accept record.]** A filing office shall refuse to accept a record for filing for a reason set forth in Section 9-516(b) and may refuse to accept a record for filing only for a reason set forth in Section 9-516(b).

(b) **[Communication concerning refusal.]** If a filing office refuses to accept a record for filing, it shall communicate to the person that presented the record the fact of and reason for the refusal and the date and time the record would have been filed had the filing office accepted it. The communication must be made at the time and in the manner prescribed by filing-office rule but [, in the case of a filing office described in Section 9-501(a)(2),] in no event more than two business days after the filing office receives the record.

(c) **[When filed financing statement effective.]** A filed financing statement satisfying Section 9-502(a) and (b) is effective, even if the filing office is required to refuse to accept it for filing under subsection (a). However, Section 9-338 applies to a filed financing statement providing information described in Section 9-516(b)(5) which is incorrect at the time the financing statement is filed.

(d) **[Separate application to multiple debtors.]** If a record communicated to a filing office provides information that relates to more than one debtor, this part applies as to each debtor separately.

§9-521. Uniform Form of Written Financing Statement and Amendment.

(a) **[Initial financing statement form.]** A filing office that accepts written records may not refuse to accept a written initial financing statement in the following form and format except for a reason set forth in Section 9-516(b):

(b) **[Amendment form.]** A filing office that accepts written records may not refuse to accept a written record in the following form and format except for a reason set forth in Section 9-516(b):

§9-522. Maintenance and Destruction of Records.

[Alternative A]

(a) **[Post-lapse maintenance and retrieval of information.]** The filing office shall maintain a record of the information provided in a filed financing statement for at least one year after the effectiveness of the financing statement has lapsed under Section 9-515 with respect to all secured parties of record. The record must be retrievable by using the name of the debtor and by using the file number assigned to the initial financing statement to which the record relates.

[Alternative B]

(a) **[Post-lapse maintenance and retrieval of information.]** The filing office shall maintain a record of the information provided in a filed financing statement for at least one year after the effectiveness of the financing statement has lapsed under Section 9-515 with respect to all secured parties of record. The record must be retrievable by using the name of the debtor and:

(1) if the record was filed [or recorded] in the filing office described in Section 9-501(a)(1), by using the file number assigned to the initial financing statement to which the record relates and the date [and time] that the record was filed [or recorded]; or

(2) if the record was filed in the filing office described in Section 9-501(a)(2), by using the file number assigned to the initial financing statement to which the record relates.

[End of Alternatives]

(b) **[Destruction of written records.]** Except to the extent that a statute governing disposition of public records provides otherwise, the filing office immediately may destroy any written record evidencing a financing statement. However, if the filing office destroys a written record, it shall maintain another record of the financing statement which complies with subsection (a).

§9-523. Information from Filing Office; Sale or License of Records.

(a) **[Acknowledgment of filing written record.]** If a person that files a written record requests an acknowledgment of the filing, the filing office shall send to the person an image of the record showing the number assigned to the record pursuant to Section 9-519(a)(1) and the date and time of the filing of the record. However, if the person furnishes a copy of the record to the filing office, the filing office may instead:

(1) note upon the copy the number assigned to the record pursuant to Section 9-519(a)(1) and the date and time of the filing of the record; and

(2) send the copy to the person.

(b) **[Acknowledgment of filing other record.]** If a person files a record other than a written record, the filing office shall communicate to the person an acknowledgment that provides:

(1) the information in the record;

(2) the number assigned to the record pursuant to Section 9-519(a)(1); and

(3) the date and time of the filing of the record.

(c) **[Communication of requested information.]** The filing office shall communicate or otherwise make available in a record the following information to any person that requests it:

(1) whether there is on file on a date and time specified by the filing office, but not a date earlier than three business days before the filing office receives the request, any financing statement that:

(A) designates a particular debtor [or, if the request so states, designates a particular debtor at the address specified in the request];

(B) has not lapsed under Section 9-515 with respect to all secured parties of record; and

(C) if the request so states, has lapsed under Section 9-515 and a record of which is maintained by the filing office under Section 9-522(a);

(2) the date and time of filing of each financing statement; and

(3) the information provided in each financing statement.

(d) **[Medium for communicating information.]** In complying with its duty under subsection (c), the filing office may communicate information in any medium. However, if requested, the filing office shall communicate information by issuing [its written certificate] [a record that can be admitted into evidence in the courts of this State without extrinsic evidence of its authenticity].

(e) **[Timeliness of filing office performance.]** The filing office shall perform the acts required by subsections (a) through (d) at the time and in the manner prescribed by filing-office rule, but not later than two business days after the filing office receives the request.

(f) **[Public availability of records.]** At least weekly, the [insert appropriate official or governmental agency] [filing office] shall offer to sell or license to the public on a nonexclusive basis, in bulk, copies of all records filed in it under this part, in every medium from time to time available to the filing office.

§9-524. Delay by Filing Office.

Delay by the filing office beyond a time limit prescribed by this part is excused if:

(1) the delay is caused by interruption of communication or computer facilities, war, emergency conditions, failure of equipment, or other circumstances beyond control of the filing office; and

(2) the filing office exercises reasonable diligence under the circumstances.

§9-525. Fees.

§9-526. Filing-Office Rules.

(a) **[Adoption of filing-office rules.]** The [insert appropriate governmental official or agency] shall adopt and publish rules to implement this article. The filing-office rules must be[:

(1)] consistent with this article[; and

(2) adopted and published in accordance with the [insert any applicable state administrative procedure act]].

(b) **[Harmonization of rules.]** To keep the filing-office rules and practices of the filing office in harmony with the rules and practices of filing offices in other jurisdictions that enact substantially this part, and to keep the technology used by the filing office compatible with the technology used by filing offices in other jurisdictions that enact substantially this part, the [insert appropriate governmental official or agency], so far as is consistent with the purposes, policies, and provisions of this article, in adopting, amending, and repealing filing-office rules, shall:

(1) consult with filing offices in other jurisdictions that enact substantially this part; and

(2) consult the most recent version of the Model Rules promulgated by the International Association of Corporate Administrators or any successor organization; and

(3) take into consideration the rules and practices of, and the technology used by, filing offices in other jurisdictions that enact substantially this part.

§9-527. Duty to Report.

The [insert appropriate governmental official or agency] shall report [annually on or before _____ Ê] to the [Governor and Legislature] on the operation of the filing office. The report must contain a statement of the extent to which:

(1) the filing-office rules are not in harmony with the rules of filing offices in other jurisdictions that enact substantially this part and the reasons for these variations; and

(2) the filing-office rules are not in harmony with the most recent version of the Model Rules promulgated by the International Association of Corporate Administrators, or any successor organization, and the reasons for these variations.

Part 6—Default

§9-601. Rights after Default; Judicial Enforcement; Consignor or Buyer of Accounts, Chattel Paper, Payment Intangibles, or Promissory Notes.

(a) **[Rights of secured party after default.]** After default, a secured party has the rights provided in this part and, except as otherwise provided in Section 9-602, those provided by agreement of the parties. A secured party:

(1) may reduce a claim to judgment, foreclose, or otherwise enforce the claim, security interest, or agricultural lien by any available judicial procedure; and

(2) if the collateral is documents, may proceed either as to the documents or as to the goods they cover.

(b) **[Rights and duties of secured party in possession or control.]** A secured party in possession of collateral or control of collateral under Section 9-104, 9-105, 9-106, or 9-107 has the rights and duties provided in Section 9-207.

(c) **[Rights cumulative; simultaneous exercise.]** The rights under subsections (a) and (b) are cumulative and may be exercised simultaneously.

(d) **[Rights of debtor and obligor.]** Except as otherwise provided in subsection (g) and Section 9-605, after default, a debtor and an obligor have the rights provided in this part and by agreement of the parties.

(e) **[Lien of levy after judgment.]** If a secured party has reduced its claim to judgment, the lien of any levy that may be made upon the collateral by virtue of an execution based upon the judgment relates back to the earliest of:

(1) the date of perfection of the security interest or agricultural lien in the collateral;

(2) the date of filing a financing statement covering the collateral; or

(3) any date specified in a statute under which the agricultural lien was created.

(f) **[Execution sale.]** A sale pursuant to an execution is a foreclosure of the security interest or agricultural lien by judicial procedure within the meaning of this section. A secured party may purchase at the sale and thereafter hold the collateral free of any other requirements of this article.

(g) **[Consignor or buyer of certain rights to payment.]** Except as otherwise provided in Section 9-607(c), this part imposes no duties upon a secured party that is a consignor or is a buyer of accounts, chattel paper, payment intangibles, or promissory notes.

§9-602. Waiver and Variance of Rights and Duties.

Except as otherwise provided in Section 9-624, to the extent that they give rights to a debtor or obligor and impose duties on a secured party, the debtor or obligor may not waive or vary the rules stated in the following listed sections:

(1) Section 9-207(b)(4)(C), which deals with use and operation of the collateral by the secured party;

(2) Section 9-210, which deals with requests for an accounting and requests concerning a list of collateral and statement of account;

(3) Section 9-607(c), which deals with collection and enforcement of collateral;

(4) Sections 9-608(a) and 9-615(c) to the extent that they deal with application or payment of noncash proceeds of collection, enforcement, or disposition;

(5) Sections 9-608(a) and 9-615(d) to the extent that they require accounting for or payment of surplus proceeds of collateral;

(6) Section 9-609 to the extent that it imposes upon a secured party that takes possession of collateral without judicial process the duty to do so without breach of the peace;

(7) Sections 9-610(b), 9-611, 9-613, and 9-614, which deal with disposition of collateral;

(8) Section 9-615(f), which deals with calculation of a deficiency or surplus when a disposition is made to the secured party, a person related to the secured party, or a secondary obligor;

(9) Section 9-616, which deals with explanation of the calculation of a surplus or deficiency;

(10) Sections 9-620, 9-621, and 9-622, which deal with acceptance of collateral in satisfaction of obligation;

(11) Section 9-623, which deals with redemption of collateral;

(12) Section 9-624, which deals with permissible waivers; and

(13) Sections 9-625 and 9-626, which deal with the secured party's liability for failure to comply with this article.

§9-603. Agreement on Standards Concerning Rights and Duties.

(a) **[Agreed standards.]** The parties may determine by agreement the standards measuring the fulfillment of the rights of a debtor or obligor and the duties of a secured party under a rule stated in Section 9-602 if the standards are not manifestly unreasonable.

(b) **[Agreed standards inapplicable to breach of peace.]** Subsection (a) does not apply to the duty under Section 9-609 to refrain from breaching the peace.

§9-604. Procedure if Security Agreement Covers Real Property or Fixtures.

(a) **[Enforcement: personal and real property.]** If a security agreement covers both personal and real property, a secured party may proceed:

(1) under this part as to the personal property without prejudicing any rights with respect to the real property; or

(2) as to both the personal property and the real property in accordance with the rights with respect to the real property, in which case the other provisions of this part do not apply.

(b) **[Enforcement: fixtures.]** Subject to subsection (c), if a security agreement covers goods that are or become fixtures, a secured party may proceed:

(1) under this part; or

(2) in accordance with the rights with respect to real property, in which case the other provisions of this part do not apply.

(c) **[Removal of fixtures.]** Subject to the other provisions of this part, if a secured party holding a security interest in fixtures has priority over all owners and encumbrancers of the real property, the secured party, after default, may remove the collateral from the real property.

(d) **[Injury caused by removal.]** A secured party that removes collateral shall promptly reimburse any encumbrancer or owner of the real property, other than the debtor, for the cost of repair of any physical injury caused by the removal. The secured party need not reimburse the encumbrancer or owner for any diminution in value of the real property caused by the absence of the goods removed or by any necessity of replacing them. A person entitled to reimbursement may refuse permission to remove until the secured party gives adequate assurance for the performance of the obligation to reimburse.

§9-605. Unknown Debtor or Secondary Obligor.

A secured party does not owe a duty based on its status as secured party:

(1) to a person that is a debtor or obligor, unless the secured party knows:

(A) that the person is a debtor or obligor;

(B) the identity of the person; and

(C) how to communicate with the person; or

(2) to a secured party or lienholder that has filed a financing statement against a person, unless the secured party knows:

(A) that the person is a debtor; and

(B) the identity of the person.

§9-606. Time of Default for Agricultural Lien.

For purposes of this part, a default occurs in connection with an agricultural lien at the time the secured party becomes entitled to enforce the lien in accordance with the statute under which it was created.

§9-607. Collection and Enforcement by Secured Party.

(a) **[Collection and enforcement generally.]** If so agreed, and in any event after default, a secured party:

(1) may notify an account debtor or other person obligated on collateral to make payment or otherwise render performance to or for the benefit of the secured party;

(2) may take any proceeds to which the secured party is entitled under Section 9-315;

(3) may enforce the obligations of an account debtor or other person obligated on collateral and exercise the rights of the debtor with respect to the obligation of the account debtor or other person obligated on collateral to make payment or otherwise render performance to the debtor, and with respect to any property that secures the obligations of the account debtor or other person obligated on the collateral;

(4) if it holds a security interest in a deposit account perfected by control under Section 9-104(a)(1), may apply the balance of the deposit account to the obligation secured by the deposit account; and

(5) if it holds a security interest in a deposit account perfected by control under Section 9-104(a)(2) or (3), may instruct the bank to pay the balance of the deposit account to or for the benefit of the secured party.

(b) [**Nonjudicial enforcement of mortgage.**] If necessary to enable a secured party to exercise under subsection (a)(3) the right of a debtor to enforce a mortgage nonjudicially, the secured party may record in the office in which a record of the mortgage is recorded:

(1) a copy of the security agreement that creates or provides for a security interest in the obligation secured by the mortgage; and

(2) the secured party's sworn affidavit in recordable form stating that:

(A) a default has occurred; and

(B) the secured party is entitled to enforce the mortgage non-judicially.

(c) [**Commercially reasonable collection and enforcement.**] A secured party shall proceed in a commercially reasonable manner if the secured party:

(1) undertakes to collect from or enforce an obligation of an account debtor or other person obligated on collateral; and

(2) is entitled to charge back uncollected collateral or otherwise to full or limited recourse against the debtor or a secondary obligor.

(d) [**Expenses of collection and enforcement.**] A secured party may deduct from the collections made pursuant to subsection (c) reasonable expenses of collection and enforcement, including reasonable attorney's fees and legal expenses incurred by the secured party.

(e) [**Duties to secured party not affected.**] This section does not determine whether an account debtor, bank, or other person obligated on collateral owes a duty to a secured party.

§9-608. Application of Proceeds of Collection or Enforcement; Liability for Deficiency and Right to Surplus.

(a) [**Application of proceeds, surplus, and deficiency if obligation secured.**] If a security interest or agricultural lien secures payment or performance of an obligation, the following rules apply:

(1) A secured party shall apply or pay over for application the cash proceeds of collection or enforcement under Section 9-607 in the following order to:

(A) the reasonable expenses of collection and enforcement and, to the extent provided for by agreement and not prohibited by law, reasonable attorney's fees and legal expenses incurred by the secured party;

(B) the satisfaction of obligations secured by the security interest or agricultural lien under which the collection or enforcement is made; and

(C) the satisfaction of obligations secured by any subordinate security interest in or other lien on the collateral subject to the security interest or agricultural lien under which the collection or enforcement is made if the secured party receives an authenticated demand for proceeds before distribution of the proceeds is completed.

(2) If requested by a secured party, a holder of a subordinate security interest or other lien shall furnish reasonable proof of the interest or lien within a reasonable time. Unless the holder complies, the secured party need not comply with the holder's demand under paragraph (1)(C).

(3) A secured party need not apply or pay over for application noncash proceeds of collection and enforcement under Section 9-607 unless the failure to do so would be commercially unreasonable. A secured party that applies or pays over for application noncash proceeds shall do so in a commercially reasonable manner.

(4) A secured party shall account to and pay a debtor for any surplus, and the obligor is liable for any deficiency.

(b) [**No surplus or deficiency in sales of certain rights to payment.**] If the underlying transaction is a sale of accounts, chattel paper, payment intangibles, or promissory notes, the debtor is not entitled to any surplus, and the obligor is not liable for any deficiency.

§9-609. Secured Party's Right to Take Possession after Default.

(a) [**Possession; rendering equipment unusable; disposition on debtor's premises.**] After default, a secured party:

(1) may take possession of the collateral; and

(2) without removal, may render equipment unusable and dispose of collateral on a debtor's premises under Section 9-610.

(b) [**Judicial and nonjudicial process.**] A secured party may proceed under subsection (a):

(1) pursuant to judicial process; or

(2) without judicial process, if it proceeds without breach of the peace.

(c) [**Assembly of collateral.**] If so agreed, and in any event after default, a secured party may require the debtor to assemble the collateral and make it available to the secured party at a place to be designated by the secured party which is reasonably convenient to both parties.

§9-610. Disposition of Collateral after Default.

(a) [**Disposition after default.**] After default, a secured party may sell, lease, license, or otherwise dispose of any or all of the collateral in its present condition or following any commercially reasonable preparation or processing.

(b) [**Commercially reasonable disposition.**] Every aspect of a disposition of collateral, including the method, manner, time, place, and other terms, must be commercially reasonable. If commercially reasonable, a secured party may dispose of collateral by public or private proceedings, by one or more contracts, as a unit or in parcels, and at any time and place and on any terms.

(c) [**Purchase by secured party.**] A secured party may purchase collateral:

(1) at a public disposition; or

(2) at a private disposition only if the collateral is of a kind that is customarily sold on a recognized market or the subject of widely distributed standard price quotations.

(d) [**Warranties on disposition.**] A contract for sale, lease, license, or other disposition includes the warranties relating to title, possession, quiet enjoyment, and the like which by operation of law accompany a voluntary disposition of property of the kind subject to the contract.

(e) [**Disclaimer of warranties.**] A secured party may disclaim or modify warranties under subsection (d):

(1) in a manner that would be effective to disclaim or modify the warranties in a voluntary disposition of property of the kind subject to the contract of disposition; or

(2) by communicating to the purchaser a record evidencing the contract for disposition and including an express disclaimer or modification of the warranties.

(f) [**Record sufficient to disclaim warranties.**] A record is sufficient to disclaim warranties under subsection (e) if it indicates "There is no warranty relating to title, possession, quiet enjoyment, or the like in this disposition" or uses words of similar import.

§9-611. Notification Before Disposition of Collateral.

(a) [**"Notification date."**] In this section, "notification date" means the earlier of the date on which:

(1) a secured party sends to the debtor and any secondary obligor an authenticated notification of disposition; or

(2) the debtor and any secondary obligor waive the right to notification.

(b) **[Notification of disposition required.]** Except as otherwise provided in subsection (d), a secured party that disposes of collateral under Section 9-610 shall send to the persons specified in subsection (c) a reasonable authenticated notification of disposition.

(c) **[Persons to be notified.]** To comply with subsection (b), the secured party shall send an authenticated notification of disposition to:

(1) the debtor;

(2) any secondary obligor; and

(3) if the collateral is other than consumer goods:

(A) any other person from which the secured party has received, before the notification date, an authenticated notification of a claim of an interest in the collateral;

(B) any other secured party or lienholder that, 10 days before the notification date, held a security interest in or other lien on the collateral perfected by the filing of a financing statement that:

(i) identified the collateral;

(ii) was indexed under the debtor's name as of that date; and

(iii) was filed in the office in which to file a financing statement against the debtor covering the collateral as of that date; and

(C) any other secured party that, 10 days before the notification date, held a security interest in the collateral perfected by compliance with a statute, regulation, or treaty described in Section 9-311(a).

(d) **[Subsection (b) inapplicable: perishable collateral; recognized market.]** Subsection (b) does not apply if the collateral is perishable or threatens to decline speedily in value or is of a type customarily sold on a recognized market.

(e) **[Compliance with subsection (c)(3)(B).]** A secured party complies with the requirement for notification prescribed by subsection (c)(3)(B) if:

(1) not later than 20 days or earlier than 30 days before the notification date, the secured party requests, in a commercially reasonable manner, information concerning financing statements indexed under the debtor's name in the office indicated in subsection (c)(3)(B); and

(2) before the notification date, the secured party:

(A) did not receive a response to the request for information; or

(B) received a response to the request for information and sent an authenticated notification of disposition to each secured party or other lienholder named in that response whose financing statement covered the collateral.

§9-612. Timelines of Notification Before Disposition of Collateral.

(a) **[Reasonable time is question of fact.]** Except as otherwise provided in subsection (b), whether a notification is sent within a reasonable time is a question of fact.

(b) **[10-day period sufficient in non-consumer transaction.]** In a transaction other than a consumer transaction, a notification of disposition sent after default and 10 days or more before the earliest time of disposition set forth in the notification is sent within a reasonable time before the disposition.

§9-613. Contents and Form of Notification Before Disposition of Collateral: General.

Except in a consumer-goods transaction, the following rules apply:

(1) The contents of a notification of disposition are sufficient if the notification:

(A) describes the debtor and the secured party;

(B) describes the collateral that is the subject of the intended disposition;

(C) states the method of intended disposition;

(D) states that the debtor is entitled to an accounting of the unpaid indebtedness and states the charge, if any, for an accounting; and

(E) states the time and place of a public disposition or the time after which any other disposition is to be made.

(2) Whether the contents of a notification that lacks any of the information specified in paragraph (1) are nevertheless sufficient is a question of fact.

(3) The contents of a notification providing substantially the information specified in paragraph (1) are sufficient, even if the notification includes:

(A) information not specified by that paragraph; or

(B) minor errors that are not seriously misleading.

(4) A particular phrasing of the notification is not required.

(5) The following form of notification and the form appearing in Section 9-614(3), when completed, each provides sufficient information:

* * *

§9-614. Contents and Form of Notification Before Disposition of Collateral: Consumer-Goods Transaction.

In a consumer-goods transaction, the following rules apply:

(1) A notification of disposition must provide the following information:

(A) the information specified in Section 9-613(1);

(B) a description of any liability for a deficiency of the person to which the notification is sent;

(C) a telephone number from which the amount that must be paid to the secured party to redeem the collateral under Section 9-623 is available; and

(D) a telephone number or mailing address from which additional information concerning the disposition and the obligation secured is available.

(2) A particular phrasing of the notification is not required.

(3) The following form of notification, when completed, provides sufficient information:

* * *

(4) A notification in the form of paragraph (3) is sufficient, even if additional information appears at the end of the form.

(5) A notification in the form of paragraph (3) is sufficient, even if it includes errors in information not required by paragraph (1), unless the error is misleading with respect to rights arising under this article.

(6) If a notification under this section is not in the form of paragraph (3), law other than this article determines the effect of including information not required by paragraph (1).

§9-615. Application of Proceeds of Disposition; Liability for Deficiency and Right to Surplus.

(a) **[Application of proceeds.]** A secured party shall apply or pay over for application the cash proceeds of disposition under Section 9-610 in the following order to:

(1) the reasonable expenses of retaking, holding, preparing for disposition, processing, and disposing, and, to the extent provided for by agreement and not prohibited by law, reasonable attorney's fees and legal expenses incurred by the secured party;

(2) the satisfaction of obligations secured by the security interest or agricultural lien under which the disposition is made;

(3) the satisfaction of obligations secured by any subordinate security interest in or other subordinate lien on the collateral if:

(A) the secured party receives from the holder of the subordinate security interest or other lien an authenticated demand for proceeds before distribution of the proceeds is completed; and

(B) in a case in which a consignor has an interest in the collateral, the subordinate security interest or other lien is senior to the interest of the consignor; and

(4) a secured party that is a consignor of the collateral if the secured party receives from the consignor an authenticated demand for proceeds before distribution of the proceeds is completed.

(b) **[Proof of subordinate interest.]** If requested by a secured party, a holder of a subordinate security interest or other lien shall furnish reasonable proof of the interest or lien within a reasonable time. Unless the holder does so, the secured party need not comply with the holder's demand under subsection (a)(3).

(c) [**Application of noncash proceeds.**] A secured party need not apply or pay over for application noncash proceeds of disposition under Section 9-610 unless the failure to do so would be commercially unreasonable. A secured party that applies or pays over for application noncash proceeds shall do so in a commercially reasonable manner.

(d) [**Surplus or deficiency if obligation secured.**] If the security interest under which a disposition is made secures payment or performance of an obligation, after making the payments and applications required by subsection (a) and permitted by subsection (c):

(1) unless subsection (a)(4) requires the secured party to apply or pay over cash proceeds to a consignor, the secured party shall account to and pay a debtor for any surplus; and

(2) the obligor is liable for any deficiency.

(e) [**No surplus or deficiency in sales of certain rights to payment.**] If the underlying transaction is a sale of accounts, chattel paper, payment intangibles, or promissory notes:

(1) the debtor is not entitled to any surplus; and

(2) the obligor is not liable for any deficiency.

(f) [**Calculation of surplus or deficiency in disposition to person related to secured party.**] The surplus or deficiency following a disposition is calculated based on the amount of proceeds that would have been realized in a disposition complying with this part to a transferee other than the secured party, a person related to the secured party, or a secondary obligor if:

(1) the transferee in the disposition is the secured party, a person related to the secured party, or a secondary obligor; and

(2) the amount of proceeds of the disposition is significantly below the range of proceeds that a complying disposition to a person other than the secured party, a person related to the secured party, or a secondary obligor would have brought.

(g) [**Cash proceeds received by junior secured party.**] A secured party that receives cash proceeds of a disposition in good faith and without knowledge that the receipt violates the rights of the holder of a security interest or other lien that is not subordinate to the security interest or agricultural lien under which the disposition is made:

(1) takes the cash proceeds free of the security interest or other lien;

(2) is not obligated to apply the proceeds of the disposition to the satisfaction of obligations secured by the security interest or other lien; and

(3) is not obligated to account to or pay the holder of the security interest or other lien for any surplus.

§9-616. Explanation of Calculation of Surplus or Deficiency.

(a) [**Definitions.**] In this section:

(1) "Explanation" means a writing that:

(A) states the amount of the surplus or deficiency;

(B) provides an explanation in accordance with subsection (c) of how the secured party calculated the surplus or deficiency;

(C) states, if applicable, that future debits, credits, charges, including additional credit service charges or interest, rebates, and expenses may affect the amount of the surplus or deficiency; and

(D) provides a telephone number or mailing address from which additional information concerning the transaction is available.

(2) "Request" means a record:

(A) authenticated by a debtor or consumer obligor;

(B) requesting that the recipient provide an explanation; and

(C) sent after disposition of the collateral under Section 9-610.

(b) [**Explanation of calculation.**] In a consumer-goods transaction in which the debtor is entitled to a surplus or a consumer obligor is liable for a deficiency under Section 9-615, the secured party shall:

(1) send an explanation to the debtor or consumer obligor, as applicable, after the disposition and:

(A) before or when the secured party accounts to the debtor and pays any surplus or first makes written demand on the consumer obligor after the disposition for payment of the deficiency; and

(B) within 14 days after receipt of a request; or

(2) in the case of a consumer obligor who is liable for a deficiency, within 14 days after receipt of a request, send to the consumer obligor a record waiving the secured party's right to a deficiency.

(c) [**Required information.**] To comply with subsection (a)(1)(B), a writing must provide the following information in the following order:

(1) the aggregate amount of obligations secured by the security interest under which the disposition was made, and, if the amount reflects a rebate of unearned interest or credit service charge, an indication of that fact, calculated as of a specified date:

(A) if the secured party takes or receives possession of the collateral after default, not more than 35 days before the secured party takes or receives possession; or

(B) if the secured party takes or receives possession of the collateral before default or does not take possession of the collateral, not more than 35 days before the disposition;

(2) the amount of proceeds of the disposition;

(3) the aggregate amount of the obligations after deducting the amount of proceeds;

(4) the amount, in the aggregate or by type, and types of expenses, including expenses of retaking, holding, preparing for disposition, processing, and disposing of the collateral, and attorney's fees secured by the collateral which are known to the secured party and relate to the current disposition;

(5) the amount, in the aggregate or by type, and types of credits, including rebates of interest or credit service charges, to which the obligor is known to be entitled and which are not reflected in the amount in paragraph (1); and

(6) the amount of the surplus or deficiency.

(d) [**Substantial compliance.**] A particular phrasing of the explanation is not required. An explanation complying substantially with the requirements of subsection (a) is sufficient, even if it includes minor errors that are not seriously misleading.

(e) [**Charges for responses.**] A debtor or consumer obligor is entitled without charge to one response to a request under this section during any six-month period in which the secured party did not send to the debtor or consumer obligor an explanation pursuant to subsection (b)(1). The secured party may require payment of a charge not exceeding $25 for each additional response.

§9-617. Rights of Transferee of Collateral.

(a) [**Effects of disposition.**] A secured party's disposition of collateral after default:

(1) transfers to a transferee for value all of the debtor's rights in the collateral;

(2) discharges the security interest under which the disposition is made; and

(3) discharges any subordinate security interest or other subordinate lien [other than liens created under [cite acts or statutes providing for liens, if any, that are not to be discharged]].

(b) [**Rights of good-faith transferee.**] A transferee that acts in good faith takes free of the rights and interests described in subsection (a), even if the secured party fails to comply with this article or the requirements of any judicial proceeding.

(c) [**Rights of other transferee.**] If a transferee does not take free of the rights and interests described in subsection (a), the transferee takes the collateral subject to:

(1) the debtor's rights in the collateral;

(2) the security interest or agricultural lien under which the disposition is made; and

(3) any other security interest or other lien.

§9-618. Rights and Duties of Certain Secondary Obligors.

(a) **[Rights and duties of secondary obligor.]** A secondary obligor acquires the rights and becomes obligated to perform the duties of the secured party after the secondary obligor:

(1) receives an assignment of a secured obligation from the secured party;

(2) receives a transfer of collateral from the secured party and agrees to accept the rights and assume the duties of the secured party; or

(3) is subrogated to the rights of a secured party with respect to collateral.

(b) **[Effect of assignment, transfer, or subrogation.]** An assignment, transfer, or subrogation described in subsection (a):

(1) is not a disposition of collateral under Section 9-610; and

(2) relieves the secured party of further duties under this article.

§9-619. Transfer of Record or Legal Title.

(a) **["Transfer statement."]** In this section, "transfer statement" means a record authenticated by a secured party stating:

(1) that the debtor has defaulted in connection with an obligation secured by specified collateral;

(2) that the secured party has exercised its post-default remedies with respect to the collateral;

(3) that, by reason of the exercise, a transferee has acquired the rights of the debtor in the collateral; and

(4) the name and mailing address of the secured party, debtor, and transferee.

(b) **[Effect of transfer statement.]** A transfer statement entitles the transferee to the transfer of record of all rights of the debtor in the collateral specified in the statement in any official filing, recording, registration, or certificate-of-title system covering the collateral. If a transfer statement is presented with the applicable fee and request form to the official or office responsible for maintaining the system, the official or office shall:

(1) accept the transfer statement;

(2) promptly amend its records to reflect the transfer; and

(3) if applicable, issue a new appropriate certificate of title in the name of the transferee.

(c) **[Transfer not a disposition; no relief of secured party's duties.]** A transfer of the record or legal title to collateral to a secured party under subsection (b) or otherwise is not of itself a disposition of collateral under this article and does not of itself relieve the secured party of its duties under this article.

§9-620. Acceptance of Collateral in Full or Partial Satisfaction of Obligation; Compulsory Disposition of Collateral.

(a) **[Conditions to acceptance in satisfaction.]** Except as otherwise provided in subsection (g), a secured party may accept collateral in full or partial satisfaction of the obligation it secures only if:

(1) the debtor consents to the acceptance under subsection (c);

(2) the secured party does not receive, within the time set forth in subsection (d), a notification of objection to the proposal authenticated by:

(A) a person to which the secured party was required to send a proposal under Section 9-621; or

(B) any other person, other than the debtor, holding an interest in the collateral subordinate to the security interest that is the subject of the proposal;

(3) if the collateral is consumer goods, the collateral is not in the possession of the debtor when the debtor consents to the acceptance; and

(4) subsection (e) does not require the secured party to dispose of the collateral or the debtor waives the requirement pursuant to Section 9-624.

(b) **[Purported acceptance ineffective.]** A purported or apparent acceptance of collateral under this section is ineffective unless:

(1) the secured party consents to the acceptance in an authenticated record or sends a proposal to the debtor; and

(2) the conditions of subsection (a) are met.

(c) **[Debtor's consent.]** For purposes of this section:

(1) a debtor consents to an acceptance of collateral in partial satisfaction of the obligation it secures only if the debtor agrees to the terms of the acceptance in a record authenticated after default; and

(2) a debtor consents to an acceptance of collateral in full satisfaction of the obligation it secures only if the debtor agrees to the terms of the acceptance in a record authenticated after default or the secured party:

(A) sends to the debtor after default a proposal that is unconditional or subject only to a condition that collateral not in the possession of the secured party be preserved or maintained;

(B) in the proposal, proposes to accept collateral in full satisfaction of the obligation it secures; and

(C) does not receive a notification of objection authenticated by the debtor within 20 days after the proposal is sent.

(d) **[Effectiveness of notification.]** To be effective under subsection (a)(2), a notification of objection must be received by the secured party:

(1) in the case of a person to which the proposal was sent pursuant to Section 9-621, within 20 days after notification was sent to that person; and

(2) in other cases:

(A) within 20 days after the last notification was sent pursuant to Section 9-621; or

(B) if a notification was not sent, before the debtor consents to the acceptance under subsection (c).

(e) **[Mandatory disposition of consumer goods.]** A secured party that has taken possession of collateral shall dispose of the collateral pursuant to Section 9-610 within the time specified in subsection (f) if:

(1) 60 percent of the cash price has been paid in the case of a purchase-money security interest in consumer goods; or

(2) 60 percent of the principal amount of the obligation secured has been paid in the case of a non-purchase-money security interest in consumer goods.

(f) **[Compliance with mandatory disposition requirement.]** To comply with subsection (e), the secured party shall dispose of the collateral:

(1) within 90 days after taking possession; or

(2) within any longer period to which the debtor and all secondary obligors have agreed in an agreement to that effect entered into and authenticated after default.

(g) **[No partial satisfaction in consumer transaction.]** In a consumer transaction, a secured party may not accept collateral in partial satisfaction of the obligation it secures.

§9-621. Notification of Proposal to Accept Collateral.

(a) **[Persons to which proposal to be sent.]** A secured party that desires to accept collateral in full or partial satisfaction of the obligation it secures shall send its proposal to:

(1) any person from which the secured party has received, before the debtor consented to the acceptance, an authenticated notification of a claim of an interest in the collateral;

(2) any other secured party or lienholder that, 10 days before the debtor consented to the acceptance, held a security interest in or other lien on the collateral perfected by the filing of a financing statement that:

(A) identified the collateral;

(B) was indexed under the debtor's name as of that date; and

(C) was filed in the office or offices in which to file a financing statement against the debtor covering the collateral as of that date; and

(3) any other secured party that, 10 days before the debtor consented to the acceptance, held a security interest in the collateral perfected by compliance with a statute, regulation, or treaty described in Section 9-311(a).

(b) **[Proposal to be sent to secondary obligor in partial satisfaction.]** A secured party that desires to accept collateral in partial satisfaction of the obligation it secures shall send its proposal to any secondary obligor in addition to the persons described in subsection (a).

§9-622. Effect of Acceptance of Collateral.

(a) [**Effect of acceptance.**] A secured party's acceptance of collateral in full or partial satisfaction of the obligation it secures:

(1) discharges the obligation to the extent consented to by the debtor;

(2) transfers to the secured party all of a debtor's rights in the collateral;

(3) discharges the security interest or agricultural lien that is the subject of the debtor's consent and any subordinate security interest or other subordinate lien; and

(4) terminates any other subordinate interest.

(b) [**Discharge of subordinate interest notwithstanding noncompliance.**] A subordinate interest is discharged or terminated under subsection (a), even if the secured party fails to comply with this article.

§9-623. Right to Redeem Collateral.

(a) [**Persons that may redeem.**] A debtor, any secondary obligor, or any other secured party or lienholder may redeem collateral.

(b) [**Requirements for redemption.**] To redeem collateral, a person shall tender:

(1) fulfillment of all obligations secured by the collateral; and

(2) the reasonable expenses and attorney's fees described in Section 9-615(a)(1).

(c) [**When redemption may occur.**] A redemption may occur at any time before a secured party:

(1) has collected collateral under Section 9-607;

(2) has disposed of collateral or entered into a contract for its disposition under Section 9-610; or

(3) has accepted collateral in full or partial satisfaction of the obligation it secures under Section 9-622.

§9-624. Waiver.

(a) [**Waiver of disposition notification**.] A debtor or secondary obligor may waive the right to notification of disposition of collateral under Section 9-611 only by an agreement to that effect entered into and authenticated after default.

(b) [**Waiver of mandatory disposition.**] A debtor may waive the right to require disposition of collateral under Section 9-620(e) only by an agreement to that effect entered into and authenticated after default.

(c) [**Waiver of redemption right.**] Except in a consumer-goods transaction, a debtor or secondary obligor may waive the right to redeem collateral under Section 9-623 only by an agreement to that effect entered into and authenticated after default.

§9-625. Remedies for Secured Party's Failure to Comply with Article.

(a) [**Judicial orders concerning noncompliance.**] If it is established that a secured party is not proceeding in accordance with this article, a court may order or restrain collection, enforcement, or disposition of collateral on appropriate terms and conditions.

(b) [**Damages for noncompliance.**] Subject to subsections (c), (d), and (f), a person is liable for damages in the amount of any loss caused by a failure to comply with this article. Loss caused by a failure to comply may include loss resulting from the debtor's inability to obtain, or increased costs of, alternative financing.

(c) [**Persons entitled to recover damages; statutory damages in consumer-goods transaction.**] Except as otherwise provided in Section 9-628:

(1) a person that, at the time of the failure, was a debtor, was an obligor, or held a security interest in or other lien on the collateral may recover damages under subsection (b) for its loss; and

(2) if the collateral is consumer goods, a person that was a debtor or a secondary obligor at the time a secured party failed to comply with this part may recover for that failure in any event an amount not less than the credit service charge plus 10 percent of the principal amount of the

obligation or the time-price differential plus 10 percent of the cash price.

(d) [**Recovery when deficiency eliminated or reduced.**] A debtor whose deficiency is eliminated under Section 9-626 may recover damages for the loss of any surplus. However, a debtor or secondary obligor whose deficiency is eliminated or reduced under Section 9-626 may not otherwise recover under subsection (b) for noncompliance with the provisions of this part relating to collection, enforcement, disposition, or acceptance.

(e) [**Statutory damages: noncompliance with specified provisions.**] In addition to any damages recoverable under subsection (b), the debtor, consumer obligor, or person named as a debtor in a filed record, as applicable, may recover $500 in each case from a person that:

(1) fails to comply with Section 9-208;

(2) fails to comply with Section 9-209;

(3) files a record that the person is not entitled to file under Section 9-509(a);

(4) fails to cause the secured party of record to file or send a termination statement as required by Section 9-513(a) or (c);

(5) fails to comply with Section 9-616(b)(1) and whose failure is part of a pattern, or consistent with a practice, of noncompliance; or

(6) fails to comply with Section 9-616(b)(2).

(f) [**Statutory damages: noncompliance with Section 9-210.**] A debtor or consumer obligor may recover damages under subsection (b) and, in addition, $500 in each case from a person that, without reasonable cause, fails to comply with a request under Section 9-210. A recipient of a request under Section 9-210 which never claimed an interest in the collateral or obligations that are the subject of a request under that section has a reasonable excuse for failure to comply with the request within the meaning of this subsection.

(g) [**Limitation of security interest: noncompliance with Section 9-210.**] If a secured party fails to comply with a request regarding a list of collateral or a statement of account under Section 9-210, the secured party may claim a security interest only as shown in the list or statement included in the request as against a person that is reasonably misled by the failure.

§9-626. Action in Which Deficiency or Surplus Is in Issue.

(a) [**Applicable rules if amount of deficiency or surplus in issue.**] In an action arising from a transaction, other than a consumer transaction, in which the amount of a deficiency or surplus is in issue, the following rules apply:

(1) A secured party need not prove compliance with the provisions of this part relating to collection, enforcement, disposition, or acceptance unless the debtor or a secondary obligor places the secured party's compliance in issue.

(2) If the secured party's compliance is placed in issue, the secured party has the burden of establishing that the collection, enforcement, disposition, or acceptance was conducted in accordance with this part.

(3) Except as otherwise provided in Section 9-628, if a secured party fails to prove that the collection, enforcement, disposition, or acceptance was conducted in accordance with the provisions of this part relating to collection, enforcement, disposition, or acceptance, the liability of a debtor or a secondary obligor for a deficiency is limited to an amount by which the sum of the secured obligation, expenses, and attorney's fees exceeds the greater of:

(A) the proceeds of the collection, enforcement, disposition, or acceptance; or

(B) the amount of proceeds that would have been realized had the noncomplying secured party proceeded in accordance with the provisions of this part relating to collection, enforcement, disposition, or acceptance.

(4) For purposes of paragraph (3)(B), the amount of proceeds that would have been realized is equal to the sum of the secured obligation, expenses, and attorney's fees unless the secured party proves that the amount is less than that sum.

(5) If a deficiency or surplus is calculated under Section 9-615(f), the debtor or obligor has the burden of establishing that the amount of proceeds of the disposition is significantly below the range of prices that a complying disposition to a person other than the secured party, a person related to the secured party, or a secondary obligor would have brought.

(b) **[Non-consumer transactions; no inference.]** The limitation of the rules in subsection (a) to transactions other than consumer transactions is intended to leave to the court the determination of the proper rules in consumer transactions. The court may not infer from that limitation the nature of the proper rule in consumer transactions and may continue to apply established approaches.

§9-627. Determination of Whether Conduct Was Commercially Reasonable.

(a) **[Greater amount obtainable under other circumstances; no preclusion of commercial reasonableness.]** The fact that a greater amount could have been obtained by a collection, enforcement, disposition, or acceptance at a different time or in a different method from that selected by the secured party is not of itself sufficient to preclude the secured party from establishing that the collection, enforcement, disposition, or acceptance was made in a commercially reasonable manner.

(b) **[Dispositions that are commercially reasonable.]** A disposition of collateral is made in a commercially reasonable manner if the disposition is made:

(1) in the usual manner on any recognized market;

(2) at the price current in any recognized market at the time of the disposition; or

(3) otherwise in conformity with reasonable commercial practices among dealers in the type of property that was the subject of the disposition.

(c) **[Approval by court or on behalf of creditors.]** A collection, enforcement, disposition, or acceptance is commercially reasonable if it has been approved:

(1) in a judicial proceeding;

(2) by a bona fide creditors' committee;

(3) by a representative of creditors; or

(4) by an assignee for the benefit of creditors.

(d) **[Approval under subsection (c) not necessary; absence of approval has no effect.]** Approval under subsection (c) need not be obtained, and lack of approval does not mean that the collection, enforcement, disposition, or acceptance is not commercially reasonable.

§9-628. Nonliability and Limitation on Liability of Secured Party; Liability of Secondary Obligor.

(a) **[Limitation of liability of secured party for noncompliance with article.]** Unless a secured party knows that a person is a debtor or obligor, knows the identity of the person, and knows how to communicate with the person:

(1) the secured party is not liable to the person, or to a secured party or lienholder that has filed a financing statement against the person, for failure to comply with this article; and

(2) the secured party's failure to comply with this article does not affect the liability of the person for a deficiency.

(b) **[Limitation of liability based on status as secured party.]** A secured party is not liable because of its status as secured party:

(1) to a person that is a debtor or obligor, unless the secured party knows:

(A) that the person is a debtor or obligor;

(B) the identity of the person; and

(C) how to communicate with the person; or

(2) to a secured party or lienholder that has filed a financing statement against a person, unless the secured party knows:

(A) that the person is a debtor; and

(B) the identity of the person.

(c) **[Limitation of liability if reasonable belief that transaction not a consumer-goods transaction or consumer transaction.]** A secured party is not liable to any person, and a person's liability for a deficiency is not affected, because of any act or omission arising out of the secured party's reasonable belief that a transaction is not a consumer-goods transaction or a consumer transaction or that goods are not consumer goods, if the secured party's belief is based on its reasonable reliance on:

(1) a debtor's representation concerning the purpose for which collateral was to be used, acquired, or held; or

(2) an obligor's representation concerning the purpose for which a secured obligation was incurred.

(d) **[Limitation of liability for statutory damages.]** A secured party is not liable to any person under Section 9-625(c)(2) for its failure to comply with Section 9-616.

(e) **[Limitation of multiple liability for statutory damages.]** A secured party is not liable under Section 9-625(c)(2) more than once with respect to any one secured obligation.

Part 7—Transition

§9-701. Effective Date.

This [Act] takes effect on July 1, 2001.

§9-702. Savings Clause.

(a) **[Pre-effective-date transactions or liens.]** Except as otherwise provided in this part, this [Act] applies to a transaction or lien within its scope, even if the transaction or lien was entered into or created before this [Act] takes effect.

(b) **[Continuing validity.]** Except as otherwise provided in subsection (c) and Sections 9-703 through 9-709:

(1) transactions and liens that were not governed by [former Article 9], were validly entered into or created before this [Act] takes effect, and would be subject to this [Act] if they had been entered into or created after this [Act] takes effect, and the rights, duties, and interests flowing from those transactions and liens remain valid after this [Act] takes effect; and

(2) the transactions and liens may be terminated, completed, consummated, and enforced as required or permitted by this [Act] or by the law that otherwise would apply if this [Act] had not taken effect.

(c) **[Pre-effective-date proceedings.]** This [Act] does not affect an action, case, or proceeding commenced before this [Act] takes effect.

§9-703. Security Interest Perfected Before Effective Date.

(a) **[Continuing priority over lien creditor: perfection requirements satisfied.]** A security interest that is enforceable immediately before this [Act] takes effect and would have priority over the rights of a person that becomes a lien creditor at that time is a perfected security interest under this [Act] if, when this [Act] takes effect, the applicable requirements for enforceability and perfection under this [Act] are satisfied without further action.

(b) **[Continuing priority over lien creditor: perfection requirements not satisfied.]** Except as otherwise provided in Section 9-705, if, immediately before this [Act] takes effect, a security interest is enforceable and would have priority over the rights of a person that becomes a lien creditor at that time, but the applicable requirements for enforceability or perfection under this [Act] are not satisfied when this [Act] takes effect, the security interest:

(1) is a perfected security interest for one year after this [Act] takes effect;

(2) remains enforceable thereafter only if the security interest becomes enforceable under Section 9-203 before the year expires; and

(3) remains perfected thereafter only if the applicable requirements for perfection under this [Act] are satisfied before the year expires.

§9-704. Security Interest Unperfected Before Effective Date.

A security interest that is enforceable immediately before this [Act] takes effect but which would be subordinate to the rights of a person that becomes a lien creditor at that time:

(1) remains an enforceable security interest for one year after this [Act] takes effect;

(2) remains enforceable thereafter if the security interest becomes enforceable under Section 9-203 when this [Act] takes effect or within one year thereafter; and

(3) becomes perfected:

(A) without further action, when this [Act] takes effect if the applicable requirements for perfection under this [Act] are satisfied before or at that time; or

(B) when the applicable requirements for perfection are satisfied if the requirements are satisfied after that time.

§9-705. Effectiveness of Action Taken Before Effective Date.

(a) **[Pre-effective-date action; one-year perfection period unless reperfected.]** If action, other than the filing of a financing statement, is taken before this [Act] takes effect and the action would have resulted in priority of a security interest over the rights of a person that becomes a lien creditor had the security interest become enforceable before this [Act] takes effect, the action is effective to perfect a security interest that attaches under this [Act] within one year after this [Act] takes effect. An attached security interest becomes unperfected one year after this [Act] takes effect unless the security interest becomes a perfected security interest under this [Act] before the expiration of that period.

(b) **[Pre-effective-date filing.]** The filing of a financing statement before this [Act] takes effect is effective to perfect a security interest to the extent the filing would satisfy the applicable requirements for perfection under this [Act].

(c) **[Pre-effective-date filing in jurisdiction formerly governing perfection.]** This [Act] does not render ineffective an effective financing statement that, before this [Act] takes effect, is filed and satisfies the applicable requirements for perfection under the law of the jurisdiction governing perfection as provided in [former Section 9-103]. However, except as otherwise provided in subsections (d) and (e) and Section 9-706, the financing statement ceases to be effective at the earlier of:

(1) the time the financing statement would have ceased to be effective under the law of the jurisdiction in which it is filed; or

(2) June 30, 2006.

(d) **[Continuation statement.]** The filing of a continuation statement after this [Act] takes effect does not continue the effectiveness of the financing statement filed before this [Act] takes effect. However, upon the timely filing of a continuation statement after this [Act] takes effect and in accordance with the law of the jurisdiction governing perfection as provided in Part 3, the effectiveness of a financing statement filed in the same office in that jurisdiction before this [Act] takes effect continues for the period provided by the law of that jurisdiction.

(e) **[Application of subsection (c)(2) to transmitting utility financing statement.]** Subsection (c)(2) applies to a financing statement that, before this [Act] takes effect, is filed against a transmitting utility and satisfies the applicable requirements for perfection under the law of the jurisdiction governing perfection as provided in [former Section 9-103] only to the extent that Part 3 provides that the law of a jurisdiction other than the jurisdiction in which the financing statement is filed governs perfection of a security interest in collateral covered by the financing statement.

(f) **[Application of Part 5.]** A financing statement that includes a financing statement filed before this [Act] takes effect and a continuation statement filed after this [Act] takes effect is effective only to the extent that it satisfies the requirements of Part 5 for an initial financing statement.

§9-706. When Initial Financing Statement Suffices to Continue Effectiveness of Financing Statement.

(a) **[Initial financing statement in lieu of continuation statement.]** The filing of an initial financing statement in the office specified in Section 9-501 continues the effectiveness of a financing statement filed before this [Act] takes effect if:

(1) the filing of an initial financing statement in that office would be effective to perfect a security interest under this [Act];

(2) the pre-effective-date financing statement was filed in an office in another State or another office in this State; and

(3) the initial financing statement satisfies subsection (c).

(b) **[Period of continued effectiveness.]** The filing of an initial financing statement under subsection (a) continues the effectiveness of the pre-effective-date financing statement:

(1) if the initial financing statement is filed before this [Act] takes effect, for the period provided in [former Section 9-403] with respect to a financing statement; and

(2) if the initial financing statement is filed after this [Act] takes effect, for the period provided in Section 9-515 with respect to an initial financing statement.

(c) **[Requirements for initial financing statement under subsection (a).]** To be effective for purposes of subsection (a), an initial financing statement must:

(1) satisfy the requirements of Part 5 for an initial financing statement;

(2) identify the pre-effective-date financing statement by indicating the office in which the financing statement was filed and providing the dates of filing and file numbers, if any, of the financing statement and of the most recent continuation statement filed with respect to the financing statement; and

(3) indicate that the pre-effective-date financing statement remains effective.

§9-707. Amendment of Pre-Effective-Date Financing Statement.

(a) **["Pre-effective-date financing statement".]** In this section, "pre-effective-date financing statement" means a financing statement filed before this [Act] takes effect.

(b) **[Applicable law.]** After this [Act] takes effect, a person may add or delete collateral covered by, continue or terminate the effectiveness of, or otherwise amend the information provided in, a pre-effective-date financing statement only in accordance with the law of the jurisdiction governing perfection as provided in Part 3. However, the effectiveness of a pre-effective-date financing statement also may be terminated in accordance with the law of the jurisdiction in which the financing statement is filed.

(c) **[Method of amending: general rule.]** Except as otherwise provided in subsection (d), if the law of this State governs perfection of a security interest, the information in a pre-effective-date financing statement may be amended after this [Act] takes effect only if:

(1) the pre-effective-date financing statement and an amendment are filed in the office specified in Section 9-501;

(2) an amendment is filed in the office specified in Section 9-501 concurrently with, or after the filing in that office of, an initial financing statement that satisfies Section 9-706(c); or

(3) an initial financing statement that provides the information as amended and satisfies Section 9-706(c) is filed in the office specified in Section 9-501.

(d) **[Method of amending: continuation.]** If the law of this State governs perfection of a security interest, the effectiveness of a pre-effective-date financing statement may be continued only under Section 9-705(d) and (f) or 9-706.

(e) **[Method of amending: additional termination rule.]** Whether or not the law of this State governs perfection of a security interest, the effectiveness of a pre-effective-date financing statement filed in this State may be terminated after this [Act] takes effect by filing a termination statement in the office in which the pre-effective-date financing statement is filed, unless an initial financing statement that satisfies Section 9-706(c) has been filed in the office specified by the law of the jurisdiction governing perfection as provided in Part 3 as the office in which to file a financing statement.

§9-708. Persons Entitled to File Initial Financing Statement or Continuation Statement.

A person may file an initial financing statement or a continuation statement under this part if:

(1) the secured party of record authorizes the filing; and

(2) the filing is necessary under this part:

(A) to continue the effectiveness of a financing statement filed before this [Act] takes effect; or

(B) to perfect or continue the perfection of a security interest.

§9-709. Priority.

(a) **[Law governing priority.]** This [Act] determines the priority of conflicting claims to collateral. However, if the relative priorities of the claims were established before this [Act] takes effect, [former Article 9] determines priority.

(b) **[Priority if security interest becomes enforceable under Section 9-203.]** For purposes of Section 9-322(a), the priority of a security interest that becomes enforceable under Section 9-203 of this [Act] dates from the time this [Act] takes effect if the security interest is perfected under this [Act] by the filing of a financing statement before this [Act] takes effect which would not have been effective to perfect the security interest under [former Article 9]. This subsection does not apply to conflicting security interests each of which is perfected by the filing of such a financing statement.

PART I. PRELIMINARY PROVISIONS

§1. Name of Act

This act may be cited as Uniform Partnership Act.

§2. Definition of Terms

In this act, "Court" includes every court and judge having jurisdiction in the case.

"Business" includes every trade, occupation, or profession.

"Person" includes individuals, partnerships, corporations, and other associations.

"Bankrupt" includes bankrupt under the Federal Bankruptcy Act or insolvent under any state insolvent act.

"Conveyance" includes every assignment, lease, mortgage, or encumbrance.

"Real property" includes land and any interest or estate in land.

§3. Interpretation of Knowledge and Notice

(1) A person has "knowledge" of a fact within the meaning of this act not only when he has actual knowledge thereof, but also when he has knowledge of such other facts as in the circumstances shows bad faith.

(2) A person has "notice" of a fact within the meaning of this act when the person who claims the benefit of the notice

   (a) States the fact to such person, or

   (b) Delivers through the mail, or by other means of communication, a written statement of the fact to such person or to a proper person at his place of business or residence.

§4. Rules of Construction

(1) The rule that statutes in derogation of the common law are to be strictly construed shall have no application to this act.

(2) The law of estoppel shall apply under this act.

(3) The law of agency shall apply under this act.

(4) This act shall be so interpreted and construed as to effect its general purpose to make uniform the law of those states which enact it.

(5) This act shall not be construed so as to impair the obligations of any contract existing when the act goes into effect, nor to affect any action or proceedings begun or right accrued before this act takes effect.

§5. Rules for Cases Not Provided for in This Act

In any case not provided for in this act the rules of law and equity, including the law merchant, shall govern.

PART II. NATURE OF PARTNERSHIP

§6. Partnership Defined

(1) A partnership is an association of two or more persons to carry on as co-owners a business for profit.

COLUMN: © PHOTOGRAPHEROLYMPUS   CLOUDS: © KERTLIS

(2) But any association formed under any other statute of this state, or any statute adopted by authority, other than the authority of this state, is not a partnership under this act, unless such association would have been a partnership in this state prior to the adoption of this act; but this act shall apply to limited partnerships except in so far as the statutes relating to such partnerships are inconsistent herewith.

§7. Rules for Determining the Existence of a Partnership

In determining whether a partnership exists, these rules shall apply:

(1) Except as provided by Section 16 persons who are not partners as to each other are not partners as to third persons.

(2) Joint tenancy, tenancy in common, tenancy by the entireties, joint property, common property, or part ownership does not of itself establish a partnership, whether such co-owners do or do not share any profits made by the use of the property.

(3) The sharing of gross returns does not of itself establish a partnership, whether or not the persons sharing them have a joint or common right or interest in any property from which the returns are derived.

(4) The receipt by a person of a share of the profits of a business is prima facie evidence that he is a partner in the business, but no such inference shall be drawn if such profits were received in payment:

   (a) As a debt by installments or otherwise,

   (b) As wages of an employee or rent to a landlord,

   (c) As an annuity to a widow or representative of a deceased partner,

   (d) As interest on a loan, though the amount of payment vary with the profits of the business.

   (e) As the consideration for the sale of a good will of a business or other property by installments or otherwise.

§8. Partnership Property

(1) All property originally brought into the partnership stock or subsequently acquired by purchase or otherwise, on account of the partnership, is partnership property.

(2) Unless the contrary intention appears, property acquired with partnership funds is partnership property.

(3) Any estate in real property may be acquired in the partnership name. Title so acquired can be conveyed only in the partnership name.

(4) A conveyance to a partnership in the partnership name, though without words of inheritance, passes the entire estate of the grantor unless a contrary intent appears.

PART III. RELATIONS OF PARTNERS TO PERSONS DEALING WITH THE PARTNERSHIP

§9. Partner Agent of Partnership as to Partnership Business

(1) Every partner is an agent of the partnership for the purpose of its business, and the act of every partner, including the execution in the partnership

name of any instrument, for apparently carrying on in the usual way the business of the partnership of which he is a member binds the partnership, unless the partner so acting has in fact no authority to act for the partnership in the particular matter, and the person with whom he is dealing has knowledge of the fact that he has no such authority.

(2) An act of a partner which is not apparently for the carrying on of the business of the partnership in the usual way does not bind the partnership unless authorized by the other partners.

(3) Unless authorized by the other partners or unless they have abandoned the business, one or more but less than all the partners have no authority to:

(a) Assign the partnership property in trust for creditors or on the assignee's promise to pay the debts of the partnership,

(b) Dispose of the good will of the business,

(c) Do any other act which would make it impossible to carry on the ordinary business of a partnership,

(d) Confess a judgment,

(e) Submit a partnership claim or liability to arbitration or reference.

(4) No act of a partner in contravention of a restriction on authority shall bind the partnership to persons having knowledge of the restriction.

§10. Conveyance of Real Property of the Partnership

(1) Where title to real property is in the partnership name, any partner may convey title to such property by a conveyance executed in the partnership name; but the partnership may recover such property unless the partner's act binds the partnership under the provisions of paragraph (1) of section 9 or unless such property has been conveyed by the grantee or a person claiming through such grantee to a holder for value without knowledge that the partner, in making the conveyance, has exceeded his authority.

(2) Where title to real property is in the name of the partnership, a conveyance executed by a partner, in his own name, passes the equitable interest of the partnership, provided the act is one within the authority of the partner under the provisions of paragraph (1) of section 9.

(3) Where title to real property is in the name of one or more but not all the partners, and the record does not disclose the right of the partnership, the partners in whose name the title stands may convey title to such property, but the partnership may recover such property if the partners' act does not bind the partnership under the provisions of paragraph (1) of section 9, unless the purchaser or his assignee, is a holder for value, without knowledge.

(4) Where the title to real property is in the name of one or more or all the partners, or in a third person in trust for the partnership, a conveyance executed by a partner in the partnership name, or in his own name, passes the equitable interest of the partnership, provided the act is one within the authority of the partner under the provisions of paragraph (1) of section 9.

(5) Where the title to real property is in the names of all the partners a conveyance executed by all the partners passes all their rights in such property.

§11. Partnership Bound by Admission of Partner

An admission or representation made by any partner concerning partnership affairs within the scope of his authority as conferred by this act is evidence against the partnership.

§12. Partnership Charged With Knowledge of or Notice to Partner

Notice to any partner of any matter relating to partnership affairs, and the knowledge of the partner acting in the particular matter, acquired while a partner or then present to his mind, and the knowledge of any other partner who reasonably could and should have communicated it to the acting partner, operate as notice to or knowledge of the partnership, except in the case of a fraud on the partnership committed by or with the consent of that partner.

§13. Partnership Bound by Partner's Wrongful Act

Where, by any wrongful act or omission of any partner acting in the ordinary course of the business of the partnership or with the authority of his co-partners, loss or injury is caused to any person, not being a partner in the partnership, or any penalty is incurred, the partnership is liable therefor to the same extent as the partner so acting or omitting to act.

§14. Partnership Bound by Partner's Breach of Trust

The partnership is bound to make good the loss:

(a) Where one partner acting within the scope of his apparent authority receives money or property of a third person and misapplies it; and

(b) Where the partnership in the course of its business receives money or property of a third person and the money or property so received is misapplied by any partner while it is in the custody of the partnership.

§15. Nature of Partner's Liability

All partners are liable

(a) Jointly and severally for everything chargeable to the partnership under sections 13 and 14.

(b) Jointly for all other debts and obligations of the partnership; but any partner may enter into a separate obligation to perform a partnership contract.

§16. Partner by Estoppel

(1) When a person, by words spoken or written or by conduct, represents himself, or consents to another representing him to any one, as a partner in an existing partnership or with one or more persons not actual partners, he is liable to any such person to whom such representation has been made, who has, on the faith of such representation, given credit to the actual or apparent partnership, and if he has made such representation or consented to its being made in a public manner he is liable to such person, whether the representation has or has not been made or communicated to such person so giving credit by or with the knowledge of the apparent partner making the representation or consenting to its being made.

(a) When a partnership liability results, he is liable as though he were an actual member of the partnership.

(b) When no partnership liability results, he is liable jointly with the other persons, if any, so consenting to the contract or representation as to incur liability, otherwise separately.

(2) When a person has been thus represented to be a partner in an existing partnership, or with one or more persons not actual partners, he is an agent of the persons consenting to such representation to bind them to the same extent and in the same manner as though he were a partner in fact, with respect to persons who rely upon the representation. Where all the members of the existing partnership consent to the representation, a partnership act or obligation results; but in all other cases it is the joint act or obligation of the person acting and the persons consenting to the representation.

§17. Liability of Incoming Partner

A person admitted as a partner into an existing partnership is liable for all the obligations of the partnership arising before his admission as though he had been a partner when such obligations were incurred, except that this liability shall be satisfied only out of partnership property.

PART IV. RELATIONS OF PARTNERS TO ONE ANOTHER

§18. Rules Determining Rights and Duties of Partners

The rights and duties of the partners in relation to the partnership shall be determined, subject to any agreement between them, by the following rules:

(a) Each partner shall be repaid his contributions, whether by way of capital or advances to the partnership property and share equally in the profits and surplus remaining after all liabilities, including those to partners, are satisfied; and must contribute towards the losses, whether of capital or otherwise, sustained by the partnership according to his share in the profits.

(b) The partnership must indemnify every partner in respect of payments made and personal liabilities reasonably incurred by him in the ordinary and proper conduct of its business, or for the preservation of its business or property.

(c) A partner, who in aid of the partnership makes any payment or advance beyond the amount of capital which he agreed to contribute, shall be paid interest from the date of the payment or advance.

(d) A partner shall receive interest on the capital contributed by him only from the date when repayment should be made.

(e) All partners have equal rights in the management and conduct of the partnership business.

(f) No partner is entitled to remuneration for acting in the partnership business, except that a surviving partner is entitled to reasonable compensation for his services in winding up the partnership affairs.

(g) No person can become a member of a partnership without the consent of all the partners.

(h) Any difference arising as to ordinary matters connected with the partnership business may be decided by a majority of the partners; but no act in contravention of any agreement between the partners may be done rightfully without the consent of all the partners.

§19. Partnership Books

The partnership books shall be kept, subject to any agreement between the partners, at the principal place of business of the partnership, and every partner shall at all times have access to and may inspect and copy any of them.

§20. Duty of Partners to Render Information

Partners shall render on demand true and full information of all things affecting the partnership to any partner or the legal representative of any deceased partner or partner under legal disability.

§21. Partner Accountable as a Fiduciary

(1) Every partner must account to the partnership for any benefit, and hold as trustee for it any profits derived by him without the consent of the other partners from any transaction connected with the formation, conduct, or liquidation of the partnership or from any use by him of its property.

(2) This section applies also to the representatives of a deceased partner engaged in the liquidation of the affairs of the partnership as the personal representatives of the last surviving partner.

§22. Right to an Account

Any partner shall have the right to a formal account as to partnership affairs:

(a) If he is wrongfully excluded from the partnership business or possession of its property by his co-partners,

(b) If the right exists under the terms of any agreement,

(c) As provided by section 21,

(d) Whenever other circumstances render it just and reasonable.

§23. Continuation of Partnership Beyond Fixed Term

(1) When a partnership for a fixed term or particular undertaking is continued after the termination of such term or particular undertaking without any express agreement, the rights and duties of the partners remain the same as they were at such termination, so far as is consistent with a partnership at will.

(2) A continuation of the business by the partners or such of them as habitually acted therein during the term, without any settlement or liquidation of the partnership affairs, is prima facie evidence of a continuation of the partnership.

PART V. PROPERTY RIGHTS OF A PARTNER

§24. Extent of Property Rights of a Partner

The property rights of a partner are (1) his rights in specific partnership property, (2) his interest in the partnership, and (3) his right to participate in the management.

§25. Nature of a Partner's Right in Specific Partnership Property

(1) A partner is co-owner with his partners of specific partnership property holding as a tenant in partnership.

(2) The incidents of this tenancy are such that:

(a) A partner, subject to the provisions of this act and to any agreement between the partners, has an equal right with his partners to possess specific partnership property for partnership purposes; but he has no right to possess such property for any other purpose without the consent of his partners.

(b) A partner's right in specific partnership property is not assignable except in connection with the assignment of rights of all the partners in the same property.

(c) A partner's right in specific partnership property is not subject to attachment or execution, except on a claim against the partnership. When partnership property is attached for a partnership debt the partners, or any of them, or the representatives of a deceased partner, cannot claim any right under the homestead or exemption laws.

(d) On the death of a partner his right in specific partnership property vests in the surviving partner or partners, except where the deceased was the last surviving partner, when his right in such property vests in his legal representative. Such surviving partner or partners, or the legal representative of the last surviving partner, has no right to possess the partnership property for any but a partnership purpose.

(e) A partner's right in specific partnership property is not subject to dower, curtesy, or allowances to widows, heirs, or next of kin.

§26. Nature of Partner's Interest in the Partnership

A partner's interest in the partnership is his share of the profits and surplus, and the same is personal property.

§27. Assignment of Partner's Interest

(1) A conveyance by a partner of his interest in the partnership does not of itself dissolve the partnership, nor, as against the other partners in the absence of agreement, entitle the assignee, during the continuance of the partnership to interfere in the management or administration of the partnership business or affairs, or to require any information or account of partnership transactions, or to inspect the partnership books; but it merely entitles the assignee to receive in accordance with his contract the profits to which the assigning partner would otherwise be entitled.

(2) In case of a dissolution of the partnership, the assignee is entitled to receive his assignor's interest and may require an account from the date only of the last account agreed to by all the partners.

§28. Partner's Interest Subject to Charging Order

(1) On due application to a competent court by any judgment creditor of a partner, the court which entered the judgment, order, or decree, or any other court, may charge the interest of the debtor partner with payment of the unsatisfied amount of such judgment debt with interest thereon; and may then or later appoint a receiver of his share of the profits, and of any other money due or to fall due to him in respect of the partnership, and make all other orders, directions, accounts and inquiries which the debtor partner might have made, or which the circumstances of the case may require.

(2) The interest charged may be redeemed at any time before foreclosure, or in case of a sale being directed by the court may be purchased without thereby causing a dissolution:

(a) With separate property, by any one or more of the partners, or

(b) With partnership property, by any one or more of the partners with the consent of all the partners whose interests are not so charged or sold.

(3) Nothing in this act shall be held to deprive a partner of his right, if any, under the exemption laws, as regards his interest in the partnership.

PART VI. DISSOLUTION AND WINDING UP

§29. Dissolution Defined

The dissolution of a partnership is the change in the relation of the partners caused by any partner ceasing to be associated in the carrying on as distinguished from the winding up of the business.

§30. Partnership Not Terminated by Dissolution

On dissolution the partnership is not terminated, but continues until the winding up of partnership affairs is completed.

§31. Causes of Dissolution

Dissolution is caused:

(1) Without violation of the agreement between the partners,

(a) By the termination of the definite term or particular undertaking specified in the agreement,

(b) By the express will of any partner when no definite term or particular undertaking is specified,

(c) By the express will of all the partners who have not assigned their interests or suffered them to be charged for their separate debts, either before or after the termination of any specified term or particular undertaking,

(d) By the expulsion of any partner from the business bona fide in accordance with such a power conferred by the agreement between the partners;

(2) In contravention of the agreement between the partners, where the circumstances do not permit a dissolution under any other provision of this section, by the express will of any partner at any time;

(3) By any event which makes it unlawful for the business of the partnership to be carried on or for the members to carry it on in partnership;

(4) By the death of any partner;

(5) By the bankruptcy of any partner or the partnership;

(6) By decree of court under section 32.

§32. Dissolution by Decree of Court

(1) On application by or for a partner the court shall decree a dissolution whenever:

(a) A partner has been declared a lunatic in any judicial proceeding or is shown to be of unsound mind,

(b) A partner becomes in any other way incapable of performing his part of the partnership contract,

(c) A partner has been guilty of such conduct as tends to affect prejudicially the carrying on of the business,

(d) A partner wilfully or persistently commits a breach of the partnership agreement, or otherwise so conducts himself in matters relating to the partnership business that it is not reasonably practicable to carry on the business in partnership with him,

(e) The business of the partnership can only be carried on at a loss,

(f) Other circumstances render a dissolution equitable.

(2) On the application of the purchaser of a partner's interest under sections 27 or 28:

(a) After the termination of the specified term or particular undertaking,

(b) At any time if the partnership was a partnership at will when the interest was assigned or when the charging order was issued.

§33. General Effect of Dissolution on Authority of Partner

Except so far as may be necessary to wind up partnership affairs or to complete transactions begun but not then finished, dissolution terminates all authority of any partner to act for the partnership,

(1) With respect to the partners,

(a) When the dissolution is not by the act, bankruptcy or death of a partner; or

(b) When the dissolution is by such act, bankruptcy or death of a partner, in cases where section 34 so requires.

(2) With respect to persons not partners, as declared in section 35.

§34. Right of Partner to Contribution From Copartners After Dissolution

Where the dissolution is caused by the act, death or bankruptcy of a partner, each partner is liable to his copartners for his share of any liability created by any partner acting for the partnership as if the partnership had not been dissolved unless

(a) The dissolution being by act of any partner, the partner acting for the partnership had knowledge of the dissolution, or

(b) The dissolution being by the death or bankruptcy of a partner, the partner acting for the partnership had knowledge or notice of the death or bankruptcy.

§35. Power of Partner to Bind Partnership to Third Persons After Dissolution

(1) After dissolution a partner can bind the partnership except as provided in Paragraph (3)

(a) By any act appropriate for winding up partnership affairs or completing transactions unfinished at dissolution;

(b) By any transaction which would bind the partnership if dissolution had not taken place, provided the other party to the transaction.

(I) Had extended credit to the partnership prior to dissolution and had no knowledge or notice of the dissolution; or

(II) Though he had not so extended credit, had nevertheless known of the partnership prior to dissolution, and, having no knowledge or notice of dissolution, the fact of dissolution had not been advertised in a newspaper of general circulation in the place (or in each place if more than one) at which the partnership business was regularly carried on.

(2) The liability of a partner under paragraph (1b) shall be satisfied out of partnership assets alone when such partner had been prior to dissolution

(a) Unknown as a partner to the person with whom the contract is made; and

(b) So far unknown and inactive in partnership affairs that the business reputation of the partnership could not be said to have been in any degree due to his connection with it.

(3) The partnership is in no case bound by any act of a partner after dissolution

(a) Where the partnership is dissolved because it is unlawful to carry on the business, unless the act is appropriate for winding up partnership affairs; or

(b) Where the partner has become bankrupt; or

(c) Where the partner has no authority to wind up partnership affairs; except by a transaction with one who

(I) Had extended credit to the partnership prior to dissolution and had no knowledge or notice of his want of authority; or

(II) Had not extended credit to the partnership prior to dissolution, and, having no knowledge or notice of his want of authority, the fact of his want of authority has not been advertised in the manner provided for advertising the fact of dissolution in paragraph (1bII).

(4) Nothing in this section shall affect the liability under section 16 of any person who after dissolution represents himself or consents to another representing him as a partner in a partnership engaged in carrying on business.

§36. Effect of Dissolution on Partner's Existing Liability

(1) The dissolution of the partnership does not of itself discharge the existing liability of any partner.

(2) A partner is discharged from any existing liability upon dissolution of the partnership by an agreement to that effect between himself, the partnership creditor and the person or partnership continuing the business; and such agreement may be inferred from the course of dealing between the creditor having knowledge of the dissolution and the person or partnership continuing the business.

(3) Where a person agrees to assume the existing obligations of a dissolved partnership, the partners whose obligations have been assumed shall be discharged from any liability to any creditor of the partnership who, knowing of the agreement, consents to a material alteration in the nature or time of payment of such obligations.

(4) The individual property of a deceased partner shall be liable for all obligations of the partnership incurred while he was a partner but subject to the prior payment of his separate debts.

§37. Right to Wind Up

Unless otherwise agreed the partners who have not wrongfully dissolved the partnership or the legal representative of the last surviving partner, not bankrupt, has the right to wind up the partnership affairs; provided, however, that any partner, his legal representative or his assignee, upon cause shown, may obtain winding up by the court.

§38. Rights of Partners to Application of Partnership Property

(1) When dissolution is caused in any way, except in contravention of the partnership agreement, each partner as against his co-partners and all persons claiming through them in respect of their interests in the partnership, unless otherwise agreed, may have the partnership property applied to discharge its liabilities, and the surplus applied to pay in cash the net amount owing to the respective partners. But if dissolution is caused by expulsion of a partner, bona fide under the partnership agreement and if the expelled partner is discharged from all partnership liabilities, either by payment or agreement under section 36(2), he shall receive in cash only the net amount due him from the partnership.

(2) When dissolution is caused in contravention of the partnership agreement the rights of the partners shall be as follows:

(a Each partner who has not caused dissolution wrongfully shall have,

(I) All the rights specified in paragr

aph (1) of this section, and

(II) The right, as against each partner who has caused the dissolution wrongfully, to damages for breach of the agreement.

(b) The partners who have not caused the dissolution wrongfully, if they all desire to continue the business in the same name, either by themselves or jointly with others, may do so, during the agreed term for the partnership and for that purpose may possess the partnership property, provided they secure the payment by bond approved by the court, or pay to any partner who has caused the dissolution wrongfully, the value of his interest in the partnership at the dissolution, less any damages recoverable under clause (2aII) of the section, and in like manner indemnify him against all present or future partnership liabilities.

(c) A partner who has caused the dissolution wrongfully shall have:

(I) If the business is not continued under the provisions of paragraph (2b) all the rights of a partner under paragraph (1), subject to clause (2aII), of this section,

(II) If the business is continued under paragraph (2b) of this section the right as against his co-partners and all claiming through them in respect of their interests in the partnership, to have the value of his interest in the partnership, less any damages caused to his co-partners by the dissolution, ascertained and paid to him in cash, or the payment secured by bond approved by the court, and to be released from all existing liabilities of the partnership; but in ascertaining the value of the partner's interest the value of the good will of the business shall not be considered.

§39. Rights Where Partnership Is Dissolved for Fraud or Misrepresentation

Where a partnership contract is rescinded on the ground of the fraud or misrepresentation of one of the parties thereto, the party entitled to rescind is, without prejudice to any other right, entitled,

(a) To a lien on, or right of retention of, the surplus of the partnership property after satisfying the partnership liabilities to third persons for any sum of money paid by him for the purchase of an interest in the partnership and for any capital or advances contributed by him; and

(b) To stand, after all liabilities to third persons have been satisfied, in the place of the creditors of the partnership for any payments made by him in respect of the partnership liabilities; and

(c) To be indemnified by the person guilty of the fraud or making the representation against all debts and liabilities of the partnership.

§40. Rules for Distribution

In settling accounts between the partners after dissolution, the following rules shall be observed, subject to any agreement to the contrary:

(a) The assets of the partnership are:

(I) The partnership property,

(II) The contributions of the partners necessary for the payment of all the liabilities specified in clause (b) of this paragraph.

(b) The liabilities of the partnership shall rank in order of payment, as follows:

(I) Those owing to creditors other than partners,

(II) Those owing to partners other than for capital and profits,

(III) Those owing to partners in respect of capital,

(IV) Those owing to partners in respect of profits.

(c) The assets shall be applied in the order of their declaration in clause (a) of this paragraph to the satisfaction of the liabilities.

(d) The partners shall contribute, as provided by section 18(a) the amount necessary to satisfy the liabilities; but if any, but not all, of the partners are insolvent, or, not being subject to process, refuse to contribute, the other parties shall contribute their share of the liabilities, and, in the relative proportions in which they share the profits, the additional amount necessary to pay the liabilities.

(e) An assignee for the benefit of creditors or any person appointed by the court shall have the right to enforce the contributions specified in clause (d) of this paragraph.

(f) Any partner or his legal representative shall have the right to enforce the contributions specified in clause (d) of this paragraph, to the extent of the amount which he has paid in excess of his share of the liability.

(g) The individual property of a deceased partner shall be liable for the contributions specified in clause (d) of this paragraph.

(h) When partnership property and the individual properties of the partners are in possession of a court for distribution, partnership creditors shall have priority on partnership property and separate creditors on individual property, saving the rights of lien or secured creditors as heretofore.

(i) Where a partner has become bankrupt or his estate is insolvent the claims against his separate property shall rank in the following order:

(I) Those owing to separate creditors,

(II) Those owing to partnership creditors,

(III) Those owing to partners by way of contribution.

§41. Liability of Persons Continuing the Business in Certain Cases

(1) When any new partner is admitted into an existing partnership, or when any partner retires and assigns (or the representative of the deceased partner assigns) his rights in partnership property to two or more of the partners, or to one or more of the partners and one or more third persons, if the business is continued without liquidation of the partnership affairs, creditors of the first or dissolved partnership are also creditors of the person or partnership so continuing the business.

(2) When all but one partner retire and assign (or the representative of a deceased partner assigns) their rights in partnership property to the remaining partner, who continues the business without liquidation of partnership affairs, either alone or with others, creditors of the dissolved partnership are also creditors of the person or partnership so continuing the business.

(3) When any partner retires or dies and the business of the dissolved partnership is continued as set forth in paragraphs (1) and (2) of this section, with the consent of the retired partners or the representative of the deceased partner, but without any assignment of his right in partnership property, rights of creditors of the dissolved partnership and of the creditors of the person or partnership continuing the business shall be as if such assignment had been made.

(4) When all the partners or their representatives assign their rights in partnership property to one or more third persons who promise to pay the debts and who continue the business of the dissolved partnership, creditors of the dissolved partnership are also creditors of the person or partnership continuing the business.

(5) When any partner wrongfully causes a dissolution and the remaining partners continue the business under the provisions of section 38(2b), either alone or with others, and without liquidation of the partnership affairs, creditors of the dissolved partnership are also creditors of the person or partnership continuing the business.

(6) When a partner is expelled and the remaining partners continue the business either alone or with others, without liquidation of the partnership

affairs, creditors of the dissolved partnership are also creditors of the person or partnership continuing the business.

(7) The liability of a third person becoming a partner in the partnership continuing the business, under this section, to the creditors of the dissolved partnership shall be satisfied out of partnership property only.

(8) When the business of a partnership after dissolution is continued under any conditions set forth in this section the creditors of the dissolved partnership, as against the separate creditors of the retiring or deceased partner or the representative of the deceased partner, have a prior right to any claim of the retired partner or the representative of the deceased partner against the person or partnership continuing the business, on account of the retired or deceased partner's interest in the dissolved partnership or on account of any consideration promised for such interest or for his right in partnership property.

(9) Nothing in this section shall be held to modify any right of creditors to set aside any assignment on the ground of fraud.

(10) The use by the person or partnership continuing the business of the partnership name, or the name of a deceased partner as part thereof, shall not of itself make the individual property of the deceased partner liable for any debts contracted by such person or partnership.

§42. Rights of Retiring or Estate of Deceased Partner When the Business Is Continued

When any partner retires or dies, and the business is continued under any of the conditions set forth in section 41(1, 2, 3, 5, 6), or section 38(2b), without any settlement of accounts as between him or his estate and the person or partnership continuing the business, unless otherwise agreed, he or his legal representative as against such persons or partnership may have the value of his interest at the date of dissolution ascertained, and shall receive as an ordinary creditor an amount equal to the value of his interest in the dissolved partnership with interest, or, at his option or at the option of his legal representative, in lieu of interest, the profits attributable to the use of his right in the property of the dissolved partnership; provided that the creditors of the dissolved partnership as against the separate creditors, or the representative of the retired or deceased partner, shall have priority on any claim arising under this section, as provided by section 41(8) of this act.

§43. Accrual of Actions

The right to an account of his interest shall accrue to any partner, or his legal representative, as against the winding up partners or the surviving partners or the person or partnership continuing the business, at the date of dissolution, in the absence of any agreement to the contrary.

PART VII. MISCELLANEOUS PROVISIONS

§44. When Act Takes Effect

This act shall take effect on the _____ day of _____ one thousand nine hundred and _____.

§45. Legislation Repealed

All acts or parts of acts inconsistent with this act are hereby repealed.

Revised Uniform Partnership Act (Selected Provisions)

[ARTICLE] 1
GENERAL PROVISIONS
SECTION 101. DEFINITIONS.

In this [Act]:

(1) "Business" includes every trade, occupation, and profession.

(2) "Debtor in bankruptcy" means a person who is the subject of:

(i) an order for relief under Title 11 of the United States Code or a comparable order under a successor statute of general application; or

(ii) a comparable order under federal, state, or foreign law governing insolvency.

(3) "Distribution" means a transfer of money or other property from a partnership to a partner in the partner's capacity as a partner or to the partner's transferee.

(4) "Foreign limited liability partnership" means a partnership that:

(i) is formed under laws other than the laws of this State; and

(ii) has the status of a limited liability partnership under those laws.

(5) "Limited liability partnership" means a partnership that has filed a statement of qualification under Section 1001 and does not have a similar statement in effect in any other jurisdiction.

(6) "Partnership" means an association of two or more persons to carry on as co-owners a business for profit formed under Section 202, predecessor law, or comparable law of another jurisdiction.

(7) "Partnership agreement" means the agreement, whether written, oral, or implied, among the partners concerning the partnership, including amendments to the partnership agreement.

(8) "Partnership at will" means a partnership in which the partners have not agreed to remain partners until the expiration of a definite term or the completion of a particular undertaking.

(9) "Partnership interest" or "partner's interest in the partnership" means all of a partner's interests in the partnership, including the partner's transferable interest and all management and other rights.

(10) "Person" means an individual, corporation, business trust, estate, trust, partnership, association, joint venture, government, governmental subdivision, agency, or instrumentality, or any other legal or commercial entity.

(11) "Property" means all property, real, personal, or mixed, tangible or intangible, or any interest therein.

(12) "State" means a State of the United States, the District of Columbia, the Commonwealth of Puerto Rico, or any territory or insular possession subject to the jurisdiction of the United States.

(13) "Statement" means a statement of partnership authority under Section 303, a statement of denial under Section 304, a statement of dissociation under Section 704, a statement of dissolution under Section 805, a statement of merger under Section 907, a statement of qualification under Section 1001, a statement of foreign qualification under Section 1102, or an amendment or cancellation of any of the foregoing.

(14) "Transfer" includes an assignment, conveyance, lease, mortgage, deed, and encumbrance.

SECTION 102. KNOWLEDGE AND NOTICE.

(a) A person knows a fact if the person has actual knowledge of it.

(b) A person has notice of a fact if the person:

(1) knows of it;

(2) has received a notification of it; or

(3) has reason to know it exists from all of the facts known to the person at the time in question.

(c) A person notifies or gives a notification to another by taking steps reasonably required to inform the other person in ordinary course, whether or not the other person learns of it.

(d) A person receives a notification when the notification:

(1) comes to the person's attention; or

(2) is duly delivered at the person's place of business or at any other place held out by the person as a place for receiving communications.

(e) Except as otherwise provided in subsection (f), a person other than an individual knows, has notice, or receives a notification of a fact for purposes of a particular transaction when the individual conducting the transaction knows, has notice, or receives a notification of the fact, or in any event when the fact would have been brought to the individual's attention if the person had exercised reasonable diligence. The person exercises reasonable diligence if it maintains reasonable routines for communicating significant information to the individual conducting the transaction and there is reasonable compliance with the routines. Reasonable diligence does not require an individual acting for the person to communicate information unless the communication is part of the individual's regular duties or the individual has reason to know of the transaction and that the transaction would be materially affected by the information.

(f) A partner's knowledge, notice, or receipt of a notification of a fact relating to the partnership is effective immediately as knowledge by, notice to, or receipt of a notification by the partnership, except in the case of a fraud on the partnership committed by or with the consent of that partner.

SECTION 103. EFFECT OF PARTNERSHIP AGREEMENT; NONWAIVABLE PROVISIONS.

(a) Except as otherwise provided in subsection (b), relations among the partners and between the partners and the partnership are governed by the partnership agreement. To the extent the partnership agreement does not otherwise provide, this [Act] governs relations among the partners and between the partners and the partnership.

(b) The partnership agreement may not:

(1) vary the rights and duties under Section 105 except to eliminate the duty to provide copies of statements to all of the partners;

(2) unreasonably restrict the right of access to books and records under Section 403(b);

(3) eliminate the duty of loyalty under Section 404(b) or 603(b)(3), but:

(i) the partnership agreement may identify specific types or categories of activities that do not violate the duty of loyalty, if not manifestly unreasonable; or

(ii) all of the partners or a number or percentage specified in the partnership agreement may authorize or ratify, after full disclosure of all material facts, a specific act or transaction that otherwise would violate the duty of loyalty;

(4) unreasonably reduce the duty of care under Section 404(c) or 603(b)(3);

(5) eliminate the obligation of good faith and fair dealing under Section 404(d), but the partnership agreement may prescribe the standards by which the performance of the obligation is to be measured, if the standards are not manifestly unreasonable;

(6) vary the power to dissociate as a partner under Section 602(a), except to require the notice under Section 601(1) to be in writing;

(7) vary the right of a court to expel a partner in the events specified in Section 601(5);

(8) vary the requirement to wind up the partnership business in cases specified in Section 801(4), (5), or (6);

(9) vary the law applicable to a limited liability partnership under Section 106(b); or

(10) restrict rights of third parties under this [Act].

SECTION 104. SUPPLEMENTAL PRINCIPLES OF LAW.

(a) Unless displaced by particular provisions of this [Act], the principles of law and equity supplement this [Act].

(b) If an obligation to pay interest arises under this [Act] and the rate is not specified, the rate is that specified in [applicable statute].

[ARTICLE] 2

NATURE OF PARTNERSHIP

SECTION 201. PARTNERSHIP AS ENTITY.

(a) A partnership is an entity distinct from its partners.

(b) A limited liability partnership continues to be the same entity that existed before the filing of a statement of qualification under Section 1001.

SECTION 202. FORMATION OF PARTNERSHIP.

(a) Except as otherwise provided in subsection (b), the association of two or more persons to carry on as co-owners a business for profit forms a partnership, whether or not the persons intend to form a partnership.

(b) An association formed under a statute other than this [Act], a predecessor statute, or a comparable statute of another jurisdiction is not a partnership under this [Act].

(c) In determining whether a partnership is formed, the following rules apply:

(1) Joint tenancy, tenancy in common, tenancy by the entireties, joint property, common property, or part ownership does not by itself establish a partnership, even if the co-owners share profits made by the use of the property.

(2) The sharing of gross returns does not by itself establish a partnership, even if the persons sharing them have a joint or common right or interest in property from which the returns are derived.

(3) A person who receives a share of the profits of a business is presumed to be a partner in the business, unless the profits were received in payment:

(i) of a debt by installments or otherwise;

(ii) for services as an independent contractor or of wages or other compensation to an employee;

(iii) of rent;

(iv) of an annuity or other retirement or health benefit to a beneficiary, representative, or designee of a deceased or retired partner;

(v) of interest or other charge on a loan, even if the amount of payment varies with the profits of the business, including a direct or indirect present or future ownership of the collateral, or rights to income, proceeds, or increase in value derived from the collateral; or

(vi) for the sale of the goodwill of a business or other property by installments or otherwise.

SECTION 203. PARTNERSHIP PROPERTY.

Property acquired by a partnership is property of the partnership and not of the partners individually.

SECTION 204. WHEN PROPERTY IS PARTNERSHIP PROPERTY.

(a) Property is partnership property if acquired in the name of:

(1) the partnership; or

(2) one or more partners with an indication in the instrument transferring title to the property of the person's capacity as a partner or of the existence of a partnership but without an indication of the name of the partnership.

(b) Property is acquired in the name of the partnership by a transfer to:

(1) the partnership in its name; or

(2) one or more partners in their capacity as partners in the partnership, if the name of the partnership is indicated in the instrument transferring title to the property.

(c) Property is presumed to be partnership property if purchased with partnership assets, even if not acquired in the name of the partnership or of one or more partners with an indication in the instrument transferring title to the property of the person's capacity as a partner or of the existence of a partnership.

(d) Property acquired in the name of one or more of the partners, without an indication in the instrument transferring title to the property of the person's capacity as a partner or of the existence of a partnership and without use of partnership assets, is presumed to be separate property, even if used for partnership purposes.

[ARTICLE] 3

RELATIONS OF PARTNERS TO PERSONS DEALING WITH PARTNERSHIP

SECTION 301. PARTNER AGENT OF PARTNERSHIP.

Subject to the effect of a statement of partnership authority under Section 303:

(1) Each partner is an agent of the partnership for the purpose of its business. An act of a partner, including the execution of an instrument in the partnership name, for apparently carrying on in the ordinary course the partnership business or business of the kind carried on by the partnership binds the partnership, unless the partner had no authority to act for the partnership in the particular matter and the person with whom the partner was dealing knew or had received a notification that the partner lacked authority.

(2) An act of a partner which is not apparently for carrying on in the ordinary course the partnership business or business of the kind carried on by the partnership binds the partnership only if the act was authorized by the other partners.

SECTION 303. STATEMENT OF PARTNERSHIP AUTHORITY.

(a) A partnership may file a statement of partnership authority, which:

(1) must include:

(i) the name of the partnership;

(ii) the street address of its chief executive office and of one office in this State, if there is one;

(iii) the names and mailing addresses of all of the partners or of an agent appointed and maintained by the partnership for the purpose of subsection (b); and

(iv) the names of the partners authorized to execute an instrument transferring real property held in the name of the partnership; and

(2) may state the authority, or limitations on the authority, of some or all of the partners to enter into other transactions on behalf of the partnership and any other matter.

(b) If a statement of partnership authority names an agent, the agent shall maintain a list of the names and mailing addresses of all of the partners and make it available to any person on request for good cause shown.

(c) If a filed statement of partnership authority is executed pursuant to Section 105(c) and states the name of the partnership but does not contain all of the other information required by subsection (a), the statement nevertheless operates with respect to a person not a partner as provided in subsections (d) and (e).

(d) Except as otherwise provided in subsection (g), a filed statement of partnership authority supplements the authority of a partner to enter into transactions on behalf of the partnership as follows:

(1) Except for transfers of real property, a grant of authority contained in a filed statement of partnership authority is conclusive in favor of a person who gives value without knowledge to the contrary, so long as and to the extent that a limitation on that authority is not then contained in another filed statement. A filed cancellation of a limitation on authority revives the previous grant of authority.

(2) A grant of authority to transfer real property held in the name of the partnership contained in a certified copy of a filed statement of partnership authority recorded in the office for recording transfers of that real property is conclusive in favor of a person who gives value without knowledge to the contrary, so long as and to the extent that a certified copy of a filed statement containing a limitation on that authority is not then of record in the office for recording transfers of that real property. The recording in the office for recording transfers of that real property of a certified copy of a filed cancellation of a limitation on authority revives the previous grant of authority.

(e) A person not a partner is deemed to know of a limitation on the authority of a partner to transfer real property held in the name of the partnership if a certified copy of the filed statement containing the limitation on authority is of record in the office for recording transfers of that real property.

(f) Except as otherwise provided in subsections (d) and (e) and Sections 704 and 805, a person not a partner is not deemed to know of a limitation on the authority of a partner merely because the limitation is contained in a filed statement.

(g) Unless earlier canceled, a filed statement of partnership authority is canceled by operation of law five years after the date on which the statement, or the most recent amendment, was filed with the [Secretary of State].

SECTION 305. PARTNERSHIP LIABLE FOR PARTNER'S ACTIONABLE CONDUCT.

(a) A partnership is liable for loss or injury caused to a person, or for a penalty incurred, as a result of a wrongful act or omission, or other actionable conduct, of a partner acting in the ordinary course of business of the partnership or with authority of the partnership.

(b) If, in the course of the partnership's business or while acting with authority of the partnership, a partner receives or causes the partnership to receive money or property of a person not a partner, and the money or property is misapplied by a partner, the partnership is liable for the loss.

SECTION 306. PARTNER'S LIABILITY.

(a) Except as otherwise provided in subsections (b) and (c), all partners are liable jointly and severally for all obligations of the partnership unless otherwise agreed by the claimant or provided by law.

(b) A person admitted as a partner into an existing partnership is not personally liable for any partnership obligation incurred before the person's admission as a partner.

(c) An obligation of a partnership incurred while the partnership is a limited liability partnership, whether arising in contract, tort, or otherwise, is solely the obligation of the partnership. A partner is not personally liable, directly or indirectly, by way of contribution or otherwise, for such an obligation solely by reason of being or so acting as a partner. This subsection applies notwithstanding anything inconsistent in the partnership agreement that existed immediately before the vote required to become a limited liability partnership under Section 1001(b).

SECTION 307. ACTIONS BY AND AGAINST PARTNERSHIP AND PARTNERS.

(a) A partnership may sue and be sued in the name of the partnership.

(b) An action may be brought against the partnership and, to the extent not inconsistent with Section 306, any or all of the partners in the same action or in separate actions.

(c) A judgment against a partnership is not by itself a judgment against a partner. A judgment against a partnership may not be satisfied from a partner's assets unless there is also a judgment against the partner.

(d) A judgment creditor of a partner may not levy execution against the assets of the partner to satisfy a judgment based on a claim against the partnership unless the partner is personally liable for the claim under Section 306 and:

(1) a judgment based on the same claim has been obtained against the partnership and a writ of execution on the judgment has been returned unsatisfied in whole or in part;

(2) the partnership is a debtor in bankruptcy;

(3) the partner has agreed that the creditor need not exhaust partnership assets;

(4) a court grants permission to the judgment creditor to levy execution against the assets of a partner based on a finding that partnership assets subject to execution are clearly insufficient to satisfy the judgment, that exhaustion of partnership assets is excessively burdensome, or that the grant of permission is an appropriate exercise of the court's equitable powers; or

(5) liability is imposed on the partner by law or contract independent of the existence of the partnership.

(e) This section applies to any partnership liability or obligation resulting from a representation by a partner or purported partner under Section 308.

SECTION 308. LIABILITY OF PURPORTED PARTNER.

(a) If a person, by words or conduct, purports to be a partner, or consents to being represented by another as a partner, in a partnership or with one or more persons not partners, the purported partner is liable to a person to whom the representation is made, if that person, relying on the representation, enters into a transaction with the actual or purported partnership. If the representation, either by the purported partner or by a person with the purported partner's consent, is made in a public manner, the purported partner is liable to a person who relies upon the purported partnership even if the purported partner is not aware of being held out as a partner to the claimant. If partnership liability results, the purported partner is liable with respect to that liability as if the purported partner were a partner. If no partnership liability results, the purported partner is liable with respect to that liability jointly and severally with any other person consenting to the representation.

(b) If a person is thus represented to be a partner in an existing partnership, or with one or more persons not partners, the purported partner is an agent of persons consenting to the representation to bind them to the same extent and in the same manner as if the purported partner were a partner, with respect to persons who enter into transactions in reliance upon the representation. If all of the partners of the existing partnership consent to the representation, a partnership act or obligation results. If fewer than all of the partners of the existing partnership consent to the representation, the person acting and the partners consenting to the representation are jointly and severally liable.

(c) A person is not liable as a partner merely because the person is named by another in a statement of partnership authority.

(d) A person does not continue to be liable as a partner merely because of a failure to file a statement of dissociation or to amend a statement of partnership authority to indicate the partner's dissociation from the partnership.

(e) Except as otherwise provided in subsections (a) and (b), persons who are not partners as to each other are not liable as partners to other persons.

[ARTICLE] 4

RELATIONS OF PARTNERS TO EACH OTHER AND TO PARTNERSHIP

SECTION 401. PARTNER'S RIGHTS AND DUTIES.

(a) Each partner is deemed to have an account that is:

(1) credited with an amount equal to the money plus the value of any other property, net of the amount of any liabilities, the partner contributes to the partnership and the partner's share of the partnership profits; and

(2) charged with an amount equal to the money plus the value of any other property, net of the amount of any liabilities, distributed by the partnership to the partner and the partner's share of the partnership losses.

(b) Each partner is entitled to an equal share of the partnership profits and is chargeable with a share of the partnership losses in proportion to the partner's share of the profits.

(c) A partnership shall reimburse a partner for payments made and indemnify a partner for liabilities incurred by the partner in the ordinary course of the business of the partnership or for the preservation of its business or property.

(d) A partnership shall reimburse a partner for an advance to the partnership beyond the amount of capital the partner agreed to contribute.

(e) A payment or advance made by a partner which gives rise to a partnership obligation under subsection (c) or (d) constitutes a loan to the partnership which accrues interest from the date of the payment or advance.

(f) Each partner has equal rights in the management and conduct of the partnership business.

(g) A partner may use or possess partnership property only on behalf of the partnership.

(h) A partner is not entitled to remuneration for services performed for the partnership, except for reasonable compensation for services rendered in winding up the business of the partnership.

(i) A person may become a partner only with the consent of all of the partners.

(j) A difference arising as to a matter in the ordinary course of business of a partnership may be decided by a majority of the partners. An act outside the ordinary course of business of a partnership and an amendment to the partnership agreement may be undertaken only with the consent of all of the partners.

(k) This section does not affect the obligations of a partnership to other persons under Section 301.

SECTION 402. DISTRIBUTIONS IN KIND.

A partner has no right to receive, and may not be required to accept, a distribution in kind.

SECTION 403. PARTNER'S RIGHTS AND DUTIES WITH RESPECT TO INFORMATION.

(a) A partnership shall keep its books and records, if any, at its chief executive office.

(b) A partnership shall provide partners and their agents and attorneys access to its books and records. It shall provide former partners and their agents and attorneys access to books and records pertaining to the period during which they were partners. The right of access provides the opportunity to inspect and copy books and records during ordinary business hours. A partnership may impose a reasonable charge, covering the costs of labor and material, for copies of documents furnished.

(c) Each partner and the partnership shall furnish to a partner, and to the legal representative of a deceased partner or partner under legal disability:

(1) without demand, any information concerning the partnership's business and affairs reasonably required for the proper exercise of the partner's rights and duties under the partnership agreement or this [Act]; and

(2) on demand, any other information concerning the partnership's business and affairs, except to the extent the demand or the information demanded is unreasonable or otherwise improper under the circumstances.

SECTION 404. GENERAL STANDARDS OF PARTNER'S CONDUCT.

(a) The only fiduciary duties a partner owes to the partnership and the other partners are the duty of loyalty and the duty of care set forth in subsections (b) and (c).

(b) A partner's duty of loyalty to the partnership and the other partners is limited to the following:

(1) to account to the partnership and hold as trustee for it any property, profit, or benefit derived by the partner in the conduct and winding up of the partnership business or derived from a use by the partner of partnership property, including the appropriation of a partnership opportunity;

(2) to refrain from dealing with the partnership in the conduct or winding up of the partnership business as or on behalf of a party having an interest adverse to the partnership; and

(3) to refrain from competing with the partnership in the conduct of the partnership business before the dissolution of the partnership.

(c) A partner's duty of care to the partnership and the other partners in the conduct and winding up of the partnership business is limited to refraining from engaging in grossly negligent or reckless conduct, intentional misconduct, or a knowing violation of law.

(d) A partner shall discharge the duties to the partnership and the other partners under this [Act] or under the partnership agreement and exercise any rights consistently with the obligation of good faith and fair dealing.

(e) A partner does not violate a duty or obligation under this [Act] or under the partnership agreement merely because the partner's conduct furthers the partner's own interest.

(f) A partner may lend money to and transact other business with the partnership, and as to each loan or transaction the rights and obligations of the partner are the same as those of a person who is not a partner, subject to other applicable law.

(g) This section applies to a person winding up the partnership business as the personal or legal representative of the last surviving partner as if the person were a partner.

SECTION 405. ACTIONS BY PARTNERSHIP AND PARTNERS.

(a) A partnership may maintain an action against a partner for a breach of the partnership agreement, or for the violation of a duty to the partnership, causing harm to the partnership.

(b) A partner may maintain an action against the partnership or another partner for legal or equitable relief, with or without an accounting as to partnership business, to:

(1) enforce the partner's rights under the partnership agreement;

(2) enforce the partner's rights under this [Act], including:

(i) the partner's rights under Sections 401, 403, or 404;

(ii) the partner's right on dissociation to have the partner's interest in the partnership purchased pursuant to Section 701 or enforce any other right under [Article] 6 or 7; or

(iii) the partner's right to compel a dissolution and winding up of the partnership business under or enforce any other right under [Article] 8; or

(3) enforce the rights and otherwise protect the interests of the partner, including rights and interests arising independently of the partnership relationship.

(c) The accrual of, and any time limitation on, a right of action for a remedy under this section is governed by other law. A right to an accounting upon a dissolution and winding up does not revive a claim barred by law.

SECTION 406. CONTINUATION OF PARTNERSHIP BEYOND DEFINITE TERM OR PARTICULAR UNDERTAKING.

(a) If a partnership for a definite term or particular undertaking is continued, without an express agreement, after the expiration of the term or completion of the undertaking, the rights and duties of the partners remain the same as they were at the expiration or completion, so far as is consistent with a partnership at will.

(b) If the partners, or those of them who habitually acted in the business during the term or undertaking, continue the business without any settlement or liquidation of the partnership, they are presumed to have agreed that the partnership will continue.

[ARTICLE] 5
TRANSFEREES AND CREDITORS OF PARTNER

SECTION 501. PARTNER NOT CO-OWNER OF PARTNERSHIP PROPERTY.

A partner is not a co-owner of partnership property and has no interest in partnership property which can be transferred, either voluntarily or involuntarily.

SECTION 502. PARTNER'S TRANSFERABLE INTEREST IN PARTNERSHIP.

The only transferable interest of a partner in the partnership is the partner's share of the profits and losses of the partnership and the partner's right to receive distributions. The interest is personal property.

SECTION 503. TRANSFER OF PARTNER'S TRANSFERABLE INTEREST.

(a) A transfer, in whole or in part, of a partner's transferable interest in the partnership:

    (1) is permissible;

    (2) does not by itself cause the partner's dissociation or a dissolution and winding up of the partnership business; and

    (3) does not, as against the other partners or the partnership, entitle the transferee, during the continuance of the partnership, to participate in the management or conduct of the partnership business, to require access to information concerning partnership transactions, or to inspect or copy the partnership books or records.

(b) A transferee of a partner's transferable interest in the partnership has a right:

    (1) to receive, in accordance with the transfer, distributions to which the transferor would otherwise be entitled;

    (2) to receive upon the dissolution and winding up of the partnership business, in accordance with the transfer, the net amount otherwise distributable to the transferor; and

    (3) to seek under (6) a judicial determination that it is equitable to wind up the partnership business.

(c) In a dissolution and winding up, a transferee is entitled to an account of partnership transactions only from the date of the latest account agreed to by all of the partners.

(d) Upon transfer, the transferor retains the rights and duties of a partner other than the interest in distributions transferred.

(e) A partnership need not give effect to a transferee's rights under this section until it has notice of the transfer.

(f) A transfer of a partner's transferable interest in the partnership in violation of a restriction on transfer contained in the partnership agreement is ineffective as to a person having notice of the restriction at the time of transfer.

SECTION 504. PARTNER'S TRANSFERABLE INTEREST SUBJECT TO CHARGING ORDER.

(a) On application by a judgment creditor of a partner or of a partner's transferee, a court having jurisdiction may charge the transferable interest of the judgment debtor to satisfy the judgment. The court may appoint a receiver of the share of the distributions due or to become due to the judgment debtor in respect of the partnership and make all other orders, directions, accounts, and inquiries the judgment debtor might have made or which the circumstances of the case may require.

(b) A charging order constitutes a lien on the judgment debtor's transferable interest in the partnership. The court may order a foreclosure of the interest subject to the charging order at any time. The purchaser at the foreclosure sale has the rights of a transferee.

(c) At any time before foreclosure, an interest charged may be redeemed:

    (1) by the judgment debtor;

    (2) with property other than partnership property, by one or more of the other partners; or

    (3) with partnership property, by one or more of the other partners with the consent of all of the partners whose interests are not so charged.

(d) This [Act] does not deprive a partner of a right under exemption laws with respect to the partner's interest in the partnership.

(e) This section provides the exclusive remedy by which a judgment creditor of a partner or partner's transferee may satisfy a judgment out of the judgment debtor's transferable interest in the partnership.

[ARTICLE] 6
PARTNER'S DISSOCIATION

SECTION 601. EVENTS CAUSING PARTNER'S DISSOCIATION.

A partner is dissociated from a partnership upon the occurrence of any of the following events:

    (1) the partnership's having notice of the partner's express will to withdraw as a partner or on a later date specified by the partner;

    (2) an event agreed to in the partnership agreement as causing the partner's dissociation;

    (3) the partner's expulsion pursuant to the partnership agreement;

    (4) the partner's expulsion by the unanimous vote of the other partners if:

        (i) it is unlawful to carry on the partnership business with that partner;

        (ii) there has been a transfer of all or substantially all of that partner's transferable interest in the partnership, other than a transfer for security purposes, or a court order charging the partner's interest, which has not been foreclosed;

        (iii) within 90 days after the partnership notifies a corporate partner that it will be expelled because it has filed a certificate of dissolution or the equivalent, its charter has been revoked, or its right to conduct business has been suspended by the jurisdiction of its incorporation, there is no revocation of the certificate of dissolution or no reinstatement of its charter or its right to conduct business; or

        (iv) a partnership that is a partner has been dissolved and its business is being wound up;

    (5) on application by the partnership or another partner, the partner's expulsion by judicial determination because:

        (i) the partner engaged in wrongful conduct that adversely and materially affected the partnership business;

        (ii) the partner willfully or persistently committed a material breach of the partnership agreement or of a duty owed to the partnership or the other partners under Section 404; or

        (iii) the partner engaged in conduct relating to the partnership business which makes it not reasonably practicable to carry on the business in partnership with the partner;

    (6) the partner's:

        (i) becoming a debtor in bankruptcy;

        (ii) executing an assignment for the benefit of creditors;

        (iii) seeking, consenting to, or acquiescing in the appointment of a trustee, receiver, or liquidator of that partner or of all or substantially all of that partner's property; or

(iv) failing, within 90 days after the appointment, to have vacated or stayed the appointment of a trustee, receiver, or liquidator of the partner or of all or substantially all of the partner's property obtained without the partner's consent or acquiescence, or failing within 90 days after the expiration of a stay to have the appointment vacated;

(7) in the case of a partner who is an individual:

(i) the partner's death;

(ii) the appointment of a guardian or general conservator for the partner; or

(iii) a judicial determination that the partner has otherwise become incapable of performing the partner's duties under the partnership agreement;

(8) in the case of a partner that is a trust or is acting as a partner by virtue of being a trustee of a trust, distribution of the trust's entire transferable interest in the partnership, but not merely by reason of the substitution of a successor trustee;

(9) in the case of a partner that is an estate or is acting as a partner by virtue of being a personal representative of an estate, distribution of the estate's entire transferable interest in the partnership, but not merely by reason of the substitution of a successor personal representative; or

(10) termination of a partner who is not an individual, partnership, corporation, trust, or estate.

SECTION 602. PARTNER'S POWER TO DISSOCIATE; WRONGFUL DISSOCIATION.

(a) A partner has the power to dissociate at any time, rightfully or wrongfully, by express will pursuant to Section 601(1).

(b) A partner's dissociation is wrongful only if:

(1) it is in breach of an express provision of the partnership agreement; or

(2) in the case of a partnership for a definite term or particular undertaking, before the expiration of the term or the completion of the undertaking:

(i) the partner withdraws by express will, unless the withdrawal follows within 90 days after another partner's dissociation by death or otherwise under Section 601(6) through (10) or wrongful dissociation under this subsection;

(ii) the partner is expelled by judicial determination under Section 601(5);

(iii) the partner is dissociated by becoming a debtor in bankruptcy; or

(iv) in the case of a partner who is not an individual, trust other than a business trust, or estate, the partner is expelled or otherwise dissociated because it willfully dissolved or terminated.

(c) A partner who wrongfully dissociates is liable to the partnership and to the other partners for damages caused by the dissociation. The liability is in addition to any other obligation of the partner to the partnership or to the other partners.

SECTION 603. EFFECT OF PARTNER'S DISSOCIATION.

(a) If a partner's dissociation results in a dissolution and winding up of the partnership business, [Article] 8 applies; otherwise, [Article] 7 applies.

(b) Upon a partner's dissociation:

(1) the partner's right to participate in the management and conduct of the partnership business terminates, except as otherwise provided in Section 803;

(2) the partner's duty of loyalty under Section 404(b)(3) terminates; and

(3) the partner's duty of loyalty under Section 404(b)(1) and (2) and duty of care under Section 404(c) continue only with regard to matters arising and events occurring before the partner's dissociation, unless the partner participates in winding up the partnership's business pursuant to Section 803.

[ARTICLE] 7

PARTNER'S DISSOCIATION WHEN BUSINESS NOT WOUND UP

SECTION 701. PURCHASE OF DISSOCIATED PARTNER'S INTEREST.

(a) If a partner is dissociated from a partnership without resulting in a dissolution and winding up of the partnership business under Section 801, the partnership shall cause the dissociated partner's interest in the partnership to be purchased for a buyout price determined pursuant to subsection (b).

(b) The buyout price of a dissociated partner's interest is the amount that would have been distributable to the dissociating partner under Section 807(b) if, on the date of dissociation, the assets of the partnership were sold at a price equal to the greater of the liquidation value or the value based on a sale of the entire business as a going concern without the dissociated partner and the partnership were wound up as of that date. Interest must be paid from the date of dissociation to the date of payment.

(c) Damages for wrongful dissociation under Section 602(b), and all other amounts owing, whether or not presently due, from the dissociated partner to the partnership, must be offset against the buyout price. Interest must be paid from the date the amount owed becomes due to the date of payment.

(d) A partnership shall indemnify a dissociated partner whose interest is being purchased against all partnership liabilities, whether incurred before or after the dissociation, except liabilities incurred by an act of the dissociated partner under Section 702.

(e) If no agreement for the purchase of a dissociated partner's interest is reached within 120 days after a written demand for payment, the partnership shall pay, or cause to be paid, in cash to the dissociated partner the amount the partnership estimates to be the buyout price and accrued interest, reduced by any offsets and accrued interest under subsection (c).

(f) If a deferred payment is authorized under subsection (h), the partnership may tender a written offer to pay the amount it estimates to be the buyout price and accrued interest, reduced by any offsets under subsection (c), stating the time of payment, the amount and type of security for payment, and the other terms and conditions of the obligation.

(g) The payment or tender required by subsection (e) or (f) must be accompanied by the following:

(1) a statement of partnership assets and liabilities as of the date of dissociation;

(2) the latest available partnership balance sheet and income statement, if any;

(3) an explanation of how the estimated amount of the payment was calculated; and

(4) written notice that the payment is in full satisfaction of the obligation to purchase unless, within 120 days after the written notice, the dissociated partner commences an action to determine the buyout price, any offsets under subsection (c), or other terms of the obligation to purchase.

(h) A partner who wrongfully dissociates before the expiration of a definite term or the completion of a particular undertaking is not entitled to payment of any portion of the buyout price until the expiration of the term or completion of the undertaking, unless the partner establishes to the satisfaction of the court that earlier payment will not cause undue hardship to the business of the partnership. A deferred payment must be adequately secured and bear interest.

(i) A dissociated partner may maintain an action against the partnership, pursuant to Section 405(b)(2)(ii), to determine the buyout price of that partner's interest, any offsets under subsection (c), or other terms of the obligation to purchase. The action must be commenced within 120 days after the partnership has tendered payment or an offer to pay or within one year after written demand for payment if no payment or offer to pay is tendered. The court shall determine the buyout price of the dissociated partner's interest, any offset due under subsection (c), and accrued interest, and enter judgment for any additional payment or refund. If deferred payment is authorized under subsection (h), the court shall also determine the security for payment and other terms of the obligation to purchase. The court may assess reasonable attorney's fees and the fees and expenses of appraisers or other experts for a party to the action, in amounts the court finds equitable, against a party that the court finds acted arbitrarily, vexatiously, or not in good faith. The finding may be based on the partnership's failure to tender payment or an offer to pay or to comply with subsection (g).

SECTION 702. DISSOCIATED PARTNER'S POWER TO BIND AND LIABILITY TO PARTNERSHIP.

(a) For two years after a partner dissociates without resulting in a dissolution and winding up of the partnership business, the partnership, including a surviving partnership under [Article] 9, is bound by an act of the dissociated partner which would have bound the partnership under Section 301 before dissociation only if at the time of entering into the transaction the other party:

(1) reasonably believed that the dissociated partner was then a partner;

(2) did not have notice of the partner's dissociation; and

(3) is not deemed to have had knowledge under Section 303(e) or notice under Section 704(c).

(b) A dissociated partner is liable to the partnership for any damage caused to the partnership arising from an obligation incurred by the dissociated partner after dissociation for which the partnership is liable under subsection (a).

SECTION 703. DISSOCIATED PARTNER'S LIABILITY TO OTHER PERSONS.

(a) A partner's dissociation does not of itself discharge the partner's liability for a partnership obligation incurred before dissociation. A dissociated partner is not liable for a partnership obligation incurred after dissociation, except as otherwise provided in subsection (b).

(b) A partner who dissociates without resulting in a dissolution and winding up of the partnership business is liable as a partner to the other party in a transaction entered into by the partnership, or a surviving partnership under [Article] 9, within two years after the partner's dissociation, only if the partner is liable for the obligation under Section 306 and at the time of entering into the transaction the other party:

(1) reasonably believed that the dissociated partner was then a partner;

(2) did not have notice of the partner's dissociation; and

(3) is not deemed to have had knowledge under Section 303(e) or notice under Section 704(c).

(c) By agreement with the partnership creditor and the partners continuing the business, a dissociated partner may be released from liability for a partnership obligation.

(d) A dissociated partner is released from liability for a partnership obligation if a partnership creditor, with notice of the partner's dissociation but without the partner's consent, agrees to a material alteration in the nature or time of payment of a partnership obligation.

SECTION 704. STATEMENT OF DISSOCIATION.

(a) A dissociated partner or the partnership may file a statement of dissociation stating the name of the partnership and that the partner is dissociated from the partnership.

(b) A statement of dissociation is a limitation on the authority of a dissociated partner for the purposes of Section 303(d) and (e).

(c) For the purposes of Sections 702(a)(3) and 703(b)(3), a person not a partner is deemed to have notice of the dissociation 90 days after the statement of dissociation is filed.

[ARTICLE] 8
WINDING UP PARTNERSHIP BUSINESS

SECTION 801. EVENTS CAUSING DISSOLUTION AND WINDING UP OF PARTNERSHIP BUSINESS.

A partnership is dissolved, and its business must be wound up, only upon the occurrence of any of the following events:

(1) in a partnership at will, the partnership's having notice from a partner, other than a partner who is dissociated under Section 601(2) through (10), of that partner's express will to withdraw as a partner, or on a later date specified by the partner;

(2) in a partnership for a definite term or particular undertaking:

(i) within 90 days after a partner's dissociation by death or otherwise under Section 601(6) through (10) or wrongful dissociation under Section 602(b), the express will of at least half of the remaining partners to wind up the partnership business, for which purpose a partner's rightful dissociation pursuant to Section 602(b)(2)(i) constitutes the expression of that partner's will to wind up the partnership business;

(ii) the express will of all of the partners to wind up the partnership business; or

(iii) the expiration of the term or the completion of the undertaking;

(3) an event agreed to in the partnership agreement resulting in the winding up of the partnership business;

(4) an event that makes it unlawful for all or substantially all of the business of the partnership to be continued, but a cure of illegality within 90 days after notice to the partnership of the event is effective retroactively to the date of the event for purposes of this section;

(5) on application by a partner, a judicial determination that:

(i) the economic purpose of the partnership is likely to be unreasonably frustrated;

(ii) another partner has engaged in conduct relating to the partnership business which makes it not reasonably practicable to carry on the business in partnership with that partner; or

(iii) it is not otherwise reasonably practicable to carry on the partnership business in conformity with the partnership agreement; or

(6) on application by a transferee of a partner's transferable interest, a judicial determination that it is equitable to wind up the partnership business:

(i) after the expiration of the term or completion of the undertaking, if the partnership was for a definite term or particular undertaking at the time of the transfer or entry of the charging order that gave rise to the transfer; or

(ii) at any time, if the partnership was a partnership at will at the time of the transfer or entry of the charging order that gave rise to the transfer.

SECTION 802. PARTNERSHIP CONTINUES AFTER DISSOLUTION.

(a) Subject to subsection (b), a partnership continues after dissolution only for the purpose of winding up its business. The partnership is terminated when the winding up of its business is completed.

(b) At any time after the dissolution of a partnership and before the winding up of its business is completed, all of the partners, including any dissociating partner other than a wrongfully dissociating partner, may waive the right to have the partnership's business wound up and the partnership terminated. In that event:

(1) the partnership resumes carrying on its business as if dissolution had never occurred, and any liability incurred by the partnership or a partner after the dissolution and before the waiver is determined as if dissolution had never occurred; and

(2) the rights of a third party accruing under Section 804(1) or arising out of conduct in reliance on the dissolution before the third party knew or received a notification of the waiver may not be adversely affected.

SECTION 803. RIGHT TO WIND UP PARTNERSHIP BUSINESS.

(a) After dissolution, a partner who has not wrongfully dissociated may participate in winding up the partnership's business, but on application of any partner, partner's legal representative, or transferee, the [designate the appropriate court], for good cause shown, may order judicial supervision of the winding up.

(b) The legal representative of the last surviving partner may wind up a partnership's business.

(c) A person winding up a partnership's business may preserve the partnership business or property as a going concern for a reasonable time, prosecute and defend actions and proceedings, whether civil, criminal, or administrative, settle and close the partnership's business, dispose of and transfer the partnership's property, discharge the partnership's liabilities, distribute the assets of the partnership pursuant to Section 807, settle disputes by mediation or arbitration, and perform other necessary acts.

SECTION 804. PARTNER'S POWER TO BIND PARTNERSHIP AFTER DISSOLUTION.

Subject to Section 805, a partnership is bound by a partner's act after dissolution that:

(1) is appropriate for winding up the partnership business; or

(2) would have bound the partnership under Section 301 before dissolution, if the other party to the transaction did not have notice of the dissolution.

SECTION 805. STATEMENT OF DISSOLUTION.

(a) After dissolution, a partner who has not wrongfully dissociated may file a statement of dissolution stating the name of the partnership and that the partnership has dissolved and is winding up its business.

(b) A statement of dissolution cancels a filed statement of partnership authority for the purposes of Section 303(d) and is a limitation on authority for the purposes of Section 303(e).

(c) For the purposes of Sections 301 and 804, a person not a partner is deemed to have notice of the dissolution and the limitation on the partners' authority as a result of the statement of dissolution 90 days after it is filed.

(d) After filing and, if appropriate, recording a statement of dissolution, a dissolved partnership may file and, if appropriate, record a statement of partnership authority which will operate with respect to a person not a partner as provided in Section 303(d) and (e) in any transaction, whether or not the transaction is appropriate for winding up the partnership business.

SECTION 806. PARTNER'S LIABILITY TO OTHER PARTNERS AFTER DISSOLUTION.

(a) Except as otherwise provided in subsection (b) and Section 306, after dissolution a partner is liable to the other partners for the partner's share of any partnership liability incurred under Section 804.

(b) A partner who, with knowledge of the dissolution, incurs a partnership liability under Section 804(2) by an act that is not appropriate for winding up the partnership business is liable to the partnership for any damage caused to the partnership arising from the liability.

SECTION 807. SETTLEMENT OF ACCOUNTS AND CONTRIBUTIONS AMONG PARTNERS.

(a) In winding up a partnership's business, the assets of the partnership, including the contributions of the partners required by this section, must be applied to discharge its obligations to creditors, including, to the extent permitted by law, partners who are creditors. Any surplus must be applied to pay in cash the net amount distributable to partners in accordance with their right to distributions under subsection (b).

(b) Each partner is entitled to a settlement of all partnership accounts upon winding up the partnership business. In settling accounts among the partners, profits and losses that result from the liquidation of the partnership assets must be credited and charged to the partners' accounts. The partnership shall make a distribution to a partner in an amount equal to any excess of the credits over the charges in the partner's account. A partner shall contribute to the partnership an amount equal to any excess of the charges over the credits in the partner's account but excluding from the calculation charges attributable to an obligation for which the partner is not personally liable under Section 306.

(c) If a partner fails to contribute the full amount required under subsection (b), all of the other partners shall contribute, in the proportions in which those partners share partnership losses, the additional amount necessary to satisfy the partnership obligations for which they are personally liable under Section 306. A partner or partner's legal representative may recover from the other partners any contributions the partner makes to the extent the amount contributed exceeds that partner's share of the partnership obligations for which the partner is personally liable under Section 306.

(d) After the settlement of accounts, each partner shall contribute, in the proportion in which the partner shares partnership losses, the amount necessary to satisfy partnership obligations that were not known at the time of the settlement and for which the partner is personally liable under Section 306.

(e) The estate of a deceased partner is liable for the partner's obligation to contribute to the partnership.

(f) An assignee for the benefit of creditors of a partnership or a partner, or a person appointed by a court to represent creditors of a partnership or a partner, may enforce a partner's obligation to contribute to the partnership.

[ARTICLE] 10
LIMITED LIABILITY PARTNERSHIP
SECTION 1001. STATEMENT OF QUALIFICATION.

(a) A partnership may become a limited liability partnership pursuant to this section.

(b) The terms and conditions on which a partnership becomes a limited liability partnership must be approved by the vote necessary to amend the partnership agreement except, in the case of a partnership agreement that expressly considers obligations to contribute to the partnership, the vote necessary to amend those provisions.

(c) After the approval required by subsection (b), a partnership may become a limited liability partnership by filing a statement of qualification. The statement must contain:

(1) the name of the partnership;

(2) the street address of the partnership's chief executive office and, if different, the street address of an office in this State, if any;

(3) if the partnership does not have an office in this State, the name and street address of the partnership's agent for service of process;

(4) a statement that the partnership elects to be a limited liability partnership; and

(5) a deferred effective date, if any.

(d) The agent of a limited liability partnership for service of process must be an individual who is a resident of this State or other person authorized to do business in this State.

(e) The status of a partnership as a limited liability partnership is effective on the later of the filing of the statement or a date specified in the statement. The status remains effective, regardless of changes in the partnership, until it is canceled pursuant to Section 105(d) or revoked pursuant to Section 1003.

(f) The status of a partnership as a limited liability partnership and the liability of its partners is not affected by errors or later changes in the information required to be contained in the statement of qualification under subsection (c).

(g) The filing of a statement of qualification establishes that a partnership has satisfied all conditions precedent to the qualification of the partnership as a limited liability partnership.

(h) An amendment or cancellation of a statement of qualification is effective when it is filed or on a deferred effective date specified in the amendment or cancellation.

SECTION 1002. NAME.

The name of a limited liability partnership must end with "Registered Limited Liability Partnership", "Limited Liability Partnership", "R.L.L.P.", "L.L.P.", "RLLP," or "LLP".

SECTION 1003. ANNUAL REPORT.

(a) A limited liability partnership, and a foreign limited liability partnership authorized to transact business in this State, shall file an annual report in the office of the [Secretary of State] which contains:

(1) the name of the limited liability partnership and the State or other jurisdiction under whose laws the foreign limited liability partnership is formed;

(2) the street address of the partnership's chief executive office and, if different, the street address of an office of the partnership in this State, if any; and

(3) if the partnership does not have an office in this State, the name and street address of the partnership's current agent for service of process.

(b) An annual report must be filed between [January 1 and April 1] of each year following the calendar year in which a partnership files a statement of qualification or a foreign partnership becomes authorized to transact business in this State.

(c) The [Secretary of State] may revoke the statement of qualification of a partnership that fails to file an annual report when due or pay the required filing fee. To do so, the [Secretary of State] shall provide the partnership at least 60 days' written notice of intent to revoke the statement. The notice must be mailed to the partnership at its chief executive office set forth in the last filed statement of qualification or annual report. The notice must specify the annual report that has not been filed, the fee that has not been paid, and the effective date of the revocation. The revocation is not effective if the annual report is filed and the fee is paid before the effective date of the revocation.

(d) A revocation under subsection (c) only affects a partnership's status as a limited liability partnership and is not an event of dissolution of the partnership.

(e) A partnership whose statement of qualification has been revoked may apply to the [Secretary of State] for reinstatement within two years after the effective date of the revocation. The application must state:

(1) the name of the partnership and the effective date of the revocation; and

(2) that the ground for revocation either did not exist or has been corrected.

(f) A reinstatement under subsection (e) relates back to and takes effect as of the effective date of the revocation, and the partnership's status as a limited liability partnership continues as if the revocation had never occurred.

[ARTICLE] 11

FOREIGN LIMITED LIABILITY PARTNERSHIP

SECTION 1101. LAW GOVERNING FOREIGN LIMITED LIABILITY PARTNERSHIP.

(a) The law under which a foreign limited liability partnership is formed governs relations among the partners and between the partners and the partnership and the liability of partners for obligations of the partnership.

(b) A foreign limited liability partnership may not be denied a statement of foreign qualification by reason of any difference between the law under which the partnership was formed and the law of this State.

(c) A statement of foreign qualification does not authorize a foreign limited liability partnership to engage in any business or exercise any power that a partnership may not engage in or exercise in this State as a limited liability partnership.

SECTION 1102. STATEMENT OF FOREIGN QUALIFICATION.

(a) Before transacting business in this State, a foreign limited liability partnership must file a statement of foreign qualification. The statement must contain:

(1) the name of the foreign limited liability partnership which satisfies the requirements of the State or other jurisdiction under whose law it is formed and ends with "Registered Limited Liability Partnership", "Limited Liability Partnership", "R.L.L.P.", "L.L.P.", "RLLP," or "LLP";

(2) the street address of the partnership's chief executive office and, if different, the street address of an office of the partnership in this State, if any;

(3) if there is no office of the partnership in this State, the name and street address of the partnership's agent for service of process; and

(4) a deferred effective date, if any.

(b) The agent of a foreign limited liability company for service of process must be an individual who is a resident of this State or other person authorized to do business in this State.

(c) The status of a partnership as a foreign limited liability partnership is effective on the later of the filing of the statement of foreign qualification or a date specified in the statement. The status remains effective, regardless of changes in the partnership, until it is canceled pursuant to Section 105(d) or revoked pursuant to Section 1003.

(d) An amendment or cancellation of a statement of foreign qualification is effective when it is filed or on a deferred effective date specified in the amendment or cancellation.

Revised Model Business Corporation Act

CHAPTER 1. GENERAL PROVISIONS

Subchapter A. Short Title and Reservation of Power

§1.01 Short Title

This Act shall be known and may be cited as the "[name of state] Business Corporation Act."

§1.02 Reservation of Power to Amend or Repeal

The [name of state legislature] has power to amend or repeal all or part of this Act at any time and all domestic and foreign corporations subject to this Act are governed by the amendment or repeal.

Subchapter B. Filing Documents

§1.20 Filing Requirements

(a) A document must satisfy the requirements of this section, and of any other section that adds to or varies these requirements, to be entitled to filing by the secretary of state.

(b) This Act must require or permit filing the document in the office of the secretary of state.

(c) The document must contain the information required by this Act. It may contain other information as well.

(d) The document must be typewritten or printed.

(e) The document must be in the English language. A corporate name need not be in English if written in English letters or Arabic or Roman numerals, and the certificate of existence required of foreign corporations need not be in English if accompanied by a reasonably authenticated English translation.

(f) The document must be executed:

    (1) by the chairman of the board of directors of a domestic or foreign corporation, by its president, or by another of its officers;

    (2) if directors have not been selected or the corporation has not been formed, by an incorporator; or

    (3) if the corporation is in the hands of a receiver, trustee, or other court-appointed fiduciary, by that fiduciary.

(g) The person executing the document shall sign it and state beneath or opposite his signature his name and the capacity in which he signs. The document may but need not contain: (1) the corporate seal, (2) an attestation by the secretary or an assistant secretary, (3) an acknowledgement, verification, or proof.

(h) If the secretary of state has prescribed a mandatory form for the document under section 1.21, the document must be in or on the prescribed form.

(i) The document must be delivered to the office of the secretary of state for filing and must be accompanied by one exact or conformed copy (except as provided in sections 5.03 and 15.09), the correct filing fee, and any franchise tax, license fee, or penalty required by this Act or other law.

§1.21 Forms

(a) The secretary of state may prescribe and furnish on request forms for: (1) an application for a certificate of existence, (2) a foreign corporation's application for a certificate of authority to transact business in this state, (3) a foreign corporation's application for a certificate of withdrawal, and (4) the annual report. If the secretary of state so requires, use of these forms is mandatory.

(b) The secretary of state may prescribe and furnish on request forms for other documents required or permitted to be filed by this Act but their use is not mandatory.

§1.22 Filing, Service and Copying Fees

[Text omitted.]

§1.23 Effective Time and Date of Document

(a) Except as provided in subsection (b) and section 1.24(c), a document accepted for filing is effective:

    (1) at the time of filing on the date it is filed, as evidenced by the secretary of state's date and time endorsement on the original document; or

    (2) at the time specified in the document as its effective time on the date it is filed.

(b) A document may specify a delayed effective time and date, and if it does so the document becomes effective at the time and date specified. If a delayed effective date but no time is specified, the document is effective at the close of business on that date. A delayed effective date for a document may not be later than the 90th day after the date it is filed.

§1.24 Correcting Filed Document

(a) A domestic or foreign corporation may correct a document filed by the secretary of state if the document (1) contains an incorrect statement or (2) was defectively executed, attested, sealed, verified, or acknowledged.

(b) A document is corrected:

    (1) by preparing articles of correction that (i) describe the document (including its filing date) or attach a copy of it to the articles, (ii) specify the incorrect statement and the reason it is incorrect or the manner in which the execution was defective, and (iii) correct the incorrect statement or defective execution; and

    (2) by delivering the articles to the secretary of state for filing.

(c) Articles of correction are effective on the effective date of the document they correct except as to persons relying on the uncorrected document and adversely affected by the correction. As to those persons, articles of correction are effective when filed.

§1.25 Filing Duty of Secretary of State

(a) If a document delivered to the office of the secretary of state for filing satisfies the requirements of section 1.20, the secretary of state shall file it.

(b) The secretary of state files a document by stamping or otherwise endorsing "Filed," together with his name and official title and the date and time of receipt, on both the original and the document copy and on the receipt for the filing fee. After filing a document, except as provided in sections 5.03 and 15.10, the secretary of state shall deliver the document copy, with the filing fee receipt (or acknowledgement of receipt if no fee is required) attached, to the domestic or foreign corporation or its representative.

(c) If the secretary of state refuses to file a document, he shall return it to the domestic or foreign corporation or its representative within five days after the document was delivered, together with a brief, written explanation of the reason for his refusal.

(d) The secretary of state's duty to file documents under this section is ministerial. His filing or refusing to file a document does not:

(1) affect the validity or invalidity of the document in whole or part;

(2) relate to the correctness or incorrectness of information contained in the document;

(3) create a presumption that the document is valid or invalid or that information contained in the document is correct or incorrect.

§1.26 Appeal From Secretary of State's Refusal to File Document

(a) If the secretary of state refuses to file a document delivered to his office for filing, the domestic or foreign corporation may appeal the refusal to the [name or describe] court [of the county where the corporation's principal office (or, if none in this state, its registered office) is or will be located] [of county]. The appeal is commenced by petitioning the court to compel filing the document and by attaching to the petition the document and the secretary of state's explanation of his refusal to file.

(b) The court may summarily order the secretary of state to file the document or take other action the court considers appropriate.

(c) The court's final decision may be appealed as in other civil proceedings.

§1.27 Evidentiary Effect of Copy of Filed Document

A certificate attached to a copy of the document filed by the secretary of state, bearing his signature (which may be in facsimile) and the seal of this state, is conclusive evidence that the original document is on file with the secretary of state.

§1.28 Certificate of Existence

(a) Anyone may apply to the secretary of state to furnish a certificate of existence for a domestic corporation or a certificate of authorization for a foreign corporation.

(b) A certificate of existence or authorization sets forth:

(1) the domestic corporation's corporate name or the foreign corporation's corporate name used in this state;

(2) that (i) the domestic corporation is duly incorporated under the law of this state, the date of its incorporation, and the period of its duration if less than perpetual; or (ii) that the foreign corporation is authorized to transact business in this state;

(3) that all fees, taxes, and penalties owed to this state have been paid, if (i) payment is reflected in the records of the secretary of state and (ii) nonpayment affects the existence or authorization of the domestic or foreign corporation;

(4) that its most recent annual report required by section 16.22 has been delivered to the secretary of state;

(5) that articles of dissolution have not been filed; and

(6) other facts of record in the office of the secretary of state that may be requested by the applicant.

(c) Subject to any qualification stated in the certificate, a certificate of existence or authorization issued by the secretary of state may be relied upon as conclusive evidence that the domestic or foreign corporation is in existence or is authorized to transact business in this state.

§1.29 Penalty for Signing False Document

(a) A person commits an offense if he signs a document he knows is false in any material respect with intent that the document be delivered to the secretary of state for filing.

(b) An offense under this section is a [_____] misdemeanor [punishable by a fine of not to exceed $_____].

Subchapter C. Secretary of State

§1.30 Powers

The secretary of state has the power reasonably necessary to perform the duties required of him by this Act.

Subchapter D. Definitions

§1.40 Act Definitions

In this Act:

(1) "Articles of incorporation" include amended and restated articles of incorporation and articles of merger.

(2) "Authorized shares" means the shares of all classes a domestic or foreign corporation is authorized to issue.

(3) "Conspicuous" means so written that a reasonable person against whom the writing is to operate should have noticed it. For example, printing in italics or boldface or contrasting color, or typing in capitals or underlined, is conspicuous.

(4) "Corporation" or "domestic corporation" means a corporation for profit, which is not a foreign corporation, incorporated under or subject to the provisions of this Act.

(5) "Deliver" includes mail.

(6) "Distribution" means a direct or indirect transfer of money or other property (except its own shares) or incurrence of indebtedness by a corporation to or for the benefit of its shareholders in respect of any of its shares. A distribution may be in the form of a declaration or payment of a dividend; a purchase, redemption, or other acquisition of shares; a distribution of indebtedness; or otherwise.

(7) "Effective date of notice" is defined in section 1.41.

(8) "Employee" includes an officer but not a director. A director may accept duties that make him also an employee.

(9) "Entity" includes corporation and foreign corporation; not-for-profit corporation; profit and not-for-profit unincorporated association; business trust, estate, partnership, trust, and two or more persons having a joint or common economic interest; and state, United States, and foreign government.

(10) "Foreign corporation" means a corporation for profit incorporated under a law other than the law of this state.

(11) "Governmental subdivision" includes authority, county, district, and municipality.

(12) "Includes" denotes a partial definition.

(13) "Individual" includes the estate of an incompetent or deceased individual.

(14) "Means" denotes an exhaustive definition.

(15) "Notice" is defined in section 1.41.

(16) "Person" includes individual and entity.

(17) "Principal office" means the office (in or out of this state) so designated in the annual report where the principal executive offices of a domestic or foreign corporation are located.

(18) "Proceeding" includes civil suit and criminal, administrative, and investigatory action.

(19) "Record date" means the date established under chapter 6 or 7 on which a corporation determines the identity of its shareholders and their shareholdings for purposes of this Act. The determinations shall be made as of the close of business on the record date unless another time for doing so is specified when the record date is fixed.

(20) "Secretary" means the corporate officer to whom the board of directors has delegated responsibility under section 8.40(c) for custody

of the minutes of the meetings of the board of directors and of the shareholders and for authenticating records of the corporation.

(21) "Share" means the unit into which the proprietary interests in a corporation are divided.

(22) "Shareholder" means the person in whose name shares are registered in the records of a corporation or the beneficial owner of shares to the extent of the rights granted by a nominee certificate on file with a corporation.

(23) "State," when referring to a part of the United States, includes a state and commonwealth (and their agencies and governmental subdivisions) and a territory, and insular possession (and their agencies and governmental subdivisions) of the United States.

(24) "Subscriber" means a person who subscribes for shares in a corporation, whether before or after incorporation.

(25) "United States" includes district, authority, bureau, commission, department, and any other agency of the United States.

(26) "Voting group" means all shares of one or more classes or series that under the articles of incorporation or this Act are entitled to vote and be counted together collectively on a matter at a meeting of shareholders. All shares entitled by the articles of incorporation or this Act to vote generally on the matter are for that purpose a single voting group.

§1.41 Notice

(a) Notice under this Act shall be in writing unless oral notice is reasonable under the circumstances.

(b) Notice may be communicated in person; by telephone, telegraph, teletype, or other form of wire or wireless communication; or by mail or private carrier. If these forms of personal notice are impracticable, notice may be communicated by a newspaper of general circulation in the area where published; or by radio, television, or other form of public broadcast communication.

(c) Written notice by a domestic or foreign corporation to its shareholder, if in a comprehensible form, is effective when mailed, if mailed postpaid and correctly addressed to the shareholder's address shown in the corporation's current record of shareholders.

(d) Written notice to a domestic or foreign corporation (authorized to transact business in this state) may be addressed to its registered agent at its registered office or to the corporation or its secretary at its principal office shown in its most recent annual report or, in the case of a foreign corporation that has not yet delivered an annual report, in its application for a certificate of authority.

(e) Except as provided in subsections (c) and (d), written notice, if in a comprehensible form, is effective at the earliest of the following:

(1) when received;

(2) five days after its deposit in the United States Mail, as evidenced by the postmark, if mailed postpaid and correctly addressed;

(3) on the date shown on the return receipt, if sent by registered or certified mail, return receipt requested, and the receipt is signed by or on behalf of the addressee.

(f) Oral notice is effective when communicated if communicated in a comprehensible manner.

(g) If this Act prescribes notice requirements for particular circumstances, those requirements govern. If articles of incorporation or bylaws prescribe notice requirements, not inconsistent with this section or other provisions of this Act, those requirements govern.

§1.42 Number of Shareholders

(a) For purposes of this Act, the following identified as a shareholder in a corporation's current record of shareholders constitutes one shareholder:

(1) three or fewer co-owners;

(2) a corporation, partnership, trust, estate, or other entity;

(3) the trustees, guardians, custodians, or other fiduciaries of a single trust, estate, or account.

(b) For purposes of this Act, shareholdings registered in substantially similar names constitute one shareholder if it is reasonable to believe that the names represent the same person.

CHAPTER 2. INCORPORATION

§2.01 Incorporators

One or more persons may act as the incorporator or incorporators of a corporation by delivering articles of incorporation to the secretary of state for filing.

§2.02 Articles of Incorporation

(a) The articles of incorporation must set forth:

(1) a corporate name for the corporation that satisfies the requirements of section 4.01;

(2) the number of shares the corporation is authorized to issue;

(3) the street address of the corporation's initial registered office and the name of its initial registered agent at that office; and

(4) the name and address of each incorporator.

(b) The articles of incorporation may set forth:

(1) the names and addresses of the individuals who are to serve as the initial directors;

(2) provisions not inconsistent with law regarding:

(i) the purpose or purposes for which the corporation is organized;

(ii) managing the business and regulating the affairs of the corporation;

(iii) defining, limiting, and regulating the powers of the corporation, its board of directors, and shareholders;

(iv) a par value for authorized shares or classes of shares;

(v) the imposition of personal liability on shareholders for the debts of the corporation to a specified extent and upon specified conditions;

(3) any provision that under this Act is required or permitted to be set forth in the bylaws; and

(4) a provision eliminating or limiting the liability of a director to the corporation or its shareholders for money damages for any action taken, or any failure to take any action, as a director, except liability for (A) the amount of a financial benefit received by a director to which he is not entitled; (B) an intentional infliction of harm on the corporation or the shareholders; (C) a violation of section 8.33; or (D) an intentional violation of criminal law.

(c) The articles of incorporation need not set forth any of the corporate powers enumerated in this Act.

§2.03 Incorporation

(a) Unless a delayed effective date is specified, the corporate existence begins when the articles of incorporation are filed.

(b) The secretary of state's filing of the articles of incorporation is conclusive proof that the incorporators satisfied all conditions precedent to incorporation except in a proceeding by the state to cancel or revoke the incorporation or involuntarily dissolve the corporation.

§2.04 Liability for Preincorporation Transactions

All persons purporting to act as or on behalf of a corporation, knowing there was no incorporation under this Act, are jointly and severally liable for all liabilities created while so acting.

§2.05 Organization of Corporation

(a) After incorporation:

(1) if initial directors are named in the articles of incorporation, the initial directors shall hold an organizational meeting, at the call of a majority of the directors, to complete the organization of the corporation by appointing officers, adopting bylaws, and carrying on any other business brought before the meeting;

(2) if initial directors are not named in the articles, the incorporator or incorporators shall hold an organizational meeting at the call of a majority of the incorporators:

(i) to elect directors and complete the organization of the corporation; or

(ii) to elect a board of directors who shall complete the organization of the corporation.

(b) Action required or permitted by this Act to be taken by incorporators at an organizational meeting may be taken without a meeting if the action taken is evidenced by one or more written consents describing the action taken and signed by each incorporator.

(c) An organizational meeting may be held in or out of this state.

§2.06 Bylaws

(a) The incorporators or board of directors of a corporation shall adopt initial bylaws for the corporation.

(b) The bylaws of a corporation may contain any provision for managing the business and regulating the affairs of the corporation that is not inconsistent with law or the articles of incorporation.

§2.07 Emergency Bylaws

(a) Unless the articles of incorporation provide otherwise, the board of directors of a corporation may adopt bylaws to be effective only in an emergency defined in subsection (d). The emergency bylaws, which are subject to amendment or repeal by the shareholders, may make all provisions necessary for managing the corporation during the emergency, including:

(1) procedures for calling a meeting of the board of directors;

(2) quorum requirements for the meeting; and

(3) designation of additional or substitute directors.

(b) All provisions of the regular bylaws consistent with the emergency bylaws remain effective during the emergency. The emergency bylaws are not effective after the emergency ends.

(c) Corporate action taken in good faith in accordance with the emergency bylaws:

(1) binds the corporation; and

(2) may not be used to impose liability on a corporate director, officer, employee, or agent.

(d) An emergency exists for purposes of this section if a quorum of the corporation's directors cannot readily be assembled because of some catastrophic event.

CHAPTER 3. PURPOSES AND POWERS

§3.01 Purposes

(a) Every corporation incorporated under this Act has the purpose of engaging in any lawful business unless a more limited purpose is set forth in the articles of incorporation.

(b) A corporation engaging in a business that is subject to regulation under another statute of this state may incorporate under this Act only if permitted by, and subject to all limitations of, the other statute.

§3.02 General Powers

Unless its articles of incorporation provide otherwise, every corporation has perpetual duration and succession in its corporate name and has the same powers as an individual to do all things necessary or convenient to carry out its business and affairs, including without limitation power:

(1) to sue and be sued, complain and defend in its corporate name;

(2) to have a corporate seal, which may be altered at will, and to use it, or a facsimile of it, by impressing or affixing it or in any other manner reproducing it;

(3) to make and amend bylaws, not inconsistent with its articles of incorporation or with the laws of this state, for managing the business and regulating the affairs of the corporation;

(4) to purchase, receive, lease, or otherwise acquire, and own, hold, improve, use, and otherwise deal with, real or personal property, or any legal or equitable interest in property, wherever located;

(5) to sell, convey, mortgage, pledge, lease, exchange, and otherwise dispose of all or any part of its property;

(6) to purchase, receive, subscribe for, or otherwise acquire; own, hold, vote, use, sell, mortgage, lend, pledge, or otherwise dispose of; and deal in and with shares or other interests in, or obligations of, any other entity;

(7) to make contracts and guarantees, incur liabilities, borrow money, issue its notes, bonds, and other obligations, (which may be convertible into or include the option to purchase other securities of the corporation), and secure any of its obligations by mortgage or pledge of any of its property, franchises, or income;

(8) to lend money, invest and reinvest its funds, and receive and hold real and personal property as security for repayment;

(9) to be a promoter, partner, member, associate, or manager of any partnership, joint venture, trust, or other entity;

(10) to conduct its business, locate offices, and exercise the powers granted by this Act within or without this state;

(11) to elect directors and appoint officers, employees, and agents of the corporation, define their duties, fix their compensation, and lend them money and credit;

(12) to pay pensions and establish pension plans, pension trusts, profit sharing plans, share bonus plans, share option plans, and benefit or incentive plans for any or all of its current or former directors, officers, employees, and agents;

(13) to make donations for the public welfare or for charitable, scientific, or educational purposes;

(14) to transact any lawful business that will aid governmental policy;

(15) to make payments or donations, or do any other act, not inconsistent with law, that furthers the business and affairs of the corporation.

§3.03 Emergency Powers

(a) In anticipation of or during an emergency defined in subsection (d), the board of directors of a corporation may:

(1) modify lines of succession to accommodate the incapacity of any director, officer, employee, or agent; and

(2) relocate the principal office, designate alternative principal offices or regional offices, or authorize the officers to do so.

(b) During an emergency defined in subsection (d), unless emergency bylaws provide otherwise:

(1) notice of a meeting of the board of directors need be given only to those directors whom it is practicable to reach and may be given in any practicable manner, including by publication and radio; and

(2) one or more officers of the corporation present at a meeting of the board of directors may be deemed to be directors for the meeting, in order of rank and within the same rank in order of seniority, as necessary to achieve a quorum.

(c) Corporate action taken in good faith during an emergency under this section to further the ordinary business affairs of the corporation:

(1) binds the corporation; and

(2) may not be used to impose liability on a corporate director, officer, employee, or agent.

(d) An emergency exists for purposes of this section if a quorum of the corporation's directors cannot readily be assembled because of some catastrophic event.

§3.04 Ultra Vires

(a) Except as provided in subsection (b), the validity of corporate action may not be challenged on the ground that the corporation lacks or lacked power to act.

(b) A corporation's power to act may be challenged:

(1) in a proceeding by a shareholder against the corporation to enjoin the act;

(2) in a proceeding by the corporation, directly, derivatively, or through a receiver, trustee, or other legal representative, against an incumbent or former director, officer, employee, or agent of the corporation; or

(3) in a proceeding by the Attorney General under section 14.30.

(c) In a shareholder's proceeding under subsection (b) (1) to enjoin an unauthorized corporate act, the court may enjoin or set aside the act, if equitable and if all affected persons are parties to the proceeding, and may award damages for loss (other than anticipated profits) suffered by the corporation or another party because of enjoining the unauthorized act.

CHAPTER 4. NAME

§4.01 Corporate Name

(a) A corporate name:

(1) must contain the word "corporation," "incorporated," "company," or "limited," or the abbreviation "corp.," "inc.," "co.," or "ltd.," or words or abbreviations of like import in another language; and

(2) may not contain language stating or implying that the corporation is organized for a purpose other than that permitted by section 3.01 and its articles of incorporation.

(b) Except as authorized by subsections (c) and (d), a corporate name must be distinguishable upon the records of the secretary of state from:

(1) the corporate name of a corporation incorporated or authorized to transact business in this state;

(2) a corporate name reserved or registered under section 4.02 or 4.03;

(3) the fictitious name adopted by a foreign corporation authorized to transact business in this state because its real name is unavailable; and

(4) the corporate name of a not-for-profit corporation incorporated or authorized to transact business in this state.

(c) A corporation may apply to the secretary of state for authorization to use a name that is not distinguishable upon his records from one or more of the names described in subsection (b). The secretary of state shall authorize use of the name applied for if:

(1) the other corporation consents to the use in writing and submits an undertaking in form satisfactory to the secretary of state to change its name to a name that is distinguishable upon the records of the secretary of state from the name of the applying corporation; or

(2) the applicant delivers to the secretary of state a certified copy of the final judgment of a court of competent jurisdiction establishing the applicant's right to use the name applied for in this state.

(d) A corporation may use the name (including the fictitious name) of another domestic or foreign corporation that is used in this state if the other corporation is incorporated or authorized to transact business in this state and the proposed user corporation:

(1) has merged with the other corporation;

(2) has been formed by reorganization of the other corporation; or

(3) has acquired all or substantially all of the assets, including the corporate name, of the other corporation.

(e) This Act does not control the use of fictitious names.

§4.02 Reserved Name

(a) A person may reserve the exclusive use of a corporate name, including a fictitious name for a foreign corporation whose corporate name is not available, by delivering an application to the secretary of state for filing. The application must set forth the name and address of the applicant and the name proposed to be reserved. If the secretary of state finds that the corporate name applied for is available, he shall reserve the name for the applicant's exclusive use for a nonrenewable 120-day period.

(b) The owner of a reserved corporate name may transfer the reservation to another person by delivering to the secretary of state a signed notice of the transfer that states the name and address of the transferee.

§4.03 Registered Name

(a) A foreign corporation may register its corporate name, or its corporate name with any addition required by section 15.06, if the name is distinguishable upon the records of the secretary of state from the corporate names that are not available under section 4.01(b)(3).

(b) A foreign corporation registers its corporate name, or its corporate name with any addition required by section 15.06, by delivering to the secretary of state for filing an application:

(1) setting forth its corporate name, or its corporate name with any addition required by section 15.06, the state or country and date of its incorporation, and a brief description of the nature of the business in which it is engaged; and

(2) accompanied by a certificate of existence (or a document of similar import) from the state or country of incorporation.

(c) The name is registered for the applicant's exclusive use upon the effective date of the application.

(d) A foreign corporation whose registration is effective may renew it for successive years by delivering to the secretary of state for filing a renewal application, which complies with the requirements of subsection (b), between October 1 and December 31 of the preceding year. The renewal application renews the registration for the following calendar year.

(e) A foreign corporation whose registration is effective may thereafter qualify as a foreign corporation under that name or consent in writing to the use of that name by a corporation thereafter incorporated under this Act or by another foreign corporation thereafter authorized to transact business in this state. The registration terminates when the domestic corporation is incorporated or the foreign corporation qualifies or consents to the qualification of another foreign corporation under the registered name.

CHAPTER 5. OFFICE AND AGENT

§5.01 Registered Office and Registered Agent

Each corporation must continuously maintain in this state:

(1) a registered office that may be the same as any of its places of business; and

(2) a registered agent, who may be:

(i) an individual who resides in this state and whose business office is identical with the registered office;

(ii) a domestic corporation or not-for-profit domestic corporation whose business office is identical with the registered office; or

(iii) a foreign corporation or not-for-profit foreign corporation authorized to transact business in this state whose business office is identical with the registered office.

§5.02 Change of Registered Office or Registered Agent

(a) A corporation may change its registered office or registered agent by delivering to the secretary of state for filing a statement of change that sets forth:

(1) the name of the corporation,

(2) the street address of its current registered office;

(3) if the current registered office is to be changed, the street address of the new registered office;

(4) the name of its current registered agent;

(5) if the current registered agent is to be changed, the name of the new registered agent and the new agent's written consent (either on the statement or attached to it) to the appointment; and

(6) that after the change or changes are made, the street addresses of its registered office and the business office of its registered agent will be identical.

(b) If a registered agent changes the street address of his business office, he may change the street address of the registered office of any corporation for which he is the registered agent by notifying the corporation in writing of the change and signing (either manually or in facsimile) and delivering to the secretary of state for filing a statement that complies with the requirements of subsection (a) and recites that the corporation has been notified of the change.

§5.03 Resignation of Registered Agent

(a) A registered agent may resign his agency appointment by signing and delivering to the secretary of state for filing the signed original and two exact or conformed copies of a statement of resignation. The statement may include a statement that the registered office is also discontinued.

(b) After filing the statement the secretary of state shall mail one copy to the registered office (if not discontinued) and the other copy to the corporation at its principal office.

(c) The agency appointment is terminated, and the registered office discontinued if so provided, on the 31st day after the date on which the statement was filed.

§5.04 Service on Corporation

(a) A corporation's registered agent is the corporation's agent for service of process, notice, or demand required or permitted by law to be served on the corporation.

(b) If a corporation has no registered agent, or the agent cannot with reasonable diligence be served, the corporation may be served by registered or certified mail, return receipt requested, addressed to the secretary of the corporation at its principal office. Service is perfected under this subsection at the earliest of:

(1) the date the corporation receives the mail;

(2) the date shown on the return receipt, if signed on behalf of the corporation; or

(3) five days after its deposit in the United States Mail, if mailed postpaid and correctly addressed.

(c) This section does not prescribe the only means, or necessarily the required means, of serving a corporation.

CHAPTER 6. SHARES AND DISTRIBUTIONS

Subchapter A. Shares

§6.01 Authorized Shares

(a) The articles of incorporation must prescribe the classes of shares and the number of shares of each class that the corporation is authorized to issue. If more than one class of shares is authorized, the articles of incorporation must prescribe a distinguishing designation for each class, and prior to the issuance of shares of a class the preferences, limitations, and relative rights of that class must be described in the articles of incorporation. All shares of a class must have preferences, limitations, and relative rights identical with those of other shares of the same class except to the extent otherwise permitted by section 6.02.

(b) The articles of incorporation must authorize: (1) one or more classes of shares that together have unlimited voting rights, and (2) one or more classes of shares (which may be the same class or classes as those with voting rights) that together are entitled to receive the net assets of the corporation upon dissolution.

(c) The articles of incorporation may authorize one or more classes of shares that:

(1) have special, conditional, or limited voting rights, or no right to vote, except to the extent prohibited by this Act;

(2) are redeemable or convertible as specified in the articles of incorporation (i) at the option of the corporation, the shareholder, or another person or upon the occurrence of a designated event; (ii) for cash, indebtedness, securities, or other property; (iii) in a designated amount or in an amount determined in accordance with a designated formula or by reference to extrinsic data or events;

(3) entitle the holders to distributions calculated in any manner, including dividends that may be cumulative, noncumulative, or partially cumulative;

(4) have preference over any other class of shares with respect to distributions, including dividends and distributions upon the dissolution of the corporation.

(d) The description of the designations, preferences, limitations, and relative rights of share classes in subsection (c) is not exhaustive.

§6.02 Terms of Class or Series Determined by Board of Directors

(a) If the articles of incorporation so provide, the board of directors may determine, in whole or part, the preferences, limitations, and relative rights (within the limits set forth in section 6.01) of (1) any class of shares before

the issuance of any shares of that class or (2) one or more series within a class before the issuance of any shares of that series.

(b) Each series of a class must be given a distinguishing designation.

(c) All shares of a series must have preferences, limitations, and relative rights identical with those of other shares of the same series and, except to the extent otherwise provided in the description of the series, of those of other series of the same class.

(d) Before issuing any shares of a class or series created under this section, the corporation must deliver to the secretary of state for filing articles of amendment, which are effective without shareholder action, that set forth:

(1) the name of the corporation;

(2) the text of the amendment determining the terms of the class or series of shares;

(3) the date it was adopted; and

(4) a statement that the amendment was duly adopted by the board of directors.

§6.03 Issued and Outstanding Shares

(a) A corporation may issue the number of shares of each class or series authorized by the articles of incorporation. Shares that are issued are outstanding shares until they are reacquired, redeemed, converted, or cancelled.

(b) The reacquisition, redemption, or conversion of outstanding shares is subject to the limitations of subsection (c) of this section and to section 6.40.

(c) At all times that shares of the corporation are outstanding, one or more shares that together have unlimited voting rights and one or more shares that together are entitled to receive the net assets of the corporation upon dissolution must be outstanding.

§6.04 Fractional Shares

(a) A corporation may:

(1) issue fractions of a share or pay in money the value of fractions of a share;

(2) arrange for disposition of fractional shares by the shareholders;

(3) issue scrip in registered or bearer form entitling the holder to receive a full share upon surrendering enough scrip to equal a full share.

(b) Each certificate representing scrip must be conspicuously labeled "scrip" and must contain the information required by section 6.25(b).

(c) The holder of a fractional share is entitled to exercise the rights of a shareholder, including the right to vote, to receive dividends, and to participate in the assets of the corporation upon liquidation. The holder of scrip is not entitled to any of these rights unless the scrip provides for them.

(d) The board of directors may authorize the issuance of scrip subject to any condition considered desirable, including:

(1) that the scrip will become void if not exchanged for full shares before a specified date; and

(2) that the shares for which the scrip is exchangeable may be sold and the proceeds paid to the scripholders.

Subchapter B. Issuance of Shares

§6.20 Subscription for Shares Before Incorporation

(a) A subscription for shares entered into before incorporation is irrevocable for six months unless the subscription agreement provides a longer or shorter period or all the subscribers agree to revocation.

(b) The board of directors may determine the payment terms of subscriptions for shares that were entered into before incorporation, unless the subscription agreement specifies them. A call for payment by the board of directors must be uniform so far as practicable as to all shares of the same class or series, unless the subscription agreement specifies otherwise.

(c) Shares issued pursuant to subscriptions entered into before incorporation are fully paid and nonassessable when the corporation receives the consideration specified in the subscription agreement.

(d) If a subscriber defaults in payment of money or property under a subscription agreement entered into before incorporation, the corporation may collect the amount owed as any other debt. Alternatively, unless the subscription agreement provides otherwise, the corporation may rescind the agreement and may sell the shares if the debt remains unpaid more than 20 days after the corporation sends written demand for payment to the subscriber.

(e) A subscription agreement entered into after incorporation is a contract between the subscriber and the corporation subject to section 6.21.

§6.21 Issuance of Shares

(a) The powers granted in this section to the board of directors may be reserved to the shareholders by the articles of incorporation.

(b) The board of directors may authorize shares to be issued for consideration consisting of any tangible or intangible property or benefit to the corporation, including cash, promissory notes, services performed, contracts for services to be performed, or other securities of the corporation.

(c) Before the corporation issues shares, the board of directors must determine that the consideration received or to be received for shares to be issued is adequate. That determination by the board of directors is conclusive insofar as the adequacy of consideration for the issuance of shares relates to whether the shares are validly issued, fully paid, and nonassessable.

(d) When the corporation receives the consideration for which the board of directors authorized the issuance of shares, the shares issued therefor are fully paid and nonassessable.

(e) The corporation may place in escrow shares issued for a contract for future services or benefits or a promissory note, or make other arrangements to restrict the transfer of the shares, and may credit distributions in respect of the shares against their purchase price, until the services are performed, the note is paid, or the benefits received. If the services are not performed, the note is not paid, or the benefits are not received, the shares escrowed or restricted and the distributions credited may be cancelled in whole or part.

§6.22 Liability of Shareholders

(a) A purchaser from a corporation of its own shares is not liable to the corporation or its creditors with respect to the shares except to pay the consideration for which the shares were authorized to be issued (section 6.21) or specified in the subscription agreement (section 6.20).

(b) Unless otherwise provided in the articles of incorporation, a shareholder of a corporation is not personally liable for the acts or debts of the corporation except that he may become personally liable by reason of his own acts or conduct.

§6.23 Share Dividends

(a) Unless the articles of incorporation provide otherwise, shares may be issued pro rata and without consideration to the corporation's shareholders or to the shareholders of one or more classes or series. An issuance of shares under this subsection is a share dividend.

(b) Shares of one class or series may not be issued as a share dividend in respect of shares of another class or series unless (1) the articles of incorporation so authorize, (2) a majority of the votes entitled to be cast by the class or series to be issued approve the issue, or (3) there are no outstanding shares of the class or series to be issued.

(c) If the board of directors does not fix the record date for determining shareholders entitled to a share dividend, it is the date the board of directors authorizes the share dividend.

§6.24 Share Options

A corporation may issue rights, options, or warrants for the purchase of shares of the corporation. The board of directors shall determine the terms upon which the rights, options, or warrants are issued, their form and content, and the consideration for which the shares are to be issued.

§6.25 Form and Content of Certificates

(a) Shares may but need not be represented by certificates. Unless this Act or another statute expressly provides otherwise, the rights and obligations of shareholders are identical whether or not their shares are represented by certificates.

(b) At a minimum each share certificate must state on its face:

(1) the name of the issuing corporation and that it is organized under the law of this state;

(2) the name of the person to whom issued; and

(3) the number and class of shares and the designation of the series, if any, the certificate represents.

(c) If the issuing corporation is authorized to issue different classes of shares or different series within a class, the designations, relative rights, preferences, and limitations applicable to each class and the variations in rights, preferences, and limitations determined for each series (and the authority of the board of directors to determine variations for future series) must be summarized on the front or back of each certificate. Alternatively, each certificate may state conspicuously on its front or back that the corporation will furnish the shareholder this information on request in writing and without charge.

(d) Each share certificate (1) must be signed (either manually or in facsimile) by two officers designated in the bylaws or by the board of directors and (2) may bear the corporate seal or its facsimile.

(e) If the person who signed (either manually or in facsimile) a share certificate no longer holds office when the certificate is issued, the certificate is nevertheless valid.

§6.26 Shares Without Certificates

(a) Unless the articles of incorporation or bylaws provide otherwise, the board of directors of a corporation may authorize the issue of some or all of the shares of any or all of its classes or series without certificates. The authorization does not affect shares already represented by certificates until they are surrendered to the corporation.

(b) Within a reasonable time after the issue or transfer of shares without certificates, the corporation shall send the shareholder a written statement of the information required on certificates by section 6.25(b) and (c), and, if applicable, section 6.27.

§6.27 Restriction on Transfer or Registration of Shares and Other Securities

(a) The articles of incorporation, bylaws, an agreement among shareholders, or an agreement between shareholders and the corporation may impose restrictions on the transfer or registration of transfer of shares of the corporation. A restriction does not affect shares issued before the restriction was adopted unless the holders of the shares are parties to the restriction agreement or voted in favor of the restriction.

(b) A restriction on the transfer or registration of transfer of shares is valid and enforceable against the holder or a transferee of the holder if the restriction is authorized by this section and its existence is noted conspicuously on the front or back of the certificate or is contained in the information statement required by section 6.26(b). Unless so noted, a restriction is not enforceable against a person without knowledge of the restriction.

(c) A restriction on the transfer or registration of transfer of shares is authorized:

(1) to maintain the corporation's status when it is dependent on the number or identity of its shareholders;

(2) to preserve exemptions under federal or state securities law;

(3) for any other reasonable purpose.

(d) A restriction on the transfer or registration of transfer of shares may:

(1) obligate the shareholder first to offer the corporation or other persons (separately, consecutively, or simultaneously) an opportunity to acquire the restricted shares;

(2) obligate the corporation or other persons (separately, consecutively, or simultaneously) to acquire the restricted shares;

(3) require the corporation, the holders of any class of its shares, or another person to approve the transfer of the restricted shares, if the requirement is not manifestly unreasonable;

(4) prohibit the transfer of the restricted shares to designated persons or classes of persons, if the prohibition is not manifestly unreasonable.

(e) For purposes of this section, "shares" includes a security convertible into or carrying a right to subscribe for or acquire shares.

§6.28 Expense of Issue

A corporation may pay the expenses of selling or underwriting its shares, and of organizing or reorganizing the corporation, from the consideration received for shares.

Subchapter C. Subsequent Acquisition of Shares by Shareholders and Corporation

§6.30 Shareholders' Preemptive Rights

(a) The shareholders of a corporation do not have a preemptive right to acquire the corporation's unissued shares except to the extent the articles of incorporation so provide.

(b) A statement included in the articles of incorporation that "the corporation elects to have preemptive rights" (or words of similar import) means that the following principles apply except to the extent the articles of incorporation expressly provide otherwise:

(1) The shareholders of the corporation have a preemptive right, granted on uniform terms and conditions prescribed by the board of directors to provide a fair and reasonable opportunity to exercise the right, to acquire proportional amounts of the corporation's unissued shares upon the decision of the board of directors to issue them.

(2) A shareholder may waive his preemptive right. A waiver evidenced by a writing is irrevocable even though it is not supported by consideration.

(3) There is no preemptive right with respect to:

(i) shares issued as compensation to directors, officers, agents, or employees of the corporation, its subsidiaries or affiliates;

(ii) shares issued to satisfy conversion or option rights created to provide compensation to directors, officers, agents, or employees of the corporation, its subsidiaries or affiliates;

(iii) shares authorized in articles of incorporation that are issued within six months from the effective date of incorporation;

(iv) shares sold otherwise than for money.

(4) Holders of shares of any class without general voting rights but with preferential rights to distributions or assets have no preemptive rights with respect to shares of any class.

(5) Holders of shares of any class with general voting rights but without preferential rights to distributions or assets have no preemptive rights with respect to shares of any class with preferential rights to distributions or assets unless the shares with preferential rights are convertible into or carry a right to subscribe for or acquire shares without preferential rights.

(6) Shares subject to preemptive rights that are not acquired by shareholders may be issued to any person for a period of one year after being offered to shareholders at a consideration set by the board of directors that is not lower than the consideration set for the exercise of preemptive rights. An offer at a lower consideration or after the expiration of one year is subject to the shareholders' preemptive rights.

(c) For purposes of this section, "shares" includes a security convertible into or carrying a right to subscribe for or acquire shares.

§6.31 Corporation's Acquisition of Its Own Shares

(a) A corporation may acquire its own shares and shares so acquired constitute authorized but unissued shares.

(b) If the articles of incorporation prohibit the reissue of acquired shares, the number of authorized shares is reduced by the number of shares acquired, effective upon amendment of the articles of incorporation.

(c) Articles of amendment may be adopted by the board of directors without shareholder action, shall be delivered to the secretary of state for filing, and shall set forth:

(1) the name of the corporation;

(2) the reduction in the number of authorized shares, itemized by class and series; and

(3) the total number of authorized shares, itemized by class and series, remaining after reduction of the shares.

Subchapter D. Distributions

§6.40 Distributions to Shareholders

(a) A board of directors may authorize and the corporation may make distributions to its shareholders subject to restriction by the articles of incorporation and the limitation in subsection (c).

(b) If the board of directors does not fix the record date for determining shareholders entitled to a distribution (other than one involving a purchase, redemption, or other acquisition of the corporation's shares), it is the date the board of directors authorizes the distribution.

(c) No distribution may be made if, after giving it effect:

(1) the corporation would not be able to pay its debts as they become due in the usual course of business; or

(2) the corporation's total assets would be less than the sum of its total liabilities plus (unless the articles of incorporation permit otherwise) the amount that would be needed, if the corporation were to be dissolved at the time of the distribution, to satisfy the preferential rights upon dissolution of shareholders whose preferential rights are superior to those receiving the distribution.

(d) The board of directors may base a determination that a distribution is not prohibited under subsection (c) either on financial statements prepared on the basis of accounting practices and principles that are reasonable in the circumstances or on a fair valuation or other method that is reasonable in the circumstances.

(e) Except as provided in subsection (g), the effect of a distribution under subsection (c) is measured:

(1) in the case of distribution by purchase, redemption, or other acquisition of the corporation's shares, as of the earlier of (i) the date money or other property is transferred or debt incurred by the corporation or (ii) the date the shareholder ceases to be a shareholder with respect to the acquired shares;

(2) in the case of any other distribution of indebtedness, as of the date the indebtedness is distributed;

(3) in all other cases, as of (i) the date the distribution is authorized if the payment occurs within 120 days after the date of authorization or (ii) the date the payment is made if it occurs more than 120 days after the date of authorization.

(f) A corporation's indebtedness to a shareholder incurred by reason of a distribution made in accordance with this section is at parity with the corporation's indebtedness to its general, unsecured creditors except to the extent subordinated by agreement.

(g) Indebtedness of a corporation, including indebtedness issued as a distribution, is not considered a liability for purposes of determinations under subsection (c) if its terms provide that payment of principal and interest are made only if and to the extent that payment of a distribution to shareholders could then be made under this section. If the indebtedness is issued as a distribution, each payment of principal or interest is treated as a distribution, the effect of which is measured on the date the payment is actually made.

CHAPTER 7. SHAREHOLDERS

Subchapter A. Meetings

§7.01 Annual Meeting

(a) A corporation shall hold annually at a time stated in or fixed in accordance with the bylaws a meeting of shareholders.

(b) Annual shareholders' meetings may be held in or out of this state at the place stated in or fixed in accordance with the bylaws. If no place is stated in or fixed in accordance with the bylaws, annual meetings shall be held at the corporation's principal office.

(c) The failure to hold an annual meeting at the time stated in or fixed in accordance with a corporation's bylaws does not affect the validity of any corporate action.

§7.02 Special Meeting

(a) A corporation shall hold a special meeting of shareholders:

(1) on call of its board of directors or the person or persons authorized to do so by the articles of incorporation or bylaws; or

(2) if the holders of at least 10 percent of all the votes entitled to be cast on any issue proposed to be considered at the proposed special meeting sign, date, and deliver to the corporation's secretary one or more written demands for the meeting describing the purpose or purposes for which it is to be held.

(b) If not otherwise fixed under sections 7.03 or 7.07, the record date for determining shareholders entitled to demand a special meeting is the date the first shareholder signs the demand.

(c) Special shareholders' meetings may be held in or out of this state at the place stated in or fixed in accordance with the bylaws. If no place is stated or fixed in accordance with the bylaws, special meetings shall be held at the corporation's principal office.

(d) Only business within the purpose or purposes described in the meeting notice required by section 7.05(c) may be conducted at a special shareholders' meeting.

§7.03 Court-Ordered Meeting

(a) The [name or describe] court of the county where a corporation's principal office (or, if none in this state, its registered office) is located may summarily order a meeting to be held:

(1) on application of any shareholder of the corporation entitled to participate in an annual meeting if an annual meeting was not held within the earlier of 6 months after the end of the corporation's fiscal year or 15 months after its last annual meeting; or

(2) on application of a shareholder who signed a demand for a special meeting valid under section 7.02 if:

(i) notice of the special meeting was not given within 30 days after the date the demand was delivered to the corporation's secretary; or

(ii) the special meeting was not held in accordance with the notice.

(b) The court may fix the time and place of the meeting, determine the shares entitled to participate in the meeting, specify a record date for determining shareholders entitled to notice of and to vote at the meeting, prescribe the form and content of the meeting notice, fix the quorum required for specific matters to be considered at the meeting (or direct that the votes represented at the meeting constitute a quorum for action on those matters), and enter other orders necessary to accomplish the purpose or purposes of the meeting.

§7.04 Action Without Meeting

(a) Action required or permitted by this Act to be taken at a shareholders' meeting may be taken without a meeting if the action is taken by all the shareholders entitled to vote on the action. The action must be evidenced by one or more written consents describing the action taken, signed by all the shareholders entitled to vote on the action, and delivered to the corporation for inclusion in the minutes or filing with the corporate records.

(b) If not otherwise determined under sections 7.03 or 7.07, the record date for determining shareholders entitled to take action without a meeting is the date the first shareholder signs the consent under subsection (a).

(c) A consent signed under this section has the effect of a meeting vote and may be described as such in any document.

(d) If this Act requires that notice of proposed action be given to nonvoting shareholders and the action is to be taken by unanimous consent of the voting shareholders, the corporation must give its nonvoting shareholders written notice of the proposed action at least 10 days before the action is taken. The notice must contain or be accompanied by the same material that, under this Act, would have been required to be sent to non-

voting shareholders in a notice of meeting at which the proposed action would have been submitted to the shareholders for action.

§7.05 Notice of Meeting

(a) A corporation shall notify shareholders of the date, time, and place of each annual and special shareholders' meeting no fewer than 10 nor more than 60 days before the meeting date. Unless this Act or the articles of incorporation require otherwise, the corporation is required to give notice only to shareholders entitled to vote at the meeting.

(b) Unless this Act or the articles of incorporation require otherwise, notice of an annual meeting need not include a description of the purpose or purposes for which the meeting is called.

(c) Notice of a special meeting must include a description of the purpose or purposes for which the meeting is called.

(d) If not otherwise fixed under sections 7.03 or 7.07, the record date for determining shareholders entitled to notice of and to vote at an annual or special shareholders' meeting is the day before the first notice is delivered to shareholders.

(e) Unless the bylaws require otherwise, if an annual or special shareholders' meeting is adjourned to a different date, time, or place, notice need not be given of the new date, time, or place if the new date, time, or place is announced at the meeting before adjournment. If a new record date for the adjourned meeting is or must be fixed under section 7.07, however, notice of the adjourned meeting must be given under this section to persons who are shareholders as of the new record date.

§7.06 Waiver of Notice

(a) A shareholder may waive any notice required by this Act, the articles of incorporation, or bylaws before or after the date and time stated in the notice. The waiver must be in writing, be signed by the shareholder entitled to the notice, and be delivered to the corporation for inclusion in the minutes or filing with the corporate records.

(b) A shareholder's attendance at a meeting:

(1) waives objection to lack of notice or defective notice of the meeting, unless the shareholder at the beginning of the meeting objects to holding the meeting or transacting business at the meeting;

(2) waives objection to consideration of a particular matter at the meeting that is not within the purpose or purposes described in the meeting notice, unless the shareholder objects to considering the matter when it is presented.

§7.07 Record Date

(a) The bylaws may fix or provide the manner of fixing the record date for one or more voting groups in order to determine the shareholders entitled to notice of a shareholders' meeting, to demand a special meeting, to vote, or to take any other action. If the bylaws do not fix or provide for fixing a record date, the board of directors of the corporation may fix a future date as the record date.

(b) A record date fixed under this section may not be more than 70 days before the meeting or action requiring a determination of shareholders.

(c) A determination of shareholders entitled to notice of or to vote at a shareholders' meeting is effective for any adjournment of the meeting unless the board of directors fixes a new record date, which it must do if the meeting is adjourned to a date more than 120 days after the date fixed for the original meeting.

(d) If a court orders a meeting adjourned to a date more than 120 days after the date fixed for the original meeting, it may provide that the original record date continues in effect or it may fix a new record date.

Subchapter B. Voting

§7.20 Shareholders' List for Meeting

(a) After fixing a record date for a meeting, a corporation shall prepare an alphabetical list of the names of all its shareholders who are entitled to notice of a shareholders' meeting. The list must be arranged by voting group (and within each voting group by class or series of shares) and show the address of and number of shares held by each shareholder.

(b) The shareholders' list must be available for inspection by any shareholder, beginning two business days after notice of the meeting is given for which the list was prepared and continuing through the meeting, at the corporation's principal office or at a place identified in the meeting notice in the city where the meeting will be held. A shareholder, his agent, or attorney is entitled on written demand to inspect and, subject to the requirements of section 16.02(c), to copy the list, during regular business hours and at his expense, during the period it is available for inspection.

(c) The corporation shall make the shareholders' list available at the meeting, and any shareholder, his agent, or attorney is entitled to inspect the list at any time during the meeting or any adjournment.

(d) If the corporation refuses to allow a shareholder, his agent, or attorney to inspect the shareholders' list before or at the meeting (or copy the list as permitted by subsection (b)), the [name or describe] court of the county where a corporation's principal office (or, if none in this state, its registered office) is located, on application of the shareholder, may summarily order the inspection or copying at the corporation's expense and may postpone the meeting for which the list was prepared until the inspection or copying is complete.

(e) Refusal or failure to prepare or make available the shareholders' list does not affect the validity of action taken at the meeting.

§7.21 Voting Entitlement of Shares

(a) Except as provided in subsections (b) and (c) or unless the articles of incorporation provide otherwise, each outstanding share, regardless of class, is entitled to one vote on each matter voted on at a shareholders' meeting. Only shares are entitled to vote.

(b) Absent special circumstances, the shares of a corporation are not entitled to vote if they are owned, directly or indirectly, by a second corporation, domestic or foreign, and the first corporation owns, directly or indirectly, a majority of the shares entitled to vote for directors of the second corporation.

(c) Subsection (b) does not limit the power of a corporation to vote any shares, including its own shares, held by it in a fiduciary capacity.

(d) Redeemable shares are not entitled to vote after notice of redemption is mailed to the holders and a sum sufficient to redeem the shares has been deposited with a bank, trust company, or other financial institution under an irrevocable obligation to pay the holders the redemption price on surrender of the shares.

§7.22 Proxies

(a) A shareholder may vote his shares in person or by proxy.

(b) A shareholder may appoint a proxy to vote or otherwise act for him by signing an appointment form, either personally or by his attorney-in-fact.

(c) An appointment of a proxy is effective when received by the secretary or other officer or agent authorized to tabulate votes. An appointment is valid for 11 months unless a longer period is expressly provided in the appointment form.

(d) An appointment of a proxy is revocable by the shareholder unless the appointment form conspicuously states that it is irrevocable and the appointment is coupled with an interest. Appointments coupled with an interest include the appointment of:

(1) a pledgee;

(2) a person who purchased or agreed to purchase the shares;

(3) a creditor of the corporation who extended it credit under terms requiring the appointment;

(4) an employee of the corporation whose employment contract requires the appointment; or

(5) a party to a voting agreement created under section 7.31.

(e) The death or incapacity of the shareholder appointing a proxy does not affect the right of the corporation to accept the proxy's authority unless notice of the death or incapacity is received by the secretary or other officer or agent authorized to tabulate votes before the proxy exercises his authority under the appointment.

(f) An appointment made irrevocable under subsection (d) is revoked when the interest with which it is coupled is extinguished.

(g) A transferee for value of shares subject to an irrevocable appointment may revoke the appointment if he did not know of its existence when he acquired the shares and the existence of the irrevocable appointment was not noted conspicuously on the certificate representing the shares or on the information statement for shares without certificates.

(h) Subject to section 7.24 and to any express limitation on the proxy's authority appearing on the face of the appointment form, a corporation is entitled to accept the proxy's vote or other action as that of the shareholder making the appointment.

§7.23 Shares Held by Nominees

(a) A corporation may establish a procedure by which the beneficial owner of shares that are registered in the name of a nominee is recognized by the corporation as the shareholder. The extent of this recognition may be determined in the procedure.

(b) The procedure may set forth:

(1) the types of nominees to which it applies;

(2) the rights or privileges that the corporation recognizes in a beneficial owner;

(3) the manner in which the procedure is selected by the nominee;

(4) the information that must be provided when the procedure is selected;

(5) the period for which selection of the procedure is effective; and

(6) other aspects of the rights and duties created.

§7.24 Corporation's Acceptance of Votes

(a) If the name signed on a vote, consent, waiver, or proxy appointment corresponds to the name of a shareholder, the corporation if acting in good faith is entitled to accept the vote, consent, waiver, or proxy appointment and give it effect as the act of the shareholder.

(b) If the name signed on a vote, consent, waiver, or proxy appointment does not correspond to the name of its shareholder, the corporation if acting in good faith is nevertheless entitled to accept the vote, consent, waiver, or proxy appointment and give it effect as the act of the shareholder if:

(1) the shareholder is an entity and the name signed purports to be that of an officer or agent of the entity;

(2) the name signed purports to be that of an administrator, executor, guardian, or conservator representing the shareholder and, if the corporation requests, evidence of fiduciary status acceptable to the corporation has been presented with respect to the vote, consent, waiver, or proxy appointment;

(3) the name signed purports to be that of a receiver or trustee in bankruptcy of the shareholder and, if the corporation requests, evidence of this status acceptable to the corporation has been presented with respect to the vote, consent, waiver, or proxy appointment;

(4) the name signed purports to be that of a pledgee, beneficial owner, or attorney-in-fact of the shareholder and, if the corporation requests, evidence acceptable to the corporation of the signatory's authority to sign for the shareholder has been presented with respect to the vote, consent, waiver, or proxy appointment;

(5) two or more persons are the shareholder as cotenants or fiduciaries and the name signed purports to be the name of at least one of the coowners and the person signing appears to be acting on behalf of all the coowners.

(c) The corporation is entitled to reject a vote, consent, waiver, or proxy appointment if the secretary or other officer or agent authorized to tabulate votes, acting in good faith, has reasonable basis for doubt about the validity of the signature on it or about the signatory's authority to sign for the shareholder.

(d) The corporation and its officer or agent who accepts or rejects a vote, consent, waiver, or proxy appointment in good faith and in accordance with the standards of this section are not liable in damages to the shareholder for the consequences of the acceptance or rejection.

(e) Corporate action based on the acceptance or rejection of a vote, consent, waiver, or proxy appointment under this section is valid unless a court of competent jurisdiction determines otherwise.

§7.25 Quorum and Voting Requirements for Voting Groups

(a) Shares entitled to vote as a separate voting group may take action on a matter at a meeting only if a quorum of those shares exists with respect to that matter. Unless the articles of incorporation or this Act provide otherwise, a majority of the votes entitled to be cast on the matter by the voting group constitutes a quorum of that voting group for action on that matter.

(b) Once a share is represented for any purpose at a meeting, it is deemed present for quorum purposes for the remainder of the meeting and for any adjournment of that meeting unless a new record date is or must be set for that adjourned meeting.

(c) If a quorum exists, action on a matter (other than the election of directors) by a voting group is approved if the votes cast within the voting group favoring the action exceed the votes cast opposing the action, unless the articles of incorporation or this Act require a greater number of affirmative votes.

(d) An amendment of articles of incorporation adding, changing, or deleting a quorum or voting requirement for a voting group greater than specified in subsection (b) or (c) is governed by section 7.27.

(e) The election of directors is governed by section 7.28.

§7.26 Action by Single and Multiple Voting Groups

(a) If the articles of incorporation or this Act provide for voting by a single voting group on a matter, action on that matter is taken when voted upon by that voting group as provided in section 7.25.

(b) If the articles of incorporation or this Act provide for voting by two or more voting groups on a matter, action on that matter is taken only when voted upon by each of those voting groups counted separately as provided in section 7.25. Action may be taken by one voting group on a matter even though no action is taken by another voting group entitled to vote on the matter.

§7.27 Greater Quorum or Voting Requirements

(a) The articles of incorporation may provide for a greater quorum or voting requirement for shareholders (or voting groups of shareholders) than is provided for by this Act.

(b) An amendment to the articles of incorporation that adds, changes, or deletes a greater quorum or voting requirement must meet the same quorum requirement and be adopted by the same vote and voting groups required to take action under the quorum and voting requirements then in effect or proposed to be adopted, whichever is greater.

§7.28 Voting for Directors; Cumulative Voting

(a) Unless otherwise provided in the articles of incorporation, directors are elected by a plurality of the votes cast by the shares entitled to vote in the election at a meeting at which a quorum is present.

(b) Shareholders do not have a right to cumulate their votes for directors unless the articles of incorporation so provide.

(c) A statement included in the articles of incorporation that "[all] [a designated voting group of] shareholders are entitled to cumulate their votes for directors" (or words of similar import) means that the shareholders designated are entitled to multiply the number of votes they are entitled to cast by the number of directors for whom they are entitled to vote and cast the product for a single candidate or distribute the product among two or more candidates.

(d) Shares otherwise entitled to vote cumulatively may not be voted cumulatively at a particular meeting unless:

(1) the meeting notice or proxy statement accompanying the notice states conspicuously that cumulative voting is authorized; or

(2) a shareholder who has the right to cumulate his votes gives notice to the corporation not less than 48 hours before the time set for the meeting of his intent to cumulate his votes during the meeting, and if

one shareholder gives this notice all other shareholders in the same voting group participating in the election are entitled to cumulate their votes without giving further notice.

Subchapter C. Voting Trusts and Agreements

§7.30 Voting Trusts

(a) One or more shareholders may create a voting trust, conferring on a trustee the right to vote or otherwise act for them, by signing an agreement setting out the provisions of the trust (which may include anything consistent with its purpose) and transferring their shares to the trustee. When a voting trust agreement is signed, the trustee shall prepare a list of the names and addresses of all owners of beneficial interests in the trust, together with the number and class of shares each transferred to the trust, and deliver copies of the list and agreement to the corporation's principal office.

(b) A voting trust becomes effective on the date the first shares subject to the trust are registered in the trustee's name. A voting trust is valid for not more than 10 years after its effective date unless extended under subsection (c).

(c) All or some of the parties to a voting trust may extend it for additional terms of not more than 10 years each by signing an extension agreement and obtaining the voting trustee's written consent to the extension. An extension is valid for 10 years from the date the first shareholder signs the extension agreement. The voting trustee must deliver copies of the extension agreement and list of beneficial owners to the corporation's principal office. An extension agreement binds only those parties signing it.

§7.31 Voting Agreements

(a) Two or more shareholders may provide for the manner in which they will vote their shares by signing an agreement for that purpose. A voting agreement created under this section is not subject to the provisions of section 7.30.

(b) A voting agreement created under this section is specifically enforceable.

§7.32 Shareholder Agreements

(a) An agreement among the shareholders of a corporation that complies with this section is effective among the shareholders and the corporation even though it is inconsistent with one or more other provisions of this Act in that it:

(1) eliminates the board of directors or restricts the discretion or powers of the board of directors;

(2) governs the authorization or making of distributions whether or not in proportion to ownership of shares, subject to the limitations in section 6.40;

(3) establishes who shall be directors or officers of the corporation, or their terms of office or manner of selection or removal;

(4) governs, in general or in regard to specific matters, the exercise or division of voting power by or between the shareholders and directors or by or among any of them, including use of weighted voting rights or director proxies;

(5) establishes the terms and conditions of any agreement for the transfer or use of property or the provision of services between the corporation and any shareholder, director, officer or employee of the corporation or among any of them;

(6) transfers to one or more shareholders or other persons all or part of the authority to exercise the corporate powers or to manage the business and affairs of the corporation, including the resolution of any issue about which there exists a deadlock among directors or shareholders;

(7) requires dissolution of the corporation at the request of one or more of the shareholders or upon the occurrence of a specified event or contingency; or

(8) otherwise governs the exercise of the corporate powers or the management of the business and affairs of the corporation or the relationship among the shareholders, the directors and the corporation, or among any of them, and is not contrary to public policy.

(b) An agreement authorized by this section shall be:

(1) set forth (A) in the articles of incorporation or bylaws and approved by all persons who are shareholders at the time of the agreement or (B) in a written agreement that is signed by all persons who are shareholders at the time of the agreement and is made known to the corporation;

(2) subject to amendment only by all persons who are shareholders at the time of the amendment, unless the agreement provides otherwise; and

(3) valid for 10 years, unless the agreement provides otherwise.

(c) The existence of an agreement authorized by this section shall be noted conspicuously on the front or back of each certificate for outstanding shares or on the information statement required by section 6.26(b). If at the time of the agreement the corporation has shares outstanding represented by certificates, the corporation shall recall the outstanding certificates and issue substitute certificates that comply with this subsection. The failure to note the existence of the agreement on the certificate or information statement shall not affect the validity of the agreement or any action taken pursuant to it. Any purchaser of shares who, at the time of purchase, did not have knowledge of the existence of the agreement shall be entitled to rescission of the purchase. A purchaser shall be deemed to have knowledge of the existence of the agreement if its existence is noted on the certificate or information statement for the shares in compliance with this subsection and, if the shares are not represented by a certificate, the information statement is delivered to the purchaser at or prior to the time of purchase of the shares. An action to enforce the right of rescission authorized by this subsection must be commenced within the earlier of 90 days after discovery of the existence of the agreement or two years after the time of purchase of the shares.

(d) An agreement authorized by this section shall cease to be effective when shares of the corporation are listed on a national securities exchange or regularly traded in a market maintained by one or more members of a national or affiliated securities association. If the agreement ceases to be effective for any reason, the board of directors may, if the agreement is contained or referred to in the corporation's articles of incorporation or bylaws, adopt an amendment to the articles of incorporation or bylaws, without shareholder action, to delete the agreement and any references to it.

(e) An agreement authorized by this section that limits the discretion or powers of the board of directors shall relieve the directors of, and impose upon the person or persons in whom such discretion or powers are vested, liability for acts or omissions imposed by law on directors to the extent that the discretion or powers of the directors are limited by the agreement.

(f) The existence or performance of an agreement authorized by this section shall not be a ground for imposing personal liability on any shareholder for the acts or debts of the corporation even if the agreement or its performance treats the corporation as if it were a partnership or results in failure to observe the corporate formalities otherwise applicable to the matters governed by the agreement.

(g) Incorporators or subscribers for shares may act as shareholders with respect to an agreement authorized by this section if no shares have been issued when the agreement is made.

Subchapter D. Derivative Proceedings

§7.40 Subchapter Definitions

In this subchapter:

(1) "Derivative proceeding" means a civil suit in the right of a domestic corporation or, to the extent provided in section 7.47, in the right of a foreign corporation.

(2) "Shareholder" includes a beneficial owner whose shares are held in a voting trust or held by a nominee on the beneficial owner's behalf.

§7.41 Standing

A shareholder may not commence or maintain a derivative proceeding unless the shareholder:

(1) was a shareholder of the corporation at the time of the act or omission complained of or became a shareholder through transfer by operation of law from one who was a shareholder at that time; and

(2) fairly and adequately represents the interests of the corporation in enforcing the right of the corporation.

§7.42 Demand

No shareholder may commence a derivative proceeding until:

(1) a written demand has been made upon the corporation to take suitable action; and

(2) 90 days have expired from the date the demand was made unless the shareholder has earlier been notified that the demand has been rejected by the corporation or unless irreparable injury to the corporation would result by waiting for the expiration of the 90 day period.

§7.43 Stay of Proceedings

If the corporation commences an inquiry into the allegations made in the demand or complaint, the court may stay any derivative proceeding for such period as the court deems appropriate.

§7.44 Dismissal

(a) A derivative proceeding shall be dismissed by the court on motion by the corporation if one of the groups specified in subsections (b) or (f) has determined in good faith after conducting a reasonable inquiry upon which its conclusions are based that the maintenance of the derivative proceeding is not in the best interests of the corporation.

(b) Unless a panel is appointed pursuant to subsection (f), the determination in subsection (a) shall be made by:

(1) a majority vote of independent directors present at a meeting of the board of directors if the independent directors constitute a quorum; or

(2) a majority vote of a committee consisting of two or more independent directors appointed by majority vote of independent directors present at a meeting of the board of directors, whether or not such independent directors constituted a quorum.

(c) None of the following shall by itself cause a director to be considered not independent for purposes of this section:

(1) the nomination or election of the director by persons who are defendants in the derivative proceeding or against whom action is demanded;

(2) the naming of the director as a defendant in the derivative proceeding or as a person against whom action is demanded; or

(3) the approval by the director of the act being challenged in the derivative proceeding or demand if the act resulted in no personal benefit to the director.

(d) If a derivative proceeding is commenced after a determination has been made rejecting a demand by a shareholder, the complaint shall allege with particularity facts establishing either (1) that a majority of the board of directors did not consist of independent directors at the time the determination was made or (2) that the requirements of subsection (a) have not been met.

(e) If a majority of the board of directors does not consist of independent directors at the time the determination is made, the corporation shall have the burden of proving that the requirements of subsection (a) have been met. If a majority of the board of directors consists of independent directors at the time the determination is made, the plaintiff shall have the burden of proving that the requirements of subsection (a) have not been met.

(f) The court may appoint a panel of one or more independent persons upon motion by the corporation to make a determination whether the maintenance of the derivative proceeding is in the best interests of the corporation. In such case, the plaintiff shall have the burden of proving that the requirements of subsection (a) have not been met.

§7.45 Discontinuance or Settlement

A derivative proceeding may not be discontinued or settled without the court's approval. If the court determines that a proposed discontinuance or settlement will substantially affect the interests of the corporation's shareholders or a class of shareholders, the court shall direct that notice be given to the shareholders affected.

§7.46 Payment of Expenses

On termination of the derivative proceeding the court may:

(1) order the corporation to pay the plaintiff's reasonable expenses (including counsel fees) incurred in the proceeding if it finds that the proceeding has resulted in a substantial benefit to the corporation;

(2) order the plaintiff to pay any defendant's reasonable expenses (including counsel fees) incurred in defending the proceeding if it finds that the proceeding was commenced or maintained without reasonable cause or for an improper purpose; or

(3) order a party to pay an opposing party's reasonable expenses (including counsel fees) incurred because of the filing of a pleading, motion or other paper, if it finds that the pleading, motion or other paper was not well grounded in fact, after reasonable inquiry, or warranted by existing law or a good faith argument for the extension, modification or reversal of existing law and was interposed for an improper purpose, such as to harass or to cause unnecessary delay or needless increase in the cost of litigation.

§7.47 Applicability to Foreign Corporations

In any derivative proceeding in the right of a foreign corporation, the matters covered by this subchapter shall be governed by the laws of the jurisdiction of incorporation of the foreign corporation except for sections 7.43, 7.45 and 7.46.

CHAPTER 8. DIRECTORS AND OFFICERS

Subchapter A. Board of Directors

§8.01 Requirements for and Duties of Board of Directors

(a) Except as provided is section 7.32, each corporation must have a board of directors.

(b) All corporate powers shall be exercised by or under the authority of, and the business and affairs of the corporation managed under the direction of, its board of directors, subject to any limitation set forth in the articles of incorporation or in an agreement authorized under section 7.32.

§8.02 Qualifications of Directors

The articles of incorporation or bylaws may prescribe qualifications for directors. A director need not be a resident of this state or a shareholder of the corporation unless the articles of incorporation or bylaws so prescribe.

§8.03 Number and Election of Directors

(a) A board of directors must consist of one or more individuals, with the number specified in or fixed in accordance with the articles of incorporation or bylaws.

(b) If a board of directors has power to fix or change the number of directors, the board may increase or decrease by 30 percent or less the number of directors last approved by the shareholders, but only the shareholders may increase or decrease by more than 30 percent the number of directors last approved by the shareholders.

(c) The articles of incorporation or bylaws may establish a variable range for the size of the board of directors by fixing a minimum and maximum number of directors. If a variable range is established, the number of directors may be fixed or changed from time to time, within the minimum and maximum, by the shareholders or the board of directors. After shares are issued, only the shareholders may change the range for the size of the board or change from a fixed to a variable-range size board or vice versa.

(d) Directors are elected at the first annual shareholders' meeting and at each annual meeting thereafter unless their terms are staggered under section 8.06.

§8.04 Election of Directors by Certain Classes of Shareholders

If the articles of incorporation authorize dividing the shares into classes, the articles may also authorize the election of all or a specified number of directors by the holders of one or more authorized classes of shares. Each class (or classes) of shares entitled to elect one or more directors is a separate voting group for purposes of the election of directors.

§8.05 Terms of Directors Generally

(a) The terms of the initial directors of a corporation expire at the first shareholders' meeting at which directors are elected.

(b) The terms of all other directors expire at the next annual shareholders' meeting following their election unless their terms are staggered under section 8.06.

(c) A decrease in the number of directors does not shorten an incumbent director's term.

(d) The term of a director elected to fill a vacancy expires at the next shareholders' meeting at which directors are elected.

(e) Despite the expiration of a director's term, he continues to serve until his successor is elected and qualifies or until there is a decrease in the number of directors.

§8.06 Staggered Terms for Directors

If there are nine or more directors, the articles of incorporation may provide for staggering their terms by dividing the total number of directors into two or three groups, with each group containing one-half or one-third of the total, as near as may be. In that event, the terms of directors in the first group expire at the first annual shareholders' meeting after their election, the terms of the second group expire at the second annual shareholders' meeting after their election, and the terms of the third group, if any, expire at the third annual shareholders' meeting after their election. At each annual shareholders' meeting held thereafter, directors shall be chosen for a term of two years or three years, as the case may be, to succeed those whose terms expire.

§8.07 Resignation of Directors

(a) A director may resign at any time by delivering written notice to the board of directors, its chairman, or to the corporation.

(b) A resignation is effective when the notice is delivered unless the notice specifies a later effective date.

§8.08 Removal of Directors by Shareholders

(a) The shareholders may remove one or more directors with or without cause unless the articles of incorporation provide that directors may be removed only for cause.

(b) If a director is elected by a voting group of shareholders, only the shareholders of that voting group may participate in the vote to remove him.

(c) If cumulative voting is authorized, a director may not be removed if the number of votes sufficient to elect him under cumulative voting is voted against his removal. If cumulative voting is not authorized, a director may be removed only if the number of votes cast to remove him exceeds the number of votes cast not to remove him.

(d) A director may be removed by the shareholders only at a meeting called for the purpose of removing him and the meeting notice must state that the purpose, or one of the purposes, of the meeting is removal of the director.

§8.09 Removal of Directors by Judicial Proceeding

(a) The [name or describe] court of the county where a corporation's principal office (or, if none in this state, its registered office) is located may remove a director of the corporation from office in a proceeding commenced either by the corporation or by its shareholders holding at least 10 percent of the outstanding shares of any class if the court finds that (1) the director engaged in fraudulent or dishonest conduct, or gross abuse of authority or discretion, with respect to the corporation and (2) removal is in the best interest of the corporation.

(b) The court that removes a director may bar the director from reelection for a period prescribed by the court.

(c) If shareholders commence a proceeding under subsection (a), they shall make the corporation a party defendant.

§8.10 Vacancy on Board

(a) Unless the articles of incorporation provide otherwise, if a vacancy occurs on a board of directors, including a vacancy resulting from an increase in the number of directors:

(1) the shareholders may fill the vacancy;

(2) the board of directors may fill the vacancy; or

(3) if the directors remaining in office constitute fewer than a quorum of the board, they may fill the vacancy by the affirmative vote of a majority of all the directors remaining in office.

(b) If the vacant office was held by a director elected by a voting group of shareholders, only the holders of shares of that voting group are entitled to vote to fill the vacancy if it is filled by the shareholders.

(c) A vacancy that will occur at a specific later date (by reason of a resignation effective at a later date under section 8.07(b) or otherwise) may be filled before the vacancy occurs but the new director may not take office until the vacancy occurs.

§8.11 Compensation of Directors

Unless the articles of incorporation or bylaws provide otherwise, the board of directors may fix the compensation of directors.

Subchapter B. Meetings and Action of the Board

§8.20 Meetings

(a) The board of directors may hold regular or special meetings in or out of this state.

(b) Unless the articles of incorporation or bylaws provide otherwise, the board of directors may permit any or all directors to participate in a regular or special meeting by, or conduct the meeting through the use of, any means of communication by which all directors participating may simultaneously hear each other during the meeting. A director participating in a meeting by this means is deemed to be present in person at the meeting.

§8.21 Action Without Meeting

(a) Unless the articles of incorporation or bylaws provide otherwise, action required or permitted by this Act to be taken at a board of directors' meeting may be taken without a meeting if the action is taken by all members of the board. The action must be evidenced by one or more written consents describing the action taken, signed by each director, and included in the minutes or filed with the corporate records reflecting the action taken.

(b) Action taken under this section is effective when the last director signs the consent, unless the consent specifies a different effective date.

(c) A consent signed under this section has the effect of a meeting vote and may be described as such in any document.

§8.22 Notice of Meeting

(a) Unless the articles of incorporation or bylaws provide otherwise, regular meetings of the board of directors may be held without notice of the date, time, place, or purpose of the meeting.

(b) Unless the articles of incorporation or bylaws provide for a longer or shorter period, special meetings of the board of directors must be preceded by at least two days' notice of the date, time, and place of the meeting. The notice need not describe the purpose of the special meeting unless required by the articles of incorporation or bylaws.

§8.23 Waiver of Notice

(a) A director may waive any notice required by this Act, the articles of incorporation, or bylaws before or after the date and time stated in the notice. Except as provided by subsection (b), the waiver must be in writing, signed by the director entitled to the notice, and filed with the minutes or corporate records.

(b) A director's attendance at or participation in a meeting waives any required notice to him of the meeting unless the director at the beginning of the meeting (or promptly upon his arrival) objects to holding the meeting or transacting business at the meeting and does not thereafter vote for or assent to action taken at the meeting.

§8.24 Quorum and Voting

(a) Unless the articles of incorporation or bylaws require a greater number, a quorum of a board of directors consists of:

(1) a majority of the fixed number of directors if the corporation has a fixed board size; or

(2) a majority of the number of directors prescribed, or if no number is prescribed the number in office immediately before the meeting begins, if the corporation has a variable-range size board.

(b) The articles of incorporation or bylaws may authorize a quorum of a board of directors to consist of no fewer than one-third of the fixed or prescribed number of directors determined under subsection (a).

(c) If a quorum is present when a vote is taken, the affirmative vote of a majority of directors present is the act of the board of directors unless the articles of incorporation or bylaws require the vote of a greater number of directors.

(d) A director who is present at a meeting of the board of directors or a committee of the board of directors when corporate action is taken is deemed to have assented to the action taken unless: (1) he objects at the beginning of the meeting (or promptly upon his arrival) to holding it or transacting business at the meeting; (2) his dissent or abstention from the action taken is entered in the minutes of the meeting; or (3) he delivers written notice of his dissent or abstention to the presiding officer of the meeting before its adjournment or to the corporation immediately after adjournment of the meeting. The right of dissent or abstention is not available to a director who votes in favor of the action taken.

§8.25 Committees

(a) Unless the articles of incorporation or bylaws provide otherwise, a board of directors may create one or more committees and appoint members of the board of directors to serve on them. Each committee may have two or more members, who serve at the pleasure of the board of directors.

(b) The creation of a committee and appointment of members to it must be approved by the greater of (1) a majority of all the directors in office when the action is taken or (2) the number of directors required by the articles of incorporation or bylaws to take action under section 8.24.

(c) Sections 8.20 through 8.24, which govern meetings, action without meetings, notice and waiver of notice, and quorum and voting requirements of the board of directors, apply to committees and their members as well.

(d) To the extent specified by the board of directors or in the articles of incorporation or bylaws, each committee may exercise the authority of the board of directors under section 8.01.

(e) A committee may not, however:

(1) authorize distributions;

(2) approve or propose to shareholders action that this Act requires to be approved by shareholders;

(3) fill vacancies on the board of directors or on any of its committees;

(4) amend articles of incorporation pursuant to section 10.02;

(5) adopt, amend, or repeal bylaws;

(6) approve a plan of merger not requiring shareholder approval;

(7) authorize or approve reacquisition of shares, except according to a formula or method prescribed by the board of directors; or

(8) authorize or approve the issuance or sale or contract for sale of shares, or determine the designation and relative rights, preferences, and limitations of a class or series of shares, except that the board of directors may authorize a committee (or a senior executive officer of the corporation) to do so within limits specifically prescribed by the board of directors.

(f) The creation of, delegation of authority to, or action by a committee does not alone constitute compliance by a director with the standards of conduct described in section 8.30.

Subchapter C. Standards of Conduct

§8.30 General Standards for Directors

(a) A director shall discharge his duties as a director, including his duties as a member of a committee:

(1) in good faith;

(2) with the care an ordinarily prudent person in a like position would exercise under similar circumstances; and

(3) in a manner he reasonably believes to be in the best interests of the corporation.

(b) In discharging his duties a director is entitled to rely on information, opinions, reports, or statements, including financial statements and other financial data, if prepared or presented by:

(1) one or more officers or employees of the corporation whom the director reasonably believes to be reliable and competent in the matters presented;

(2) legal counsel, public accountants, or other persons as to matters the director reasonably believes are within the person's professional or expert competence; or

(3) a committee of the board of directors of which he is not a member if the director reasonably believes the committee merits confidence.

(c) A director is not acting in good faith if he has knowledge concerning the matter in question that makes reliance otherwise permitted by subsection (b) unwarranted.

(d) A director is not liable for any action taken as a director, or any failure to take any action, if he performed the duties of his office in compliance with this section.

§8.31 Director Conflict of Interest*

(a) A conflict of interest transaction is a transaction with the corporation in which a director of the corporation has a direct or indirect interest. A conflict of interest transaction is not voidable by the corporation solely because of the director's interest in the transaction if any one of the following is true:

(1) the material facts of the transaction and the director's interest were disclosed or known to the board of directors or a committee of the board of directors and the board of directors or committee authorized, approved, or ratified the transaction;

(2) the material facts of the transaction and the director's interest were disclosed or known to the shareholders entitled to vote and they authorized, approved, or ratified the transaction; or

(3) the transaction was fair to the corporation.

(b) For purposes of this section, a director of the corporation has an indirect interest in a transaction if (1) another entity in which he has a material financial interest or in which he is a general partner is a party to the transaction or (2) another entity of which he is a director, officer, or trustee is a party to the transaction and the transaction is or should be considered by the board of directors of the corporation.

(c) For purposes of subsection (a)(1), a conflict of interest transaction is authorized, approved, or ratified if it receives the affirmative vote of a majority of the directors on the board of directors (or on the committee) who have no direct or indirect interest in the transaction, but a transaction may not be authorized, approved, or ratified under this section by a single director. If a majority of the directors who have no direct or indirect interest in the transaction vote to authorize, approve, or ratify the transaction, a quorum is present for the purpose of taking action under this section. The presence of, or a vote cast by, a director with a direct or indirect interest in the transaction does not affect the validity of any action taken under subsection (a)(1) if the transaction is otherwise authorized, approved, or ratified as provided in that subsection.

(d) For purposes of subsection (a)(2), a conflict of interest transaction is authorized, approved, or ratified if it receives the vote of a majority of the shares entitled to be counted under this subsection. Shares owned by or

voted under the control of a director who has a direct or indirect interest in the transaction, and shares owned by or voted under the control of an entity described in subsection (b)(1), may not be counted in a vote of shareholders to determine whether to authorize, approve, or ratify a conflict of interest transaction under subsection (a)(2). The vote of those shares, however, shall be counted in determining whether the transaction is approved under other sections of this Act. A majority of the shares, whether or not present, that are entitled to be counted in a vote on the transaction under this subsection constitutes a quorum for the purpose of taking action under this section.

§8.32 Loans to Directors

(a) Except as provided by subsection (c), a corporation may not lend money to or guarantee the obligation of a director of the corporation unless:

(1) the particular loan or guarantee is approved by a majority of the votes represented by the outstanding voting shares of all classes, voting as a single voting group, except the votes of shares owned by or voted under the control of the benefited director; or

(2) the corporation's board of directors determines that the loan or guarantee benefits the corporation and either approves the specific loan or guarantee or a general plan authorizing loans and guarantees.

(b) The fact that a loan or guarantee is made in violation of this section does not affect the borrower's liability on the loan.

(c) This section does not apply to loans and guarantees authorized by statute regulating any special class of corporations.

§8.33 Liability for Unlawful Distributions

(a) A director who votes for or assents to a distribution made in violation of section 6.40 or the articles of incorporation is personally liable to the corporation for the amount of the distribution that exceeds what could have been distributed without violating section 6.40 or the articles of incorporation if it is established that he did not perform his duties in compliance with section 8.30. In any proceeding commenced under this section, a director has all of the defenses ordinarily available to a director.

(b) A director held liable under subsection (a) for an unlawful distribution is entitled to contribution:

(1) from every other director who could be held liable under subsection (a) for the unlawful distribution; and

(2) from each shareholder for the amount the shareholder accepted knowing the distribution was made in violation of section 6.40 or the articles of incorporation.

(c) A proceeding under this section is barred unless it is commenced within two years after the date on which the effect of the distribution was measured under section 6.40(e) or (g).

Subchapter D. Officers

§8.40 Required Officers

(a) A corporation has the officers described in its bylaws or appointed by the board of directors in accordance with the bylaws.

(b) A duly appointed officer may appoint one or more officers or assistant officers if authorized by the bylaws or the board of directors.

(c) The bylaws or the board of directors shall delegate to one of the officers responsibility for preparing minutes of the directors' and shareholders' meetings and for authenticating records of the corporation.

(d) The same individual may simultaneously hold more than one office in a corporation.

§8.41 Duties of Officers

Each officer has the authority and shall perform the duties set forth in the bylaws or, to the extent consistent with the bylaws, the duties prescribed

*[Editors' Note: In 1989, the Revised Model Business Corporation Act was amended by deleting Sections 8.31 and 8.32 and replacing them with a new Subchapter F, consisting of Sections 8.60–8.63. Because of the relatively short period of time since the adoption of Subchapter F, this volume retains the deleted sections as well as the new material.]

by the board of directors or by direction of an officer authorized by the board of directors to prescribe the duties of other officers.

§8.42 Standards of Conduct for Officers

(a) An officer with discretionary authority shall discharge his duties under that authority:

(1) in good faith;

(2) with the care an ordinarily prudent person in a like position would exercise under similar circumstances; and

(3) in a manner he reasonably believes to be in the best interests of the corporation.

(b) In discharging his duties an officer is entitled to rely on information, opinions, reports, or statements, including financial statements and other financial data, if prepared or presented by:

(1) one or more officers or employees of the corporation whom the officer reasonably believes to be reliable and competent in the matters presented; or

(2) legal counsel, public accountants, or other persons as to matters the officer reasonably believes are within the person's professional or expert competence.

(c) An officer is not acting in good faith if he has knowledge concerning the matter in question that makes reliance otherwise permitted by subsection (b) unwarranted.

(d) An officer is not liable for any action taken as an officer, or any failure to take any action, if he performed the duties of his office in compliance with this section.

§8.43 Resignation and Removal of Officers

(a) An officer may resign at any time by delivering notice to the corporation. A resignation is effective when the notice is delivered unless the notice specifies a later effective date. If a resignation is made effective at a later date and the corporation accepts the future effective date, its board of directors may fill the pending vacancy before the effective date if the board of directors provides that the successor does not take office until the effective date.

(b) A board of directors may remove any officer at any time with or without cause.

§8.44 Contract Rights of Officers

(a) The appointment of an officer does not itself create contract rights.

(b) An officer's removal does not affect the officer's contract rights, if any, with the corporation. An officer's resignation does not affect the corporation's contract rights, if any, with the officer.

Subchapter E. Indemnification

§8.50 Subchapter Definitions

In this subchapter:

(1) "Corporation" includes any domestic or foreign predecessor entity of a corporation in a merger or other transaction in which the predecessor's existence ceased upon consummation of the transaction.

(2) "Director" means an individual who is or was a director of a corporation or an individual who, while a director of a corporation, is or was serving at the corporation's request as a director, officer, partner, trustee, employee, or agent of another foreign or domestic corporation, partnership, joint venture, trust, employee benefit plan, or other enterprise. A director is considered to be serving an employee benefit plan at the corporation's request if his duties to the corporation also impose duties on, or otherwise involve services by, him to the plan or to participants in or beneficiaries of the plan. "Director" includes, unless the context requires otherwise, the estate or personal representative of a director.

(3) "Expenses" include counsel fees.

(4) "Liability" means the obligation to pay a judgment, settlement, penalty, fine (including an excise tax assessed with respect to an em-

ployee benefit plan), or reasonable expenses incurred with respect to a proceeding.

(5) "Official capacity" means: (i) when used with respect to a director, the office of director in a corporation; and (ii) when used with respect to an individual other than a director, as contemplated in section 8.56, the office in a corporation held by the officer or the employment or agency relationship undertaken by the employee or agent on behalf of the corporation. "Official capacity" does not include service for any other foreign or domestic corporation or any partnership, joint venture, trust, employee benefit plan, or other enterprise.

(6) "Party" includes an individual who was, is, or is threatened to be made a named defendant or respondent in a proceeding.

(7) "Proceeding" means any threatened, pending, or completed action, suit, or proceeding, whether civil, criminal, administrative, or investigative and whether formal or informal.

§8.51 Authority to Indemnify

(a) Except as provided in subsection (d), a corporation may indemnify an individual made a party to a proceeding because he is or was a director against liability incurred in the proceeding if:

(1) he conducted himself in good faith; and

(2) he reasonably believed:

(i) in the case of conduct in his official capacity with the corporation, that his conduct was in its best interests; and

(ii) in all other cases, that his conduct was at least not opposed to its best interests; and

(3) in the case of any criminal proceeding, he had no reasonable cause to believe his conduct was unlawful.

(b) A director's conduct with respect to an employee benefit plan for a purpose he reasonably believed to be in the interests of the participants in and beneficiaries of the plan is conduct that satisfies the requirement of subsection (a)(2)(ii).

(c) The termination of a proceeding by judgment, order, settlement, conviction, or upon a plea of nolo contendere or its equivalent is not, of itself, determinative that the director did not meet the standard of conduct described in this section.

(d) A corporation may not indemnify a director under this section:

(1) in connection with a proceeding by or in the right of the corporation in which the director was adjudged liable to the corporation; or

(2) in connection with any other proceeding charging improper personal benefit to him, whether or not involving action in his official capacity, in which he was adjudged liable on the basis that personal benefit was improperly received by him.

(e) Indemnification permitted under this section in connection with a proceeding by or in the right of the corporation is limited to reasonable expenses incurred in connection with the proceeding.

§8.52 Mandatory Indemnification

Unless limited by its articles of incorporation, a corporation shall indemnify a director who was wholly successful, on the merits or otherwise, in the defense of any proceeding to which he was a party because he is or was a director of the corporation against reasonable expenses incurred by him in connection with the proceeding.

§8.53 Advance for Expenses

(a) A corporation may pay for or reimburse the reasonable expenses incurred by a director who is a party to a proceeding in advance of final disposition of the proceeding if:

(1) the director furnishes the corporation a written affirmation of his good faith belief that he has met the standard of conduct described in section 8.51;

(2) the director furnishes the corporation a written undertaking, executed personally or on his behalf, to repay the advance if it is ultimately determined that he did not meet the standard of conduct; and

(3) a determination is made that the facts then known to those making the determination would not preclude indemnification under this subchapter.

(b) The undertaking required by subsection (a)(2) must be an unlimited general obligation of the director but need not be secured and may be accepted without reference to financial ability to make repayment.

(c) Determinations and authorizations of payments under this section shall be made in the manner specified in section 8.55.

§8.54 Court-Ordered Indemnification

Unless a corporation's articles of incorporation provide otherwise, a director of the corporation who is a party to a proceeding may apply for indemnification to the court conducting the proceeding or to another court of competent jurisdiction. On receipt of an application, the court after giving any notice the court considers necessary may order indemnification if it determines:

(1) the director is entitled to mandatory indemnification under section 8.52, in which case the court shall also order the corporation to pay the director's reasonable expenses incurred to obtain court-ordered indemnification; or

(2) the director is fairly and reasonably entitled to indemnification in view of all the relevant circumstances, whether or not he met the standard of conduct set forth in section 8.51 or was adjudged liable as described in section 8.51(d), but if he was adjudged so liable his indemnification is limited to reasonable expenses incurred.

§8.55 Determination and Authorization of Indemnification

(a) A corporation may not indemnify a director under section 8.51 unless authorized in the specific case after a determination has been made that indemnification of the director is permissible in the circumstances because he has met the standard of conduct set forth in section 8.51.

(b) The determination shall be made:

(1) by the board of directors by majority vote of a quorum consisting of directors not at the time parties to the proceeding;

(2) if a quorum cannot be obtained under subdivision (1), by majority vote of a committee duly designated by the board of directors (in which designation directors who are parties may participate), consisting solely of two or more directors not at the time parties to the proceeding;

(3) by special legal counsel:

(i) selected by the board of directors or its committee in the manner prescribed in subdivision (1) or (2); or

(ii) if a quorum of the board of directors cannot be obtained under subdivision (1) and a committee cannot be designated under subdivision (2), selected by majority vote of the full board of directors (in which selection directors who are parties may participate); or

(4) by the shareholders, but shares owned by or voted under the control of directors who are at the time parties to the proceeding may not be voted on the determination.

(c) Authorization of indemnification and evaluation as to reasonableness of expenses shall be made in the same manner as the determination that indemnification is permissible, except that if the determination is made by special legal counsel, authorization of indemnification and evaluation as to reasonableness of expenses shall be made by those entitled under subsection (b)(3) to select counsel.

§8.56 Indemnification of Officers, Employees, and Agents

Unless a corporation's articles of incorporation provide otherwise:

(1) an officer of the corporation who is not a director is entitled to mandatory indemnification under section 8.52, and is entitled to apply for court-ordered indemnification under section 8.54, in each case to the same extent as a director;

(2) the corporation may indemnify and advance expenses under this subchapter to an officer, employee, or agent of the corporation who is not a director to the same extent as to a director; and

(3) a corporation may also indemnify and advance expenses to an officer, employee, or agent who is not a director to the extent, consistent with public policy, that may be provided by its articles of incorporation, bylaws, general or specific action of its board of directors, or contract.

§8.57 Insurance

A corporation may purchase and maintain insurance on behalf of an individual who is or was a director, officer, employee, or agent of the corporation, or who, while a director, officer, employee, or agent of the corporation, is or was serving at the request of the corporation as a director, officer, partner, trustee, employee, or agent of another foreign or domestic corporation, partnership, joint venture, trust, employee benefit plan, or other enterprise, against liability asserted against or incurred by him in that capacity or arising from his status as a director, officer, employee, or agent, whether or not the corporation would have power to indemnify him against the same liability under section 8.51 or 8.52.

§8.58 Application of Subchapter

(a) A provision treating a corporation's indemnification of or advance for expenses to directors that is contained in its articles of incorporation, bylaws, a resolution of its shareholders or board of directors, or in a contract or otherwise, is valid only if and to the extent the provision is consistent with this subchapter. If articles of incorporation limit indemnification or advance for expenses, indemnification and advance for expenses are valid only to the extent consistent with the articles.

(b) This subchapter does not limit a corporation's power to pay or reimburse expenses incurred by a director in connection with his appearance as a witness in a proceeding at a time when he has not been made a named defendant or respondent to the proceeding.

Subchapter F. Directors' Conflicting Interest Transactions*

§8.60 Subchapter Definitions

In this subchapter:

(1) "Conflicting interest" with respect to a corporation means the interest a director of the corporation has respecting a transaction effected or proposed to be effected by the corporation (or by a subsidiary of the corporation or any other entity in which the corporation has a controlling interest) if

(i) whether or not the transaction is brought before the board of directors of the corporation for action, the director knows at the time of commitment that he or a related person is a party to the transaction or has a beneficial financial interest in or so closely linked to the transaction and of such financial significance to the director or a related person that the interest would reasonably be expected to exert an influence on the director's judgment if he were called upon to vote on the transaction; or

(ii) the transaction is brought (or is of such character and significance to the corporation that it would in the normal course be brought) before the board of directors of the corporation for action, and the director knows at the time of commitment that any of the following persons is either a party to the transaction or has a beneficial financial interest in or so closely linked to the transaction and of such financial significance to the person that the interest would reasonably be expected to exert an influence on the director's judgment if he were called upon to vote on the transaction: (A) an entity (other than the corporation) of which the director is a director, general partner, agent, or employee; (B) a person that controls one or more of the entities specified in subclause (A) or an entity that is controlled by, or is under common

*[Editors' Note: In 1989, the Revised Model Business Corporation Act was amended by deleting Sections 8.31 and 8.32 and replacing them with a new Subchapter F, consisting of Sections 8.60–8.63. Because of the relatively short period of time since the adoption of Subchapter F, this volume retains the deleted sections as well as the new material.]

control with, one or more of the entities specified in subclause (A); or (C) an individual who is a general partner, principal, or employer of the director.

(2) "Director's conflicting interest transaction" with respect to a corporation means a transaction effected or proposed to be effected by the corporation (or by a subsidiary of the corporation or any other entity in which the corporation has a controlling interest) respecting which a director of the corporation has a conflicting interest.

(3) "Related person" of a director means (i) the spouse (or a parent or sibling thereof) of the director, or a child, grandchild, sibling, parent (or spouse of any thereof) of the director, or an individual having the same home as the director, or a trust or estate of which an individual specified in this clause (i) is a substantial beneficiary; or (ii) a trust, estate, incompetent, conservatee, or minor of which the director is a fiduciary.

(4) "Required disclosure" means disclosure by the director who has a conflicting interest of (i) the existence and nature of his conflicting interest, and (ii) all facts known to him respecting the subject matter of the transaction that an ordinarily prudent person would reasonably believe to be material to a judgment about whether or not to proceed with the transaction.

(5) "Time of commitment" respecting a transaction means the time when the transaction is consummated or, if made pursuant to contract, the time when the corporation (or its subsidiary or the entity in which it has a controlling interest) becomes contractually obligated so that its unilateral withdrawal from the transaction would entail significant loss, liability, or other damage.

§8.61 Judicial Action

(a) A transaction effected or proposed to be effected by a corporation (or by a subsidiary of the corporation or any other entity in which the corporation has a controlling interest) that is not a director's conflicting interest transaction may not be enjoined, set aside, or give rise to an award of damages or other sanctions, in a proceeding by a shareholder or by or in the right of the corporation, because a director of the corporation, or any person with whom or which he has a personal, economic, or other association, has an interest in the transaction.

(b) A director's conflicting interest transaction may not be enjoined, set aside, or give rise to an award of damages or other sanctions, in a proceeding by a shareholder or by or in the right of the corporation, because the director, or any person with whom or which he has a personal, economic, or other association, has an interest in the transaction, if:

(1) directors' action respecting the transaction was at any time taken in compliance with section 8.62;

(2) shareholders' action respecting the transaction was at any time taken in compliance with section 8.63; or

(3) the transaction, judged according to the circumstances at the time of commitment, is established to have been fair to the corporation.

§8.62 Directors' Action

(a) Directors' action respecting a transaction is effective for purposes of section 8.61(b)(1) if the transaction received the affirmative vote of a majority (but no fewer than two) of those qualified directors on the board of directors or on a duly empowered committee of the board who voted on the transaction after either required disclosure to them (to the extent the information was not known by them) or compliance with subsection (b); provided that action by a committee is so effective only if:

(1) all its members are qualified directors; and

(2) its members are either all the qualified directors on the board or are appointed by the affirmative vote of a majority of the qualified directors on the board.

(b) If a director has a conflicting interest respecting a transaction, but neither he nor a related person of the director specified in section 8.60(3)(i) is a party to the transaction, and if the director has a duty under law or professional canon, or a duty of confidentiality to another person, respecting information relating to the transaction such that the director may not make the disclosure described in section 8.60(4)(ii), then disclosure is sufficient for purposes of subsection (a) if the director (1) discloses to the directors voting on the transaction the existence and nature of his conflicting interest and informs them of the character and limitations imposed by that duty before their vote on the transaction, and (2) plays no part, directly or indirectly, in their deliberations or vote.

(c) A majority (but no fewer than two) of all the qualified directors on the board of directors, or on the committee, constitutes a quorum for purposes of action that complies with this section. Directors' action that otherwise complies with this section is not affected by the presence or vote of a director who is not a qualified director.

(d) For purposes of this section, "qualified director" means, with respect to a director's conflicting interest transaction, any director who does not have either (1) a conflicting interest respecting the transaction, or (2) a familial, financial, professional, or employment relationship with a second director who does have a conflicting interest respecting the transaction, which relationship would, in the circumstances, reasonably be expected to exert an influence on the first director's judgment when voting on the transaction.

§8.63 Shareholders' Action

(a) Shareholders' action respecting a transaction is effective for purposes of section 8.61(b)(2) if a majority of the votes entitled to be cast by the holders of all qualified shares were cast in favor of the transaction after (1) notice to shareholders describing the director's conflicting interest transaction, (2) provision of the information referred to in subsection (d), and (3) required disclosure to the shareholders who voted on the transaction (to the extent the information was not known by them).

(b) For purposes of this section, "qualified shares" means any shares entitled to vote with respect to the director's conflicting interest transaction except shares that, to the knowledge, before the vote, of the secretary (or other officer or agent of the corporation authorized to tabulate votes), are beneficially owned (or the voting of which is controlled) by a director who has a conflicting interest respecting the transaction or by a related person of the director, or both.

(c) A majority of the votes entitled to be cast by the holders of all qualified shares constitutes a quorum for purposes of action that complies with this section. Subject to the provisions of subsections (d) and (e), shareholders' action that otherwise complies with this section is not affected by the presence of holders, or the voting, of shares that are not qualified shares.

(d) For purposes of compliance with subsection (a), a director who has a conflicting interest respecting the transaction shall, before the shareholders' vote, inform the secretary (or other office or agent of the corporation authorized to tabulate votes) of the number, and the identity of persons holding or controlling the vote, of all shares that the director knows are beneficially owned (or the voting of which is controlled) by the director or by a related person of the director, or both.

(e) If a shareholders' vote does not comply with subsection (a) solely because of a failure of a director to comply with subsection (d), and if the director establishes that his failure did not determine and was not intended by him to influence the outcome of the vote, the court may, with or without further proceedings respecting section 8.61(b)(3), take such action respecting the transaction and the director, and give such effect, if any, to the shareholders' vote, as it considers appropriate in the circumstances.

CHAPTER 9. [RESERVED]

CHAPTER 10. AMENDMENT OF ARTICLES OF INCORPORATION AND BYLAWS

Subchapter A. Amendment of Articles of Incorporation

§10.01 Authority to Amend

(a) A corporation may amend its articles of incorporation at any time to add or change a provision that is required or permitted in the articles of incorporation or to delete a provision not required in the articles of incorporation. Whether a provision is required or permitted in the articles of incorporation is determined as of the effective date of the amendment.

(b) A shareholder of the corporation does not have a vested property right resulting from any provision in the articles of incorporation, including provisions relating to management, control, capital structure, dividend entitlement, or purpose or duration of the corporation.

§10.02 Amendment by Board of Directors

Unless the articles of incorporation provide otherwise, a corporation's board of directors may adopt one or more amendments to the corporation's articles of incorporation without shareholder action:

(1) to extend the duration of the corporation if it was incorporated at a time when limited duration was required by law;

(2) to delete the names and addresses of the initial directors;

(3) to delete the name and address of the initial registered agent or registered office, if a statement of change is on file with the secretary of state;

(4) to change each issued and unissued authorized share of an outstanding class into a greater number of whole shares if the corporation has only shares of that class outstanding;

(5) to change the corporate name by substituting the word "corporation," "incorporated," "company," "limited," or the abbreviation "corp.," "inc.," "co.," or "ltd.," for a similar word or abbreviation in the name, or by adding, deleting, or changing a geographical attribution for the name; or

(6) to make any other change expressly permitted by this Act to be made without shareholder action.

§10.03 Amendment by Board of Directors and Shareholders

(a) A corporation's board of directors may propose one or more amendments to the articles of incorporation for submission to the shareholders.

(b) For the amendment to be adopted:

(1) the board of directors must recommend the amendment to the shareholders unless the board of directors determines that because of conflict of interest or other special circumstances it should make no recommendation and communicates the basis for its determination to the shareholders with the amendment; and

(2) the shareholders entitled to vote on the amendment must approve the amendment as provided in subsection (e).

(c) The board of directors may condition its submission of the proposed amendment on any basis.

(d) The corporation shall notify each shareholder, whether or not entitled to vote, of the proposed shareholders' meeting in accordance with section 7.05. The notice of meeting must also state that the purpose, or one of the purposes, of the meeting is to consider the proposed amendment and contain or be accompanied by a copy or summary of the amendment.

(e) Unless this Act, the articles of incorporation, or the board of directors (acting pursuant to subsection (c)) require a greater vote or a vote by voting groups, the amendment to be adopted must be approved by:

(1) a majority of the votes entitled to be cast on the amendment by any voting group with respect to which the amendment would create dissenters' rights; and

(2) the votes required by sections 7.25 and 7.26 by every other voting group entitled to vote on the amendment.

§10.04 Voting on Amendments by Voting Groups

(a) The holders of the outstanding shares of a class are entitled to vote as a separate voting group (if shareholder voting is otherwise required by this Act) on a proposed amendment if the amendment would:

(1) increase or decrease the aggregate number of authorized shares of the class;

(2) effect an exchange or reclassification of all or part of the shares of the class into shares of another class;

(3) effect an exchange or reclassification, or create the right of exchange, of all or part of the shares of another class into shares of the class;

(4) change the designation, rights, preferences, or limitations of all or part of the shares of the class;

(5) change the shares of all or part of the class into a different number of shares of the same class;

(6) create a new class of shares having rights or preferences with respect to distributions or to dissolution that are prior, superior, or substantially equal to the shares of the class;

(7) increase the rights, preferences, or number of authorized shares of any class that, after giving effect to the amendment, have rights or preferences with respect to distributions or to dissolution that are prior, superior, or substantially equal to the shares of the class;

(8) limit or deny an existing preemptive right of all or part of the shares of the class; or

(9) cancel or otherwise affect rights to distributions or dividends that have accumulated but not yet been declared on all or part of the shares of the class.

(b) If a proposed amendment would affect a series of a class of shares in one or more of the ways described in subsection (a), the shares of that series are entitled to vote as a separate voting group on the proposed amendment.

(c) If a proposed amendment that entitles two or more series of shares to vote as separate voting groups under this section would affect those two or more series in the same or a substantially similar way, the shares of all the series so affected must vote together as a single voting group on the proposed amendment.

(d) A class or series of shares is entitled to the voting rights granted by this section although the articles of incorporation provide that the shares are nonvoting shares.

§10.05 Amendment Before Issuance of Shares

If a corporation has not yet issued shares, its incorporators or board of directors may adopt one or more amendments to the corporation's articles of incorporation.

§10.06 Articles of Amendment

A corporation amending its articles of incorporation shall deliver to the secretary of state for filing articles of amendment setting forth:

(1) the name of the corporation;

(2) the text of each amendment adopted;

(3) if an amendment provides for an exchange, reclassification, or cancellation of issued shares, provisions for implementing the amendment if not contained in the amendment itself;

(4) the date of each amendment's adoption;

(5) if an amendment was adopted by the incorporators or board of directors without shareholder action, a statement to that effect and that shareholder action was not required;

(6) if an amendment was approved by the shareholders:

(i) the designation, number of outstanding shares, number of votes entitled to be cast by each voting group entitled to vote separately on the amendment, and number of votes of each voting group indisputably represented at the meeting;

(ii) either the total number of votes cast for and against the amendment by each voting group entitled to vote separately on the amendment or the total number of undisputed votes cast for the amendment by each voting group and a statement that the number cast for the amendment by each voting group was sufficient for approval by that voting group.

§10.07 Restated Articles of Incorporation

(a) A corporation's board of directors may restate its articles of incorporation at any time with or without shareholder action.

(b) The restatement may include one or more amendments to the articles. If the restatement includes an amendment requiring shareholder approval, it must be adopted as provided in section 10.03.

(c) If the board of directors submits a restatement for shareholder action, the corporation shall notify each shareholder, whether or not entitled to vote, of the proposed shareholders' meeting in accordance with section 7.05. The notice must also state that the purpose, or one of the purposes, of the meeting is to consider the proposed restatement and contain or be accompanied by a copy of the restatement that identifies any amendment or other change it would make in the articles.

(d) A corporation restating its articles of incorporation shall deliver to the secretary of state for filing articles of restatement setting forth the name of the corporation and the text of the restated articles of incorporation together with a certificate setting forth:

(1) whether the restatement contains an amendment to the articles requiring shareholder approval and, if it does not, that the board of directors adopted the restatement; or

(2) if the restatement contains an amendment to the articles requiring shareholder approval, the information required by section 10.06.

(e) Duly adopted restated articles of incorporation supersede the original articles of incorporation and all amendments to them.

(f) The secretary of state may certify restated articles of incorporation, as the articles of incorporation currently in effect, without including the certificate information required by subsection (d).

§10.08 Amendment Pursuant to Reorganization

(a) A corporation's articles of incorporation may be amended without action by the board of directors or shareholders to carry out a plan of reorganization ordered or decreed by a court of competent jurisdiction under federal statute if the articles of incorporation after amendment contain only provisions required or permitted by section 2.02.

(b) The individual or individuals designated by the court shall deliver to the secretary of state for filing articles of amendment setting forth:

(1) the name of the corporation;

(2) the text of each amendment approved by the court;

(3) the date of the court's order or decree approving the articles of amendment;

(4) the title of the reorganization proceeding in which the order or decree was entered; and

(5) a statement that the court had jurisdiction of the proceeding under federal statute.

(c) Shareholders of a corporation undergoing reorganization do not have dissenters' rights except as and to the extent provided in the reorganization plan.

(d) This section does not apply after entry of a final decree in the reorganization proceeding even though the court retains jurisdiction of the proceeding for limited purposes unrelated to consummation of the reorganization plan.

§10.09 Effect of Amendment

An amendment to articles of incorporation does not affect a cause of action existing against or in favor of the corporation, a proceeding to which the corporation is a party, or the existing rights of persons other than shareholders of the corporation. An amendment changing a corporation's name does not abate a proceeding brought by or against the corporation in its former name.

Subchapter B. Amendment of Bylaws

§10.20 Amendment by Board of Directors or Shareholders

(a) A corporation's board of directors may amend or repeal the corporation's bylaws unless:

(1) the articles of incorporation or this Act reserve this power exclusively to the shareholders in whole or part; or

(2) the shareholders in amending or repealing a particular bylaw provide expressly that the board of directors may not amend or repeal that bylaw.

(b) A corporation's shareholders may amend or repeal the corporation's bylaws even though the bylaws may also be amended or repealed by its board of directors.

§10.21 Bylaw Increasing Quorum or Voting Requirement for Shareholders

(a) If expressly authorized by the articles of incorporation, the shareholders may adopt or amend a bylaw that fixes a greater quorum or voting requirement for shareholders (or voting groups of shareholders) than is required by this Act. The adoption or amendment of a bylaw that adds, changes, or deletes a greater quorum or voting requirement for shareholders must meet the same quorum requirement and be adopted by the same vote and voting groups required to take action under the quorum and voting requirement then in effect or proposed to be adopted, whichever is greater.

(b) A bylaw that fixes a greater quorum or voting requirement for shareholders under subsection (a) may not be adopted, amended, or repealed by the board of directors.

§10.22 Bylaw Increasing Quorum or Voting Requirement for Directors

(a) A bylaw that fixes a greater quorum or voting requirement for the board of directors may be amended or repealed:

(1) if originally adopted by the shareholders, only by the shareholders;

(2) if originally adopted by the board of directors, either by the shareholders or by the board of directors.

(b) A bylaw adopted or amended by the shareholders that fixes a greater quorum or voting requirement for the board of directors may provide that it may be amended or repealed only by a specified vote of either the shareholders or the board of directors.

(c) Action by the board of directors under subsection (a)(2) to adopt or amend a bylaw that changes the quorum or voting requirement for the board of directors must meet the same quorum requirement and be adopted by the same vote required to take action under the quorum and voting requirement then in effect or proposed to be adopted, whichever is greater.

CHAPTER 11. MERGER AND SHARE EXCHANGE

§11.01 Merger

(a) One or more corporations may merge into another corporation if the board of directors of each corporation adopts and its shareholders (if required by section 11.03) approve a plan of merger.

(b) The plan of merger must set forth:

(1) the name of each corporation planning to merge and the name of the surviving corporation into which each other corporation plans to merge;

(2) the terms and conditions of the merger; and

(3) the manner and basis of converting the shares of each corporation into shares, obligations, or other securities of the surviving or any other corporation or into cash or other property in whole or part.

(c) The plan of merger may set forth:

(1) amendments to the articles of incorporation of the surviving corporation; and

(2) other provisions relating to the merger.

§11.02 Share Exchange

(a) A corporation may acquire all of the outstanding shares of one or more classes or series of another corporation if the board of directors of each corporation adopts and its shareholders (if required by section 11.03) approve the exchange.

(b) The plan of exchange must set forth:

(1) the name of the corporation whose shares will be acquired and the name of the acquiring corporation;

(2) the terms and conditions of the exchange;

(3) the manner and basis of exchanging the shares to be acquired for shares, obligations, or other securities of the acquiring or any other corporation or for cash or other property in whole or part.

(c) The plan of exchange may set forth other provisions relating to the exchange.

(d) This section does not limit the power of a corporation to acquire all or part of the shares of one or more classes or series of another corporation through a voluntary exchange or otherwise.

§11.03 Action on Plan

(a) After adopting a plan of merger or share exchange, the board of directors of each corporation party to the merger, and the board of directors of the corporation whose shares will be acquired in the share exchange, shall submit the plan of merger (except as provided in subsection (g)) or share exchange for approval by its shareholders.

(b) For a plan of merger or share exchange to be approved:

(1) the board of directors must recommend the plan of merger or share exchange to the shareholders, unless the board of directors determines that because of conflict of interest or other special circumstances it should make no recommendation and communicates the basis for its determination to the shareholders with the plan; and

(2) the shareholders entitled to vote must approve the plan.

(c) The board of directors may condition its submission of the proposed merger or share exchange on any basis.

(d) The corporation shall notify each shareholder, whether or not entitled to vote, of the proposed shareholders' meeting in accordance with section 7.05. The notice must also state that the purpose, or one of the purposes, of the meeting is to consider the plan of merger or share exchange and contain or be accompanied by a copy or summary of the plan.

(e) Unless this Act, the articles of incorporation, or the board of directors (acting pursuant to subsection (c)) require a greater vote or a vote by voting groups, the plan of merger or share exchange to be authorized must be approved by each voting group entitled to vote separately on the plan by a majority of all the votes entitled to be cast on the plan by that voting group.

(f) Separate voting by voting groups is required:

(1) on a plan of merger if the plan contains a provision that, if contained in a proposed amendment to articles of incorporation, would require action by one or more separate voting groups on the proposed amendment under section 10.04;

(2) on a plan of share exchange by each class or series of shares included in the exchange, with each class or series constituting a separate voting group.

(g) Action by the shareholders of the surviving corporation on a plan of merger is not required if:

(1) the articles of incorporation of the surviving corporation will not differ (except for amendments enumerated in section 10.02) from its articles before the merger;

(2) each shareholder of the surviving corporation whose shares were outstanding immediately before the effective date of the merger will hold the same number of shares, with identical designations, preferences, limitations, and relative rights, immediately after;

(3) the number of voting shares outstanding immediately after the merger, plus the number of voting shares issuable as a result of the merger (either by the conversion of securities issued pursuant to the merger or the exercise of rights and warrants issued pursuant to the merger), will not exceed by more than 20 percent the total number of voting shares of the surviving corporation outstanding immediately before the merger; and

(4) the number of participating shares outstanding immediately after the merger, plus the number of participating shares issuable as a result of the merger (either by the conversion of securities issued pursuant to the merger or the exercise of rights and warrants issued pursuant to the merger), will not exceed by more than 20 percent the total number of participating shares outstanding immediately before the merger.

(h) As used in subsection (g):

(1) "Participating shares" means shares that entitle their holders to participate without limitation in distributions.

(2) "Voting shares" means shares that entitle their holders to vote unconditionally in elections of directors.

(i) After a merger or share exchange is authorized, and at any time before articles of merger or share exchange are filed, the planned merger or share exchange may be abandoned (subject to any contractual rights), without further shareholder action, in accordance with the procedure set forth in the plan of merger or share exchange or, if none is set forth, in the manner determined by the board of directors.

§11.04 Merger of Subsidiary

(a) A parent corporation owning at least 90 percent of the outstanding shares of each class of a subsidiary corporation may merge the subsidiary into itself without approval of the shareholders of the parent or subsidiary.

(b) The board of directors of the parent shall adopt a plan of merger that sets forth:

(1) the names of the parent and subsidiary; and

(2) the manner and basis of converting the shares of the subsidiary into shares, obligations, or other securities of the parent or any other corporation or into cash or other property in whole or part.

(c) The parent shall mail a copy or summary of the plan of merger to each shareholder of the subsidiary who does not waive the mailing requirement in writing.

(d) The parent may not deliver articles of merger to the secretary of state for filing until at least 30 days after the date it mailed a copy of the plan of merger to each shareholder of the subsidiary who did not waive the mailing requirement.

(e) Articles of merger under this section may not contain amendments to the articles of incorporation of the parent corporation (except for amendments enumerated in section 10.02).

§11.05 Articles of Merger or Share Exchange

(a) After a plan of merger or share exchange is approved by the shareholders, or adopted by the board of directors if shareholder approval is not required, the surviving or acquiring corporation shall deliver to the secretary of state for filing articles of merger or share exchange setting forth:

(1) the plan of merger or share exchange;

(2) if shareholder approval was not required, a statement to that effect;

(3) if approval of the shareholders of one or more corporations party to the merger or share exchange was required:

(i) the designation, number of outstanding shares, and number of votes entitled to be cast by each voting group entitled to vote separately on the plan as to each corporation; and

(ii) either the total number of votes cast for and against the plan by each voting group entitled to vote separately on the plan or the total number of undisputed votes cast for the plan separately by each voting group and a statement that the number cast for the plan by each voting group was sufficient for approval by that voting group.

(b) Unless a delayed effective date is specified, a merger or share exchange takes effect when the articles of merger or share exchange are filed.

§11.06 Effect of Merger or Share Exchange

(a) When a merger takes effect:

(1) every other corporation party to the merger merges into the surviving corporation and the separate existence of every corporation except the surviving corporation ceases;

(2) the title to all real estate and other property owned by each corporation party to the merger is vested in the surviving corporation without reversion or impairment;

(3) the surviving corporation has all liabilities of each corporation party to the merger;

(4) a proceeding pending against any corporation party to the merger may be continued as if the merger did not occur or the surviving corporation may be substituted in the proceeding for the corporation whose existence ceased;

(5) the articles of incorporation of the surviving corporation are amended to the extent provided in the plan of merger; and

(6) the shares of each corporation party to the merger that are to be converted into shares, obligations, or other securities of the surviving or any other corporation or into cash or other property are converted and the former holders of the shares are entitled only to the rights provided in the articles of merger or to their rights under chapter 13.

(b) When a share exchange takes effect, the shares of each acquired corporation are exchanged as provided in the plan, and the former holders of the shares are entitled only to the exchange rights provided in the articles of share exchange or to their rights under chapter 13.

§11.07 Merger or Share Exchange With Foreign Corporation

(a) One or more foreign corporations may merge or enter into a share exchange with one or more domestic corporations if:

(1) in a merger, the merger is permitted by the law of the state or country under whose law each foreign corporation is incorporated and each foreign corporation complies with that law in effecting the merger;

(2) in a share exchange, the corporation whose shares will be acquired is a domestic corporation, whether or not a share exchange is permitted by the law of the state or country under whose law the acquiring corporation is incorporated;

(3) the foreign corporation complies with section 11.05 if it is the surviving corporation of the merger or acquiring corporation of the share exchange; and

(4) each domestic corporation complies with the applicable provisions of sections 11.01 through 11.04 and, if it is the surviving corporation of the merger or acquiring corporation of the share exchange, with section 11.05.

(b) Upon the merger or share exchange taking effect, the surviving foreign corporation of a merger and the acquiring foreign corporation of a share exchange is deemed:

(1) to appoint the secretary of state as its agent for service of process in a proceeding to enforce any obligation or the rights of dissenting shareholders of each domestic corporation party to the merger or share exchange; and

(2) to agree that it will promptly pay to the dissenting shareholders of each domestic corporation party to the merger or share exchange the amount, if any, to which they are entitled under chapter 13.

(c) This section does not limit the power of a foreign corporation to acquire all or part of the shares of one or more classes or series of a domestic corporation through a voluntary exchange or otherwise.

CHAPTER 12. SALE OF ASSETS

§12.01 Sale of Assets in Regular Course of Business and Mortgage of Assets

(a) A corporation may, on the terms and conditions and for the consideration determined by the board of directors:

(1) sell, lease, exchange, or otherwise dispose of all, or substantially all, of its property in the usual and regular course of business,

(2) mortgage, pledge, dedicate to the repayment of indebtedness (whether with or without recourse), or otherwise encumber any or all of its property whether or not in the usual and regular course of business, or

(3) transfer any or all of its property to a corporation all the shares of which are owned by the corporation.

(b) Unless the articles of incorporation require it, approval by the shareholders of a transaction described in subsection (a) is not required.

§12.02 Sale of Assets Other Than in Regular Course of Business

(a) A corporation may sell, lease, exchange, or otherwise dispose of all, or substantially all, of its property (with or without the good will), otherwise than in the usual and regular course of business, on the terms and conditions and for the consideration determined by the corporation's board of directors, if the board of directors proposes and its shareholders approve the proposed transaction.

(b) For a transaction to be authorized:

(1) the board of directors must recommend the proposed transaction to the shareholders unless the board of directors determines that because of conflict of interest or other special circumstances it should make no recommendation and communicates the basis for its determination to the shareholders with the submission of the proposed transaction; and

(2) the shareholders entitled to vote must approve the transaction.

(c) The board of directors may condition its submission of the proposed transaction on any basis.

(d) The corporation shall notify each shareholder, whether or not entitled to vote, of the proposed shareholders' meeting in accordance with section 7.05. The notice must also state that the purpose, or one of the purposes, of the meeting is to consider the sale, lease, exchange, or other disposition of all, or substantially all, the property of the corporation and contain or be accompanied by a description of the transaction.

(e) Unless the articles of incorporation or the board of directors (acting pursuant to subsection (c)) require a greater vote or a vote by voting groups, the transaction to be authorized must be approved by a majority of all the votes entitled to be cast on the transaction.

(f) After a sale, lease, exchange, or other disposition of property is authorized, the transaction may be abandoned (subject to any contractual rights) without further shareholder action.

(g) A transaction that constitutes a distribution is governed by section 6.40 and not by this section.

CHAPTER 13. DISSENTERS' RIGHTS

Subchapter A. Right to Dissent and Obtain Payment for Shares

§13.01 Definitions

In this chapter:

(1) "Corporation" means the issuer of the shares held by a dissenter before the corporate action, or the surviving or acquiring corporation by merger or share exchange of that issuer.

(2) "Dissenter" means a shareholder who is entitled to dissent from corporate action under section 13.02 and who exercises that right when and in the manner required by sections 13.20 through 13.28.

(3) "Fair value," with respect to a dissenter's shares, means the value of the shares immediately before the effectuation of the corporate action to which the dissenter objects, excluding any appreciation or depreciation in anticipation of the corporate action unless exclusion would be inequitable.

(4) "Interest" means interest from the effective date of the corporate action until the date of payment, at the average rate currently paid by the corporation on its principal bank loans or, if none, at a rate that is fair and equitable under all the circumstances.

(5) "Record shareholder" means the person in whose name shares are registered in the records of a corporation or the beneficial owner of shares to the extent of the rights granted by a nominee certificate on file with a corporation.

(6) "Beneficial shareholder" means the person who is a beneficial owner of shares held in a voting trust or by a nominee as the record shareholder.

(7) "Shareholder" means the record shareholder or the beneficial shareholder.

§13.02 Right to Dissent

(a) A shareholder is entitled to dissent from, and obtain payment of the fair value of his shares in the event of, any of the following corporate actions:

(1) consummation of a plan of merger to which the corporation is a party (i) if shareholder approval is required for the merger by section 11.03 or the articles of incorporation and the shareholder is entitled to vote on the merger or (ii) if the corporation is a subsidiary that is merged with its parent under section 11.04;

(2) consummation of a plan of share exchange to which the corporation is a party as the corporation whose shares will be acquired, if the shareholder is entitled to vote on the plan;

(3) consummation of a sale or exchange of all, or substantially all, of the property of the corporation other than in the usual and regular course of business, if the shareholder is entitled to vote on the sale or exchange, including a sale in dissolution, but not including a sale pursuant to court order or a sale for cash pursuant to a plan by which all or substantially all of the net proceeds of the sale will be distributed to the shareholders within one year after the date of sale;

(4) an amendment of the articles of incorporation that materially and adversely affects rights in respect of a dissenter's shares because it:

(i) alters or abolishes a preferential right of the shares;

(ii) creates, alters, or abolishes a right in respect of redemption, including a provision respecting a sinking fund for the redemption or repurchase, of the shares;

(iii) alters or abolishes a preemptive right of the holder of the shares to acquire shares or other securities;

(iv) excludes or limits the right of the shares to vote on any matter, or to cumulate votes, other than a limitation by dilution through issuance of shares or other securities with similar voting rights; or

(v) reduces the number of shares owned by the shareholder to a fraction of a share if the fractional share so created is to be acquired for cash under section 6.04; or

(5) any corporate action taken pursuant to a shareholder vote to the extent the articles of incorporation, bylaws, or a resolution of the board of directors provides that voting or nonvoting shareholders are entitled to dissent and obtain payment for their shares.

(b) A shareholder entitled to dissent and obtain payment for his shares under this chapter may not challenge the corporate action creating his entitlement unless the action is unlawful or fraudulent with respect to the shareholder or the corporation.

§13.03 Dissent by Nominees and Beneficial Owners

(a) A record shareholder may assert dissenters' rights as to fewer than all the shares registered in his name only if he dissents with respect to all shares beneficially owned by any one person and notifies the corporation in writing of the name and address of each person on whose behalf he asserts dissenters' rights. The rights of a partial dissenter under this subsection are determined as if the shares as to which he dissents and his other shares were registered in the names of different shareholders.

(b) A beneficial shareholder may assert dissenters' rights as to shares held on his behalf only if:

(1) he submits to the corporation the record shareholder's written consent to the dissent not later than the time the beneficial shareholder asserts dissenters' rights; and

(2) he does so with respect to all shares of which he is the beneficial shareholder or over which he has power to direct the vote.

Subchapter B. Procedure for Exercise of Dissenters' Rights

§13.20 Notice of Dissenters' Rights

(a) If proposed corporate action creating dissenters' rights under section 13.02 is submitted to a vote at a shareholders' meeting, the meeting notice must state that shareholders are or may be entitled to assert dissenters' rights under this chapter and be accompanied by a copy of this chapter.

(b) If corporate action creating dissenters' rights under section 13.02 is taken without a vote of shareholders, the corporation shall notify in writing all shareholders entitled to assert dissenters' rights that the action was taken and send them the dissenters' notice described in section 13.22.

§13.21 Notice of Intent to Demand Payment

(a) If proposed corporate action creating dissenters' rights under section 13.02 is submitted to a vote at a shareholders' meeting, a shareholder who wishes to assert dissenters' rights (1) must deliver to the corporation before the vote is taken written notice of his intent to demand payment for his shares if the proposed action is effectuated and (2) must not vote his shares in favor of the proposed action.

(b) A shareholder who does not satisfy the requirements of subsection (a) is not entitled to payment for his shares under this chapter.

§13.22 Dissenters' Notice

(a) If proposed corporate action creating dissenters' rights under section 13.02 is authorized at a shareholders' meeting, the corporation shall deliver a written dissenters' notice to all shareholders who satisfied the requirements of section 13.21.

(b) The dissenters' notice must be sent no later than 10 days after the corporate action was taken, and must:

(1) state where the payment demand must be sent and where and when certificates for certificated shares must be deposited;

(2) inform holders of uncertificated shares to what extent transfer of the shares will be restricted after the payment demand is received;

(3) supply a form for demanding payment that includes the date of the first announcement to news media or to shareholders of the terms of the proposed corporate action and requires that the person asserting dissenters' rights certify whether or not he acquired beneficial ownership of the shares before that date;

(4) set a date by which the corporation must receive the payment demand, which date may not be fewer than 30 nor more than 60 days after the date the subsection (a) notice is delivered; and

(5) be accompanied by a copy of this chapter.

§13.23 Duty to Demand Payment

(a) A shareholder sent a dissenters' notice described in section 13.22 must demand payment, certify whether he acquired beneficial ownership of the shares before the date required to be set forth in the dissenter's notice pursuant to section 13.22(b)(3), and deposit his certificates in accordance with the terms of the notice.

(b) The shareholder who demands payment and deposits his shares under section (a) retains all other rights of a shareholder until these rights are cancelled or modified by the taking of the proposed corporate action.

(c) A shareholder who does not demand payment or deposit his share certificates where required, each by the date set in the dissenters' notice, is not entitled to payment for his shares under this chapter.

§13.24 Share Restrictions

(a) The corporation may restrict the transfer of uncertificated shares from the date the demand for their payment is received until the proposed corporate action is taken or the restrictions released under section 13.26.

(b) The person for whom dissenters' rights are asserted as to uncertificated shares retains all other rights of a shareholder until these rights are cancelled or modified by the taking of the proposed corporate action.

§13.25 Payment

(a) Except as provided in section 13.27, as soon as the proposed corporate action is taken, or upon receipt of a payment demand, the corporation shall pay each dissenter who complied with section 13.23 the amount the corporation estimates to be the fair value of his shares, plus accrued interest.

(b) The payment must be accompanied by:

(1) the corporation's balance sheet as of the end of a fiscal year ending not more than 16 months before the date of payment, an income statement for that year, a statement of changes in shareholders' equity for that year, and the latest available interim financial statements, if any;

(2) a statement of the corporation's estimate of the fair value of the shares;

(3) an explanation of how the interest was calculated;

(4) a statement of the dissenter's right to demand payment under section 13.28; and

(5) a copy of this chapter.

§13.26 Failure to Take Action

(a) If the corporation does not take the proposed action within 60 days after the date set for demanding payment and depositing share certificates, the corporation shall return the deposited certificates and release the transfer restrictions imposed on uncertificated shares.

(b) If after returning deposited certificates and releasing transfer restrictions, the corporation takes the proposed action, it must send a new dissenters' notice under section 13.22 and repeat the payment demand procedure.

§13.27 After-Acquired Shares

(a) A corporation may elect to withhold payment required by section 13.25 from a dissenter unless he was the beneficial owner of the shares before the date set forth in the dissenters' notice as the date of the first announcement to news media or to shareholders of the terms of the proposed corporate action.

(b) To the extent the corporation elects to withhold payment under subsection (a), after taking the proposed corporate action, it shall estimate the fair value of the shares, plus accrued interest, and shall pay this amount to each dissenter who agrees to accept it in full satisfaction of his demand. The corporation shall send with its offer a statement of its estimate of the fair value of the shares, an explanation of how the interest was calculated, and a statement of the dissenter's right to demand payment under section 13.28.

§13.28 Procedure if Shareholder Dissatisfied With Payment or Offer

(a) A dissenter may notify the corporation in writing of his own estimate of the fair value of his shares and amount of interest due, and demand payment of his estimate (less any payment under section 13.25), or reject the corporation's offer under section 13.27 and demand payment of the fair value of his shares and interest due, if:

(1) the dissenter believes that the amount paid under section 13.25 or offered under section 13.27 is less than the fair value of his shares or that the interest due is incorrectly calculated;

(2) the corporation fails to make payment under section 13.25 within 60 days after the date set for demanding payment; or

(3) the corporation, having failed to take the proposed action, does not return the deposited certificates or release the transfer restrictions imposed on uncertificated shares within 60 days after the date set for demanding payment.

(b) A dissenter waives his right to demand payment under this section unless he notifies the corporation of his demand in writing under subsection (a) within 30 days after the corporation made or offered payment for his shares.

Subchapter C. Judicial Appraisal of Shares

§13.30 Court Action

(a) If a demand for payment under section 13.28 remains unsettled, the corporation shall commence a proceeding within 60 days after receiving the payment demand and petition the court to determine the fair value of the shares and accrued interest. If the corporation does not commence the proceeding within the 60-day period, it shall pay each dissenter whose demand remains unsettled the amount demanded.

(b) The corporation shall commence the proceeding in the [name or describe] court of the county where a corporation's principal office (or, if none in this state, its registered office) is located. If the corporation is a foreign corporation without a registered office in this state, it shall commence the proceeding in the county in this state where the registered office of the domestic corporation merged with or whose shares were acquired by the foreign corporation was located.

(c) The corporation shall make all dissenters (whether or not residents of this state) whose demands remain unsettled parties to the proceeding as in an action against their shares and all parties must be served with a copy of the petition. Nonresidents may be served by registered or certified mail or by publication as provided by law.

(d) The jurisdiction of the court in which the proceeding is commenced under subsection (b) is plenary and exclusive. The court may appoint one or more persons as appraisers to receive evidence and recommend decision on the question of fair value. The appraisers have the powers described in the order appointing them, or in any amendment to it. The dissenters are entitled to the same discovery rights as parties in other civil proceedings.

(e) Each dissenter made a party to the proceeding is entitled to judgment (1) for the amount, if any, by which the court finds the fair value of his shares, plus interest, exceeds the amount paid by the corporation or (2) for the fair value, plus accrued interest, of his after-acquired shares for which the corporation elected to withhold payment under section 13.27.

§13.31 Court Costs and Counsel Fees

(a) The court in an appraisal proceeding commenced under section 13.30 shall determine all costs of the proceeding, including the reasonable compensation and expenses of appraisers appointed by the court. The court shall assess the costs against the corporation, except that the court may assess costs against all or some of the dissenters, in amounts the court finds equitable, to the extent the court finds dissenters acted arbitrarily, vexatiously, or not in good faith in demanding payment under section 13.28.

(b) The court may also assess the fees and expenses of counsel and experts for the respective parties, in amounts the court finds equitable:

(1) against the corporation and in favor of any or all dissenters if the court finds the corporation did not substantially comply with the requirements of sections 13.20 through 13.28; or

(2) against either the corporation or a dissenter, in favor of any other party, if the court finds that the party against whom the fees and expenses are assessed acted arbitrarily, vexatiously, or not in good faith with respect to the rights provided by this chapter.

(c) If the court finds that the services of counsel for any dissenter were of substantial benefit to other dissenters similarly situated, and that the fees for those services should not be assessed against the corporation, the court may award to these counsel reasonable fees to be paid out of the amounts awarded the dissenters who were benefited.

CHAPTER 14. DISSOLUTION

Subchapter A. Voluntary Dissolution

§14.01 Dissolution by Incorporators or Initial Directors

A majority of the incorporators or initial directors of a corporation that has not issued shares or has not commenced business may dissolve the corporation by delivering to the secretary of state for filing articles of dissolution that set forth:

(1) the name of the corporation;

(2) the date of its incorporation;

(3) either (i) that none of the corporation's shares has been issued or (ii) that the corporation has not commenced business;

(4) that no debt of the corporation remains unpaid;

(5) that the net assets of the corporation remaining after winding up have been distributed to the shareholders, if shares were issued; and

(6) that a majority of the incorporators or initial directors authorized the dissolution.

§14.02 Dissolution by Board of Directors and Shareholders

(a) A corporation's board of directors may propose dissolution for submission to the shareholders.

(b) For a proposal to dissolve to be adopted:

(1) the board of directors must recommend dissolution to the shareholders unless the board of directors determines that because of conflict

of interest or other special circumstances it should make no recommendation and communicates the basis for its determination to the shareholders; and

(2) the shareholders entitled to vote must approve the proposal to dissolve as provided in subsection (e).

(c) The board of directors may condition its submission of the proposal for dissolution on any basis.

(d) The corporation shall notify each shareholder, whether or not entitled to vote, of the proposed shareholders' meeting in accordance with section 7.05. The notice must also state that the purpose, or one of the purposes, of the meeting is to consider dissolving the corporation.

(e) Unless the articles of incorporation or the board of directors (acting pursuant to subsection (c)) require a greater vote or a vote by voting groups, the proposal to dissolve to be adopted must be approved by a majority of all the votes entitled to be cast on that proposal.

§14.03 Articles of Dissolution

(a) At any time after dissolution is authorized, the corporation may dissolve by delivering to the secretary of state for filing articles of dissolution setting forth:

(1) the name of the corporation;

(2) the date dissolution was authorized;

(3) if dissolution was approved by the shareholders:

(i) the number of votes entitled to be cast on the proposal to dissolve; and

(ii) either the total number of votes cast for and against dissolution or the total number of undisputed votes cast for dissolution and a statement that the number cast for dissolution was sufficient for approval.

(4) If voting by voting groups is required, the information required by subparagraph (3) shall be separately provided for each voting group entitled to vote separately on the plan to dissolve.

(b) A corporation is dissolved upon the effective date of its articles of dissolution.

§14.04 Revocation of Dissolution

(a) A corporation may revoke its dissolution within 120 days of its effective date.

(b) Revocation of dissolution must be authorized in the same manner as the dissolution was authorized unless that authorization permitted revocation by action by the board of directors alone, in which event the board of directors may revoke the dissolution without shareholder action.

(c) After the revocation of dissolution is authorized, the corporation may revoke the dissolution by delivering to the secretary of state for filing articles of revocation of dissolution, together with a copy of its articles of dissolution, that set forth:

(1) the name of the corporation;

(2) the effective date of the dissolution that was revoked;

(3) the date that the revocation of dissolution was authorized;

(4) if the corporation's board of directors (or incorporators) revoked the dissolution, a statement to that effect;

(5) if the corporation's board of directors revoked a dissolution authorized by the shareholders, a statement that revocation was permitted by action by the board of directors alone pursuant to that authorization; and

(6) if shareholder action was required to revoke the dissolution, the information required by section 14.03(3) or (4).

(d) Unless a delayed effective date is specified, revocation of dissolution is effective when articles of revocation of dissolution are filed.

(e) When the revocation of dissolution is effective, it relates back to and takes effect as of the effective date of the dissolution and the corporation resumes carrying on its business as if dissolution had never occurred.

§14.05 Effect of Dissolution

(a) A dissolved corporation continues its corporate existence but may not carry on any business except that appropriate to wind up and liquidate its business and affairs, including:

(1) collecting its assets;

(2) disposing of its properties that will not be distributed in kind to its shareholders;

(3) discharging or making provision for discharging its liabilities;

(4) distributing its remaining property among its shareholders according to their interests; and

(5) doing every other act necessary to wind up and liquidate its business and affairs.

(b) Dissolution of a corporation does not:

(1) transfer title to the corporation's property;

(2) prevent transfer of its shares or securities, although the authorization to dissolve may provide for closing the corporation's share transfer records;

(3) subject its directors or officers to standards of conduct different from those prescribed in chapter 8;

(4) change quorum or voting requirements for its board of directors or shareholders; change provisions for selection, resignation, or removal of its directors or officers or both; or change provisions for amending its bylaws;

(5) prevent commencement of a proceeding by or against the corporation in its corporate name;

(6) abate or suspend a proceeding pending by or against the corporation on the effective date of dissolution; or

(7) terminate the authority of the registered agent of the corporation.

§14.06 Known Claims Against Dissolved Corporation

(a) A dissolved corporation may dispose of the known claims against it by following the procedure described in this section.

(b) The dissolved corporation shall notify its known claimants in writing of the dissolution at any time after its effective date. The written notice must:

(1) describe information that must be included in a claim;

(2) provide a mailing address where a claim may be sent;

(3) state the deadline, which may not be fewer than 120 days from the effective date of the written notice, by which the dissolved corporation must receive the claim; and

(4) state that the claim will be barred if not received by the deadline.

(c) A claim against the dissolved corporation is barred:

(1) if a claimant who was given written notice under subsection (b) does not deliver the claim to the dissolved corporation by the deadline;

(2) if a claimant whose claim was rejected by the dissolved corporation does not commence a proceeding to enforce the claim within 90 days from the effective date of the rejection notice.

(d) For purposes of this section, "claim" does not include a contingent liability or a claim based on an event occurring after the effective date of dissolution.

§14.07 Unknown Claims Against Dissolved Corporation

(a) A dissolved corporation may also publish notice of its dissolution and request that persons with claims against the corporation present them in accordance with the notice.

(b) The notice must:

(1) be published one time in a newspaper of general circulation in the county where the dissolved corporation's principal office (or, if none in this state, its registered office) is or was last located;

(2) describe the information that must be included in a claim and provide a mailing address where the claim may be sent; and

(3) state that a claim against the corporation will be barred unless a proceeding to enforce the claim is commenced within five years after the publication of the notice.

(c) If the dissolved corporation publishes a newspaper notice in accordance with subsection (b), the claim of each of the following claimants is barred unless the claimant commences a proceeding to enforce the claim against the dissolved corporation within five years after the publication date of the newspaper notice:

(1) a claimant who did not receive written notice under section 14.06;

(2) a claimant whose claim was timely sent to the dissolved corporation but not acted on;

(3) a claimant whose claim is contingent or based on an event occurring after the effective date of dissolution.

(d) A claim may be enforced under this section:

(1) against the dissolved corporation, to the extent of its undistributed assets; or

(2) if the assets have been distributed in liquidation, against a shareholder of the dissolved corporation to the extent of his pro rata share of the claim or the corporate assets distributed to him in liquidation, whichever is less, but a shareholder's total liability for all claims under this section may not exceed the total amount of assets distributed to him.

Subchapter B. Administrative Dissolution

§14.20 Grounds for Administrative Dissolution

The secretary of state may commence a proceeding under section 14.21 to administratively dissolve a corporation if:

(1) the corporation does not pay within 60 days after they are due any franchise taxes or penalties imposed by this Act or other law;

(2) the corporation does not deliver its annual report to the secretary of state within 60 days after it is due;

(3) the corporation is without a registered agent or registered office in this state for 60 days or more;

(4) the corporation does not notify the secretary of state within 60 days that its registered agent or registered office has been changed, that its registered agent has resigned, or that its registered office has been discontinued; or

(5) the corporation's period of duration stated in its articles of incorporation expires.

§14.21 Procedure for and Effect of Administrative Dissolution

(a) If the secretary of state determines that one or more grounds exist under section 14.20 for dissolving a corporation, he shall serve the corporation with written notice of his determination under section 5.04.

(b) If the corporation does not correct each ground for dissolution or demonstrate to the reasonable satisfaction of the secretary of state that each ground determined by the secretary of state does not exist within 60 days after service of the notice is perfected under section 5.04, the secretary of state shall administratively dissolve the corporation by signing a certificate of dissolution that recites the ground or grounds for dissolution and its effective date. The secretary of state shall file the original of the certificate and serve a copy on the corporation under section 5.04.

(c) A corporation administratively dissolved continues its corporate existence but may not carry on any business except that necessary to wind up and liquidate its business and affairs under section 14.05 and notify claimants under sections 14.06 and 14.07.

(d) The administrative dissolution of a corporation does not terminate the authority of its registered agent.

§14.22 Reinstatement Following Administrative Dissolution

(a) A corporation administratively dissolved under section 14.21 may apply to the secretary of state for reinstatement within two years after the effective date of dissolution. The application must:

(1) recite the name of the corporation and the effective date of its administrative dissolution;

(2) state that the ground or grounds for dissolution either did not exist or have been eliminated;

(3) state that the corporation's name satisfies the requirements of section 4.01; and

(4) contain a certificate from the [taxing authority] reciting that all taxes owed by the corporation have been paid.

(b) If the secretary of state determines that the application contains the information required by subsection (a) and that the information is correct, he shall cancel the certificate of dissolution and prepare a certificate of reinstatement that recites his determination and the effective date of reinstatement, file the original of the certificate, and serve a copy on the corporation under section 5.04.

(c) When the reinstatement is effective, it relates back to and takes effect as of the effective date of the administrative dissolution and the corporation resumes carrying on its business as if the administrative dissolution had never occurred.

§14.23 Appeal From Denial of Reinstatement

(a) If the secretary of state denies a corporation's application for reinstatement following administrative dissolution, he shall serve the corporation under section 5.04 with a written notice that explains the reason or reasons for denial.

(b) The corporation may appeal the denial of reinstatement to the [name or describe] court within 30 days after service of the notice of denial is perfected. The corporation appeals by petitioning the court to set aside the dissolution and attaching to the petition copies of the secretary of state's certificate of dissolution, the corporation's application for reinstatement, and the secretary of state's notice of denial.

(c) The court may summarily order the secretary of state to reinstate the dissolved corporation or may take other action the court considers appropriate.

(d) The court's final decision may be appealed as in other civil proceedings.

Subchapter C. Judicial Dissolution

§14.30 Grounds for Judicial Dissolution

The [name or describe court or courts] may dissolve a corporation:

(1) in a proceeding by the attorney general if it is established that:

(i) the corporation obtained its articles of incorporation through fraud; or

(ii) the corporation has continued to exceed or abuse the authority conferred upon it by law;

(2) in a proceeding by a shareholder if it is established that:

(i) the directors are deadlocked in the management of the corporate affairs, the shareholders are unable to break the deadlock, and irreparable injury to the corporation is threatened or being suffered, or the business and affairs of the corporation can no longer be conducted to the advantage of the shareholders generally, because of the deadlock;

(ii) the directors or those in control of the corporation have acted, are acting, or will act in a manner that is illegal, oppressive, or fraudulent;

(iii) the shareholders are deadlocked in voting power and have failed, for a period that includes at least two consecutive annual meeting dates, to elect successors to directors whose terms have expired; or

(iv) the corporate assets are being misapplied or wasted;

(3) in a proceeding by a creditor if it is established that:

(i) the creditor's claim has been reduced to judgment, the execution on the judgment returned unsatisfied, and the corporation is insolvent; or

(ii) the corporation has admitted in writing that the creditor's claim is due and owing and the corporation is insolvent; or

(4) in a proceeding by the corporation to have its voluntary dissolution continued under court supervision.

§14.31 Procedure for Judicial Dissolution

(a) Venue for a proceeding by the attorney general to dissolve a corporation lies in [name the county or counties]. Venue for a proceeding brought by any other party named in section 14.30 lies in the county where a corporation's principal office (or, if none in this state, its registered office) is or was last located.

(b) It is not necessary to make shareholders parties to a proceeding to dissolve a corporation unless relief is sought against them individually.

(c) A court in a proceeding brought to dissolve a corporation may issue injunctions, appoint a receiver or custodian pendente lite with all powers and duties the court directs, take other action required to preserve the corporate assets wherever located, and carry on the business of the corporation until a full hearing can be held.

(d) Within 10 days of the commencement of a proceeding under section 14.30(2) to dissolve a corporation that has no shares listed on a national securities exchange or regularly traded in a market maintained by one or more members of a national securities exchange, the corporation must send to all shareholders, other than the petitioner, a notice stating that the shareholders are entitled to avoid the dissolution of the corporation by electing to purchase the petitioner's shares under section 14.34 and accompanied by a copy of section 14.34.

§14.32 Receivership or Custodianship

(a) A court in a judicial proceeding brought to dissolve a corporation may appoint one or more receivers to wind up and liquidate, or one or more custodians to manage, the business and affairs of the corporation. The court shall hold a hearing, after notifying all parties to the proceeding and any interested persons designated by the court, before appointing a receiver or custodian. The court appointing a receiver or custodian has exclusive jurisdiction over the corporation and all its property wherever located.

(b) The court may appoint an individual or a domestic or foreign corporation (authorized to transact business in this state) as a receiver or custodian. The court may require the receiver or custodian to post bond, with or without sureties, in an amount the court directs.

(c) The court shall describe the powers and duties of the receiver or custodian in its appointing order, which may be amended from time to time. Among other powers:

(1) the receiver (i) may dispose of all or any part of the assets of the corporation wherever located, at a public or private sale, if authorized by the court; and (ii) may sue and defend in his own name as receiver of the corporation in all courts of this state;

(2) the custodian may exercise all of the powers of the corporation, through or in place of its board of directors or officers, to the extent necessary to manage the affairs of the corporation in the best interests of its shareholders and creditors.

(d) The court during a receivership may redesignate the receiver a custodian, and during a custodianship may redesignate the custodian a receiver, if doing so is in the best interests of the corporation, its shareholders, and creditors.

(e) The court from time to time during the receivership or custodianship may order compensation paid and expense disbursements or reimbursements made to the receiver or custodian and his counsel from the assets of the corporation or proceeds from the sale of the assets.

§14.33 Decree of Dissolution

(a) If after a hearing the court determines that one or more grounds for judicial dissolution described in section 14.30 exist, it may enter a decree dissolving the corporation and specifying the effective date of the dissolution, and the clerk of the court shall deliver a certified copy of the decree to the secretary of state, who shall file it.

(b) After entering the decree of dissolution, the court shall direct the winding up and liquidation of the corporation's business and affairs in accordance with section 14.05 and the notification of claimants in accordance with sections 14.06 and 14.07.

§14.34 Election to Purchase in Lieu of Dissolution

(a) In a proceeding under section 14.30(2) to dissolve a corporation that has no shares listed on a national securities exchange or regularly traded in a market maintained by one or more members of a national or affiliated securities association, the corporation may elect or, if it fails to elect, one or more shareholders may elect to purchase all shares owned by the petitioning shareholder at the fair value of the shares. An election pursuant to this section shall be irrevocable unless the court determines that it is equitable to set aside or modify the election.

(b) An election to purchase pursuant to this section may be filed with the court at any time within 90 days after the filing of the petition under section 14.30(2) or at such later time as the court in its discretion may allow. If the election to purchase is filed by one or more shareholders, the corporation shall, within 10 days thereafter, give written notice to all shareholders, other than the petitioner. The notice must state the name and number of shares owned by the petitioner and the name and number of shares owned by each electing shareholder and must advise the recipients of their right to join in the election to purchase shares in accordance with this section. Shareholders who wish to participate must file notice of their intention to join in the purchase no later than 30 days after the effective date of the notice to them. All shareholders who have filed an election or notice of their intention to participate in the election to purchase thereby become parties to ownership of shares as of the date the first election was filed, unless they otherwise agree or the court otherwise directs. After an election has been filed by the corporation or one or more shareholders, the proceeding under section 14.30(2) may not be discontinued or settled, nor may the petitioning shareholder sell or otherwise dispose of his shares, unless the court determines that it would be equitable to the corporation and the shareholders, other than the petitioner, to permit such discontinuance, settlement, sale, or other disposition.

(c) If, within 60 days of the filing of the first election, the parties reach agreement as to the fair value and terms of purchase of the petitioner's shares, the court shall enter an order directing the purchase of petitioner's shares upon the terms and conditions agreed to by the parties.

(d) If the parties are unable to reach an agreement as provided for in subsection (c), the court, upon application of any party, shall stay the section 14.30(2) proceedings and determine the fair value of the petitioner's shares as of the day before the date on which the petition under section 14.30(2) was filed or as of such other date as the court deems appropriate under the circumstances.

(e) Upon determining the fair value of the shares, the court shall enter an order directing the purchase upon such terms and conditions as the court deems appropriate, which may include payment of the purchase price in installments, where necessary in the interests of equity, provision for security to assure payment of the purchase price and any additional costs, fees, and expenses as may have been awarded, and, if the shares are to be purchased by shareholders, the allocation of shares among them. In allocating petitioner's shares among holders of different classes of shares, the court should attempt to preserve the existing distribution of voting rights among holders of different classes insofar as practicable and may direct that holders of a specific class or classes shall not participate in the purchase. Interest may be allowed at the rate and from the date determined by the court to be equitable, but if the court finds that the refusal of the petitioning shareholder to accept an offer of payment was arbitrary or otherwise not in good faith, no interest shall be allowed. If the court finds that the petitioning shareholder had probable grounds for relief under paragraphs (ii) or (iv) of section 14.30(2), it may award to the petitioning shareholder reasonable fees and expenses of counsel and of any experts employed by him.

(f) Upon entry of an order under subsections (c) or (e), the court shall dismiss the petition to dissolve the corporation under section 14.30, and the petitioning shareholder shall no longer have any rights or status as a shareholder of the corporation, except the right to receive the amounts awarded to him by the order of the court which shall be enforceable in the same manner as any other judgment.

(g) The purchase ordered pursuant to subsection (e), shall be made within 10 days after the date the order becomes final unless before that time the corporation files with the court a notice of its intention to adopt articles of dissolution pursuant to sections 14.02 and 14.03, which articles must then be adopted and filed within 50 days thereafter. Upon filing of such articles of dissolution, the corporation shall be dissolved in accordance with the provisions of sections 14.05 through 07, and the order entered pursuant to subsection (e) shall no longer be of any force or effect, except that the court may award the petitioning shareholder reasonable fees and expenses in accordance with the provisions of the last sentence of subsection (e) and the petitioner may continue to pursue any claims previously asserted on behalf of the corporation.

(h) Any payment by the corporation pursuant to an order under subsections (c) or (e), other than an award of fees and expenses pursuant to subsection (e), is subject to the provisions of section 6.40.

Subchapter D. Miscellaneous

§14.40 Deposit With State Treasurer

Assets of a dissolved corporation that should be transferred to a creditor, claimant, or shareholder of the corporation who cannot be found or who is not competent to receive them shall be reduced to cash and deposited with the state treasurer or other appropriate state official for safekeeping. When the creditor, claimant, or shareholder furnishes satisfactory proof of entitlement to the amount deposited, the state treasurer or other appropriate state official shall pay him or his representative that amount.

CHAPTER 15. FOREIGN CORPORATIONS

Subchapter A. Certificate of Authority

§15.01 Authority to Transact Business Required

(a) A foreign corporation may not transact business in this state until it obtains a certificate of authority from the secretary of state.

(b) The following activities, among others, do not constitute transacting business within the meaning of subsection (a):

(1) maintaining, defending, or settling any proceeding;

(2) holding meetings of the board of directors or shareholders or carrying on other activities concerning internal corporate affairs;

(3) maintaining bank accounts;

(4) maintaining offices or agencies for the transfer, exchange, and registration of the corporation's own securities or maintaining trustees or depositaries with respect to those securities;

(5) selling through independent contractors;

(6) soliciting or obtaining orders, whether by mail or through employees or agents or otherwise, if the orders require acceptance outside this state before they become contracts;

(7) creating or acquiring indebtedness, mortgages, and security interests in real or personal property;

(8) securing or collecting debts or enforcing mortgages and security interests in property securing the debts;

(9) owning, without more, real or personal property;

(10) conducting an isolated transaction that is completed within 30 days and that is not one in the course of repeated transactions of a like nature;

(11) transacting business in interstate commerce.

(c) The list of activities in subsection (b) is not exhaustive.

§15.02 Consequences of Transacting Business Without Authority

(a) A foreign corporation transacting business in this state without a certificate of authority may not maintain a proceeding in any court in this state until it obtains a certificate of authority.

(b) The successor to a foreign corporation that transacted business in this state without a certificate of authority and the assignee of a cause of action arising out of that business may not maintain a proceeding based on that cause of action in any court in this state until the foreign corporation or its successor obtains a certificate of authority.

(c) A court may stay a proceeding commenced by a foreign corporation, its successor, or assignee until it determines whether the foreign corporation or its successor requires a certificate of authority. If it so determines, the court may further stay the proceeding until the foreign corporation or its successor obtains the certificate.

(d) A foreign corporation is liable for a civil penalty of $ for each day, but not to exceed a total of $ for each year, it transacts business in this state without a certificate of authority. The attorney general may collect all penalties due under this subsection.

(e) Notwithstanding subsections (a) and (b), the failure of a foreign corporation to obtain a certificate of authority does not impair the validity of its corporate acts or prevent it from defending any proceeding in this state.

§15.03 Application for Certificate of Authority

(a) A foreign corporation may apply for a certificate of authority to transact business in this state by delivering an application to the secretary of state for filing. The application must set forth:

(1) the name of the foreign corporation or, if its name is unavailable for use in this state, a corporate name that satisfies the requirements of section 15.06;

(2) the name of the state or country under whose law it is incorporated;

(3) its date of incorporation and period of duration;

(4) the street address of its principal office;

(5) the address of its registered office in this state and the name of its registered agent at that office; and

(6) the names and usual business addresses of its current directors and officers.

(b) The foreign corporation shall deliver with the completed application a certificate of existence (or a document of similar import) duly authenticated by the secretary of state or other official having custody of corporate records in the state or country under whose law it is incorporated.

§15.04 Amended Certificate of Authority

(a) A foreign corporation authorized to transact business in this state must obtain an amended certificate of authority from the secretary of state if it changes:

(1) its corporate name;

(2) the period of its duration; or

(3) the state or country of its incorporation.

(b) The requirements of section 15.03 for obtaining an original certificate of authority apply to obtaining an amended certificate under this section.

§15.05 Effect of Certificate of Authority

(a) A certificate of authority authorizes the foreign corporation to which it is issued to transact business in this state subject, however, to the right of the state to revoke the certificate as provided in this Act.

(b) A foreign corporation with a valid certificate of authority has the same but no greater rights and has the same but no greater privileges as, and except as otherwise provided by this Act is subject to the same duties, restrictions, penalties, and liabilities now or later imposed on, a domestic corporation of like character.

(c) This Act does not authorize this state to regulate the organization or internal affairs of a foreign corporation authorized to transact business in this state.

§15.06 Corporate Name of Foreign Corporation

(a) If the corporate name of a foreign corporation does not satisfy the requirements of section 4.01, the foreign corporation to obtain or maintain a certificate of authority to transact business in this state:

(1) may add the word "corporation," "incorporated," "company," or "limited," or the abbreviation "corp.," "inc.," "co.," or "ltd.," to its corporate name for use in this state; or

(2) may use a fictitious name to transact business in this state if its real name is unavailable and it delivers to the secretary of state for filing a copy of the resolution of its board of directors, certified by its secretary, adopting the fictitious name.

(b) Except as authorized by subsections (c) and (d), the corporate name (including a fictitious name) of a foreign corporation must be distinguishable upon the records of the secretary of state from:

(1) the corporate name of a corporation incorporated or authorized to transact business in this state;

(2) a corporate name reserved or registered under section 4.02 or 4.03;

(3) the fictitious name of another foreign corporation authorized to transact business in this state; and

(4) the corporate name of a not-for-profit corporation incorporated or authorized to transact business in this state.

(c) A foreign corporation may apply to the secretary of state for authorization to use in this state the name of another corporation (incorporated or authorized to transact business in this state) that is not distinguishable upon his records from the name applied for. The secretary of state shall authorize use of the name applied for if:

(1) the other corporation consents to the use in writing and submits an undertaking in form satisfactory to the secretary of state to change its name to a name that is distinguishable upon the records of the secretary of state from the name of the applying corporation; or

(2) the applicant delivers to the secretary of state a certified copy of a final judgment of a court of competent jurisdiction establishing the applicant's right to use the name applied for in this state.

(d) A foreign corporation may use in this state the name (including the fictitious name) of another domestic or foreign corporation that is used in this state if the other corporation is incorporated or authorized to transact business in this state and the foreign corporation:

(1) has merged with the other corporation;

(2) has been formed by reorganization of the other corporation; or

(3) has acquired all or substantially all of the assets, including the corporate name, of the other corporation.

(e) If a foreign corporation authorized to transact business in this state changes its corporate name to one that does not satisfy the requirements of section 4.01, it may not transact business in this state under the changed name until it adopts a name satisfying the requirements of section 4.01 and obtains an amended certificate of authority under section 15.04.

§15.07 Registered Office and Registered Agent of Foreign Corporation

Each foreign corporation authorized to transact business in this state must continuously maintain in this state:

(1) a registered office that may be the same as any of its places of business; and

(2) a registered agent, who may be:

(i) an individual who resides in this state and whose business office is identical with the registered office;

(ii) a domestic corporation or not-for-profit domestic corporation whose business office is identical with the registered office; or

(iii) a foreign corporation or foreign not-for-profit corporation authorized to transact business in this state whose business office is identical with the registered office.

§15.08 Change of Registered Office or Registered Agent of Foreign Corporation

(a) A foreign corporation authorized to transact business in this state may change its registered office or registered agent by delivering to the secretary of state for filing a statement of change that sets forth:

(1) its name;

(2) the street address of its current registered office;

(3) if the current registered office is to be changed, the street address of its new registered office;

(4) the name of its current registered agent;

(5) if the current registered agent is to be changed, the name of its new registered agent and the new agent's written consent (either on the statement or attached to it) to the appointment; and

(6) that after the change or changes are made, the street addresses of its registered office and the business office of its registered agent will be identical.

(b) If a registered agent changes the street address of his business office, he may change the street address of the registered office of any foreign corporation for which he is the registered agent by notifying the corporation in writing of the change and signing (either manually or in facsimile) and delivering to the secretary of state for filing a statement of change that complies with the requirements of subsection (a) and recites that the corporation has been notified of the change.

§15.09 Resignation of Registered Agent of Foreign Corporation

(a) The registered agent of a foreign corporation may resign his agency appointment by signing and delivering to the secretary of state for filing the original and two exact or conformed copies of a statement of resignation. The statement of resignation may include a statement that the registered office is also discontinued.

(b) After filing the statement, the secretary of state shall attach the filing receipt to one copy and mail the copy and receipt to the registered office if not discontinued. The secretary of state shall mail the other copy to the foreign corporation at its principal office address shown in its most recent annual report.

(c) The agency appointment is terminated, and the registered office discontinued if so provided, on the 31st day after the date on which the statement was filed.

§15.10 Service on Foreign Corporation

(a) The registered agent of a foreign corporation authorized to transact business in this state is the corporation's agent for service of process, notice, or demand required or permitted by law to be served on the foreign corporation.

(b) A foreign corporation may be served by registered or certified mail, return receipt requested, addressed to the secretary of the foreign corporation at its principal office shown in its application for a certificate of authority or in its most recent annual report if the foreign corporation:

(1) has no registered agent or its registered agent cannot with reasonable diligence be served;

(2) has withdrawn from transacting business in this state under section 15.20; or

(3) has had its certificate of authority revoked under section 15.31.

(c) Service is perfected under subsection (b) at the earliest of:

(1) the date the foreign corporation receives the mail;

(2) the date shown on the return receipt, if signed on behalf of the foreign corporation; or

(3) five days after its deposit in the United States Mail, as evidenced by the postmark, if mailed postpaid and correctly addressed.

(d) This section does not prescribe the only means, or necessarily the required means, of serving a foreign corporation.

Subchapter B. Withdrawal

§15.20 Withdrawal of Foreign Corporation

(a) A foreign corporation authorized to transact business in this state may not withdraw from this state until it obtains a certificate of withdrawal from the secretary of state.

(b) A foreign corporation authorized to transact business in this state may apply for a certificate of withdrawal by delivering an application to the secretary of state for filing. The application must set forth:

(1) the name of the foreign corporation and the name of the state or country under whose law it is incorporated;

(2) that it is not transacting business in this state and that it surrenders its authority to transact business in this state;

(3) that it revokes the authority of its registered agent to accept service on its behalf and appoints the secretary of state as its agent for service of process in any proceeding based on a cause of action arising during the time it was authorized to transact business in this state;

(4) a mailing address to which the secretary of state may mail a copy of any process served on him under subdivision (3); and

(5) a commitment to notify the secretary of state in the future of any change in its mailing address.

(c) After the withdrawal of the corporation is effective, service of process on the secretary of state under this section is service on the foreign corporation. Upon receipt of process, the secretary of state shall mail a copy of the process to the foreign corporation at the mailing address set forth under subsection (b).

Subchapter C. Revocation of Certificate of Authority

§15.30 Grounds for Revocation

The secretary of state may commence a proceeding under section 15.31 to revoke the certificate of authority of a foreign corporation authorized to transact business in this state if:

(1) the foreign corporation does not deliver its annual report to the secretary of state within 60 days after it is due;

(2) the foreign corporation does not pay within 60 days after they are due any franchise taxes or penalties imposed by this Act or other law;

(3) the foreign corporation is without a registered agent or registered office in this state for 60 days or more;

(4) the foreign corporation does not inform the secretary of state under section 15.08 or 15.09 that its registered agent or registered office has changed, that its registered agent has resigned, or that its registered office has been discontinued within 60 days of the change, resignation, or discontinuance;

(5) an incorporator, director, officer, or agent of the foreign corporation signed a document he knew was false in any material respect with intent that the document be delivered to the secretary of state for filing;

(6) the secretary of state receives a duly authenticated certificate from the secretary of state or other official having custody of corporate records in the state or country under whose law the foreign corporation is incorporated stating that it has been dissolved or disappeared as a result of a merger.

§15.31 Procedure for and Effect of Revocation

(a) If the secretary of state determines that one or more grounds exist under section 15.30 for revocation of a certificate of authority, he shall serve the foreign corporation with written notice of his determination under section 15.10.

(b) If the foreign corporation does not correct each ground for revocation or demonstrate to the reasonable satisfaction of the secretary of state that each ground determined by the secretary of state does not exist within 60 days after service of the notice is perfected under section 15.10, the secretary of state may revoke the foreign corporation's certificate of authority by signing a certificate of revocation that recites the ground or grounds for revocation and its effective date. The secretary of state shall file the original of the certificate and serve a copy on the foreign corporation under section 15.10.

(c) The authority of a foreign corporation to transact business in this state ceases on the date shown on the certificate revoking its certificate of authority.

(d) The secretary of state's revocation of a foreign corporation's certificate of authority appoints the secretary of state the foreign corporation's agent for service of process in any proceeding based on a cause of action which arose during the time the foreign corporation was authorized to transact business in this state. Service of process on the secretary of state under this subsection is service on the foreign corporation. Upon receipt of process, the secretary of state shall mail a copy of the process to the secretary of the foreign corporation at its principal office shown in its most recent annual report or in any subsequent communication received from the corporation stating the current mailing address of its principal office, or, if none are on file, in its application for a certificate of authority.

(e) Revocation of a foreign corporation's certificate of authority does not terminate the authority of the registered agent of the corporation.

§15.32 Appeal From Revocation

(a) A foreign corporation may appeal the secretary of state's revocation of its certificate of authority to the [name or describe] court within 30 days after service of the certificate of revocation is perfected under section 15.10. The foreign corporation appeals by petitioning the court to set aside the revocation and attaching to the petition copies of its certificate of authority and the secretary of state's certificate of revocation.

(b) The court may summarily order the secretary of state to reinstate the certificate of authority or may take any other action the court considers appropriate.

(c) The court's final decision may be appealed as in other civil proceedings.

CHAPTER 16. RECORDS AND REPORTS

Subchapter A. Records

§16.01 Corporate Records

(a) A corporation shall keep as permanent records minutes of all meetings of its shareholders and board of directors, a record of all actions taken by the shareholders or board of directors without a meeting, and a record of all actions taken by a committee of the board of directors in place of the board of directors on behalf of the corporation.

(b) A corporation shall maintain appropriate accounting records.

(c) A corporation or its agent shall maintain a record of its shareholders, in a form that permits preparation of a list of the names and addresses of all shareholders, in alphabetical order by class of shares showing the number and class of shares held by each.

(d) A corporation shall maintain its records in written form or in another form capable of conversion into written form within a reasonable time.

(e) A corporation shall keep a copy of the following records at its principal office:

(1) its articles or restated articles of incorporation and all amendments to them currently in effect;

(2) its bylaws or restated bylaws and all amendments to them currently in effect;

(3) resolutions adopted by its board of directors creating one or more classes or series of shares, and fixing their relative rights, preferences, and limitations, if shares issued pursuant to those resolutions are outstanding;

(4) the minutes of all shareholders' meetings, and records of all action taken by shareholders without a meeting, for the past three years;

(5) all written communications to shareholders generally within the past three years, including the financial statements furnished for the past three years under section 16.20;

(6) a list of the names and business addresses of its current directors and officers; and

(7) its most recent annual report delivered to the secretary of state under section 16.22.

§16.02 Inspection of Records by Shareholders

(a) Subject to section 16.03(c), a shareholder of a corporation is entitled to inspect and copy, during regular business hours at the corporation's principal office, any of the records of the corporation described in section 16.01(e) if he gives the corporation written notice of his demand at least five business days before the date on which he wishes to inspect and copy.

(b) A shareholder of a corporation is entitled to inspect and copy, during regular business hours at a reasonable location specified by the corporation, any of the following records of the corporation if the shareholder meets the requirements of subsection (c) and gives the corporation written notice of his demand at least five business days before the date on which he wishes to inspect and copy:

(1) excerpts from minutes of any meeting of the board of directors, records of any action of a committee of the board of directors while acting in place of the board of directors on behalf of the corporation, minutes of any meeting of the shareholders, and records of action taken

by the shareholders or board of directors without a meeting, to the extent not subject to inspection under section 16.02(a);

(2) accounting records of the corporation; and

(3) the record of shareholders.

(c) A shareholder may inspect and copy the records identified in subsection (b) only if:

(1) his demand is made in good faith and for a proper purpose;

(2) he describes with reasonable particularity his purpose and the records he desires to inspect; and

(3) the records are directly connected with his purpose.

(d) The right of inspection granted by this section may not be abolished or limited by a corporation's articles of incorporation or bylaws.

(e) This section does not affect:

(1) the right of a shareholder to inspect records under section 7.20 or, if the shareholder is in litigation with the corporation, to the same extent as any other litigant;

(2) the power of a court, independently of this Act, to compel the production of corporate records for examination.

(f) For purposes of this section, "shareholder" includes a beneficial owner whose shares are held in a voting trust or by a nominee on his behalf.

§16.03 Scope of Inspection Right

(a) A shareholder's agent or attorney has the same inspection and copying rights as the shareholder he represents.

(b) The right to copy records under section 16.02 includes, if reasonable, the right to receive copies made by photographic, xerographic, or other means.

(c) The corporation may impose a reasonable charge, covering the costs of labor and material, for copies of any documents provided to the shareholder. The charge may not exceed the estimated cost of production or reproduction of the records.

(d) The corporation may comply with a shareholder's demand to inspect the record of shareholders under section 16.02(b)(3) by providing him with a list of its shareholders that was compiled no earlier than the date of the shareholder's demand.

§16.04 Court-Ordered Inspection

(a) If a corporation does not allow a shareholder who complies with section 16.02(a) to inspect and copy any records required by that subsection to be available for inspection, the [name or describe court] of the county where the corporation's principal office (or, if none in this state, its registered office) is located may summarily order inspection and copying of the records demanded at the corporation's expense upon application of the shareholder.

(b) If a corporation does not within a reasonable time allow a shareholder to inspect and copy any other record, the shareholder who complies with section 16.02(b) and (c) may apply to the [name or describe court] in the county where the corporation's principal office (or, if none in this state, its registered office) is located for an order to permit inspection and copying of the records demanded. The court shall dispose of an application under this subsection on an expedited basis.

(c) If the court orders inspection and copying of the records demanded, it shall also order the corporation to pay the shareholder's costs (including reasonable counsel fees) incurred to obtain the order unless the corporation proves that it refused inspection in good faith because it had a reasonable basis for doubt about the right of the shareholder to inspect the records demanded.

(d) If the court orders inspection and copying of the records demanded, it may impose reasonable restrictions on the use or distribution of the records by the demanding shareholder.

Subchapter B. Reports

§16.20 Financial Statements for Shareholders

(a) A corporation shall furnish its shareholders annual financial statements, which may be consolidated or combined statements of the corporation and one or more of its subsidiaries, as appropriate, that include a balance sheet as of the end of the fiscal year, an income statement for that year, and a statement of changes in shareholders' equity for the year unless that information appears elsewhere in the financial statements. If financial statements are prepared for the corporation on the basis of generally accepted accounting principles, the annual financial statements must also be prepared on that basis.

(b) If the annual financial statements are reported upon by a public accountant, his report must accompany them. If not, the statements must be accompanied by a statement of the president or the person responsible for the corporation's accounting records:

(1) stating his reasonable belief whether the statements were prepared on the basis of generally accepted accounting principles and, if not, describing the basis of preparation; and

(2) describing any respects in which the statements were not prepared on a basis of accounting consistent with the statements prepared for the preceding year.

(c) A corporation shall mail the annual financial statements to each shareholder within 120 days after the close of each fiscal year. Thereafter, on written request from a shareholder who was not mailed the statements, the corporation shall mail him the latest financial statements.

§16.21 Other Reports to Shareholders

(a) If a corporation indemnifies or advances expenses to a director under section 8.51, 8.52, 8.53, or 8.54 in connection with a proceeding by or in the right of the corporation, the corporation shall report the indemnification or advance in writing to the shareholders with or before the notice of the next shareholders' meeting.

(b) If a corporation issues or authorizes the issuance of shares for promissory notes or for promises to render services in the future, the corporation shall report in writing to the shareholders the number of shares authorized or issued, and the consideration received by the corporation, with or before the notice of the next shareholders' meeting.

§16.22 Annual Report for Secretary of State

(a) Each domestic corporation, and each foreign corporation authorized to transact business in this state, shall deliver to the secretary of state for filing an annual report that sets forth:

(1) the name of the corporation and the state or country under whose law it is incorporated;

(2) the address of its registered office and the name of its registered agent at that office in this state;

(3) the address of its principal office;

(4) the names and business addresses of its directors and principal officers;

(5) a brief description of the nature of its business;

(6) the total number of authorized shares, itemized by class and series, if any, within each class; and

(7) the total number of issued and outstanding shares, itemized by class and series, if any, within each class.

(b) Information in the annual report must be current as of the date the annual report is executed on behalf of the corporation.

(c) The first annual report must be delivered to the secretary of state between January 1 and April 1 of the year following the calendar year in which a domestic corporation was incorporated or a foreign corporation was authorized to transact business. Subsequent annual reports must be delivered to the secretary of state between January 1 and April 1 of the following calendar years.

(d) If an annual report does not contain the information required by this section, the secretary of state shall promptly notify the reporting domestic or foreign corporation in writing and return the report to it for correction. If the report is corrected to contain the information required by this section and delivered to the secretary of state within 30 days after the effective date of notice, it is deemed to be timely filed.

CHAPTER 17. TRANSITION PROVISIONS

§17.01 Application to Existing Domestic Corporations

This Act applies to all domestic corporations in existence on its effective date that were incorporated under any general statute of this state providing for incorporation of corporations for profit if power to amend or repeal the statute under which the corporation was incorporated was reserved.

§17.02 Application to Qualified Foreign Corporations

A foreign corporation authorized to transact business in this state on the effective date of this Act is subject to this Act but is not required to obtain a new certificate of authority to transact business under this Act.

§17.03 Saving Provisions

(a) Except as provided in subsection (b), the repeal of a statute by this Act does not affect:

(1) the operation of the statute or any action taken under it before its repeal;

(2) any ratification, right, remedy, privilege, obligation, or liability acquired, accrued, or incurred under the statute before its repeal;

(3) any violation of the statute, or any penalty, forfeiture, or punishment incurred because of the violation, before its repeal;

(4) any proceeding, reorganization, or dissolution commenced under the statute before its repeal, and the proceeding, reorganization, or dissolution may be completed in accordance with the statute as if it had not been repealed.

(b) If a penalty or punishment imposed for violation of a statute repealed by this Act is reduced by this Act, the penalty or punishment if not already imposed shall be imposed in accordance with this Act.

§17.04 Severability

If any provision of this Act or its application to any person or circumstance is held invalid by a court of competent jurisdiction, the invalidity does not affect other provisions or applications of the Act that can be given effect without the invalid provision or application, and to this end the provisions of the Act are severable.

§17.05 Repeal

The following laws and parts of laws are repealed: [to be inserted].

§17.06 Effective Date

This Act takes effect _____.

Dictionary of Legal Terms*

abatement Reduction or elimination of gifts by category upon the reduction in value of the estate.

absolute surety Surety liable to a creditor immediately upon the default of the principal debtor.

acceptance

Commercial paper Acceptance is the drawee's signed engagement to honor the draft as presented. It becomes operative when completed by delivery or notification. UCC §3-410.

Contracts Compliance by offeree with terms and conditions of offer.

Sale of goods UCC §2-606 provides three ways a buyer can accept goods: (1) by signifying to the seller that the goods are conforming or that he will accept them in spite of their nonconformity, (2) by failing to make an effective rejection, and (3) by doing an act inconsistent with the seller's ownership.

acceptor Drawee who has accepted an instrument.

accession An addition to one's property by increase of the original property or by production from such property. *E.g.,* A innocently converts the wheat of B into bread. UCC §9-315 changes the common law where a perfected security interest is involved.

accident and health insurance Provides protection from losses due to accident or sickness.

accommodation An arrangement made as a favor to another, usually involving a loan of money or commercial paper. While a party's intent may be to aid a maker of a note by lending his credit, if he seeks to accomplish thereby legitimate objects of his own and not simply to aid the maker, the act is not for accommodation.

accommodation indorser Signer not in the chain of title.

accommodation party A person who signs commercial paper in any capacity for the purpose of lending his name to another party to an instrument. UCC §3-415.

accord and satisfaction A method of discharging a claim whereby the parties agree to accept something in settlement, the "accord" being the agreement and the "satisfaction" its execution or performance. It is a new contract that is substituted for an old contract, which is thereby discharged, or for an obligation or cause of action and that must have all of the elements of a valid contract.

account Any account with a bank, including a checking, time, interest or savings account. UCC §4-194. Also, any right to payment, for goods or services, that is not evidenced by an instrument or chattel paper. *E.g.,* account receivable.

accounting Equitable proceeding for a complete settlement of all partnership affairs.

act of state doctrine Rule that a court should not question the validity of actions taken by a foreign government in its own country.

actual authority Power conferred upon agent by actual consent given by principal.

actual express authority Actual authority derived from written or spoken words of principal.

actual implied authority Actual authority inferred from words or conduct manifested to agent by principal.

actual notice Knowledge actually and expressly communicated.

actus reas Wrongful or overt act.

ademption The removal or extinction of a devise by act of the testator.

adequacy of consideration Not required where parties have freely agreed to the exchange.

adhesion contract Standard "form" contract, usually between a large retailer and a consumer, in which the weaker party has no realistic choice or opportunity to bargain.

adjudication The giving or pronouncing of a judgment in a case; also, the judgment given.

administrative agency Governmental entity (other than courts and legislatures) having authority to affect the rights of private parties.

administrative law Law dealing with the establishment, duties, and powers of agencies in the executive branch of government.

administrative process Entire set of activities engaged in by administrative agencies while carrying out their rulemaking, enforcement, and adjudicative functions.

administrator A person appointed by the court to manage the assets and liabilities of an intestate (a person dying without a will). A person named in the will of a testator (a person dying with a will) is called the executor. Female designations are administratrix and executrix.

adversary system System in which opposing parties initiate and present their cases.

adverse possession A method of acquiring title to real property by possession for a statutory period under certain conditions. The periods of time may differ, depending on whether the adverse possessor has color of title.

affidavit A written statement of facts, made voluntarily, confirmed by oath or affirmation of the party making it, and taken before an authorized officer.

affiliate Person who controls, is controlled by, or is under common control with the issuer.

affirm Uphold the lower court's judgment.

affirmative action Active recruitment of minority applicants.

affirmative defense A response that attacks the plaintiff's legal right to bring an action as opposed to attacking the truth of the claim. *E.g.,* accord and satisfaction; assumption of risk; contributory negligence; duress; estoppel.

affirmative disclosure Requirement that an advertiser include certain information in its advertisement so that the ad is not deceptive.

after-acquired property Property the debtor may acquire at some time after the security interest attaches.

agency Relation in which one person acts for or represents another by the latter's authority.

*Many of the definitions are abridged and adapted from *Black's Law Dictionary*, 5th edition, West Publishing Company, 1979.

Actual agency Exists where the agent is really employed by the principal.

Agency by estoppel One created by operation of law and established by proof of such acts of the principal as reasonably lead to the conclusion of its existence.

Implied agency One created by acts of the parties and deduced from proof of other facts.

agent Person authorized to act on another's behalf.

allegation A statement of a party setting out what he expects to prove.

allonge Piece of paper firmly affixed to the instrument.

annuity contract Agreement to pay periodic sums to insured upon reaching a designated age.

annul To annul a judgment or judicial proceeding is to deprive it of all force and operation.

answer The answer is the formal written statement made by a defendant setting forth the ground of his defense.

antecedent debt Preexisting obligation.

anticipatory breach of contract (or **anticipatory repudiation**) The unjustified assertion by a party that he will not perform an obligation that he is contractually obligated to perform at a future time. See UCC §§610 & 611.

apparent authority Such principal power that a reasonable person would assume an agent has in light of the principal's conduct.

appeal Resort to a superior (appellate) court to review the decision of an inferior (trial) court or administrative agency.

appeal by right Mandatory review by a higher court.

appellant A party who takes an appeal from one court to another. He may be either the plaintiff or defendant in the original court proceeding.

appellee The party in a cause against whom an appeal is taken; that is, the party who has an interest adverse to setting aside or reversing the judgment. Sometimes also called the "respondent."

appropriation Unauthorized use of another person's name or likeness for one's own benefit.

appurtenances Things appurtenant pass as incident to the principal thing. Sometimes an easement consisting of a right of way over one piece of land will pass with another piece of land as being appurtenant to it.

APR Annual percentage rate.

arbitration The reference of a dispute to an impartial (third) person chosen by the parties, who agree in advance to abide by the arbitrator's award issued after a hearing at which both parties have an opportunity to be heard.

arraignment Accused is informed of the crime against him and enters a plea.

articles of incorporation (or **certificate of incorporation**) The instrument under which a corporation is formed. The contents are prescribed in the particular state's general incorporation statute.

articles of partnership A written agreement by which parties enter into a partnership, to be governed by the terms set forth therein.

as is Disclaimer of implied warranties.

assault Unlawful attempted battery; intentional infliction of apprehension of immediate bodily harm or offensive contact.

assignee Party to whom contract rights are assigned.

assignment A transfer of the rights to real or personal property, usually intangible property such as rights in a lease, mortgage, sale agreement, or partnership.

assignment of rights Voluntary transfer to a third party of the rights arising from a contract.

assignor Party making an assignment.

assumes Delegatee agrees to perform the contractual obligation of the delegator.

assumes the mortgage Purchaser of mortgaged property becomes personally liable to pay the debt.

assumption of risk Plaintiff's express or implied consent to encounter a known danger.

attachment The process of seizing property, by virtue of a writ, summons, or other judicial order, and bringing the same into the custody of the court for the purpose of securing satisfaction of the judgment ultimately to be entered in the action. While formerly the main objective was to coerce the defendant debtor to appear in court, today the writ of attachment is used primarily to seize the debtor's property in the event a judgment is rendered.

Distinguished from execution See **execution**.

Also, the process by which a security interest becomes enforceable. Attachment may occur upon the taking of possession or upon the signing of a security agreement by the person who is pledging the property as collateral.

authority Power of an agent to change the legal status of his principal.

authorized means Any reasonable means of communication.

automatic perfection Perfection upon attachment.

award The decision of an arbitrator.

bad checks Issuing a check with funds insufficient to cover it.

bailee The party to whom personal property is delivered under a contract of bailment.

Extraordinary bailee Absolutely liable for the safety of the bailed property without regard to the cause of loss.

Ordinary bailee Must exercise due care.

bailment A delivery of personal property in trust for the execution of a special object in relation to such goods, beneficial either to the bailor or bailee or both, and upon a contract to either redeliver the goods to the bailor or otherwise dispose of the same in conformity with the purpose of the trust.

bailor The party who delivers goods to another in the contract of bailment.

bankrupt The state or condition of one who is unable to pay his debts as they are, or become, due.

Bankruptcy Code The Act was substantially revised in 1978, effective October 1, 1979. Straight bankruptcy is in the nature of a liquidation proceeding and involves the collection and distribution to creditors of all the bankrupt's nonexempt property by the trustee in the manner provided by the Act. The debtor rehabilitation provisions of the Act (Chapters 11 and 13) differ from straight bankruptcy in that the debtor looks to rehabilitation, rather than liquidation, and the creditors look to future earnings of the bankrupt, rather than to property held by the bankrupt, to satisfy their claims.

bargain Negotiated exchange.

bargained exchange Mutually agreed-upon exchange.

basis of the bargain Part of the buyer's assumption underlying the sale.

battery Unlawful touching of another; intentional infliction of harmful or offensive bodily contact.

bearer Person in possession of an instrument.

bearer paper Payable to holder of the instrument.

beneficiary One who benefits from act of another. See also **third-party beneficiary**.

Incidental A person who may derive benefit from performance on contract, though he is neither the promisee nor the one to whom performance is to be rendered. Since the incidental beneficiary is not a donee or creditor beneficiary (see **third-party beneficiary**), he has no right to enforce the contract.

Intended beneficiary Third party intended by the two contracted parties to receive a benefit from their contract.

Trust As it relates to trust beneficiaries, includes a person who has any present or future interest, vested or contingent, and also includes the owner of an interest by assignment or other transfer and, as it relates to a charitable trust, includes any person entitled to enforce the trust.

beyond a reasonable doubt Proof that is entirely convincing and satisfying to a moral certainty; criminal law standard.

bilateral contract Contract in which both parties exchange promises.

bill of lading Document evidencing receipt of goods for shipment issued by person engaged in business of transporting or forwarding goods; includes airbill. UCC §1-201(6).

Through bill of lading A bill of lading which specifies at least one connecting carrier.

bill of sale A written agreement, formerly limited to one under seal, by which one person assigns or transfers his right to or interest in goods and personal chattels to another.

binder A written memorandum of the important terms of a contract of insurance which gives temporary protection to an insured pending investigation of risk by the insurance company or until a formal policy is issued.

blue law Prohibition of certain types of commercial activity on Sunday.

blue sky laws A popular name for state statutes providing for the regulation and supervision of securities offerings and sales, to protect citizen-investors from investing in fraudulent companies.

bona fide In good faith.

bond A certificate or evidence of a debt on which the issuing company or governmental body promises to pay the bondholders a specified amount of interest for a specified length of time and to repay the loan on the expiration date. In every case, a bond represents debt—its holder is a creditor of the corporation, not a part owner, as the shareholder is.

boycott Agreement among parties not to deal with a third party.

breach Wrongful failure to perform the terms of a contract.

Material breach Nonperformance which significantly impairs the aggrieved party's rights under the contract.

bribery Offering property to a public official to influence the official's decision.

bulk transfer Transfer not in the ordinary course of the transferor's business of a major part of his inventory.

burglary Breaking and entering the home of another at night with intent to commit a felony.

business judgment rule Protects directors from liability for honest mistakes of judgment.

business trust A trust (managed by a trustee for the benefit of a beneficiary) established to conduct a business for a profit.

but for rule Person's negligent conduct is a cause of an event if the event would not have occurred in the absence of that conduct.

buyer in ordinary course of business Person who buys in ordinary course, in good faith, and without knowledge that the sale to him is in violation of anyone's ownership rights or of a security interest.

by-laws Regulations, ordinances, rules, or laws adopted by an association or corporation for its government.

callable bond Bond that is subject to redemption (reacquisition) by the corporation.

cancellation One party's putting an end to a contract because of a breach by other party.

capital Accumulated goods, possessions, and assets, used for the production of profits and wealth. Owners' equity in a business. Also used to refer to the total assets of a business or to capital assets.

capital surplus Surplus other than earned surplus.

carrier Transporter of goods.

casualty insurance Covers property loss due to causes other than fire or the elements.

cause of action The ground on which an action may be sustained.

caveat emptor "Let the buyer beware." This maxim is more applicable to judicial sales, auctions, and the like than to sales of consumer goods, where strict liability, warranty, and other laws protect.

certificate of deposit A written acknowledgment by a bank or banker of a deposit with promise to pay to depositor, to his order, or to some other person or to his order. UCC §3-104(2)(c).

certificate of title Official representation of ownership.

certification Acceptance of a check by a drawee bank.

certification of incorporation See **articles of incorporation**.

certification mark Distinctive symbol, word, or design used with goods or services to certify specific characteristics.

certiorari "To be informed of." A writ of common law origin issued by a superior to an inferior court requiring the latter to produce a certified record of a particular case tried therein. It is most commonly used to refer to the Supreme Court of the United States, which uses the writ of certiorari as a discretionary device to choose the cases it wishes to hear.

chancery Equity; equitable jurisdiction; a court of equity; the system of jurisprudence administered in courts of equity.

charging order Judicial lien against a partner's interest in the partnership.

charter An instrument emanating from the sovereign power, in the nature of a grant. A charter differs from a constitution in that the former is granted by the sovereign, while the latter is established by the people themselves.

Corporate law An act of a legislature creating a corporation or creating and defining the franchise of a corporation. Also a corporation's constitution or organic law; that is to say, the articles of incorporation taken in connection with the law under which the corporation was organized.

chattel mortgage A pre-Uniform Commercial Code security device whereby the mortgagee took a security interest in personal property of the mortgagor. Such security device has generally been superseded by other types of security agreements under UCC Article 9 (Secured Transactions).

chattel paper Writings that evidence both a debt and a security interest.

check A draft drawn upon a bank and payable on demand, signed by the maker or drawer, containing an unconditional promise to pay a sum certain in money to the order of the payee. UCC §3-104(2)(b).

Cashier's check A bank's own check drawn on itself and signed by the cashier or other authorized official. It is a direct obligation of the bank.

C. & F. Cost and freight; a shipping contract.

C.I.F. Cost, insurance, and freight; a shipping contract.

civil law Laws concerned with civil or private rights and remedies, as contrasted with criminal laws.

The system of jurisprudence administered in the Roman empire, particularly as set forth in the compilation of Justinian and his successors, as distinguished from the common law of England and the canon law. The civil law (Civil Code) is followed by Louisiana.

claim A right to payment.

clearinghouse An association of banks for the purpose of settling accounts on a daily basis.

close corporation See **corporation**.

closed-ended credit Credit extended to debtor for a specific period of time.

closed shop Employer can only hire union members.

C.O.D. Collect on delivery; generally a shipping contract.

code A compilation of all permanent laws in force consolidated and classified according to subject matter. Many states have published official codes of all laws in force, including the common law and statutes as judicially interpreted, which have been compiled by code commissions and enacted by the legislatures.

codicil A supplement or an addition to a will; it may explain, modify, add to, subtract from, qualify, alter, restrain, or revoke provisions in an existing will. It must be executed with the same formalities as a will.

cognovit judgment Written authority by debtor for entry of judgment against him in the event he defaults in payment. Such provision in a debt instrument on default confers judgment against the debtor.

collateral Secondarily liable; liable only if the party with primary liability does not perform.

collateral (security) Personal property subject to security interest.

Banking Some form of security in addition to the personal obligation of the borrower.

collateral promise Undertaking to be secondarily liable, that is, liable if the principal debtor does not perform.

collecting bank Any bank, except the payor bank, handling the item for collection. UCC §4-105(d).

collective mark Distinctive symbol used to indicate membership in an organization.

collision insurance Protects the owner of an automobile against damage due to contact with other vehicles or objects.

commerce power Exclusive power granted by the U.S. Constitution to the federal government to regulate commerce with foreign countries and among the states.

commercial bailment Bailment in which parties derive a mutual benefit.

commercial impracticability Performance can only be accomplished with unforeseen and unjust hardship.

commercial law A phrase used to designate the whole body of substantive jurisprudence (*e.g.,* Uniform Commercial Code; Truth in Lending Act) applicable to the rights, intercourse, and relations of persons engaged in commerce, trade, or mercantile pursuits. See **Uniform Commercial Code**.

commercial paper Bills of exchange (*i.e.,* drafts), promissory notes, bank checks, and other negotiable instruments for the payment of money, which, by their form and on their face, purport to be such instruments. UCC Article 3 is the general law governing commercial paper.

commercial reasonableness Judgment of reasonable persons familiar with the business transaction.

commercial speech Expression related to the economic interests of the speaker and its audience.

common carrier Carrier open to the general public.

common law Body of law originating in England and derived from judicial decisions. As distinguished from statutory law created by the enactment of legislatures, the common law comprises the judgments and decrees of the courts recognizing, affirming, and enforcing usages and customs of immemorial antiquity.

community property Rights of a spouse in property acquired by the other during marriage.

comparable worth Equal pay for jobs of equal value to the employer.

comparative negligence Under comparative negligence statutes or doctrines, negligence is measured in terms of percentage, and any damages allowed shall be diminished in proportion to amount of negligence attributable to the person for whose injury, damage, or death recovery is sought.

complainant One who applies to the courts for legal redress by filing a complaint (*i.e.,* plaintiff).

complaint The pleading which sets forth a claim for relief. Such complaint (whether it be the original claim, counterclaim, cross-claim, or third-party claim) shall contain (1) a short, plain statement of the grounds upon which the court's jurisdiction depends, unless the court already has jurisdiction and the claim needs no new grounds of jurisdiction to support it, (2) a short, plain statement of the claim showing that the pleader is entitled to relief, and (3) a demand for judgment for the relief to which he deems himself entitled. Fed.R. Civil P. 8(a). The complaint, together with the summons, is required to be served on the defendant. Rule 4.

composition Agreement between debtor and two or more of her creditors that each will take a portion of his claim as full payment.

compulsory arbitration Arbitration required by statute for specific types of disputes.

computer crime Crime committed against or through the use of a computer or computer/services.

concealment Fraudulent failure to disclose a material fact.

conciliation Nonbinding process in which a third party acts as an intermediary between disputing parties.

concurrent jurisdiction Authority of more than one court to hear the same case.

condition An uncertain event which affects the duty of performance.

> *Concurrent conditions* The parties are to perform simultaneously.
>
> *Express condition* Performance is contingent on the happening or nonhappening of a stated event.

condition precedent An event which must occur or not occur before performance is due; event or events (presentment, dishonor, notice of dishonor) which must occur to hold a secondary party liable to commercial paper.

condition subsequent An event which terminates a duty of performance.

conditional acceptance An acceptance of an offer contingent upon the acceptance of an additional or different term.

conditional contract Obligations are contingent upon a stated event.

conditional guarantor of collection Surety liable to creditor only after creditor exhausts his legal remedies against the principal debtor.

confession of judgment Written agreement by debtor authorizing creditor to obtain a court judgment in the event debtor defaults. See also **cognovit judgment**.

confiscation Governmental taking of foreign-owned property without payment.

conflict of laws That branch of jurisprudence, arising from the diversity of the laws of different nations, states, or jurisdictions, that reconciles the inconsistencies, or decides which law is to govern in a particular case.

confusion Results when goods belonging to two or more owners become so intermixed that the property of any of them no longer can be identified except as part of a mass of like goods.

consanguinity Kinship; blood relationship; the connection or relation of persons descended from the same stock or common ancestor.

consensual arbitration Arbitration voluntarily entered into by the parties.

consent Voluntary and knowing willingness that an act should be done.

conservator Appointed by court to manage affairs of incompetent or to liquidate business.

consideration The cause, motive, price, or impelling influence which induces a contracting party to enter into a contract. Some right, interest, profit, or benefit accruing to one party or some forbearance, detriment, loss, or responsibility given, suffered, or undertaken by the other.

consignee One to whom a consignment is made. Person named in bill of lading to whom or to whose order the bill promises delivery. UCC §7-102(b).

consignment Ordinarily implies an agency; denotes that property is committed to the consignee for care or sale.

consignor One who sends or makes a consignment; a shipper of goods. The person named in a bill of lading as the person from whom the goods have been received for shipment. UCC §7-102(c).

consolidation In *corporate law*, the combination of two or more corporations into a newly created corporation. Thus, A Corporation and B Corporation consolidate to form C Corporation.

constitution Fundamental law of a government establishing its powers and limitations.

constructive That which is established by the mind of the law in its act of *construing* facts, conduct, circumstances, or instruments. That which has not in its essential nature the character assigned to it, but acquires such character in consequence of the way in which it is regarded by a rule or policy of law; hence, inferred, implied, or made out by legal interpretation; the word "legal" being sometimes used here in lieu of "constructive."

constructive assent An assent or consent imputed to a party from a construction or interpretation of his conduct; as distinguished from one which he actually expresses.

constructive conditions Conditions in contracts which are neither expressed nor implied but rather are imposed by law to meet the ends of justice.

constructive delivery Term comprehending all those acts which, although not truly conferring a real possession of the vendee, have been held by construction of law to be equivalent to acts of real delivery.

constructive eviction Failure by the landlord in any obligation under the lease that causes a substantial and lasting injury to the tenant's enjoyment of the premises.

constructive notice Knowledge imputed by law.

constructive trust Arising by operation of law to prevent unjust enrichment. See also **trustee**.

consumer goods Goods bought or used for personal, family, or household purposes.

consumer product Tangible personal property normally used for family, household, or personal purposes.

contingent remainder Remainder interest, conditional upon the happening of an event in addition to the termination of the preceding estate.

contract An agreement between two or more persons which creates an obligation to do or not to do a particular thing. Its essentials are competent parties, subject matter, a legal consideration, mutuality of agreement, and mutuality of obligation.

Destination contract Seller is required to tender delivery of the goods at a particular destination; seller bears the expense and risk of loss.

Executed contract Fully performed by all of the parties.

Executory contract Contract partially or entirely unperformed by one or more of the parties.

Express contract Agreement of parties that is expressed in words either in writing or orally.

Formal contract Agreement which is legally binding because of its particular form or mode or expression.

Implied-in-fact contract Contract where agreement of the parties is inferred from their conduct.

Informal contract All oral or written contracts other than formal contracts.

Installment contract Goods are delivered in separate lots.

Integrated contract Complete and total agreement.

Output contract A contract in which one party agrees to sell his entire output and the other agrees to buy it; it is not illusory, though it may be indefinite.

Quasi contract Obligation not based upon contract that is imposed to avoid injustice.

Requirements contract A contract in which one party agrees to purchase his total requirements from the other party; hence, such a contract is binding, not illusory.

Substituted contract An agreement between the parties to rescind their old contract and replace it with a new contract.

Unconscionable contract One which no sensible person not under delusion, duress, or in distress would make, and such as no honest and fair person would accept. A contract the terms of which are excessively unreasonable, overreaching, and one-sided.

Unenforceable contract Contract for the breach of which the law does not provide a remedy.

Unilateral and bilateral A unilateral contract is one in which one party makes an express engagement or undertakes a performance, without receiving in return any express engagement or promise of performance from the other. Bilateral (or reciprocal) contracts are those by which the parties expressly enter into mutual engagements.

contract clause Prohibition against the states' retroactively modifying public and private contracts.

contractual liability Obligation on a negotiable instrument, based upon signing the instrument.

contribution Payment from cosureties of their proportionate share.

contributory negligence An act or omission amounting to a want of ordinary care on the part of the complaining party, which, concurring with defendant's negligence, is proximate cause of injury.

The defense of contributory negligence is an absolute bar to any recovery in some states; because of this, it has been replaced by the doctrine of comparative negligence in many other states.

conversion Unauthorized and wrongful exercise of dominion and control over another's personal property, to exclusion of or inconsistent with rights of the owner.

convertible bond Bond that may be exchanged for other securities of the corporation.

copyright Exclusive right granted by federal government to authors of original works including literary, musical, dramatic, pictorial, graphic, sculptural, and film works.

corporation A legal entity ordinarily consisting of an association of numerous individuals. Such entity is regarded as having a personality and existence distinct from that of its several members and is vested with the capacity of continuous succession, irrespective of changes in its membership, either in perpetuity or for a limited term of years.

Closely held or close corporation Corporation that is owned by few shareholders and whose shares are not actively traded.

Corporation de facto One existing under color of law and in pursuance of an effort made in good faith to organize a corporation under the statute. Such a corporation is not subject to collateral attack.

Corporation de jure That which exists by reason of full compliance with requirements of an existing law permitting organization of such corporation.

Domestic corporation Corporation created under the laws of a given state.

Foreign corporation Corporation created under the laws of any other state, government, or country.

Publicly held corporation Corporation whose shares are owned by a large number of people and are widely traded.

Subchapter S corporation A small business corporation which, under certain conditions, may elect to have its undistributed taxable income taxed to its shareholders. I.R.C. §1371 et seq. Of major significance is the fact that Subchapter S status usually avoids the corporate income tax, and corporate losses can be claimed by the shareholders.

Subsidiary and parent Subsidiary corporation is one in which another corporation (called parent corporation) owns at least a majority of the shares and over which it thus has control.

corrective advertising Disclosure in an advertisement that previous ads were deceptive.

costs A pecuniary allowance, made to the successful party (and recoverable from the losing party), for his expenses in prosecuting or defending an action or a distinct proceeding within an action. Generally, "costs" do not include attorneys' fees unless such fees are by a statute denominated costs or are by statute allowed to be recovered as costs in the case.

cosureties Two or more sureties bound for the same debt of a principal debtor.

co-tenants Persons who hold title concurrently.

counterclaim A claim presented by a defendant in opposition to or deduction from the claim of the plaintiff.

counteroffer A statement by the offeree which has the legal effect of rejecting the offer and of proposing a new offer to the offeror. However, the provisions of UCC §2-207(2) modify this principle by providing that the "additional terms are to be construed as proposals for addition to the contract."

course of dealing A sequence of previous acts and conduct between the parties to a particular transaction which is fairly to be regarded as establishing a common basis of understanding for interpreting their expressions and other conduct. UCC §1-205(1).

course of performance Conduct between the parties concerning performance of the particular contract.

court above—court below In appellate practice, the "court above" is the one to which a cause is removed for review, whether by appeal, writ of error, or certiorari, while the "court below" is the one from which the case is being removed.

covenant Used primarily with respect to promises in conveyances or other instruments dealing with real estate.

Covenants against encumbrances A stipulation against all rights to or interests in the land which may subsist in third persons to the diminution of the value of the estate granted.

Covenant appurtenant A covenant which is connected with land of the grantor, not in gross. A covenant running with the land and binding heirs, executors, and assigns of the immediate parties.

Covenant for further assurance An undertaking, in the form of a covenant, on the part of the vendor of real estate to do such further acts for the purpose of perfecting the purchaser's title as the latter may reasonably require.

Covenant for possession A covenant by which the grantee or lessee is granted possession.

Covenant for quiet enjoyment An assurance against the consequences of a defective title, and against any disturbances thereupon.

Covenants for title Covenants usually inserted in a conveyance of land, on the part of the grantor, and binding him for the completeness, security, and continuance of the title transferred to the grantee. They comprise covenants for seisin, for right to convey, against encumbrances, or quiet enjoyment, sometimes for further assurance, and almost always of warranty.

Covenant in gross Such as do not run with the land.

Covenant of right to convey An assurance by the covenantor that the grantor has sufficient capacity and title to convey the estate which he by his deed undertakes to convey.

Covenant of seisin An assurance to the purchaser that the grantor has the very estate in quantity and quality which he purports to convey.

Covenant of warranty An assurance by the grantor of an estate that the grantee shall enjoy the same without interruption by virtue of paramount title.

Covenant running with land A covenant which goes with the land, as being annexed to the estate, and which cannot be separated from the land or transferred without it. A covenant is said to run with the land when not only the original parties or their representatives, but each successive owner of the land, will be entitled to its benefit, or be liable (as the case may be) to its obligation. Such a covenant is said to be one which "touches and concerns" the land itself, so that its benefit or obligation passes with the ownership. Essentials are that the grantor and grantee must have intended that the covenant run with the land, the covenant must affect or concern the land with which it runs, and there must be privity of estate between the party claiming the benefit and the party who rests under the burden.

covenant not to compete Agreement to refrain from entering into a competing trade, profession, or business.

cover Buyer's purchase of goods in substitution for those not delivered by breaching seller.

credit beneficiary See **third-party beneficiary**.

creditor Any entity having a claim against the debtor.

crime An act or omission in violation of a public law and punishable by the government.

criminal duress Coercion by threat of serious bodily injury.

criminal intent Desired or virtually certain consequences of one's conduct.

criminal law The law that involves offenses against the entire community.

cure The right of a seller under the UCC to correct a nonconforming delivery of goods to buyer within the contract period. §2-508.

curtesy Husband's estate in the real property of his wife.

cy-pres As near (as possible). Rule for the construction of instruments in equity, by which the intention of the party is carried out *as near as may be*, when it would be impossible or illegal to give it literal effect.

damage Loss, injury, or deterioration caused by the negligence, design, or accident of one person, with respect to another's person or property. The word is to be distinguished from its plural, "damages," which means a compensation in money for a loss or damage.

damages Money sought as a remedy for breach of contract or for tortious acts.

Actual damages Real, substantial, and just damages, or the amount awarded to a complainant in compensation for his actual and real loss or injury, as opposed, on the one hand, to "nominal" damages and, on the other, to "exemplary" or "punitive" damages. Synonymous with "compensatory damages" and "general damages."

Benefit-of-the-bargain damages Difference between the value received and the value of the fraudulent party's performance as represented.

Compensatory damages Compensatory damages are such as will compensate the injured party for the injury sustained, and nothing more; such as will simply make good or replace the loss caused by the wrong or injury.

Consequential damages Such damage, loss, or injury as does not flow directly and immediately from the act of the party, but only from some of the consequences or results of such act. Consequential damages resulting from a seller's breach of contract include any loss resulting from general or particular requirements and needs of which the seller at the time of contracting had reason to know and which could not reasonably be prevented by cover or otherwise, and injury to person or property proximately resulting from any breach of warranty. UCC §2-715(2).

Exemplary or punitive damages Damages other than compensatory damages which may be awarded against a person to punish him for outrageous conduct.

Expectancy damages Calculable by subtracting the injured party's actual dollar position as a result of the breach from that party's projected dollar position had performance occurred.

Foreseeable damages Loss of which the party in breach had reason to know when the contract was made.

Incidental damages Under UCC §2-710, such damages include any commercially reasonable charges, expenses, or commissions incurred in stopping delivery, in the transportation, care, and custody of goods after the buyer's breach, in connection with the return or resale of the goods, or otherwise resulting from the breach. Also, such damages, resulting from a seller's breach of contract, include expenses reasonably incurred in inspection, receipt, transportation, and care and custody of goods rightfully rejected, any commercially reasonable charges, expenses, or commissions in connection with effecting cover, and any other reasonable expense incident to the delay or other breach. UCC §2-715(1).

Irreparable damages In the law pertaining to injunctions, damages for which no certain pecuniary standard exists for measurement.

Liquidated damages and penalties Damages for breach by either party may be liquidated in the agreement but only at an amount which is reasonable in the light of the anticipated or actual harm caused by the breach, the difficulties of proof of loss, and the inconvenience or nonfeasibility of otherwise obtaining an adequate remedy. A term fixing unreasonably large liquidated damages is void as a penalty. UCC §2-718(1).

Mitigation of damages A plaintiff may not recover damages for the effects of an injury which she reasonably could have avoided or substantially ameliorated. This limitation on recovery is generally denominated as "mitigation of damages" or "avoidance of consequences."

Nominal damages A small sum awarded where a contract has been breached but the loss is negligible or unproven.

Out-of-pocket damages Difference between the value received and the value given.

Reliance damages Contract damages placing the injured party in as good a position as he would have been in had the contract not been made.

Treble damages Three times actual loss.

de facto "In fact, in deed, actually." This phrase is used to characterize an officer, a government, a past action, or a state of affairs which must be accepted for all practical purposes but which is illegal or illegitimate. See also **corporation**, *corporation de facto*.

de jure Descriptive of a condition in which there has been total compliance with all requirements of law. In this sense it is the contrary of *de facto*. See also **corporation**, *corporation de jure*.

de novo Anew; afresh; a second time.

debenture Unsecured bond.

debt security Any form of corporate security reflected as debt on the books of the corporation in contrast to equity securities such as stock; *e.g.*, bonds, notes, and debentures are debt securities.

debtor Person who owes payment or performance of an obligation.

deceit A fraudulent and cheating misrepresentation, artifice, or device used to deceive and trick one who is ignorant of the true facts, to the prejudice and damage of the party imposed upon. See also **fraud**; **misrepresentation**.

decree Decision of a court of equity.

deed A conveyance of realty; a writing, signed by a grantor, whereby title to realty is transferred from one party to another.

deed of trust Interest in real property which is conveyed to a third person as trustee for the creditor.

defamation Injury of a person's reputation by publication of false statements.

default judgment Judgment against a defendant who fails to respond to a complaint.

defendant The party against whom legal action is sought.

definite term Lease that automatically expires at end of the term.

delectus personae Partner's right to choose who may become a member of the partnership.

delegatee Third party to whom the delegator's duty is delegated.

delegation of duties Transferring to another all or part of one's duties arising under a contract.

delegator Party delegating his duty to a third party.

delivery The physical or constructive transfer of an instrument or of goods from one person to another. See also **constructive delivery**.

demand Request for payment made by the holder of the instrument.

demand paper Payable on request.

demurrer An allegation of a defendant that even if the facts as stated in the pleading to which objection is taken be true, their legal consequences are not such as to require the demurring party to answer them or to proceed further with the cause.

The Federal Rules of Civil Procedure do not provide for the use of a demurrer, but provide an equivalent to a general demurrer in the motion to dismiss for failure to state a claim on which relief may be granted. Fed.R. Civil P. 12(b).

deposition The testimony of a witness taken upon interrogatories, not in court, but intended to be used in court. See also **discovery**.

depository bank The first bank to which an item is transferred for collection even though it may also be the payor bank. UCC §4-105(a).

descent Succession to the ownership of an estate by inheritance or by any act of law, as distinguished from "purchase."

Descents are of two sorts, *lineal* and *collateral*. Lineal descent is descent in a direct or right line, as from father or grandfather to son or grandson. Collateral descent is descent in a collateral or oblique line, that is, up to the common ancestor and then down from him, as from brother to brother, or between cousins.

design defect Plans or specifications inadequate to ensure the product's safety.

devise A testamentary disposition of land or realty; a gift of real property by the last will and testament of the donor. When used as a noun, means a testamentary disposition of real or personal property; when used as a verb, means to dispose of real or personal property by will.

dictum Generally used as an abbreviated form of *obiter dictum*, "a remark by the way"; that is, an observation or remark made by a judge which does not embody the resolution or determination of the court and which is made without argument or full consideration of the point.

directed verdict In a case in which the party with the burden of proof has failed to present a prima facie case for jury consideration, the trial judge may order the entry of a verdict without allowing the jury to consider it because, as a matter of law, there can be only one such verdict. Fed.R. Civil P. 50(a).

disaffirmance Avoidance of a contract.

discharge Termination of certain allowed claims against a debtor.

disclaimer Negation of warranty.

discount A discount by a bank means a drawback or deduction made upon its advances or loans of money, upon negotiable paper or other evidences of debt payable at a future day, which are transferred to the bank.

discovery The pretrial devices that can be used by one party to obtain facts and information about the case from the other party in order to assist the party's preparation for trial. Under the Federal Rules of Civil Procedure, tools of discovery include depositions upon oral and written questions, written interrogatories, production of documents or things, permission to enter upon land or other property, physical and mental examinations, and requests for admission. Rules 26–37.

dishonor To refuse to accept or pay a draft or to pay a promissory note when duly presented. UCC §3-507(1); §4-210. See also **protest**.

disparagement Publication of false statements resulting in harm to another's monetary interests.

disputed debt Obligation whose existence or amount is contested.

dissenting shareholder One who opposes a fundamental change and has the right to receive the fair value of her shares.

dissolution The dissolution of a partnership is the change in the relation of the partners caused by any partner's ceasing to be associated with the carrying on, as distinguished from the winding up, of the business. See also **winding up**.

distribution Transfer of partnership property from the partnership to a partner; transfer of property from a corporation to any of its shareholders.

dividend The payment designated by the board of directors of a corporation to be distributed *pro rata* among a class or classes of the shares outstanding.

document Document of title.

document of title Instrument evidencing ownership of the document and the goods it covers.

domicile That place where a person has his true, fixed, and permanent home and principal establishment, and to which whenever he is absent he has the intention of returning.

dominant Land whose owner has rights in other land.

donee Recipient of a gift.

donee beneficiary See **third-party beneficiary**.

donor Maker of a gift.

dormant partner One who is both a silent and a secret partner.

dower A species of life-estate which a woman is, by law, entitled to claim on the death of her husband, in the lands and tenements of which he was seised in fee during the marriage, and which her issue, if any, might by possibility have inherited.

Dower has been abolished in the majority of the states and materially altered in most of the others.

draft A written order by the first party, called the drawer, instructing a second party, called the drawee (such as a bank), to pay a third party, called the payee. An order to pay a sum certain in money, signed by a drawer, payable on demand or at a definite time, and to order or bearer. UCC §3-104.

drawee A person to whom a bill of exchange or draft is directed, and who is requested to pay the amount of money therein mentioned. The drawee of a check is the bank on which it is drawn.

When a drawee accepts, he engages that he will pay the instrument according to its tenor at the time of his engagement or as completed. UCC §3-413(1).

drawer The person who draws a bill or draft. The drawer of a check is the person who signs it.

The drawer engages that upon dishonor of the draft and any necessary notice of dishonor or protest, he will pay the amount of the draft to the holder or to any indorser who takes it up. The drawer may disclaim this liability by drawing without recourse. UCC §3-413(2).

due negotiation Transfer of a negotiable document in the regular course of business to a holder, who takes in good faith, without notice of any defense or claim, and for value.

duress Unlawful constraint exercised upon a person, whereby he is forced to do some act against his will.

Physical duress Coercion involving physical force or the threat of physical force.

duty Legal obligation requiring a person to perform or refrain from performing an act.

earned surplus Undistributed net profits, income, gains, and losses.

earnest The payment of a part of the price of goods sold, or the delivery of part of such goods, for the purpose of binding the contract.

easement A right in the owner of one parcel of land, by reason of such ownership, to use the land of another for a special purpose not inconsistent with a general property right in the owner. This right is distinguishable from a "license," which merely confers a personal privilege to do some act on the land.

Affirmative easement One where the servient estate must permit something to be done thereon, as to pass over it, or to discharge water on it.

Appurtenant easement An incorporeal right which is attached to a superior right and inheres in land to which it is attached and is in the nature of a covenant running with the land.

Easement by necessity Such arises by operation of law when land conveyed is completely shut off from access to any road by land retained by the grantor or by land of the grantor and that of a stranger.

Easement by prescription A mode of acquiring title to property by immemorial or long-continued enjoyment; refers to personal usage restricted to claimant and his ancestors or grantors.

Easement in gross An easement in gross is not appurtenant to any estate in land or does not belong to any person by virtue of ownership of an estate in other land but is a mere personal interest in or a right to use the land of another; it is purely personal and usually ends with death of grantee.

Easement of access Right of ingress and egress to and from the premises of a lot owner to a street appurtenant to the land of the lot owner.

ejectment An action to determine whether the title to certain land is in the plaintiff or is in the defendant.

electronic funds transfer A transaction with a financial institution by means of computer, telephone, or other electronic instrument.

emancipation The act by which an infant is liberated from the control of a parent or guardian and made his own master.

embezzlement The taking, in violation of a trust, of the property of one's employer.

emergency Sudden, unexpected event calling for immediate action.

eminent domain Right of the people or government to take private property for public use upon giving fair consideration.

employment discrimination Hiring, firing, compensating, promoting, or training of employees based on race, color, sex, religion, or national origin.

employment relationship One in which employer has right to control the physical conduct of employee.

endowment contract Agreement to pay insured a lump sum upon reaching a specified age or in event of death.

entirety Used to designate that which the law considers as a single whole incapable of being divided into parts.

entrapment Induced by a government official into committing a crime.

entrusting Transfer of possession of goods to a merchant who deals in goods of that kind and who may in turn transfer valid title to a buyer in the ordinary course of business.

equal pay Equivalent pay for the same work.

equal protection Requirement that similarly situated persons be treated similarly by government action.

equipment Goods used primarily in business.

equitable Just, fair, and right. Existing in equity; available or sustainable only in equity, or only upon the rules and principles of equity.

equity Justice administered according to fairness, as contrasted with the strictly formulated rules of common law. It is based on a system of rules and principles which originated in England as an alternative to the harsh rules of common law and which were based on what was fair in a particular situation.

equity of redemption The right of the mortgagor of an estate to redeem the same after it has been forfeited, at law, by a breach of the condition of the mortgage, upon paying the amount of debt, interest, and costs.

equity securities Stock or similar security, in contrast to debt securities such as bonds, notes, and debentures.

error A mistake of law, or a false or irregular application of it, such as vitiates legal proceedings and warrants reversal of the judgment.

Harmless error In appellate practice, an error committed in the progress of the trial below which was not prejudicial to the rights of the party assigning it and for which, therefore, the appellate court will not reverse the judgment.

Reversible error In appellate practice, such an error as warrants the appellate court's reversal of the judgment before it.

escrow A system of document transfer in which a deed, bond, or funds is or are delivered to a third person to hold until all conditions in a contract are fulfilled; *e.g.,* delivery of deed to escrow agent under installment land sale contract until full payment for land is made.

estate The degree, quantity, nature, and extent of interest which a person has in real and personal property. An estate in lands, tenements, and hereditaments signifies such interest as the tenant has therein.

Also, the total property of whatever kind that is owned by a decedent prior to the distribution of that property in accordance with the terms of a will or, when there is no will, by the laws of inheritance in the state of domicile of the decedent.

Future estate An estate limited to commence in possession at a future day, either without the intervention of a precedent estate or on the determination by lapse of time, or otherwise, of a precedent estate created at the same time. Examples include reversions and remainders.

estoppel A bar or impediment raised by the law which precludes a person from alleging or from denying a certain fact or state of facts, in consequence of his or her previous allegation, denial, conduct, or admission, or in consequence of a final adjudication of the matter in a court of law. See also **waiver**.

eviction Dispossession by process of law; the act of depriving a person of the possession of lands which he has held, pursuant to the judgment of a court.

evidence Any species of proof or probative matter legally presented at the trial of an issue by the act of the parties and through the medium of witnesses, records, documents, concrete objects, etc., for the purpose of inducing belief in the minds of the court or jury as to the parties' contention.

exception A formal objection to the action of the court, during the trial of a cause, in refusing a request or overruling an objection; implying that the party excepting does not acquiesce in the decision of the court but will seek to procure its reversal, and that he means to save the benefit of his request or objection in some future proceeding.

exclusionary rule Prohibition of illegally obtained evidence.

exclusive dealing Sole right to sell goods in a defined market.

exclusive jurisdiction Such jurisdiction that permits only one court (state or federal) to hear a case.

exculpatory clause Excusing oneself from fault or liability.

execution *Execution of contract* includes performance of all acts necessary to render it complete as an instrument; implies that nothing more need be done to make the contract complete and effective.

Execution upon a money judgment is the legal process of enforcing the judgment, usually by seizing and selling property of the debtor.

executive order Legislation issued by the president or a governor.

executor A person appointed by a testator to carry out the directions and requests in his will and to dispose of the property according to his testamentary provisions after his decease. The female designation is executrix. A person appointed by the court in an intestacy situation is called the administrator(rix).

executory That which is yet to be executed or performed; that which remains to be carried into operation or effect; incomplete; depending upon a future performance or event. The opposite of executed.

executory contract See **contracts**.

executory promise Unperformed obligation.

exemplary damages See **damages**.

exoneration Relieved of liability.

express Manifested by direct and appropriate language, as distinguished from that which is inferred from conduct. The word is usually contrasted with "implied."

express warranty Explicitly made contractual promise regarding property or contract rights transferred; in a sale of goods, an affirmation of fact or a promise about the goods or a description, including a sample, of goods which becomes part of the basis of the bargain.

expropriation Governmental taking of foreign-owned property for a public purpose and with payment.

ex-ship Risk of loss passes to buyer when the goods leaving the ship. See UCC §2-322. See also **F.A.S.**

extortion Making threats to obtain property.

fact An event that took place or a thing that exists.

false imprisonment Intentional interference with a person's freedom of movement by unlawful confinement.

false light Offensive publicity placing another in a false light.

false pretenses Intentional misrepresentation of fact in order to cheat another.

farm products Crops, livestock, or stock used or produced in farming.

F.A.S. Free alongside. Term used in sales price quotations indicating that the price includes all costs of transportation and delivery of the goods alongside the ship. See UCC §2-319(2).

federal preemption First right of the federal government to regulate matters within its powers to the possible exclusion of state regulation.

federal question Any case arising under the Constitution, statutes, or treaties of the United States.

fee simple

Absolute A fee simple absolute is an estate that is unlimited as to duration, disposition, and descendibility. It is the largest estate and most extensive interest that can be enjoyed in land.

Conditional Type of transfer in which grantor conveys fee simple on condition that something be done or not done.

Defeasible Type of fee grant which may be defeated on the happening of an event. An estate which may last forever, but which may end upon the happening of a specified event, is a "fee simple defeasible."

Determinable Created by conveyance which contains words effective to create a fee simple and, in addition, a provision for automatic expiration of the estate on occurrence of stated event.

fee tail An estate of inheritance, descending only to a certain class or classes of heirs; *e.g.*, an estate is conveyed or devised "to A. and the heirs of his body," or "to A. and the heirs male of his body," or "to A., and the heirs female of his body."

fellow servant rule Common law defense relieving employer from liability to an employee for injuries caused by negligence of fellow employee.

felony Serious crime.

fiduciary A person or institution who manages money or property for another and who must exercise in such management activity a standard of care imposed by law or contract; *e.g.*, executor of estate; receiver in bankruptcy; trustee.

fiduciary duty Duty of utmost loyalty and good faith, such as that owed by a fiduciary such as an agent to her principal.

field warehouse Secured party takes possession of the goods but the debtor has access to the goods.

final credit Payment of the instrument by the payor bank.

financing statement Under the Uniform Commercial Code, a financing statement is used under Article 9 to reflect a public record that there is a

security interest or claim to the goods in question to secure a debt. The financing statement is filed by the security holder with the secretary of state or with a similar public body; thus filed, it becomes public record. See also **secured transaction**.

fire (property) insurance Provides protection against loss due to fire or other related perils.

firm offer Irrevocable offer to sell or buy goods by a merchant in a signed writing which gives assurance that it will not be rescinded for up to three months.

fitness for a particular purpose Goods are fit for a stated purpose, provided that the seller selects the product knowing the buyer's intended use and that the buyer is relying on the seller's judgment.

fixture An article in the nature of personal property which has been so annexed to realty that it is regarded as a part of the land. Examples include a furnace affixed to a house or other building, counters permanently affixed to the floor of a store, and a sprinkler system installed in a building. UCC §9-313(1)(a).

Trade fixtures Such chattels as merchants usually possess and annex to the premises occupied by them to enable them to store, handle, and display their goods, which generally are removable without material injury to the premises.

F.O.B. Free on board at some location (for example, F.O.B shipping point; F.O.B destination); the invoice price includes delivery at seller's expense to that location. Title to goods usually passes from seller to buyer at the F.O.B location. UCC §2-319(1).

foreclosure Procedure by which mortgaged property is sold on default of mortgagor in satisfaction of mortgage debt.

forgery Intentional falsification of a document with intent to defraud.

four unities Time, title, interest, and possession.

franchise A privilege granted or sold, such as to use a name or to sell products or services. The right given by a manufacturer or supplier to a retailer to use his products and name on terms and conditions mutually agreed upon.

fraud Elements include false representation; of a present or past fact; made by defendant; action in reliance thereon by plaintiff; and damage resulting to plaintiff from such misrepresentation.

fraud in the execution Misrepresentation that deceives the other party as to the nature of a document evidencing the contract.

fraud in the inducement Misrepresentation regarding the subject matter of a contract that induces the other party to enter into the contract.

fraudulent misrepresentation False statement made with knowledge of its falsity and intent to mislead.

freehold An estate for life or in fee. It must possess two qualities: (1) immobility, that is, the property must be either land or some interest issuing out of or annexed to land; and (2) indeterminate duration.

friendly fire Fire contained where it is intended to be.

frustration of purpose doctrine Excuses a promisor in certain situations when the objectives of contract have been utterly defeated by circumstances arising after formation of the agreement, and performance is excused under this rule even though there is no impediment to actual performance.

full warranty One under which warrantor will repair the product and, if unsuccessful, will replace it or refund its cost.

fungibles With respect to goods or securities, those of which any unit is, by nature or usage of trade, the equivalent of any other like unit. UCC §1-201(17); *e.g.,* a bushel of wheat or other grain.

future estate See **estate**.

garnishment A statutory proceeding whereby a person's property, money, or credits in the possession or control of another are applied to payment of the former's debt to a third person.

general intangible Catchall category for collateral not otherwise covered.

general partner Member of either a general or limited partnership with unlimited liability for its debts, full management powers, and a right to share in the profits.

gift A voluntary transfer of property to another made gratuitously and without consideration. Essential requisites of "gift" are capacity of donor, intention of donor to make gift, completed delivery to or for donee, and acceptance of gift by donee.

gift causa mortis A gift in view of death is one which is made in contemplation, fear, or peril of death and with the intent that it shall take effect only in case of the death of the giver.

good faith Honesty in fact in conduct or in a transaction.

good faith purchaser Buyer who acts honestly, gives value, and takes the goods without notice or knowledge of any defect in the title of his transferor.

goods A term of variable content and meaning. It may include every species of personal property, or it may be given a very restricted meaning. Sometimes the meaning of "goods" is extended to include all tangible items, as in the phrase "goods and services."

All things (including specially manufactured goods) which are movable at the time of identification to a contract for sale other than the money in which the price is to be paid, investment securities, and things in action. UCC §2-105(1).

grantee Transferee of property.

grantor A transferor of property. The creator of a trust is usually designated as the grantor of the trust.

gratuitous promise Promise made without consideration.

group insurance Covers a number of individuals.

guaranty A promise to answer for the payment of some debt, or the performance of some duty, in case of the failure of another person who, in the first instance, is liable for such payment or performance.

The terms *guaranty* and *suretyship* are sometimes used interchangeably; but they should not be confounded. The distinction between contract of suretyship and contract of guaranty is whether or not the undertaking is a joint undertaking with the principal or a separate and distinct contract; if it is the former, it is one of "suretyship," and if the latter, it is one of "guaranty." See also **surety**.

guardianship The relationship under which a person (the guardian) is appointed by a court to preserve and control the property of another (the ward).

heir A person who succeeds, by the rules of law, to an estate in lands, tenements, or hereditaments, upon the death of his ancestor, by descent and right of relationship.

holder Person who is in possession of a document of title or an instrument or an investment security drawn, issued, or indorsed to him or to his order, or to bearer, or in blank. UCC §1-201(20).

holder in due course A holder who takes an instrument for value, in good faith, and without notice that it is overdue or has been dishonored or of any defense against or claim to it on the part of any person.

holograph A will or deed written entirely by the testator or grantor with his own hand and not witnessed (attested). State laws vary with respect to the validity of the holographic will.

homicide Unlawful taking of another's life.

horizontal privity Who may bring a cause of action.

horizontal restraints Agreements among competitors.

hostile fire Any fire outside its intended or usual place.

identified goods Designated goods as a part of a particular contract.

illegal per se Conclusively presumed unreasonable and therefore illegal.

illusory promise Promise imposing no obligation on the promisor.

implied-in-fact condition Contingencies understood but not expressed by the parties.

implied-in-law condition Contingency that arises from operation of law.

implied warranty Obligation imposed by law upon the transferor of property or contract rights; implicit in the sale arising out of certain circumstances.

implied warranty of habitability Leased premises are fit for ordinary residential purposes.

impossibility Performance that cannot be done.

in personam "Against the person." Action seeking judgment against a person involving his personal rights and based on jurisdiction of his person, as distinguished from a judgment against property (*i.e.*, in rem).

in personam jurisdiction Jurisdiction based on claims against a person, in contrast to jurisdiction over his property.

in re In the affair; in the matter of; concerning; regarding. This is the usual method of entitling a judicial proceeding in which there are no adversary parties, but merely some res concerning which judicial action is to be taken, such as a bankrupt's estate, an estate in the probate court, a proposed public highway, etc.

in rem A technical term used to designate proceedings or actions instituted *against the thing*, in contradistinction to personal actions, which are said to be *in personam*.

Quasi in rem A term applied to proceedings which are not strictly and purely *in rem*, but are brought against the defendant personally, though the real object is to deal with particular property or subject property to the discharge of claims asserted; for example, foreign attachment, or proceedings to foreclose a mortgage, remove a cloud from title, or effect a partition.

in rem jurisdiction Jurisdiction based on claims against property.

incidental beneficiary Third party whom the two parties to a contract have no intention of benefiting by their contract.

income bond Bond that conditions payment of interest on corporate earnings.

incontestability clause The prohibition of an insurer to avoid an insurance policy after a specified period of time.

indemnification Duty owed by principal to agent to pay agent for losses incurred while acting as directed by principal.

indemnify To reimburse one for a loss already incurred.

indenture A written agreement under which bonds and debentures are issued, setting forth maturity date, interest rate, and other terms.

independent contractor Person who contracts with another to do a particular job and who is not subject to the control of the other.

indicia Signs; indications. Circumstances which point to the existence of a given fact as probable, but not certain.

indictment Grand jury charge that the defendant should stand trial.

indispensable paper Chattel paper, instruments, and documents.

indorsee The person to whom a negotiable instrument, promissory note, bill of lading, etc., is assigned by indorsement.

indorsement The act of a payee, drawee, accommodation indorser, or holder of a bill, note, check, or other negotiable instrument, in writing his name upon the back of the same, with or without further or qualifying words, whereby the property in the same is assigned and transferred to another. UCC §3-202 *et seq.*

Blank indorsement No indorsee is specified.

Qualified indorsement Without recourse, limiting one's liability on the instrument.

Restrictive indorsement Limits the rights of the indorser in some manner.

Special indorsement Designates an indorsee to be paid.

infliction of emotional distress Extreme and outrageous conduct intentionally or recklessly causing severe emotional distress.

information Formal accusation of a crime brought by a prosecutor.

infringement Unauthorized use.

injunction An equitable remedy forbidding the party defendant from doing some act which he is threatening or attempting to commit, or restraining him in the continuance thereof, such act being unjust and inequitable, injurious to the plaintiff, and not such as can be adequately redressed by an action at law.

innkeeper Hotel or motel operator.

inquisitorial system System in which the judiciary initiates, conducts, and decides cases.

insider Relative or general partner of debtor, partnership in which debtor is a partner, or corporation in which debtor is an officer, director, or controlling person.

insiders Directors, officers, employees, and agents of the issuer as well as those the issuer has entrusted with information solely for corporate purposes.

insolvency Under the UCC, a person is insolvent who either has ceased to pay his debts in the ordinary course of business or cannot pay his debts as they fall due or is insolvent within the meaning of the Federal Bankruptcy Law. UCC §1-201(23).

    Insolvency (bankruptcy) Total liabilities exceed total value of assets.

    Insolvency (equity) Inability to pay debts in ordinary course of business or as they become due.

inspection Examination of goods to determine whether they conform to a contract.

instrument Negotiable instruments, stocks, bonds, and other investment securities.

insurable interest Exists where insured derives pecuniary benefit or advantage by preservation and continued existence of property or would sustain pecuniary loss from its destruction.

insurance A contract whereby, for a stipulated consideration, one party undertakes to compensate the other for loss on a specified subject by specified perils. The party agreeing to make the compensation is usually called the "insurer" or "underwriter"; the other, the "insured" or "assured"; the written contract, a "policy"; the events insured against, "risks" or "perils"; and the subject, right, or interest to be protected, the "insurable interest." Insurance is a contract whereby one undertakes to indemnify another against loss, damage, or liability arising from an unknown or contingent event.

    Co-insurance A form of insurance in which a person insures property for less than its full or stated value and agrees to share the risk of loss.

    Life insurance Payment of a specific sum of money to a designated beneficiary upon the death of the insured.

    Ordinary life Life insurance with a savings component that runs for the life of the insured.

    Term life Life insurance issued for a limited number of years that does not have a savings component.

intangible property Protected interests that are not physical.

intangibles Accounts and general intangibles.

intent Desire to cause the consequences of an act or knowledge that the consequences are substantially certain to result from the act.

inter alia Among other things.

inter se or **inter sese** "Among or between themselves." Used to distinguish rights or duties between two or more parties from their rights or duties to others.

interest in land Any right, privilege, power, or immunity in real property.

interest in partnership Partner's share in the partnership's profits and surplus.

interference with contractual relations Intentionally causing one of the parties to a contract not to perform the contract.

intermediary bank Any bank, except the depositary or payor bank, to which an item is transferred in the course of collection. UCC §4-105(c).

intermediate test Requirement that legislation have a substantial relationship to an important governmental objective.

international law Deals with the conduct and relations of nation-states and international organizations.

interpretation Construction or meaning of a contract.

interpretative rules Statements issued by an administrative agency indicating its construction of its governing statute.

intestate A person is said to die intestate when he dies without making a will. The word is also often used to signify the person himself. *Compare* **testator**.

intrusion Unreasonable and highly offensive interference with the seclusion of another.

inventory Goods held for sale or lease or consumed in a business.

invitee A person is an "invitee" on land of another if (1) he enters by invitation, express or implied, (2) his entry is connected with the owner's business or with an activity the owner conducts or permits to be conducted on his land, and (3) there is mutual benefit or a benefit to the owner.

joint liability Liability where creditor must sue all of the partners as a group.

joint and several liability Liability where creditor may sue partners jointly as a group or separately as individuals.

joint stock company A general partnership with some corporate attributes.

joint tenancy See **tenancy**.

joint venture An association of two or more persons to carry on a single business transaction for profit.

judgment The official and authentic decision of a court of justice upon the respective rights and claims of the parties to an action or suit therein litigated and submitted to its determination.

judgment in personam A judgment against a particular person, as distinguished from a judgment against a thing or a right or *status*.

judgment in rem An adjudication pronounced upon the status of some particular thing or subject matter, by a tribunal having competent authority.

judgment n.o.v. Judgment *non obstante veredicto* in its broadest sense is a judgment rendered in favor of one party notwithstanding the finding of a verdict in favor of the other party.

judgment notwithstanding the verdict A final binding determination on the merits made by the judge after and contrary to the jury's verdict.

judgment on the pleadings Final binding determination on the merits made by the judge after the pleadings.

judicial lien Interest in property that is obtained by court action to secure payment of a debt.

judicial review Power of the courts to determine the constitutionality of legislative and executive acts.

jurisdiction The right and power of a court to adjudicate concerning the subject matter in a given case.

jurisdiction over the parties Power of a court to bind the parties to a suit.

jury A body of persons selected and summoned by law and sworn to try the facts of a case and to find according to the law and the evidence. In general, the province of the jury is to find the facts in a case, while the judge passes upon pure questions of law. As a matter of fact, however, the jury must often pass upon mixed questions of law and fact in determining the case, and in all such cases the instructions of the judge as to the law become very important.

justifiable reliance Reasonably influenced by a misrepresentation.

labor dispute Any controversy concerning terms or conditions of employment or union representation.

laches Based upon maxim that equity aids the vigilant and not those who slumber on their rights. It is defined as neglect to assert a right or claim which, taken together with a lapse of time and other circumstances causing prejudice to the adverse party, operates as a bar in a court of equity.

landlord The owner of an estate in land, or a rental property, who has leased it to another person, called the "tenant." Also called "lessor."

larceny Trespassory taking and carrying away of the goods of another with the intent to permanently deprive.

last clear chance Final opportunity to avoid an injury.

lease Any agreement which gives rise to relationship of landlord and tenant (real property) or lessor and lessee (real or personal property).

    The person who conveys is termed the "lessor," and the person to whom conveyed is the "lessee"; and when the lessor conveys land or tenements to a lessee, he is said to lease, demise, or let them.

    Sublease, or *underlease* One executed by the lessee of an estate to a third person, conveying the same estate for a shorter term than that for which the lessee holds it.

leasehold An estate in realty held under a lease. The four principal types of leasehold estates are the estate for years, periodic tenancy, tenancy at will, and tenancy at sufferance.

leasehold estate Right to possess real property.

legacy A legacy is a gift or bequest by will of personal property, whereas a devise is a testamentary disposition of real estate.

Demonstrative legacy A bequest of a certain sum of money, with a direction that it shall be paid out of a particular fund. It differs from a specific legacy in this respect: that, if the fund out of which it is payable fails for any cause, it is nevertheless entitled to come on the estate as a general legacy. And it differs from a general legacy in this: that it does not abate in that class, but in the class of specific legacies.

General legacy A pecuniary legacy, payable out of the general assets of a testator.

Residuary legacy A bequest of all the testator's personal estate not otherwise effectually disposed of by his will.

Specific legacy One which operates on property particularly designated. A legacy or gift by will of a particular specified thing, as of a horse, a piece of furniture, a term of years, and the like.

legal aggregate A group of individuals not having a legal existence separate from its members.

legal benefit Obtaining something to which one had no legal right.

legal detriment Doing an act one is not legally obligated to do or not doing an act one has a legal right to do.

legal entity An organization having a legal existence separate from that of its members.

legal sufficiency Benefit to promisor or detriment to promisee.

legislative rules Substantive rules issued by an administrative agency under the authority delegated to it by the legislature.

letter of credit An engagement by a bank or other person made at the request of a customer that the issuer will honor drafts or other demands for payment upon compliance with the conditions specified in the credit.

letters of administration Formal document issued by probate court appointing one an administrator of an estate.

letters testamentary The formal instrument of authority and appointment given to an executor by the proper court, empowering him to enter upon the discharge of his office as executor. It corresponds to letters of administration granted to an administrator.

levy To assess; raise; execute; exact; tax; collect; gather; take up; seize. Thus, to levy (assess, exact, raise, or collect) a tax; to levy an execution, *i.e.*, to levy or collect a sum of money on an execution.

liability insurance Covers liability to others by reason of damage resulting from injuries to another's person or property.

liability without fault Crime to do a specific act or cause a certain result without regard to the care exercised.

libel Defamation communicated by writing, television, radio, or the like.

liberty Ability of individuals to engage in freedom of action and choice regarding their personal lives.

license License with respect to real property is a privilege to go on premises for a certain purpose, but does not operate to confer on or vest in the licensee any title, interest, or estate in such property.

licensee Person privileged to enter or remain on land by virtue of the consent of the lawful possessor.

lien A qualified right of property which a creditor has in or over specific property of his debtor, as security for the debt or charge or for performance of some act.

lien creditor A creditor who has acquired a lien on the property by attachment.

life estate An estate whose duration is limited to the life of the party holding it or of some other person. Upon the death of the life tenant, the property will go to the holder of the remainder interest or to the grantor by reversion.

limited liability Liability limited to amount invested in a business enterprise.

limited partner Member of a limited partnership with liability for its debts only to the extent of her capital contribution.

limited partnership See **partnership**.

limited partnership association A partnership which closely resembles a corporation.

liquidated Ascertained; determined; fixed; settled; made clear or manifest. Cleared away; paid; discharged.

liquidated damages See **damages**.

liquidated debt Obligation that is certain in amount.

liquidation The settling of financial affairs of a business or individual, usually by liquidating (turning to cash) all assets for distribution to creditors, heirs, etc. To be distinguished from dissolution.

loss of value Value of promised performance minus value of actual performance.

lost property Property with which the owner has involuntarily parted and which she does not know where to find or recover, not including property which she has intentionally concealed or deposited in a secret place for safekeeping. Distinguishable from mislaid property, which has been deliberately placed somewhere and forgotten.

main purpose rule Where object of promisor/surety is to provide an economic benefit for herself, the promise is considered outside of the statute of frauds.

maker One who makes or executes; as the maker of a promissory note. One who signs a check; in this context, synonymous with drawer. See **draft**.

mala in se Morally wrong.

mala prohibita Wrong by law.

mandamus "We command." A legal writ compelling the defendant to do an official duty.

manslaughter Unlawful taking of another's life without malice.

Involuntary manslaughter Taking the life of another by criminal negligence or during the course of a misdemeanor.

Voluntary manslaughter Intentional killing of another under extenuating circumstances.

manufacturing defect Not produced according to specifications.

mark Trade symbol.

market allocations Division of market by customers, geographic location, or products.

marketable title Free from any defects, encumbrances, or reasonable objections to one's ownership.

marshaling of assets Segregating the assets and liabilities of a partnership from the assets and liabilities of the individual partners.

master See **principal**.

material Matters to which a reasonable investor would attach importance in deciding whether to purchase a security.

material alteration Any change that changes the contract of any party to an instrument.

maturity The date at which an obligation, such as the principal of a bond or a note, becomes due.

maxim A general legal principle.

mechanic's lien A claim created by state statutes for the purpose of securing priority of payment of the price or value of work performed and materials furnished in erecting or repairing a building or other structure; as such, attaches to the land as well as buildings and improvements erected thereon.

mediation Nonbinding process in which a third party acts as an intermediary between the disputing parties and proposes solutions for them to consider.

mens rea Criminal intent.

mentally incompetent Unable to understand the nature and effect of one's acts.

mercantile law An expression substantially equivalent to commercial law. It designates the system of rules, customs, and usages generally recognized and adopted by merchants and traders that, either in its simplicity or as modified by common law or statutes, constitutes the law for the regulation of their transactions and the solution of their controversies. The Uniform Commercial Code is the general body of law governing commercial or mercantile transactions.

merchant A person who deals in goods of the kind involved in a transaction or who otherwise by his occupation holds himself out as having knowledge or skill peculiar to the practices or goods involved in the transaction or to whom such knowledge or skill may be attributed by his employment of an agent or broker or other intermediary who by his occupation holds himself out as having such knowledge or skill. UCC §2-104(1).

merchantability Merchant seller guarantees that the goods are fit for their ordinary purpose.

merger The fusion or absorption of one thing or right into another. In corporate law, the absorption of one company by another, the latter retaining its own name and identity and acquiring the assets, liabilities, franchises, and powers of the former, which ceases to exist as separate business entity. It differs from a consolidation, wherein all the corporations terminate their separate existences and become parties to a new one.

   Conglomerate merger An acquisition, which is not horizontal or vertical, by one company of another.

   Horizontal merger Merger between business competitors, such as manufacturers of the same type of products or distributors selling competing products in the same market area.

   Short-form merger Merger of a 90 percent subsidiary into its parent.

   Vertical merger Union with corporate customer or supplier.

midnight deadline Midnight of the next banking day after receiving an item.

mining partnership A specific type of partnership for the purpose of extracting raw minerals.

minor Under the age of legal majority (usually eighteen).

mirror image rule An acceptance cannot deviate from the terms of the offer.

misdemeanor Less serious crime.

mislaid property Property which an owner has put deliberately in a certain place that she is unable to remember, as distinguished from lost property, which the owner has left unwittingly in a location she has forgotten. See also **lost property**.

misrepresentation Any manifestation by words or other conduct by one person to another that, under the circumstances, amounts to an assertion not in accordance with the facts. A "misrepresentation" that justifies the rescission of a contract is a false statement of a substantive fact, or any conduct which leads to a belief of a substantive fact material to proper understanding of the matter in hand. See also **deceit**; **fraud**.

   Fraudulent misrepresentation False statement made with knowledge of its falsity and intent to mislead.

   Innocent misrepresentation Misrepresentation made without knowledge of its falsity but with due care.

   Negligent misrepresentation Misrepresentation made without due care in ascertaining its falsity.

M'Naughten Rule Right/wrong test for criminal insanity.

modify Change the lower court's judgment.

money Medium of exchange issued by a government body.

monopoly Ability to control price or exclude others from the marketplace.

mortgage A mortgage is an interest in land created by a written instrument providing security for the performance of a duty or the payment of a debt.

mortgagor Debtor who uses real estate to secure an obligation.

multinational enterprise Business that engages in transactions involving the movement of goods, information, money, people, or services across national borders.

multiple product order Order requiring an advertiser to cease and desist from deceptive statements on all products it sells.

murder Unlawful and premeditated taking of another's life.

mutual mistake Where the common but erroneous belief of both parties forms the basis of a contract.

necessaries Items needed to maintain a person's station in life.

negligence The omission to do something which a reasonable person, guided by those ordinary considerations which ordinarily regulate human affairs, would do, or the doing of something which a reasonable and prudent person would not do.

   Culpable negligence Greater than ordinary negligence but less than gross negligence.

negligence per se Conclusive on the issue of negligence (duty of care and breach).

negotiable Legally capable of being transferred by indorsement or delivery. Usually said of checks and notes and sometimes of stocks and bearer bonds.

negotiable instrument Signed document (such as a check or promissory note) containing an unconditional promise to pay a "sum certain" of money at a definite time to order or bearer.

negotiation Transferee becomes a holder.

net assets Total assets minus total debts.

no arrival, no sale A destination contract, but if goods do not arrive, seller is excused from liability unless such is due to the seller's fault.

no-fault insurance Compensates victims of automobile accidents regardless of fault.

nonconforming use Preexisting use not in accordance with a zoning ordinance.

nonprofit corporation One whose profits must be used exclusively for the charitable, educational, or scientific purpose for which it was formed.

nonsuit Action in form of a judgment taken against a plaintiff who has failed to appear to prosecute his action or failed to prove his case.

note   See **promissory note**.

novation A novation substitutes a new party and discharges one of the original parties to a contract by agreement of all three parties. A new contract is created with the same terms as the original one; only the parties have changed.

nuisance Nuisance is that activity which arises from the unreasonable, unwarranted, or unlawful use by a person of his own property, working obstruction or injury to the right of another or to the public, and producing such material annoyance, inconvenience, and discomfort that law will presume resulting damage.

obiter dictum See **dictum**.

objective fault Gross deviation from reasonable conduct.

objective manifestation What a reasonable person under the circumstances would believe.

objective satisfaction Approval based upon whether a reasonable person would be satisfied.

objective standard What a reasonable person under the circumstances would reasonably believe or do.

obligee Party to whom a duty of performance is owed (by delegator and delegatee).

obligor Party owing a duty (to the assignor).

offer A manifestation of willingness to enter into a bargain, so made as to justify another person in understanding that his assent to that bargain is invited and will conclude it. Restatement, Second, Contracts, §24.

offeree Recipient of the offer.

offeror Person making the offer.

open-ended credit Credit arrangement under which debtor has rights to enter into a series of credit transactions.

opinion Belief in the existence of a fact or a judgment as to value.

option Contract providing that an offer will stay open for a specified period of time.

order A final disposition made by an agency.

order paper Payable to a named person or to anyone designated by that person.

order to pay Direction or command to pay.

original promise Promise to become primarily liable.

output contract See **contracts**.

palpable unilateral mistake Erroneous belief by one party that is recognized by the other.

parent corporation Corporation which controls another corporation.

parol evidence Literally oral evidence, but now includes prior to and contemporaneous, oral, and written evidence.

parol evidence rule Under this rule, when parties put their agreement in writing, all previous oral agreements merge in the writing and the contract as written cannot be modified or changed by parol evidence, in the absence of a plea of mistake or fraud in the preparation of the writing. But the rule does not forbid a resort to parol evidence not inconsistent with the matters stated in the writing. Also, as regards sales of goods, such written agreement may be explained or supplemented by course of dealing, usage of trade, or course of conduct, and by evidence of consistent additional terms, unless the court finds the writing to have been intended also as a complete and exclusive statement of the terms of the agreement. UCC §2-202.

part performance In order to establish part performance taking an oral contract for the sale of realty out of the statute of frauds, the acts relied upon as part performance must be of such a character that they reasonably can be naturally accounted for in no other way than that they were performed in pursuance of the contract, and they must be in conformity with its provisions. See UCC §2-201(3).

partial assignment Transfer of a portion of contractual rights to one or more assignees.

partition The dividing of lands held by joint tenants, copartners, or tenants in common into distinct portions, so that the parties may hold those lands in severalty.

partnership An association of two or more persons to carry on, as co-owners, a business for profit.

Partnerships are treated as a conduit and are, therefore, not subject to taxation. The various items of partnership income (gains and losses, etc.) flow through to the individual partners and are reported on their personal income tax returns.

Limited partnership Type of partnership comprised of one or more general partners who manage business and who are personally liable for partnership debts, and one or more limited partners who contribute capital and share in profits but who take no part in running business and incur no liability with respect to partnership obligations beyond contribution.

Partnership at will One with no definite term or specific undertaking.

partnership capital Total money and property contributed by partners for permanent use by the partnership.

partnership property Sum of all of the partnership's assets.

past consideration An act done before the contract is made.

patent Exclusive right to an invention.

payee The person in whose favor a bill of exchange, promissory note, or check is made or drawn.

payer or **payor** One who pays or who is to make a payment, particularly the person who is to make payment of a check, bill, or note. Correlative to "payee."

payor bank A bank by which an item is payable as drawn or accepted. UCC §4-105(b). Correlative to "Drawee bank."

per capita This term, derived from the civil law and much used in the law of descent and distribution, denotes that method of dividing an intestate estate by which an equal share is given to each of a number of persons, all of whom stand in equal degree to the decedent, without reference to their stocks or the right of representation. The opposite of *per stirpes.*

per stirpes This term, derived from the civil law and much used in the law of descent and distribution, denotes that method of dividing an intestate estate where a class or group of distributees takes the share to which its deceased would have been entitled, taking thus by its right of representing such ancestor and not as so many individuals. The opposite of *per capita.*

perfect tender rule Seller's tender of delivery must conform exactly to the contract.

perfection of security interest Acts required of a secured party in the way of giving at least constructive notice so as to make his security interest effective at least against lien creditors of the debtor. See UCC §§9-302 through 9-306. In most cases, the secured party may obtain perfection either by filing with the secretary of state or by taking possession of the collateral.

performance Fulfillment of one's contractual obligations. See also **part performance; specific performance**.

periodic tenancy Lease with a definite term that is to be continued.

personal defenses Contractual defenses which are good against holders but not holders in due course.

personal property Any property other than an interest in land.

petty crime Misdemeanor punishable by imprisonment of six months or less.

plaintiff The party who initiates a civil suit.

pleadings The formal allegations by the parties of their respective claims and defenses.

Rules or codes of civil procedure Unlike the rigid technical system of common law pleading, pleadings under federal and state rules or codes of civil procedure have a far more limited function, with determination and narrowing of facts and issues being left to discovery devices and pretrial conferences. In addition, the rules and codes permit liberal amendment and supplementation of pleadings. Under rules of civil procedure, the pleadings consist of a complaint, an answer, a reply to a counterclaim, an answer to a cross-claim, a third-party complaint, and a third-party answer.

pledge A bailment of goods to a creditor as security for some debt or engagement.

Much of the law of pledges has been replaced by the provisions for secured transactions in Article 9 of the UCC.

possibility of reverter The interest which remains in a grantor or testator after the conveyance or devise of a fee simple determinable and which permits the grantor to be revested automatically of his estate on breach of the condition.

possibility test Under the statute of frauds, asks whether performance could possibly be completed within one year.

power of appointment A power of authority conferred by one person by deed or will upon another (called the "donee") to appoint, that is, to select and nominate, the person or persons who is or are to receive and enjoy an estate or an income therefrom or from a fund, after the testator's death, or the donee's death, or after the termination of an existing right or interest.

power of attorney An instrument authorizing a person to act as the agent or attorney of the person granting it.

power of termination The interest left in the grantor or testator after the conveyance or devise of a fee simple on condition subsequent or conditional fee.

precatory Expressing a wish.

precedent An adjudged case or decision of a court, considered as furnishing an example or authority for an identical or similar case afterwards arising or a similar question of law. See also **stare decisis.**

preemptive right The privilege of a stockholder to maintain a proportionate share of ownership by purchasing a proportionate share of any new stock issues.

preference The act of an insolvent debtor who, in distributing his property or in assigning it for the benefit of his creditors, pays or secures to one or more creditors the full amount of their claims or a larger amount than they would be entitled to receive on a *pro rata* distribution. The treatment of such preferential payments in bankruptcy is governed by the Bankruptcy Act, §547.

preliminary hearing Determines whether there is probable cause.

premium The price for insurance protection for a specified period of exposure.

preponderance of the evidence Greater weight of the evidence; standard used in civil cases.

prescription Acquisition of a personal right to use a way, water, light, and air by reason of continuous usage. See also **easement**.

presenter's warranty Warranty given to any payor or acceptor of an instrument.

presentment The production of a negotiable instrument to the drawee for his acceptance, or to the drawer or acceptor for payment; or of a promissory note to the party liable, for payment of the same. UCC §3-504(1).

presumption A presumption is a rule of law, statutory or judicial, by which a finding of a basic fact gives rise to the existence of presumed fact, until presumption is rebutted. A presumption imposes on the party against whom it is directed the burden of going forward with evidence to rebut or meet the presumption, but does not shift to such party the burden of proof in the sense of the risk of nonpersuasion, which remains throughout the trial upon the party on whom it was originally cast.

price discrimination Price differential.

price fixing Any agreement for the purpose and effect of raising, depressing, fixing, pegging, or stabilizing prices.

prima facie (Latin) At first sight; on the first appearance; on the face of it; so far as can be judged from the first disclosure; presumably; a fact presumed to be true unless disproved by some evidence to the contrary.

primary liability Absolute obligation to pay a negotiable instrument.

principal

Law of agency The term "principal" describes one who has permitted or directed another (*i.e.*, an agent or a servant) to act for his benefit and subject to his direction and control. Principal includes in its meaning the term "master" or employer, a species of principal who, in addition to other control, has a right to control the physical conduct of the species of agents known as servants or employees, as to whom special rules are applicable with reference to harm caused by their physical acts.

Disclosed principal One whose existence and identity are known.

Partially disclosed principal One whose existence is known but whose identity is not known.

Undisclosed principal One whose existence and identity are not known.

principal debtor Person whose debt is being supported by a surety.

priority Precedence in order of right.

private carrier Carrier which limits its service and is not open to the general public.

private corporation One organized to conduct either a privately owned business enterprise for profit or a nonprofit corporation.

private law The law involving relationships among individuals and legal entities.

privilege Immunity from tort liability.

privity Contractual relationship.

privity of contract That connection or relationship which exists between two or more contracting parties. The absence of privity as a defense in actions for damages in contract and tort actions is generally no longer viable with the enactment of warranty statutes (*e.g.*, UCC §2-318), acceptance by states of the doctrine of strict liability, and court decisions which have extended the right to sue to third-party beneficiaries and even innocent bystanders.

probable cause Reasonable belief of the offense charged.

probate Court procedure by which a will is proved to be valid or invalid, though in current usage this term has been expanded to include generally all matters and proceedings pertaining to administration of estates, guardianships, etc.

procedural due process Requirement that governmental action depriving a person of life, liberty, or property be done through a fair procedure.

procedural law Rules for enforcing substantive law.

procedural rules Rules issued by an administrative agency establishing its organization, method of operation, and rules of conduct for practice before it.

procedural unconscionability Unfair or irregular bargaining.

proceeds Consideration for the sale, exchange, or other disposition of collateral.

process

Judicial process In a wide sense, this term may include all the acts of a court from the beginning to the end of its proceedings in a given cause; more specifically, it means the writ, summons, mandate, or other process which is used to inform the defendant of the institution of proceedings against him and to compel his appearance, in either civil or criminal cases.

Legal process This term is sometimes used as equivalent to "lawful process." Thus, it is said that legal process means process not merely fair on its face but valid in fact. But properly it means a summons, writ, warrant, mandate, or other process issuing from a court.

profit corporation One founded for the purpose of operating a business for profit.

profit à prendre Right to make some use of the soil of another, such as a right to mine metals; carries with it the right of entry and the right to remove.

promise to pay Undertaking to pay an existing obligation.

promisee Person to whom a promise is made.

promisor Person making a promise.

promissory estoppel Arises where there is a promise which promisor should reasonably expect to induce action or forbearance on part of promisee and which does induce such action or forbearance, and where injustice can be avoided only by enforcement of the promise.

promissory note An unconditional written promise to pay a specified sum of money on demand or at a specified date. Such a note is negotiable if signed by the maker and containing an unconditional promise to pay a sum certain in money either on demand or at a definite time and payable to order or bearer. UCC §3-104.

promoters In the law relating to corporations, those persons who first associate themselves for the purpose of organizing a company, issuing its prospectus, procuring subscriptions to the stock, securing a charter, etc.

property Interest that is legally protected.

Abandoned property Intentionally disposed of by the owner.

Lost property Unintentionally left by the owner.

Mislaid property Intentionally placed by the owner but unintentionally left.

prosecute To bring a criminal proceeding.

protest A formal declaration made by a person interested or concerned in some act about to be done, or already performed, whereby he expresses his dissent or disapproval or affirms the act against his will. The object of such a declaration usually is to preserve some right which would be lost to the protester if his assent could be implied, or to exonerate him from some responsibility which would attach to him unless he expressly negatived his assent.

Notice of protest A notice given by the holder of a bill or note to the drawer or indorser that the bill has been protested for refusal of payment or acceptance. UCC §3-509.

provisional credit Tentative credit for the deposit of an instrument until final credit is given.

proximate cause Where the act or omission played a substantial part in bringing about or actually causing the injury or damage and where the injury or damage was either a direct result or a reasonably probable consequence of the act or omission.

proxy (Contracted from "procuracy.") Written authorization given by one person to another so that the second person can act for the first, such as that given by a shareholder to someone else to represent him and vote his shares at a shareholders' meeting.

public corporation One created to administer a unit of local civil government or one created by the United States to conduct public business.

public disclosure of private facts Offensive publicity given to private information about another person.

public law The law dealing with the relationship between government and individuals.

puffery Sales talk that is considered general bragging or overstatement.

punitive damages Damages awarded in excess of normal compensation to punish a defendant for a serious civil wrong.

purchase money security interest Security interest retained by a seller of goods in goods purchased with the loaned money.

qualified fee Ownership subject to its being taken away upon the happening of an event.

quantum meruit "As much as he deserves." Describes the extent of liability on a contract implied by law. Elements essential to recovery under quantum meruit are (1) valuable services rendered or materials furnished (2) for the person sought to be charged, (3) which services and materials such person accepted, used, and enjoyed, (4) under such circumstances as reasonably notified her that plaintiff, in performing such services, was expected to be paid by the person sought to be charged.

quasi As if; almost as it were; analogous to. Negatives the idea of identity but points out that the conceptions are sufficiently similar to be classed as equals of one another.

quasi contract Legal fiction invented by common law courts to permit recovery by contractual remedy in cases where, in fact, there is no contract, but where circumstances are such that justice warrants a recovery as though a promise had been made.

quasi in rem See **in rem**.

quasi in rem jurisdiction Jurisdiction over property not based on claims against it.

quiet enjoyment Right of a tenant not to have his physical possession of premises interfered with by the landlord.

quitclaim deed A deed of conveyance operating by way of release; that is, intended to pass any title, interest, or claim which the grantor may have in the premises but neither professing that such title is valid nor containing any warranty or covenants for title.

quorum When a committee, board of directors, meeting of shareholders, legislature, or other body of persons cannot act unless at least a certain number of them are present.

rape Unlawful, nonconsensual sexual intercourse.

ratification In a broad sense, the confirmation of a previous act done either by the party himself or by another; as, for example, confirmation of a voidable act.

In the law of principal and agent, the adoption and confirmation by one person, with knowledge of all material facts, of an act or contract performed or entered into in his behalf by another who at the time assumed without authority to act as his agent.

rational relationship test Requirement that legislation bear a rational relationship to a legitimate governmental interest.

real defenses Defenses that are valid against all holders, including holders in due course.

real property Land, and generally whatever is erected or growing upon or affixed to land. Also, rights issuing out of, annexed to, and exercisable within or about land. See also **fixture**.

reasonable man standard Duty of care required to avoid being negligent; one who is careful, diligent, and prudent.

receiver A fiduciary of the court, whose appointment is incident to other proceedings wherein certain ultimate relief is prayed. He is a trustee or ministerial officer representing the court, all parties in interest in the litigation, and the property or funds entrusted to him.

recognizance Formal acknowledgment of indebtedness made in court.

redemption The realization of a right to have the title of property restored free and clear of a mortgage, performance of the mortgage obligation being essential for such purpose. (b) Repurchase by corporation of its own shares.

reformation Equitable remedy used to reframe written contracts to reflect accurately real agreement between contracting parties when, either through mutual mistake or unilateral mistake coupled with actual or equitable fraud by the other party, the writing does not embody the contract as actually made.

regulatory license Requirement to protect the public interest.

reimbursement Duty owed by principal to pay back authorized payments agent has made on principal's behalf. Duty owed by a principal debtor to repay surety who pays principal debtor's obligation.

rejection The refusal to accept an offer; manifestation of an unwillingness to accept the goods (sales).

release The relinquishment, concession, or giving up of a right, claim, or privilege, by the person in whom it exists or to whom it accrues, to the person against whom it might have been demanded or enforced.

remainder An estate limited to take effect and be enjoyed after another estate is determined.

remand To send back. The sending by the appellate court of a cause back to the same court out of which it came, for the purpose of having some further action taken on it there.

remedy The means by which the violation of a right is prevented, redressed, or compensated. Though a remedy may be by the act of the party injured, by operation of law, or by agreement between the injurer and the injured, we are chiefly concerned with one kind of remedy, the judicial remedy, which is by action or suit.

rent Consideration paid for use or occupation of property. In a broader sense, it is the compensation or fee paid, usually periodically, for the use of any property, land, buildings, equipment, etc.

replevin An action whereby the owner or person entitled to repossession of goods or chattels may recover those goods or chattels from one who has wrongfully distrained or taken such goods or chattels or who wrongfully detains them.

reply Plaintiff's pleading in response to the defendant's answer.

repudiation Repudiation of a contract means refusal to perform duty or obligation owed to other party.

requirements contract See **contracts**.

res ipsa loquitur "The thing speaks for itself." Permits the jury to infer both negligent conduct and causation.

rescission An equitable action in which a party seeks to be relieved of his obligations under a contract on the grounds of mutual mistake, fraud, impossibility, etc.

residuary Pertaining to the residue; constituting the residue; giving or bequeathing the residue; receiving or entitled to the residue. See also **legacy, residuary legacy**.

respondeat superior "Let the master answer." This maxim means that a master or employer is liable in certain cases for the wrongful acts of his servant or employee, and a principal for those of his agent.

respondent In equity practice, the party who makes an answer to a bill or other proceeding. In appellate practice, the party who contends against an appeal; i.e., the appellee. The party who appeals is called the "appellant."

restitution An equitable remedy under which a person who has rendered services to another seeks to be reimbursed for the costs of his acts (but not his profits) even though there was never a contract between the parties.

restraint on alienation A provision in an instrument of conveyance which prohibits the grantee from selling or transferring the property which is the subject of the conveyance. Many such restraints are unenforceable as against public policy and the law's policy of free alienability of land.

restraint of trade Agreement that eliminates or tends to eliminate competition.

restrictive covenant Private restriction on property contained in a conveyance.

revenue license Measure to raise money.

reverse An appellate court uses the term "reversed" to indicate that it annuls or avoids the judgment, or vacates the decree, of the trial court.

reverse discrimination Employment decisions taking into account race or gender in order to remedy past discrimination.

reversion The term reversion has two meanings. First, it designates the estate left in the grantor during the continuance of a particular estate; second, it denotes the residue left in grantor or his heirs after termination of a particular estate. It differs from a remainder in that it arises by an act of law, whereas a remainder arises by an act of the parties. A reversion, moreover, is the remnant left in the grantor, while a remainder is the remnant of the whole estate disposed of after a preceding part of the same has been given away.

revocation The recall of some power, authority, or thing granted, or a destroying or making void of some deed that had existence until the act of revocation made it void.

revocation of acceptance Rescission of one's acceptance of goods based upon a nonconformity of the goods which substantially impairs their value.

right Legal capacity to require another person to perform or refrain from performing an act.

right of entry The right to take or resume possession of land by entering on it in a peaceable manner.

right of redemption The right (granted by statute only) to free property from the encumbrance of a foreclosure or other judicial sale, or to recover the title passing thereby, by paying what is due, with interest, costs, etc. Not to be confounded with the "equity of redemption," which exists independently of statute but must be exercised before sale. See also **equity of redemption**.

right to work law State statute that prohibits union shop contracts.

rights in collateral Personal property the debtor owns, possesses, or is in the process of acquiring.

risk of loss Allocation of loss between seller and buyer where the goods have been damaged, destroyed, or lost.

robbery Larceny from a person by force or threat of force.

rule Agency statement of general or particular applicability designed to implement, interpret, or process law or policy.

rule against perpetuities Principle that no interest in property is good unless it must vest, if at all, not later than twenty-one years, plus period of gestation, after some life or lives in being at time of creation of interest.

rule of reason Balancing the anticompetitive effects of a restraint against its procompetitive effects.

sale Transfer of title to goods from seller to buyer for a price.

sale on approval Transfer of possession without title to buyer for trial period.

sale or return Sale where buyer has option to return goods to seller.

sanction Means of enforcing legal judgments.

satisfaction The discharge of an obligation by paying a party what is due to him (as on a mortgage, lien, or contract) or what has been awarded to him by the judgment of a court or otherwise. Thus, a judgment is satisfied by the payment of the amount due to the party who has recovered such judgment, or by his levying the amount. See also **accord and satisfaction**.

scienter Knowingly.

seal Symbol that authenticates a document.

secondary liability Obligation to pay is subject to the conditions of presentment, dishonor, notice of dishonor, and sometimes protest.

secret partner Partner whose membership in the partnership is not disclosed.

Section 402A Strict liability in tort.

secured bond A bond having a lien on specific property.

secured claim Claim with a lien on property of the debtor.

secured party Creditor who possesses a security interest in collateral.

secured transaction A transaction founded on a security agreement. Such agreement creates or provides for a security interest. UCC §9-105(h).

securities Stocks, bonds, notes, convertible debentures, warrants, or other documents that represent a share in a company or a debt owed by a company.

> *Certificated security* Security represented by a certificate.
>
> *Exempt security* Security not subject to registration requirements of 1933 Act.
>
> *Exempt transaction* Issuance of securities not subject to the registration requirements of 1933 Act.
>
> *Restricted securities* Securities issued under an exempt transaction.
>
> *Uncertificated security* Security not represented by a certificate.

security agreement Agreement that grants a security interest.

security interest Right in personal property securing payment or performance of an obligation.

seisin Possession with an intent on the part of him who holds it to claim a freehold interest.

self-defense Force to protect oneself against attack.

separation of powers Allocation of powers among the legislative, executive, and judicial branches of government.

service mark Distinctive symbol, word, or design that is used to identify the services of a provider.

servient Land subject to an easement.

setoff A counterclaim demand which defendant holds against plaintiff, arising out of a transaction extrinsic to plaintiff's cause of action.

settlor Creator of a trust.

severance The destruction of any one of the unities of a joint tenancy. It is so called because the estate is no longer a joint tenancy, but is severed.

Term may also refer to the cutting of crops, such as corn, wheat, etc., or to the separation of anything from realty.

share A proportionate ownership interest in a corporation.

Shelley's case, rule in Where a person takes an estate of freehold, legally or equitably, under a deed, will, or other writing, and in the same instrument there is a limitation by way of remainder of any interest of the same legal or equitable quality to his heirs, or heirs of his body, as a class of persons to take in succession from generation to generation, the limitation to the heirs entitles the ancestor to the whole estate.

The rule was adopted as a part of the common law of this country, though it has long since been abolished by most states.

shelter rule Transferee gets rights of transferor.

shipment contract Seller is authorized or required only to bear the expense of placing goods with the common carrier and bears the risk of loss only up to such point.

short-swing profits Profits made by insider through sale or other disposition of corporate stock within six months after purchase.

sight draft An instrument payable on presentment.

signature Any symbol executed with intent to validate a writing.

silent partner Partner who takes no part in the partnership business.

slander Oral defamation.

small claims courts Inferior civil courts with jurisdiction limited by dollar amount.

social security Measures by which the government provides economic assistance to disabled or retired employees and their dependents.

sole proprietorship A form of business in which one person owns all the assets of the business, in contrast to a partnership or a corporation.

sovereign immunity Foreign country's freedom from a host country's laws.

special warranty deed Seller promises that he has not impaired title.

specific performance The doctrine of specific performance is that where damages would compensate inadequately for the breach of an agreement, the contractor or vendor will be compelled to perform specifically what he has agreed to do; *e.g.*, ordered to execute a specific conveyance of land.

With respect to the sale of goods, specific performance may be decreed where the goods are unique or in other proper circumstances. The decree for specific performance may include such terms and conditions as to payment of the price, damages, or other relief as the court may deem just. UCC §§2-711(2)(b), 2-716.

standardized business form A preprinted contract.

stare decisis Doctrine that once a court has laid down a principle of law as applicable to a certain state of facts, it will adhere to that principle and apply it to all future cases having substantially the same facts, regardless of whether the parties and property are the same or not.

state action Actions by governments, as opposed to actions taken by private individuals.

state-of-the-art Made in accordance with the level of technology at the time the product is made.

stated capital Consideration, other than that allocated to capital surplus, received for issued stock.

statute of frauds A celebrated English statute, passed in 1677, which has been adopted, in a more or less modified form, in nearly all of the United States. Its chief characteristic is the provision that no action shall be brought on certain contracts unless there be a note or memorandum thereof in writing, signed by the party to be charged or by his authorized agent.

statute of limitation A statute prescribing limitations to the right of action on certain described causes of action; that is, declaring that no suit shall be maintained on such causes of action unless brought within a specified period after the right accrued.

statutory lien Interest in property, arising solely by statute, to secure payment of a debt.

stock "Stock" is distinguished from "bonds" and, ordinarily, from "debentures" in that it gives a right of ownership in part of the assets of a corporation and a right to interest in any surplus after the payment of debt. "Stock" in a corporation is an equity, representing an ownership interest. It is to be distinguished from obligations such as notes or bonds, which are not equities and represent no ownership interest.

Capital stock See **capital**.

Common stock Securities which represent an ownership interest in a corporation. If the company has also issued preferred stock, both common and preferred have ownership rights. Claims of both common and preferred stockholders are junior to claims of bondholders or other creditors of the company. Common stockholders assume the greater risk, but generally exercise the greater control and may gain the greater reward in the form of dividends and capital appreciation.

Convertible stock Stock which may be changed or converted into common stock.

Cumulative preferred Stock having a provision that if one or more dividends are omitted, the omitted dividends must be paid before dividends may be paid on the company's common stock.

Preferred stock is a separate portion or class of the stock of a corporation that is accorded, by the charter or by-laws, a preference or priority in respect to dividends, over the remainder of the stock of the corporation, which in that case is called *common stock*.

Stock warrant A certificate entitling the owner to buy a specified amount of stock at a specified time(s) for a specified price. Differs from a stock option only in that options are granted to employees and warrants are sold to the public.

Treasury stock Shares reacquired by a corporation.

stock option Contractual right to purchase stock from a corporation.

stop payment Order for a drawee not to pay an instrument.

strict liability A concept applied by the courts in product liability cases in which a seller is liable for any and all defective or hazardous products which unduly threaten a consumer's personal safety. This concept applies to all members involved in the manufacture and sale of any facet of the product.

strict scrutiny test Requirement that legislation be necessary to promote a compelling governmental interest.

subagent Person appointed by agent to perform agent's duties.

subject matter jurisdiction Authority of a court to decide a particular kind of case.

subject to the mortgage Purchaser is not personally obligated to pay the debt, but the property remains subject to the mortgage.

subjective fault Desired or virtually certain consequences of one's conduct.

subjective satisfaction Approval based upon a party's honestly held opinion.

sublease Transfer of less than all of a tenant's interest in a leasehold.

subpoena A subpoena is a command to appear at a certain time and place to give testimony upon a certain matter. A subpoena duces tecum requires production of books, papers, and other things.

subrogation The substitution of one thing for another, or of one person into the place of another with respect to rights, claims, or securities.

Subrogation denotes the putting of a third person who has paid a debt in the place of the creditor to whom he has paid it, so that he may exercise against the debtor all the rights which the creditor, if unpaid, might have exercised.

subscribe Literally, to write underneath, as one's name. To sign at the end of a document. Also, to agree in writing to furnish money or its equivalent, or to agree to purchase some initial stock in a corporation.

subscriber Person who agrees to purchase initial stock in a corporation.

subsidiary corporation Corporation controlled by another corporation.

substantial performance Equitable doctrine protects against forfeiture for technical inadvertence, trivial variations, or omissions in performance.

substantive due process Requirement that governmental action be compatible with individual liberties.

substantive law The basic law of rights and duties (contract law, criminal law, tort law, law of wills, etc.), as opposed to procedural law (law of pleading, law of evidence, law of jurisdiction, etc.).

substantive unconscionability Oppressive or grossly unfair contractual terms.

sue To begin a lawsuit in a court.

suit A generic term of comprehensive signification that applies to any proceeding in a court of justice in which the plaintiff pursues, in such court, the remedy which the law affords him for the redress of an injury or the recovery of a right.

Derivative suit Suit brought by a shareholder on behalf of a corporation to enforce a right belonging to the corporation.

Direct suit Suit brought by a shareholder against a corporation based upon his ownership of shares.

summary judgment Rule of Civil Procedure 56 permits any party to a civil action to move for a summary judgment on a claim, counterclaim, or cross-claim when he believes that there is no genuine issue of material fact and that he is entitled to prevail as a matter of law.

summons Writ or process directed to the sheriff or other proper officer, requiring him to notify the person named that an action has been commenced against him in the court from which the process has issued and that he is required to appear, on a day named, and answer the complaint in such action.

superseding cause Intervening event that occurs after the defendant's negligent conduct and relieves him of liability.

supreme law A law that takes precedence over all conflicting laws.

surety One who undertakes to pay money or to do any other act in event that his principal debtor fails therein.

suretyship A guarantee of debts of another.

surplus Excess of net assets over stated capital.

tangible property Physical objects.

tariff Duty or tax imposed on goods moving into or out of a country.

tenancy Possession or occupancy of land or premises under lease.

Joint tenancy Joint tenants have one and the same interest, accruing by one and the same conveyance, commencing at one and the same time, and held by one and the same undivided possession. The primary incident of joint tenancy is survivorship, by which the entire tenancy on the decease of any joint tenant remains to the survivors, and at length to the last survivor.

Tenancy at sufferance Only naked possession which continues after tenant's right of possession has terminated.

Tenancy at will Possession of premises by permission of owner or landlord, but without a fixed term.

Tenancy by the entirety A tenancy which is created between a husband and wife and by which together they hold title to the whole with right of survivorship so that, upon death of either, the other takes the whole to the exclusion of the deceased's heirs. It is essentially a "joint tenancy," modified by the common law theory that husband and wife are one person.

Tenancy for a period A tenancy for years or for some fixed period.

Tenancy in common A form of ownership whereby each tenant (*i.e.*, owner) holds an undivided interest in property. Unlike the interest of a joint tenant or a tenant by the entirety, the interest of a tenant in common does not terminate upon his or her prior death (*i.e.*, there is no right of survivorship).

tenancy in partnership Type of joint ownership that determines partners' rights in specific partnership property.

tenant Possessor of a leasehold interest.

tender An offer of money; the act by which one produces and offers to a person holding a claim or demand against him the amount of money which he considers and admits to be due, in satisfaction of such claim or demand, without any stipulation or condition.

Also, there may be a tender of performance of a duty other than the payment of money.

tender of delivery Seller makes available to buyer goods conforming to the contract and so notifies the buyer.

tender offer General invitation to all shareholders to purchase their shares at a specified price.

testament Will.

testator One who makes or has made a testament or will; one who dies leaving a will.

third-party beneficiary One for whose benefit a promise is made in a contract but who is not a party to the contract.

Creditor beneficiary Where performance of a promise in a contract will benefit a person other than the promisee, that person is a creditor beneficiary if no purpose to make a gift appears from the terms of the promise, in view of the accompanying circumstances, and performance of the promise will satisfy an actual, supposed, or asserted duty of the promisee to the beneficiary.

Donee beneficiary The person who takes the benefit of the contract even though there is no privity between him and the contracting parties. A third-party beneficiary who is not a creditor beneficiary. See also **beneficiary**.

time paper Payable at definite time.

time-price doctrine Permits sellers to have different prices for cash sales and credit sales.

title The means whereby the owner of lands or of personalty has the just possession of his property.

title insurance Provides protection against defect in title to real property.

tort A private or civil wrong or injury, other than breach of contract, for which a court will provide a remedy in the form of an action for damages.

Three elements of every tort action are the existence of a legal duty from defendant to plaintiff, breach of that duty, and damage as proximate result.

tortfeasor One who commits a tort.

trade acceptance A draft drawn by a seller which is presented for signature (acceptance) to the buyer at the time goods are purchased and which then becomes the equivalent of a note receivable of the seller and the note payable of the buyer.

trade name Name used in trade or business to identify a particular business or manufacturer.

trade secrets Private business information.

trademark Distinctive insignia, word, or design of a good that is used to identify the manufacturer.

transferor's warranty Warranty given by any person who transfers an instrument and receives consideration.

treaty An agreement between or among independent nations.

treble damages Three times actual loss.

trespass At common law, trespass was a form of action brought to recover damages for any injury to one's person or property or relationship with another.

Trespass to chattels or personal property An unlawful and serious interference with the possessory rights of another to personal property.

Trespass to land At common law, every unauthorized and direct breach of the boundaries of another's land was an actionable trespass. The present prevailing position of the courts finds liability for trespass only in the case of intentional intrusion, or negligence, or some "abnormally dangerous activity" on the part of the defendant. *Compare* **nuisance**.

trespasser Person who enters or remains on the land of another without permission or privilege to do so.

trust Any arrangement whereby property is transferred with the intention that it be administered by a trustee for another's benefit.

A trust, as the term is used in the Restatement, when not qualified by the word "charitable," "resulting," or "constructive," is a fiduciary relationship with respect to property, subjecting the person by whom the title to the property is held to equitable duties to deal with the property for the benefit of another person, which arises through a manifestation of an intention to create such benefit. Restatement, Second, Trusts §2.

Charitable trust To benefit humankind.

Constructive trust Wherever the circumstances of a transaction are such that the person who takes the legal estate in property cannot also enjoy the beneficial interest without necessarily violating some established principle of equity, the court will immediately raise a *constructive trust* and fasten it upon the conscience of the legal owner, so as to convert him into a trustee for the parties who in equity are entitled to the beneficial enjoyment.

Inter vivos trust Established during the settlor's lifetime.

Resulting trust One that arises by implication of law, where the legal estate in property is disposed of, conveyed, or transferred, but the intent appears or is inferred from the terms of the disposition, or from the accompanying facts and circumstances, that the beneficial interest is not to go or be enjoyed with the legal title.

Spendthrift trust Removal of the trust estate from the beneficiary's control.

Testamentary trust Established by a will.

Totten trust A tentative trust which is a joint bank account opened by the settlor.

Voting trust A trust which holds the voting rights to stock in a corporation. It is a useful device when a majority of the shareholders in a corporation cannot agree on corporate policy.

trustee In a strict sense, a "trustee" is one who holds the legal title to property for the benefit of another, while, in a broad sense, the term is sometimes applied to anyone standing in a fiduciary or confidential relation to another, such as agent, attorney, bailee, etc.

trustee in bankruptcy Representative of the estate in bankruptcy who is responsible for collecting, liquidating, and distributing the debtor's assets.

tying arrangement Conditioning a sale of a desired product (tying product) on the buyer's purchasing a second product (tied product).

ultra vires Acts beyond the scope of the powers of a corporation, as defined by its charter or by the laws of its state of incorporation. By the doctrine of ultra vires, a contract made by a corporation beyond the scope of its corporate powers is unlawful.

unconscionable Unfair or unduly harsh.

unconscionable contract See **contracts**.

underwriter Any person, banker, or syndicate that guarantees to furnish a definite sum of money by a definite date to a business or government in return for an issue of bonds or stock. In insurance, the one assuming a risk in return for the payment of a premium.

undisputed debt Obligation whose existence and amount are not contested.

undue influence Term refers to conduct by which a person, through his power over the mind of a testator, makes the latter's desires conform to his own, thereby overmastering the volition of the testator.

unemployment compensation Compensation awarded to workers who have lost their jobs and cannot find other employment.

unenforceable Contract under which neither party can recover.

unfair employer practice Conduct in which an employer is prohibited from engaging.

unfair labor practice Conduct in which an employer or union is prohibited from engaging.

unfair union practice Conduct in which a union is prohibited from engaging.

Uniform Commercial Code One of the Uniform Laws, drafted by the National Conference of Commissioners on Uniform State Laws, governing commercial transactions (sales of goods, commercial paper, bank deposits and collections, letters of credit, bulk transfers, warehouse receipts, bills of lading, investment securities, and secured transactions).

unilateral mistake Erroneous belief on the part of only one of the parties to a contract.

union shop Employer can hire nonunion members, but such employees must then join the union.

universal life Ordinary life divided into two components, a renewable term insurance policy and an investment portfolio.

unliquidated debt Obligation that is uncertain or contested in amount.

unqualified indorsement (see **indorsement**) One that imposes liability upon the indorser.

unreasonably dangerous Danger beyond that which the ordinary consumer contemplates.

unrestrictive indorsement (see **indorsement**) One that does not attempt to restrict the rights of the indorsee.

usage of trade Any practice or method of dealing having such regularity of observance in a place, vocation, or trade as to justify an expectation that it will be observed with respect to the transaction in question.

usury Collectively, the laws of a jurisdiction regulating the charging of interest rates. A usurious loan is one whose interest rates are determined to be in excess of those permitted by the usury laws.

value The performance of legal consideration, the forgiveness of an antecedent debt, the giving of a negotiable instrument, or the giving of an irrevocable commitment to a third party. UCC §1-201(44).

variance A use differing from that provided in a zoning ordinance in order to avoid undue hardship.

vendee A purchaser or buyer; one to whom anything is sold. See also **vendor**.

vendor The person who transfers property by sale, particularly real estate; "seller" being more commonly used for one who sells personalty. See also **vendee**.

venue "Jurisdiction" of the court means the inherent power to decide a case, whereas "venue" designates the particular county or city in which a court with jurisdiction may hear and determine the case.

verdict The formal and unanimous decision or finding of a jury, impaneled and sworn for the trial of a cause, upon the matters or questions duly submitted to it upon the trial.

vertical privity Who is liable to the plaintiff.

vertical restraints Agreements among parties at different levels of the distribution chain.

vested Fixed; accrued; settled; absolute. To be "vested," a right must be more than a mere expectation based on an anticipation of the continuance of an existing law; it must have become a title, legal or equitable, to the present or future enforcement of a demand, or a legal exemption from the demand of another.

vested remainder Unconditional remainder that is a fixed present interest to be enjoyed in the future.

vicarious liability Indirect legal responsibility; for example, the liability of an employer for the acts of an employee or that of a principal for the torts and contracts of an agent.

void Null; ineffectual; nugatory; having no legal force or binding effect; unable, in law, to support the purpose for which it was intended.

This difference separates the words "void" and "voidable": *void* in the strict sense means that an instrument or transaction is nugatory and ineffectual, so that nothing can cure it; *voidable* exists when an imperfection or defect can be cured by the act or confirmation of the person who could take advantage of it.

Frequently, the word "void" is used and construed as having the more liberal meaning of "voidable."

voidable Capable of being made void. See also **void**.

voir dire Preliminary examination of potential jurors.

voluntary Resulting from free choice. The word, especially in statutes, often implies knowledge of essential facts.

voting trust Transfer of corporate shares' voting rights to a trustee.

wager (gambling) Agreement that one party will win or lose depending upon the outcome of an event in which the only interest is the gain or loss.

waiver Terms "estoppel" and "waiver" are not synonymous; "waiver" means the voluntary, intentional relinquishment of a known right, and "estoppel" rests upon principle that, where anyone has done an act or made a statement that would be a fraud on his part to controvert or impair, because the other party has acted upon it in belief that what was done or said was true, conscience and honest dealing require that he not be permitted to repudiate his act or gainsay his statement. See also **estoppel**.

ward An infant or insane person placed by authority of law under the care of a guardian.

warehouse receipt Receipt issued by a person storing goods.

warehouser Storer of goods for compensation.

warrant, v. In contracts, to engage or promise that a certain fact or state of facts, in relation to the subject matter, is, or shall be, as it is represented to be.

In conveyancing, to assure the title to property sold, by an express covenant to that effect in the deed of conveyance.

warranty A warranty is a statement or representation made by a seller of goods, contemporaneously with and as a part of a contract of sale, though collateral to express the object of the sale, having reference to the character, quality, or title of goods, and by which the seller promises or undertakes to ensure that certain facts are or shall be as he then represents them.

The general statutory law governing warranties on sales of goods is provided in UCC §2-312 *et seq.* The three main types of warranties are (1) express warranty; (2) implied warranty of fitness; (3) implied warranty of merchantability.

warranty deed Deed in which grantor warrants good clear title. The usual covenants of title are warranties of seisin, quiet enjoyment, right to convey, freedom from encumbrances, and defense of title as to all claims.

Special warranty deed Seller warrants that he has not impaired title.

warranty liability Applies to persons who transfer an instrument or receive payment or acceptance.

warranty of title Obligation to convey the right to ownership without any lien.

waste Any act or omission that does permanent injury to the realty or unreasonably changes its value.

white-collar crime Corporate crime.

will A written instrument executed with the formalities required by statutes, whereby a person makes a disposition of his property to take effect after his death.

winding up To settle the accounts and liquidate the assets of a partnership or corporation, for the purpose of making distribution and terminating the concern.

without reserve Auctioneer may not withdraw the goods from the auction.

workers' compensation Compensation awarded to an employee who is injured, when the injury arose out of and in the course of his employment.

writ of certiorari Discretionary review by a higher court. See also **certiorari**.

writ of execution Order served by sheriff upon debtor demanding payment of a court judgment against debtor.

zoning Public control over land use.

Index

Index